Frequently Asked Questions

Ten Best Tips

Ed Bott, *Award-winning computer journalist*

Carl Siechert, *Windows documentation expert*

Craig Stinson, *Contributing Editor, PC Magazine*

Microsoft

Microsoft®

Windows® XP

INSIDE

DELUXE EDITION

OUT

- **Hundreds of timesaving solutions—easy to find, easy to use!**
- **All-new information on Windows XP Service Pack 1**
- **Expanded coverage of Windows XP Home Edition, Windows XP Professional, security, and more**

PUBLISHED BY
Microsoft Press
A Division of Microsoft Corporation
One Microsoft Way
Redmond, Washington 98052-6399

Library of Congress Cataloging-in-Publication Data
Bott, Ed.
    Microsoft Windows XP Inside Out / Ed Bott, Carl Siechert, Craig Stinson.--Deluxe ed.
        p. cm.
    Includes index.
    ISBN 0-7356-1805-4 (Deluxe ed.)
    1. Microsoft Windows (Computer file) 2. Operating systems (Computers). I. Siechert,
Carl. II. Stinson, Craig. III. Title.

    QA76.76.O63 B6444   2002
    005.4'44769--dc21   2002033817

Printed and bound in the United States of America.

5 6 7 8 9   QWT   7 6 5 4

Distributed in Canada by H.B. Fenn and Company Ltd.

A CIP catalogue record for this book is available from the British Library.

Microsoft Press books are available through booksellers and distributors worldwide. For further information about international editions, contact your local Microsoft Corporation office or contact Microsoft Press International directly at fax (425) 936-7329. Visit our Web site at www.microsoft.com/mspress. Send comments to *mspinput@microsoft.com*.

Acquisitions Editor: Alex Blanton
Project Editor: Sandra Haynes
Technical Editor: Curtis Philips

Body Part No. X08-95154

*This book is dedicated to the person with whom
I share my life, that special woman whose
name begins with J.*

—*Ed Bott, for* Judy
—*Carl Siechert, for* Jan
—*Craig Stinson, for* Jean

Contents at a Glance

Table of Contents

Part 1
Setup, Startup, Tune-Up   1

Chapter 1
Introducing Windows XP   3

Chapter 2
Installing and Configuring Windows XP   23

Chapter 4
Help and Support Options   141

Chapter 5
Installing, Uninstalling, and Managing Programs   171

Chapter 10
Automating Windows XP   355

Part 3
Managing Files   409

Chapter 11
Windows Explorer for Experts   411

newfeature!

Chapter 12
Managing and Finding Files   **451**

newfeature!

Part 4
Mastering Digital Media   571

Chapter 16
Customizing Windows Media Player   573

Chapter 17
Using Windows Media Player   597

Table of Contents

Table of Contents

Chapter 23
Securing Your Internet Connection   801

Chapter 24
Hosting a Web or FTP Site   831

Chapter 27
Managing Disks and Drives   915

Chapter 28
Troubleshooting Windows Errors   957

Chapter 29
Editing the Registry   971

Part 8
Networking   989

Chapter 30
Setting Up a Small Network   991

Chapter 31
Tweaking and Troubleshooting a Small Network 1031

Chapter 32
Managing Shared Folders and Printers 1049

Chapter 33
Remote Access Options 1093

Appendix C
Working with the Command Prompt 1243

Acknowledgments

Many skilled hands contributed to this book. We would like to thank all the contributors in the Business Product Group at Microsoft Press for designing the *Inside Out* series and Casey Doyle and Kong Cheung for getting the first edition of this book under way. We owe an additional debt to Alex Blanton, the Microsoft Press acquisitions editor who conceived the Deluxe Edition.

Erin Milnes and Andrea Fox were responsible for eliminating typos, inconsistencies, and stylistic errors. Lisa Bellomo put in long hours to turn our words into typeset pages. Curtis Philips, of Publishing.com, edited every chapter for technical accuracy and kept track of a long list of production details under difficult scheduling constraints. Our imperturbable project editor at Microsoft Press, Sandra Haynes, coordinated the efforts of all with style, grace, and good humor. Thanks to John Pierce for uncovering the mysteries of Windows XP Tablet PC Edition and sharing them in Appendix B. We also owe a profound debt of gratitude to our fellow Windows XP beta testers, with whom we shared questions, answers, and amazing discoveries, and to the many technical experts and product managers at Microsoft, who shared their inside information about Windows XP with us.

Many, many thanks!

Ed Bott, Carl Siechert, Craig Stinson

We'd Like to Hear from You!

Our goal at Microsoft Press is to create books that help you find the information you need to get the most out of your software.

The INSIDE OUT series was created with you in mind. As part of an effort to ensure that we're creating the best, most useful books we can, we talked to our customers and asked them to tell us what they need from a Microsoft Press series. Help us continue to help you. Let us know what you like about this book and what we can do to make it better. When you write, please include the title and author of this book in your e-mail, as well as your name and contact information. We look forward to hearing from you.

How to Reach Us

E-mail:	nsideout@microsoft.com
Mail:	Inside Out Series Editor
	Microsoft Press
	One Microsoft Way
	Redmond, WA 98052

Note: Unfortunately, we can't provide support for any software problems you might experience. Please go to http://support.microsoft.com *for help with any software issues.*

About the CD

The companion CD that ships with this book contains many tools and resources to help you get the most out of your Inside Out book.

What's on the Deluxe Edition CD

Your INSIDE OUT CD includes the following:

- **Microsoft Software.** In this section you'll find a copy of Windows XP SP1 and Windows Media Bonus Pack for your use.

- **Microsoft Partner Software.** In this section you'll find helpful tools and utilities for your use.

- **The Windows Catalog.** Here you'll find a list of great products built especially for the Microsoft Windows XP operating system.

- **Author Extras.** This section includes sample files and programs referenced in the book.

- **Complete eBook and Sample Chapters.** In this section you'll find the entire electronic version of this title as well as a set of sample chapters from other Inside Out books.

- **Computer Dictionary eBook.** Here you'll find the full electronic version of the Microsoft Computer Dictionary, Fifth Edition.

- **Networking Encyclopedia eBook.** Here you'll find the full electronic version of the Microsoft Encyclopedia of Networking, Second Edition.

The companion CD provides detailed information about the files on this CD, and links to Microsoft and third-party sites on the Internet. The companion CD's HTML interface is designed to be accessed through Microsoft Internet Explorer (version 4.01 or later). The electronic books that have been included on the CD require Internet Explorer 5.01 or later. The Setup program for the eBooks will offer to install Internet Explorer 5.5 for you if it detects that your system does not meet the minimum eBook requirements.

---

note Please note that the third-party software and links to third-party sites are not under the control of Microsoft Corporation and Microsoft is therefore not responsible for their content, nor should their inclusion on this CD be construed as an endorsement of the product or the site. Please check third-party Web sites for the latest version of their software.

Software provided on this CD is in English language only and may be incompatible with non-English language operating systems and software.

Using the CD

To use this companion CD, insert it into your CD-ROM drive. If AutoRun is not enabled on your computer, click on Index.htm in the WebSite folder of the CD.

System Requirements

Following are the minimum system requirements necessary to run the CD:

- Microsoft Windows 95 or later operating system (including Windows 98, Windows Millennium Edition, Windows NT 4.0 with Service Pack 3, Windows 2000, or Windows XP)
- 266-MHz or higher Pentium-compatible CPU
- 64 megabytes (MB) RAM
- 8X CD-ROM drive or faster
- 80 MB of free hard disk space (to install the eBook files)
- Microsoft Windows–compatible sound card and speakers
- Microsoft Internet Explorer 4.01 or later; Internet Explorer 5.01 or later is required to view the eBooks.
- Microsoft Mouse or compatible pointing device

note System requirements might be higher for the add-ins available on the CD. Individual add-in system requirements are specified on the CD. An Internet connection is necessary to access some of the hyperlinks. Connect time charges might apply.

Support Information

Every effort has been made to ensure the accuracy of the book and the contents of this companion CD. For feedback on the book content or this companion CD, please contact us by using any of the addresses listed in the "We'd Like to Hear From You" section.

Microsoft Press provides corrections for books through the World Wide Web at *http://www.microsoft.com/mspress/support/*. To connect directly to the Microsoft Press Knowledge Base and enter a query regarding a question or issue that you may have, go to *http://www.microsoft.com/mspress/support/search.asp*.

For support information regarding Windows XP, you can connect to Microsoft Technical Support on the Web at *http://support.microsoft.com/*.

Conventions and Features Used in This Book

This book uses special text and design conventions to make it easier for you to find the information you need.

Text Conventions

Convention	Meaning
Abbreviated menu commands	For your convenience, this book uses abbreviated menu commands. For example, "Choose Tools, Track Changes, Highlight Changes" means that you should click the Tools menu, point to Track Changes, and select the Highlight Changes command.
Boldface type	**Boldface** type is used to indicate text that you enter or type.
Initial Capital Letters	The first letters of the names of menus, dialog boxes, dialog box elements, and commands are capitalized. Example: the Save As dialog box.
Italicized type	*Italicized* type is used to indicate new terms.
Plus sign (+) in text	Keyboard shortcuts are indicated by a plus sign (+) separating two key names. For example, Ctrl+Alt+Delete means that you press the Ctrl, Alt, and Delete keys at the same time.

Design Conventions

newfeature!

This text identifies a new or significantly updated feature in this version of the software.

InsideOut

These are the book's signature tips. In these tips, you'll get the straight scoop on what's going on with the software—inside information on why a feature works the way it does. You'll also find handy workarounds to different software problems.

tip Tips provide helpful hints, timesaving tricks, or alternative procedures related to the task being discussed.

Troubleshooting

Look for these sidebars to find solutions to common problems you might encounter. Troubleshooting sidebars appear next to related information in the chapters. You can also use the Troubleshooting Topics index at the back of the book to look up problems by topic.

Cross-references point you to other locations in the book that offer additional information on the topic being discussed.

 This icon indicates sample files or text found on the companion CD.

caution Cautions identify potential problems that you should look out for when you're completing a task or problems that you must address before you can complete a task.

note Notes offer additional information related to the task being discussed.

Sidebar

The sidebars sprinkled throughout these chapters provide ancillary information on the topic being discussed. Go to sidebars to learn more about the technology or a feature.

Part 1

Setup, Startup, Tune-Up

Chapter 1

Introducing Windows XP

Think you know Microsoft Windows inside out? Think again.

For more than a decade, power users have obsessed over ways to make Windows run faster, work smarter, and crash less often. Through books, magazine articles, and the Web, Windows users have amassed huge collections of keyboard shortcuts, registry hacks, elegant workarounds, and undocumented secrets to help master each succeeding Windows version. And now that Microsoft Windows XP has arrived, much of that hard-earned knowledge is irrelevant or obsolete.

Sorry to have to deliver the bad news, but it's true: From top to bottom, Windows XP is dramatically different from previous Windows versions. The more you think you know about Windows, the more likely you'll feel at least a little disoriented when you begin working with Windows XP. That's especially true if you've spent the past few years mastering Windows 95 and its successors, Windows 98 and Windows Me (Millennium Edition).

Now for the good news: The changes in Windows XP are well worth the time and effort you'll spend unlearning old habits and mastering a new operating system. After you learn your way around Windows XP, we predict you'll appreciate its reliability, security, and smoother way of handling everyday tasks. Our mission in this book is to help you take full advantage of the rich new features in Windows XP while working around this complex operating system's quirks, rough edges, and annoyances. And although the book is published by Microsoft Press, we've taken advantage of our editorial freedom to tell you when we've found a better way than the Windows way.

At Home with Windows XP

This book describes two different versions of Windows XP: Windows XP Professional and Windows XP Home Edition. The two versions are largely identical; Windows XP Professional includes everything in Windows XP Home Edition, plus some additional features targeted toward corporate network users and power users. Near the beginning of each chapter in this book, you'll find a sidebar like this one that points out any version differences in the topics covered by the chapter. The differences are also identified in the chapter's text, but the sidebar gives the Home Edition user a quick rundown of any significant limitations.

This book brings you the detailed, inside information you need to quickly get your bearings in Windows XP and make the right setup and configuration choices the first time. Don't like the default settings? Don't worry. We've uncovered the fastest, easiest ways to get things done, and we also show you how to tweak the radically redesigned Windows XP interface so it works the way you want it to work. We've found plenty of registry hacks and undocumented secrets, too.

For the sake of this book, we assume that you have plenty of experience with Windows 95/98/Me and at least a nodding familiarity with Windows 2000. If that description fits you, read this chapter carefully to learn about the major changes in Windows XP that will most affect you. If you're an experienced Windows 2000 user, some of the information in this chapter may seem familiar, but we recommend that you skim through it anyway, because some changes that aren't immediately obvious can have a big impact on your PC and network. (Pay particular attention to the tricky new security and file-sharing system, which is dramatically different from its Windows 2000 predecessor on home and small business PCs.)

newfeature!
What's New in Windows XP

Windows XP brings together two product families that were previously separate and decidedly unequal. From Windows 2000, it inherits a reliable, generally crash-proof foundation. It adds a host of user-friendly features and system utilities that were previously available only in Windows 98 or Windows Me. For good measure, it tosses in some interface enhancements and new capabilities that were previously available only as third-party add-ins.

Most importantly, Windows XP comes in two distinctly different versions:

- **Windows XP Home Edition.** This budget-priced version is typically bundled with consumer PCs sold for use in homes and very small businesses. It's intended for nontechnical users who don't need to connect to corporate networks and don't want to fuss with complicated system and security options. It's compatible with any desktop or notebook PC that has a single CPU and a single video display.

Chapter 1: Introducing Windows XP

● **Windows XP Professional.** This version includes everything in the Home Edition, plus all the networking and security components required to join a Windows NT/2000/XP domain. If your system configuration includes certain types of high-performance hardware, such as a dual-processor motherboard, you'll need Windows XP Professional to fully utilize it.

Before you read any further, check to see which version of Windows XP is installed on your PC. Open Control Panel's System option and look on the General tab. Figure 1-1 shows what you should expect to see if you're running the initial release of Windows XP Professional. If you've installed a service pack, you'll see its details here, too. (You can read more details about the differences between Windows XP Home Edition and Professional in Appendix A, "Professional or Home Edition: What's the Difference?")

Figure 1-1. The System Properties dialog box supplies detailed information about your Windows version and your hardware configuration.

---

tip **Get fast access to system settings**

You don't have to pass through Control Panel to get to the System Properties dialog box. Hold down the Windows logo key and press Break to open this handy dialog box immediately. No Windows logo key? Create a shortcut to Sysdm.cpl (you'll find it in the %SystemRoot%\System32 folder) and place it anywhere in the Programs menu. Then open the shortcut's properties dialog box and assign it an easy-to-remember keyboard shortcut such as Ctrl+Alt+Shift+S. Another alternative: simply right-click My Computer (on the desktop, on the Start menu, or in a Windows Explorer window) and choose Properties.

Windows XP Professional is a massive collection of code that tries to be all things to all people, from performance-obsessed gamers to buttoned-down corporate executives and spreadsheet jockeys. For the most part, it succeeds. In this book, we cover a broad range of tasks that a well-rounded Windows XP user might tackle at home or at work.

newfeature!
Increased Reliability and Security

If you're upgrading from Windows 2000, the architectural changes in Windows XP are subtle and in some instances practically invisible. But if you're moving up from Windows 95/98 or Windows Me, you'll have to deal with new system utilities (using the Disk Management snap-in instead of Fdisk to create and format hard disk partitions, for instance). You'll also face unfamiliar setup options, such as whether to choose NTFS or stick with FAT32 as the file system for hard disk partitions. And you'll need to understand the new file-sharing system, which is considerably more secure than the minimal password protection used in Windows 95/98 and Windows Me.

For a full explanation of your file-sharing options, see Chapter 13, "Securing Files and Folders."

The payoff for this added complexity is a dramatic decrease in system crashes, hangs, lockups, and mysterious error messages—thanks to the following improvements:

- **New Windows engine.** The designers of Windows XP tossed out every last vestige of the MS-DOS-compatible core code used in Windows 95/98 (and, despite some attempts to hide it, in Windows Me as well). At the heart of both versions of Windows XP is the robust and reliable kernel introduced in Windows 2000. With its fully protected memory model, tightly integrated security, and a hardware abstraction layer (HAL) that protects key system components from poorly written programs, Windows XP is far less likely to crash in everyday use. And when crashes do occur, you can choose from a more powerful set of troubleshooting utilities than those available for earlier Windows versions.

- **Robust system protection tools.** A common source of problems in previous Windows versions is "DLL hell"—the irritating instability that results when poorly written applications replace crucial system files with outdated or incorrect versions. Windows XP monitors these crucial system files, preserving the correct version of the system file while allowing the program you just installed to use its own DLL file. For additional protection, you can use the System Restore utility (shown in Figure 1-2) to create a snapshot of system files and settings so that you can "roll back" to a previous configuration when a new application or device driver causes problems.

Chapter 1: Introducing Windows XP

> **caution**   System Restore is an integral part of a comprehensive data-protection program that should also include a regular backup schedule. Although this utility can help you recover from common configuration errors, it will not protect data files from corruption or accidental deletion, and it can't do anything to recover data that's damaged by a hard drive failure or electrical spike.

> For detailed instructions on how to keep crashes from occurring, see Chapter 25, "Performing Routine Maintenance." To minimize damage caused by crashes that happen in spite of your best efforts, see Chapter 26, "Recovering After a Computer Crash."

● **Device driver rollback.** Windows veterans know that buggy device drivers can make a mess of even the most meticulously maintained system. Windows XP protects you from driver-related woes by warning you when you try to install an unsigned driver that has not been certified as compatible with Windows XP. It also offers the capability to uninstall a driver and restore the previous version—from Safe Mode, if necessary.

> For more information about hardware and Windows XP, see Chapter 6, "Setting Up and Troubleshooting Hardware."

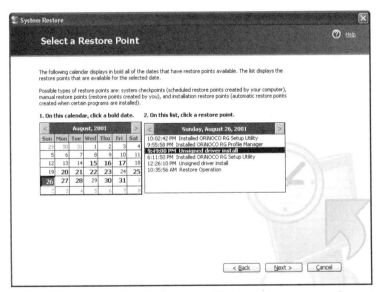

Figure 1-2.   Use the System Restore utility to undo system configuration changes that cause headaches. Windows XP automatically saves files and settings (called restore points) at regular intervals; you can create checkpoints manually as well.

Part 1: Setup, Startup, Tune-Up

- **Security features.** Password-protected logins and the ability to set permissions on files and folders make it possible for you to share a PC with others without allowing them to install unwelcome software (including viruses) or delete important files. A friendly Welcome screen and easy-to-use administrative tools make it especially easy to set up a shared PC at home or in a small office, with each user having a customized desktop and Start menu, plus secure access to protected files.

> For a detailed explanation of how Windows XP lets you control what each user can and can't do, see Chapter 3, "Controlling Access to Your Computer." To learn how to restrict access to personal and sensitive files and folders, see Chapter 13, "Securing Files and Folders." Need instructions on how to share files and printers over a network? You'll find those details in Chapter 32, "Managing Shared Folders and Printers."

newfeature!
Fresh Visual Design

Windows XP offers the most sweeping overhaul of the Windows interface since the introduction of Windows 95. If you choose the new Windows XP interface, you'll notice the following changes right away:

- **Brighter colors.** The default Windows XP color scheme is bolder and edgier than the relatively sedate color combinations used in previous Windows versions. Windows XP takes full advantage of video hardware that is capable of 24-bit and 32-bit true color settings.

- **3-D windows and buttons.** When you choose the Windows XP style, windows and buttons take on a 3-D appearance with rounded edges and sleek shadows. In addition, you'll see subtle shifts in color as you pass the mouse pointer over buttons, tabs, and other interface elements, much the same as those that characterize hot spots on a Web page.

- **Sharper icons.** Every system icon has been reworked for Windows XP. The new icons are brighter and richer looking, because they support color resolutions up to 24-bit (true color). In addition, each icon is available in three sizes, including a super-size 48×48 pixel version that's more than twice as large as the standard 32×32 icons used in previous Windows versions. The extra detail is most useful in the new Tiles view, where two or three lines of annotation can appear alongside the icon to provide additional information.

- **Integrated themes.** Microsoft first introduced desktop themes in the Microsoft Plus! add-in for Windows 95 as a way to save sets of color schemes, fonts, font sizes, sounds, and other interface elements. In Windows XP, theme support is tightly integrated into Control Panel's Display utility and supports changes to common controls, window borders, and menus as well.

newfeature!
Improved Usability for Everyday Tasks

Most of the basic building blocks of the Windows XP user interface are familiar from previous Windows versions—you'll find the desktop, Start button, and taskbar, for example, right where you expect them to be. But dig deeper into menus and dialog boxes and you'll discover hundreds of changes that grew out of testing in Microsoft's usability laboratory. Many of these changes are intended to make Windows computing easier for novice users, but in some cases the hand-holding and extra explanation can unnecessarily slow down power users.

For instance, the default Control Panel view organizes icons into a task-based Category view that requires drilling down an extra level to get to advanced options. As an experienced Windows user, you'll probably prefer the Classic view of Control Panel, where every icon appears in a single folder window. Throughout this book, we'll point out similar places where you can adjust default settings to give yourself faster access to the features you use most.

You can configure Windows XP to use the Classic Start menu style, which is practically indistinguishable from the Windows 2000 interface. But if you're a power user, we recommend that you try out the new Windows XP interface for at least a week. You may discover that some of the interface changes cure long-standing Windows annoyances. Among the productivity-boosting improvements in Windows XP are the following:

- **Friendly Welcome screen.** As the administrator of a Windows XP machine, you define a user account for each person allowed to use that computer. The Welcome screen lists each authorized user; each user clicks his or her name and enters a password (if required) to jump to a personalized desktop and unlock access to private files. On a shared PC, you can switch between users without having to close down running programs or stop a download. You can drop in and check your e-mail or send a quick instant message, for instance, while another user takes a brief break.

- **Fast User Switching.** On a shared home computer, the capability to switch quickly between accounts without having to log off is an absolute killer feature and the single best reason to prefer either edition of Windows XP over previous Windows versions. When you step away from the computer, you can leave documents open and keep your e-mail program running in the background, checking for new messages at regular intervals. The default Windows XP screen saver switches to the Welcome screen after 10 minutes with no keyboard or mouse activity.

- **Start menu improvements.** The redesigned Windows XP Start menu, shown in Figure 1-3 on the next page, uses more on-screen real estate than the Start menu you know so well. By using two columns instead of one, it organizes shortcuts to the programs you use most often, to locations where your personal files are stored, and to system folders and tools.

Part 1: Setup, Startup, Tune-Up

Figure 1-3. The new two-column Start menu offers quicker access to common locations and maintains a dynamic list of shortcuts to the programs you use most often.

- **A cleaner desktop.** In a clean installation, the Windows XP desktop is downright Spartan, with only the Recycle Bin installed there by default. A wizard periodically sweeps across the desktop, offering to move icons that haven't been used recently into an Unused Desktop Shortcuts folder. In a similar vein, Windows XP groups taskbar buttons to avoid the common problem of buttons being so small as to be unusable. If you have five browser windows open, for instance, all those windows will be grouped under a single Internet Explorer button, with a number on the button to tell you how many separate windows are grouped there; click that button to choose from a menu that lists the titles of each individual window.

- **Easier file management.** Windows Explorer gets a thorough overhaul in Windows XP. When a folder window is open, clicking the Folders button toggles the left pane between the familiar Folders tree and the new task pane, containing a set of links that offer quick access to common tasks, shortcuts to related locations, and details about the current selection. The new Tiles view offers an alternate organization of common locations; this view is particularly effective in the My Computer window, as Figure 1-4 shows. Windows Explorer in Windows XP is also much smarter about file associations than earlier versions.

Chapter 1: Introducing Windows XP

Click button to collapse and expand menu

Displays details about the current selection

Figure 1-4. Collapsible menus (left) let you see details about the current selection and choose common actions without having to right-click.

---

tip   **Toggle the Folders tree**

Regardless of which view you use for a given folder, you can click the Folders button to toggle between Windows Explorer's Folders bar and the task pane. Use the double arrows at the right of each menu to collapse or expand the choices shown in that box; in the Details box, the double arrow toggles the display of information about the currently selected file or folder (including previews of image files).

● **Extensive Help and support resources.** As you would expect, the online Help files are filled with tutorials, troubleshooters, and step-by-step instructions, but those static resources are just a start. The HTML-based Help And Support Center shown in Figure 1-5 on the next page takes advantage of your Internet connection to update Help files with headlines from Microsoft's support site. From the Help And Support Center window, you can also search the Microsoft Knowledge Base, access Windows XP newsgroups, connect to Microsoft support, and even run your own help desk using the Remote Assistance feature.

Part 1: Setup, Startup, Tune-Up

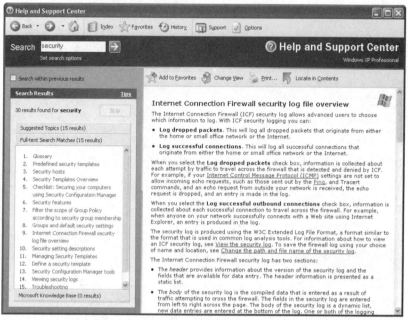

Figure 1-5. The Help And Support Center provides direct access to system utilities and information, including articles from Microsoft's Knowledge Base.

---

tip **Provide personal support**

It never fails: When friends, coworkers, or family members discover that you're a Windows expert, you get pressed into service as an unpaid support technician. If the party asking for help is running any edition of Windows XP and has an active Internet connection, your job is much easier. Have the other person send you a Remote Assistance request; when you accept the request, you connect directly to their computer and can edit registry settings, fix file associations, set System options, and perform just about any other troubleshooting or repair task, just as if you were sitting at the other person's desk.

For more details on how to configure the Help And Support Center and use Remote Assistance, see Chapter 4, "Help and Support Options."

---

newfeature!
Internet Enhancements

As befits a twenty-first-century operating system, Windows XP includes an extensive array of Internet features that go far beyond basic browsing. Three improvements are worthy of special note:

Internet Explorer 6   Windows XP incorporates the most recent version of Microsoft's browser. It gets the same visual overhaul as the rest of Windows, with bright toolbar button images, and it integrates streaming media playback tools into the task pane on the left. But its most worthwhile new capability is "under the hood," where Internet Explorer 6 incorporates controls you can use to protect your privacy. By default, the browser uses privacy policies to determine what personally identifiable information can be stored by a Web site; if you want greater control over your personal data, you can build a custom policy that determines on a site-by-site basis which cookies are allowed and which are blocked.

> To learn how privacy policies and cookie controls work, see "Managing Cookies," page 782.

Internet Connection Firewall   The explosion in popularity of "always on" Internet connections, such as cable modems and DSL hook-ups, has a dark side. Even a technically unsophisticated hacker can break into a poorly secured computer and access private files or plant a Trojan horse program. Unlike any previous Windows version, Windows XP includes a bare-bones firewall that stops the most common attacks.

> If you already use a third-party firewall program such as ZoneAlarm, see "Limitations of Internet Connection Firewall," page 809.

Internet Connection Sharing   Every version of Windows since Windows 98 Second Edition has included software that allows you to share a single Internet connection over a home or small business network. Windows XP streamlines the setup process and adds the capability for remote users to stop and start a dial-up connection on the gateway PC.

newfeature!
Integrated Tools for Working with Digital Media

If you've used previous Windows versions to work with digital images or music files, you've no doubt struggled with cumbersome third-party utilities and complex file-transfer procedures. With an assortment of wizards and new features, Windows XP streamlines the experience of working with all types of digital media.

Digital Music

Windows Media Player 8 is included in both editions of Windows XP. As Figure 1-6 on the next page shows, it's especially adept at managing your music collection. (Some computers that come with Windows pre-installed do not include Windows Media Player. You can download the latest version from *http://www.microsoft.com/windows/windowsmedia/players.asp.*)

Part 1: Setup, Startup, Tune-Up

Figure 1-6. Use Windows Media Player 8 to copy tracks from music CDs to files on your hard disk. Then create custom playlists and copy the music to portable players and even custom CDs.

Use Windows Media Player to accomplish any of these everyday tasks:

- Play music CDs and download information about the artist, album, and tracks from the Internet.

- Copy ("rip") tracks from a CD and store them as digital music files on your hard disk. Windows Media Player 8 supports the popular MP3 format and Windows Media Audio (WMA) files.

- Organize digital media files in the My Music folder. Windows XP stores downloaded information about each track in the properties for the digital music file and uses downloaded CD cover images to identify each folder.

- Copy music files from your hard drive to a portable music player, or use a CD-R/CD-RW drive to create custom CDs.

> For detailed information about digital music features in Windows XP, see Chapter 17, "Using Windows Media Player."

Digital Pictures

Thanks to digital cameras, you no longer have to pay for expensive film developing. Figure 1-7 shows the Scanner And Camera Wizard, which does a superb job of connecting to newer digital cameras and flash memory cards so that you can quickly preview captured images and transfer them to your hard drive. By adjusting a few options, you can automate this process so that transferring digital images requires almost no extra effort from you.

Chapter 1: Introducing Windows XP

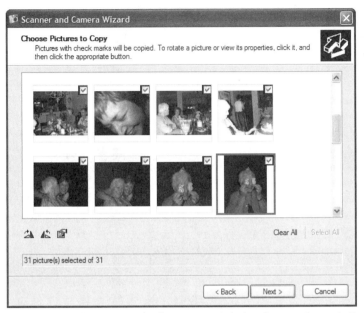

Figure 1-7. The Scanner And Camera Wizard walks you through the process of transferring images from an external device to your hard disk.

Managing a large collection of digital photos is easier, too, thanks to file viewing tools built into Windows Explorer. Figure 1-8 shows the new Filmstrip view of the My Pictures folder. Each image in the folder appears as a thumbnail along the bottom of

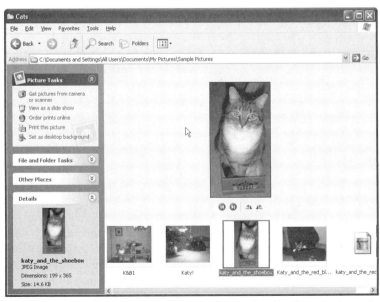

Figure 1-8. The new Filmstrip view combines thumbnails and a large Preview area to make it easy to quickly inspect the contents of a folder full of digital photos.

the window, with the currently selected image visible in a much larger preview area that occupies the top of the folder window. You can also view the contents of a folder as a slide show.

The My Pictures folder includes links to commercial services where you can order professionally printed copies of digital images. If you have a color printer, use the Photo Printing Wizard (shown in Figure 1-9) to crop and resize images; then use the layout tools to combine multiple images on a single sheet of paper.

Select a predefined layout here

Preview the results here

Figure 1-9. The Photo Printing Wizard allows you to lay out multiple images on a single sheet, to avoid wasting expensive paper and other supplies.

To learn how to set up a digital camera or scanner and manage image files in Windows XP, see Chapter 18, "Organizing and Editing Images."

Digital Video

If you have the correct hardware, Windows XP gives you access to a passable set of video playback and editing tools.

● On any system equipped with a DVD drive and a compatible decoder (software or hardware), you can play back prerecorded DVD discs in Windows Media Player. This feature is especially useful for frequent travelers with Windows XP-equipped notebooks; skip the in-flight movie and watch a DVD from your own collection instead.

- Use the Windows Movie Maker program to capture video from a camcorder or VCR; then edit it and add titles, narration, and other effects. No one will confuse Movie Maker with a professional strength video editing package, but its capabilities are good enough for casual use. It's particularly effective at compressing video clips down to sizes that can be sent easily via e-mail or posted on a Web page.

newfeature!
Network Smarts

Windows XP was designed from the ground up to work well on networks of all sizes. In most cases, setting up a simple home network is automatic.

- **Network Setup Wizard.** Although you can choose to configure networking components manually, Windows XP automates most network configuration tasks with a simple straightforward wizard. Use the wizard to set up a simple home network, configure Internet Connection Sharing, create connections to dial-up Internet accounts, or connect to a corporate network over a virtual private network (VPN).

---

tip   **Quickly fix connectivity problems**

Are you having trouble connecting to other computers on your local area network? If your network uses a hardware firewall that assigns IP addresses to each machine and you're certain you've configured all other components correctly, check to see whether the Internet Connection Firewall is enabled. That component can effectively block communication between PCs on the network.

For step-by-step network setup instructions, see Chapter 30, "Setting Up a Small Network."

- **Wireless access.** Out of the box, both editions of Windows XP support wireless networks that follow the IEEE 802.11b standard, including Agere's (formerly Lucent) Orinoco and Cisco's Aironet systems. These solutions are appropriate in homes and small businesses where stringing Category 5 cable is impractical; they also allow notebook users to access public wireless systems such as those found in an increasing number of airports and coffee shops.

- **Remote Desktop connections.** One of the coolest features in Windows XP Professional is its support for remote connections to another PC. When you allow remote connections (this feature is disabled by default), anyone with an authorized user account can log in to the machine over a local area network or across the Internet, using the dialog box shown in Figure 1-10 on the next page. Use this feature to access your work PC from home

Chapter 1

(eliminating the need to keep files in sync between two PCs). On a home network, you might use this feature to connect to a Windows XP Professional computer from another PC so that you can run an application without having to install it on the remote computer.

> For full instructions on how to set up and use the Remote Desktop feature, see "Setting Up a Remote Desktop Connection to Another Computer," page 1095.

Figure 1-10. Using the Remote Desktop feature, you can connect to a Windows XP Professional machine from another PC, even if the remote computer is using an earlier Windows version.

What's New in Service Pack 1

In the fall of 2002, about a year following the release of Windows XP, Microsoft released Service Pack 1 (more commonly called SP1) for Windows XP. A service pack is a collection of program updates, bug fixes, and security patches all rolled into a single package that you can install on a computer running Windows XP.

The changes that are outwardly visible in SP1 are few and generally subtle. For example, in a security-related enhancement the message that appears when you download a file using Internet Explorer has been modified to provide a clearer warning of the potential dangers of downloaded files, as shown in Figure 1-11.

Chapter 1: Introducing Windows XP

> **note** New computers should have SP1 pre-installed, but if your computer does not yet have SP1, don't despair; SP1 is included on this book's companion CD. If you don't have the CD,you can download and install SP1 using Windows Update. (For information about Windows Update, see "Service Packs, Patches, and Windows Update," page 64.) If you don't have a fast Internet connection, you can order the service pack on CD directly from Microsoft.
>
> How can you tell whether you already have SP1? Right-click My Computer and choose Properties to open the System Properties dialog box; the General tab shows "Service Pack 1" under the System heading if SP1 has been installed.

Figure 1-11.   The download warning in SP1 (right) provides more information about the file and a caution about files from unknown sources.

Another noticeable change in SP1 is the addition of a Set Program Access And Defaults option in Add Or Remove Programs on the Start menu. This option, shown in Figure 1-12 on the next page, eases access to your favorite Web browser, e-mail program, media player, and other components while hiding the others. Before the release of SP1, Microsoft components often opened by default even after you installed components from another company. For details about Set Program Access And Defaults, see "Selecting a Web Browser and Other Middleware Components," page 76.

Most of the other, less visible changes fall in one of the following categories:

● **Improvements in security and reliability.** SP1 includes literally hundreds of fixes to a variety of problems and security vulnerabilities—everything from "contact information for Epson Stylus Photo is incorrect" to "unchecked buffer in Universal Plug and Play can lead to system compromise." Patches for many of these problems were available as individual "hotfixes" through Windows Update prior to SP1's release; the service pack rolls up all these patches. Although most of the fixes apply to core Windows files, some of the accessory programs included with Windows (such as Windows Messenger and Windows Movie Maker) have new versions with a handful of perceptible differences.

Chapter 1

Figure 1-12. With this new option in Add Or Remove Programs, you can specify default programs, whether they're from Microsoft or another company.

When a program crashes ("terminates abnormally" in polite company), the Online Crash Analysis feature offers to send information about the crash to Microsoft for examination. Although some users decline to send information because of privacy concerns, many users have participated to the benefit of all. Microsoft engineers have collected the information needed to solve many of the reported problems; these solutions are incorporated into SP1. Furthermore, they have a large sampling of data that enables them to concentrate development efforts on actual errors instead of perceived problems. For information about Online Crash Analysis, see "When It's Time to Ask for Outside Help…," page 970.

In addition, Windows has undergone a thorough code review as part of Microsoft's Trustworthy Computing initiative announced by Bill Gates in January 2002. Changes resulting from this code review are incorporated in SP1.

● **Support for new types of hardware.** In addition to drivers for more devices than were included with the original release of Windows XP, SP1 includes support for a whole new class of devices that use USB 2.0, the latest version of universal serial bus technology. SP1 also includes the underpinnings for Windows XP Media Center Edition (a version for PCs that form the hub of a home entertainment center), Windows XP Tablet PC Edition (a version for portable computers with stylus input), and Windows CE for Smart Displays (a version for portable secondary display monitors). Each of these hardware types requires Windows XP with SP1, but without the accompanying hardware and the software that comes with it, you won't see any difference in Windows XP.

Chapter 1: Introducing Windows XP

● **Changes in Windows Product Activation (WPA).** WPA was implemented with Windows XP to combat software piracy—the use of unlicensed versions of Windows. With SP1, a change has been made to thwart the misuse of a particular volume license key (one that can be used an unlimited number of times) that has been widely distributed in the warez (illicit software) community. Users who have installed Windows XP using that key will not be able to install SP1, nor will they be able to install any future service packs or hotfixes from Microsoft.

The other change to WPA removes an obstacle that sometimes impeded legitimate Windows users. With the original version of WPA, if you change a number of hardware components beyond a certain threshold, Windows requires you to activate your copy of Windows (via an Internet connection or by telephone) before it allows you to log on. (This is done because Windows presumes that a computer with that many different components must be a different machine.) This immediate lockout can be a great inconvenience if it happens to occur while you're unable to activate (for example, on an airplane with no phone or Internet access) or if you're repeatedly swapping hardware in and out to troubleshoot a hardware problem. With SP1, you now have a three-day grace period for so-called "out-of-tolerance" situations.

For more information about WPA, see "Activating Windows XP," page 38.

● **Support for the .NET Framework.** At the time of this book's publication, the .NET Framework, which is an optional component of SP1, is of interest primarily to software developers, who are using it as the foundation for a new generation of software applications. When those applications are more widely available, however, everyone will need the .NET Framework, which provides the common elements used by all .NET programs. The .NET Framework is roughly analogous to the Visual Basic runtime library (Vbrun*xx*.dll) required by most compiled Visual Basic programs.

Chapter 2

Installing and Configuring Windows XP

Some Windows users never have to deal with the Windows Setup program. If you buy a new computer with Microsoft Windows XP pre-installed, you may be able to use it forever without having to do anything more than minor maintenance.

For upgraders, hobbyists, and inveterate tinkerers, however, the Windows XP Setup program is inescapable. Knowing how to upgrade properly or perform a clean install can spell the difference between a smooth-running system and a box of troubles. And if you're responsible for multiple Windows installations, you'll want to delve into the Deployment Tools package (which resides on the Windows XP CD) for time-saving strategies.

In this chapter, we'll explain the subtleties and intricacies of the Windows Setup program, explore the workings of the Files And Settings Transfer Wizard, and show you how to set up a computer with multiple versions of Windows.

Avoiding Compatibility Problems

Many programs originally written for Windows 95, Windows 98, or Windows Me won't run properly under Windows XP. Likewise, some hardware devices use drivers that aren't compatible with Windows XP. The worst possible time to find out about either type of compatibility problem is right after you complete the setup process, when you try to use a favorite program or device.

At Home with Windows XP

Windows XP Home Edition is indistinguishable from the Professional edition when it comes to the core tasks of installing the operating system, updating system files, transferring files and settings between computers, and configuring startup options. Some of the advanced setup options described in this chapter, including the use of answer files and disk imaging, are most commonly used in corporate settings, where Windows XP Professional is a better choice than Home Edition.

To spare yourself unnecessary headaches, run the Windows XP Upgrade Advisor before installing Windows XP on a system on which a previous version of Windows is already installed. You can start this abbreviated version of Setup directly from the menu that appears when you insert the Windows XP CD—choose Check System Compatibility, and then click Check My System Automatically. If the CD's opening menu doesn't appear, type *d*:\i386\winnt32 -checkupgradeonly (replacing *d* with the correct drive letter, of course) at any command prompt.

When you start the Windows Setup program on a system running Windows 98 or Windows Me, it asks you to enter the product ID, checks for dynamic updates, and then runs a slightly different version of the Upgrade Advisor, giving you the option to check hardware only or to check all installed programs as well. The full option produces the same report you'd see if you had run this utility on its own. If you discover a serious incompatibility, you can (and should) cancel Setup; if the Upgrade Report lists only minor problems, you can continue with confidence.

---

tip   **Use dynamic updates**

When you upgrade over an existing Windows version, Setup offers to check for dynamic updates. If you have an active Internet connection, be sure to take advantage of this option. Dynamic updates can include service packs, updated drivers for hardware detected on your system, and upgrade packs for programs you're currently running. Rolling these updates into Windows Setup saves you time and hassle and ensures that you don't have to install a bunch of updates immediately after you boot Windows XP for the first time.

The resulting report lists problems that you might encounter during the upgrade process, including hardware and software incompatibilities. For some programs, you might be instructed to download upgrade packs. When upgrading over Windows 98 or Windows Me, you might need to uninstall a program before setting up Windows XP, and then reinstall the program after Setup is complete.

Figure 2-1 shows a typical Upgrade Advisor report. Scroll through the entire list to identify any urgent warnings or compatibility issues that require your immediate attention.

Chapter 2: Installing and Configuring Windows XP

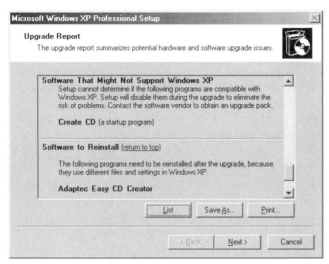

Figure 2-1. Read this upgrade report carefully before continuing with Setup. In some cases, you might need to uninstall programs or find new drivers before going any further.

For the most part, you can safely follow these general guidelines: Business and consumer applications that are compatible with Windows 2000 should work with Windows XP. Applications that were written for Windows 98 or Windows Me are more likely to cause problems, especially if they use virtual device drivers (VxDs). In addition, some programs install differently on Windows 98 and Windows Me than on Windows 2000 and Windows XP—they use different program files or write values to different registry locations, for example. The Upgrade Advisor should flag any such programs, and if they're available, Windows will automatically download upgrade packs as part of the dynamic update process.

When upgrading, be especially vigilant with utility software that works at the system level. If you use a disk partitioning tool, antivirus program, personal firewall software, or other system utility that was originally written for a previous Windows version, it's prudent to assume that it won't work properly with Windows XP. Always look for upgraded versions that are certified to be compatible with Windows XP before continuing with Setup.

InsideOut

The Upgrade Advisor is thorough, but it's not exhaustive. If you've installed a program or hardware device that is absolutely essential to your daily productivity, don't assume that it passes muster just because the Upgrade Advisor doesn't flag it as a problem device. Microsoft's hardware compatibility list (*http://www.microsoft.com/hcl*) is regularly updated, and it often includes links to additional information and updated drivers. For software, check the manufacturer's Web site for a definitive assurance of compatibility with Windows XP.

Chapter 2

Preparing to Install Windows XP

Before you install Windows XP, run through this simple checklist:

Confirm that your hardware satisfies the system requirements
Microsoft's official spec sheet says the bare minimum configuration includes a 233 MHz processor from the Pentium/Celeron family or the AMD K6/ Athlon/Duron family (or compatible); 64 MB of RAM; 1.5 GB of spare disk space; and a video adapter capable of Super VGA (800×600) resolution. The recommended configuration is at least a 300 MHz CPU with 128 MB of RAM. You'll also need a mouse or other pointing device, a keyboard, and a CD-ROM or DVD drive.

Chapter 2

> **tip**   Don't skimp on RAM
>
> Defining an acceptable level of performance is strictly a matter of personal preference. The speed of the CPU is probably the least critical element of a Windows XP system. A fast hard disk and gobs of memory will do much more to keep a system running smoothly with multiple applications and multiple users. If you plan to use memory-intensive programs such as Microsoft Outlook, Adobe PhotoShop, or Macromedia's Shockwave, don't settle for less than 256 MB of RAM. And if you plan to take advantage of Fast User Switching to allow multiple users to log on simultaneously, you'll need still more RAM—figure on 64 MB for each additional user.

Gather network details   If you need to supply a static IP address and subnet mask, collect this information and have it at hand. Likewise, be sure you know the name of your workgroup or domain. If you plan to set up your network along with the rest of Windows, be sure you're physically connected to the network or that your wireless hardware is working properly.

Check hardware and software compatibility   If you need any updated drivers or upgrade packs, download them before you run Setup, and burn them to CD or copy them to floppy disks so they'll be available when you need them.

Back up your data files and system settings   If you're planning an upgrade, don't underestimate Murphy's Law. Use a reliable backup program or the Files And Settings Transfer Wizard (described in "Moving Windows Settings and Files," page 51) to make a safe copy of important data.

Disable antivirus software and other system utilities   The Upgrade Report should identify utilities that might interfere with Setup. To be on the safe side, disable any system utility before getting started.

Chapter 2: Installing and Configuring Windows XP

Setting Up Windows XP

When setting up either edition of Windows XP, you need to first choose one of three installation strategies, each with its own set of pros and cons:

- **Clean install.** As the name implies, this installation option sets up a fresh new copy of Windows XP, completely replacing any previous version of Windows on the partition where it's set up and erasing all other files on that partition. Although you can start a clean install by running Setup from an earlier version of Windows, it is much simpler to do so by booting directly from the CD. In either case, you can use an existing partition or define and format partitions during Setup.

- **Upgrade over an existing Windows version.** You can upgrade to Windows XP Home Edition or Professional from Windows 98, Windows 98 Second Edition, or Windows Millennium Edition. You can also upgrade to Windows XP Professional from Windows NT Workstation 4 (Service Pack 6) or Windows 2000 Professional (with or without service packs). If you're currently running Windows 3.1 or Windows 95, you cannot upgrade to any version of Windows XP and must perform a clean install. In all upgrade scenarios, Setup preserves most user settings and installed programs and attempts to upgrade device drivers to Windows XP–compatible versions.

- **Side-by-side (multiboot) installation.** Use this option (a variation of the clean install process) when you want to preserve an existing copy of Windows. When Setup is finished, you'll be able to choose your OS from a boot menu. You must install the new version on a separate partition; installing multiple Windows versions on a single partition is a recipe for disaster.

Choosing between a clean install and an upgrade is not a cut-and-dried decision. Even on systems that meet the requirements for upgrading, a clean install offers the assurance that you're wiping out all traces of any previous Windows problems caused by installing and uninstalling programs, downloading Web-based components, and over-tweaking the computer's settings. Starting with a clean registry and a solid base of Windows system files should give your computer an opportunity to deliver full performance, unburdened by the past.

On the other hand, an upgrade is sometimes the only way to guarantee that a specific program or driver will work properly. We've seen software and hardware drivers that work well under Windows 2000 but refuse to install properly after a clean Windows XP setup; in many cases, these programs and drivers will continue to work if you upgrade to Windows XP. If you're experiencing this problem, the best choice may be a hybrid of the two approaches. Start with a clean install of Windows 2000 and add any required programs and drivers. After verifying that everything works properly, upgrade to Windows XP.

Troubleshooting

During setup, some peripherals don't work properly.

Check your system BIOS. An outdated BIOS can cause problems with disk partitioning, power management, peripheral configuration, and other crucial low-level functions. To find out whether an update is available, check with the manufacturer of your computer or its motherboard. Identifying the BIOS and tracking down the appropriate source for updates isn't always easy; you'll find detailed information at the indispensable (and thoroughly independent) Wim's BIOS (*http://www.wimsbios.com*).

After verifying that you're running the most recent BIOS version, use the BIOS setup program to select the "non–Plug and Play operating system" option. This advice may seem counterintuitive—after all, Windows XP is indeed a Plug and Play operating system. However, this setting was intended for use with earlier Windows versions, and if it's set incorrectly it can prevent the Windows XP boot loader from accessing devices at startup.

Most Windows Setup options are fairly straightforward. A clean setup consists of the following four distinct steps:

- **File copy.** This step copies the Windows Setup files to a folder on the partition where they can run when you restart the system. If you boot from CD, Setup skips this step and loads the files directly from the CD.

- **Text mode setup.** On a clean install, this step is where you select (and if necessary, create and format) the partition you want to use for the Windows XP system files.

- **GUI mode setup.** This is the graphical portion of Windows Setup. In a clean interactive installation, this is where you select regional settings (language and time zone, for instance) and enter details such as the product key, computer name, and administrator password.

- **Windows Welcome.** This is the final portion of Setup, where you have the option to create user accounts and activate Windows. System manufacturers sometimes modify these options to add their own logos, custom registration screens, and additional options or features. In previous versions, this stage was also known as Out Of Box Experience, or OOBE. The OOBE label refers to your experience when you take a new computer out of the box and set it up for the first time.

Chapter 2: Installing and Configuring Windows XP

> **note** All the files used for this portion of Setup are included in the Oobe folder in the System32 folder. If you like the mood music that runs during this portion of Setup, for instance, you can add it to your list of favorite Media Clips. Open the %SystemRoot%\System32\Oobe\Images folder, right-click Title.wma, and choose Add To Playlist.

Performing a Clean Install

The simplest setup scenario of all is installing Windows XP in a newly created partition on a system that does not currently have any version of Windows installed (or, as an alternative, to wipe out a partition containing an existing version of Windows and completely replace it with a clean install of Windows XP). The safest way to embark on a clean install is to boot from the Windows XP CD. Insert the Windows CD and restart your computer. Watch for a boot prompt; typically, you need to press a key to boot from the CD; after the setup process begins, you can follow the instructions as outlined in this section.

> **note** For a bootable CD to work properly, you must set the boot order in the BIOS so that the CD drive appears ahead of the hard disk drive and any other bootable media; we recommend setting the CD drive as the first boot device, followed by the hard disk, floppy disk, and any other bootable devices, in whichever order you prefer. The boot options available for every computer are different, as is the technique for accessing the BIOS setup program. During boot, watch for a message that tells you which key to press for setup. If you're lucky, the BIOS setup program on your computer includes a Boot tab where you can specify the order of boot devices; if this option isn't immediately apparent, look for a page called Advanced CMOS Settings or something similar.

Most computers that meet the minimum requirements for Windows XP include the capability to boot from a CD-ROM drive. In some relatively uncommon configurations, however, this option isn't available. This problem is most likely to affect you if your CD-ROM is connected to a SCSI adapter that doesn't allow booting from a CD, or if you're trying to install Windows XP on a notebook computer that doesn't include an integrated CD drive. Try one of these alternatives to work around the problem:

- Start your computer from a Windows 98/Me emergency boot disk. This floppy disk includes generic CD drivers that allow you to access most IDE and SCSI drives. From the MS-DOS prompt, run the SmartDrive disk-caching utility (Smartdrv.exe), and then start Windows Setup using the Winnt.exe command. (Because this program is running from MS-DOS, you can't use the 32-bit Setup program, Winnt32.exe.)

---

tip **Don't skip SmartDrive**

If you have to copy files from a CD to your hard disk using MS-DOS, the SmartDrive utility is essential. Without this helper, copying the Setup files can take hours; with SmartDrive installed, the process practically flies by. Look for the Smartdrv.exe file on the MS-DOS startup disk. If it's not there, you can copy it to your boot floppy from the \Windows\Command folder of any version of Windows 95/98/Me.

- If you can access the Windows XP CD from your previous Windows version and you have a FAT32 partition that is separate from the one on which you plan to install Windows XP, copy the i386 folder from the CD to that partition. (If you have only a single partition available, you'll be unable to perform a clean install using this technique, because you won't be able to wipe out the current system partition without also erasing your Setup files. Likewise, if the second partition is formatted using NTFS, you will not be able to access it from a Windows 98/Me boot floppy.) Then restart the computer using the Windows 98/Me emergency boot disk and run Setup from a command prompt, again using the Winnt command.

---

note Where does Setup install Windows XP system files? The exact name of the folder varies. On a clean install, Setup creates a top-level folder called Windows on the drive you designate and then copies system files there. On an upgrade, Setup uses the current path for %WinDir%—for Windows 98 or Windows Me, that's typically C:\Windows; for Windows NT 4 and Windows 2000, the drive letter may vary, but the name of the system folder is usually \Winnt. When performing a clean install, you can specify a different folder name, but your safest choice is to use the default name.

Whether you started from a previous Windows version or booted from a CD, your next stop (after Setup restarts, of course) will be a series of text-mode Setup screens. If your system currently contains a working version of Windows XP, you'll see a screen that offers to repair the installation for you. Press Esc to bypass this screen and reach a disk setup screen similar to the one shown in Figure 2-2.

From this screen, you can do any of the following tasks:

Select an existing partition on which to install Windows XP   Use this option if you already created and formatted an empty partition in preparation for setting up Windows, or if you plan to install Windows XP on a preexisting partition that currently contains data or programs but no operating system. Do not choose this option if a previous version of Windows is already installed on the selected partition. The result in that case might be to leave behind unwanted system files and leftovers from previously installed programs, defeating the purpose of doing a clean install.

Chapter 2: Installing and Configuring Windows XP

```
Windows XP Professional Setup

    The following list shows the existing partitions and
    unpartitioned space on this computer.

    Use the UP and DOWN ARROW keys to select an item in the list.

        • To set up Windows XP on the selected item, press ENTER.
        • To create a partition in the unpartitioned space, press C.
        • To delete the selected partition, press D.

    1999 MB Disk 0 at Id 0 on bus 0 on atapi [MBR]
            Unpartitioned space                    1998 MB








    ENTER=Install  C=Create Partition  F3=Quit
```

Figure 2-2. This disk management screen is visible only if you boot from the Windows XP CD or choose the option to specify the installation partition.

Create a new partition from unpartitioned space Use this option to set up one or more partitions on a new drive or on an existing drive after deleting partitions. By default, Setup offers to use all unpartitioned space on the current disk. You can specify a smaller partition size if you want to subdivide the disk into multiple drives.

Delete an existing partition Choose this option if you want to do a clean install on a drive that currently contains an earlier version of Windows. Because this operation deletes data irretrievably, you must respond to at least two "Are you sure?" confirmation requests. After deleting the partition, you can create a new one and select it as the destination for your Windows XP installation.

Troubleshooting

Your system crashes after text-mode Setup is complete.

The most common cause of a Stop error (also known as the *Blue Screen of Death*, or *BSOD*) during Setup is a missing or incompatible driver for a disk subsystem. If your computer includes a high-performance IDE controller (typically identified in the BIOS as ATA-66 or ATA-100) or a SCSI boot device, Windows XP might not include a compatible driver for that controller.

The best solution to this dilemma is to download a driver that is compatible with Windows XP (in most cases, a driver designed for Windows 2000 will work just as well). Copy the driver files to a floppy disk, and restart your system. When text mode Setup begins, look for a prompt along the bottom of the screen that asks you whether you

(continued)

> **Troubleshooting** *(continued)* have a storage device that uses a custom driver. Press F6 at this point; when Setup finishes loading its files, it will prompt you to supply the floppy disk containing the custom driver.
>
> If you can't find a compatible driver for your high-speed IDE controller, you can usually continue with Setup by shutting down your system and switching the drive cables to the standard IDE controller (you may need to adjust BIOS options as well). Disk performance will suffer somewhat, but you'll be able to complete Setup using the built-in IDE drivers. You can supply the correct drivers (and switch the controller cables) later.

Upgrading a Previous Windows Version

To upgrade to Windows XP, start your current version of Windows, insert the Windows XP CD, and choose Install Windows XP from the Welcome To Microsoft Windows XP menu. Do not boot from the CD and try to perform an upgrade; that won't work. (If you prefer working at a command prompt in Windows, skip the CD menu and type *d*:\i386\Winnt32.exe, substituting the correct letter of your CD-ROM drive for *d*.) On the first page of the Windows Setup Wizard, select Upgrade (Recommended) and click Next.

If you choose to upgrade, the Windows Setup program asks you to enter a few pieces of information, including the product key; the remainder of the process continues completely unattended. Setup replaces your existing Windows files, but it preserves user settings, such as desktop appearance, color schemes, network connections, and so on. It also retains the programs you have installed and all their settings. (As noted earlier in this chapter, the Upgrade Advisor report identifies any programs that are incompatible with Windows XP.) After several reboots that typically require no attention from you, the upgrade installation completes, and you're ready to pick up where you left off—with Windows XP as your new operating system.

After the upgrade is complete, run through the following checklist to confirm that the process went smoothly and to clean up any loose ends:

1 **Reset passwords for migrated user accounts.** When upgrading over an installation of Windows 98 or Windows Me, Setup adds an account for each user that had a profile in the previous operating system, but discards the passwords for each such account. As administrator, you can manually add each user's password.

2 **Run the Network Setup Wizard.** The upgrade should preserve your network and Internet settings. The Network Setup Wizard helps set up file sharing and enables Internet Connection Firewall.

3 **Check that all essential programs and devices work properly.** Don't assume that the Upgrade Advisor was 100 percent accurate. Be sure to test each of your programs and devices to make sure they're operating as you expect. If you encounter serious problems, you can try to fix them or uninstall Windows XP and restore your previous operating system.

4 **Consider upgrading your system drive to NTFS.** On an upgrade from Windows 98 or Windows Me, the Setup program does not automatically convert drives to NTFS but leaves them in FAT32 format. If you're satisfied that your system is working properly, you can significantly tighten security by using the Convert utility to change the format to NTFS.

> For more details about converting drives to NTFS, see "NTFS or FAT32: Which Disk Format Should You Choose?" page 920.

5 **Save your Administrator password.** On an upgrade to Windows XP Professional, you're required to set a password for the built-in Administrator account (in Home Edition, this password is intentionally left blank). Write this password down and squirrel it away in a safe place. (And, no, a sticky note on the side of your monitor is not a safe place!)

Installing Windows XP on a Computer with Other Operating Systems

If your computer already has a 32-bit version of Windows installed *and* you have at least two disk partitions defined, you can install a clean copy of Windows XP without disturbing your existing Windows installation. At boot time, you choose your Windows version from a startup menu. Although this is typically called a dual-boot system, it's more accurate to call it a multiboot configuration, because you can install multiple copies of Windows NT, Windows 2000, and Windows XP.

Having the capability to choose your operating system at startup is handy if you have a program or device that simply won't work under Windows XP. When you need to use the legacy program or device, you can boot into your other Windows version without too much fuss. This capability is also useful for software developers, who need to be able to test how their programs work under different operating systems. For experienced Windows users, installing a second copy of Windows XP in its own partition can also be helpful as a way to experiment with a program or device driver that is not certified to be compatible with Windows XP without possibly compromising a working system. After you finish setting up the second, clean version of Windows XP, you'll see an additional entry on the startup menu that corresponds to your new installation. (The newly installed version is the default menu choice; it runs automatically if 30 seconds pass and you don't make a choice.) Experiment with the program or driver and see how well it works. If, after testing thoroughly, you're satisfied that the program is safe to use, you can add it to the Windows XP installation you use every day. If it causes problems, you can remove the program or driver.

> **tip** Use third-party utilities to manage partitions
>
> Although you can install multiple copies of Windows NT, Windows 2000, and Windows XP, you can have only one copy of Windows 95, Windows 98, or Windows Me on a multiboot system that is managed by the Windows XP boot manager. If you want to be able to choose from two or more Windows versions from the Windows 95/98/Me product line in addition to Windows XP, you need to use a third-party boot manager program. PowerQuest's highly regarded PartitionMagic (*http://www.powerquest.com/ partitionmagic*) includes a capable utility called BootMagic. (Be sure to check compatibility carefully; PartitionMagic version 6.0 and earlier will not work properly with Windows XP.) If you want an alternate boot manager and don't need partition management software, BootIt NG from Terabyte Unlimited (*http://www.terabyteunlimited.com*) is compatible with Windows XP.

To add Windows XP to a system where an existing version of Windows is already installed, first make sure that you have an available partition (or unformatted disk space) separate from the partition that contains the system files for your current Windows version.

InsideOut

There is one (and only one) circumstance in which it is desirable to install a fresh copy of Windows XP on a partition that already contains Windows system files. This option is relevant if you have only a single disk partition available and you're unable to start your existing installation of Windows XP even after using all the repair techniques described in Chapter 26, "Recovering After a Computer Crash." In that case, you might choose to boot from your Windows XP CD and perform a clean install in a new folder on the same partition. After Setup is complete, you should be able to access your data files through the new Windows XP installation. Use this option as a last resort, and then only to recover data so that you can restore it after fixing the underlying problem, wiping the hard drive clean, and reinstalling Windows XP.

The target partition can be a separate partition on the same physical disk, or it can be on a different hard disk. If your system contains a single disk with a single partition used as drive C, you cannot safely create a multiboot system unless you add a new disk or use third-party software such as PartitionMagic to shrink the existing partition and create a new partition from the free space. The new partition does not need to be empty; however, it should not contain system files for another Windows installation.

Follow these steps to set up Windows XP on a multiboot system:

1 After starting your current Windows version, insert the Windows XP CD.

2 From the Welcome To Microsoft Windows XP menu, choose Install Windows XP.

Chapter 2: Installing and Configuring Windows XP

If the Welcome menu doesn't appear, CD AutoPlay is probably disabled on your computer. In that case, open the Run dialog box and then type *d*:**\i386 \Winnt32.exe** (substitute the correct letter of your CD-ROM drive for *d*).

3 From the first Windows Setup dialog box, select New Installation (Advanced) from the Installation Type list. Click Next to continue.

4 When prompted, accept the End User License Agreement (EULA) and enter the 25-character product key.

5 In the Setup Options dialog box, click the Advanced Options button.

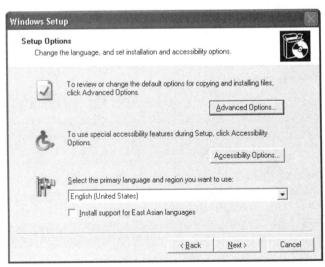

6 In the Advanced Options dialog box, select I Want To Choose The Install Drive Letter And Partition During Setup, as shown on the next page.

Part 1: Setup, Startup, Tune-Up

caution This option is crucial to a successful multiboot installation! If you get distracted and forget to select this option, the Setup program will automatically upgrade your existing Windows installation and you will lose your current operating system.

7 Click through the remaining steps of the wizard and allow the computer to restart. At that point, you will start in text-mode Setup, where you can specify the disk and partition on which you want to install Windows XP.

The Setup program automatically handles details of adding the newly installed operating system to the startup menu.

Avoiding Dual-Boot Disasters

We can't say it strongly enough: Do not install two or more versions of Windows on a single partition! Doing so can cause serious problems with applications, many of which reside in the \Program Files folder on the boot partition (the partition where the operating system is installed).

Many programs use different versions of executable files and dynamic link libraries for Windows 95/98/Me and Windows NT/2000/XP. If you try to share such a program between two Windows versions, it won't work properly in at least one Windows version. In addition, you may experience these problems:

● Program preferences, options, and settings you've chosen in one operating system don't show up when you use the other operating system because each stores its own registry entries.

● If you uninstall an application, its entries still show up on the Start menu, on the Add/Remove Programs list, and throughout the registry of the other operating system—yet the program files are gone.

You might encounter still other problems with multiple operating systems on a single partition. And if you call Microsoft Product Support Services for help with such problems, you'll be told—politely, to be sure—that you need to reformat your drive and start over. Microsoft does not support such installations. That alone should be a clear indication that it's not a good idea!

Although we recommend that you use separate partitions for each operating system, there's no reason you can't share data on a common drive that's available to all operating systems. In fact, you might want to change the target folder location of your My Documents folder in each operating system so that it points to the same folder.

Controlling Setup with Switches

When using the Winnt32.exe command to start the Windows Setup program, you can modify the program's behavior with a number of command-line switches. Table 2-1 lists the most useful of these switches.

Table 2-1. Command-Line Setup Switches for Winnt32.exe

Switch	What It Does
/checkupgradeonly	Runs the Upgrade Advisor without installing Windows XP
/cmd:*command_line*	Specifies a command to be carried out after the graphical portion of Setup has completed; often used to install applications as part of the Windows XP Setup
/cmdcons	Adds the Recovery Console to the Windows XP startup menu (see "Adding the Recovery Console," page 87)
/copydir:*folder_name*	Creates a subfolder within the Windows XP folder and copies the contents of the specified folder there; useful if you need to make drivers available for later installation
/copysource:*folder_name*	Creates a temporary subfolder within the Windows XP folder; this subfolder is deleted when Setup finishes
/makelocalsource	Instructs Setup to copy installation source files to your local hard disk; use this option if the CD will be unavailable during installation
/noreboot	Eliminates forced reboot after file-copying phase of Setup; useful if you need to execute another command before restarting

(continued)

Table 2-1. *(continued)*

Switch	What It Does
/s:*sourcepath*	Specifies source location of Windows XP Setup files, typically on a server; repeat this switch up to eight times to specify multiple servers
/syspart:*drive_letter*	Allows you to copy Setup files to a hard disk, mark the disk as active, move it to another machine, and restart to continue Setup on the new computer; must be used with /tempdrive and can be run only on Windows NT/2000/XP machines
/tempdrive:*drive_letter*	Used in conjunction with /syspart to specify the primary partition to be used for storing Windows XP Setup files and installing a new copy of Windows XP; an upgrade installation will be placed on the partition from which Winnt32.exe is run
/udf:*ID[,UDB_file]*	Identifies a Uniqueness Database (UDB) file that modifies an answer file (see "Using Answer Files for Automated Installation," page 43)
/unattend[*seconds*][:*answer_file*]	Used in conjunction with an unattended Setup, as described in the next section; optional [*seconds*] parameter is only required on Windows NT 4 upgrades, and the file name can be omitted if the default name Unattend.txt is used

newfeature!
Activating Windows XP

Windows XP includes a new antipiracy feature called Windows Product Activation (WPA). As in previous Windows versions, you must enter a 25-character product key during the Setup process. WPA adds a new requirement: After Setup completes, you must activate your installation within 30 days, either by connecting to a Microsoft activation server over the Internet, or by calling a toll-free number and speaking with a customer service representative at a WPA clearinghouse.

WPA is a mechanism designed to enforce license restrictions by preventing the most common form of software piracy, casual copying. Typically, a Microsoft Windows XP license entitles you to install the operating system software on a single computer. If you

Chapter 2: Installing and Configuring Windows XP

use the same CD and product key to install Windows XP on a different system, you'll be unable to activate the software automatically. Here's what you need to know about WPA:

- **Under most circumstances, activation is automatic and instantaneous.** If you purchase a shrink-wrapped copy of Windows XP and install it on a new computer, you can activate over the Internet, and the process should take no more than a few seconds. If you need to use the phone, the process takes longer, because you have to read a 50-digit identification key to the customer service representative and then input the 42-digit confirmation ID supplied by the clearinghouse representative, as shown in Figure 2-3.

- **Within 30 days of installing Windows XP, you must activate the software.** If you choose the phone option, you'll see a list of toll-free numbers.

- **Activation is not registration.** The activation process is completely anonymous and does not require that you divulge any personal information. If you choose to register your copy of Windows XP, this is a completely separate (and optional) task.

- **You're allowed to reinstall Windows an unlimited number of times on the same hardware.** During the activation process, Windows XP transmits an encrypted file that serves as a "fingerprint" of key components in your system. If you reinstall Windows XP on the same hardware, the activation server checks the new fingerprint against the one stored in its database. If they match, activation is automatic.

Figure 2-3. Activating a copy of Windows over the phone is considerably more complex than doing it over the Internet.

> **tip** **Don't rush to activate**
>
> When you install a retail copy of Windows XP, you're prompted during the final stage of Setup to activate the product. We recommend that you choose not to activate it immediately. Instead, give yourself at least a week to verify that Windows XP works properly on your hardware and that you won't be required to replace any hardware or the entire computer. After you're confident that Windows XP is completely compatible with your hardware, you can safely activate. Use the persistent reminder balloons in the notification area, or click the Start button and choose the Activate Windows short-cut at the top of the All Programs menu.

- **Multiple hardware upgrades may require you to reactivate Windows.** The activation software is designed to prevent attempts to "clone" an activated copy of Windows and install it on another computer. If you replace or upgrade four or more components from a list of 10 components on your computer in a period of 120 days or less, the activation mechanism may mistakenly assume that you've installed the operating system on a new computer. In that case, you'll be required to call the WPA clearinghouse and get a new activation code. The list of components included in the hardware "fingerprint" includes your display adapter, primary hard disk, volume serial number, SCSI adapter, IDE disk controller, CD-ROM drive, network adapter (based on its MAC address), CPU type, CPU serial number, and the amount of installed RAM. It does not include Zip drives, digital cameras, or similar peripheral devices. If the computer is marked as dockable, however (as most notebook computers are), the requirements are relaxed significantly, and you can safely upgrade seven of the components on the list (including the network adapter) or nine components (if the network adapter remains unchanged) before being forced to activate Windows again.

- **Copies of Windows XP sold with new computers may be exempt from WPA.** If you purchase a new computer on which Windows XP is pre-installed, the activation process may have been completed before you took delivery. In addition, copies of Windows sold this way are frequently tied via software to the BIOS of that computer (this method of installation is called System Locked Pre-Installation, or SLP). You may reinstall that copy of Windows XP an unlimited number of times on the computer it came with, regardless of how many upgrades you make as long as you don't change the BIOS. In fact, you can replace the motherboard on a system activated with SLP as long as the new part is from the same manufacturer and uses the same BIOS identifier. However, you may be prohibited by the license agreement from transferring that copy of Windows to another computer.

- **Many corporations are also exempt from WPA requirements.** Businesses that purchase as few as five copies of qualified Microsoft software, including Windows XP, through a Microsoft volume licensing (VL) program

Chapter 2: Installing and Configuring Windows XP

receive VL media and product keys that do not require activation. Under the terms of a volume license agreement, each computer with a copy of Windows XP must have a valid license.

For more details on volume licensing programs for Windows and other Microsoft software, read the Microsoft Licensing FAQ at *http://www.microsoft.com/business/ licensing/faq.asp*. For an exhaustive technical discussion of Product Activation, read the white paper at *http://www.microsoft.com/technet/prodtechnol/winxppro/evaluate/ xpactiv.asp*.

InsideOut

Want to prevent at least some activation headaches? Make a backup copy of Wpa.dbl, a tiny file stored in the %SystemRoot%\System32 folder. This file contains the hardware "fingerprint" information used to determine whether activation is required. If you need to reinstall Windows XP on a system that has already been activated, you can restore this file and bypass the need for activation—if your hardware hasn't changed appreciably since the original activation. Windows also creates a backup copy of this file, called Wpa.bak, at startup. This backup copy can be a lifesaver if you encounter problems after a hardware upgrade. If Windows refuses to run because your new hardware has triggered the activation code, you may be able to recover using this workaround: Restore your old hardware, start your computer in Networked Safe Mode, and rename Wpa.bak to Wpa.dbl. If all goes as it should, you'll be reactivated and able to continue working.

Automated Setup Options

If you plan to install Windows XP on one or two computers, running the Setup program from the CD is your best choice. But if you're planning to upgrade an entire office full of computers, you can save a substantial amount of time by automating the installation. The two most popular options are

- **Unattended setup.** This option uses a batch file and a script (called an answer file) to bypass the Setup program's prompts and fill in answers automatically. You can choose from five unattended modes.

- **Disk imaging (cloning).** In this option, you set up Windows on a sample computer and then run the System Preparation utility (Sysprep.exe), which removes the unique security identifier (SID). You can then use a disk cloning program such as Symantec's Ghost (*http://www.symantec.com/ghost*) or PowerQuest's DriveImage (*http://www.powerquest.com/driveimage*) to copy the entire partition to a new computer; when it starts up, it runs a Mini-Setup program that completes in 5–10 minutes instead of the hour or more that a full Setup requires.

> **note** Large organizations with existing networks built around Windows 2000 Server or Windows .NET Server can deploy Windows XP on hundreds or thousands of machines with relative ease using Remote Installation Services (RIS) and Microsoft Systems Management Server (SMS). These options require substantial up-front preparation by information technology specialists, but the payoff can be dramatic. You can find more information about RIS at the Windows 2000/.NET Server Web site (*http:// www.microsoft.com/windows/server*). SMS allows an administrator to manage and monitor installations from a central location. For information about SMS, visit *http:// www.microsoft.com/smsmgmt*.

Installing the Deployment Tools

The Windows XP Professional and Home Edition CDs include a selection of utilities and Help files that make it possible to use the automated installation processes described in this section. The Microsoft Windows Corporate Deployment Tools are located in a compressed Cabinet file (a compressed archive that is similar to a .zip file but uses the .cab extension). Before you can use these utilities, you have to copy them to your hard disk.

From Windows Explorer, open the \Support\Tools folder on the Windows XP CD, and double-click Deploy.cab. Select all files in this compressed folder, and copy them to a folder on your hard disk.

> **tip** Keep support files together
>
> If you've already installed the Support Tools, why not keep the Deployment Tools in the same location? Create a new subfolder called Deploy in the %ProgramFiles%\Support Tools folder and use it to store the deployment utilities.

The following files are included in Deploy.cab:

- **Setupmgr.exe.** This executable file opens the Microsoft Setup Manager Wizard, which is used for creating answer files. It includes a help file (Setupmgr.chm), which is accessible only from within the Setup Manager Wizard.

- **Sysprep.exe.** This executable file runs the System Preparation Tool, which is used for creating and deploying disk images.

> **caution** Do not run Sysprep.exe on any system unless you intend to make an image of that system. Sysprep is a powerful tool that removes unique security identifiers from a Windows computer. If you run it by mistake on a working system, you will wipe out the security settings on that computer and may suffer unintended consequences, such as losing the ability to access files in your user profile.

- **Setupcl.exe.** A small program used by Sysprep.exe to create unique security identifiers (SIDs).

- **Deploy.chm.** Microsoft Windows Corporate Deployment Tools User's Guide, in Compiled HTML Help format, provides detailed instructions and technical information about the deployment process. You can double-click to browse its contents.

- **Ref.chm.** Compiled HTML Help file that contains reference information about the utilities and support files used in the deployment process. You can double-click to browse its contents.

In addition, three specialized utilities that are intended primarily for use by computer manufacturers are included within the Deploy.cab collection on the Windows XP CD:

- **Cvtarea.exe.** Used in conjunction with Convert.exe (the utility that converts a drive to NTFS format) to create an unfragmented placeholder file for NTFS system files. The file is overwritten by the Master File Table during the conversion to NTFS.

- **Oformat.com.** An enhanced version of the Windows 98 Format.exe program (an MS-DOS application) that creates a FAT32 volume with clusters that are aligned optimally for conversion to NTFS format.

- **Factory.exe.** Helper program used with Sysprep.exe to make changes to a standard configuration before delivering it to end users.

For more information about these files, read the descriptions in the Deployment Tools User's Guide (Deploy.chm).

Using Answer Files for Automated Installation

The most tedious part of performing a clean Windows XP installation is waiting. At several points during the installation process, the Setup program stops and waits for you to fill in essential information—your name, the computer's name, network settings, and so on. Instead of waiting around for those dialog boxes to appear, you can create an *answer file*—a text file that automatically fills in the blanks for you and allows Setup to continue unattended. An answer file can also contain answers to a number of questions that aren't posed by the interactive Setup program, which means that you actually have much greater control over installations. You can use an answer file whether you install from the Windows XP CD or from a shared network folder.

InsideOut

The automated setup solutions we discuss in this chapter were designed for offices, but they may be ideal for you even if you only have one or two computers. If you're a dyed-in-the-wool hardware tinkerer and you regularly strip your system to bare metal and rebuild it with new components, use an answer file to take the tedium out of rerunning Setup each time. If you store your favorite customizations in .reg files or save them using the Files And Settings Transfer Wizard, you can be up and running in no time.

Creating an Answer File

To create an answer file, open the Windows Setup Manager Wizard (Setupmgr.exe) and follow its prompts. Most of the wizard's dialog boxes are self-explanatory, with fill-in-the-blank forms that match up neatly with questions that are familiar to anyone who has interactively run Setup from the Windows XP CD. If this is the first time you're using the wizard, you'll probably want to create a new answer file and designate it for Windows unattended installation. If you already have an answer file and you need to change one or more details in that file (such as the product key or computer name), choose the Modify An Existing Answer File option.

note The Windows Setup Manager Wizard on the Windows XP CD runs on Windows XP Professional or Home Edition and on Windows 2000. It will not run on any earlier version of Windows.

The following list describes some of the more interesting options:

- **User Interaction Level.** This page, shown in Figure 2-4, lets you choose one of five options that control how much the user sees during installation (for example, you can hide Windows Setup pages for which you've provided the answers) and whether you want the user to be able to override the answers you provide in the answer file. If you choose anything other than the Fully Automated option, you can leave selected answers blank; this technique is useful when you want the user to provide specific information (such as a user name) during Setup.

- **Distribution Folder.** If you plan to install from CD, you can ignore this option. However, if you want to install from a network share, you can specify it here; this option gives you the flexibility to add other files as well, such as drivers not found on the Windows XP CD.

44

Chapter 2: Installing and Configuring Windows XP

Figure 2-4. Check the Description panel at the bottom of this dialog box to see how each script-based option works.

● **Computer Names.** This page, shown in Figure 2-5, allows you to enter the name of each computer individually, or you can import a text file that contains the names. You can specify more than one computer name here if you want to use this answer file to automate installation of Windows XP on multiple computers. If you're willing to accept computer names that follow no pattern, you can allow Setup to create each computer's name on the fly by appending seemingly random letters and numbers to the first few letters of your organization's name.

Figure 2-5. If you need to set up multiple computers, specify a group of names in this dialog box and then use the same answer file for each installation.

> **tip** **Learn how to create custom names**
>
> If you enter multiple computer names in the Setup Manager Wizard, you need to customize the batch file used to start the Setup program. Add the /udf switch after either Winnt32.exe or Winnt.exe, and copy the .udf file (which is automatically created by Setup Manager) to the same location as the answer file.

After you finish filling in the blanks in the Setup Manager Wizard, it creates an answer file and stores it using the name and location you specify. Saving the answer file to a floppy disk makes it especially easy to use if you plan to install from CD.

> **tip** **Use descriptive names**
>
> The Setup Manager Wizard uses Unattend.txt as its default file name, but you can choose a different name if you prefer. Descriptive names can be helpful if you create multiple answer files to handle different hardware configurations—you might choose Notebook.txt as the name of the answer file you use for portable configurations, for instance.

Customizing an Answer File

The easiest way to customize an answer file—if you simply need to modify some settings you made with Setup Manager—is to restart Setup Manager. On the wizard's second page, select Modify An Existing Answer File and specify the file name.

But there's much more you can do with an answer file; the Setup Manager Wizard guides you through only the most commonly used settings. If you want to get more creative with your automated installations, open Ref.chm, the online reference guide that is included as part of the Deployment Tools collection. This Compiled HTML Help file provides a complete reference to all the answer file parameters in the Unattend.txt section. The information is well organized and clearly presented, although its sheer bulk can be overwhelming. You might consider some of these additions or modifications:

- Use the [Components] section to specify which accessory programs are installed. You can use this option to prevent distractions like the Pinball game from being installed, for example.

- Consider adding Win9xUpgrade=Yes to the [Unattended] section if you're upgrading computers that are currently running Windows 98 or Windows Me. Without these keys (which Setup Manager does not add), Setup installs Windows XP on the same partition as the existing operating system, but in a separate folder. This produces an improperly configured dual-boot system that's practically guaranteed to cause problems later.

- Use the [Win9xUpg] section to control how user accounts and passwords on Windows 95/98/Me computers are migrated to Windows 2000.

- Edit the [SystemRestore] section to configure System Restore options, including the percentage of disk space reserved for saved configuration information.

- Use the [Fax] section to configure the fax service.

Answer files are plain ASCII text files that follow a consistent organization and syntax. The file consists of section headers—a section header is a word enclosed in square brackets on a line by itself—followed by keys and values. Each key begins on a new line, and it's usually followed by an equal sign and a value for the key. If a value contains any spaces, it must be enclosed in quotation marks. You can include comments in an answer file by putting a semicolon at the beginning of each comment line. The Windows XP Preinstallation Reference includes three sample Unattend.txt files that you can examine in more detail.

---

note In previous versions of the Setup Manager Wizard, passwords were stored in the answer file as ordinary text. In the Windows XP version of this utility, your passwords are considerably more secure. When you enter the Administrator password for the target computer, be sure to select the Encrypt Administrator Password In Answer File check box. This option eliminates the chance that a snoop can peek into the answer file and steal the password for the Administrator account.

Using an Answer File During Setup

To use an answer file, include the /Unattend switch (along with the file specification for the answer file) on the command line for Winnt32.exe, the Windows XP Setup program. For example, if you're installing from the Windows XP Professional CD and you want to use an answer file named Unattend.txt that's stored on a floppy disk, enter this command line:

```
d:\i386\winnt32 /unattend:a:\unattend.txt
```

---

tip **Combine a CD and floppy for a clean install**

Of course, you can also use an answer file to automate the installation on a new computer—and you don't have to enter any command lines at all. If your computer can boot from the Windows XP Professional or Home Edition CD, save the answer file on a floppy disk and name it Winnt.sif. Insert the CD and the floppy disk and turn on the computer. Setup runs from the CD and uses Winnt.sif as its answer file.

If you used the Setup Manager Wizard to create the answer file, the process of using the resulting Unattend.txt file is even simpler. Setup Manager creates a batch file using the same file name (but with a .bat extension) and location that you specified for the answer file. Simply navigate to the folder where you saved the answer file (usually the distribution folder, if you set one up, or a floppy disk) and open the batch file. If you copy the batch file, the answer file, or both from the location where Setup Manager originally stored them, you might need to edit the batch file to update the path information.

Troubleshooting

Unattended Setup stops unexpectedly.

Even simple errors in answer files can cause Setup to stop before it ever gets started—and you won't get any hints about where the problem lies. If you receive a message saying that your Setup script file is "inaccessible or invalid," check each line to see that it follows the proper format. Be sure that all values with spaces are enclosed in quotation marks, and be especially vigilant for stray commas.

Using Disk Imaging

Windows XP, like its predecessor Windows 2000, includes Sysprep, a program that allows you to install a system, complete with Windows applications, and then duplicate it to other systems. After the system has been duplicated, the end user starts up the new system and run either the Windows Welcome portion of Windows Setup (if you choose the Disk Duplication option) or an abbreviated "Mini-Setup" routine that requires only about five minutes to run (if you choose the Automating Mini-Setup option). Because Sysprep duplicates an entire hard disk partition, you can use it to copy complete systems that include additional customizations and installed applications.

note Why is Sysprep necessary? Unlike Windows 98 and Windows Me, each computer running any member of the Windows NT family (including Windows XP and Windows 2000) must have a unique security identifier, or SID. If two computers on a network have identical SIDs, the result is chaos. Because the Setup program automatically creates a unique SID for each Windows installation, cloning a running Windows XP system won't work—the clone would have the same SID as the original computer. Sysprep solves this problem by removing the SID on the master system, before you create the clone. When you transfer the image to the new system and start it up for the first time, Sysprep generates a unique SID.

Using Automated Installations: The Simplest Way

If you have a small office—a few dozen computers or less—you don't need to pass an MCSE (Microsoft Certified Systems Engineer) exam to become a Setup wiz. Instead, you can follow this simple, straightforward method for automating your installations:

1 Install Windows XP on one computer.

2 Install the Deployment Tools on the same computer.

3 Use the Windows Setup Manager Wizard to create an answer file. If you already have a network set up, use Setup Manager to create a distribution folder. Otherwise, tell Setup Manager that you'll install from the CD.

4 Using the information in Ref.chm, edit the answer file you created to include any additional customizations you want.

5 If the computers you're targeting for installation don't have a working network connection, copy the answer file, the batch file, and the .udf file (if any) created by Setup Manager to a floppy disk.

6 At each computer, connect to the distribution folder (if you already have a working network) and run the batch file, or run it from the floppy disk. (If you specified more than one computer name in the answer file, you'll need to append the specific computer name to the command line when you run the batch file.)

The process of creating an answer file should take a few minutes—an hour if you decide to customize it extensively. You can easily save 30 minutes or more on each unattended installation, compared to the time it would take to sit in front of the computer and respond to its prompts. That's a healthy return on your investment of time.

Sysprep might not be right for you. Although this utility makes it easy to duplicate fully configured systems, it has the following restrictions and limitations:

- Most important, the master and target computers must have identical hard drive controllers, identical hardware abstraction layers (HALs), and identical BIOS versions. Although other components—such as modems, sound cards, network cards, and so on—need not be identical, this limitation effectively restricts the use of Sysprep to fleets of identical computers. If you have a varied collection of computers of different ages and manufacturers, chances are good that Sysprep won't work for all of them.

- You'll need third-party software (or a hardware device) for disk duplication. Sysprep merely prepares the image for copying and then runs a version of Setup after the image has been copied to a new computer. But to actually make the copy, you'll need a program such as Ghost (from Symantec) or DriveImage (from PowerQuest) or a disk-duplicating device.

● The hard disk on the target computer must be at least as big as the one on the master computer.

● The master computer on which you prepare the Sysprep partition must be a clean install with no user accounts or profiles and no encrypted data. The user will be able to set up accounts when he or she turns on the computer and completes the setup process.

If these restrictions aren't a problem for you, you can follow these steps to use Sysprep:

1 Install Windows XP on a master computer. (Because you might go through this process several times before you get everything set up just the way you want, you should create an answer file and use it for setting up the master computer. See the preceding section, "Using Answer Files for Automated Installation," page 43.)

---

note Do not join a domain during this initial setup—even if you intend to do so later— because running Sysprep removes the SID that allows the computer to connect to the domain. Set up the master computer in a workgroup. When Windows Welcome or the Mini-Setup program runs on each target computer, you can choose to join a domain.

---

2 Log on to the computer using the Administrator account.

3 Customize the computer as desired, and install applications that you want to be included on all target computers.

4 Create a folder named \Sysprep on the system partition. Extract Sysprep.exe and Setupcl.exe from the Deploy.cab file in the \Support\Tools folder on the Windows XP CD and copy them to this folder.

5 Run Sysprep.exe. In a few moments, the system will shut down by itself (if it's ACPI-compliant) or display a message stating that it's safe to turn off the computer.

6 Duplicate the hard disk. Depending on the duplication method, you might need to remove the hard disk from the system or you might need to boot from a floppy disk that starts the third-party disk-duplication software.

When you start a computer that contains a duplicated disk (or, for that matter, when you turn on the master computer, if it still contains the master disk), Sysprep automatically

1 Detects Plug and Play devices.

2 Runs the Windows Welcome portion of Windows Setup, which lets you set up user accounts and activate Windows.

3 Deletes the \Sysprep folder and its contents.

4 Reboots the computer.

This entire process takes only a few minutes, much less time than Setup normally requires.

If you chose the Automating Mini-Setup option, the process takes slightly longer but is still quite speedy. You can automate Mini-Setup by creating an answer file to provide some (or all) of the requested information. Use the Setup Manager Wizard to create the answer file, being sure to select Sysprep Install on the Product To Install page. The file uses the same format, sections, keys, and values as an ordinary answer file. Settings that are unnecessary or inappropriate in the disk-imaging process are ignored. You must name the answer file Sysprep.inf, and you must place it in the \Sysprep folder before you run Sysprep.exe. Table 2-2 shows the information that Mini-Setup requests, along with the answer file sections and keys that you can use to automate the process.

Table 2-2. **Answer File Keys for Automating Mini-Setup**

Mini-Setup Requests This Information	Unless You Use These Keys
Your agreement to the terms of the End User License Agreement (EULA)	[Unattended] OemSkipEula
Regional settings	[GuiUnattended] OemSkipRegional (provide settings in the [RegionalSettings] section)
Name and organization	[UserData] FullName, OrgName
Product key	[UserData] ProductID
Computer name	[UserData] ComputerName
Administrator password	[GuiUnattended] AdminPassword
Modem dialing information	[TapiLocation] AreaCode, CountryCode, Dialing, LongDistanceAccess
Date, time, and time zone	[GuiUnattended] TimeZone
Network identification	[Identification] DomainAdmin, DomainAdminPassword, JoinDomain, JoinWorkgroup

newfeature!
Moving Windows Settings and Files

If you upgrade an existing computer to Windows XP, all of your data and most of your programs should survive Setup intact. But what do you do if Windows XP is already installed on a new computer, or if you've decided to do a clean install on your existing system? In previous versions, you would have had to use third-party utilities or go through a tedious backup and restore process. With Windows XP, you can use a new utility called the Files And Settings Transfer Wizard to handle most of the grunt work.

InsideOut

Although you might be tempted to use the Files And Settings Transfer Wizard immediately after installing Windows XP, we suggest you curb your enthusiasm. Run Windows Update first, and install all necessary updates. Be on the lookout for an update to the Files And Settings Transfer Wizard that fixes a handful of bugs; this fix is in the Recommended Updates category and is included with Service Pack 1. After you've made sure the new computer is up to date, fire up the wizard and transfer your files and settings.

With the help of this wizard, you can migrate settings and files from your old computer to the new one. Although the wizard has its limitations, it's highly flexible and offers an impressive number of customization options. You can save settings from any 32-bit version of Windows (including Windows 95), and you can restore the saved files and settings on Windows XP Home Edition or Professional, using either of these options:

- **Make a direct connection.** You can connect two computers over a local area network or using a serial cable and transfer settings directly from the old computer to the new one. A Fast Ethernet connection is by far your best choice, especially if you want to transfer a large number of data files. Direct cable connections are significantly slower.

- **Save your settings to a file.** If a direct connection isn't practical or possible (if you're planning to wipe out an existing partition so you can do a clean install on the same computer, for example), you can save the wizard's output to a compressed file and then restore it after you finish Setup. Save the file to a floppy disk, to removable media such as a Zip disk or CD-RW, or to a network folder.

tip   Migrate multiple users

If the "old" computer is set up with multiple user profiles, you must run the Files And Settings Transfer Wizard separately for each user when saving and restoring files. If the original system is running Windows NT/2000/XP, start by migrating all settings and files for a user with an account in the Administrators group. This ensures that file associations and other common settings are captured. Then, for each succeeding user, customize the migration settings so you collect only personal data and settings. Be sure to restore the files and settings in the same order. Log on as the first user and restore the first, complete set. Then log on using a different user account and migrate that user's files and settings, repeating this process until all files and settings are restored.

By default, the Files And Settings Transfer Wizard migrates the following items:

- **User-specific settings.** This category includes visual settings, such as your current theme, wallpaper, and screen saver; folder and taskbar options; accessibility options; phone, modem, and dial-up networking connections; and network printers and drives (as defined in the My Network Places folder).

- **Internet settings.** The wizard copies the contents of your Favorites folder and cookies to the new computer. It does not, however, retain user names, passwords, and other details saved by Internet Explorer's AutoComplete feature.

- **E-mail.** The wizard collects mail account settings, messages, and address books from Microsoft Outlook Express and Microsoft Outlook. It does not keep track of individual identities in Outlook Express; all mail for all identities is merged during the transfer.

- **Application settings.** Registry settings and preference files for a long list of programs are copied automatically. Naturally, this list is heavy on Microsoft programs—Office 97/2000/XP, Works 2001, and Money 2001, among many others. But the list also includes more than 30 third-party programs, including Netscape Communicator, AOL Instant Messenger and ICQ, Eudora, Adobe Photoshop and Acrobat Reader, Lotus SmartSuite, Quicken, WordPerfect Office 2000, WinZip, WinAmp, and RealPlayer. The wizard does not migrate program files; instead, it copies the settings and preference files to the correct location on the new computer and uses them when you install the program.

---

tip **See the full list of migrated programs**

Is your favorite program on the list of programs whose settings are migrated by the Files And Settings Transfer Wizard? You can view the full list by opening a text file called Migapp.inf, which is stored in the Valueadd\Msft\Usmt folder on the Windows XP CD. (After installation, this and other setting files are available in %SystemRoot%\ System32\Usmt.) Entries here define the registry settings and user files that are migrated for each program.

- **Files and folders.** In folders that are typically used for data files—My Documents, My Pictures, and Shared Documents, for instance—all files are migrated automatically, regardless of extension. In all other locations, the wizard uses a long list of extensions to identify which data files should be transferred. You can add or remove extensions from this list and specify additional folders that you want the wizard to copy to the new computer.

Pay careful attention to the wizard's options when moving data. The transfer method and options you choose can have a profound effect on how long the process takes and how successful you are. The following sections contain detailed instructions and tips on how to migrate files and settings safely and successfully.

Transferring Files and Settings Between Computers

If you're replacing your old computer with a new one running Windows XP, your best bet is to connect the two computers over a local area network and use the Files And Settings Transfer Wizard. This technique is not only the fastest way to get your new computer up and running, it's also the best way to avoid losing data. Because your existing data files remain intact on the old computer, you can recover easily if the wizard inadvertently leaves behind a crucial data file.

To get started, install Windows XP on the new computer and ensure that the old and new computers can successfully connect over your network. Then follow these steps to run the Files And Settings Transfer Wizard:

1 On the new computer, click the Start button and then choose All Programs, Accessories, System Tools, Files And Settings Transfer Wizard. (To skip the cascading menus, you can also type **migwiz** at any command prompt, including the Run dialog box.) Click Next at the opening page.

2 When prompted, choose the New Computer option and click Next.

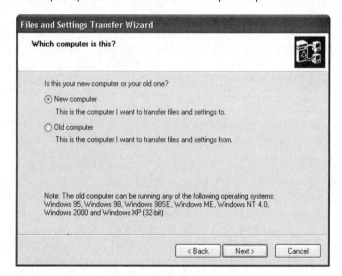

3 In the following dialog box, choose the I Will Use The Wizard From The Windows XP CD option and click Next.

4 At the old computer, insert the Windows XP CD into the CD-ROM drive. From the Welcome To Microsoft Windows XP menu, choose Perform Additional Tasks and then click Transfer Files And Settings. Click Next.

5 Choose the Old Computer option and click Next. If your old computer is not running Windows XP, the Old Computer option is automatically selected and this page does not appear. Proceed to step 6.

Chapter 2: Installing and Configuring Windows XP

6 In the Select A Transfer Method dialog box, choose the Home Or Small Office Network option and click Next. (If this option is not available, verify that your network connection is working properly and start over with the new computer.)

You can now complete the wizard using the procedures in "Choosing Files and Settings to Transfer," page 57.

---

tip **Avoid the direct cable option**

The Direct Cable option in the Select A Transfer Method page of the Files And Settings Transfer Wizard sounds promising. Trust us, it's not. To connect two computers using this technique, you must use a null modem cable—a specially wired serial cable popularized by the venerable LapLink program. Serial connections are painfully slow; even at their theoretical top speed of 115,200 bits per second, they're only marginally faster than a decent dial-up Internet connection. If all you're transferring is settings, you'll find it easier to use ordinary floppy disks. If you have several hundred megabytes of data, beg, borrow, or buy a Zip drive and use it instead.

Saving Files and Settings to a Folder or Drive

If it's impossible or impractical to connect the old and new computers directly, use the Files And Settings Transfer Wizard to store your saved settings in one or more files. Follow these steps to do so:

1 At the old computer, insert the Windows XP CD into the CD-ROM drive. From the Welcome To Microsoft Windows XP menu, choose Perform Additional Tasks and then click Transfer Files And Settings. Click Next.

Part 1: Setup, Startup, Tune-Up

2 When prompted, choose the Old Computer option and click Next. If your old computer is not running Windows XP, this option is automatically selected and this page does not appear. Proceed to step 3.

3 In the Select A Transfer Method dialog box, choose either of the following options:

- **Floppy Drive Or Other Removable Media.** The drive list shows all removable drives that are identified by letter, including standard 3.5-inch (1.44 MB) floppy drives, Zip drives (100 MB and 250 MB capacity), Compact Flash and other memory card readers, and CD-RW drives, if you have packet-writing software such as Adaptec's DirectCD installed. If you choose a floppy drive from this list, the What Do You Want To Transfer page of the wizard defaults to the Settings Only option, eliminates the option to transfer e-mail messages and settings, and warns you that transferring files may require a large number of floppy disks.

- **Other (For Example, A Removable Drive Or Network Drive).** Choose this option if you want to save files and settings to a folder on a local or network drive. When you select this option, the What Do You Want To Transfer page of the wizard defaults to the Both Files And Settings option.

You can now complete the wizard using the procedures in the following section.

> **note** When you choose the Other option, the Files And Settings Transfer Wizard creates a folder called Usmt2.unc in the location you specify. It then stores the files and settings to be migrated in one or more files, using the names Img00001, Img00002, and so on. The maximum size of each such file is 2 GB.

Choosing Files and Settings to Transfer

When you reach the point in the Files And Settings Transfer Wizard where you actually begin saving data, you can choose Settings Only, Files Only, or Files And Settings from the What Do You Want To Transfer? page of the wizard. It's also possible to customize the options you choose here. Pay very close attention to these options, because they might not behave as you expect.

Settings Only

Generally speaking, you should choose the Settings Only option when you want to minimize the amount of data you need to move from the old computer to the new one. Unfortunately, the Settings Only option can drag along a startling amount of data if you don't understand the inner workings of the Files And Settings Transfer Wizard. The wizard behaves differently, depending on which transfer method you've chosen. For instance, if you choose a 3.5-inch floppy drive as the destination on a system running Windows 98, the list on the right side of the page should resemble the example in Figure 2-6.

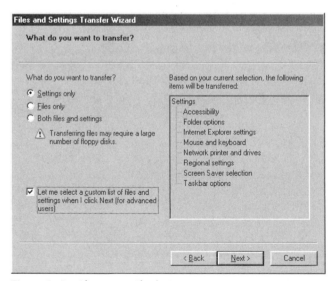

Figure 2-6. If you specify that you want to save settings to a floppy drive, the Files And Settings Transfer Wizard offers this minimal list.

Chapter 2

That selection doesn't take up much room at all—in this example, the total amount of data to be transferred fits easily on two floppy disks, as the message that appears informs us.

But when you change the destination to a folder on a local hard drive, the list of items under the Settings heading changes, as you can see in Figure 2-7. The new list includes 11 new entries, including settings for such items as Microsoft Office, Outlook Express, RealJukebox 2, and Windows Media Player. (The list of settings is dynamically created, so the entries for Microsoft Office and RealPlayer/RealJukebox appear only if those programs are installed on the computer where you're running the Files And Settings Transfer Wizard.)

Although the Settings Only option is still selected, just as before, the list of settings is greatly expanded, and this time it includes some data files. The resulting data file in this example adds up to a whopping 131 MB—most of it consisting of e-mail messages from Outlook Express and the Personal Store file from Outlook 2002.

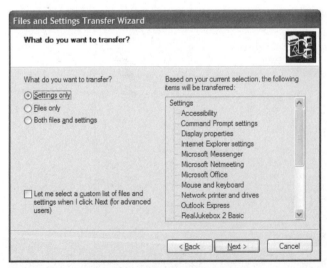

Figure 2-7. When you choose to save settings on a local or network drive, the Settings Only list gets considerably longer.

---

tip **Calculate how much space you need**

If you choose Other on the Select A Transfer Method page and then specify a location other than a removable drive, the Files And Settings Transfer Wizard starts saving files without giving you the slightest indication of how much space you'll need. The only way to get a reliable indication of how much disk space you'll gobble up is through a two-step process. Specify a floppy drive as your destination, even if you intend to save your files and settings to a local or network drive instead. After the wizard completes its preliminary calculations, it displays a message that tells you how much space you're about to use. If the result is what you expected, cancel the wizard and start over, this time specifying the location where you really want to save your files and settings.

If you're unsatisfied with either of these options—for instance, if you don't want to transfer your e-mail messages to the new computer—you must choose the option to customize your files and settings, as described in "Customizing the List of Saved Files and Settings" on the next page.

Files Only

When you use the Files And Settings Transfer Wizard to move files from one computer to another, the wizard actually performs two distinct operations, although this division is not immediately apparent. The list of items to be transferred consists of two groups, as the example in Figure 2-8 shows:

- **Specific Folders.** By default, this category identifies commonly used storage locations and migrates *all* files it finds in those locations, regardless of their extension.

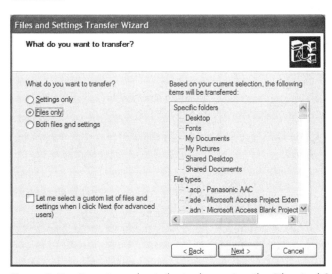

Figure 2-8.   Be extremely vigilant when using the Files And Settings Transfer Wizard to move files, or you could end up moving several gigabytes of data.

Chapter 2

- **File Types.** Scroll through this category and you'll see that it consists of a long list of file extensions—more than 160 in all. Using this option, the wizard searches every folder on every local drive for files with those extensions. You cannot exclude any drive or folder from this search.

The Specific Folders category works exactly as expected. The wizard grabs all files in your My Documents and My Pictures folder, for example, and restores them to the same location on the new computer. The wizard uses class identifiers (CLSIDs) to identify the proper location of these folders, so your files should end up in the correct location even if you've installed Windows XP on a different drive or changed the location of the My Documents folder on either the old or new computer.

The File Types category, however, can have unexpected (and unwelcome) results. The list of file extensions includes a long list of media file types, including music files in the MP3 and Windows Media Audio formats. If you have a large collection of songs you've copied from CDs or downloaded from the Internet and those files are stored on a separate drive, the Files And Settings Transfer Wizard will dutifully try to gather them up and move them to your new computer. If your collection is measured in multiple gigabytes, the process will seem to take forever, and if you're storing the saved settings to a local drive, you'll probably run out of disk space during the process.

The only solution is to use the option to create a custom list of your files and settings, as described later in this section.

Both Files And Settings

No surprises here: This option combines the default settings from the Settings Only and Files Only options.

Customizing the List of Saved Files and Settings

You can safely get away with using the default settings for the Files And Settings Transfer Wizard if you satisfy the following conditions:

- Your old and new computers are networked and you plan to transfer files and settings over that network connection.

- You have at least as much total disk space on the new computer as on the old one.

If the partitioning scheme on the new computer is different from that on the old one, however, or if your data files are meticulously organized in folders other than My Documents, you should consider customizing the way the Files And Settings Transfer Wizard works. When you reach the What Do You Want To Transfer? page on the old computer, select the options shown in Figure 2-9. Choose Both Files And Settings, and then select the Let Me Select A Custom List of Files check box.

Chapter 2: Installing and Configuring Windows XP

Click here to customize transfer options

Figure 2-9. Select this check box to tell the wizard you want to choose which files and settings are transferred.

After choosing this option, click Next to display the Select Custom Files And Settings page. On this page, you can add or remove settings, files, file types, and folders to customize the way the Files And Settings Transfer Wizard works. Figure 2-10 shows this page after customizing some settings.

Figure 2-10. If the Files And Settings Transfer Wizard is too aggressive, rein it in by removing some options from this list.

You can customize the Files And Settings Transfer Wizard using these five buttons:

- **Add Setting.** This option shows items you've removed from the Settings list. It's also useful if the wizard is displaying a shortened list of settings because you've chosen to save settings to a floppy disk. You cannot create custom settings here.

- **Add Folder.** Use this option if you store data in a location other than the default system folders and you want the wizard to migrate all files and subfolders from that folder, regardless of their extension. In Figure 2-10, for example, we've added the Downloads folder from drive D. You can add an unlimited number of folders to this list.

- **Add File.** Choose this option if you want to be certain that you migrate a specific file from a specific location without also transferring other files in that folder. You can add an unlimited number of files to this list.

- **Add File Type.** If you use an application that produces data files with an extension that is not on the list of file types migrated by the Files And Settings Transfer Wizard, choose that file type here. Note that you can hold down the Ctrl key to select multiple file types.

- **Remove.** Select any setting, folder, file, or file type, and click this button to remove it from the list.

Here are some pointers to help you use the Files And Settings Transfer Wizard more effectively:

Check the list of file types carefully   The default list of file types includes a huge number of file types that most people never use. In addition, it includes some file types that you might prefer not to migrate, such as music or video files. By trimming this list so it includes only the file types you want to collect, you can speed up the collection process and keep the size of the transferred files manageable.

InsideOut

In the Files And Settings Transfer Wizard, the Specific Folders and File Types settings are combined in the Files Only option. If you want to transfer only files from locations that you define, you have to clear the entire File Types list, one entry at a time; the interface doesn't allow you to eliminate the entire group, as you might expect. Fortunately, there's an easy (if less than intuitive) shortcut. Click to select the first item under the File Types heading. Hold down the Alt key and then press and hold the R key. This deletes the selected item and immediately starts removing the remaining items as well, a process that takes only a few seconds using this shortcut.

Always prefer folders over file types   If you're highly organized and you know that all your MP3 and WMA files are in a specific location, add that folder to the Specific Folders list and remove those entries from the File Types list. This also helps ensure that all your files go to the location you prefer on the new computer instead of being automatically moved into the My Music folder.

Know where applications store their data and preferences   Many small Windows utilities keep settings and preferences in specific files in specific locations. If you use any such utilities, use the Add File button to specify that you want those files transferred.

Use custom settings to back up parts of your system   If you use custom settings in the Files And Settings Transfer Wizard, you can save specific groups of settings and files. By removing all options from the wizard and then adding back only those you want to keep, you can save a specific group of settings in a single file on a floppy or network drive.

Restoring Files and Settings on Your New Computer

If you use a network or cable connection to transfer files between two computers with the Files And Settings Transfer Wizard, you control both ends of the process. After you establish a connection and finish collecting files from the old computer, the new computer will generate a random password as a security measure. You'll be prompted to enter that password on the old computer. (This is an essential security precaution to prevent an intruder from using the Files And Settings Transfer Wizard to steal information over a network.) The transfer proceeds automatically after you supply the correct password.

If you've saved the files and settings to a floppy disk or a local or network drive, follow these steps to continue the transfer process:

1 Run the Files And Settings Transfer Wizard on the new computer and then choose New Computer from the Which Computer Is This page. Click Next.

Part 1: Setup, Startup, Tune-Up

2 When prompted on the next page, choose I Don't Need The Wizard Disk, as shown here. Click Next.

3 On the next page, specify the location where the files and settings are stored. Choose a floppy drive or other removable media from the removable media list, or choose Other and click the Browse button to locate the local or network drive on which the saved files reside.

4 Click Next to begin the transfer.

Service Packs, Patches, and Windows Update

Over time, Microsoft publishes changes to Windows. Some changes are minor additions to the Windows feature set. Other changes are designated as critical updates; these patches (also known as *hotfixes*) repair bugs that can hamper your system's performance, compromise its security, or cause system crashes. At regular intervals, Microsoft gathers these patches into collections called service packs and makes them available for download. Applying a service pack to your computer is functionally equivalent to (but much simpler than) individually installing all the fixes it contains.

note The CD included with this book includes a full copy of Service Pack 1, suitable for installation on the original release of Windows XP Professional or Home Edition. If you haven't applied this service pack yet, save yourself a hefty download and use the CD copy instead. Afterward, be sure to use Windows Update to find and install any updates that have appeared since the release of Service Pack 1.

Using Windows Update Manually

The most reliable way to install these updates to your computer is with the help of Windows Update. This online service provides one-stop access to the entire collection of updates for Windows and the various programs included with it. The list of available updates includes service packs, updated device drivers, and security updates. To run Windows Update, use any of the following techniques:

- In the Help And Support Center, under Pick A Task, click Keep Your Computer Up-To-Date With Windows Update.

- Open the Start menu and choose All Programs, Windows Update.

- At a command prompt, type **wupdmgr**.

- In Internet Explorer, open the Tools menu and choose Windows Update.

- In Internet Explorer, browse to *http://windowsupdate.microsoft.com*.

The first method displays Windows Update within the Help And Support Center window, as shown in Figure 2-11. If you use any of the other methods, Windows Update appears in an Internet Explorer window.

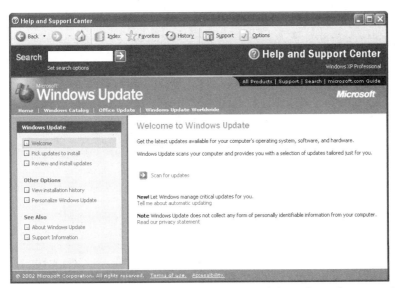

Figure 2-11. Windows Update can run as part of the Help And Support Center, as shown here, or in an ordinary Internet Explorer window.

To complete the update process, follow these steps:

1 Click Scan For Updates.

65

2 Click each of the three links on the left side—Critical Updates, Windows XP, and Driver Updates—to view information about and select available updates in those categories.

3 Read the description for each item, and then use the Add and Remove buttons to customize the list of updates to be installed. Because you'll almost certainly want to install all critical updates, they're selected by default.

4 After you finish adding items to the list, click Review And Install Updates.

InsideOut

Recommended Updates (which appear in the Windows XP category) include a slew of updates that you probably have no need for, including patches designed to fix problems with hardware you don't own, updates to components you don't use (Windows Movie Maker, for instance), and regional updates that don't apply to you. If you skip an update, though, it's waiting for you the next time you check Windows Update, unless you customize the display to eliminate individual unwanted items—or, for that matter, entire sections.

To customize Windows Update, perform a scan as usual, and then click Personalize Windows Update (under Other Options in the left pane).

newfeature!
Automating Your Updates

Windows Updates are not distributed on a regular basis. Instead, they're published when the need arises, such as when a patch is developed for a newly discovered security vulnerability. In Windows XP, you can eliminate the necessity to check for updates manually by using a new feature called Automatic Updates. With this feature enabled, you can instruct Windows to periodically check for critical updates. Using the preferences you define, Automatic Updates checks for new critical updates, downloads them in the background, using a small segment of your available Internet connection bandwidth, and—with your permission—installs them automatically.

note Automatic Update retrieves only critical updates. To view, download, and install other Windows updates and newly released drivers, you need to visit the Windows Update site.

Windows XP Service Pack 1 includes a major overhaul of the Automatic Updates feature, which was first released (naturally) through Windows Update, as a Recommended Update in June 2002. In the original release of Windows XP, you could choose to be alerted when new updates were available, and Windows would download them for you to install, but the operating system wouldn't actually perform the updates. With Service

Chapter 2: Installing and Configuring Windows XP

Pack 1 installed, the Automatic Updates dialog box includes the option to install critical updates on a specified schedule.

After you first install Windows XP, the operating system is persistent about reminding you to set up the Automatic Updates feature. You can adjust these options at any time by opening System in Control Panel (in the Performance And Maintenance group) and clicking the Automatic Updates tab. To enable Automatic Updates, select the Keep My Computer Up To Date check box at the top of the dialog box. Then select one of the three options available to you here, as shown in Figure 2-12:

Notify Me Before Downloading Any Updates And Notify Me Again Before Installing Them On My Computer   If you don't want to tie up your dial-up Internet connection downloading updates, choose this option. An icon in the notification area alerts you when a download is available; you decide whether and when to download and install it. If you decide not to install an update that has been downloaded, Windows deletes the downloaded files from your computer. If you later change your mind, open Automatic Updates and choose Declined Updates.

Download The Updates Automatically And Notify Me When They Are Ready To Be Installed   This option is most appropriate for users with high-speed, always-on Internet connections—cable modems and DSL, for instance. An icon in the notification area alerts you when a download has arrived. You can accept or reject any download.

Figure 2-12.   To choose how Windows checks for updates, choose one of the three options under Settings.

Automatically Download The Updates, And Install Them On The Schedule That I Specify   Choose this option if you want the Automatic Updates process to live up to its name completely. In this "set it and forget it" configuration, Windows Update checks for critical updates on the schedule you specify (by default at 3:00 A.M. every day, although you can change the schedule to weekly and change the time as well), downloads each one as soon as it appears, and installs the update for you. Beware, however: If an update requires restarting your computer, Windows will do so with no regard to whether any applications are open. This option is most appropriate if you leave your computer turned on.

Clearing the Keep My Computer Up To Date check box disables Automatic Updates. Doing so is appropriate if you want to manage updates from a network location instead of having each computer download and install updates individually. (For details, see the following section.)

At any time, you can review the history of updates installed on your computer; you can also see the entire list of available updates. Both options are available from the Windows Update link in the Help And Support Center.

To install an update that you previously rejected, open the System Properties dialog box and click the Automatic Updates tab; then click the Restore Declined Updates button. This button will be unavailable until at least one update has been declined.

Downloading the Update Files for Multiple Computers

Some of the available updates are quite large, often exceeding 5 MB of data. And sometimes the file size shown in Windows Update is misleading; it indicates only the size of the installer for the update, not the update itself, which might be considerably larger. Particularly if you have a slow Internet connection, you'll want to minimize the bandwidth consumed by downloads from Windows Update.

Although it's not very well advertised (compared to the myriad ways to start Windows Update—only a portion of which are enumerated earlier in this chapter), Microsoft maintains Web sites where you can download stand-alone installable versions of the security patches and other updates for Windows. After downloading these patches and updates, you can burn them to CD or make them available on a network server for installation on multiple computers. A site called Windows Update Catalog offers updates for Windows XP, Windows 2000, and Microsoft Windows .NET Server.

The easiest way to access Windows Update Catalog is to open Windows Update, click Personalize Windows Update (in the left pane), and then select Display The Link To The Windows Update Catalog Under See Also. Click Save Settings to have a link to Windows Update Catalog appear in the left pane each time you visit Windows Update. Alternatively, you can use this direct link:

http://v4.windowsupdate.microsoft.com/en/default.asp?corporate=true

Troubleshooting

Windows Update doesn't work.

When you start Windows Update, it might display a "software update incomplete" message. (This message appears before you have an opportunity to scan or select updates to install.)

Windows Update requires the use of an ActiveX control, which is installed automatically with Service Pack 1. If you have not yet installed Service Pack 1, this control is downloaded and installed the first time you access the Windows Update site. To successfully install the ActiveX control, you must

● Be logged on as a member of the Administrators group.

● Enable (with prompting) the download and running of signed ActiveX controls. (Use settings on the Security tab of the Internet Options dialog box; for more information, see "Using Security Zones," page 818.)

● Click Yes in the Security Warning dialog box that asks whether you want to install the Windows Update control.

Once the ActiveX control is installed, an explanatory message appears if a nonadministrative user tries to run Windows Update.

Disabling Windows Update

Windows Update gives any Windows user with administrative rights the ability to locate, download, and install security fixes, drivers, and other updates. That's fine on a personal computer, but in a business setting you might decide that you prefer to give a single network administrator the right to install updates rather than relying on individual users to keep their systems up-to-date. If the computers in question are running Windows XP Professional, you can set a policy that prevents individual users (even administrators) from using the Internet version of Windows Update. With this configuration, you can (and should) download and save individual updates and install them manually on each computer.

The following procedure disables manual access to Windows Update on a local computer running Windows XP Professional, shuts down automatic updates, and removes all links to the Windows Update site:

1 At a command prompt, type **gpedit.msc** to open the Group Policy console.

2 In the folder pane, open User Configuration\Administrative Templates\Windows Components\Windows Update.

3 Double-click Remove Access To Use All Windows Update Features.

4 Select Enabled. This option eliminates all manual access to Windows Update for all local users. (Select Disabled to restore access to Windows Update.)

5 In the folder pane, open User Configuration\Administrative Templates\System.

6 Double-click Windows Automatic Updates.

7 Select Disabled. This option completely removes the Automatic Updates tab from the System option in Control Panel.

Several other Windows features also trigger Windows Update. Specifically, the operating system may access Windows Update on its own in any of the following three circumstances:

- When you install a Plug and Play device that does not have a signed driver already installed

- When any user clicks the Update Driver button from the properties dialog box for an installed device

- When you run the Add Printer wizard

If you decide you want to lock these back doors to Windows Update with a policy, follow these steps:

1 At a command prompt, type **gpedit.msc** to open the Group Policy console.

2 In the folder pane, open User Configuration\Administrative Templates\System.

3 Double-click Configure Driver Search Locations.

4 Select Enabled and then choose the Don't Search Windows Update option.

For more information about group policy, see Appendix E, "Group Policy."

Accessibility Options

As in previous versions, Windows XP includes three accessibility options designed to make the operating system more usable for persons with vision, hearing, or mobility impairments. These tools are available for use during Setup—when using Windows Setup, click the Accessibility Options button; from a command prompt, add the /a switch to the Winnt.exe command. These options can also be adjusted after Setup on a per-user basis. You can use any of the following tools alone or in combination:

- **Magnifier** enlarges part of the screen, making it easier for persons with vision impairments to see objects and read text.

- **Narrator** converts on-screen text to speech and sends it to your computer's speakers. This option allows people who are blind or have severe vision impairments to use Windows.

---

tip   **Let the Magnifier window float**

The Magnifier tool can be useful for anyone whose vision is less than perfect. You don't have to use it all the time to benefit from it. Normally, the Magnifier window sits in a fixed location at the top of the screen and tracks the movement of the mouse pointer. That default location is extremely wide and short; in this configuration, you can adjust its height, but only by reducing the size of the window you're actually working in. You may find it easier to work with the viewing window by undocking it and adjusting its dimensions. Point to the Magnifier pane, click, and drag to the location where you want it to appear. Drag the window borders to change the height or width of the Magnifier pane.

- **On-Screen Keyboard** provides an alternate means for Windows users with impaired mobility to enter text using a pointing device. Options on the Keyboard menu let you change keyboard layouts; options on the Settings menu let you control how the on-screen keyboard works—you can choose whether to select a letter by clicking, for example, or by allowing the pointer to pause over a key for a specific amount of time.

All three accessibility tools are available to any user, at any time, by choosing All Programs, Accessories, Accessibility. The Accessibility Wizard, also found on this menu, walks you through the process of adjusting Windows Display settings and configuring accessibility options.

Troubleshooting

After experimenting with the Accessibility Wizard, your visual settings are changed unexpectedly.

During its Q&A process, this wizard makes changes to the size of objects such as fonts and icons used in the Windows interface. Even if you back out of the wizard and tell it not to apply any changes, you may find that your taskbar and tray icons have been changed. To restore your preferred settings, open Control Panel's Display option and click the Themes tab. If you previously saved your settings, choose the saved theme here; otherwise, choose one of the default Windows Themes.

If you want accessibility options to be available at all times, even before logging on to the computer, you need to enable the Utility Manager. This option (shown below) allows you to quickly start or stop an accessibility option. Although the Utility Manager is available from the Accessibility group on the Accessories menu, you can access it more quickly by using its built-in keyboard shortcut: Windows logo key + U. This shortcut is the only way to display the Utility Manager before logging on.

Adding and Removing Windows Components

In previous Windows versions, you could select a Custom Setup option, which allowed you to pick and choose from a lengthy menu of available components during the initial Windows installation. In Windows XP, no such option is available. When you run the Setup program from a CD, you get the standard complement of Windows components, including multimedia tools, games, wallpaper, and other frills you might prefer to do without. In addition, some optional components (mostly advanced services) are left out. In this section, we'll show you how to tweak a Windows installation so that you end up with the pieces you want and no more.

After you complete the Setup process, open Add Or Remove Programs from Control Panel and then click Add/Remove Windows Components. This opens the Windows Components Wizard, shown in Figure 2-13.

By selecting or clearing boxes shown here, you can add or remove any of a small list of optional Windows components. In some cases, a component includes subcomponents that can be individually installed or removed; click the component name (instead of the check box) and click the Details button to see a list of available subcomponents. If you're setting up an office computer, for instance, you can navigate to Accessories And Utilities and uninstall the entire Games group, or, on the next sublevel, individually remove Solitaire, Pinball, and other time-wasters.

Figure 2-13. This dialog box lets you install or remove a limited number of Windows options.

Table 2-3 lists the optional components available in a default installation of Windows XP.

Table 2-3. **Optional Windows Components**

Component	Installed by Default?	Comments
Accessories And Utilities	Yes	Click the Details button to remove some or all accessories (including desktop wallpaper and document templates) and games.
Fax Services	No	The best way to add fax capabilities to Windows XP is to open the Printers And Faxes folder and click the Set Up Faxing link under Printer Tasks.
Indexing Service	Yes	To enable, disable, or configure this service, use the Search pane in Windows Explorer. Clear this box only if you want to completely remove the service. (For more details, see "Using Indexing Service and Query Language," page 480.)
Internet Explorer	Yes	Clear this box to remove the Internet Explorer icon from the Desktop and Start Menu. This option does not remove any Internet Explorer components.
Internet Information Services (Professional Only)	No	Select this box to add a personal Web server to Windows XP. Click the Details button to select individual subcomponents. (For more details, see Chapter 24, "Hosting a Web or FTP Site.")
Management And Monitoring Tools	No	This option adds two Simple Network Management Protocol (SNMP) agents designed for use with centralized administration tools.
Message Queuing (Professional Only)	No	This option adds software that allows applications to communicate with other applications over a corporate network.
MSN Explorer	Yes	Microsoft's all-in-one Web package integrates a browser with e-mail and messaging capabilities. If you're comfortable with Internet Explorer and a full-strength e-mail program, you can remove this option and reclaim 13 MB of disk space.

Table 2-3. *(continued)*

Component	Installed by Default?	Comments
Networking Services	No	Click the Details button to see the three options listed here. Most Windows users don't need the RIP Listener or Simple TCP/IP Services. Choose the Universal Plug And Play (UPnP) option to enable communications between your computer and stand-alone UPnP devices.
Other Network File And Print Services	No	Install this option to add Print Services for UNIX, which allows UNIX-based network clients to connect to Windows printers.
Update Root Certificates	Yes	Automatically downloads the most current security certificates for secure e-mail, Web browsing, and software delivery.

A handful of additional Windows components that are part of a full Windows XP Professional installation can actually be removed as well, although they're initially hidden from the list in the Windows Components Wizard. To unhide these components so that you can remove them if needed, you need to edit the Setup Information file that contains details about that component. To add Windows Messenger to the list of optional components, for instance, follow these steps:

1 Open Windows Explorer, navigate to the %SystemRoot%\Inf folder, and then select the Sysoc.inf file. (Before making any changes, make a backup copy.)

2 In Notepad or a similar text editor, open Sysoc.inf.

3 Each hidden component has its own line in this file, with the word *hide* at the end of the line. For the Windows Messenger service, this line reads as follows:

```
msmsgs=msgrocm.dll,OcEntry,msmsgs.inf,hide,7
```

Edit the line to read:

```
msmsgs=msgrocm.dll,OcEntry,msmsgs.inf, ,7
```

4 Save Sysoc.inf and reopen the Windows Components Wizard. Scroll to the bottom of the list to see the newly available component.

Chapter 2

> **caution** By removing the word *hide* from other entries in Sysoc.inf, you can add them to the list of Windows components that can be removed. If you're not 100 percent certain of the consequences, don't do it! Removing Windows Messenger, for instance, makes it more difficult to connect with another Windows XP user via the Remote Assistance feature. In some cases, restoring an option to the list of components that can be removed has no practical effect. Even after adding Terminal Server to the list, for example, you cannot select or remove it. The check box simply doesn't respond to clicks.

Selecting a Web Browser and Other Middleware Components

When you install Windows XP Service Pack 1, a new option appears in the Add Or Remove Programs dialog box. This option, imposed as a condition of settlement of the antitrust suit brought by the United States Department of Justice, gives Windows users the option to remove access to a number of Microsoft programs that were previously tightly integrated into Windows. This list of "middleware" components includes the following:

- **Web Browser.** The Microsoft default program is Internet Explorer.

- **E-mail Program.** Unless you specify otherwise, Windows uses Outlook Express for this function.

- **Media Player.** In Windows XP, Windows Media Player 8 is the default utility for playing sounds, videos, and media files.

- **Instant Messaging Program.** Windows Messenger is integrated into a number of places in Windows XP, including Internet Explorer and Outlook Express.

- **Virtual Machine for Java.** Microsoft includes its own Java VM, which can be downloaded from Windows Update.

Clicking the Set Program Access And Defaults icon on the left reveals the options shown in Figure 2-14. With the help of options in this dialog box, you can change the default program used for any of the five tasks listed here. You can also remove easy access to any or all of the Microsoft programs used to perform these tasks.

If you installed a retail copy of Windows XP and then added Service Pack 1, the first option, Microsoft Windows, is selected. This option maintains the status quo, with all five categories being assigned to their default Microsoft programs.

Choosing the Non-Microsoft options removes access to all five Microsoft programs listed above. If you previously had icons for Internet Explorer, Outlook Express, and other programs on the Start menu, the Quick Launch bar, or the desktop, they are

Chapter 2: Installing and Configuring Windows XP

Figure 2-14. Use this dialog box to change default programs used with Windows and to hide access to Microsoft programs and utilities.

removed. If you have not installed alternative programs for e-mail and Web access, the E-mail and Internet choices at the top of the Start menu change to generic icons, and clicking either one opens the Internet Options dialog box.

InsideOut

When you choose the drastic Non-Microsoft option, the code that runs Internet Explorer, Outlook Express, and other utilities is still available on your computer. If you don't install an alternative Web browser, Internet Explorer will still start up when you double-click an Internet shortcut or type a Web address in the Run box. Likewise, you can launch any program by typing the name of its executable file in the Run box: **msimn** for Outlook Express, **wmplayer** for Windows Media Player.

Finally, you can banish some Microsoft programs while keeping others available. After installing the alternate software (the Mozilla Web browser, for instance, or RealPlayer), open the Set Program Access And Defaults dialog box and choose the Custom option. For each category, you can choose whether to use the currently installed program or the Microsoft default. In addition, you can choose to hide access to one or more of the Microsoft programs while allowing access to others.

note Because this option is new, not all alternative programs work with it yet. If your favorite non-Microsoft Web browser or media player doesn't respond when you select these options, check with the developer and see if a new version is in the works.

Configuring System Restore Options

When a rogue program or buggy driver causes your computer to crash, the System Restore feature can be a lifesaver. (For details on how you can use System Restore, see "Undoing Configuration Mistakes with System Restore," page 900.) If you accept its default settings this feature will gobble up a hefty chunk of disk space and can have unexpected (and unpleasant) side effects, including the deletion of recently downloaded files with no warning. Before you need to use System Restore, familiarize yourself with its workings and learn how to customize it so it doesn't take you by surprise. You can take charge of System Restore in several ways.

To access the full set of System Restore options, open System in Control Panel and click the System Restore tab, shown in Figure 2-15.

Click here to completely disable System Restore

Click here to adjust settings (or disable System Restore) for the selected drive

Figure 2-15. By default, System Restore monitors changes to every drive on your system and sets aside up to 12 percent of each drive for storing its data.

Using this dialog box, you can adjust any of the following settings:

● **Drive space used.** By default, System Restore reserves 12 percent of available disk space on every drive. On a 30-GB drive, that adds up to an excessive 3.6 GB of storage space. To rein in space usage for a specific drive, click the Settings button to the right of that drive and move the slider control to the left, as shown in Figure 2-16.

Chapter 2: Installing and Configuring Windows XP

Figure 2-16.   Use this slider to reduce the appetite of System Restore. The setting shown here is one-third the normal 12 percent allocation, but should be sufficient for most uses.

> **note**   The default location for System Restore data is *d*:\System Volume Information, where *d* is the letter of each drive. Each restore point is stored in its own subfolder, under the name _restore*GUID*, where *GUID* is a unique 32-character alphanumeric identifier. This location cannot be changed. On an NTFS drive, these files are not accessible to users, even those in the Administrators group; the default NTFS permissions grant access only to the System account.

● **Drives to be monitored.** By design, System Restore keeps tabs on every drive on your system. If you've set aside one or more drives exclusively for data, you can safely turn off System Restore monitoring on those drives. This action has the effect of reclaiming the space used for restore points; it also prevents System Restore from inadvertently wiping out files on those drives. To exclude a drive from monitoring, open the System Properties dialog box and click the System Restore tab. Select the drive to exclude, click the Settings button, and select Turn Off System Restore On This Drive. Note that this option is not available on the drive that contains your system files.

> **caution**   System Restore is a powerful tool, and you shouldn't disable it without a good reason. If you're extremely low on disk space and a hard disk upgrade is impractical or impossible (as on some notebook computers), you might choose to do so. Otherwise, let it run.

● **Files and folders to be monitored.** By default, System Restore maintains a strict hands-off policy on all files stored in your My Documents folder and in the %SystemRoot%\Downloaded Program Files folder. Every other folder on your system is fair game, however, and the results can be disconcerting. After you use System Restore to roll back your system to a previous configuration, you may discover that the utility wiped out executable files, scripts, dynamic link libraries (DLLs), TrueType fonts, VBScript (.vbs) files, and files using other monitored formats that were stored outside of your My Documents folder and that had been downloaded after the date of the restore point you selected. If you routinely download programs or create PDF files in a non-protected location, you may want to specifically declare that location to be exempt from System Restore monitoring. To do so, you must add a value to the registry. Follow these steps:

1 Open Registry Editor (Regedit.exe) and select the following key:

HKLM\System\CurrentControlSet\Control\BackupRestore\FilesNotToBackup

2 Choose Edit, New, Multi-String Value.

3 Give the new value a name that describes the location you're about to specify: My Downloads, for instance.

4 Double-click the newly created value. Enter the full path of the folder you want to protect from monitoring and then click OK.

Note that the change you just made will not go into effect until after you set your next restore point manually or Windows creates a system checkpoint. Therefore, it's good practice to set a fresh restore point after making changes.

If you ever receive a "low disk space" warning for any drive, check your System Restore settings immediately. The utility will shut down on its own if free disk space drops below 200 MB on any single partition. When this happens, you receive no warning. The only indication appears when you open the System Restore properties dialog box, where each drive letter's status is listed as Suspended.

Windows might not turn System Restore back on automatically. To do so manually, try the following workaround:

1 From Control Panel, open the System tool and click the System Restore tab.

2 Select the Turn Off System Restore On All Drives option and click Apply. This completely shuts down System Restore.

Chapter 2: Installing and Configuring Windows XP

3 Clear the Turn Off System Restore On All Drives option and click Apply. The Status column for each drive changes to Monitoring, an indication that System Restore is working again.

Part 1: Setup, Startup, Tune-Up

4 From the Available Drives list, select the entry for any drive that you want to exclude from System Restore protection and click the Settings button.

5 Select the Turn Off System Restore On This Drive option, and click OK. Repeat for other drives you want to exclude from System Restore.

6 Click OK to close the System Restore dialog box.

If the drive that produced the "low disk space" warning is normally full (as might be the case on a drive used to store a large archive of media files that never change), be sure to exclude that drive so that it doesn't continually disable System Restore.

Configuring Startup Options

For most users, most of the time, starting up Windows is a simple process: turn on the computer, wait for the Welcome screen to appear, click your logon name, and away you go.

For more details about customizing the Windows logon process, see "Controlling How Users Log On," page 107.

On multiboot configurations, the process gets slightly more complicated, thanks to a startup menu that allows you to choose from different operating systems.

Customizing Multiboot Menus

If more than one operating system is installed on your computer, a boot menu appears each time you start the machine. This boot menu lets you choose which operating system you want to run. (For information about setting up multiple operating systems, see "Installing Windows XP on a Computer with Other Operating Systems," page 33.) By default, the boot menu stays on screen for 30 seconds; an on-screen timer lets you know how much time you have left. If you don't choose an option before the timer runs out, the default operating system (usually the most recent installation of Windows XP) starts

Chapter 2: Installing and Configuring Windows XP

up. While the boot menu is visible, you can press the Up or Down Arrow key to high-light a different operating system, which also stops the timer's countdown. Press Enter to start the selected operating system.

At any time, you can change the menu's display time and specify which operating system starts by default. To adjust boot menu settings, follow these steps:

1 Open System in Control Panel and click the Advanced tab. (Alternatively, click the Start button, right-click My Computer, and choose Properties.)

2 In the Startup And Recovery section, click Settings to display the dialog box shown in Figure 2-17.

3 In the Default Operating System list, select the operating system that you want to be initially highlighted on the boot menu and started by default.

4 To adjust the length of time (in seconds) that the boot menu is displayed, change the number to the right of Time To Display List Of Operating Systems. Choose any number between 1 and 99. To set the boot menu so that the default operating system starts automatically, clear the check box at the left, or enter 0.

Figure 2-17. Control the boot menu by setting options in the System Startup section of this dialog box.

Choices you make in this dialog box actually write changes to the Boot.ini file, which is stored in the root of the system drive. You can also click the Edit button to open the file in Notepad and edit it directly.

> **note** You can't rename the operating systems in the Default Operating System list from this dialog box; to do that, you must edit Boot.ini, as described in the following section, "Modifying Boot.ini."

Overview of the Startup Process

When you turn on your computer, it goes through an elaborate startup process. The process begins when your computer performs its power-on self test (POST), which is followed by the POST for each adapter card that has a BIOS, such as SCSI adapters and video cards. The system BIOS then reads the master boot record (MBR)—the first sector on the first hard disk—and transfers control to the code in the MBR, which is created by Windows XP Setup. This is where Windows takes over the startup process. Here's what happens next:

1 The MBR reads the boot sector—the first sector of the active partition—which contains code that starts Ntldr, the bootstrap loader for Windows XP. The initial role of Ntldr is to switch the system to protected mode with paging enabled (to allow full memory addressing), start the file system, read the Boot.ini file, and display the boot menu.

Note that Ntldr must be located in the root folder of the active partition, along with Ntdetect.com, Boot.ini, Bootsect.dos (if you're going to dual boot), and Ntbootdd.sys (if you're using certain SCSI adapters for the drive with the boot partition). For more information about sectors, partitions, and drives, see Chapter 27, "Managing Disks and Drives."

2 If you select Windows XP from the boot menu, Ntldr runs Ntdetect.com to gather information about the currently installed hardware. Ntldr then uses the Advanced RISC Computing (ARC) path specified in Boot.ini to find the boot partition—the one where Windows XP is installed—and loads the two files that constitute the Windows XP core: Ntoskrnl.exe and Hal.dll. Both files must be located in the %SystemRoot%\System32 folder.

3 Ntldr continues by reading the files that make up the registry, selecting a hardware profile and control set, and loading device drivers.

4 At this point, Ntoskrnl.exe takes over and starts Winlogon.exe, which in turn starts Lsass.exe (Local Security Administration), the program that displays the Welcome screen (or the Windows logon dialog box) and allows you to log on with your user name and password.

Understanding the boot process can help you to pinpoint problems that occur during startup. For more information, see "Using Advanced Startup Options," page 897.

Chapter 2: Installing and Configuring Windows XP

Modifying Boot.ini

To adjust some startup options, you might need to open Boot.ini and edit it manually. Because this file is set with the hidden and system attributes, it doesn't ordinarily appear in Windows Explorer; to edit it, use either of these techniques:

- Open the Run dialog box and type **C:\boot.ini**. (This assumes that drive C contains your startup files.)

- Open System in Control Panel, click the Advanced tab, click the Settings button under Startup And Recovery, and click the Edit button in the System Startup section.

ARC Paths in Boot.ini

In the [operating systems] section of the Boot.ini file, you'll find a somewhat cryptic line for each installed copy of Windows XP, Windows 2000, or Windows NT. This line uses Advanced RISC Computing (ARC) paths to specify the location of the boot partition. On a system that uses standard IDE drives, the ARC path in Boot.ini looks like this:

multi(0)disk(0)rdisk(0)partition(2)\WINDOWS

The first parameter identifies the disk controller. In the multi() form, it should always be 0.

The disk parameter is not used in the multi() form and should always be 0.

The rdisk parameter in the multi() form specifies the ordinal number on the controller (starting with 0) of the disk that contains the boot partition. Thus, if multiple hard disks are installed, the first disk is 0, the second is 1, and so on.

The partition parameter identifies the partition number of the boot partition. Partitions on a disk are numbered starting with 1.

The last part of the ARC path (usually \WINDOWS or \WINNT) identifies the path to the folder where that version of Windows is installed.

Two additional ARC structures identify disks using scsi() and signature() as the beginning of the ARC path, as described in Knowledge Base articles Q227704 and Q102873. It's rare that you'd ever need (or want) to edit any of the ARC paths in Boot.ini. (The most likely reason is if you've used a third-party utility like PartitionMagic to add or remove partitions on your boot or system drive.) In fact, if you don't have a deep understanding of disk structures, you can render your system unable to start by editing these settings incorrectly. But if you need to revive a system that's lost its Boot.ini and other key startup files, you might need this information.

In either case, the Boot.ini file opens in Notepad. A typical Boot.ini file might look like this:

```
[boot loader]
timeout=30
default=multi(0)disk(0)rdisk(0)partition(2)\WINDOWS
[operating systems]
multi(0)disk(0)rdisk(0)partition(2)\WINDOWS="Microsoft Windows XP
    Professional" /fastdetect
C:\="Microsoft Windows Millennium Edition"
```

With two exceptions, the [boot loader] section contains items that are more easily changed through the Startup And Recovery dialog box, as explained in the previous section. One exception is if you want the boot menu to be displayed until you press Enter, regardless of how much time elapses. To configure your boot menu to work that way, set the timeout value to –1. (You can't set that value in the Startup And Recovery dialog box.)

The other exception that requires you to edit Boot.ini is when you want to change the descriptions or optional parameters in the [operating systems] section. Each line represents a boot menu item and includes the ARC path of the operating system's boot partition (see "ARC Paths in Boot.ini" on the preceding page), the text that appears on the boot menu (enclosed in quotation marks), and optional parameters. You can adjust each item as follows:

● Change the text description for each operating system—particularly if multiple copies of the same operating system are installed on your computer. If you've installed a clean copy of Windows XP to test a few new programs, for instance, you might want to change its description to "Windows XP Pro – Clean Install."

● Append a parameter to the Windows 2000 or Windows XP line (following /Fastdetect, a parameter that disables serial mouse detection). Most parameters are for development and debugging purposes only. *Microsoft Windows XP Professional Resource Kit Documentation* (Microsoft Press, 2001) contains a more complete list. Here are two parameters you might want to try:

   ■ /Noguiboot eliminates the Windows splash screen during startup. Instead you get to continue staring at the horizontal bar at the bottom of the screen.

   ■ /Sos displays the name of each driver as it loads and provides additional text descriptions of what's occurring during startup. It also shows the Windows XP build number, service pack level, number of processors, and amount of installed memory, providing a quick confirmation that Windows is installed correctly and that it's properly recognizing your computer's configuration.

● Remove an item from the menu. Doing so won't free the space used by the operating system whose line you remove; it simply removes the item from the menu. However, you can subsequently remove that operating system's files after you boot into one of the remaining operating systems in the list.

> **caution**   Don't remove the line that matches the default setting in the [boot loader] section.

Adding the Recovery Console

The Recovery Console is a no-frills command-line environment that you can use to recover from serious startup problems. With Recovery Console, you can log in as a member of the Administrators group and access files and folders on your hard drives, format drives, start and stop services, replace corrupt files, and so on.

> **For details about how to use the Recovery Console in case of disaster, see "Making Repairs from the Recovery Console," page 907.**

Although you can run the Recovery Console by booting directly from the Windows XP CD, it's much more convenient to set it up as a startup option on your boot menu. Do it now, before you need it, by following these steps:

1   Insert the Windows XP CD into your drive.

2   At a command prompt, type *d*:**\i386\winnt32.exe /cmdcons** (replacing *d* with the letter of your CD drive).

A Windows Setup message appears, describing the Recovery Console option.

3   Click Yes to install the console.

The next time you start your computer, you'll see a "Microsoft Windows Recovery Console" entry on the boot menu.

If you decide for whatever reason that you no longer want the Recovery Console on the boot menu, follow these steps to remove it:

1 Edit the Boot.ini file to remove the Recovery Console entry (as described in "Modifying Boot.ini," page 85.) The entry should look like this:

```
C:\cmdcons\bootsect.dat="Microsoft Windows Recovery Console
    " /cmdcons
```

2 Open Windows Explorer, browse to the root directory of the drive specified in the Boot.ini entry for Recovery Console, and then delete the Cmdcons folder. (Because this is a hidden system folder, you might need to adjust folder options to make it visible, as described in "Hidden Files and Folders," page 435.)

3 In the root directory, delete the file Cmldr.

Removing the Recovery Console will recover about 7 MB of disk space.

Chapter 3

Controlling Access to Your Computer

Using security concepts that are central to the industrial-strength security in Microsoft Windows NT and Windows 2000, Windows XP allows you to restrict access to your computer so that only people you authorize can use the computer or view its files. This is a sharp departure from Windows 95/98/Me, in which bypassing security was as simple as pressing Esc when Windows asked you for a password. With Windows XP, you can

- Require each user to identify himself or herself when logging on

- Control access to files and other resources that you own

- Audit system events, such as logons and the use of files and other resources

For information about auditing, see Chapter 38, "Auditing Security."

Of course, if your computer is in a secure location where only people you trust have physical access to it, you might not have such concerns. Because the designers of Windows XP were able to provide for the needs of those who want convenience as well as those who need security, Windows XP works for you too. You'll still probably want to create a user account for each person who uses the computer, because associated with each account is a user profile that stores all manner of information unique to that user: favorite Web sites, desktop background, document folders, and so on. With features such as the Welcome screen and Fast User Switching, described in this chapter, you can log on or switch between user accounts with only a few clicks.

At Home with Windows XP

With respect to features described in this chapter, the most significant differences between Windows XP Professional and Windows XP Home Edition are the following:

- In Windows XP Home Edition, Simple File Sharing is the only available file-sharing mode. Simple File Sharing provides Windows XP Home Edition users with an easier-to-understand user interface, but it reduces the granularity with which you can assign permissions to shared resources. For an overview of the differences between Simple File Sharing and the alternative sharing mode available to Professional users, see "Simple File Sharing vs. Windows 2000–Style Sharing," page 98. For more details about these differences, see "Simple File Sharing vs. Advanced Permissions," page 499.

- In Windows XP Home Edition, you can't log on to the Administrator account except in Safe Mode. For information about the Administrator account, see "What Happened to the Administrator Account?" page 117.

Certain of the procedures described in this chapter are available only in Windows XP Professional, because they involve the use of MMC snap-ins that are not included in Windows XP Home Edition. Wherever possible, we describe workarounds that are available to Home Edition users. For example, the Local Users And Groups snap-in (lusrmgr.msc) is not included in Windows XP Home Edition. The Net User and Net Localgroup commands are available in both versions of Windows XP, however, and you can do the same things (and more) with these command-line utilities that you can do with Local Users And Groups.

Introducing Windows XP Security

The Windows XP approach to security is discretionary. That is, each securable system resource—each file or printer, for example—has an owner, who has discretion over who can and cannot access the resource. Usually, a resource is owned by the user who created it. If you create a file, for example, you are the file's owner under ordinary circumstances. (Computer administrators, however, can take ownership of resources they didn't create.)

note To exercise full discretionary control over individual files, you must store those files on an NTFS volume. Windows XP supports the FAT and FAT32 file systems used by MS-DOS and Windows 95, Windows 98, and Windows Me for the sake of compatibility. However, the FAT and FAT32 systems were not designed with security in mind. To enjoy the full benefits of Windows XP security, you must use NTFS. For more information, see "NTFS or FAT32: Which Disk Format Should You Choose?" on page 920.

To determine which users have access to a resource, Windows assigns a *security ID* (SID) to each user account. Your SID (a gigantic number guaranteed to be unique) follows you around wherever you go in Windows. When you log on, the operating system first validates your user name and password. Then it creates a *security access token*. You can think of this as the electronic equivalent of an ID badge. It includes your user name and SID, plus information about any security groups to which your account belongs. (Security groups are described later in this chapter.) Any program you start gets a copy of your security access token.

Whenever you attempt to walk through a controlled "door" in Windows (for example, when you connect to a shared printer), or any time a program attempts to do that on your behalf, the operating system examines your security access token and decides whether to let you pass. If access is permitted, you notice nothing. If access is denied, you see an unavailable menu or dialog box control or, in some cases, you get to hear a beep and read a refusal message.

In determining whom to pass and whom to block, Windows consults the resource's *access control list* (ACL). This is simply a list of SIDs and the access privileges associated with each one. Every resource subject to access control has an ACL.

Permissions and Rights

Windows distinguishes two types of access privileges: permissions and rights. A *permission* is the ability to access a particular object in some defined manner—for example, to write to an NTFS file or to modify a printer queue. A *right* is the ability to perform a particular systemwide action, such as logging on or resetting the clock.

The owner of a resource (or an administrator) assigns permissions to the resource via its properties dialog box. For example, if you are the printer owner or have administrative privileges, you can restrict someone from using a particular printer by visiting the properties dialog box for that printer. Administrators set rights via the Local Security Policy console in the Administrative Tools folder. If you have an administrative account and you're using Windows XP Professional, you can use Local Security Policy to grant someone the right to load a device driver.

> **note** In this book, as in many of the Windows XP messages and dialog boxes, *privileges* serves as an informal term encompassing both permissions and rights.

Chapter 3

In Depth: Security Identifiers

Windows XP security relies on the use of a security identifier (SID) to identify a user. When you create a user account, Windows assigns a unique SID to that account. The SID remains uniquely associated with that user account until the account is deleted, whereupon the SID is never used again—for that user or any other user. Even if you re-create an account with identical information, a new SID is created.

A SID is a variable-length value that contains a revision level, a 48-bit Identifier Authority value, and a number of 32-bit subauthority values. The SID takes the form S-1-*x*-*y1*-*y2*-.... S-1 identifies it as a revision 1 SID; *x* is the value for the IdentifierAuthority; and *y1*, *y2*, and so on are values for subauthorities.

You'll sometimes see the SID in a security dialog box (for example, on the Security tab of a file's properties dialog box while Simple File Sharing is not enabled) before Windows has had time to look up the user account name. If a SID on a Security tab doesn't change to a name, it's because it's a SID for an account that has been deleted; you can safely delete it from the permissions list because it'll never be used again. You'll also see SIDs in the hidden protected operating system folder \Recycler (each SID you see in this folder represents the Recycle Bin for a particular user), in the registry (the HKEY_USERS hive contains a key, identified by SID, for each user account on the computer), and deep in the %UserProfile%\Application Data\Microsoft folder structure, among other places.

Not all SIDs are unique. A number of commonly used SIDs are constant among all Windows XP installations. For example, S-1-5-18 is the SID for the built-in System account, a hidden member of the Administrators group that is used by the operating system and by services that log on using the System account. *Microsoft Windows XP Professional Resource Kit Documentation* (Microsoft Press, 2001) contains a complete list of such SIDs, called *well-known SIDs*.

User Accounts

The backbone of Windows XP security is the ability to uniquely identify each user. During setup—or at any time later—a computer administrator creates a user account for each user. The *user account* is identified by a user name and (optionally) a password, which the user provides when logging on to the system. Windows then controls, monitors, and restricts access to system resources based on the permissions and rights associated with each user account by the resource owners and the system administrator.

In addition to such "normal" user accounts, Windows provides two special accounts that have predefined sets of permissions and rights associated with them: the Administrator account and the Guest account.

- **Administrator account.** Every computer running Windows XP has a special account named Administrator. This account has full rights over the entire computer. It can create other user accounts and is generally responsible for managing the computer. Many system features and rights are off limits to accounts other than Administrator (or another account that belongs to the Administrators group).

- **Guest account.** The Guest account resides at the other end of the privilege spectrum. It is designed to allow an infrequent or temporary user such as a visitor to log on to the system without providing a password and use the system in a restricted manner. (By default, the Guest account is disabled on a clean install of Windows XP; no one can use an account that's disabled.) The Guest account is also used for access to shared network resources on your computer when Simple File Sharing is enabled.

> For information about using the Administrator account, see "What Happened to the Administrator Account?" on page 117. For information about using the Guest account, see "Setting Up a Secure Guest Account," page 139.

Local Accounts and Groups vs. Domain Accounts and Groups

Windows stores information about user accounts and security groups in a security database. Where the security database resides depends on whether your computer is part of a workgroup or a domain.

A workgroup setup (or a standalone computer) uses only local user accounts and local groups—the type described in this chapter. The security database on each computer stores the local user accounts and local groups that are specific to that computer. Local user accounts allow users to log on only to the computer where you create the local account. Likewise, a local account allows users to access resources only on that same computer. (This doesn't mean that you can't share your resources with other network users, even if you're not part of a domain. For details, see Chapter 32, "Managing Shared Folders and Printers.") With such a setup, you avoid the initial expense of purchasing and configuring Microsoft Windows .NET Server—but because you must manage user accounts on each individual computer, this process becomes unwieldy with more than five or ten computers.

The alternative is to set up the network as a domain. A Windows *domain* is a network that has at least one machine running Windows .NET Server, Windows 2000 Server,

(continued)

Chapter 3

Local Accounts and Groups vs. Domain Accounts and Groups (continued)

or Windows NT Server as a domain controller. A *domain controller* is a computer that maintains the security database, including user accounts and groups, for the domain. With a *domain user account,* you can log on to any computer in the domain (subject to your privileges set at the domain level and on individual computers), and you can gain access to permitted resources anywhere on the network.

In general, if your computer is part of a Windows domain, you shouldn't need to concern yourself with local user accounts. Instead, all user accounts should be managed at the domain controller. But you might want to add certain domain user accounts or groups to your local groups. By default, the Domain Admins group is a member of the local Administrators group, and Domain Users is a member of the local Users group; members of those domain groups thereby assume the rights and permissions afforded to the local groups to which they belong.

Domain-based accounts and groups are also known as *global accounts* and *global groups*.

For more information about working with domains, see Chapter 34, "Working with Windows Domains."

newfeature!
Account Types

Account type is a simplified way—new in Windows XP—of describing membership in a security group, a collection of user accounts. Groups allow a system administrator to create classes of users who share common privileges. For example, if everyone in the accounting department needs access to the Payables folder, the administrator can create a group called Accounting and grant the entire group access to that folder. If the administrator then adds all user accounts belonging to employees in the accounting department to the Accounting group, these users will automatically have access to the Payables folder. A user account can belong to one group, more than one group, or no group at all.

Groups are a valuable administrative tool. They simplify the job of ensuring that all members with common access needs have an identical set of privileges. Although you can grant privileges to each user account individually, doing so is tedious and prone to errors—and usually considered poor practice. You're better off assigning permissions and rights to groups, and then adding user accounts to the group with the appropriate privileges.

Permissions and rights for group members are cumulative. That means that if a user account belongs to more than one group, the user enjoys all the privileges accorded to all groups of which the user account is a member.

Chapter 3: Controlling Access to Your Computer

Windows XP classifies each user account as one of four account types:

- **Computer administrator.** Members of the Administrators group are classified as computer administrator accounts. The Administrators group, which
by default includes the Administrator account and all accounts you create
during Windows XP setup, has more control over the system than any
other group. Computer administrators can

    - Create, change, and delete user accounts and groups

    - Install programs

    - Share folders

    - Set permissions

    - Access all files

    - Take ownership of files

    - Grant rights to other user accounts and to themselves

    - Install or remove hardware devices

    - Log on in Safe Mode

- **Limited.** Members of the Users group are classified as limited accounts. By
default, limited accounts can

    - Change the password, picture, and associated .NET Passport for their
own user account

    - Use programs that have been installed on the computer

    - View permissions (if Simple File Sharing is disabled)

    - Create, change, and delete files in their document folders

    - View files in shared document folders

- **Guest.** Members of the Guests group are shown as guest accounts. Guest
accounts have privileges similar to limited accounts. A user logged on with
the Guest account (but not any other account that is a member of the
Guests group) cannot create a password for the account.

- **Unknown.** The account type for a user account that is not a member of the
Administrators, Users, or Guests group is shown as Unknown. Because accounts
you create with User Accounts in Control Panel are automatically assigned to
the Administrators group or the Users group, you'll see the Unknown account
type only if you upgraded your computer from an earlier version of Windows
(for example, new users in Windows 2000 are assigned by default to the Power
Users group) or if you use the Local Users And Groups console or the Net
Localgroup command to manage group membership. (The Local Users And
Groups console is not available in Windows XP Home Edition.)

> **tip** **Reserve administrator accounts for special occasions**
>
> A limited account is the best and safest type for everyday use. Limited accounts and their limited privileges provide fewer opportunities for malicious hackers to cause problems; a limited account also prevents some self-inflicted damage, such as accidentally deleting shared files. Unfortunately, some programs don't work properly when accessed by a limited account. Try making your own account a limited account (or, if you use Windows XP Professional, a member of the Power Users group) and see whether you can perform all your normal computing activities. When you need to run a program that doesn't work with limited accounts or you need to make administrative changes, use a separate administrator account you set up for the purpose. (Log on using your administrator account or use the Run As command. For details about Run As, see "Running a Program as Another User," page 188.) If this becomes too cumbersome, change your everyday account back to an administrator account.

There's nothing wrong with accounts of this type, and if you need to use other security groups to classify the accounts on your computer you should do so. In User Accounts, all the usual account-management tasks are available for accounts of Unknown type, but if you want to view or change group membership, you'll need to use Local Users And Groups or the Net Localgroup command.

> **For information about the User Accounts option in Control Panel, see "Working with User Accounts," page 100. For information about Local Users And Groups and Net Localgroup management tools, see "Advanced Account Setup Options," page 120.**

A clean installation of Windows XP Professional creates the following groups—each with predefined rights and permissions—in addition to the Administrators, Users, and Guests groups:

● **Backup Operators.** Members of the Backup Operators group have the right to back up and restore folders and files—even ones that they don't otherwise have permission to access. Backup operators also have access to the Backup Utility program.

● **HelpServicesGroup.** This group is used by Microsoft and computer manufacturers for Remote Assistance, enabling technical support personnel to connect to your computer (only with your permission, of course!).

> **For information about Remote Assistance, see "Connecting to Another PC with Remote Assistance," page 154.**

● **Network Configuration Operators.** Members of this group have administrative privileges in areas that relate to setting up and configuring networking components.

- **Power Users.** The Power Users group is intended for those who need many, but not all, of the privileges of the Administrators group. Power Users can't take ownership of files, back up or restore files, load or unload device drivers, or manage the security and auditing logs. Unlike ordinary users, however, Power Users can share folders; create, manage, delete, and share local printers; and create local users and groups.

- **Remote Desktop Users.** Users in this group can connect to the computer via the Remote Desktop feature, if it is enabled.

For information about Remote Desktop, see Chapter 33, "Remote Access Options."

- **Replicator.** Members of the Replicator group can manage the replication of files on the domain, workstation, or server. (File replication, a feature of Windows .NET Server and its predecessors, Windows 2000 Server and Windows NT Server, is beyond the scope of this book.)

Except for HelpServicesGroup, these additional groups are not included on a computer running Windows XP Home Edition. Applications that you install might create additional security groups.

note A computer that is a member of a domain offers two standard account types, and they're slightly different from the ones that appear on a workgroup computer. A *standard user* is one that is a member of the Power Users group, and a *restricted user* is one that is a member of the Users group.

User Profiles

Windows limits access to information through the use of user profiles. A *user profile* contains all the desktop settings for a user's work environment. But it's much more than that. In addition to storing the user's personal registry settings for everything from desktop background to the author initials used in Microsoft Word, the profile contains a number of files that are specific to a user, such as cookies the user receives while using Microsoft Internet Explorer, documents in the My Documents folder and its subfolders, and shortcuts to network places.

By default, each user who logs on to a computer has a local user profile, which is created when the user logs on for the first time. Local user profiles are stored in %SystemDrive%\Documents And Settings. Each user's profile is stored in a subfolder with the user name as the folder name. The full path of one of the profiles on a computer in our office is C:\Documents And Settings\Cheryl, for example. (The entire path for the current user's profile is stored in another commonly used environment variable, %UserProfile%.)

Chapter 3

In general, each user account has full access to its own user profile and can create, change, and delete files within the profile as well as make settings that are stored in the profile. Nonadministrative accounts have only limited access to profiles belonging to other users; by default, they can view files but not make any changes to another user's profile.

> For more information about the content of user profiles and managing them, see Chapter 35, "Managing User Profiles."

newfeature!

Simple File Sharing vs. Windows 2000–Style Sharing

A primary feature of Windows XP is the ability to securely allow or deny access to files, printers, and other resources. Maximum flexibility—the ability to specify permissions at a granular level (for example, separate permissions for reading a folder directory, reading a file, changing a file, adding a new file, deleting a file, and so on) for individual users or groups—requires an option-filled user interface that many users find daunting.

Windows XP addresses this potential confusion by introducing *Simple File Sharing,* a stripped-down interface that makes it easy to set up common security arrangements. Simple File Sharing differs from classic (Windows 2000–style) file sharing in the following ways:

- The Sharing tab in a folder's properties dialog box provides fewer, simpler options, as shown in Figure 3-1. This simplified Sharing tab controls share permissions *and* NTFS file permissions. (Many Windows NT and Windows 2000 users were confused by this subtle, yet important, distinction; placing all the controls on this tab makes it clear what you need to do to share with other local users and network users.)

- The properties dialog box for a folder, file, or printer does not have a Security tab. Figure 3-2, on page 100, shows the Security tab revealed when Simple File Sharing is disabled.

- Permissions are set only at the folder level; you can't apply permissions to individual files (except with the arcane Cacls and Xcacls command-line utilities).

- Your options for sharing folders and the files they contain are few: you can share with all other local users; you can share with network users; and you can prevent other users from viewing one or more of your private folders.

- Network users who connect to your computer are authenticated using your computer's Guest account. This means that network users who access a shared folder on your computer have only those privileges and permissions that are specifically granted to the Guest account.

> For information about setting permissions, see Chapter 13, "Securing Files and Folders." For information about sharing with other users on your network, see Chapter 32, "Managing Shared Folders and Printers."

Chapter 3: Controlling Access to Your Computer

Sharing tab with Simple
File Sharing enabled

Sharing tab with classic
file sharing model

Figure 3-1. Simple File Sharing consolidates the small number of sharing and security options on a single tab.

If you use Windows XP Home Edition, you don't have a choice: Simple File Sharing is your only option.

If you use Windows XP Professional, you can choose to use Simple File Sharing or the classic sharing and security interface. To switch between them, open Folder Options (in Control Panel's Appearance And Themes category), click the View tab, and select or clear the last item in the Advanced Settings box, Use Simple File Sharing (Recommended). Simple File Sharing is enabled by default on computers that are not members of a domain.

InsideOut

Even power users sometimes appreciate the cleaner, simpler approach provided by Simple File Sharing. It's one of those settings that you might like to be able to switch to and from quickly and easily—using Simple File Sharing most of the time and disabling it when you need to set special permissions for a particular object. Making the change through the user interface requires, at a minimum, six clicks. To switch back

(continued)

> **Inside Out** *(continued)*   and forth rapidly, you might want to create a script that
> changes the ForceGuest value of the HKLM\System\CurrentControlSet\Control\Lsa
> registry key. Setting ForceGuest to 0 disables Simple File Sharing; setting it to 1
> enables the feature. You can find such a script, called ToggleSharingOptions.vbs, on
> the companion CD. (For a program listing of ToggleSharingOptions.vbs, see "Control-
> ling Access with NTFS Permissions," page 507.) After you have a registry-toggling
> switch, you might want to assign a shortcut key to it or place a shortcut in an easily
> accessible location. (For general information about scripts, see "Automating Tasks
> with Windows Script Host," page 390. You'll find a sample script that toggles registry
> settings in the sidebar titled "Batch Programs vs. Scripts: Which Should You Use?"
> page 387.)

Figure 3-2. With classic sharing, the Security tab for a file (as shown here) or a folder
lets you specify various permissions for individual users and groups.

newfeature!
Working with User Accounts

When you install Windows XP, its setup program requires you to create at least one user
account (in addition to the Administrator and Guest accounts that Windows Setup creates). If you upgrade to Windows XP and you had local accounts set up in your previous
operating system (that is, you were using Windows NT or Windows 2000, or you had

enabled user profiles in Windows 95/98/Me), Windows Setup migrates those accounts to your Windows XP installation. Accounts that you migrate from Windows NT/2000 maintain their group memberships and passwords. Accounts you create during setup, as well as accounts you migrate from Windows 95/98/Me, are members of the Administrators group and they have no password.

---

caution An administrator account with a blank password creates a security risk! (Note that when you upgrade from Windows 95/98/Me, Windows XP retains the user accounts you had set up in your previous operating system, but it removes the password associated with those accounts.) Although new security features in Windows XP prevent network logon by an account with a blank password, someone with physical access to your computer can log on without providing a password. And because they have administrative privileges, they have full access to your computer. In other words, until you assign a password to each account that Windows Setup creates in Windows XP, anyone can log on and can view or modify your files and settings.

Through User Accounts in Control Panel, Windows XP provides a simple method for creating new accounts, making routine changes to existing accounts, and deleting accounts. If your computer is not a member of a domain, when you launch User Accounts in Control Panel you'll see a window similar to the one shown in Figure 3-3.

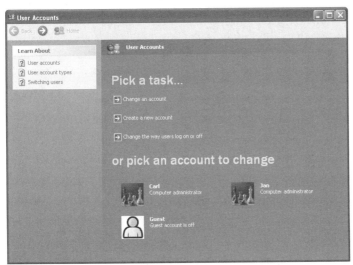

Figure 3-3. User Accounts on a workgroup computer has a clean, simple interface.

If your computer is a member of a domain, the version of User Accounts that appears looks nothing like the one shown in Figure 3-3. Rather, it's similar to Users And Passwords in Windows 2000. For more information, see "Advanced Account Setup Options," page 120.

Chapter 3

> **note** To create accounts or make changes to other accounts, you must be logged on as an administrator. Users without administrative privileges can use User Accounts only to create, change, or remove their own password; change their picture; or link their account to a .NET Passport.

Creating a New User Account

User Accounts offers a convenient Create A New Account link on its home page and it lets you create a new account with a minimum of fuss. You need to supply only a name for the account and decide whether you want the account to be a computer administrator account or a limited account.

> **note** The name you provide when you create a new account with Windows is used for both the user name and the full name. The *user name* is the primary name used internally by Windows. You use it when you log on without the benefit of the Welcome screen and when you specify the account name in various commands and dialog boxes for setting permissions. The *full name* is the name that appears on the Welcome screen, at the top of the Start menu, and in User Accounts. You can change either name later.

If you want to specify any other information about the account—including setting a password—you must make changes after you create the account, as described in the following section. Alternatively, you can use the Local Users And Groups snap-in or the Net User /Add command, both of which allow you to create an account and make several other settings simultaneously. For more information, see "Advanced Account Setup Options," page 120.

> **tip** **Don't use spaces in the user name**
>
> User Accounts allows you to include spaces in the user name when you create an account. Don't do it. Spaces in user names cause complications with some applications and when you use command-line tools for managing user accounts. If you want a space to appear (for example, if you want your full name, including first and last name) on the Welcome screen and on the Start menu, create your account name without a space. (For example, use just your first name or, if that's the same as another account name, use your first name and last initial without a space.) After you create the account, you can change the full name without changing the user name, as described in the following section.

Chapter 3: Controlling Access to Your Computer

Changing Account Settings

Making routine changes is easy with User Accounts. Don't bother clicking the Change An Account link, which leads to a window that shows all the accounts that you can change. Instead, at the bottom of the User Accounts home page, simply click the name of the account you want to change. You'll see a window similar to the one shown in Figure 3-4.

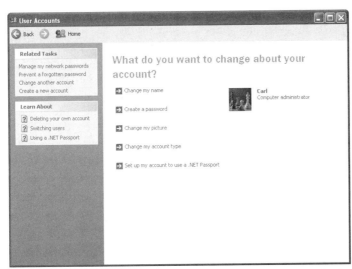

Figure 3-4. User Accounts provides easy access to commonly changed account information.

> **note** If you choose Control Panel, User Accounts while logged on as a limited user, you bypass the first User Accounts window—the one shown in Figure 3-3—which shows all the user accounts and lets an administrator perform certain other tasks. Instead, you go directly to a pared-down version of the account-change window shown in Figure 3-4. In that window, you can create, change, or remove your password; change your picture; or link your account to a .NET Passport. A limited user cannot change the name or account type, nor can a limited user modify other accounts.

In this window, you can make the following account changes to your own account or other accounts on your computer:

- **Name.** Although User Accounts doesn't explain the distinction, when you change the name here you're changing the full name (the one that appears on the Welcome screen, on the Start menu, and in User Accounts), not the user name. Changing the name here—after creating a short user name without spaces—allows you to create a friendly name that appears on-screen.

103

- **Password.** You can create a password and store a hint that will provide a reminder for a forgotten password. If the account is already password protected, User Accounts allows you to change the password or remove the password. For more information about passwords, see "Setting Logon Passwords," page 128.

- **Picture.** If you don't want a user to be identified as a rubber ducky (or whatever icon Windows selects for the account), you can change the picture associated with the account name at the top of the Start menu and in User Accounts. (The picture doesn't appear if your computer is a member of a domain or if you use the classic Start menu.) As shown in Figure 3-5, clicking the change-picture link shows all the pictures stored in AllUsersProfile%\ Application Data\Microsoft\User Account Pictures\Default Pictures, but you're not limited to those choices (most of which are no more or less appropriate than the rubber ducky icon). Click Browse For More Pictures, and you can select any picture in bitmap format (.bmp extension), Graphics Interchange Format (GIF), Joint Photographic Experts Group (JPEG) format, or Portable Network Graphics (PNG) format, such as a picture of yourself or a favorite scene. Windows reduces the picture to fit the picture box and stores the resulting file in %AllUsersProfile%\Application Data\Microsoft\User Account Pictures with the account's user name as the file name.

Click to select one of your own pictures

Click to snap a picture with an attached camera

Figure 3-5. Select a picture that reflects your personality.

- **Account type.** With User Accounts, you can change the account type to Computer Administrator (which adds the account to the Administrators group) or Limited (which adds the account to the Users group). If you want to add the account to other groups, you must use Local Users And Groups or the Net Localgroup command. For more information about those alternatives, see "Advanced Account Setup Options," page 120.

---

tip   **Access the account change windows quickly**

If you want to change your own picture, you can jump directly to the picture-changing window shown in Figure 3-5 by opening the Start menu and clicking your picture. Then, if you want to change other settings for your account, click the Back button to display the window shown in Figure 3-4. To display the window shown in Figure 3-3 on page 101 (so you can make changes to other accounts), click Home.

For your own account (that is, the one with which you're currently logged on), you can make the following additional changes:

- **.NET Passport.** You can set up your own account to use a .NET Passport or to change the Passport currently associated with your account. For more information about .NET Passport settings, see "Setting Up a .NET Passport," page 136.

- **Network passwords.** Under Related Tasks, you'll find the Manage My Network Passwords link, which lets you manage stored user names and passwords that you use to access network resources and Web sites. For more information, see "Gaining Access to Shared Folders on Another Computer," page 1072.

- **Password reset disk.** The Prevent A Forgotten Password link, also under Related Tasks, launches a wizard from which you can create a password reset disk. For more information, see "Recovering from a Lost Password," page 134.

Deleting an Account

You can delete any account except one that is currently logged on. To delete an account, open User Accounts and click the name of the account you want to delete. Then click Delete The Account. User Accounts gives you a choice, shown in Figure 3-6 on the next page, about what to do with the account's files:

- **Keep Files.** Windows copies certain parts of the user's profile—specifically, files and folders stored on the desktop and in the My Documents folder—to a folder on your desktop, where they become part of your profile and remain under your control. The rest of the user profile, such as e-mail messages and other data stored in the Application Data folder, Internet favorites, and settings stored in the registry, will be deleted after you confirm your intention in the next window that appears.

- **Delete Files.** After you select Delete Files and confirm your intention in the next window, Windows deletes the account, its user profile, and all files associated with the account, including those in its My Documents folder.

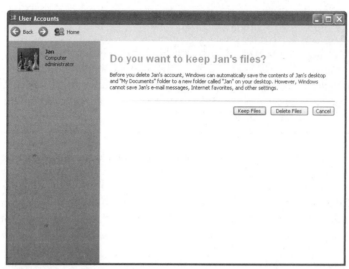

Figure 3-6. Select Keep Files to avoid losing files in the account's My Documents folder.

---

note User Accounts won't let you delete the last account on the computer, even if you're logged on as Administrator. This limitation helps to enforce the sound security practice of using an account other than Administrator for your everyday computing.

After you delete an account, of course, that user can no longer log on. Deleting an account also has other effects you should be aware of. You cannot restore access to resources that currently list the user in their access control lists simply by re-creating the account. This includes files to which the user has permission and the user's encrypted files, personal certificates, and stored passwords for Web sites and network resources. That's because those permissions are linked to the user's original SID—not the user name. Even if you create a new account with the same name, password, and so on, it will have a new SID, which will not gain access to anything that was restricted to the original user account.

You might encounter another predicament if you delete an account. If you use a tool other than User Accounts to delete the account, the user's original profile remains in the Documents And Settings folder. If you later create a new account with the same name, Windows creates a new profile folder, but because a folder already exists with that user's name (for example, C:\Documents And Settings\Josie), it appends the computer name to the user name to create a convoluted folder name (for example, C:\Documents And Settings\Josie.SEQUOIA). The extra folder not only consumes disk space, but leads to confusion about which is the correct profile folder. (In general, the one with the longest name is the most recent. But you can be certain only by examining files in the profile folder.) To avoid this problem, use User Accounts to delete accounts because it properly deletes the old profile along with the account.

InsideOut

If you delete an account with a tool other than User Accounts, the account's profile continues to occupy space in the Documents And Settings folder and in the registry. You
don't want to delete the files or registry entries directly because a simple mistake could
affect other accounts. Instead, right-click My Computer and choose Properties. Click the
Advanced tab and then click Settings under User Profiles. Select the account named
Account Unknown (the deleted account) and click Delete.

Controlling How Users Log On

If your computer is not part of a domain, Windows XP offers two different methods
for users to log on:

newfeature!

● **Welcome screen.** The Welcome screen, shown in Figure 3-7, offers an easy way
for users to log on. Users simply click their name and, if required, type their
password. For more information, see "Using the Welcome Screen," page 110.

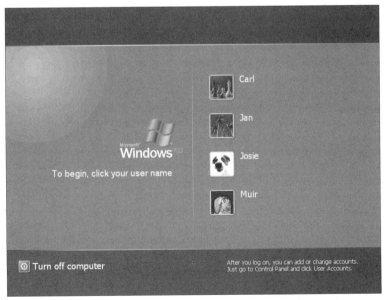

Figure 3-7. The Welcome screen provides the simplest logons for computers shared by only a handful of users.

Part 1: Setup, Startup, Tune-Up

> **note** Don't be misled by the fact that the word *Welcome* appears nowhere on the Welcome screen, yet the classic logon screen shows a Welcome To Windows dialog box. In dialog boxes and in help, references to the Welcome screen refer to the logon screen shown in Figure 3-7.

● **Classic logon.** The alternative to the Welcome screen is the sequence of logon screens used in Windows NT and Windows 2000. When the Welcome screen is disabled (or on a domain-based computer, which doesn't support the Welcome screen), after Windows completes its startup tasks you'll see one of the following dialog boxes: Welcome To Windows, shown in Figure 3-8, or Log On To Windows, shown in Figure 3-9.

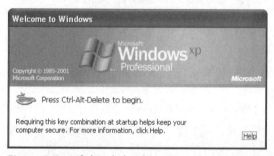

Figure 3-8. If this dialog box appears, press Ctrl+Alt+Delete to initiate the logon process.

Figure 3-9. Ordinarily, the User Name box is filled in with the name of the last user who logged on.

Chapter 3: Controlling Access to Your Computer

---

tip   **Hide the name of the last user to log on**

Local Security Settings contains a policy that you might want to enable if you don't use the Welcome screen. Ordinarily, the name of the last user who logged on appears in the Log On To Windows dialog box. On a system that's used primarily by a single user, this is a convenient feature that allows the user to log on again without typing his or her name each time. But it's also a bit of a security hole, because anyone can learn a valid user name just by looking at this dialog box. If you're using Windows XP Professional, you can prevent the last-used name from appearing by typing **secpol.msc** at a command prompt to open Local Security Settings. In Local Security Settings, open Local Policies\Security Options. Enable the policy named Interactive Logon: Do Not Display Last User Name.

Systems set up for the greatest security initially display a Welcome To Windows dialog box that invites you to log on by pressing Ctrl+Alt+Delete. When you do so, the Log On To Windows dialog box appears. Type your name and password to log on.

---

tip   **Skip the Ctrl+Alt+Delete requirement**

If you don't want to be bothered by the Welcome To Windows dialog box or pressing Ctrl+Alt+Delete to reach the Log On To Windows dialog box, make the following change:

1   At a command prompt, type **control userpasswords2** and press Enter. (If your computer is joined to a domain, you can simply open User Accounts in Control Panel.)

2   In the User Accounts dialog box that appears, click the Advanced tab.

3   Under Secure Logon, clear the Require Users To Press Ctrl+Alt+Delete check box.

Be aware that doing so removes a security feature. Because a component of the Windows XP security system prevents any other application from capturing this particular key combination, pressing Ctrl+Alt+Delete ensures that the next dialog box that appears, Log On To Windows, is displayed by the operating system and not by a rogue application that's trying to capture your password, for example.

Chapter 3

newfeature!

Using the Welcome Screen

Except on computers that are part of a domain (a configuration that doesn't support the Welcome screen), Windows XP is configured by default to use the Welcome screen.

---

tip   **Log on using hidden accounts**

While the Welcome screen is displayed, you can display the Log On To Windows dialog box shown in Figure 3-9 by pressing Ctrl+Alt+Delete two times. This allows you to log on using an account that isn't shown on the Welcome screen (Administrator, for example). Note, however, that this trick works only when no other users are logged on.

If your system is not using the Welcome screen and you want it to, follow these steps:

1 While logged on as an administrator, open User Accounts in Control Panel.

2 Click the Change The Way Users Log On Or Off link.

If a warning message about offline files appears, simply click Cancel. As the message points out, offline files and Fast User Switching are incompatible, but you don't need to disable offline files to enable only the Welcome screen.

3 Select Use The Welcome Screen and then click Apply Options.

By default, whenever the screen saver kicks in and you subsequently press a key or move the mouse, you'll find yourself back at the Welcome screen. This provides some protection against someone using your computer when you've stepped away. To resume working, you'll need to click your name and enter your password. If you'd rather return to work without going through these extra steps, do the following:

1 Right-click the desktop and choose Properties to open the Display Properties dialog box.

2 Click the Screen Saver tab.

3 Clear the check box labeled On Resume, Display Welcome Screen (if Fast User Switching is enabled) or On Resume, Password Protect (if Fast User Switching is disabled).

Your decision to use the Welcome screen has other, perhaps unexpected, effects as well. For example, if you use the Welcome screen, pressing Ctrl+Alt+Delete after you're logged on displays Windows Task Manager, an invaluable little program that lets you end hung applications and shows running tasks and processes, how much memory and processor time each is using, and a concise summary of several performance metrics, among other information. If you have disabled the Welcome screen, however, pressing Ctrl+Alt+Delete displays the Windows Security dialog box, shown in Figure 3-10.

Chapter 3

Troubleshooting

You can't enable (or disable) the Welcome screen.

If you have problems enabling or disabling the Welcome screen with User Accounts, you can edit the registry or set a policy that implements the logon style you want to use.

In either Windows XP Professional or Windows XP Home Edition, you can enable or disable the Welcome screen with a registry setting. Use Registry Editor to change the LogonType value in the HKLM\Software\Microsoft\Windows NT\CurrentVersion\ WinLogon key. Set it to 0 to use the classic logon or 1 to use the Welcome screen.

In Windows XP Professional, you can also enable or disable the Welcome screen with a policy. Follow these steps:

1 At a command prompt, type **gpedit.msc** to open the Group Policy console.

2 Open the Computer Configuration\Administrative Templates\System\Logon folder.

3 Double-click the Always Use Classic Logon policy.

4 Select Enabled to use the classic logon, Disabled to use the Welcome screen, or Not Configured to cede control to the registry setting.

A policy setting overrides the setting you make in User Accounts or in the registry. For more information about group policy, see Chapter 35, "Managing User Profiles."

Chapter 3

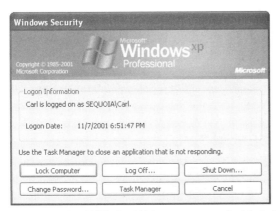

Figure 3-10. With the Welcome screen disabled, Ctrl+Alt+Delete displays this dialog box instead of Task Manager.

tip Whether you use the Welcome screen or not, you can get to Task Manager with a single keystroke: Ctrl+Shift+Esc.

InsideOut

You can prevent an account from appearing on the Welcome screen, thereby creating a "hidden" account. (It's not completely hidden, because the account is visible to administrators in Local Users And Groups and the account's profile in the Documents And Settings folder is visible to all users.) Use Registry Editor to open HKLM\Software\ Microsoft\Windows NT\CurrentVersion\Winlogon\SpecialAccounts\UserList. Create a new DWORD value, setting its name to the user name of the account you want to hide and leaving its value set to 0.

But be careful with this trick: you won't be able to get to the account with Fast User Switching because the account doesn't appear on the Welcome screen. Pressing Ctrl+Alt+Delete two times at the Welcome screen to display the Log On To Windows dialog box works only when no other users are logged on. Therefore, if you want to use this type of hidden account, you should either disable Fast User Switching or resign yourself to using the account only when no one else is logged on.

Other minor changes also mimic the behavior of Windows 2000 and Windows XP when your computer is part of a domain. For example, the button at the bottom of the Start menu changes from Turn Off Computer to Shut Down. And the dialog box that appears after you click that button provides a list of shutdown options instead of separate buttons for each option.

Troubleshooting

The Welcome screen doesn't display any accounts.

You might find yourself staring at a Welcome screen that asks you to click a user name—but there are no user names to click. This can occur if you manage to delete all local user accounts (User Accounts won't let you do this, but other account-management tools aren't as protective) or, in some cases, if you upgrade your computer from an earlier version of Windows.

If you're using Windows XP Professional, press Ctrl+Alt+Delete two times to display the Log On To Windows dialog box. Type **Administrator** in the User Name box, and enter the password you created for the Administrator account during setup. Logged on as Administrator, you can run User Accounts and create one or more new accounts, which will thereafter show up on the Welcome screen.

Windows XP Home Edition users can't log on using the Administrator account, which is prevented by account restrictions from logging on. Instead, you must start Windows XP in Safe Mode by pressing F8 at the beginning of the startup process. After you're up and running in Safe Mode, you can run User Accounts to create one or more new accounts.

Chapter 3: Controlling Access to Your Computer

Bypassing the Logon Screen

If your computer has only one account (aside from Administrator and Guest) and if that account doesn't have a password, Windows XP automatically logs on as that user during startup. You won't see the Welcome screen or any other logon screens; Windows launches straight to your desktop.

You might want to set up your computer to log on this way even if it has more than one user account. This kind of logon could be convenient in several situations: if you're the primary user of the computer but other people occasionally need to use it; if you occasionally need to log on as a different user to install software or perform other tasks; or if you have set up a password for your account (so that you could use scheduled tasks or connect remotely, operations that are available only to accounts with passwords), but you still want it to log you on automatically at startup.

> **caution** Automatically logging on means that the system effectively enters your user name and password when you turn on the power. Anyone who has physical access to your computer can then log on as "you" and have access to all computer resources (including Web sites for which you've saved passwords) that you normally have.

You can set up your computer to log on automatically by following these steps:

1 At a command prompt, type **control userpasswords2** and press Enter. Doing so launches the Windows 2000–style User Accounts application.

2 On the Users tab, clear the Users Must Enter A User Name And Password To Use This Computer check box and then click OK. Note that the Users Must Enter A User Name And Password To Use This Computer check box doesn't appear if your computer is a member of a domain. Only computers that aren't part of a network or are part of a workgroup can bypass this dialog box. Domain users must enter a user name and password, even to log on locally.

The Automatically Log On dialog box appears.

3 Type the user name and password for the account that you want to be logged on each time you start your computer.

After you make this change, you can use other accounts on the computer by logging off and then logging on to another account or by using Fast User Switching.

> **tip** If you've configured your system to log on automatically, you can suppress the automatic logon by holding down the left Shift key as the system boots. If you want to prevent users from bypassing the automatic logon (thereby ensuring that your system always starts with a particular account), you can use a registry setting to make the system ignore the Shift key. Use Registry Editor to navigate to HKLM\Software\Microsoft\ WindowsNT\CurrentVersion\Winlogon. If the string value IgnoreShiftOverride doesn't exist, create it. Set this value to 1 to ensure that your system always starts with its auto-logon account.

newfeature! Configuring Fast User Switching

Fast User Switching, one of the most exciting new features in Windows XP, allows multiple users to be logged on to the computer at the same time. As the feature name suggests, you can quickly switch among users. This might be convenient, for example, if one user logs on, opens several documents, and begins downloading a huge file from the Internet. Meanwhile, another user comes along and wants to quickly check e-mail. With Fast User Switching enabled, it's no problem. The second user can log on, log off, and return control to the first user. While the second user is logged on, the first user's applications (such as the download process) continue to run.

Chapter 3: Controlling Access to Your Computer

To switch to another user account, press the Windows logo key+L. This displays the Welcome screen, from which the second user can click his or her name and enter the password, if required.

---

note If your keyboard doesn't have a Windows logo key (or you prefer using the mouse), you can get to the Welcome screen by clicking Start, Log Off. In the Log Off Windows dialog box, click Switch User.

Fast User Switching won't work in every situation. To enable the feature you must observe the following requirements:

- The Welcome screen must be enabled.

- The computer must not be joined to a domain.

- Offline files must be disabled.

- Although it's not an absolute requirement, the computer should have more than 64 MB of memory. By default, Fast User Switching is disabled on computers that have only 64 MB. (To run Windows XP effectively, you should have at least 128 MB in any case.)

To enable Fast User Switching, follow these steps:

1 While logged on as an administrator, open User Accounts in Control Panel.

2 Click the Change The Way Users Log On Or Off link to see the following screen.

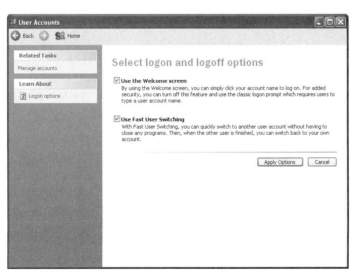

3 Select Use Fast User Switching and then click Apply Options.

---

note If a warning message about offline files appears, open the Folder Options dialog box by clicking OK. You must disable offline files before you can enable Fast User Switching.

---

tip **Check your e-mail without switching**

The logon screen for Fast User Switching shows which users are logged on (a note under each name indicates the number of programs each has running or, for users who are logged on but have no programs running, their logon status). In addition, the logon screen displays the number of unread messages below the name of each user whose e-mail program is running. To use this feature, simply start Outlook Express or Windows Messenger and leave it running when you switch users.

Logging Off or Locking Your Computer

When you're finished using your computer, you want to be sure that you don't leave it in a condition in which others can use your credentials to access your files. To do that, you need to log off, switch users, or lock your computer.

- **Log off.** With this option, all your programs close and dial-up connections are ended. To log off, choose Start, Log Off and click Log Off.

- **Switch users.** With this option, which is available only if Fast User Switching is enabled, your programs continue to run. Your account is still logged on, but (if it's protected by a password) only you can return to your session. To switch users, press the Windows logo key+L or choose Start, Log Off and then click Switch Users. Either method takes you to the Welcome screen for Fast User Switching.

- **Lock your computer.** With this option, which is available only when Fast User Switching is disabled, your programs continue to run. However, only you or another administrator can unlock the computer. If another administrator unlocks the computer, he or she can do so only by closing your programs (without saving any open documents) and logging you off. To lock a computer, press the Windows logo key+L or (if the Welcome screen is disabled) press Ctrl+Alt+Delete and click Lock Computer. If you press Ctrl+Alt+Delete when the Welcome screen is enabled, choose Lock Computer from the Windows Task Manager Shut Down menu.

Chapter 3

---

tip   Create a shortcut for switching users or locking your computer

The Windows logo key+L is a terrific shortcut for switching users or locking your computer. But if your keyboard doesn't have a Windows logo key or you prefer using a mouse, you can create a program shortcut that provides single-click access to the same feature. Follow these steps to create a switch/lock shortcut on your desktop:

1   Right-click the desktop and choose New, Shortcut.

2   On the first page of the Create Shortcut wizard, type **rundll32.exe user32.dll,LockWorkStation** and click Next.

3   Type a name for the shortcut (**Lock Workstation** would be appropriate) and click Finish.

4   Right-click the new shortcut and choose Properties.

5   On the Shortcut tab, click Change Icon.

6   In the text box, type **shell32.dll** and press Enter.

7   Select an icon that tickles your fancy; you'll find several with lock, key, and user images. Then click OK.

8   In the Shortcut Key box, type the shortcut key you want to use (for example, Ctrl+Alt+L).

To immediately display the logon screen (if Fast User Switching is enabled) or lock your computer (if Fast User Switching is disabled), simply double-click your new shortcut or type the shortcut key you assigned. To make it accessible with a single click, even when your desktop is covered with other windows, move the shortcut to the Quick Launch bar.

In any case, if you want to prevent others from using your account, you must protect your account with a password. When you choose any of these options, Windows hides whatever you were working on. Your computer continues to run (subject to power management settings), and any resources shared by your computer remain available to other users on the network.

newfeature!

What Happened to the Administrator Account?

Ordinarily, the Administrator account is hidden from view. It appears on the Welcome screen only in the following situations:

● No other administrative user accounts exist.

● You start your computer in Safe Mode (by pressing F8 during startup).

● The Administrator account is logged on and you're using Fast User Switching.

117

Nonetheless, the account does exist, and it takes care of some important functions. First, because it can't be deleted, it provides a safety net in case you somehow manage to delete all other accounts. You can log on as Administrator and then create other accounts. Second, it's the only account that can log on to the Recovery Console, your last-ditch opportunity for repairing a damaged system.

> **note** By default, the Administrator password in Windows XP Home Edition is blank. This isn't the gaping security hole that you might imagine, however, because in Home Edition the Administrator account is barred from logging on locally or through a network connection. You do, however, need to know that the password is blank if you ever need to run Recovery Console, which requires the Administrator password. If the blank password concerns you, you can change it. For details, see "Securing the Administrator Account," on the facing page.

Logging On as Administrator

If you're using Windows XP Professional, you can log on as Administrator. If the Welcome screen is enabled, press Ctrl+Alt+Delete twice at the Welcome screen to display the Log On To Windows dialog box. (Be sure that no other account is logged on when you do this.) If the Welcome screen is disabled, press Ctrl+Alt+Delete one time as you would to log on with any other account. Type **Administrator** in the User Name box, and enter the password you created for the Administrator account during setup.

> **note** Except in Safe Mode, Windows XP Home Edition users can't log on using the Administrator account, because it is prevented by account restrictions from logging on. To log on to the Administrator account using Windows XP Home Edition, first make sure that your system is not set up to bypass the screen. (See "Bypassing the Logon Screen," page 113.) Then press F8 while booting and choose Safe Mode from the menu that appears.

Making Administrator the Only Administrative Account

If your applications support it, you're better off using a limited account (or a Power Users account) as your everyday logon account and using an administrator account only when you need to perform administrative tasks. You can use any administrator account for those tasks, but if you prefer, you can use the Administrator account. Here's how you can set up your system to easily use Administrator in this way:

1 At a command prompt, type **lusrmgr.msc** to open Local Users And Groups.

2 In the console tree, click Groups.

3 Double-click the Administrators group and remove all accounts except Administrator.

4 Open the Users or Power Users groups and then click Add to add each of the accounts you removed.

With all administrative accounts except Administrator removed, the Administrator account becomes accessible from the Welcome screen.

---

caution Use this procedure only with Windows XP Professional. With Windows XP Home Edition, you can't use Local Users And Groups (although you can make the group membership changes with the Net Localgroup command). But more important, the Administrator account is not allowed to log on in Windows XP Home Edition, so even if you get it to appear on the Welcome screen, you won't be able to use it.

InsideOut

If you're using Windows XP Professional, you can add Administrator to the Welcome screen, without eliminating all other administrative accounts, by modifying the registry. Use Registry Editor to navigate to HKLM\Software\Microsoft\WindowsNT\ CurrentVersion\Winlogon\SpecialAccounts\UserList. In this subkey, create the new DWORD value *Administrator*. Then set this value to 1. To remove Administrator from the Welcome screen, return to the registry and set the Administrator value to 0.

Securing the Administrator Account

Because an account named Administrator exists on almost every computer running Windows XP, and because this account is all-powerful, malevolent hackers might attempt to break into a computer using the Administrator account. After all, they already know the user name, so they just need to figure out the password. You can make your Administrator account more secure in two ways:

- **Use a secure password.** If you're logged on as Administrator, you can use User Accounts to set a password. But if you want to create a randomly generated secure password, open a Command Prompt window and type this command:

```
net user administrator /random
```

Windows displays the new password it creates. Be sure to write it down and store it in a safe place!

● **Change the name of the account.** It doesn't need to be cryptic like a password; it just needs to be something other than "Administrator," the name that every hacker already knows and expects to find. To change the name, follow these steps:

1 At a command prompt, type **secpol.msc** to open Local Security Settings. (Alternatively, you can double-click the Local Security Policy shortcut in Control Panel's Administrative Tools folder.)

2 Open Local Policies\Security Options.

3 In the details pane, double-click Accounts: Rename Administrator Account.

4 Type the new name for the Administrator account.

---

note Because the Local Security Settings snap-in isn't available in Windows XP Home Edition, you can't use it to change the name of the Administrator account. However, you can change the user name by launching the Windows 2000–style User Accounts. At a command prompt, type **control userpasswords2**. Then select Administrator and click Properties. Be sure you change the user name, not the full name.

Advanced Account Setup Options

Windows XP includes no fewer than four different interfaces for managing users and groups:

● **User Accounts.** Located in Control Panel, User Accounts provides the simplest method to perform common tasks. For more information, see "Working with User Accounts," page 100.

● **User Accounts (Windows 2000 style).** If your computer is joined to a domain, opening User Accounts in Control Panel displays a different version, as shown in Figure 3-11. If your computer is not joined to a domain, you can open this version by typing **control userpasswords2** at a command prompt.

The capabilities of this version of User Accounts are few (you can add or remove local user accounts, set passwords, and place a user account in a single security group), but it has a handful of unique features that you might find compelling. With this version, you can

■ Change an account's user name

■ Configure automatic logon (for more information, see "Bypassing the Logon Screen," page 113)

■ Eliminate the Ctrl+Alt+Delete requirement if you're not using the Welcome screen

Chapter 3: Controlling Access to Your Computer

Figure 3-11. On a domain member computer, User Accounts looks like Users And Passwords in Windows 2000.

---

tip **Create a shortcut to User Accounts**

If your computer is not a domain member, yet you find yourself using this version of User Accounts frequently, create a shortcut to it. Store the shortcut in Control Panel's Administrative Tools folder.

- **Local Users And Groups.** This Microsoft Management Console (MMC) snap-in provides access to more account-management features than User Accounts and is friendlier than command-line utilities. For more information, see "Using the Local Users And Groups Snap-In," page 123.

- **Command-line utilities.** The Net User and Net Localgroup commands, though not particularly intuitive (starting with the name—we're talking about local accounts and groups, not network-based accounts!), provide the most complete and direct access to various account tasks. For more information, see "Using the Net User and Net Localgroup Commands," page 125.

With varying degrees of ease, all of these options allow an administrator to create, modify, and delete local user accounts and security groups. The availability and appearance of each of these options depends on which version of Windows XP you have (the Local Users And Groups console is not available in Windows XP Home Edition) and whether your computer is a member of a domain (Users And Passwords in Control Panel is completely different for domain members). Which interface you choose depends in part on whether you prefer a graphical interface or a command prompt.

121

But you'll also find that each tool offers capabilities that the others do not. To help you decide which tool to use for a particular task, Table 3-1 shows which common account-management tasks can be performed with each interface.

Table 3-1. **Account-Management Tool Tasks**

Task	User Accounts in Control Panel (Workgroup)	User Accounts in Control Panel (Domain)	Local Users And Groups Console	Command-Line Utilities
Local User Accounts				
Create user account	✓	✓	✓	✓
Delete user account	✓	✓	✓	✓
Place account in a group	✓[1]	✓[1]	✓	✓
Change user name		✓	✓	
Change full name	✓	✓	✓	✓
Change description		✓	✓	✓
Change picture	✓			
Set a password	✓	✓[2]	✓	✓
Set a password hint	✓			
Set password restrictions			✓	✓
Set logon hours				✓
Enable or disable account	✓[3]		✓	✓
Unlock account			✓	✓

Table 3-1. *(continued)*

Task	User Accounts in Control Panel (Workgroup)	User Accounts in Control Panel (Domain)	Local Users And Groups Console	Command-Line Utilities
Local User Accounts *(continued)*				
Set account expiration date				✓
Specify profile and logon script			✓	✓
Link account to .NET Passport	✓	✓		
Security Groups				
Create			✓	✓
Delete			✓	✓
Rename			✓	✓
Set group membership			✓	✓
Add a domain account to a group		✓[1]	✓	✓

[1] With User Accounts, you can add an account to only one group. The workgroup version of User Accounts can add an account only to the Administrators or Users group.

[2] With User Accounts, you can set the password only for a local account other than the one with which you're currently logged on.

[3] With User Accounts, you can enable or disable the Guest account, but not other user accounts.

Using the Local Users And Groups Snap-In

Local Users And Groups, an MMC snap-in, offers more advanced capabilities than either version of User Accounts. Local Users And Groups is not available in Windows XP Home Edition. You can start Local Users And Groups, shown in Figure 3-12 on the next page, in any of the following ways:

- In Computer Management, open System Tools, Local Users And Groups.

- At a command prompt, type **lusrmgr.msc**.

- If your computer is a domain member, in User Accounts click the Advanced tab and then click the Advanced button.

A red *X* identifies accounts that have been disabled

Figure 3-12.   Through its Spartan interface, Local Users And Groups offers more capabilities than User Accounts.

Table 3-2 lists the procedures for performing various tasks with the Local Users And Groups snap-in.

Table 3-2. **Local Users And Groups Procedures**

Task	Procedure
Local User Accounts	
Create	Right-click Users and choose New User.
Delete	In Users, right-click the account and choose Delete.
Change user name	In Users, right-click the account and choose Rename.
Change full name or description	In Users, double-click the account to display the General tab of the properties dialog box.
Set or change password	In Users, right-click the account and choose Set Password.
Set password restrictions	In Users, double-click the account to display the General tab of the properties dialog box.
Enable or disable	In Users, double-click the account to display the General tab of the properties dialog box, and then clear or select the Account Is Disabled check box. (When an account is disabled, the user can't log on or access resources on the computer.)
Unlock after too many unsuccessful logon attempts	In Users, double-click the account to display the General tab of the properties dialog box, and then clear the Account Is Locked Out check box.

Table 3-2. *(continued)*

Task	Procedure
Set group membership	In Users, double-click the account and then click the Member Of tab.
Specify profile and logon script	In Users, double-click the account and then click the Profile tab. For details, see "Working with User Profiles," page 1157.
Local Groups	
Create	Right-click Groups and choose New Group.
Delete	In Groups, right-click the group and choose Delete.
Rename	In Groups, right-click the group and choose Rename.
Set group membership	In Groups, double-click the group to display the properties dialog box. You can add local user accounts, domain user accounts, and domain groups to a local group. In the Select Users dialog box that appears when you click Add, use the Locations button to specify the computer name (for local users) or domain name (for domain users and groups).

Using the Net User and Net Localgroup Commands

If you prefer a terse Command Prompt window to a gooey utility, you'll want to use Net.exe for managing local users and groups. To change any local user account or group information, you need to be logged on as a member of the local Administrators group. (Alternatively, you can use Run As to launch the Command Prompt window, or you can precede each command you enter in a Command Prompt window with **runas /user:administrator**.)

In the following sections, we describe only the most common Net commands (and their most common parameters) for managing local users and groups. This isn't an exhaustive reference, however. You can get that information from online help or by typing **net help** *command,* replacing *command* with the word that follows Net in the examples. For instance, to get more information about the Net Localgroup command, type **net help localgroup**. This provides more help than typing **net localgroup /?**, which shows only the command syntax.

Net User

The Net User command lets you view, add, modify, or delete user accounts.

Viewing user account information   Typing **net user** with no parameters causes the program to display the name of your computer and a list of local user accounts. If you follow Net User with the name of a local user account (for example, **net user jan**), Net User displays all information about the user account, as shown in the sample that follows.

```
C:\>net user

User accounts for \\SEQUOIA

-----------------------------------------------------------------
Administrator            Carl                   Guest
HelpAssistant            Jan                    SUPPORT_388945a0
The command completed successfully.


C:\>net user jan
User name                        Jan
Full Name                        Jan
Comment
User's comment
Country code                     000 (System Default)
Account active                   Yes
Account expires                  Never

Password last set                7/4/2001 12:43 PM
Password expires                 Never
Password changeable              7/4/2001 12:43 PM
Password required                Yes
User may change password         Yes

Workstations allowed             All
Logon script
User profile
Home directory
Last logon                       7/4/2001 11:54 AM

Logon hours allowed              All

Local Group Memberships          *Users
Global Group memberships         *None
The command completed successfully.
```

Adding or modifying a user account   Following Net User *username*, you can append any or all of the parameters shown in Table 3-3. For example, you can add a new account for a user named Josie, create a complex password, and prevent Josie from changing the password with the following command:

```
C:\>net user Josie /add /random /passwordchg:no
Password for Josie is: nkHRE$oU

The command completed successfully.
```

126

Chapter 3: Controlling Access to Your Computer

Table 3-3. **Useful Parameters for the Net User Command**

Parameter	Description
password or * or /Random	Sets the password. If you type an asterisk (*), Net User prompts for the password you want to assign; it does not display the password as you type it. The /Random switch generates a hard-to-crack, eight-character password.
/Add	Creates a new user account. The user name must be 20 characters or fewer and can't contain any of these characters: " / \ [ ] : ; l = , + * ? < >
/Fullname:"*name*"	Specifies the user's full name.
/Comment:"*text*"	Provides a descriptive comment (maximum length of 48 characters).
/Passwordchg:yes or /Passwordchg:no	Specifies whether the user is allowed to change the password.
/Active:no or /Active:yes	Disables or enables the account. (When an account is disabled, the user can't log on or access resources on the computer.)
/Expires:*date* or /Expires:never	Sets the expiration date for an account. For *date,* use the short date format set in Regional Options. The account expires at the beginning of the day on the specified date; from that time on, the user can't log on or access resources on the computer until an administrator sets a new expiration date.
/Passwordreq:yes or /Passwordreq:no	Specifies whether the user account is required to have a nonblank password.
/Times:*times* or /Times:all	Sets the times when an account is allowed to log on. For *times,* enter the days of the week you want to allow logon. Use a hyphen to specify a range of days or use a comma to list separate days. Following each day entry, specify the allowable logon times. For example, type **M-F,8am-6pm; Sa,9am-1pm** to restrict logon times to normal working hours. Use All to allow logon at any time; a blank value prevents the user from ever logging on.

note The last three switches in Table 3-3 (/Expires, /Passwordreq, and /Times) allow you to make settings that you can't make (or even view) using Local Users And Groups. These switches provide some powerful options that are otherwise available only with Windows 2000 Server or Windows .NET Server.

Deleting a user account   To remove a user account from the local security database, simply use the /Delete switch with the Net User command, like this:

```
C:\>net user josie /delete
The command completed successfully.
```

Net Localgroup

The Net Localgroup command lets you view, add, modify, or delete local security groups.

Viewing group information   Type **net localgroup** with no parameters to display the name of your computer and a list of local groups. If you follow Net Localgroup with the name of a group (for example, **net localgroup "power users"**), Net Localgroup lists the members of the group.

Adding or deleting a group   Following Net Localgroup *groupname*, append /Add to create a new group or append /Delete to remove an existing group. When you add a group or view its information, you can optionally add a descriptive comment (maximum length of 48 characters) by appending the /Comment:"*text*" switch.

Adding or deleting group members   You can add local user accounts, domain user accounts, and global groups to a local group (though you can't add other local groups). To do so, enter the names of the users or groups to add after the group name (separate multiple names with a space) and include the /Add switch. For example, to add Jan and Josie to the Power Users group, use this command:

```
C:\>net localgroup "power users" jan josie /add
The command completed successfully.
```

To delete one or more group members, use the same syntax, replacing the /Add switch with /Delete.

Working with Domain Accounts

By appending the /Domain switch to any of the Net User or Net Localgroup commands described in this chapter, you can view, add, modify, or delete domain user accounts and global groups—as long as you log on as a member of the Domain Admins group. You don't need to specify the domain name; the Net User and Net Localgroup commands always work with the primary domain controller of your computer's primary domain.

Setting Logon Passwords

By default, Windows XP is somewhat insecure. User accounts that you create during setup (as well as user accounts that are migrated from Windows 95/98/Me during an upgrade) have administrative privileges and they have no password. Because the Welcome screen shows every defined user account, anyone who has physical access to your computer can log on as an administrator by simply clicking a name on the Welcome screen. Requiring a password for each account (particularly administrator accounts) goes a long way toward securing your computer.

---

newfeature!

note You needn't worry about someone logging on to your computer remotely (over the network, the Internet, or with Remote Desktop Connection, for example) if your account doesn't have a password. New security features in Windows XP prevent remote logon by any account with a blank password. When you don't have a password in Windows XP, the risk comes only from people who have physical access to your computer.

This feature is enforced by a policy. If you have Windows XP Professional, you can confirm that the policy is enabled, as follows. At a command prompt, type **secpol.msc** to open Local Security Settings. Open Local Policies\Security Options and be sure that the Accounts: Limit Local Account Use Of Blank Passwords To Console Logon Only policy is enabled. (If you use Windows XP Home Edition, you needn't worry; the policy can't be disabled.)

Troubleshooting

Windows requires a logon password but you don't have one.

Ordinarily, a user who has no logon password assigned can log on simply by clicking her or his name on the Welcome screen. In some cases, clicking the name displays a request for a password, and nothing you type (even just pressing Enter) satisfies the request.

This sometimes occurs when auditing is enabled. You can solve the problem by disabling auditing (for details, see "Keeping an Eye on Who Uses Your Computer," page 1202), but a much better solution is to assign a logon password—even a short one— to the user.

Creating a Secure Password

A password is of little value if it's easily guessed by an intruder. Obviously, you shouldn't use your name or something equally transparent. However, even a random word provides little security against a determined intruder because some hackers use tools that try every word in the dictionary. By observing the following guidelines, you can create a password that's difficult to crack:

● Use at least seven characters.

● Use a mixture of uppercase letters, lowercase letters, numbers, and punctuation (for example, OneWorld7).

- Use random sequences instead of words, or intersperse numbers and punctuation within words (for example, oNe6Wo7RlD).

- Consider using the initials of a phrase that you can easily remember. For example, you could remember the password WdYw2gT as "Where do you want to go today?"

Troubleshooting

You can't log on.

Even when you're *certain* you know the password, you might have trouble logging on. First, be aware that passwords are case sensitive: you must type capital letters and lowercase letters exactly as you did when you created the password. If you still can't get on, be sure the Caps Lock key is not on.

Setting a Password

The simplest way to set a password for yourself or for another user (if you're logged on as an administrator) is with User Accounts in Control Panel. Click the name of the user for which you want to set a password and then click Create A Password. A window like the one shown in Figure 3-13 appears.

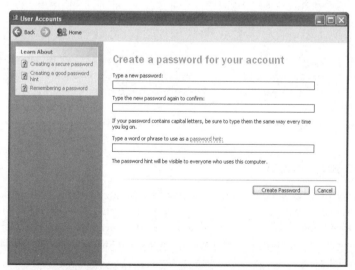

Figure 3-13. User Accounts allows you to provide a reminder hint that becomes available on the Welcome screen.

You can set a password with the other account management tools, but User Accounts is the only tool that lets you specify a password hint. The password hint is available by clicking the question mark icon that appears after you click your name on the Welcome screen. Be sure your hint is only a subtle reminder—not the password itself—because any user can click your name and then view the hint.

---

caution   You can safely set the initial password for another user, as described here, or you can use any of the other account-management tools to set the password. But do not remove or change a user's password using any of these methods unless the user has forgotten the password and has absolutely no other way to access the account. (For more information, see "Recovering from a Lost Password," page 134.) If you change or remove another user's password, that user loses all personal certificates and stored passwords for Web sites and network resources. Without the personal certificates, the user loses access to all of his or her encrypted files (for information about encrypted files, see Chapter 14, "Encrypting Confidential Information") and all e-mail messages encrypted with the user's private key. Windows deletes the certificates and passwords to prevent the administrator who makes a password change from gaining access to them—but this security comes at a cost!

Troubleshooting

You can't access encrypted files because an administrator changed your password.

When an administrator removes or changes the password for your local account, you no longer have access to your encrypted files and e-mail messages. That's because your master key, which is needed to unlock your personal encryption certificate (which, in turn, is needed to unlock your encrypted files), is encrypted with a hash of your password. When the password changes, the master key is no longer accessible. To regain access to the master key (and, by extension, your encrypted files and e-mail messages), change your password back to your old password. Alternatively, use your Password Reset Disk to change your password.

When you change your own password (through User Accounts or with your Password Reset Disk), Windows uses your old password to decrypt the master key and then re-encrypts it with the new password, so your encrypted files and e-mail messages remain accessible.

Tightening Password Security

Even if you convince everyone who uses your computer to use passwords, you can be sure that they won't always follow the secure practices of choosing a difficult-to-crack password and changing it periodically. If security is a serious concern in your organization, you can take the following measures to help ensure that users don't make it easy for hackers to guess their passwords:

- You can use the Net User command to generate a complex password. In a Command Prompt window, type **net user** *username* **/random**.

- If you have Windows XP Professional, you can set password policies that place restrictions on the types of passwords users can provide and how often users can (or must) change them.

The easiest way to set password policies is with the Local Security Settings console, shown in Figure 3-14. To open Local Security Settings, in Control Panel open Administrative Tools, Local Security Policy. (If you use Category view, Administrative Tools is under Performance And Maintenance.) Alternatively, type **secpol.msc** at a command prompt.

To see the policies that set password behavior for all accounts, open Account Policies\Password Policy. Table 3-4 describes each of these policies.

As an alternative to the Local Security Settings console, you can set a number of these policies using the Net Accounts command. In Table 3-4, the appropriate switch to set a policy is shown next to the policy name as it appears in Local Security Settings. For example, to set the maximum password age to 21 days, you type **net accounts /maxpwage:21** at a command prompt.

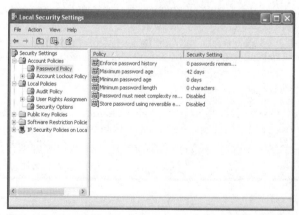

Figure 3-14. With Local Security Settings, you can set password requirements for all local user accounts.

132

Table 3-4. **Account Policies**

Policy	Net Accounts Switch	Description
Enforce password history	/Uniquepw:*number*	Specifying a number greater than 0 (the maximum is 24) causes Windows to remember that number of previous passwords and forces users to pick a password different from any of the remembered ones.
Maximum password age	/Maxpwage:*days*	Specifying a number greater than 0 (the maximum is 999) dictates how long a password remains valid before it expires. (To override this setting for certain user accounts, open the account's properties dialog box in Local Users And Groups and select the Password Never Expires check box.) Selecting 0 means passwords never expire. (With the Net Accounts command, use the /Maxpwage: unlimited switch if you want passwords to never expire; 0 is not an acceptable value.)
Minimum password age	/Minpwage:*days*	Specifying a number greater than 0 (the maximum is 999) lets you set the amount of time a password must be used before a user is allowed to change it. Selecting 0 means that users can change passwords as often as they like.
Minimum password length	/Minpwlen:*length*	Specifying a number greater than 0 (the maximum is 14) forces passwords to be longer than a certain number of characters. Specifying 0 permits users to have no password at all. *Note: Changes to the minimum password length setting do not apply to current passwords.*

(continued)

Table 3-4. *(continued)*

Policy	Net Accounts Switch	Description
Password must meet complexity requirements	N/A	Enabling this policy requires that new passwords be at least six characters long; that the password contain a mix of uppercase letters, lowercase letters, numbers, and punctuation (at least one character from three of these four classes); and that the password does not contain the user name or any part of the full name. *Note: Enabling password complexity does not affect current passwords.*
Store password using reversible encryption for all users in the domain	N/A	Enabling this policy effectively stores passwords as clear text instead of encrypting them, which is much more secure. The only situation in which you should even consider enabling this policy is when you have a particular application that needs access to the user password for authentication.

> **note** If you set a maximum password age so that passwords expire automatically, Windows reminds the user to change the password at each logon, beginning 14 days before the password expires. If you want to change the reminder period, in Local Security Settings open Local Policies\Security Options. Double-click the Interactive Logon: Prompt User To Change Password Before Expiration policy, and set the number of days before the expiration date that you'd like the warning to begin appearing.

newfeature!

Recovering from a Lost Password

It's bound to happen: Someday when you try to log on to your computer and are faced with the password prompt, you will draw a blank. Windows XP offers two tools that help you to deal with this dilemma:

- **Password hint.** The hint is available by clicking the question mark icon that appears after you click your name on the Welcome screen. (It's not available if you don't use the Welcome screen.) For more information, see "Setting a Password," page 130.

- **Password Reset Disk.** The Password Reset Disk allows you (or anyone with your Password Reset Disk) to change your password—without needing to know your old password. As standard practice, each user should create a Password Reset Disk and keep it in a secure location. Then, if a user forgets the password, he or she can reset it using the Password Reset Disk.

> **note**   You can make a Password Reset Disk only for your local user account. If your computer is joined to a domain, you can't create a Password Reset Disk as a back door to your domain logon password. However, in a domain environment a domain administrator can safely change your password and you'll still have access to your encrypted files.

Both require a little forethought on your part. You must create the hint when you set your password, and you must create the Password Reset Disk before you actually need it.

To create a Password Reset Disk, you'll need to know your current password and you'll need to have a floppy disk available. Follow these steps:

1 Log on using the account for which you want to create a Password Reset Disk.

2 In Control Panel, click User Accounts.

3 If you're logged on as an administrator, click your account name.

4 Click Prevent A Forgotten Password (in the task pane under Related Tasks) to launch the Forgotten Password Wizard.

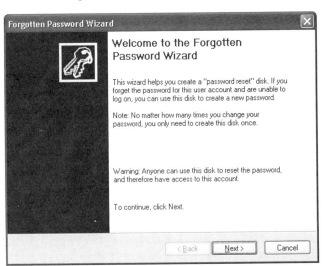

5 Follow the wizard's instructions.

You can have only one Password Reset Disk for each user account. If you make a new one, the old one is no longer usable.

Chapter 3

Setting Up a .NET Passport

Your user account can be linked to a .NET Passport—a service that provides single sign-on access to a number of Web sites and a secure way to make online payments. With Passport, you provide your user name and password one time and gain access to your Hotmail account, Windows Messenger, and a large number of Web sites. Your Passport profile can contain (at your option and control, of course) your credit card numbers so that you can easily make online payments. This is much easier than the systems used by early e-commerce sites, where you needed a different user name and password for each site you visited. If you used credit cards for online payments, you had to make changes at each site if your credit card number changed.

You'll need to use a Passport if you plan to use Windows Messenger to communicate with other Internet users or use the built-in Web publishing and photo-print ordering features of Windows XP. Microsoft and other businesses that use the .NET Passport technology intend to offer many more services as well.

To create a Passport (if you don't already have one) and link it to your user account so that you're automatically logged on to Passport when you log on to your computer, follow these steps:

1 Open User Accounts in Control Panel.

2 If you're logged on as an administrator, click your user name.

3 Click Set Up My Account To Use A .NET Passport, which launches the .NET Passport Wizard.

4 Follow the wizard's instructions. You can link your Passport to one of your existing e-mail addresses or you can obtain a new, free e-mail account; the wizard leads you either way.

> **note** Even if your computer is a domain member, you might want to create a Password Reset Disk for a local user account on your computer. To do that, log on as the local user. Press Ctrl+Alt+Delete to open the Windows Security dialog box. Click Change Password, and then click Backup to launch the Forgotten Password Wizard.

When you attempt to log on, one of two things happens if you don't provide the correct password:

- If you have created a Password Reset Disk, Windows displays a message that includes either a Use Your Password Reset Disk link (if your computer is configured to use the Welcome screen) or a Reset button (if you're not using the Welcome screen).

  Click the link or the button to launch the Password Reset Wizard. You'll need your Password Reset Disk, of course. The Password Reset Wizard asks you to create a new password and hint. Log on with your new password, and then return your Password Reset Disk to its safe storage place. You do not need to make a new Password Reset Disk.

- If you have not created a Password Reset Disk, Windows displays a message that tells you, in effect, to type your password correctly.

  In this situation, if you can't remember the password and the hint doesn't jog your memory, you're out of luck. An administrator can log on and change or remove your password for you, but you'll lose access to your encrypted files and e-mail messages.

Setting Up Windows XP on a Shared Computer

Whether you're setting up a computer for your family to use at home or to be used in a business, it's prudent to set it up securely. Doing so helps to protect each user's data from inadvertent deletions and changes as well as malicious damage and theft. When you set up your computer, consider these suggestions:

- **Control who can log on.** Create accounts only for users who need to log on locally (that is, at your computer as opposed to over a network). Delete or disable other accounts (except the built-in accounts created by Windows).

- **Change all user accounts except one to limited accounts.** You'll need one administrative account for installing programs, creating and managing accounts, and so on. All other accounts—including your own everyday account—can run with limited privileges.

> **note** You'll find that certain programs—particularly programs written for earlier versions of Windows—won't run for users with limited accounts. If that's the case, try adding the users who need the affected programs to the Power Users group. (If your computer is not joined to a domain, you'll need to use Local Users And Groups or the Net Localgroup command to add users to this group. For details, see "Advanced Account Setup Options," page 120.) If the programs still won't run, change the affected users to administrators.

- **Be sure all accounts are password protected.** This is especially important for administrator accounts and for other accounts whose profiles contain important or sensitive documents. You might not want to set a password on your toddler's account, but all other accounts should be protected from the tyke accidentally clicking the wrong name on the Welcome screen.

- **Restrict logon times.** You might want to limit the computing hours for some users. You can limit logon times with the Net User *username* /Times command. (For details, see "Using the Net User and Net Localgroup Commands," page 125.) And if you use Windows XP Professional, you can forcibly log off users if they are still logged on at the end of their allowable logon time. To do that, at a command prompt, type **secpol.msc** to open Local Security Settings. Open Local Policies\Security Options and enable the policy named Network Security: Force Logoff When Logon Hours Expire.

- **Restrict access to certain files.** You'll want to be sure that some files are available to all users, whereas other files are available only to the person who created them. You can implement such protections with all versions of Windows XP. If you have Windows XP Professional, you can further refine your file protection scheme by selectively applying permissions to varying combinations of files, folders, and users. For details, see Chapter 13, "Securing Files and Folders."

- **Restrict the amount of disk space available to each user.** If you have Windows XP Professional, you can set disk quotas for each user, thereby preventing your teenager from filling the whole hard drive with downloaded music files or a coworker from gobbling up disk space with scanned photographs, for example. For details, see "Setting Quotas for Disk Space Use," page 948.

- **Turn on the Guest account only when necessary.** You might occasionally have a visitor who needs to use your computer. Rather than logging on with your own account and exposing all your own files and settings to the visitor, turn on the Guest account in such situations. To do that, log on as an administrator. In Control Panel, open User Accounts, click Guest, and then click Turn On The Guest Account. To disable the account, return to the same window and click Turn Off The Guest Account.

Setting Up a Secure Guest Account

By default, the Guest account has access to your computer's programs, to files in the Shared Documents folder, and to files in the Guest profile. But no password is required to use the account, so you'll want to be sure that the Guest account doesn't expose items that a casual user shouldn't see or modify. In fact, the default settings place pretty tight restrictions on the Guest account, but you should ensure that these rather obscure settings are still in place:

- **Prevent network logon by the Guest account.** This prevents a user at another computer from using the Guest account to log on over the network. In Local Security Settings (Secpol.msc), open Local Policies, User Rights Assignment. Be sure that Guest is listed in the Deny Access To This Computer From The Network policy.

  Do not include Guest in this policy if you use Simple File Sharing and you are sharing your computer's folders or printers. Simple File Sharing requires the use of the Guest account for network access.

- **Prevent a Guest user from shutting down the computer.** In Local Security Settings, open Local Policies, User Rights Assignment. Be sure that Guest is not listed in the Shut Down The System policy. (Even with this policy in place, anyone—including guests—can shut down the computer from the Welcome screen. You can set a policy that allows only a logged-on user to shut down the computer. To do that, open Local Policies, Security Options and disable the Shutdown: Allow System To Be Shut Down Without Having To Log On policy.)

- **Prevent a Guest user from viewing event logs.** In Registry Editor, open HKLM\System\CurrentControlSet\Services\Eventlog. Visit each of the three subkeys—Application, Security, and System—and be sure that each contains a DWORD value named RestrictGuestAccess set to 1.

Chapter 4

Help and Support Options

Did you give up on the Windows Help system years ago? Most experienced Windows users quickly learned to skip right past the Help files in Windows 95 and 98, which are aimed squarely at novices and are hampered by a Help engine that's extremely awkward to navigate. The reservoir of Help content in Windows Me and Windows 2000 is much deeper, and the HTML-based interfaces are slicker and easier to use, but in both of those Windows versions the online Help file is still essentially a user manual that's been carved into small pieces and grows increasingly outdated with each Windows update.

Not so in Microsoft Windows XP. The Help And Support Center in both the Home and Professional editions includes a tremendous collection of resources for Windows users at every level of experience. Besides the traditional tutorials and reference material, you'll find the following extras integrated into the Help And Support Center in Windows XP:

- Links to system tools and utilities, including Disk Defragmenter, System Configuration Utility (Msconfig), Network Diagnostics, and Windows Update, all of which run within the Help And Support Center window.

- Syntax and usage information for 175 command-line options, organized alphabetically.

- Dozens of troubleshooters, covering a huge assortment of common and not-so-common problems.

- Links that collect up-to-date information about your system and its current configuration, with details about all installed hardware, software, and services.

141

Part 1: Setup, Startup, Tune-Up

At Home with Windows XP

For the most part, the Help And Support Center in Windows XP Home Edition looks and works just like the one in Windows XP Professional. Topics that relate only to Professional, of course, are omitted, as are links to tools that are available only in Professional. If you use the Command Prompt window, you'll be disappointed to discover that, although both editions support most of the same commands, Home Edition does not include help for the commands.

Two features of the Help And Support Center are not available in Home Edition:

- The ability to install and use Help files from different versions of Windows.
- The ability for an expert to initiate a Remote Assistance session instead of depending on the novice to get things going.

- Easy access to error logs, status of services, and other advanced system information.

- Access to Group Policy settings (Windows XP Professional only).

- Links to external information sources, including the Microsoft Knowledge Base and an assortment of Windows-focused newsgroups.

- Access to Remote Assistance, which allows a Windows XP user to ask a friend for help; the more experienced user can connect directly to the machine experiencing the problem via the Internet or a local area network and make needed repairs or configuration changes directly.

newfeature!
Using the Help And Support Center

When you open the Help And Support Center, your first stop is always the Home page. Figure 4-1 shows the options available from this page.

The left-hand column lists common Help topics. (This list replaces the Help Contents page found in previous Windows versions.) The links in the two groups on the right, each identified by a green arrow, lead to tools and support resources. The Did You Know? list in the lower right contains headlines provided by Microsoft support. This area can be customized by third parties as well; if your copy of Windows was included with a new PC, the system manufacturer might have customized the Help And Support Center with links to its support site here.

The toolbar at the top of the Help And Support Center window provides basic browser-style navigation tools. Back and Forward buttons move through recently viewed topics. Although the toolbar icons closely resemble those used in Internet

Chapter 4: Help and Support Options

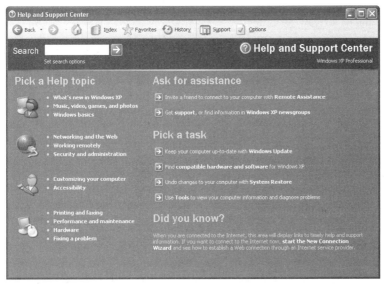

Figure 4-1. The Help And Support Center home page includes links to basic information, troubleshooting tools, and external support resources.

Explorer, note that the Home, Favorites, and History buttons take you to the respective pages within the Help And Support Center.

Troubleshooting

There's no Help And Support command on the Start menu.

Ordinarily, you open the Help And Support Center by choosing Start, Help And Support. If the command doesn't appear on your Start menu, you can always open the Help And Support Center by choosing Start, Run and typing **helpctr**. But if you want to restore the command to your Start menu, right-click the Start button and choose Properties. On the Start Menu tab of the Taskbar And Start Menu Properties dialog box, click Customize. In the Customize Start Menu dialog box, click Advanced, and then, in the Start Menu Items list, select Help And Support.

If the Help And Support check box is selected but you still have no Help And Support command on the Start menu, then the command has been disabled by policy. Choose Start, Run and type **gpedit.msc** to open Group Policy. In the console tree, select User Configuration\Administrative Templates\Start Menu And Taskbar. Then, in the details pane, double-click Remove Help Menu From Start Menu and select Not Configured or Disabled. (Either choice restores the command to the Start menu.)

> **tip** **Save time by playing Favorites**
>
> The Windows XP Professional Help file is truly massive, consisting of nearly 10,000 individual topics drawn from more than 200 Compiled Help (.chm) files. When you uncover a particularly useful topic that you know you'll want to refer to later, click the Add To Favorites button just above the topic window and spare yourself the hassle of searching for it again. By default, each entry in the Help And Support Center Favorites list uses the title of the topic as its name. Use the Rename button at the bottom of the Favorites list to give a list item a name that's more meaningful to you. (This is especially important with Glossary entries, which are all initially named *Glossary* in the Favorites list.) Items in the Favorites list appear in the order in which you add them; unfortunately, there's no way to reorder these items.

> **caution**   Avoid adding items to the Favorites list when you have multiple instances of the Help And Support Center open. Changes you make in one window may not be reflected in the other, and the list of Favorites visible in the last window you close will be saved, possibly wiping out any entries you saved in other windows.

Troubleshooting

Help has stopped working.

The Help And Support Center uses two related modules: the Microsoft Help Center Service (Helpsvc.exe) and the Help And Support Center executable (Helpctr.exe). Under some circumstances, clicking the Help And Support Center icon might not produce a result. If you look in the Windows Task Manager, you'll see that both modules are running; you might also see multiple instances of Helpctr.exe, which could be causing your Help problems. To solve this problem, follow these steps:

1 Press Ctrl+Shift+Esc to open Windows Task Manager.

2 Click the Processes tab and then click the Image Name heading to sort the list in alphabetical order.

3 Highlight each instance of Helpctr.exe in the list and click the End Process button. Repeat until all instances are gone from the list and then close Task Manager.

4 Open Control Panel's Services option (in the Administrative Tools group, under Performance And Maintenance Options).

5 Select Help And Support from the list of services, right-click, and then choose Restart.

After completing this procedure, you should be able to restart the Help And Support Center.

Searching for Help Topics

Need a refresher on a basic Windows feature or task? Sometimes a well-written, step-by-step tutorial from the Help files is just the thing you need to help a friend or relative who's struggling with Windows XP. Sending them detailed instructions saves you time and increases the chance that they'll get the results they need.

To find tutorials and instructions, you could navigate through the categories, scanning each list until you find the topic you're looking for. But there's a faster way: Choose a general category from the Help And Support Center home page and then use the Search box to locate the exact topic you need.

Follow these steps to search for specific topics:

1 Click a category from the Pick A Help Topic list on the home page to display its list of topics.

2 On the next page, enter a word or phrase in the Search box. Look just below the Search box and you'll see an option (already selected) that restricts your search to the category you chose on the home page.

3 Click the green arrow to the right of the Search box to perform the search.

4 Click a topic title from the list on the left to display its contents in the pane on the right.

---

tip   **Keep drilling to maximize Search efficiency**

You can customize search options to display a much longer list of topics than the default of 15. (For more information, see "Customizing the Help And Support Center," page 149.) Giving yourself a long list of topics from which to choose is the best way to ensure that your search covers enough ground, but it can also produce information overload. If your initial search returns too many hits and quickly scrolling through the list doesn't turn up the topic you want, enter additional search terms and check the Search Within Previous Results option to narrow the topics list. It might take several such searches to find exactly the right topic, but this search technique is extremely effective.

Figure 4-2 on the next page shows the results of one such search. Note that the search terms you entered are highlighted in each topic.

Part 1: Setup, Startup, Tune-Up

By default, Windows highlights each occurrence of your search terms.

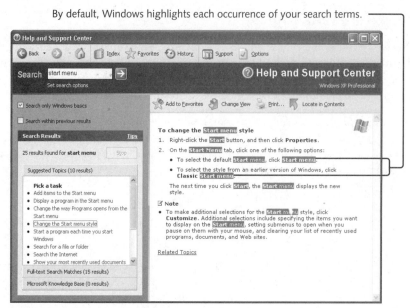

Figure 4-2. The two check boxes just below the Search box appear only if you choose a category from the home page before starting your search.

Search results are broken down into the following three groups:

Suggested Topics   This group is based on a comparison between the search terms you entered and keywords defined in the Help files. Because the search is performed against a relatively small index file, this list appears almost immediately; however, the quality of the results depends on the keywords assigned by the Help file authors.

Full-Text Search Matches   This group displays topics where the content of the Help information matches the word or phrase you entered. Although these files are also indexed, the search universe is much larger, and it typically takes longer to display the results.

Microsoft Knowledge Base   This group searches Microsoft's extensive collection of documentation for bug fixes and technical explanations that aren't available in the local Help files. The list of found articles matches the search terms and uses settings defined in the Options dialog box.

To launch a search that uses the entire Help file, enter the text in the Search box on the home page. Search terms are not case sensitive, and if you enter two or more words, the Search algorithm looks for topics containing that exact combination before looking for topics that contain the individual words. To set Search options so that results display only topics containing a specific phrase, enclose that phrase in quotation marks. Search ignores a long list of common insignificant words, such as *a, for, from,* and *like.*

Chapter 4

---

tip   **Fast lane to the Knowledge Base**

If you have the article ID (the letter Q followed by a number) for a specific entry in the Knowledge Base, an expert trick can help you jump straight to that page using Internet Explorer: Click in the Address bar and enter **mskb** followed by a space and the article ID number (with or without the Q). This technique takes you straight to the correct article, using the MSN search engine. This trick may stop working if you customize Internet Explorer's AutoSearch settings.

According to the Help And Support Center documentation, you can use Boolean syntax to narrow down searches using the AND, OR, NOT, and NEAR operators to tell the Help And Support Center how you want it to handle multiple search terms. If you're experienced with Boolean syntax, you can use this type of search string to fine-tune the list of results. For instance, searching for **Internet NOT sharing** finds topics related to Internet Explorer and the basics of connecting to the Internet, while filtering out topics that cover Internet Connection Sharing. These operators work inconsistently in some cases, so be prepared to experiment a bit. If you search for **Start NOT menu**, for instance, you'll turn up some topics containing the phrase *Start menu,* which should be rejected by this syntax.

Using the Help Index

 If you're not sure of the exact term you're looking for, Search can be frustrating. In that case, you might have better results scrolling through the Index, which lists the keyword entries for each topic. To switch to this view, click the Index button. Figure 4-3 on the next page shows what you'll see next.

The text box in the Index list resembles the Search box, but it behaves quite differently. As you enter text in this box, the Index selection jumps to the first topic that matches the characters you entered. The comparison is based on the beginning of the description; if you enter **networking**, for instance, you'll jump to the group of topics that begin with that keyword, skipping over the Home Networking entry.

---

tip   **Get wizards on demand**

If you want a quick overview of every wizard in Windows XP, open the Help And Support Center, click the Index button, and then jump to the group of topics under the keyword *wizards.* You'll find documentation for more than two dozen Windows XP wizards listed here, with step-by-step instructions for a wide range of common tasks.

Figure 4-3. Use the Index to scroll through a lengthy list of topics, organized alphabetically by keyword.

Save Help Topics as Shortcuts

Because the Internet Explorer engine is at the heart of the Help And Support Center, each topic has its own URL. If you know how to manipulate these URLs, you can save a specific Help topic as an external shortcut. Using that shortcut, you can jump directly to a specific topic without having to go through the Help And Support Center first. Unfortunately, Windows XP does not let you create a shortcut to a Help topic directly. To do so, follow the process outlined below:

1 Open the topic for which you want to create a shortcut, right-click anywhere on the page (except on a link), and choose Properties.

2 Select the entire URL from the Address field (be sure to scroll down to select the full address).

3 Press Ctrl+C to copy it to the Clipboard.

4 Right-click the desktop (or in a folder where you want to save the shortcut) and choose New, Shortcut.

5 In the Create Shortcut dialog box, type **%systemroot%\pchealth\helpctr\ binaries\helpctr /url** followed by a space, and then paste the copied URL.

6 Click Next, give the shortcut a name, and click Finish.

Chapter 4: Help and Support Options

> Shortcuts you create in this fashion work with URLs in two common Help formats:
>
> ● The Help Center Pluggable protocol (with the prefix *hcp://*) is less common and is typically used for Help topics that link to external applications and locations, such as Remote Assistance or Windows Newsgroups.
>
> ● HTML Help protocol (with the prefix *ms-its://*) is used for access to information in Compiled Help (.chm) files. If you just want quick access and don't mind opening this type of URL in the Windows 2000–style HTML Help viewer, you can use the Hh.exe Help engine. Open the Create Shortcut wizard and type **hh** followed by a space and the Help topic's URL. The resulting shortcut opens the selected topic in a window that lists only topics from the same Help file.
>
> For more information about HTML Help URLs, see Knowledge Base article Q235226, "INFO: HTML Help URL Protocols."

Customizing the Help And Support Center

You can customize the look and feel of the Windows XP Help And Support Center window; you can also adjust search options. To work with these settings, click the Options button on the Help And Support Center toolbar.

Clicking the Change Help And Support Center Options link from the left pane displays the dialog box shown in Figure 4-4. To squeeze the maximum amount of information

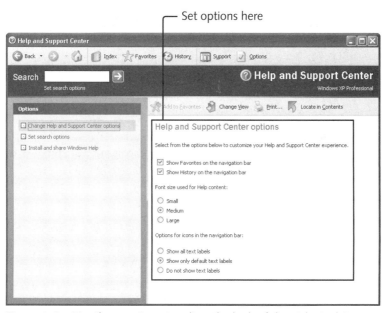

Figure 4-4. Use these options to adjust the look of the Help And Support Center window.

Chapter 4

into each Help topic window, set the font size to small. (If your vision is less than perfect, however, the small font size might be too small to be comfortably readable.) To reduce the amount of space used by the navigation toolbar and the options buttons at the top of the topic window, choose the Do Not Show Text Labels option. Although you can hide the Favorites and History buttons, it is not possible to hide the navigation toolbar itself.

> **note** In Windows Me and Windows 2000, the only way to change the font size used in Help windows was to globally change the fonts used throughout Internet Explorer. The Windows XP design decouples these two settings so that you can separately control font settings for the Help And Support Center and full browser windows.

To change default search settings for the Help And Support Center, click the Set Search Options link, and work with the dialog box shown in Figure 4-5.

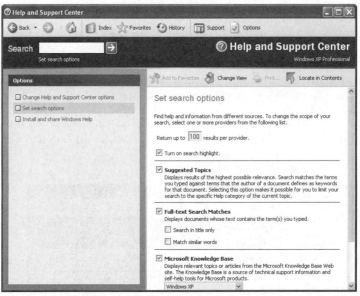

Figure 4-5. Most power users will want to adjust the number of entries returned by a search from its default value of 15; a value of 100 should be plenty.

The following Search options are adjustable:

Return Up To nnn Results Per Provider The default value of 15 is too small for any wide-ranging search. Although you can enter any number up to 999, a value in the 50–100 range should be adequate.

Turn On Search Highlight When this option is selected, Windows highlights each occurrence of your search term in topics that appear as a result of a search. Figure 4-2 on page 146 shows an example.

Chapter 4

Chapter 4: Help and Support Options

---

tip   **Turn off the search highlight**

The search highlight can be helpful in drawing your focus to the section of a topic in which you're most interested. Unfortunately, it can be a distraction as well. If it's too much for you, click the Set Search Options link right below the Search box. Clear the Turn On Search Highlight check box, and then click the Back button in the navigation bar to return to your now-pristine topic.

Suggested Topics   When this option is selected (the default setting), Windows uses the index of keywords for every search. Note that clearing this check box removes the capability to restrict a search to a specific topic, as described in the previous section.

Full-Text Search Matches   This check box is also selected by default, although the two options beneath it are not. Use the Search In Title Only option to ignore the body text of Help topics; in general this option has little to recommend it. Choose Match Similar Words if you want to extend searches to alternate forms of a word—for instance, if you enter **network**, the search results will also include topics that contain the word *networking*.

Microsoft Knowledge Base   The options here are similar to those on Microsoft's Knowledge Base Web page—if you prefer the Help And Support Center interface, you can use the Select A Product Or Topic list to conduct searches for information about related products (such as Outlook Express and Internet Explorer) or technology areas (keyboards and device drivers, for example). To maximize your chances of getting answers, select All Windows Products from this list.

Sharing Help Files

In Windows XP Professional only, a third link in the Help And Support Center Options pane offers you the choice to Share Windows Help. This option is most useful if you're responsible for multiple computers running different versions of Windows XP or Windows .NET Server. This capability is of obvious benefit to Help Desk professionals, but it can also be useful on a home network that includes a mix of PCs running Windows XP Professional and Home Edition. By switching to the Home Edition Help content, you can look up answers to troubleshooting questions without having to exit Windows XP Professional and without risk of being confused by the differences between the two editions.

---

note   Don't overestimate the capabilities of the Share Windows Help feature. Only systems running Windows XP and Windows .NET servers can share Help files. A Windows XP machine cannot install Help files for earlier Windows versions such as Windows Me or Windows 2000, nor can earlier Windows versions install Help files from Windows XP.

Part 1: Setup, Startup, Tune-Up

To set up the capability to access Help files from Windows XP Home Edition on a system running Windows XP Professional, first make sure you have the Windows XP Home Edition CD handy, and then follow these steps:

1 From a PC running Windows XP Professional, open the Help And Support Center and then click the Options button.

2 Choose Install And Share Windows Help from the Options pane on the left.

3 In the Share Windows Help pane on the right, click Install Help Content From A CD Or Disk Image.

4 Click the Browse button, select the \I386 folder on the Windows XP Home Edition CD, and then click the Find button.

5 Select Windows XP Home Edition from the list of available Help versions and then click the Install button. Windows XP copies a number of files from the CD to your hard disk. When the process is complete, the Status column reads Already Installed.

After you've successfully added the extra Help files to your system, you can return to the Help And Support Center at any time to switch between Help versions. Choose Install And Share Windows Help again, and then select the Switch From One Operating System's Help Content To Another option. The Switch Help Version dialog box shows a list of available Help files. Click the Switch button to load the Home Edition Help files. When you've found the answers you were looking for, repeat this process and switch back to the Professional Help files.

Chapter 4: Help and Support Options

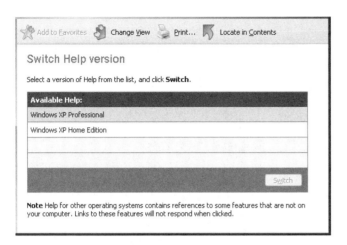

If your local area network includes several Windows XP Professional machines, you can set up shared Help files on each one without having to shuffle CDs between multiple machines. After installing the Help files for Windows XP Home Edition or Windows .NET Server, click the Install And Share Windows Help option again and then select the Share Your Help Content With Others On Your Network option to make the newly shared files available over the network.

From another networked machine running Windows XP Professional (or any version of a Windows .NET Server), select the Install Help Content From Another Windows Computer option. Enter the name of the machine containing the shared Help files and then click the Install button to load those files. This procedure has the same result as if you had installed the Help files from the CD—the full Help database is copied to the second PC.

The final menu choice in the Install And Share Windows Help pane allows you to remove installed Help files belonging to another Windows version. Use this option if you no longer need the extra Help files and you want to reclaim the disk space they're gobbling up.

newfeature!
Connecting to Another PC with Remote Assistance

If you've ever tried to help a novice user troubleshoot a Windows problem over the phone, you know how frustrating the entire process can be. It's usually difficult for an inexperienced user to accurately communicate detailed configuration information, especially if the problem involves technically challenging areas such as hardware drivers or network protocols. Because you're not looking over the user's shoulder, you can't see error messages or informational dialog boxes, so you have to rely on the user to read this crucial information back to you. Even when you successfully pin down the problem and find a solution, you have to walk the user through a repair process that can be daunting.

And if the registry needs editing…well, good luck. With Windows XP, on the other hand, you can eliminate most of those headaches using a new (and very cool) support tool called Remote Assistance. This feature, available in both Windows XP Professional and Home Edition, lets you open a direct connection between two machines over the Internet or over a local area network. Even if you're hundreds or thousands of miles away, you can watch as the user demonstrates the problem and take control of the screen to make repairs quickly and accurately. You can investigate Control Panel settings, run diagnostic tools, install updates, and even edit the registry of the problem-plagued PC. Repairs that might have taken hours the old-fashioned way can be accomplished in a few minutes using this tool.

note Behind the scenes, Remote Assistance uses Windows XP Terminal Services to share a desktop and other resources between two PCs. Although this is the same underlying code used in the Remote Desktop feature, Remote Assistance is fundamentally different in two ways. First, in a Remote Assistance session, both users must be present at their respective PCs and must agree to establish the connection. Second, you can use Remote Assistance to connect to a PC running Windows XP Home Edition, whereas incoming Remote Desktop connections can only be enabled on Windows XP Professional.

Remote Assistance is designed for informal, peer-to-peer use by Windows users without an extensive technical background. Although the user interface hides most of its complexities, a basic understanding of how Remote Assistance connections work can help you make reliable connections without compromising the security of either computer.

Chapter 4

How Remote Assistance Works

The two parties in a Remote Assistance session are called the *novice* and the *expert*. To use Remote Assistance, both parties must be using Windows XP, both must have active Internet connections or be on the same local area network, and neither can be blocked by firewalls. Creating a complete Remote Assistance session is a three-step process:

1 The novice sends a Remote Assistance invitation, typically using Windows Messenger or e-mail.

2 The expert accepts the invitation, opening a terminal window that displays the desktop of the novice's machine.

3 The expert can view the desktop in a read-only window and exchange messages with the novice using text or voice chat. Before the expert can work with objects on the remote PC, the novice must enable the Allow Expert Interaction option.

At the heart of each Remote Assistance connection is a small text file called an *RA ticket*. (More formally, its type is Microsoft Remote Assistance Incident and its extension is .msrcincident.) This file uses XML fields to define the parameters of a Remote Assistance connection. When you use Windows Messenger to manage the connection, the RA ticket is never visible. When a novice sends a Remote Assistance request via e-mail, however, the RA ticket rides along as an attachment to the message. The expert has to double-click this file to launch the Remote Assistance session.

Remote Assistance works by creating a direct connection between two computers using the TCP/IP protocol. For this connection to be successful, both computers involved must be able to communicate using their respective IP addresses.

Troubleshooting

Double-clicking an RA ticket results in an error message.

If you're experiencing problems with a Remote Assistance connection and you're using an RA ticket file (not Windows Messenger), make sure the ticket file is pointing to the correct IP address. If you received the invitation via e-mail, save the rcBuddy.MsRcIncident file and open it using Notepad or another text editor.

Look at the RCTICKET field, which follows this format:

```
RCTICKET="65538,1,ip_address:3389;machine_name:3389,encrypted_connection_info
```

Check the *ip address* value to be certain it points to the current IP address of the novice's machine and, if necessary, edit it. But don't tamper with the *encrypted connection info* data.

A Remote Assistance connection is relatively easy when both parties have public IP addresses provided by an Internet service provider. In that scenario, the computers connect directly, sending and receiving data on TCP port 3389. Routers along the Internet connection between the two computers are able to recognize the addresses of the two computers and send the respective packets to their correct destination. Internet Connection Firewall in Windows XP automatically opens this port when you request a Remote Assistance connection.

Remote Assistance connections are also straightforward and typically trouble-free on a private network such as a workgroup in a home or small office. In that case, each machine can communicate directly with the other without having to pass through any routers.

> **tip** Use a VPN if possible
>
> On a corporate network, the preferred way to work around firewalls is to establish a virtual private network (VPN) connection. This allows all traffic to pass through the firewall and eliminates the need to create possible security holes by opening specific ports. For more information, see "Connecting to a Virtual Private Network," page 1123.

What happens if one or both sides of the connection are using private IP addresses assigned through Network Address Translation (NAT)? That's when Remote Assistance gets complicated. Because these addresses are reserved for exclusive use on private networks, they cannot be routed over the Internet. Instead, a software or hardware-based NAT device handles the grunt work of passing data between the single public IP address it uses to communicate with the Internet and the private IP addresses on the local network. How it performs that job determines whether the Remote Assistance connection will succeed or fail. The exact outcome depends on how the computer acquired the private IP address:

- **Internet Connection Sharing.** When you use Internet Connection Sharing (ICS) from Windows XP or Windows Me, the ICS server hands out private IP addresses to all other computers on the network. The ICS server listens for Remote Assistance traffic on TCP port 5001 and forwards it to port 3389, allowing the connection to succeed on its end, regardless of whether the computer in question is playing the role of novice or expert. If computers on both ends of the connection are using any combination of public IP addresses and private addresses supplied by ICS, the Remote Assistance session should work perfectly.

> **note** If your network includes an Internet Connection Sharing server running Windows 98 Second Edition or Windows 2000, Remote Assistance will not work properly.

Chapter 4: Help and Support Options

- **UPnP-compatible hardware router or residential gateway.** If the source of the private IP address is a hardware router or residential gateway, the connection will be successful if the router supports the Universal Plug and Play (UPnP) standard. Most routers manufactured in 2001 or earlier do not support UPnP, although a firmware upgrade may add this capability.

- **Non-UPnP-compatible hardware router or residential gateway.** If both computers are behind NAT devices that are not UPnP compatible, it is not possible to complete a Remote Assistance connection. If only one computer is using a private IP address whose source is a hardware router or residential gateway that is not UPnP compatible, making a successful connection is often possible, although it requires jumping through some hoops. In this configuration, your best bet is to use Windows Messenger to create the Remote Assistance connection. The novice initiates the connection to the expert on a random port; the expert then uses this port to initiate a connection back to the novice.

The trickiest connection of all involves a novice who is behind a non-UPnP NAT device, such as a router or residential gateway on a cable or DSL connection, and who is unable or unwilling to use Windows Messenger. In that case, you may be able to make a Remote Assistance connection work by editing the RA ticket file. Find the address of the NAT device (the public IP address it uses to connect to the Internet) and the private address of the novice's computer; then follow these steps:

1 On the NAT device attached to the novice's network, open port 3389. Traffic on this port must be able to reach the novice machine before it can complete the Remote Assistance connection. On the popular Linksys router product family, for example, you accomplish this goal by using the Forwarding option in the router's Control Panel.

2 Open the Help And Support Center and create a Remote Assistance invitation, saving it as a file on your desktop or another convenient location. This ticket file includes a pointer to your private IP address; if you send this ticket to an expert who is not on the same private network as you, it will fail because his computer will not be able to find a route to your IP address.

3 Open Notepad or another text editor and edit the RCTICKET field, adding the external IP address of the NAT device before the internal IP address. For instance, if your NAT device uses an external IP address of 24.100.255.255 and your private address is 192.168.1.105 and your machine name is Groucho, this field should read as follows (the added information is shown in bold):

```
RCTICKET="65538,1,24.100.255.255:3389;192.168.1.105:3389;groucho:3389,
encrypted connection info
```

4 Send the RA ticket file to the expert. When he or she double-clicks this file, the information you added will allow it to work its way over the Internet to your NAT device and then into your computer on port 3389.

> **tip** **Watch for disconnected dial-up connections**
>
> Dynamic IP addresses assigned by a dial-up Internet service provider pose special problems. When you create an invitation and send it via e-mail, Remote Assistance embeds the current IP address in that invitation. If you lose the dial-up connection and have to reconnect, the ISP will almost certainly assign a new IP address, rendering the invitation unusable. At that point, you have two options: Cancel the invitation and issue a new one, or use a text editor to change the existing invitation so that it points to the newly assigned IP address. To discover the new IP address, enter the **ipconfig** command at a command prompt.

Sending a Remote Assistance Invitation

By default, Windows XP requires that a user request assistance before a Remote Assistance connection is made. From the Help And Support Center home page, click Invite A Friend To Connect To Your Computer With Remote Assistance. (You can also reach this page from the Remote Assistance shortcut on the All Programs menu.) Click Invite Someone To Help You. The Remote Assistance pane, shown in Figure 4-6, offers three methods to send an invitation for assistance.

● **Windows Messenger.** If you're currently signed on to Windows Messenger, a list of available contacts appears in the Remote Assistance pane. Choose a name and click Invite This Person. Because each user is authenticated through a .NET Passport, there's no need to provide a separate password for this request. The expert sees the request directly in the Messenger window and can click a link to launch the connection.

InsideOut

If you need to send a Remote Assistance invitation (or help someone else send an invitation to you), Windows Messenger is by far the quickest and easiest option. You get immediate confirmation that the invitation has been received and accepted, and the Messenger window handles the connection details without requiring any file attachments. Skip the extra steps in the Help And Support Center, and send the invitation directly from Messenger by choosing Tools, Ask For Remote Assistance. The next best option? Pick up the phone. The person requesting assistance can advise the expert to be on the lookout for an e-mail request, negotiate a mutually agreeable time, provide the expert with the Remote Assistance password, and give a general description of the problem. After making contact via telephone, send the Remote Assistance request via e-mail.

Chapter 4: Help and Support Options

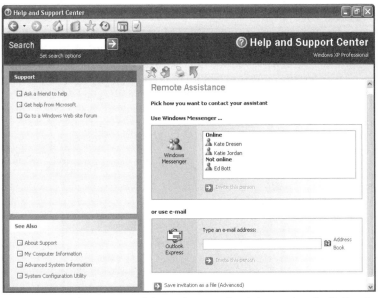

Figure 4-6. Choose any of these three methods to send an invitation for Remote Assistance.

● **E-mail.** To send an invitation via e-mail, enter an e-mail address or click the Address Book icon to select a name from the Windows Address Book; then click Invite This Person. You can enter the text you want to appear in the body of the message, as shown here, and then click Continue to set an expiration time and password. Click the Send Invitation button when you've filled in all the details.

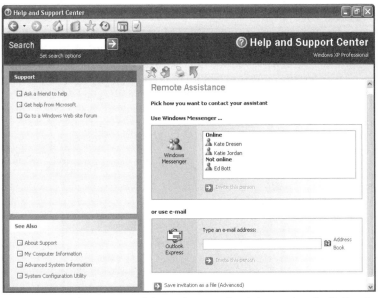

Chapter 4

Part 1: Setup, Startup, Tune-Up

● **Save Invitation as a File (Advanced).** This option is for use when another connection type is impossible or impractical. As with the e-mail option, you can define an expiration time and password. After saving the file locally, you're responsible for transferring it to the remote assistant, typically by attaching it to an e-mail message or saving it on a floppy disk or a shared network location.

Initiating a Remote Assistance Session as the Expert

A weakness of Remote Assistance is that it ordinarily depends on the novice—someone who is having trouble using his or her computer—to initiate a Remote Assistance session by sending an invitation. Depending on how the novice and expert computers are connected and the novice's general computer aptitude, this hurdle might prevent the novice from ever getting the needed help.

An expert running Windows XP Professional (but not Windows XP Home Edition) can initiate a session with another Windows XP Professional user on the same local area network. To do that, the expert must first configure the novice's computer to accept unsolicited Remote Assistance requests, as follows:

1 On the novice's computer, type **gpedit.msc** to open Group Policy. (Alternatively, from the expert's computer, open the novice computer's Group Policy remotely. For details, see "Starting Group Policy for a Remote Computer," page 1281.)

2 In Group Policy, open Computer Configuration\Administrative Templates\System\Remote Assistance, and then double-click Offer Remote Assistance.

Chapter 4

Chapter 4: Help and Support Options

3 On the Setting tab, select Enabled.

4 Specify whether you want helpers to be able to remotely control the computer or simply to view it remotely.

5 Click the Show button to display the list of permitted helpers. In the Show Contents dialog box, shown in Figure 4-7, click Add to add a user account or security group to the list. In the Add Item dialog box, type the name of the account or group. Then click OK to close each dialog box.

note If your computers are not joined to a domain, you must enter the name of a user account that exists on both the novice's and expert's machines. The account's password must be the same on both computers. For this reason, you'll probably find it most convenient to add a user account to the novice machine, using the name that the expert uses to log on to his or her machine. For details, see "Creating a New User Account," page 102.

Figure 4-7. Specify the names of users and groups who are allowed to initiate a Remote Assistance session with this computer.

6 Turn off Simple File Sharing.

In Control Panel, open Folder Options (in the Appearance And Themes category). On the View tab, clear the Use Simple File Sharing (Recommended) check box.

caution Disabling Simple File Sharing has effects that reach far beyond Remote Assistance. For information about the differences between Simple File Sharing and classic sharing, see "Simple File Sharing vs. Advanced Permissions," page 499.

Once the novice's computer is set up in this way, an expert can initiate an unsolicited Remote Assistance session by following these steps:

1 On the Help And Support Center home page, click Use Tools To View Your Computer Information And Diagnose Problems (under Pick A Task in the right column).

note The expert must be logged on using an account that has the same user name and password as a "permitted helpers" account on the novice's computer. Alternatively, the expert can use the Runas command to open the Help And Support Center. For example, if both computers have an account named Smartypants, a user on the expert machine could open the Help And Support Center by entering the following command in a Command Prompt window:

```
runas /user:smartypants "%systemroot%\pchealth\helpctr\binaries\helpctr"
```

2 In the Tools box on the left side, click Offer Remote Assistance.

3 Type the name or IP address of the novice's computer, and click Connect.

4 If Windows prompts you to do so, select the name of a user on the novice's computer.

5 Click the Start Remote Assistance button.

A dialog box appears on the novice's screen; if the novice accepts your invitation, the Remote Assistance session begins.

Troubleshooting

An error appears when the expert tries to connect.

If you, as expert, offer Remote Assistance as described in the preceding procedure, you might receive an error message ("Access to the requested resource has been disabled by your administrator") after you click Connect. This message appears when the novice's computer has not been configured to accept unsolicited Remote Assistance requests. You must use Group Policy on the novice's computer to enable the Offer Remote Assistance setting.

If the error message reads "Permission denied," be sure that Help And Support Center on the expert's computer is running in the context of a user account that matches one on the novice's computer (that is, it has the same user name and password on both machines). In addition, be sure that Simple File Sharing is disabled on the novice's computer.

Working in a Remote Assistance Session

After the expert launches the connection request and the novice grants permission, a two-pane Remote Assistance window opens on the expert's machine. The left pane is used for text chat; the pane on the right displays the novice's desktop, as shown in Figure 4-8 on the next page.

As the expert, you'll use the toolbar at the top of the Remote Assistance window, shown here, to take control of the remote desktop, send a file, or disconnect when the session is complete. (The novice has similar options available on a toolbar whose format is slightly different.)

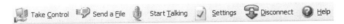

For obvious security reasons, clicking the Take Control button sends a request to the novice, who has to grant permission before you can actually begin working with the remote desktop. At any time, the novice can cut off your ability to control the session by tapping the Esc key, or you can click the Release Control button on the Remote Assistance toolbar.

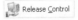

Part 1: Setup, Startup, Tune-Up

Ed and Katy can discuss the problem in this chat pane

Ed can work on Katy's screen in this window

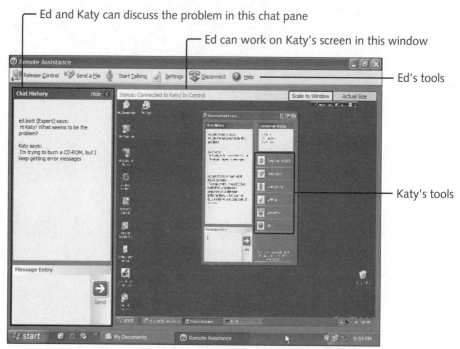

Ed's tools

Katy's tools

Figure 4-8. Use the two tabs in the top right corner of this window to switch between zoomed and actual views of the remote desktop.

Regardless of your expert credentials, your actions in a Remote Assistance session are governed by the privileges assigned to the novice user's account. When connecting to a machine belonging to a user with a limited account, for instance, you might be unable to edit the registry or make necessary configuration changes unless you can supply an administrator's password (using the Run As dialog box).

Chapter 4

For more details about running an application or utility with a different user's account privileges, see "Running a Program as Another User," page 188.

Maintaining Security

Remote Assistance is a powerful tool. In the wrong hands, it's also potentially dangerous, because it allows a remote user to install software and tamper with a system configuration. In a worst-case scenario, someone could trick an unsuspecting novice into allowing access to his or her machine, and then plant a Trojan application or gain access to sensitive files.

Four essential security precautions can slam the door on security breaches:

- Set a short expiration time on Remote Assistance invitations sent via e-mail. A time of 1 hour should be sufficient for most requests. (Note that the invitation must be *accepted* within the specified time; you don't need to specify enough time to complete the Remote Assistance session.) An expired RA ticket file is worthless to a potential hacker.

- Assign a strong password to Remote Assistance invitations. Because e-mail is fundamentally insecure, never send a Remote Assistance invitation without password-protecting it first. This option is selected by default when you create an invitation. Communicate the password by telephone or in a separate e-mail message; don't include it with the RA ticket.

Part 1: Setup, Startup, Tune-Up

● Manually expire invitations when they're no longer needed. To do so, open the Remote Assistance page in the Help And Support Center and then choose the View Invitation Status link. The resulting window shows all recently issued invitations and allows you to resend, delete, or change the expiration date of an invitation.

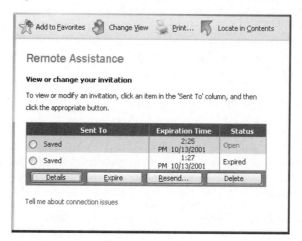

● Disable Remote Assistance on any machine where its possible benefits are outweighed by potential security risks. To completely disable Remote Assistance on a given machine, open System in Control Panel, click the Remote tab, and then clear the Allow Remote Assistance Invitations To Be Sent From This Computer check box. If that step is too drastic, you can limit Remote Assistance capabilities so that an expert cannot take control of the remote machine. Click the Advanced button on the Remote tab and then clear the Allow This Computer To Be Controlled Remotely check box.

---

tip   **Use Group Policy to control Remote Assistance**

With Group Policy (Gpedit.msc), you can disable or restrict the ability of users on a computer to request Remote Assistance. In Group Policy, open the Computer Configuration\Administrative Templates\System\Remote Assistance folder, and double-click Solicited Remote Assistance. To prevent users from sending invitations, select Disabled. To restrict users, select Enabled, and then set the options that determine whether experts can control or view the computer and the maximum allowable ticket time. Settings you make here override any settings you make in the System Properties dialog box.

InsideOut

In some cases, you may want to create a long-term Remote Assistance invitation. If you're the expert for a friend or family member, for instance, there's no need to create a new invitation each time the novice gets stuck. Instead, have that person create an invitation and save it as a file. From the novice's machine, open the Help And Support Center, select the Save Invitation As A File option, and specify the maximum expiration time of 99 days. Store the invitation in a convenient place on your system, and use it each time you get a call for help. Note that this option will not work if the novice has a dial-up Internet account whose IP address changes with each new connection; it's most effective when the novice has a cable modem or other always-on connection with a fixed IP address.

Improving Remote Assistance Performance

You might shudder at the thought of accessing another desktop over a dial-up connection. Surprisingly, the performance can be quite usable. You wouldn't want to use this sort of connection for everyday work, but for troubleshooting, it's good enough. You can maximize Remote Assistance performance over a dial-up link by observing these precautions:

- Try to connect at 56 Kbps, if possible.

- Reduce the visual complexity of the novice machine as much as possible: Reduce the display resolution to 800×600 and use only as many colors as is absolutely necessary. (Remote Assistance automatically disables wallpaper and other nonessential graphics.)

- Turn off desktop animations and other sophisticated visual effects, and avoid opening windows that contain complex graphics unless absolutely necessary.

- Close any unnecessary applications on the novice machine.

- Don't move the mouse on the novice machine, if possible, when the expert is in control of the screen.

Chapter 4

Other Support Resources

Official Help resources are the first line of support, but they're not the only source of answers. Windows-related newsgroups can be a gold mine of information and are particularly useful when your problem involves an unusual error message or a specific combination of hardware. If you can find a post from another user who has experienced the same problem, you might also find a solution, or at least get clues that will point you in the right direction.

To search newsgroups from the Help And Support Center, start at the home page, and click the Get Support, Or Find Information In Windows XP Newsgroups link; then choose Go To A Windows Web Site Forum, and click Go To Windows Newsgroups. This opens a browser window with a Web-based interface to Windows XP–related newsgroups.

> If you want to maintain an archive of newsgroup posts, skip this Web view and use Outlook Express, as described in "Saving Messages Before They're Deleted from the Server," page 700.

Contacting Microsoft Support

The Help And Support Center includes a variety of tools you can use to initiate support requests directly with Microsoft. From the home page, click the Get Support link, and then choose Get Help From Microsoft. If you have an active Internet connection, you can submit a support request directly to Microsoft.

Before initiating a support request, be sure to check your support eligibility. You may be eligible for free support, or you may be required to pay a per-incident fee. The details vary depending on how and when you purchased your copy of Windows.

If you're eligible for support but do not currently have access to an Internet connection, you can save configuration information to a file and submit it later, when you're connected to the Internet again. To use this tool, follow these steps:

1 Open the Help And Support Center and click Get Support, Or Find Information In Windows XP Newsgroups.

2 Click the Get Help From Microsoft link.

3 Sign in using your .NET Passport and supply any required personal information.

4 At the Microsoft Online Assisted Support page, click the View Other Support Options link.

5 Click Save Information About This Computer To Submit To Microsoft Online Assisted Support.

6 Specify a location for the file and save the resulting file. Later, when you connect to the Internet, you can transmit the file to a support engineer.

Chapter 4: Help and Support Options

As Figure 4-9 shows, this procedure is almost completely automatic.

Figure 4-9. When you submit an online support request, Windows gathers all necessary files and submits them automatically.

Chapter 5

Installing, Uninstalling, and Managing Programs

Compared to most earlier versions of Windows, the process of adding a new program is simpler and safer in Windows XP. For anyone upgrading from Windows 2000, the changes are mostly in the area of compatibility: Many programs that refuse to run properly under Windows 2000 (especially games) do better under Windows XP. On the other hand, programs that depend on virtual device drivers (VxDs) simply won't run under Windows XP (or Windows 2000, for that matter).

If you're accustomed to Windows 95, Windows 98, or Windows Me, you'll notice two dramatic improvements in the way the operating system manages installed programs. Windows XP file protection prevents a rogue program from compromising your operating system by installing outdated or incorrect versions of crucial system files; and a greatly improved Add Or Remove Programs dialog box in Control Panel makes it easier to manage installed programs.

How User Rights Affect Program Setup Options

When you attempt to install a program under Windows XP, your setup options depend on the permissions available to you through the account you used to log on. If you're running under an administrator account, you can install any program without restrictions (barring compatibility problems, of course). You can also choose to remove, modify, or repair that program at any time.

171

At Home with Windows XP

The program-management actions described in this chapter work exactly the same way whether you use Windows XP Professional or Windows XP Home Edition. The only part of this chapter that does not apply to Home Edition users are references to the Power Users group, a security group with privileges between those granted to computer administrators and limited users. The Power Users group is not available in Home Edition.

For instructions on how to manage users and groups, including a computer administrator account, see "Working with User Accounts," page 100.

If you log on with a limited user account, however, you will be blocked from installing any program that can be run by other users—in other words, most programs. You can start the Setup program, but it will typically stop before successfully completing. Setup problems can be especially vexing with older applications that aren't certified for use with Windows 2000/XP. With most certified programs, the error message will be easy to understand, like the message that appears when a limited user tries to install a new copy of Microsoft Office XP.

tip   Use Run As to install from your everyday limited account

When Windows blocks installation with the dialog box shown above, you can complete the installation by selecting the name of an administrator account and providing its password; the Setup program then runs in the context of that user. This option is often more convenient than logging off and logging back on, particularly if you use a limited account as your everyday account.

Chapter 5: Installing, Uninstalling, and Managing Programs

Legacy applications that assume the user is running Windows 95/98 behave unpredict-ably when confronted with the more stringent security model of Windows XP. Like the following example, in these cases, the error message that appears when a limited user is blocked from setting up a program can be bafflingly irrelevant.

The program might squawk when Setup tries to copy files to protected folders, where limited users lack appropriate permissions, or it might complain that it couldn't create a specific registry key or value. The only programs that can successfully be installed under a limited user account are those that copy files only to the user's profile, modify only registry settings in the HKEY_CURRENT_USER hive, and install shortcuts only for the currently logged-on user. If the Setup program tries to step outside these bounds, it fails.

On a system that has been upgraded from Windows 2000, some accounts might belong to the Power Users group. This type of user account should be able to install most applications, but any Setup program that replaces operating system files or installs a service will fail; the system blocks access to these crucial parts of the file system and registry by all users except administrators. Security purists recommend that you log on for everyday computing tasks using an account in the Power Users group and use a computer administrator account only when the task requires it.

The Power Users group is on the list of default groups in Windows XP Professional, but it's not available when you create or change an account using Control Panel's User Accounts dialog box. To work with this group, use the Local Users And Groups snap-in from the Computer Management console.

Troubleshooting

You're having trouble installing a program for a user with a limited account.

Unfortunately, many applications that were originally designed for Windows 95/98 and Windows Me stumble when they encounter the multi-user environment of Windows 2000 and Windows XP. Sooner or later (probably sooner), you'll run into problems setting up a third-party program for a user with a limited account. Even after you successfully install the software, you might discover that the program refuses to run. Here's where to look for possible solutions:

● **Is an upgrade available?** A later version of the program might work properly under Windows XP.

(continued)

Troubleshooting *(continued)*

● **Is there a published workaround?** Contact the support department for the software developer and search public newsgroups. An experienced support professional or another user of the product might be able to suggest a way to bypass the problem. If the company has its own support database, don't restrict your search to Windows XP–related issues; a workaround for Windows 2000 is likely to succeed under Windows XP as well.

● **Can you adjust permissions in the registry?** The program might be encountering a problem because it requires that the current user be allowed to modify keys or values in a protected part of the registry. If you can determine which keys are causing the problem, you might be able to log on using an administrator's account, adjust permissions using Registry Editor, and solve the problem.

● **Temporarily "promote" the user.** Try changing the user's account type from Limited to Computer Administrator, and then run Setup for the program. After Setup completes successfully and you confirm that the program will run, see if any user data files are being stored in a system location. If so, move those files to the user's profile and change the account back to Limited. This technique might help get past a glitch caused strictly by a simple design flaw in the Setup program. (For example, some Setup programs are designed to prevent installation by any user who is not a member of the Administrators group—even if the account has all the requisite privileges.)

In some cases, you might discover that the best solution to the problem is to sidestep it completely. Find a Windows XP–compatible program that accomplishes the same goal as the one that's giving you problems. If you can't find a suitable replacement, allow the user to run that program with an administrator's account as described in the final section of this chapter.

caution   Don't be lulled into a false sense of security by the fact that you're logged on using an account in the Power Users group instead of an administrator's account. Running under a limited account provides excellent protection, but is too restrictive for most experienced Windows users to tolerate. The modest restrictions on Power Users still leave your system open to tremendous damage. They can inadvertently install a virus or Trojan horse program, for instance, or trigger the "blue screen of death" by replacing signed drivers with newer, untested versions (buggy video or disk drivers are especially troublesome). They can also create problems by editing keys and values in the HKLM\Software registry hive.

Installing Programs

The Add Or Remove Programs dialog box used in Windows XP is similar to the one introduced in Windows 2000 and dramatically different from its bare-bones predecessor in Windows 95/98 and Windows Me. As Figure 5-1 shows, the list of currently installed programs provides detailed information about each one, including the amount of disk space the program occupies, how often it's been used, and the date the program was last started. You'll also find buttons to uninstall or modify the program.

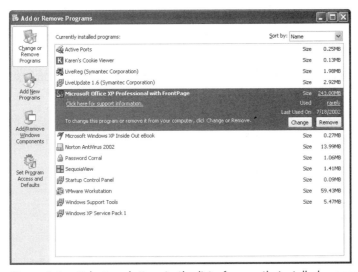

Figure 5-1. Select each item in the list of currently installed programs for detailed information; note the link to additional support information.

Indiscriminately installing software is rarely a good idea. A poorly written program can create system instabilities, cause conflicts with other programs, and impede system performance by using excessive amounts of RAM or CPU time. Before installing a new program, ask the following questions:

● **Is it compatible with Windows XP?** Look for a definitive statement of compatibility on the software package or on the software developer's Web site. Also, check Microsoft's database of compatible applications, available via the Find Compatible Hardware And Software For Windows XP link on the Help And Support Center's home page. For more information about compatibility issues, see the next section in this chapter.

● **Are any patches available?** Checking for updates before installing a new program can spare you painful installation headaches.

● **Are there known problems with the program?** A quick search through public newsgroups via Google's online Usenet archive (*http://groups.google.com*) might turn up valuable setup hints or convince you not to even try to install a particular program.

● **Can it be uninstalled easily?** If the program's setup routine was written with a recent version of InstallShield, Wise Install, or Microsoft's Windows Installer, it will almost certainly include tools that allow you to remove it completely. The older the program, the more likely its uninstall procedure is incomplete.

---

tip   **Set a restore point first**

Even if you're absolutely convinced that a new program is well tested and completely safe, it's *always* a good idea to manually create a System Restore checkpoint first. Give the restore point a descriptive name that clearly identifies it. If you run into unforeseen problems, uninstall the program and then use System Restore to remove any leftover program files and registry entries. For more details, see "Undoing Configuration Mistakes with System Restore," page 900.

Looking for Support Shortcuts

Thoughtful software developers embed links to support resources and tools directly in the program's listing in the Add Or Remove Programs dialog box. If you've installed Microsoft Office XP, for example, the support link leads to the dialog box shown here. Programs that use Windows Installer (including Office 2000 and Office XP) might also include a Repair button like the one shown here, which can be used to quickly fix problems caused by missing or damaged program files.

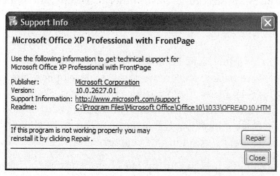

Installing 32-Bit Windows Programs

Virtually all modern 32-bit Windows programs start the Setup process through a file called Setup.exe. Windows can track down the proper Setup file automatically when you use the Add New Programs tab on the Add Or Remove Programs dialog box, shown in Figure 5-2. Click the CD Or Floppy button to search removable media. Use the Browse button on the resulting dialog box to search in other locations (including your default downloads folder or a shared network folder).

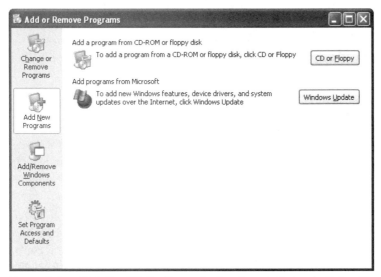

Figure 5-2. Click the CD Or Floppy button to quickly locate Setup files. Programs appear in the bottom of this window only when configured by a network administrator.

On corporate networks, the Add New Programs tab also lists applications that a network administrator has made available to authorized users and groups over a network built around Windows 2000 or Windows .NET servers. Using Windows Installer, administrators can configure a program so that it installs automatically when the user needs it. A program installed this way will appear in either of these two configurations:

- When an application has been *assigned* to a user, shortcuts to the program appear on the user's Start menu or desktop, and relevant file types are preassociated with the application. As soon as the user chooses the menu item, activates the shortcut, or opens an associated document, the application is installed. An application assigned to a specific user is available to that user wherever he or she logs on. An application can also be assigned to a computer, in which case the application is automatically installed when the computer starts up. (And if someone uninstalls the assigned application, it is automatically reinstalled at the next logon.)

177

- An application that is *published* to a user is installed only when the user chooses that option from the list of available programs at the bottom of the Add New Programs window.

To learn more about using Windows Update to automatically install new features or drivers, see "Service Packs, Patches, and Windows Update," page 64.

Installing and Running 16-Bit Windows Programs

Windows XP does an impressive job of running programs that were originally written years ago for Windows 3.*x*. To run these older 16-bit programs under a 32-bit operating system, Windows XP launches a subsystem—a *virtual machine*—that mimics "386 enhanced mode" in the older Windows 3.*x* environment.

Although Windows XP allows you to run these 16-bit programs, you'll encounter a few glitches:

- Most 16-bit programs do not support long file names. (Windows XP maintains the links between short and long file names, however, so that long file names are preserved when a 16-bit application modifies a file and saves it using the same name.)

- In general, 16-bit applications do not run as fast as comparable 32-bit applications. The 16-bit programs are restricted to using a single thread, even on a multithreaded operating system such as Windows XP. And calls made by a 16-bit application must be translated for the 32-bit operating system. This translation process, called *thunking,* adds to execution time.

- Some 16-bit applications require 16-bit device drivers, which are not supported in Windows XP. Applications that directly access hardware must supply a Windows XP virtual device driver and a Windows XP 32-bit device driver, or they won't run.

- Dynamic link libraries (DLLs) written for 16-bit applications cannot be used by 32-bit applications, and vice versa. Because the setup program for most applications installs all the DLLs needed by the application, you won't be aware of this distinction most of the time. But if, for example, you have a macro written for Microsoft Word 6 (a 16-bit application) that accesses one or more DLLs, it won't work with Word 2002 (a 32-bit application).

Many 16-bit programs use the Windows 3.*x*–vintage Win.ini and System.ini files to store program-specific configuration information (some programs use private .ini files as well). Windows XP retains bare-bones copies of Win.ini and System.ini in the %SystemRoot% folder. If you encounter problems with a 16-bit application, you might find clues in these two files.

Chapter 5: Installing, Uninstalling, and Managing Programs

---

tip **Learn how to spot a 16-bit application**

Because most Windows 3.x–based programs run properly under Windows XP, it's sometimes difficult to tell 16-bit and 32-bit applications apart. Here are two methods for determining whether an application is 16-bit or 32-bit: right-click the program's executable file and then choose Properties. If you see a Version tab, it's a 32-bit program. Or, if the program is running, press Ctrl+Alt+Del to open Windows Task Manager. On the Processes tab, look in the Image Name column for the name of the program's executable file. If any 16-bit programs are running, you'll find an entry for Ntvdm.exe, the virtual DOS machine. Just above it in the list, you'll see indented entries for Wowexec.exe (the Windows on Windows subsystem) and the executable name of each 16-bit program running in that virtual machine.

By default, Windows XP treats each running 16-bit application as a thread within a single virtual machine. If you're running multiple 16-bit applications, they share a common memory space, and a crash in one Windows 3.x–based application will typically bring down all the others with it—causing you to lose any unsaved information in all 16-bit applications. If you regularly run multiple 16-bit applications and one of them hangs or crashes frequently, you should run it in a separate memory space. To do so, follow these steps:

1 Create a shortcut to the program, right-click the shortcut icon, and then choose Properties.

2 On the Shortcut tab, click the Advanced button.

3 Select the Run In Separate Memory Space check box. (See Figure 5-3.)

4 Click OK, and then close all open dialog boxes to apply the change.

Select this check box to force a 16-bit program to run in its own virtual machine

Figure 5-3. A program running in separate memory space can't cause problems for other 16-bit programs running at the same time.

Before deciding to run multiple 16-bit applications in separate virtual machines, you should weigh the tradeoffs. The downside is that this approach uses extra memory. (Windows Task Manager can help you measure the exact differences in RAM consumption for each scenario as explained in "Monitoring Memory Usage," page 231.) However, there are several benefits, including preemptive multitasking, better responsiveness, and the ability to run multiple instances of applications that normally do not allow you to do so. In general, this option is best reserved for mission-critical legacy applications.

> **note**   Command.com, the MS-DOS command processor, is a 16-bit application included with Windows XP. If you type **command** in the Run box, Windows starts a new MS-DOS virtual machine. Don't confuse this option with Cmd.exe, the 32-bit Windows XP Command Prompt program. For most command-line tasks, Cmd is preferred; reserve Command.com for those rare occasions when you want to run a 16-bit MS-DOS program.

Installing and Configuring MS-DOS Programs

By definition, all programs originally written for MS-DOS are 16-bit programs. As such, they run in a virtual machine alongside their 16-bit counterparts developed for Windows 3.*x*.

To control the behavior of MS-DOS-based programs, you use a properties dialog box whose design hasn't changed much since Windows 95. Custom property settings for each program are stored in a shortcut file called a program information file (PIF).

> **tip**   **Set global PIF options**
>
> Is the default MS-DOS environment not quite right? You can adjust the default settings that apply to all MS-DOS programs by editing the settings stored in %SystemRoot%_default.pif. When you double-click the icon for an MS-DOS-based program and Windows can't find a matching PIF, it uses the settings recorded here. Likewise, when you create a new PIF, it starts with these default settings. If you want an MS-DOS batch file to run each time any MS-DOS program starts up, save the file as %SystemRoot%_default.bat.

You can create multiple shortcuts (PIFs) for a single MS-DOS program, each with its own custom settings, such as a default data file or working directory. When you right-click the icon for an MS-DOS executable file and make any changes to its properties, Windows saves your changes in the same folder, creating or updating a file with the same name as the executable file and the extension .pif. You can change the name of the shortcut file or move it to another folder.

The PIF format is binary and can't be edited except through the properties dialog box. Right-click the icon for the MS-DOS program's executable file to display this dialog

Chapter 5: Installing, Uninstalling, and Managing Programs

box, which adds four tabs containing options that are exclusively available to MS-DOS programs. Using the Misc tab, shown in Figure 5-4, for instance, you can disable Windows shortcut keys that conflict with shortcuts in the MS-DOS program. Other options on other tabs allow you to adjust the amount of memory allocated to a program, specify the program's initial display mode (full-screen or windowed), the icon associated with the program, and other options.

Figure 5-4. The Font, Memory, Screen, and Misc tabs in this dialog box control settings that are exclusive to MS-DOS programs.

> **note** For a concise explanation of each option in the properties dialog box for an MS-DOS program, right-click the option and then use the context-sensitive What's This? menu. Alternatively, click the title bar's question mark icon and then click the option that needs explanation.

You can run any character-based program written for MS-DOS either in full-screen mode or in a window. (Graphics-based programs run only in full-screen mode.) If you run a program in full-screen mode, it looks exactly like it does when you run it under MS-DOS. If you run it in a window, it has a title bar, a Control menu, and other familiar window management features.

Chapter 5

> **tip**   **Switch to full screen and back again**
>
> To switch an MS-DOS program window between full-screen and windowed views, use the keyboard shortcut Alt+Enter. If the Alt+Enter shortcut is disabled (because it's used for another purpose by the MS-DOS program) and the program is currently in full-screen view, press Alt+Tab or Ctrl+Esc to switch to another program, or tap the Windows logo key to display the Start menu. Then right-click the taskbar button for the program you switched away from. Choose Properties from the shortcut menu, click the Options tab in the properties dialog box, and then select the Window option button.

Running some MS-DOS programs properly might require that you change the system configuration used by the MS-DOS virtual machine. Two files, Autoexec.nt and Config.nt, serve this function in Windows XP. These two files serve a purpose similar to that of Autoexec.bat and Config.sys in MS-DOS and Windows 95/98, with several important differences:

- Autoexec.nt and Config.nt are located by default in the %SystemRoot% \System32 folder. (The corresponding files on an MS-DOS or Windows 95/98 machine are in the root folder of drive C.)

- In Windows XP (as in Windows 2000), you can create custom versions of Autoexec.nt and Config.nt for specific applications. To associate your custom configuration files with a specific application, copy the default files to a separate location and edit them as needed. Next, open the properties dialog box for the MS-DOS program, click the Advanced button on the Program tab, and then enter the correct locations as shown below. (Note that this dialog box includes a Compatible Timer Hardware Emulation check box. This option imposes a performance penalty, so you should select it only if your application won't run with the box cleared.)

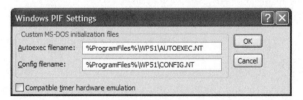

- Commands you enter in these two files affect only the MS-DOS subsystem. Many commands, such as Buffers and Break, are ignored, although they can be entered for compatibility purposes when an MS-DOS program insists that they be present. Windows XP includes its own versions of Himem.sys, Ansi.sys, Country.sys, and Setver.exe. Avoid using the following unsupported and unnecessary Windows 95/98 drivers in Config.nt: Emm386.exe, Smartdrv.sys, Ramdrive.sys, and Dblspace.sys/Drvspace.sys. Windows XP ignores all entries in Autoexec.nt except those defined by Set or Path commands, which it adds to the startup environment for that MS-DOS virtual machine.

Chapter 5: Installing, Uninstalling, and Managing Programs

Making a Program Available to All Users

Most of the time, when you install a Windows program from an administrator's account, its shortcuts are placed in %AllUsersProfile%\Start Menu\Programs, so that any user who wants to run that program can do so. Exceptionally well-written programs ask you whether you want to install the program for all users or only for the currently logged-on user. (This option is especially appropriate when you're installing a utility program that you don't want other users to be able to run.)

What should you do when Setup installs a program only for the currently logged-on user? If you want other users to have access to the program, you have two choices:

● Log on using each user account and rerun Setup. This option gives you the flexibility to make a program available to selected users, but it has one significant drawback: you have to remember to run that Setup program again every time you create a new user account.

● For simple programs that don't require per-user settings to be added to the registry before running, you might be able to simply add a shortcut to %AllUsersProfile%\Start Menu\Programs. To ensure that a program is available to all current and future users, move the program's shortcut from your personal profile to the All Users folder.

To move the program's shortcut, follow these steps:

1 Click the Start button, right-click the shortcut or group you want to move, and then choose Cut from the shortcut menu.

2 Right-click the Start menu and then choose Explore All Users.

3 Select the Programs folder, right-click, and then choose Paste.

Use the same basic procedure, only in reverse, if you want to move a program shortcut or group from the All Users folder to your personal profile so that it is no longer available to other users. They will still be able to launch the program from the Run box or from an Explorer window, but you will have removed the most visible means of access to the program.

newfeature!
Forcing Older Programs to Run Properly

Windows XP goes to heroic lengths to run many 32-bit Windows applications that refused to run under Windows 2000. The list of compatible software includes thousands of productivity titles and games. Unfortunately, not all programs that ran correctly under previous Windows versions will run under Windows XP, and some can cause serious problems. When you attempt to install a program that is known to have compatibility problems, Windows XP should display a message like the one shown here. Don't take this message lightly! If a patch is available, download and install it immediately. If no patch is available, do not install the program.

If you run across a program that worked flawlessly under a previous Windows version but refuses to install or run under Windows XP, you might be able to run the program by adjusting its compatibility options. (This functionality was available in Windows 2000 via a Resource Kit utility called Apcompat.exe.) In Windows XP, you can reset compatibility options with a wizard or via the properties dialog box for a program shortcut. Both options have the same effect—they try to fool the underlying program into believing that it's running on an earlier version of Windows. This strategy is especially effective at getting around a Setup program that stops when it finds a Windows version number it doesn't understand.

caution   Tinkering with compatibility options is a risky strategy, especially when the program in question is a low-level utility such as an antivirus program or disk partitioning tool that was not specifically designed for Windows XP. Even a seemingly innocuous CD-burning program can be a major troublemaker if it tries to install an incompatible device driver. When in doubt, your best bet is to do more research before trying to tweak compatibility options.

To use the Program Compatibility Wizard, open the All Programs menu and then click Accessories. Click the program shortcut to launch the wizard and follow its step-by-step instructions. This is the only way to adjust compatibility settings on programs that are on removable media (including CDs) or on shared network drives.

If you've successfully set up a program but it refuses to run, the easiest and fastest way to set compatibility options is to work directly with a program shortcut. Right-click the shortcut icon and choose Properties, and then click the Compatibility tab, as shown in Figure 5-5. Select the Run This Program In Compatibility Mode For check box, and choose one of the four available operating systems: Windows 95, Windows 98/Windows Me, Windows NT 4.0 (Service Pack 5), or Windows 2000. Use the Display

Chapter 5: Installing, Uninstalling, and Managing Programs

Settings options to deal with programs that have video problems when run at higher resolutions and color depths. The Input Settings option (which appears only if you've installed Service Pack 1 for Windows XP) disables "advanced text services," which include handwriting recognition and speech recognition. Because advanced text services reduce performance, you should disable them for your older programs that can't use these cutting-edge input methods.

This option appears only if SP1 is installed

Figure 5-5. Use these compatibility options to fool an older Windows program into running on Windows XP.

Managing Installed Programs

In its default view, the Add Or Remove Programs dialog box lists installed programs in alphabetical order by program name. If you're ready to do some spring cleaning, use the drop-down Sort By list in the upper right corner to sort by the date last used. Programs you haven't used recently are possible candidates for removal. If your goal is to free up disk space, sort by size; the biggest disk hogs appear at the top of the resulting list.

For programs that include multiple Setup options, use the Add Or Remove Programs dialog box to rerun Setup and remove installed components or add options that you previously bypassed. Programs that use Windows Installer as their Setup engine typically offer a Change button for this purpose. Installer-based applications (including major Internet Explorer upgrades) may also offer a Repair option, typically buried under a Support link. In theory, Windows Installer should be able to detect problems caused by a damaged or deleted DLL and repair the component automatically when you run the application—prompting you for installation media if necessary. Use the Repair button to completely refresh the set of installed program files and accompanying registry keys and values.

Uninstalling Programs

To remove an installed Windows program, open the Add Or Remove Programs dialog box from Control Panel, select the program's entry in the list on the Change Or Remove Programs page, and click the Remove or Change/Remove button.

> **caution** Click the Remove button at your own risk. Although most installer programs are courteous enough to ask your permission before launching the uninstaller program, a small number of programs will simply remove themselves, immediately and without any further prompting.

Here are some basic facts you should know about uninstalling programs:

- Windows XP warns you if you attempt to remove a program while other users are logged on. For safety's sake, you should always completely log off any other user accounts before attempting to remove a program.

- Most uninstall programs leave at least a few traces of the program behind, either inadvertently or by design. For instance, programs that create data files typically do not remove custom user settings and data files as part of the uninstall process.

- You can only remove programs from the Add Or Remove Programs dialog box if they were originally installed with a Windows-compatible Setup program. Some programs (typically utilities) work by copying their files to a folder. In this case, you uninstall the program by manually removing its files and any shortcuts.

- In some cases, a poorly written uninstall routine may leave a phantom entry behind in the list of installed programs, even after it has successfully removed all traces of the program itself. To remove an item from the list in this case, you can use Microsoft's unsupported (but highly recommended) Tweak UI utility. For details about Tweak UI, see "Customizing Windows XP with Tweak UI," page 327. You can also remove entries manually, using Registry Editor. Detailed instructions are available in Knowledge Base article Q247501, "How to Manually Remove Programs from the Add/Remove Programs List."

Managing Program Shortcuts

During Setup, most Windows programs typically create one or more shortcuts on the Start menu (and occasionally on the desktop and Quick Launch toolbar as well). By tweaking shortcuts, you can control exactly how and when programs start up. Here are some useful improvements you can make to a generic program shortcut:

- **Specify startup options.** Create multiple versions of a program shortcut for special purposes. Many programs allow command-line arguments (the name of a file or startup folder, for instance) or startup switches that control default settings. With Microsoft Word, for instance, you can use the /T switch followed by a template name (don't add a space) to create a new document using that template. Open the shortcut's properties dialog box, and enter the arguments or switches immediately after the command name in the Target box, as shown in Figure 5-6. (Note in this example that we've also adjusted the Start In location and added a shortcut key.)

Figure 5-6. Tweak the properties of program shortcuts to enter command-line arguments, assign shortcut keys, and add ScreenTips.

- **Assign a keyboard shortcut.** Click in the Shortcut Key field and press a keyboard combination that you want to use for launching or switching to this program. The shortcut key you assign must consist of one character key (a letter, number, or symbol) plus at least two of the following three keys: Ctrl, Alt, and Shift. (If you press a character key only, Windows automatically adds Ctrl+Alt.) Shortcut keys work only when assigned to a program shortcut on the Start menu, the All Programs menu, or the desktop. The shortcut you define will not work if it conflicts with a combination used in the program whose window has the focus.

---

tip   **Put the Windows logo key to work**

Most keyboards sold with Windows PCs include a Windows logo key that's hardwired to several useful system functions. (For a complete list of Windows logo key shortcuts, search the Help And Support Center for "Natural Keyboard Shortcuts.") Windows doesn't allow you to use the Windows logo key as part of user-defined shortcuts, but a free utility called WinKey adds this capability. Download it from Copernic Technologies at *http://www.copernic.com/winkey.*

● **Add a ScreenTip.** The text in the shortcut's Comments field appears in the ScreenTip when you hover the mouse pointer over the shortcut. You can add comments to your custom shortcuts to explain their purpose; if you would like to remove the comment text of an existing shortcut, delete it here.

For tips on how to customize the Start menu and Quick Launch bar, see "Making It Easy to Start Your Favorite Programs," page 267.

Running a Program as Another User

In some situations, you might not be able to run a program using the account under which you're currently logged on. This is most likely if you're logged on using an account in the Power Users group and the program you want to use requires administrative privileges. You have three options:

● If Fast User Switching is enabled on your computer, click the Start button, choose Log Off, and then click the Switch User button. Log on using an administrative account and run the program. If the program will take some time to complete, you can allow it to remain running in the background while you switch back to your regular user account. Fast User Switching is not available on a Windows XP Professional machine that is joined to a domain. For more information, see "Configuring Fast User Switching," page 114.

● For immediate access to a program without leaving your currently logged-on account, use the Run As option. The Run As menu choice is available when you right-click any shortcut or program icon. On some special-purpose shortcuts—most notably shortcuts placed on the All

Chapter 5: Installing, Uninstalling, and Managing Programs

Programs menu by Microsoft Office—you have to hold down the Shift key as you right-click to display the Run As option. Select the option shown here, The Following User, and enter the user name and password of an account that has the desired permissions.

---

tip   Choose an account each time

You can configure any program shortcut so that Windows prompts you for logon credentials every time you double-click that shortcut. This is an ideal solution for the Computer Management option in the Administrative Tools folder, for instance. To specify this option, right-click the shortcut icon and choose Properties. On the Shortcut tab, click the Advanced button and select the Run With Different Credentials check box.

● Use the Runas command from a command window, from the Run dialog box, or in the Target field of a shortcut's properties dialog box to specify that you want a program to start with a specific user account. For instance, you can create a shortcut that opens a Command Prompt window using another user's permissions by typing the following syntax in the Target field of the shortcut's properties dialog box (substituting the actual user name, of course):

```
runas /user:username cmd
```

After you issue the command or activate the shortcut, you'll be prompted to enter the password for the specified user account. For security reasons, you cannot save the password with the shortcut. Note that the Runas command does not work with Microsoft Management Console (MMC) shortcuts; if you're logged in as a limited user and you want to start the Computer Management console using an administrator's account, right-click and use the Run As command on the shortcut menu.

InsideOut

In Windows XP, you can prevent a program from taking advantage of administrative permissions by using an option in the Run As dialog box. Right-click the program shortcut and choose Run As from the shortcut menu. In the Run As dialog box, select Current User, and then select the Protect My Computer And Data From Unauthorized Program Activity check box. This option runs the program using the credentials of the current user (and, therefore, that user's privileges), with one glaring restriction: It prevents the program from making any changes to the registry. This option is especially effective when you're trying out a new program that is untrusted; by selecting this check box, you can safely run the program and see if it generates any error messages or displays any unusual behavior.

The Run As menu choice works with most third-party programs and many Windows utilities and Control Panel options. (Hold down the Shift key when right-clicking a Control Panel icon to use this option.) A handful of applications that are started indirectly by Windows XP cannot be started with the Run As menu choice. You'll strike out if you try to use Run As with Windows Explorer, for instance. The option is also unavailable for desktop items created by the system and for objects in the Network Connections folder. Interestingly, a full menu of options is available when you press Shift and right-click any icon in the Printers And Faxes folder, and then choose Run As. Use this option if you're running under an ordinary user account and need to delete or pause items in the print queue that were created by another user.

Chapter 6

Setting Up and Troubleshooting Hardware

It's probably only a slight exaggeration to say that no two computers are alike. Motherboards, disk controllers, video and network adapters, and peripherals of all shapes and sizes combine to create a nearly infinite number of possible computer configurations.

Although Microsoft Windows XP doesn't work with every computer peripheral ever made, the list of compatible devices is extensive and impressive. On new hardware and with popular upgrades, Windows detects the device automatically and installs the correct driver software so that you can use the device and its full array of features.

If Windows has a problem with a device, you can take your choice of troubleshooting tools. Although the basic Device Manager interface closely resembles its predecessors, the Windows XP version of this essential utility is more versatile.

A Crash Course in Device Drivers

Before Windows can work with any piece of hardware, it requires a compatible, properly configured device driver. *Drivers* are compact control programs that hook directly into Windows and handle the essential tasks of communicating your instructions to a hardware device and then relaying data back to you. After you set up a hardware device, its driver loads automatically and runs as part of the operating system, without requiring any further intervention on your part.

191

At Home with Windows XP

You'll encounter no differences in working with hardware devices whether you use Windows XP Home Edition or Windows XP Professional. The procedures for installing devices, working with device drivers, and troubleshooting hardware problems are the same in both versions of Windows. Windows XP Professional includes a command-line utility called Driverquery that is not available in Home Edition.

Windows XP includes an enormous library of drivers—for printers, keyboards, scanners, mice and related pointing devices, digital cameras, and other devices—in a single compressed file called Driver.cab. (You'll find this file located in the %SystemRoot%\ Driver Cache\i386 folder.) All the drivers in this file are certified to be fully compatible with Windows XP and are digitally signed by Microsoft. When you install a new Plug and Play–compatible device, Windows checks this location first. If it finds a suitable driver, installation proceeds automatically. In addition, Microsoft regularly makes new, certified drivers available through Windows Update.

To be properly installed in Windows XP, a hardware driver must have a Setup Information file (with the extension .inf). This is a text file that contains detailed information about the device to be installed, including the names of its driver files, the locations where they are to be installed, any required registry settings, and version information. All devices with drivers included in Driver.cab include corresponding Setup information files, which can be found in %SystemRoot%\Inf. When you install a new driver, it might also add a Setup Information file in this location.

The basic structure of a Setup Information file is similar to an old-fashioned Windows 3.x–style .ini file; each piece of setup information appears on its own line under a bracketed section heading, as in the following example (taken from a much larger .inf file for Kodak digital cameras):

```
;
; DC240 and compatible USB camera
;
[DC240]
Include=sti.inf
Needs=STI.USBSection

CopyFiles=DC240.Files,Kodak.Color
AddReg=DC240.AddReg
DeviceData=DC240.DeviceData
SubClass=StillImage
DeviceType=2
Capabilities=0x35
UninstallSection=
Events=DC240.Events
ICMProfiles=kodak_dc.icm
```

Chapter 6: Setting Up and Troubleshooting Hardware

```
[DC240.Services]
Include=sti.inf
Needs=STI.USBSection.Services

[DC240.DeviceData]
Server=local
UI DLL=sti.dll
UI Class ID={4DB1AD10-3391-11D2-9A33-00C04FA36145}
```

Although the Setup Information file is a crucial part of the driver installation process for a specific piece of hardware, you don't work with it directly. Instead, this file supplies instructions that the operating system uses during Plug and Play detection, or when you use the Add Hardware Wizard or a Setup program to install a device.

> **caution**   The syntax of Setup Information files is complex, and the intricacies of .inf files can trip up even experienced software developers. If you find that a driver setup routine isn't working properly, you might be tempted to try editing the Setup Information file to work around the hang-up. Trust us: That approach is almost certain to fail. In fact, by tinkering with .inf files, you run the risk of corrupting registry settings and crashing your system.

newfeature!
Are Signed Drivers Safer?

Windows XP includes a mechanism for attaching a digital signature to a driver file. A digitally signed driver is relatively easy to spot, because it's marked at every turn by the logo shown here.

In its default settings, Windows XP warns you if you're attempting to install a driver that isn't digitally signed. During the driver setup process, you'll see a strongly worded message like the one shown in Figure 6-1 on the next page.

In general, you should prefer signed drivers for two reasons:

- The digital signature confirms that the driver has undergone extensive compatibility testing in Microsoft's Windows Hardware Quality Labs (WHQL). It represents a strong assurance that the driver follows installation guidelines and that you can count on it not to cause your system to crash or become unstable.

- The signature means that the driver hasn't been tampered with by other installation programs or by a virus or Trojan horse program.

Chapter 6

Part 1: Setup, Startup, Tune-Up

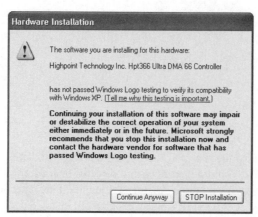

Figure 6-1. Take this warning seriously. Unsigned, incompatible drivers can cause performance and stability problems.

Don't underestimate the negative consequences that can result from installing an unsigned, faulty driver. Because hardware drivers access low-level functions in the operating system, a badly written driver is much more likely to cause blue-screen errors than a buggy program. Even a seemingly innocuous driver can result in sudden crashes that result in loss of data and can prevent you from restarting your computer.

Sometimes, you have to make the difficult decision of whether to install an unsigned driver or give up the use of a piece of hardware. If the hardware device is essential and replacing it would be prohibitively expensive, you might decide that the risk is worth it. In other cases, the choice is more difficult, as is the case when you have to choose between a signed driver that offers a minimal set of features or an unsigned alternative driver that allows you to take advantage of special features that are specific to your hardware.

> **tip** **Give unsigned drivers a workout**
>
> If you decide to take a chance on an unsigned driver, your best strategy is to back up your data and then thoroughly test the new driver right away. (Windows automatically sets a System Restore point when you install an unsigned driver.) Run every application that's installed on your computer. Try to get a few CPU-intensive and disk-intensive tasks going at the same time. Open and save files, especially big, complex ones. Try running disk utilities such as Chkdsk and Defrag. If the new driver is going to cause problems with the hardware and software you currently use, you want to find out immediately after installing it so you can roll back to your previous configuration with as little hassle as possible.

As noted earlier, the default setting warns you if you're about to install an unsigned driver. If you're an experienced Windows user and you're confident of your ability to identify and select compatible drivers, you can eliminate this warning completely. You can also change system settings to prevent users from installing any unsigned drivers, a

Chapter 6: Setting Up and Troubleshooting Hardware

strategy that might be appropriate on a shared machine where you're concerned that kids or coworkers will undermine system stability by trying to install an incompatible device. To adjust driver-signing policies, follow these steps:

1 From Control Panel, open System and click the Hardware tab.

2 Click the Driver Signing button.

3 In the Driver Signing Options dialog box, shown in Figure 6-2, choose the action you want Windows to take whenever a user is about to install an unsigned driver.

■ **Ignore.** This option allows the user to install any unsigned driver without having to click through a warning message.

■ **Warn.** This is the Windows XP default. Users can choose to override the warning and install an unsigned driver.

■ **Block.** When this option is selected, Windows will not allow any unsigned driver to be installed.

4 To apply the selected option only to the current user, clear the Make This Action The System Default check box. Select this check box to set the selected action for all users. (This option is available only if you're logged on as an administrator.)

5 Click OK to apply the changes.

Figure 6-2. Take your choice: You can tighten or loosen driver security with this dialog box.

195

InsideOut

The Make This Action The System Default option is equivalent to using Local Security Policy to set driver-signing policies. (Local Security Policy is an MMC console that's available only in Windows XP Professional.) Security policies provide an effective way to prevent users from making unwanted changes to the driver-signing policy you establish; the setting you make determines which Driver Signing Options dialog box options are available to nonadministrative users. After you make a setting with the system default option selected or in Local Security Policy, only settings that are at least as strict appear in the Driver Signing Options dialog box when displayed by a nonadministrative user. (All three options are always available to administrators, although an administrator must select Make This Action The System Default to select an option less strict than the current default.)

If you'd prefer to make this setting in the Local Security Settings policy editor (there's no advantage to doing so, unless you have other policies to set) follow these steps: In Control Panel choose Administrative Tools (in the Performance And Maintenance category), Local Security Policy. In the Local Security Settings console, open Security Settings\Local Policies\Security Options. Double-click Devices: Unsigned Driver Installation Behavior. Select one of the three options, which—despite the different wording—correspond to the options in the Driver Signing Options dialog box: Silently Succeed (Ignore), Warn But Allow Installation (Warn), or Do Not Allow Installation (Block).

In the case of specific drivers that are known to cause serious problems, a Windows XP feature called Windows Driver Protection will refuse to install that driver regardless of the policy you've set. When you run the Add Hardware Wizard and point to a driver that is in the database of blocked drivers, you see a dialog box like the one shown in Figure 6-3.

Windows provides multiple warnings and notifications when it takes the drastic step of blocking a driver. The Add Hardware Wizard concludes with a Cannot Install This

Figure 6-3. Windows Driver Protection blocks installation of drivers that are known to cause serious stability problems.

Hardware message, which includes the text "This driver has been blocked from loading." The pop-up message in the notification area also displays a failure message, as shown here. However, failed driver installations are not recorded in Event Viewer.

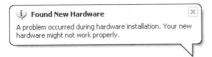

Will Drivers Written for Other Windows Versions Work with Windows XP?

If a signed, Windows XP–compatible driver is not available for a given device, you might be able to use a driver originally written for a previous version of Windows.

For the best chance of success, find a driver written for Microsoft Windows 2000. Many (but certainly not all) Windows 2000 drivers will work properly in Windows XP.

Some Windows Driver Model (WDM) drivers that were originally written for Windows Me might also work under Windows XP, but only if the accompanying Setup Information (.inf) file includes specific instructions for Windows 2000/XP.

Drivers originally written for Windows 95/98 or Windows NT 4 or earlier are unlikely to work properly with Windows XP, because the architectural differences between those operating systems and Windows XP are just too great.

---

tip   **Dig deep for drivers**

It's not always clear from the labeling on the outside of a floppy disk or CD that the drivers it contains are for multiple Windows versions. Sometimes the structure of the disk itself can offer important clues. Look for a Win2000 or W2K subdirectory, for example, and point the Add Hardware Wizard to that location when prompted. If a suitable .inf file is available, you may be able to complete the installation.

Setting Up a New Device

Since its introduction in Windows 95, Plug and Play technology has evolved tremendously. Early incarnations of this technology were notoriously unreliable, leading some users to dismiss the feature as "plug and pray." In recent years, however, hardware and software standards have converged to make most device configuration tasks completely automatic. With true Plug and Play devices, Windows XP handles virtually all of the work of configuring computer hardware and attached devices.

For Plug and Play to work properly, all the pieces of a computer system must be capable of working together to perform hardware configuration tasks. Specifically:

- The system BIOS must be capable of responding to Plug and Play and power management events. By definition, any system with an ACPI BIOS includes this capability.

- The operating system must be capable of responding to Plug and Play events. Windows XP fully supports the Plug and Play standard.

- The device must be capable of identifying itself, listing its required resources (including drivers), and allowing software to configure it. The Microsoft "Designed for Windows" logo identifies hardware that meets all these requirements.

- The device driver must be capable of interacting with the operating system and responding to device notification and power management events. A Plug and Play driver can load automatically when Windows detects that a device has been plugged in, and can suspend and resume properly along with the system.

---

tip　**Run setup software first**

In many cases, new hardware devices include a setup CD that includes driver files and utility software. The best time to run this CD is *before* plugging in the device. If the drivers are signed, the setup program copies the driver files and setup Information file to your hard disk so that installation can proceed automatically when you plug in the device.

In Windows XP, Plug and Play support is optimized for USB, IEEE 1394 (FireWire), PCMCIA (PC Card), and PCI devices. By definition, any USB or PCMCIA device is a Plug and Play device, as are virtually all PCI devices. Devices that connect to a parallel or serial port may or may not be fully Plug and Play compatible, and legacy devices that use the ISA bus are by definition not capable of being managed by Plug and Play.

Managing the Plug and Play Process

When you install a Plug and Play device for the first time, Windows reads the Plug and Play identification tag contained in the hardware's BIOS or firmware. It then compares that ID tag with a master list of corresponding tags drawn from all the Setup Information files in the hidden Inf folder. If it finds a signed driver with a matching tag, it installs the correct driver file (or files) and makes other necessary system modifications with no intervention required from you. Unlike previous Windows versions, which display the

Chapter 6: Setting Up and Troubleshooting Hardware

progress of Plug and Play operations in dialog boxes, Windows XP provides more subtle indications in the form of pop-up balloon tips in the notification area. You might see a series of these notifications, culminating with the final message shown here.

When Windows detects a Plug and Play device (after you've plugged it into a USB port, for instance) but cannot locate a suitable signed device driver, it starts the Found New Hardware Wizard.

> **note** You must be logged on as a member of the Administrators group to install hardware drivers. If you're logged on using an account without administrative permissions, you'll be prompted to supply an administrator's user name and password during hardware setup.

The basic workings of the Found New Hardware Wizard should be familiar to anyone who's ever installed a device in any version of Windows. As Figure 6-4 shows, the wizard's opening screen offers two choices.

Figure 6-4. Select the second option instead of this default choice if you've downloaded a new hardware driver and don't plan to use a CD or floppy disk.

The exact procedure to follow varies, depending on where the driver you plan to install is located:

The new device came with an installation CD or floppy disk containing Windows XP–compatible drivers   Choose the first option, Install The Software Automatically (Recommended), and then click Next. This option searches all removable drives and looks for suitable Setup Information files. If only one compatible driver is available, the wizard installs it automatically; if the wizard finds more than one compatible driver, it presents a list of drivers that match the Plug and Play ID of the new device and allows you to choose.

You've downloaded a Windows XP–compatible driver to a local or network drive   Choose the second option, Install From A List Or Specific Location (Advanced). After you click Next, you see the dialog box shown in Figure 6-5.

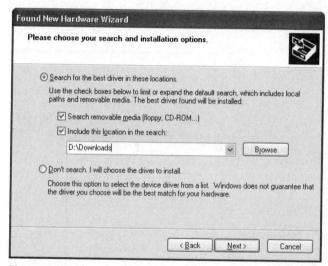

Figure 6-5.   If you've downloaded a new driver, use this dialog box to specify its location.

Follow these steps to point the wizard to the correct driver files:

1   Select the first option, Search For The Best Driver In These Locations.

2   Select the Include This Location In The Search option.

3   Enter the full path of the folder that contains the downloaded driver and Setup Information file, or use the Browse button to point to this location.

4   Click Next to search the specified location and follow the prompts to complete the installation.

Chapter 6: Setting Up and Troubleshooting Hardware

You want to choose a specific driver for the new hardware   Use this option to select a specific driver from several choices that might be compatible with the new device. For instance, you might want to bypass a signed driver included with Windows XP and instead use the manufacturer's unsigned driver, so that you can enable specific features of the new device.

To install an unsigned driver in place of a signed driver, follow these steps:

1   From the Found New Hardware Wizard, choose the second option, Install From A List Or Specific Location (Advanced). Click Next.

2   Select the Don't Search. I Will Choose The Driver To Install option and click Next. The wizard displays a list of compatible drivers like the one shown here.

3   To expand the list so that all drivers in the selected device class are available, clear the Show Compatible Hardware check box.

4   Choose a device from the list and click Next to complete the installation.

Configuring Non–Plug and Play Devices

As you might suspect, Windows will not automatically set up a non–Plug and Play device. The Windows XP driver cache contains hundreds of drivers for such devices, however, most of them relatively old but still worthwhile. Other such devices have Windows 2000 drivers that are compatible with Windows XP and can be downloaded. If you own such a device, use the Add Hardware Wizard to complete the hardware

Part 1: Setup, Startup, Tune-Up

setup process. After downloading compatible hardware drivers (or verifying that Windows XP includes built-in drivers for the device in question), follow these steps:

1 If the device includes a CD or a downloadable Setup program, run it now. This option places the driver files on your hard disk and simplifies later installation steps.

2 Connect the new hardware to your computer. In the case of an internal device such as an add-in card, power down the system, add the device, and then restart.

note Although you can try to run the Add Hardware Wizard without first installing the device, you're wasting your time. The wizard will shut down without completing its assigned task if you try to take this shortcut.

3 Open Control Panel, double-click the System icon, and then click the Add Hardware Wizard button on the Hardware tab.

4 Click Next to skip past the Welcome screen and begin searching for the installed device.

If the wizard finds the new device, you can select it to install the correct driver and finish the wizard. In most cases, the wizard won't find the new device and will instead prompt you to search for the device.

5 Click Yes when asked whether you've already installed the new device, and click Next to continue. The wizard displays a list of devices currently installed on the computer, similar to the one shown here.

Chapter 6: Setting Up and Troubleshooting Hardware

6 If the device you're trying to install is in this list, select it. Otherwise, scroll to the bottom of the list and choose Add A New Hardware Device. Click Next to continue.

7 In the wizard's next step, choose how you want to select the device to be installed:

- For printers, network cards, modems, and other devices that can be detected mechanically, choose Search For And Install The Hardware Automatically (Recommended). After you click Next, the wizard quickly runs a detection module that searches for anything on its list of non–Plug and Play devices. If it finds the new device, it installs the driver automatically, and your work is finished. If the wizard doesn't find any new hardware, you'll be prompted to click Next and look manually; in this case proceed to step 8.

- If you'd prefer to skip the detection process, choose Install The Hardware That I Manually Select From A List (Advanced) and click Next.

8 From the Common Hardware Types list, choose a hardware category (or the inclusive Show All Devices category) and click Next.

9 From the master list of available drivers, which will look similar to the one shown in Figure 6-6, select the device manufacturer and the correct model. Click Next to continue.

10 Follow the prompts to complete the wizard.

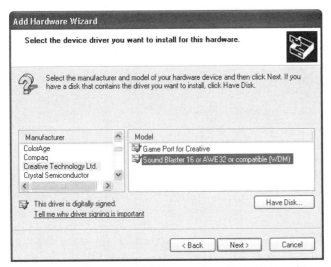

Figure 6-6. This master list shows all available device drivers, broken down by category and by manufacturer.

On the final page, the wizard reports on the result of the installation. If you encounter any problems, follow the troubleshooting links listed there.

203

Finding Information About an Installed Driver

Knowing which hardware drivers are installed on your computer can make a huge difference when it comes to troubleshooting problems or configuring advanced features
for a device. In every case, your starting point is Device Manager, a graphical utility
that provides detailed information about all installed hardware, along with controls
that you can use to configure devices, assign resources, and set advanced options. To
open Device Manager, use any of the following techniques:

- From any command prompt, enter **devmgmt.msc**.

- Right-click the My Computer icon on the Start menu or the desktop,
  choose Manage, and then select Device Manager from the left pane of the
  Computer Management console, under System Tools.

- From Control Panel, double-click the System icon and click the Device
  Manager button on the Hardware tab.

As Figure 6-7 shows, Device Manager is organized as a hierarchical list that inventories
every piece of hardware within or connected to your computer. The default view shows
devices by type.

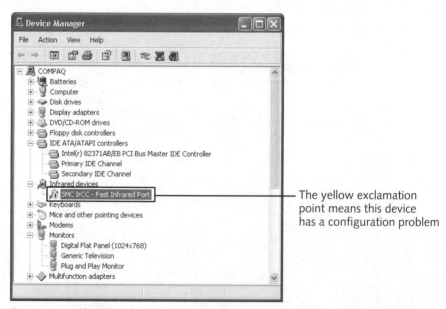

The yellow exclamation
point means this device
has a configuration problem

Figure 6-7. Click the plus sign to the left of each category to see individual devices
within that category.

---

tip   **Change the Device Manager view**

You can change the default view of Device Manager to organize entries in the list by resource or by connection. Use Device Manager's View menu to switch between any of the four built-in views. Resource views are especially useful when you're trying to track down problems caused by IRQ conflicts. Choosing either Resources By Type or Resources By Connection shows a list of all devices in which you can see how DMA, IO addresses, and IRQs are assigned. Another option on the View menu lets you show hidden devices.

Viewing Device and Driver Details

To view information about a specific device, double-click its entry in the device list. Each device has its own multitabbed Properties dialog box. At a minimum, each device includes two tabs, General and Driver. The General tab lists basic facts about the device, including the device name, the name of its manufacturer, and its current status, as shown in Figure 6-8.

Figure 6-8. The General tab supplies basic information about a device and whether it's currently functioning properly.

Part 1: Setup, Startup, Tune-Up

The Driver tab, shown in Figure 6-9, lists version information about the currently installed driver for the selected device. Although the information shown here is sparse, it covers the essentials: You can tell at a glance who supplied the driver and whether it's digitally signed; you can also determine the date and version number of the driver, which is important when deciding whether you should download and install an available update.

Figure 6-9. The Driver tab, which is available for every installed device, offers crucial information and troubleshooting tools.

To view additional information about an installed driver, click the Driver Details button. As you can see from Figure 6-10, this dialog box provides far more comprehensive information, including the names and locations of all associated files. Selecting any file name from this list displays details for that file in the lower portion of the dialog box.

In addition to this basic information, the Properties dialog box for a given device can include any number of custom tabs. The Lucent Win Modem shown in Figure 6-11 is an extreme example, with a total of seven tabs, including the basic information on the General and Driver tabs. (Settings for modems are also available from the Phone And Modem Options dialog box in Control Panel.)

Chapter 6: Setting Up and Troubleshooting Hardware

This icon indicates a signed driver file

The driver selected above is unsigned

Figure 6-10. This detailed view of installed drivers provides important information about each file the device uses. In this example, a number of files are not digitally signed.

Figure 6-11. Any device that requires system resources includes the Resources tab in its Device Manager entry.

InsideOut

If you're running Windows XP Professional and want a more compact record of installed drivers in a format that you can review later, use the Driverquery command. Entering this command with no switches produces a simple list of installed devices and drivers. You can modify the output of the command with a variety of switches, and you can redirect the output of the command to a file so that you can load it in another program. For instance, you can use the /V switch to produce a detailed (verbose) listing, and add the /Fo switch with the Csv parameter to generate the output in a format suitable for use in Microsoft Excel:

```
driverquery /v /fo csv > drvlist.csv
```

Open Drvlist.csv in Excel to see a neatly formatted and highly detailed list of all your hardware. (For a full list of the switches available for the Driverquery command, add the /? switch or search in the Help And Support Center for Driverquery.)

By design, the information displayed in Device Manager is dynamic. When you add or remove or reconfigure a device, the information stored here changes as well. To save a permanent record of the settings for one or more devices, open Device Manager and choose Action, Print. For the most complete record of device settings and installed drivers, choose the All Devices And System Summary option in the Print dialog box. But make sure you're prepared for the output, which can easily run to more than 20 pages!

InsideOut

A nifty shareware program offers another solution to managing installed device drivers. Instead of simply displaying or printing all the pertinent information about drivers, WinDriver Ghost collects all the files that comprise your device drivers and stores them so that they can be reinstalled easily. It backs up all your device drivers—whether they came from the original Windows installation, from the CD that came with the device, or from a downloaded file—into a single location for easy retrieval. At the time this book was written, WinDriver Ghost (originally known as WinDriver Expert) was being updated frequently, but the author's Web site was unavailable. However, an Internet search for "WinDriver Ghost" should turn up plenty of locations where you can download the latest version of this handy tool.

Chapter 6: Setting Up and Troubleshooting Hardware

Adjusting Advanced Settings

Some devices include specialized tabs on the Properties dialog box available from Device Manager. Controls on these additional tabs allow you to change advanced settings and properties for devices. For instance:

- Network cards and modems typically include a power management tab that allows you to control whether the device can force the computer to wake up from standby mode. This option is useful if you have fax capabilities enabled for a modem, or if you use the Remote Desktop feature over the Internet on a machine that isn't always running at full power. On portable computers, you can also use this option to allow Windows to turn off a device to save power.

- On disk drives, the Volumes tab contains no information when you first display the Properties dialog box for that device. Click the Populate button to read the volume information for the selected disk; you can then choose any of the listed volumes, as shown in Figure 6-12, and click the Properties button to check the disk for errors, run the Defrag utility, or perform other maintenance tasks. Although you can perform these same tasks by right-clicking a drive icon in the My Computer window, this option may be useful in situations where you have multiple hard disks installed and you suspect that one of those disks is having mechanical problems. Using this option lets you quickly see which physical disk a given volume is stored on.

Figure 6-12. After you click the Populate button, this tab lists volumes on the selected drive and gives you full access to troubleshooting and maintenance tools.

● DVD drives offer an option to change the DVD region, which controls what disks can be played on that drive, as shown here.

caution　The DVD Region setting actually increments a counter on the physical drive itself, and that counter can be changed only a limited number of times. Be extremely careful with this setting, or you might end up losing the capability to play any DVDs in your collection.

● Network cards often allow you to work with a plethora of settings on an Advanced tab, as shown in this example. Randomly tinkering with these settings is almost always counterproductive; however, you may be able to solve specific performance or connectivity problems by adjusting settings as directed by the device manufacturer or a Knowledge Base article.

Chapter 6: Setting Up and Troubleshooting Hardware

- Self-powered USB hubs (those that are connected to an AC power source) include a Power tab like the one shown on the next page. Use this information to calculate the amount of power required by devices that draw power from the hub. If the total power requirement is more than the hub can supply, you might need a new hub.

> **tip** **View devices over the network**
>
> You can use Device Manager to inspect settings on a remote computer. This option can be useful when troubleshooting from a distance. To view devices on another computer, open the Computer Management console (Compmgmt.msc), select the Computer Management icon at the top of the left pane, and choose Action, Connect To Another Computer. This option allows you to view information but not change device settings. If you need to troubleshoot device problems over a network, use Remote Assistance (described in "Connecting to Another PC with Remote Assistance," page 154) or a Remote Desktop connection ("Using Remote Desktop Connection," page 1102).

Viewing and Changing Resource Assignments

If you've worked with MS-DOS and early versions of Windows, you've probably struggled with device conflicts, most often when two or more pieces of hardware lay claim to the same IRQ. On modern computers with an ACPI BIOS and Windows XP, those sorts of conflicts are mercifully rare. In the original design of the IBM Personal Computer, IRQs were in short supply, with a total of 15 available and many of those reserved by system devices, such as communications ports, keyboards, and disk controllers. With older Windows versions, problems could occur when adding a new device such as a sound card or network adapter. If the new device was hardwired to a specific IRQ that was already in use, or if there were no free IRQs, the device simply would not work.

On computers running Windows 2000 and Windows XP with a mix of PCI add-in cards, the operating system takes advantage of the ACPI features on the motherboard to share scarce IRQs among multiple devices. In Device Manager, you can see resource allocations at a glance by choosing Resources By Type or Resources By Connection from the View menu. In the example shown here, IRQ 9 is being managed by the Microsoft ACPI-Compliant system (an ISA device) and shared successfully by two PCI devices; a pair of video cards are peacefully coexisting on IRQ 11.

Chapter 6: Setting Up and Troubleshooting Hardware

Under most circumstances, you cannot use Device Manager to change resource settings for a specific PCI or USB device. Resources are allocated automatically by the operating system at startup, and the controls to change resource settings are unavailable. Resource conflicts are most common with legacy devices such as ISA-based sound cards that are not fully compatible with Plug and Play. Figure 6-13, for instance, shows the resource settings for a Plug and Play device that is in conflict with a legacy device. In this example, you might be able to adjust resource settings manually from the Resources tab: Clear the Use Automatic Settings check box and cycle through different settings to see if any of the alternate configurations resolve the conflict.

Figure 6-13. The message at the bottom of this dialog box identifies a resource conflict. To resolve the problem, adjust settings for the non–Plug and Play device.

If you suspect that a hardware problem is caused by a resource conflict, you can get an overview of resource usage by opening the System Information utility (Msinfo32.exe), which is found on the All Programs menu under Accessories, System Tools. Open Hardware Resources in the console pane and pay special attention to the Conflicts/Sharing entry, shown in Figure 6-14 on the next page, and the Forced Hardware item. Don't be alarmed if you see a number of devices sharing a single IRQ; that's perfectly normal.

For more information about System Information, see "Digging Deeper with Dedicated System Information Tools," page 1324.

For legacy devices whose resources can't be assigned by Windows, you'll need to adjust jumpers on the card or device, or use a software-based setup/configuration utility to change resource settings for that device.

Chapter 6

213

Part 1: Setup, Startup, Tune-Up

Figure 6-14. All the devices shown in this example are sharing resources properly. If two unrelated devices try to share a resource other than an IRQ, you may need to adjust device settings manually.

Troubleshooting

Resource conflicts prevent a device from working.

If two devices are in conflict for a system resource, try any of these strategies to resolve the problem:

1 With PCI devices, try swapping cards, two at a time, between PCI slots. On some motherboards, IRQs and other resources are assigned on a per-slot basis, and moving a card can free up the proper resources. Check the motherboard documentation to see which IRQs are assigned to each slot and experiment until you find an arrangement that works.

2 If the conflict is caused by a legacy (ISA) device, replace it with a Plug and Play–compatible PCI device.

3 Use jumpers or a software utility to change settings on a legacy device so that it reserves a different set of resources. You will need documentation from the manufacturer to accomplish this goal.

If you have problems with PCI devices, the device itself might not be to blame. When drivers and ACPI BIOS code interact improperly, conflicts can result. Check for an updated hardware driver (especially if the current driver is unsigned) and look for a BIOS update as well.

Managing Installed Drivers

If you're having a hardware problem that you suspect is caused by a device driver, your first stop should be Device Manager. Open the Properties dialog box for the device, and use the following buttons on the Driver tab to perform maintenance tasks:

- **Update Driver.** This choice starts the Hardware Update Wizard.

- **Roll Back Driver.** This option uninstalls a recently updated driver and "rolls back" your system configuration to the previously installed driver. Unlike System Restore, this option affects only the selected device. If you have never updated the selected driver, Windows will offer to run a trouble-shooter when you click this button.

- **Uninstall.** This button completely removes driver files and registry settings for the selected device. This option is available from Safe Mode if you need to remove a driver that is causing blue-screen (Stop) errors. You can also use this capability to remove and then reinstall or update a driver that you suspect was incorrectly installed.

---

tip   **Double-check System Restore settings**

When you install a new, unsigned hardware driver, Windows XP automatically attempts to create a new System Restore checkpoint. That doesn't mean it will be successful, especially if a problem with your System Restore settings has caused this utility to suspend operations temporarily. To make certain that you can roll back your changes if necessary, set a new System Restore checkpoint manually before making any kind of hardware configuration change. (For more details, see "Undoing Configuration Mistakes with System Restore," page 900.)

Updating a Device Driver

Microsoft and third-party device manufacturers frequently issue upgrades to device drivers. In some cases, the updates enable new features; in other cases, the newer version swats a bug that might or might not affect you. If you've downloaded a new driver for a device that's currently installed on your computer, use the Upgrade Hardware Wizard to install it properly.

If the new driver includes a setup program, run it first, so that the proper files are copied to your system. Then start the wizard from Device Manager by double-clicking the entry for the device you want to upgrade and clicking the Update Driver button on the Driver tab. This wizard uses the identical procedures as the Add Hardware Wizard. Follow the procedures outline in "Setting Up a New Device," page 197, to point the wizard to the correct location for the driver and complete the update.

> **tip**   **Check driver versions**
>
> How do you know whether a downloaded version is newer than the currently installed driver on your system? A good Readme file should provide this information and is the preferred option. In the absence of documentation, file dates offer some clues, but are not always reliable. A better indicator is to inspect the properties of the driver files themselves. After unzipping the downloaded driver files to a folder on a local or network drive, right-click any file with a .dll or .sys extension and choose Properties. On the Version tab, you should be able to find details about the specific driver version, which you can compare to the driver details shown in Device Manager.

Rolling Back to a Previous Driver Version

newfeature!

Unfortunately, updated drivers can sometimes cause new problems that are worse than the woes they were intended to fix. This is especially true if you're experimenting with unsigned drivers or beta versions of new drivers. If your troubleshooting leads you to suspect that a specific driver is the cause of recent crashes or system instability, consider removing that driver and rolling your system configuration back to the previously installed driver.

In earlier Windows versions, this process was cumbersome and tricky. In Windows XP, it's as easy as clicking a button. Open Device Manager and double-click the entry for the device you want to roll back. Then go to the Driver tab and click the Roll Back Driver button. The procedure is straightforward and self-explanatory.

Uninstalling a Driver

There are at least three circumstances under which you might want to remove a device driver completely from your system:

- You're no longer using the device, and you want to prevent the previously installed drivers from loading or using any resources.

- You've determined that the only drivers available for the device are not stable enough to use on your system.

- The currently installed driver is not working correctly, and you want to reinstall it from scratch.

To remove the driver permanently, open Device Manager and double-click the entry for the device in question. On the Driver tab, click the Uninstall button. Click OK when prompted to confirm that you want to remove the driver, and Windows will remove files and registry settings completely.

InsideOut

Removing and reinstalling the driver for a Plug and Play device requires a little extra effort. Because these drivers are loaded and unloaded dynamically, you can only remove the driver if the device in question is plugged in. Use the Uninstall button to remove the driver before unplugging the device. To reinstall the device drivers without unplugging, open Device Manager and choose Action, Scan For Hardware Changes.

Troubleshooting

Your computer experiences sporadic blue screens, lockups, or other strange behavior.

When your computer acts unpredictably, chances are good that a buggy device driver is at fault.

If you're experiencing unexplained computer problems, a powerful troubleshooting tool called Driver Verifier Manager (commonly called Verifier) is a terrific way to identify flawed device drivers. Instead of your computer locking up at a most inopportune time with a misleading Blue Screen of Death (BSOD), with Verifier your computer stops predictably at startup with a BSOD that accurately explains the true problem. Although this doesn't sound like a huge improvement (your system still doesn't work, after all), Verifier performs a critical troubleshooting step: identifying the problem. You can then correct the problem by removing or replacing the offending driver. (If you're satisfied that the driver really is okay despite Verifier's warning, you can turn off Verifier for all drivers or for a specific driver. Any driver that Verifier chokes on should be regarded with suspicion, but some legitimate drivers bend the rules without causing problems.)

Verifier works at startup to thoroughly exercise each driver. It performs many of the same tests that are done by WHQL as part of the certification and signing process, such as checking for the way the driver accesses memory.

Beware: If Driver Verifier Manager finds a nonconforming driver—even one that seems not to cause any problems—it will prevent your system from starting. Use Verifier only if you're having problems. In other words, if it ain't broke…

To use Driver Verifier Manager, at a command prompt type **verifier**. In Verifier's initial dialog box, shown on the next page, select Create Standard Settings. In the next dialog box, select the type of drivers you want to verify; unsigned drivers are a likely cause of problems. Complete the wizard and restart your computer.

(continued)

Troubleshooting *(continued)*

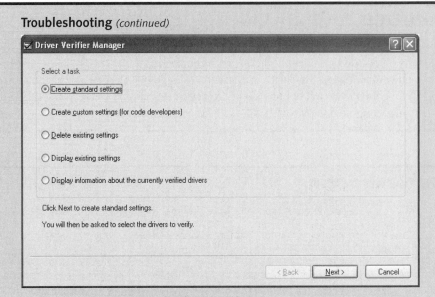

If your computer stops with a blue screen when you next log on, you've identified a problem driver! The error message includes the name of the offending driver and an error code. For information about the error codes, see Microsoft Knowledge Base article Q315252, "A Partial List of Driver Error Codes That the Driver Verifier Tool Uses to Report Problems." To resolve the problem, boot into Safe Mode (press F8 during startup) and disable or uninstall the problem driver. You'll then want to check with the device vendor to get a working driver that you can install.

To disable Driver Verifier Manager so that it no longer performs its verification checks at startup, run Verifier and select Delete Existing Settings in its initial dialog box. Alternatively, at a command prompt type **verifier /reset**. (If you haven't yet solved the driver problem, of course, you'll be stopped at a BSOD—unable to disable Verifier. In that case, boot into Safe Mode and then disable Verifier.)

You can configure Verifier so that it checks only certain drivers. To do that, after you select Create Standard Settings and click Next, select the last option, Select Driver Names From A List. This option lets you exempt a particular driver from Verifier's scrutiny—such as one that Verifier flags but you are certain is not the cause of your problem.

You can read more about Verifier online at *http://www.microsoft.com/hwdev/driver/ verifier.asp* and *http://www.compuware.co.jp/drivercentral/resources/ win2k_driverver.asp*.

Enabling and Disabling Specific Devices

Installing and uninstalling device drivers can be a hassle. If all you want to do is enable or disable a specific device, you can do so from Device Manager. Open the properties dialog box for the selected device, click the General tab, and toggle the Device Usage setting between Use This Device (Enable) and Do Not Use This Device (Disable). The drivers for a disabled device remain available, but Windows does not load them.

You might choose to disable the driver for a device if you use it infrequently and want to avoid having it use resources or cause stability problems at other times. Enable the device when you want to use it, and keep it disabled the rest of the time. For the most part, however, the capability to enable and disable devices is used in conjunction with hardware profiles.

This capability is most common with notebook computers attached to docking stations, where your video settings, storage devices, and other hardware options vary depending on whether the notebook is in the docking station or not. However, you can also use profiles to set up specialized configurations on a desktop computer. For instance, on a graphics workstation with multiple imaging devices, you might want to avoid conflicts by choosing different combinations of enabled devices for different user profiles. If you use multiple network devices to manage connections to different networks, you might want to use hardware profiles for this task as well.

By default, Windows creates a single user profile, Profile 1, when you first install Windows. If you have a notebook computer with a Plug and Play–compatible docking station, Windows automatically creates Docked and Undocked configurations for you and loads the proper configuration when you connect or disconnect from the docking station. To work with hardware profiles, open the System icon in Control Panel, click the Hardware tab, and then click Hardware Profiles. Figure 6-15 on the next page shows the available options.

The best way to create a new profile is to copy an existing profile and then enable or disable devices as needed. Follow these steps to create a second profile on a system that currently has only one:

1 Open Control Panel, double-click System and click the Hardware Profiles button on the Hardware tab.

2 In the Hardware Profiles dialog box, select Profile 1 and click the Copy button.

3 In the Copy Profile dialog box, enter a descriptive name for the new profile or accept the default, Profile 2. Click OK.

Part 1: Setup, Startup, Tune-Up

Use these arrows to move your preferred profile to the top of the list

Click here to give each profile a descriptive name

Figure 6-15. On Plug and Play notebook docking stations, Windows creates profiles automatically. To create a new profile, click the Copy button.

4 In the Hardware Profiles section, specify which profile you want Windows to use at startup:

- ■ To always choose from a menu of available profiles, choose Wait Until I Select A Hardware Profile.

- ■ To set a default profile, use the up and down arrows to arrange the Available Hardware Profiles list so that your preferred profile is at the top. Then choose Select The First Profile Listed If I Don't Select A Profile In *nn* Seconds and specify a default waiting period (in seconds).

5 Restart your computer and choose the profile you want to modify. Open Device Manager and adjust the Device Usage settings for each device you want to enable or disable, as follows:

- ■ Choose Use This Device (Enable) for any device you want to make available for that profile.

- ■ Choose Do Not Use This Device In The Current Hardware Profile (Disable) for any device that should remain disabled in the current profile.

- ■ Choose Do Not Use This Device In Any Hardware Profiles (Disable) to disable a device regardless of which profile you select.

6 After configuring all devices in the current profile, close Device Manager.

7 To adjust other profiles, log on using the selected profile and repeat step 5.

Chapter 6: Setting Up and Troubleshooting Hardware

Decoding Hardware Errors

When Windows encounters a problem with a device or its driver, it changes the icon in Device Manager and displays an error code on the General tab of the device's properties dialog box. Each code is identified by a number and a brief text description. Table 6-1 contains a partial list of error codes and suggested actions you should take to try to resolve them.

Table 6-1. Common Device Manager Error Codes

Error Code	Error Message	What to Do About It
1	*This device is not configured correctly. (Code 1)*	After downloading a compatible driver for the device, click the Update Driver button and follow the wizard's prompts to install the new driver.
10	*This device cannot start. (Code 10)*	Device failed to start. Click the Update Driver button to install updated drivers if available.
		The Troubleshoot button may provide useful information as well.
12	*This device cannot find enough free resources that it can use. If you want to use this device, you will need to disable one of the other devices on this system. (Code 12)*	The device has been assigned one or more I/O ports, IRQs, or DMA channels used by another device. This error message can also appear if the BIOS is configured incorrectly (for example, if a USB controller doesn't get an IRQ from the BIOS).
		Check BIOS settings. Use the Resources tab to identify the conflicting device.
14	*This device cannot work properly until you restart your computer. (Code 14)*	The driver has probably been installed correctly, but will not be started until you reboot the system.
16	*Windows cannot identify all the resources this device uses. (Code 16)*	A legacy device is improperly configured. Use the Resources tab to fill in the missing details.
18	*Reinstall the drivers for this device. (Code 18)*	Click the Update Driver button to start the Update Hardware Wizard and reinstall the driver.

(continued)

Chapter 6

Table 6-1. *(continued)*

Error Code	Error Message	What to Do About It
19	*Your registry might be corrupted. (Code 19)*	Incorrect or conflicting information is entered in the registry settings for this device. Try using the Troubleshooting Wizard to identify the specific problem. If that is unsuccessful, uninstall and then reinstall the driver. Try using System Restore to roll back the configuration to a point where the device worked properly.
21	*Windows is removing this device. (Code 21)*	The system will remove the device. Wait a few seconds, and then refresh the Device Manager view. If the device continues to display, restart the computer.
22	*This device is disabled. (Code 22)*	The device has been disabled using Device Manager. To enable it, click the Enable Device button.
24	*This device is not present, is not working properly, or does not have all its drivers installed. (Code 24)*	A catch-all error that can be caused by bad hardware or corrupt or incompatible drivers. This message also appears after you use the Remove Device option. Use the Troubleshooting Wizard to identify the specific problem.
28	*The drivers for this device are not installed. (Code 28)*	After downloading a compatible driver for the device, click the Update Driver button and follow the wizard's prompts to install the new driver.
29	*This device is disabled because the firmware of the device did not give it the required resources. (Code 29)*	Most commonly seen with SCSI adapters, third-party disk controllers, and other devices that supply their own BIOS. Check the documentation for the device to learn how to re-enable it.
31	*This device is not working properly because Windows cannot load the drivers required for this device. (Code 31)*	Windows was unable to load the driver, probably because it is not compatible with Windows XP. After downloading a compatible driver for the device, click the Update Driver button and follow the wizard's prompts to install the new driver.

Chapter 6: Setting Up and Troubleshooting Hardware

Table 6-1. *(continued)*

Error Code	Error Message	What to Do About It
32	*A driver service for this device was not required, and has been disabled. (Code 32)*	The driver has been disabled.
		The start type for this service is set to Disabled in the registry. If the driver really is required, change the start type in the BIOS, using the BIOS setup utility as defined in the documentation for the device.
		If the device previously worked properly, use System Restore to return to a working configuration.
33	*Windows cannot determine which resources are required for this device. (Code 33)*	Typically indicates a misconfigured legacy device or a hardware failure. See the documentation for the device for more information.
34	*Windows cannot determine the settings for this device. Consult the documentation that came with this device and use the Resource tab to set the configuration. (Code 34)*	This legacy device requires a forced configuration. Change the hardware settings (using jumpers or a software utility), and then use Device Manager's Resources tab to set the forced configuration.
35	*Your computer's system BIOS does not include enough information to properly configure and use this device. To use this device, contact your computer manufacturer to obtain a firmware or BIOS update. (Code 35)*	This error is specific to multiprocessor systems. Check with the system manufacturer for a BIOS upgrade.
36	*This device is requesting a PCI interrupt but is configured for an ISA interrupt (or vice versa). Please use the computer's system setup program to reconfigure the interrupt for this device. (Code 36)*	IRQ translation failed. This error usually occurs on Advanced Power Management (APM) machines. Check BIOS settings to see if certain IRQs have been reserved incorrectly. Upgrade to an ACPI BIOS if possible.

(continued)

Chapter 6

Table 6-1. *(continued)*

Error Code	Error Message	What to Do About It
37	*Windows cannot initialize the device driver for this hardware. (Code 37)*	After downloading a compatible driver for the device, click the Update Driver button and follow the wizard's prompts to install the new driver.
38	*Windows cannot load the device driver for this hardware because a previous instance of the device driver is still in memory. (Code 38)*	Restart the computer.
39	*Windows cannot load the device driver for this hardware. The driver may be corrupted. (Code 39)*	The driver is missing or corrupted, or is in conflict with another driver. Look for an updated driver or reinstall the current driver. If the device worked previously, use System Restore to roll back to a working configuration.
40	*Windows cannot access this hardware because its service key information in the registry is missing or recorded incorrectly. (Code 40)*	Information in the registry's service key for the driver is invalid. Reinstall the driver.
41	*Windows successfully loaded the device driver for this hardware but cannot find the hardware device. (Code 41)*	Windows loaded the driver but cannot find the device. This error occurs with legacy devices because Plug and Play cannot detect the legacy device. Use Device Manager to uninstall the driver and then use the Add Hardware Wizard to reinstall it.
42	*Windows cannot load the device driver for this hardware because there is a duplicate device already running in the system. (Code 42)*	Restart the computer.

Chapter 6: Setting Up and Troubleshooting Hardware

Table 6-1. *(continued)*

Error Code	Error Message	What to Do About It
43	*Windows has stopped this device because it has reported problems. (Code 43)*	A driver has reported a device failure. Uninstall and reinstall the device. If that doesn't work, contact the device manufacturer.
44	*An application or service has shut down this hardware device. (Code 44)*	The device has been halted by an application or service. Restart the computer.
47	*Windows cannot use this hardware device because it has been prepared for "safe removal," but it has not been removed from the computer. (Code 47)*	The device has been prepared for ejection from a PCMCIA slot, a USB port, or a docking station. Unplug the device and plug it in again, or restart the computer.
48	*The software for this device has been blocked from starting because it is known to have problems with Windows. Contact the hardware vendor for a new driver. (Code 48)*	Contact the hardware vendor for a compatible driver.

Chapter 7

Tuning Up System Performance

Every Windows user has experienced sudden, unexplained slowdowns in system performance. Routine actions that normally take a few microseconds suddenly cause your computer to stop responding. Your hard disk chatters incessantly. You're forced to wait when switching between programs. Surprisingly, you don't need an engineering degree, an oscilloscope, or expensive third-party software to track down the cause of these performance problems and solve them.

With one quick keyboard combination, you can open the Windows XP Task Manager, which helps you monitor essential hardware resources, including your central processing unit (CPU), memory, and network adapter. You can quickly spot programs that are using excessive amounts of system resources and quickly determine whether a sudden slowdown is caused by too little memory. Sometimes the reason a system turns sluggish is because too many programs or services are running in the background. We'll show you how to trim the fat using some well-hidden Windows utilities.

To monitor performance over time, you can use the Performance Console, a sophisticated and extraordinarily customizable tool that gives you a more detailed look at your computer's overall performance. In this chapter, we'll provide detailed instructions to help you master this expert tool as well.

At Home with Windows XP

All of the tools for monitoring and adjusting system performance described in this chapter are available in both editions of Windows XP. The System Configuration utility (Msconfig.exe) is also available in both editions. The Group Policy console (Gpedit.msc), which can be used to enable or disable particular startup applications, is not included with Windows XP Home Edition, however.

Detecting Common Performance Bottlenecks

Most performance problems can be traced to a handful of common bottlenecks that boil down to the same basic problem: trying to do too much work with too few resources. Fortunately, Microsoft Windows XP includes a wonderful utility that makes it easy to spot problems and in some cases fix them immediately. Veterans of Windows 2000 and Windows NT know the Windows Task Manager well; if you're accustomed to the bare-bones Task Manager from Windows 95, Windows 98, or Windows Me, you'll be impressed with the greatly expanded capabilities in the Windows XP version.

note One performance problem that affects users of Windows 95/98/Me is gone from all editions of Windows XP. After upgrading, you no longer need to worry about system resource limitations caused by the infamous 64-KB User and GDI heaps in those Windows versions. Windows XP is immune from the crashes and forced reboots that result when individual programs drain system resources; with enough memory, you'll find that you can run multiple applications safely and reliably, without holding your breath in fear that opening one more window will cause the system to lock up.

The Windows Task Manager provides a continuously updated display of exactly what's going on with your system's key internal resources. You can see at a glance which applications and processes are running, along with information about how much memory and what percentage of the CPU each process is using. (We discuss these essential capabilities later in this chapter, in "Managing Programs and Processes," page 241.) You can keep tabs on your network connection to determine whether your network adapter is a bottleneck. And if you're willing to customize the Task Manager, you can dig into a wealth of esoteric performance indicators as well, some of which can be extremely useful in helping you find and fix performance problems.

Chapter 7: Tuning Up System Performance

---

tip   **Match programs with processes**

A *process* is the technical term for any program code that runs in its own address space. In Windows Task Manager, the Processes list includes applications that you start from the All Programs menu, as well as subsystems and services that are managed by the operating system. To match a running program with the specific process it's using, right-click the program name on the Applications tab of Windows Task Manager and then choose Go To Process.

If you're using the Welcome screen to log on to Windows, you can open the Windows Task Manager at any time by pressing Ctrl+Alt+Delete. If you're not using the Welcome screen or you're joined to a Windows domain, press Ctrl+Alt+Delete and then click the Task Manager button in the Windows Security dialog box. Regardless of your system configuration, you can always go directly to Task Manager by pressing Ctrl+Shift+Esc.

As Figure 7-1 shows, Windows Task Manager is a multitabbed dialog box. The Applications, Processes, and Performance tabs are visible on all Windows XP systems. The Networking tab is visible only if the computer is configured with a network adapter, and the Users tab is shown only if Fast User Switching is enabled. A status bar at the bottom of the window, visible on all tabs, displays the number of processes that are currently running, the percentage of your CPU's processing capacity that's currently in use, and some information about your system's current memory usage.

Figure 7-1. Each entry on the Processes tab of Windows Task Manager provides useful details about memory and CPU usage for that process.

Troubleshooting

Windows Task Manager is missing its menus.

If Windows Task Manager mysteriously appears without its title bar, menu bar, tabs, and status bar, don't be alarmed. You inadvertently double-clicked in the Task Manager window and switched to this stripped-down interface. It's not a bug; it's a feature, designed to give you a clearer, less cluttered picture of system information. To toggle between this resizable window and the normal view, double-click anywhere except within the list box that displays the names of programs and processes.

The Performance tab, shown in Figure 7-2, provides four graphs and some tabular data. The CPU Usage and PF Usage graphs display the percentage of your CPU's processing capacity and the amount of virtual memory (page file) capacity that your system has reserved for future use as of the most recent update of Windows Task Manager. The CPU Usage History and Page File Usage History sections provide line graphs of the same performance measures over time. (For more details about page file usage, see "Making the Most of Virtual Memory," page 238.)

Figure 7-2. Click the Performance tab to get a big-picture view of CPU, memory, and page file usage.

How much history the history graphs record depends on Windows Task Manager's current update speed and the width of its window. Each vertical gridline in these graphs represents six update intervals. If you widen the window, you see more history.

By default, Windows Task Manager updates its data once every two seconds. To increase the frequency to twice per second, choose View, Update Speed and then change the frequency from Normal to High. To reduce the update frequency to once every four seconds, choose the Low setting from the Update Speed menu. If you want to study the graph of the most recent history, you can stop all updates by choosing View, Update Speed, Paused. At any frequency, you can force an immediate update by pressing F5 (the systemwide shortcut for the Refresh command) or choosing Refresh Now from the View menu.

On the vertical axis, all four graphs are scaled from 0 to 100 percent. Increasing the height of the window expands the axis without changing its end points, making the graphs easier to read.

---

tip   **Get a close-up of CPU usage**

Double-clicking anywhere within the Performance tab—on the graphs themselves or the surrounding matter—removes everything but the CPU Usage and CPU Usage History graphs, allowing you to see more detail without expanding the window itself. With the window thus altered, you can resize the display and keep it on top as you work. To move to the Processes or Applications tab, press Ctrl+Tab. To return Windows Task Manager to its normal display, double-click again.

The remainder of the Performance tab provides some "snapshot" statistics about the current state of your computer's memory, which are discussed in the following section.

---

caution   The numbers you see throughout Windows Task Manager can provide useful general information about your system, but they can also mislead you. In some cases, the numbers are technically accurate, but don't actually provide meaningful information that you can use to solve performance problems. For instance, despite its name, the Page File Usage History graph actually indicates when space in the page file has been committed or reserved, not when Windows has actually begun swapping data between physical memory and your hard disk. If you're planning to make changes on the basis of numbers you see here, be sure to test the effect of those changes carefully to ensure that the results are as you expect.

Monitoring Memory Usage

The most common reason a Windows system slows down is that you've filled every bit of physical memory. When this happens, Windows begins a process called *paging*—that is, moving blocks of program code and data files (each block is called a *page*) out of memory and onto disk. A modest amount of paging is perfectly normal, but excessive paging can take a terrible toll on overall system performance. This type of performance problem is especially noticeable when trying to switch between several memory-intensive programs on a computer that doesn't have enough RAM to keep up. The result is nearly nonstop "thrashing" as the disk tries in vain to shuffle data to and from the much faster memory chips.

For a quick snapshot of current memory usage, open Windows Task Manager and look along the bottom of any tab. The statistic at the far right, Commit Charge, lists two numbers, presented as a fraction. The first number (the numerator) represents your current *total commit charge*—the total amount of physical and virtual memory in use by all running processes. (*Virtual memory* is memory backed by your page file.) The denominator represents your total available memory, physical and virtual. By itself, this number will only tell you whether you're about to run completely out of memory—in other words, when commit charge is nearly equal to available memory.

To uncover more details about your current memory usage, click the Performance tab and look at the series of tables in the bottom half of the dialog box. Beware: the numbers and labels here can be absolutely baffling and can steer even an expert Windows user into the wrong conclusions. Table 7-1 explains how you can use this data to answer common questions about memory usage.

Table 7-1. **Decoding Task Manager Performance Data**

Category	Value	What It Means
Totals	Handles	Unique identifiers that allow a program to access system resources such as files, registry keys, fonts, and bitmaps. In theory, this value can be used to identify programs that fail to restore memory properly after being shut down. In practice, this information is mostly useful to developers who are using specialized debugging tools to troubleshoot memory leaks in applications.
	Threads	An object within a process that runs program instructions. Multithreaded programs can perform multiple operations simultaneously. As with handles, this value is generally most useful to a software developer while testing an application for memory leaks.
	Processes	Total number of processes (programs, subsystems, and services) running for all users of the local computer. (This number is also displayed in the lower left corner of the Task Manager window.)

Chapter 7: Tuning Up System Performance

Table 7-1. *(continued)*

Category	Value	What It Means
Commit Charge (K)	Total	Total amount of physical and virtual memory currently in use by the operating system and all programs, measured in kilobytes. (This value is also displayed in the lower right corner of the Task Manager window.) Commit charge increases as you open additional programs and data files and should decrease when you close programs and files.
	Limit	Total amount of physical and virtual memory available for use by the operating system and all programs, measured in kilobytes. (This value is also displayed in the lower right corner of the Task Manager window.) To raise this limit, add more RAM or increase the size of the page file, or both.
	Peak	The highest amount of memory that has been in use during the current session, measured in kilobytes. If this value regularly approaches or equals the Limit value, your system might need more memory.
Physical Memory (K)	Total	The total amount of physical RAM installed in the computer, measured in kilobytes. Divide by 1024 to convert to megabytes.
	Available	The total amount of physical RAM, measured in kilobytes, that Windows will make available to programs before swapping data to virtual memory. Windows will always try to reserve some physical RAM for additional applications, even when the total commit charge exceeds the total amount of physical RAM installed.
	System Cache	The total amount of physical RAM, measured in kilobytes, used to store recently accessed programs and data. Windows will try to use as much physical RAM as possible for this function, but will release RAM from the file system cache when needed for programs and operating system functions.
Kernel Memory (K)	Total	The total amount of RAM, measured in kilobytes, used by core components of the operating system, including device drivers.

(continued)

233

Table 7-1. *(continued)*

Category	Value	What It Means
	Paged	The total amount of memory, measured in kilobytes, used by Windows core components and mapped to pages in virtual memory.
	Nonpaged	Amount of operating system and driver code, measured in kilobytes, that must be run in physical memory and cannot be paged to virtual memory.

If your system starts to slow down and you suspect that memory is the issue, a quick scan of the Performance tab can provide important clues. If Total Commit Charge is higher than Total Physical Memory, for instance, Windows must swap pages between fast RAM chips and the much slower virtual memory in the page file, causing the system to slow down. Figure 7-3 shows a computer that barely meets Microsoft's minimum RAM requirements; its performance is under severe stress as the numbers here clearly illustrate.

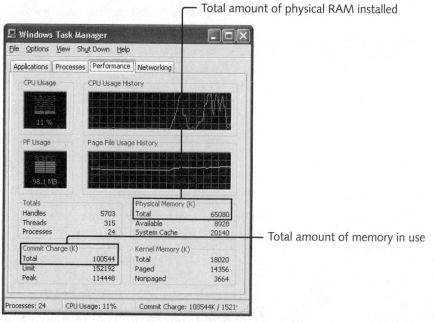

Figure 7-3. When Total Commit Charge is higher than Total Physical Memory, the result is excessive paging—and reduced performance.

In this example, the Total Commit Charge is 100544 KB (roughly 98 MB), well over the computer's physical RAM of 65080 KB (64 MB). In this configuration, a significant percentage of the programs and data currently used by the system are running from

Chapter 7: Tuning Up System Performance

slow, disk-based virtual memory, and excessive paging will occur each time the user switches between running programs.

Now look at Figure 7-4, which depicts a system that is loaded with 1 GB of physical RAM—roughly eight times the amount of memory that Microsoft recommends for satisfactory use with Windows XP.

Despite running 35 separate processes, including a number of demanding Microsoft Office XP applications, this computer is currently using less than a quarter of its total physical memory for programs and data, as evidenced by the Total Commit Charge of 238952 KB. The excess RAM is not going to waste, however, because Windows has devoted a huge portion of it to caching previously loaded programs and data files. The result is a tremendous boost in apparent speed in everyday use. Each time you start a program or load a file, Windows first checks to see whether that file is already stored in the cache; if the file is there, it loads in a fraction of the time it would take to access the file from the hard disk. An operation that might take 8–10 seconds when running from the hard disk can complete in 2–3 seconds if the necessary files are already in the cache.

Even if you're not experiencing noticeable performance slowdowns, it's a good idea to check memory usage occasionally. Pay special attention to the Commit Charge Peak setting, which tells you the maximum amount of memory you've used during the current Windows session. If this number is consistently higher than the amount of physical RAM installed on your machine, your system cache is being starved of the physical memory it needs to run properly.

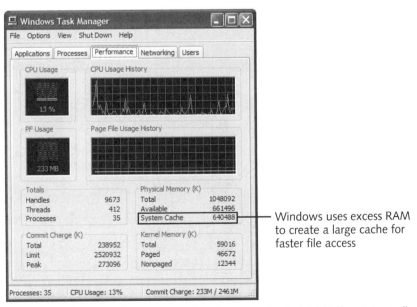

Windows uses excess RAM to create a large cache for faster file access

Figure 7-4. Because this computer has far more physical RAM than it typically uses, Windows is able to allocate a huge amount of memory to the system cache.

InsideOut

If you use applications that routinely load and reload extremely large data files, such as video editing programs, computer-aided drafting (CAD) tools, or database management software, you stand to get an especially large boost from the Windows file cache. For systems running this type of software, there's no such thing as too much RAM. The improvement in performance from a simple RAM upgrade can be breathtaking, especially on a computer whose CPU and hard disk are relatively slow.

Not surprisingly, the best cure for memory-related performance problems is usually to add more RAM. You can also delay the onset of paging by shutting down unneeded programs and services to free up memory. To identify the specific programs that are gobbling memory, open Windows Task Manager, click the Processes tab, and click the Mem Usage column heading twice to sort the list in descending order, so that processes using the most RAM float to the top of the list, as shown in Figure 7-5.

This view of running programs and processes is especially useful when you're about to start a memory-intensive program on a system that is nearly out of physical RAM. By shutting down applications that are presently using more than their fair share of RAM, you can often reclaim enough memory to avoid the slowdown caused by excessive paging.

Figure 7-5. Click any heading to sort by that column. In this example, clicking the Mem Usage heading twice lets you see which applications are memory hogs.

Avoiding CPU Overload

For most home and business computing tasks, the central processing unit (CPU) chip is rarely a source of anything more than momentary slowdowns. A sudden burst of CPU activity might cause your computer to temporarily slow to a crawl, but it should normally snap back to life in a few seconds. The two most common CPU-related problems occur when a program consistently asks more than your computer can deliver:

- **CPU-intensive software.** Programs designed for transforming and editing digital media often make inordinate demands on the CPU. Programming tools, CAD software, and even some games can have the same effect, which is especially noticeable when you try to run other tasks in the background. With these types of programs, a faster CPU can make a noticeable difference.

- **Poorly written programs.** In some cases, a program grabs onto the CPU with the tenacity of a puppy protecting its favorite chew toy and won't let go. As a result, the program uses a high percentage of the processor even when it's apparently doing nothing. If you spot a program that hogs the CPU in this fashion, contact the software developer to see if an updated version is available.

To see how much processor time each process is consuming at any given moment, open Windows Task Manager and click the Processes tab. Find the name of the program or service in the Image Name column and select that row; then observe the value in the CPU column. This value should change dynamically as a program works its way through tasks. Compressing a file using the popular WinZip program, for instance, might use a high percentage of your CPU's available cycles, but this should settle down to zero after the program has completed its work. This value is expressed as a percentage, where the total of all running processes always adds up to 100.

> **note** If the CPU column has to add up to 100, what happens when your system is doing nothing? Windows XP uses a "placeholder" process called System Idle Process that indicates when the CPU is not handling other threads. If this value isn't visible, select the Show Processes From All Users box in the bottom left corner of the Processes tab.

If you display the Processes tab and sort the resulting list in descending order using the CPU column, you can quickly see how much work an individual task requires. Armed with this information, you can determine whether and when to multitask, and when you should allow a program to run on its own. Using Windows Media Player to copy a track from a CD to disk, for instance, can practically take over some CPUs, using 90% or more of available CPU cycles. If that's the case on your system, you'll get best results by avoiding any other background activity while the CD is being copied.

> **tip**   **Keep an eye on your CPU**
>
> It's difficult to know when your CPU is under stress until you discover it the hard way—by watching an application struggle to get started. Here's a trick that can give you a quick graphic display of current CPU usage: Open Windows Task Manager. From the Options menu, choose Hide When Minimized. Now minimize the Task Manager and watch as it takes an unobtrusive place in the notification area at the right of the taskbar (sometimes referred to as the system tray). This icon serves as a bar-style CPU graph, glowing bright green to indicate when the CPU is in use. To see the exact percentage of CPU usage, let the mouse pointer rest over the Task Manager icon briefly. To restore the Task Manager, double-click the tray icon or press Ctrl+Alt+Delete.

Making the Most of Virtual Memory

As noted earlier, Windows does not live on RAM chips alone. In addition to using physical RAM to store programs and working data, Windows creates a hidden file on your hard disk and uses that file to swap data out of physical memory when necessary. This page file is also sometimes referred to as a *swap file* or *paging file*. (In fact, different dialog boxes throughout Windows XP use different terms to refer to this file.) In the interest of convenience and consistency, we will use the term *page file*.

In a default Windows XP installation, Windows creates the page file in the root folder on the same drive that holds the Windows system files. The size of the page file is determined by the amount of RAM in your system: By default, the minimum size is 1.5 times the amount of physical RAM on your system, and the maximum size is 3 times that value. You can see the page file in a Windows Explorer window if you configure Windows to show hidden and system files; look for Pagefile.sys in the root of your system drive.

An option in the System Control Panel lets you see your current page file settings and adjust them as needed. You can change the size of the page file, move it to another drive, or split it over several physical drives to improve performance.

To view and change page file settings, follow these steps:

1   Log on using an account in the Administrators group and open System in Control Panel.

2   On the Advanced tab, click the Settings button in the Performance section.

3   In the Performance Options dialog box, click the Advanced tab.

4   Click the Change button to display the Virtual Memory dialog box, shown in Figure 7-6.

Chapter 7: Tuning Up System Performance

Figure 7-6.   If you're careful, you can tweak the size of the page file to improve system performance.

5 Look in the Total Paging File Size For All Drives box to see the current settings for the page file.

6 Select any drive from the list at the top of the dialog box to adjust the settings for that drive. The following options are available:

■ **Custom Size.** Enter a value in the Initial Size box to specify the starting size (in MB) for the Pagefile.sys on the selected drive. In the Maximum Size box, enter a value (also in MB) that is at least as large as the initial size but is smaller than 4096 MB (4 GB).

■ **System Managed Size.** Select this option to instruct Windows XP to dynamically manage the size of the page file for that drive. This is the preferred option if you intend to override the default Windows settings.

■ **No Paging File.** Choose this option for any drive where you don't want to create a page file. Make sure that a page file exists on at least one drive.

7 After making changes for an individual drive, click the Set button to record your changes.

8 Repeat steps 6 and 7 for other drives, as needed. Click OK to close the dialog box when you're finished.

How big should your page file be? A large page file is appropriate for systems with relatively low RAM configurations—on a system with 128 MB of RAM, for instance, a page file of 192 MB to 384 MB makes perfect sense. With higher RAM counts, overly large page files simply waste disk space. If you have 512 MB or more of RAM and your Total Commit Charge never approaches the total physical memory installed on your computer and you're short of free disk space, you might want to set your page file to a fixed size, where the initial and maximum sizes are identical and are equal to your total amount of installed RAM. Be aware, however, that this option can result in out-of-memory error messages if your computing requirements change over time.

Do you have two or more physical drives? Moving the page file to a fast drive that doesn't contain your Windows system files is a good idea. Splitting the page file over two or more physical drives is an even better idea, because your disk controller can process multiple requests to read or write data concurrently. Don't make the mistake of splitting the page file over multiple drive letters on a single physical disk, however. If you have a single hard disk that contains C, D, and E drives and you split the page file over two or more of these partitions, you might actually make your computer run more slowly than before. In that configuration, the magnetic heads on the physical disk have to do more work, loading pages from different portions of the same disk sequentially, rather than loading data from a single contiguous region of the hard disk.

If you decrease the size of either the minimum or maximum page file settings, or if you create a new page file on a drive, you must restart your computer to make the change effective. Increasing the size of a page file typically does not require that you restart your computer.

---

caution   If you have plenty of physical memory installed in your computer, you might be tempted to completely disable your page file. Don't do it! By design, Windows XP requires a page file for a number of core functions, and several third-party programs will cause out-of-memory errors if you try to get rid of all virtual memory. Remember, Windows doesn't actually use the page file until it's needed, so you won't gain any performance advantage by tweaking your system in this fashion.

Windows XP is capable of dynamically increasing the size of your page file if needed. This option works only if you have selected the System Managed Size option or if you have specified a maximum size that is larger than the current size of the page file.

Based on experiences with previous versions, some Windows users advocate creating a fixed-size page file, where the initial size and maximum size are identical. In theory, this strategy should improve performance by preventing Windows from storing the page file in fragments on a single physical disk. In practice, however, the design of the page file is such that it tends to use large blocks of disk space, and as a result the impact of fragmentation on the page file is minimal. You might notice a very small performance hit when Windows increases the size of the page file, but that's a one-time operation and won't affect everyday performance.

> **tip** **Play it safe with your page file**
>
> On systems with 512 MB or more of physical memory, the large initial size of the
> page file can consume excessive amounts of disk space. On a system with 1 GB of
> RAM, for instance, the starting page file size is 1.5 GB, and under normal circum-
> stances it's likely that this file will never be used. The best strategy for page-file
> management in this configuration is to set Initial Size to be relatively small—say,
> 512 MB—while setting a large maximum size so that Windows can increase the
> page file size if necessary. This setting keeps disk space use in check but prevents
> the possibility of experiencing out-of-memory errors. If disk space is really tight,
> set the initial page-file size to its minimum of 2 MB and set the maximum size to a
> value that is at least as large as the amount of installed memory. Use your computer
> normally for a few weeks and allow Windows to create a page file of the proper
> size. Use Task Manager to monitor the size of the page file and make certain that
> it's below the maximum size you specified.

For more details about improving performance of hard disks, see "Defragmenting Disks for
Better Performance," page 870.

Managing Programs and Processes

In Windows Task Manager, the Applications tab lists all running programs that have
corresponding taskbar buttons. The entries you see here are approximately the same as
the ones presented by the Windows Alt+Tab task switcher. As Figure 7-7 on the next
page illustrates, the name of each entry in the Task column is identical to the text displayed in its title bar.

In its default Details view, the Applications tab includes a Status column. Most of the
time, the entry in this list will read *Running*. If an application hangs or freezes for any
reason, you see the words *Not Responding* in this column instead. In that case, you
can attempt to shut down the misbehaving program by selecting its entry and clicking
End Task. Don't be too quick on the trigger, however: Not Responding doesn't necessarily mean that an application is irredeemably lost. If the program in question is
using every bit of resources to handle a difficult task, it might simply be too busy to
communicate with Windows Task Manager. Before you decide to end the program,
give it a chance to finish whatever it's doing. How long should you wait? That depends
on the task. If the operation involves a large data file (doing a global search and
replace in a big Microsoft Access database, for instance), it's appropriate to wait
several minutes, especially if you can hear the hard disk chattering or see the disk
activity light flickering. But if the task you selected normally completes in a few seconds, you needn't wait more than a minute.

Part 1: Setup, Startup, Tune-Up

Figure 7-7. The Applications tab lists all running programs with a corresponding taskbar button; it doesn't include hidden programs and system processes.

---

tip **Be smart about shutdowns**

When you shut down an application by clicking the End Task button on the Applications tab, the effect is the same as if you had chosen to shut down the program using its menus or by right-clicking its taskbar button and choosing Close. If the program can respond to the shutdown request, it should prompt you for confirmation or give you a chance to save open files, if necessary. By contrast, the End Process button on the Processes tab zaps a process immediately and irrevocably, closing any open files without giving you a chance to save them. Whenever possible, you should try the End Task option first and reserve the drastic End Process option for situations when you have no alternative.

As noted earlier, the items listed on the Applications tab represent only a portion of the total number of programs and services running on a Windows computer at any given time. To see the entire list of running processes and gain access to a broader selection of tools for managing them, click the Processes tab.

In its default view, the Processes tab lists programs and services that are directly accessible to the user. Note in the example shown here that 30 processes are currently running (as evidenced by the value in the lower left corner of the dialog box). So why does the list display only a dozen entries?

Chapter 7: Tuning Up System Performance

The short list shows only processes that are directly accessible to control by the user. If you select the Show Processes From All Users check box, the list expands to include all currently running processes. In this case, the list of all users includes the built-in System, Network Service, and Local Service accounts.

For each process, Windows Task Manager includes the following information by default: Image Name (the name of the process), User Name (which user started the process), CPU (the percentage of the CPU's capacity that the process is currently using), and Mem Usage (the amount of memory the process requires to perform its regular functions, sometimes referred to as its *working set*).

InsideOut

If you add the figures in the Mem Usage column, you'll notice that the total does not correspond to any figure on the Performance tab. That's perfectly normal. In the curious language of software developers, the number to the right of each entry in the Processes list represents the sum of the memory pages in its current working set. Those pages might not have been used in days or weeks, but Windows doesn't remove them until it needs the pages for something else. In addition, some chunks of code are shareable. Two or more programs in the list might be using the same code, stored in the same physical location in memory; but each entry in the Processes list will count that amount of memory separately. Use the numbers in the Mem Usage column as a general guideline, but don't assume that they're completely accurate.

Processes are sorted initially by the order in which they were started, with the most recent entries at the top. You can sort by any other column by clicking the column heading (click a second time to reverse the sort order). As noted earlier, this is a good way to identify processes that are using more than their fair share of memory or CPU time.

With a modest amount of work, you can customize the Processes tab so that it shows far more information about each running process than the lean default view. To change the columns displayed on this tab, choose View, Select Columns and then add or remove entries from the dialog box shown here.

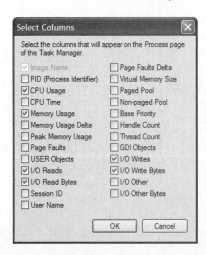

Most of these columns correspond to entries available in the Performance console (described later in this chapter, in "Advanced System Performance Measurement," page 253). After selecting the columns you want to see, click OK. You can then rearrange the display by dragging column headings to the left or right and dragging the border of any column heading to change its width. If necessary, resize the Task Manager window to see more data. Figure 7-8, for instance, adds four columns that measure disk reads and writes on a per-program basis. If your hard disk starts thrashing for no apparent reason, switching to a view like this one can help you quickly determine which program is responsible.

Figure 7-8. Customize the display of data on the Processes tab to identify other performance bottlenecks, such as disk input/output, as shown here.

Configuring Programs That Run Automatically

An extremely common performance problem occurs when Windows loads an excessive number of programs automatically at startup. The result, especially on systems with minimal memory, is unpleasant: Startup takes unnecessarily long, applications that you never use steal memory from programs you use frequently, and the page file gets more of a workout than it should. Some programs, such as antivirus utilities, need to start up automatically. But in most cases you're better served by running programs when you need them and closing them when they're not needed.

Overcrowded startups are most common on computer systems sold in retail outlets, where Windows XP is pre-installed along with a heaping helping of applications. In some cases, the bundled programs are welcome; but a free software program is no bargain if it takes up memory and you never use it. After purchasing a new PC, it's always a good idea to look through the list of bundled software so that you can keep the programs you plan to use and discard the ones you don't want or need. In previous versions, you could spot

Giving Programs an Extra Dose of CPU

For each running process, Windows assigns a *base priority*—a ranking that determines how that process shares CPU cycles with other processes. By default, the base priority for most processes is Normal. A handful of essential system services run with a base priority of High, including Task Manager (Taskmgr.exe), the Windows Logon process (Winlogon.exe), and the Client/Server Runtime Subsystem (Csrss.exe). These settings help ensure that these processes take priority even when another program is hogging the CPU.

You can add the Base Priority column to the display of data on the Processes tab of Windows Task Manager. You can also change the base priority of any process by selecting the name of the process, right-clicking, and choosing Set Priority. The six available settings appear on a submenu, as shown here.

Because the base priority for any process is set by its program code, any changes you make using Windows Task Manager remain in effect for the current session only. If you always want to run an application at a priority level other than its default, you can create a shortcut that uses the Start command to start the application. Type **start /?** in a command prompt window to display the arguments that let you run a program at a priority level other than its default.

Like so many performance-related tweaks, this one should be used sparingly, and only when you're absolutely certain of the consequences. For the most part, we suggest that you avoid tinkering with this feature, because its headache-generating capability far outweighs its potential to solve problems. Consider using this option to assign a

Chapter 7: Tuning Up System Performance

lower-than-normal priority to a CPU-hogging task that otherwise interrupts other essential activities, for example, but be certain to test the consequences carefully before employing this technique on a regular basis. Be extremely cautious when using the Realtime priority, however, which can allow a process to lock up a system so tightly that not even Task Manager can break in, and the result can be data loss. This option is not recommended for normal use; in theory, it might be useful on a dedicated machine that runs only a single, critical CPU-intensive task.

On a dual-CPU system running Windows XP Professional, you have one additional option: you can assign a process that is normally shared by both processors to a single processor by right-clicking its entry in the Processes list and choosing Set Affinity from the shortcut menu. This command does not appear on the shortcut menu on single-processor systems. This option too should be used sparingly, and only when a particular task uses all available CPU cycles from both processors and interferes with performance of other programs.

the symptoms of an overstuffed system by looking at the long line of icons in the notification area at the right of the taskbar. Because Windows XP tidies these icons regularly, you might not realize that you have a problem on your system.

For more details about customizing the taskbar and notification area, see "Removing Unneeded Icons from the Notification Area," page 320.

Tracking down programs that start automatically isn't as easy as it sounds. A program can be configured to run at startup by any of the following methods:

- **Startup folder (User).** The %UserProfile%\Start Menu\Programs\Startup folder contains shortcuts that run when a specific user account logs on.

- **Startup folder (Common).** Shortcuts in the %AllUsersProfile%\Start Menu\ Programs\Startup folder run automatically whenever any user logs on.

- **Run key (Machine).** Programs listed in the registry's HKLM\Software\ Microsoft\Windows\CurrentVersion\Run key are available for all users.

- **Run key (User).** Programs listed in the HKCU\Software\Microsoft\Windows\ CurrentVersion\Run registry key run when the current user logs on.

- **Load value.** Programs listed in the load value of the registry key HKCU\Software\Microsoft\Windows NT\CurrentVersion\Windows run when anyone logs on.

- **Scheduled Tasks folders.** You can use Scheduled Tasks to specify per-user tasks that run at startup. In addition, an administrator can set up startup tasks for your user account; by default such tasks are listed only in the administrator's Scheduled Tasks folder, not your own. Other users can also schedule tasks that run when you log on; these tasks run as background processes only.

- **Win.ini.** Programs written for 16-bit Windows versions may add commands to the Load= and Run= lines in the [Windows] section of this startup file located in %SystemRoot%, a legacy of the Windows 3.1 era.

- **RunOnce and RunOnceEx keys.** This group of registry keys identifies programs that run once and only once at startup. These keys may be assigned to a specific user account or to the machine.

  HKLM\Software\Microsoft\Windows\CurrentVersion\RunOnce
  HKLM\Software\Microsoft\Windows\CurrentVersion\RunOnceEx
  HKCU\Software\Microsoft\Windows\CurrentVersion\RunOnce
  HKCU\Software\Microsoft\Windows\CurrentVersion\RunOnceEx

- **Group Policy.** The Group Policy console includes two policies called Run These Programs At User Logon that specify a list of programs to be run whenever anyone logs on. (For more information, see "Using Policies to Control Startup Applications," page 251.)

- **Policies\Explorer\Run keys.** Using policies to specify startup programs, as described in the previous paragraph, creates corresponding values in either of two registry keys: HKLM\Software\Microsoft\Windows\CurrentVersion\ Policies\Explorer\Run or HKCU\Software\Microsoft\Windows\ CurrentVersion\Policies\Explorer\Run. It is possible for a legitimate program or rogue process to create or modify these registry values directly— that is, without using the Group Policy object. Note that disabling the Run These Programs At User Logon policies in Group Policy Editor does not prevent Windows from launching the items listed in the Policies\Explorer\Run registry keys.

- **BootExecute value.** By default, the multi-string BootExecute value of the registry key HKLM\System\CurrentControlSet\Control\Session Manager is set to *autocheck autochk* *. This value causes Windows, at startup, to check the file-system integrity of your hard disks if your system has been shut down abnormally. It is possible for other programs or processes to add themselves to this registry value. (Note: Microsoft warns against deleting the default BootExecute value. For information about what to do if your system hangs while Autocheck is running, see Microsoft Knowledge Base article Q151376, "How to Disable Autochk If It Stops Responding During Reboot.")

- **Logon scripts.** Logon scripts, which run automatically at startup, can open other programs. Logon scripts are specified in Group Policy in Computer Configuration\Windows Settings\Scripts and User Configuration\Windows Settings\Scripts (Logon/Logoff).

newfeature!

Windows XP includes a System Configuration Utility, Msconfig.exe, which allows you to see most of the programs that run at startup. Although it resembles the Windows 98/Me utility of the same name, it adds important features not found in those operating systems. For Windows 2000 users, it is a completely new addition. To start the System Configuration Utility, type **msconfig** at any command prompt.

Chapter 7: Tuning Up System Performance

> **note** Neither the System Configuration Utility nor either of the third-party startup managers recommended later in this section recognizes startup applications specified via the Group Policy console. (See "Using Policies to Control Startup Applications," page 251.)

Figure 7-9 shows the System Configuration Utility's Startup tab, which lists each startup item, the name and full path of the command used to start that item, and the location of the startup entry.

Figure 7-9. To stop a program from starting up automatically, clear the check box next to its entry.

The Startup tab of the System Configuration Utility is intended for use as a troubleshooting tool. By clicking the Disable All button, you can clear every check box in the list, preventing Windows from starting any programs automatically at startup; then, through an iterative process of restoring one or two programs at a time to the list, you can restart and see which one is causing a particular problem.

To test whether it's safe to remove a single program from the list of those that start automatically with Windows, clear the check box to the left of the program's name on the System Configuration Utility's Startup tab and restart. After verifying that your system works properly without that program starting automatically, you can safely remove it, following these guidelines:

- **Look first for an option in the program itself.** Most programs that start automatically allow you to change this behavior by clearing a check box in an Options or Preferences dialog box. It might take some digging around, but this is always the preferred option.

- **Remove the program shortcut from the Startup folder.** This option is the preferred technique for preventing a program from starting up automatically;

Chapter 7

Part 1: Setup, Startup, Tune-Up

it won't work if the auto-start option is set in the registry. You can move the shortcut to another location if you think you might want to restore it later.

● **As a last resort, edit the registry manually.** This technique is messy, risky, and not always successful; some particularly persistent programs restore the startup values in the registry the next time you run the program itself.

---

tip   **Get a more powerful startup manager**

Although the System Configuration Utility is a priceless troubleshooting tool, it lacks a few features. For instance, although you can disable a shortcut or registry entry using the System Configuration Utility, this utility won't allow you to permanently remove entries from your startup configuration or to choose from a menu of startup configurations each time you begin working with Windows. Fortunately, a quick search on the Web can help you find several useful free alternatives. Our favorites are Startup Control Panel, written by Mike Lin and available at *http://www.mlin.net/StartupCPL.shtml,* and Startup Cop, written by Neil J. Rubenking and available at *http://www.pcmag.com/utilities.*

No matter how you choose to control programs that auto-start, resist the temptation to use the System Configuration Utility as a permanent startup manager. Doing so impairs its ability to work effectively as a troubleshooting tool; if you experience a startup problem, you'll have to keep careful records to tell which programs have been disabled for troubleshooting purposes and which should be permanently shut down. In addition, using the System Configuration Utility causes the dialog box shown here to appear the next time you start your computer; after you click OK, the System Configuration Utility opens.

If you used the utility for troubleshooting and you've successfully resolved the issue you were testing, choose the Normal Startup option and click OK to close the System Configuration Utility. The next time you start your computer, it will run through its complete startup routine and all the options you cleared will be enabled again.

If you choose to use the System Configuration Utility as a startup manager, disable the warning dialog box to avoid accidentally restoring the full startup configuration. After restarting your computer, select the Don't Show This Message Or Launch The System

Configuration Utility When Windows Starts check box and then click OK. The startup options you disabled using the System Configuration Utility remain disabled until you restore them. If you open the System Configuration Utility without making changes, you must click Cancel to close it, or it will prompt you to restart your computer.

Using Policies to Control Startup Applications

The Group Policy console (Gpedit.msc) includes three policies that affect startup applications (and documents):

- Run These Programs At User Logon
- Do Not Process The Run Once List
- Do Not Process The Legacy Run List

Each of these policies appears in two places in Group Policy:

- Computer Configuration\Administrative Templates\System\Logon
- User Configuration\Administrative Templates\System\Logon

Changes at either node affect all users of the current computer. If startup programs are specified in both Run These Programs At User Logon policies, all such programs are run at startup—the Computer Configuration programs first, followed by the User Configuration programs. If policies at the two nodes conflict, the Computer Configuration settings take priority. To view or modify any of these policy settings, log on as a member of the Administrators group and run Gpedit.msc. Note that the Group Policy console is not available in Windows XP Home Edition.

For more information about Group Policy, see Appendix E, "Group Policy."

Run These Programs At User Logon

This policy lets you specify a list of startup applications. To implement the policy, double-click Run These Programs At User Logon, in the details pane of the Group Policy console. Then select Enabled, click Show, and click Add. In the Add Item dialog box, type the name of an executable, or a document associated with an executable. If necessary, specify the complete path of the item, so that Windows can find it at startup. (If you're not sure whether the full path is necessary, try using the Start menu's Run command to run the item. If the Run command requires the path, Group Policy requires it as well.)

Do Not Process The Run Once List

Enabling this policy prevents Windows from processing the contents of HKLM\ SOFTWARE\Microsoft\Windows\CurrentVersion\RunOnce. Windows includes the policy as a security measure. If you're concerned that a virus or Trojan horse might use the RunOnce key to launch some malicious code on your system, enable the policy. Be aware, though, that many legitimate programs rely on this key to complete their setup routines.

Do Not Process The Legacy Run List

What Group Policy calls the "legacy run list" is the list of programs launched at startup via the registry keys HKLM\SOFTWARE\Microsoft\Windows\CurrentVersion\Run and HKCU\SOFTWARE\Microsoft\Windows\CurrentVersion\Run. Like the policy described in the previous paragraph, this one appears to be included as a security measure. If you're concerned about the possibility that a rogue application might infiltrate your system via one of these registry keys, enable the policy. Be aware, though, that many legitimate programs—virus checkers, for example—rely on one of these registry keys for startup launch. If you decide to enable the policy, you will need to find another way to launch such programs. Startup Control Panel, described earlier in this section— see "Get a More Powerful Startup Manager," page 250—provides an easy way to move startup programs from registry keys to your Startup folder. Simply right-click an item in Startup Control Panel, choose Send To, and then choose either Startup (Common) or Startup (User).

Controlling Services at Startup

Services are software components that perform specific system functions, typically working closely with key operating system code and hardware. On a typical system running Windows XP Home Edition or Professional, 50 processes may be running at any given time, performing tasks as diverse as managing Plug and Play activities, monitoring hard disks, overseeing security accounts, and synchronizing the system clock with Internet-based time servers.

> For more details about Windows XP services, see Appendix F, "Managing Services."

Some services are essential to the operation of Windows; others are optional and can safely be disabled to free up memory and other resources. The Services tab of the System Configuration Utility, shown in Figure 7-10, allows you to temporarily disable one or more services so that you can test how your system runs without that service.

The four columns on the Services tab list the name of the service, the manufacturer, its current status (running, stopped, or paused), and whether it's essential to the operation of Windows.

Although this tab includes a Disable All button, this option is not recommended for anything except the most drastic troubleshooting. This tool is most appropriately used very sparingly.

Figure 7-10. As with the Startup tab, you can clear check boxes here to stop specific services from loading when Windows starts.

---

tip **Look for third-party services**

The Hide All Microsoft Services check box at the bottom of the Services tab serves an important function by highlighting added services (such as third-party disk defragmenters and antivirus programs) that are not part of the Windows operating system. If you're experiencing performance or stability problems, choose this option to see the short list of third-party services. By temporarily disabling one or more of these services, you might be able to identify the cause of a problem quickly.

Advanced System Performance Measurement

As noted earlier, the Windows Task Manager provides a quick snapshot of system performance. A more robust system tool, the Performance console, allows you to monitor a much longer list of performance metrics than is available in Windows Task Manager. You can also log performance data to disk files or export it to programs like Microsoft Excel for detailed analysis, set "alerts" that cause Windows XP to take specified actions when performance thresholds are crossed, and monitor remote systems as well as your local machine.

---

note The Performance console is a snap-in to Microsoft Management Console. For more information about MMC-based utilities, see Appendix D, "Using and Customizing Microsoft Management Console."

Using the Performance Console

To begin using the Performance console, open the Administrative Tools option in Control Panel and then double-click the Performance icon. (Or, if you're comfortable at the command line, type **perfmon.msc** to open it directly.)

The Performance console, shown in Figure 7-11, has two components: System Monitor and Performance Logs And Alerts. The latter is subdivided into Counter Logs, Trace Logs, and Alerts. System Monitor provides graphical displays and textual information about your system's current state and recent history. Performance Logs And Alerts lets you track your system over longer periods of time, recording data in disk files for subsequent analysis. You can use the Alerts section of Performance Logs And Alerts to indicate actions that your computer should take if performance measures meet specified thresholds. In this chapter, we focus exclusively on using the System Monitor component. For details on how to create and reuse system logs and set up alerts, see *Microsoft Windows XP Professional Resource Kit Documentation* (Microsoft Press, 2001).

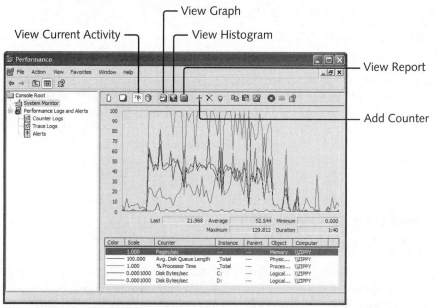

Figure 7-11. The System Monitor component of the Performance console can provide graphical information about your system's current and recent status.

The Performance console can track everything from relatively mundane but core activities, such as processor time and disk access, to exotic and highly technical measurements, such as the number of nonpaging read bytes per second handled by the network redirector. Whatever you decide to track, you add it to the Performance console in the form of an *object* and a *counter*:

- **Object.** This is any portion of a computer's resources that can be assigned characteristics and manipulated as a single identifiable element. Typical objects on most computers include the processor, memory, page file, and physical and logical disks. The complete list of objects varies from one system to another, depending on what hardware is installed, what network protocols are used, and so on.

- **Counter.** This tracks various types of information about the objects to which they are assigned. The available counters vary from object to object. For the Processor object, for example, the available counters include % Interrupt Time, % Processor Time, Interrupts/sec, and several others.

Some counters report instantaneous values. Others report the average of the current value and the value at the previous sampling interval. Still others report the difference between the current value and the previous value. If you're uncertain about what a particular counter represents, click Explain in the Add Counters dialog box, as explained in "Adding Counters" below.

Some objects can appear more than once in the Performance console; each such counter is considered a separate *instance*, allowing you to measure and compare the same type of performance using different software processes or hardware devices. The Process object has an instance for each process that's running. The PhysicalDisk object has an instance for each physical disk installed in the computer, and so on. Objects that have multiple instances typically include an instance that supplies information about the total of all the individual instances. So, for example, you could create multiple instances of the IO Data Bytes/sec counter, which measures all data that a process reads and writes from all sources (disk, network, and devices). In this example, the counter that tracks total IO Data for all running processes would give you an accurate measurement of overall system performance; by adding counters for each running process, you could see if a particular process is responsible for more than its fair share of this total.

Monitoring Current and Recent Information with System Monitor

In its Chart view, System Monitor shows the current state of one or more counters, along with a certain amount of very recent history. (At the default sampling interval of 1 second, the duration of a System Monitor chart is 1 minute and 40 seconds.) Alternative views show the current state of counters as a histogram or a textual report. To switch between Chart, Histogram, and Report views, use the View Graph, View Histogram, and View Report buttons on the toolbar (see Figure 7-11). Alternatively, right-click anywhere on the chart, choose Properties from the shortcut menu, and then select the view you want on the General tab of the System Monitor Properties dialog box.

Adding Counters

In any view, System Monitor's details pane is initially blank, waiting for you to select one or more of its myriad available performance measures. (A red vertical bar appears at the left side of the chart. If you do not see this bar, click the View Current Activity button on System Monitor's toolbar.) To make your selection, click the Add button on the toolbar or right-click the chart and choose Add Counters from the shortcut menu. The Add Counters dialog box, shown in Figure 7-12, appears.

To monitor your own computer, choose Use Local Computer Counters. To monitor a remote computer, choose Select Counters From Computer and then select the name of the computer you want to watch.

To specify what you want to monitor, begin by selecting an object from the Performance Object list. The remaining two lists in the dialog box then show the counters and instances available for the selected object. You can select counters and instances singly, or you can make multiple selections. (Hold down the Shift key to select adjacent items or the Ctrl key to select ones that are not adjacent.) You can also use the All Counters and All Instances option buttons to select all the items in a list.

If you're not sure what a particular counter counts (more than a remote possibility, given the number of available counters), select it in the counters list and then click Explain. A paragraph of descriptive prose will descend from the bottom of the dialog box.

After you've selected a combination of object, counter, and instance, you can click Add to add the combination to your chart, histogram, or report. After you're through adding counters, click Close to return to the Performance console. You can add as many counters as you like to your chart, histogram, or report. Note, however, that a chart with many counters can be difficult to read. If you need to track a large number of performance measures at one time, consider using multiple instances of the Performance console and putting some of the counters on the second or subsequent instance.

Figure 7-12. To tell System Monitor what you want to monitor, select an object, a counter, and an instance from the lists in this dialog box.

Changing the Chart's Display Characteristics

System Monitor's Chart and Histogram views plot all counters against a single vertical axis scaled, by default, from 0 to 100. A default scaling factor is applied to each counter so that counters with large values (such as PhysicalDisk(_Total)\Disk Read Bytes/sec, which measures the number of bytes per second read from all physical disks and might reach the high hundreds of thousands or more) can coexist meaningfully in a chart with low-value counters (such as PhysicalDisk(_Total)\Disk Reads/sec, which measures the number of read operations per second).

It's quite possible that, in order to make a chart intelligible, you will need to adjust its scale or the scaling factor for one or more counters (or both the scale and one or more scaling factors). In particular, you will need to make some kind of adjustment if System Monitor represents one or more of your counters as a horizontal line along the top edge of the chart. That's System Monitor's way of saying that your data, given its current scaling factor, exceeds the highest value of the vertical axis.

Changing the vertical axis scale   To change the scale, right-click the chart or histogram and choose Properties from the shortcut menu. On the Graph tab of the System Monitor Properties dialog box, type values in the Maximum and Minimum fields. Note that because all of System Monitor's many counters return positive values exclusively, you cannot set the minimum scale point to less than 0. On this tab, you can also add horizontal or vertical gridlines, supply a descriptive label for the vertical axis, and give the chart a title. These options are especially useful if you create special-purpose Performance consoles designed to zero in on specific performance characteristics of a system.

Changing a counter's scaling factor   To change the scaling factor for a counter, go to the Data tab of the System Monitor Properties dialog box, select the counter, and then adjust the value of the Scale field. The default scaling factor is called Default, which tells you nothing about the value that System Monitor has chosen to use. To see what the default value actually is, check the Scale column in the chart's legend. For help in deciding what scaling factor might be appropriate, check the Minimum and Maximum values in the Value bar—the numeric fields that appear directly below the chart, above the legend.

Note, however, that the Value bar displays information only about the counter that's currently selected in the legend. Therefore, when adjusting the scaling factor for a particular counter, it's a good idea to select it in the legend *before* you open the System Monitor Properties dialog box as shown here.

Changing colors, fonts, and titles   Other options on the various tabs of the System Monitor Properties dialog box let you change colors and fonts for your chart or histogram, add a main title or a vertical-axis title, and change the fonts and colors used for chart elements. You can also use Width, Color, and Style lists on the Data tab to modify the appearance of selected counters. Be aware, though, that the Style options are available only for the default line width. If you choose a nondefault width, you get the default (solid) line style.

Emphasizing a particular line   With several counters displayed on the same chart, it can sometimes be hard to tell which is which. If you double-click a line on the chart, System Monitor selects the associated counter in the legend. But when lines are close

Chapter 7: Tuning Up System Performance

together, it can be difficult to be sure that you've double-clicked the right one. The Highlight button (the light bulb) on the toolbar can help. When you click the Highlight tool (or use its keyboard shortcut Ctrl+H), System Monitor displays the current chart line in a bold width and contrasting color. With highlighting on, you can move up and down through the legend and see at a glance which chart line belongs to which legend entry.

Changing the sampling interval   By default, System Monitor samples counters at 1-second intervals. System Monitor always adjusts its display to show 100 sampling intervals, so at any resolution or window size the default-sampled chart shows 1 minute and 40 seconds' worth of data. You can alter the sampling interval by going to the General tab of the System Monitor Properties dialog box. Integers from 1 to 3888000 (1 second to 45 days) are accepted. To set up a console that shows page-file usage over a two-hour period, for instance, enter 72.

To freeze the current chart (stop sampling), clear the Sample Automatically Every check box on the General tab of the System Monitor Properties dialog box. Alternatively, click the Freeze Display button (the red "X") on the toolbar, or use its keyboard shortcut, Ctrl+F.

Saving and Reusing System Monitor Settings

To copy the current chart's properties to the Clipboard, press Ctrl+C, or click the Copy Properties button on System Monitor's toolbar. To paste properties from the Clipboard, press Ctrl+V, or use the Paste Counter List button. By using the Clipboard in this fashion, you can replicate a chart in a separate instance of System Monitor. Alternatively, you can use the Clipboard to restore the current state of a chart after making changes to it—provided, of course, that you haven't cleared the Clipboard in the meantime. Note that the Paste Counter List tool pastes all properties stored on the Clipboard, not just the counter list.

Advanced System Tweaks

A handful of advanced features in Windows XP allow you to tune performance settings to match your computing needs. In some cases, these options happen automatically, and knowing how to tune them can be useful.

Troubleshooting

Multiple instances of Svchost.exe appear in Task Manager.

That's perfectly normal. Service Host (Svchost.exe) is a core piece of Windows XP code that collects a number of lower-level system-critical services and runs them in a common environment. By gathering multiple functions together, this arrangement reduces boot time and system overhead and eliminates the need to run dozens of separate low-level services. Because different groups of services have different requirements in terms of system access and security, Windows XP creates a number of different groups.

Several interesting ways to adjust performance characteristics appear when you open System in Control Panel, click the Advanced tab, click Settings in the Performance section, and then select the Advanced tab. In the resulting Performance Options dialog box, shown in Figure 7-13, the two top options let you tune CPU and memory usage.

In the Processor Scheduling section, Programs is selected by default. If you multitask heavily and you're willing to sacrifice some zip in foreground program execution in exchange for faster background processing, select the Background Services option.

In the Memory Usage section, you can also shift the default settings, which are optimized for running programs. Choosing the System Cache option reserves a much larger percentage of available physical memory for use in the cache. This option is most useful if you use extremely data-intensive applications, such as video editing programs or large databases.

To improve the speed of starting applications, Windows XP continually monitors files that are used when the computer starts and when you start applications. It then creates an index (in the %SystemRoot%\Prefetch folder) that lists segments of frequently used programs and the order they're loaded in. This prefetching process improves performance by allowing the operating system to quickly grab program files.

Chapter 7: Tuning Up System Performance

Figure 7-13. By default, the two options highlighted here are optimized to help you run programs most effectively under Windows XP.

The prefetching code is even more effective when used in conjunction with the built-in defragmenting tool. Every three days, during idle times, this utility rearranges program code, moving it to the outside of the disk to make it more efficient when loading. To force Windows to perform this optimization without having to do a full defragmentation, use the Defrag.exe command with the –b switch. For instance: **defrag c: -b.**

This command forces the command-line version of Defrag.exe to run, optimizing boot files and applications while leaving the rest of the drive undisturbed.

Part 2

Customizing Windows XP

Tweaking the Windows XP Interface

In the development of Microsoft Windows XP, the *user interface*—everything that connects you, the user, to the computer—underwent its first major overhaul since the introduction of Windows 95. The basic elements remain in place, and most of the tips and techniques you used in earlier versions of Windows work equally well in the bold new interface of Windows XP. But you'll also discover much that is new.

As in previous versions of Windows, the default configuration provided by the Setup program provides a decent color arrangement, a serviceable screen resolution, appropriately sized buttons and icons, and so on. But because one size does not fit all, Windows gives you many choices about the appearance and behavior of your Start menu, desktop, taskbar, and other elements. In this chapter, we explore those choices and offer suggestions on setting up your system so that it works best for *you*.

User profiles allow two or more users of a machine to establish individual settings that will be remembered and restored each time they log on. You're free to paint your workspace purple without offending someone else who also needs to use your machine. Nearly all the customizing steps described in this chapter are profile-specific, which means that they affect only the current user account.

At Home with Windows XP

When it comes to customization of the user interface, Windows XP Professional and Windows XP Home Edition are essentially alike: what you can do in one, you can do in the other as well. A couple of tweaks involving the My Recent Documents menu (the Start menu section that provides shortcuts to your fifteen most recently opened documents) require the use of the Group Policy snap-in (Gpedit.msc), which is not available in Windows XP Home Edition. You can work around that small limitation easily enough, however, by downloading the free Tweak UI utility from *www.microsoft.com/ windowsxp/pro/downloads/powertoys.asp*. A description of Tweak UI appears at the end of this chapter.

note The default interface described in this chapter is the one you see if you install a retail version of Windows XP. If Windows came pre-installed on your computer, the computer manufacturer might provide a desktop and Start menu that's different from what you see here. The procedures for changing those defaults, however, should be the same on any computer.

A Road Map to the Windows XP User Interface

Figure 8-1 shows some of the elements of a typical Windows XP desktop. The first thing you'll notice, if you're familiar with earlier versions of Windows, is the distinct lack of clutter.

- A default configuration of Windows XP has only one desktop icon, Recycle Bin, but you can add as many as you like. If you upgraded from an earlier version of Windows, your old desktop icons are still in place.

- The notification area (some people call it the system tray) displays only the icons you choose. Windows hides the icons you seldom use (but which some programs insist on putting there), displaying only the ones that you're actively using. The others are available with a single click.

- The taskbar doesn't squeeze on a button for every open window. Instead, when enough windows are open to fill the taskbar, Windows combines buttons from the same application (such as multiple Microsoft Word documents) into a single button that you can expand with a quick click.

- By default, the taskbar doesn't include the Quick Launch toolbar or any other toolbar.

266

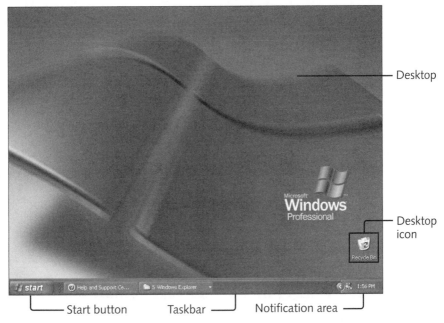

Desktop

Desktop icon

Start button   Taskbar   Notification area

Figure 8-1. A default Windows XP desktop includes these elements.

Making It Easy to Start Your Favorite Programs

The purpose of an operating system is not to impress you with its snazzy looks or nifty animated menus and sounds. Although these adornments might enhance your experience, the real purpose is to run the programs you need for work or play. Windows offers a number of different methods for starting a program:

- Click the program's shortcut on the Start menu. This is, by far, the most common method and usually the easiest. The following sections are devoted to tuning up the Start menu to work the way you work.

- Click the program's icon on the Quick Launch toolbar or another toolbar. Toolbars are extremely handy, yet little understood. For details, see "Using the Quick Launch Bar and Other Desktop Toolbars," page 281.

- Double-click the program's icon on the desktop or in another folder.

- Type the name of the program's executable file in any of these locations:

    - In the Run dialog box (choose Start, Run or press the Windows logo key+R)

    - In the Address toolbar (include the file's path)

    - In the Address bar in Windows Explorer (include the file's path)

- Press the shortcut key assigned to a program shortcut.

---

tip   **Open a document to start a program**

You can also start a program by using any of the techniques listed here to open one of the program's documents. Instead of clicking the program's icon or typing its name, click a document icon or type the document's name to open the specified document in its associated program.

---

newfeature!

Setting the Appearance of the Start Menu

It all begins (and ends, as some wags are fond of pointing out) with the Start menu, which provides access to nearly everything you need to do in Windows. This invaluable command post appears at a single click or keystroke. (On newer keyboards, press the Windows logo key; or on any keyboard, press Ctrl+Esc.) Windows XP now offers two different versions of the Start menu, as shown in Figures 8-2 and 8-3.

As these figures demonstrate, the layout of the new default Start menu is completely different from the compact one that appeared in earlier versions of Windows (now called the classic Start menu). The default Start menu makes it easy to access items (such as My Computer) that were on the desktop in earlier versions. (Although the desktop seems like a convenient place to store such icons, they're usually covered by windows when you need them, so you must first get the windows out of the way to use desktop icons.) The default menu offers prominent shortcuts to your Web browser and e-mail program, along with shortcuts to your most-used programs.

To switch between the two Start menu options, right-click the Start button and choose Properties. The Taskbar And Start Menu Properties dialog box appears, as shown in Figure 8-4 on page 270. Select either Start Menu or Classic Start Menu.

Click All Programs to display a cascading menu of all your installed programs

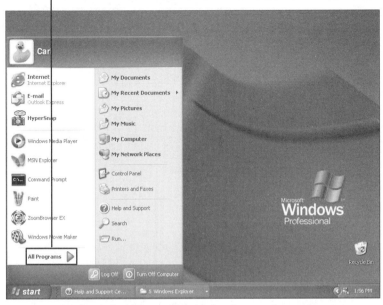

Figure 8-2. The default Start menu places frequently used programs on the left side and frequently used folders on the right side.

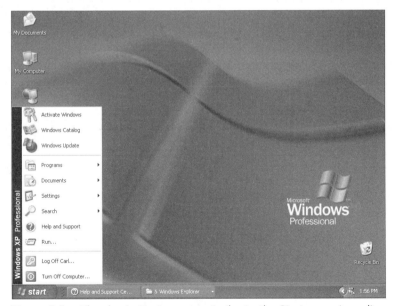

Figure 8-3. The classic Start menu is similar to the Start menu in earlier versions of Windows.

269

Figure 8-4. You can also reach the Taskbar And Start Menu Properties dialog box via Control Panel. (If you use Category view, you'll find Taskbar And Start Menu under Appearance And Themes.)

> **note** By default, when you switch to the classic Start menu, icons for My Documents, My Computer, My Network Places, and Internet Explorer appear on the desktop. And when you switch back, these icons disappear. Whichever you select, however, you can override this default and choose which icons you want on your desktop. For details, see "Controlling Desktop Icons," page 293. Tweak UI also provides check-box control over the standard desktop icons. For more information, see "Customizing Windows XP with Tweak UI," page 327.

While you're in the Taskbar And Start Menu Properties dialog box, you might want to make one other appearance-related change that allows more items to fit on the menu:

- If you choose the default Start menu, click Customize and then, on the General tab of the Customize Start Menu dialog box, select Small Icons.

- If you choose Classic Start Menu, click Customize and then, in the Customize Classic Start Menu dialog box, select Show Small Icons In Start Menu (near the bottom of the Advanced Start Menu Options list).

With either menu version, choosing small icons changes only the appearance of the main Start menu. Cascading submenus always use small icons, and there's no option to display them with large icons.

This glimpse beyond the Customize button shows lots of other customization options, which is the topic of the following section.

---

tip **Change your name and icon**

One advantage of the default Start menu over the classic Start menu is that the top of the menu shows at a glance who is currently logged on. You can change the name and the icon that appears alongside it. (The same name and icon appear on the Welcome screen.) To change the name or icon, visit User Accounts in Control Panel. For more information, see "Changing Account Settings," page 103.

Controlling the Content of the Start Menu

newfeature!

Regardless of which Start menu you choose, much of the menu is customizable. You can add, delete, move, copy, sort, and rename most menu items. You can turn some into cascading menus, which allow you to navigate to a particular item of interest without even clicking; all you need to do is point at an item to open its submenu.

The default Start menu, shown in Figure 8-5 on the next page, shows programs on its left side. Closer inspection shows that the left side is further divided into three areas:

- **Pinned items list.** Items at the top of the menu always appear on the menu. You decide which programs you want here, and in which order.

- **Most frequently used programs list.** Windows monitors which programs you use most often and adds them to this list automatically. Each program that is added knocks off a less-used program. You can control the number of items that appear here and you can remove items from this list, but you can't add items or change their order.

- **All Programs button.** This is the entry point to a traditional menu of all installed programs. The content that appears here is the same content you see when you click Programs on the classic Start menu, plus any items that appear at the top of the classic Start menu (above Programs). You're free to rearrange these links in whatever way works best for you.

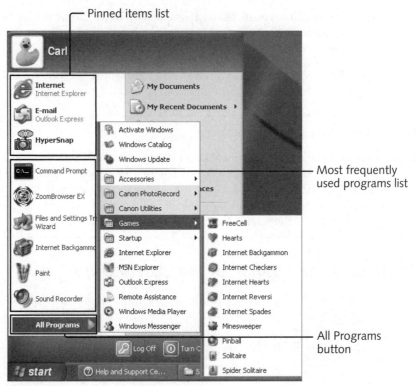

Figure 8-5. The menu that appears when you click All Programs includes items from the top of the classic Start menu as well as the classic menu's Programs menu.

> **note** Items on the pinned items list and most frequently used programs list do not appear anywhere on the classic Start menu. A close replacement for the pinned items list, however, is the top of the Start menu, above the Programs folder. You can add any items you like to this part of the classic Start menu.

Adding an Item to the Menu

To add a program to the pinned items list, right-click it and choose Pin To Start Menu. You can right-click a program wherever it appears—on the Start menu, in Windows Explorer, or on the desktop. Alternatively, you can drag a program icon (or a document icon) to the Start button.

To add a program or document to any part of the All Programs menu, drag it there. If you have a shortcut on your desktop, for example, that you would also like to appear somewhere on the Start menu, simply click it, hold down the mouse button, and move your mouse pointer to the Start button. When the Start menu opens, after a moment's delay, you can drag the desktop shortcut to the pinned items list or to some other location within the All Programs menu. As you move the mouse, a dark line shows where the new item will appear when you release the button.

> **note** If you drag a shortcut to the Start button and release the mouse button before the Start menu opens, the new item will appear in the pinned items list. If you're using the classic Start menu, items you drop on the Start button appear at the top of the menu.

You can use the same technique to drag items from Windows Explorer windows to the Start menu. Windows leaves the dragged item where you got it and plants a copy on the Start menu. If the dragged item isn't a shortcut to begin with, Windows creates a shortcut to it on the Start menu. Thus, for example, you can drag a folder to the Start menu without changing the folder structure of your drive in any way; on the menu, Windows simply creates a pointer (a shortcut) to the folder.

> **note** Windows creates a shortcut only if you drag a file or folder to the pinned items list or the All Programs menu (or to the top of the Start menu or Programs menu if you're using the classic Start menu). Dragging a file or folder to one of the document links, such as My Documents or My Pictures, causes Windows to *move* the item to that folder instead of creating a shortcut. Just as you can when dragging items in Windows Explorer, you can determine what Windows will do by noticing the icon as you drag it: If it's going to create a shortcut, the mouse pointer includes a small boxed arrow.

If you're not sure how to get to a Windows Explorer window that displays the item you want on the Start menu, you can use the Search command to locate it—and then drag the item from the Search Results window to the menu. For example, suppose you want to put Notepad at the top of your Start menu, but you're not quite sure where Notepad lives. Open the Start menu and click Search. Tell Search to find Notepad, and when Notepad.exe appears in the Search Results pane, simply drag it to the Start button.

> **tip** **Remove the orange highlight from new program shortcuts**
>
> When you install a new program, by default Windows highlights in orange the additions to your Start menu for a few days. This makes it easier to find the new items and makes you aware of added items that you might have otherwise overlooked. Some users find the highlights distracting, however. If you want to remove the highlights, open the Taskbar And Start Menu Properties dialog box. On the Start Menu tab, click Customize. Click the Advanced tab and clear the Highlight Newly Installed Programs check box.

newfeature!

Controlling the Pinned Internet and E-Mail Items

By default, the Start menu includes two links in the pinned items list: one for your Web browser and one for your e-mail program. If you don't use these links, you can remove them in the same way that you remove other links: Right-click and choose Remove From This List.

To change the program that is started by each of these items or to restore either one if you removed it in error, follow these steps:

1 Right-click the Start button and choose Properties to open the Taskbar And Start Menu Properties dialog box.

2 On the Start Menu tab, click Customize to open the Customize Start Menu dialog box.

3 Under Show On Start Menu, select the check box for each item that you want to appear. Then select which of your installed Web browsers and e-mail programs you want the pinned item to start.

Deleting an Item from the Menu

To remove a program or document from the Start menu, follow these steps:

1 Click the Start button and then release the mouse button.

2 Right-click the item you want to delete.

3 For an item on the pinned items list or most frequently used programs list, choose Remove From This List from the shortcut menu. For an item in the All Programs menu, choose Delete from the shortcut menu and then click Yes in the Confirm File Delete or Confirm Shortcut Delete dialog box.

The shortcut menu that appears when you right-click a pinned item also includes an Unpin From Start Menu command. Choosing this command deletes the program from the pinned items list, but if it happens to be one of your most frequently used programs, it instantly reappears on the most frequently used programs list. To ensure that the program doesn't appear on either list, choose Remove From This List.

---

note Deleting a shortcut from the Start menu does not uninstall the program; it deletes only the shortcut to the program.

Moving or Copying a Menu Item

To move an item from one part of the Start menu to another, simply grab it and drag it. Click the Start button, release the mouse button, move the mouse pointer to the item you want to move, and then click again and hold down the mouse button. Now move the mouse in the direction of the item's new destination. As you do, Windows draws a thick line to show where the item will land if you release the mouse button.

To copy an item to a new location, follow the same steps as for moving, but hold down the Ctrl key while you drag. A plus sign (+) next to the mouse pointer confirms that you're copying, not moving. Release the mouse button first, and then release the Ctrl key.

Dragging items from the left side of the default Start menu to the All Programs menu always copies the item; you don't need to hold down the Ctrl key. The same is true for items you drag from the All Programs menu to the pinned items list.

Troubleshooting

You can't drag items on the Start menu.

You might find that you can't drag items to, from, or within the Start menu; when you drag items over the Start menu, an "unavailable" symbol appears instead of a black line that indicates the destination. In this case, you need to enable the Start menu's drag-and-drop capability. To do that, right-click the Start button, choose Properties, and click Customize. If you're using the default Start menu, click the Advanced tab and then, in the Start Menu Items box, select Enable Dragging And Dropping. (If you're using the classic Start menu, in the Advanced Start Menu Options box in the Customize Classic Start Menu dialog box, select Enable Dragging And Dropping.)

The drag-and-drop techniques that let you rearrange menu items also work for moving and copying items to off-menu locations. Thus, for example, if your menu gets crowded, you can move some items from the menu to your desktop, to a toolbar, or to a folder. In all cases, Windows creates a shortcut in the new location.

Sorting Menu Items

Windows lets you move or copy menu items to any location on the All Programs submenu, as described in the previous section. Although this allows you to place them in any order that suits you, you might prefer to revert to a more orderly approach. You can ask Windows to re-sort a single submenu in its default order: folders in alphabetical order, followed by menu items in alphabetical order.

To sort a single submenu, follow these steps:

1 Click the Start button and then release the mouse button.

2 Move the mouse pointer to the submenu you want to sort.

3 Right-click an item on the submenu and choose Sort By Name from the shortcut menu.

If you use the classic Start menu, you can sort all submenus within the Programs submenu at once, as follows:

1 Right-click the Start button and choose Properties.

2 On the Start Menu tab, click Customize.

3 In the Customize Classic Start Menu dialog box shown here, click Sort.

> **note** Windows maintains the sort order for the default Start menu and the classic Start menu separately. Therefore, changes you make to one Start menu—whether you change the order by dragging or sort the items with a sort command—do not appear if you switch to the other menu style. The sort orders for both menus are stored in the HKCU\Software\Microsoft\Windows\CurrentVersion\Explorer\MenuOrder registry key. The classic-menu order is stored in the Start Menu subkey, and the default-menu order is stored in the Start Menu2 subkey.

InsideOut

Even if you never change the menu order manually, your menu can soon become jumbled because new programs you install ordinarily place their shortcuts at the bottom of the menu. If you prefer to have your menus always sorted alphabetically, you can use a registry trick to force alphabetical sorts: remove permissions to the registry key that controls menu order.

1 Open Registry Editor and select HKCU\Software\Microsoft\Windows\CurrentVersion\Explorer\MenuOrder.

2 On the Edit menu, choose Permissions.

3 In the Permissions For MenuOrder dialog box, click Advanced.

4 In the Advanced Security Settings For MenuOrder dialog box, clear the Inherit From Parent check box.

5 In the Security dialog box that appears, click Copy.

6 Click OK to return to the Permissions For MenuOrder dialog box, and then clear the Full Control access control entry for your own account and for any security groups that you're a member of, leaving the Read access control entry in place.

Without Full Control permissions, Windows is prevented from rearranging menu items. Your programs remain in alphabetical order, even when new items are installed. The downside to this change is that you can no longer make your own ad hoc rearrangements, and any such arrangements you had made previously are lost. To revert to default behavior, reinstate Full Control permissions, then log off and log on again.

Renaming a Menu Item

In earlier versions of Windows it wasn't easy to rename an item on the Start menu. In Windows XP it is, thanks to an additional shortcut menu command. To rename a menu item, follow these steps:

1 Click the Start button and then release the mouse button.

277

2 Right-click the menu item you want to rename and choose Rename.

3 Edit the name (or type a new one) and then click OK.

Troubleshooting

No shortcut menu appears when you right-click.

When you right-click an item on the Start menu, a shortcut menu should appear. If instead the menu flashes and no shortcut menu appears, the Enable Dragging And Dropping check box has been cleared. Although it's not apparent from the name, this option enables shortcut menus as well as drag-and-drop capability. To enable the option, right-click the Start button, choose Properties, and then click Customize. If you're using the default Start menu, click the Advanced tab and then, in the Start Menu Items box, select Enable Dragging And Dropping. (If you're using the classic Start menu, the option appears in the Advanced Start Menu Options box in the Customize Classic Start Menu dialog box.)

newfeature!
Managing the Most Frequently Used Programs List

The list of most frequently used programs —the items that appear on the default Start menu between the pinned items list and the All Programs link—is controlled by Windows. It keeps track of your program usage so that the programs you use most appear here automatically. The most frequently used programs list does not appear anywhere on the classic Start menu.

The most frequently used programs list includes only shortcuts to .exe files; other executable files you open do not appear, regardless of how often you run them. In addition, the following items are excluded by default (for more information, see Knowledge Base article Q282066, "Frequently Used Programs Not Automatically Added to the Start Menu"):

● Programs listed in the AddRemoveApps value of the registry key HKLM\Software\Microsoft\Windows\CurrentVersion\Explorer\FileAssociation. By default, the following items are excluded here: Setup.exe, Install.exe, Isuninst.exe, Unwise.exe, Unwise32.exe, St5unst.exe, Rundll32.exe, Msoobe.exe, and Lnkstub.exe. You can add items to the list.

● Programs whose HKCR\Applications*Appname* registry key include the string value NoStartPage. For example, the registry key HKCU\Applications\ Explorer.exe includes the string value NoStartPage, so shortcuts to Explorer.exe never appear on the most frequently used programs list. By default, the items excluded here are Explorer.exe, Icwconn1.exe, Inoculan.exe,

Mobsync.exe, Navwnt.exe, Realmon.exe, and Sndvol32.exe. You can add an item to this exclusion list by finding its HKCU\Applications*Appname* key and adding the string value NoStartPage.

● Items whose shortcut names include any of the following text: Documentation, Help, Install, More Info, Readme, Read me, Read First, Setup, Support, What's New, Remove. This list of exclusion strings is specified in the AddRemoveNames value of HKLM\Software\Microsoft\Windows\CurrentVersion\Explorer\FileAssocation.

To specify the number of programs that appear on the most frequently used programs list, right-click the Start button, choose Properties, and click Customize. On the General tab of the Customize Start Menu dialog box, enter the value you want in the

Using Windows Explorer to Modify the All Programs Menu

The All Programs submenu of the Start menu is merely a representation of a collection of shortcuts stored on your computer. Therefore, you can use Windows Explorer to add, delete, move, and copy items in the All Programs menu instead of using the procedures described in the preceding sections. (You can't use Windows Explorer to establish the sort order, however. That information is stored in the registry, and it's best modified by working in the Start menu.)

The All Programs submenu contains the links stored in two different folders (along with all their subfolders, which create the cascading menu structure): %UserProfile%\Start Menu and %AllUsersProfile%\Start Menu. The items in your own user profile appear only when you're logged on, whereas those in the All Users profile appear no matter who is logged on. Items from the two folders are merged into a seamless list.

Store the items that you want to appear at the top of the All Programs menu in the Start Menu folders. (If you use the classic Start menu, items in the Start Menu folders appear at the top of the Start menu, above the Programs menu.) Store the shortcuts and folders that you want to appear in the lower part of the All Programs menu in the Start Menu\Programs folders. (In the classic Start menu, these items appear on the Programs menu.)

To work with these items in Windows Explorer, you can use the usual techniques to navigate to the folders. But an easier way is to right-click the Start button and choose Open (to open %UserProfile%\Start Menu) or Open All Users (to open %AllUsersProfile%\Start Menu). If you prefer to display the Folders bar in Windows Explorer, choose the Explore or Explore All Users command instead.

Number Of Programs On Start Menu box. You can specify any number from 0 (if you hate the feature) through 30 (if you have a gigantic screen, high resolution, and lots of different programs).

The Clear List button gives you an opportunity to wipe the slate clean. After you click it, Windows begins monitoring your program usage anew, adding a program to the list each time you start one.

Unlike the folders and items in the All Programs menu, the most frequently used programs list is buried deep in the registry, and there's no practical way to edit it directly. Instead, let Windows add programs as it sees fit, use the Remove From This List command and the Clear List button to remove items, and use Pin To Start Menu to be sure that your most-favorite programs remain at easy reach.

Using Personalized Menus

With personalized menus, a feature that's available only when you use the classic Start menu, Windows displays the menu items you use most frequently and hides the others. This reduces clutter and leads to shorter menus, which are easier to scan and use. A double arrow at the bottom of a submenu indicates the presence of seldom-used items. To display these items, click the double arrow. Or if you simply wait a few seconds, Windows senses your momentary confusion and expands the menus, as shown in Figure 8-6. The newly visible items appear on a light-colored background so that they're easier to spot.

Figure 8-6. Personalized menus hide seldom-used menu items.

Some users love personalized menus and others loathe this feature. Fortunately, Windows gives you a choice. To enable or disable personalized menus, follow these steps:

1 Right-click the Start button and choose Properties.

280

2 On the Start Menu tab, click Customize.

3 In the Advanced Start Menu Options list in the Customize Classic Start Menu dialog box, select or clear the Use Personalized Menus check box.

---

note The personalized menu setting in the Customize Classic Start Menu dialog box affects only the Start menu. To enable or disable personalized menus in other programs that use them, such as Internet Explorer or Microsoft Office, set the option within that program.

---

tip **Scroll your Programs menu if it gets too long**

Windows has another trick for dealing with an overgrown Programs menu. If your Programs menu is too tall for your screen, Windows normally displays it in multiple columns, which can quickly outgrow the screen's width. For a cleaner alternative, select Scroll Programs in the Advanced Start Menu Options box. This option appends an arrow at the top or bottom of a menu if it won't fit vertically; point to the arrow to scroll the menu in that direction.

This same option is available to users of the default Start menu. Right-click the Start button, choose Properties, and click Customize. In the Customize Start Menu dialog box, click the Advanced tab and then select Scroll Programs in the Start Menu Items box.

Using the Quick Launch Bar and Other Desktop Toolbars

A *toolbar* is a collection of icons that simplify commonplace tasks. Windows includes a toolbar called Quick Launch that adds three icons to your taskbar: Internet Explorer, Show Desktop, and Windows Media Player. With the toolbar in place, a single click of an icon initiates an action. The Show Desktop icon displays the desktop, in the process minimizing whatever windows might be open; clicking Show Desktop again restores all windows to their previous size and position. The other icons simply start their corresponding programs.

In addition to the Quick Launch toolbar, the following toolbars can be displayed on the taskbar or elsewhere on your desktop:

● **Address.** The Address toolbar provides a place where you can enter an Internet address or the name and path of a program, document, or folder. When you press Enter or click the Go button, Windows takes you to the Internet address, starts the program, opens the document, or displays the folder in a Windows Explorer window. The Address toolbar is functionally equivalent to the Start menu's Run command or the Address bar in Windows Explorer or Internet Explorer.

Chapter 8

- **Links.** The Links toolbar provides a set of shortcuts to selected Internet sites. It's equivalent to the Links toolbar in Internet Explorer or Windows Explorer.

- **Desktop.** The Desktop toolbar provides copies of all the icons currently displayed on your desktop. You might find this toolbar handy if you're using an HTML page as background for your desktop and your normal desktop icons get in the way.

To give you an idea of the flexibility of toolbars, Figure 8-7 shows an unrealistically cluttered collection of them. It's unlikely that anyone would want all these toolbars displayed at once—at least in the fashion shown here—but you might want to use one or more on your own desktop.

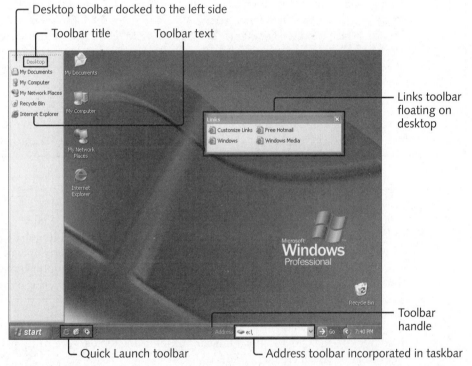

Figure 8-7. You can customize these four standard toolbars and create your own new toolbars.

You can customize any of the supplied toolbars except for Address. So, for example, you can add icons for your own programs or shortcuts to the Quick Launch toolbar, remove from the Links toolbar links that you don't find useful (or add links to your own favorite sites), and so on. You can also create entirely new toolbars.

Desktop toolbars appear initially on the taskbar, but you can *float* them on the desktop or *dock* them against any side of the desktop. Thus, for example, you can have your taskbar docked against the bottom edge of the desktop and line the other three edges with toolbars.

Installing and Removing Toolbars

To install a new toolbar or remove one you're currently using, right-click any unoccupied part of the taskbar or any existing toolbar. Choose Toolbars from the shortcut menu that appears, and then choose from the ensuing submenu. A check mark beside a toolbar's name means that it is already displayed on the taskbar. Clicking a checked toolbar name removes that toolbar from the taskbar. To remove a toolbar that is not on the taskbar—or to add another toolbar to it—right-click an unoccupied part of the toolbar, choose Toolbars, and then choose from the submenu. You can also click the Close button on a floating toolbar to remove it from the desktop.

Troubleshooting

The Show Desktop tool is missing.

The Show Desktop tool is not an ordinary program shortcut. If it is deleted, the procedure for re-creating it is not obvious. Follow these steps:

1 Open Notepad and type the following text:

```
[Shell]
Command=2
IconFile=explorer.exe,3
[Taskbar]
Command=ToggleDesktop
```

2 Save the new file as Show Desktop.scf.

3 Drag the file's icon to the Quick Launch bar or other location where you want the shortcut to appear.

Sizing and Positioning Toolbars

Before you can move or resize toolbars that are on the taskbar, the taskbar must be unlocked. To do that, right-click an unoccupied area of the taskbar and, if a check mark appears next to the Lock The Taskbar command, choose the command to clear the check mark. Alternatively, open the Taskbar And Start Menu Properties dialog box and, on the Taskbar tab, clear the Lock The Taskbar check box.

> **note** When the taskbar is locked, you can add or remove toolbars and icons and you can make other changes in toolbar appearance. Locking only prevents you from moving or resizing toolbars or the taskbar itself. Locking the taskbar does not affect toolbars that are not on the taskbar.

When the taskbar is not locked, a dotted vertical bar appears at the left edge of every toolbar positioned on the taskbar. (If the taskbar is displayed vertically against the left or right edge of the desktop, the bar is horizontal and appears at the top of the toolbar.) This is the toolbar's *handle* (shown in Figure 8-7 on page 282). To move a toolbar out onto the desktop, position the mouse pointer on the handle. When the pointer changes shape, drag the toolbar. (If the toolbar title is displayed, you can grab it instead.) To dock a toolbar against a different edge of the desktop, drag it all the way to that edge. When you release the mouse button, the toolbar will dock.

On the desktop, the toolbar takes the form of a simple window, with a title bar and a Close button.

> **note** You can dock toolbars only against the edges of the whole desktop. If your desktop spans two or more monitors, you can't dock a toolbar against a screen edge that's adjacent to the edge of another screen.

You can move the toolbar around by dragging its title bar or close it by clicking the Close button. To reposition a toolbar on the taskbar, simply drag its title bar to the taskbar. You can also use the handle to change a toolbar's size or position on the taskbar. Assuming your taskbar is horizontal, dragging the handle to the right decreases the width of the toolbar and makes more room for the toolbar on the left. Dragging to the left has the opposite effect.

To change the size of a desktop toolbar, simply drag one of its borders.

> **note** A toolbar that's too large to fit in its taskbar space displays its remaining contents in a pop-up menu if you click the double arrow that appears at its right or bottom edge.

Any toolbar that's docked to the edge of the desktop can be set to auto-hide. To do that, right-click the toolbar's title or any unoccupied space and choose Auto-Hide. With that setting in place, the toolbar retreats into the side of the desktop, leaving only a thin line as a reminder of its presence. When you want to use the toolbar, simply move the mouse pointer to the edge of the desktop, and the toolbar springs into view.

Customizing Toolbars

To remove a tool from a toolbar, right-click it and choose Delete from the shortcut menu. To add to a toolbar a tool that starts a program or opens a document, drag the

Chapter 8

item's icon from the desktop or a Windows Explorer window and deposit it wherever you want it to appear on the toolbar. To change the properties for a particular tool, right-click and choose Properties; you'll see the familiar properties dialog box for a shortcut file.

Troubleshooting

You can't modify a toolbar icon.

When you modify certain toolbar icons, you might get a message that your changes can't be saved and that access is denied. This can occur if a Quick Launch icon has to have its read-only attribute set. The solution, which you're not likely to intuit from the error message, is quite simple: right-click the icon, choose Properties, click the General tab, and clear the Read-Only check box.

Toolbars can be displayed with or without their titles, and their tools can be displayed with either large or small icons, and with or without identifying text. To avail yourself of any of these customizing options, right-click the toolbar you want to modify (not on a tool, however). Choose View followed by Show Title to suppress or display the toolbar title; choose Large Icons or Small Icons to change the icon size; or choose Show Text to suppress or display tool text.

Note that if you don't display tool text, you can still see the name of any tool simply by moving your mouse pointer over it and pausing for a moment.

InsideOut

When set up in a certain way, the Desktop toolbar can provide a cascading menu of all the folders and files on your system. Follow these steps to set up this handy feature:

1 Display the Desktop toolbar somewhere on the taskbar, and be sure its toolbar title is displayed.

2 Reduce the Desktop toolbar's size by dragging its handle (and the handles of surrounding toolbars, if necessary) until it displays only the toolbar title ("Desktop") and a double arrow.

Now when you click the double arrow, a menu of desktop items appears. Desktop items that contain other folders and files (such as My Computer, My Documents, and My Network Places) cascade to show their contents when you point at them.

285

Creating a New Toolbar

Any folder on your system can become a toolbar. This includes Windows system folders such as Printers And Faxes or Control Panel. To create a new toolbar, right-click an existing toolbar or a spot on the taskbar, choose Toolbars, and then choose New Toolbar. In the next dialog box, navigate to a folder and click OK.

The folder's name becomes the name of the new toolbar, and each item within the folder becomes a tool.

> **tip** Create a toolbar by dragging a folder
>
> You can quickly and easily make a toolbar of any folder by dragging the folder to the edge of the desktop and releasing it. Doing so docks the toolbar to the edge where you dropped it. You can change whether the toolbar title or button text appear and the size of the icons, and you can move the toolbar to another location.

With the exception of the Address toolbar, every toolbar is a representation of a folder that exists somewhere on your system. To see a toolbar's underlying folder in a Windows Explorer window, right-click the toolbar and choose Open Folder. If you prefer to make your additions, deletions, and other changes in Windows Explorer instead of working directly on the toolbar, you can do so. Table 8-1 shows the file locations for the three standard toolbars.

Table 8-1. Folder Locations of Standard Toolbars

Toolbar	Location
Quick Launch	%AppData%\Microsoft\Internet Explorer\Quick Launch
Links	%UserProfile%\Favorites\Links
Desktop	%UserProfile%\Desktop and %AllUsersProfile%\Desktop

Making It Easy to Open Your Favorite Documents

When Microsoft introduced the My Documents folder in Windows 98, many longtime computer users with roots in MS-DOS and the earliest versions of Windows objected vociferously. Aside from the name, which some found cloying, they didn't want to be told where to store their documents. (By the way, you can change the name of My Documents in the same way that you change the name of any other folder: right-click and choose Rename.) But the implementation of My Documents has been greatly improved in subsequent versions of Windows, and it provides the easiest and best place to organize and store your documents. Its advantages include the following:

- Windows provides easy access to the My Documents folder (and its subfolders) through the Start menu, the task pane in Windows Explorer, common File Open and File Save dialog boxes, and other places.

- Using My Documents makes it easy to share the documents you want to share and keep private the ones you don't want to share (particularly if you use Windows XP Home Edition, in which it's difficult to modify the default share permissions and NTFS permissions).

- Keeping your documents in My Documents and its subfolders makes it much easier to back up your documents or move them to another computer en masse. Gathering all your documents from their far-flung locations all over your drive is an essential first step in developing a practical backup strategy.

Of course, you're still free to store your documents where you want, but there's really no reason *not* to use My Documents. In short, My Documents has come a long way since its introduction and is the best place to store your documents. Clicking a link to My Documents—and you'll see lots of them in Windows XP—leads you directly to your document storage location, where you can open your document of choice with a simple double-click.

For information about moving the My Documents folder, see "Moving Folders from the Standard Profile Locations," page 1162.

To access documents that you share with others, either in the Shared Documents folder or in a folder on a network drive, simply create a shortcut to the shared folder in your My Documents folder. That way My Documents becomes the single access point for all your documents—private, shared locally, and shared on the network.

Many programs, by default, store the documents they create in a folder other than My Documents. If the program allows it, override those defaults! For example, unless you use roaming user profiles, move your Outlook Express message store to My Documents. (In Outlook Express, choose Tools, Options, Maintenance, Store Folder, Change.)

tip   **Archive your old documents in a different folder**

To keep the My Documents folder from becoming unwieldy—both in the number of folders and files you need to wade through to find the one you want and in the amount of data you must back up—use it only for documents that you're actively working with. Every month or so, move the documents you no longer use regularly to a folder (not in My Documents) named Archives (or something equally descriptive). This speeds up your backup routine considerably: your My Documents folder, which you should back up frequently, remains relatively small, and you need to back up the Archives folder only when you add files to it.

Chapter 8

Working with Recently Opened Documents

The Start menu contains an item called My Recent Documents (on the classic Start menu, its name is simply Documents) that contains shortcuts to 15 of your most recently used documents. To reopen one of these documents, simply click its name.

> **note** By default, My Recent Documents doesn't appear on the Start menu in Windows XP Home Edition. To display it, right-click the Start button, choose Properties, and click Customize. On the Advanced tab of the Customize Start Menu dialog box, select List My Most Recently Opened Documents.

Troubleshooting

Recent documents don't appear on the Start menu or on the File menu in Microsoft Office applications.

Ordinarily, documents you open are added to the My Recent Documents list on the Start menu. In addition, recent documents you open in Office applications (such as Microsoft Word and Microsoft Excel) appear at the bottom of the application's File menu, for easy reuse. You might find that documents you open are not added to either location. Furthermore, the Options dialog box settings that control this feature in Office applications is unavailable. This problem occurs when a policy prevents the creation of shortcuts to recently opened documents. The policy can be set through Group Policy (Gpedit.msc), but most people make the setting (inadvertently) through Tweak UI, a popular utility available from Microsoft. You can solve the problem—and resume adding recently opened documents to the menus—in either of two ways:

● **Use Tweak UI.** Open Tweak UI and click Explorer. In the Settings box, select Maintain Document History. For more information about Tweak UI, see "Customizing Windows XP with Tweak UI," page 327.

● **Use Group Policy.** At a command prompt, type **gpedit.msc** to open Group Policy. Navigate to User Configuration\AdministrativeTemplates\Start Menu And Taskbar. In the details pane, double-click Do Not Keep History Of Recently Opened Documents. Select Disabled and then click OK. (Group Policy is not available in Windows XP Home Edition.)

If your purpose in setting the policy initially was to prevent the appearance of recent documents on the Start menu but you want recent documents listed on your applications' File menus, make the policy change explained above. Then remove the Recent Documents menu from the Start menu. For details, see "Removing the Recent Documents Menu" on page 290.

Removing Items from the Documents Menu

You can prune individual items from the My Recent Documents menu in the same way that you remove items from other parts of the Start menu: right-click an item and choose Delete from the shortcut menu. Notice when you remove an item in this way, however, that My Recent Documents still contains 15 items! That's because the My Recent Documents menu reflects the contents of a hidden folder called Recent, which is stored as part of your user profile. Windows keeps shortcuts to all recently used documents in the %UserProfile%\Recent folder but displays only the most recent 15 on the My Recent Documents menu.

To clear the whole menu, including the backup supply of shortcuts, follow these steps:

1 Right-click the Start button, choose Properties, and click Customize.

2 If you're using the default Start menu, click the Advanced tab and click Clear List. If you're using the classic Start menu, click the Clear button.

Note that you can't add items to the My Recent Documents menu by making direct additions to the Recent folder. For the purposes of building this menu, Windows simply ignores anything in the Recent folder that it didn't put there itself. When you use the Clear List command, however, *everything* in the Recent folder is deleted, no matter how it got there.

If you have privacy concerns about the recently opened documents list—specifically, the ability of others to snoop in your Recent folder after you log off to see what you've been up to—you'll want to enable a policy that clears the list automatically each time you log off. Follow these steps:

1 At a command prompt, type **gpedit.msc** to open Group Policy.

2 Open User Configuration\Administrative Templates\Start Menu And Taskbar.

3 Double-click the Clear History Of Recently Opened Documents On Exit policy.

4 On the Setting tab, select Enabled.

> **note** Changes you make with Group Policy affect all users on your computer. Group Policy is not available in Windows XP Home Edition. However, you can use Tweak UI, in either Windows XP Professional or Windows XP Home Edition, to clear your document history on exit. (Click Explorer, then select Clear Document History On Exit). Note that this Tweak UI setting affects the current user only. For more information about Tweak UI, see "Customizing Windows XP with Tweak UI," page 327.

Removing the Recent Documents Menu

If you find that you have no use for the list of recently opened documents, you can remove it from the Start menu. The method you use depends on which Start menu you use, and whether you're working with Windows XP Professional or Windows XP Home Edition.

- To remove My Recent Documents from the default Start menu, in either edition of Windows XP, right-click the Start button, choose Properties, and click Customize. On the Advanced tab of the Customize Start Menu dialog box, clear the List My Most Recently Opened Documents check box. This change affects only the default Start menu.

- In Windows XP Professional, you can remove the Documents menu from the classic Start menu, by using Group Policy. At a command prompt, type **gpedit.msc** to start Group Policy. Open User Configuration\Administrative Templates\Start Menu And Taskbar. Double-click Remove Documents Menu From Start Menu and select Enabled. This change affects the default Start menu as well as the classic Start menu.

- To remove the Documents menu from the classic Start menu in Windows XP Home Edition, you need Tweak UI. In Tweak UI, click Explorer, and then clear Allow Recent Documents On Start Menu. If necessary to make the change take effect, either log off and log back on or switch to the default Start menu and then back to the classic Start menu. For more information about Tweak UI, see "Customizing Windows XP with Tweak UI," page 327.

> **note** Removing the list of recently opened documents from the Start menu does not remove existing shortcuts from the Recent folder, nor does it prevent the creation of new shortcuts. Therefore, if you reenable the list's appearance on the Start menu, the list will be up to date. Also note that disabling the My Recent Documents menu via Tweak UI removes the Recent Documents section from the Advanced tab of the Customize Start Menu dialog box. To reinstate My Recent Documents after you have taken this step, you must first return to Tweak UI and select Allow Recent Documents On Start Menu. Then go back to the Advanced tab of the Customize Start Menu dialog box and select List My Most Recently Opened Documents.

Customizing the Start Menu with Shortcuts to Other Folders

In addition to shortcuts to programs and recently opened documents, both versions of the Start menu provide links to a handful of other common folders and destinations. But the links that appear by default are only a compact subset of the available links.

You can add others or delete the ones you don't want. In addition, you can set up certain Start menu items as cascading menus. Instead of opening Control Panel in its own window and then double-clicking one of its icons, for example, you can configure it as a cascading menu with its utilities available as a submenu of the Start menu, as shown in Figure 8-8.

Figure 8-8. Control Panel is one of several items that can be set up as a cascading menu.

newfeature!

The following items can be included or excluded as top-level items on the default Start menu, at your option:

- Links to folders and files

  - Favorites

  - My Computer

  - My Documents

  - My Music

  - My Network Places

  - My Pictures

- Settings and configuration items

  - Administrative Tools

  - Control Panel

Chapter 8

■ Network Connections

■ Printers And Faxes

● Links to other tasks

■ Help And Support

■ Run

■ Search

To select the items you want to appear and, in some cases, specify whether you want a link or a cascading menu, right-click the Start button and choose Properties to open Taskbar And Start Menu Properties. Click Customize and then click the Advanced tab. Make your selections in the Start Menu Items box, shown in Figure 8-9.

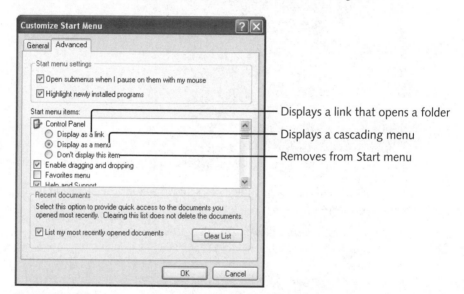

Figure 8-9. You can make your Start menu as comprehensive or Spartan as you like.

If you use the classic Start menu, your choices are similar, yet fewer. The Customize Classic Start Menu dialog box (right-click the Start button, choose Properties, and click Customize) lets you choose three optional items:

● Administrative Tools

● Favorites

● Run

In addition, the dialog boxes include several "expand" check boxes, which display the following items as cascading menus:

- Control Panel (on the Settings menu)

- My Documents (on the Documents menu)

- My Pictures (on the Documents menu)

- Network Connections (on the Settings menu)

- Printers And Faxes (on the Settings menu)

Managing Desktop Clutter

Usability studies at Microsoft show that desktop clutter—accumulated icons from various program installations, stored documents, and from Windows itself—stifles productivity. The designers of Windows XP have taken to heart those study results and produced a desktop that, by default, contains only a single desktop icon (Recycle Bin). Key system icons are now located where they're more accessible, on the Start menu. The Desktop Cleanup Wizard automates the process of relocating other seldom-used desktop icons. But in the words of a Windows XP product manager, "The desktop is yours to abuse as you see fit." Windows XP makes it easier to restore system icons to the desktop should you decide that location works best for you.

With a desktop that's no longer littered with icons, you might want to choose a more interesting background or put some useful Web content on your desktop. The following sections describe these desktop-management options in detail.

newfeature! Controlling Desktop Icons

The desktop icons that appear by default depend upon your choice of Start menu. With the default menu, you get only a Recycle Bin icon. Switching to the classic menu adds icons for My Documents, My Computer, My Network Places, and Internet Explorer. (If you upgraded from an earlier version of Windows or migrated from another computer using the File And Settings Transfer Wizard, your desktop might have additional icons.)

To control which of these system icons appears on your desktop, follow these steps:

1 Right-click an unoccupied area of the desktop and choose Properties. Alternatively, open Display (in the Appearance And Themes category) in Control Panel. Either action opens the Display Properties dialog box.

2 In Display Properties, click the Desktop tab and then click Customize Desktop.

3 In the Desktop Icons section of the General tab, select the items you want to appear.

While you've got the Desktop Items dialog box open, you might want to examine its other features:

● If you're really into customization, you can change the icon used for any of the system folders displayed in the center of the dialog box. If you upgraded from Windows 98, you'll find an interesting collection of icons in your %ProgramFiles%\Plus!\Themes folder. A clean installation of Windows XP doesn't have too many interesting alternatives (you might, however, want to check the hodgepodge of icons in %SystemRoot%\System32\Shell32.dll), but the capability exists nonetheless.

> **note** If you're interested in creating your own icons for the desktop or for use elsewhere in Windows, you'll find an excellent description of the process on the Internet at *http://msdn.microsoft.com/library/en-us/dnwxp/html/winxpicons.asp*.

● A more interesting option is the Desktop Cleanup Wizard. This wizard, which you invoke by clicking Clean Desktop Now, displays a list of all the shortcuts on your desktop, along with the date each shortcut was last used, as shown in Figure 8-10. You select the items you no longer need to have on your desktop, and the wizard moves the selected items to a desktop folder it creates named Unused Desktop Shortcuts. Your seldom-used shortcuts are still available; you just need to dig into the folder to use them instead of searching for them on the desktop. You should delete shortcuts you'll never need again. That's a task

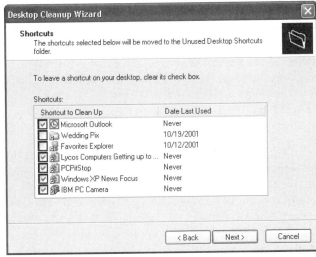

Figure 8-10. The wizard selects shortcuts that haven't been used in a long time (or ever), but you can override its choices on this page.

you'll need to do manually; Windows doesn't presume to know which ones can be safely deleted altogether.

InsideOut

If you want the ultimate clean desktop, you have the following options:

- You can toggle the display of all desktop icons in one fell swoop by right-clicking the desktop and choosing Arrange Icons By, Show Desktop Icons.

- In Windows XP Professional, you can remove the Recycle Bin icon—but you must use a policy to do so. At a command prompt, type **gpedit.msc** to open Group Policy. Open User Configuration\Administrative Templates\Desktop. Double-click the Remove Recycle Bin Icon From Desktop policy and select Enabled. Your deleted files continue to collect in the Recycle Bin (depending on your Recycle Bin settings, of course), but its icon is no longer available on the desktop or in Windows Explorer. Note that, like all local group policies, settings you make here affect all users of your computer. In the Desktop policy folder, you'll notice policies that remove other desktop items. Policy settings override any settings a user makes in the Desktop Items dialog box. For more information about policies, see Appendix E, "Group Policy."

- In either edition of Windows XP, you can use Tweak UI to enable or disable the display of icons for Internet Explorer, My Computer, My Documents, My Network Places, and Recycle Bin. Click Desktop, and then select or clear check boxes as desired. For more information about Tweak UI, see "Customizing Windows XP with Tweak UI," page 327.

After you've populated your desktop with icons, you might want to control the arrangement of those icons. Right-clicking the desktop and choosing Arrange Icons By produces a submenu with a number of useful commands. The Name, Size, Type, Modified, Auto Arrange, and Align To Grid commands work just as they do in Windows Explorer to sort and lay out your icons. (For details, see "Sorting and Grouping Icons," page 428.) Show Desktop Icons hides or displays all desktop icons. The last two commands on the menu—Lock Web Items On The Desktop and Run Desktop Cleanup Wizard—provide handy shortcuts to options in the Desktop Items dialog box.

As an ordinary folder, the desktop, of course, can store much more than system icons and program shortcuts. If you're not careful, it can become a repository for all manner of documents, downloaded files, shortcuts, and so on. Although it's nice to have some such items in this convenient location, you'll probably want to avoid the clutter created by injudicious use of the desktop as a storage depot. Instead, use My Documents and its subfolders, which provide a good way to organize your documents and, in fact, are just as accessible.

InsideOut

The Desktop Items dialog box includes a check box that allows you to schedule the Desktop Cleanup Wizard every 60 days. (The wizard itself doesn't run automatically. Instead, at the designated schedule interval, a reminder appears if your desktop has any unused shortcuts. Clicking the reminder starts the wizard.) Selecting the check box is the easiest way to ensure that you run the wizard periodically. But you're not stuck with a 60-day recurrence. To have the wizard reminder appear more or less frequently, open Registry Editor and navigate to HKCU\Software\Microsoft\Windows\CurrentVersion\Explorer\Desktop\CleanupWiz. Double-click the Days Between Clean Up value, select the Decimal option, and enter the number of days between reminders. (If the value doesn't exist, create a new DWORD value named Days Between Clean Up.)

Troubleshooting

When you delete a desktop item it also disappears from other users' desktops.

The items that appear on your desktop (aside from the My Documents, My Computer, My Network Places, and Internet Explorer icons) come from two sources: %UserProfile%\Desktop (your own profile) and %AllUsersProfile%\Desktop (the All Users profile). Items in the latter folder appear on the desktop of everyone who uses your computer. Ordinarily, items that you place on your desktop are stored as part of your profile. But the setup routines for some programs add a shortcut to the All Users

Chapter 8

desktop so that everyone can access the program. When you delete a desktop item, if it's stored in the All Users profile, your deletion affects everyone's desktop—not just your own. Windows gives no indication that your change might affect others, nor is there any visual indication of an item's actual location. Before you delete an item from your desktop—whether manually or with the Desktop Cleanup Wizard—you might want to confirm its location. Right-click its icon and choose Properties. On the General tab, see whether the Location field shows All Users or your own user name.

To recover shared items that you've already deleted, move them from your Unused Desktop Shortcuts folder to %AllUsersProfile%\Desktop (if you used the Desktop Cleanup Wizard to remove them) or restore them from your Recycle Bin (if you deleted them manually). To remove a shortcut from your desktop but keep it on others, you'll need to copy it to the Desktop folder in each user's profile and then delete it from the All Users profile.

Making Desktop Icons Easier to See

If your vision is impaired or if you use a high display resolution on a small monitor, you might find it difficult to see desktop icons or the label that appears below each one.

To change the size of the icons, right-click the desktop, choose Properties, click the Appearance tab, and click Effects. In the Effects dialog box, select Use Large Icons. For more precise control of icon size, on the Appearance tab of the Display Properties dialog box, click Advanced. In the Advanced Appearance dialog box, shown in Figure 8-11,

Figure 8-11. If your icon settings go too far afield, you can return to the default settings shown here.

select Icon in the Item box. Then adjust the size of the icon (in pixels) and the text below the icon. If you make significant changes from the default settings, you might also need to adjust the space between icons so they don't overlap. In the Item box, select Icon Spacing (Horizontal) and change the size; repeat with Icon Spacing (Vertical).

> **note** Whether you use the Effects dialog box or the Advanced Appearance dialog box to modify the icon size, your change affects Icons view in Windows Explorer as well as desktop icons.

Your difficulty in reading icon labels might be resolved by disabling a particular visual effect instead of modifying their size. To find out, follow these steps:

1 Right-click My Computer and choose Properties. (Alternatively, open System in Control Panel's Performance And Maintenance category.)

2 In the System Properties dialog box, click the Advanced tab and then, under Performance, click Settings. This opens the Performance Options dialog box.

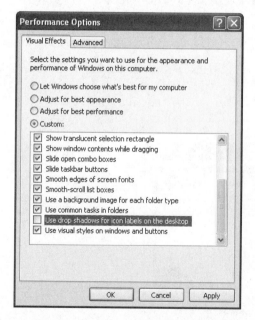

3 On the Visual Effects tab, clear the Use Drop Shadows For Icon Labels On The Desktop check box.

With this option disabled, icon labels appear on a solid rectangular background, which provides better contrast (as well as giving your computer a tiny performance boost).

Changing the Background

You can perk up any desktop with a background image. You can use a small image repeated (*tiled*) to fill the desktop, a centered image, or an image stretched to cover the entire desktop. Your background can be supplied by a graphics file in any of several common formats: bitmap (.bmp or .dib extension), Graphics Interchange Format (.gif), Joint Photographic Experts Group (.jpg or .jpeg), or Portable Network Graphics (.png). Alternatively, you can drape your desktop with a Hypertext Markup Language (HTML) file stored on your computer or on a network drive, complete with live links. (HTML is the programming language used to encode Web pages.)

To select a background, right-click the desktop, choose Properties from the shortcut menu, and click the Desktop tab. This takes you to the dialog box shown in Figure 8-12.

Figure 8-12. The Desktop tab in the Display Properties dialog box lets you use a picture or an HTML page as your desktop background.

Select an image file from the Background list, or click the Browse button to find an HTML file or an image that's not in the list. (The list initially includes image files from your My Pictures folder, %SystemRoot%, and %SystemRoot%\Web\Wallpaper.) If you don't want a background image, select (None), which appears at the top of the list.

After choosing an image file, you can choose either Center, Tile, or Stretch from the Position list. If you choose Center, the color indicated in the Color box surrounds the image if it's not big enough to fill the screen. If you choose Tile, your image is repeated as often as needed to fill the screen. If you choose Stretch, Windows resizes your image to fit the screen (in the process possibly distorting it beyond recognition).

InsideOut

If more than one monitor is connected to your computer, you might want to have a different background image appear on each monitor. You can't do that with an ordinary desktop background—the type you select on the Desktop tab. If you use the Desktop tab to make your selection, Windows repeats the image on each monitor. However, you can achieve the desired effect by placing an image as a Web item on each monitor. Then click each Web item's maximize button, or open its Control menu and choose Cover The Desktop. (This command, in fact, causes the image to cover the monitor, not the entire desktop.) For information about Web items, see "Displaying Web Content on Your Desktop" on the facing page.

note If you choose an HTML file, it covers the entire desktop except for the space occupied by the taskbar and any other desktop toolbars. Any desktop icons you have displayed overlay the HTML document. An HTML document you display this way won't have any scroll bars. Therefore, an HTML file to be used as your desktop background should be designed so that the entire page fits on your screen and so that its text and images don't interfere with your desktop icons. If you want an HTML document on your desktop but you don't want these constraints, use the procedures in the following section, "Displaying Web Content on Your Desktop."

InsideOut

You might find it useful to have a visual indication of which version of Windows you're currently running, particularly if you administer several computers or if you boot among several operating systems on your own computer. A minor change to the registry displays this information in the lower right corner of your desktop. To enable this feature, use Registry Editor to navigate to the HKCU\Control Panel\Desktop key. Open the PaintDesktopVersion value and set it to 1. To remove the text, change the value back to 0. You'll need to log off and back on for the change to take effect. (If you don't see the version number when PaintDesktopVersion is set to 1, right-click the desktop, choose Properties, click the Desktop tab, and click Customize Desktop. On the Web tab of the Desktop Items dialog box, clear Lock Desktop Items.)

Note that if you're using an evaluation version of Windows, this version information is always displayed on the desktop—regardless of the setting of this registry value—as a reminder that you're using a version that will expire after a period of time.

An alternative method for applying an image to the background exists for pictures stored on your computer and for pictures on Web pages.

newfeature!

- **Windows Explorer.** Any image stored in a picture folder can be applied to the background by selecting it and then clicking Set As Desktop Background in the Picture Tasks section of the task pane. Alternatively, right-click the image and choose Set As Desktop Background. (A picture folder is one to which the Pictures or Photo Albums template has been applied using the Customize tab in the folder's properties dialog box.)

- **Internet Explorer.** If you see an image on a Web page that you'd like to use as your desktop background, right-click the image and choose Set As Background.

InsideOut

Earlier versions of Windows offered a different type of background: patterns. A pattern is a small bitmapped image that is repeated over the entire screen. It's only two colors, but it lets you dress up the display for a minimum amount of memory. Support for patterns is now gone from the Display Properties dialog box, but you can implement them through the registry by following these steps:

1 Start Registry Editor and open HKCU\Control Panel\Patterns.

2 Find the value for the pattern you want, double-click the value, and copy its data.

3 Open HKCU\Control Panel\Desktop and create a new string value named Pattern.

4 Double-click the Pattern value and paste the value data you copied in step 2.

5 On the Desktop tab of the Display Properties dialog box, select (None) as the background.

6 Log off and log back on.

Displaying Web Content on Your Desktop

You can choose to display Web content on your desktop. The Web content—sometimes called Active Desktop items—can include items such as stock or news tickers that can be updated from the Internet automatically at scheduled times. Your desktop can also contain an HTML document, complete with links to other HTML documents.

Figure 8-13 on the next page shows a desktop with two Web items—a stock market ticker and a webcam image. These items are updated periodically from the Internet.

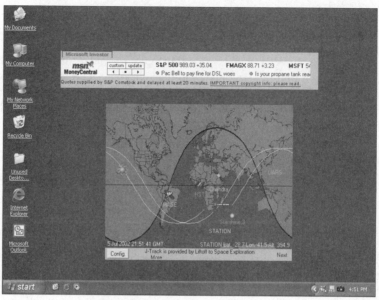

Figure 8-13. This stock market ticker and webcam image provide updated information.

To add Web content to your desktop, follow these steps:

1 Right-click the desktop, choose Properties, click the Desktop tab, and click Customize Desktop.

2 In the Desktop Items dialog box, click the Web tab and then click New. The New Desktop Item dialog box appears.

From this dialog box, you have three choices:

■ If you know the Uniform Resource Locator (*URL*—an item's address on the Internet or your intranet) of the item you want to add, type it in the Location box and click OK.

302

■ If you want to display a local file (such as a picture or an HTML document) or the target of an Internet shortcut, click Browse and navigate to the item you want.

■ Click Visit Gallery to display the Desktop Gallery Web site. (When you go to this page, you might see a security warning window asking whether you want to download an ActiveX control. Go ahead and click Yes if you see this message.) The Desktop Gallery Web site provides a list of Web sites that offer content designed expressly for display on your desktop. The Web sites made available via Microsoft's Desktop Gallery are good ones to try because their content has been tailored for desktop display. But you can display any Web site's contents on your desktop.

3 After you click OK in the New Desktop Item dialog box or add an item from the Desktop Gallery, you might be asked to confirm that you want to add the item to your desktop. After you confirm, you'll see a dialog box that looks something like this.

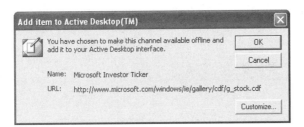

To add the item to your desktop and accept the vendor's default update schedule, simply click OK. If you want to set up your own schedule, click Customize. This starts the Offline Favorite Wizard, which lets you specify the schedule for updating the content.

---

tip **Display folder contents on your desktop**

Displaying a folder as a desktop item provides convenient access to a folder's contents because it's always on the desktop. You can choose any view available in Windows Explorer, and the desktop item displays any folder customization you've created. To add a folder to your desktop, type the complete path of the folder you want to display in the Location text box in the New Desktop Item dialog box. (This is one place where you can't use environment variables like %UserProfile%.)

After your Web content has arrived on your desktop, you can interact with it exactly as you would if you were working within a Web browser. When you click a link, Windows activates your browser, connects to the Internet if you're not already online, and then performs the action stipulated by that link.

> **tip**   **Add Web content to your desktop quickly**
>
> If you want to add an image (such as a webcam image) from a Web page to your desktop, the easiest way to do so is to right-click the image and choose Set As Desktop Item.
>
> You can turn any Web page or link into desktop Web content directly from Internet Explorer. To use the current page, right-drag the icon from the Address bar to the desktop, and then choose Create Active Desktop Items Here from the shortcut menu. To use the target of a link, right-drag the link from your browser window to the desktop.

Moving and Sizing Web Content

Web items displayed on your desktop are windows, albeit unconventional ones. You can move them around, change their sizes, and close them. You can't minimize them, however. You can lock them in place so that they can't be moved or resized.

To move one of these windows, follow these steps:

1   Make sure the windows aren't locked in place. Right-click the desktop and choose Arrange Icons By. If a check mark appears by Lock Web Items On Desktop, choose the command to clear the check mark.

2   Move your mouse pointer somewhere near the window's top edge and pause there.

After a moment, a border pops up from the top edge.

3   Drag this border to move the window.

To change a window's size, point to one of the window's borders. When your mouse pointer changes to a two-headed arrow, drag.

The icons in the top border are similar in operation to the icons in an ordinary window's title bar.

▾	Displays the Control menu
☐	Expands window to cover the entire desktop (or the current screen if you're using multiple monitors)
◻	Expands window to cover the entire desktop except for a resizable area at the left side, where desktop icons appear
▣	Restores window to normal size
✕	Closes window

Updating Web Content

Web content on your desktop doesn't update continuously; it updates only at scheduled intervals and when you request an update. To update all items immediately, open Display Properties, select the Desktop tab, click Customize Desktop, and then click Synchronize. Alternatively, open the Start menu and choose All Programs, Accessories, Synchronize; in the Items To Synchronize dialog box, select one or more items and click Synchronize. To update a single item, point to the top edge of the item, click the down arrow that appears in the upper left corner to open the Control menu, and choose Synchronize.

To change an item's update schedule, visit its properties dialog box. Here are some ways to get there:

- Point to the top edge of the item, click the down arrow that appears in the upper left corner to open the Control menu, and choose Properties. (This method is available only when the Lock Desktop Items check box isn't selected.)

- Right-click the desktop, choose Properties, and click Desktop, Customize Desktop, Web. In the Desktop Items dialog box that appears, select the item whose schedule you want to change and click the Properties button.

- On the Start menu, point to All Programs, Accessories, and then choose Synchronize. Select the item whose schedule you want to change and click the Properties button.

> **tip** To see when an item was last updated, choose Synchronize from the Accessories folder of the Start menu. In the Last Updated column, you'll find the date and time of the most recent update for each item.

Removing Web Content from Your Desktop

What do you do when you're tired of looking at that news ticker, weather map, or other desktop item? You can suppress its display by simply closing it, which you can do in any of the following ways:

● Point to the top edge of the Web item and then click the Close button (the X icon that appears in the upper right corner). (This method is available only when the Lock Desktop Items check box isn't selected.)

● Point to the top edge of the item and then choose Close from the Control menu that appears when you click the down arrow in the upper left corner of the border. (This method is available only when the Lock Desktop Items check box isn't selected.)

● In the Desktop Items dialog box, click the Web tab and then clear the check box next to the window name. (Select the check box to reopen the window.)

InsideOut

Throughout this chapter, we explain lots of options, but offer few specific recommendations. That's because every user's needs and tastes are different. The authors of this book each have different desktop layouts, and we change them occasionally as requirements or whims move us. In case you're wondering how we set up our own systems, here's the desktop of one of our computers.

- After having the taskbar on the right side for many months, we've moved it back to the bottom of the screen, and it's two buttons high. This allows room for plenty of taskbar buttons—this computer typically has 10–15 open windows—and it makes room for a dozen Quick Launch buttons. The extra height also makes room for the complete date and time to appear in the notification area.

- The Quick Launch bar is on the taskbar, and it's sized to just accommodate buttons for 12 frequently used tasks. Though some users prefer shortcut keys or a carefully arranged Start menu—and many dislike the clutter imposed by the Quick Launch bar—it works well for us.

- The Desktop toolbar appears as just a title at the right end of the taskbar. Because My Computer and My Documents icons are on the desktop, clicking the double-arrow yields a cascading menu of all documents and other files on the system.

- The Address toolbar—which we use often—is docked to the top of the screen. It's rolled down in the preceding illustration, but it's set to auto-hide.

- The desktop is littered with icons. (We've been meaning to clean it up, honest.)

- We've customized the notification area to always show the new-mail icon and a couple of others that we use regularly. The rest are hidden—some permanently, others when inactive.

- We use the new-style Start menu (not shown in the illustration), but have removed several items (My Pictures, My Music, and so on) that we don't use and added a few others (such as Favorites).

To meet the publishing requirements of this book, we reduced the resolution to 800×600 for this illustration. Ordinarily, we run at 1152×864. At that resolution, the toolbar, taskbar, icons, and even the webcam picture of Yosemite's Half Dome occupy much less relative space than this illustration suggests. Nonetheless, the screen is quite cluttered.

Note that most of these settings on this heavily used system are wildly different from the austere default Windows settings. (They're probably also wildly different from what you would choose!) Don't be afraid to experiment.

Windows continues to update a Web item even if it's not being displayed. To prevent further updates, open the Desktop Items dialog box. Select the item, click Properties, and then clear the Make This Page Available Offline check box on the Web Document tab.

If you want to permanently delete an item, click the Web tab in the Desktop Items dialog box. Select the item you want to delete and then click Delete.

newfeature!
Changing Colors, Fonts, and Visual Effects

One of the most talked-about features in Windows XP is its bright (some say cartoonish) new look. The new visual style—which includes rounded corners on windows and buttons, new desktop icons, bright colors, and more legible fonts—is one part of a theme that was dubbed Luna during its development. A desktop *theme* is a predefined set of colors, fonts, sounds, and other elements. Themes are not new to Windows, of course; they've been around since Microsoft Plus! was released for Windows 95. But Windows XP implements themes through a new visual styles engine that allows much greater customization. Instead of merely changing the color of a title bar, theme developers can change its texture, pattern, and shape!

Out of the box, Windows XP includes two distinct visual styles:

- **Windows XP style.** This is the new style that you see in illustrations throughout this book.

- **Windows classic style.** This style, marked by rigidly rectangular windows and solid colors, is the style that appears in Windows 95/98/Me and Windows NT/2000.

> **note** Certain windows—notably command prompt windows and windows for some earlier programs—don't conform to the new Windows XP style. Instead, they have square borders, along with title bar buttons, scroll bars, and other elements that follow the Windows classic style. That's because they run outside the control of the Themes service. It's perfectly normal—and unchangeable.

To select a theme based on one of these visual styles, open Display Properties, shown in Figure 8-14. You can get there by right-clicking the desktop and choosing Properties, or by choosing Display in Control Panel's Appearance And Themes category. Make your selection in the Theme box.

Both styles permit considerable customization. You can create your own theme by making changes to the items shown in Table 8-2. When you have everything set the way you like, return to the Themes tab in Display Properties and click Save As. Themes you save in My Documents or in %SystemRoot%\Resources\Themes appear on the Theme list.

> **tip** **Use ClearType**
>
> ClearType can sharpen text for easier reading. It's intended for use on LCD monitors, but it improves text appearance on some CRT displays too. Try it; if you don't like it, switch back. To enable ClearType, open Display Properties and click Appearance, Effects. Then select Use The Following Method To Smooth Edges Of Screen Fonts and click ClearType in the box below. You can also try the Standard setting, designed for CRT users. For information about how ClearType works, visit *http://grc.com/cleartype.htm*.

308

Figure 8-14. The bulk of the Themes tab is devoted to showing a preview of the selected theme.

Table 8-2. **Theme Components You Can Change**

Component	How to Change
Background	In Display Properties, click the Desktop tab and specify Background, Position, and Color.
Colors	In Display Properties, click the Appearance tab and select a Color Scheme. If none of the predefined schemes pleases your eye, click Advanced, where you can select your own color for each item. Note that the list of color schemes changes depending on your choice of Windows And Buttons style. Note also that many choices you make in the Advanced Appearance dialog box (such as the color of the active title bar) have no effect on ordinary windows if you choose the Windows XP visual style.
Fonts	In Display Properties, click the Appearance tab and select a Font Size. If you want to use a different font or size, click Advanced, where you can select your own font for each item that displays text.

(continued)

Table 8-2. *(continued)*

Component	How to Change
Icons for My Computer, My Documents, My Network Places, and Recycle Bin	In Display Properties, click Desktop, Customize Desktop and select images for the desktop icons. Note that a theme doesn't record your choices of which icons appear on the desktop; it includes only your choice of icon for each item.
Mouse pointers	In Mouse Properties (open Mouse in Control Panel's Printers And Other Hardware category), click the Pointers tab and select individual pointers or a preset scheme.
Screen saver	In Display Properties, click the Screen Saver tab and select a screen saver.
Sounds	In Sounds And Audio Devices Properties (in Control Panel's Sounds, Speech, And Audio Devices category), click the Sounds tab and then select sounds for various events.
Visual style	In Display Properties, click the Appearance tab and select a Windows And Buttons style.

tip If you come up with a combination of sights and sounds that you particularly like, be sure to save it. If you don't, your changes are discarded when you select another theme.

Modifying the Predefined Color Schemes

To modify one of the supplied color schemes (a group of settings that also includes fonts and sizes of certain interface elements), open Display Properties and click the Appearance tab, shown in Figure 8-15. In the Windows And Buttons box, select a visual style and then select a scheme in the Color Scheme box.

Click Advanced to display the Advanced Appearance dialog box, shown in Figure 8-11 on page 297. In the sample window, click the screen element you want to change. Then use the boxes and buttons at the bottom of the dialog box to make your color, font, and size selections. For title bars, you can specify two colors; Windows creates a gradation from Color 1 (at the left end of the title bar) to Color 2 (at the right end). The Item list includes some items that don't appear in the sample window, so you might want to review it in its entirety before you move on.

Figure 8-15. The available color schemes depend on your choice of visual style in the Windows And Buttons box.

The Color button for each item opens a selection of 20 standard colors. If you don't see the one you're looking for, click the Other button. Windows then displays a Color dialog box, as shown in Figure 8-16. Should you fail to find exactly the color you want in the Basic Colors palette, you can define your own custom colors. Change the color that

Figure 8-16. If you know a color's RGB specification, you can enter the values directly in the Red, Green, and Blue boxes.

appears in the Color|Solid box, either by adjusting the positions of the hue/saturation crosshair and the luminosity arrow or by specifying numeric values. When you have the color you want, click Add To Custom Colors. If you want to replace an existing custom color, select it before you specify your new color.

> **note** If you select Windows XP Style in the Windows And Buttons box on the Appearance tab, some settings you make in the Advanced Appearance dialog box will have no effect on most windows. Though it's bound to cause some confusion, this is intentional. By design, the Windows XP visual style settings override some of these settings. How do you know which settings and which windows? Experiment. If you manage to make your screen illegible, you can always return to one of the original themes or color schemes.

Troubleshooting

Windows and buttons have square corners, even with the Windows XP theme selected.

If your display looks more like one from an earlier version of windows—for example, the windows and buttons don't have round corners, the Close button doesn't stand out from other title bar buttons, and the Start button doesn't stand out on the taskbar—the first thing to check is that Windows XP Style is selected in the Windows And Buttons box on the Appearance tab of Display Properties. But what if the Windows XP Style choice isn't available? Visual styles are implemented by the Themes service. If the service isn't running, Windows reverts to the classic Windows styles, which don't rely on the Themes service.

To restore the Windows XP styles, open the Services console (at a command prompt, type **services.msc**), select Themes in the right pane, and then click the Start link on the Extended tab or the Start Service button on the toolbar.

If that doesn't fix the problem, right-click My Computer and choose Properties to open System Properties. Click the Advanced tab and then click Settings under Performance. On the Visual Effects tab, select Use Visual Styles On Windows And Buttons (the last item in the Custom box).

Installing Additional Themes

If you click the Theme box on the Themes tab of Display Properties, near the bottom of the list you'll find the item More Themes Online. This is a link that takes you to *www.microsoft.com/windows/plus*, a site where you can read about, sample, and buy

312

Plus! for Windows XP. Priced at $29.95, Plus! includes four additional themes: Aquarium, da Vinci, Nature, and Space—along with various other attractions. The four Plus! themes, like their predecessors in earlier Plus! editions, supply thematically related wallpaper, animated pointers, sound schemes, and screen savers.

Figure 8-17 provides a look at the wallpaper, color scheme, and Normal Select pointer (note the space-shuttle image resting on the OK button) for the Space theme. Unfortunately, a silent, motionless, black-and-white screen shot can't begin to convey the full effect of this theme or any of the others that come with Plus! The stunning three-dimensional graphics of the Plus! screen savers, in particular, have to be seen to be appreciated. The package includes eight such screen savers, four of which are not attached to themes. You can, of course, apply any of the screen savers without opting for any of the related thematic material.

Figure 8-17. Microsoft's Plus! package comes with four new themes: Space (shown here), Nature, da Vinci, and Aquarium.

As additional inducement for you to part with $29.95, Plus! provides three games and assorted other media-oriented goodies: a voice interface for Windows Media Player, a CD label creator, a tool for creating custom playlists in Windows Media Player, and a utility for converting MP3 files to WMA. Plus! runs in both editions of Windows XP. Minimum requirements are a 500 MHz processor (750 MHz recommended), 64 MB of memory (128 MB recommended), and 300 MB of hard disk space. To install the screen savers and games, you need a 3-D graphics accelerator card with at least 16 MB of memory.

Skinning Windows XP

Prior to the initial release of Windows XP, rumors were flying that Microsoft was going to make the newest version of the operating system completely "skinnable"—that is, that users would be able to overhaul the appearance and behavior of windows, menus, and controls in ways that go well beyond switching wallpaper and color schemes. In the end, however, in the interest of maintaining consistency and relative simplicity, Microsoft chose not to integrate skinning features into Windows XP, but instead to provide "hooks" for skinning products from third parties.

The most widely used of such products is WindowBlinds, from Stardock. Priced at $19.95, WindowBlinds is one component of a suite of customizing products called Object Desktop ($49.95). If your taste for novelty goes way beyond what you can do with the native Windows XP interface, you'll want to investigate WindowBlinds and Object Desktop—at *www.stardock.com*. With a complete set of skinning tools, you'll be able to do such things as reposition buttons and controls, add rollup buttons to windows (buttons that shrink windows into their title bars instead of collapsing them onto the taskbar), add background images to the Start menu—and much, much more.

Stardock also maintains a Web site (*www.wincustomize.com*) where users can upload their latest creations and download those of fellow skinners. Figure 8-18 shows a sample skin downloaded from wincustomize.com.

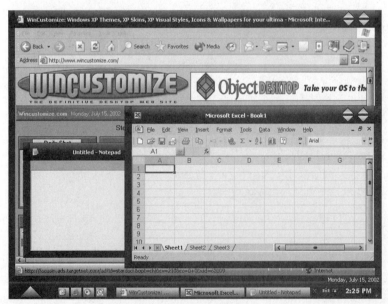

Figure 8-18. This WindowBlinds skin, downloaded from *www.wincustomize.com*, features bright blue pinstriped window borders, rollup buttons, a close button where the control menu normally resides, and a black-and-white gradient-filled Start menu button that doesn't say "Start."

Going Retro: Reverting to Windows 2000 (or Earlier)

You might decide that the new look of Windows is not for you. Because old habits die hard, you might find it easier for yourself (or other users in your organization) to stay with the familiar interface of earlier Windows versions. To do that, you really need to change only two settings:

1 In Display Properties, click the Themes tab and select Windows Classic in the Theme box. (Optionally, you can select your favorite color scheme on the Appearance tab.)

2 In Taskbar And Start Menu Properties, click the Start Menu tab and select Classic Start Menu. (If you want to go all the way, click the Taskbar tab and clear Group Similar Taskbar Buttons and Hide Inactive Icons.)

Before you do this, however, try the new interface for a while. You might find the improvements helpful. If you are really sure you want to recreate the look and feel of earlier versions of Windows, you should probably take the following additional steps:

1 Open User Accounts in Control Panel, click Change The Way Users Log On Or Off, and clear Use The Welcome Screen.

(continued)

Going Retro: Reverting to Windows 2000 (or Earlier)   *(continued)*

2 Right-click My Computer and choose Properties. In the Performance section of the Advanced tab of the System Properties dialog box, click Settings. Then select Adjust For Best Performance.

3 Run Services.msc, double-click Themes, change Startup Type to Manual, and click Stop.

If your goal is to recreate the Windows 2000 ambience, you won't need to have the Themes service running. Stopping the service will make some additional memory available to your system.

Customizing Visual Effects for Better Performance

Before you leave the topic of colors, fonts, and visual effects, you might want to consider what impact these snazzy visual effects have on performance. With a late-model, high-powered computer, you're not likely to notice any slowdown. But if you're using a computer that's more than a few years old, you can probably improve its performance by eliminating some visual effects. It's nice that menus fade in and fade out, that windows perceptibly shrink to the taskbar when minimized, and so on. But it is just eye candy, after all, and it's not worth slowing your computing experience for.

You'll find a collection of performance-related settings for visual effects by following these steps:

1 Right-click My Computer (on the Start menu, the desktop, or in a Windows Explorer window) and choose Properties to open the System Properties dialog box. Alternatively, open System in Control Panel (Performance And Maintenance category).

2 Click the Advanced tab and then click Settings under Performance. The Performance Options dialog box appears.

Customizing the Taskbar

The taskbar houses the Start button, the notification area, and a button for each running program. You can use these task buttons to switch from one running program to another. You can also click a task button to minimize an open window or to reopen a minimized one. Your taskbar might also hold one or more toolbars—collections of icons that let you start programs quickly.

For information about toolbars, see "Using the Quick Launch Bar and Other Desktop Toolbars," page 281.

Changing the Taskbar's Size and Appearance

The default location of the taskbar is along the bottom edge of the desktop. Before you can move or resize the taskbar, it must be unlocked. Right-click an unoccupied area of the taskbar and, if a check mark appears next to the Lock The Taskbar command, choose the command to clear the check mark. You can move the taskbar to any other edge of the desktop if you want to try something a little different. Point to an unoccupied area of the taskbar and drag toward another edge of the desktop.

By default, the taskbar shows one row of buttons (or one column, if your taskbar is docked against the left or right edge of the desktop). If you keep toolbars on the taskbar, you might find it convenient to expand the taskbar to two or even three rows. Simply position the mouse along the inner border of the taskbar (the edge closest to the center of the screen). When the mouse pointer becomes a two-headed arrow, drag toward the center of the screen to expand the taskbar.

Making More Room on the Taskbar

In previous versions of Windows, active users who like to keep many windows open simultaneously had to figure out which tiny taskbar button represented which window. As new windows opened, each taskbar button was reduced to fit, leaving no room for the taskbar title.

Windows XP offers a better way: taskbar grouping. With this feature, when the taskbar fills up, Windows consolidates taskbar buttons from a single application (for example, several Internet Explorer windows) under one taskbar button. A number on the button indicates how many application instances it contains. Clicking the button displays a list of windows, as shown in Figure 8-19. As you might expect, right-clicking an item in the list displays the same shortcut menu that you'd see if the window had its own button; with this menu, you can move, resize, or close the window.

Figure 8-19. Click a list item to select its window.

In addition to reducing taskbar clutter, task grouping offers some other benefits that aren't immediately apparent. The menu that appears when you right-click the group button provides several useful commands. With a single click, you can:

- Display all windows in the group (choose Cascade, Tile Horizontally, or Tile Vertically), without affecting any other open windows

- Minimize all windows in the group

- Close all windows in the group

To enable taskbar grouping, open the Taskbar And Start Menu Properties dialog box, shown in Figure 8-20. You can find it in Control Panel (in the Appearance And Themes category) or, more simply, by right-clicking an unoccupied area of the taskbar and choosing Properties. Select Group Similar Taskbar Buttons.

Figure 8-20. Reduce clutter and gain window-management features by selecting taskbar grouping.

InsideOut

By default, taskbar grouping comes into play only when the taskbar fills up. Even if you have multiple windows open from the same application, if there's room for a separate button for each window, that's what you get.

You might prefer to have all similar windows grouped together all the time. To do that, you'll need to edit the registry. Use Registry Editor to open HKCU\Software\Microsoft\Windows\CurrentVersion\Explorer\Advanced. Create a new DWORD value named TaskbarGroupSize.

This setting controls how many windows are allowed before Windows starts grouping them under a single taskbar button. A setting of 2 groups related windows as soon as you open a second window, even if there's plenty of room on the taskbar; 3 enables grouping as soon as you have three or more similar windows, and so on. If you prefer to prevent taskbar grouping unless your taskbar gets *really* crowded, use a higher setting (say, 5). You must log off and then back on before this setting takes effect.

You can also increase button space by removing the clock from the taskbar. If you don't need Windows to display the time of day, you can probably squeeze at least one more button onto the bar by unloading the clock. In the Taskbar And Start Menu Properties dialog box, clear Show The Clock.

Getting the Taskbar Out of Your Way

By default, the taskbar remains visible even when you're working in a maximized program. If that's inconvenient for any reason, you can tell it to get out of the way. The Taskbar And Start Menu Properties dialog box, shown in Figure 8-20 on the preceding page, offers two options to control this behavior.

- **Keep The Taskbar On Top Of Other Windows.** Clearing this check box means you'll be able to see the taskbar at all times *except* when a window is maximized or placed over the taskbar.

- **Auto-Hide The Taskbar.** With this option selected, the taskbar retreats into the edge of the desktop. To display the taskbar, move the mouse pointer to the edge of the desktop where the taskbar is located.

> **tip** Regardless of how you set options in the Taskbar And Start Menu Properties dialog box, you can make the taskbar visible at any time by pressing the Windows logo key or Ctrl+Esc.

> **note** Locking the taskbar (an option in the Taskbar And Start Menu Properties dialog box and on the shortcut menu that appears when you right-click the taskbar) does not prevent you from using either of the preceding options. Locking merely prevents you from inadvertently moving or resizing the taskbar or any toolbars in the taskbar.

newfeature!
Removing Unneeded Icons from the Notification Area

The notification area (formerly known as the system tray or the status area) can become crowded with tiny icons—many of which don't "notify" you of anything. A variety of programs use the notification area to provide program-starting icons. But many of those programs seldom need to be started; they continue to do their job without any intervention from you. Windows XP adds a new feature that hides icons you don't use. Like the programs on the left side of the Start menu, the notification area adapts to the way you work. And also like the Start menu, you can specify your own preferences that override the adaptive behavior of Windows XP.

With this feature enabled, only active icons and icons you specify appear in the notification area. Others are only a click away: Click the arrow at the left end of the notification area to display the hidden icons, as shown in Figure 8-21.

Click to display hidden icons

Figure 8-21. Clicking the arrow expands the notification area to reveal all icons.

To enable this feature, select Hide Inactive Icons in the Taskbar And Start Menu Properties dialog box. To specify which icons should be hidden, click Customize to display the dialog box shown in Figure 8-22. For each icon—including icons that have been displayed in the past as well as ones that are currently in the notification area—you can choose whether to hide or show.

Figure 8-22. You determine which icons you want to be visible and which ones you want to be accessible only when you expand the notification area.

newfeature!
Streamlining Control Panel

Earlier versions of Windows had a single Control Panel—a collection of icons that led to assorted configuration tools and settings. As computers became more complex, the number of icons in Control Panel grew, giving pause to users plunging into Control Panel for the first time. Windows XP addresses this confusion by dividing Control Panel icons into categories, and putting a friendly face on the new Control Panel, shown in Figure 8-23 on the next page.

Click to see items that aren't in any category

Click to switch to a single-level Control Panel

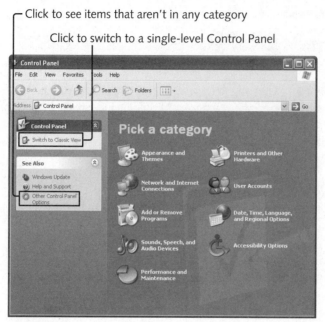

Figure 8-22. The new Control Panel is pretty, but requires an extra step to reach your destination.

Experienced users are likely to find the new Control Panel more of a hindrance than an aid, but fortunately, it's easy to revert to the single-level Control Panel of old, shown in Figure 8-24. Resetting Control Panel will probably be one of the first changes you'll make on a new computer.

Figure 8-24. With classic view, all your Control Panel icons are in one place.

InsideOut

Some programs and devices install their own Control Panel applications. These applications should go into the proper category if you use Category view, but applications not written to Windows XP specifications might not. If you want to change the category in which a Control Panel application appears, you can do so with a registry edit.

The HKLM\Software\Microsoft\Windows\CurrentVersion\Control Panel\Extended Properties\{305CA226-D286-468e-B848-2B2E8E697B74} 2 key contains the category information. Each DWORD value, which uses the full path to a .cpl (Control Panel) file as its name, should have one of the following settings:

Category	Value Data
Accessibility Options	0x00000007
Add or Remove Programs	0x00000008
Appearance and Themes	0x00000001
Date, Time, Language, and Regional Options	0x00000006
Network and Internet Connections	0x00000003
Other Control Panel Options	0x00000000
Performance and Maintenance	0x00000005
Printers and Other Hardware	0x00000002
Sounds, Speech, and Audio Devices	0x00000004
User Accounts	0x00000009
No category	0xFFFFFFFF

Although Control Panel provides a suitable means of access to settings you make only occasionally, you might prefer a more direct way to open certain configuration tools. Table 8-3 on the next page shows the command line you can use to reach each of the standard Control Panel applications. In many cases, you can use a command line to go directly to a particular tab of interest, saving another click. You can use these command lines at a command prompt, of course, but for frequently used items they'll be of more use encapsulated in a shortcut or used in a batch program or script.

note As an alternative to using Control.exe to start Control Panel items—the method used in most Table 8-3 entries—you can run a dynamic-link library (DLL) as an application. In each instance, replace **control** with **rundll32.exe shell32.dll,Control_RunDLL**. (Note that the second parameter—Control_RunDLL—is case sensitive.) This method works better in some programming languages.

Table 8-3. **Commands to Open Control Panel Items**

Control Panel Option	Command
Accessibility Options	**control access.cpl,,x** where *x* is replaced by one of these values:

Control Panel Option	Command
Add Hardware	**control hdwwiz.cpl**
Add or Remove Programs	Change or Remove Programs **control appwiz.cpl** Add New Programs **control appwiz.cpl,,1** Add/Remove Windows Components **control appwiz.cpl,,2** Set Program Access and Defaults **control appwiz.cpl,,3**
Administrative Tools	**control admintools**
Date and Time	**control timedate.cpl,,x** where *x* is replaced by one of these values:

Control Panel Option	Command
Display	**control desk.cpl,,x** where *x* is replaced by one of these values:

Note: You would expect the value 2 to display the Appearance tab, but a bug in Windows causes it to display the Screen Saver tab instead. This might be fixed by the time you read this.

Table 8-3. *(continued)*

Control Panel Option	Command
Folder Options	**control folders**
Fonts	**control fonts**
Game Controllers	**control joy.cpl**
Internet Options	**control inetcpl.cpl,,*x*** where *x* is replaced by one of these values:

Internet Properties	? X
General	Security	Privacy	Content	Connections	Programs	Advanced
0	1	2	3	4	5	6

Keyboard	**control main.cpl,@1,*x*** where *x* is replaced by one of these values:

Keyboard Properties	? X
Speed	Hardware
0	1

Mouse	**control main.cpl,,*x*** where *x* is replaced by one of these values:

Mouse Properties	? X
Buttons	Pointers	Pointer Options	Wheel	Hardware
0	1	2	3	4

Network Connections	**control netconnections**
Phone and Modem Options	**control telephon.cpl,,*x*** where *x* is replaced by one of these values:

Phone and Modem Options	? X
Dialing Rules	Modems	Advanced
0	1	2

(continued)

Chapter 8

Table 8-3. *(continued)*

Control Panel Option	Command
Power Options	**control powercfg.cpl**
Printers and Faxes	**control printers**
Regional and Language Options	**control intl.cpl,,*x*** where *x* is replaced by one of these values:

Scanners and Cameras	**control scannercamera**
Scheduled Tasks	**control schedtasks**
Sounds and Audio Devices	**control mmsys.cpl,,*x*** where *x* is replaced by one of these values:

Speech	**control speech**
System	**control sysdm.cpl,,*x*** where *x* is replaced by one of these values:

Taskbar and Start Menu	**rundll32.exe shell32.dll,Options_RunDLL 1**
User Accounts	Workgroup version (not available in domain environment) **control userpasswords** Windows 2000/domain version **control userpasswords2**

Table 8-3. *(continued)*

Control Panel Option	Command
Wireless Link	**control irprops.cpl,,x** where *x* is replaced by one of these values:

Customizing Windows XP with Tweak UI

Tweak UI, shown in Figure 8-25, is one of a set of PowerToys created by Microsoft to enhance the functionality of Windows XP. You can download any or all of the PowerToys, free of charge, from *www.microsoft.com/windowsxp/pro/downloads/powertoys.asp.*

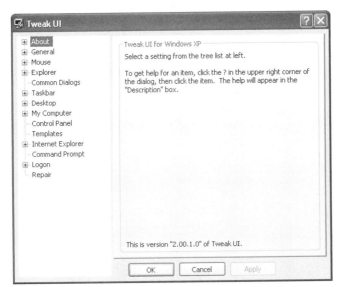

Figure 8-25. Tweak UI, a free but unsupported utility from Microsoft, gives you many additional ways to customize the appearance and behavior of Windows XP.

As its name suggests, Tweak UI provides all sorts of ways to tweak the Windows user interface. You can use Tweak UI, for example, to change the appearance of shortcut icons, prevent particular applications from appearing on the most-frequently-used-programs section of the Start menu, add folders of your choice to the Places bar that appears along the left side of the common File, Open and File, Save dialog boxes—and much, much more.

Some of Tweak UI's options (such as the one that lets you change the threshold at which Windows groups similar items on the taskbar) are alternatives for procedures described elsewhere in this chapter. A few provide functionality that would otherwise be inaccessible to users of Windows XP Home Edition. Many others are simple menu-pick avenues to customizations that would otherwise require you to edit the registry.

If you have used the version of Tweak UI that was available at the time when Windows XP first shipped, be aware that Microsoft has withdrawn that version and replaced it with another. If you plan to download the newest version, you must uninstall the old one first. You'll find that, in the latest incarnation, each of the PowerToys can now be downloaded and installed (as well as uninstalled) individually.

Because Microsoft does not officially support Tweak UI, you won't be able to call Product Support Services if you run into difficulty with it or any of the other PowerToys. It's not likely that you will need support, however. We consider them safe, reliable, and extremely useful.

Chapter 9

Configuring Shutdown and Power Management Options

In the past, power management has been the concern primarily of laptop-toting road warriors and others who use battery-powered portable computers. Those computers' short battery life—as little as one hour between charges—demanded that users monitor battery charge levels closely and do everything possible to minimize battery consumption. Systems were designed to turn off certain components when not in use and to switch the whole system to a low-power state after a period of inactivity.

Recent years have seen tremendous advances in battery technology. In addition, current models of devices such as displays and hard drives draw less power than their predecessors. This combination of technology advances has led to greatly increased battery life for portable computers—suggesting that power management is no longer an important topic. In fact, it has become even more important.

The dawn of the new millennium brought rolling blackouts to California and soaring electricity prices for nearly everyone. Now proper power management is as important for desktop computers as it is for battery-powered computers. (Although the advances in hardware technology have achieved considerable power savings, operating system power management features still provide a significant boost in battery life for portable computers.)

329

At Home with Windows XP

Windows XP Professional and Windows XP Home Edition are both adept at managing power. All descriptions and procedures in this chapter apply equally to both editions of the operating system.

The power management and shutdown features provide three primary benefits to users of all computers:

- Minimizes power consumption, which lowers power costs for desktop users and increases battery life for portable users

- Provides "instant-on" capability

- Provides an orderly shutdown in case of power outage

How Does Your Computer Manage Power?

Microsoft Windows XP—along with an OnNow-capable computer and suitable applications—manages a computer's power in such a way that power usage (and noise) is minimized, but the computer and its peripherals are instantly available when needed. Based on settings you make, Windows XP switches the computer and its peripherals to a low-power state when they're not in use. Such a system can be wakened by events received from an application, a modem, a network connection, or other devices. This capability allows scenarios such as these:

- You have a computer set up as a host for Internet Connection Sharing and a shared printer. It can be in a quiet, low-power sleep state until another computer on your network needs an Internet connection or a printer, whereupon the computer becomes instantly available.

- You have a computer set up as a telephone answering device. It wakes from a low-power state whenever the phone rings.

- You have security devices such as break-in detectors or a camera. They can wake the computer so it will automatically send e-mail or pager alerts.

- You have maintenance and other tasks scheduled to run when the computer's not being used. Tasks in the Scheduled Tasks folder can be configured to wake the computer at the appointed time and perform the task.

Some of these capabilities are dependent upon your computer being compliant with the Advanced Configuration and Power Interface (ACPI) specification.

For information about ACPI, see "ACPI vs. APM," page 348.

What Is OnNow?

OnNow is a Microsoft initiative to advance PC hardware so it supports instant-on capability, yet appears to be off (that is, it's quiet and uses little or no power) when it's not in use. This has ramifications beyond eliminating the need to go get a cup of coffee to occupy the time after you switch on your computer: it allows devices and applications to wake the computer from a low-power state and immediately get to work. Microsoft set the following design goals for a typical consumer PC running Windows XP:

- Boot from power off to a usable state in 30 seconds.
- Resume from hibernation in 20 seconds.
- Resume from standby in 5 seconds.

newfeature!

Although these goals are met only by compliant hardware, meeting them relies on several under-the-hood improvements in Windows XP. For example, changes were made in the boot loader that greatly reduce the time spent seeking data on hard disks. The boot process was also optimized to perform certain steps concurrently and to avoid or postpone the loading of processes and services that aren't needed at boot time.

Configuring Your Computer's BIOS

For Windows XP power management features to work properly, you should disable all power management features in your computer's BIOS (Basic Input/Output System). Run its setup program (usually accessed by pressing Del or F1 during the computer's power-on self test; watch the screen for a message explaining how to enter setup), and browse the menus for all settings related to power management. With ACPI, power management should be under the exclusive control of the operating system. When the operating system and the BIOS contend for control, problems often result.

Conserving Power on All Computers—Even Desktops!

There used to be an ongoing debate: should you turn your computer off when you're not using it or leave it on all the time? Proponents of leaving it on claimed that turning the power on and off—causing motors to start and stop and other components to heat up and cool down—would shorten its life. This assertion was never widely accepted and, in fact, others argued that leaving the computer on all the time would wear out bearings and other moving parts more quickly. So the issue of whether your computer will last longer if it's turned off or left on when not in use has never been satisfactorily resolved. (Besides, no matter which routine wears out your computer faster, it's likely to become obsolete long before it wears out.) With that issue out of consideration then, it makes sense to turn off your computer (or switch to a low-power state) simply for the energy savings.

Chapter 9

331

> **note** Screen savers—programs that display varying patterns on your computer's screen while you're not using it—can be fun, but they don't save energy. In fact, by keeping the monitor on and by using CPU cycles, they actually consume more energy than if you didn't use a screen saver at all.

How much power does a desktop computer consume? Unlike many appliances, you won't find on the back of a computer a sticker that specifies power consumption. And specifications for most computers don't indicate power consumption because so many variables exist. Each expansion card or other device you install in the computer consumes power; more power is consumed when the computer is in use than when it's inactive; power management features control power consumption; and so on. You can use an ammeter to get an idea of how much your computer uses. Or you can visit the Web page of American Power Conversion Corp., a company that makes uninterruptible power supplies and surge protectors. You can find a page that calculates the power needs of your computer at *http://www.apcc.com/template/size/apc*.

How much could you save? Suppose your computer uses 300 watts and you use it 8 hours a day. Without power management (in other words, if you leave it on at full power), during the other 16 hours it consumes 4.8 kilowatt-hours (KWH). If power in your area costs, say, 15 cents per KWH, you'd save 72 cents per day. And if you pay the bill for several computers, the potential savings are significant.

Of course, you can realize these savings with any computer and with any operating system: you simply remember to turn the system off when you're not using it. Windows XP and an OnNow-capable computer, however, switch to low-power (or no-power) states automatically after a period of inactivity. Besides turning off your computer at night, ACPI can reduce power consumption while you're away at lunch or working away from your computer. But there's another key difference between the power-saving states used by Windows XP and simply switching off the power: using Windows power management enables the computer to return to a working state much more quickly.

InsideOut

Navigating through menus to get to Control Panel options can be tedious. Here's a fast way to get to Power Options if part of the desktop is visible: right-click the desktop and choose Properties. In the Display Properties dialog box, click the Screen Saver tab and click Power.

And for command prompt aficionados, here's an even quicker method: at a command prompt, type **powercfg.cpl**.

If you find the need to visit Power Options Properties often, you can include its icon in the notification area so that it's only a click away. To do that, select Always Show Icon On The Taskbar on the Advanced tab of the Power Options Properties dialog box.

To configure any of the Windows XP power management features, open Power Options in Control Panel. (If you use Category view in Control Panel, you'll find Power Options under Performance And Maintenance.) Figure 9-1 shows the Power Schemes tab of the Power Options dialog box.

Figure 9-1. The appearance of your Power Options Properties dialog box depends on your system—whether it's ACPI-compliant, whether it has a battery, whether it has power backup in the form of an uninterruptible power supply (UPS), and so on.

Using Standby to Reduce Power Use

Standby uses only enough power to preserve the contents of memory—typically only a few watts. Its advantages over hibernation are that it doesn't require free disk space and it allows nearly instant system reactivation. Use standby when you're planning to not use your computer for a few minutes or a few hours; use hibernation for longer periods of disuse.

On systems that support standby, you can allow the system to switch to standby automatically after a period of inactivity or you can switch to standby manually.

To enable automatic switching, follow these steps:

1 In the Power Options Properties dialog box shown in Figure 9-1, click the Power Schemes tab.

2 Specify a time in the System Standby box.

Power States: Standby vs. Hibernation

Although your computer appears to be either on or off, the ACPI specification actually defines six different power states, which are described in the following table.

State	Description
S0 Working	On. The CPU is fully up and running. Under the direction of the operating system or device settings, other devices may be running in a low-power state.
S1 Standby	Appears off. (Some systems have a blinking light to indicate they're in a sleep state.) The display and drives are powered off, but power remains for the CPU, memory, and fans.
S2 Standby	Appears off. Same as S1, but the CPU and cache are powered off.
S3 Standby	Appears off. Minimal power is provided to refresh RAM; all other devices are powered off.
S4 Hibernate	Appears off. The system is completely powered off, but the contents of RAM have been saved to disk.
S5 Off	Off. The system is completely powered off and nothing has been saved.

Not all computers support all six states and, in fact, Windows XP presents only four choices to users. (S1, S2, and S3 are all variants of the condition called *standby*.) The two power-saving states that you'll encounter in Windows XP are *standby* and *hibernation*.

What's the difference between standby and hibernation? In a nutshell, standby simply shifts to a low-power state by shutting down hard drives, fans, the CPU, and other power-hungry components—but it continues to draw some power to retain the contents of memory and to be ready to spring back to life quickly. Hibernation saves the contents of memory to the hard disk and then shuts off all power. The following table shows the features that differentiate standby and hibernation.

Advantage	Standby	Hibernation
Uses no power		✓
Powers down more quickly	✓	
Returns to work state more quickly	✓	
Doesn't require disk space	✓	
Preserves data even if power goes off		✓

InsideOut

If the power goes out while your computer is on standby, you lose whatever is in memory. If you have any unsaved documents, for example, they're gone. With an uninterruptible power supply (UPS), however, you can prevent data loss during blackouts. Although the blackout might last longer than the battery run time provided by the UPS, you can prevent loss, even if your computer happens to be on standby and you're away when the power goes out. To do so, make the following settings in Power Options:

● Enable hibernation. (On the Hibernate tab, select Enable Hibernate Support.)

● Specify a time—less than the battery run time—for the computer to switch to hibernation. (On the Power Schemes tab, set a time for System Hibernates under Running On Batteries.)

Thereafter, your computer switches to standby after the specified amount of time has elapsed without any input from keyboard, mouse, or other devices.

To configure other standby options, follow these steps:

1 In the Power Options Properties dialog box shown in Figure 9-2, click the Advanced tab.

Figure 9-2. Use the Advanced tab to specify button actions.

2 If you're concerned about somebody else waking your computer from standby, select Prompt For Password When Computer Resumes From Standby. This option has no effect if your account doesn't need a password to log on to Windows.

3 For each button under Power Buttons, select Standby—or another action if you prefer. (Despite its possible appearance in the dialog box, not all computers have a sleep button.)

tip If you configure your power button to do something other than shut down (its traditional function), you can still force the computer to power off completely. Simply press and hold the power button for several seconds.

Troubleshooting

Your computer won't enter standby or hibernation.

Power management features—in particular standby and hibernation—rely on device drivers that support power management in addition to compatible hardware. In particular, incompatible video drivers prevent these features from working. The built-in VGA driver, for example, is a bare-bones driver that doesn't support power management. If standby and hibernate don't work, install an updated driver for your display adapter.

To switch to standby manually, use either of these methods:

● Press the button on your computer or keyboard (for example, the power button or sleep button) that you've configured to switch to standby.

● On the Start menu, choose Turn Off Computer. In the window that appears (Figure 9-3), click Stand By.

Figure 9-3. A fourth option—Hibernate—is hidden. Hold down the Shift key to see it.

If your computer is a member of a domain, the procedure is slightly different: On the Start menu, choose Shut Down. A dialog box like the one
shown in Figure 9-4 appears. Select Stand By in the list and then click OK.

Figure 9-4. Domain members see this window instead of the one shown
in Figure 9-3.

Shutting Down Your Computer

Despite the quick-resume advantages provided by standby and hibernation, you'll still
want to shut down your computer completely on occasion. You can do this in either of
two ways:

- On the Start menu, choose Turn Off Computer, Turn Off. (If your computer is part of a domain, click Start, Shut Down, select Shut Down, and
  then click OK.)

- Press the computer's power button. (If you've configured it to switch to
  standby or hibernation, press and hold the button for several seconds to
  perform a complete shutdown.)

newfeature!
In Windows XP, these two methods perform a controlled shutdown in exactly the same
way: the operating system notifies applications that it's going to shut down (giving
them an opportunity to save unsaved work), waits for responses, and then shuts down.
This is a departure from Windows 2000, in which pressing the power switch performs
a "critical action" shutdown. In this type of shutdown, Windows notifies applications
and devices about the impending shutdown—but doesn't wait for a response. Some
people discovered this difference in Windows 2000 and used the power switch to shut
down more quickly. What they didn't realize is that they risked losing unsaved data
with this method; Windows XP now eliminates that confusing distinction.

Troubleshooting

A hung application prevents shutdown.

If you need to shut down in a hurry—or if a frozen application prevents you from shutting down in the normal ways—you can use the following procedure. Be aware, however, that you won't get an opportunity to save open documents. Windows shuts down immediately—no "Windows is shutting down" or other messages. To perform an emergency shutdown, press Ctrl+Alt+Del to display Task Manager. Open the Shut Down menu and hold down the Ctrl key as you click the Turn Off command. Poof!

If your computer is part of a domain, the procedure is similar. Press Ctrl+Alt+Del and then hold down Ctrl when you click Shut Down. In this situation, you'll get a warning message pointing out—quite correctly—that this should be used only as a last resort.

Hibernating for Maximum Power Savings

Hibernation is a way of shutting down your computer without shutting down the operating system. Hibernation is an option on many systems, even if they're neither APM (Advanced Power Management) nor ACPI-compliant. When you hibernate, Windows XP copies everything in memory to disk and then powers down all components of your computer. When you emerge from hibernation (by pressing your computer's power switch), the memory image that was copied to disk is restored, and you're ready to go back to work.

Hibernation saves time because it relieves Windows of all the housekeeping chores it would normally perform during shutdown and restart. Instead of having to close files on shutdown, redetect hardware, reconstitute the hardware-specific sections of your registry, reload drivers, and restart programs, the operating system simply saves and restores the state of your computer.

caution *Never* boot into another operating system while your computer is hibernating. That is, if your computer is set up so that it can boot into an operating system other than Windows XP, do not hibernate Windows XP and then boot into another operating system. Doing so can corrupt or destroy your stored data. When Windows hibernates, it stores the contents of RAM—which usually includes part of the hard disk's MFT (master file table). If you boot to another file system, make some changes to the data on disk, and then resume from hibernation, Windows restores the MFT from the stored hibernation file—which likely means your changes will be overwritten.

If you want to boot to another operating system, be sure you *shut down* or *restart* your computer rather than hibernating.

Chapter 9

InsideOut

When you hibernate, Windows stores the contents of memory on your computer's boot partition in a file named Hiberfil.sys. As long as hibernation is enabled, you can't delete it, rename it, or move it to another disk or partition. That's because of its integral role in the boot process. When you turn on the power, Ntldr (the bootstrap loader program for Windows XP) looks for the existence of Hiberfil.sys on the boot partition. (At that point in the boot process, no other programs or drivers are running and the registry isn't accessible—so it's not possible to specify another location.) If the file exists, Ntldr then checks to see whether a flag is set to indicate that the computer is in hibernation. If so, its contents are restored to memory. (If the file doesn't exist or the hibernation flag isn't set, Ntldr then proceeds to run the normal boot sequence.)

If you need the space occupied by Hiberfil.sys, you must disable hibernation by clearing the check box on the Hibernate tab.

Because hibernation puts your work into nonvolatile storage, it's a safer way to reduce power during periods of inactivity than standby. If you experience a power failure while your computer is hibernating, you won't lose anything because your computer's memory has been copied to disk. On the other hand, hibernation requires an amount of free disk space equivalent to the amount of your computer's random access memory. If you have a 128-MB system, for example, you need 128 MB of free disk space to hibernate. Moreover, it takes longer to emerge from hibernation than to come off standby, because the operating system has to restore data from disk.

To configure your system for hibernation, in the Power Options Properties dialog box, click the Hibernate tab and select Enable Hibernation.

You can configure other hibernation options to

- Set an inactive time limit to automatically switch to hibernation (Power Schemes tab).

- Assign a button on the computer to switch the computer to hibernation (Advanced tab).

- Require a password to resume from hibernation (Advanced tab). Although the check box mentions only standby, it affects emergence from hibernation also.

Chapter 9

InsideOut

If you use password security on your computer—and, unless it's in a locked closet that's not connected to a network or the Internet, you probably should—you might also use policies that cause passwords to expire periodically. If your password happens to expire while your computer is in hibernation (and you've enabled the password prompt on resume option), you've got a problem: Windows won't let you resume from hibernation. Therefore, you can't set a new password. Granted, it's an unusual set of circumstances, but we know from personal experience that it's possible. There is a workaround: using Safe Mode (press F8 at startup and choose Safe Mode), log on as Administrator. As Administrator, you can change the password for the hibernated account and then reboot.

To hibernate manually, use either of these methods:

- Press the button on your computer or keyboard (for example, the power button or sleep button) that you've configured to hibernate.

- On the Start menu, click Turn Off Computer. In the window that appears (see Figure 9-3 on page 336)—here's the tricky part—hold down the Shift key. The Stand By button changes to Hibernate; click it before releasing Shift and the computer will hibernate rather than enter standby mode. (If your computer doesn't support standby, then the button always appears as Hibernate, and you won't need to press the Shift key.)

Troubleshooting

Your system reboots or shuts down instead of hibernating.

A faulty device driver is probably causing a blue-screen error during the hibernation process. To see whether that's the case, open the System Properties dialog box (press Windows+Break or, in Control Panel, open Performance And Maintenance, System) and click the Advanced tab. Under Startup And Recovery, click Settings. In the Startup And Recovery dialog box, select the Write An Event To The System Log check box and clear Automatically Restart. Close the dialog boxes and try to hibernate. Now, if a blue-screen error occurs, it remains on-screen and you can use it to help pinpoint which driver is causing the problem.

If you have an APM system that shuts down instead of hibernating, try the following. Open Device Manager (Devmgmt.msc) and choose View, Show Hidden Devices. Open NT Apm/Legacy Support and be sure that the NT Apm/Legacy Interface Node device is enabled.

Waking Up Your Computer

You can bring your computer back from standby or hibernation simply by pressing the power button. In a few seconds, you'll be back to where you were when the computer powered down—or at a dialog box asking for your password before allowing access. But you can also configure various devices and applications to wake the computer. For example, if the keyboard device is configured to wake the computer, pressing any key powers up the computer.

Troubleshooting

Your system won't emerge from standby.

First check with your system vendor to be sure you have the latest BIOS. If that doesn't fix it, the problem is likely to be with a device driver. Try removing or disabling all your peripheral devices. If you can then emerge from standby properly, add devices back one at a time and test whether your system emerges from standby after adding each one. When you find the device that causes the problem, check with its vendor to see whether an updated driver is available.

In some cases, a problematic device driver prevents a particular device from waking. For example, your computer resumes from standby, but the mouse doesn't work. You can sometimes fix this problem by *disabling* the option that allows the problem device to wake the computer. If the mouse doesn't work, for example, go to the properties dialog box for the mouse as described next and clear the check boxes on the Power Management tab.

To enable a hardware device—such as the keyboard, mouse, modem, network card, and so on—to wake the computer, follow these steps:

1 In Device Manager (type **devmgmt.msc** at a command prompt), double-click the name of the device for which you want to enable power management.

2 In the device's properties dialog box, click the Power Management tab, shown in Figure 9-5 on the next page. (If the dialog box has no Power Management tab, the device can't be used to wake the computer.)

3 Select the appropriate check boxes for your situation.

This option allows a device to wake the computer

Figure 9-5. On the Power Management tab, you direct your computer to wake from a low-power state when it receives a signal from a device.

newfeature!

OnNow-aware applications can also be configured to wake the computer. For example, items in the Scheduled Tasks folder can be configured to run at predetermined times, even if the computer is on standby.

InsideOut

Does your computer wake up in the middle of the night, even when no one touches it? Some broadband Internet providers periodically probe your computer to see whether it's still connected. If your network interface card is configured to wake the computer, one of these probes will do it. If you don't want to disable the wake-on-LAN feature, you can ensure that probes from your Internet connection don't rouse your computer by turning off the computer's power completely before you and your computer retire: shut down Windows and flip off the switch on your power strip or UPS. (Be sure, however, that your computer is not on standby when you do this.)

Follow these steps to enable power management for a scheduled task:

1 Open the Scheduled Tasks folder (choose Start, All Programs, Accessories, System Tools, Scheduled Tasks).

2 Create a new task or select an existing one.

3 Double-click the task to open its properties dialog box and click the Settings tab.

4 Select the appropriate check boxes under Power Management, shown in Figure 9-6.

342

Figure 9-6. You can configure tasks to wake the computer if it's sleeping or prevent them from running if the computer isn't running on AC power.

Chapter 9

Troubleshooting

Your APM machine has problems emerging from standby.

If your computer uses APM for power management and sometimes fails to come out of standby, check the time-out settings in your BIOS Setup program. If these thresholds are lower than the ones set in the Power Options Properties dialog box, you might sometimes be unable to emerge from standby. To resolve the problem, set the BIOS time-out settings to their maximum values.

Using Power Schemes

A power scheme is a named combination of power-reduction settings. Windows XP provides a number of predefined schemes, which appear on the Power Schemes tab in Power Options. (See Figure 9-1 on page 334.) You can alter the supplied schemes or add your own.

To modify an existing power scheme, simply select it in the Power Schemes list, adjust the settings below, and then click OK. To create a new scheme, edit an existing one. Then click Save As and supply a new name.

343

Conserving Power on Portable Computers

All of the power-management features that reduce power consumption on desktop computers work equally well on portable computers. In addition, several other features benefit users of late-model, battery-powered portable computers:

newfeature!

- When the computer's lid is closed, the display is switched off.

newfeature!

- When a portable computer is running on battery power, the display is dimmed; it automatically returns to full brightness when the computer is plugged in.

newfeature!

- A portable computer can be configured so that when it's running on battery power, the processor runs at a lower speed, which consumes less power. (To configure this option, visit the Advanced tab in the Power Options Properties dialog box.)

- A portable computer can be configured so that when it's running on battery power and it enters a low-battery or critical-battery condition, it automatically raises an alarm, switches to a low-power state, or runs a program. This feature is useful especially when, for example, your computer is on standby and you're not around; it can automatically hibernate to preserve your data when the batteries run down. (To configure this option, visit the Alarms tab in the Power Options Properties dialog box, shown below.)

Displaying a Power Status Indicator

As in many corners of the Windows XP user interface, the Advanced tab of the Power Options Properties dialog box presents nothing the least bit advanced. It's simply a catch-all location for miscellaneous user-interface elements.

One of those elements in the Power Options Properties dialog box is an option to display a power status icon in your taskbar's notification area. Should you accept, a battery icon appears while you're running on batteries, and a power-cord icon appears when you're not. When your battery power falls below about 50 percent, the battery icon changes to a "half-full" appearance.

Double-clicking the icon provides more detailed information about your battery's condition. Right-clicking the icon generates a shortcut menu, from which you can return to the Power Options Properties dialog box.

Protecting Your Data During a Power Outage

You've been working on an important document—your doctoral thesis, a new musical composition, a financial projection—for several hours. Suddenly the screen goes blank and the room becomes dark. Amazingly, it's *then* that the proverbial light bulb blinks on above your head: "I should have saved that document!" If the power goes off, the computer's memory—including any changes to unsaved files—is erased.

The first way to protect your data is to back it up frequently:

- Use your program's autosave feature if it has one. For example, you can configure Microsoft Word to save AutoRecover information every few minutes. (On the Tools menu, choose Options and then click the Save tab.) The next time you start Word (after the power comes back on), it opens your document with the last-saved AutoRecover information.

- Get in the habit of saving frequently. In most programs, Ctrl+S is the keyboard shortcut for saving the current document. Press Ctrl+S every few minutes, whenever you get up from your desk, or even each time you pause to think about what to type next. This action should become so instinctive that you do it automatically.

- Establish—and follow—a regular backup routine. Should the lights go dim and your files somehow become scrambled, you'll at least be able to restore the document as it existed at the time of your most recent backup. It beats starting over. For more information, see "Smart Backup Strategies," page 882.

Of course, these precautions defend against disasters other than power outages. For real protection against data loss in the event of a power outage, you need a UPS—an uninterruptible power supply. A UPS is essentially a battery backup system. When the lights go off, the battery kicks in to provide power. Most UPSs also provide some form of power conditioning, which reduces or eliminates surges, spikes, and brownouts (low voltage). Any of these conditions can damage electronic equipment as well as your data.

Configuring a UPS

The easiest type of UPS to configure is the kind that connects to your computer's USB port. If you have this type, plug it into one of the USB ports on your computer—not to a USB hub. When you do that, it installs its driver and modifies the Power Options Properties dialog box appropriately: It adds an Alarms tab and a Power Meter tab, as shown in Figure 9-7. It also adds to the Power Schemes tab settings for shutdown times while running on batteries. (Don't be concerned that the UPS tab has disappeared; it's needed only for UPSs that connect to a standard serial port.)

Figure 9-7. A USB-interface UPS typically adds a Power Meter tab, with which you can monitor your battery's charge.

> **tip** **Save open documents before you leave your computer**
>
> Even if you have a UPS, you should save your open documents and close your applications before you leave your computer. Most UPSs designed for personal computers keep the computer running for only a few minutes before it's forced to shut down—and any documents left open at that time are lost just as if you had no UPS protection at all. By saving open documents before you leave your computer, you avoid data loss in the case of a blackout that lasts longer than your batteries.
>
> Of course, the one time you neglect to follow that advice will be right before the power goes out. Windows XP offers a better solution: configure your computer to hibernate when the UPS battery reaches a critically low level. To do that, in Power Options click Configure on the UPS tab or click the Alarms tab. (Where you find the setting depends on which UPS model you have.)

If your computer uses a serial-interface UPS, a UPS tab appears in your Power Options Properties dialog box, as shown in Figure 9-8. You should visit this corner of the power-management UI to make sure that your UPS is properly identified and configured. If the UPS tab doesn't already identify the make and model of your UPS, click Select. In the ensuing dialog box, you can specify a manufacturer and model as well as the port to which the UPS is connected.

Figure 9-8. Use the UPS tab to configure and monitor a serial-interface UPS.

To configure the actions taken by your UPS and by Windows XP should your normal power become unavailable, click the Configure button. In the UPS Configuration dialog box, shown in Figure 9-9, you can specify such things as a program that should run either when the UPS battery is close to exhaustion or when your system has been running on UPS battery power for a specified period of time.

Figure 9-9. In the UPS Configuration dialog box, you can tell Windows XP what you want it to do when the power is out and the UPS battery is approaching exhaustion.

ACPI vs. APM

Windows provides three levels of power-management support:

- On computers that are fully compliant with the Advanced Configuration and Power Interface (ACPI) specification—a requirement of OnNow-capable computers—the operating system maintains efficient and reliable control of the power supplied to your monitor, disk drives, peripherals, and motherboard components, reducing power to those components appropriately when your computer is inactive.

- On many systems that are not ACPI-compliant but that use an Advanced Power Management (APM) 1.2 BIOS, Windows can provide a serviceable, if somewhat less versatile, form of power management.

● On some earlier systems that do not have an APM 1.2 BIOS, the operating system can still conserve power by having the operating system shut down the monitor and disk drives during periods of inactivity. If you have a pre-APM BIOS, you might also be able to put your system manually into hibernation when you don't plan to use it again for a while.

The advantage of ACPI over APM is that ACPI puts power management completely in the control of the operating system. Because ACPI is an operating-system specification, Windows XP can provide a consistent approach to power management across all ACPI-compliant systems, thereby ensuring reliability while reducing training costs and user perplexity. With applications that are designed for ACPI, an ACPI-compliant system can also track the status of running or scheduled programs and coordinate power transitions with applications as well as hardware.

APM, on the other hand, is a BIOS specification. (The Basic Input/Output System, or *BIOS,* is a low-level interface that stands between the operating system and the various hardware components of your system.) To manage power on a system that incorporates an APM BIOS but is not fully compliant with ACPI, Windows must work cooperatively with the BIOS. Because differences exist between the various APM BIOSs that are in use, APM-enabled systems differ considerably in their power-management behavior. Therefore it's impossible to say with certainty what power-management features will be available on your own APM system, exactly how those features will be implemented, and whether all your power-management features will work with 100 percent reliability.

In addition to reliability and consistency, other advantages of ACPI include the following:

● **Control of USB and FireWire devices.** ACPI systems can track the status of devices connected to your computer via Universal Serial Bus or IEEE 1394 (FireWire). Because APM cannot monitor such devices, an APM system might attempt to go into standby or hibernation when a peripheral is active.

● **Support for wake-on-LAN and wake-on-ring.** An ACPI system can be configured to emerge from standby or hibernation when data arrives over the local area network or modem. Windows cannot take advantage of wake-on-LAN or wake-on-ring with systems that use APM.

● **User definition of the power and reset buttons.** On an ACPI system, you can configure the power and reset buttons to do what you want them to do. You can set the power button so that it puts the system into standby or hibernation, for example, rather than turning the computer off—thereby making it less likely that you'll inadvertently cut the power to your system.

Chapter 9

- **Better battery management.** Under ACPI, Windows can provide separate meters for each battery on the system. Under APM, Windows represents multiple batteries as though they were a single composite battery.

- **Dynamic configuration of PC cards.** On ACPI systems, you can insert and remove PC (PCMCIA) cards, and the operating system responds appropriately without requiring you to reboot.

- **Multiprocessor support.** APM power management is not available on multiprocessor systems.

Determining Whether Your System Is ACPI-Compliant

During setup, Windows XP decides whether your computer is ACPI-compliant. If it is (according to the Setup program's judgment), Setup installs an ACPI hardware abstraction layer (HAL). Otherwise, Setup installs a standard APM (non-ACPI) HAL. The decision algorithm is as follows:

1. Setup looks to see whether your BIOS is on a list of BIOSs known to be incompatible with ACPI. (This list is in the [NWACL] section of a file named Txtsetup.sif, which is located in the \i386 folder of the Windows XP CD-ROM.) If your BIOS is on the list, you get the non-ACPI HAL.

2. If your BIOS isn't on the known-to-be-incompatible list, Setup checks the BIOS date. If it's later than January 1, 1999, you get the ACPI HAL.

3. If the BIOS date is prior to January 1, 1999, Setup checks a known-to-be-good BIOS list (located in the [GoodACPIBios] section of Txtsetup.sif). If yours is there, you get the ACPI HAL. If it's not, Setup installs the non-ACPI HAL.

How do you know whether Setup deemed your computer to be ACPI-compliant? You can use Device Manager to determine whether your computer is using ACPI for power management, by following these steps:

1. Open Device Manager. (At a command prompt, type **devmgmt.msc**).

   You can also reach Device Manager from the System Properties dialog box. Press the Windows logo key+Break, click the Hardware tab, and then click Device Manager.

2. Open the System Devices entry.

   If your system is ACPI-compliant (and the Windows XP Setup program has installed an ACPI HAL), you'll find an item called Microsoft ACPI-Compliant System.

> **tip** You can also check for ACPI compliance in the Power Options Properties dialog box. If it includes an APM tab, your system is not ACPI-compliant. (The absence of an APM tab, however, does not necessarily mean that your system *is* ACPI-compliant.)

Upgrading to ACPI Support

In some cases, a BIOS update can make a standard PC ACPI-compliant. If your computer is shown in Device Manager as a Standard PC and you want to upgrade to ACPI support, your first step is to check with your computer vendor to get the latest BIOS. In most cases, updating the BIOS doesn't require swapping out the BIOS chip (as it did on early PCs); rather, you copy a vendor-provided program to a floppy disk and boot the computer from the floppy disk. The program writes new data to the BIOS.

If you use a BIOS update to upgrade a system from APM to ACPI support, you must reinstall Windows XP after performing the upgrade. That's because ACPI support is dependent on an ACPI HAL, which you can get only by reinstalling Windows. You can perform an upgrade installation. (In other words, you don't need to perform a clean install.) This is a relatively painless operation that retains your existing settings, programs, and files.

InsideOut

Do not use the Hardware Update Wizard or any other driver update procedure to change from Standard PC to an ACPI HAL (or the reverse). There's a good chance that your computer won't boot after making such a change. Even if it does boot, other severe problems could occur later. That's because changing the HAL is much more complex than simply changing a driver; all hardware must be redetected, support for Plug and Play and other hardware must be changed, and the part of the registry that stores information about installed hardware must be modified. The only supported way to make these changes is by rerunning Setup, as described above.

If you've already made this mistake, there's hope. Boot from your Windows XP CD and let Setup find the existing Windows installation. It should ask if you want to repair it. Answer in the affirmative, and Setup will reinstall the correct HAL while leaving all your other files and settings in place.

During setup, you can force Windows to install the standard PC HAL or an ACPI HAL rather than relying on the Setup program's judgment about your computer's level of ACPI support. There's seldom reason to do so—although symptoms of noncompliance might not be immediately apparent, Setup is usually right about which computers properly adhere to the ACPI specification—but you might need to do this if you encounter power-related problems with one HAL or the other. To specify which HAL to install, follow these steps:

1 Boot from the Windows XP CD to initiate Setup.

2 At the point in text-mode setup where a message at the bottom of the screen reads "Press F6 if you need to install a third party SCSI or RAID driver," press F5. (That's right: press F5 at the F6 prompt.)

3 Use the Up Arrow key and Down Arrow key to scroll through the list of computer types. Highlight the one you want and then press Enter.

Enabling APM Power Management

If your system is not ACPI-compliant and an APM tab appears in the Power Options Properties dialog box, you can use APM for power management. On some systems, the Windows XP Setup program enables APM power management automatically. These are systems with BIOSs known to cooperate effectively with Windows XP. On other systems, Windows provides support for APM power management, but you have to enable it yourself. You do that by going to the APM tab in Power Options and selecting the Enable Advanced Power Management Support check box. You do not have to restart your system after enabling APM power management. If you subsequently disable APM, however, you do need to restart.

Troubleshooting

Windows won't allow you to enable APM.

If you can't enable APM, installing the NT Apm/Legacy Interface Node device might solve the problem. To do that, run the Add Hardware Wizard. In the wizard's list of installed hardware, select Add A New Hardware Device. Select manual installation and then, in the list of common hardware types, select NT Apm/Legacy Interface Node. For more information about the Add Hardware Wizard, see Chapter 6, "Setting Up and Troubleshooting Hardware."

APM is designed to monitor hardware interrupts and I/O port data traffic at the BIOS level to determine whether your system is active or inactive. The BIOS measures periods of inactivity against thresholds that you set via your system's BIOS Setup program. If the BIOS timer arrives at a preset threshold, the BIOS sends a message to Windows requesting some form of power transition (standby, for example). Windows verifies that your computer is ready for the requested power reduction and then tells the BIOS to go ahead with the requested transition. On a portable computer, the BIOS might

Troubleshooting

The Power Options Properties dialog box doesn't have an APM tab.

If you think Windows should provide APM support for your computer, but there's no APM tab in Power Options, the first thing to investigate is your computer's BIOS setup program. If APM is disabled in the BIOS when Windows is installed, the Windows XP Setup program does not install APM support. If APM is disabled in your system's BIOS, try reenabling it and reinstalling Windows XP.

If you still don't have APM support after taking these measures, your BIOS might be one that Windows XP regards as troublesome and declines to support. You can confirm this by running the program Apmstat.exe, which is one of the support tools included on your Windows XP CD-ROM. To install the support tools, navigate to the \Support\Tools folder on the CD, and then run Setup.

It's best to run Apmstat with the *verbose* switch in a Command Prompt window, like this:

```
apmstat -v
```

If the news from Apmstat is disagreeable, your next step is to contact your hardware vendor and see whether a BIOS upgrade is available. Microsoft strongly recommends that you do not try to circumvent its decision not to support your current BIOS.

also monitor battery status and send Windows a power-reduction request when battery strength falls below a specified threshold.

Unfortunately, Windows cannot discriminate between the various possible reasons for an APM power-transition request. It cannot tell, for example, whether the BIOS is asking for power reduction because the system is idle, because battery power is low, or because the user has pressed the computer's sleep button.

InsideOut

Because Windows tries to honor the BIOS request under all circumstances, the system might attempt to go into standby or hibernation at a time when the computer is not actually idle. To avoid such problems, if you're using an APM system, set the BIOS inactivity thresholds to their highest possible values or disable these thresholds altogether. (On some systems, APM will not work if you disable the BIOS power-reduction thresholds.) With BIOS thresholds disabled or set to high values, you can rely on activity timers provided by Windows for power management. (For information about adjusting BIOS power-management settings, consult the documentation that came with your computer.)

Chapter 9

Chapter 10

Automating Windows XP

If you use your computer very much—and if you're reading this book you probably do—you probably find yourself repeatedly performing the same steps to accomplish a number of ordinary tasks. The task might be a routine maintenance activity, such as backing up your data or cleaning detritus from your hard disk, or it might be a job that requires many steps. Computers excel at repetitive actions, and Microsoft Windows XP provides several ways to automate such tasks:

- **Task Scheduler.** This service launches programs on a regular schedule or upon certain events, such as logging on to your computer.

- **Batch programs.** These programs, a throwback to the earliest days of MS-DOS, still provide an easy, reliable way to run a sequence of programs and commands. Most programs can be started from a command prompt, which means they can be started from a batch program.

- **Windows Script Host.** This feature allows you to run scripts written in VBScript, JScript, and other languages. Although learning how to use Windows Script Host is more difficult than learning how to create batch programs, scripts can interact with the operating system and with other programs in much more powerful ways.

In some cases, you'll find it useful to combine these techniques. For example, suppose your computer has two hard disks and you want to defragment them weekly. You can set up a scheduled task to run the Defrag command, but it can defragment only a single drive. Rather than setting up a separate task for each hard disk—and having to manage multiple

355

At Home with Windows XP

All of the ways to automate Windows XP described in this chapter can be used in both editions of the operating system. To curtail the capabilities of the Task Scheduler by means of policies, however, you need to use Windows XP Professional.

---

schedules—create a batch program that includes a command to defragment each hard disk, and then create a scheduled task to run the batch program once a week.

For more information about defragmenting, see "Defragmenting Disks for Better Performance," page 870.

Scheduling Tasks to Run Automatically

Windows XP includes a flexible, easy-to-use scheduling tool that allows you to automate chores that need to be performed at regular intervals. You can view, create, modify, and delete scheduled tasks with a visit to the Scheduled Tasks folder: In Control Panel, choose Performance And Maintenance, Scheduled Tasks.

---

tip **Finding the Scheduled Tasks tool**

If you prefer navigating the Start menu—or if you want to find a shortcut to the Scheduled Tasks folder that you can put in a more convenient location—choose Start, All Programs, Accessories, System Tools, Scheduled Tasks. Alternatively, in Windows Explorer you can navigate to %SystemRoot%\Tasks.

Running a Program at a Scheduled Time

Task Scheduler, the name of the service that runs scheduled tasks, can be used to launch any program, script, or document on a schedule you specify. To create a scheduled task, open Add Scheduled Task in the Scheduled Tasks folder. The Scheduled Task Wizard that appears when you choose Add Scheduled Task is mostly, but not entirely, self-explanatory. Here are some aspects of the wizard that might not be apparent at first glance:

- You can schedule any application, script, batch program, shortcut, or linked document—anything that you can execute on a command line. You can also specify command-line arguments, but doing so requires a visit to the task's properties dialog box after you have created the task.

- If you schedule a task to run "when my computer starts," that task will run as a noninteractive process when the computer starts and will continue to run, regardless of who is logged on, until the system is shut down or you terminate the task. (Because you are the task's owner, only you or a member of the Administrators group can terminate it. To terminate a noninteractive process, right-click its name in the Scheduled Tasks folder, and choose End Task. Alternatively, press Ctrl+Shift+Esc to open Windows Task Manager, click the Processes tab, select the process, and then click End Process.)

● If you schedule a task to run "when I log on," the task actually runs when *anyone* logs on. If you log on, the task runs interactively (provided, of course, that it was designed to run that way). If someone else logs on, the task runs as a noninteractive process.

InsideOut

If you set up a logon task for your own use, expecting it to run interactively, and someone else logs on before you, that task will run noninteractively when you log on. Windows XP leaves the task running when the other user logs off (because you own it) and does not start a second, interactive, instance when you log on. The quickest way to get your task running the way you intended is to open Scheduled Tasks, right-click the task and choose End Task, and then right-click it again and choose Run.

note Logon tasks do not run when you use Fast User Switching to switch to another person's profile—even if the new user has not already logged on. Logon tasks that are not already running run only when someone logs on while all users are logged off.

● The screen shown in Figure 10-1 prompts you for a user account name and a password. If you're logged on as a member of the Administrators group, you can specify a user account and password other than your own here,

Figure 10-1. If you're an administrator, you can use this screen to schedule interactive tasks for other accounts.

thereby creating an interactive task for another user. Even if you're merely scheduling a task for your own account, however, you must supply your account name and password (the latter twice) in this dialog box—despite the fact that you've already given your password at logon.

InsideOut

You can create a scheduled task by simply dragging an executable (program or document) from Windows Explorer or the desktop to %SystemRoot%\Tasks. Windows XP sets up a .job (scheduled task) file for the object you drop and gives it a default schedule—every day at 9 A.M. Note, however, that this new scheduled task will not run until you authenticate it with a user name and password. To do that, right-click the new .job file in the Tasks folder and choose Properties from the shortcut menu. On the Task tab of the properties dialog box, fill out the Run As box, click Set Password, and supply the appropriate password. You can also delete existing .job files by dragging them from the Tasks folder to the desktop.

● If you schedule a recurring task or one that will run at some distant point in the future, be aware that the password you specify must be valid at the time the task runs. If you change your password periodically, or if you set up a task for a user account that changes its password periodically, you might need to reenter the password down the line. You can do that by right-clicking the task in the Scheduled Tasks folder and choosing Properties from the shortcut menu.

Troubleshooting

Your logon task appears not to run.

Because they might run as noninteractive tasks, the best use for logon tasks is for background tasks, such as checking for viruses or monitoring computer usage remotely. If you want a particular interactive program to start whenever you log on—say, for example, you would like a to-do list to open in Notepad—place a shortcut to the program in the Startup group instead of using a logon task.

● Unless the Remove Advanced Menu policy has been enabled (see "Restricting the Task Scheduler with Policies," page 362), the wizard's last page includes a check box that asks whether you want to open "advanced properties" for the new task when you click Finish. What appears if you select this check box is actually the normal properties dialog box for the task. To set advanced properties, click the Schedule tab, and then click Advanced. In the Advanced Schedule Options dialog box, you can do such things as set repeat parameters and an end date for your new task. You can always come back to these options later by right-clicking the task in the Scheduled Tasks folder and choosing Properties from the shortcut menu. (For more information about advanced scheduling options, see "Advanced Scheduling Options" on the next page.)

InsideOut

A new security feature in Windows XP prevents accounts with no password (that is, a blank password) from logging on except at the Welcome screen. (This prevents easy access to the user's profile from a nefarious Internet hacker, for example.) Because Task Scheduler uses Run As capability (which is also locked out by this security restriction) to launch tasks, you must use an account that has a password to run scheduled tasks.

If your computer is in a location where you can safely use it without password-protecting your account, there is a simple workaround: create a separate user account for running scheduled tasks and assign a password to that account.

Monitoring Scheduled Tasks

You can get useful information about the status of a scheduled task by displaying the Scheduled Tasks folder in Details view. Among other things, you can learn when the task last ran (or was scheduled to run), when it's scheduled to run again, and who created the task.

If a task fails to run, Details view will tell you so but won't tell you why. To get diagnostic information, choose View Log from the Scheduled Tasks folder's Advanced menu. The log (%SystemRoot%\Schedlgu.txt) appears as a plain-text file in Notepad.

A Note About Security

The behavior of the Windows XP Scheduled Tasks facility points up a fact that you should always keep in mind when working on a network or sharing your own machine with other user accounts: It's possible for someone else to start a process that runs invisibly while you're logged on to your own account. Even though a process started by someone else is limited by the privileges available to that other user, it's possible for such a process to monitor your activities. If you work with data that you don't want others to see, keep that data on an NTFS volume, and use NTFS file security to restrict others' access.

Chapter 10

Tasks that fail to run because the computer is off at the appointed hour, or because the computer is on battery power and you've stipulated that the task shouldn't run in that condition, are recorded as missed tasks. You can be notified about missed tasks by choosing Notify Me Of Missed Tasks from the Scheduled Tasks folder's Advanced menu. If you miss a task because your computer is off, a message to that effect appears at your next logon.

InsideOut

Task Scheduler doesn't add new events to the end of the log file. Rather, it creates a sort of circular log file: When it records a new entry after reaching the log's size limit, it replaces the oldest entry still in the log. To find the most recent entry, use Notepad's Find command to search for *****. The newest entry precedes a line that reads "[***** Most recent entry is above this line *****]."

Advanced Scheduling Options

Visiting the properties dialog box for a task lets you modify the task's schedule, change the password or user name associated with the task, add command-line arguments for the task, or even change the application that is scheduled to run. The properties dialog box also provides some useful advanced scheduling options.

The Show Multiple Schedules check box, on the Schedule tab, lets you assign more than one schedule to the same task. You could, for example, arrange to have your task run every Friday at 5 P.M. and also at 5 P.M. on the 30th day of every month. When you select this check box, a New button appears. Click New to enter a second or subsequent schedule.

Figure 10-2 shows the dialog box that is displayed when you click Advanced on the Schedule tab. Here you can specify an end date for a recurrent task or specify a repeat interval for a recurrent task. If you select Repeat Task, you can use the Time or Duration option to tell the system when to quit repeating. To repeat every two hours until 11 P.M., for example, you could select Repeat Task, set the Every fields to 2 and Hours, select Time, and specify 11 P.M. To run at 30-minute intervals for four hours, you could set the Every fields to 30 and Minutes, select Duration, and then specify 4 hours and 0 minutes.

On the Settings tab, shown in Figure 10-3, you can provide a termination order for a task that has run too long, stipulate that a task not run if the computer is in use at the scheduled time (or stop running if someone begins using the computer), and tell the system not to run a task if the computer is running on battery power. On ACPI-compliant computers, the Power Management section of this dialog box includes a Wake The Computer To Run This Task check box. Selecting this check box ensures that your task will run at the scheduled time, even if it's in standby at the time. (For information about ACPI, see "ACPI vs. APM," page 348.)

On the Settings tab, you can also select a check box that will remove the task object from the Scheduled Tasks folder if, on the current schedule, it's never going to run again.

Figure 10-2. Click Advanced on the Schedule tab to produce the Advanced Schedule Options dialog box, where you can set end dates and recurrence parameters.

Figure 10-3. The Settings tab of a task's properties dialog box provides power-management control and other useful options.

---

note The computer is considered to be "idle" when there's no keyboard or mouse activity.

Chapter 10

Restricting the Task Scheduler with Policies

The Task Scheduler node in the Group Policy console (Gpedit.msc) includes seven policies that you can use to curtail features relating to scheduled tasks. These policies are listed in Table 10-1. (The Group Policy console is available in Windows XP Professional only.)

Table 10-1. Task Scheduler Policies

Policy	Effect When Enabled
Hide Property Pages	Prevents users from viewing and changing the properties of new and existing tasks, including their schedules, Run As accounts, and passwords.
Prevent Task Run Or End	Prevents users from running or stopping a task manually.
Prohibit Drag-and-Drop	Prevents users from creating a task by dragging an executable to the Tasks folder.
Prohibit New Task Creation	Eliminates the Add Scheduled Task item from the Tasks folder. Administrators can still use the Schtasks command to create new tasks.
Prohibit Task Deletion	Prevents users from deleting tasks from the Tasks folder. Administrators can still use the Schtasks command to delete tasks.
Remove Advanced Menu	Simplifies the Scheduled Task Wizard by eliminating the option to set advanced scheduling properties.
Prohibit Browse	Eliminates the Browse button from the Scheduled Task Wizard and from the Task tab of a task's properties dialog box.

Note the following:

● All of the policies affect task scheduling via the Scheduled Tasks folder only. None of them restrict your ability to use the Schtasks command.

● Hide Property Pages prevents users from changing the characteristics of tasks once they have been scheduled. Unless you also enable Prohibit New Task Creation, users can still set task properties while creating new tasks.

● The purpose of Remove Advanced Menu is to simplify the Scheduled Task Wizard. You can still set a task's advanced properties by returning to the properties dialog box after the task has been created.

If you choose to enable any of these policies, be aware that your settings apply to all users of the current computer, regardless of whether you work within Computer Configuration\Administrative Templates\Windows Components\Task Scheduler or User Configuration\Administrative Templates\Windows Components\Task Scheduler. (If you make differing changes to both Group Policy nodes, the Computer Configuration changes take priority.) For more information about policies and the Group Policy console, see Appendix E, "Group Policy."

newfeature! Scheduling Tasks with the Schtasks Command

The Scheduled Tasks facility provides a friendly and versatile method of creating and managing scheduled tasks. In some instances, however, you might find it easier to manage scheduled tasks from a command prompt. For those occasions, Windows XP provides the Schtasks command, a replacement for the venerable At command that was included with previous versions of the Windows NT platform.

note You can continue to enter At commands at the command prompt or in batch programs; tasks that you set up this way appear in the Scheduled Tasks folder, identified as At*n*, where *n* is a task ID supplied by the system. If you edit an At task in Scheduled Tasks, however, the task is upgraded to a "normal" scheduled task. At that point, you can no longer delete the task at a command prompt, and you must supply user credentials (account name and password) before the task can run.

With Schtasks, you can create, modify, delete, end, view, and run scheduled tasks, on your own computer or on another computer on your network. The Schtasks command is a boon not only for Windows XP users who prefer working at an MS-DOS-style prompt, but more importantly, for you to manage scheduled tasks from batch files.

note The Schtasks command is available only to computer administrators. Others who attempt to use it are rebuffed with the message, "ERROR: Access is denied."

Schtasks is a rather complex command with lots of command-line switches and other parameters (its description in the Help And Support Center runs to 16 densely packed pages of text), but it has only six main variants:

- **Schtasks /Create.** This variant, which you use to create a new scheduled task, is the most complex because of all the scheduling flexibility. You can, for example, set up a schedule at an interval expressed in minutes, hours, days, weeks, or months—in addition to the event-based schedules, such as on startup, on logon, and when the system is idle.

- **Schtasks /Change.** This variant allows you to modify an existing task. You can change the program that the task runs, the user account under which the task runs, or the password for the user account.

363

- **Schtasks /Delete.** This variant deletes an existing scheduled task or, optionally, all scheduled tasks on a computer.

- **Schtasks /End.** This variant stops a program that was started by a scheduled task.

- **Schtasks /Query.** This variant displays all scheduled tasks on a computer, including those that were created by other users.

- **Schtasks /Run.** This variant immediately starts a scheduled task, ignoring the schedule that was created for the task.

You can get more help about each of these variants of the Schtasks by viewing the descriptions in the Help And Support Center or by appending /? to one of these commands at a command prompt. For example, for detailed information about Schtasks /Run, at a command prompt type:

```
schtasks /run /?
```

A few examples should give you an idea of the power of the Schtasks command. Suppose, for example, you want to take a break every four hours at 20 minutes past the hour to play a bit of Solitaire. The following command sets up a task that launches Solitaire on that schedule:

```
schtasks /create /tn "Solitaire break" /tr sol.exe /sc hourly /mo 4 /st 00:20:00
```

In this example, the /Tn switch specifies the name of the task, /Tr specifies the name of the executable program (if the program is not stored in the %SystemRoot%\System32 folder, you must specify the complete path to the program), /Sc specifies the schedule type, /Mo specifies the interval, and /St specifies the starting time.

When you create a task as shown in this example, you'll see that Schtasks prompts you for the password for your account. You can bypass this prompt by appending /rp *password* to the command, where *password* is your logon password.

The following example creates a scheduled task that runs a script on the last Friday of each calendar quarter. (This isn't a script that's included with Windows; it's a made-up name intended to spark ideas on your part!)

```
schtasks /create /tn "Quarterly wrap-up" /tr c:\apps\qtrwrap.vbs
    /sc monthly /mo last /d fri /m mar,jun,sep,dec
```

By default, tasks scheduled via the Schtasks command run under the user account that's currently logged on. To make them run under a different user account, use the /Ru switch followed by the user account name you want to use; you'll also need to know the logon password for that account. To use the built-in System account, append **/ru "System"** to the command. No password is required for the System account, but because only administrators can use Schtasks, this doesn't present a security problem.

Because the System account cannot log on interactively, you can't see or interact with programs run by the System account.

If you're familiar with the At command from Windows NT and Windows 2000, you'll see that Schtasks offers several improvements:

- You specify tasks using a friendly name rather than a serial ID number.

- You have many more options in setting up schedules, including specifying the last (or first, second, and so on) day of a month, specific times of day, and various other intervals.

- You can view, modify, run, or end an existing scheduled task.

caution Don't disable the Task Scheduler service by stopping it in the Services snap-in or with the Stop Using Task Scheduler command on the Advanced menu. Although they don't appear as scheduled tasks, several behind-the-scenes optimizations rely on the Task Scheduler service. In particular, optimizations that improve disk layout (by moving files around on disk for the best performance), boot time, and application opening time run as scheduled tasks.

Downloading Web Pages at a Scheduled Time

Most of the time, you'll use Internet Explorer or another browser while you're connected to the Internet. If you prefer, you can have Internet Explorer visit your favorite Web sites at night (for example) and then deliver the goods for you to read offline the following morning.

To schedule a page for automatic download, it must be in your list of Favorites. Pages included on the Favorites menu have a Make Available Offline option; enabling this option (and specifying a schedule) causes Internet Explorer to fetch pages at the appointed time.

note Making a page available offline—with or without specifying a schedule—makes it possible for you to view the page even when your computer isn't connected to the Internet.

Adding a Page to Your Offline Web Pages List

You can add the page to your offline Web pages list (that is, make it available offline) when you create the favorite or at any time later on.

Follow these steps to add a page to your Favorites folder, make it available offline, and specify a download schedule:

1 Display the page, and then choose Favorites, Add To Favorites.

2 In the Add Favorite dialog box, select Make Available Offline.

Chapter 10

365

3 Click the Customize button to start the Offline Favorite Wizard.

With this wizard, you can specify the following:

- Whether Internet Explorer should also download pages that are linked from the page you're saving as a favorite

- When Internet Explorer should download the pages

  If you choose to use an existing named schedule, Windows doesn't show you exactly what that schedule is. The best course of action is to select an existing schedule and proceed blindly ahead. After you've saved the favorite, open its properties dialog box (right-click its entry in the Favorites menu and choose Properties), click the Schedule tab, and then make any necessary adjustments.

- Whether the page requires a user name and password for access

4 Change the name and location of the favorite if you like, and then click OK.

To set up a download schedule for an existing favorite, follow these steps:

1 Open the existing favorite page's properties dialog box. (Right-click its entry on the Favorites menu or on the Favorites bar and then choose Properties from the shortcut menu.)

Don't bother using the shortcut menu's Make Available Offline command. It launches the Offline Favorite Wizard—forcing you to step through several pages even if you don't want to change any default settings—and it doesn't offer many of the options that are available in the properties dialog box.

2 On the Web Document tab of the page's properties dialog box, select Make This Page Available Offline.

3 Click the Schedule and Download tabs, and make settings as described in the following section.

> For more information about adding favorites and organizing the list, see "Managing Your Favorites," page 773.

Changing Offline Web Page Settings

The properties dialog box for an offline Web page is the place where you can set up a synchronization schedule, determine exactly what is downloaded, and set up e-mail notification of changes. Do one of the following to view the properties dialog box:

- Right-click its entry on the Favorites menu or on the Favorites bar, and then choose Properties from the shortcut menu.

- Choose Organize Favorites from the Favorites menu, right-click the page, and then click Properties.

366

Setting up a synchronization schedule   By default, Internet Explorer synchronizes your locally stored copy of an offline Web page with the original version only when you choose Synchronize from the Tools menu. Using the Schedule tab in the properties dialog box, you can set up a schedule for synchronizations. At the appointed times, Internet Explorer connects to the Internet (if you're not already connected) and updates the offline page by downloading the current version of the online page.

Take these steps to set up a synchronization schedule:

1   On the Schedule tab of the page's properties dialog box, select Use The Following Schedule(s).

2   If the schedule you want to use isn't in the list, click Add. The New Schedule dialog box appears.

3   Specify the number of days between updates and the time you want the updates to occur, and give the schedule a name. Select the check box if you want to connect to the Internet at the appointed time. (If you don't select the box and you're not already connected to the Internet, the connection dialog box waits for your go-ahead.) Then click OK.

4   Select the check box next to each named schedule you want to use for this page.

tip   **Create complex schedules**

The New Schedule dialog box allows you to set up schedules that update, at most, once per day. To update more frequently, you can create several schedules. But there's a better way: Set up a daily schedule, and then, on the Schedule tab, select the schedule and click Edit. In the schedule's properties dialog box that appears, click the Schedule tab. Here you can schedule updates at any of several intervals, upon certain events, or on certain days of the week or month; you can even create multiple schedules. And by clicking the Advanced button, you can schedule updates as often as every minute and set an ending time for scheduled updates. For more information about advanced scheduling options, see "Advanced Scheduling Options," page 360.

---

tip **Prevent synchronization while traveling**

Futile attempts by Internet Explorer to make a dial-up connection while you're away from a phone line can be annoying. To prevent such interruptions, on the Schedule tab of the properties dialog box for the offline page, select the synchronization schedule and click Edit. Then, on the Settings tab, select Don't Start The Task If The Computer Is Running On Batteries.

Setting up download and e-mail notification options   Visit the Download tab in the properties dialog box (shown in Figure 10-4) in the following circumstances:

● You want to change the level to which Internet Explorer downloads linked pages.

The default is zero, which means you download only the offline page—but not any pages that are reached by links on the original page. You can specify up to three levels, but be aware that the amount of material that Internet Explorer will have to download increases exponentially as you select deeper levels of links.

If you choose to include linked pages, you can limit the download to include only links to other pages at the same site (this prevents downloading pages

Figure 10-4.   The Download tab allows you to determine what is down-loaded automatically. Clicking Advanced displays the Advanced Download Options dialog box.

linked to banner ads, for example) or only links to HTML pages. (Click Advanced to set the latter option.)

● You want to change the kinds of items that Internet Explorer downloads—for example, to exclude images or add sound and video. (Click the Advanced button to set these options.)

● You want to impose a maximum download size for the page.

● You want to receive e-mail notification when the page changes. (Enter your e-mail address and the name of your mail server; this feature works only with SMTP-based (Simple Mail Transfer Protocol) mail systems, which excludes many Internet mail accounts.)

● The page requires a user name and password for access. (Click the Login button to enter this information.)

Recording Keyboard and Mouse Actions as Macros

As an alternative to learning a programming language (such as the batch language or a script language you can use with Windows Script Host), your needs might be met by a simple macro recorder—a program that records keystrokes and mouse actions and then plays them back upon demand. A number of macro recorder programs are available at little or no cost on the Internet. You might want to try the following:

● Aldo's Macro Recorder (*http://www.aldostools.com/macro.html*)

● EZ Macros (*http://www.americansys.com/ezmacros.htm*)

● Macro Magic (*http://www.iolo.com/*)

A search for "macro" or "macro recorder" on any search engine or shareware download site is likely to turn up dozens of programs in this category.

Automating Command Sequences with Batch Programs

A *batch program* (also commonly called a *batch file*) is a text file that contains a sequence of commands to be executed. You define the sequence of commands, name the sequence, and then execute the commands by entering the name at a command prompt. Any action you can take by typing a command at a command prompt can be encapsulated in a batch program.

InsideOut

In Windows XP, you can name your batch programs with a .bat or .cmd file name extension. The Windows XP command interpreter, Cmd.exe, attempts to execute commands from any file with either of these extensions. When you type the name of a batch program at a command prompt, Cmd.exe looks first for a file with a .bat extension. If you have two batch programs in the same folder with the same base name but different extensions, the .bat file will be executed—not the .cmd file. You can override this behavior by including the extension when you type the file name.

When you type the name of your batch program at the command prompt, the command interpreter opens the file and starts reading the statements. It reads the first line, executes the command, and then goes on to the next line. On the surface, this seems to operate just as if you were typing each line yourself at the command prompt. In fact, however, it can be much more complicated because you can use parameters with batch programs to vary their behavior just as you can with other types of programs. Batch programs can also respond to values returned by programs and to the values of environment variables.

The rules for capitalization in batch programs are the same as at the command prompt—there are none. Commands and labels are not case sensitive, and you can mix capital and lowercase letters at will. (With certain commands, however, switches and parameters are case sensitive.) In the examples in this book, we show commands in lowercase because that's the easiest to type (although we capitalize command names in explanatory text). On the other hand, we use uppercase for labels so that they stand out clearly. We use mixed case for messages that appear on the screen and for names used when creating folders or files, because the capitalization is retained when the text is transferred to screen or disk.

> **note** Several examples in this chapter include commands that won't fit on a single line on the printed page of this book. The second and subsequent lines of such commands are indented. You, however, should type these commands on a single line.

Using Batch Commands

Batch commands are the commands that generally make sense only when used within a batch program. With a few exceptions, Windows XP has the same batch program commands as MS-DOS. We start by summarizing all the batch commands, in Table 10-2, and then look at some Windows XP batch programs. We explain some of the commands, but for most of them, this table—along with the command reference in Windows XP—should suffice.

Table 10-2. **Batch Commands**

Command	Purpose
@	Prevents the line from being displayed on the screen when used as the first character in a line.
Echo [Off I On]	Turns screen echoing off or on.
Echo *msg*	Displays *msg* on the screen.
Echo.	Displays a blank line on the screen.
Rem *msg*	Identifies *msg* as a comment.
If [Not] Errorlevel *num cmd*	Executes *cmd* if the error level value returned from the previous command is less than or equal to *num*. (*Not* reverses the logic.)
If [Not] Exist *file cmd*	Executes *cmd* if *file* exists. (*Not* reverses the logic.)
If [Not] *txt1* == *txt2 cmd*	Executes *cmd* if *txt1* is the same as *txt2*, including case. (*Not* reverses the logic.)
Goto *label*	Transfers control to the line marked by *label*.
: *label*	Names the line to be reached by a Goto command.
For %%*var* In (*set*) Do [*cmd*] %%*var*	Loops through the items in *set*, executing *cmd* for each loop and replacing any instances of *var* with the matching item from *set*, which can be a list separated by spaces or can contain the wildcard characters * and ?.
Shift	Shifts command-line parameters one place so that %2 becomes %1, %3 becomes %2, and so on.
Call *batfile args*	Executes *batfile* with *args* and then returns to the calling batch program.
Setlocal	Makes current environment variables local to this batch program; any changes to variables are known only in this batch program until Endlocal is executed.
Endlocal	Makes environment variables known to the system; any changes made after Endlocal remain in effect when the batch program terminates.
Pushd *path*	Saves the current folder on a stack and changes to *path*.

(continued)

Chapter 10

371

Table 10-2. *(continued)*

Command	Purpose
Popd	Changes to the last folder saved by Pushd and removes it from the stack.
Pause	Suspends processing until a key is pressed.
Title	Sets the title of the Command Prompt window.

Getting More Information About Command-Line Tools

Windows XP Professional includes information about command-line tools in its graphical Help And Support Center, but it's hard to find. (The help is also available in Windows XP Home Edition, but it's even harder to find because there's no direct link to it.) In either version, however, you can get a complete list of supported commands by typing **help** at a command prompt. For help on a particular command, type **help** followed by the name of the command (for example, **help xcopy**) or type the name of the command followed by **/?** (for example, **xcopy /?**).

If you prefer the graphical help, which provides more information, you can get to it via this path in Windows XP Professional:

1 Click Start, Help And Support.

2 On the Help And Support Center home page, under Pick A Task, click Use Tools To View Your Computer Information And Diagnose Problems.

3 Under Tools in the contents pane, click Command-Line Reference A-Z.

If you use the graphical help frequently, you'll want to add this page to your Help And Support favorites list. (Click Add To Favorites.) But you can also get to detailed graphical help quickly from a command prompt—the place where you're most likely to be when you need the information. This is the only way for Windows XP Home Edition users to open graphical help about command-line tools. You can get directly to this help page by typing this unwieldy command at a prompt:

```
%systemroot%\pchealth\helpctr\binaries\helpctr
      /url ms-its:%systemroot%\Help\ntcmds.chm::/ntcmds.htm
```

You can go directly to the help for a particular command by replacing the last occurrence of "ntcmds" with the name of the command you're interested in. Typing this cryptic string, of course, is no easier than navigating through the pages of the Help And Support Center. But with a couple of tricks, you can eliminate all the messy typing and make it much easier to get right to the help you want.

First, use Doskey—a program that creates command-line macros—to encapsulate the preceding command in a macro named *h*. To create the macro, at a command prompt type:

```
doskey h=%systemroot%\pchealth\helpctr\binaries\helpctr
    /url ms-its:%systemroot%\Help\ntcmds.chm::/$1.htm
```

With this macro—which includes $1 as a replaceable parameter—you type **h** followed by a space and the name of the command about which you want information. For example, to get information about Doskey, you'd type **h doskey**. To display the index page that lists all the commands, type **h ntcmds**.

A Doskey macro that you enter at a command prompt works only within that session. Your macro won't work in other command prompt windows you open, and it's gone altogether when you close the window in which you created it. You can save your macros to a file and load them with a short command each time you open a command prompt window, but there's a better way:

Employ the second trick, which uses the registry's AutoRun value to cause the macro to be automatically created in *every* command prompt session you open. Follow these steps:

1 Open Registry Editor. (For information about Registry Editor, see Chapter 29, "Editing the Registry.")

2 Navigate to HKLM\Software\Microsoft\Command Processor. (This key affects all users who log on to your computer. If you want the help macro to be available only for your user account, go to HKCU\Software\Microsoft\ Command Processor instead.)

3 Double-click the AutoRun value (if it doesn't exist, create a string value called AutoRun) and type the following command (the same one described above) in the Value Data box:

```
doskey h=%systemroot%\pchealth\helpctr\binaries\helpctr
    /url ms-its:%systemroot%\Help\ntcmds.chm::/$1.htm
```

4 Click OK and close Registry Editor.

 If you don't want to get your hands dirty by delving into the registry, the companion CD contains a script called Command-line help.vbs that makes this registry change for you.

InsideOut

Using the Rem command is the documented way to put comments in your batch programs, but it is intrusive because the command looks like part of the comment. Furthermore, if you leave echoing on while debugging a batch program, all your comments are echoed, making it harder to read commands. A better way to add comments to code is to use two colons:

```
:: This line is for humans; computers ignore it
```

This kind of comment is never echoed. Be sure to use two colons; using only one creates a label that might conflict with a legitimate label. Although this commenting style is handy, we use the conventional Rem statement in this book's examples to avoid confusing readers who miss this tip.

Creating a Simple Batch Program

The most important step in writing a batch program (or any other kind of computer program) is to state the problem correctly. In this example, the problem is to connect to a dial-up connection by repeatedly dialing different connections until a successful connection is made. If a connection fails (because the line is busy or you enter the wrong password, for example), the program should try another dial-up connection.

This batch program relies on Rasdial.exe, the command-line version of the dialing component used by dial-up connections. The program uses dial-up connections that you have previously created in the Network Connections folder.

To create a batch program, use a plain-text editor, such as Notepad. (When you save the file, be sure to give it a .bat or .cmd file name extension.) The following listing shows Dial.bat in its entirety:

```
@echo off
rem Connects to a Dial-up Connection
title Dialing Connections

:START
echo Connecting to MSN
rasdial msn pct_hiker *
if not errorlevel 1 goto end

echo Connecting to Earthlink
rasdial earthlink swdocs *
if not errorlevel 1 goto end
```

```
echo Connecting to local ISP
rasdial "pasadena isp" swdocs *
if errorlevel 1 goto start

:END
title Command Prompt
```

You'll find Dial.bat—along with several other example batch programs—on the companion CD.

You execute a batch program by typing its name at the command prompt, like this:

```
C:\>dial
```

By default, batch programs display each line on the screen before attempting to execute it. Because this is seldom desirable, most batch programs start with the same line that ours starts with:

```
@echo off
```

The at sign (@) says not to display the Echo Off command. The Echo Off command says not to display any more lines for the rest of the batch program.

The line that follows the descriptive Rem statement

```
title Dialing Connections
```

sets the title of the Command Prompt window to Dialing Connections, as shown in Figure 10-5. This title helps orient users to the task at hand.

Figure 10-5. The Title command sets the title of the Command Prompt window.

Between the Start and End labels are three sets of dialing commands—one for each Internet service provider (ISP) for which we've created a dial-up connection. As we've used it here, the parameters following Rasdial are the connection name (the name that appears in the Network Connections folder) and the user name. The asterisk causes

Rasdial to prompt for your password; you could put the password in your batch program (in plain text) if you're sure that it won't be compromised. Like many programs, when Rasdial exits, it sets an error level, which is simply a numeric result code. The If statement in Dial.bat tests the error level for values of 1 *or greater*. An error level of 0 indicates a successful connection. (Rasdial uses many other values to indicate various error conditions. For a list of error codes, type **hh netcfg.chm** to open Network Connections help; on the Contents tab, open Troubleshooting and select Error Messages.)

Each of the If commands includes a Goto command that directs processing to the correct part of the batch program. When a Goto is executed, the command interpreter jumps to the line with the matching label and starts executing the lines it finds following the label. (A label is a line starting with a colon.) Following the first two connection attempts, if the error level value is *not* greater than or equal to 1, the command processor transfers control to the End label; otherwise, it drops down to the next statement. In the final If statement, the program jumps back up to the Start label if the error level is greater than or equal to 1.

The Goto End statement prevents the subsequent commands from being executed by directing processing to the End label. Without these statements, Rasdial would dial the second and third connections, even if the first one was successful.

The single statement that follows the End label simply resets the window title.

Better Options for Testing Error Level Values

If you want your batch program to take different actions based on different error level values, you can use successive If statements to test for each value. With MS-DOS and earlier versions of Windows, it was necessary to test error level values in decreasing order, because the condition is true if the error level value is equal to or greater than the value you specify. But if you're writing a batch program for use only on computers running Windows 2000 or Windows XP, you can use comparison operators to more easily act on different error level values. To do that, you must use the %ErrorLevel% environment variable, which expands into the current error level value. For example, you might use a statement like the following to jump to a certain section of the program if Rasdial sets the error level to 676—the result code that indicates the line is busy:

```
if %errorlevel% equ 676 goto busy
```

The available comparison operators are Equ (equal to), Neq (not equal to), Lss (less than), Leq (less than or equal to), Gtr (greater than), and Geq (greater than or equal to). You can use comparison operators only if command extensions are enabled. For information about command extensions, see "Using Command Extensions," page 1248.

Using Advanced Techniques

This section offers a few example batch programs that illustrate some additional programming techniques.

You can find these batch programs—Rsbackup.bat, CleanRecent.bat, and Alphabetize.bat—on the companion CD.

Backing Up the Removable Storage Database

This batch program creates a backup copy of the Removable Storage database. It illustrates some commonly used techniques, including stopping and starting services and using environment variables. The following program is called Rsbackup.bat:

```
@echo off
rem Backs up the Removable Storage database
title Removable Storage Backup
echo Removable Storage database backup in process...

echo Stopping the Removable Storage service
net stop "removable storage" > nul

echo Copying the Removable Storage database
xcopy /y %systemroot%\system32\ntmsdata %systemroot%\system32\ntmsdata
    \backup\ > nul

echo Starting the Removable Storage service
net start "removable storage" > nul

echo.
echo Removable Storage database was backed up to
echo %SystemRoot%\System32\NtmsData\Backup\
title Command Prompt
```

The first command to examine is Net Stop:

```
net stop "removable storage" > nul
```

The Net command is frequently included in batch programs because it can be used to control so many functions in Windows. In this case, we are stopping the Removable Storage service to ensure that it doesn't have the database files open when we try to copy them. To stop or start a service, you can use the service's "friendly name" (that is, the name that appears in the Services snap-in), as we've done here, or you can use the actual service name if you know it. (In the case of Removable Storage, the service name is Ntmssvc.)

Throughout the program, Echo statements keep the user informed of the progress. Therefore, we use > Nul to redirect the output of the Net statement to the Nul device—colloquially known as the "bit bucket"—because its output is redundant.

The Xcopy command then makes a copy of the files:

```
xcopy /y %systemroot%\system32\ntmsdata systemroot%\system32\ntmsdata\
    backup\ > nul
```

On most computers, the Removable Storage database files are stored in C:\Windows\System32\Ntmsdata. However, if you installed Windows to a different folder, the files will be in a different location. In this Xcopy statement, %SystemRoot% is an environment variable that specifies where Windows is installed on the local computer. By using environment variables, we can ensure that our batch programs work on any computer that is running Windows XP.

Table 10-3 lists some useful environment variables. You can see the current environment variables for your computer by typing **set** at the command prompt. To use an environment variable in a batch program or at the command prompt, precede and follow its name with a percent sign (%). When the batch program executes, the value of the environment variable replaces its name in the batch program. (For more information, see "Using Environment Variables," page 1257.)

Table 10-3. **Useful Environment Variables**

Environment Variable	Value
AppData	Location of the Application Data folder for the current user (for example, C:\Documents And Settings \CarlS\Application Data).
CommonProgramFiles	Location of the Common Files folder (typically C:\Program Files\Common Files).
ComSpec	Executable file for the command processor (typically C:\Windows\System32\Cmd.exe).
HomeDrive	Drive letter that's mapped to the home folder for a user profile. By default, it's the same as the letter of the system volume (typically C).
HomePath	Folder for a user profile on the home drive (for example, \Documents And Settings\CarlS). Together, HomeDrive and HomePath specify the default folder for a user profile.
OS	Operating system on the user's workstation (Windows_NT on a system running Windows XP, Windows 2000, or Windows NT).

Table 10-3. *(continued)*

Environment Variable	Value
Path	Application search path. When you type the name of an executable at a command prompt, Windows looks in each folder in the search path if the executable file is not in the current folder.
ProgramFiles	Location of the Program Files folder (typically C:\Program Files).
SystemDrive	Drive on which the system folder resides (typically C).
SystemRoot	System folder; the folder that contains the Windows XP operating system files (typically C:\Windows).
Temp	Folder for storing temporary files (for example, C:\Docume~1\CarlS\Locals~1\Temp—the short path name for C:\Documents and Settings\CarlS \Local Settings\Temp).
UserDomain	Domain the user is logged into (for example, SWDOCS) or, if the computer is not logged in to a domain, the name of the computer (for example, SEQUOIA).
UserName	User's logon name (for example, CarlS).
UserProfile	Location of the current user's profile (for example, C:\Documents And Settings\CarlS).
Windir	Same as SystemRoot; included for compatibility with earlier versions of Windows.

When the database files have been copied, another Net command restarts the Removable Storage service:

```
net start "removable storage" > nul
```

Cleaning Out the Recent Documents List

The batch program that follows, called CleanRecent.bat, removes some of the files from the recently used documents list that you see if you select My Recent Documents from the Start menu. Removing document types that you don't want on this list allows room for more of the documents that you do want to see.

379

```
@echo off
rem Cleans unwanted file types from the Recent folder
title Clean Recent
echo Cleaning Recent folder...

for %%t in (wav log ini) do del "%userprofile%\recent\*.%%t.lnk"

echo.
echo Done cleaning Recent folder.
title Command Prompt
```

> **note** CleanRecent.bat is effective only if you have cleared the option to hide file name extensions on the View tab in Folder Options before you opened the documents that appear on the Recent menu. If extensions don't appear on the Recent menu, this program can't identify the files to be deleted.

This batch program uses the For...In...Do command to repeatedly execute the Del command. The document type file name extensions that you want to remove from the list are enclosed in the parentheses. The For command executes the Del command once for each entry in this list. The variable %%T contains the current extension and is substituted in the Del command. This is effectively the same as typing three Del commands.

Note that the file names have an .lnk extension added. This is because the Recent folder contains shortcuts (which have the extension .lnk) rather than containing the actual recently used files.

Alphabetizing Your Favorites Menu and Your Start Menu

This batch program is somewhat more complex than the ones we have looked at so far. It uses more advanced techniques to control program flow.

Alphabetize.bat alphabetizes your Favorites menu and the Programs branch of your Start menu. (You can have it act on your Favorites menu, your Start menu, or both.) The menus become unsorted as you add new items—which are appended to the bottom of the menu—or manually reorder them by dragging menu items. Windows XP includes a Sort By Name command on the shortcut menu that appears if you right-click one of these menus. But Alphabetize.bat offers something more: If you decide you like the previous order better, Alphabetize.bat can restore the previous order—giving it an "undo" capability. Furthermore, Alphabetize.bat reorders the entire menu, including its submenus, whereas the Sort By Name command doesn't sort the contents of submenus.

> **note** Alphabetize.bat works only with the classic Start menu, not the default Start menu.

380

The order information for the Start and Favorites menus is kept in the registry. To alphabetize, this batch program exports the current settings to a file and then simply deletes the appropriate keys from the registry. Without an order specified in the registry, Windows alphabetizes the lists. As you add or move menu items, Windows re-creates the order information in the registry.

In the Alphabetize.bat listing that follows, we've included line numbers for reference. Note that you can't use line numbers in an actual batch program.

```
 1 @echo off
 2 rem Alphabetizes Favorites and/or Start menu
 3 setlocal
 4 if not exist "%appdata%\inside out\" md "%appdata%\Inside Out\"
 5
 6 if "%1" == "" goto usage
 7 if "%1" == "/?" goto usage
 8 if /i %1 == help goto usage
 9 set type=%1
10 set action=%2
11 if "%2" == "" set action=sort
12
13 set startmenu=false
14 set favorites=false
15 goto %type%
16 :STARTMENU
17 set startmenu=true
18 goto %action%
19 :FAVORITES
20 set favorites=true
21 goto %action%
22 :BOTH
23 set startmenu=true
24 set favorites=true
25 goto %action%
26
27 :SORT
28 :SORTFAVORITES
29 if not %favorites% == true goto sortstartmenu
30 reg export "HKCU\Software\Microsoft\Windows\CurrentVersion\Explorer\
   MenuOrder\Favorites" "%AppData%\Inside Out\Favorites.reg" > nul
31 reg delete "HKCU\Software\Microsoft\Windows\CurrentVersion\Explorer\
   MenuOrder\Favorites" /f > nul
32 if %errorlevel% equ 0 echo Favorites alphabetized.
33
34 :SORTSTARTMENU
35 if not %startmenu% == true goto :eof
36 reg export "HKCU\Software\Microsoft\Windows\CurrentVersion\Explorer\
   MenuOrder\Start Menu" "%AppData%\Inside Out\Start Menu.reg" > nul
```

```
37 reg delete "HKCU\Software\Microsoft\Windows\CurrentVersion\Explorer\
   MenuOrder\Start Menu" /f > nul
38 if %errorlevel% equ 0 echo Start Menu alphabetized.
39 goto :eof
40
41 :UNDO
42 :UNDOFAVORITES
43 if not %favorites% == true goto undostartmenu
44 if not exist "%appdata%\inside out\favorites.reg" goto noundofile
45 reg import "%appdata%\inside out\favorites.reg" > nul
46 echo Favorites order restored.
47
48 :UNDOSTARTMENU
49 if not %startmenu% == true goto :eof
50 if not exist "%appdata%\inside out\start menu.reg" goto noundofile
51 reg import "%appdata%\inside out\start menu.reg" > nul
52 echo Start menu order restored.
53 goto :eof
54
55 :NOUNDOFILE
56 echo No file exists to restore.
57 goto :eof
58
59 :USAGE
60 echo.
61 echo Usage:
62 echo Alphabetize StartMenu^|Favorites^|Both [Undo]
63 echo.
64 echo Example:
65 echo Alphabetize Favorites
66 echo.
67 echo Add Undo to restore previous settings.
```

Lines 1 through 3 take care of some basic setup functions. They identify what this batch program does and turn echoing off. The Setlocal command specifies that environment variables created or changed by this batch program should be "local" to this batch program and should not affect other programs.

Line 4 creates a folder under the Application Data folder called Inside Out. Because the Md (make directory) command displays an error if the folder already exists, we use If Not Exist so that the Md command is executed only if the folder does not exist.

The second section of the batch program, lines 6 through 11, checks for command-line parameters. The %1 that appears in several of these lines represents the first argument on the command line. %2 represents the second, and so on up to %9. If you type the command **alphabetize a**, for example, the command interpreter sees this as the first line in this section of the batch program:

```
if "a" == "" goto usage
```

382

Using Local Environment Variables

In many cases, a batch program needs to change a standard environment variable, such as Path. But changing this critical variable without restoring it when you are finished could cause problems for other programs. If you're writing the batch program for your own use, it's not difficult to restore modified variables, although it gets tiresome after awhile. But if you're writing a batch program to be run by others, you probably won't even know what settings to restore.

Windows XP addresses this problem with the Setlocal and Endlocal commands. Setlocal makes any further settings or changes to environment variables local to the current batch program. Endlocal returns handling of environment variables back to normal mode—any further changes remain after the batch program terminates.

You might want to use a batch program to modify environment variables for either of two reasons. First, this might be the primary purpose of the batch program, as it is in the following short batch program (call it Addpath.bat), which adds a folder to the end of the search path:

```
@echo off
set Path=%Path%;%1
```

But more often, you will use environment variables to save values or change program behavior within the batch program. The simple rule is to use Setlocal at the start of the batch program and Endlocal at the end. Even if your batch program sets only a temporary environment variable, you want to be sure that the variable is cleared on termination. For example:

```
Setlocal
rem Set new path
set Path=D:\BIN
rem Do something with the new path
  .
  .
  .
endlocal
rem Path goes back to its original value after EndLocal
```

The test for equality would not be True, so the Goto statement would not be executed. But if you type **alphabetize** (without any arguments), the command interpreter would see

```
if "" == "" goto usage
```

and the Goto statement would be executed.

Notice in Alphabetize.bat that %1 is surrounded by quotation marks. This isn't a requirement. We could just as easily have written %1$==$. All we're doing is making sure that the command interpreter always sees something on both sides of the equal signs. Without a character there, it sees the line as

```
if == goto usage
```

The result would be a syntax error, causing the batch program to terminate. The quotation marks are a readable way to be sure neither side is ever empty.

The first line of this section (line 6), therefore, is for the case when no command-line parameters are used, and it sends the command processor to the Usage label (line 59), where the program displays instructions for using Alphabetize.

Lines 7 and 8 do the same thing: They answer calls for help. Because the comparison in an If statement requires an exact match, in line 8 we used the /I switch, which causes the If statement to ignore case. This switch is available only if command extensions are enabled. The /I switch overcomes a major limitation of earlier versions of MS-DOS and Windows, in which you'd need to set up several If statements to test for capitalization variants of the word *help*. For example, you might test for *help*, *HELP*, and *Help*—and you still wouldn't catch every possible form.

If the command line includes parameters that are not requests for help, lines 9 through 11 come into play. The Set commands assign the command-line parameters to environment variables that we can use later in the batch program. If the second command-line parameter is blank ("%2" == ""), the action is assumed to be Sort and is set to that value.

In lines 13 through 25, we set a group of environment variables that are used to tell the remainder of the batch program what to do.

Replaceable Parameters

Besides %1 through %9, you should be aware of two other useful replaceable parameters: %* and %0.

%* represents *all* the command-line arguments. One useful place for this parameter is in a For...In...Do statement. For example, you could enhance CleanRecent.bat (the batch program described in the preceding section) by changing its For statement to read

```
for %%t in (%*) do del "%userprofile%"\recent\*.%%t.lnk
```

You would then type the extensions you want to delete (separated by spaces) on the command line. You could type any number of extensions.

%0 represents the command name (in other words, the name of the batch program).

Lines 13 and 14 set the environment variables StartMenu and Favorites to their default value of False. The Goto %Type% command (line 15) sends processing to the label that matches the Type variable set earlier. Because labels are not case sensitive, it doesn't matter whether the user types **both, Both,** or some other variant. The rest of this section sets the StartMenu and Favorites variables to True if they are to be processed. They remain set to False if they are not to be processed. The Goto %Action% commands (lines 18, 21, and 25) send processing to the proper section of the batch program—to the Sort label (line 27) or the Undo label (line 41).

Now we are ready to start the actual work. Lines 27 through 39 sort the menus, and lines 41 through 57 restore the old menu arrangements.

The Sort section starts by checking that the value of the variable Favorites is True, in line 29. If it is not, the processing of Favorites is skipped. Next, the Reg Export command (line 30) creates a file that contains the current Favorites order. The environment variable AppData is used to locate the Inside Out folder that was created at the beginning of the

Using Pushd and Popd to Change to a Different Folder

A common sequence of events in a batch program is to move to a specific folder, do some work there, and then return to the original folder. The problem is that your batch program can be run from any folder. If you don't know where you are, you can't go back. Pushd and Popd to the rescue.

The Pushd command saves the current folder and changes to a new one. The Popd command restores the original. Normally, you need these commands only in batch programs, but an example from the command line shows how they work:

```
C:\bat>pushd \data
C:\data>pushd sales
C:\data\sales>popd
C:\data>popd
C:\bat>
```

You can probably figure out intuitively what's going on here, but if you're not a programmer, you might wonder what "push" and "pop" in the command names mean. *Push* means to put something onto a *stack,* in this case a stack of folder names. *Pop* means to take the top item—the only one you can get at—off the stack.

In the example, we first push the Bat folder onto the stack. If we popped now, we would return to the Bat folder. Instead we push another folder, Data. We have to pop it off the stack before we can get to the Bat folder. Of course, in a batch program we would be doing some work in each folder before we pushed another one or popped to restore the old one.

Chapter 10

batch program. After the backup file is made, the Reg Delete command (line 31) removes all the Favorites order information from the registry. Without this information in the registry, the menu reverts to its default alphabetical order. The /F switch does this without confirmation, and > Nul eliminates the completion message.

Reg sets the error level value to 0 upon successful completion or to 1 if an error occurs. The If statement in line 32 echoes a message of success if the error level is 0. This form of the If statement works only with Windows 2000 and Windows XP; if you want to create a program for use on computers running earlier versions of Windows, you could instead use the more traditional form:

```
if not errorlevel 1 echo Favorites alphabetized.
```

The SortStartMenu section (lines 34 through 39) performs the same process on the Start menu. Lines 35 and 39 demonstrate another feature introduced in Windows 2000: the Goto :EOF command. This special label, which must include the colon, causes the command processor to jump to the end of the batch program—in other words, to end execution. With MS-DOS and earlier versions of Windows, you must create a label at the end of the file and use it as the target of the Goto command to achieve the same result.

The Undo section of the batch program, lines 41 through 57, restores the original menu order. Again, the first check is to be sure that the Favorites are supposed to be processed (line 43). Then the If Not Exist command in line 44 checks to be sure that a backup file exists. If the file doesn't exist, the NoUndoFile section (lines 55 through 57) displays a message to that effect.

The Reg Import command (line 45) does the actual work. It imports the contents of the backup file to the registry, restoring the previous order.

The UndoStartMenu section (lines 48 through 53) performs the same process on the Start menu.

It's a good idea to make batch programs self-documenting. The Usage section, lines 59 through 67, does just that. This section consists of a series of Echo commands that display the correct usage of this batch program. Note the use of the Echo command followed by a dot, which displays a blank line for improved legibility. (If you use Echo alone, it reports the state of the echoing function—on or off.)

The interesting thing about line 62 is the use of the escape symbol (^) to indicate that the pipe symbol (|) should be treated as a character and not interpreted as a pipe symbol. Without the escape symbol, the command interpreter would try to pipe the Echo command and the first few words to whatever follows the pipe symbol, which would cause a syntax error. You must use the escape symbol any time you want to echo a pipe symbol (|), a greater than sign (>), a less than sign (<), an ampersand (&), or a caret (^).

Although this batch program illustrates some advanced techniques of batch processing, it also demonstrates some limitations.

If you misspell the first parameter, which should be Favorites, StartMenu, or Both, the batch program will fail. For example, if you type **alphabetize favorits**, the batch program displays this message:

```
The system cannot find the batch label specified - favorits
```

There is no way to trap for this error or to change the message to something more meaningful.

Likewise, if you happen to type one of the options for the first parameter as the second parameter, the batch program goes into an endless loop. For example, if you type **alphabetize favorites both**, the batch program appears to hang. It is actually very busy jumping back and forth between various labels, but the only way to stop it is to press Ctrl+Break.

These limitations are typical of complex batch programs. Batch programs provide a quick way to do simple tasks, but other tools (such as Windows Script Host) are better for more complex tasks.

A final word about debugging batch programs: You usually have to do some experimenting to get your batch programs to work exactly the way you want. You can write the batch program in one Command Prompt window and test it in another. To see exactly what the command interpreter sees, change the first line to

```
rem @echo off
```

This "comments out" the Echo Off command so that each line echoes to the screen with parameters and environment variables filled in before it is executed. In our sample file, you would probably also want to temporarily remove the redirection to Nul from each command so that you could see all the output.

Batch Programs vs. Scripts: Which Should You Use?

This chapter describes two rather different methods for automating repetitive tasks, batch programs and scripts. Which you should use depends in part on your comfort level. For tasks that can be performed by either method, choose the one that's easiest for you. Batch programs are generally easier to write and debug, particularly if you're already familiar with the batch command language used in MS-DOS and earlier versions of Windows. You'll find, however, that many tasks can't be performed by batch programs. And even those that can are often done better with a script, which provides better program logic, user feedback, and error handling.

(continued)

Batch Programs vs. Scripts: Which Should You Use? *(continued)*   To give you an idea of how batch programs and scripts compare for a simple procedure, examine the following examples. As you can see, it's sometimes possible to use nearly identical program logic in both languages. These programs examine the registry to see whether hidden files (those with the hidden attribute set) are displayed in Windows Explorer. If not, the programs modify the registry so that hidden files, super hidden files (those with the system and hidden attributes set), and all file name extensions are displayed. If hidden files are already displayed, the programs modify the registry so that these items are not displayed. Of course, you can make these display changes with a trip to the Folder Options dialog box instead of modifying the registry directly. But that's rather tedious, and these settings are ones that you may want to switch between frequently—the perfect application for a batch program or a script.

Here's the batch program, called ToggleHiddenExplorerStuff.bat:

```
:: Script to toggle Windows Explorer display of hidden files,
:: super-hidden files, and file name extensions

@echo off
setlocal

set key = HKCU\Software\Microsoft\Windows\CurrentVersion\Explorer\Advanced
set hiddenvalue=Hidden
set superhiddenvalue=ShowSuperHidden
set fileextvalue=HideFileExt

reg query %key% /v %hiddenvalue% | find "0x2" > NUL

if errorlevel 1 goto Hide

:Show
reg add %key% /v %hiddenvalue% /t REG_DWORD /d 1 /f > NUL
reg add %key% /v %superhiddenvalue% /t REG_DWORD /d 1 /f > NUL
reg add %key% /v %fileextvalue% /t REG_DWORD /d 0 /f > NUL
echo.
echo Windows Explorer will show hidden files and file name extensions.
echo You might need to change to another folder or press F5 to refresh
echo the view for the change to take effect.
goto :eof

:Hide
reg add %key% /v %hiddenvalue% /t REG_DWORD /d 2 /f > NUL
reg add %key% /v %superhiddenvalue% /t REG_DWORD /d 0 /f > NUL
reg add %key% /v %fileextvalue% /t REG_DWORD /d 1 /f > NUL
```

Chapter 10

```
echo.
echo Windows Explorer will not show hidden files and file name extensions.
echo (These are the default settings.) You might need to change to another
echo folder or press F5 to refresh the view for the change to take effect.
```

Here's the equivalent script version, ToggleHiddenExplorerStuff.vbs, written in VBScript:

```
' Script to toggle Windows Explorer display of hidden files,
' super-hidden files, and file name extensions

Option Explicit
Dim dblHiddenData, strHiddenKey, strSuperHiddenKey, strFileExtKey
Dim strKey, WshShell
On Error Resume Next

strKey = "HKCU\Software\Microsoft\Windows\CurrentVersion\Explorer\Advanced"
strHiddenKey = strKey & "\Hidden"
strSuperHiddenKey = strKey & "\ShowSuperHidden"
strFileExtKey = strKey & "\HideFileExt"

Set WshShell = WScript.CreateObject("WScript.Shell")
dblHiddenData = WshShell.RegRead(strHiddenKey)

If dblHiddenData = 2 Then
    WshShell.RegWrite strHiddenKey, 1, "REG_DWORD"
    WshShell.RegWrite strSuperHiddenKey, 1, "REG_DWORD"
    WshShell.RegWrite strFileExtKey, 0, "REG_DWORD"
    WScript.Echo "Windows Explorer will show hidden files and file " & _
        "name extensions. You might need to change to another folder " & _
        "or press F5 to refresh the view for the change to take effect."

Else
    WshShell.RegWrite strHiddenKey, 2, "REG_DWORD"
    WshShell.RegWrite strSuperHiddenKey, 0, "REG_DWORD"
    WshShell.RegWrite strFileExtKey, 1, "REG_DWORD"
    WScript.Echo "Windows Explorer will not show hidden files or file " & _
        "name extensions. (These are the default settings.) You might " & _
        "need to change to another folder or press F5 to refresh the " & _
        "view for the change to take effect."
End If
```

 Both programs are included on the companion CD.

Automating Tasks with Windows Script Host

Microsoft Windows Script Host (WSH) provides a way to perform more sophisticated tasks than the simple jobs that batch programs are able to handle. You can control virtually any component of Microsoft Windows and of many Windows-based programs with Windows Script Host scripts.

To run a script, you can type a script name at a command prompt or simply double-click the script's icon in Windows Explorer. Windows Script Host has two nearly equivalent programs—Wscript.exe and Cscript.exe—that, with the help of a language interpreter dynamic-link library such as Vbscript.dll, execute scripts written in VBScript or other scripting languages.

With WSH, the files can be written in several different languages, including VBScript (a scripting language similar to Microsoft Visual Basic) and JScript (a form of JavaScript). Windows Script Host is, in fact, just what its name says: a host for script languages. VBScript and JScript interpreters come with Windows XP; interpreters for Perl and other languages are available elsewhere.

Because WSH scripts can access ActiveX controls, they provide great flexibility. Several objects are provided with Windows Script Host that allow you basic control of Windows and your computer. By using ActiveX, you can control many of the programs on your computer. For example, you can create a WSH script to display a chart in Microsoft Excel.

As an introduction, here's the WSH "Hello World" script. It's as short as it can get in any programming language:

```
WScript.Echo "Hello World"
```

Using a plain-text editor such as Notepad, put this line in a file with a .vbs file name extension (Hello.vbs, for example), and you have a working WSH script. Simply double-click the file's icon in Windows Explorer to run your script.

Finding Scripting Resources

You won't learn how to write a script in this chapter. You must know a scripting language, or else use the resources described in the following paragraphs to learn one. (If you know Visual Basic, you already know a scripting language.) Our intent is to show you some of what you can do with Windows Script Host and help you find the widely scattered information you need to use it effectively.

One of the biggest hurdles to learning to use WSH is finding the information you need. The scripting language, whether it is VBScript or JScript, is separate from the objects you use in your scripts, and each piece has separate documentation. You must find the

Wscript vs. Cscript

Windows XP includes two programs that run WSH scripts. Cscript.exe is the command-line version, and Wscript.exe is the GUI version. Although this sounds like a big distinction, for most scripts the differences are pretty small. Try running Hello.vbs—a one-line program described on the previous page—with each program to see the difference. At the command prompt, type these two lines:

```
cscript hello.vbs
wscript hello.vbs
```

Figure 10-6 shows the results. Cscript displays the words "Hello World" in a Command Prompt window. Wscript displays a small dialog box with the message "Hello World" and an OK button. With Cscript, you use command-line parameters to change the properties of a script file. Wscript, in contrast, provides a dialog box to set the properties. Type **wscript** at a command prompt to display the properties dialog box.

— Output from Cscript.exe

— Graphical output from Wscript.exe

Figure 10-6. Cscript.exe, the console version, displays its result in a Command Prompt window, whereas with Wscript.exe a dialog box appears.

Note that Cscript and Wscript command-line options use two slashes. This differentiates them from command-line options for the script being executed, which use a single slash. To see all the command-line options, type **cscript //?** (or **wscript //?**) at a command prompt.

reference guide for both the scripting language you choose and the objects you use. Throughout this chapter, we tell you where to find the relevant documentation, most of which is available on Microsoft's Web site. Microsoft has an entire subsite for scripting at *http://msdn.microsoft.com/scripting*. Browsing this site can be confusing, however. The site describes the use of the scripting languages and their associated objects, but it also provides information for software developers who want to add scripting capabilities to their programs—which is another topic altogether.

Chapter 10

> **tip** For a wealth of third-party information about scripting and batch programming, visit *www.robvanderwoude.com*. Replete with instruction, examples, and links to Microsoft and other third-party information sources, Van der Woude's site covers Kix, Perl, and Rexx, as well as batch files and WSH.

Scripts and Security

Much has been made about the security risks posed by Windows Script Host. The power and flexibility afforded by WSH can be used by forces of evil just as easily as they can be used to make your life simpler. Indeed, the infamous I Love You and Anna Kournikova e-mail worms were powered by VBScript attachments.

You can make some simple changes that reduce the chance that you'll accidentally run a nefarious script.

As a first line of defense, be sure that the file name extension is always displayed for script files. (This would have tipped off many people who opened an e-mail attachment named Anna Kournikova.jpg.vbs. Because the extension is not displayed by default, many hopeful fans expected to see a picture of the tennis star.) Second, change the default action for scripts from Open to Edit. This causes the files to open harmlessly in Notepad if you double-click a file. To make these changes, follow these steps:

1 In Windows Explorer choose Tools, Folder Options.
2 Click the File Types tab.
3 Select the JS (JScript Script File) file type and then click Advanced.
4 Select the Always Show Extension check box.
5 In the Actions list, select Edit and click Set Default. Then click OK.
6 Repeat steps 3 through 5 for JSE (JScript Encoded Script File), VBE (VBScript Encoded Script File), VBS (VBScript Script File), and WSF (Windows Script File) file types.
7 Click Close when you've secured all the script file types.

Changing the default action to Edit makes it more difficult to run scripts that show up as e-mail attachments, which is one of the most likely places to find a malevolent script. However, it also makes it more difficult to execute legitimate scripts from trusted sources: You must save the attachment and then, in Windows Explorer, right-click it and choose Open. You can use this same technique (right-click and choose Open) to run any script stored on your computer, but if you want to avoid that inconvenience for a script that you *know* to be harmless, simply create a shortcut to the script. (Be sure the Target text in the shortcut's properties dialog box begins with *wscript.exe* or *cscript.exe*; if you include only the script name, this trick won't work.) Double-clicking the shortcut runs the script without further ado.

Choosing a Scripting Language

Windows Script Host doesn't care whether you use VBScript, JScript, or some other scripting language. All the objects are available to any language, and in most situations, you can choose to use the language with which you are most comfortable. In this book, we use VBScript. You can actually mix languages in the same program.

VBScript is a major subset of Visual Basic. If you know Visual Basic, there is little that you can't do in VBScript. One of the biggest differences is that VBScript has only Variant variables. You simply use Dim and the variable name; you can't add a variable type because they are all the same. You can find documentation of VBScript at *http://msdn.microsoft.com/scripting/vbscript/techinfo/vbsdocs.htm.*

Here is a short script, called Folders.vbs, that shows some of the elements of a script written in VBScript:

```
Option Explicit

Dim objWSShell
Dim strMsg
Dim intCtr

Set objWSShell = WScript.CreateObject("WScript.Shell")
WScript.Echo "Your desktop is " & objWSShell.SpecialFolders("Desktop") _
    & vbNewLine

strMsg = "All your special folders are:" & vbNewLine
For intCtr = 0 To objWSShell.SpecialFolders.Count - 1
    strMsg = strMsg & objWSShell.SpecialFolders.Item(intCtr) & vbNewLine
Next
WScript.Echo strMsg
```

 You can find Folders.vbs—and all the other example scripts from this chapter—on the companion CD.

The script starts with an Option Explicit statement, which tells the VBScript interpreter to require you to use a Dim statement for every variable in the script. This helps to prevent errors from misspelled variable names and is accepted as good programming practice.

The Set statement creates a WScript Shell object, which is used to access the special folders. One of the properties of the Shell object is the SpecialFolders object. The SpecialFolders object lets you retrieve the path and file name of any of the special folders on your system. For example, this script retrieves the Desktop folder, as shown in Figure 10-7 on the next page.

2: Customizing Windows XP

Chapter 10

Figure 10-7. Folders.vbs initially displays the location of your Desktop folder.

The next section of the script, the For...Next loop, displays all the special folders. This section demonstrates a technique that makes scripts work well with both Wscript and Cscript. Instead of putting a WScript.Echo statement inside the loop, we add each result to the strMsg string and then display this string after the loop is finished. When run with Cscript, the results are the same. However, when run with Wscript, accumulating the results into a string and using one WScript.Echo statement means that one dialog box is displayed for the entire loop (as shown in Figure 10-8), rather than one dialog box for each special folder.

Figure 10-8. The For...Next loop builds a string that is displayed in a single dialog box.

Using the Script File Format

For WSH scripts, you can use VBScript in files with the .vbs extension and JScript in files with the .js extension. Windows Script Host adds another level of tags that provide more flexibility and power. In fact, WSH files, which use the .wsf extension, are actually Extensible Markup Language (XML) files that use tags, as shown in the following example (Hello.wsf):

```
<?XML version="1.0"?>
<package>
<job id="job1">
<?job debug="true"?>
<script language="VBScript" src="MyScript.vbs"/>
```

```
<script language="VBScript">
<![CDATA[
    WScript.Echo "Hello World"
]]>
</script>
</job>
</package>
```

Table 10-4 describes the function of each of these tags, plus a few others.

Table 10-4. Useful XML Tags

Tag	Description
<?XML version="1.0"?>	Marks your code as compliant with XML 1.0. This tag is optional now but might be required by future XML tools.
<package> </package>	Encloses multiple jobs in a single file. The <package> tag is optional if you have only one pair of <job> tags.
<job id="job1"> </job>	Identifies jobs in a file. When you have multiple jobs in a file, you can run any one with this syntax: Cscript //Job:MyFirstJob MyScripts.wsf
<?job debug="true"?>	Allows use of the script debugger. You can add error="true" to this tag to allow error messages for syntax or run-time errors.
<script language= "VBScript" src= "MyScript.vbs"/>	Includes, or merges, another file into the current one when the script runs. This tag allows you to easily reuse code.
<script language= "VBScript"> </script>	Encloses a script. In a single job, you might have several scripts—even in different scripting languages.
<![CDATA[ ]]>	Indicates that the parser should treat your code as character data and not interpret the characters in it. Use this tag if you use the XML tag.
<object>	Defines objects that can be referenced by the script.
<reference>	Provides a reference to an external type library, allowing you to use defined constants from that type library.
<resource>	Isolates text or numeric data that should not be hard-coded in a script.

Debugging Scripts

To debug scripts, you first need to install Microsoft Script Debugger. You can download it from *http://msdn.microsoft.com/scripting/debugger/*.

Also, if you want to debug a .wsf file, you must add the line *<?job debug="true"?>* to your script file. (It goes right below the <job> tag.) Without this line, the debugger will not open.

---

note After you have installed the debugger, the messages you see when you encounter a script error while you browse the Internet are different. At the bottom, the message asks, "Do you want to debug the current page?" If you click Yes, the debugger appears with the page loaded. Because you are probably looking at someone else's site, however, you probably want to click No!

You can find the documentation for Script Debugger at *http://msdn.microsoft.com/scripting/debugger*. Keep in mind that you can use this same debugger to debug both client and server scripts for Web pages; most of the documentation is focused on those activities. (In fact, Windows Script Host might not be mentioned in the debugger documentation at all.)

You start the debugger using command-line switches with the Cscript or Wscript commands. The //X switch starts the debugger, loads the script into the debugger, and stops at the first line of the script. The //D switch starts the debugger only when an error is encountered. It also loads the program in the debugger and stops at the line where it encountered the error.

Here's an example of debugging a very simple script, which we call Debug.vbs:

```
main()

Function main()
x = 99
WScript.echo "Hello once"
WScript.echox "Error 1 here"
WScript.echo "Hello twice"
End Function
```

After creating this script, at the command prompt type

```
wscript //d debug.vbs
```

The words "Hello once" should appear in a small dialog box. When you click OK, Script Debugger appears, with the error highlighted, as shown in Figure 10-9.

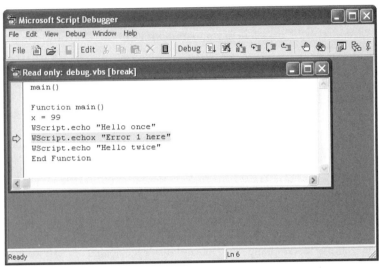

Figure 10-9. When you run a script with the //D switch and an error occurs, Script Debugger appears and highlights the error.

The debugger helps you find your error, but you can't fix errors here. As you notice at the top of the document window, the file is identified as read-only. You can open another instance of the file in the debugger and edit that file. The debugger provides an editor that is on a par with Notepad.

Using Other Debugger Windows

At this point, the debugger can provide some additional information, but you are effectively done with running the script. Three additional windows, all available both from the View menu and from the right side of the toolbar, allow you to see more information about your script:

- **Running Documents.** This window shows you scripts that are currently running. Besides Windows Script Host, you are likely to see Microsoft Internet Explorer here. If you right-click a script in this window, one command appears on the menu: Break At Next Statement. This command provides a way to "invite" a script into the debugger.

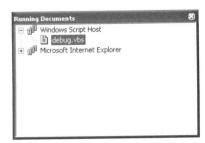

Chapter 10

● **Call Stack.** This window displays the call history to the current point in the current script. This can help you figure out just how you got where you are.

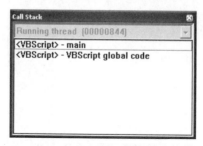

● **Command.** This window allows you to view and manipulate variables in your script. In the following example, the first line "printed" the value of *x*. (A question mark is shorthand for the Visual Basic Print command.) Then the value of *x* was changed to 100 and displayed again.

When you work in the Command window, you must use the same language as the currently running script. If you are running a VBScript file, for example, type a question mark followed by a space and the variable name to display a variable's value. If you are running a JScript file, simply enter the name of the variable. You can also view and change an object's properties in the Command window.

Stepping Through Scripts

When you start the debugger using the //X command-line switch, the debugger opens with the first line of the script highlighted. You can move through the script and see how the program flow works. All the debugging information is available so that you can check the value of variables and object properties and see how they are changed by the operation of the script.

The Debug toolbar—one of three toolbars in Script Debugger—contains the tools you need to step through a script. Table 10-5 describes the buttons on the Debug toolbar.

The debugging process is to step through the script, line by line, until you find an error. When you determine that a specific part of the script works, you can set a breakpoint at the beginning of the untested part and then click Run to get to that point quickly.

Table 10-5. **Script Debugger's Debug Toolbar**

Button	Name	Description
	Run	Executes the script until it hits a break-point, an error, or comes to the end of the script
	Stop Debugging	Runs the script outside the debugger
	Break At Next Statement	Activates an open server script in the debugger; not useful for WSH files
	Step Into	Advances the script by one statement; steps into functions and subroutines
	Step Over	Advances the script by one statement; executes but does not display functions and subroutines
	Step Out	Advances the script until it exits the current function or subroutine
	Toggle Breakpoint	Inserts or removes a breakpoint at the line containing the insertion point
	Clear All Breakpoints	Clears all breakpoints
	Running Documents	Displays the Running Documents window
	Call Stack	Displays the Call Stack window
	Command Window	Displays the Command window

When you believe that your functions and subroutines are working correctly, you can speed up debugging by clicking Step Over to execute them as one step, instead of using the Step Into button.

Introducing Objects

You can't do much with WSH without using objects. An *object* is a variable comprising both routines and data that is treated as a discrete entity. Some objects are built into the scripting language; others are provided by the operating system. One of the previous script examples used the WScript.Shell object to gain access to the Windows shell.

399

Table 10-6 describes the objects that are built into VBScript. They are documented, along with the VBScript language, at *http://msdn.microsoft.com/scripting/vbscript/ techinfo/vbsdocs.htm*.

Table 10-6. **VBScript Objects**

Object	Description
Class object	Provides access to the events of a created class
Dictionary object	Stores data in key/item pairs
Drive object	Provides access to the properties of a disk drive or network share
Drives collection	Collection of all available Drive objects
Err object	Provides information about run-time errors
File object	Provides access to all the properties of a file
Files collection	Collection of all File objects within a folder
FileSystemObject object	Provides access to your computer's file system
Folder object	Provides access to all the properties of a folder
Folders collection	Collection of all Folder objects contained within a Folder object
Match object	Provides access to the read-only properties of a regular expression match
Matches collection	Collection of regular expression Match objects
RegExp object	Provides simple regular expression support
TextStream object	Facilitates sequential access to a file

Windows Script Host provides the objects shown in Table 10-7. They are documented, along with Windows Script Host, at *http://msdn.microsoft.com/scripting/*. On that page, click Windows Script Host Documentation.

Table 10-7. **Windows Script Host Objects**

Object	Description
WScript object	Exposes properties that specify the path of the running scripting host (Wscript.exe or Cscript.exe), its arguments, and the working mode (interactive or batch); also provides methods to create and read objects
WshArguments object	Returns a pointer to the collection of command-line parameters
WshEnvironment object	Retrieves system environment variables
WshNetwork object	Maps the network, making it easy to connect and disconnect remote drives and printers
WshShell object	Starts new processes, creates shortcuts, and provides the Environment collection to handle environment variables such as SystemRoot, Path, and Prompt
WshShortcut object	Creates an object reference to a shortcut
WshSpecialFolders object	Accesses the Windows shell folders such as the Desktop folder, the Start Menu folder, and the My Documents folder
WshUrlShortcut object	Creates an object reference to a URL shortcut

Using the FileSystemObject

One of the objects you will probably use often is FileSystemObject. This object gives you access to the files and folders on your computer. The following example, called FileProp.vbs, shows how to use this object; Figure 10-10 on the next page shows the result.

```
' Displays properties of file on command line

    Option Explicit
    Dim strArg, objFileSys, objFile, strMsg

    If WScript.Arguments.Count < 1 Then
        WScript.Echo "Usage: FileProp <filename>" & vbNewLine & _
            "Or drag and drop a file on this file."
        WScript.Quit (1)
    End If
```

```
Set objFileSys = CreateObject("Scripting.FileSystemObject")

strArg = objFileSys.GetAbsolutePathName(WScript.Arguments(0))

Set objFile = objFileSys.GetFile(strArg)
strMsg = "Name: " & vbTab & objFile.Name & vbNewLine
strMsg = strMsg & "Short: " & vbTab
strMsg = strMsg & objFile.ShortName & vbNewLine
strMsg = strMsg & "Folder: " & vbTab
strMsg = strMsg & objFile.ParentFolder & vbNewLine
strMsg = strMsg & "Size: " & vbTab
strMsg = strMsg & objFile.Size & vbNewLine
strMsg = strMsg & "Created: " & vbTab
strMsg = strMsg & objFile.DateCreated & vbNewLine
strMsg = strMsg & "Modified:" & vbTab
strMsg = strMsg & objFile.DateLastModified & vbNewLine
strMsg = strMsg & "Type: " & vbTab
strMsg = strMsg & objFile.Type & vbNewLine
WScript.Echo strMsg
Set objFile = Nothing
Set objFileSys = Nothing
```

This script first checks to see whether the command line contains any parameters. If none are found, it displays a usage message and quits. The script works with drag and drop because Windows adds the name of dropped files to the command line. If you drop more than one file on this script, it displays information about only the first one.

After the error checking is out of the way, the script creates a FileSystemObject object and then uses that object to get the full path name of the file. Using the full path name, it gets a File object.

The script then builds a string by concatenating various properties of the File object. When the entire string is built, the script displays it with the Echo method of the WScript object. You can also use the MsgBox function to display strings. It allows you to specify which buttons appear, to change the title from Windows Script Host to a message you specify, and to respond to the button a user clicks. Whereas the WScript.Echo method works differently in Cscript and Wscript, the MsgBox function

Figure 10-10. The FileProp.vbs script quickly displays some file properties that aren't easily viewed in Windows Explorer.

402

works the same way in both: It always displays a dialog box. To see the difference, try replacing the WScript.Echo line in the previous script with the following line:

```
MsgBox strMsg, vbOKOnly, "File Properties"
```

Finally, the script releases the FileSystemObject object and the File object by setting the variables to the built-in value Nothing, which releases the resources used by the objects. It's not important to do this in a small script such as this one because it happens anyway when the script ends, but in more involved scripts, releasing the objects when you've finished with them can reduce the resources your script requires.

Example Scripts

In this section, we present two sample scripts that demonstrate some of the techniques you can use with Windows Script Host.

Viewing Knowledge Base Articles

The first script displays a Microsoft Knowledge Base (MSKB) article in Internet Explorer. You can find references to MSKB articles in lots of places: books like this one, magazines, and Web sites. The references are easily recognized—they consist of the letter Q followed by a six-digit number—but it's not so easy to display an article on the Microsoft Web site because you must follow several links in succession or type a lengthy URL. This simple script, named Kbquick.vbs, opens a Microsoft Knowledge Base article in Internet Explorer. It asks for the Article ID, creates the URL for the article, and launches Internet Explorer with that URL.

```
'****************************************************************
'* File: KBquick.vbs
'*
'* Function: Opens a specified Microsoft Knowledge Base article.
'*
'* Usage: Prompts for an Article ID, then launches Internet
'* Explorer displaying that article.
'*
'****************************************************************
Option Explicit

Dim shell
Dim strKBID
Dim strURL
Dim strPrompt
Dim strTitle
Dim strDefault
```

```
' Ask for the Article ID.

strPrompt = "Enter the Article ID of the Microsoft Knowledge " & _
    "Base article."
strTitle = "Knowledge Base Assistant"
strDefault = "Q"
strKBID = InputBox(strPrompt, strTitle, strDefault)
' If the user clicks Cancel or enters nothing, exit.
if strKBID = "" Then
    WScript.Quit
End If


' Check the length and first character.
While len(strKBID) <> 7 or UCase(left(strKBID, 1)) <> "Q
    strPrompt = "Knowledge Base IDs start with the letter Q,
    strPrompt = strPrompt & "which is followed by 6 digits."
    strKBID = InputBox(strPrompt, strTitle, strKBID)
    if strKBID = "" Then
        WScript.Quit
    End If
Wend


' Create a URL from the Article ID
strURL = "http://support.microsoft.com/support/kb/articles/"
strURL = strURL & left(strKBID, 4) & "/"
strURL = strURL & mid(strKBID, 5, 1) & "/"strURL = strURL & _
    right(strKBID, 2) & ".asp"


' Open the article in Internet Explorer
Set shell = CreateObject("WScript.Shell")
shell.Run("IEXPLORE" & " " & strURL)
shell.AppActivate "IExplore"
```

The InputBox function is used to request the Article ID. Because the Article ID always starts with the letter Q, it is placed in the text box by default. The InputBox function returns the Article ID to the script.

After the Article ID is in hand, some simple error checking is performed. The script checks to see whether the Article ID is seven characters long and that the first character is the letter Q. If an error is found, the InputBox function is used again to request a different Article ID. The While … Wend loop keeps asking until the user gets it right or clicks Cancel.

The next step is to parse the Article ID and create a URL. The URL for article Q123456, for example, is *http://support.microsoft.com/support/kb/articles/q123/4/56.asp*.

With a full URL, the script launches Internet Explorer, and the Knowledge Base article appears on the screen, as shown in Figure 10-11.

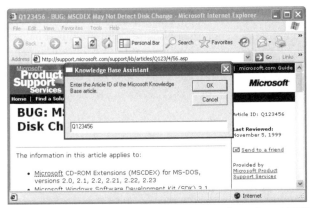

Figure 10-11. The script asks for the number of an MSKB article and then displays the article in Windows Explorer.

---

tip **Use another shortcut to Knowledge Base articles**

If you have Internet Explorer configured to use MSN as the search provider for Address bar searches, it offers a built-in alternative to this Knowledge Base Assistant script. In Internet Explorer's Address bar, simply type **mskb** followed by a space and the article ID. If you have problems using this trick, see "Searching from the Address Bar," page 795.

Keeping a Journal

The following script, named Journal.vbs, helps keep an ad hoc journal by opening a text file and adding a time stamp, as shown in Figure 10-12. For consistency with other

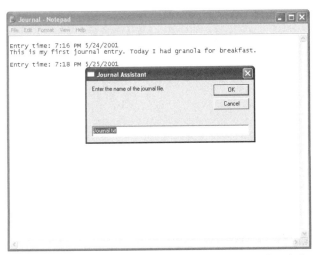

Figure 10-12. Journal.vbs opens a file in Notepad and then types the time and date at the end of the file.

scripts in this chapter, we've included comments, used standard naming conventions, included error-checking routines, and otherwise dressed it up. But at its heart, this script demonstrates how you can use scripting to perform simple automation tasks merely by having a script launch a program or play back keystrokes.

```
'******************************************************************************
'*
'* File: Journal.vbs
'*
'* Function: Opens a text file and adds a time stamp.
'*
'* Usage: Uses a command-line argument for the file name to open.
'* If there is no command-line argument, prompts for it.
'*
'******************************************************************************
Option Explicit

Dim shell
Dim strFileName
Dim strPrompt
Dim strTitle
Dim strDefault

' Check for a command-line argument.
If WScript.Arguments.Count Then
    ' Use the command-line argument for the file name.
    strFileName = WScript.Arguments(0)
Else
    ' No command-line argument. Ask for a file name.
    strPrompt = "Enter the name of the journal file."
    strTitle = "Journal Assistant"
    strDefault = "Journal.txt" ' propose a name
    strFileName = InputBox(strPrompt, strTitle, strDefault)
    ' If the user clicks Cancel or enters nothing, exit.
    If strFileName = "" Then
        WScript.Quit
    End If
End If

' Start Notepad with the specified file.
Set shell = CreateObject("WScript.Shell")
shell.Run("Notepad " & strFileName)
shell.AppActivate "Notepad"
WScript.Sleep 100 ' allow time for Notepad to get going

' Move to the end of the file and add the time stamp.
shell.SendKeys "^{END}{ENTER}{ENTER}" ' move to end of file
shell.SendKeys "Entry time: " ' add a text string
shell.SendKeys "{F5}{ENTER}" ' add the time stamp
```

There are four ways to specify the text file you want to use as a journal:

● Enter the file name at the prompt that the script presents.

● Start the script from a command prompt and include the file name on the command line.

● Use a shortcut to the script that includes the file name in the shortcut's Target box.

● Drag the file from Windows Explorer and drop it on the script or a shortcut to the script. (If you drop a file onto a shortcut to which you have added a file name, the dropped file overrides the file in the shortcut and the dropped file is opened.)

When the script starts, it checks to see whether there is a command-line argument. If so, it is used as a file name. If not, the script uses the InputBox function to request a file name.

After the script has a file name, it opens Notepad and displays that file. Then it uses the SendKeys method to manipulate Notepad.

SendKeys does as its name implies, and sends keystrokes to a program. In the SendKeys syntax, most keys are represented by the normal character. Keys that don't produce characters, such as Enter or Backspace, are represented by special character codes, as shown in Table 10-8. Keys you use in combination with other characters (Shift, for example) are also represented by codes.

Table 10-8. **Codes for SendKeys Method**

Key	Code
Backspace	{BACKSPACE}, {BS}, or {BKSP}
Break	{BREAK}
Caps Lock	{CAPSLOCK}
Delete	{DELETE} or {DEL}
Down Arrow	{DOWN}
End	{END}
Enter	{ENTER} or ~
Esc	{ESCAPE} or {ESC}
Help	{HELP}

(continued)

Table 10-8. *(continued)*

Key	Code
Home	{HOME}
Insert	{INSERT} or {INS}
Left Arrow	{LEFT}
Num Lock	{NUMLOCK}
Page Down	{PGDN}
Page Up	{PGUP}
Print Screen	{PRTSC}
Right Arrow	{RIGHT}
Scroll Lock	{SCROLLLOCK}
Tab	{TAB}
Up Arrow	{UP}
Function keys F1 through F16	{F1} through {F16}
Shift	+
Ctrl	^
Alt	%

Part 3

Managing Files

Windows Explorer for Experts

Getting Windows Explorer and the other components of the Microsoft Windows XP user interface to look and work in a manner that's congenial and congruent with your level of expertise is critical to your satisfaction in Windows XP. Fortunately, Microsoft made Windows Explorer highly customizable. You don't need to use it the way it came out of the box (although you certainly may). To help you tailor the interface to suit your working style, this chapter presents a brief expert's tour of Windows Explorer.

newfeature!
Choosing Between Common Tasks and Classic Folders

One of the first customizing decisions you'll probably want to make in working with Windows Explorer in Windows XP is whether or not to retain the pane of links to common tasks that Windows Explorer can display along the left side of your folder windows, shown in Figure 11-1 on the next page. Displaying these links can be useful. You can use them to copy and move files, attach files to e-mail messages, display pictures as slide shows, play music, and so on; you can also use links in the Other Places section of the pane to move quickly to other folders. But this "task pane" does consume screen space, so there might be times when you'd rather not see it. Unfortunately, your decision about whether to use or lose the task pane is global—that is, you can't have it on in some folders and off in others. Fortunately, you can switch between one mode and the other quickly and easily.

At Home with Windows XP

Windows Explorer works exactly the same way in both versions of Windows XP. The Folder Options dialog box, which is described in this chapter, contains one option that's not available in Windows XP Home Edition—the option to disable Simple File Sharing.

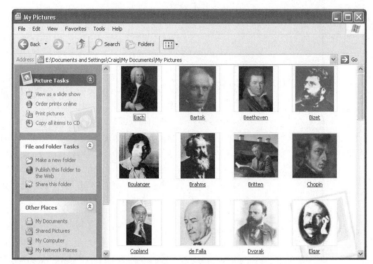

Figure 11-1. Viewing common tasks in the left pane provides links relevant to current folder content.

The task pane is on by default. To turn it off, follow these steps:

1 In Windows Explorer, choose Tools, Folder Options.

2 On the General pane of the Folder Options dialog box, shown in Figure 11-2, select Use Windows Classic Folders.

---

note Another way to get to the Folder Options dialog box is via Control Panel. Open Control Panel, choose Appearance And Themes if you're using Category View, and then click Folder Options. A better alternative for frequent Folder Options users: create a shortcut (on your desktop or in another convenient location) using the command **control folders**.

---

tip **If you use it often, put it on the toolbar**

If you make frequent trips to the Folder Options dialog box, you can save time by putting a Folder Options button on the toolbar. For details, see "Customizing the Toolbars," page 414.

Figure 11-2. Select Use Windows Classic Folders to remove the task panes from all windows.

Toggling Between Folder Views

Unlike the Explorer bars that can also take up residence along the left edge of your Windows Explorer windows, the task pane does not come with a Close button. If you want to see it some of the time but not all the time, you have to toggle it in and out of view by returning to the Folder Options dialog box. That's not too onerous if you put the Folder Options command on your toolbar, but it's still less convenient than you might like.

Here's an alternative approach: Toggle the task pane by clicking the Folders button on the toolbar. Clicking the Folders button replaces the task pane with the Folders bar, which shows an outline of your computer's storage resources. A second click removes the Folders bar and replaces it with the task pane. (For more information about the Folders bar, see "Using the Folders Bar," page 421.) With the Folders bar displayed, you still don't have the maximum space available for files, but the left side of your screen is given over to something just as useful as the task pane. And you can switch between the task pane and Folders bar with a single click.

Using the Details Section of the Task Pane

The lowest section of the task pane is like a miniature properties dialog box—it provides useful information about the currently selected item or items. For example, with the Bach item selected, as shown in Figure 11-1, the Details pane looks like this.

If all the items in the folder displayed in Figure 11-1 were selected, the details section would look like this.

In 800×600 resolution, you might not see the details section without scrolling the task pane. If you find it more useful than one or more of the sections that appear above it, you can bring it into view by collapsing the sections you don't need to see. Click the double-arrow in the upper right corner of a section to collapse it. (Click again to expand it.)

Customizing the Toolbars

Windows Explorer offers three toolbars: Standard Buttons, Address bar, and Links. You can display these toolbars in any combination. To display or hide a toolbar, choose View, Toolbars, and then select the toolbar you want (or don't want) from the submenu.

---

note The Radio toolbar that was available in earlier versions of Windows has been replaced by the Media Explorer bar. For information about the Media Explorer bar, see "Using Explorer Bars," page 417.

---

tip As a quicker way to display or hide a toolbar, right-click any toolbar. This action displays the View, Toolbars submenu.

Chapter 11: Windows Explorer for Experts

You can change the size or position of any toolbar by dragging the handle that appears at the left edge of the toolbar, shown here.

——— Drag these handles to resize
or reposition the toolbars

To put a toolbar on a new line, drag it downward by its handle. If two toolbars appear on the same line and you want to reverse their order, drag one of them down, and then drag it up on the other side of the second toolbar.

note If you can't move or resize the toolbars, they are probably locked. Open the View menu, select Toolbars, and click Lock The Toolbars to unlock them.

Note that the menu bar can also be repositioned. If you want to see it below the toolbars, simply drag it downward. To eliminate the menu bar altogether (and fill the screen with Windows Explorer), press F11. Press F11 again to return Windows Explorer to its previous appearance.

tip Lock the toolbars

After you have arranged the toolbars to your satisfaction, you can lock them so that you don't inadvertently change their current sizes and positions. Choose View, Toolbars, Lock The Toolbars. The handles at the left edges of the toolbars become solid when locked. To unlock the toolbars so that you can move them around again, choose View, Toolbars, Lock The Toolbars again.

If a toolbar is too wide to be displayed entirely in its current position (and given the current window size), Windows Explorer displays a chevron at the right edge. Click the chevron to display the toolbar items that don't fit.

In addition to repositioning and resizing the toolbars, you can customize the content of the Standard Buttons toolbar. You can specify which buttons to include, what order they should appear in, how big the icons should be, and whether and how to display text labels for the icons.

Chapter 11

415

> **tip**   **Go button, be gone!**
>
> The Go button at the right side of the Address Bar toolbar is a bit of a redundancy. If you select an address from the Address bar list, Windows Explorer takes you to that address directly. If you type an address in the Address bar, Windows Explorer takes you to that address as soon as you press Enter. The only time you would need the Go button would be if you typed an address and, for some reason, didn't care to press the Enter key. Clicking Go would then accomplish the same feat as pressing Enter. To remove the Go button and make more room for other items, right-click the Go button and select Go Button from the shortcut menu.

To customize the Standard Buttons toolbar, follow these steps:

1 Choose View, Toolbars, Customize. The following dialog box appears.

2 To add a button, select it in the left box and click Add. To remove a button, select it in the right box and click Remove.

3 To change the position of a button, select it in the right box and click Move Up or Move Down. Alternatively, you can drag a button to its desired position.

4 To change the position of or eliminate descriptive text, select from the Text Options list.

5 To change the size of toolbar icons, choose from the Icon Options list.

Displaying the Status Bar

Unlike earlier versions, the Windows XP version of Windows Explorer does not display the status bar by default. To make the status bar visible, choose View, Status Bar. The status bar, shown here, provides useful information, such as the number of objects selected (or the total number of objects in the displayed folder) and their total size.

Chapter 11: Windows Explorer for Experts

Total size of selection — Number of items selected — Source of selection

Using Explorer Bars

The View, Explorer Bar command opens a menu on which you can choose from five Explorer bars: Search, Favorites, Media, History, and Folders. You might have additional Explorer bars, courtesy of applications that you have installed (Microsoft Encarta, for example, installs an Explorer bar for Encarta Researcher). If so, these additional Explorer bars will also be listed on the Explorer Bar submenu.

The Explorer bar you select appears along the left edge of the Windows Explorer window, replacing the task pane, if you have chosen to display task panes. Figure 11-3 shows a Windows Explorer view of My Computer with the History bar in place.

Figure 11-3. The History bar is most commonly used in Microsoft Internet Explorer but can be useful in Windows Explorer as well.

You can use the same Explorer bars in both Internet Explorer and Windows Explorer. Some of the Explorer bars (History, for example) are more commonly used in the Internet context. But all have some utility in Windows Explorer as well. The following paragraphs offer brief descriptions of the Explorer bars and the use to which they can be put in Windows Explorer.

Chapter 11

417

Part 3: Managing Files

Using the Search Bar

Choosing the Search Explorer bar displays the Search Assistant, which helps you search for files and folders. This action is equivalent to choosing Search from the Start menu, except that the Search Assistant is set by default to look in the current folder. When you search using the Explorer bar, the results of your search appear in the main part of the Windows Explorer window. To return to the normal folder display, click Back on the Standard Buttons toolbar.

The Search bar can be opened by either of two keyboard shortcuts: F3 and Ctrl+E. It can also be opened and closed by clicking the Search button that appears by default in the Standard Buttons toolbar.

Using the Favorites Bar

The Favorites Explorer bar displays the contents of your Favorites folder, located at %UserProfile%\Favorites. The contents of this folder also determine what appears in Windows Explorer's Favorites menu.

Most users store links to commonly visited Internet sites in their Favorites folder, but you can put any kind of shortcut (or folder or file) there. For example, if there's a folder or document you need frequently for a project you're currently working on, you can create a shortcut to it, store the shortcut in your Favorites folder, and then use the Favorites Explorer bar as a way to move to the folder or open the file. Figure 11-4 shows the Favorites Explorer bar with the folder containing files for this chapter at the top.

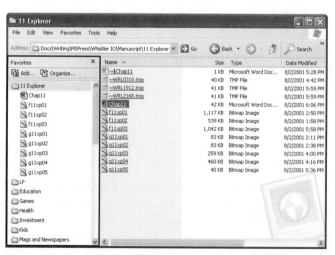

Figure 11-4. For easy navigation, we've added a shortcut to the Chapter 11 folder at the top of our Favorites bar. We could also get to this folder now via the Favorites menu.

Chapter 11: Windows Explorer for Experts

The simplest way to add a folder to your Favorites bar (and Favorites menu) is as follows:

1 Display the folder you want to add in Windows Explorer.

2 Display the Favorites Explorer bar.

3 Click the Add To Favorites button at the top of the Favorites bar. The following dialog box appears.

4 Click Create In to expand the dialog box if you want to place the new favorite in an existing Favorites subfolder or to place it in a new folder (click the New Folder button in the expanded dialog box to do that). Otherwise, click OK.

To add a file to the Favorites bar, hold down the Alt key while dragging the file to the Favorites bar.

The new item is placed at the bottom of your Favorites bar. If you're going to be using it frequently, you might want to drag it toward the top of the list.

The keyboard shortcut for the Favorites bar is Ctrl+I. Unlike the Search and Folders buttons, the Favorites bar has no buttons on the Standard Buttons toolbar by default, but you can add one by customizing the toolbar.

Using the Media Bar

The Media Explorer bar provides links to various places within WindowsMedia.com. (To go straight to the home page of WindowsMedia.com, click the Play button at the bottom of the Media bar. For more information about WindowsMedia.com, see Chapter 16, "Customizing Windows Media Player.") The Media bar has no keyboard shortcut and no toolbar button in Windows Explorer.

Using the History Bar

The History Explorer bar shows you what Web sites you've visited and what document files (local and networked) you've opened recently. Like the Favorites bar, it's used mostly in the Internet Explorer context, but it can also help you find your way back to a recently used document. It's particularly useful in that connection if the document you want is no longer available via the Start menu's My Recent Documents folder. It's

Part 3: Managing Files

also a help if you want to go back to a recently visited Web site and you don't want to open Internet Explorer to do it. When you open a Web site in Windows Explorer, Windows Explorer effectively becomes Internet Explorer.

> **tip** To see the names of recently opened local documents in the History bar, open the folder named My Computer. To see the names of networked documents, open the name of the remote computer.

You can sort the History bar in any of the following ways:

- **By Date.** In chronological order by date

- **By Site.** In alphabetical order by site name

- **By Most Visited.** In order of most visited (most visited sites at the top, least visited at the bottom)

- **By Order Visited Today.** In order of sites most visited today

To select a sorting order, click the View button at the top of the History bar.

You can also filter the History bar to show only items that meet a search criterion. This can be quite useful. If you've visited hundreds of Web sites in the last two weeks but you only want to know about the ones containing the text *Windows XP,* you can use the History bar's Search tool. Click the Search button at the top of the History bar, enter your search string, and then click Search now, as shown here.

To return to the full history, click View and then select a sort order.

The History bar's handy keyboard shortcut is Ctrl+H, and you can add a History button to your Standard Buttons toolbar.

Using the Folders Bar

Folders is probably the most useful Explorer bar from a file-management perspective. The Folders bar displays all your storage resources, both local and remote, in a hierarchical tree. You can use the tree as a navigational tool (hop straight to a distant folder by expanding and selecting that branch of the tree) and as a copy or move target (drag an item from a folder window and drop it on the appropriate entry in the Folders bar).

---

tip **Hold down the right mouse button while you drag**

Windows has logical and consistent defaults for whether it copies or moves when you drag an item onto the Folders bar. In most cases, it moves when the source and destination are on the same disk, and it copies if source and destination are on different disks. But it's easy to forget and move when you mean to copy—or vice versa. To avoid mishap, form the habit of right-dragging. When you drop the item on its target, you can choose the action you want from the shortcut menu that appears.

The Folders bar is so useful that the shortcut menu for every folder includes a command that opens the selected folder in Windows Explorer with the Folders bar displayed. Right-click any folder or shortcut to a folder and choose Explorer (instead of Open), and Windows Explorer displays the selected folder as well as the Folders bar.

---

newfeature!
Navigating the Folders Bar in Simple Folder View

Windows XP introduces a friendlier Folders bar. Now, if you click a folder name in the Folders bar, Windows Explorer displays the folder's contents and expands the folder branch you clicked. Click another folder name, and Windows Explorer closes the branch where you were, opening the one you just clicked in its place. If you want to expand a branch without closing a previous one, click the item's plus-sign icon, not its name.

This new navigational mode is a big help when you're working with folders that have a lot of subfolders. In previous versions of Windows, it was easy to get lost in the details (the subfolders) and lose track of the larger structure (the top-level set of folders). If you prefer the previous ways, however, you can restore them by following these steps:

1 Choose Tools, Folder Options.

2 Click the View tab.

3 In the Advanced Settings list, clear Display Simple Folder View In Explorer's Folders List.

Choosing View Options

Windows Explorer provides six distinct ways of viewing items in a folder:

- Details
- List
- Thumbnails
- Tiles
- Icons
- Filmstrip

You can choose these options either from the View menu or by clicking the Views button on the Standard Buttons toolbar.

> **note** Filmstrip view is available only in *picture folders*—that is, folders that use either the Pictures or Photo Album template. (For more information about folder templates, see "Choosing a Folder Template," page 430.) Filmstrip view also requires that you choose Show Common Tasks In Folders, on the General tab of the Folder Options dialog box. You don't have to be displaying the task pane; you can display an Explorer bar instead (shown in Figure 11-5 on the next page).

If you've used earlier versions of Windows, you're probably familiar with Details and List views, and perhaps also with Thumbnails view. (Details view presents a columnar display of file names and attributes. List view offers a compact display, consisting only of small icons and file names. In Thumbnails view, Windows Explorer displays previews of file contents, if it can; you see miniature images of graphics and HTML files, for example.) Windows veterans will also notice that the Small Icons view of yore is no more.

newfeature!

The new Tiles view generates larger and more colorful icons than the previous Large Icons view. In Tiles view, Windows Explorer also displays a generous three lines of text to describe each file. This allows it to give you more information about each file than you would see in Icons view. The information that appears depends on the file type. With WMA (Windows Media Audio) files, for example, Windows Explorer displays performer names as well as file names.

In Filmstrip view, shown in Figure 11-5, the currently selected picture (or the first picture, if none is selected) appears in a larger size in the center of the window (with the help of the Windows Picture And Fax Viewer accessory). Below the selected image, Windows Explorer displays four buttons. The first two buttons let you change which picture is displayed in the larger frame by clicking backward and forward through the folder. The other two buttons allow you to rotate the current picture clockwise or counterclockwise. If you rotate a picture, the Windows Picture And Fax Viewer saves

Chapter 11: Windows Explorer for Experts

Figure 11-5. In Filmstrip view, the Windows Picture And Fax Viewer accessory shows a larger version of the selected file. You can also turn your folder into a slide show.

the rotated image under the current file name, overwriting the image that was saved under that name before. To keep the original and create a rotated copy, use the task pane to copy the original first.

As Figure 11-5 shows, you don't have to have the task pane visible to use Filmstrip view. But if you do display the task pane, you can use its first Picture Tasks link to generate a slide show from all the pictures in your folder by clicking View As A Slide Show.

Making All Folders Use the Same View

If you want all your folders to use the same view—Details or Tiles, for example—set up one folder the way you want it. Then do the following:

1 Choose Tools, Folder Options.

2 Click the View tab.

3 Click Apply To All Folders.

After you have made all your folders look more or less the same, you can still apply distinct views to individual folders. For example, you might want to have 90 percent of your folders use Details view but still display your picture folders in Thumbnails or Filmstrip view. No problem; use the Apply To All Folders command to make all the folders use Details view. Then go to your pictures folders and override the default by applying Thumbnails or Filmstrip view.

To return all of your folders to their default views, go back to the Folder Options dialog box, click the View tab, and then click Reset All Folders.

Chapter 11

Changing Views in Common Dialog Boxes

You can change from one view to another inside the common dialog boxes used by most Windows applications—the Open and Save dialog boxes, for example. To select a different view in one of these dialog boxes, click the arrow on the dialog box's Views button and then choose a view from the menu that appears.

The common dialog boxes open in List view by default in all but certain system folders. Unfortunately, you can't make a view change for a particular folder persistent. You can switch from List to Details when you open a file, for example, but the next time you open a file, you'll be back in List view again.

The places bar that appears along the left edge of the common dialog boxes provides a one-click shortcut to five storage locations. By default, the five locations in the places bar are My Recent Documents, Desktop, My Documents, My Computer, and My Network Places. Using either of two tools—Group Policy and Tweak UI—you can replace these standard locations with ones that are more useful to you.

newfeature!

Customizing the Common Dialog Boxes with Group Policy

To customize the places bar using Group Policy, you need Windows XP Professional, and you must be logged on as an administrator. With those prerequisites in place, follow these steps:

1 At a command prompt, type **gpedit.msc** to open Group Policy.

2 In the tree pane, select User Configuration\Administrative Templates\Windows Components\Windows Explorer\Common Open File Dialog.

3 In the details pane, double-click Items Displayed In Places Bar.

4 Select Enabled, and then make entries in each of the five item boxes. You can enter any of the following:

- The path to a local folder or mapped network folder (for example, **c:\work**)

- The UNC path to a shared network folder (for example, **\\sequoia\projectx**)

- **CommonDocuments**, which displays Shared Documents (%AllUsersProfile%\Documents)

- **CommonMusic**, which displays Shared Music (%AllUsersProfile%\Documents\My Music)

- **CommonPictures**, which displays Shared Pictures (%AllUsersProfile%\Documents\My Pictures)

Chapter 11: Windows Explorer for Experts

- **Desktop**, which displays %UserProfile%\Desktop

- **MyComputer**, which displays My Computer

- **MyDocuments**, which displays My Documents (%UserProfile%\My Documents)

- **MyFavorites**, which displays Favorites (%UserProfile%\Favorites)

- **MyMusic**, which displays My Music (%UserProfile%\My Documents\My Music)

- **MyNetworkPlaces**, which displays My Network Places (%UserProfile%\Nethood)

- **MyPictures**, which displays My Pictures (%UserProfile%\My Documents\My Pictures)

- **Printers**, which displays Printers And Faxes

- **ProgramFiles**, which displays %ProgramFiles% (by default, C:\Program Files)

- **Recent**, which displays My Recent Documents (%UserProfile%\Recent)

Chapter 11

If you use Group Policy to configure the places bar, you should make entries in all five text boxes. If you don't, Windows inserts for each missing item a placeholder icon that doesn't work properly.

> **tip** Put links to shared network folders on the places bar only if your computer and the computer with the shared folder are always connected to the network. If either computer is disconnected when you choose File Open or File Save, you'll have to endure a lengthy wait while Windows tries to find the folder.

If you prefer to get rid of the places bar altogether, you can do that with Group Policy. Open Group Policy as described in steps 1 and 2 of the preceding procedure, double-click Hide The Common Dialog Places Bar, and select Enabled.

Customizing the Common Dialog Boxes with Tweak UI

Tweak UI for Windows XP, a program you can download from *http://www.microsoft.com/ windowsxp/pro/downloads/powertoys.asp*, also lets you customize the Open and Save dialog boxes.

Tweak UI for Windows XP is an application created by Microsoft for expert *tweakers,* but it is not a program formally supported by Microsoft. If you're comfortable with that arrangement, you'll find a lot to like in Tweak UI. You can use it to customize all kinds of details about the Windows user interface that are otherwise inaccessible to end users. When it comes to customizing the places bar, Tweak UI offers a couple of advantages over Group Policy:

- It works in Windows XP Home Edition as well as Professional.
- Its <none> option allows you to have fewer than five icons on the places bar.

To configure the places bar with Tweak UI, start Tweak UI (if you use the default setup, you'll find an icon for it in the Start, All Programs, Powertoys For Windows XP folder) and select Common Dialogs in the left pane. As shown in Figure 11-6, you can use any of the valid entries permitted by Group Policy (listed in the preceding section) or you can select from a short list of common places.

Chapter 11: Windows Explorer for Experts

Figure 11-6. Microsoft's Tweak UI program lets you modify the places bar in the common Open and Save dialog boxes.

---

note If you are a Microsoft Office user, you've undoubtedly noticed that the Open and Save dialog boxes used by the Office applications provide far more customizing capability than the ones used by most other Windows programs. (For example, you can put more than five icons on the places bar.) The reason is that Office doesn't use the common dialog boxes.

Customizing Details View

In Details view, Windows Explorer presents a table of properties for each folder and file. The properties that appear by default in this table depend on the kind of files the folder contains. With picture folders, for example, Details view includes columns that report the dimensions of each picture and the date the picture was taken. In music folders, the default columns include Artist, Album Title, Duration, and so on.

You can customize the columns that appear in any folder's Details view by choosing View, Choose Details. As Figure 11-7 on the next page shows, the list of available properties is extensive.

Figure 11-7. You can show any of these properties in a folder's Details view.

With the Choose Details dialog box, you can also rearrange the order in which columns appear, and change the width of any column. You'll probably find it easier to make these kinds of changes directly, however—by adjusting columns with your mouse in Windows Explorer. Drag a heading to the left or right to reposition it. Drag the right edge of a column heading to change that column's width.

> **tip** You can also choose which columns to display in Details view by right-clicking any column heading.

Sorting and Grouping Icons

In Details view, you can sort the contents of a folder by clicking a column heading. For example, to arrange a folder's contents by file size (smallest to largest), click the Size heading. Click the column heading again to reverse the sort order.

In other views, you can sort the contents by choosing View, Arrange Icons By, and then selecting a sort key from the submenu. The available sort keys depend on the folder type. As Figure 11-8 shows, with a music folder you can sort by Artist, Album Title, Year, Track Number, and Duration, as well as by Name, Size, and Type.

newfeature! Figure 11-8 also illustrates a nifty new feature of Windows Explorer in Windows XP. In all views except List and Filmstrip, you can use the Show In Groups command

Chapter 11: Windows Explorer for Experts

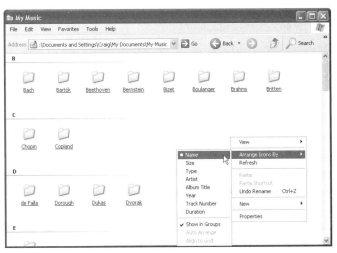

Figure 11-8. The Show In Groups command makes it easier to find files and folders.

(on the Arrange Icons By submenu) to organize your folders by some category of your choosing—size, date, name, or type, for example. When you have a lot of items in a folder, displaying the contents in groups can help you locate the one you need. The Show In Groups command can also make it more pleasant to look at a small folder that contains significantly different kinds of items—such as My Computer, as shown in Figure 11-9.

Figure 11-9. Grouping items by type makes a more pleasant display, even in a folder with relatively few items.

---

tip   **Remove the Files Stored On This Computer group**

Some users prefer not to take up space in My Computer with the Files Stored On This Computer group. You can eliminate that group from My Computer as follows:

1 Open Registry Editor.

2 Navigate to HKLM\Software\Microsoft\Windows\CurrentVersion\ Explorer\My Computer\NameSpace\Delegate Folders.

3 Below this key, you'll see a subkey called {59031a47-3f72-44a7-89c5-5595fe6b30ee}. Delete this subkey and close Registry Editor.

(As always, exercise extreme caution when editing the registry. For more information about editing the registry and using Regedit, see Chapter 29, "Editing the Registry.")

---

newfeature!
Choosing a Folder Template

Windows XP does not include the Customize This Folder Wizard, which let you assign pictures and HTML templates as backgrounds to folders in earlier versions of Windows Explorer. Instead of taking you to the wizard, the View, Customize This Folder command now puts you on the Customize tab of the folder's properties dialog box, as shown in Figure 11-10, where you can choose one of the folder templates that Windows supplies, put a picture on a folder's Thumbnails-view icon, or change a folder's icon altogether.

Figure 11-10. On the Customize tab of a folder's properties dialog box, you can choose a template, assign a picture, and change the folder icon.

Chapter 11: Windows Explorer for Experts

The seven supplied templates are as follows:

- Documents (for any file type)
- Pictures (best for many files)
- Photo Album (best for fewer files)
- Music (best for audio files and playlists)
- Music Artist (best for works by one artist)
- Music Album (best for tracks from one album)
- Videos

Most of the time, you'll find that Windows applies an appropriate template without any help from you. If you use Windows Media Player to copy tracks from an audio CD to your hard disk, for example, Windows Media Player (by default) creates an artist folder, stores an album folder within that artist folder, and stores the individual audio tracks in that album folder. The artist folder is given the Music Artist template, and the album folder gets the Music Album template—as you would expect. If Windows finds ordinary documents in a folder (that is, not media files), it assigns it the Documents template, and so on.

To choose a template other than the one Windows assigns by default, follow these steps:

1 Right-click a blank space in the folder.

2 Choose Customize This Folder.

3 In the Use This Folder Type As A Template list, choose a template.

Your choice of template (or, more typically, the choice that Windows makes) affects the following:

- The tasks that appear at the top of the task pane
- The default view (Filmstrip for a Photo Album template, for example)
- Whether Windows can display four pictures or only one on the folder icon in Thumbnails view
- The background image for the folder

---

note The Customize This Folder command is not available for certain system folders, such as My Documents, My Music, Shared Music, and Shared Pictures.

Chapter 11

newfeature!
Putting Pictures on Folder Icons

Folder icons that appear in a folder displayed in Thumbnails view can be decorated with pictures. Windows XP uses this feature to "preview" the contents of picture, video, music album, and music artist folders. When you copy audio tracks to your hard disk with Windows Media Player, Windows adorns the artist folder with album art from the albums contained within that folder. When Windows discerns that a folder contains pictures, it plants up to four of those pictures on the folder icon, as shown in Figure 11-11. When it sees videos, it displays the first frame of up to four videos.

Figure 11-11. Windows automatically displays up to four pictures on folder icons for folders containing image files.

Windows fancies up your folder icons for media folders automatically. All you need to do to take advantage of this feature is make sure the parent folder (the one containing the adorned folder icons) is displayed in Thumbnails view.

You can also put your own pictures on folder icons, and they don't have to be pictures contained within the folder in question. To dress up an icon yourself, return to the Customize tab of the folder's properties dialog box (shown in Figure 11-10 on page 430), click Choose Picture, and specify. If you change your mind and want to remove the picture, click Restore Default.

Choosing Advanced Folder Options

The View tab of the Folder Options dialog box, shown in Figure 11-12, offers a potpourri of advanced options that govern various aspects of Windows Explorer's behavior. Some of these are self-explanatory and relatively inconsequential. Others are less obvious and can have a significant impact on how you work in Windows XP. The following sections provide brief descriptions of these options.

Chapter 11: Windows Explorer for Experts

Figure 11-12. The Advanced Settings list includes obvious and obscure miscellany.

Automatically Search for Network Folders and Printers

By default, Windows scans your network periodically for newly shared printers and folders, adding those that it finds to My Network Places and your Printers And Faxes folder. You might want to clear this check box if you're disconnected from the network most of your day. Otherwise, leave it selected; it's a convenience you might as well enjoy.

Display File Size Information in Folder Tips

If you pause your mouse pointer over a folder icon, Windows Explorer normally displays a "folder tip" that describes the contents of the folder and tells you how much space the folder's contents consume.

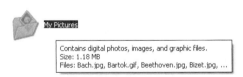

If you'd rather skip the file size information and see only a description of the folder contents, clear Display File Size Information In Folder Tips. If you'd rather see no folder tips at all, clear Show Pop-Up Description For Folder And Desktop Items. Clearing the latter check box also suppresses the file size information, regardless of how the former check box is configured.

Chapter 11

433

Part 3: Managing Files

newfeature!
Display Simple Folder View in Explorer's Folders List

This check box enables the simple-folder navigational method described earlier in this chapter (see "Navigating the Folders Bar in Simple Folder View," page 421.

newfeature!
Display the Contents of System Folders

One of the ways that Windows XP tries to protect you from damaging your operating system is by discouraging you from even opening folders containing system files—such as %ProgramFiles%, %SystemRoot%, and %SystemRoot%\System32. If the Display The Contents Of System Folders check box is clear (its default state), Windows displays this message when you try to display a system folder.

If you're an experienced Windows user, you might object to being shut out of the system folders. You can display system files by selecting Display The Contents Of System Folders. You can also enable the display of system folders selectively. If you leave the Display The Contents Of System Folders check box clear, you'll see the warning screen the first time you visit a system folder. Click Show The Contents Of This Folder, and the folder's contents will be visible thereafter, regardless of how the check box is set. Note that this is a per-user setting; other user accounts will still find the system folders blocked—unless they too click the link that lets them in.

Display the Full Path in the Address Bar and Title Bar

By default, Windows Explorer displays the full path of the current folder in the Address bar but only the folder name in the Windows Explorer title bar. You can shuffle these options any way you like by manipulating two Advanced Settings options. If you like to display the Address bar alongside the Standard Buttons toolbar, you might find that you seldom have room for the full path in the Address bar. The title bar for the Windows Explorer window, on the other hand, typically has room for long paths. So, it's possible you'll want to reverse the defaults. On the other hand, if you use the Folders bar, you might find that you don't need the full path

Chapter 11: Windows Explorer for Experts

specification in either location. Experiment to see what works best for you. Be aware that if you display the full path on the title bar, Windows also displays it in your taskbar buttons. These typically do not have room for full paths; when necessary, Windows simply truncates text in the taskbar buttons, though if you pause the pointer over the button the full path and name will appear.

newfeature!

Do Not Cache Thumbnails

Windows normally stores the images that appear in Thumbnails view in a *cache*; that is, it keeps them in a hidden file named Thumbs.db so that it can redisplay the images more quickly each time you reopen a folder in Thumbnails view. Selecting the Do Not Cache Thumbnails check box can free up a bit of disk space, but it might cause delays when you open folders.

> **note** Changing this setting does not delete any existing instances of Thumbs.db; it merely prevents the creation of new cache files.

Hidden Files and Folders

By default, Windows Explorer hides files and folders that have either the hidden attribute or the system attribute set. The operating system keeps these items out of sight, on the assumption that what you can't see you can't delete, rename, or corrupt.

To make hidden files and folders visible, select Show Hidden Files And Folders. (If you don't see this option, double-click Hidden Files And Folders.) To make visible files and folders with both the system and the hidden attributes set (the so-called "super-hidden" items), clear Hide Protected Operating System Files (Recommended).

> **tip** **Search for hidden files**
>
> In earlier versions of Windows, if hidden files were not displayed in Windows Explorer, they were also invisible to the Search command. In Windows XP, you can search for hidden items, regardless of your settings in the Folder Options dialog box. For more information, see "Locating Files with Search Companion," page 474.

Hide Extensions for Known File Types

Windows Explorer normally displays file name extensions only for file types unknown to the registry, leaving you to discern the type of most files by their icons, screen tips, the tags that appear below file names in Tiles view, or the Type column in Details view. This behavior results in cleaner, leaner displays in Windows Explorer as well as in the dialog boxes that you use to open and save files.

The disadvantage of hiding extensions is that it makes it harder for you to change a file's extension. For example, suppose you want to change the name of the file *Notes.txt* to *Notes.doc*—so that it will open automatically in WordPad (or Microsoft Word) instead of Notepad. If the extension is hidden, you will see the entry *Notes* in Windows Explorer. If you simply add **.doc** to the end of this entry, you will see *Notes.doc* in Windows Explorer. But the new name of the file will be *Notes.doc.txt*, and the file will still be associated with Notepad. To change the extension, you must first make the extension visible.

---

tip   **Use Open With to see a file's extension**

If you just want to know what a file's extension is, and Windows Explorer is hiding extensions for known file types, right-click the file name and choose Open With. (If Open With presents a submenu, select Choose Program on the submenu.) Near the top of the Open With dialog box, you'll find the full name of the file, extension included.

 The companion CD included with this book includes a batch file and a VBScript file, both of which toggle all of Windows Explorer's "hide" settings on or off. Run ToggleHiddenExplorerStuff.bat or ToggleHiddenExplorerStuff.vbs once to make hidden and super-hidden files visible and to show extensions; run it a second time to return these settings to their defaults.

---

tip   **Show extensions for particular files only**

To see the extensions for a particular known file type, while hiding all the others, use the File Types tab in the Folder Options dialog box. Select the file type whose extension you want to see, click Advanced, and then select the Always Show Extension check box.

Hide Protected Operating System Files (Recommended)

If this option is selected (as it is by default), Windows Explorer hides files that have both the system attribute and the hidden attribute set.

Launch Folder Windows in a Separate Process

Windows Explorer normally uses the same memory space for all open folder windows. If you set the Launch Folder Window In A Separate Process check box, the memory used by each window will be segregated. (The name of the option is misleading; you'll still have only one Explorer.exe process running, but that process will use separate memory spaces for each window.) If Windows Explorer is prone to crashing on your system, you might want to try selecting this check box. Otherwise, there's no good reason to do so, and you'll conserve memory by leaving it clear.

Chapter 11: Windows Explorer for Experts

newfeature!
Managing Pairs of Web Pages and Folders

If you save a Web page using Internet Explorer's Web Page, Complete option (choose Web Page, Complete (*.htm, *.html) in the Save As Type list), Internet Explorer saves the Web page's text in one file and puts all the associated graphics and other supporting documents in a folder with the same name. For example, if you save the MSN home page (*http://www.msn.com*) under its default name, Welcome to MSN_com, you will get a file named Welcome to MSN_com.htm and a folder called Welcome to MSN_com, the latter containing various GIF and JPEG images and perhaps a script or two.

By default, Windows Explorer handles such file-and-folder pairs as a single entity. The file and folder are shown as separate items, but any action taken upon one is automatically taken upon both. Delete or move either the file or the folder, for example, and Windows Explorer moves or deletes both items. This behavior makes it less likely that you'll "break" a saved Web page by separating its component parts.

Provided you have Microsoft Office installed, you can choose two alternatives to the default behavior:

● Show And Manage The Pair As A Single File

● Show Both Parts And Manage Them Individually

(If you don't see these options, double-click Managing Pairs Of Web Pages And Folders.) If you change Windows Explorer's behavior after saving a file-and-folder pair, Windows Explorer applies the new behavior to the existing pair. For example, if you save a page using the Show Both Parts And Manage Them Individually option, your file and folder are initially independent. But if you then switch back to the default behavior, the file and folder become linked, as though you had saved them that way in the first place.

Remember Each Folder's View Settings

By default, Windows Explorer remembers the view settings you assign to a folder. That is, the next time you open a folder, it looks the same way it did the last time you were there. Not everyone prefers this behavior. If you like to maintain a consistent look in all your folders (for information about how to do this, see "Making All Folders Use the Same View," page 423), and change the view only occasionally for some special situations, you might rather have Windows restore your preferred view when you close a folder. If that's the case, clear Remember Each Folder's View Settings.

newfeature!
Restore Previous Folder Windows at Logon

When you logged on to previous versions of Windows, Windows Explorer reopened any folders that were open when you logged off. Because many users found the convenience of reopening folders more than outweighed by the extra time required to complete the logon, Windows XP has made this behavior optional—and has disabled it by default.

To have your previously opened windows reopened at logon, set Restore Previous Folder Windows At Logon.

newfeature!
Show Control Panel in My Computer

Earlier versions of Windows included the Control Panel folder in My Computer. Windows XP, by default, eschews the folder-style presentation of Control Panel options in favor of a Control Panel menu, but lets you switch back to the "classic view" Control Panel if you prefer the old ways. With either the new style or the old, however, you have the option of including Control Panel in the My Computer folder. To put it there, select Show Control Panel In My Computer.

Note that Control Panel appears in the Folders bar under My Computer, regardless of how this option is set, as shown in Figure 11-13.

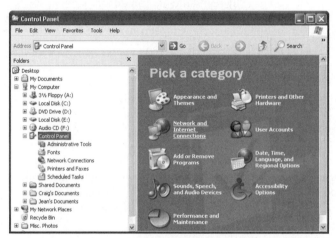

Figure 11-13. Regardless of whether Control Panel appears in your My Computer folder, it appears under My Computer in the Folders bar.

Show Encrypted or Compressed NTFS Files in Color

By default, the names of encrypted NTFS files and folders are displayed in green; those of compressed files and folders appear in blue. If you like black better, clear Show Encrypted Or Compressed NTFS Files In Color. (For information about using encryption, see Chapter 14, "Encrypting Confidential Information." For information about using NTFS compression, see "Implementing NTFS Compression," page 462.)

newfeature!
Show Pop-Up Descriptions for Folder and Desktop Items

This option enables pop-up descriptions when you select folders or desktop items. If you don't need the information or the pop-up information becomes distracting or gets in your way, clear this check box to disable it.

newfeature!

Use Simple File Sharing (Recommended)

The last check box in the Advanced Settings list enables or disables Simple File Sharing. For additional information about Simple File Sharing, see "Simple File Sharing vs. Windows 2000–Style Sharing," page 98.

Because you can't disable Simple File Sharing in Windows XP Home Edition, this option appears only in Windows XP Professional.

Using Cascading Folder Menus

Most users know that you can put a shortcut to any folder on your Start menu (or desktop) and then use the shortcut as a simple way of opening that folder in Windows Explorer. Less obvious is the fact that you can put a whole branch of your file system on the Start menu, and then use cascading submenus to get to any point within the branch. Figure 11-14 shows an example in which a remote folder (running on a Windows 2000 system) has been added to the local Start menu. When you add a system of subfolders to the menu this way, you can open any subfolder by navigating to it in the menu, right-clicking it, and then choosing either Open or Explore from the shortcut menu. (Choose Explore to open the folder with the Folders bar.)

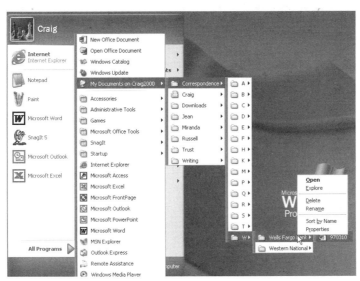

Figure 11-14. Adding a branch of your file system to your Start menu lets you navigate quickly to distant folders.

To add a branch of your folder structure to the Start menu, follow these steps:

1 In Windows Explorer, open the parent of the folder that you want to be the root of the cascading system.

2 Drag the icon for the root folder to the Start menu, and hold it there while the Start menu opens.

■ If you're using the Windows XP–style Start menu, drag the folder to All Programs, and wait while the All Programs menu opens. Drag the folder to the place where you want it, and then release the mouse button.

■ If you're using the classic Start menu, drag the folder to the top portion of the menu, position it where you want it, and then release the mouse button.

Windows creates a shortcut to your folder in the place where you release the mouse button. Note that if you're using the Windows XP–style Start menu, you *can* create that shortcut at the top of the left portion of the menu, but if you put it there, the shortcut opens the root folder only. If you want to be able to cascade the subfolder structure, you need to position the root folder within All Programs.

Working with File Types and File Associations

The File Types tab of the Folder Options dialog box (choose Tools, Folder Options, File Types) displays a list of your registered document file types. A few entries from this long list are visible in Figure 11-15.

By selecting file types from the Registered File Types list, you can perform a number of tasks:

● Change the default action for a file type

● Change the application associated with a file type

● Change a file type's icon

● Specify whether the file type's extension should be displayed in Windows Explorer

● Specify whether a file type should be opened immediately after being downloaded

● Add commands to the file type's shortcut menu

Chapter 11: Windows Explorer for Experts

Figure 11-15. On the File Types tab you can change such things as the default actions for document types.

Changing the Default Action for a File Type

A file type's default action is the one that occurs when you double-click it (or single-click it if you've set up Windows Explorer for single-click starting). If you right-click a file in Windows Explorer, the default action is shown in boldface on the shortcut menu. Most commonly, the default action for a document is to open it for editing or display in its parent application—the application with which it is associated. There are exceptions, however. The default action for a .reg file, for example, is to merge the file's data with the registry. To edit the .reg file, you need to choose a nondefault command (Edit) from the shortcut menu. (Alternatively, you can change the default action to Edit.)

To change a file type's default action, follow these steps:

1 In the File Types list, select the file whose default action you want to change.

2 Click Advanced.

3 In the list of available actions, select the action you want to be the default.

4 Click Set Default. This figure shows the result of setting .tif files to be opened by default.

Changing the Application Associated with a File Type

Perhaps the simplest way to change the application associated with a file type is to right-click it in Windows Explorer and choose Open With from the shortcut menu. In the Open With dialog box, select the application you want associated with the file type, and then select Always Use The Selected Program To Open This Kind Of File.

Alternatively, you can accomplish this change in the File Types list. Select the file you want to change, click the Change button, and then select the program you want associated with the file type, as shown next.

Changing a File Type's Icon

To change the icon used for a file type, follow these steps:

1 Select the file type in the File Types list.

2 Click Advanced.

3 Click Change Icon.

4 Choose a new icon from the Change Icon dialog box, shown on the next page.

If you don't find an icon to your liking in the Change Icon dialog box, click Browse and navigate to another program that might offer something you prefer. Icons are commonly stored within .exe, .dll, and .ico files.

Making the Extension of a Particular File Type Visible

If you have set Windows Explorer to hide extensions for known file types (that is, if you have left its default behavior in place), you can still display extensions for particular kinds of files. In the File Types list, select the file type whose extension you want to see. Then click Advanced and select Always Show Extension.

Specifying Download Behavior

To specify that files of a particular type should always be opened as soon as you have finished downloading them, select the file type in the File Types list. Click Advanced and then clear Confirm Open After Download.

Chapter 11

> **caution** Indiscriminately opening certain types of files you download could be disastrous to the health of your computer if those files contain viruses or worms. Files with extensions that indicate they are executable files are the ones you need to watch most carefully, such as .bat, .vbs, .exe, or .com.

Editing a File Type's Shortcut Menu

When you right-click a file or folder in Windows Explorer, you get the familiar shortcut menu of commands available for that object. The commands that appear on this menu can be derived from the following locations:

- HCKR*class*\Shell (where *class* is a descriptor of the file—such as txtfile for files with the extensions .dic, .exc, .log, .scp, .txt, .wtx, and possibly others on your system)

- HKCR*\Shell

- HKCR\Unknown\Shell

- HKCR*class*\Shellex\ContextMenuHandlers

- HKCR*\Shellex\ContextMenuHandlers

- The file %SystemRoot%\System32\Shell32.dll

Those that appear under HKCR*class*\Shell are file-type specific. Those that appear under HKCR*\Shell and HKCR\Unknown\Shell work just like the ones under HCKR*class*\Shell except that they apply to all file types (*) or to unregistered file types (Unknown).

Those that appear under either of the ContextMenuHandlers keys are shell extensions provided by .exe or .dll files. And those that come from Shell32.dll are the so-called *canonical verbs*—Cut, Copy, Paste, Delete, Rename, and Properties.

You can edit the commands that appear under the Shell keys or add new commands there. But you don't need to go to the registry to do this unless you want to manipulate the *\Shell or \Unknown\Shell keys. To modify shortcut-menu commands for registered file types, use the File Types list in Windows Explorer. It's safer and just as effective.

To edit an existing command, follow these steps:

1 Select the file type in the File Types list.

2 Click Advanced.

3 In the Actions list, select the command you want to edit.

4 Click Edit.

5 Make your changes on the Action line, and then click OK.

To add a new command, select the file type in the File Types list, click Advanced, and then click New. On the Action line of the New Action dialog box, type the command as you want it to appear on the shortcut menu. On the Application Used To Perform Action line, type the command string you want to use.

For example, .log files are associated with Notepad, by default. Suppose you would like to open them occasionally in WordPad instead—perhaps in order to apply some formatting for reporting purposes. You can use Open With to open the files in WordPad, of course, but let's assume that you'd like to streamline the process by having an Open With WordPad command on the shortcut menu. Here's how to do it:

1 In the Extensions column of the File Types list, select LOG.

2 Click Advanced.

3 In the Edit File Type dialog box, click New.

4 Fill out the New Action dialog box as shown here.

The ampersand before *WordPad* is optional; it makes the letter *W* a shortcut key for the new command. The %1 at the end of the command string is a placeholder for the name of the file that you right-click.

> **note** Because .log files belong to the class txtfile, making this shortcut-menu change for .log files also adds the new command to the shortcut menus for the other txtfile types—.txt, .dic, and so on.

To add a command for the * or Unknown file types, follow these steps:

1 Open Registry Editor.

2 Navigate to HKCR* or HKCR\Unknown.

3 If the Shell subkey doesn't exist, create it.

4 Create a subkey under Shell and then give it the name of your new command.

5 Make the default value of your new command subkey the text that you want to appear on the shortcut menu.

6 Create a new subkey called Command under the subkey you just created.

7 Make the default value for this new subkey the command string that you want your command to execute.

Figure 11-16 shows the result in the registry of the Open With WordPad command described earlier in this section. You would use a similar subkey structure to add commands to either HKCR* or HKCR\Unknown.

Figure 11-16. Adding a command to the shortcut menu for .log and other txtfile types generates these new registry entries.

---

caution Use extreme care when editing the registry directly. Don't make changes in the registry when an alternative method exists. To modify shortcut menus, use the File Types list in Windows Explorer if possible. For more information about working directly with the registry, see Chapter 29, "Editing the Registry."

Using Windows Explorer's Command-Line Syntax

Cascading folder menus, as described earlier in this chapter, are one way to open Windows Explorer with a particular folder in view. But they might not be the ideal way. Compare the two views of the System32 folder shown in Figure 11-17 on the next page. The one on the left was generated by a Start menu item; the one on the right was produced by means of Windows Explorer's command-line syntax.

Part 3: Managing Files

Figure 11-17. The view on the right, produced by a command string, restricts the Folders bar to a particular branch of the file structure.

The difference between the two is all in the Folders bar. The command-line string in this case puts the selected folder (System32) at the top of the folder hierarchy, eliminating all folders at higher levels and letting you focus your attention on System32.

This is one example of the usefulness of the Windows Explorer command-line syntax. You can probably find others in your own work. You can use Windows Explorer command strings in shortcuts, with the Start menu's Run command, at the command prompt, or in batch programs or scripts. The syntax is as follows:

```
explorer [/n | /e][,/root,object][[,/select],subobject]
```

The switches, all of which are optional, have the following effects:

Switch	Effect
/N	Opens without displaying the Folders bar.
/E	Opens with the Folders bar displayed.
/Root,*object*	Restricts Windows Explorer to *object* and all folders contained within object.
/Select,*subobject*	Gives the initial focus to the parent folder of *subobject* and selects *subobject*. If /Select is omitted, *subobject* specifies the folder that gets the initial focus.

Let's look at some examples. To begin,

```
explorer /e,/root,%systemroot%\system32
```

opens Windows Explorer and displays the Folders bar, restricting the namespace to %SystemRoot%\System32 and its subfolders. (This is the syntax used to generate the window on the right side of Figure 11-17.)

To open %SystemRoot%\Cursors in Windows Explorer, with the Folders bar displayed and the file Appstart.ini selected, you must include the file name and extension in the command string, as follows:

```
explorer /e, /select,%systemroot%\cursors\appstart.ani
```

Typing the following opens %SystemRoot% without the Folders bar:

```
explorer %systemroot%
```

The folder is loaded as the subobject focus, not as the root folder—which means that you can navigate upward from %SystemRoot% in the folder hierarchy.

The string

```
explorer /n
```

opens the drive on which Windows XP is installed without displaying the Folders bar, whereas

```
explorer /e,.
```

opens %UserProfile% and displays the Folders bar.

Using GUIDs to Open Shell Folders in Windows Explorer

A GUID, or *globally unique identifier,* is a string of 32 hexadecimal digits enclosed within braces, with hyphens separating the digits into groups of eight, four, four, four, and twelve—like this:

```
{nnnnnnnn-nnnn-nnnn-nnnn-nnnnnnnnnnnn}
```

Windows XP uses GUIDs to identify all kinds of objects, including certain system folders. You can open the following GUIDs in Windows Explorer.

{208D2C60-3AEA-1069-A2D7-08002B30309D}	My Network Places
{20D04FE0-3AEA-1069-A2D8-08002B30309D}	My Computer
{2227A280-3AEA-1069-A2DE-08002B30309D}	Printers And Faxes
{645FF040-5081-101B-9F08-00AA002F954E}	Recycle Bin
{7007ACC7-3202-11D1-AAD2-00805FC1270E}	Network Connections
{D6277990-4C6A-11CF-8D87-00AA0060F5BF}	Scheduled Tasks

You might find it convenient to incorporate command strings that use GUIDs in short-cuts for opening Windows Explorer, or in batch programs or in scripts. When you construct the command string, put a space after the word *explorer,* and then two colons. Follow the colons immediately with the GUID, like this:

```
explorer ::{208D2C60-3AEA-1069-A2D7-08002B30309D}
```

If you use one or more of the optional switches (for example, /root,), follow the last character in the string with a space, then two colons, then the GUID, like this:

```
explorer /root, ::{208D2C60-3AEA-1069-A2D7-08002B30309D}
```

If you don't like typing GUIDs, you can copy them from the registry. In Registry Editor, navigate to HKCR\CLSID. Then search for the folder you want to open—My Network Places, for example. Registry Editor should locate a key that has the GUID you want. (Compare it with the text in this book to make sure you have the right one.) When you find it, select it and choose Edit, Copy Key Name. You'll be copying the full key path, of course, including My Computer\HKEY_CLASSES_ROOT\CLSID\. But you can edit out the parts you don't need when you paste this text into your command string. If you type the GUID yourself, you can use either capital or lowercase letters. The strings 3AEA and 3aea are equivalent, for example.

Chapter 12

Managing and Finding Files

Not long ago, when hard disk capacity was still measured in megabytes, the most serious file management problem facing the typical computer user was how to keep from running out of disk space. Now that disks offering tens of gigabytes are commonplace (and the operating system itself consumes nearly a gigabyte), different issues have come to the fore. Although it's still true, perhaps, that there's no such thing as a large enough hard disk, for most users running out of space is a significantly smaller concern than it once was. What matters now is learning how to use storage resources effectively and knowing how to find crucial documents saved in these vast warehouses.

This chapter presents strategies for managing files effectively, discusses some of the file management tools provided by Microsoft Windows XP, and describes the operating system's powerful indexing and search facility. Windows XP Indexing Service comes with an elaborate query language that allows you to locate documents quickly based on their content or other properties. You don't have to master every detail of this language to make good use of the service, but the more you know about it the less likely it is that you'll ever lose an important document.

Seven Principles of Effective File Management

It's fashionable to present principles in multiples of seven. So here are our picks:

Use My Documents   For all the reasons outlined in Chapter 8 (see "Making It Easy to Open Your Favorite Documents," page 286), it's smart to take advantage of My Documents. Most of your

451

At Home with Windows XP

All the features described in this chapter work identically in Windows XP Professional and Windows XP Home Edition. A number of the illustrations in this chapter show a Security tab in the properties dialog box. The tab, which appears only when Simple File Sharing is disabled, is not available in Windows XP Home Edition. (The workings of the Security tab are described in Chapter 13, "Securing Files and Folders.")

applications will expect to save and retrieve documents from this folder anyway, so it's best to build your *document storage structure* (that is, your folders and subfolders) within the framework of My Documents. If you don't like where Windows XP has set up My Documents (the default location is %UserProfile%\My Documents, which is a subfolder on the drive where Windows is installed), you can move it (see "Moving Folders from the Standard Profile Locations," page 1162).

Another virtue of My Documents is that it enforces a prudent separation of documents and executables. Documents stored where programs are stored are at risk for accidental deletion when programs are uninstalled or upgraded. My Documents also discourages you from using your desktop as a document repository. You should use your Windows desktop the way you use your regular desktop—as a temporary surface. It's fine to store something there momentarily (an item downloaded from the Internet, for example, to be read or installed and then deleted or relocated). But if you pile up your everyday work there, you'll not only create visual clutter, you'll also deprive yourself of the organizational services (Details View and the Folders bar, for example) available in ordinary Windows Explorer folders.

Adopt consistent methods for file and folder naming   Both Windows XP Search Companion and Indexing Service can help you find anything. But you can save yourself a lot of trouble by working out a naming scheme for the kinds of documents you create most often, and then sticking to that scheme.

Keep names short   The long file names that Windows began allowing years ago brought welcome relief from the eight-character constraints of MS-DOS and early Windows days. But that doesn't mean you should use descriptive sentences in place of easy-to-recognize names. Long names produce cluttered or truncated displays. Brevity promotes clarity.

Let your folders do some of the naming. Rather than create a file called Great American Novel Chapter One Fumbling First Effort.doc, why not build a folder structure like this?

Chapter 12: Managing and Finding Files

A structure like this can alleviate the temptation to use verbose file names.

Segregate current and completed work   One way to simplify your storage system is to remove completed work, either by archiving it to an offline storage medium (a backup tape or recordable CD disc, for example) or by moving it to an archival subfolder. It's also an excellent idea to compress archived documents; even a huge hard disk eventually fills to capacity. For information about using file compression, see "Maximizing Storage Space with NTFS Compression and Compressed (Zipped) Folders," page 460.

Store like with like   Restricting folders to a single document type (or predominantly one type) allows you to take advantage of Windows Explorer's new folder templates and makes it easier for you to find documents you need later on. With all your pictures for a given trip or time period in a single folder (and nothing else), for example, it's easy to use the new Filmstrip view and slide show feature to find the right picture for your newsletter.

Avoid flat folder structures   If you need to put so many subfolders in a folder that you can't see all of them at a glance in the Folders bar, consider creating an alphabetic menu, like the one shown in Figure 12-1.

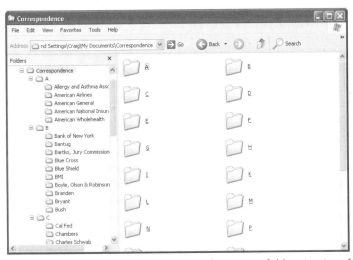

Figure 12-1.   An alphabetic menu can keep your folder structure from becoming too "flat."

Use shortcuts and OLE links instead of multiple document copies
If you need to be able to get to the same document from multiple locations, don't create copies of the document. Create shortcuts to it instead. For details, see "Creating and Customizing Document Shortcuts," page 458. Similarly, if you need to reuse boilerplate text in multiple documents, use your application's Paste Link command, instead of its normal Paste

command. The resulting OLE link stores a pointer in your document to the boilerplate source. If you change the source, all the documents with links to the source are updated automatically.

Using Tools for File Management

You can move and copy files the same way you move and copy text within a document—by copying or cutting to the Clipboard and then pasting in a new location. But Windows provides a wealth of tools that make file transfer even simpler, help you track document statistics, enable you to compress and decompress files, and perform other vital document management tasks.

Manipulating Files with the Folders Bar

When you're moving or copying files from one folder to another, particularly if the folders are widely separated in your folder hierarchy, the simplest method is often to display the Folders bar and drag the file or files with your mouse. Any folder in the Folders bar can serve as a "drop target." To move an item from Folder A to Folder B, display it in Folder A, display the Folders bar, drag the item from Folder A, and then drop it on Folder B in the Folders bar.

Windows Explorer doesn't display the Folders bar by default. You can make it appear by clicking Folders on the Standard Buttons toolbar or by choosing View, Explorer Bar, Folders.

note The Folders bar is a little easier to work with in Windows XP than it was in earlier versions of Windows. For more information, see "Navigating the Folders Bar in Simple Folder View," page 421.

InsideOut

If you select a group of items in Windows Explorer and then choose File, Rename or press F2, it will appear as though you are about to rename only the last item you selected. After you type a new name and press Enter, however, you will find that all items in the selection have acquired the new name—with numbers in parentheses to distinguish one renamed item from another. For example, select three files with dissimilar names, press F2, type **NewName**, and then press Enter. Your three files will be named *NewName*, *NewName (1)*, and *NewName (2)*.

This bulk-renaming behavior is new in Windows XP and might come as a surprise to some users. If you accidentally rename a folder full of files when you mean to rename only one, press Ctrl+Z (or choose Edit, Undo Rename). The last of your files to be renamed (*NewName (2)* in the example just given) will regain its former name. Press Ctrl+Z again and another file will revert. Continue in this manner until all but the intended file have shed their new names.

Inspecting and Setting File Properties

The properties dialog box for a file or folder (or a selection of files or folders) provides a wealth of useful information about the selected item or items. To display this information, right-click the item and choose Properties from the shortcut menu. The kind of information you will see depends on the type of item you have selected. Figure 12-2 shows the General tab of the properties dialog box for the Microsoft Word document used to generate this chapter (while the chapter was still under construction).

Figure 12-2. The General tab of a document's properties dialog box reports file size, creation date, attributes, and parent application.

As you can see, this part of the properties dialog box provides information about the file's size, location, dates, parent application, and other attributes. There's even a button you can use to change the parent application, should you need to do that. For other and simpler ways to change the association between a document and an application, see "Changing the Application Associated with a File Type," page 442.

Most of the properties shown on the General tab are *read-only* (that is, they're set by the operating system and can't be changed by you), and you can get most of this information easily enough in Windows Explorer, without displaying the properties dialog box. The Summary and Custom tabs, for documents whose properties dialog box includes these tabs, provide less readily available details and include properties whose value you can set yourself. On the next page, Figure 12-3 shows the Advanced view of the Summary tab and Figure 12-4 shows the Custom tab for our Chapter 12 Word document.

> **note** If the Summary tab for a properties dialog box looks significantly different from Figure 12-3 and you see an Advanced button, click Advanced. The Advanced presentation of the Summary tab provides access to more properties than does the Simple presentation. Also, note that the Security tab does not appear if you are using Simple File Sharing, if you are running Windows XP Home Edition, or if the document is not stored on an NTFS drive.

It might not be obvious from looking at a Summary tab which properties are read-only and which can be set or changed by you. If you're not sure about a property, click on it in the Value column. If the property can be set, an edit box will appear.

As Figure 12-4 shows, the Custom tab lets you create your own properties and set their values. The Name list, shown open in Figure 12-4, enumerates suggested custom properties. But you can type whatever name you want in the Name box. After you provide a value for the item the Add button becomes available for you to add the property to the file.

Applications that provide user-editable properties, such as Microsoft Word, provide access to those properties within their own menu systems. In Word, for example, you can choose File, Properties to set the value of properties, such as Title, Subject, and Category, for the current document. But the properties dialog box provides another route to those properties, one that is worth knowing about from a file management perspective.

> **tip** **Use Indexing Service to locate files**
>
> You can use Indexing Service and its query language to look for files on the basis of property values. For example, you can search for all files whose Category property has the value *Manuscript*. For more information, see "Using Indexing Service and Query Language," page 480.

Chapter 12: Managing and Finding Files

Click these fields to enter new information

Figure 12-3. Some of the properties on the Summary tab can be modified at will.

Figure 12-4. You can use the Custom tab to create your own properties and set their values.

Using Details View to See and Compare Properties of Many Files

The most important properties available via the properties dialog box can also be displayed as columns in Windows Explorer's Details view. Details view also lets you sort files on the basis of their property values—from largest to smallest, oldest to newest, and so on.

For more information about customizing Details view, see "Customizing Details View," page 427.

Creating and Customizing Document Shortcuts

Document shortcuts let you open documents from places other than where those documents are stored—from your desktop, for example. (We don't advocate storing documents on the desktop, but using the desktop for shortcuts to documents you're currently involved with is not a bad idea—provided you get rid of the shortcuts when you no longer need them, and provided you don't have security concerns about others who might have access to your computer!)

The simplest way to create a desktop shortcut to a document is as follows:

1 Display the document in Windows Explorer (with Windows Explorer not maximized).

2 Hold down the Alt key and drag the document to your desktop.

3 Rename the shortcut, removing the words *Shortcut to* (an optional step). The small arrow at the lower left of the icon indicates you're looking at a shortcut.

After you have a shortcut on your desktop, you can assign a keyboard shortcut to it. (As you see, the word *shortcut* can mean many things in Windows.) This keyboard shortcut to your shortcut is a keystroke combination that lets you "run" the shortcut (that is, open the document in its parent application) without your having to hunt for it on the desktop. To assign a keyboard shortcut, follow these steps:

1 Right-click the shortcut, choose Properties from the shortcut menu, and then click the Shortcut tab.

2 Type a letter or other character in the Shortcut Key box. (Windows will prefix your keystroke with Ctrl+Alt+.) If you prefer another key combination, you're free to type combinations of Ctrl, Alt, and Shift with your keyboard character.

Chapter 12: Managing and Finding Files

3 While you're in the properties dialog box, you can also use the Run box to tell Windows how you want the document and its parent application to open—minimized, normal, or maximized.

---

tip **Test your shortcut's shortcut**

Not all combinations of Ctrl and Alt and a letter or function key can be used in keyboard shortcuts. Those that conflict with existing shortcuts, for example, are disallowed. Rather than try to learn and memorize which ones you can and can't use, just test your shortcut before relying on it. If nothing happens when you type the combination, try another.

---

note Windows will let you assign keyboard shortcuts to document shortcuts stored in folders other than the desktop. But they won't work.

Protecting Files with the Read-Only Attribute

If you have documents on your hard disk that you keep only for reference—documents that you have no need to change or that must not be changed, it's a good idea to make them read-only. If you edit and then attempt to save a read-only document, your application will present its Save As dialog box, prompting you to supply a new file name and ensuring that the original file remains unmodified.

To give a file read-only status, right-click it and choose Properties from the shortcut menu. On the General tab of the properties dialog box, select Read-Only.

---

caution   Read-only files can be renamed, moved, deleted—and, of course, read. To keep other users from opening or deleting particular files, use the powerful security features built into Windows XP. (For information about securing files, see Chapter 13, "Securing Files and Folders." For information about encrypting files, see Chapter 14, "Encrypting Confidential Information.") To protect against accidental deletion by yourself, make a backup! (For more information about avoiding accidental erasure of files, see "Using and Configuring the Recycle Bin," page 471.)

InsideOut

A folder itself cannot be made read-only. Nevertheless, the properties dialog box for a folder does include a read-only check box. You can use this check box to set or clear the read-only attribute for all *existing* files in the selected folder. This action has no bearing on files that you create subsequently.

In most cases, when you open the properties dialog box for a folder, the Read-Only check box will contain a green square. This indicates either a mixed or undetermined condition. Windows displays the green square in a folder's properties dialog box because it would take too long to check the state of the read-only attribute for every file in the folder. To apply the read-only attribute to the contents of a folder, click the check box until a check mark appears. To clear the attribute, click the check box until it is empty. In both cases, when you leave the dialog box, Windows will ask whether you want to apply your action to subfolders of the selected folder or only to the selected folder's files.

newfeature!
Maximizing Storage Space with NTFS Compression and Compressed (Zipped) Folders

Even a huge hard disk eventually fills to capacity. To help you avoid running out of room, Windows XP supports two forms of file compression, NTFS file compression and compressed (zipped) folders. The former, available only on disks formatted with the NTFS file system, is the same compression option offered in Windows 2000. The latter is an implementation of the industry-standard ZIP format (the compression format used by WinZip and other third-party programs). You can use either compression option or both.

Here are some essential points to note about NTFS compression and compressed (zipped) folders:

- NTFS compression achieves only a modest degree of compression but is extremely easy to use. After you have compressed a set of files and folders (or an entire NTFS disk), files look and behave exactly as before, in both Windows Explorer and in the dialog boxes of the applications you use. The only outwardly visible difference is that the names of your files are shown in blue. However, if you look at the properties dialog box for a compressed file, you'll see on the General tab that the Size On Disk value is (usually) considerably smaller than the Size value; with uncompressed files, the Size On Disk value is the same or slightly larger (because of the way disk space is allocated).

- Windows Explorer and your applications decompress NTFS-compressed files when you open them and recompress them when you save. This on-the-fly compression and decompression occurs so quickly you probably won't notice any performance effect.

- Files compressed via NTFS compression remain compressed only as long as they stay on NTFS disks. If you move a compressed file to a FAT32 disk or e-mail it to a colleague, the file on the FAT32 disk or the one attached to your e-mail is expanded to normal size, making it compatible with other machines and other viewers' software.

- NTFS compression is incompatible with NTFS encryption. A file can be compressed or encrypted (or neither), but not both.

- You can get more dramatic compression with zipped folders than with NTFS compression. Moreover, a zipped folder stays compressed, no matter where it is. Thus zipped folders are an ideal way to compress large files for e-mailing or uploading to Internet sites.

- Because zipped folders use an industry-standard compression format, many of your associates will be able to work with your zipped folders, even if they don't use any version of Windows.

- Windows Explorer compresses and decompresses files in zipped folders on the fly. But your applications do not. Therefore, you can open a ZIP-compressed file in its parent application by double-clicking it in Windows Explorer, but you can't open it using an application's Open command.

Because of the differences between the two compression methods, zipped folders are best used for the following purposes:

- For creating compressed archives of files that you no longer need on a regular basis

- For e-mailing large attachments or uploading documents to FTP or Web sites

- For squeezing the maximum amount of free space out of a disk that's getting close to full

NTFS compression, on the other hand, is great for everyday work. You won't get a huge amount of space gain with it, but it's easy to set up and so simple to use you'll probably forget you're using it.

Implementing NTFS Compression

NTFS compression is implemented by means of a file attribute, much as read-only status is. To compress a file or folder using NTFS compression, follow these steps:

1 Right-click the file or folder (or selection of files or folders) in Windows Explorer and choose Properties from the shortcut menu.

2 On the General tab of the properties dialog box, click Advanced.

3 Select Compress Contents To Save Disk Space and then click OK in both dialog boxes.

If you've selected a folder, you'll see this dialog box.

In most cases, you'll want to select the second option. If you apply the compression attribute to the current folder only, files that you subsequently add to the folder will be compressed, but the files that are already there will not be.

You can compress an entire NTFS drive at once. Doing this might tie up your computer for several hours (during which time performance in other programs will be seriously degraded), but you need to do it only once. If you plan to leave the computer unattended while Windows is compressing files, be sure to close all running programs. Windows can't compress files that are open, and if it comes to one that it can't compress, it will sit idle until you tell it what to do (you can close the file and tell it to try again, or you can ask it to skip the open file and go on). You don't want to come back in the morning and find that the system has been waiting all night for your verdict.

Using Zipped Folders

If you have experience with the WinZip program, you're probably familiar with the concept of an archive—a collection of files that are compressed and combined into a single file. In WinZip, you can extract (decompress) files from an archive individually or all at once, and you can add new files to existing archives. The archive itself, in Windows Explorer, might look like this.

Using zipped folders, the same archive looks like this.

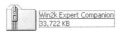

Windows Explorer represents the archive as a folder, displaying the folder with a special icon. To see what's in the archive, simply open the folder. To read a file in the archive, double-click it, just as you would double-click a file in a normal Windows Explorer folder. If the file is a document associated with an application, Windows Explorer starts the application, and the application opens a read-only copy of your document. If the item you double-click is an executable, it runs—unless it requires additional files that are also compressed. In that situation, you need to *extract* (decompress) all the necessary files first, and then run or install the compressed program (see "Extracting Files and Folders from an Archive," page 467).

Creating a new zipped folder   To create a new archive using zipped folders, follow these steps:

1 In Windows Explorer, display the folder in which you want the new archive to reside.

2 Right-click empty space in the folder.

3 From the shortcut menu, choose New, Compressed (Zipped) Folder.

4 Type a meaningful name for the folder, but keep the .zip extension so it will function correctly.

Adding files and folders to a zipped folder   To add files and folders to your archive, simply copy or move them into the zipped folder. If you copy, you then have a compressed version of the copied object inside the zipped folder and the original version outside. If you move, you have only the compressed version—and you free up some space on your disk.

Chapter 12

463

Archiving files with the Send To command   You can create an archive and copy one or more files or folders to it in one step by using the Send To command. To compress a single file or folder, follow these steps:

1 Right-click the file or folder.

2 From the shortcut menu, choose Send To, Compressed (Zipped) Folder.

 Windows creates an archive with the same name as the selected object.

To compress a group of files or folders, follow these steps:

1 Select everything you want to compress.

2 Right-click one of the selected objects.

3 From the shortcut menu, choose Send To, Compressed (Zipped) Folder.

The new archive will have the same name as the object you right-clicked. You can then use the Rename command (press F2) if that's not the name you want to use.

Protecting an archive with a password   The ZIP format supports the use of passwords to prevent unauthorized parties from extracting compressed objects from an archive. If you have used WinZip to assign passwords to archives, Windows XP recognizes and enforces those passwords when you extract objects from the protected archive.

To password-protect a new archive that you create using zipped folders, follow these steps:

1 Select any file in the zipped folder (not the folder itself).

2 Choose File, Add a Password, and then complete the Add Password dialog box.

These steps apply the same password to every file in the archive. If the archive includes folders, their contents are password protected as well.

Be aware that new files added to a password-protected zipped folder do not inherit the password. To add password protection to a new file, first remove the current password from all other files in the archive (select any file, choose File, Remove Password, and then complete the Password Needed dialog box). Then reinstate your password, using the same procedure you used to create it in the first place.

---

caution   Assigning a password to an archive prevents unauthorized users from extracting (opening) its files. But it does not prevent anyone from opening the zipped folder itself and reading the file names. If the file names reveal confidential information, don't rely on zipped-folder password protection. Password-protecting an archive also does not prevent anyone from deleting objects from the archive. Note, too, that files deleted from a zipped folder do not go to the Recycle Bin, so they are not retrievable.

Using WinZip and Zipped Folders

You can use WinZip *and* zipped folders. If you have WinZip installed on your system, your archives will be displayed either with the WinZip icon or the zipped-folder icon, depending on how you have the association for ZIP files set. If your archives look like folders with zippers, then the default application for ZIP files is Compressed (Zipped) Folder. You can change it to WinZip as follows:

1 In Windows Explorer, choose Tools, Folder Options.

2 Click the File Types tab.

3 In the Extensions column, select ZIP. You'll see the following screen.

4 Click Restore. (Alternatively, click Change. Then click WinZip Executable in the Open With dialog box.)

If you have WinZip installed and you leave Compressed (Zipped) Folder as the default application for archives, you will still have access to all the commands that WinZip adds to the shortcut menu for files and folders. And you can still open a zipped folder in WinZip—by right-clicking the folder and choosing Open With, WinZip Executable.

Windows creates temporary hidden folders during the extraction process. These folders, which contain uncompressed versions of the extracted items, are deleted when you close the zipped folder. If Windows Explorer stops responding for any reason before you have closed an archive, the temporary folders remain on your hard disk, in the parent folder of the zipped folder. Files that were password protected in the archive are not protected in these temporary folders. If Windows Explorer crashes while you work with a zipped folder, be sure to delete the hidden temporary folders.

Working with files and folders in a zipped folder Figure 12-5 shows a zipped folder containing a few files and many subfolders (which themselves contain additional files and subfolders). In the figure, the task pane has been replaced by the Folders bar.

As you can see by looking at the Address bar, the zipped folder is really a file with the extension .zip. The zipped-folder feature enables Windows Explorer to display the archive as though it were a folder, and you can use any of Windows Explorer's normal features to inspect the contents of the archive. If you display the archive in Details view, Windows Explorer displays information about the original and compressed sizes of each object. (You can get the same information for any individual object by right-clicking it and opening its properties dialog box.)

The Folders bar does not maintain the folder metaphor as well as the rest of Windows Explorer, however. The names of compressed subfolders contained in the archive do not appear there unless you first open those folders. You'll also notice that if you display a folder that contains normal subfolders, zipped folders, and files, the zipped folders are sorted with the files, not the ordinary folders.

Figure 12-5. A zipped folder looks like a folder, but it's really a file with the extension .zip.

Chapter 12: Managing and Finding Files

As mentioned, you can open a read-only copy of a compressed document by double-clicking it in the zipped folder. Windows Explorer creates a temporary hidden folder when you do this, extracts the document to the temporary folder, and then passes the uncompressed document to its parent application. If you then edit and save the document, your application presents its Save As dialog box, because the document is read-only. Unfortunately, it also invites you to save the document (under a new name) in this temporary folder. If you save it there, Windows Explorer will refrain from deleting the temporary folder when you eventually close the zipped folder. But the folder will remain hidden, and if you don't happen to have Windows Explorer set to show hidden files and folders, your file will be invisible. To avoid cluttering your disk with hidden temporary files and losing track of files you do want to keep, remember to change the path to one of your document folders when you save your edits.

If you need to edit a document after opening it from a zipped folder, the best thing to do is save it, under its original name, in a different folder (the desktop is a good location in this case). Then, when you have finished, drag the document from its new location back into the zipped folder. Windows will present a dialog box, asking permission to overwrite the existing compressed file.

> **note** You can use Search Companion to look for file names within zipped folders. But you can't search for file *content* (specific words or phrases within files) in zipped folders. (For more information about Search Companion, see "Locating Files with Search Companion," page 474.)

Extracting Files and Folders from an Archive To extract a single object or selection of objects from a zipped folder, drag the selection out of the folder—onto your desktop or into another folder. To delete the compressed copy or copies at the same time, right-drag the selection and then choose Move Here from the shortcut menu. To extract all items from a zipped folder, select the folder and choose File, Extract All. A wizard will prompt you for a destination folder.

Copying Files to CDs

You don't need special software to write files to a disk in your CD-R or CD-RW drive. The simplest procedure is as follows:

1 Insert a blank CD in the drive (or a CD-RW disk that you're ready to erase and overwrite).

2 Right-click a file or folder, or a selection of files or folders, that you want to copy to a CD.

3 From the shortcut menu, choose Send To, CD Drive.

4 Repeat these steps for all the items that you want to copy.

Chapter 12

5 Open your CD drive in My Computer.

6 Click Write These Files To CD on the task pane, or choose File, Write These Files To CD.

For information about setting up and configuring a writable or rewritable CD drive, as well as information about using third-party CD burning software, see "Working with Writable and Rewritable CD Drives," page 953.

As an alternative to using the Send To command, you can drag files into the Windows Explorer folder for your CD. Or you can use the Copy and Paste commands.

When you copy files and folders into the CD drive's folder, by whatever means, Windows prepares them for transfer to a writable CD. The CD folder becomes, in effect, a staging area for the eventual CD burn. While files are being copied to the staging area, you might see a dialog box like this one.

InsideOut

Burning CDs with Windows XP gobbles up alarming amounts of disk space and demands careful attention if you want to avoid "low disk space" errors. When you drag files or folders into the CD window and add them to the Files Ready To Be Written To The CD list, Windows makes a copy of each file in the %UserProfile%\Local Settings\ Application Data\Microsoft\CD Burning folder. If you're planning to fill a 700-MB CD with files that are already stored on your computer, that means you'll use up an additional 700 MB of space just making these copies. Then, when you go to write the CD, Windows creates a CD image from the files stored in the CD Burning folder, using an additional chunk of space on a drive or volume you specify in the CD Drive properties dialog box. This file, which is hidden, appears in the root of the specified drive under the name CD Burning Stash File. Although Windows cleans up after itself after writing the CD, the net effect causes your system to use temporary space equal to approximately twice the size of the files you plan to copy.

With some files, Windows Explorer maintains *metadata*—data about the file's data. This information—the dimensions of a graphic image, for example, or the bit rate of an audio file—cannot be copied to the CD. When you see a dialog box like this, your choices are to skip the file or copy it without its metadata. You can also select the check box to keep Windows from displaying similar messages during the current copy process.

After you have moved some files to the CD folder, the folder will look something like Figure 12-6.

Click one of these links to write the CD or to clear files and start over

This banner appears regardless of the view you select

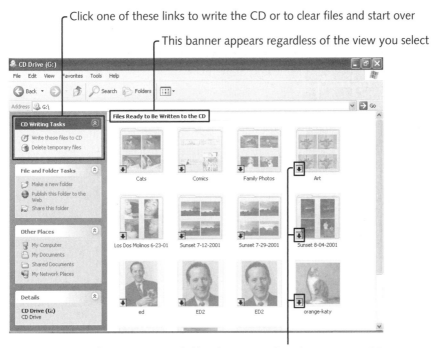

These arrows mark files that are ready to be written to CD

Figure 12-6. Windows adds a downward arrow to the icons for files and folders about to be written to a CD.

Notice that the CD folder does not tell you the total size of the objects in the staging area. (Even if you display the status bar and select everything in the folder, it doesn't provide this information.) To find out whether you're about to try copying more data than will fit, press Ctrl+A, and then right-click an item and choose Properties from the shortcut menu. For your files to fit on a standard CD, this total should be less than 650 MB. With a high-capacity CD, you can go as high as 850 MB.

Windows XP writes audio CDs in the Red Book format and data CDs in a combination of the ISO 9660 and Joliet formats. This means that audio CDs can be played in conventional audio CD players and data CDs can be read on systems running other operating systems (Macintosh, for example) and older versions of Windows or MS-DOS.

> **tip** **Calculate total data size before you start copying**
>
> If you try to copy more data than will fit, the CD Writing Wizard, which manages the burning process, will complain immediately and make you remove some files from the staging folder. In other words, the wizard isn't able to copy as many files as will fit, saving the rest for a second CD. So you might as well save yourself some hassle and figure out in advance whether you've overshot the limit.

When you click Write These Files To CD, the CD Writing Wizard appears.

On the wizard's first page, you can type a name for the CD. The name you supply—it can be up to 16 characters in length—will help you identify the CD's contents when you open it later in Windows Explorer.

InsideOut

If you save photos or other images to a CD, you can view them as a slide show, just as you can with photos on your hard disk—by clicking View As A Slide Show in the task pane. Users of earlier versions of Windows don't have this snazzy feature, so if you share the CD with them, they'll need an image-viewing application. However, if you install the CD Slide Show Generator, a free PowerToy you can download from *http://www.microsoft.com/windowsxp/pro/downloads/powertoys.asp*, the CD Writing Wizard includes an extra step, which offers to add a picture viewer to the CD. If you choose to include it on the CD, the picture viewer runs automatically when the CD is inserted in a computer running Windows 95 or later. If you want to share your pictures with someone using a non-Windows computer, another PowerToy can assist. Use the HTML Slide Show Wizard (available from the same site as CD Slide Show Generator) to create a slide show that runs in a Web browser. Then copy the resulting Web folders to the CD.

Using and Configuring the Recycle Bin

The Recycle Bin provides protection against accidental erasure of files. In most cases, when you delete one or more files or folders, the deleted items go to the Recycle Bin, not into the ether. If you change your mind, you can go to the bin and recover the thrown-out items. Eventually, when the bin fills up, Windows begins emptying it, permanently deleting the files that have been there the longest.

The following kinds of deletions do not go to the Recycle Bin:

- Files stored on removable disks
- Files stored on network drives
- Files deleted from compressed (zipped) folders

You can bypass the Recycle Bin yourself, permanently deleting an item, by holding down the Shift key while you press the Delete key. You might want to do this if you need to get rid of some very large files and you're sure you'll never want these files back. Skipping the Recycle Bin in this case will reclaim some disk space.

You can also turn off the Recycle Bin's services permanently. (For more details, see "Disabling the Recycle Bin," on the next page.)

tip   **Search the Recycle Bin**

In earlier versions of Windows, Search Assistant ignored the Recycle Bin. It no longer does. To include deleted files in your search, be sure to choose Search Companion's All Files And Folders option. For more information, see "Locating Files with Search Companion," page 435.

Changing the Amount of Space Allocated to the Recycle Bin

Although the Recycle Bin folder (the place where you can see which files have been deleted and from which you can restore deleted files) lists deletions from all local hard drives together, Windows actually maintains separate recycling stores for each drive. By default, when a drive's recycling store reaches 10 percent of the overall capacity of the drive, Windows begins deleting the oldest files from that store permanently.

Part 3: Managing Files

If 10 percent seems like too much (or too little) space to devote to accident prevention, you can specify a different figure, following these steps:

1 Right-click the Recycle Bin icon on the desktop.

2 Choose Properties from the shortcut menu.

3 To specify a new maximum that will be applied to all local hard disk drives, make sure that Use One Setting For All Drives is selected on the Global tab, as shown in Figure 12-7. Then move the slider to the left or right.

4 If instead you want to configure your drives' recycling capacities independently, clear Use One Setting For All Drives. Then adjust the slider on each drive's own tab. The sliders won't be available unless you cleared the Use One Setting For All Drives check box first.

Figure 12-7. Windows normally devotes a maximum of 10 percent of a disk's size to the Recycle Bin.

Disabling the Recycle Bin

If you'd rather do without the Recycle Bin, select Do Not Move Files To The Recycle Bin in the Recycle Bin's properties dialog box. This action is equivalent to setting the maximum capacity to 0 percent, and you can do this for all drives or only particular ones.

Suppressing Confirmation Prompts

Whether the Recycle Bin is enabled or disabled, Windows normally displays a confirmation prompt when you delete something. If that prompt annoys you, go to the

Global tab of the Recycle Bin Properties dialog box and clear Display Delete Confirmation Dialog. Unlike the actions just described, disabling the confirmation prompt is something you can do globally only.

Restoring Files and Folders

When you open the Recycle Bin, Windows displays the names of recently deleted items in an ordinary Windows Explorer window, as shown in Figure 12-8. In Details view, you can see when each item was deleted and which folder it was deleted from. You can use the column headings to sort the folder—for example, to display the items that have been in the bin the longest at the top, with more recent arrivals below.

Figure 12-8. You can get useful information about deleted items by looking at the Recycle Bin's columns in Details View.

Note that deleted folders are shown only as folders; you don't see the names of items contained within the folder. If you restore a deleted folder, however, Windows re-creates the folder and its contents.

To restore an item, select it and then click Restore This Item in the task pane. (If the task pane isn't visible, choose File, Restore.)

The Restore command puts the item back in the folder from which it was deleted. If that folder doesn't currently exist, Windows asks your permission to re-create it.

If you want, you can restore a file or folder to a different location. Select the item, choose Edit, Move To Folder, and then specify the new location. (Alternatively, you can drag an item out of the Recycle Bin and drop it wherever you want it.)

Purging the Recycle Bin

A deleted file sitting in your Recycle Bin takes up as much space as it did before it was deleted. If you're deleting files to free up space for new programs and documents, transferring them to the Recycle Bin won't help. You need to remove them permanently. The safest way to do this is to move the items to another storage medium—a different hard disk or a removable disk, for example.

If you're sure you'll never need a particular file again, however, you can delete it in the normal way and then purge it from the Recycle Bin. Display the Recycle Bin, select the item, and then press Delete.

To empty the Recycle Bin entirely, right-click the Recycle Bin icon on your desktop and choose Empty Recycle Bin from the shortcut menu. Or display the Recycle Bin and click Empty The Recycle Bin in the task pane.

newfeature! Locating Files with Search Companion

The first time you call upon Search Companion—by choosing Start, Search, or by pressing F3 in a Windows Explorer window—you might be greeted by Rover, the search dog. He is friendly—and, he's optional. If you'd rather go it alone, without Rover's assistance, click Change Preferences. (You might have to scroll the search pane to find this command; it's at the bottom of the menu.) Then click Without An Animated Screen Character.

On the other hand, if you like animated screen characters, you can retain Rover or try one of the several other characters that Windows offers. To review the cast, click Change Preferences, then click With A Different Character. Use the Next and Back buttons to move through the list.

Your decision about whether or not to use an animated character has no bearing on available search options. If you choose Without An Animated Screen Character, the choices in the task pane stay the same as they were before. About the only link you'll not find is the Do A Trick link you see when you click on an animated character.

If you're used to searching in earlier versions of Windows, the searching options presented by Windows XP Search Companion will be a bit unfamiliar to you. You can re-create a look that more closely resembles that of Windows 2000 Search Assistant as follows.

1 Click Change Preferences.

2 Click Change Files And Folders Search Behavior.

3 Choose the Advanced option.

Chapter 12: Managing and Finding Files

In the advanced mode, the user interface is different (and perhaps more congenial, if you're a Windows veteran). But the standard and advanced styles both offer the same choices. Only the presentation is different. (The examples in the remainder of this chapter assume that you chose the standard mode.)

Specifying a Search Type

Search Companion can perform three basic kinds of file searches:

- Digital media
- Documents
- All files and folders

Each of these search types entails a set of defaults about where and how the companion should do its work. You can override some of the defaults. In addition, you can perform any search with or without the help of Indexing Service. We'll look at indexed searches later in this chapter (see "Using Indexing Service and Query Language," page 480).

Searching for Digital Media

To search for digital media, choose Start, Search. Then click Pictures, Music, or Video. The following search pane appears.

Part 3: Managing Files

You can select any, all, or none of these three check boxes. If you select zero, two, or three check boxes, Search Companion searches all digital media folders before looking at other folders on your hard disk. If you select one, the companion looks first at folders of the selected type. For example, if you select Music, the companion begins by searching music folders.

Other default characteristics of a media search include the following:

- Search Companion examines all document and system folders on all local hard disks, after first looking at folders of the specified media type.

- Search Companion does not look at hidden files and folders.

- Search Companion looks at metadata as well as file names.

The last of these attributes is extremely useful. Although the names of performing artists might not appear in the file names of your music files, for example, you can search for all tracks by a given performer by entering the performer's name in the All Or Part Of The File Name box. You can also enter a genre description in this box or a phrase from a song's lyrics (if lyrics appear in the song's properties dialog box). Figure 12-9 shows the results of a genre search. When searching for photos, you can specify the dimensions of the photo. Type **162 x 200** in the All Or Part Of The File Name box, for example, and the companion will find all pictures measuring 162 pixels by 200 pixels. (Be sure to leave a single space before and after the *x* in the size specification.)

Figure 12-9. Search Companion can locate all music files of a given genre or by a specified performer.

Chapter 12: Managing and Finding Files

Searching for Documents

To search for documents, choose Search on the Start menu. Then click Documents (Word Processing, Spreadsheet, Etc.). You'll see the following search pane.

The option buttons let you restrict the search to documents last modified within a particular time range. Leave Don't Remember selected to search without regard for modification date. A document search has the following default characteristics:

- Search Companion begins with My Documents and its subfolders and then searches the remainder of your local hard disks.

- Search Companion omits system folders.

- Search Companion omits hidden files.

- Search Companion looks only for files that can be created by end users employing registered applications.

The last point is the crucial difference between a document search and a search for all files. When you search for documents, you get documents only—no folders, no executables, no configuration files, no help files. Use this option to look for your own work, Web pages that you've downloaded, saved e-mail files, and so on. If, for some reason, the companion fails to turn up a file that you think the Documents option should find, then try searching for all files.

InsideOut

In our tests, Search Companion consistently generated duplicate entries for files using its Documents option. Typically a file located in My Documents appeared once in the folder My Documents and a second time in the folder %UserProfile%\My Documents. These are, of course, alternative formulations for the same folder, but Search Companion apparently insisted on searching the folder and reporting its contents twice.

Searching for All Files and Folders

To search for anything and everything, choose Search from the Start menu. Then click All Files And Folders. The following search pane appears.

You can search by file name or by file content—or both. If you specify a file name, Search Companion locates items whose names include your search string. (In other words, there's an implicit asterisk wildcard before and after whatever you type.) If you search for content, you'll find the going slow, unless Indexing Service is turned on and has had time to complete the catalog of your disks. For more information about Indexing Service, see "Using Indexing Service and Query Language," page 480. A search for all files and folders has the following default characteristics:

- Search Companion searches all local hard disks.

- Search Companion searches system folders and the Recycle Bin.

In short, an "all files" search is truly an all-points bulletin—by default. Note, however, that an "all files" search does not look at metadata associated with media files.

Troubleshooting

Windows Search doesn't find a file—even when you know it's there.

When you search based on file content by entering text in the A Word Or Phrase In The File box, the results might be incomplete. That's because, for this type of search, Windows relies on Indexing Service, which catalogs only certain types of files. (For a list of the file types, see "Limitations of Indexing Service," page 481.) In the initial release of Windows XP, even text files with certain common extensions were not cataloged; this problem is resolved with the installation of Service Pack 1 for Windows XP. For more information, including a registry workaround to enable searching of other file types, see Microsoft Knowledge Base article Q309173, "Using the 'A Word or Phrase in the File' Search Criterion May Not Work."

Overriding Defaults

You can change the search characteristics for a media search or document search by clicking Use Advanced Search Options. The search pane changes when you do this, revealing an expanded list of options that let you do the following:

- Specify file content (a word or phrase contained in the file)
- Specify particular folders or disks to search, excluding others
- Specify a date range (the companion examines the date the file was most recently modified and returns files that fall within your specified range)
- Specify file size parameters
- Include or exclude system folders
- Include or exclude hidden files and folders
- Include or exclude subfolders of the disk or folders you ask to search
- Make the search case sensitive (it is not, by default)
- Search a backup tape

When you choose an "all files" search, these options are already displayed. One additional option also appears—the option to specify a file type. You can limit your search to any of the file types registered on your system.

Refining a Search

After Search Companion finishes carrying out a search for you, it asks whether you'd like to "refine" your search. You might expect that a refined search would search the current search results, using more restrictive criteria. In Search Companion, that's not what it means. Search Companion is simply giving you the opportunity to search again. It retains your previous criteria, on the assumption that you will give it additional criteria (looking in more locations, for example), but it doesn't limit the search to the current result set.

Saving and Reusing Search Criteria

To preserve the criteria that you've used in a search operation for future use, choose File, Save Search. Search Companion creates a Saved Search file (by default in My Documents). To search again with the same criteria, double-click this file, and then click Search.

Using Indexing Service and Query Language

Created for and first delivered with Microsoft Internet Information Services (IIS), Indexing Service is a feature originally designed to facilitate fast and flexible searches for information stored on Web sites. Because its query technology can be applied to ordinary disk storage as well as to Web sites, Indexing Service has become a core component of Windows (beginning with Windows 2000) and is integrated with Search Companion.

Indexing Service extends the power of Search Companion in several ways. First, it can speed up searching dramatically. How much performance gain you'll see depends on many circumstances. But in tests for this book, we often found that content searches ran on the order of a hundred times faster with Indexing Service than without it.

Second, Indexing Service's query language lets you find files on the basis of many different properties in addition to the size, date, and file type. With Indexing Service enabled, Search Companion can locate a file on the basis of word count, most recent editor, most recent printing time, and many other attributes.

For a list of the most useful properties that can be included in Indexing Service queries, see Table 12-1, page 485.

In addition, the query language offers Boolean operators and the ability to find inflected forms of search strings. The Boolean operators allow you to specify more than one criterion in a search (all files written by Bill containing the words *Windows XP*, for example). The ability to find inflected word forms means that, for example, a search for *swim* will also show instances of *swimming*, *swam*, and *swum*.

Security and Indexing Service

Indexing Service obeys the rules of NTFS file security. If a *catalog* (the collection of files used by Indexing Service to record the contents and properties of your files) resides on a local NTFS disk, the access privileges of the user executing a search determine the results of that search. The service will not return the names of files for which the user does not have at least Read access permission. If the catalog is stored on a network drive accessed by means of a Universal Naming Convention (UNC) path, the user might see the names of files for which he or she lacks Read permission but will not be able to open any such files.

By default, Indexing Service creates its catalogs in folders to which only the System account has access. This precaution prevents accidental deletion. More important, it helps maintain security. As long as the default access permissions for the catalog folder are not changed by an administrator, you can be assured that the catalog files themselves are not subject to unauthorized inspection.

Indexing Service never indexes encrypted documents. If a file is encrypted after being indexed, the service removes it from the catalog.

Limitations of Indexing Service

Does using Indexing Service have drawbacks? Not many. But here are some things you should know:

- **Indexing Service requires disk space.** Because Indexing Service catalogs your disks in the background, during periods when your computer is idle, you don't pay a performance penalty for having the service running. You do, however, sacrifice some disk space. Microsoft estimates that the catalog will consume from 15 to 30 percent of the size of the indexed files. Prudence suggests assuming the higher figure is more accurate.

- **Indexing Service catalogs the content of only certain kinds of files.** By default, Indexing Service catalogs the content of the following document types:

  - HTML files (their text)

  - Text files

  - Documents created by Microsoft Office (version 95 and later)

  - Any other document type for which a suitable filter is installed

  A *filter* tells Indexing Service how to separate meaningful text from file headers, formatting information, and all other nontextual elements. Microsoft provides filters for HTML, text, Office, and mail and news documents. Third parties might provide filters for their own documents. If

481

you use a non-Microsoft office suite, you might want to check with that product's vendor to see whether an Indexing Service filter is available.

With an optional setting available via Indexing Service MMC console, you can set the service to index files with unknown extensions. (For details, see "Indexing Files with Unknown Extensions," page 491.) If you index files with unknown extensions, the service tries to extract meaningful content from file types other than the ones it catalogs by default.

- **Indexing Service ignores "noise" words.** The list of words ignored by Indexing Service appears in the file %SystemRoot%\System32\Noise.*xxx*, where *xxx* is a three-letter abbreviation for the language you use. The file is plain text, and you can edit it with Notepad. The noise filter for English, Noise.eng, includes common prepositions and conjunctions, articles, relative pronouns, various forms of the verb *to be* and other common verbs, individual numerals, individual letters, and a handful of other frequently occurring words.

  If you include a noise word in a search string, the service treats that word as a placeholder. For example, in the search string "age before beauty," *before* is a noise word. Indexing Service will treat this string as equivalent to "age after beauty," "age without beauty," and so on.

- **Indexing Service ignores case.** If Indexing Service is not running, Search Companion can perform case-sensitive searches. With Indexing Service running, it can't.

- **Indexed searching is not always available, even if you have enabled Indexing Service.** If the service hasn't finished building its initial catalog, or if it's busy updating the catalog, Search Companion simply dispenses with it, performing an ordinary (unindexed) search.

Activating Indexing Service

The simplest way to start Indexing Service (if it's not already started) is as follows:

1 Choose Search from the Start menu.

2 Click Change Preferences.

3 Click With Indexing Service.

If With Indexing Service doesn't appear on the menu (and Without Indexing Service appears instead), the service is already running. If the menu includes both With Indexing Service and Without Indexing Service, you don't have permission to start (or stop) the service. You need to have an administrator account to configure the service.

Before you can use Indexing Service for queries, the service needs time to generate a catalog. You should let it run overnight before relying on it for queries.

Submitting Queries

To use Indexing Service to look for files containing a particular word or phrase, type that word or phrase in the A Word Or Phrase In The File box. (If you're doing a media or document search, you will need to click Use Advanced Search Options to display this box.) To submit a more complex query, enter the query in this same box, but use the syntax of the query language, described in the following sections. Figure 12-10 shows an example of a query that returns all files whose DocAuthor property is Craig.

Figure 12-10. To submit a query, type in the A Word Or Phrase In The File box.

When Search Companion begins searching, it should display the words *Searching by Index*. If it does not, your catalog is not ready for an indexed search. The companion, in that case, will search your files one by one, not its catalog. If the catalog was recently available (that is, if you've already allowed plenty of time for the service to create its initial catalog), then you can assume Indexing Service is merely busy updating the catalog and that it will be available again shortly.

Phrase and Free-Text Query Expressions

Query expressions involving text can take either of two forms, called *phrase* and *free-text*. In a phrase expression, the service looks for exact matches. For example, given the query

```
{phrase} John's debugger eats bugs {/phrase}
```

the service returns only those files that include exactly that four-word string.

In a free-text expression, the service treats the text as though each word were separated from the next by a Boolean OR—that is, it returns files that match any of the words. It also looks for inflected forms of verbs. So the query

```
{freetext} John's debugger eats bugs {/freetext}
```

would cause the service to look for files that contain any of the following words: *John's, debugger, eats, bugs, ate, eating, eaten.*

Phrase queries are the default. Therefore, if you simply type some text as your query, without tags such as {freetext} or {phrase}, Search Companion performs a phrase query.

Restrictions on Content Queries

Note the following about query expressions that include text:

- Free-text and phrase expressions cannot be mixed in a single query; that is, you cannot use a Boolean or proximity operator to connect a free-text expression to a phrase expression

- Enclose your text in quotation marks if it contains any of the following characters: % | ^ # @ $

- Enclose your text in quotation marks if the text you're looking for contains any of the following words: *and, or, not, near, equals, contains*

- Indexing Service always ignores case

- You can't use relational operators (>, <, =, and so forth) in content queries

Working with Properties

Technically, all queries are property queries. When you look for files that contain particular words, you're searching on the basis of the Contents property. Contents is Indexing Service's default property—which is why you can look for a particular word or phrase without having to use a {prop} tag. Table 12-1 lists the most important additional properties that you can use in your queries. Note that not all of these properties are available for every document type.

In addition to the properties listed in Table 12-1, Indexing Service can catalog custom properties associated with a document.

To specify a property in a query, you use the {prop} tag, following this syntax:

```
{prop name=property name} query_expression {/prop}
```

where *property name* is a property like those listed in the left column of Table 12-1, and where *query expression* is the content to be searched for. As an example, to search for documents located in the C:\Press Releases\01 directory, you would type the following:

```
{prop name=directory} C:\Press Releases\01 {/prop}
```

If the query expression (the text between the opening and closing tags) includes wildcard characters, you must also use the {regex} tag. For details, see "Pattern-Matching Queries," page 489.

If the property name includes spaces (this might be the case for a custom property), enclose the property name within quotation marks.

Table 12-1. **Useful Document Properties Available for Indexing Service Queries**

Property Name	Description
Access	The last time the document was accessed
All	All properties, including Contents; works only for text queries, not numeric queries
AllocSize	The amount of disk space allocated to the document
Created	The time the document was created
Directory	The physical path to the document, not including the document name
DocAppName	The name of the application that created the document
DocAuthor	The author of the document
DocByteCount	The number of bytes in the document
DocCategory	The document type
DocCharCount	The number of characters in the document
DocComments	Comments about the document
DocCompany	The name of the company for which the document was written
DocCreatedTm	The time the document was created
DocEditTime	The total time spent editing the document
DocHiddenCount	The number of hidden slides in a Microsoft PowerPoint document

(continued)

Chapter 12

Table 12-1. *(continued)*

Property Name	Description
DocKeywords	Key words associated with the document
DocLastAuthor	The user who most recently edited the document
DocLastPrinted	The time the document was last printed
DocLastSavedTm	The time the document was last saved
DocManager	The name of the manager of the document's author
DocNoteCount	The number of pages with notes in a PowerPoint document
DocPageCount	The number of pages in the document
DocParaCount	The number of paragraphs in the document
DocPartTitles	The names of document parts, such as worksheet names in a Microsoft Excel document or slide titles in a PowerPoint document
DocRevNumber	The current version number of the document
DocSlideCount	The number of slides in a PowerPoint document
DocTemplate	The name of the template used by the document
DocTitle	The title of the document
DocWordCount	The number of words in the document
Filename	The name of the document
Path	The physical path to the document, including the document name
ShortFileName	The 8.3-format name of the document
Size	The size of the document, in bytes
Write	The date and time the document was last modified

The EQUALS and CONTAINS Operators

In query expressions involving text, use the EQUALS operator when you require an exact match. For example, this query

```
{prop name=docTitle} equals Queen's Gambit Declined {/prop}
```

locates all files whose DocTitle property value is exactly *Queen's Gambit Declined*.

When you care only whether a particular word appears in a property value (no matter what else may be there), use the CONTAINS operator (or no operator; CONTAINS is the default). For example, to find documents in which the phrase *Queen's Gambit Declined* appears somewhere within any property (including the contents), you could write either of the following:

```
{prop name=all} contains Queen's Gambit Declined {/prop}

{prop name=all} Queen's Gambit Declined {/prop}
```

To find documents in which any of those words (or any of the inflected forms of *declined*) appear, express the text in free-text mode:

```
{prop name=all} contains {freetext} Queen's Gambit Declined
    {/freetext} {/prop}

{prop name=all} {freetext} Queen's Gambit Declined {/freetext}
    {/prop}
```

Relational Operators

Indexing Service offers the following relational operators.

Operator	Description
=	Equal to
!=	Not equal to
<	Less than
<=	Less than or equal to
>	Greater than
>=	Greater than or equal to

Date and Time Expressions

Dates and times should be expressed in one of the following formats:

```
yyyy/mm/dd hh:mm:ss
yyyy-mm-dd hh:mm:ss
```

The first two year digits are optional. If you omit them, Indexing Service regards all years as falling between 1930 and 2029. You can add an optional three-digit millisecond value to the time value (for example, 2000/04/12 14:54:23.456). All times are recorded in coordinated universal time format (UTC, or Universal Time Coordinate), which is essentially the same as Greenwich mean time.

Chapter 12

In conjunction with relational operators, you can express times as offsets relative to the current time, using the following abbreviations.

Abbreviation	Meaning
y	Year
q	Quarter (three months)
m	Month
w	Week
d	Day
h	Hour
n	Minute
s	Second

For example, the query

```
{prop name=write} >-1d12h {/prop}
```

returns files last modified within the previous 36 hours.

Boolean Operators

Indexing Service offers the following Boolean operators.

Operator	Short Form	Long Form
AND	&	AND
OR	|	OR
Binary NOT	&!	AND NOT
Unary NOT	!	NOT

The binary NOT operator is used between two properties. For example, in the query

```
{prop name=DocAuthor} Carl {/prop} &! {prop name=DocSubject} Windows {/prop}
```

the binary NOT operator returns documents whose author is Carl and whose subject is not Windows.

The unary NOT operator is used to negate a single query expression. For example, the query

```
{prop name=size} not > 1000
```

returns documents whose size is not greater than 1,000 bytes. The only reason the distinction matters is that the unary NOT is permitted only in queries in which the query expression is a numeric value.

Order of Operator Precedence

The Boolean operators are evaluated in the following order:

1 NOT

2 AND

3 OR

Operators at the same precedence level are evaluated in left-to-right order. You can use parentheses to override the default precedence.

Pattern-Matching Queries

Indexing Service supports three types of pattern-matching queries:

- Queries that use MS-DOS-style wildcard characters (* and ?)
- UNIX-style regular-expression queries
- Queries that look for alternative word forms

Queries That Use MS-DOS-Style Wildcard Characters

Indexing Service recognizes both of the standard MS-DOS wildcard characters, * and ?. The asterisk represents any number of characters, and the question mark represents any single character.

For example, file names with the pattern *.do? can be found with this query:

```
{prop name=filename} {regex} *.do? {/regex} {/prop}
```

Do not omit the {regex} tag. If you do, Indexing Service returns only those files with the characters *do?* before the extension!

Queries That Use UNIX-Style Regular Expressions

Indexing Service supports the UNIX regular-expression syntax. A full treatment of the possibilities this affords is beyond the scope of this chapter. Here, however, is one potentially useful example. The query

```
{prop name=filename} {regex} *.|(do?|,xl?|,mdb|) {/regex} {/prop}
```

returns all files with any of the following extensions: *.do?*, *.xl?*, or *.mdb*.

Queries That Look for Alternative Word Forms

To find words that begin with particular letters, use the asterisk wildcard. For example, the query

```
{prop name=contents} dog* {/prop}
```

returns documents with *dog*, *doghouse*, *doggerel*, *dogmatic*, *doggone*, and so forth.

To find inflected forms of verbs, use the double-asterisk wildcard. For example,

```
{prop name=contents} swim** {/prop}
```

locates files containing *swim*, *swam*, and *swum*—but not *swimmer*.

Administering Indexing Service

The MMC console for administering Indexing Service is Ciadv.msc, shown in Figure 12-11. You can get there by either of the following routes:

- Type **ciadv.msc** at a command prompt.

- Right-click My Computer and choose Manage. In Computer Management, open Services And Applications. Under Services And Applications, select Indexing Service.

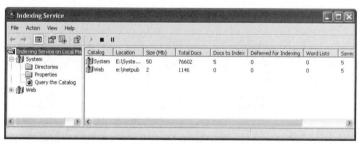

Figure 12-11. You can use this MMC console to administer Indexing Service.

You must be logged on as an administrator to use Indexing Service console.

If the Indexing Service console does not display the console tree (the left pane), you might want to do the following to display it:

1 Choose View, Customize.

2 Select the Console Tree check box and then click OK.

Chapter 12: Managing and Finding Files

The console tree displays an entry for each catalog created by Indexing Service. By default, that includes a System catalog and, if IIS is installed, a Web catalog. You can also create additional catalogs or delete existing ones in the Indexing Service console.

> For information about creating additional catalogs, see Microsoft Knowledge Base article Q308202, "HOW TO: Create and Configure a Catalog for Indexing."

Opening the entry for a catalog reveals the three subentries shown in Figure 12-11: Directories, Properties, and Query The Catalog. Directories shows which folders are indexed by the selected catalog (and lets you make changes to that list). Properties shows which properties are being indexed, and Query The Catalog provides a query form that you can use as an alternative to Search Companion. Queries submitted with this query form generate the same list of files as queries submitted via Search Companion, but the files arrive as hyperlinks rather than as Windows Explorer entries.

When you select a catalog name in the console tree, the details pane of Indexing Service provides status information about the selected catalog.

An Overview of the Indexing Process

Indexing Service creates and maintains its catalogs through the following processes:

1 **Scanning.** The service scans the disks and folders to be indexed to determine which files have changed and thus need to be reindexed. A full scan takes place the first time you turn on the service, whenever you add a folder to a catalog, and whenever a serious error occurs. Incremental scans take place whenever the service is restarted (for example, when you restart your computer) and at least once a day.

2 **The creation of word lists.** A word list is a small temporary index maintained in memory. Documents in a word list are automatically reindexed whenever the service is restarted.

3 **The creation of saved indexes.** A saved index is a highly compressed temporary disk file optimized for fast response to searches. The service combines word list data into saved indexes whenever a large enough number of word lists have accumulated.

4 **Merging.** Merging is the combining of data from multiple word lists and saved indexes into a permanent master index.

Indexing Files with Unknown Extensions

To include files with unknown extensions in all your catalogs, right-click Indexing Service On Local Machine, at the top of the console tree, and choose Properties from the shortcut menu. The dialog box shown in Figure 12-12 on the next page appears.

Figure 12-12. Use this properties dialog box to add unknown file types to your catalog.

On the Generation tab, select the Index Files With Unknown Extensions check box. Indexing Service will then do its best to extract meaningful content from file types for which it lacks a filter. After you've made this change, you must stop and restart Indexing Service for your change to take effect.

To index unknown file types only in a particular catalog, right-click that catalog's name, such as System or Web, in the console tree and then choose Properties. On the Tracking tab, clear the Inherit Above Settings From Service check box. Then go to the Generation tab and select Index Files With Unknown Extensions. (If you don't first clear Inherit Above Settings From Service, the catalog you've selected uses whatever setting you've applied to the service as a whole.) After making this change, stop and restart the catalog to have your change take effect.

Supplying an Alias for a Folder Name

By default, Indexing Service identifies remote folders by their share names and their full UNC paths. The UNC paths appear in the Alias column in the details pane of the Indexing Service console. If this default alias is not to your liking, follow these steps:

1 Right-click Indexing Service On Local Machine.

2 Choose Properties from the shortcut menu.

3 Click the Tracking tab.

4 Clear the Add Network Share Alias Automatically check box.

Chapter 12: Managing and Finding Files

You can then supply your own alias (if you want) by expanding the catalog entry in the console tree, selecting Directories in the console tree, double-clicking the directory (folder) name in the details pane, and filling out the ensuing dialog box.

You can also clear the alias default at the catalog level rather than the service level. To do so, right-click the catalog name, choose Properties, go to the Tracking tab, clear the Inherit Above Settings From Service check box, and then clear Add Network Share Alias Automatically.

Stopping, Pausing, and Restarting

To stop the service, right-click Indexing Service On Local Machine and choose Stop from the shortcut menu. To stop the processing of a particular catalog, right-click that catalog's name, choose All Tasks from the shortcut menu, and then choose Stop.

To pause the service or pause the processing of a catalog, follow the same steps, but choose Pause instead of Stop. While the service or a catalog is paused, you can still execute queries, but no further catalog processing occurs. To restart after a pause or a stop, retrace your steps and choose Start.

Changing the Folders Included in a Catalog

To see which folders are included in a catalog, open the catalog's entry in the console tree and select Directories. Figure 12-13 shows a sample of what you might see.

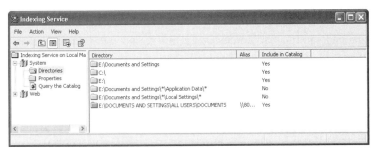

Figure 12-13. The Directories list shows which folders a catalog includes.

Folders with a Yes in the Include In Catalog column are part of that catalog—as are all their subfolders, with the exception of subfolders explicitly excluded by entries that have a No in the Include In Catalog column.

To add a folder to a catalog, right-click Directories in the console tree, choose New, and then choose Directory. In the ensuing dialog box, supply the path and alias of the folder you want to add. To delete a folder, right-click it in the details pane and choose Delete from the shortcut menu. To change a folder's status—from included to excluded, or vice versa—double-click the folder in the details pane. In the ensuing dialog box, select Yes or No as appropriate.

493

Excluding Specific Files on NTFS Disks

To explicitly include or exclude a file on an NTFS-formatted disk from your catalog(s), right-click the file in a Windows Explorer window and choose Properties from the shortcut menu. On the General tab of the properties dialog box, click the Advanced button to display the Advanced Attributes dialog box, shown in Figure 12-14. Clear the For Fast Searching, Allow Indexing Service To Index This File check box to exclude this file from all catalogs.

Figure 12-14. You can use this Advanced Attributes dialog box to explicitly exclude a file from your catalog(s).

Manually Rescanning a Folder

You can manually initiate an incremental or full scan of any folder by right-clicking the folder name in the Indexing Service details pane, choosing All Tasks, and then choosing Rescan (Full) or Rescan (Incremental). Microsoft recommends that you do a full rescan if you install a new filter, start or stop the indexing of unknown file types, or edit the noise word file.

Adjusting Indexing Service's Performance Parameters

To adjust Indexing Service's performance parameters, first stop the service. Right-click Indexing Service On Local Machine in the console tree, choose All Tasks, and then choose Tune Performance. These steps take you to Indexing Service Usage dialog box, shown in Figure 12-15.

Chapter 12: Managing and Finding Files

Figure 12-15. The Indexing Service Usage dialog box lets you choose a broad performance category.

If none of the first four options listed in this dialog box quite describes your situation, choose Customize, and then click the Customize button. The Desired Performance dialog box, shown in Figure 12-16, appears.

Figure 12-16. The Desired Performance dialog box allows fine-tuning.

The sliders here control the processing priority that Windows will give to the service's catalog building (Indexing) and query processing (Querying). Moving either slider to the right makes the service more responsive while reducing the performance of whatever applications you might be running concurrently with Indexing Service.

Chapter 13

Securing Files and Folders

When two or more people use the same computer, how do you keep each user from snooping in files and folders that should be private? How do you allow easy access to files that should be shared? And how do you keep untrained users from accidentally wiping out important files? Out of the box, anyone with a user account on a Microsoft Windows XP computer has virtually unlimited access to files and folders. In either edition of Windows XP, you can lock up your personal files and folders by selecting a single check box, even if you know nothing about security. Or, with Windows XP Professional and some advanced access control options, you can exercise precise control over who gets to access any file or folder on any drive.

If the bulk of your previous computing experience is with Windows 95, Windows 98, or Windows Me, the entire notion of file and folder security is probably an alien concept. Those consumer-based operating systems offer only the most rudimentary security. On the other hand, if you're a seasoned Windows NT or Windows 2000 user, you probably already understand the basics of access control; your challenge with Windows XP is understanding its new and radically different Simple File Sharing interface.

This chapter focuses exclusively on sharing and securing files among users who log on to the same computer. If you're interested in learning how to share files and folders over a network, see "Converting a FAT32 Disk to NTFS," page 922.

497

At Home with Windows XP

Because Simple File Sharing is the only file-sharing mode available in Windows XP Home Edition, users of Home Edition will be concerned mostly with the first third of this chapter. The material beginning on page 507 ("Controlling Access with NTFS Permissions") addresses the more granular form of permission-setting available to users of Windows XP Professional.

It is possible, but not easy, to apply NTFS permissions to NTFS-formatted disks on Home Edition systems. To do this you need either to start Windows XP in Safe Mode or use the terse syntax of the Cacls command. If you're an administrator who manages file-sharing on Home Edition systems and requires the full set of security features available via NTFS, the entire chapter will be relevant to you. In particular, be sure to read the description of the Safe Mode "back door" in the Inside Out tip on page 507, and the section on Cacls ("Setting Permissions from a Command Prompt," page 525).

How Setup Decisions Dictate Your Security Options

Three factors dictate how much control you have over access to shared files and folders on a computer running Windows XP:

- **Disk format.** Access controls, which determine whether a given user can open a folder, read a file, create new files, and perform other file operations, are available only on NTFS-formatted drives. On drives formatted with FAT32, most local security options are unavailable. Any user can access any file without restriction.

For more details about the differences between NTFS and FAT32, see "NTFS or FAT32: Which Disk Format Should You Choose?" page 920.

- **Windows XP edition.** By default, Windows XP Home Edition and Windows XP Professional share a simplified security interface that allows you to set a limited number of access controls based on built-in group memberships. If you use Windows XP Professional, you can configure your system to use more complex security options that closely resemble those found in Windows 2000. We discuss the differences between these options fully in this section.

- **User account settings.** During setup, Windows XP creates a group of shared folders specifically designed to hold files for all users of that computer. (If your computer is joined to a Windows domain, these shared locations are unavailable.) In addition, each user with an account on the machine can designate certain folders as private.

For more details about differences in security options and the Windows interface when running under a domain, see "Domains vs. Workgroups," page 1128.

NTFS vs. FAT32

When it comes to security, the single most important factor is the file system you've chosen for the drive containing the Windows system files and user profiles. If the drive is formatted using the FAT32 file system, none of the options discussed in this section apply to you. The only way to enable file system permissions is to convert the drive to NTFS format.

For instructions on how to convert a FAT32 partition to NTFS, see "Converting a FAT32 Disk to NTFS," page 922.

tip **Access NTFS permissions from Home Edition**

Throughout this book, we note that users of Windows XP Home Edition are locked out of the full range of file-security options. That's true, with one noteworthy exception: When you restart Home Edition in Safe Mode (as described in "Using Safe Mode," page 898), you'll find the full Windows 2000–style access control editor. This back door is designed for recovery of protected files after a system crash, but a determined Home Edition user can take advantage of it to set permissions on files and folders. Our take? If you understand NTFS permissions and need to use them, get Windows XP Professional.

newfeature!
Simple File Sharing vs. Advanced Permissions

On a clean installation or an upgrade over Windows 98/Me, Windows XP assigns default security settings that work like on/off switches. This Simple File Sharing interface initially makes all the files in your user profile (including your My Documents folder, desktop, Start menu, and Favorites) visible to anyone who has an administrator's account on your computer (users with limited accounts are restricted from viewing files in other profiles). As Figure 13-1 on the next page shows, opening the My Computer window displays a separate icon for the folder that holds each user's personal documents, along with an icon for a Shared Documents folder. (See the following section for a full discussion of how the Shared Documents folder works.)

This low-security configuration is similar to the standard setup on a machine running Windows 95/98/Me. In an environment where all users trust each other completely, it makes collaborating easy: If you and a coworker share a computer, you can each keep your personal files organized in your My Documents folder for convenience; if you need to look at a file that your coworker created, you open his or her My Documents folder. Likewise, at home, you and your spouse can browse each other's files.

Figure 13-1. By default, the My Computer window shows an icon for every user's My Documents folder.

But some environments demand less trust and more protection. On a home computer, for example, parents might want to keep financial data and other private files locked out of the reach of children—not just to ensure privacy, but also to protect them from accidental changes or deletion. By selecting a check box on the Sharing tab of a folder's properties dialog box, you can designate as private all or part of your user profile. After you've selected that option, your files are visible only when you log on using your account.

It's certainly easy to make a folder private—all you do is right-click a folder, choose Sharing And Security, and select the Make This Folder Private check box—but this Simple File Sharing option suffers from some significant limitations:

- The Make This Folder Private option is available only within your user profile. If you use a program that stores its user data in any other location, you cannot protect that folder from unauthorized access. Likewise, if you've created a second partition on which you store digital images, media files, or other space-gobbling data, you have no way to protect those files from unauthorized access or accidental deletion.

- Protection applies to all files and subfolders within a folder where you select this option. You cannot protect an individual file, nor can you single out files or subfolders within a protected folder and make them available to others.

- The "private" setting is an all-or-nothing proposition. When you select the Make This Folder Private check box, Windows sets permissions on that folder so that you and only you can access files stored in that location. Clear the check box, and any user who logs on to the computer can view the files stored there.

Chapter 13: Securing Files and Folders

● When Simple File Sharing is enabled and you move or copy files or folders between a private folder and a shared location, the moved or copied objects always take on the security attributes of the destination folder. This behavior changes if you disable Simple File Sharing. See "Troubleshooting Permission Problems," page 528, for more details.

---

caution   The Make This Folder Private option is ineffective unless you've configured your account with a password. If you neglect this step, any other user can go to the Welcome screen, click your logon name, and gain complete access to your files. A dialog box reminds you of this basic fact and offers to help you set a password if you try to make a folder private on an account that has no password.

How Simple File Sharing Works

There's nothing magical about Simple File Sharing. This user interface hides the full set of NTFS permissions and applies a strictly defined set of permissions to selected objects. If you have a basic understanding of NTFS permissions, here is what's happening behind the scenes:

● **Default permissions.** When you create a new user account and log on for the first time, Windows XP creates an empty set of user profile folders and assigns Full Control permissions for the new user. In addition, Windows assigns Full Control permissions to the built-in Administrators group and the System account. Windows designates the logged-on user as the Creator Owner of these folders; the owner has full rights to work with the files and folders and to change the access controls on these files. (For more details on what ownership means, see "Taking Ownership of Files and Folders," page 526.)

● **Private folders.** Selecting the Make This Folder Private option removes the Administrators group from the list of permitted users, leaving only the user's account and the built-in System account on the Permissions list. (A member of the Administrators group can regain access only by taking ownership of the folder, a drastic action that is recorded in the computer's event logs and is immediately obvious to the previous owner.)

● **Shared folders.** As the name implies, the Shared Documents folder and its subfolders are available for use by anyone with an account on the computer. Members of the Administrators group have Full Control permissions over this folder and all its subfolders. Members of the built-in Power Users group (available only in Windows XP Professional) have all rights except the ability to change permissions or take ownership of files in this folder. Finally, those with limited accounts (members of the built-in Users group) can read and open files in the Shared Documents folder but cannot create new files, modify existing files, or copy or move files to this location.

Part 3: Managing Files

If you want to break through any of these limitations, you can disable the Simple File Sharing interface and use the full complement of Windows 2000–style file permissions. As noted previously, these options are available only if you're running Windows XP Professional, and only on NTFS-formatted drives. To make the switch, open any Windows Explorer window (the My Documents or My Computer window will do) and choose Tools, Folder Options. Click the View tab, scroll to the bottom of the list, and then clear the Use Simple File Sharing (Recommended) check box.

> **note** You must be a member of the Administrators group to change file-sharing options.

After you make this change, you'll notice a new Security tab on the properties dialog box for any folder stored on an NTFS drive. Figure 13-2, for example, shows the Security settings for a subfolder in the My Documents folder for the user Ed. The check boxes are unavailable because these settings are inherited from a higher-level folder. For details, see "Applying Advanced Security Settings," page 509.

When you turn off Simple File Sharing, you plunge into a confusing and potentially dangerous set of options. Even expert Windows users struggle with the proper use of NTFS permissions, and if you make a mistake you can lock yourself and other authorized users out. Before you decide to forego the Simple File Sharing interface, make sure you understand the consequences completely. Read the rest of this chapter carefully, and if you share files and folders over a network, read Chapter 32, "Managing Shared Folders and Printers," as well, because these settings have a profound impact on network security, too.

Figure 13-2. When you disable Simple File Sharing, you expose the full range of NTFS permissions for files and folders.

Default Locations for Shared Files

As noted in the previous section, Windows XP sets aside a group of folders for users to share documents with one another. By default, these folders are located in the All Users profile (on a default setup, the path is C:\Documents And Settings\All Users). File and folder permissions are set so that administrators have full access to these folders.

> **note** If you belong to a Windows domain, the shared folder shortcuts referred to in this section aren't available at all. In workgroup setups and on standalone computers, the exact location of each shared folder is defined in the registry using values under the following key: HKLM\SOFTWARE\Microsoft\Windows\CurrentVersion\Explorer\Shell Folders.

Sorting out the exact location and behavior of shared folders can be confusing. When you open a shared folder in a Windows Explorer window, the folder name that appears in the Address bar doesn't always match the label that appears under the folder icon and in the title bar of the open window. The registry values that define shared folders use completely different names as well. In addition, some shared folders are hidden and at least one doesn't work as you might expect. Confused? The following list is not exhaustive, but it should help you make sense of the most frequently used shared folders:

- **Shared Documents.** To access this folder icon, open the My Computer window. The Shared Documents shortcut actually points to the Documents folder in the All Users profile. Its location is stored in the registry using the value Common Documents.

- **Shared Pictures.** You'll find this subfolder in the Shared Documents folder. Its actual name, confusingly, is My Pictures. Its location is stored in the registry using the value CommonPictures.

Shared Pictures

- **Shared Music.** This subfolder is also found in the Shared Documents folder. The actual name of this folder is My Music, and its location is stored in the registry using the value CommonMusic.

Shared Music

503

- **Desktop.** Any files you copy or move to the Desktop folder in the All Users profile show up on the desktop of all users on the system. Users with limited accounts can view and open these files but cannot rename or delete them. This location is stored in the registry as Common Desktop.

- **Start Menu.** As is the case with the Desktop folder, shortcuts or files you add to this common location appear on the Start menu for all users and can only be changed by members of the Administrators or Power Users group. This location is stored in the registry as Common Start Menu.

- **Favorites.** You might expect this folder to behave like the Desktop and Start Menu folders, merging its contents with the user's personal Favorites collection. Unfortunately, it doesn't. In fact, this folder does nothing at all.

---

tip   **Get to shared folders faster**

Instead of typing the full path to the All Users profile every time you want to work with files and shortcuts stored there, get in the habit of using shortcuts based on the system variable %AllUsersProfile%. That variable works in all shortcuts and is especially useful on systems on which you have multiple versions of Windows XP installed. By using this system variable, you don't have to remember whether the current system is using the copy of Windows on drive C or drive D. If you're logged on as an administrator, you can also right-click the Start button and choose Open All Users or Explore All Users to get to the shared Start Menu folder.

---

newfeature!
Keeping Your Own Files Private

If you create a new account during setup, or if the Windows Setup program automatically creates your user account when you upgrade from Windows 98 or Windows Me, your account starts out with no password. As the final step when you add a password to your own account from User Accounts in Control Panel, Windows displays the dialog box shown in Figure 13-3, which offers to help you make your files and folders private. (This option appears only with Simple File Sharing in effect and does not appear with limited accounts or accounts whose user profiles are stored on a FAT32 drive.)

Using this option to make your files private is convenient, but it's not the only way to exercise your right to privacy. Regardless of which choice you make when presented with this dialog box, you can change your mind later. You can add or remove protection from your entire profile, or apply the Make This Folder Private option to selected subfolders in your profile.

Chapter 13: Securing Files and Folders

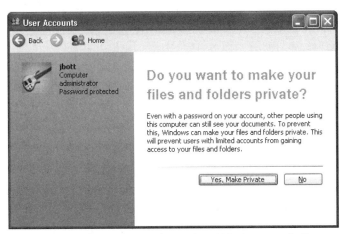

Figure 13-3. If you choose this option, Windows resets the permissions on your user profile so that only you can view or open your files and folders.

To protect your entire profile, follow these steps:

1 In the Run box or from any command prompt, type **%systemdrive%\ documents and settings**.

2 Right-click the icon labeled with your user name and choose Sharing And Security.

3 Under Local Sharing And Security, select the Make This Folder Private check box, as shown in Figure 13-4.

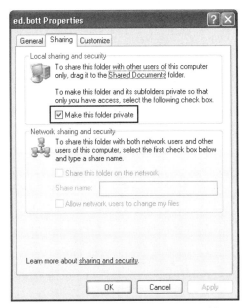

Figure 13-4. Select the Make This Folder Private check box to prevent other users from accessing files in your user profile.

505

4 Click OK to close the dialog box and apply your changes.

Other users who log on to the same computer and open the My Computer window can no longer see the folder icon that represents your My Documents folder if you've made your user profile private. Other users who try to access your profile by opening the Documents And Settings folder will receive an "access denied" error message when they double-click the folder that contains your profile. The result is the same if another user tries to open a subfolder that you've made private.

Troubleshooting

The Make This Folder Private option can't be selected.

The Sharing And Security command is available when you right-click any folder icon. Under some circumstances, however, the Make This Folder Private option appears dimmed and you are unable to select this check box (or clear it, if it's already checked). If you encounter this problem, run through the following checklist:

Is the drive formatted using NTFS? The Make This Folder Private option will always be unavailable on FAT32 partitions.

Is the folder in your user profile? You cannot use the Make This Folder Private option on any other folder, including those in another user's profile.

Is a parent folder already set as private? If you're trying to protect a subfolder in your user profile and the dimmed box is checked, you almost certainly have already used the Make This Folder Private option on a parent folder or on the entire profile. Work your way up the folder tree until you find the folder where you set this option.

You can apply protection to selected subfolders within your user profile. For instance, you might want other users to be able to work with some files in your My Documents folder while keeping other files protected. To set up this sort of partial protection, create a subfolder and give it a descriptive name like Private. Then move the files and folders you want to protect into that subfolder, and select the Make This Folder Private option for that folder only.

To remove protection from a folder, clear the Make This Folder Private check box. You might have to log off and log back on again before other accounts recognize the change in permissions.

InsideOut

An undocumented loophole in Windows XP Home Edition makes it possible (although not easy) to set individual file and folder permissions by starting in Safe Mode. On a home computer where the drive containing the Documents And Settings folder is formatted with NTFS, for instance, you might have three accounts, all in the Administrators group: Mom, Dad, and Katy. Mom and Dad each need to be able to do online banking with Quicken or Microsoft Money, but daughter Katy isn't allowed near those files. If Mom stores the data file in her private My Documents folder both Katy and Dad are locked out. If she stores the data file in the Shared Documents folder, Katy can access it. The solution? Mom needs to take the following steps:

1 Create the data file in her (Mom's) My Documents folder.

2 Copy the data file to the Shared Documents folder. (Leave the existing file in the My Documents folder as a backup in case of problems.)

3 Restart the computer in Safe Mode (see "Using Safe Mode," page 898, for instructions) and log on from the Welcome screen.

4 Open Windows Explorer and navigate to the Shared Documents folder.

5 Right-click the file whose permissions are to be adjusted and choose Properties from the shortcut menu. Click the Security tab and remove all accounts except Mom, Dad, and System, each of which should have Full Control. (You may need to change inheritance settings, as described in "Applying Permissions to Subfolders Through Inheritance," page 517.)

6 Restart the computer, log on using each account, and try to access the file. If the permissions work as expected, delete the backup copy.

You can use this same technique to restrict access to any folder stored on an NTFS-formatted volume.

Controlling Access with NTFS Permissions

If you're frustrated by the limitations of Simple File Sharing, you do have an alternative—that is, if you're running Windows XP Professional and if the drive that contains the files you want to protect is formatted with the NTFS file system. (On a machine running Windows XP Home Edition, the only way to adjust permissions on individual files or folders is by restarting in Safe Mode or using the Cacls utility from a command prompt, an option we describe in "Setting Permissions from a Command Prompt," page 525.)

By disabling Simple File Sharing and using the full range of NTFS access controls, you can accomplish any or all of the following goals:

Control access to any file or folder on any NTFS-formatted drive This is a dramatic improvement over Simple File Sharing, which allows you to protect files in your user profile only.

Allow different types of access for different users or groups of users For instance, you might allow your teenagers read-only access to your collection of digital music files, so they can play them but not erase them to make room for their own downloaded tunes. You and your spouse, on the other hand, get full rights to add or delete any files. This is a significant change from the all-or-nothing access controls available via Simple File Sharing.

Fine-tune permissions on specific files or folders In a folder that contains the templates you use to create new documents or Web pages, you might want to restrict users to read-only access, while blocking their ability to overwrite or delete files. Anyone can open a new file based on an existing template, but you can be certain that the revised file won't inadvertently replace one of your carefully crafted templates.

> **caution** Setting NTFS permissions without understanding the full consequences can lead to unexpected and unwelcome results, including a complete loss of access to files and folders. Working with the built-in permission sets—Full Control, Modify, and so on— is the safest strategy. If you plan to tinker with special permissions, set up a folder and fill it with test files so that you can experiment safely. When you're certain you've worked out the correct mix of permissions, apply them to the folder containing your real working files and delete the test folder.

The best way to begin working with permissions is to start by using the Make This Folder Private option on any folders you want to protect in your user profile. This sets a baseline of default permissions that guarantee you'll have exclusive access to those files. After completing that process, you're ready to turn off the Simple File Sharing interface and reveal the more complex Security tab, with its full array of NTFS permissions. To do so, from any Windows Explorer window, click Tools and then click Folder Options. On the View tab, clear the Use Simple File Sharing (Recommended) check box.

As a general practice, you should be consistent in your use of either the Simple File Sharing interface or the full NTFS permissions. Switching back and forth indiscriminately can wreak havoc with network shares, for instance, as we point out in Chapter 32, "Managing Shared Folders and Printers." If you normally use Simple File Sharing, but

Chapter 13: Securing Files and Folders

occasionally need to work with the full set of permissions, you can bypass the dialog boxes with this simple script, which toggles between the two modes. Open Notepad or any plain text editor and enter the following text:

```
'' ToggleSharingOptions.vbs

' Toggles between Simple Sharing and full NTFS permissions

Option Explicit
Dim strOldForceGuestValue, WshShell

On Error Resume Next

Set WshShell = WScript.CreateObject("WScript.Shell")
strOldForceGuestValue = _
    WshShell.RegRead("HKLM\SYSTEM\CurrentControlSet\Control\Lsa\forceguest")

If strOldForceGuestValue = "1" Then
    WshShell.RegWrite _
        "HKLM\SYSTEM\CurrentControlSet\Control\Lsa\forceguest", 0, "REG_DWORD"
    WScript.Echo "Full permissions are now available"
Else
    WshShell.RegWrite _
        "HKLM\SYSTEM\CurrentControlSet\Control\Lsa\forceguest", 1, "REG_DWORD"
    WScript.Echo "Simple sharing is now on"
End If
```

Alternatively you can copy the ToggleSharingOptions.vbs file from the companion CD included with this book.

Save the file in the Windows folder or in the All Users\Desktop folder as ToggleSharingOptions.vbs. Create a shortcut to the script and add it to the All Programs menu; for even faster access, assign a keyboard shortcut to the script.

Applying Advanced Security Settings

To view and edit NTFS permissions for a file or folder, right-click its icon, choose Properties, and then click the Security tab. This dialog box lists all the groups and users with permissions set for the selected object. As the example in Figure 13-5 on the next page shows, you can assign different permissions to each user—in this case, Katy can read and play (Execute) files in the Music Downloads folder but is forbidden to change existing files (Modify) or create new ones (Write).

Part 3: Managing Files

Select a user or group name from this box

View permissions for the selected user here

Figure 13-5. View and edit permissions for the selected user in the list at the bottom of this dialog box; each user or group can have a different set of permissions.

In Windows XP, the owner of a file or folder (typically the person who creates the file) has the right to allow or deny access to that resource. In addition, members of the Administrators group and other authorized users can grant or deny permissions. You can add individual users to the list of users and allow or deny specific types of file and folder actions. You can also assign permissions to built-in groups (Administrators, for instance) or create your own groups and assign permissions that way. As we'll explain later in this section, some permissions don't need to be explicitly defined but instead are inherited based on permissions from a parent folder. All permissions are stored in the file system as part of the access control list (ACL).

> For more details about creating and managing user accounts and groups, see "Working with User Accounts," page 100.

If the user or group whose permissions you want to edit is already listed at the top of the Security dialog box, you can select check boxes in the Allow column to add permissions, or clear boxes to remove permissions. Select check boxes in the Deny column only if you want to explicitly forbid certain users from exercising a specific permission. Deny access control entries take precedence over any other permission settings that apply to an account, such as those granted through membership in a group. If you want to completely lock out a specific user or group from access to a selected file or folder, select the Deny check box on the Full Control line.

> **tip** **Be careful with the Deny box**
>
> On the average home or small business computer, resist the temptation to select any of the check boxes in the Deny column on the Security tab. This option is typically used on large, complex networks where many groups of users are defined (individual departments, for example) and administrators want to exercise tight control over sensitive files in specific locations. Unraveling the interactions between Allow and Deny permissions can be a daunting task. On a machine with a handful of users, it's almost always simpler to define permissions by selecting and clearing check boxes in the Allow column.

In most cases, you can safely assign permissions by selecting a user or group name and then selecting one or more of the predefined groups of permissions listed in the bottom of the Security dialog box. Table 13-1 describes the basic function of each of these entries.

Table 13-1. How Permissions Control File and Folder Access

Permission	How It Controls Access to Files and Folders
Full Control	Gives the designated user or group full control over the selected file or folder, as the name implies. Selecting this box selects all check boxes below it as well. These users can list contents of a folder, read and open files, create new files, delete files and subfolders, change permissions on files and subfolders, and take ownership of files.
Modify	Allows users to read, change, create, and delete files, but not to change permissions or take ownership of files. Selecting this check box selects all the options listed below it and is equivalent to choosing the Write and Read & Execute permissions.
Read & Execute	Allows the user to view files and execute programs. Selecting this check box selects the List Folder Contents and Read boxes as well.
List Folder Contents (folders only)	Provides the same individual permissions as Read & Execute and is available only on the Security tab for a folder. The only difference between the two permissions is in the way they are inherited.[1]
Read	Allows users to list the contents of a folder, view file attributes, read permissions, and synchronize files. This is the most basic permission of all.

(continued)

Part 3: Managing Files

Table 13-1. *(continued)*

Permission	How It Controls Access to Files and Folders
Write	Allows users to create files, write data, read attributes and permissions, and synchronize files.
Special Permissions	If this permission is selected, the assigned permissions don't match any of the built-in templates shown here. Click the Advanced button to see details.

[1] When the Read & Execute permission is applied to a folder, this permission is inherited by all files and subfolders within the folder. The List Folder Contents permission, on the other hand, though functionally identical, is inherited by subfolders but not by files within the folder or subfolders. For details about inherited permissions, see "Applying Permissions to Subfolders Through Inheritance," page 517.

To set permissions for a group or user that isn't listed in the Group Or User Names box, follow these steps:

1 Open the properties dialog box for the file or folder and click the Security tab.

2 Click the Add button.

3 Type the name in the Select User Or Group dialog box shown here; when entering multiple names, separate them with semicolons. (Note that you must type the user name, which may be different from the full name that appears on the Welcome screen.)

4 Click the Check Names button to confirm that you entered the names correctly.

5 Click OK to return to the Security dialog box and set permissions for the newly added user(s).

Chapter 13

InsideOut

On a standalone computer or on a computer that is part of a workgroup and is not joined to a Windows domain, the list of available names is drawn only from the account database on the local computer—that is, the computer at which you're logged on. If your machine is a domain member, you can click the Locations button and choose whether you want to specify permissions based on users of the local computer or those in the domain's directory. If you're entering names of users on a Windows domain, enter a portion of the name and then click the Check Names button. Unfortunately, you can't use the same shortcut to select users and groups defined in the local computer's account database; instead, you have to enter the user's name in full, and if you're off by even a single letter you'll get an error message. (Windows will, however, fill in the computer or domain name for you automatically.) To see a list of available local users and groups, click the Advanced button, and then click Find Now. The resulting list includes all user accounts, groups, and special accounts on the local computer.

When adding or removing permissions, follow these basic principles:

Start from the top and work down   By default, permissions you set on a folder apply to all files and subfolders within that folder. (For more details, see "Applying Permissions to Subfolders Through Inheritance," page 517.) Managing file access is much easier when you have a consistent set of permissions for all files in a location, with exceptions only where needed.

Organize shared data files into common locations   If shared data is scattered over multiple drives and folders, it's too easy to inadvertently let permissions get out of sync. Try to consolidate shared data files into a single group of folders. When data is all in one place, you'll find it easier to manage permissions and make proper backups.

Use groups whenever possible   This is especially important in a small business setting. Take advantage of the built-in Administrators, Power Users, and Users groups for basic permissions. If you need to define custom permissions so that several users can access files stored in multiple folders, use group-based permissions to simplify the process. Create a new local group and add the users who need access to the files in question. (For details, see "Using the Local Users and Groups Snap-In," page 123.) Open the properties dialog box for the first folder, click the Security tab, add the newly created group, and grant the appropriate permissions to that group. Repeat this process for each additional folder. Later, when one member of the group leaves and another one joins, you can change the group membership and automatically update the permissions for all folders without having to go through each folder's properties dialog box again.

513

Chapter 13

For more information about how to create and manage local groups, see "Working with User Accounts," page 100.

Steer clear of Special permissions   Unless you're a wizard at understanding the interplay of NTFS permissions, resist the temptation to tweak special permissions for individual files or folders. The built-in security settings (Full Control, Modify, Read & Execute) cover most needs adequately.

Grant only the level of access that users require   If a specific user needs to read files stored in a certain location, but does not need to create new files or edit existing ones, grant that user only the Read permission. This precaution is especially important to prevent novices and untrained users from wiping out important data files accidentally.

Troubleshooting

You can't change file or folder permissions.

If you're unable to set custom permissions, look for the symptom in this list and try the following problem-solving techniques:

- **The Security tab is not visible.** Do you see only a Sharing tab? If so, choose Tools, Folder Options and clear the Use Simple File Sharing (Recommended) check box. If, after making this change, you still see only a Sharing tab, check the properties for the drive; the most likely explanation is that the drive is formatted using the FAT32 file system. The Security tab is visible only on NTFS drives.

- **You've made changes, but the check marks disappear.** This may not be a problem at all. If you set permissions and apply them to anything other than the default location—This Folder, Subfolder, And Files—Windows adds a check mark in the Special Permissions box (when viewing permissions for a folder, you have to scroll to the bottom of the Permissions list to see this box). You can view the applied permissions by clicking the Advanced button, selecting the user or group, and clicking the Edit button.

- **Permission settings are unavailable.** Check your user account rights. You must be logged on as a member of the Administrators group or be the owner of an object to set its permissions. These settings will also be unavailable if the selected object is inheriting its permissions from a parent folder. To set custom permissions on such an object, you have to remove the inheritance, as described later in this chapter, in "Applying Permissions to Subfolders Through Inheritance," page 517.

Chapter 13: Securing Files and Folders

Working with Built-in Users and Groups

In addition to the standard local groups (Administrators and Users, for instance), Windows XP includes a number of special identities. These users and groups, which are built into the system and can't be deleted, are used to apply special permissions to system resources (including files and folders); in many cases, these identities are place-holders that apply to user accounts based on the way a given account uses the system.

> **note** Special identities are often referred to as well-known security identifiers (SIDs).

The most common special identity you're likely to encounter in everyday use is the Everyone group, which includes all users who log onto the system. On a drive that's been newly converted to NTFS, the Everyone group is assigned the Full Control permission—as you would expect, this has the effect of allowing anyone who logs on to the computer to do anything with files and folders on that drive, unless further restrictions are placed on subfolders and files.

Understanding these built-in accounts and groups is crucial to using advanced NTFS permissions effectively. Table 13-2 lists the most common special identities.

Table 13-2. **Special Identities Available in Windows XP**

Special Identity	Description
Everyone	Includes every user who accesses the computer, including Guests. This group does not include Anonymous logons.
Creator Owner	Identifies the user who created the selected file or folder or who has taken ownership of it since it was created.
Authenticated User	Includes any user who logs on with a user name and pass-word. Unlike the Everyone identity, this group does not include users who log on as Guest, even if the Guest account has been assigned a password.
Interactive	Includes any user that logs on locally or through a Remote Desktop connection.
Anonymous Logon	Identifies network logons for which credentials are not pro-vided, such as connections to a Web server. Anonymous and Interactive logons are mutually exclusive.
Dialup	Includes any user who accesses the computer over a dial-up connection.
Network	Includes any user that logs on over the network. Does not include Interactive logons that use Remote Desktop over a network.

Some of these special identities are esoteric, and the average user will never need to apply them. But others can be extremely powerful additions to your security toolkit. For instance, you can use the following combinations of permissions to tighten security on your computer:

- For shared data folders, assign the Read & Execute permission and the Write permission to the Users group, and the Full Control permission to the Creator Owner special identity. In this configuration, every user who creates a file or folder becomes that object's owner and has the ability to read, modify, and delete it. Other users can read and modify documents created by other users but can't accidentally delete them.

- If you have a second drive in your system and you want to prevent all access to files on that drive by anyone using the Guest account, change the default permissions on the root of the drive. Add the Authenticated Users group and give it Full Control, and then remove the default Everyone group.

caution One of the most common mistakes made by users who are inexperienced with NTFS permissions is to remove the Everyone group from the root of a drive—or worse, to select the Deny box next to Full Control for this group. If you try to take either of these drastic measures in Windows XP Professional, the system displays a dialog box warning you that you're about to deny all access to all files on the drive by all users—which is almost certainly not the intended result! Remember, more restrictive permissions always override more lenient permissions. As a rule of thumb, the best strategy for the permissions on the top-level folder for any drive is to make sure that all users who will access files on that drive have the proper level of access. After you've organized data on that drive, tighten up permissions on each subfolder so that it's accessible by the correct users and groups.

Windows XP includes three special identities that are reserved for software and system processes and are never used by human users. The Batch identity provides permissions for any batch process (such as a job launched via Task Scheduler) that needs to access a resource on the computer. The Service identity is used by system services and is controlled by the operating system. The System identity allows the operating system itself to access protected resources. As a general rule, permissions for these three groups are set by the operating system and should never be adjusted by users.

Chapter 13: Securing Files and Folders

> **caution** Tampering with the default permissions on the drive that contains Windows system files is a bad idea. As part of the setup process, Windows XP applies specific permissions to the root of the system drive; to the Windows, System32, and Documents And Settings folders; and to specific subfolders within each of these locations. Changing the default permissions will not improve security and will almost certainly cause some users or programs to have problems. If you've made a mess of permissions in a system folder and you need to know how to put things right again, search the Knowledge Base for a Windows XP–specific update to article Q244600, "Default NTFS Permissions in Windows 2000."

Applying Permissions to Subfolders Through Inheritance

Files and subfolders can inherit permissions from a parent folder. By default, any new permissions you assign to a folder are passed on to subfolders as well. Thus, when you create a new subfolder in your My Documents folder, it inherits the permissions you've set for your profile. If you made your user profile private, the new subfolder and any files you create or store within it will be private as well.

You can prevent permissions from being inherited by changing the inheritance options for a folder. You can specify that subfolders or files (or both) no longer inherit permissions that have been assigned to the parent folder containing them. Instead, only permissions you explicitly apply to files and subfolders will apply.

To see the inheritance options for a selected folder, right-click the folder icon, choose Properties, and then click the Security tab. Click the Advanced button to display the Advanced Security Settings dialog box. The Inherited From column in the Permission Entries list shows the parent folder from which a given set of permissions is inherited. In the example shown in Figure 13-6 on the next page, the Everyone group inherits Full Control permissions from the access control list on the root folder of drive E, whereas the other permissions, designated as <not inherited>, have been applied directly on this folder.

In this example, the inherited permissions are getting in the way of the tight security we want to apply to this folder. To remove the inherited permissions, clear the option labeled Inherit From Parent The Permission Entries That Apply To Child Objects. When you clear this check box, you see the following dialog box, which warns you to specify how you want to reset the permissions on the selected folder.

Part 3: Managing Files

Choose one of the following three options:

- **Copy.** This option copies the permissions from the parent folder to the current file or folder and then breaks the inheritance link to the parent folder. After choosing this option, you can adjust the permissions to suit your security needs.

- **Remove.** This option completely removes the inherited permissions and keeps only the permissions you've explicitly assigned to the file or folder.

- **Cancel.** This option closes the warning dialog box and leaves the inheritance options intact.

These permissions are applied directly to the current folder

Figure 13-6. The list of permissions shown here helps you identify which are inherited from parent folders.

When you remove inherited permissions from a folder, it becomes a new top-level folder. By default, any permissions you assign to this folder ripple down the hierarchy of subfolders and to files within those subfolders as well.

For an excellent illustration of how these settings all work together, look at the permissions on your user profile after you choose the Simple File Sharing option to make the folder private. Using Simple File Sharing, click the Make This Folder Private option, and then turn off Simple File Sharing. When you click the Advanced button on the Security tab of the "private" folder, you'll see that the Inherit From Parent The Permission Entries That Apply To Child Objects check box has been cleared and that the permissions on the folder now include only the System account and your user account, both with Full Control permissions. The net effect is to block out every user except you.

In some cases, you may want to apply two or more sets of permissions to the same folder for the same group, with each set of permissions having different inheritance settings. For instance, say that you and several coworkers on a shared computer are working on a top-secret project. You've set up a shared folder called Project X Files for use by everyone who has an account on your computer. In the main folder, you've stored a handful of document templates that you want members of the team to use when creating new documents; you've also set up subfolders to hold files that are currently being worked on.

In this scenario, you might want the Everyone group to have Read & Execute access to files within a top-level folder, and Full Control over subfolders. Using this arrangement of permissions, you can allow users to open templates stored in the top-level folder, while protecting those templates from accidental changes or deletions. By using a different set of permissions on subfolders, you can allow users to create new files and modify previously saved documents. To apply permissions with this level of fine-grain control, follow these steps:

1 Open the properties dialog box for the top-level folder you want to adjust (Project X Files in this example), and click the Security tab.

2 Click the Add button.

3 In the Select Users Or Groups dialog box, enter **Administrators** and click OK.

4 Choose Administrators from the Group Or User Names List at the top of the properties dialog box, and then select the Allow box to the right of the Full Control entry in the Permissions list.

5 Click the Add button again.

6 This time, enter **Everyone** in the Select Users Or Groups dialog box and click OK.

7 Select Everyone and then select the Allow box to the right of the Read & Execute entry.

8 Click the Advanced button to open the Advanced Security Settings dialog box.

9 If necessary, clear the Inherit From Parent The Permission Entries That Apply To Child Objects check box (and then select Copy when the Security message appears).

10 Select the entry for Everyone and click the Edit button to open the Permission Entry dialog box (shown here). Open the Apply Onto list, choose This Folder And Files, and click OK.

11 From the Advanced Security Settings dialog box, click the Add button.

12 In the Select User Or Group box, enter **Everyone** and click OK.

13 In the Permission Entry dialog box, check the Full Control box, choose Subfolders Only from the Apply Onto list, and then click OK.

The resulting set of permissions should look like the one shown in Figure 13-7 on the next page. With these settings, you and other members of the Administrators group can add and change files in the main folder; you can also add subfolders. All other users can view and open files in the main folder but can't create new files, change existing files, or delete files or subfolders. They can, however, save files in the subfolders you create.

Figure 13-7. By applying different sets of permissions to files and subfolders, you can fine-tune permissions for a group of folders all at once.

What's the advantage of using inherited permissions in this fashion? Each time you create a subfolder, Windows automatically applies the proper permissions to it, using the inheritance settings you defined. Without these settings, you would be forced to define permissions from scratch for each new subfolder. That's a lot of needless work, with the potential for errors and inconsistencies. More importantly, if you decide to change the permissions later—by changing the Full Control permission for subfolders from the Everyone group to a more limited group of users, for instance—you can make a single change and have the changes apply to all the child folders automatically.

Testing the Effect of Permissions

Because file and folder permissions can come from a variety of settings, it's sometimes difficult to figure out exactly what each user can and can't do with a given file or folder. As a general rule, you can figure out *effective permissions* by combining all the NTFS permissions assigned to an individual user account and to all of the groups to which that user belongs. Thus, if a user has Read & Execute permission for a folder set through her user account and is also a member of a group that has been assigned Write permissions for that folder, she has both Read and Write permissions for the folder.

newfeature!

On a scale of complexity, calculating effective permissions is more difficult than programming a VCR and only slightly less taxing than quantum physics. Fortunately, Windows XP Professional includes a new tool that does the calculations for you.

To see what the effect of all NTFS permissions will be on a given user or group, follow these steps:

1 Right-click the file or folder in question and then choose Properties.

2 On the Security tab, click the Advanced button and then click the Effective Permissions tab.

3 Click the Select button to open the Select User or Group dialog box.

4 Enter the name of the user or group for which you want to check effective permissions and then click OK.

InsideOut

Anyone who's ever struggled trying to figure out Windows 2000 permissions will really appreciate the Effective Permissions dialog box in Windows XP. It's a wonderful addition, and if you're going to use NTFS permissions you should learn its ins and outs. Unfortunately, it also includes one potentially confusing interface element. The Group Or User Name box looks like a place to enter text directly, but it doesn't work that way in practice. You have to display the Select User Or Group dialog box to enter a name.

The resulting dialog box shows the effective permissions that apply to the user or group you selected. These permissions are presented using the complete list of available permissions from the Advanced Security Settings dialog box, which are far more detailed than those shown on the Security tab. This level of detail can be difficult to decipher, but it's crucial in identifying subtle changes that can compromise security. In the example in Figure 13-8 on the next page, for instance, the user named Ed has permissions that are equivalent to Read & Execute; in addition, he can change permissions on the selected object.

The Effective Permissions calculation looks up all local and domain groups to which a user or group belongs and takes those permissions into account in its summary. A check mark identifies permissions that have been assigned. The resulting display is a snapshot of permissions based on other settings. You can't change any permissions from this dialog box.

note The effective permissions calculation does not include the Anonymous Logon or Authenticated Users group, nor does it include settings granted because a user is the Creator Owner of an object. In addition, the calculation does not consider whether you're logging on interactively or over a network. If you've customized any of these permissions, you'll need to account for the differences.

Figure 13-8. Use this dialog box to see how permissions through user accounts and groups combine for a given user. Check marks indicate which permissions are assigned.

Using Special Permissions

Don't be misled by the long list of so-called special permissions that you see when you click the Advanced button, select a user or group name, and then click the Edit button. Whenever you use NTFS permissions, whether it's through the Simple File Sharing model or the more full featured Security dialog box, your actions result in changes to this list. Using the built-in permission options—Full Control, Modify, and so on—actually sets predetermined groups of permissions here. Figure 13-9, for instance, shows the results when you select the Allow box next to the Read & Execute entry—Windows actually sets five individual permissions in response to the single click.

When dealing with unusual access control situations, the best solution is usually to start by applying the predefined basic permission that comes closest to the desired result. Then add or remove special permissions as needed. Table 13-3 lists the full set of special permissions that are applied when you set each of the predefined permission options.

Table 13-3. Special Permissions Applied by Basic Permissions

Basic Permission	Special Permissions
Read	● List Folder / Read Data
	● Read Attributes
	● Read Extended Attributes
	● Read Permissions

(continued)

Table 13-3. *(continued)*

Basic Permission	Special Permissions
Read & Execute *or* List Folder Contents	● All Read permissions listed above ● Traverse Folder / Execute File
Write	● Create Files / Write Data ● Create Folders / Append Data ● Write Attributes ● Write Extended Attributes
Modify	● All Read & Execute permissions listed above ● All Write permissions listed above ● Delete
Full Control	● All permissions listed above ● Delete Subfolders And Files ● Change Permissions ● Take Ownership

Figure 13-9. In general, you don't need to adjust these so-called special permissions. Using the check boxes on the Security dialog box makes the adjustments for you.

Setting Permissions from a Command Prompt

Cacls.exe, a command-line utility available in both Windows XP Professional and Home Edition, provides another way to view and edit permissions. With Cacls (short for *Control ACLs*), you can view existing permissions by typing **cacls** *filename* at a command prompt, replacing *filename* with the name of the file or folder you're interested in (wildcards are acceptable as well). The resulting list of permissions is terse, to say the least. Next to each user account name, Cacls displays a single letter for any of three standard permission settings: F for Full Control, C for Change, R for Read. Any other combination of settings from the Security tab or the Advanced Security Settings dialog box generates output only a programmer could love.

Cacls is useful for quickly finding the permissions for an object—particularly if you're already working in a Command Prompt window. As an administrator, especially when working with Windows XP Home Edition, it's an indispensable part of your toolkit.

> **tip** **Get a more powerful permission tool**
>
> If you like Cacls, you'll love Xcacls. As the name suggests, it's an extended version of the basic utility included with Windows 2000 and Windows XP. This utility is included in the Support Tools collection found on the Windows XP CD in \Support\Tools\Support.cab.

You can also set permissions with Cacls. In fact, in Windows XP Home Edition, using this utility is the only way to adjust individual permissions without restarting in Safe Mode. Use the switches listed in Table 13-4 to modify the effects of Cacls.

Table 13-4. **Command-line Switches for Cacls.exe**

Switch	What It Does
/T	Changes permissions of specified files in the current directory and all subdirectories
/E	Edits access control list instead of replacing it
/C	Continues on "access denied" errors
/G *user:perm*	Grants specified user access rights; if used without /E, completely replaces existing permissions
/R *user*	Revokes specified user's access rights (must be used with /E)
/P *user:perm*	Replaces specified user's access rights
/D *user*	Denies access to specified user

In conjunction with the /G and /P switches, use one of the following four letters where indicated by the *perm* placeholder:

- F (for *full control*) is equivalent to selecting the Allow box next to Full Control on the Security tab.
- C (for *change*) is equivalent to selecting the Allow box for Modify.
- R (for *read*) is equivalent to selecting the Allow box for Read & Execute.
- W (for *write*) is equivalent to selecting the Allow box for Write.

Note that wildcards can be used to specify more than one file in a command and that you can specify more than one user in a command. For instance, if you've created a subfolder called Archives in the Shared Documents folder and you want Carl to have Full Control and Craig to have Read permissions in that folder, open a command prompt window, navigate to the Shared Documents folder, and type the following command:

```
cacls archives /g carl:f craig:r
```

If you then decide that you want to revoke Craig's access rights and give Read permissions to the Administrators group, type this command:

```
cacls archives /e /r craig /g administrators:r
```

> **caution**   Just because you *can* set permissions with Cacls doesn't mean you should. It's easy to make a mistake that causes you to lose existing permissions on a file. If you're using Windows XP Professional, there's no reason to use Cacls to set permissions. If you're using Windows XP Home Edition, try the Cacls command on a test folder first and make sure that your settings have the desired effect before you use this command on your actual working files.

Taking Ownership of Files and Folders

When you create a file or folder on an NTFS drive, Windows XP designates your user account as the owner of that object. That status gives you the right to allow or deny permission for other users and groups to access the file or folder. As owner, you can lock out every other user, including all members of the Administrators group.

So what happens if you turn over responsibility for a document (or an entire folder full of documents) to another user? As the owner, you can allow the other user to take ownership of the object. In addition, any member of the Administrators group can take ownership of any file or folder, although he or she cannot transfer ownership to other users.

Chapter 13: Securing Files and Folders

Turning over the ownership of a file or folder makes sense when you want someone else to be responsible for setting permissions for that object. To ensure a smooth transition of power, use either of the following techniques.

- If you're a member of the Administrators group, follow these steps:

  1 Right-click the file or folder icon and choose Properties.

  2 On the Security tab, click the Advanced button to open the Advanced Security Settings dialog box for the file or folder.

  3 Click the Owner tab. As the example in Figure 13-10 shows, this dialog box shows the current owner and allows you to transfer ownership to the Administrators group or to your account.

  4 Select either name from the Change Owner To list and click OK.

Figure 13-10. Only members of the Administrators group have the right to take ownership of files and folders.

- If you're not an administrator, you must first be granted the right to take ownership of a file or folder explicitly. To do this, ask the current owner or any member of the Administrators group to add your account to the access control list for the file or folder and give you the Take Ownership permission. This permission can be found at the bottom of the list of special permissions available by clicking Edit from the Advanced Security Settings dialog box.

Ultimately, the ability for an administrator to take ownership of files and folders means that you can't count on absolute privacy for any files stored on an NTFS drive. No matter how securely you lock them up, an administrator can break through the lock by taking ownership of the files. This is a brute force solution, however, and it's not something that can be easily hidden. If you're concerned about security and you want to monitor changes in ownership of file-system objects, configure your system so that Take Ownership events in a particular location are audited. You'll find step-by-step instructions in "Seeing Who Has Tried to Access Your Files and Folders," page 1206.

new feature!

Troubleshooting Permission Problems

NTFS permissions are straightforward and uncomplicated when the Simple File Sharing interface is enabled. In this configuration, users do not have the ability to manipulate file and folder access controls directly. You can select one or more folders within your user profile and make those locations private, but no other security settings are available for customization. With Simple File Sharing enabled, when you move or copy files or folders from a folder you've made private into any other location on an NTFS volume, the moved or copied objects take on the security attributes of the destination folder—in most cases, that means they're freely available to all other users. When you drag a file out of your private My Documents folder and drop it in the Shared Documents folder, for instance, that file is accessible by all other users of the local computer. Conversely, when you move a file from the Shared Documents folder into your private My Documents folder, it becomes a private file accessible only to you.

But if you disable Simple File Sharing and work directly with NTFS permissions, ordinary file management tasks can have unintended and confusing consequences. In fact, even when a user has been granted Full Control permissions for a given folder, he or she may encounter an "access denied" error message when trying to open, rename, delete, or copy a file or folder.

To understand why this problem occurs, you need to understand what happens when you move or copy files or folders from one location to another. During the move, the permissions for the files or folders may change. With Simple File Sharing disabled, Windows XP follows a strict set of rules when applying permissions during a move or copy operation. Note the different results that apply depending on whether you're moving or copying the object and whether the destination is on the same drive or on a different drive:

When you copy a file or folder to an NTFS drive... The newly created folder or file takes on the permissions of the destination folder, and the original object retains its permissions. This is true regardless of whether the destination is on the same NTFS drive as the original file or on a separate NTFS drive. You become the Creator Owner of the new file or folder, which means you can change its permissions.

Chapter 13: Securing Files and Folders

When you move a file or folder within a single NTFS drive...   The moved folder or file retains its original permissions and you become the Creator Owner.

When you move a file or folder from one NTFS drive to another...   The moved folder or file picks up the permissions of the destination folder and you become the Creator Owner.

When you copy or move a file or folder from a FAT32 drive to an NTFS drive...   The newly created folder or file picks up the permissions of the destination folder and you become the Creator Owner.

When you copy or move a file or folder from an NTFS drive to a FAT32 drive...   The moved or copied folder or file in the new destination loses all permission settings, because the FAT32 file system is incapable of storing these details.

When Simple File Sharing is disabled, you may discover, after dragging a file from your My Documents folder into the Shared Documents folder, that other users are unable to access that file. This result will occur if the following conditions apply:

- The drive that contains the Documents And Settings folder is formatted using the NTFS file system.

- You've made your entire user profile private (as you were prompted to do when you added a password to your account).

- You've disabled Simple File Sharing.

- You've created a group of files (or a subfolder) in your My Documents, My Music, or My Pictures folder, and you want to share those files with other users by dragging them to the Shared Documents folder.

Because both locations are on the same NTFS-formatted drive, dragging any file or folder from your user profile to the Shared Documents folder moves the selected object without making any changes to its access control list. As a result, other users can see the icon for the file or folder but are greeted with an "access denied" error message when they double-click it. Frustrating, isn't it? The solution to this dilemma is simple. If you've disabled Simple File Sharing, never *move* a file from your personal profile to a shared location. Instead, get in the habit of *copying* the file. The new copy inherits the permissions from the destination folder (Shared Documents), and is therefore available to every user. After copying the file or folder, you can safely delete the original from your private folder.

Another common cause of permission problems has an equally simple solution. After you add a user account to a group that has been assigned permissions for a file or folder, the user must log off and log back on to have access to the files.

> **tip**   **Don't overlook inherited permissions**
>
> When trying to sort out why a user is having problems accessing a given file or folder, look first in the Advanced Security Settings dialog box. Pay particular attention to the Inherited From column in the Permission Entries list. The data here will often show you the exact source of an unexpected permission problem.

Chapter 14

Encrypting Confidential Information

Organizations of all sizes—and even home computer users—are likely to have sensitive data that must never be available to others. Financial data—your accounting data, personal finance data files, and so on—certainly falls into this category. But your computer might also be the repository for marketing plans, trade secrets, medical history, diaries, phone books, and similar information. Two popular trends in computing—interconnected computers (on a local area network or on the Internet) and portable computers—put this data at risk. If someone can obtain a file by downloading it from your computer or by borrowing (or stealing) your portable computer, they will know your secrets.

Microsoft Windows XP provides a way to prevent the loss of such confidential data. The Encrypting File System (EFS) encodes your files so that, even if someone is able to obtain the file, they can't read it. The files are readable only when you log on to the computer using your user account (which, presumably, you have protected with a strong password). In fact, even someone else logging on to your computer won't have access to your encrypted files, which provides protection on systems that are shared by more than one user.

At Home with Windows XP

To take advantage of the Encrypting File System (EFS), you must be using Windows XP Professional. EFS is not available on computers running Windows XP Home Edition.

Encryption is the process of encoding sensitive data using a key algorithm. Without the correct key, the data can't be decrypted. Microsoft Windows XP uses encryption for several purposes:

- Encrypting files on an NTFS volume (a disk partition formatted with the NTFS file system) (see "Encrypting Folders and Files" on the next page)

- Encrypting data sent between a Web browser and a server using Secure Sockets Layer (SSL) (see "Enabling a Secure (Encrypted) Connection," page 854)

- Encrypting data sent between computers using a virtual private network (VPN)

- Encrypting or signing e-mail messages

Beware the Dangers of EFS!

EFS provides secure encryption of your most important information. The encryption is so secure that if you lose the key to decrypt your data, the information is effectively lost. By default, Microsoft Windows XP provides no "back door" if your private key is lost.

You can innocently lose your key in a number of ways. Among the worst:

- Working with the Certificates dialog box or the Certificates console (Certmgr.msc), you can inadvertently delete the encryption certificate, which contains the key.

- You might have your data stored in encrypted folders on a second volume (drive D, for example). You notice that your computer is running sluggishly and its hard drive is overflowing with junk files—so you decide to reinstall Windows from scratch. Not worrying about your files on another partition, you format drive C and reinstall Windows. Although it's not apparent, reinstalling Windows creates new security identifiers (SIDs) for each user, even if you do everything exactly the same way each time you run Setup. As a result, each user's encryption certificates are also different from the ones they replaced, and they can't be used to access the encrypted data stored on drive D. Even the Administrator account—which also has a new SID—can't decrypt the files from a different Windows installation.

Fortunately, with a little care, these drastic scenarios can be prevented. To learn about EFS and then begin safely using it for your important files, we recommend that you follow this approach:

1 Create an empty folder and encrypt it. (For details, see "Encrypting Folders and Files" below.)

2 Create a nonessential file in the encrypted folder (or copy a file to the folder)—and verify that you can use it as you would any ordinary file.

3 If your computer is not part of a domain, create a data recovery agent, a second user account that can be used to decrypt files should your personal encryption certificate become lost or corrupt. (For details, see "Creating a Data Recovery Agent," page 542.)

4 Back up your recovery agent certificate and your personal encryption certificate. (For details, see "Backing Up Your Certificates," page 546.)

Note that you won't have a certificate to back up until after you have encrypted at least one folder or file. A new Windows installation doesn't have encryption certificates; one is created the first time a user encrypts a folder or file.

5 Begin using EFS for your important confidential files.

In summary: if you encrypt files, be sure to set up a recovery agent. Back up both your personal certificate and the recovery agent's certificate. Review the best practices listed at the end of this chapter to ensure that you don't leave any loopholes in your security.

Encrypting Folders and Files

The Encrypting File System allows you to encrypt files on a local NTFS volume so that only you can use them. This offers an additional level of protection beyond that provided by NTFS permissions, which you can use to restrict access to your files by others who log on to your computer. NTFS permissions are vulnerable in a couple of ways. First, all those with administrative privileges can grant themselves (or others) permission to access your files. What's worse, anyone who gains physical access to your computer can boot from a floppy disk (or from another operating system, if your computer is set up for dual booting), and use a utility such as NTFSDOS (from *http://www.sysinternals.com*) to read the files on your hard drive—without having to provide a user name or password. Portable computers, which are more easily stolen, are especially vulnerable to this type of information loss.

> **note** On most computers, you can use BIOS settings as another protection against this type of loss. Set your BIOS so that a password is required to start the computer or to enter the BIOS setup program, and set the boot options so that the computer can't be booted from a floppy disk. Unfortunately, this type of protection can also be circumvented. For example, removing the hard drive and installing it in another computer makes its files available to someone with the proper tools.

EFS provides a secure way to store your sensitive data. It uses your public key to create a randomly generated file encryption key (FEK). Although transparent to the user, Windows automatically encrypts the data using this FEK as data is written to disk. The data can be decrypted only with your certificate and its associated private key, which are available only when you log on with your user name and password. (Designated recovery agents can also decrypt your data.) Other users who attempt to use your encrypted files receive an "access denied" message.

For information about recovery agents, see "Recovering Encrypted Files and Folders," page 551.

You can encrypt individual files or folders. We recommend that you encrypt folders instead of individual files. That way, not only are the existing files in the folder encrypted, but new files that you create in the folder are also encrypted automatically. This includes temporary files that your applications create in the folder. (For example, Microsoft Word creates a copy of a document when you open it for editing. If the document's folder isn't encrypted, the temporary copy isn't encrypted—giving prying eyes a potential opportunity to view your data.) For this reason, you should consider encrypting your %Temp% and %Tmp% folders, which many applications use to store temporary copies of documents that are open for editing, in addition to the folder where your sensitive documents are stored.

Securing the Paging File

If you're truly concerned about the possibility of your computer falling into the wrong hands, you should be sure that you don't leave any tracks in the paging file. By default, when you shut down your system, the paging file remains intact. People who have access to your computer could conceivably look through the unencrypted paging file to find information they shouldn't have.

You can foil such snooping by changing a registry entry. Use a registry editor to navigate to the HKLM\System\CurrentControlSet\Control\Session Manager\Memory Management key and set the value of ClearPageFileAtShutdown to 1. After you do that, Windows fills inactive pages in the paging file with zeros whenever you shut down. Because this could slow down your system, don't make this change unless your security needs demand it.

Chapter 14: Encrypting Confidential Information

---

caution Before you encrypt anything important, you should back up your personal encryption certificate (with its associated private key) and the recovery agent certificate to a floppy disk and store it in a secure location. If you ever lose your original certificate (because of a hard disk failure, for example), you can restore the backup copy and regain access to your files. If you lose all copies of your certificate (and no recovery agent certificates exist), you won't be able to use your encrypted files. No back door exists, nor is there any practical way to hack these files. (If there were, it wouldn't be very good encryption.) For details, see "Backing Up Your Certificates," page 546.

To encrypt a folder, follow these steps:

1 Right-click the folder, choose Properties, click the General tab, and then click the Advanced button, as shown below. (If the properties dialog box doesn't have an Advanced button, the folder is not on an NTFS-formatted volume, and you can't use EFS.)

> **tip** Your important files are likely to be in your My Documents folder; other at-risk files can be in a Temp folder. Ordinarily, these folders are on your boot partition. If the boot partition is not an NTFS volume, you can't encrypt those folders. If it's not feasible to convert your boot partition to NTFS (if you need FAT format for dual-boot capabilities, for example), there is a solution if your computer has more than one volume: format another volume as NTFS and move your important folders there. Because My Documents and Temp are special folders, simply moving them with Windows Explorer won't do the job, however. (In fact, doing so will cause severe problems; don't even try.) You can safely move these folders using other methods, however. For details, see "Moving Folders from the Standard Profile Locations," page 1162.

2 Select Encrypt Contents To Secure Data. (Note that you can't encrypt compressed files. If the files are already compressed, Windows clears the Compressed attribute. Because encryption and compression are mutually exclusive, this section of the dialog box really should contain option buttons rather than check boxes—with the addition of a "Neither" option button.)

3 Click OK twice. If the folder contains any files or subfolders, Windows then displays a confirmation message.

> **note** If you select Apply Changes To This Folder Only, Windows doesn't encrypt any of the files currently in the folder. Any new files that you create in the folder, including files that you copy or move to the folder, will be encrypted.

To encrypt a file, follow the same procedure. You'll see a different confirmation message (shown in Figure 14-1) to remind you that the file's folder is not encrypted and to give you an opportunity to encrypt it. You generally don't want to encrypt individual files, because the information you intend to protect can too easily become decrypted without your knowledge. For example, with some applications, when you open a document for editing, the application creates a copy of the original document. When you save the

Chapter 14: Encrypting Confidential Information

Figure 14-1. In this dialog box, a message advises you to encrypt folders rather than individual files.

document after editing, the application saves the copy—which is not encrypted—and deletes the original, encrypted document. Static files that you use for reference only— but never for editing—can safely be encrypted without encrypting the parent folder. Even in that situation, however, you'll probably find it simpler to encrypt the whole folder.

note You can't encrypt any files that have the system attribute, nor any files located in %SystemRoot% or its subfolders. (Those files are usually system files, and the system might be rendered unusable if some of its essential files were encrypted.) Also you can't encrypt any files or folders in a roaming profile.

If you see a message box like the one shown here when you try to encrypt a file or folder, EFS has been disabled on your computer. Although its four buttons might lead you to believe that you have a choice in the matter, you don't. Regardless of which button you click, Windows refuses to encrypt your files—just as if you clicked Cancel.

To solve this problem, you need to enable the Encrypting File System. For details, see "Disabling or Reenabling EFS," page 552.

Other than the fact that their names in Windows Explorer are green (instead of the black text used for ordinary uncompressed files), you'll notice no significant difference in working with encrypted folders or files while you're logged on using the same account as when you encrypted them. But encrypted files do act differently in several subtle ways. Table 14-1 describes the important differences.

Table 14-1. **Behavior of Encrypted Files**

When You Do This	This Happens
Log on using a different account	• If you try to open an encrypted file, you get an "access denied" message. • If you try to decrypt an encrypted file by clearing the encryption attribute, you get an "access denied" message. • If you have Modify or Full Control permission, you can delete or rename an encrypted file.
Copy or move an unencrypted file to an encrypted folder	• The copy in the encrypted folder becomes encrypted.
Copy an encrypted file	• If you copy an encrypted file to an NTFS volume on your computer or another computer running Windows XP or Windows 2000, it remains encrypted. (If EFS is disabled on the target computer, Windows warns that the copied file will lose its encryption.) • If you copy to a FAT volume (including floppy disks) or to an NTFS volume on a computer that is running Windows NT, the file becomes decrypted.
Move an encrypted file	• If you move to another folder on the same volume, the file remains encrypted. • Moving the file to another volume is essentially a "copy and then delete" process; moving your own encrypted files is handled as in copy operations, described above. • If you move someone else's encrypted file to a FAT volume, you get an "access denied" message.
Rename an encrypted file	• The file is renamed and it remains encrypted.
Delete an encrypted file	• If you delete to the Recycle Bin, the restorable file remains encrypted.

Table 14-1. *(continued)*

When You Do This	This Happens
Back up an encrypted file using Backup	• You've picked the best way to back up encrypted files or move them between systems! The files in the backup media remain encrypted, whether they're on disk or tape. (Because most removable media can't be formatted as NTFS, an ordinary copy becomes decrypted.)
Use encrypted files on a different computer	• Your personal encryption certificate and its private key must be available on the computer. You can copy the keys manually. For details, see "Backing Up Your Certificates," page 546.
	• If you use roaming profiles, your encryption keys are automatically available on all computers you log on to with that user account. For more information, see "Using Roaming User Profiles," page 1165.

> **caution**   Other users with permission to delete a file (that is, users with Modify or Full Control permission) can't use your encrypted files—but they can make them difficult for you to use. Any such user can rename your files, which can make them difficult to find, and also can delete your files. (Even if the user merely deletes them to the Recycle Bin and doesn't remove them altogether, the deleted files are unavailable to you because you don't have access to any other user's Recycle Bin.) Therefore, if you're concerned about protecting your files from other authorized users as well as from a thief who steals your computer, you should modify the NTFS permissions to prevent any type of modification by other users. For more information, see "Applying Advanced Security Settings," page 509.

Decrypting Folders and Files

Like the encryption process, decryption is done transparently. That is, you simply work with your encrypted files exactly the same way you work with unencrypted files. When Windows detects that a file you're accessing is encrypted, it finds your certificate and uses its private key to decrypt the data as it is read from the disk.

To permanently decrypt a folder or file, simply clear the Encrypt Contents To Secure Data check box in the Advanced Attributes dialog box. If you decrypt a folder, Windows asks whether you want to decrypt only the folder or the folder and its contents. If you choose the latter option, Windows prohibits you from decrypting any files for which you don't hold a valid encryption certificate. If you change the attribute for a file that you encrypted, Windows decrypts it without further ado. If you attempt to decrypt a file that someone else encrypted, you get an *access denied* message.

Chapter 14

InsideOut

Unless you use a command-line utility like Cipher.exe, it's difficult to see at a glance which files are encrypted and which are not. Right-clicking each file and then choosing Properties, General, Advanced (followed by Cancel, Cancel) is tedious. Fortunately, there's an easier way. In Windows Explorer, use Details view. Choose View, choose Details, and then select Attributes. Encrypted files show a letter *E* in the Attributes column. You can also set an option so that the names of encrypted files appear in a different color from other file names. In Folder Options, click the View tab, and select Show Encrypted Or Compressed NTFS Files In Color.

newfeature!
Allowing Others to Use Your Encrypted Files

After you have encrypted a file, you can allow others to access the file transparently, just as you can. This capability, which is new in Windows XP, lets you secure a file with EFS, yet make it available to other users you select. The other users you specify may be users with whom you share your computer, or they can access the file over the network. To enable another user to use one of your encrypted files, follow these steps:

1 Right-click an encrypted file and choose Properties. On the General tab, click Advanced.

2 In the Advanced Attributes dialog box, click Details.

> **note** The Details button is unavailable when you initially encrypt a file. You must encrypt the file and then return to the Advanced Attributes dialog box to use Details. Note also that the Details button is available only when you select a single file; if you select a folder or multiple files, the button is unavailable.

3 In the Encryption Details dialog box, click Add. The Select User dialog box appears, as shown in Figure 14-2.

4 Select the name of the user to whom you want to give access, and then click OK.

> **note** Only users who have an EFS certificate on your computer appear in the Select User dialog box. The easiest way for a user who shares your computer to create a certificate (and, therefore, appear in this list) is for that user to log on and encrypt a file. Network users should export their own certificate (for details, see "Exporting a Personal Encryption Certificate," page 548); you can then import the certificate on your computer.

Chapter 14: Encrypting Confidential Information

Figure 14-2. You can provide access to any account that has an Encrypting File System certificate on your computer.

Using the Cipher Command

If you prefer to use the command line, a non-GUI alternative to the Advanced Attributes dialog box is available for encrypting and decrypting folders and files. Like the Windows Explorer methods described earlier in this chapter, Cipher.exe allows you to encrypt or decrypt folders or individual files. If you specify a folder, you can choose whether to include existing files and subfolders.

Type **cipher** with no parameters to display the encryption state of the current folder and its files.

To encrypt or decrypt a folder or file, include the path and the appropriate switches. Use the /E switch to encrypt the folders or files you specify or the /D switch to decrypt. For example, to encrypt the My Documents folder, including its files and subfolders, type **cipher /e /a /s:"%userprofile%\my documents"** at a command prompt.

In the file specification, you can use wildcards. You can also specify multiple folders and files in a single instance of the command; simply separate each name with a space. Table 14-2 on the next page shows the most commonly used switches for Cipher; for a complete list, type **cipher /?** at a command prompt.

Table 14-2. **Command-Line Switches for Cipher.exe**

Switch	Description
/E	Encrypts the specified folders.
/D	Decrypts the specified folders.
/S:*folder*	Performs the operation on *folder* and its subfolders (but not files).
/A	Performs the operation on specified files and files in specified folders.
/K	Creates a new file encryption key for the user running Cipher. If this option is used, all others are ignored.
/R	Generates a recovery agent key and certificate. The key and certificate are placed in a .pfx file, and the certificate alone is placed in a .cer file.
/U	Updates the user's file encryption key or recovery agent's key on every encrypted file on local drives.
/U /N	Lists every encrypted file on local drives without changing anything.

Creating a Data Recovery Agent

A *data recovery* agent is another user, usually Administrator, that can access your encrypted files. This allows you to recover encrypted files if something happens to your private key.

Microsoft Windows XP does not create a default recovery agent on standalone computers. If you are a member of a domain, the domain administrator is the default recovery agent.

> **note** A data recovery agent can only recover files that are encrypted *after* the recovery certificate is created and the recovery agent is designated, as described in the following sections. The agent won't have access to preexisting encrypted files. That's because when a file is encrypted, EFS uses the public key of the account that's encrypting the file and of each designated recovery agent. Therefore, only the recovery agents whose certificates are installed at the time a file is encrypted can decrypt the file.

To create a data recovery agent you must create a data recovery certificate and then designate a user to be the data recovery agent.

Generating a Recovery Agent Certificate

To generate a recovery agent certificate, follow these steps:

1 Log on as Administrator.

2 At a command prompt, type **cipher /r:*filename***.

3 When prompted, type a password that will be used to protect the files you create.

This generates both a .pfx file and a .cer file with the file name you specify.

> **caution**   These files allow anyone to become a recovery agent. Be sure to copy them to a disk and put it in a secure, safe place. Then erase these files from your hard drive.

Designating Data Recovery Agents

You can designate any user as a data recovery agent. We recommend that you use the Administrator account.

> **note**   Do not designate the account you use to create encrypted files as a recovery agent. Doing so provides little or no protection. If the user profile is damaged or deleted you will lose all the keys that allow decryption of the files.

Follow these steps to designate a data recovery agent:

1 Log on to the account that you want to designate as a data recovery agent.

2 In Certificates (Certmgr.msc), go to Certificates – Current User\Personal.

3 Choose Action, All Tasks, Import to launch the Certificate Import Wizard. Click Next. The File To Import page appears.

Chapter 14

4 Enter the path and file name of the encryption certificate (a .pfx file) you exported and click Next. If you click Browse, you must select Personal Information Exchange in the Files Of Type box to see .pfx files. Click Next.

5 Enter the password for this certificate and then select Mark This Key As Exportable. Click Next.

6 Select Automatically Select The Certificate Store Based On The Type Of Certificate and then click Next. Click Finish.

7 In Local Security Settings (Secpol.msc) go to Security Settings\Public Key Policies\Encrypting File System.

8 Choose Action, Add Data Recovery Agent. Click Next.

9 On the Select Recovery Agents page, click Browse Folders and then navigate to the folder that contains the .cer file that you created. (The Browse Directory button searches Active Directory, a feature of domains based on the Windows 2000 Server and Windows .NET Server families.) Select the file and click Open.

The Select Recovery Agents page now shows the new agent as USER_UNKNOWN. This is normal, because the name is not stored in the file.

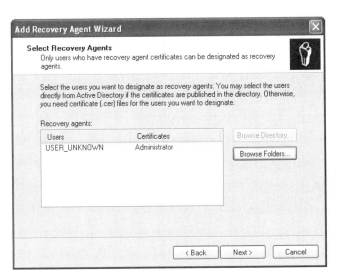

10 Simply click Next and then click Finish.

The current user is now the recovery agent for all encrypted files on this system.

Removing the Private Key

To prevent someone from simply logging on as Administrator and viewing another user's encrypted files, you can export and remove the recovery agent's private key. Keep the key in a secure location—without it you can't use the recovery agent.

To remove the recovery agent's private key, follow these steps:

1 Log on to the account you designated as a recovery agent.

2 In Certificates (Certmgr.msc), under Certificates–Current User, open Personal, Certificates.

3 Right-click the File Recovery certificate (so identified in the Intended Purposes column), and then choose All Tasks, Export to launch the Certificate Export Wizard. Click Next.

4 Select Yes, Export The Private Key, and then click Next.

5 Select Enable Strong Protection and Delete The Private Key If The Export Is Successful. Click Next.

6 Enter a password twice, and then click Next.

7 Specify the path and file name for the exported file.

8 Click Next and then click Finish.

As with the recovery agent certificates, you should copy the file to a removable disk, store it in a secure location, and then remove the file from your hard disk.

The recovery agent's public key is now added to each encrypted file, but because the private key is not available, the recovery agent can't view the files. To reestablish the recovery agent's access to encrypted files, import the private key you just exported, using the same procedure as for importing a personal certificate.

For details, see "Importing a Personal Encryption Certificate," page 549.

Backing Up Your Certificates

When you use encryption for the first time, Windows automatically creates a self-signed certificate for EFS. (*Self-signed* means that it's not granted by a trusted certification authority that can confirm your identity. Such verification is unnecessary for this purpose; it's merely confirming that the certificate was created while your account was logged on.) This certificate becomes your *personal encryption certificate,* and it contains the public/private key pair used for encrypting and decrypting files while you're logged on.

Each user who encrypts files on a system has a personal encryption certificate. In addition, Windows can create a certificate for the designated recovery agent. This certificate, whose purpose is File Recovery, is not the same as that user's personal encryption certificate, whose purpose is shown as Encrypting File System.

All users should have a backup of their personal encryption certificate. More important, the system administrator should have a backup of the recovery agent certificate. Without one or the other, encrypted files are unusable.

Backing Up the Recovery Agent Certificate

The recovery agent certificate provides an administrative alternative for decrypting files if a user's personal encryption certificate is unavailable for any reason. Having a backup of this certificate is essential if you plan to use EFS.

To back up the recovery agent certificate, follow these steps:

1 Log on as a member of the Administrators group.

2 In Local Security Settings (Secpol.msc), go to Security Settings\Public Key Policies\Encrypting File System.

tip If you have an aversion to command prompts, you can open Local Security Settings by going to Control Panel, Performance And Maintenance, Administrative Tools, Local Security Policy.

3 Right-click the certificate issued to Administrator for the purpose of File Recovery, choose All Tasks, Export to launch the Certificate Export Wizard, and then click Next. The Export File Format page opens.

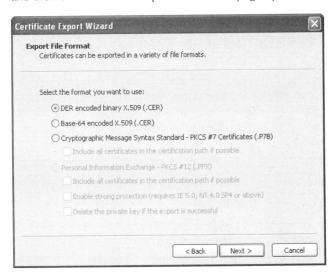

4 Select DER Encoded Binary X.509 (.CER), and then click Next.

5 Specify the path and file name for the exported file.

6 Click Next and then click Finish.

Chapter 14

Exporting a Personal Encryption Certificate

To back up a personal encryption certificate, take these steps:

1 Log on as the user whose certificate you want to back up.

2 On the Content tab of the Internet Options dialog box (in Internet Explorer, choose Tools, Internet Options), click Certificates to open the Certificates dialog box.

> **note** If you prefer, you can use the Certificates snap-in for Microsoft Management Console for this procedure. We chose to open the Certificates dialog box via Internet Options because this route is available and easily understandable to all users; no special privileges are required.

3 On the Personal tab, select the certificate that shows Encrypting File System in the Certificate Intended Purposes box at the bottom of the dialog box.

> **note** Windows creates this certificate the first time you encrypt a folder or file. Unless you have encrypted something—or you created an encryption certificate in some other way—the certificate won't exist.

4 Click Export to launch the Certificate Export Wizard, and then click Next.

5 Select Yes, Export The Private Key, and then click Next two times.

6 Specify a password for the .pfx file. It doesn't need to be the same as your logon password. Click Next.

7 Specify the path and file name for the exported file.

8 Click Next and then click Finish.

As you'll see in the next section, the import process makes it very easy to install your certificate on another computer—and thereby provide access to your encrypted files. For that reason, be careful to observe these guidelines:

- When you export your certificate, be sure to protect it with a password that can't be guessed easily. Unlike the case of logon attempts, no policies exist to prevent further attempts after a certain number of incorrect guesses. (On the other hand, be sure to use a password that *you* can remember when the need arises!)

- Be sure to keep your certificate files—whether they're on a floppy disk, a hard disk, or some other medium—in a secure place.

Importing a Personal Encryption Certificate

You will need to import your personal certificate—one that you exported to disk using the procedure in the preceding section—in either of the following situations:

- You want to use your encrypted files on a different computer.

- Your original personal certificate is accidentally lost or becomes corrupt.

To import a personal encryption certificate, follow these steps:

1 On the Content tab of the Internet Properties dialog box (choose Control Panel, Network And Internet Connections, Internet Options), click Certificates to open the Certificates dialog box.

2 Click Import to launch the Certificate Import Wizard, and then click Next.

3 Enter the path and file name of the encryption certificate (a .pfx file) you exported, and then click Next. If you click Browse, you need to select Personal Information Exchange in the Files Of Type box to see .pfx files.

4 Enter the password, select other options if you want, and then click Next.

5 Select Place All Certificates In The Following Store, click Browse, and then select Personal. Click OK, Next, and then Finish.

Creating a New Personal Encryption Certificate

If you lose your personal encryption certificate, you can create a new one using Cipher.exe, the command-line encryption utility. At a command prompt, simply type **cipher /k**, and it creates a new personal encryption certificate for the user running Cipher. (By using the Runas command to launch Cipher, you can create certificates for other users.) Of course, you can't use the new certificate to decrypt files that were encrypted using the public key from your old certificate.

Recovering Encrypted Files and Folders

The security policy for a computer or a domain includes a data recovery policy. This policy designates one or more users as data recovery agents; these users can decrypt encrypted files even if the personal encryption certificate that was used to encrypt the file is no longer available. This makes it possible to recover encrypted files after an employee leaves a company, for example.

If your computer is not part of a domain, there is no default recovery agent and you should create one, as described earlier in this chapter. In a Windows 2000 Server or Windows .NET Server domain environment, the default recovery agent is the Administrator account for the domain.

If your computer is a member of a domain, the domain administrator can designate additional users as recovery agents. Using the domain's Enterprise Certificate Authority, the domain administrator creates recovery agent certificates for these users and adds them to Public Key Policies\Encrypted Data Recovery Agents in Local Security Settings or, more likely, in the domain security policy.

To restore the recovery agent's file recovery certificate when it's needed, take the following steps:

1   Log on as Administrator.

2   Use the Certificates dialog box to import the file recovery certificate. Use the same procedure as for importing a personal encryption certificate. For details, see "Importing a Personal Encryption Certificate," page 549.

---

note If you don't have a domain with an Enterprise Certificate Authority and you want to use an account other than Administrator as the recovery agent, log on as that user, and then restore Administrator's file recovery certificate to the personal store. Thereafter, any time you log on with that user account, you can work with any encrypted files on the system.

If you're in a situation where you need to recover encrypted files, you need to know which user accounts are authorized to decrypt the files. For a single file, you can view its Encryption Details dialog box, as shown in Figure 14-2 on page 541. (Right-click the file and choose Properties. On the General tab, click Advanced, Details.) To learn about multiple files, you're better off with a command-line utility named Efsinfo.exe, which shows who encrypted each file and who has permission to decrypt it, including any recovery agents. Efsinfo.exe is on the Windows XP CD-ROM in \Support\Tools\ Support.cab; it's not installed by default. In addition to the help generated by typing **efsinfo /?** at a command prompt and the help available in the Help And Support Center, Microsoft Knowledge Base article Q243026 has more information about Efsinfo. A utility called EFSDump, from the good people at Sysinternals, is available at *http://www.sysinternals.com/ntw2k/source/misc.shtml*. Like Efsinfo.exe, EFS Dump shows who encrypted a file and who has access to it.

Disabling or Reenabling EFS

If you want to prevent users from encrypting files on a particular machine, you can disable the Encrypting File System.

> **caution** Disabling EFS not only prevents users from encrypting any additional folders or files, but it also prevents access to existing encrypted files.

To disable EFS on a computer that is not part of a domain, follow these steps:

1 At a command prompt, type **regedit** to open Registry Editor.

2 Open the HKLM\Software\Microsoft\Windows NT\CurrentVersion\EFS key.

3 Choose Edit, New, DWORD Value.

4 Type **EfsConfiguration** as the name for the new value.

5 Double-click the new value and change its value data to 1.

6 Restart the computer.

To reenable EFS, return to the same value and change it to 0.

> **note** Intrepid tweakers might come upon a check box called Allow Users To Encrypt Files Using Encrypting File System (EFS) and assume that clearing it disables EFS. Unfortunately, it has no effect in a workgroup environment. (If you want to check it out for yourself, open Local Security Settings (Secpol.msc), select Public Key Policies, right-click Encrypting File System, and choose Properties.)

If the computer is part of a domain, higher-level policies supersede your settings in Local Security Settings, which controls only the local Group Policy object. If the default domain policy allows the use of EFS, it continues to be available. Of course, by applying the changes to a domain-based policy instead of the local policy, you can disable EFS on all computers to which the policy is applied. *Microsoft Windows 2000 Server Resource Kit* (Microsoft Press, 2000) provides information about EFS in a domain environment.

Best Practices for Safe Encryption

If you don't implement EFS correctly you can undermine your security efforts. For example, your editing program may leave unencrypted temporary files on your drive. Or worse, you can render your encrypted files unusable. To avoid these pitfalls, follow these suggestions:

- Encrypt the My Documents folder and any other local folder you use for storing documents. This ensures that files created by Microsoft Office are encrypted.

- Encrypt the %Temp% and %Tmp% folders. This ensures that any temporary files are encrypted.

- Always encrypt folders, not files. When a folder is encrypted, all files created in that folder are encrypted. Many editing programs save a new copy of the document you are editing. This copy will be encrypted if you encrypt the folder, but it will be plain text if you only encrypt the original file.

- Export and protect the private keys for recovery accounts, and then remove them from the computer. This prevents someone from accessing your files using the recovery agent account.

- Export the personal encryption certificate for each account.

- Don't destroy recovery certificates when you change recovery agent policies. Keep them until you are sure all files that are protected by them have been updated.

- When printing, avoid using spool files, or encrypt the folder in which they are created.

- Secure your paging file so it is overwritten when Windows shuts down. (See the sidebar "Securing the Paging File," page 534.)

Chapter 15

Working with Offline Files and Folders

If you need to take work on the road—even if the road is only your daily commute—you'll appreciate the offline files feature in Microsoft Windows XP Professional. When you make a shared file or folder available for offline use, Windows *caches* (that is, stores temporarily) a copy of that file or folder on the hard disk of your local computer. While you're disconnected from the network, you can work with the copy, exactly as though it were the original. When you reconnect, Windows synchronizes your cached files with their server counterparts, so you have up-to-date versions on both your local machine and the server.

> **note** Throughout this chapter, we use the term *server* to signify the computer on which a shared file or folder resides. That computer might or might not be running one of the server editions of Windows. The features described in this chapter work the same way in a peer-to-peer network setting (such as a typical home or small business network) as in a network that uses one or more domain controllers.

If you've upgraded to Windows XP from Windows 95, Windows 98, or Windows Me, you might be accustomed to using the Briefcase feature in those versions for offline work. You can still use Briefcase. However, if you can choose to use either offline files or Briefcase, choose offline files; the newer feature is both more robust and easier to use. On the other hand, if your traveling computer isn't networked with your stationary computer(s), you don't have the option of using offline files—hence we describe the use of Briefcase later in this chapter.

555

At Home with Windows XP

Unfortunately, the offline files and folders feature is available only in Windows XP Professional. If you use Windows XP Home Edition and travel frequently with your notebook computer, you might consider this sufficient reason to upgrade to Professional. Note that only the traveling machine needs the offline files capability. If your portable computer is networked with one or more homebound computers, with each system running Windows XP Home Edition, upgrading the portable computer to Professional will give you the ability to take files on the road and synchronize them on return, even if the other computers continue to run Home Edition.

For more information about using offline files with the Briefcase, see "Synchronizing Files with Briefcase," page 568.

Even if you don't travel, you might have use for the offline files capability of Windows XP. Offline files can reduce network traffic and ensure continuity on systems that are sometimes disconnected from the network (inadvertently or intentionally). For more information, see "Setting Caching Options on the Server," page 561.

note Windows XP—both Home Edition and Professional—also allows you to mark favorite Internet sites for offline use. By right-clicking an item in your Favorites folder and choosing Make Available Offline from the shortcut menu, you can *subscribe* to the selected site. Windows then downloads current content to your local hard disk and updates the information periodically, according to the synchronization schedule you specify. For more about this form of offline work, see "Making a Favorite Available Offline," page 777.

Setting Up Your System to Use Offline Files

Before you can cache server-based files and folders on your local system, you have to make sure that the offline files feature is enabled on your local computer. And to enable offline files, you must first *disable* Fast User Switching (if that feature is currently enabled). With Fast User Switching disabled, you will need to close any running programs before switching user accounts.

To disable Fast User Switching, open Control Panel, User Accounts, and then select Change The Way Users Log On Or Off. Clear the Use Fast User Switching option. When you no longer need to use offline files, you can return to Control Panel to re-enable Fast User Switching.

Chapter 15: Working with Offline Files and Folders

To enable offline files, open Control Panel, Folder Options (if you're using Category view in Control Panel, Folder Options is in Appearance And Themes); you can also choose Folder Options from the Tools menu in Windows Explorer). On the Offline Files tab of the Folder Options dialog box, make sure that Enable Offline Files is selected. Figure 15-1 shows this dialog box with default settings.

Figure 15-1. The Offline Files tab of the Folder Options dialog box is where you turn on or off your system's ability to use offline files.

Choosing Setup Options

The most crucial option on the Offline Files tab of the Folder Options dialog box is the first check box—the one that turns the entire feature on or off. The remaining options in this dialog box govern such matters as logoff synchronization, encryption of offline files, and maximum cache size.

The second most crucial option is the third check box—Synchronize All Offline Files Before Logging Off. With this check box selected (its default state), Windows performs what it calls a *full synchronization* whenever you log off your user account. This action ensures that whenever you pack up and go, your cached files match the latest server versions. Be aware, though, that you must actually log off (or shut down) to effect this synchronization. If you simply disconnect from the network, or if you hibernate rather than shutting down, Windows doesn't have a chance to synchronize your files.

Troubleshooting

Windows can't synchronize certain files when you log off.

Some types of files cannot be synchronized for offline use, including Microsoft Outlook Personal Folders files (.pst) and files with the .dbf extension, which may be database files or Outlook Express folders. Likewise, if shared files are open (that is, in use by someone else or by another running process) when you synchronize, you'll be unable to synchronize those files. In either case, you'll see the following error message.

To view the names of the files that Windows was unable to synchronize, click the Details button. If the files are not eligible for synchronization, you can either choose not to synchronize those files, or change the file name extension for each file listed in the Details section to one that is not on the prohibited list. If the synchronization attempt was initiated by your logging off, you'll have no choice but to complete the logoff after dismissing the error message. But if the unsynchronized files are ones you'll need while you're away and they were simply skipped because the files were open, you might want to log back on, arrange to have the files closed (find out who's using them and ask them to desist momentarily), and then log off again.

If the option to synchronize at logoff is not selected, you'll get what Windows calls a *partial synchronization*. This means that Windows caches a copy of a server-based file or folder when you mark it "Make Available Offline." (For details, see "Making Files and Folders Available Offline," on the facing page.) Thus, when you head for the road you'll have *something* to work with—but it might not be the latest version available. So if your purpose in enabling offline files is to take current work with you, select Synchronize All Offline Files Before Logging Off (or get in the habit of manually synchronizing all files before you leave).

The option to synchronize all offline files when you log back on (the second check box in Figure 15-1 on the previous page) is clear by default. Leaving the option in this state gives you the chance to continue working with the offline versions of your files when you return to the office. When you're ready, you can synchronize manually by choosing Tools, Synchronize in Windows Explorer. If this isn't what you want—that is, if you want Windows to synchronize automatically when you reconnect—select the second check box.

For more information about synchronizing manually, see "Synchronizing on Demand, on Idle, or on Schedule," page 565.

If Display A Reminder Every is selected, Windows displays balloon messages in the notification area at periodic intervals when your system is disconnected from the network. You might find this notification useful if you occasionally become disconnected from your network without realizing it. Otherwise, it's likely to be a nuisance—for example, when you are traveling and know you're offline. Clear the check box if you don't fancy balloons.

When you use offline files, Windows creates a special system folder called Offline Files. You can get to this folder by clicking View Files in the Folder Options dialog box. If you want a desktop shortcut to the folder as well, select Create An Offline Files Shortcut On The Desktop.

If you carry sensitive information on your laptop, you might want to select Encrypt Offline Files To Secure Data. That way, only your own user account will be able to read the cached data. Be aware that many programs (such as Microsoft Word) create temporary files as you work. These files would not be encrypted. The program creating the temporary files would also delete them in the course of your normal work, but the temporary data would remain in an unencrypted form on your hard disk. To maximize security while you work with encrypted offline information, you should also use Windows Explorer to encrypt the folders where temporary files are stored. You can open these folders in Windows Explorer by choosing Start, Run and typing %Temp% or %Tmp%.

For more details about encrypting files and folders, see Chapter 14, "Encrypting Confidential Information."

Windows allocates 10 percent of your local hard disk, by default, for use in caching offline files. You can adjust this setting upward or downward.

Making Files and Folders Available Offline

After you have set up your computer for offline files, you make individual files and folders available for offline use by right-clicking them in Windows Explorer and choosing Make Available Offline. You select files and folders that reside on the server computer while working from the *client* computer (the one that will go offline), not the server. For example, in Figure 15-2 on the next page, we've marked the folder \\Craig2000\DDocs\Miranda for offline use by navigating to that network folder in My Network Places from the client computer.

Figure 15-2. To make a file or folder available offline, right-click it from the computer that will go offline, and then select Make Available Offline.

When you mark a folder for offline use, Windows caches all files in the folder. If the folder has subfolders, you'll be asked whether you want to cache those as well. Windows then performs a synchronization on the selected items—that is, it creates copies in the client computer's cache. Icons for cached folders and files thereafter appear in Windows Explorer with a double arrow, as shown here.

tip **Choose a larger icon size to distinguish shortcuts and cached items**

Because Windows uses the lower left corner of folder and file icons for both the single-arrow shortcut symbol and the double arrow cached item symbol, shortcuts and cached items look essentially alike in Windows Explorer's List and Details views. Try Icons or Tiles view if you have trouble telling them apart.

Working Offline

While you're offline, you can work with cached folders and files, exactly as if you were online. You can navigate to those items in My Network Places or My Computer, or you can access the files and folders from within your application in the customary ways. In Windows Explorer, you will see the cached folders and their parent folders, but not uncached "siblings." For example, in Figure 15-3, the folder Miranda is visible in \\Craig2000\DDocs, because we marked it for offline use (see Figure 15-2). The sibling folder Writing is also visible, but its icon does not bear the telltale double arrow. That's because one of Writing's subfolders is marked for offline use, but Writing itself is not.

Chapter 15: Working with Offline Files and Folders

Offline
files

As a reminder of the fact that you're disconnected, Windows displays an "offline" icon
in the notification area. You can double-click that icon to read status information.

Figure 15-3.   While you work offline, Windows Explorer shows only the folders that
you've cached, along with their parent folders.

Setting Caching Options on the Server

All discussion of the behavior of offline files and folders so far in this chapter has
assumed that the caching property of each network share accessed for offline work
is set at its default value. This value, called Manual Caching Of Documents, is one of
three possible settings. To adjust the caching property, do the following on the server
computer:

1 Type **\fsmgmt.msc** at a command prompt. This runs the Shared Folders management console.

2 In the console tree (the left pane), select Shares.

3 In the details pane (the right pane), right-click the share whose property you
want to set and then choose Properties.

4 On the General tab of the properties dialog box, click Caching. The Caching
Settings dialog box opens, as shown in Figure 15-4 on the next page.

note   The Properties dialog box for a shared folder is not available if you're using Simple
File Sharing. To turn Simple File Sharing off, choose Tools, Folder Options in Windows
Explorer. On the View tab, clear Use Simple File Sharing (Recommended). For more
information about Simple File Sharing, see "Simple File Sharing vs. Windows 2000–
Style Sharing," page 98.

Part 3: Managing Files

Figure 15-4. You can use this dialog box to control caching behavior for a network share.

The default setting, Manual Caching Of Documents, stipulates that only those files and folders explicitly marked Make Available Offline are cached. When you choose Make Available Offline on the client computer, you are guaranteed that the selected item will be available offline. This is the setting you want to use when you take work out of the office on a portable computer.

Disabling Automatic Caching on Particular Computers

If you use automatic caching as a means of maintaining continuity in an environment where network connections are sometimes broken, you can disable this functionality on particular client computers. You might want to do this, for example, if a particular user needs to know when the network is down. Follow these steps to disable automatic caching on a client:

1 Choose Tools, Options in Windows Explorer.

2 On the Offline Files tab, click Advanced.

3 In the Offline Files – Advanced Settings dialog box, select Never Allow My Computer To Go Offline.

Alternatively, in this same dialog box, you can disable offline work only when connections to particular servers are broken.

4 Select the option Notify Me And Begin Working Offline, and then add particular servers to the exception list.

5 Add specific servers by clicking Add to open the Add Custom Action dialog box.

6 Type or browse to the name of each computer you do *not* want to cache for offline work and select the option Never Allow My Computer To Go Offline.

Chapter 15

The alternative settings for the caching property are Automatic Caching Of Documents and Automatic Caching Of Programs.

Using Automatic Caching Of Documents

When Automatic Caching Of Documents is selected, Windows caches a server-based file or folder automatically as soon as you access it from the client computer. When you open a cached document from a client computer, the cached copy is used, but the original document on the server is also opened to prevent other people from changing the file while you have it open.

Because it doesn't require the separate step of copying a server resource into your cache, automatic caching is more convenient and easier to use than the default manual caching. On the other hand, with automatic caching, Windows doesn't guarantee that your server resources remain in the cache. How long they stay there, in fact, depends on usage. As the amount of disk space you've allocated to the cache is consumed, Windows discards any documents that have not been used recently to make room for newer ones.

Using Automatic Caching Of Programs

You can use the Automatic Caching Of Programs And Documents setting for folders that contain programs and documents that are read but not changed. (In fact, you should restrict permissions on such folders to read-only.) Automatic caching of programs can speed up access to programs and documents, because after a file is cached, your system does not have to retrieve it from the server again; only the local copy is opened.

Turning Off Caching for a Specific Share

You can turn the offline files feature off on a per-share basis. To disable caching for a share, clear Allow Caching Of Files In This Shared Folder, in the Caching Settings dialog box (see Figure 15-4).

How Windows Synchronizes Your Files

By default, your offline files and folders are synchronized when you log off your account and synchronized again when you log back on. This means that your work is current when you leave the office, and your server is brought up to date when you return. When you synchronize, Windows XP performs the following operations for each offline file:

- If you have changed the file while offline and the server-based copy has not been changed, Windows updates the server copy with your changes.

- If you have not made changes to your offline copy but the server copy has been changed, Windows updates the copy in your cache.

- If both the server copy and your offline copy have changed, a dialog box appears, as shown in Figure 15-5. You can keep your client version, the server version, or both. (Click the View buttons if you're not sure.)

Figure 15-5. When synchronization reveals file conflicts between server and cache, you can keep either version—or both.

- If either the offline copy or the server copy of a file is deleted, the file on the other computer is deleted as well, as long as it wasn't changed while you were offline.

- If the server copy has been deleted and you changed your offline copy, a dialog box appears. You can save your version on the server or delete your offline copy.

- If you delete your version and the server copy has been changed, a dialog box asks whether you want to delete the server copy or use the server copy. If you decide to use the server copy, the server version appears in your offline cache.

- If a new file has been added on the server to a folder that you have marked for offline availability, that new file is copied to your cache.

Synchronizing on Demand, on Idle, or on Schedule

The default logoff/logon synchronization scheme ensures that work is current when you leave the office and when you return. For most users, this is all the synchronization that's needed. You can, however, have Windows synchronize at other times as well. To do so, choose Start, All Programs, Accessories, Synchronize. Or choose Tools, Synchronize in Windows Explorer. The Items To Synchronize dialog box (also known as the Synchronization Manager) appears, as shown in Figure 15-6.

Figure 15-6. You can use this dialog box to schedule a synchronization.

To synchronize immediately, select the items you want to synchronize and click Synchronize. For other options, click Setup. The Synchronization Settings dialog box, shown in Figure 15-7 on the next page, has three tabs. Use the Logon/Logoff tab to fine-tune the way Windows synchronizes at these critical times. Use the other two tabs to set up synchronization when your computer is idle or at other scheduled times.

Figure 15-7. The Synchronization Settings dialog box includes a check box that allows you to request a confirmation prompt before synchronization occurs.

> **tip** By selecting Ask Me Before Synchronizing The Items in the Synchronization Settings dialog box, you can ensure that Windows never synchronizes files without your permission.

Managing the Cache

Windows maintains a system folder that lists all the server-based files you've made available to yourself for offline use. The Offline Files folder, shown in Figure 15-8, also includes information about the synchronization status of each file, the permissions associated with each file, the location of each file's server counterpart, whether the server is currently online or offline, and so on. Files that are stored on servers set for manual caching (see "Setting Caching Options on the Server," page 561) are identified as Always Available Offline. Those that reside on shares set for automatic caching are identified as Temporarily Available Offline. You can launch a cached item (open a document in its parent application, for example) by double-clicking it in the Offline Files folder.

Chapter 15: Working with Offline Files and Folders

Figure 15-8. The Offline Files folder shows the status of each offline file.

> **tip** If you don't have a desktop shortcut for the Offline Files folder, you can get to it by choosing Tools, Folder Options in Windows Explorer. Click the Offline Files tab and then click View Files.

Increasing or Decreasing the Maximum Cache Size

By default, Windows prevents the cache size from exceeding 10 percent of the size of the partition on which Windows is installed. You can increase or decrease that amount by dragging the slider on the Offline Files tab of the Folder Options dialog box (shown in Figure 15-1 on page 557). You cannot move or extend the cache to another partition, however.

Deleting Files from the Cache

When you no longer need offline access to a network resource, return to that resource in My Computer or My Network Places, right-click the item in question, and clear Make Available Offline. If the share involved is set for manual caching (see "Setting Caching Options on the Server," page 561), Windows purges the items from your cache in addition to turning off offline access. If the share is set for automatic caching, items that are currently in the cache remain there. To delete them, choose Tools, Options in Windows Explorer and then click the Offline Files tab. In the Folder Options dialog box (shown in Figure 15-1 on page 557), click Delete Files. Then select the shares whose items you want to delete.

Synchronizing Files with Briefcase

Briefcase allows you to create copies of files for offline use and subsequently synchronize those files with their online originals. It's not as easy to use as offline files, but it's the tool you need if you don't have a local area network connection between your portable and desktop computers.

To use Briefcase with removable media, follow these steps:

1 Put a disk (preferably freshly formatted) in a removable disk drive of the machine that holds the files you want to use offline (your desktop machine, most likely).

2 Open the removable disk in Windows Explorer.

3 Right-click in the removable disk's folder and choose New, Briefcase.

4 Rename the briefcase (an optional step, but you'll want to do this if you use more than one briefcase at a time).

5 Open the briefcase (it's a folder, almost like any other) and then close the dialog box that appears.

6 Copy files into your new briefcase until the removable disk is somewhat less than full. Don't fill the disk, because you need room for your files to grow as you work with them.

7 Insert the removable disk in your portable computer, and move or copy the briefcase to the portable's hard disk. (Move or copy the briefcase *folder,* not the individual files in the briefcase.)

8 Repeat these steps for as many removable disks as you need, giving each briefcase a unique name.

9 Upon returning to your desktop computer, copy each briefcase on your portable machine to a removable disk, and then transfer the disk's contents to your desktop computer.

10 To synchronize, open a briefcase and then choose Briefcase, Update All. (The Briefcase menu appears on the Windows Explorer menu only when a briefcase folder is selected.) To synchronize only particular files, select Details view, select the files you want to synchronize, and then choose Briefcase, Update Selection.

Chapter 15: Working with Offline Files and Folders

Getting Status Information About Briefcase Files

In Windows Explorer Details view, Briefcase provides useful information about the origin and status of your documents. As Figure 15-9 shows, the Status column shows which files are current and which need updating. The Sync Copy In column tells where the original version of each file is stored.

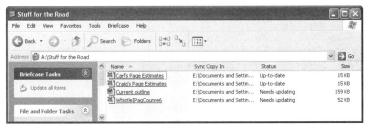

Figure 15-9. Columns in Windows Explorer show which briefcase files need updating and where each file's original version resides.

When your briefcase is online with the computer where it was created, you can also get status information about a particular file by right-clicking it, choosing Properties, and viewing the Update Status tab. Figure 15-10, for example, shows the status for a file that has been changed in the briefcase.

Figure 15-10. The properties dialog box for a briefcase file can tell you which version of the file is more current.

569

Synchronizing Files

When you're ready to synchronize your briefcase files with their originals, you can either work with one file at a time or update the whole briefcase at once. To update a single file, select it and choose Briefcase, Update Selection. To update the whole briefcase, choose Briefcase, Update All (or click its toolbar equivalent). You'll see an update dialog box similar to the one shown in Figure 15-11.

Figure 15-11. When you choose Update All from the Windows Explorer Briefcase menu, the arrows in this dialog box show you which versions of your files need updating.

The arrows in the center of the dialog box can point in either direction, depending on which versions of your files are changed and which need updating. When you click Update, Windows copies the changed version, no matter where it resides, over the unchanged one. If both files have been modified, the default action is not to update either. If a file was deleted in one location, it will be copied to the other location to replace the deleted file.

If the update action that Briefcase proposes for an item isn't the action you want, right-click its entry in the Update dialog box and then choose the action you prefer.

Separating a Briefcase File from Its Sync Copy

If you move a file from a briefcase to any other folder, the link between that file and its original version is broken. The result is an ordinary copy. You can also sever the link between a file and its sync copy without removing it from the briefcase. To do this, select the file and then choose Briefcase, Split From Original. In Briefcase's Status column, the file will then be listed as an "orphan."

Part 4

Mastering Digital Media

Chapter 16

Customizing Windows Media Player

Microsoft Windows Media Player version 8 is an all-in-one client for rendering digital media. You can use it to play sound and video files in a wide variety of formats, as well as audio and video content streamed from Internet sites. You can use it to listen to home-town radio stations (or other radio stations from all parts of the world) and (if you have a properly configured DVD drive) play your favorite movies. You can *rip* tracks from audio CDs (that is, copy them to your hard disk), create your own custom CDs (if you have a CD-R or CD-RW drive), and download songs to your portable audio player. You can use Windows Media Player as a jukebox to play all your favorite songs, in custom sequences that you devise or in random order.

Windows Media Player is also designed to serve as a gateway to media-related sites on the Internet. If you click Media Guide in Media Player's taskbar (the vertical panel of options at the left edge of the Media Player window), Windows Media Player becomes a special-purpose Web browser, focused initially on *http://www.windowsmedia.com*, an Internet "magazine" that provides access to all manner of news and entertainment content, as shown in Figure 16-1 on the next page. You can use links on this site to watch news clips, listen to music, check out previews of current movies, and, of course, purchase various kinds of media items. The content of WindowsMedia.com changes regularly. If you like to keep up with what's going on in the entertainment world, a daily visit to WindowsMedia.com is not a bad way to start. (You can also go there via Internet Explorer, of course.)

At Home with Windows XP

Windows Media Player works identically in Windows XP Home Edition and Professional. All the information in this chapter applies equally to both versions.

Figure 16-1. Windows Media Player's Media Guide (*http://www.windowsmedia.com*) is an Internet magazine, updated regularly, where you can browse, listen, watch, and buy.

Even more than most other programs you use, Windows Media Player is a highly customizable application. There's no need to stick with the standard rectangular windows when you're running Media Player. In its "full" mode, you can make the window frame and menu bar disappear, giving the program a sleek and curvy appearance. (You can also suppress other elements of the standard user interface, as we'll see later in the chapter.) If you switch to skin mode, you can change Media Player's appearance utterly by choosing from many custom visual designs, known as *skins*. Figure 16-2 shows Windows Media Player in full mode without frame and menu bar, and Figure 16-3 shows Media Player wearing the Windows XP skin. The program is playing the same audio track in both guises; all that's changed is its appearance.

tip **Skip the magazine**

By default, Windows Media Player goes straight to its Media Guide (WindowsMedia.com) each time you launch the program. This behavior can cause a delay if you have a slow Internet connection, or if you're not connected all the time. To turn it off, choose Tools, Options. On the Media Player tab, clear Start Player In Media Guide.

> **note** If you don't see Windows Media Player's menu bar because it has the appearance shown in Figure 16-2, press Alt. If Windows Media Player is currently in skin mode, press Ctrl+1 to return it to full mode. Then press Alt if necessary.

Figure 16-2. In full mode, you can eliminate Windows Media Player's frame and menu bar.

Figure 16-3. You can choose from a variety of supplied skins, download others, or even create your own.

Troubleshooting

Windows Media Player does not connect to Media Guide or to the Windows Media online artist information database.

If you find you never connect to WindowsMedia.com and that Windows Media Player is consistently unable to download track information for your CDs, even when you know you have a functioning Internet connection, you might have inadvertently set the program to stay offline. To see if this is the case, open the File menu. If Work Offline is checked, choose this command to clear the check mark and go back online.

You can also customize Windows Media Player's behavior in a variety of ways. Some of your customizing decisions have a major impact on the quality of your experience with Media Player—your choice of file format to use when copying audio tracks from CDs to hard disk, for example. Because of this, we will focus on customization in this chapter and will defer the details about using Windows Media Player—playing tracks, burning CDs, watching movies, and so on—to Chapter 17, "Using Windows Media Player."

Controlling File Type Associations

The check boxes shown in Figure 16-4 identify the types of media files that Windows Media Player can render. To get to this list, choose Tools, Options, and click the File Types tab. When you highlight an item in this list, the Description section of the dialog box enumerates the file name extensions that make up the selected file type. Check boxes that are selected in this list denote file types for which Windows Media Player is the default application. (A gray check box indicates a file type for which another program, at one time, has been registered as the default application.) If Windows Media Player is the default application for a file type, double-clicking a file of that type in Windows Explorer (or a shortcut to such a file) launches Windows Media Player, which in turn plays the file.

This file type includes files with these extensions

The gray check box indicates this file type was previously configured to launch a different player

Figure 16-4. The File Types tab in the Options dialog box lists the kinds of media files that Windows Media Player can render.

As you see, the list of file types is extensive. Not quite everything that moves or plays is there (RealAudio and QuickTime formats are notable absentees), but a great many media formats are represented.

Because the software market is well supplied with inexpensive (and in some cases free) alternatives to Windows Media Player, it's quite possible that you have other programs that can also play some of these file types. If you do use more than one media player, you'll want to decide which kinds of files should open by default with which applications. That task is not always as easy as it sounds—left to their default settings, most media players try to attach themselves to as many file types as they can handle, and the most aggressive programs include features that allow them to "reclaim" associations when another player comes along. If you want to split media-playing duties between two programs, with each one assigned to what it does best, you may need to adjust the settings for each one carefully.

If you install another media player after setting up Windows XP, it's possible that the other player will have taken over some of the file types that were originally associated with Windows Media Player. (Similarly, if you installed Windows XP as an upgrade on a computer where you had previously configured another media playing program, Windows Media Player might have assumed control over one or more of those file types, as indicated by a gray check box like the one shown in Figure 16-4.) To reinstate Windows Media Player as the default application for one or more formats, choose Tools, Options, click the File Types tab, and reselect the appropriate check boxes. Alternatively, if Windows Media Player is currently the default application for file types that you would rather play back in a different media player, you'll need to take care of the problem by adjusting options in the other player.

Changing the Default Application for Individual File Extensions

The media formats listed in Media Player's Options dialog box shown in Figure 16-4 represent types of files; some of these file types use more than one file name extension to identify themselves. The Windows Media Audio (WMA) file type, for example, uses the extensions .wma and .wax. If you change Windows Media Player's behavior by selecting or clearing a check box in the Options dialog box, you are, in most cases, changing the default application for several file name extensions.

To change the default program for a particular extension, you might need to use Windows Explorer. Follow these steps:

1 In any Windows Explorer window, locate a file with the extension whose default application you want to modify.

2 Right-click the file and choose Open With.

3 In the Open With dialog box, select the program you want to use as the default for this file name extension.

4 Select Always Use The Selected Program To Open This Kind Of File and then click OK.

Chapter 16

577

newfeature! Changing the AutoPlay Behavior for a CD or DVD Drive

Normally, Windows prompts you to choose an action each time you insert a CD or DVD—your options might include displaying the contents of the CD in Windows Explorer, playing an audio CD or DVD in Windows Media Player or another application, or transferring digital photos to your My Pictures folder. The menu that appears when you insert a CD is dynamic, and its choices are determined by the content on the CD and the applications installed on your computer. When you insert an audio CD, for instance, Windows offers you the choice of playing the CD with each of your installed media player programs that has registered itself as being capable of playing music CDs. To change the default program for a particular type of content and avoid seeing this dialog box in the future, follow these steps:

1 Open My Computer.

2 Right-click the icon for your CD or DVD drive, choose Properties, and then click the AutoPlay tab.

3 In the list at the top of the dialog box, shown in Figure 16-5, select a disc type. (In the figure, we've selected Music CD. Other options include Pictures, Video Files, Mixed Content, and DVD Movie.)

Figure 16-5. You can specify the action you want Windows to take when you insert particular kinds of discs into your CD or DVD drive.

4 In the Actions section of the dialog box, select the action that you want Windows to take when you insert a disc of the selected content type. If you want to preserve your options every time you insert a particular type of disc, select Prompt Me Each Time To Choose An Action.

5 Click OK.

newfeature!

Understanding and Protecting Your Digital Rights

Windows Media Player is designed to deal gracefully with licensed media files—that is, digital content whose use is governed by a licensing agreement with the content provider. The license associated with a file, which protects the provider against illegal distribution of the media item, specifies how you can use the file and for what period of time. The terms of the license are determined by the content vendor.

When you download a media item—a song or a movie clip, for instance—from the Internet, the content provider might provide you with a license. Alternatively, if you play an unlicensed file that requires a license, Windows Media Player tries to obtain the license. You might have to register or pay for the license at this time.

> **note** If you want to avoid acquiring licensed media, choose Tools, Options. On the Media Player tab in the Options dialog box, clear Acquire Licenses Automatically.

In some cases, a license will allow you to play the media item for an indefinite period of time but only on the computer on which the item was obtained. In other cases, a license will expire after some period of time but allow the item to be copied or moved to other computers (but not necessarily to CDs). If the protected content originated on a CD (that is, if you copied protected content from a CD to your hard disk), you typically are permitted to copy the content onto another CD but not to other computers. Copying to SDMI-compliant portable devices is typically restricted by the same terms that apply to the use of the item on the computer where it was downloaded. (SDMI stands for Secure Digital Music Initiative, a forum that seeks to establish technology specifications for protecting the property rights of digital content providers. For more information, see *http://www.sdmi.org*.)

You can find out what the terms of an item's license are by examining the item's properties dialog box. Locate the file in Windows Explorer (usually you'll find it in My Music), right-click it, choose Properties from the shortcut menu, and click the License tab. Figure 16-6 on the next page shows the License tab for a downloaded music file. Alternatively, if the file is included in your Windows Media Player Media Library, you can right-click it there, choose Properties, and click the License Information tab. The same information appears in both places.

Chapter 16

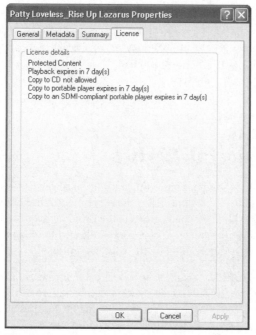

Figure 16-6. You can read the terms of a media item's license by displaying its properties dialog box, either in Windows Explorer or in Media Player's Media Library.

If you have bought licenses for items that allow you to play the items for an indefinite period of time on your own computer, that doesn't mean you can never move the media items to another computer. You can move them (giving up your privileges on the current computer, of course), but only if you have backed up your licenses. When you move the media to a new computer, you restore the licenses on the new computer.

caution Microsoft allows you to restore your licenses on a maximum of four unique computers. If you reformat your hard disk and reinstall Windows XP, Microsoft considers the new installation to be a new unique computer.

Backing Up Your Licenses

To back up all of your media licenses, follow these steps in Windows Media Player:

1 Choose Tools, License Management.

2 In the License Management dialog box, shown in Figure 16-7, click Browse and then specify a location for your backup. You might want to create at least one backup on a removable medium.

3 Click Backup Now.

Chapter 16

Figure 16-7. If you have digital licenses, back them up! Otherwise you could lose your media collection when you move to a new computer.

Restoring Your Licenses

To restore your licenses, follow these steps:

1 Choose Tools, License Management.

2 In the License Management dialog box, shown in Figure 16-7, click Restore Now. The following appears.

Restoring sends to Microsoft a globally unique identifier (GUID) that enables Microsoft to track how many times you restore your licenses. The company does this to discourage illicit replication of licensed files. (To read more about what information about your computer Windows Media Player might send over the Internet, click the Learn More button.)

3 Click OK.

581

newfeature!

Configuring Windows Media Player to Copy Music from CDs

Windows Media Player can copy, or rip, tracks from audio CDs and store them as WMA files on your hard disk. Before you start ripping, however, answer the following questions:

- Should you use copy protection or not?
- At what bit rate should you copy?
- Where should your files be stored, and what naming convention do you want to use?

Windows Media Player copies CD tracks, by default, into your My Music folder (%UserProfile%\My Documents\My Music). Windows organizes tracks into sub-folders, with a folder for each artist and a subfolder for each album by that artist. If you don't have enough room on the disk where that folder resides, you can choose an alternative location before you start copying. Windows Media Player automatically keeps track of the locations of your media files, even if you move them in Windows Explorer after adding them to the media library; as a result, you can always change your mind about file locations, and you won't have to rebuild your media library if you decide eventually to move the whole library to another drive. You should give some consideration in advance to the naming convention that Windows Media Player will use, however.

Deciding Whether to Use Copy Protection

You can copy CD tracks to your hard disk with or without copy protection. On a fresh installation of Windows XP, copy protection is enabled. When you rip a track from a CD, Windows Media Player records a license for each track that prevents you from playing the track on another computer or copying it to an SDMI-compliant portable device. (The license does not prevent you from copying tracks back to your own custom CDs, however.) For the average music lover, these restrictions are an unnecessary hassle, and you will probably find it more convenient to copy your CDs without such protection. To turn copy protection off, choose Tools, Options. On the Copy Music tab, clear Protect Content.

If you didn't choose to clear Protect Content on the Options menu, you will see the following notice the first time you copy a CD:

Make your choice and then click OK to start copying.

Choosing a Bit Rate for Your WMA Files

Files copied from audio CDs to your hard disk must be compressed, or each CD you copy will consume more than half a gigabyte of disk space. Algorithms used to compress audio (and video) files are *lossy*, which means that they achieve compression by eliminating expendable data. In the case of audio files, the expendable data consists mostly of frequencies that humans don't ordinarily hear.

InsideOut

You can't copy a CD track directly to your hard drive from Windows Explorer. If you right-click an audio CD and choose Explore from the shortcut menu, you'll see that each track is listed as a small file with the .cda extension. CDA is not a file format; instead, these pointers serve as shortcuts to the actual files, which are stored in a format that is essentially identical to a WAV file. If you want to make a perfect copy of a single music track or an entire CD, you need software that can reliably extract every bit of digital information from the disc, without allowing any data to be lost through compression. Most commercial CD-burning software includes the capability to copy CDs directly; although the copies usually include errors that are mostly imperceptible to the human ear. Perfectionists who want to extract audio from CDs without any errors should look at a program called Exact Audio Copy, written by Andre Wiethoff and available for download from *http://www.exactaudiocopy.de*.

What Happened to MP3?

Windows Media Player, as shipped with Windows XP, does not create MP3 files from CD audio tracks. It does, however, play any MP3 files that you might have or obtain, without sacrificing fidelity, and it does support the addition of MP3 encoders from third parties.

The WMA format supported by Windows Media Player achieves audio quality equivalent to that of MP3 at much higher compression. A CD track encoded via WMA will use no more than half the disk space of an MP3 file of comparable quality (in some cases, the size of the WMA file is closer to one third the size of the equivalent MP3).

If you need to generate MP3 files from CD tracks you can download an MP3 Creation Pack for Windows XP from Cyberlink Corporation, InterVideo, Inc., or Ravisent Technologies, Inc. These third-party add-ins can create MP3 files at bit rates of up to 320 Kbps, and the cost is extremely low (typically $10). To find one of these products, choose Tools, Options. On the Copy Music tab, click MP3 Information.

The MP3 Information and Compare buttons on the Copy Music tab in the Options dialog box, shown in Figure 16-8, are links to Microsoft Web sites where you can find additional information about the relative strengths and weaknesses of MP3 and WMA.

Choosing a bit rate for your copied files means deciding how much compression you want. Higher bit rates preserve more of the original sound quality of your audio tracks but result in larger files on your hard disk or portable player. Windows Media Player provides the following file copying options.

Bit Rate (Kbps)	Approximate File Size per CD (MB)
48	22
64	28
96	42
128	56
160	69
192	86

What bit rate is best for you? It depends on how big your disk is (and how many CDs you intend to copy), how much you care about preserving the full spectrum of sound recorded on your CD, and the quality of your playback equipment. An additional consideration is whether you intend to copy the tracks to a portable music device with limited storage; choosing a lower bit rate means you can pack more songs onto the device. For most users and typical computer speakers, 64 kilobits per second is the minimum acceptable choice, allowing for generally good audio quality at little expense of disk space.

Microsoft describes the quality achieved at 48 Kbps as "near-CD," claiming CD quality for all the other bit rates. If you're a discerning audiophile with high-quality playback equipment, you will almost certainly take issue with those claims and choose the minimum acceptable audio quality by performing comparative testing with your own ears and speakers.

To express your preference regarding bit rate, choose Tools, Options, and click the Copy Music tab. Then use the Copy Music At This Quality slider, shown in Figure 16-8. Moving the slider to the left produces smaller files; moving it to the right produces better quality.

Figure 16-8. Use this slider to make your selection for balancing file size and sound quality.

Deciding How to Name Your Files and Where to Store Them

By default, Windows Media Player stores CD tracks in My Music, a subfolder of My Documents. If you decide you want to store your media library in a different location, choose Tools, Options. On the Copy Music tab, shown in Figure 16-8, click Change. This capability is useful if you share a home computer with other family members and want everyone to have access to the same music library. If your songs are stored in your personal profile and you make your profile private, other users will be unable to access the tunes. In this case, move the files to the Shared Documents\Shared Music folder instead.

If you are online when you copy a CD, Windows Media Player connects to the Windows Media online database and gets whatever information is available about that CD.

Typically, that includes the names of songs and performers, album names, information about musical genres, and album art. Windows Media Player uses some of this information to create file names for your copied CD tracks. (All of the information Media Player gets from this online repository of information can be used in one way or another, even if it doesn't become part of your file names. The album art, for example, appears in Windows Explorer when you use Thumbnails view. For more information about the Windows Media online database and the Media Library, see "Viewing Media Information and Album Art," page 600.)

By default, the file names for your tracks are made up of the track number followed by a space character followed by the song title (which probably includes spaces). Such a file name might look like this:

03 I Do It For Your Love.wma

In Windows Explorer's Tiles view, a folder of CD tracks named by this convention might look like the one shown in Figure 16-9. Notice that Windows Explorer displays the artist and album title in gray below the track number and song title. This additional information, which is not part of the file name, is recorded as metadata associated with the media file. These details and others also appear in Media Player's Media Library, if you add a song to the library, and in Windows Explorer's Details view. In Windows Explorer you can control the categories of additional information that appear by choosing View, Choose Details and selecting or clearing check boxes in the Choose Details dialog box, shown in Figure 16-10.

Because Windows Explorer (and Media Player's Media Library) can display so much information about a media file by means of its metadata, it's not vital that you include a lot of detail in the actual file name. Using the track number as the beginning of the file name ensures that the tracks on an album always sort correctly, even when copied to another drive, device, or media-playing program. However, if you copy a song to a portable player, the portable player will probably display only the file name. Therefore,

Figure 16-9. In Tiles view, Windows Explorer displays metadata in gray beneath file names. This information (and more) also appears in Details view.

Figure 16-10. You can use the Choose Details dialog box to specify what kind of metadata you want to see in Windows Explorer.

when you choose a file naming convention in Windows Media Player, give some thought to how your files will look in the tiny LCD display of your portable. In that context, the most important information is probably the song name, followed perhaps by the album name; you might not need the track number at all.

In any event, you can tell Media Player how you want your files named as follows:

1 Choose Tools, Options, and click the Copy Music tab.

2 Click Advanced to open the File Name Options dialog box.

3 Select the check boxes for the information categories that you want to include in your file names, and clear the other check boxes.

4 If desired, use the Move Up and Move Down buttons to change the order in which name elements appear.

5 Use the Separator list to change the character that appears between name elements, if you don't want spaces. Your alternatives are dashes, dots, and underlines. The Preview area shows how the names will appear.

6 Click OK.

caution If Windows Media Player cannot identify your CD tracks by accessing the Windows Media online database, it uses generic names such as Unknown Album, Unknown Artist, and Track 1. To keep your files recognizable in Windows Explorer and Media Player's Media Library, do not accept these generic names. Edit the track information *before* Windows Media Player begins copying tracks and creating disk files. For more information, see "What to Do if Windows Media Doesn't Recognize Your Disc," page 605. If you've already ripped some tracks with these generic names, you can use the Media Library Management Wizard (one of the Windows Media Player PowerToys) to add album art, album title, and track details. See "Managing Your Media Library," page 609, for more details.

newfeature!
Customizing Windows Media Player's Appearance

Even without putting on a skin, you can do a great many things to modify Media Player's appearance. You can switch between a normal windowed view with menu bar and the irregularly shaped menu-less form, shown in Figure 16-2 on page 575. You can display or hide the taskbar (the vertical panel at the left). In Now Playing, you can display or hide the current playlist and switch between a windowed display and a frameless full-screen display. And you can display any of Media Player's many visualizations while your music plays. (*Visualizations* are animated designs that Windows Media Player can display while playing music.)

For more information about visualizations, see "Using Visualizations," page 591.

Figure 16-11 shows the controls that allow you to modify Media Player's appearance with your mouse while Windows Media Player is running in full (not skin) mode.

Figure 16-11. Mouse controls allow you to change Windows Media Player's appearance while the program is running in full mode.

Toggling the Menu Bar

Menu
bar

The menu bar toggle lets you switch between a normal windowed display and an irregularly shaped display that eliminates Media Player's menu bar and title bar. As an alternative to clicking this button, you can choose View, Full Mode Options, and then choose Show Menu Bar, Hide Menu Bar, or Auto Hide Menu Bar. If you choose Auto Hide, the menu bar is hidden until you put your mouse in the area where the menu bar would otherwise be. If you like the frameless look, you'll probably find this the most convenient way to implement it.

Toggling Shuffle Mode

Shuffle
mode

The shuffle mode toggle doesn't affect Media Player's appearance in any way, but because its control is nestled amongst the appearance controls, it's appropriate to mention it here. Clicking this toggle causes Windows Media Player to play the current playlist in random order. Clicking it again turns this feature off.

For more information about playback controls, see "Playing Audio CDs," page 597. For more information about playlists, see "Working with Playlists," page 612.

You can also toggle shuffle mode by choosing Play, Shuffle or by pressing Ctrl+H.

Chapter 16

Toggling the Graphic Equalizer and Other Settings

Equalizer

In Now Playing, you can turn on a ten-band graphic equalizer and adjust sliders to change the quality of sound generated by Windows Media Player. To turn the equalizer on, click the Equalizer toggle. Then click Select View and choose Graphic Equalizer from the menu that appears.

> For more information about using the graphic equalizer, see "Using the Graphic Equalizer and SRS WOW Effects," page 601.

Select view

The Select View menu, on which the Graphic Equalizer command appears, offers some other useful options as well. For example, by choosing Media Information, you can display an album cover and other bits of information about the current item, courtesy of the Windows Media online database, as shown in Figure 16-12. Clicking the More link in this display transports you to WindowsMedia.com, where you can download and buy similar items.

To turn on any of the Select View options using menu commands, choose View, Now Playing Tools.

Figure 16-12. Choosing Media Information from the Select View menu produces a display of your current item's album cover and other useful information.

Toggling the Playlist Display

Playlist

A *playlist* in Windows Media Player is a collection of related media items. For example, all the songs in a particular album could make up a playlist. So could all the songs in all albums by a particular performer, or some ad hoc collection of songs that you put together yourself. In Now Playing, Windows Media Player can display the current

590

playlist, including titles and track times, in a panel at the right side of the window. The item in the playlist that is currently being played appears highlighted in green.

If you would rather not see the playlist, click the Playlist toggle. Or choose View, Now Playing Tools, Show Playlist.

Toggling the Taskbar

Taskbar

Windows Media Player's taskbar is the panel of options that appears along the left margin of the window (Now Playing, Media Guide, and so on). It's handy for navigation, but it takes up screen space that could be used for visualizations. You can send it away by clicking the taskbar toggle—the little arrow halfway up the taskbar's right edge. With the taskbar gone, you can still navigate via commands on the View, Taskbar submenu.

Using Visualizations

Visualization

Visualizations are designs of light and color that change with the frequency and volume of your music. Windows Media Player displays visualizations in Now Playing and in many skins. (The skin has to support visualizations, but most do.) Visualizations are grouped into collections with names such as Ambience, Bars And Waves, and Spikes. To choose one of these visualization collections, click the leftmost of the three visualization controls. This action opens a menu of collections, as shown in Figure 16-13. After choosing a collection, you can use the other two visualization controls (the left

Figure 16-13. Click the leftmost visualization control to display a menu of visualization collections.

and right arrows) to move between members of the collection. Alternatively, you can pick a visualization by choosing View, Visualizations. Some visualization collections contain a randomization option that rotates among all the collection's visualizations in random order and timing patterns.

Full screen

Many, but not all, visualizations can be displayed in full-screen mode and are much more effective that way. If the current visualization allows full-screen display, the full-screen toggle appears. Click it or press Alt+Enter, and your entire monitor becomes a light show. Click again anywhere or press Alt+Enter again to return to normal display.

Troubleshooting

No visualizations appear.

If you don't see visualizations in Now Playing, choose View, Now Playing Tools. If Show Visualization is not selected, choose this command. Note that Media Player cannot display visualizations during playback of MIDI files and might not work for CD tracks when the CD player is set for analog playback.

Using Skins

Skin mode

To switch from full mode to skin mode, press Ctrl+2, choose View, Skin Mode, or click the skin mode button at the bottom of Media Player. Windows Media Player applies the current skin. To choose a skin before going into skin mode, click Skin Chooser on Media Player's feature taskbar, or choose View, Taskbar, Skin Chooser. Select the skin you want, and then click Apply Skin. Windows Media Player comes with about 20 skins, but you're not limited to that set, by any means. Additional skins are available from many sources, and if you have some expertise with XML and JavaScript, you can create your own without great difficulty. For more information about adding skins, see "Adding Skins and Visualizations," page 594.

For an excellent tutorial on creating skins, see *Microsoft Windows Media Player for Windows XP Handbook* (Microsoft Press, 2001).

All skins include the most essential controls—for playing, pausing, stopping, advancing to the next track, retreating to the previous one, adjusting volume, and so on. Beyond these, skin features vary considerably. Some can show the current playlist or the graphic equalizer. Some show the current visualization and let you move to a different one. Some show the name of the current track. You'll need to experiment to see what the different skins can do—and where each control is located.

> **tip** To return from skin mode to full mode, press Ctrl+1.

Most of the Windows Media Player menu commands are available in the skin-mode shortcut menu. Right-click anywhere on the skin to generate this menu. One item missing from this menu is a command to switch to a different skin. If Windows Media Player is displaying its "anchor window" in the lower right corner of your screen, you can click the anchor window and then choose Select A New Skin from *its* shortcut menu. The anchor window looks like this:

It's otherwise not terribly useful, because its commands (and many others) appear on the skin's own shortcut menu. You can eliminate the anchor window by clicking it and choosing Hide Anchor Window. Alternatively, choose Tools, Options. On the Media Player tab of the Options dialog box, clear Display Anchor Window When In Skin Mode. Note that closing the Anchor Window is not the way to hide it—it closes Media Player and brings your entertainment to a sudden stop.

> **tip** To make a skin stay on top of all other windows, choose Tools, Options. On the Media Player tab of the Options dialog box, select Display On Top When In Skin Mode.

Extending Windows Media Player's Capabilities

Fine as it is, Windows Media Player is still a work in progress. Microsoft provides updates periodically, and you can check for the availability of an update at any time by choosing Help, Check For Player Updates. If new components are available, a list of them will be displayed, and you can choose to install or not install any component.

To have Windows Media Player check for updates automatically at regular intervals, choose Tools, Options. On the Media Player tab, select Once A Day, Once A Week, or Once A Month. The default is Once A Month.

Troubleshooting

You suspect you have a faulty codec.

It's unlikely that an installed codec will give you trouble. But if you suspect that is happening, follow these steps to manage the codecs installed on your computer:

1 Open Sounds And Audio Devices in Control Panel.

2 On the Hardware tab, choose Audio Codecs or Video Codecs from the Devices list. Click the Properties button.

3 When the Audio Codecs or Video Codecs properties dialog box opens, go to its Properties tab.

4 Right-click the codec you're concerned about and—you guessed it—click Properties once more.

In the codec's properties dialog box you'll find a priority number. When two codecs are available to Windows Media Player for processing the same kind of media, Media Player uses the one with the lower priority number. If you want, you can change a codec's priority by entering a different number. Alternatively, you can select Do Not Use This Codec to disable the codec altogether. If doing this solves your problem, you can try contacting the codec's vendor to obtain an update. If it doesn't, you can return to this properties dialog box to reenable the codec.

In the same dialog box, directly below these three options, you'll find a check box labeled Download Codecs Automatically. A *codec* is a software component used to compress and decompress digital media. Before a sound or video clip can be streamed to your computer from an Internet site, your computer must be equipped with a suitable codec. You don't have to be concerned about finding and installing codecs yourself. If Download Codecs Automatically is selected (as it is by default), providers of streamed media will download needed codecs to you without your having to do anything. If the check box is clear, media providers will prompt for permission before downloading a new codec.

newfeature!
Adding Skins and Visualizations

The simplest way to add more skins to Windows Media Player is to click Skin Chooser on the feature taskbar, and then click More Skins. This link takes you to a page at WindowsMedia.com, where you can find a long alphabetical list of skins approved by Microsoft. Figure 16-14 shows this site as it appeared in September 2001. Downloading is straightforward, and the skins are automatically added to the Media Player's Skin Chooser list as soon as they're downloaded.

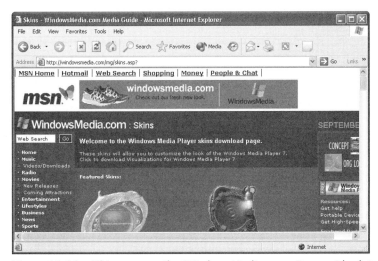

Figure 16-14. This page on the WindowsMedia.com site provides lots of new skins for your player.

For additional skins, visit Microsoft's Windows Media Bonus Pack site, *http://www.microsoft.com/windows/windowsmedia/en/download/bonuspack.asp*. For a list of links to non-Microsoft sites that offer Windows Media Player skins, see *http://www.nwlink.com/~zachd/pss/pss.html#skins*.

The simplest way to get more visualizations is to choose Tools, Download Visualizations. This takes you to WindowsMedia.com, where you can download the latest offerings from Microsoft.

Using Windows Media Player

In this chapter we'll look at the specifics of using Windows Media Player to play CDs and other audio tracks, video clips, DVD movies, and streaming media. We'll also explore Radio Tuner, which lets you listen to radio stations around the world, and Media Library, the tool for organizing your audio and video files and your lists of radio *presets* (collections of radio stations that you want to be able to return to quickly and easily).

Playing Audio CDs

Playing an audio CD in Windows Media Player is almost like playing it on any conventional CD player: insert disc, close drive, enjoy music. The *almost* has to do with your CD (or DVD) drive's AutoPlay settings. As described in Chapter 16, you can configure the way Windows responds to the insertion of CDs or DVDs containing various kinds of content. If you have set up your system so that the AutoPlay application for music CDs is Windows Media Player, Media Player starts playing your disc more or less the moment you insert it (provided it's not busy doing something else).

For more information about setting AutoPlay options, see "Changing the AutoPlay Behavior for a CD or DVD Drive," page 578.

If Windows Media Player is not the AutoPlay application for music CDs, you'll need to start Windows Media Player manually after you insert a CD, then click the Play button. Windows Media Player will begin playing the first item in the current playlist—which might or might not be your CD.

At Home with Windows XP

Windows Media Player works identically in Windows XP Home Edition and Professional. All the information in this chapter applies equally to both versions.

(For more information about playlists, see "Working with Playlists," page 612.) If Windows Media Player starts playing something other than your CD, click Stop. Then follow these steps:

1 Open the Playlist control, near the upper right corner of Windows Media Player, as shown in Figure 17-1.

2 Select your CD (it should be at the top of the list).

3 Click the Play button; press Ctrl+P; or choose Play, Play/Pause.

Figure 17-1. The Playlist control is always visible in Windows Media Player's full mode.

Windows Media Player's playback controls, shown in Figure 17-2, look and function like those on common consumer devices, such as CD players and video cassette recorders.

Figure 17-2. Windows Media Player uses playback controls like those of other consumer devices.

598

The Play button becomes a Pause button while Windows Media Player is playing. The Mute button is a toggle; click one time for silence, a second time for music. The Next and Previous buttons move ahead and back one item within the current playlist. You can drag the slider in the Seek control to move to a different place within the item that's currently playing. So, for example, to start the current track over again, you would drag the Seek slider all the way to the left.

Troubleshooting

Windows Media Player skips when you play a CD.

If you get "skippy" performance, try switching your CD drive to analog playback. Choose Tools, Options and then click the Devices tab. Select your CD drive and click Properties. In the Playback section of the properties dialog box, select Analog. If this doesn't solve the problem, select Digital again, and then try selecting Use Error Correction (in the same dialog box).

Windows Media Player plays through the current playlist in order, once, unless you turn on Shuffle or Repeat (or both):

Shuffle mode

- If you turn on Shuffle by clicking the Shuffle button, by pressing Ctrl+H, or by choosing Play, Shuffle, Windows Media Player moves through the playlist in a random order.

- If you choose Repeat by pressing Ctrl+T or by choosing Play, Repeat, Windows Media Player plays the current playlist continuously—that is, it repeats the playlist each time it finishes the final track.

Because Windows Media Player generates a different random sequence each time you start the program, the shuffle order will be different each time you insert a CD. But if you repeat the CD multiple times in a given listening session, you'll shuffle through the tracks in the same sequence each time. To deliberately change the shuffle order, turn shuffle off and then turn it on again.

While a CD is playing, the best seat in Windows Media Player's house is Now Playing (click Now Playing in the taskbar or choose View, Taskbar, Now Playing). There you can enjoy visualizations, see what tracks are coming up in the current playlist, view information about the current album, and more.

Playlist

If the playlist is not displayed along the right edge of Now Playing, click the Playlist button or choose View, Now Playing Tools, Show Playlist. If the playlist is displayed, you can switch to a different track by double-clicking the track.

Chapter 17

Troubleshooting

Your computer slows down while CDs are playing.

Visualizations might have a noticeable impact on system performance on some older computers. If your other programs slow down while you play CDs, choose View, Now Playing Tools. If Show Visualizations is checked, choose this command to turn visualizations off.

---

newfeature!
Viewing Media Information and Album Art

If you're connected to the Internet, Windows Media Player can connect to WindowsMedia.com and display information about the CD you're currently playing; details about artists and albums are provided by All Media Guide (AMG), *http://www.allmediaguide.com*). To see what it finds, choose View, Now Playing Tools, Media Information. The album art that appears is an Internet link. If you click it, you'll arrive at the Buy Now page at WindowsMedia.com, where you can do just that. (If you like the artist you're listening to, click the Copy From CD button, click Album Details, and click the Artist Profile button. Scroll to the bottom of the page, where you'll find links to information about related artists.)

Troubleshooting

Windows Media Player doesn't show media information.

If displaying Media Information in Windows Media Player doesn't show such information as track titles in the Media Information window or in the playlist, try ejecting the CD and reloading it. Also, remember that you must be connected to the Internet to retrieve media information for a CD.

Album art, once retrieved from the Internet, is cached on your computer. Thereafter, even if you're no longer online, you can display the album art in the visualization area of Now Playing. To do this, choose View, Visualizations, Album Art. Here, too, the art itself becomes a link to the Buy Now page at WindowsMedia.com. Figure 17-3 shows Now Playing with album art in the visualization area.

Figure 17-3. Windows Media Player can show album art that it retrieved from the Internet in the visualization area, even after you've logged off.

newfeature! Using the Graphic Equalizer and SRS WOW Effects

Windows Media Player includes a 10-band graphic equalizer with numerous preset equalizer settings. To adjust the balance of the various frequency bands in your playback, click Now Playing (if you're not there already). Then choose View, Now Playing Tools, Graphic Equalizer. If the frequency sliders appear dark, turn the equalizer on by clicking the Off button to toggle it on. Figure 17-4 shows the graphic equalizer.

Click these buttons to control how the graphic equalizer sliders move

Click here to choose a preset equalizer setting

Figure 17-4. Windows Media Player's graphic equalizer includes presets for many different kinds of music.

To choose one of the preset equalizer settings, click the Select Preset button, as shown in Figure 17-4, and make a selection from the menu that appears. To create your own custom setting, drag one or more frequency-band sliders upward or downward. When you drag a slider, other sliders might move with it, depending on which of the three

Chapter 17

options stacked to the left of the sliders is selected. For example, to move one slider without affecting any others, click the top slider option. To change the distribution of sound between your left and right speakers, drag the Balance slider.

If your sound equipment can take advantage of SRS WOW settings, you can control them in Windows Media Player. To learn more about SRS WOW Effects, which can provide a 3-D sound experience from only two speakers, click the SRS button to open the SRS Labs Web site. To access the effects, choose View, Now Playing Tools, SRS WOW Effects. If the controls are unavailable and you see an Off button, click the button to toggle the effects on. With SRS WOW Effects on, you can select the kind of speakers you're using (normal, large, or headphones), adjust TruBass, and adjust WOW Effect.

newfeature!
Copying Audio Tracks
from CD to Hard Disk

Windows Media Player enables you to copy CD audio tracks to your hard disk for later listening; you can also transfer the saved tracks to custom CDs you burn on a CD-R or CD-RW drive or download those tracks to your portable player. To copy an audio CD to your hard disk, first make sure that you have selected the file format that you want to use and that you have adopted an appropriate naming scheme and location for your copied files. (For details about these configuration decisions, see "Configuring Windows Media Player to Copy Music from CDs," page 582.) Next, insert the disc, and then choose Copy From CD on Windows Media Player's taskbar. Windows Media Player might also begin playing your CD. That's not a problem; Windows Media Player can play and copy at the same time.

If you're connected to the Internet, when you choose Copy From CD, Windows Media Player consults its online data sources to determine the name of your disc, as well as the names of each track and the genre of music the disc contains. Figure 17-5 shows how Windows Media Player might look after it has successfully found all this information.

By default, Windows Media Player selects the check boxes next to all track names when you choose to copy a CD to disk. To copy particular tracks only, clear the check boxes beside tracks that you don't want to copy. To clear or select all the check boxes at once, clear or select the check box at the top of the column.

When you copy a CD, the album becomes a playlist in Windows Media Player's Media Library, using the album title as the name of the playlist. If you want to be able to play the album back in a custom track order, you can create that order now, by dragging track names up and down in the copy window. Or you can do this at any time later on, by selecting the album in your Media Library.

For more information about playlists, see "Working with Playlists," page 612. For more information about Media Library, see "Managing Your Media Library," page 609.

Click here to select or clear all tracks, or click individual tracks below

Click here to start copying tracks to your disk

Figure 17-5. If your CD is among the 500,000 or more in the Windows Media database, the title of the disc will appear at the top of the copy window, and the tracks will be identified by name.

When everything is set as you want it in the Copy From CD window, click Copy Music to begin the copy process. If this is the first copy you've made, you might see a message warning you that copy protection is enabled on your computer. Select the Do Not Protect Content check box, and click OK if you want your files to be saved in a format where they can be freely transferred between computers and devices without having to hassle with licenses (of course, this presumes you're willing to take responsibility for using the copied tracks in an ethically appropriate fashion).

For more information about protected content, see "Understanding and Protecting Your Digital Rights," page 579.

As tracks are being copied, the copy window reports the progress of this operation. You can do other things in Windows Media Player while this is going on—listen to the radio, listen to the CD you're copying, or listen to something else altogether. If you have two CD drives, you can even play one CD while copying another. (Use the Play menu to choose the disc you want to play after you begin copying the first disc.)

Editing Track Information Before You Copy

If the Windows Media online database recognizes your disc but doesn't have all the track names the way you want to see them in your Media Library, click Get Names in the copy window. The downloaded information will appear in a pane at the bottom of the copy window. (You can enlarge this pane by dragging the horizontal split bar that separates it from the original track listing.) To change any part of this information, click the Edit button (just below the album cover). An editing window, similar to the one shown in Figure 17-6, will then appear.

Use the boxes at the top of the editing pane to edit the artist name, album name, or genre. Use the boxes below to edit the titles of individual tracks. The names of performers and composers for individual tracks are hidden by default; to show these details and make them available for editing, click the respective column headings.

When you've completed your edits, click the Next button. The resulting pane displays the results of your editing and gives you a chance to review it for errors. As the text at the top of the pane notes, your edits are sent to Windows Media to update the database from which it came. From a personal standpoint, however, the important thing is that editing the album information keeps your own Media Library in good order. And doing it before you begin the copy process ensures that the file names you see later, when you work with your Media Library in Windows Explorer, are correct.

Figure 17-6. If you don't agree with the album information returned by AMG, you can edit it here.

> **note** According to the experts we consulted, the information you submit when you update a Windows Media listing is indeed used to correct errors or omissions in the online database, although the process can take six weeks or more. In addition, when you submit artist/album/track information for a CD that isn't currently listed in the online database, your input is likely to end up in the database after a similar processing period. If you're an artist or CD producer in the United States, you can submit your changes directly to *artist_submissions@allmediaguide.com*; consumers can send corrections to *feedback@allmusic.com*.

> **tip** **Pay attention to genre and artist names**
>
> The Windows Media online database occasionally abbreviates musical genres in ways that are unnecessary for Windows Media Player. If you're bothered by this—if you'd rather see *Country* than *CTRY*, for example, edit the genre before you copy. Genres become playlists. You get one playlist for all your Rock tracks, another for all your Jazz tracks, and so on. So it's good to be consistent about genre names. Artists too become playlists. On albums where different artists perform on different tracks, AMG generally doesn't provide the track-by-track details. If getting the playlists right is important to you, edit before you copy.

What to Do If Windows Media Doesn't Recognize Your Disc

If the Windows Media online database doesn't recognize your disc (either because it's from an obscure artist or because you mixed the tracks and burned it yourself) or if you don't have an Internet connection to retrieve the information, Windows Media Player proposes to name it Unknown Album (followed by the current date and time). Tracks will be named by their order on the disc (Track 1, Track 2, and so on), the artist will be identified as Unknown Artist, and the genre will be called Unknown. At this point, you have three options:

- Don't worry about it; just go ahead and copy.
- Copy now, worry later.
- Fix the names before you copy.

If you accept the default names, your music will sound fine, but you'll have a hard time finding your way back to it, either in your Windows Media Player Media Library or in Windows Explorer. If you copy now, figuring that you'll edit track, album, and artist names later on, you'll be able to make your Media Library look right. But in

Windows Explorer, your file and folder names will be a jumble of Unknowns, and editing the Media Library later in Windows Media Player will not alter the file names in Windows Explorer. As your library grows, this state of affairs will almost surely come to annoy you.

To avoid confusion later, do your editing now—before you click the Copy Music button. Follow these steps:

1 At the bottom of the Copy From CD window, you should see the Search For Album Information pane. (If this pane is not visible, click Get Names.)

2 Select either Search By Artist Name or Search By Album Name. If you are certain that the CD is not listed in the Windows Media database, select Type The Information For A Personally Created (Burned) CD, click Next, and skip to step 6.

3 Enter a portion of the artist name or album name, and click Next.

4 In the Results list, select the correct artist or album information, and click Next. If you've selected a multi-disc album you'll also be prompted to specify the disc (*Disc 1*, *Disc 2*, and so on). If the correct artist or album does not appear in the list, or if Windows Media reports that it can't find a match, select Artist Not Found or Album Not Found, click Next, and skip to step 6.

5 If track information appears, review the track listings to be sure they're correct. If no track information appears or if you notice any errors, click the Edit button and enter the correct track names. Click Finish and skip to step 7.

6 If you chose to manually enter or edit any information, a form will appear that contains as much (or little) information as could be retrieved from the Web site. Fill in any empty text boxes, and then click Finish.

7 The information you retrieved and supplied now appears in the copy window. Select tracks as usual and begin the copy process.

The foregoing procedure assumes that you have an Internet connection. If you do not, you will be unable to get to the tracks editing form. In that case, you can—and should—edit your track information in Windows Media Player's copy window. Right-click the first item you want to edit and choose Edit from the shortcut menu. This will put you into an edit mode, in which you can move from column to column by pressing Tab or Shift+Tab, and move from row to row by pressing the Up Arrow or Down Arrow key.

Alternatively, you can edit a particular column for all selected rows as follows:

1 Select the rows you want to edit (or press Ctrl+A to edit all rows).

2 Right-click anywhere and choose Edit Selected Items.

3 Use Tab to move to the column you want to edit.

4 Make your changes and press Enter.

You can use this procedure as a quick way to edit the Genre column for an entire album, or the Artist column, if the same artist performs on multiple tracks.

You cannot edit the album name in Windows Media Player's copy window. And even if you change the Artist field for each track on the CD, the information displayed at the top of the window continues to read "Unknown Artist – Unknown Album (*date and time*)." As a result, when you go to copy your tracks to disk, they end up in a subfolder called "Unknown Album (*date and time*)," which you'll find inside another folder called Unknown Artist. Fortunately, the file for each track is properly named, because you went to the trouble of manually entering track names and other details first. Correcting the artist and album names in your Media Library is a two-step process:

- First, click Media Library in the taskbar (or choose View, Taskbar, Media Library). Select the Unknown Album (*date and time*) entry from the Album category. Click any track name from the list, and press Ctrl+A to select all tracks. Right-click any entry under the Album heading, and choose Edit Selected Items. Press Enter to save your changes. If necessary, repeat this process for the Artist field.

- Next, open the My Music folder in Windows Explorer, and double-click the Unknown Artist folder. Find the folder whose name starts with Unknown Album, and rename it to the correct album title. If you already have other albums by this artist, move this folder to the folder named after the artist. If this is the first album by the artist, rename the Unknown Artist folder using the artist's name.

Troubleshooting

Windows Media Player displays no title or artist information for an unknown CD.

If you see no information at all for the artist and album name—not even Unknown Artist and Unknown Album—when you insert a new CD and click the Copy From CD button, the most likely explanation is that CD AutoRun has been disabled. If you try to copy a CD to disk at this point, the tracks will end up in the top level of the My Music folder, instead of going in their own Unknown Album folder within the Unknown Artist folder. One possible explanation is that another program automatically disabled CD AutoRun; VMWare, for instance, does this. To work around this problem, you can try one of two solutions.

- After inserting the CD, close Windows Media Player and reopen it. This will refresh the drive contents and display the Unknown Artist\Unknown Album labels.

- Enable CD AutoRun. Open Registry Editor (Regedit.exe) and navigate to HKLM\SYSTEM\CurrentControlSet\Services\Cdrom. Change this setting to 1 to enable CD AutoRun (a setting of 0 disables AutoRun).

Does that procedure seem overly complicated? If you are temporarily without an Internet connection, it's probably best to wait until you can go online. Then click Get Names as described earlier, and use the edit form to fill in the information in one step.

InsideOut

The Windows Media online database uses information from a variety of suppliers, including All Media Guide (AMG) and Muze (for U.K. titles). The total number of albums listed at AMG stands well above 500,000 and is constantly growing. The service is heavily skewed in favor of pop and rock titles and has much less information about classical music CDs. If you want to copy a classical collection to your hard disk, your best bet is to find a third-party CD player that uses an alternative Internet service called CDDB. The CDDB database of classical discs is extensive, and after you have copied your discs via the other product, you can import the resulting files into your Windows Media Player Media Library.

newfeature!
Managing Your Media Library

Windows Media Player's Media Library feature lets you gather all kinds of media files into a single outlined list, where everything is easy to relocate and replay. Related items in Media Library are automatically gathered into playlists, and you can create additional custom playlists of your favorite tracks.

As Figure 17-7 shows, Media Player's Media Library uses two panes to display your library. The left pane is an outline, and the right pane displays the details of the left pane's current selection.

Figure 17-7. Windows Media Player uses an outline to organize your media library.

609

Chapter 17

Where is all this information stored? The entire Media Library is stored in a single database file, which is shared by all local users. This file, which is not directly editable using any tool except Windows Media Player, contains information about DVDs you've watched and CDs you've played, as well as details about music and video files you've added to your library, whether by recording them from CD or importing previously recorded files. In addition, the Media Library database contains custom playlists you've created and a list of featured radio stations, which is downloaded from the Windows Media Web site.

InsideOut

Although you can't edit the Media Library database, you can clean it up easily if it becomes corrupted (or if you simply want to get a fresh start). After closing Windows Media Player, open Windows Explorer and browse to %AllUsersProfile%\Application Data\Microsoft\Media Index. Delete the database file, wmplibrary_v_0_12.db. Reopen Windows Media Library, and use the Search facility to import music and other media files stored on your computer (see the following section, "Adding Items to Your Media Library," for more details). This step erases the stored details (including customizations) of any CDs and DVDs you've played; you'll need to download those details again for each CD in your collection.

Adding Items to Your Media Library

As you have seen, if you've already copied some CDs to your hard disk, those copies automatically become part of your media library. Windows Media Player creates entries in the audio section of your library for album titles, artist names, song titles, and musical genres. Adding tracks by copying CDs is, however, only one of several ways to build your library.

Using Search to Add Items

If you already have a collection of songs and other media items, you can add those to the Media Library by letting Windows Media Player search your disks for compatible media files. To do this, choose Tools, Search For Media Files, or press F3. Click the Advanced button in the Search For Media Files dialog box to reveal the full dialog box, as shown in Figure 17-8.

By default the program searches all local drives, ignoring audio files smaller than 100 KB and video files smaller than 500 KB, and ignoring Windows XP system folders. These defaults filter out sounds and videos employed by the operating system (your logon and logoff melodies, for example), while collecting media items that you're likely to want to hear or see again.

610

Figure 17-8. Windows Media Player can populate your media library by searching disks for media files.

caution If you have more than one version of Windows installed on your local hard drives, the default search parameters will *not* filter out sounds used by that other operating system. If you search all local drives using these defaults, your library will acquire such items as Tada, the Microsoft Sound, and the Windows Logon Sound. No harm is done if these and similar works find their way into your library, but you will probably want to delete them eventually. You should also be wary of running broad search-and-gather operations if you have media-rich applications such as Microsoft Encarta on board. Otherwise your library is likely to collect dozens of inscrutably named audio and video files that might not be terribly useful out of context.

To limit the search to a particular drive, open the Search On list. To focus on a particular folder and all of its subfolders, click Browse. In the Browse For Folder dialog box that appears, you can specify shared network folders as well as local folders.

tip **Decide where to store your media files**

Are your media files scattered all over your hard disk, in a mishmash of folders? Before importing them into your Media Library, why not reorganize them into a more manageable collection of folders? The best place to store your own collection of music files, of course, is in the My Music folder, which is a part of your personal profile. However, if you have a large collection of specialized media files, such as live music recordings, you might want to keep them separate from the CDs you record to disk. (Keeping these files outside of your personal profile also prevents your profile from becoming so large that you can't easily back it up.) If several users share your computer and you also want to share a music collection, try saving your files in the Shared Music folder; to locate it, open My Computer and then open the Shared Documents folder. You'll have best results if you limit the number of storage locations to no more than a handful of folders.

Adding Items When Played

If you download media from the Internet, you have a choice about whether to add such items to your library automatically. If you want every item you play to take up residence in the library, choose Tools, Options, and click the Media Player tab. Then select Add Items To Media Library When Played. Otherwise, leave this check box clear.

Adding Specific Files or URLs

If you don't add media items automatically the first time you play them, you can drag a media file from Windows Explorer (or your desktop) and drop it onto Media Player's right pane to bring the item into your library. Or you can choose File, Add To Media Library. The submenu that appears lets you specify a file, a URL, or whatever item is currently playing.

Searching for Items in Your Media Library

As your library grows, you might find it more and more difficult to locate particular items of interest. Windows Media Player's Search command can help.

> **note** Don't confuse the Search command that searches the items already in your media library with the Tools, Search For Media Files command that searches your hard disk(s) for content to add to the library.

To search your library, first click Media Library in the taskbar (if you're not already there). Then click Search in the button bar above the library. In the Search Media Library dialog box, specify words to search by and categories of media information to search, and then click the Search button.

Working with Playlists

A *playlist* is a collection of media items that Windows Media Player can play back as a unit, in either linear or random order. Each item listed at the lowest level in Media Library's left pane is a playlist. So, for example, in Figure 17-9, the Paul Simon entry listed in the Artist category is a playlist consisting of tracks from two albums, *Live Rhymin'* and *Still Crazy After All These Years*. If you want to listen only to one of the Paul Simon albums, each album is available as a playlist in the Album category. Similarly, you can listen to all items of a given genre by selecting one from the Genre category.

Playlist   Contents of the selected playlist

Figure 17-9. Each item at the lowest level of the Media Library outline constitutes a playlist.

Creating a Custom Playlist

You can create custom playlists to combine your favorite tracks, to compare several performances of the same piece, or to serve whatever purpose you choose. Follow these steps to create a custom playlist:

1 Click New Playlist at the top of the Media Library window.

2 Enter a name for your playlist in the New Playlist dialog box, and click OK.

3 To add a track to a custom playlist, select a track from the right pane of the library and drag it to the new playlist entry in the left pane, or right-click the track in the right pane and choose Add To Playlist. In the latter case the Playlists window appears, in which you select the playlist you want to add the track to. (You can also create a new playlist from this window by clicking New.)

Figure 17-10 on the next page shows a custom playlist that combines performances of the Chopin *Preludes* by four different pianists, with the tracks from the four albums interleaved to facilitate comparison.

This album's tracks are collated with
matching tracks from three other artists

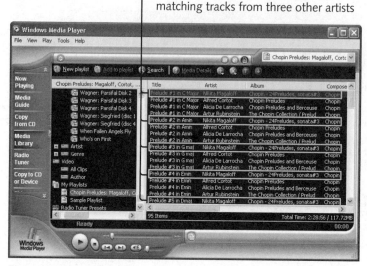

Figure 17-10. One use for a custom playlist is to compare performances of the same music by different artists.

Editing a Custom Playlist

You can change the order in which tracks appear in your custom playlists (but not in the playlists that Windows Media Player generates itself). The simplest way to rearrange a custom playlist is to display it in Media Library, and then drag tracks upward or downward with your mouse. You can also do this in Now Playing, if the playlist is displayed along the right side of your screen.

To reorder a custom playlist with menu commands, right-click an item you want to move. Then choose Move Up or Move Down from the shortcut menu.

---

tip   **Change the playlist order—temporarily**

You can change the play order of any playlist, custom or default, by sorting on a different field. Want to play an album's tracks in alphabetical order? Select the album in the left pane of the Media Library window and click the Title heading in the right pane. Click a second time to reverse the sort order (that is, change A–Z to Z–A). You can also use this technique to play an album's shortest or longest tracks first or to play the tracks according to their play counts—the number of times each track has been played. Unlike changes that you make to custom playlists with the Move Up and Move Down commands, however, sorting changes are temporary. The next time you start Windows Media Player, everything will appear in the original order.

To delete an item from a custom playlist, right-click it and choose Delete From Playlist. (Be sure not to choose Delete From Library—unless you want to remove it from the library altogether, not just from the custom playlist.)

---

tip   **Change the playlist order—permanently**

The only way to permanently customize the play order of a playlist that Windows Media Player generates is to copy it to a custom playlist. For instance, you might have copied a CD to your disk, in which case the track number defines the order in which songs on that album are played. If you want to play the tracks in a sequence that can't be set by sorting on one of the category fields in the right pane, define your preferred custom order by following these steps:

1 Select the album (or an artist if you prefer) in the left pane.

2 Click anywhere in the right pane and press Ctrl+A to select all the tracks.

3 Right-click the selected tracks and choose Add To Playlist.

4 Click the New button, and then name the new playlist.

5 Select the new playlist in the My Playlists section and arrange the tracks exactly as you like.

Your custom list will contain the same tracks as the one generated by Windows Media Player, but you can always play back your list in your custom order, and you can rearrange the order whenever you like.

Exporting and Importing Playlists

You can save a playlist in a file by selecting the playlist in Media Library's left pane and then choosing File, Export Playlist To File. These steps create a file with an .asx extension. You can replay the saved playlist by double-clicking the .asx file in Windows Explorer (provided the media files themselves are still present). An .asx file consists of a plain-text description of your playlist that can be read in Notepad or a similar text editor. (To open an .asx file, right-click it in Windows Explorer, choose Open With, and specify Notepad.) As Figure 17-11 on the next page shows, the file uses XML tags to specify the name, genre, artist, and other parameters of each track in the list.

Within each <Entry> block, the line that begins <Param Name = "SourceURL" specifies the location and name of the entry's media file. If these SourceURL lines specify paths that are valid on another computer, you can reuse your .asx file on that other computer. For example, if you've copied CDs to more than one computer and you have the same folder structure on both computers, your exported playlist will work on both computers. If the paths are not valid on the computer on which you want to use your playlist file, you can edit the SourceURL lines. For example, if your other computer is networked with the computer where the media files are stored, you can make the exported playlist file work on that other computer by replacing local paths with network paths on the SourceURL lines.

```
Chopin Preludes - Notepad
File  Edit  Format  View  Help
<Asx Version = "3.0" >
<Param Name = "Name" Value = "Chopin Preludes: Magaloff, Cortot, De Larrocha, Rubinstein" />
<Param Name = "PlaylistAttribute" Value = "0" />
<Param Name = "CreationTime" Value = "7/11/2001 9:07:41 PM" />
<Param Name = "LastModifiedTime" Value = "7/11/2001 9:25:16 PM" />
<Param Name = "AllowShuffle" Value = "yes" />

<Entry>
<Title > Prelude #1 in C Major</Title>
<Duration value = "00:00:40.684" />
<Param Name = "Name" Value = "Prelude #1 in C Major" />
<Param Name = "Genre" Value = "Classical" />
<Param Name = "Artist" Value = "Nikita Magaloff" />
<Author > Nikita Magaloff</Author>
<Param Name = "Album" Value = "Chopin - 24Preludes, sonata#3" />
<Param Name = "MediaType" Value = "audio" />
<Param Name = "MediaAttribute" Value = "0" />
<Param Name = "Bitrate" Value = "97288" />
<Param Name = "DigitallySecure" Value = "0" />
<Param Name = "PlayCount" Value = "1" />
<Param Name = "SourceURL" Value = "C:\My Music\Nikita Magaloff\Chopin - 24Preludes, sonata-3`
<Param Name = "CreationDate" Value = "7/8/2001 3:33:22 PM" />
<Param Name = "Composer" Value = "Chopin" />
<Param Name = "Size" Value = "494284" />
<Ref href = "C:\My Music\Nikita Magaloff\Chopin - 24Preludes, sonata-3\01 - 24 Preludes op.2{
</Entry>

<Entry>
<Title > Prelude #1 in C Major</Title>
<Duration value = "00:00:36.141" />
<Param Name = "Name" Value = "Prelude #1 in C Major" />
<Param Name = "Artist" Value = "Alfred Cortot" />
```

Figure 17-11. An .asx file uses XML tags to describe the items of your playlist.

Windows Media Player can also import playlists in a wide variety of formats, including formats created by other media programs. Choose File, Import Playlist To Media Library. In the Open dialog box that appears, use the Files Of Type list to specify Media Playlist (*.asx, *.wax, *.m3u, *.wvx, *.wmx) and then choose the playlist file you want to import.

Editing Metadata Tags in the Media Library

Information in the right pane of Media Library is organized in categories, the first five of which—Title, Artist, Album, Composer, and Genre—are editable (the rest are read-only). You can edit anything that appears in these first five columns by right-clicking it and choosing Edit from the shortcut menu. While you're editing, you can move from column to column by pressing Tab or Shift+Tab, and move from row to row by pressing the Up Arrow or Down Arrow key.

If you're going to make the same editing change to an entire column, select all the rows first (click the first entry and then Shift+click the last entry). Then right-click and choose Edit Selected Items. Move to the column you want to edit by pressing Tab or Shift+Tab, make the edit in one row, and then press Enter to duplicate the edit to the entire column.

All editable data in the right pane of Media Library is *metadata*. That is, what you're doing when you edit is changing the values of tags associated with your media files, not file names. To change file names, you need to work in Windows Explorer. For music files, Windows Media Player can read and write these details using *tags* stored directly in the file, using one of the following three formats:

● **ID3v1.** This relatively old format is still in wide use for MP3 files. It consists of six fields, each of fixed size, stored in 128 bytes at the end of the file. Windows Media Player can read ID3v1 tags but does not write them.

616

- **ID3v2.** Modern media players that use the MP3 format typically store metadata using these tags, which can contain dozens of fields, each holding an unlimited number of characters. Because these tags are often used to help identify streaming media, they are stored at the beginning of the media file. If you edit the details associated with an MP3 file in Windows Media Player, it writes the data to the file using this type of tag.

- **WMA.** These tags are the native format used for Windows Media Audio files. The metadata is stored at the beginning of the file, and the format is functionally equivalent to ID3v2 tags.

When you edit details of a track in your Media Library, Windows Media Player writes the information back to the file containing that track, using either an ID3v2 or WMA tag. This change is permanent. When you import files into Windows Media Player, the data stored in these tags is used to populate the fields in the Media Library.

You can also edit metadata directly in Windows Explorer. Right-click any media file and choose Properties, and then click the Summary tab (you may need to click the Advanced button to see this information). Each field shown here is editable. If you select multiple files, you can use this dialog box to edit fields such as the name of the artist or album for all selected tracks. Note that changing metadata stored within each file does not change the information displayed in your Media Library unless you remove the tracks from the Media Library and add them again using the Search tool.

Chapter 17

Troubleshooting

You can't edit track numbers in Windows Media Player.

When you view the contents of an album, the right pane shows the track number for each song. However, Windows Media Player does not allow you to edit this information directly. For albums you record using Windows Media Player, this shouldn't be a problem, because the track information is pulled directly from the Windows Media online database and is generally accurate. However, if you discover an error in the track numbering, or if you import a group of songs that were recorded using a different program, which incorrectly numbered the tracks, you need to use a fairly cumbersome workaround to fix this data. From Windows Explorer, right-click each file that contains an incorrect track number, and choose Properties. On the Summary tab, click the value to the right of the Track Number field, and change it to the correct value. Repeat for each incorrectly numbered track. Then delete the tracks from your Media Library, press F3 to open the Search box, and import the changed files.

If that seems like too much of a hassle, consider using a tag-editing utility instead. A quick search of the Internet for "ID3v2 tag editors" will turn up dozens of candidates. We highly recommend eMusic Tag Editor, available as shareware from Abyss Audio (*http://www.abyssaudio.com*). The Explorer-style interface is extremely easy to use, and it works exceptionally well with all types of metadata, regardless of format.

Adding Lyrics to Songs

You can add lyrics to a song's metadata and then display those lyrics as you play the song. Start by right-clicking your song's entry in Media Library. Choose Properties from the shortcut menu and then click the Lyrics tab. Enter or edit the lyrics there, as shown in Figure 17-12.

To display the song's lyrics in Now Playing while you play it back, choose View, Now Playing Tools, Lyrics. As Figure 17-13 shows, Windows Media Player centers the lyrics display.

Figure 17-12. Use the Lyrics tab of a song's Properties dialog box to enter or edit lyrics.

Figure 17-13. In Now Playing, you can display your song's lyrics.

Working with Your Media Library in Windows Explorer

Windows Media Player's Media Library and Windows Explorer are tightly integrated, so that you can manipulate your library easily in either context. If you rename or move a media file in Windows Explorer, Windows Media Player dutifully records the change in the Media Library database; you won't have to rebuild or edit your library in any way. If you delete an item using Windows Explorer, the item will remain in your library. But the first time you try to play it, Windows Media Player will display the deleted track in red and go on to the next track in the playlist. If you right-click the track that now appears in red, and then choose Error Details from the shortcut menu, a dialog box like this one appears.

If the item still exists somewhere (other than in your Recycle Bin) and Windows Media Player is mistaken about the deletion, click Browse and help Windows Media Player find it. If you have deleted it and want to remove the listing from your media library, select the Remove File From Media Library check box and then click OK.

By default, Windows Media Player stores copied CD tracks in My Music, a subfolder of My Documents. As Figure 17-14 shows, Windows Media Player populates My Music with artist folders, storing album folders within artist folders and individual tracks within the album folders. At the top level of this structure, Windows Explorer's thumbnails view uses album art to adorn the folders; you can display as many as four album images on a folder this way (the Paul Simon folder in Figure 17-14, for example, includes two images, because it contains two album folders—*Live Rhymin'* and *Still Crazy After All These Years*).

---

tip   **Use your own art**

To use any album image as folder art, save it in the album folder with the file name Folder.jpg.

At any level of this folder structure—My Music, an artist folder, or an album folder—Windows Explorer's left pane conveniently offers links to relevant tasks. You can

Chapter 17

Figure 17-14. Windows Explorer uses album art in thumbnails view.

play an entire folder (including all the individual media items in its subfolders) by selecting the folder and clicking Play Selection. Or you can play all media items in My Music by selecting nothing there and clicking Play All. In either case, Windows Explorer passes the list of media items to Windows Media Player, which builds and plays a temporary playlist.

If you click Shop For Music Online, Windows Explorer transports you to WindowsMedia.com, where you can do what that link implies. And if you select a folder and click Copy To Audio CD, Windows Explorer passes the selection to Windows Media Player, which builds a playlist and prepares to burn a CD.

For more information about creating custom CDs, see "Burning Custom CDs," on the next page.

Managing Media with PowerToys and Wizards

If you've built up a substantial collection of music and other media and you're having trouble keeping track of all the details, download the Windows Media Bonus Pack, and use the Media Library Management Wizard (part of the PowerToys collection) to get things under control again. The wizard allows you to synchronize data between the Media Library and your saved files—a useful shortcut for adding metadata to the Media Library without having to delete and import the changed files. A check box on the final page of the wizard lets you rename files stored on your hard disk so that they're consistent with your preferred naming scheme. This option permanently changes the file names, so use it with extreme caution!

You can download the Bonus Pack, which includes several other useful tools as well, from *http://www.microsoft.com/windows/windowsmedia/download/bppowertoys.asp.*

Deleting Items from Your Media Library

When you delete an item from your media library—by right-clicking it in the right pane and choosing Delete From Library—Windows Media Player transfers the item to the Deleted Items section of the library. If you change your mind, go to Deleted Items\All Deleted Media, right-click the item in the right pane, and choose Restore from the shortcut menu. To remove the item permanently, right-click it in All Deleted Media and choose Delete From Library. The following confirmation dialog box appears.

Click Yes, and the item is removed from your media library. Select the check box first, and Windows Media Player will also remove the music file from your hard disk.

To delete a custom playlist, right-click its name under My Playlists, in the left pane of Media Library. Then choose Delete from the shortcut menu. Windows Media Player will transfer the playlist to the Deleted Items folder. Select the playlist there, press Tab to move to the right pane, press Ctrl+A to select all items in the playlist, right-click, and then choose Delete From Library. Without asking for confirmation, Windows Media Player will transfer the individual items to All Deleted Media.

> **tip** To clean out your All Deleted Media folder all at one time, select any item in the right pane of that folder, press Ctrl+A, right-click, choose Delete From Library, and then answer the confirmation prompt.

newfeature!
Burning Custom CDs

If you have a CD recorder, Windows Media Player can use it to burn a selection of songs onto a custom CD. You don't need to use Windows Explorer or a third-party CD-burning program to do this (although you can, if you want).

If the items you want to copy to a CD already exist as a playlist—either a custom playlist or a playlist that Windows Media Player has created for you—select that playlist in your media library. Then click Copy To CD Or Device in Windows Media Player's taskbar. You'll see a display comparable to the one shown in Figure 17-15.

Your playlist appears in the left pane, with check boxes for each track. Windows Media Player initially selects all check boxes, on the assumption that you want to copy all

Figure 17-15. The left pane shows the tracks to be copied and their total playing time; the right pane shows the current content of the CD and the amount of available playing time.

tracks. The right pane shows the current content of the CD, if any. A list box at the top of the right pane identifies the drive to which Windows Media Player proposes to copy the files. If you have multiple drives and you want to copy to one other than the one displayed, choose it from this list. If you have a portable device (other than a CD recorder) installed, that device will also appear in this list.

Note the total time figure at the bottom of the left pane and the available time figure at the bottom of the right. If the total time exceeds the available time, some of your tracks will be marked Will Not Fit, as shown in Figure 17-16.

Figure 17-16. The Status column identifies tracks that will not fit onto the CD.

623

Be aware that if Windows Media Player comes to a track that's too large to fit, it continues to scan the playlist until it finds a track that will fit. That maximizes the amount of music you copy to your CD, but it can interfere with the linear order you might be expecting. If you don't want to copy any more tracks after the first one that doesn't fit, you'll need to clear all the remaining check boxes. Alternatively, you can clear all check boxes by clearing the single check box that appears at the top of the left pane (next to the word *Title*), and then select tracks until you come to one that won't fit.

If you change your mind about copying the selected playlist, or if you've accidentally selected the wrong playlist, click Media Library in the taskbar. The next time you select a playlist and click Copy To CD Or Device, the playlist you have just selected will appear in the Copy To CD Or Device window, in place of the one that was there before.

If the items you want to copy don't exist as a playlist, right-click each item in turn and choose Copy To Audio CD from the shortcut menu. (Choose this command even if you're copying to a portable device, not an audio CD.) In this scenario, Windows Media Player adds each item in turn to a special playlist called Send To. The Send To playlist, unlike any other that you copy, works *cumulatively*. That is, each time you choose Copy To Audio CD, the selected item is added to the Send To playlist; it doesn't replace the items that were there before. To remove an item from the Send To playlist, select Send To Playlist in the left pane of the Media Library window. (You'll find it under My Playlists.) Right-click the item in the right pane and choose Delete From Playlist. Alternatively, you can right-click an item in the left pane of the Copy To CD Or Device window and choose Delete From Playlist.

When you're ready to copy, click Copy Music in the Copy To CD Or Device window. The CD-burning process takes a little while. Windows Media Player first checks each track to make sure that its license (if any) permits copying. Then it converts each file in turn to a temporary .wav audio file. Because .wav files are uncompressed, you might need as much as 1 GB of temporary storage to accommodate this process. By default, Windows Media Player uses the drive on which Windows XP is installed. If you don't have enough room there, choose Tools, Options, and then click the Devices tab. Select your CD recorder and then click Properties. On the Recording tab of the properties dialog box, shown in Figure 17-17, select a different disk.

Finally, after each track is checked and converted, Windows Media Player begins copying files to the CD. You can follow the progress of all these operations by watching the Status column in the Copy To CD Or Device window, or you can return to another part of Windows Media Player and play other media.

By default, Windows Media Player ejects your disc when the copy is complete. If you don't want it to do this, go to the Recording tab of your device's properties dialog box and clear Automatically Eject The CD After Writing.

Figure 17-17. The Recording tab of your device's properties dialog box lets you specify the disk used for temporary storage while Windows Media Player burns CDs.

Troubleshooting

Tracks that play continuously in Windows Media Player don't do so on custom CDs.

This version of Windows Media Player puts two-second "spacers" between tracks on CDs that it burns, and you don't have the option of eliminating these spacers. Tracks that are intended to be played continuously thus will be discontinuous when copied to a CD. To eliminate the gaps, use a third-party CD-burning program.

newfeature!
Copying to a Portable Device

The procedure for copying music to a portable player is just like that for burning a custom CD. When you get to the copy window, be sure that the name of your device appears at the top of the right pane. If it does not (if you see a CD drive there, for example), open the list and select your portable device. For more information, see the previous section.

Chapter 17

Listening to Radio Stations

Windows Media Player's Radio Tuner lets you find radio stations from all over the world that stream music, sports, news, and weather over the Internet. Some of the stations you'll find are broadcast stations that also stream their signal on the Internet, while others are Internet-only stations.

To open the tuner, click Radio Tuner in the taskbar. Radio Tuner connects to WindowsMedia.com and, initially, presents the display shown in Figure 17-18. The left side of the screen is divided into three expandable sections, called Featured Stations, My Stations, and Recently Played Stations. The first of these is a short set of "editor's picks" to help you get started with the tuner. When you find a station you like, you can add it to the My Stations section. To return to a station you listened to previously, even one you didn't add to My Stations, visit Recently Played Stations.

To play a station in the Featured Stations list, click the green arrow to the left of its name. Alternatively, you can click the name itself to get a little more information about the station. Three new links appear when you do this: one to add the station to your My Stations list (if it isn't already there), another to visit the station's own Web site, and a third to play the station.

Figure 17-18. Radio Tuner's Featured Stations list provides a preset list of 10 news and music stations.

To move beyond the 10 featured stations, you can click one of the genre links at the right side of the screen—for example, Country, Top 40, or World Music. Don't think that the small set of genres that appear in that part of the screen is all that Radio Tuner has to offer, though. If you click Find More Stations, and then, on the ensuing screen, open the Browse By Genre list, you see the generous set of categories shown in Figure 17-19.

Figure 17-19. You can browse the world's radio stations using this impressive list of categories.

Below the Browse By Genre list, hidden by the expanded list shown in Figure 17-19, are two additional search boxes. You can use the first, labeled Search, to hunt for radio stations by one or more keywords of your choosing—the name of a syndicated talk-show host, for example. When you want to find stations in your own hometown, you'll find the second box—Zip Code (US Only)—invaluable. Don't forget the Use Advanced Search link below the two basic search options either. Clicking this link opens the Advanced Search pane from which you can open lists of stations sorted by genre, language, country, U.S. state, station speed, broadcast band, keyword, call sign, or frequency.

Using Presets

Once you add a station to your My Stations list it appears there, of course, and also in your Media Library, under the heading Radio Tuner Presets, as shown in Figure 17-20 on the next page. Thus, once you've found your favorite radio stations, you can easily switch between recorded audio tracks and radio offerings without having to return to the tuner.

InsideOut

The Radio Tuner Presets category also includes Radio Tuner's Featured Stations list. Unfortunately, you can't delete these from Media Library. You can remove your own stations, but only by first removing them from the My Stations section of Radio Tuner. (Click a station there to reveal its Remove From My Stations link.)

Chapter 17

Figure 17-20. Stations that you add to the My Stations section of Radio Tuner are also accessible from the Radio Tuner Presets section of Media Library.

Finding Stations in Your Web Browser

Windows Media Player's Station Finder is, of course, not the only way to find radio stations on the Internet. You can also use your Web browser to locate stations. If you find a station that produces a streaming signal in Windows Media format, you can add it to

---

Privacy Issues Involving Streaming Media

Whenever you download streaming media from the Internet—a radio station, a video presentation, or anything else—Windows Media Player, by default, sends your IP address and a client ID. The client ID is a GUID (a globally unique identifier—a very long number guaranteed to be unique in the world) that enables the media server to monitor the connection between it and your computer. According to Microsoft's Privacy Statement (choose Help, Privacy Statement in Windows Media Player to read it in detail), possessing this client ID enables the server to "make adjustments to provide increased playback quality and to alert you to unseen events that occur when receiving streams over the Internet." The Privacy Statement asserts that this identifier contains no "personally identifiable information." Nevertheless, if you're uncomfortable with this arrangement, you can tell Windows Media Player not to send the client ID. To do so, choose Tools, Options. On the Media Player tab, clear Allow Internet Sites To Uniquely Identify Your Player.

Suppressing the client ID in no way restricts your ability to receive streaming media. It's possible that it will impair the quality of reception that you enjoy. If you experience problems with the client ID transmission turned off, try turning it back on and see whether matters improve.

Chapter 17

your Windows Media Player media library by choosing File, Add To Media Library, Add Currently Playing Track while the station is playing. The station will then be listed in the All Audio folder of your media library.

Many Internet radio stations stream their signal in RealAudio format instead of Windows Media format. RealAudio is not supported by Windows Media Player, so you will not be able to add those stations to your library. Some stations give you a choice between RealAudio and Windows Media. Choose the latter if you want to be able to return to the station from within Windows Media Player.

newfeature!
Watching DVD Movies

DVD playback in Windows Media Player requires a supported DVD drive and a software decoder. If you bought your computer with a DVD drive and Windows XP preinstalled, the computer manufacturer may have included a DVD decoder as part of the software bundled with your new PC, in which case you can safely assume your hardware setup supports playback in Windows Media Player. If you installed Windows XP on an older computer, you might need to purchase, download, and install a decoder from the Internet. If this is the case, the first time you insert a DVD disc in your drive, Windows Media Player will display an error message with a link to its DVD Troubleshooter. Follow this link, if necessary, and you'll find a list of compatible decoders.

After all the requisite hardware and software is in place, playing a DVD movie in Windows Media Player is as transparently simple as playing an audio CD. If Windows Media Player is the AutoPlay application for DVD movies, it will start automatically and begin playing your movie. If it isn't, start Windows Media Player yourself. Then choose Play, DVD Or CD Audio. In the submenu that appears, choose your DVD drive.

While your movie is playing, its chapters appear in the Playlist section of Now Playing. This chapter list provides one means of navigation within the movie. You can jump to a particular chapter by double-clicking it in Now Playing. You can also get to the movie's own menu screen by clicking the Menu button near the lower left corner of Now Playing.

Using DVD Controls

If you choose View, Now Playing Tools, DVD Controls, the controls shown in Figure 17-21 appear at the bottom of Now Playing. You can use these to display your movie one frame at a time, to fast-forward or rewind, or to make minor adjustments in the playback speed.

Figure 17-21. The DVD controls let you fast-forward, rewind, and adjust playback speed.

629

Using Subtitles, Closed Captions, and Other Features

To take advantage of other features offered by your movie, choose View, DVD Features. Figure 17-22 shows how the DVD Features menu appears for one particular movie. On your movie, other features might be available.

Click to view movie full screen

Figure 17-22. To display closed captions, change languages, or take advantage of other features offered by your movie, choose View, DVD Features.

Watching Movies Full Screen

To fully appreciate your movie, you probably don't want to see any part of Windows Media Player. You can display the movie full screen by choosing View, Full Screen, pressing Alt+Enter, or clicking the View Full Screen button shown in Figure 17-22.

In full-screen mode, Windows Media Player's playback controls appear temporarily in the lower left corner of your screen. Information about the movie you're watching, as well as buttons providing access to its menu and chapter list, appear temporarily along the top edge of the screen. All of these controls fade from view after about three seconds and reappear whenever you move the mouse. While you're watching the movie on the full screen, you can also right-click at any time to get to the DVD Features menu.

To return to Media Player's normal windowed presentation, press Alt+Enter or Esc. Or right-click and choose Exit Full Screen.

Organizing and Editing Images

newfeature!

Microsoft Windows XP does a spectacular job with all sorts of image files, including digital photos and scanned documents. Out of the box, it works with hundreds of imaging devices to help you convert photos and documents from a scanner or digital camera into a Windows-compatible format, move the resulting files to your computer, and keep those images organized. When working with image files, you'll use the following tools:

- **Scanner And Camera Wizard.** If your imaging device includes a Windows XP–compatible driver, you're home free. This straightforward wizard makes short work of getting images into your computer.

- **Additional wizards.** Built-in wizards and dialog boxes help you shrink files so that you can send them by e-mail, publish images to Web sites, manage the details of printing pictures, and order prints from online suppliers.

- **Windows Explorer enhancements.** Throughout Windows Explorer, you'll find features designed to make working with digital image files easier, most notably a new Filmstrip view that combines thumbnails and a preview pane. These enhancements are immediately visible in the My Pictures folder, but you can customize any folder that contains image files to give yourself access to the new image-handling tools.

- **Windows Picture And Fax Viewer.** This utility, also new to Windows XP, offers an easy way to preview (and in some cases, annotate) image files.

631

At Home with Windows XP

All of the features described in this chapter are available in Windows XP Home Edition as well as Windows XP Professional.

newfeature!

Setting Up a Scanner or Digital Camera

To take advantage of the image-handling features in Windows XP, start with the right hardware. Specifically, you need a digital camera or scanner that supports the Windows Image Acquisition (WIA) standard and connects to your computer via a Universal Serial Bus (USB), SCSI, or IEEE 1394 cable. When you plug in a WIA-compliant device, Windows automatically recognizes it, installs the correct drivers, and adds an icon for the device in Control Panel's Scanners And Cameras folder. By right-clicking the device icon and opening its properties dialog box, you can configure options that are specific to that device, including color profiles and how to respond when specific actions occur, as shown in Figure 18-1.

tip   **Give new life to an old camera**

Do you have an older digital camera that doesn't include WIA drivers? If it still takes perfectly good pictures, don't toss it out. As long as it uses industry-standard memory cards (Compact Flash or SmartMedia), you can get an external memory reader that connects via the USB port on your computer. A number of companies, including SanDisk (*http://www.sandisk.com*) and Kingston (*http://www.kingston.com*), make reliable and inexpensive readers that are compatible with Windows XP. Instead of connecting the camera directly to the computer, you transfer the memory card to the reader. Windows recognizes digital memory cards as generic storage devices (look for an icon in the My Computer window) and provides the exact same image-handling features you would get with a WIA-compatible camera. Card readers also help you conserve your camera's battery power, because you don't have to leave the camera turned on while you transfer pictures; using a memory card reader allows you to take more pictures before having to recharge or change your camera's batteries.

WIA-aware imaging programs like Microsoft Office XP, Microsoft Picture It! 2000 or later, and Adobe Photoshop can communicate directly with WIA-compatible imaging devices. For Windows programs that are only compatible with TWAIN devices, WIA provides a compatibility layer that allows you to capture and transfer images without having to install extra software. When Windows makes a WIA device available through the TWAIN compatibility layer, its device name includes "WIA-" as a prefix. The TWAIN compatibility layer isn't perfect; for instance, it supports only the BMP (Windows Bitmap) file format and doesn't allow you to use the automatic document feeders found on many high-end flatbed scanners.

Figure 18-1. From the Scanners And Cameras folder, you can associate specific actions with events, such as clicking the Scan button on a flatbed scanner.

With older devices that do not have WIA drivers and communicate with Windows via a serial port, you'll be unable to take advantage of any image-handling features found in Windows XP. These devices typically hook into Windows using proprietary interfaces; any such device won't show up in the Scanners And Cameras folder and won't be available for use with Windows XP wizards.

In some cases, you may have to choose between the software and drivers that came with your device and the WIA-based features in Windows XP. If the manufacturer's software includes device-specific features, such as the ability to program buttons on a scanner or to access configuration options in a camera, it may be your best choice. When you choose this option, you'll lose the ability to work with the device through the Scanner And Camera Wizard, but for some devices the trade-off may be worth it.

---

tip **Use System Restore before experimenting**

It's impractical to switch between the WIA-based imaging features in Windows XP and those found in a device manufacturer's proprietary software. If your device works when you plug it into a Windows XP system but you want to experiment with the manufacturer's software to decide whether its features are a better fit for you, be sure to set a System Restore checkpoint before installing the software and drivers. If you decide you prefer the WIA-based tools, uninstall the software package and then use System Restore to remove the manufacturer's drivers and restore your system to its previous configuration. For full details, see "Undoing Configuration Mistakes with System Restore," page 900.

Chapter 18

633

Saving and Editing Images

To transfer images from a digital device to your computer, your simplest option is to use the Scanner And Camera Wizard. Because each class of device is inherently different, the exact choices available to you depend on your starting point.

On systems where multiple WIA-compatible devices are installed, you can begin with the Scanner And Camera Wizard menu choice (click the Start button and then choose All Programs, Accessories). You'll see a dialog box like the one in Figure 18-2. Pick a device and click OK to continue.

Figure 18-2. If you have multiple imaging devices, you can select one and adjust its properties if necessary from this dialog box.

InsideOut

When you're scanning photographs on a flatbed scanner, knowing a few simple secrets can save you hours of tedious cropping. For starters, place a sheet of clean white paper behind the image, to serve as a background. When you reach the Choose Scanning Preferences step of the wizard, don't just click Next; if you do that, the wizard will scan the entire image area, and you'll have to manually crop the resulting image file. Instead, *always* click Preview. After the preview scan is complete, the wizard displays the scan and selects the image automatically—a task that's much easier thanks to the plain white background you provided. After you verify that the selection is correct, click Next to complete the scan.

To scan a document or photo, start by double-clicking the device icon in the My Computer window or in Control Panel's Scanners And Cameras folder. (If you're using the Category view of Control Panel, you'll find this option under Printers And Other Hardware.) As Figure 18-3 shows, the controls in the Choose Scanning Preferences dialog box allow you to select the picture type, preview the image, and (if necessary) crop it to suit your needs. With scanners that include a document feeder, you can also choose the paper source and page size.

Figure 18-3. This dialog box gives you quick access to all scanning controls.

With a digital camera, the wizard behaves a bit differently. As soon as Windows detects that you've connected a camera to the computer, it fires up the Scanner And Camera Wizard, reads the images stored in the camera's memory, and displays thumbnails of the stored images, as shown in Figure 18-4 on the next page.

By default, all the stored images are selected. If you want to copy the entire group to your hard drive, click Next. If you can tell at a glance that some of the images aren't keepers, clear the check mark above those thumbnails before going to the next step. What if you only want to transfer one or two images from a memory card that contains dozens of images? Save yourself some effort by clicking Clear All at the lower right, and then check only the images you want.

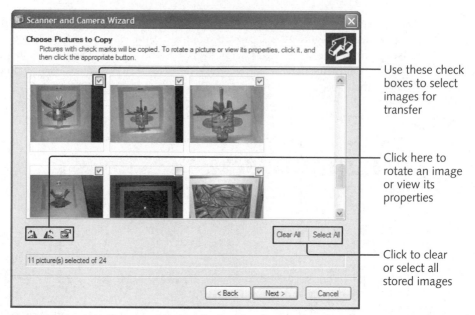

Use these check boxes to select images for transfer

Click here to rotate an image or view its properties

Click to clear or select all stored images

Figure 18-4. Use the wizard to transfer images from a digital camera's memory card to your hard drive.

---

tip   **When in doubt, copy**

It's difficult to work with the tiny thumbnail images in the Scanner And Camera Wizard. You'll generally find it most efficient to copy all images to your hard drive, where you can cull the shots you don't want to keep and then work with the rest. Although the thumbnail viewer in the Scanner And Camera Wizard includes tools for rotating images, this task is also best left for the larger Preview window on the computer.

If you're a digital camera fanatic, you can skip the wizard altogether and automatically copy all images to your hard drive every time you connect a WIA-compatible camera. (If you're using a USB-based memory-card reader, this option isn't available.)

Follow these steps to set up this option:

1 With the camera connected and powered on, open the Scanners And Cameras folder in Control Panel.

2 Right-click the camera icon and choose Properties.

3 In the properties dialog box, click the Events tab, and adjust the settings as shown next.

When you select these options, Windows automatically creates a subfolder in the My Pictures folder using the current date, copies all pictures from the camera to that folder, and deletes the images from the camera's memory so that you can start fresh.

In the final step of the Scanner And Camera Wizard, you specify the location where you want the images stored. If you've selected multiple images, you also specify a group name. The wizard tacks on consecutive numbers at the end of the group name for each individual image—Picture 001, Picture 002, and so forth.

tip   Skip the wizard for faster results

If you don't like the wizard's step-by-step approach, you can cut straight to the chase and work directly with images stored on a digital camera. After connecting the device, open the My Computer window and double-click the camera icon to display stored images directly in a Windows Explorer window. Select one or more images, and then use the Copy The Selected Items link in the File And Folder Tasks pane to copy the images to a folder of your choice using the default names supplied by your camera.

Finally, you can scan an image directly from any WIA-compatible application. In Microsoft Paint, for example, choose File, From Scanner Or Camera to open a simplified version of the Scanner And Camera Wizard. Instead of being saved to a file, the resulting image appears in the Paint window, where you can crop or edit it before saving.

Chapter 18

Choosing the Right File Format

When you capture an image with a digital camera, the camera settings define the file format used. As a result, when you transfer images, you're not given a choice of formats. But when you scan a document, the final step of the wizard uses the dialog box shown in Figure 18-5. The name and location fields are self-explanatory, but choosing the right file format isn't always so easy.

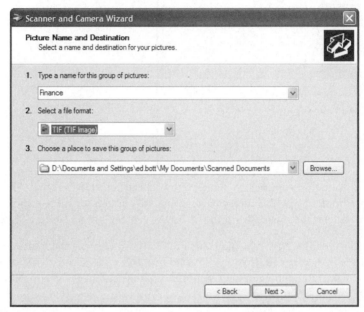

Figure 18-5. After scanning an image, save it using a descriptive name and one of four default file formats.

Select one of the following four formats:

● **BMP** saves the file in the Windows Bitmap format. Because this format does not support compression, images tend to be very large. This is rarely the right choice for scanned images unless you intend to open the image in Microsoft Paint, edit it, and save it in another format immediately.

● **JPG** is the three-letter extension used to identify images that use the Joint Photographic Experts Group (JPEG) format. Because it is highly compressible, this is one of two popular formats used for Web graphics (the other is Graphics Interchange Format, or GIF). It's an excellent choice if the scanned image is destined for use on the Web. However, the compression used to create JPEG files results in a permanent loss of detail. If you want to preserve as much detail as possible, choose a different format.

- **TIF** is the three-letter extension for the Tagged Interchange File Format, which is compatible with a large number of software applications. Although TIFF files can be compressed, the compression does not result in a loss of detail; of course, the trade-off is that TIFF files are generally larger than GIF or JPEG files. This is the best choice for graphics that will be used in desktop publishing programs. It's also the default format for faxes received through the Windows XP Fax Service. When scanning multiple pages using an automatic document feeder, choose this format to save the files in multipage TIFF format, in which all pages are merged into a single file.

- **PNG** stands for Portable Network Graphics, a format that is platform independent, highly compressible, and safe for use on Web pages because it's supported by virtually all modern browsers. Although some experts predict it will someday replace GIF, as of this writing it is still not widely used. The PNG filter used in Windows XP tends to produce relatively large images with no loss of detail.

> **note** Previous versions of Windows included a useful image viewing and editing tool called Kodak Imaging. This tool is no longer available in a clean installation of Windows XP, although it is preserved if you upgrade over Windows 98, Windows Me, or Windows 2000. You'll sorely miss Imaging if you routinely work with multipage TIFF files, because the Windows Picture And Fax Viewer doesn't offer any way to add, delete, or rearrange individual pages in such a file. If you need this capability, you'll need a third-party image-editing utility. The feature-rich, easy-to-use IrfanView (*http://www.irfanview.com*) is an excellent option; it's free for home users and costs only $10 for business use.

Need to convert a graphics file after saving it to your hard disk? Open the Microsoft Paint program, Mspaint.exe (to find its shortcut, click the Start button, choose All Programs, Accessories, and click Paint). Unlike the noticeably underpowered Paint utility in Windows 95/98/Me, which could only work with BMP files, the version in Windows XP is surprisingly robust. It still works with BMPs, of course, but you can also open and save picture files in JPEG, GIF, TIFF, and PNG formats. (You cannot, however, choose custom options such as compression levels for any of these formats.)

newfeature!
Compressing and Shrinking Image Files

When you initially capture or scan an image, the size of the file can be enormous. That's all well and good if you have a large hard drive and you intend to send the digital photo to a color printer using high-quality paper. The larger size means more detail and thus a better image. But large file size is a serious hindrance if you plan to send an image as an e-mail attachment or upload it to a Web site. In either of those cases, your most important consideration is reducing the image to a size that can be conveniently downloaded without sacrificing quality.

639

Shrinking Images for E-Mail

If you plan to send digital photos to a friend or relative via e-mail, you'll run into problems if you don't plan carefully. If the recipient has a dial-up Internet connection, for instance, they probably won't appreciate tying up the line for a half-hour as your 6-MB attachment in TIFF or BMP format trickles in. With some Internet service providers (ISPs), attachments over a specified size are summarily rejected or can exhaust the user's quota on the server, causing all incoming messages to be rejected until he or she downloads your attachment.

If you manually attach an image file to a message, Microsoft Outlook Express, Outlook 2000/2002, and other e-mail client programs will send the original, uncompressed image. However, Windows XP can help you shrink the size of the image and convert the file to a compressible format, if you use the right technique. To do so, follow these steps:

1 Open a Windows Explorer window and select one or more picture files.

2 Click the E-Mail This File link in the File And Folder Tasks pane. If you make multiple selections, the wording of this task link changes to apply to the selected items or to all items in a folder. (If this option isn't visible, right-click the selection and choose Send To, Mail Recipient from the shortcut menu.)

3 In the Send Pictures Via E-Mail dialog box, the Make My Pictures Smaller option is selected by default. Click the Show More Options link to display the expanded version of this dialog box, as shown here.

By default, this option converts BMP and TIFF images to JPEG format (because GIF and JPEG images are already compressible, using this option leaves those file formats alone). It then compresses the file substantially and resizes the image to 640×480 pixels. If you're willing to accept a larger file size in exchange for more detail, you can select the Medium (800×600) or Large (1024×768) options instead.

4 Make a selection and click OK. Windows opens your default e-mail program, creates a new message, and attaches the compressed image file(s).

5 Add message text, insert the recipient's address, and click the Send button without worrying that you'll be overloading someone's Inbox.

The results of this compression can be startling. Table 18-1 shows the before and after file sizes of four images. In all cases, the compressed file is less than half the size of the original, and in the case of large TIFF and BMP files the compression ratio is as much as 99%.

Table 18-1. How Compression Affects Graphics File Sizes

Original Picture Specifications	Original Size and Format	Compression Small (640x480)	Large (1024x768)
Scanned text document (B&W, 150 dpi, 8½×11 inches)	268 KB JPEG	36 KB JPEG	126 KB JPEG
Scanned magazine page (grayscale, 150 dpi, 8½×11 inches)	1.11 MB TIFF	16 KB JPEG (text unreadable)	85 KB JPEG (text readable)
Color photo from digital camera (24-bit color, 192 dpi, 1280×960 resolution)	556 KB JPEG	56 KB JPEG	235 KB JPEG
Scanned color photo (24-bit color, 300 dpi, 3×5 inches)	6 MB BMP	12 KB JPEG	66 KB JPEG

caution Using this technique to shrink and compress an image file invariably causes a loss of data. When you're sending a snapshot to your parents, the drop in quality is probably a fair tradeoff for the faster, slimmer e-mail attachment. But if the scanned image contains text, or if the recipient wants to be able to print a high-quality copy, check the compressed image before you click Send. Where quality is crucial, you might have better results using the Zip format to compress the original file without losing any data. Or look for a third-party image editing program such as Paint Shop Pro (*http://www.jasc.com*), which gives you greater control over compression.

Optimizing Image Files for the Web

Overly large image files are just as unwelcome on Web sites as they are in e-mail. Professional Web developers make a science out of "optimizing" graphics files for use on Web pages. Windows XP offers a limited set of tools for compressing image files and transferring them to a select number of Web-based locations, including free sites on

Chapter 18

641

MSN. The Web Publishing Wizard works only on Web sites that are specifically configured to hook into the wizard's dialog boxes. If you have a Web site hosted elsewhere,
you won't be able to access it through this wizard.

To launch the Web Publishing Wizard, select one or more graphics files (or an entire
folder) and click the Publish To The Web link in the File And Folder Tasks list. After
confirming, and if necessary, changing your file selection and choosing a Web-based
destination, you'll end up at the dialog box shown in Figure 18-6. As in the Send
Pictures Via E-Mail dialog box, you can choose from three image sizes.

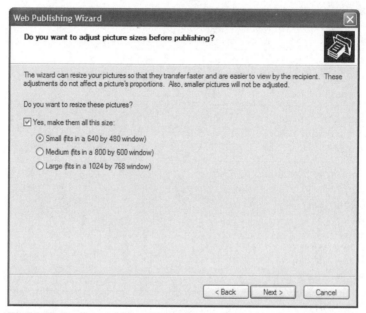

Figure 18-6. To avoid wasting Web server space and speed up page loading times,
choose the Small option when uploading image files.

If you prefer to leave all your files their original size, clear the Yes, Make Them All This
Size check box. Otherwise, choose one of the three options, and complete the wizard to
compress and upload the files in a single operation.

Compressing Image Files

The simplest way to compress a bitmap image, so you can make it more suitable for
uploading to the Web, is to open it in Paint, and then use Paint's Save As command to
convert it to a JPEG file. You can reduce the size of your BMP files by as much as 95
percent using this simple procedure.

Windows XP doesn't include any batch conversion tools, but a couple of easy workarounds let you reduce the size of many image files at once. The first method is to

download the Image Resizer PowerToy from *www.microsoft.com/windowsxp/pro/ downloads/powertoys.asp*. (Don't be concerned about the "pro" in that URL; the PowerToys work with both Windows XP Professional and Windows XP Home Edition.) Like the other PowerToys available from that site, Image Resizer is offered free but not supported by Microsoft. We can attest to its reliability, though.

Once you have downloaded and installed Image Resizer, a Resize Pictures command appears on the shortcut menu whenever you select one or more image files. Clicking the command produces the following dialog box. (Click Advanced if you don't see the full dialog box.) You can change the size of an entire folderful of images at once with this command.)

Note that the Image Resizer can change the size of your pictures, but not the file format. A BMP file resized this way remains a BMP file and still consumes far more bits than a comparably sized JPEG. If you need to make a significant reduction in the file size of a batch of images—say, if you're getting ready to upload a folder of scanned photos to a personal Web site hosted on a server that isn't compatible with the Web Publishing Wizard—you can take the following indirect route:

1 Open a Windows Explorer window, navigate to the folder that contains the images, and then select one or more files.

2 Click the E-Mail The Selected Items link in the File And Folder Task list.

3 In the Send Pictures Via E-Mail dialog box, choose the image size you want (Small, Medium, or Large), and click OK.

4 A new mail message window opens. Don't bother adding an address to the resulting e-mail. Instead, open a new Windows Explorer window and browse to the folder where you want to save the compressed files. (Don't use the original folder.)

5 Select all the attachment icons from the e-mail message, and then drag them out of the message window and into the folder you just opened.

6 Close the message window. Your files are now ready for uploading.

Chapter 18

643

Creating an HTML Slide Show

Want to turn your pictures into a slide show suitable for uploading to a Web site? The Microsoft PowerToys collection includes a tool that lets you do just that. You can download this HTML Slide Show Wizard from *www.microsoft.com/windowsxp/pro/ downloads/powertoys.asp.* (The PowerToys are a set of free utilities created by, but not supported by, Microsoft.)

Note: Slide shows created with the HTML Slide Show Wizard can be viewed on your own computer as well as on a Web site. If you show them in Microsoft Internet Explorer, your slides include attractive transition effects. The PowerToys collection also includes a CD Slide Show Generator that lets you add a viewer to custom-burned picture CDs. For information about this PowerToy, see the Inside Out tip on page 470.

The HTML Slide Show Wizard starts by walking you through the selection of individual images and folders of images to include in your show. Once you've gathered your pictures, you can put them in the order you want by dragging them in a dialog box that looks like this:

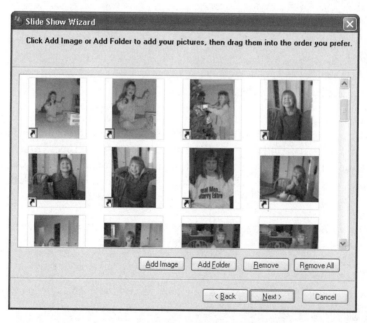

The wizard's remaining steps let you name your show, add your own name as the show's author (if you choose), provide a file name and a folder in which to store the show, and choose various options. The most important of these options lets you reduce large images to a size more suitable for Web storage—320×240, 640×480, or 800×600. You can also choose between a simple show and an advanced show. The latter gives your audience a few extra viewing options but requires additional storage.

To try out your work locally, simply navigate in Windows Explorer to the folder in which the wizard stored your show, and then double-click the file Default.htm. Figure 18-7 illustrates the wizard's output, as rendered by Internet Explorer in full-screen mode.

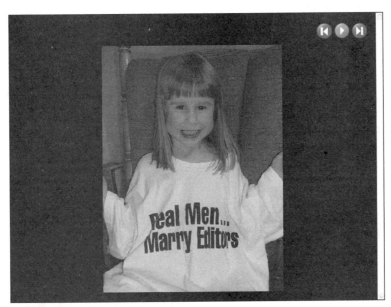

Figure 18-7. The HTML Slide Show Wizard generates attractive slide shows suitable for local viewing or uploading to the Internet.

newfeature!
Printing Digital Photos

Digital images are ideal for on-screen viewing, but they're hardly suitable for framing. That's where the Windows XP Photo Printing Wizard comes in. This new addition to Windows allows you to size, crop, and rotate images so that you get the best results on the printed page. This wizard is particularly useful when you want to make best use of expensive photo-quality paper, because it allows you to lay out multiple photos on the page for maximum coverage.

The easiest starting point for the Photo Printing Wizard is the Print This Picture link in the Picture Tasks box shown here. (This task box is visible by default in the My Pictures folder and any other location you've designated as a place to store pictures or photos.)

If the Picture Tasks pane isn't visible, you can bring up the wizard easily enough. Select one or more images in any Windows Explorer window, right-click, and choose Print from the shortcut menu. If you want to see the picture in its own window first, right-click and choose Preview to open the file in the Windows Picture And Fax Viewer. From this window, you can launch the Photo Printing Wizard by clicking the Print button.

The wizard walks you through the following three steps:

- **Picture Selection.** This window shows the files you selected or, if you didn't make a selection, all image files in the current folder. Use the check boxes above each thumbnail to select or clear an image from the list.

- **Printing Options.** Choose a printer from the drop-down list, and then click the Printing Preferences button to set printer-specific options. This step is crucial if you intend to use photo paper. Choose color and resolution options here, and specify whether you want to print multiple copies.

- **Layout Selection.** This is where you specify how you want the photos to be arranged on the page. As Figure 18-8 shows, you can mix and match photographs on each layout.

Figure 18-8. To make most efficient use of expensive photo paper, use the Photo Printing Wizard to lay out images on the page.

You'll get best results using the Photo Printing Wizard when you start with images saved using the 4:3 ratio that's standard with most cameras—digital and film. All but one of the nine available layouts crop images during the printing process. Depending on the proportions of the selected images, you could be unpleasantly surprised by the final results. Table 18-2 lists all the available layouts and offers advice for using each one most effectively.

---

tip   **Avoid wasting paper**

Make your choices carefully when choosing a print layout, or you might end up wasting paper accidentally. Pay special attention to the number of photos in your selection and on the layout; if you select three images and then choose the 5x7 in. Prints layout, which contains slots for two prints, the wizard will put the final image on a page by itself. Rather than waste half a sheet of photo paper, you might want to select a fourth image to fill the remaining space. Or, as an alternative, you could split the job in two. Select two images and print them on a single page; then run the wizard again and print the third image using the same layout, increasing the Number Of Times To Use Each Picture setting to 2.

Table 18-2. **Photo Printing Wizard Layouts**

Layout	How to Use It
Full page fax or photo prints	The Full Page Fax Print layout is the only one that doesn't crop any portion of the image away. Instead, the image is centered on the page and rotated, if necessary, leaving some white space on two sides. The Full Page Photo Print layout crops the image slightly to fill the entire space.
Contact sheet prints	Choose this layout to print out thumbnail images of all selected images, with the file name just below each image. Ideal for creating a printed index to a large library of digital images.
8×10 in. prints	Similar to the full page layouts, with slightly more severe cropping. This layout removes about 6% (cropped equally from the shorter sides of the image) of a standard 4:3 photo.
5×7 in. prints	A very efficient use of paper, with about 5% of the image cropped away; the cuts are made equally on both long edges of the image.

(continued)

Table 18-2. *(continued)*

Layout	How to Use It
4×6 in. cutout prints or album prints	Cropping removes more than 10% of the image, and the effect can be especially severe because the cuts are to the long edges—in other words, an image that is shot in normal orientation loses equally large slices from the top and bottom. For most efficient use of paper, choose the layout with three photos per 8½-by-11-inch sheet.
3.5×5 in. cutout prints	This option makes the most efficient use of paper, with less intrusive cropping than the 4x6 layout.
Wallet prints	This layout involves virtually no cropping. If you don't need nine copies of a single image, try selecting three images and printing each picture three times.

When using the Photo Printing Wizard, choose layouts carefully and pay close attention to cropping. For casual snapshots, the default cropping might not be noticeable. But for images that are carefully composed, you'll get best results by cropping the image manually so its proportions match those of the print layout you plan to use.

Organizing Your Digital Picture Collection

Most people throw their digital images into the online equivalent of a shoe box. The Scanner And Camera Wizard can automatically number image files and dump them into folders for you, but that's about the extent of its organizational expertise. If you shoot lots of pictures, learn how to take advantage of information called *metadata* to keep track of extra details.

Image metadata is nonpicture information that's captured and stored within a picture file. Metadata typically includes the width and height of the image (in pixels), the resolution (in dpi), and the color depth. Depending on the camera you use, metadata can also include technical information such as the camera model, flash mode, f-number, and exposure time. Some high-end devices even allow you to add audio annotations to images and store them in the same file. A few bits of metadata are available in the ScreenTip that appears when you pause the mouse pointer over an image file, as shown on the facing page.

Dimensions: 1280 x 960
Date Picture Taken: 3/25/2001 11:37 PM
Camera Model: KODAK DC240 ZOOM DIGITAL CAMERA
Type: JPEG Image
Size: 407 KB

Windows XP doesn't allow you to edit image metadata. But you can use it in Windows Explorer windows to sort and file images. To see all available metadata for an individual image file, right-click the file icon and then choose Properties. On the Summary tab, click Advanced to display a scrolling list of available metadata properties and values. Image data appears above the Description data, as in the example in Figure 18-9.

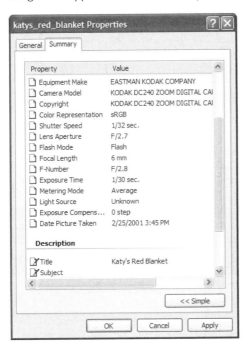

Figure 18-9. Image metadata is captured by a camera and stored within each image file; it can't be edited.

To really take advantage of metadata, you need to customize the Windows Explorer window so that metadata information is visible. To do so, switch to Details view, right-click any column heading, and then select the names of available fields to make those columns visible. Click More at the bottom of the list to see all possible fields. Here you can select multiple fields and arrange their order in one step.

(continued)

Organizing Your Digital Picture Collection (continued)

Figure 18-10 shows the results of customizing Details view for a folder filled with image files. The most noteworthy addition here is the Date Picture Taken column. Click the column heading to sort by this field and gather pictures that were taken around the same time.

Figure 18-10. Displaying image metadata in a Windows Explorer window makes it a snap to see the date when a photo was taken.

You can search for pictures on the basis of their metadata tags. To find all pictures taken with your GR-DVM90 camera, for example, choose Pictures, Music, Or Video in the Search pane, and then select Pictures And Photos. Then click Use Advanced Search Options and enter GR-DVM90 in the A Word Or Phrase In The File box.

newfeature!

Managing Images in Windows Explorer

In Windows XP, the My Pictures folder is the official storage location for image files of all sorts. When you acquire an image with a WIA-compatible device, it's stored in this folder. When you use Internet Explorer's Image toolbar, you jump straight to this folder. And any modern application that uses image files will use this folder as its default storage location.

Although the My Pictures folder itself has been around for several Windows versions, Windows XP incorporates the following new file management features that make it easier to work with image files:

- **Thumbnails view.** When you choose this view to display the contents of the My Pictures folder, Windows shows a miniature image of the image file itself. The icon for each subfolder that contains image files displays thumbnails of the last four images you created or modified in that subfolder.

- **The Picture Tasks box.** This list of links gives you quick access to common tasks you're likely to perform with images. You can order prints online, copy a group of files to a CD, view all the images in the current folder as a full-screen slide show, or launch the Photo Printing Wizard.

- **Filmstrip view.** In the My Pictures folder (and all its subfolders) this new view allows you to quickly preview images, rotate them 90 degrees at a time, and perform common image-related tasks. Figure 18-11 on the next page shows this view in action. Note that the "strip" of photos in the bottom of the window scrolls from left to right, whereas the preview pane above it stays in a fixed location.

> **tip**   Give photos some extra room
>
> Want to clear the title bar, menus, Address bar, and other space-hogging screen elements when working with a folder full of images? Press F11, the Full Screen shortcut key, to banish virtually all the clutter above the preview pane in Filmstrip view. The only thing left is a scaled-down toolbar. To return to normal view, press F11 again.

Chapter 18

Use these two buttons to quickly preview images

These buttons rotate the selected image 90 degrees left or right

Figure 18-11. In the new Filmstrip view, you can scroll through thumbnails along the bottom of the folder window and preview selected images.

Troubleshooting

Some thumbnails don't appear.

In Thumbnails or Filmstrip view, you might encounter some images that simply won't display as a proper thumbnail. A variety of technical problems can cause broken thumbnails, which typically appear as a large red X or a generic image icon. Try one of the following techniques to restore the thumbnail:

● Press F5 to refresh the folder's contents.

● Right-click the image icon and choose Refresh Thumbnail from the shortcut menu.

● Rotate the image 90 degrees clockwise and then rotate it back to its original position. This technique allows Windows to reread the image.

● Open the image file in Paint and save it under another name, using the same format.

If none of these techniques is successful, the file might be in a format that Windows Explorer's thumbnail handler doesn't recognize, even though it can preview the image when selected. If that's the case, try opening the image in Paint and saving it under a new name, using a different file format.

Customizing Folders for Images

When you create a new subfolder in the My Pictures folder, it automatically inherits all of Windows Explorer's image-handling tools. But you can customize any folder to have these tools as well. Say, for instance, that you keep a collection of logos and product pictures in a subfolder on your drive D. Here's how to customize this folder so it includes Filmstrip view and the Picture Tasks list:

1 Right-click the folder icon and choose Properties.

2 On the Customize tab, choose Pictures from the Use This Folder Type As A Template list.

3 If you want to organize image files in subfolders, select Also Apply This Template To All Subfolders.

4 To define a custom image that will appear on the folder in Thumbnails and Filmstrip views, click the Choose Picture button and select an image file. If you skip this step, Windows Explorer will display the last four images modified. Note that the image you define here will become part of the template for this folder and will appear on every subfolder you create as well.

5 To add a custom icon to identify the folder in all other views, click the Change Icon button and select an icon file. (To see an example, look at the custom My Music and My Pictures icons in the My Documents folder.)

---

tip   **Make your own icons**

Creating custom icons isn't particularly difficult. There are dozens of free and shareware icon editors available, or you can create your own. The rules for an icon are simple: Make it 32 pixels square and save it in BMP format, using the extension .ico.

When you're finished, the dialog box displays the custom image you selected, as in the example shown in Figure 18-12 on the next page. Click OK to apply your changes.

Chapter 18

Figure 18-12. Use these settings to customize any folder on any drive so that it includes image file management tools.

InsideOut

When customizing a folder, you can also choose Photo Album from the Use This Folder Type As A Template list. What's the difference? In a Photo Album folder, Filmstrip is the default view; a Pictures folder defaults to Thumbnails view. Otherwise, the two customizations are identical.

Viewing and Annotating Image Files

Unless you install a third-party program to handle image viewing, double-clicking an image file opens the Windows Picture And Fax Viewer. This utility, a Windows XP newcomer, displays images in a resizable preview window that includes a toolbar for common actions.

If you open an ordinary image file, the toolbar consists of 14 buttons that allow you to resize the image; rotate it 90 degrees in either direction; delete, print, or save the file; and open it for editing.

As Figure 18-13 shows, however, the toolbar is greatly expanded when you open a TIFF image. Nine additional buttons allow you to annotate the image, using text, simple lines and shapes, yellow "sticky notes," and a highlighter tool. Notice, too, the navigation controls in the center of the toolbar, which allow you to move from page to page within a multipage document such as a fax.

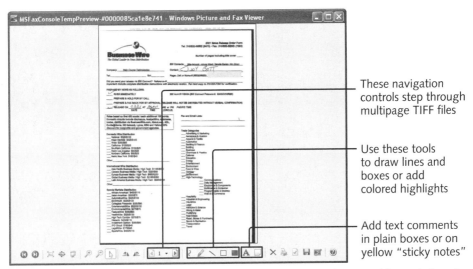

These navigation controls step through multipage TIFF files

Use these tools to draw lines and boxes or add colored highlights

Add text comments in plain boxes or on yellow "sticky notes"

Figure 18-13. Use the tools at the bottom of this Viewer window to add annotations to a TIFF file.

To open an image file in the Windows Picture And Fax Viewer, double-click the file's icon or thumbnail. If that doesn't work, right-click the icon and choose Windows Picture And Fax Viewer from the Open With menu.

Part 5

Using E-Mail, Fax, and Messaging

Chapter 19

Using and Customizing Outlook Express

Why Outlook Express? You probably use at least one suite of office applications, which means you probably already have a program to send and retrieve your e-mail. So why would you want to use Microsoft Outlook Express—especially considering that its name suggests that it's just a lightweight, scaled down, miniature version of Microsoft Outlook (the scheduling, contact-management, and e-mail client component of Microsoft Office)?

Names can be deceiving. Outlook Express might not have quite the power of Outlook, but it would be a mistake to consider it lightweight. If you've dismissed Outlook Express because you're already happily sending and receiving e-mail with another product, here are some reasons to reconsider your decision:

Identities   Outlook Express's *identities* feature allows multiple users to send and receive mail, each using separate accounts and storing their messages and address books in private sets of folders. This feature was originally intended for use with earlier versions of Windows, in which a family shares a single copy of Outlook Express running on a single computer. In Microsoft Windows XP, this feature is much less compelling, because each user can have a separate account with a private copy of Outlook Express. With the help of Fast User Switching, any user on a shared computer can easily and quickly access his or her own mail. Outlook Express identities are still useful for individuals who want to create multiple e-mail "personalities" that share a common address book. For some

At Home with Windows XP

Outlook Express 6 is absolutely identical in Windows XP Home Edition and Professional. All the information in this chapter applies to users of both editions of Windows XP.

suggestions on how you can benefit from using Outlook Express identities, see "Managing Identities," page 671. For more information about sharing contacts, see "Managing Contacts," page 673.

Newsgroups   Outlook Express is both an e-mail client and a capable newsgroup client. If you take advantage of the Internet's vast array of public and proprietary newsgroups, you might want to employ the same application for accessing both your mail account and your newsgroups. That way you can integrate e-mail and newsgroup messages into a common topic-oriented folder structure. For more details on setting up and using newsgroup accounts, see "Using Newsgroups," page 697.

Hotmail   You can use Microsoft's free Hotmail service (using either a hotmail.com or msn.com address) with any Internet connection. You don't need an e-mail client to access your Hotmail account. However, with Outlook Express, you can use Hotmail more effectively. If you have a Hotmail account as well as an industry-standard SMTP/POP3 e-mail account hosted with your ISP, Outlook Express gracefully deals with both, each in its own folder tree. Outlook Express also enables you to work with your Hotmail messages offline. You can use it to read and answer mail when you're away from your Internet connection. Then, when you reconnect, Outlook Express synchronizes your offline work with the Hotmail server, sending your replies and letting you know about additional messages that have arrived.

Getting Started with Outlook Express

Getting started with Outlook Express involves a few relatively painless steps: setting up your accounts, tailoring the program's visual presentation so that the information you need is at hand but your screen isn't overwhelmed with details you don't require, and making a few decisions in the Options dialog box.

Setting Up Accounts

The Internet Accounts dialog box (choose Tools, Accounts) is where you can set up, review, edit, and delete accounts. Accounts are organized in three categories, called Mail, News, and Directory Service. Each category gets a tab in the dialog box. For your convenience, the dialog box lists your accounts of all three types on an All tab (see Figure 19-1).

Chapter 19: Using and Customizing Outlook Express

Figure 19-1. The All tab of the Internet Accounts dialog box provides a consolidated list of your mail, news, and directory service accounts.

Mail and news accounts are presumably self-explanatory; they allow you to send and receive e-mail and newsgroup messages. Directory service accounts are different— and might better be described as connections than as accounts. A directory service is a repository of information about people and businesses. When you don't know someone's e-mail address, you can try to find it by searching your directory services. You can also set things up so that Outlook Express checks incomplete e-mail addresses in your outbound messages against one or more directory services. For more information about directory services, see "Creating a Directory Service Account," page 663.

Creating a Mail Account

If you start Outlook Express without already having established a mail account, the Internet Connection Wizard appears to guide you through the steps necessary to create your first account. If you need to create an additional account, or if you canceled out of the wizard when you first got to it and are ready now to create your first account, choose Tools, Accounts. In the Internet Accounts dialog box, click Add, and then Mail. You'll be greeted by the Your Name page of the Internet Connection Wizard. The wizard already knows your name, of course, but with this first page it gives you the chance to change the way your name is presented to recipients of your e-mail messages. For example, if your name is Prasanna Samarawickrama, but you'd rather your recipients see your messages as coming from Prasanna (without the last name), you can make the necessary changes here. When you complete the first page of the wizard, click Next to move to the second page.

> **tip**   **Keep it simple**
>
> It might be tempting to add some flourish to your name on the Your Name page—your academic or professional credentials, for example. But remember that what you put here is likely to be added to the address books of your personal and business contacts. If you want to identify yourself elaborately, do it in a signature (choose Tools, Options, and then click the Signatures tab), rather than on the Your Name page. You'll be able to change the signature over time and use personalized signatures for different audiences.

The wizard's second page is called Internet E-Mail Address. Here you specify the address that will be added to your recipients' address books if they exercise an "Add Sender to Address Book" command in their e-mail software. By default, this is also the address that your recipients will use if they click Reply to answer your e-mail. If you want replies to go to a different address, you'll need to edit the properties for your account after you've finished with the wizard.

On the wizard's E-Mail Server Names page, you'll need to supply server addresses for your inbound and outbound mail. If you're not sure what to enter on this screen, contact your ISP or network administrator. Outlook Express supports three server protocols for inbound mail: POP3, IMAP, and HTTP. If your inbound server uses POP3 or IMAP, you'll need to specify a separate server address for outbound mail. (The outbound server uses the SMTP protocol.) If your inbound mail uses HTTP (as Hotmail does, for example), you'll need to specify only one server address. The outbound server edit box will appear gray in that case, and a new box will appear in which you can specify your HTTP mail provider. If you choose Hotmail, the remaining server field will be conveniently filled in for you. If you choose Other, you'll need to fill in that box yourself.

> **note**   As of this writing, only Hotmail and MSN support HTTP mail via Outlook Express. Although many other companies offer Web-based mail services, none of them can be configured to work with Outlook Express.

On the Internet Mail Logon page of the wizard, supply your logon information—the name of your account, as given to you by your ISP or other service provider, and your password. A Remember Password option on this screen will be selected by default. If you're concerned that someone else might try to use your computer to access your e-mail account, clear this check box. You'll then be prompted for the password each time you send or retrieve mail.

After you've supplied the logon information, click Next, then Finish, and you're ready to use the new account.

> **tip** **Export a copy of your account information**
>
> If you don't ever want to be bothered re-creating an e-mail account, choose Tools, Accounts, select the account name, and then click Export. Outlook Express will save your account settings in an .iaf file. If you ever need to re-establish the account—on this computer or another—you can import that .iaf file (in encrypted format), so if you're concerned about security, store the file offline, using a suitably private backup medium such as a floppy disk locked in a filing cabinet.

Creating a News Account

Creating a newsgroup account is just like creating a mail account, except that you provide the address of an NNTP server instead of mail servers. Choose Tools, Accounts, click Add, News, and then follow the wizard. On the first two pages, provide your display name (the name that other newsgroup users will see when you post messages) and your return e-mail address. On the third page, supply the server details. If your news server does not require you to log on (many do not), leave the My News Server Requires Me To Log On option unselected. If you're setting up access to a private news server or you subscribe separately to a commercial news server—that is, a news server that does require a logon—select this option, and then supply logon details on the ensuing page.

Creating a Directory Service Account

By default, Outlook Express provides access to your Active Directory and several public Lightweight Directory Access Protocol (LDAP) servers. (The Active Directory is a service that provides information about objects available on a domain-based network. In standalone or workgroup settings, Outlook Express ignores the Active Directory account.) With these directory "accounts" established, you can look for people or businesses on the Internet (or in your Active Directory) by pressing Ctrl+E (or clicking the Find button on the toolbar and then choosing People from the Find menu). As Figure 19-2 shows, the Find People dialog box includes a drop-down list of available directory

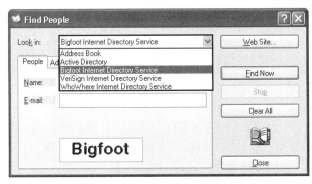

Figure 19-2. The Find People dialog box allows you to look for a contact in any of your established directory service accounts.

services (as well as your own address book). If you have the server and logon information, you can make additional LDAP servers available by choosing Tools, Accounts, and then clicking Add and Directory Service.

When you create e-mail messages, Outlook Express checks your addressees against your own address book. If you type an addressee's name on the To line, for example, Outlook Express retrieves the addressee's e-mail address from the address book. If you type part of a name and Outlook Express can't figure out who you're trying to address, it presents a list of possible matches. By default, the program does not check addressees against entries in LDAP servers. But you can add this form of lookup as follows:

1 Choose Tools, Accounts.

2 On the Directory Service tab (or All tab) of the Internet Accounts dialog box, select the name of a directory service, and then click Properties.

3 On the General tab of the directory service's properties dialog box, select Check Names Against This Server When Sending Mail.

Editing Account Information

After you've used the Internet Connection Wizard to create an account, you can use the account's properties dialog box to modify any of the information you gave the wizard. To open an account's properties dialog box, choose Tools, Accounts. Select the name of the account and then click Properties.

InsideOut

You have no choice but to use the wizard to set up a new mail account initially. However, if you're a sophisticated mail user you should visit the properties dialog box for each mail account after completing initial setup. Several options are particularly useful, including the following:

● **Mail Account (General tab).** Use this option to change the name displayed in the Accounts dialog box. By default, the account name is the same as the mail server for SMTP/POP3 accounts; Hotmail accounts use the word *Hotmail* and a number to identify multiple accounts. Change this if you've created several versions of the same account with different properties for different uses, or if you have multiple Hotmail/MSN accounts.

● **Reply Address (General tab).** Enter an e-mail address here if you want recipients to send replies to a different address than the address from which you sent the original message. Use this option, for instance, if you send messages from a Hotmail account while traveling because your regular SMTP server is unavailable but want replies to go back to your personal account.

Chapter 19: Using and Customizing Outlook Express

● **My Server Requires Authentication (Servers tab).** Select this option if you are connecting to an SMTP server that requires an extra authentication step as an anti-spam measure—many servers require that you log on to the POP3 server first (using your user name and password) before being allowed to send messages.

● **Leave A Copy Of Messages On Server (Advanced tab).** This option comes in handy if you're checking your work mail from a computer at home (or vice-versa) but you want to maintain a complete archive of messages on the other computer. You can check for new messages at home; when you return to the office, your mail program will download those messages into your Inbox.

Customizing the Look of Outlook Express

Figure 19-3 shows all of Outlook Express's optional visual elements. Unless you're using a large monitor at high resolution, you probably don't want all these elements crowding your display. Everything in Outlook Express's presentation is optional, except for the title bar, the menu bar, and the message list. To tell the program what you want to see, choose View Layout, and then select or clear check boxes in the Window Layout Properties dialog box.

Figure 19-3. Everything in this display except the title bar, menu bar, and message list is optional.

Previewing Messages

The preview pane displays the contents of the currently selected message. When you're scanning mail or newsgroup messages, you can save yourself a lot of time by scanning the first few lines of each message in the preview pane, rather than opening each message and reading it in its own window. However, using the preview pane also exposes you to the dark side of e-mail, because it allows potentially hostile scripts to run without any action on your part. It also downloads any HTML content, including "Web bugs" that can confirm to mail senders that you received their message and at least previewed it.

> **caution** A number of viruses and worms in recent years have taken advantage of vulnerabilities in the HTML-rendering capabilities of Outlook Express to automatically install hostile code. If you're diligent about applying security patches and keeping your antivirus software updated, you're generally safe from these types of attacks. However, you run a small but significant risk of infection on those rare occasions when a new virus or worm appears that exploits a previously unknown vulnerability. If your approach to computer security is extra-cautious, bordering on paranoid, you should disable the preview pane so that you can scan incoming messages and delete suspicious content before it has a chance to do any damage.

If you choose to display the preview pane, you can position it either below the message list or alongside it. You can also choose whether or not to include the preview pane header. As you can see in Figure 19-3, the header doesn't provide any information that can't also be displayed in the column headings of the message list, so if you're short of visual space, you can economize by eliminating the preview pane header.

Navigating the Folders List

Outlook Express uses folders to organize messages. The program creates one set of folders by default. Called Local Folders, these folders are used for any POP3 e-mail accounts you have. It also includes Outbox and Drafts folders that are shared by all your accounts. In addition to the Local Folders tree, Outlook Express creates a separate set of folders for each HTTP and IMAP account you use, as well as a set of folders for each of your news accounts. Figure 19-3, for example, shows two branches of folders in the Outlook Express tree—Local Folders and Hotmail. Scrolling the folders list would reveal additional branches of folders for news accounts. All these folder branches are subsumed under a heading called Outlook Express.

Figure 19-3 shows the three visual elements that you can use to navigate your folders—the folders list, the folder bar, and the Outlook bar. Of these, the Outlook bar is the least useful because it provides access to only a few folders (initially the top-level folders in the Local Folder tree; you can add other folders by right-clicking them and choosing Add To Outlook Bar). You can right-click any empty space in the Outlook bar and choose the Small Icons option to make room for more such icons, but unless you're lavishly fixed for screen real estate, you might as well pass on the option to display the Outlook bar. (The Outlook bar originated with Microsoft Outlook, which puts it to better use by including selections that take advantage of its unique personal-information–management capabilities, such as Contacts, Tasks, Notes, Journal, and Calendar.)

The folders list provides familiar controls for navigating folders and subfolders. Like the Folders bar in Windows Explorer, it comes with a convenient Close button, so you can easily bump it out of the way if you occasionally need a wider perspective on your message list and preview pane. (To redisplay it, choose View, Layout, and then select Folder List.)

The folder bar isn't as useful if you're displaying the folders list. With the folders list absent, however, it turns into a handy drop-down list. Click its heading and your entire folder structure unfolds, allowing easy navigation. Thus, if you opt to show the folder bar but not the folders list, you get a broad view of your messages without sacrificing mobility.

For an even more economical layout, you can hide the Outlook bar, the folders list, *and* the folder bar. When you want to move to a different folder, press Ctrl+Y. The Go To Folder dialog box appears, as shown in Figure 19-4, allowing you to navigate to any folder.

Figure 19-4. If you prefer not to display the folders list alongside your messages, you can navigate by pressing Ctrl+Y to summon this dialog box.

Displaying Contacts

If you choose to display Contacts, Outlook Express presents a list of everyone in your address book alongside your message list and preview pane. Having the contacts list visible can sometimes simplify message addressing. Double-click a person's name in the list, and Outlook Express opens a New Message window, with the message already addressed to that person. On the other hand, the contact list typically crowds out the folders list, so many users prefer not to display it. If you forego the contacts list, you can always find your contacts by opening your address book (press Ctrl+Shift+B; click Addresses on the toolbar; or choose Tools, Address Book).

> **tip**   **Use your contact list to send instant messages**
>
> If you use Windows Messenger and Outlook Express, your Windows Messenger contacts appear at the top of Outlook Express's contacts pane. A green icon appears next to any contacts who are currently online. If a contact is online, you can initiate an instant message conversation with that person by double-clicking his or her name in the contacts pane. For more information about Windows Messenger, see "Introducing Windows Messenger," page 730.

Setting Basic Options

The Options dialog box (choose Tools, Options) offers a great many choices, some of which you should make right away, others of which you can defer or ignore.

Checking for Mail at Regular Intervals

By default, Outlook Express checks every 30 minutes to see whether you have mail. You can change that interval (or disable automatic checking) on the General tab of the Options dialog box. Whether or not you fetch mail on a schedule, you can send and receive at any time by pressing Ctrl+M. This keyboard shortcut checks all your e-mail accounts, unless you have disabled automatic e-mail checking for a particular account (choose Tools, Accounts, select the account you want to check manually, click the Properties button, and clear the Include This Account When Receiving Mail Or Synchronizing option on the General tab). To check a particular account only, choose Tools, Send And Receive, and then select the account you want to check.

Outlook Express also ordinarily looks for mail at startup (that is, when you launch Outlook Express) and plays a sound to announce the arrival of a message. You can turn these defaults off by clearing check boxes on the General tab. If you want sound notification but prefer a different tune, choose Sounds And Audio Devices from the Control Panel (in Category view it's located in Sounds, Speech, And Audio Devices). Select the Sounds tab and then change the sound associated with the New Mail Notification event.

Minimizing Connect Time with Dial-Up Accounts

If you use a dial-up connection for e-mail, you should check a few configuration settings to make sure Outlook Express behaves the way you want it to. On the General tab of the Options dialog box, you'll find a setting labeled If My Computer Is Not

Connected At This Time. This determines what Outlook Express should do if you're checking for mail at scheduled intervals and you're offline when mail time arrives.

On the assumption that you might not always be connected to a phone line (you might be using a portable computer, for example), Outlook Express's default setting is Do Not Connect. If you're hooked up to the phone line most of the time, you might want to change to Connect Only When Not Working Offline. When you take your portable computer on the road and don't have a dial-up connection at your disposal, choose Work Offline from Outlook Express's File menu to let the program know when it would be pointless to dial.

Whether your computer is stationary or mobile, if you use the same telephone line for voice and data, if your ISP bills you by the hour, or if you incur tolls for your e-mail calls, go to the Connection tab of the Options dialog box, and select Hang Up After Sending And Receiving.

Controlling the Format of Outbound Messages

Most e-mail client programs nowadays can read HTML. Many newsgroup clients cannot. Therefore, Outlook Express formats outbound mail by default in HTML, leaving news posts in plain text. You can change these defaults on the Send tab of the Options dialog box.

If most of your correspondents have e-mail programs that can read HTML but some do not, you can set up Outlook Express so that it sends new messages in plain text to those that require it. To ensure that a particular person receives plain-text mail from you, open that person's record in Address Book by double-clicking the entry or by right-clicking it and choosing Properties. Select the Name tab and then select Send E-mail Using Plain Text Only. Be aware that if you send HTML to a recipient whose program cannot handle HTML, you'll have a disgruntled correspondent to answer to.

> For more information about using Address Book, see "Managing Contacts," page 673.

---

tip Turn HTML off while composing a message

If you forget to suppress HTML formatting in a recipient's address book entry, you can still turn it off while composing a message. In the New Message window, choose Format, Plain Text.

Making Outlook Express the Default Mail and News Handler

Near the bottom of the General tab of the Options dialog box, you'll find options for making Outlook Express the default mail handler and the default news handler. The default handlers are the programs that an Internet browser (such as Microsoft

Internet Explorer) turns to when you choose the browser's Mail or News command. For example, if you click the Mail tool on the Internet Explorer toolbar, and then choose New Message, Internet Explorer launches Outlook Express's New Message window—if Outlook Express is the default mail handler. The default mail handler is also the program that springs to life if you click a mailto link on a Web page or other document.

If you do not make Outlook Express the default handler for either mail or news, but no other mail or news client is installed on your system, Windows will treat Outlook Express as the default anyway (although it might not update the Options dialog box to say so). If you do make Outlook Express the default and decide subsequently to use a different mail or news handler, use *that* program's menus and dialog boxes to make *it* the default. Outlook Express itself does not have an "undefault" command.

> **tip** If your computer is running Windows XP Service Pack 1 and has been customized to hide access to one or more Microsoft Windows programs, you may not be able to select Outlook Express as your default e-mail program. In fact, you may not be able to find a program icon of any sort for Outlook Express. In this configuration, you can still run Outlook Express by opening the Run dialog box and entering the command **msimn.exe**. You can also manually create a shortcut to Outlook Express using **"%programfiles%\Outlook Express\msimn.exe"** as the target.
>
> For more details about the option to hide Outlook Express and other integrated Microsoft Windows programs, see "Selecting a Web Browser and Other Middleware Components," page 76.

Setting Security Options

Before you begin using Outlook Express, you should choose Tools, Options, and then select the Security tab in the Options dialog box to review your security settings. Make sure that the following options are selected:

● Restricted Sites Zone (More Secure)

● Warn Me When Other Applications Try To Send Mail As Me

Both are selected by default, but it's a good idea to check anyway.

Outlook Express shares the settings for the two most restrictive security zones available in Internet Explorer—the Internet zone and the Restricted Sites zone. By setting Outlook Express to follow the security restrictions observed in the Restricted Sites zone, you get the maximum protection that you have set for this zone in Internet Explorer. This setting goes a long way toward warding off potential viruses and Trojan horses. If something does make it past your defenses, the Warn Me option will provide protection against those viruses that replicate themselves by trying to hijack Outlook Express and its mail-sending capabilities.

It's worth noting that ActiveX controls and scripts are always disabled in Outlook Express, even if you've enabled them in the corresponding security zone for Internet Explorer. Also, the Warn Me capability is useless against modern viruses and worms that incorporate their own SMTP server to send infected messages without getting involved with Outlook Express.

note If you're concerned about e-mail security, we recommend our other book, *Microsoft Windows Security Inside Out* (Microsoft Press, 2002), which covers the topic in much greater detail than we can here, with a special emphasis on Outlook Express and Microsoft Outlook.

In Windows XP Service Pack 1, Microsoft introduced an important new security feature in Outlook Express. HTML-formatted e-mail and newsgroup messages can pose a host of problems. Pornographic spam messages, for instance, can display shocking images in your Inbox. Spam senders can confirm that your e-mail address is valid by embedding coded images in HTML-formatted messages and then checking the server logs to see which ones were downloaded in an e-mail client. You can short-circuit both types of threats by configuring Outlook Express to read all messages in plain text only. To enable this feature, choose Tools, Options, click the Read tab, and select the Read All Messages In Plain Text option.

Managing Identities

As we mentioned earlier in this chapter, the developers of Outlook Express originally devised the identities feature as a way for multiple users of the same computer to share a single copy of Outlook Express while still maintaining separate accounts, messages, and address books. With Windows XP, this feature is hardly necessary; it's much more practical for each person to have a separate user account, logging on with Fast User Switching to check their e-mail without disturbing another person's work.

But you might find it handy to switch between multiple identities, even if you're the only user of your computer. Having two or more identities is especially useful if you have multiple e-mail accounts and you want to maintain strict separation between them. For instance, you might create one identity for work, where you send and receive mail using your company's SMTP and POP3 servers. In another identity, you would send and receive personal messages from the account at your home ISP, along with two or three Hotmail accounts you use for shopping online. And you might use yet another identity for browsing newsgroups; by carefully configuring the settings in your news account, you can ensure that your "real" e-mail addresses for home and work are never published on a public newsgroup where they can be picked up by spammers.

Each identity is completely separate, with its own set of mail and news accounts, its own folders and message-handling rules, and a private address book. (A Shared Contacts folder in the Windows Address Book lets you create address book records that are visible to every identity.) When you switch between identities, Outlook Express actually shuts down and restarts, loading the new settings.

To start working with multiple identities, choose File, Identities, Manage Identities. As Figure 19-5 shows, Outlook Express initially uses a single identity, called Main Identity. You might want to replace this moniker with a real name—your own, perhaps, or a phrase that describes the purpose of the identity—Ed's Work Mail, Ed's Personal Mail, or Newsgroups Only, for instance. To change the name of the default identity, select Main Identity in the Manage Identities dialog box and click Properties. In the Identity Properties dialog box, in addition to renaming the identity, you can assign a password to it, so that only those who know the password can open the identity in Outlook Express or delete the identity if it's already open.

Figure 19-5. Outlook Express is initially set up with a single identity, called Main Identity. Use this dialog box to add others and rename Main Identity.

InsideOut

An identity password might discourage casual browsing of your mail, but it won't thwart even a modestly talented intruder. To make your e-mail inaccessible to others, password-protect your Windows XP user account, and make your store folder (the folder in which Outlook Express stores your messages) private. Be aware that your Address Book contacts can be seen by others, even if you do password-protect your user account. For information about the Outlook Express store folder, see "Relocating Your Message Store to Simplify Backup," page 702. For information about making folders private, see "Keeping Your Own Files Private," page 504.

Chapter 19: Using and Customizing Outlook Express

To create a new identity, click New, type a name, and type a password if you want one. That's all there is to it.

On opening, Outlook Express always returns to the identity that was in use when the program was closed—regardless of how the Manage Identities dialog box is filled out. To switch identities, choose File, Switch Identity. The first time you switch to a newly created identity, the Internet Connection Wizard prompts you to create a new account. If you want to use the same account settings in more than one identity, you'll need to re-create the account in each one.

---

tip **Consolidate identities**

Change your mind about using identities? You can use Outlook Express's Import command to import messages from one identity into another. Choose File, Import, Messages, Microsoft Outlook Express 6, and then specify the identity you want to import from. After you have consolidated all your messages into the main identity's folders, you can delete the identities you no longer need.

Managing Contacts

Outlook Express is tightly integrated with Address Book, a separate application designed to be shared by other programs that use contact information—fax clients, teleconferencing software, and the like. You can run Windows Address Book from Outlook Express by simply clicking Addresses on the toolbar. You can close it by pressing Esc. (If the toolbar isn't visible, choose Tools, Address Book.) You can also run Address Book from the Start menu; look for it under Accessories, or choose the Run command and type **wab**.

Figure 19-6 on the next page shows Address Book. As you can see, the program presents four columns of information, leading with name and e-mail address. You can change the order in which the four columns appear by dragging them to the left or right. You can change the sort order by clicking on the column by which you want to sort.

Names appear in Address Book, by default, in first name, last name order. You can override this when you create a new contact (click the arrow beside the Display box and choose from the list), but it's not advisable to do so. When you use Outlook Express facilities for adding contact names directly from e-mail messages (for example, the names of people you reply to via e-mail), those names almost always arrive in first-last order. If some of your contacts are listed last-first and others first-last, you wind up with a jumbled address book.

You'll also notice that Address Book doesn't know or care about the formatting of telephone numbers. If you want consistency, you have to enforce it upon yourself.

Figure 19-6. Address Book's four-column display is sorted by default by Name, with names presented in first, last order.

Organizing Contacts in Folders

The address book shown in Figure 19-6 includes two panes. The left pane contains a Shared Contacts folder for contacts shared between all identities using Outlook Express and a folder containing the current identity's contacts. The current identity's contacts are normally visible only to the current identity.

If your system does not display a left pane, choose View, Folders And Groups.

---

tip   View other identities' contacts

Address Book normally shows only the current identity's contacts and the shared contacts. This is a convenience feature, not a security feature. You can see the contacts of all the identities defined in Outlook Express by starting Address Book from a command line—type the command string **wab /a**. (If Address Book doesn't immediately display identity names in a left pane, choose View, Folders And Groups.) If you don't want other users to see your contacts, don't use identities.

The entries in the left pane—Shared Contacts and Craig's Contacts in Figure 19-6—are folders. To organize your contacts more effectively, you can add folders of your own to any existing folder. To add a folder, right-click its parent and choose New, New Folder.

To move a contact from one folder to another, select the contact's name in the right pane and then drag it to the appropriate folder in the left pane. To make a personal contact visible to other identities, for example, drag it from the right pane and drop it on the Shared Contacts heading in the left pane.

> **note** You cannot copy a contact by holding down Ctrl as you drag. Duplicate entries in Address Book create inefficiency, so Address Book doesn't encourage copying. (You can copy a contact, however, by right-clicking it, choosing Copy, moving to the destination, right-clicking again, and then choosing Paste.)

Sharing Contacts with Microsoft Outlook

Earlier versions of Address Book gave you the option of using your Microsoft Outlook Contacts folder in Outlook Express. If you accepted this option, Address Book became a front end to Outlook, visible in Outlook Express and any other applications that used Address Book. Contacts added via Outlook thus became accessible to Outlook Express, and contacts added to Address Book by means of Outlook Express options (such as Outlook Express's option to add the names of people you reply to via e-mail) became usable in Outlook.

This integration with Outlook is still available in Address Book 6 (the version shipped with Windows XP), but only via an undocumented registry edit. To share contact information between Outlook and Address Book, open Registry Editor, and go to HKCU\Software\Microsoft\WAB\WAB4. Add the DWORD value UseOutlook to this key (if it isn't already present), and set it to 1. To return to the unintegrated state, return to this registry value and either delete it or set it to 0.

The tradeoff for integration between Outlook and Address Book is that it precludes your using identities in Address Book. If you are using Outlook integration and you display the Folders And Groups pane in Address Book, you see the subfolders of your Outlook Contacts folder instead of your shared contacts and personal contacts.

Adding Individual Contacts and Distribution Lists

To add someone to your address book, right-click the folder you want the contact to appear in, and choose New, New Contact. (Alternatively, select the folder and then choose File, New Contact.) A seven-tabbed dialog box appears, in which you can enter as much or as little information as you need.

You can also add groups to your address book. When you send mail to a group, Outlook Express parses the group name into its individual member names and sends your mail to everyone in the group. To create a group, follow these steps:

1 Right-click the parent folder and choose New, New Group.

The properties dialog box for the new group opens, as shown in Figure 19-7 on the next page.

Part 5: Using E-Mail, Fax, and Messaging

2 Enter a group name (the name that you will choose when you address your outgoing mail).

3 Add names to the group. You can populate the group with contacts several ways:

- To add contacts that are already in your address book, click Select Members.

- To add a new contact to the group and also an individual entry to the address book, click New Contact.

- To add a new contact to the group but not create a separate individual entry for that contact, fill out the Name and E-Mail boxes, and then click Add.

4 Optionally enter additional information about the group itself on the Group Details tab of the Properties dialog box.

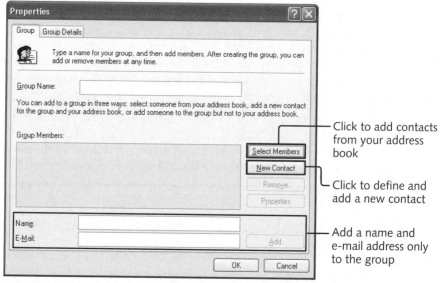

Click to add contacts from your address book

Click to define and add a new contact

Add a name and e-mail address only to the group

Figure 19-7. To create a distribution list, assign a group name and then add contacts from your address book to the group.

Adding Contacts Who Have Multiple E-Mail Addresses

You can enter multiple e-mail addresses on the Name tab of a contact's address book record. When you do this, Address Book requires that you designate one of the addresses as the default. When addressing a message to a contact with multiple e-mail addresses, if you specify the contact's name (as opposed to e-mail address) on the To line, Outlook Express looks the name up in your address book and uses the default mail address. In other words, you don't get to choose the address at the time you send the message. If you want control over which address is used, you need to specify the e-mail address, not the name, on the To line.

An alternative—and better—approach is to create separate address book entries for each of your contact's multiple e-mail addresses. You don't need to use different names when you do this (but you can if you want to). If John Doe has six e-mail addresses and you create six John Doe records in Address Book, when you create a message with John Doe on the To line, Outlook Express will present a dialog box asking you to choose an address.

Adding Contacts from E-Mail Messages

By default, when you reply to an e-mail message, Outlook Express adds the name of the person you reply to (and of everyone else who received that message, if you clicked Reply All) to your address book. For most users, this is a useful service. Junk senders don't land in your address book, because you don't reply to their spam, but contacts you find worth responding to are added. If you want to turn off this default behavior, choose Tools, Options, go to the Send tab, and clear Automatically Put People I Reply To In My Address Book.

You can also add senders to your address book without replying to their mail. In the message list, you can right-click a message and choose Add Sender To Address Book. Alternatively, you can open the message in its own window (double-click the message in the message list) and then, in the message window, choose Tools, Add To Address Book, Sender. There's a subtle but important difference between these two approaches. If you add the sender to your address book from the message list, the new contact is added forthwith. If you add the sender to your address book from the message window, you get to see and edit the new contact record before committing it to the address book. This technique gives you an opportunity to add more information about the entry while it's fresh in your mind.

From within the message window, you can also add other folks to your address book. If you receive a message that has gone to many other addressees as well, you can add them all at once by choosing Tools, Add To Address Book, Everyone On To List. (Note that this method doesn't catch recipients on the Cc line.) Or you can add any particular addressee by right-clicking that person's name—in any part of the address portion of the message—and choosing Add To Address Book.

Troubleshooting

Your address book is full of duplicates.

Over time, your address book will almost certainly accumulate some duplicate entries. The most common reason for duplication is that the people you correspond with send their messages from different systems with differing account identification. For example, suppose a friend buys a new computer and sets up an e-mail account (in Outlook Express or another e-mail client), uses the same e-mail address as before, but presents his name in a slightly different way (with a middle initial, perhaps). When you respond to mail sent from that new setup, Outlook Express will add a new entry to your address book. Fortunately, although the clutter in your address book might bother you, it has no adverse effect on Outlook Express.

You will also undoubtedly accumulate address book entries that you simply don't recognize. This can happen, for example, because you join a mailing list and receive a confirmation message from the list administrator that requires you to reply. Typically, when you reply, a new address book entry is added that consists only of an e-mail address. When you look at that entry later, you have no idea whose address it is or why the entry is there.

Again, the only negative consequence is clutter. If it bothers you, you can either turn off the automatic creation of address book entries from messages you send in reply (choose Tools, Options, go to the Send tab, and then clear Automatically Put People I Reply To In My Address Book), or you can periodically cruise through your address book, using your Delete key to clear out the clutter.

tip **Unmask mysterious senders**

Occasionally you might receive a message from someone identified only by an inscrutable e-mail address. You can look up the address in your address book by right-clicking the address and choosing Find from the shortcut menu. If you don't find the sender's identity that way, try right-clicking the address and pressing Ctrl+C to copy it. Then press Ctrl+E to open the Find People dialog box. Choose an LDAP server on the Look In line, select the E-Mail box, and press Ctrl+V to paste the address you copied. Then click Find Now to search for information over the Internet.

Exchanging Electronic Business Cards (vCards)

Address Book supports the vCard format, which allows you to exchange electronic business cards with other users via e-mail. To send your business card to another user, first create an address book record for yourself. Then select your record in Address Book, and choose File, Export, Business Card (vCard). This creates a file with the extension .vcf. Now create a message and attach this .vcf file. For information about attaching files to e-mail messages, see "Adding Attachments," page 685.

> **tip** **Keep your vCard up to date**
>
> If you created your electronic business card file a while ago and you're not sure the information is up to date, you can create one that is current each time you send it. Compose your e-mail message, open Address Book from the message's Tools menu, and then drag your name (or that of the business card you want to send) from Address Book into the body of the message and drop it there. A new .vcf file is instantly attached to the message. You can add as many of these business cards as you like before sending your message. But note that this shortcut won't update the .vcf file on your hard disk.

You can have Outlook Express include your business card in all outgoing mail or news messages. To do this, first create your card, as described in the previous paragraph. Then choose Tools, Options, and go to the Compose tab. In the Business Cards section of the dialog box, select Mail, News, or both Mail and News, and then select the contact name from the list.

To store an associate's electronic business card, double-click the attached .vcf file. The vCard appears as an address book record. Then click Add To Address Book.

> **note** If double-clicking a .vcf file does not display the vCard in Address Book, then your .vcf files are probably associated with some other application (such as Outlook). You can fix this by choosing Tools, Folder Options in Windows Explorer. Go to the File Types tab, select VCF in the Extensions column of the Registered File Types list, click Change, and then select Address Book.

Importing and Exporting Contacts

Address Book can import contacts from other Address Book files, as well as from comma-separated values (.csv) files and a few other formats. It can also write (export) your contact data in Address Book (.wab) or .csv formats, or as a Microsoft Exchange Personal Address Book.

Importing Address Book Data

To import data from another Address Book (.wab) file, choose File, Import, Address Book in Outlook Express or File, Import, Address Book (WAB) in Address Book. Address Book imports all records in the selected file. If an imported name has the same name as a record in the current file, Address Book tries to merge the data without creating a duplicate record. But if conflicts exist between imported data and existing data—say, for example, that an existing record has one business phone number and an imported record of the same name has another—Address Book does not import the conflicting record. Folder assignments in the imported data are ignored, but group assignments are preserved.

Importing Data from Other Programs

To import information from another contact manager, choose File, Import, Other Address Book in either Outlook Express or Address Book. Choose a file format from the list and then click Import.

If you specify a .csv file for import, Address Book will ask you to map the import file's fields (columns) to Address Book fields. If the .csv file doesn't include field headings (not an unlikely circumstance), you will have to use data in the first record of the .csv file as your guide for creating this mapping. Blank fields in the first record can make this difficult. To get around this problem, either make sure the first record is completely filled out before exporting to .csv from the source program (your other contact manager), or import the .csv file into a spreadsheet program and add field headings there. Then resave the file in .csv format and import it into Address Book.

If the .csv file that you're importing includes records whose names match records already in your address book, the import routine will ask whether you want to replace the existing record. If you answer no, the program will not import that entry.

Exporting the Address Book to a .wab File

To export your address book as an address book (.wab) file, choose File, Export, Address Book (WAB) in Address Book. Note that when you write Address Book data to an existing .wab file, the exported data replaces the existing data. It is not merged with the existing file. Thus, exporting to a .wab file is a good way to back up your contact list but not a method of merging your data with someone else's!

Exporting the Address Book to a .csv File

To export your address book as a .csv file, open Address Book and choose File, Export, Other Address Book. In the dialog box that appears, select Text File (Comma Separated Values), and then click Export. A wizard will prompt you for a file name, and a checkbox list of Address Book fields will appear. Select the fields you want to export and then click Finish.

---

tip **Try importing first**

Exporting to a .csv file is an excellent way of getting your contact data into a spreadsheet or database program. (It's also the simplest, most effective way we know to back up and restore the contents of your address book.) If you're trying to merge Address Book data with information in another contact management program, however, you should check first to see whether the other program can import .wab files directly. That way you can avoid potential mismatches of Address Book fields with fields in the other contact management program.

Printing Your Address Book

You can turn your address book into a handy printed phone or address list for easy access to contact information when you're away from your computer. To print, click the Print button on the Address Book toolbar. To print particular records only, select the ones you want (hold down Ctrl while selecting nonadjacent records), and then click Print.

The Print Style section of the Print dialog box offers three options:

- **Memo.** This option prints all the information you've stored for the selected contacts.

- **Business Card.** This option prints full name, job title, company name, business address, all phone numbers, and all e-mail addresses.

- **Phone List.** This option prints full name and all phone numbers. The printed list includes alphabetical separators.

Backing Up Your Address Book

As we noted earlier, the easiest way to back up your address book is to export it to a text file. To restore the backed-up addresses, open Address Book and choose File, Import, Other Address Book; choose Text File (Comma Separated Values) from the list of available formats, and browse to the previously exported file.

You can also back up the file in which your address book data resides. You'll find it in a .wab file nested many folders deep on your local hard disk. To discover its location, choose Help, About Address Book. To get to the folder containing this file (so that you can copy it), do the following:

1 Select its path in the About dialog box (select everything but the file name itself), and press Ctrl+C to copy it.

2 Choose Run from the Start menu and then press Ctrl+V to insert the path into the Open text box.

3 Click OK and the folder will be displayed in Windows Explorer.

Address Book backs up your data as you work in a file with the extension .wa~. The backup file is stored in the same folder as its companion .wab file. If your .wab file becomes corrupt, your .wa~ file might still be good. To find out, rename the .wa~ file to give it the expected .wab extension.

The location of your .wab and .wa~ files is recorded in the registry key HKCU\Software\ Microsoft\WAB\WAB4\Wab File Name. If for any reason you need to move the file, be sure to update this registry key. Otherwise, Address Book will simply create a new file in the default location.

Sending Mail

Sending e-mail is straightforward: address the message, type the message, format the message, attach files as needed, set a priority level if needed, request a receipt if desired, and click Send. To send on "plain paper," start by clicking Create Mail on Outlook Express's toolbar. To send a message on "stationery," click the arrow next to the Create Mail tool and then select your stationery from the menu. Outlook Express responds with a New Message window.

For more information about stationery, see "Using Stationery," page 684.

Addressing the Message

If you use multiple e-mail accounts, the first thing to do when you open the New Message window is make sure the program is sending from the account you want to use. If you don't see the right address on the From line, click the arrow to open the list and then choose a different address. If you have only one e-mail account the From line does not appear by default.

On the To line, you can enter either a contact's name (if the name is in your address book) or the contact's e-mail address. By default, Outlook Express will complete the address for you as soon as you have typed enough characters to make your intention unambiguous. To change this setting choose Tools, Options, open the Send tab, and select or clear Automatically Complete E-Mail Addresses When Composing.

---

tip   Create a shortcut for your pen pal

If you regularly send e-mail to the same person, you might want to create a desktop shortcut for that person. Double-clicking the shortcut will then take you to a New Message window with the envelope already addressed. To create such a shortcut, choose New, Shortcut on your desktop. In the Command Line box, type **mailto:** followed immediately (with no space) by the recipient's name or e-mail address.

To send to multiple recipients, type a comma or semicolon after each recipient's name or address. If you send to a group that you have defined in Address Book, be aware that your recipients will see the name (or address) of each member of the group, not the group name. To send to multiple recipients without making each recipient's name or address visible to all the others, use the Bcc (blind courtesy copy) line. When a Bcc recipient receives your mail, the To field in the recipient's e-mail program says Undisclosed-Recipient and all other addressees on the Bcc line are invisible.

> **tip** **Display the Bcc line**
>
> The New Message window in Outlook Express doesn't ordinarily display a Bcc line, and it can be difficult to find. To display the Bcc line, choose View, All Headers in the New Message window. The All Headers setting is persistent, though. After you have displayed the Bcc line in a new message, it appears in all subsequent new messages—until you turn it off again.

Formatting the Message

If you use HTML formatting, the New Message window displays a formatting toolbar full of rich formatting options. You can choose fonts and point sizes, create bulleted lists, indent paragraphs, and do practically anything else that you might do in a modern word processor. The toolbar even includes a style list (see Figure 19-8) that simplifies your formatting tasks.

Figure 19-8. HTML support in Outlook Express allows you to do almost anything in an e-mail message that you might do in a word processor—including using defined styles.

Choosing a Font

Outlook Express uses Arial as the default font for all your messages. That means that everyone who uses Outlook Express and accepts the default uses the same font. If you prefer something distinctive, choose Options from the Outlook Express Tools menu. On the Compose tab, click Font Settings and then choose a font. (You can do this separately for mail and news.) It's best to pick a font that most Windows users have. If you select Haettenschweiler Bold (or some other obscure font), recipients who haven't installed your off-the-beaten-track font will see whatever Windows decides to substitute. You can also set the default style, size, and color of the font.

Working Directly with HTML Code

If you're an HTML expert, you can do even more in the way of formatting than the Formatting toolbar allows. You can add animations, scripts, and anything else that you might put on a Web page. To work directly in HTML code, choose View, Source Edit in the New Message window. The tabs that appear along the bottom of the window allow you to switch views while composing your message. The Edit tab provides the same WYSIWYG view as you see when Source Edit view is turned off. The Source tab view shows HTML code along with your text, and the Preview tab attempts to show all elements of your HTML code in action, even some that might not fully display in the Edit window. However, you can't edit in Preview mode.

The Source Edit setting is persistent. If you turn it on, it stays on in subsequent messages until you turn it off again.

Using Stationery

Want a colorful background for your e-mail? Choose from one of the many stationery selections offered by Outlook Express. If you don't find one to your liking on the numbered list that appears when you click the arrow next to the Create Mail button, choose Select Stationery from that menu. You'll find a larger assortment in the Select Stationery dialog box that appears. You can click Edit to modify an existing stationery or click Create New to have the Stationery Setup Wizard help you design your own.

Inserting Hyperlinks

To insert a hyperlink in an e-mail message, choose Insert, Hyperlink in the New Message window. The most common use for a hyperlink is to point the recipient of your e-mail message to a Web site of interest. But, as Figure 19-9 shows, you can insert many other kinds of links as well.

Figure 19-9. By choosing Insert, Hyperlink, you can add links of any sort to your messages.

Chapter 19: Using and Customizing Outlook Express

Inserting Your Signature

A signature is a block of text or graphics that you add to a message. Your signature would normally contain your name and e-mail address and any other information (a favorite quotation, perhaps) that you want to include. To create a signature in Outlook Express, choose Tools, Options, click the Signatures tab, and then click New. In the Edit Signature section of the dialog box, shown in Figure 19-10, type the text of your signature. Alternatively, select the File option and use the Browse button to find a text or HTML file. You can create as many signatures as you want in this manner.

Figure 19-10. Specify the text or file you want to appear at the end of your messages.

To add your signature automatically to every message, select Add Signatures To All Outgoing Messages. If you have more than one signature, click the Set As Default button to mark the one you want used automatically.

To add your signature to some but not all messages, leave the Add Signatures To All Outgoing Messages check box clear. Then when you want to use a signature, choose Insert, Signature in the New Message window. If you have more than one signature on file, a Signature submenu will appear, from which you can choose the one you want.

Adding Attachments

An attachment is a file that's sent with your e-mail message. To add an attachment, click the Attach button on the New Message window's Standard Buttons toolbar, and then specify the file you want to attach. (Alternatively, you can simply drag a file from Windows Explorer into the New Message window.)

Setting a Priority Level

Messages are sent at normal priority by default. To flag an outgoing message as high or low priority, choose Message, Set Priority in the New Message window. Then select from the submenu that appears. How the high-priority or low-priority message appears to your recipient depends on the e-mail client program he or she is using, of course.

Requesting a Receipt

By choosing Tools, Request Read Receipt in the New Message window, you can ask your recipient to send confirmation that he or she has received your message. (To send a receipt request with every message, open Options in Outlook Express. Click the Receipts tab and select Request A Read Receipt For All Sent Messages.) Receipt requests are anything but foolproof. Depending on the e-mail client program your recipient is using, and how that program is configured, your recipient might see something comparable to the following.

If your recipient doesn't want to acknowledge receipt, there's not much you can do about it.

---

tip **You don't have to send a receipt**

It can be annoying to see a receipt request pop up when you select a message header. If you find such requests intrusive, choose Tools, Options. On the Receipts tab, choose Never Send A Receipt. Alternatively, if you want to send receipts but don't want to be bothered with the request, select Always Send A Read Receipt. Outlook Express will then send receipts to anyone who requests them—without asking permission or telling you that a receipt was requested.

Reading and Organizing Mail

When Outlook Express retrieves your mail, it puts each new message in the Inbox folder, unless you have set up a rule to move it to some other folder. Unread messages appear in the message list in boldface type, with a closed envelope icon. After you read a message, its entry changes to normal type with an open envelope icon. To read a message in a separate window, double-click it in the message list.

Chapter 19: Using and Customizing Outlook Express

Viewing and Saving Attachments

Messages with attachments are identified in the message list by a paper clip icon. In the message window, the name of the attachment appears on an Attach line in the header area, above the message text. To open an attachment, double-click it on the Attach line. To save it instead of opening it, right-click it and choose Save As—or drag it onto your desktop or into Windows Explorer. Of course, e-mail attachments can carry viruses as well, which is why anyone who uses Windows and receives e-mail should install effective antivirus software and keep it up to date. In addition, you can take a number of precautions to reduce the likelihood that a dangerous virus will sneak onto your computer by way of an e-mail attachment. For details, see "Blocking Dangerous Attachments," page 694.

Watching, Ignoring, and Flagging Messages

Figure 19-11 shows the Outlook Express message list with all four of its optional iconic columns displayed. By glancing at these columns, you can see that one message in the list (with the paper clip) includes an attachment, one (with the "no" icon—the red circle with a slash through it) is marked to be ignored, another (with the spectacles) is marked to be watched, four have been flagged for attention, two are marked with an exclamation point to indicate they are high priority, and two others show a blue arrow

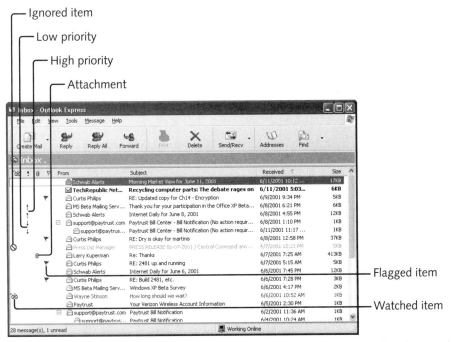

Figure 19-11. Outlook Express uses distinctive icons to identify watched and ignored messages.

indicating low priority. The remaining messages in the priority column (the second column from the left in the figure with the heading) have no icon, which means that they were sent at normal priority.

If you don't see all of these iconic columns, you can make them visible by choosing View, Columns. In the Columns dialog box, select the check boxes for the columns you want to see, clear those for the columns you don't want to see, and use the Move Up and Move Down buttons to change the order in which columns appear. To return to the default column arrangement, click Reset.

You can mark a message with a watch or ignore icon by clicking in the Watch/Ignore column. Your first click there inserts a watch icon; a second click changes that to an ignore icon, and a third click clears the column. When a message is marked to be watched, Outlook Express displays the message entry in a contrasting color (red, by default; to change that, go to the Read tab of the Options dialog box). When you mark a message to be ignored, Outlook Express displays the entry in gray.

---

tip   **Create custom views of hot (or not-so-hot) topics**

The watch/ignore icons are most useful in newsgroups, but they can also come in handy in e-mail folders. For instance, if you subscribe to several mailing lists that generate hundreds of messages, you can mark some conversation threads to be watched and others to be ignored. Then, to cut down the clutter, you can create custom views to show only watched messages or to hide ignored messages. To change the display of messages, choose View, Current View, Customize Current View, and then fill in the blanks as explained in the next section.

To flag a message (that is, to display a red flag in the Flag column), choose Message, Flag Message. (You can do this either in Outlook Express or in the Message window.) The flag means whatever you want it to mean; it's just a way of calling particular messages to your attention. If you always want to flag messages from a particular sender (your spouse, for example), you can set up a rule to do that. For more information about rules, see "Using Rules to Organize Messages," on the facing page.

Using Views to Hide Particular Kinds of Messages

Outlook Express comes with three standard message views:

- Show All Messages
- Hide Read Messages
- Hide Read Or Ignored Messages

The default is Show All Messages, and this view is applied by default to all folders. To apply a different view to a particular folder, choose View, Current View, and then select one of the views listed in the upper portion of the submenu. Or if you have the Views

Chapter 19: Using and Customizing Outlook Express

bar displayed in Outlook Express you can click the Views bar arrow and then choose the view.

To apply a view to all of your folders, follow these steps:

1 From the View menu, choose Current View, Define Views.

2 In the Define Views dialog box, select the view you want, and then click Apply View.

3 In the Apply View dialog box, choose All Of My Folders.

By creating your own custom views, you can also arrange to have particular categories of messages hidden or displayed, in all folders or in particular folders. To create a custom view, choose View, Current View, Define Views. In the Define Views dialog box, click New. At number 1 in the New View Dialog box, shown in Figure 19-12, select one or more check boxes. At number 2, click each blue link that appears and fill out the ensuing dialog box. Finally, supply a name for the new view, if you want to name it, at number 3.

Figure 19-12. You can use the New View dialog box to specify which kinds of messages should be hidden or displayed.

Using Rules to Organize Messages

Outlook Express allows you to create message rules to manage mail and newsgroup posts. You can use rules to store messages with a particular characteristic—a particular sender or subject line, for example—in a different folder, or to automatically send a reply, forward the message, or discard it without downloading it from your mail server. Rules can be a real time-saver if you receive a lot of routine (or junk) mail, if you want to forward your mail to a different address when you're not able to receive it, or if you

Part 5: Using E-Mail, Fax, and Messaging

want to reply to all incoming messages with an out-of-the-office message while you're away. Rules are similar to custom views, except that you can do much more with rules.

Creating a New Rule

To create a new rule, choose Tools, Message Rules, and then specify either Mail or News. This section describes the creation of a mail rule, but the procedure is the same for news rules. Figure 19-13 shows the New Mail Rule dialog box.

Figure 19-13. Message rules make your computer sort the mail for you.

Follow these general steps to create a new rule:

1 At number 1 of the dialog box, Select The Conditions For Your Rule, select one or more check boxes.

These check boxes define the conditions under which your rule is to be carried out.

2 At number 2, Select The Actions For Your Rule, select one or more check boxes.

These check boxes define the actions that you want Outlook Express to perform.

3 After you have selected the conditions and actions, click each blue link that appears at number 3 of the dialog box, Rule Description.

The links that appear and the dialog boxes they open help you to further define conditions and actions.

Chapter 19: Using and Customizing Outlook Express

4 Finally, at number 4, change the default name for your new rule to a more descriptive one, and click OK.

Sending an Automatic Reply

You might receive certain types of mail to which you would like to send an automatic reply. To create such a rule you choose the action Reply With Message, but you must first create and save the reply message you want to have sent:

1 Create a message without an addressee.

2 In the New Message window, choose Save As and specify a file name and path.

3 Create a new rule, specifying the conditions that will trigger the rule and specifying Reply With Message as the action that will be carried out.

This places a blue link in the Rule Description section of the New Mail Rule dialog box.

4 Click the link and specify the file name of the reply message you saved.

Using Negative Criteria

You can create a rule based on a negative criterion—for example, all messages that do *not* come from a particular sender. To do this, first set up the rule using a positive criterion (all messages that *do* come from a particular sender). After you have finished specifying your criterion, you will see an Options button (if you chose messages from a particular sender as your criterion the Options button will appear on the Select People dialog box). Click this button to open the Rule Condition Options dialog box, shown in Figure 19-14. In this dialog box, select the Message Does Not Contain The People Below option.

Figure 19-14. Message rules can use negative as well as positive criteria.

Using Multiple Criteria

In rules that involve people, content, or accounts, you can specify multiple criteria. For example, if you wanted messages that contained either "make money" or "work from home" (phrases commonly found in spam) to be deleted from the mail server, you could select Where The Message Body Contains Specific Words in the first section of the New Mail Rule dialog box, click the Contains Specific Words link, type **make money** and click Add, and then type **work from home** and click Add. The rule would then take effect if mail arrived in your Inbox that contained either phrase. (In other words, the phrases would be linked by the logical operator *or*.)

To make the rule affect only those messages containing *both* phrases, first set up the criterion in the normal way. Then click the Options button in the Type Specific Words dialog box to open the Rule Condition Options dialog box. Then select the Message Matches All Of The Words Below option.

Creating a Rule from the Selected Message

As a handy timesaver, Outlook Express allows you to create a rule based on the sender of the current message. If you receive a message from someone and you know immediately that you want all mail from that person to be handled by a rule, select the message and choose Message, Create Rule From Message. The New Mail Rule dialog box will appear, already set up to apply the new rule to messages from the selected sender.

Blocking Obnoxious Mail

Outlook Express's Blocked Senders list can help you ward off junk mail. When you get a message from someone you never want to hear from again, select the message and choose Message, Block Sender. You'll see a dialog box similar to this one.

If you make a mistake or change your mind about a blocked sender, you can restore him or her to your good graces. Choose Tools, Message Rules, Blocked Senders List. Select the sender you want to restore, and then click Remove. Alternatively, you can keep the entry in your list but clear either or both of the check boxes for blocking mail and news messages. This way, you can be selective in the kinds of blocking you apply, and you can quickly reapply blocking if it becomes appropriate again.

> **tip** **Don't rely on the Blocked Senders list to kill spam**
>
> You might be tempted to use the Blocked Senders list to block junk mail (aka spam). For the most part, this strategy is doomed to failure, because the worst forms of spam come from "throwaway" e-mail addresses that are used only once. Adding this sort of address to your Blocked Senders list has no practical effect because you're not likely to ever receive a message from that sender again. The Blocked Senders list is most effective in blocking unscrupulous junk mailers who persist in sending unwanted e-mail messages using addresses from the same domain. Most such firms claim to be using "opt-in" lists and include language that implies that you signed up for their annoying missives. To block all future messages from these pests, open the Blocked Senders dialog box and enter only the domain name. This step indiscriminately eliminates all mail from an entire domain, so use it with care! (And for many more suggestions on how to fight back against spam, see Chapter 11, "Blocking Spam," in *Microsoft Windows Security Inside Out.*)

Searching for Messages

The Edit, Find command can help you locate a lost, buried, or forgotten e-mail message. You can search the current folder or all folders. If you like keyboard shortcuts, press Shift+F3 to search the current folder, Ctrl+Shift+F (*not* Ctrl+Shift+F3) to search all folders, or F3 to repeat your last search. As Figure 19-15 shows, you can search each component of the message header as well as message text, and you can specify other qualifiers as well—the date the message was received, whether the message was flagged or whether the message included one or more attachments. Messages meeting any criterion appear at the bottom of the dialog box. You can use the Find dialog box's Message menu to read, reply to, or forward found messages.

Figure 19-15. The Find Message dialog box locates messages that match specified conditions.

---

tip   **Find a message the moment it arrives**

If you leave the Find Message dialog box open, the system continues to monitor incoming messages, adding appropriate ones to the list of found messages. This can be handy if you receive a large volume of mail and need to watch for messages covering particular topics.

Saving Messages Outside Outlook Express

You can save any message as a separate file by selecting the message and choosing File, Save As. Your file will have the extension .eml and will be associated with Outlook Express (unless you install another e-mail client that claims that extension or you change the association yourself). From your desktop or Windows Explorer, you can reread the message at any time by double-clicking it—whether or not Outlook Express is running. You can also use this technique to back up and restore one or more messages. Save the messages in a folder in Windows Explorer; to restore the messages, drag them into the Outlook Express window and drop them on a folder icon.

---

tip   **Save important messages**

It's not smart to entrust critical information exclusively to Outlook Express's message store. If your message store becomes corrupted for any reason, or if you purge old messages periodically (something you *should* do), you could inadvertently lose or destroy some vital bit of correspondence. To protect yourself, save a copy of anything you must not lose.

Blocking Dangerous Attachments

As you undoubtedly know, the most common mode of delivery for viruses and worms is in the form of e-mail attachments. The writers of hostile software use a variety of psychological techniques to induce you to run an infected attachment, such as forging e-mail headers to make it appear as though the message came from a friend or trusted business contact and making the attachment appear to be a fun and innocuous game, screen saver, or photo attachment. How can you protect yourself from the very real risks of infection?

For starters, install antivirus software, keep it up to date, and make sure that it's running at all times. A good antivirus program will detect infected e-mail attachments when they arrive; even if the antivirus program doesn't integrate with your e-mail software, it should intercept a hostile attachment if you try to save or open the file.

Chapter 19: Using and Customizing Outlook Express

Train all users of your computer in the proper handling of file attachments. *Never* open an unexpected e-mail attachment, even if it appears to come from a trustworthy source. When in doubt, pick up the phone or send an e-mail message to the sender and ask them what's in the attachment they sent. If you can't reach the sender and you still have doubts, delete the file.

For maximum security, you can use the attachment-blocking capabilities in Outlook Express 6. As in Microsoft Outlook 2002 or Outlook 2000 with the E-Mail Security Update, this feature prevents you from opening or saving certain types of file attachments that are potentially dangerous. Unfortunately, the list of files that Outlook Express considers hazardous is so sweeping that you may find this feature more frustrating than helpful. The list starts with executable files (those with the extensions .exe, .bat, .pif, and so on), which represent the bulk of potentially hostile attachments; but it also blocks a much longer list of normally useful files, including compressed file archives (.zip), Adobe Portable Document Files (.pdf), and Office documents (.doc, .xls, and so on). If you intend to use this feature and still exchange attachments via e-mail, be prepared to do a significant amount of tweaking to the default settings first.

To turn on attachment blocking, choose Tools, Options. On the Security tab, select Do Not Allow Attachments To Be Saved Or Opened That Could Potentially Be A Virus. With this option selected, Outlook Express examines all attachments and displays a warning banner when it finds one or more attachments on its prohibited list, as shown in Figure 19-16.

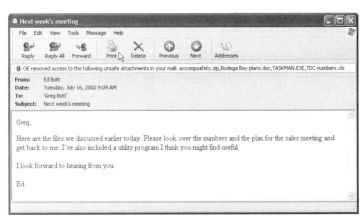

Figure 19-16. With attachment blocking turned on, Outlook Express blocks access to even these harmless .zip files and Microsoft Office documents.

To relax some of the restrictions so that Outlook Express allows certain types of attachments to pass through its filters, you need to make the following adjustments:

1 Open Windows Explorer and choose Tools, Folder Options.

2 Click the File Types tab, and then scroll through the Registered File Types list until you find the extension for the file type you want to change. Select that entry in the list.

3 Click the Advanced button.

4 In the Edit File Type dialog box, clear the Confirm Open After Download check box.

5 Click OK to close the Edit File Type dialog box, and then click Close in the Folder Options dialog box.

Repeat steps 1–4 for any other file types that you want to designate as safe. (Note that this option is not available for executable file types. Also, be aware that changing this setting for any file type might affect the way it's handled in Internet Explorer as well.)

Troubleshooting

You received an e-mail message containing an attachment you know is safe, but Outlook Express won't let you open or save it.

Unlike the similar feature in Microsoft Outlook 2000 and 2002, you can easily work around attachment blocking in Outlook Express. To temporarily restore access to a blocked attachment, choose Tools, Options, click the Security tab, and clear the Do Not Allow Attachments To Be Saved Or Opened That Could Potentially Be A Virus check box. Close the dialog box to return to the message, where you'll find that the attachment is now available for you to work with. Afterward, be certain to turn the safety feature back on again!

Using Hotmail and Other Server-Based Systems

Hotmail accounts and other e-mail accounts that use HTTP or IMAP differ from POP3 accounts in that messages are kept on the account-provider's server and can be accessed from any computer via the Internet. When you set up the account in Outlook Express, the account provider creates a folder structure for you. These folders reside on the server and are mirrored on your own system. Depending on the account provider, you might or might not have the opportunity to pick and choose which of the service's folders you want to use (in Hotmail, you do not have this choice). Your HTTP or IMAP folders appear in a separate part of the folder tree from the Local Folders section used by your POP3 accounts.

Chapter 19: Using and Customizing Outlook Express

When you send and receive mail using a server-based system (a process called *synchronization*), you have the option of downloading all messages, new messages only, message headers only, or nothing. To specify your synchronization preferences, select the root folder in the appropriate part of your folder tree. For example, with a Hotmail account, you would select the folder called Hotmail. As Figure 19-17 shows, you can then specify synchronization settings individually for each of the folders maintained by the server.

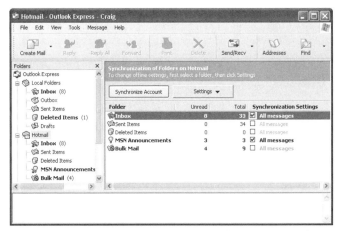

Figure 19-17. You can express your synchronization preferences individually for each folder maintained by the server.

To change a synchronization setting for a folder, select the folder and click Settings. If you get a lot of mail, only some of which you need, and you're on a slow dial-up connection, you might want to set your Inbox to download headers only. To download the message body for an item of interest, you can double-click its header. Unless you enjoy reading unsolicited commercial messages, you'll probably want to set Hotmail's Bulk Mail folder to download nothing—that is, not to synchronize. If you don't need local copies of your sent messages, you can also opt not to synchronize the Sent Items folder.

Using Newsgroups

Newsgroups function much like server-based mail systems. Messages reside on a server. You create a local mirror of the server (or a portion thereof!) and synchronize it periodically by downloading headers, new messages, or all messages. One major difference is that, rather than giving you a simple folder structure (such as the one that Hotmail downloads for you), the news server typically hosts thousands of newsgroups. You choose the ones you care about by *subscribing* to them, and these subscribed newsgroups become subfolders in the news section of your Outlook Express folder tree. Another difference is that newsgroup messages (often called *posts*) are visible to everyone who has access to the news server. Your account is not private.

The first time you select a news server in your folder tree, Outlook Express offers to download a list of newsgroups available from the server. When the downloading is complete (be patient), you will see the Newsgroup Subscriptions dialog box, which will look similar to Figure 19-18. Icons for each of your newsgroup accounts will appear in the left pane, and the All tab will display an alphabetical list of your server's many offerings. You can filter the list by typing some text on the Display Newsgroups Which Contain line.

Figure 19-18. The list of your server's newsgroups is likely to be enormous. Use the Display Newsgroups Which Contain box to zero in on groups of interest.

By default, Outlook Express downloads newsgroup names but not descriptions of the groups' content. If you need the descriptions as well, go to the Properties dialog box for your newsgroup account (choose Tools, Accounts, select the account, and click Properties). On the Advanced tab, select Use Newsgroup Descriptions. Then return to the Newsgroup Subscriptions dialog box and click Reset List (and this time be *really* patient).

After you have found a group you're interested in, select its name on the All tab and click Subscribe. You can subscribe to as many groups as you want. Outlook will create a subfolder for each. If you lose interest in a group, click its entry in the folders list and click the Unsubscribe button.

Marking Headers Offline for Later Download

The newsgroups you're interested in might well hold thousands of posts each. If you're using a dial-up connection, you probably don't want to download all of those messages. Instead, you can set Outlook Express to download the headers only. Then, while offline, you can scan the headers, marking the ones you care about for subsequent downloading. When you reconnect, you can download the full contents of the marked messages.

Setting Synchronization Options

To set your newsgroups for header download, or to choose a different synchronization option, select the news server in your folders list. You'll see a display similar to the one shown in Figure 19-17, except that you'll see a list of your subscribed newsgroups instead of a set of Hotmail folders. Select a newsgroup in the right pane, click Settings, and choose a synchronization option. As with server-based e-mail, your choices are All Messages, New Messages Only, Headers Only, and Don't Synchronize.

Selecting Headers While Offline

While you're offline, you can mark headers for subsequent full download. Select a newsgroup in the left pane and a header in your message list, and then choose Tools, Mark For Offline. From the submenu, you can then choose Download Message Later, Download Conversation Later, Download All Messages Later. Typically, you'll want to choose Download Conversation Later. Then, when you reconnect and synchronize, Outlook Express will download the marked message and all responses to it.

---

tip   **Save time by using the Mark For Offline column**

If the Mark For Offline column appears in your message list (it does, by default, when you're working with newsgroups), you can click in that column beside a header to mark that message for subsequent downloading. The Mark For Offline column is headed by a downward-pointing arrow. When you click in the column next to a message you want to download, an arrow appears beside the marked message. If you mark a message that has a plus sign beside it, Outlook Express will download the message and all responses to it when you synchronize. To remove a mark after you have clicked in the Mark For Offline column, click again.

Using Rules to Mark Newsgroup Posts for Download

Message rules work similarly with newsgroup items as with e-mail messages. (For more information about rules, see "Using Rules to Organize Messages," page 689.) One of the actions you can choose with newsgroup rules, however, is Mark It For Download. While you're offline, if you find a topic of interest in a newsgroup, but you see that there are numerous, widely scattered messages on that topic, you can create a rule that looks for a keyword in the header and marks all headers with that keyword for download. Apply the rule, and you've saved yourself the time and bother of seeking all those messages manually.

Downloading New Messages Only

If you're managing to stay current with the posts in a newsgroup, you can take advantage of the New Messages Only synchronization setting. When you connect, Outlook Express will download only those messages that you haven't already read.

What if this is your strategy, but occasionally you fall behind? For that situation, the program provides the Catch Up command. Right-click a newsgroup and choose Catch Up, and when you connect to the server, Outlook Express will consider all of its messages as read. Then you can start fresh with downloading new messages as they arrive.

InsideOut

In Windows XP Service Pack 1, Microsoft has fixed a long-standing bug in the Outlook Express news-reading capability. Want to get rid of a message you downloaded from a newsgroup? Press the Delete key. In previous versions, this key did nothing. With SP1 installed, it permanently zaps the unwanted message.

Saving Messages Before They're Deleted from the Server

Because Outlook Express mirrors the newsgroup server when you synchronize, when messages are deleted from the server (as they eventually must be, to make room for new posts), they are also removed from Outlook Express. To preserve important messages, copy them into one of your local folders, or save them as disk files. To save a message, choose File, Save As. Outlook Express gives the file the extension .nws. You can reopen a saved message by double-clicking it in Windows Explorer.

Maintaining Outlook Express

If you use Outlook Express regularly for a period of months or years, you will undoubtedly accumulate a large store of messages. Eventually, the size of your message store will begin to slow the program down. To keep it performing nimbly, you need to clean out your folders periodically.

When you delete messages, Outlook Express moves them to the Deleted Items folder. This folder functions like the Windows Recycle Bin. It holds items in case you want to see them again. To delete items permanently, you need to take the separate step of deleting them from the Deleted Items folder. Outlook Express does this for you automatically when you quit—provided you have told it to do so. To set up this behavior, choose Tools, Options. On the Maintenance tab, select Empty Messages From The 'Deleted Items' Folder On Exit.

Chapter 19: Using and Customizing Outlook Express

Simply deleting messages will not significantly reduce the size of your message store, however! When you delete a message, Outlook Express marks the item as deleted but does not remove it from the disk file in which the folder is stored. Thus, over time, you can accumulate a significant amount of wasted disk space. Under these circumstances, Outlook Express's performance will suffer, even though the apparent contents of your folders is relatively small.

To reclaim the wasted disk space, you have to take a second step, called compacting. You can set Outlook Express to do this for you automatically when the wasted space reaches some specified percentage of your overall message store. To do this, choose Tools, Options. On the Maintenance tab, shown in Figure 19-19, select Compact Messages In The Background. Then specify a value in the box next to Percent Wasted Space.

If you prefer to compact on demand, rather than having the program do it for you, click Clean Up Now on the Maintenance tab of the Options dialog box. To compact all of your folders, specify Outlook Express in the Local File(s) For list in the Local File Clean Up dialog box. To compact a particular folder, click Browse and then select the folder.

Figure 19-19.   Select Compact Messages In The Background to avoid bloat in your message store.

Part 5: Using E-Mail, Fax, and Messaging

Relocating Your Message Store to Simplify Backup

By default, Outlook Express creates your message store in a deeply nested folder. To locate yours, choose Tools, Options. On the Maintenance tab, click Store Folder. You'll see something like the following.

If you click on this path and press End you'll discover that the path is even worse than it looks! You can back up from a folder this deeply nested, but you'll find it easier to do so if you move the message store to a more reasonable location. (We recommend that you keep the message folders in your profile, but choose a location that's easier to find in your folder hierarchy.)

To move your message store to a place where your backup routine can more easily find it, follow these steps:

1 Create the folder you want to use—for example, you could create a folder called My Messages in your My Documents folder.

2 Choose Tools, Options.

3 On the Maintenance tab, click Store Folder.

4 In the Store Location dialog box, click Change to open the Browse for Folder dialog box.

5 Select the new store folder you created.

Outlook Express will move your messages the next time you start the program.

---

note Each identity uses its own message store. If you use identities and want to move your store folders to locations where they can be easily found, create new repository folders for each identity, and then repeat the change procedure for each.

Chapter 19: Using and Customizing Outlook Express

caution   If you look in your message store folder, you'll find a file named Folders.dbx and an additional .dbx file for each of your Outlook Express folders. The Folders.dbx file contains the structural information about your Outlook Express identity, and the remaining folders contain messages. Don't try to reorganize your folder tree by manipulating these files directly. If you rename or delete a file, you'll just confuse—and possibly disable— Outlook Express. Because the location of your message store is recorded in the registry (the Store Root value is in HKCU\Identities\\{*GUID*}\Software\Microsoft\Outlook Express\5.0), you're also asking for trouble if you try to move the store folder in Windows Explorer. Let Outlook Express do it for you.

Archiving Old Messages

Outlook Express does not include a command for archiving old messages. But you can accomplish the task by following these steps:

1   Create a new folder with a suitable name—such as Year 2000 Messages. If you want to keep received and sent messages separate, create one folder for each.

2   Open the Find dialog box. Use the Outlook Express Find command (choose Edit, Find, Message, or press Ctrl+Shift+F).

3   In the Find Message dialog box, use the Received Before control to locate the messages you want to archive.

4   When the messages have been found, drag them into your archival folder(s).

5   Close Outlook Express.

6   Open your message store in Windows Explorer. Look for a .dbx file with the name of your archival folder.

7   Copy the folder to a location outside the message store. Repeat for your second archival folder if you archived sent and received messages separately.

8   Reopen Outlook Express and delete the archival folder(s).

If you need to reopen the archived messages at a later date, re-create empty folder(s) in Outlook Express with the same name as the archival folders. Close Outlook Express, copy the archival folders back into your message store (overwriting the empty archival .dbx file(s) in the message store), and then reopen Outlook Express.

Moving Your Outlook Express Files to a New Computer

If your new computer is networked with your old one, it's not too hard to move your entire Outlook Express setup to the new rig. You can use the Files And Settings Transfer utility, as described in "Moving Windows Settings and Files," page 51. This option has the advantage of moving all your messages, account settings, and rules in one graceful procedure. If you prefer to do this task manually, however, follow these steps:

First, on the old machine, back up each of your accounts and your address book. To back up an account, choose Tools, Accounts, select the account name, and click Export. To back up your address book, open Address Book and choose File, Export, Address Book (WAB). Now determine the location of your message store by choosing Tools, Options, clicking the Maintenance tab, and clicking Store Folder. You might want to write this path down or copy it to the Clipboard (by pressing Ctrl+C) so that you can find the folder more easily in Windows Explorer.

On the new machine, import your accounts and address book. To import an account, choose Tools, Accounts, and click Import. To import your address book, open Address Book and choose File, Import, Address Book (WAB). Next, choose Tools, Options. On the Maintenance tab of the Options dialog box, click Store Folder to discover the location of your new store folder.

To complete the move, close Outlook Express and copy all files from your old store folder to your new one. When you reopen Outlook Express, everything should be there.

Chapter 20

Sending and Receiving Faxes

Microsoft Windows XP includes a fax component (Microsoft Fax, or Fax for short) that lets you send, receive, and manage faxes using your computer's fax modem. With Fax installed, you can transmit documents directly from the applications that create them (your word processor, for example), send a scanned image, or address a fax recipient directly from a supported e-mail client (Microsoft Outlook, for example). You can use one of the four cover page templates that come with Fax, or you can use the program's cover page editor to design your own.

If you've worked with earlier Windows fax components (Personal Fax for Windows in Windows 2000 or At Work Fax in Windows 95/98), you'll probably find the user interface of the current version an improvement. Management tasks that used to be dispersed between various interface elements, for example, are now consolidated into a single console, and the integration between Fax and Outlook (and with the rest of Microsoft Office) is smoother than before. Office users, for example, will appreciate the fact that Fax now uses the Office Address Book or Contacts folder, instead of requiring you to maintain a separate list of fax recipients in Windows Address Book.

Installing Fax

If you perform a clean setup of Windows XP, Fax is not installed, even if your computer has a supported fax device. You need to install the fax component as a separate step. (If you upgrade to Windows XP from a Windows 2000 or Windows 95/98 system that has an earlier Windows fax component installed, Windows XP installs the Windows XP fax component and preserves your earlier configuration. For more information, see "Upgrading an Earlier Windows Fax Component," page 707.)

705

At Home with Windows XP

All of the features for sending, receiving, and managing faxes, as well as those for designing and managing cover pages, are available in both editions of Windows XP. Because Windows XP Home Edition always uses Simple File Sharing, Home Edition users might notice one minor difference between Fax on their systems and Fax on a Windows XP Professional system that is not using Simple File Sharing. With Simple File Sharing in effect, the Fax Security tab in the Fax Properties dialog box is not normally visible. Home Edition users can make that tab visible and work with fax security settings, however, simply by holding down the Ctrl key when opening the properties dialog box. (For more information about fax security settings, see "Managing Security," page 727. For information about Simple File Sharing, see "Simple File Sharing vs. Windows 2000–Style Sharing," page 98, and "Simple File Sharing vs. Advanced Permissions," page 499.)

To install Fax, log on to an account in the Administrators group, open Add Or Remove Programs in Control Panel, and then click Add/Remove Windows Components. In the Windows Components Wizard (shown in Figure 20-1), select Fax Services. Then click Next and be prepared to insert your Windows XP CD if requested.

Figure 20-1. Fax is not installed by default on a clean setup. Use Add Or Remove Programs in Control Panel to install it.

Installing Fax adds the following items to your Start menu (choose All Programs, Accessories, Communications, Fax):

● Fax Console

● Fax Cover Page Editor

● Send A Fax

The first of these, Fax Console, is the principal tool for configuring and managing fax activities in Windows XP. Note that it is not an MMC console; the MMC-hosted Fax Management Console of Windows 2000 has been eliminated in Windows XP.

Installing Fax also adds the Fax service to the list of services that appears in the Services MMC console (Services.msc) and, provided you have a supported fax device installed on the local computer, creates a new printer named Fax. This new Fax printer appears alongside other local and remote printers in your Printers And Faxes folder, as well as in your applications' Print dialog boxes. In general, faxing a document in Windows XP is as simple as directing output to the Fax printer.

Upgrading an Earlier Windows Fax Component

If you have been using At Work Fax in Windows 95/98 or Personal Fax for Windows in Windows 2000, and you upgrade to Windows XP, the Windows XP Setup program installs Fax and preserves as much as possible of your earlier fax configuration and archives. In the case of the Windows 2000 upgrade, Fax will retain your device configuration, sender information, and cover pages. The first time you open Fax Console, you'll be given the opportunity to import your Windows 2000 fax archives. If you decline, you can import them later by choosing File, Import, Sent Faxes or File, Import, Received Faxes in Fax Console. In the case of the Windows 95/98 upgrade, your device configuration, sender information, and cover pages will be preserved, but you will not be able to import your Windows 95/98 archives into Fax Console. Your existing faxes will be preserved as TIFF files, however, and you will be able to review them in Windows Explorer or using any application that reads TIFF files.

Configuring Fax

To configure Fax—that is, to specify your sender information, answering parameters, and other details governing the behavior of the fax application—log on to an administrator account. Then start by running Fax Console. The first time you do this, the Fax Configuration Wizard appears. The wizard guides you through most of the essential configuration steps, as described in the following paragraphs. When you've completed the wizard's questionnaire, you'll want to open the Fax Properties dialog box to take care of a few additional configuration details.

(If the Fax Configuration Wizard does not appear when you run Fax Console, you—or someone else—have already been through the wizard process. You can return to the wizard, if necessary, by choosing Tools, Configure Fax from Fax Console.)

Sharing Fax Among Users at the Same Computer

If you share a fax device with other users of your computer, keep in mind the following details:

● Each user can supply his or her own personal data for use on cover pages. Fax Cover Page Editor comes with four generic cover page templates that are available to all users. Users can create personally customized versions of these templates or design new personal templates from scratch. But regardless of whether you transmit with a generic cover page template or one that you have tailored in some way, the resulting cover page will incorporate your own information, not that of another user at your computer. (For more about Fax Cover Page Editor, see "Creating Personal Cover Pages," page 724.)

● Each user has access to his or her own address book for specifying addressee fax numbers.

● Each user can set his or her own default "printing" characteristics. For example, one user can set Fax to transmit in portrait mode at letter size, and another can opt for landscape mode at Quarto, and Fax will maintain these per-user settings. (For details, see "Choosing Paper Size, Image Quality, and Orientation," page 711.)

● Users can express individual preferences about how they are to be notified of fax events—whether an icon should appear in the notification area, whether Fax Console should appear when a fax is being sent or received, and whether fax events should be announced with certain sounds. (For details, see "Setting Tracking Preferences," page 713.)

● All other configuration details are maintained in common for all users. Under default security settings, these common configuration details are accessible only to administrative accounts. (For more information, see "Managing Security," page 727.)

● All users share a common set of archival folders in Windows Explorer for sent and received faxes.

Providing Information About Yourself

The information solicited by the Fax Configuration Wizard's Sender Information page, shown in Figure 20-2, is used by Fax Cover Page Editor to generate appropriately filled-out cover pages. Include as many or as few details as you want to appear on your cover pages. Note that the Tools, Sender Information command in Fax Console returns you to a slightly reorganized version of this dialog box, in case you want to make changes without going through the whole wizard process again.

Figure 20-2. The fields on the wizard's Sender Information page supply data to Fax Cover Page Editor.

Selecting a Fax Device and Configuring Send and Receive Settings

By default, Fax is set up to allow you to send but not to receive. You can adjust these settings on the wizard's Select Device For Sending Or Receiving Faxes page, shown in Figure 20-3. In the Please Select The Fax Device list, indicate the device you want to enable (if it isn't already selected). Note that if your system has multiple local fax

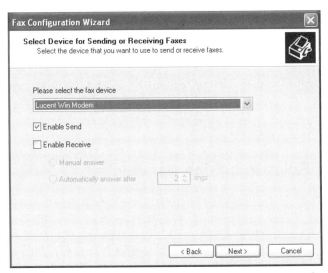

Figure 20-3. Fax can support one local device at a time; if you have more than one, select the device you want to use on this page of the wizard.

Chapter 20

devices, you can switch between them on this screen. Fax can support only one local device at a time, however.

If you select Enable Receive, Fax defaults to answering automatically on the second ring. You can adjust that ring parameter or opt to answer manually. If you choose Manual Answer, you can use a simple menu command or command button to make your modem pick up the phone.

Specifying Your Transmitting Station Identifier (TSID)

If you have selected Enable Send on the Select Device For Sending Or Receiving Faxes page, the wizard asks next for your transmitting station identifier (TSID). The TSID is a string of up to 20 characters that tells your fax recipients where your faxes are coming from. (If your fax modem and telephone service support Caller ID, your outbound transmissions might also identify you in this way. For Caller ID to work, however, your recipient must also have phone service and a fax device that support Caller ID.) When you send a fax, the receiving device prints your TSID at the top of each page (unless it has been set up not to do so). It is customary, but not essential, to put your fax number in the TSID.

If you have more than one local fax device, you can set a separate TSID string for each. For details, see "Making Other Device-Specific Settings," page 713.

Specifying Your Called Subscriber Identification (CSID)

Provided you have selected Enable Receive on the Select Device For Sending Or Receiving Faxes page, the wizard next prompts for your Called Subscriber Identification (CSID). Like the TSID, the CSID is a string of up to 20 characters. The CSID provides information to senders about the person they have reached. When someone sends you a fax, the fax application on your system sends back your CSID. It's customary, but not required, to put your fax number in the CSID.

Like the TSID, described in the preceding section, the CSID string is device-specific. The Fax Configuration Wizard assigns a common CSID to all local devices. If you have more than one device and want to individualize their CSIDs, see "Making Other Device-Specific Settings," page 713.

Routing Received Faxes to a Printer or Folder

If you have enabled your fax modem to receive, the Fax Configuration Wizard's Routing Options page, shown in Figure 20-4, gives you the option of copying incoming faxes to a printer and a file folder. Received faxes are stored as TIFF files in a folder specified on the Archives tab of the Fax Properties dialog box. (To get to this dialog box, choose Tools, Fax Printer Configuration in Fax Console, and then click the Archives tab.) By default, the archive folder is %AllUsersProfile%\Application Data\Microsoft\Windows NT\MSFax\Inbox. The wizard's Routing Options page gives you a way to create a duplicate set of files for faxes you receive.

Figure 20-4. The wizard's Routing Options page gives you the opportunity to copy incoming faxes to a printer and folder.

---

tip **Keep track of your received faxes**

The default archive location for received faxes is in the lower depths of your file system, five levels below the All Users profile. You're likely to miss this remote folder when setting up backup routines. To ensure that you don't lose important faxes, consider using the Routing Options page to create copies in a folder that you can more easily incorporate into a backup routine, such as My Documents\Faxes. (Alternatively, you can change the default archive location.)

Troubleshooting

Your faxes can't be routed to an Outlook Inbox.

Unfortunately, the option to route incoming faxes to an Outlook Inbox has been eliminated from Fax in Windows XP. For more information and a suggested workaround, see Microsoft Knowledge Base article Q311794, "The Windows XP-Based Fax Service Does Not Transfer Incoming Faxes to Your Inbox in Outlook 2000 or Outlook 2002." There's also no longer an option to have Fax notify you by e-mail if a fax arrives.

Choosing Paper Size, Image Quality, and Orientation

By default, the fax driver is set to deliver output at letter size, 200×200 dpi, and portrait orientation. You can change any of these details by visiting the General tab of the Fax

Part 5: Using E-Mail, Fax, and Messaging

Properties dialog box. To get to the Fax Properties dialog box, choose Tools, Fax Printer Configuration in Fax Console, or open Printers And Faxes in Control Panel, right-click Fax, and choose Properties from the shortcut menu. Then click the Printing Preferences button to open the Fax Printing Preferences dialog box. Paper size, image quality, and orientation are per-user settings, and non-administrative accounts can make changes on the Fax Preferences tab.

Setting Retry Characteristics and Discount Hours

The retry parameter, which tells Fax how often and how frequently to keep trying to send a fax if the first attempt fails, is a device-specific setting. If you have multiple fax devices, you can assign different retry values to each. Because the setting is device-specific, it's a little harder to find than some of the other Fax configuration options.

The default retry values are three attempts at 10-minute intervals. If you want more retries or a shorter interval, open the Fax Properties dialog box. Click the Devices tab, select the device you want to configure, and then click Properties to open the properties dialog box for the selected device (as shown in Figure 20-5). On the Send tab of this dialog box, you can express your retry preferences.

Figure 20-5. Open the Fax Properties dialog box to set retry characteristics and discount hours for a local fax device.

If your telephone service costs less at particular hours of the day, or if you simply prefer sending faxes at off-peak hours (because they're more likely to get through without encountering busy signals, for example), you can indicate those discount hours on the Send tab of the device-specific properties dialog box (shown in Figure 20-5). When you send a fax, you'll have the opportunity to schedule it to begin during the discount period.

Making Other Device-Specific Settings

Fax uses a common device driver for all local fax devices. If you have more than one local device, you can make several device-specific settings, in addition to the retry parameters and discount hours described in the previous section. To make any of these settings, choose Tools, Fax Printer Configuration in Fax Console, click the Devices tab, select a device, and click Properties. The following device-specific settings are available:

- TSID (on the Send tab)
- CSID, answer mode, and routing of received faxes (on the Receive tab)
- Scheduled removal of failed faxes from Fax Console's Outbox folder (on the Cleanup tab)

Setting Tracking Preferences

By default, Fax provides both sound and visual feedback of its activities. When either sending or receiving, for example, Fax normally displays Fax Monitor, shown in Figure 20-6. Fax Monitor can help you recognize and correct an error condition, such as the absence of a dial tone, or let you know how many pages of your outbound fax have been sent successfully, in case the transmission is interrupted.

Additionally, Fax's tracking defaults include an icon in the notification area that appears while a document is coming or going (and stays visible, marked with a red *X*, if an

Figure 20-6. Fax Monitor, displayed by default while Fax is sending or receiving, gives feedback about success and failure.

Part 5: Using E-Mail, Fax, and Messaging

outbound fax fails) and various sound events—a ringing tone when someone dials your fax number, for example, and a "ta-da" to signal a successful send. All these items can be configured—on a per-user basis—on the Tracking tab of the Fax Properties dialog box. (Click Configure Sound Settings on the Tracking tab to turn sound notification on or off for particular sound events.)

You'll notice that Fax Monitor includes an Answer Now button. If you have your fax device set up to answer manually (for example, if you use the line for both voice and fax), clicking this button is an easy way to get your modem to pick up the phone. It's not the only way, however. If you want to answer manually, but don't like having Fax Monitor pop up when the phone rings, you can use the File, Receive A Fax Now command in Fax Console instead.

If you decide to keep the sound events active but don't care for the sounds that Windows has chosen, open Sounds And Audio Devices in Control Panel and go to the Sounds tab. You'll find the four fax events—Fax Error, Fax Line Rings, Fax Sent, and New Fax—not under a Fax heading, where you would probably expect to see them, but under the Windows Explorer heading.

Specifying the Locations of Fax Console's Inbox and Sent Items Folders

The Archives tab in the Fax Properties dialog box, shown in Figure 20-7, lets you override the default storage locations for received and sent faxes. As mentioned earlier,

Figure 20-7. You can choose to archive faxes in any folders you like, including ones easier to find than the default locations shown here.

these default locations, subfolders of %AllUsersProfile%\Application Data\Microsoft\ Windows NT\MSFax seem almost calculated to discourage browsing and easy backup.

You don't have to rely on Windows Explorer for browsing, of course; you can do it from within Fax Console, instead. But backup is another matter. If you want to include your fax archives in a regular backup routine, consider moving the vault to a more accessible location.

Faxing a Document or Cover Page

To fax a document, simply print it—using Fax (or whatever you have renamed your fax device) as the "printer." You can do this from your word processor or spreadsheet, from the Photo Printing Wizard (if, for example, you want to fax a scanned image), or from any other application. When output is directed to the fax device, the Send Fax Wizard appears. The wizard begins by asking for the names and fax numbers of your recipients, as shown in Figure 20-8.

Figure 20-8. You can specify as many recipients as you like on the Send Fax Wizard's Recipient Information page. Click Address Book to fetch addressees and distribution groups from your Windows Address Book or Office Address Book.

---

tip Sending multiple pictures via Fax

You can use the Photo Printing Wizard to transmit multiple images as successive pages of a multi-page fax. In Windows Explorer, open the folder containing the images you want to send. Then choose Print Pictures in the task pane, select each image you want to transmit in the Photo Printing Wizard, and select your fax device as the printer to use.

On the Recipient Information page, you can specify as many recipients as you like, either by entering names and telephone numbers directly (clicking Add after each entry) or by clicking Address Book and selecting addressees from your Windows Address Book or Office Address Book (if Office is installed, Fax uses the Office Address Book or Contacts folder). Addressees fetched from an address book can either be individuals or distribution groups. If you select a distribution group, the Send Fax Wizard parses the group into individual addressees and displays each name and fax number in the window at the bottom of the dialog box. If you select an address book entry that does not include a fax number, the Send Fax Wizard warns you that it has rejected the entry when you try to complete the send.

If you're entering names directly on the Recipient Information page, you will usually find it easiest to select the Use Dialing Rules check box. Then when you enter an area code in the first box adjacent to Fax Number, Windows will supply the appropriate dialing prefixes, according to whatever rules you have set up in Control Panel, Phone And Modem Options. (If you have not yet set up dialing rules or you need to edit your dialing rules, click the Dialing Rules button on the Recipient Information page.)

Once you have finished addressing your fax, click Next to get to the wizard's next page, Preparing The Cover Page (shown in Figure 20-9). If you want to send a cover page, enable the Select A Cover Page Template With The Following Information option and

Figure 20-9. The list of available cover page templates includes the four that Fax Cover Page Editor supplies by default, any templates that the Windows XP Setup program has brought over from an earlier fax component, as well as any personal templates you have created.

Chapter 20: Sending and Receiving Faxes

then select from the list of available templates in the Cover Page Template list. Then fill in the Subject Line and Note boxes. You can also click Sender Information to check or edit the data that Cover Page Editor will feed to your selected template. (For more about cover pages, see "Creating Personal Cover Pages," page 724.)

Finally, click Next to schedule your fax (as shown in Figure 20-10). You can send it immediately, during discount hours, or at a specific time during the next 24 hours.

The bottom of the wizard's Schedule page gives you three priority options. When you have multiple jobs in an outbound fax queue, jobs of a given priority in a given time status (Now, for example, or When Discount Rates Apply) are sent in the order created. If you're going to create a queue of documents to be sent later in the day, you can ensure that particular items are transmitted ahead of the others by giving them High priority.

On the wizard's final page, you can review your settings. You can also click the Preview Fax button to look over the document and cover page that Fax is preparing to send, make sure the cover page includes the appropriate information, and so on. If anything's amiss, you can back out, fix, and resend.

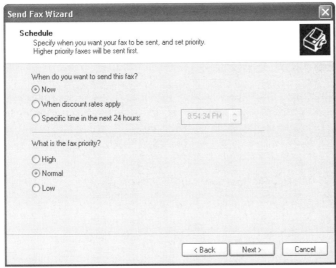

Figure 20-10. You can send now, during discount hours, or at a specific time of day.

> ## Troubleshooting
>
> **Fax won't send to a remote fax device.**
>
> If you read the section entitled "Using Remote Fax Resources" in the Help file for Fax Console (in Fax Console, choose Help, Help Topics, and find the topic on the Contents tab), you might easily conclude that Fax can use both local fax devices and fax devices shared by other computers in your workgroup. That, unfortunately, is not the case. The only remote fax resources that Fax can use are those provided by a supported fax server product, such as Microsoft Small Business Server or .NET Server. The properties dialog box for your local fax device includes a Sharing tab, but, for now, at any rate, the sole purpose of that tab is to let you know that you can't share the device.

Faxing a Cover Page Only

To send only a cover page, with or without a note, choose File, Send A Fax, in Fax Console. The process is the same as for sending a document, except that the Send Fax Wizard requires you to supply a subject line on your cover page. (You can leave the subject line blank when you print a document to Fax but not when the only page you're faxing is the cover page.)

Faxing from Microsoft Outlook

You can create messages in Outlook (and other supported e-mail programs) and transmit them as faxes from your Outlook Outbox. To do this, you must first install the fax mail transport. In Outlook 2002, follow these steps:

1 Choose Tools, E-Mail Accounts.

2 Select Add A New E-Mail Account, and click Next.

3 Select Additional Server Types, and click Next.

4 Select Fax Mail Transport, and click Next.

5 Close and reopen Outlook.

To include cover pages with the faxes you transmit from Outlook, perform these steps:

1 Choose Tools, E-Mail Accounts.

2 Select View Or Change Existing E-Mail Accounts, and click Next.

3 Select Fax Mail Transport, and click Change.

4 In the Fax Mail Transport dialog box (shown in Figure 20-11), select Include A Cover Page With Faxes, select the cover page template you want to use as a default (you'll still be able to use other cover page templates for particular messages), and then click OK.

Figure 20-11. You can configure Outlook to use a particular cover page template by default, but you can't change the font used by your Outlook faxes.

Addressing Faxes in Outlook

Once you have installed Fax Mail Transport in Outlook, you can address messages to fax recipients by selecting their names from your Office Address Book or Contacts folder. Outlook will recognize fax numbers and route your messages to Fax. If you include both e-mail addressees and fax addressees, Outlook will process the e-mail first, and then deliver the fax addressees to Fax.

As an alternative to selecting names from an address book, you can enter fax addressees directly on the To: line, using either of the following formats:

● [Fax:*name@faxnumber*]
● [Fax:*faxnumber*]

For example, any of the following would be acceptable:

- [Fax:Ed Bott@+1 (480) 555-0101]

- [Fax:+1 (480) 555-0101]

- [Fax:Ed@555-0101]

- [Fax:555-0101]

Note that the square brackets are essential. If you include the name of your addressee and you're using a cover page template, Fax will feed the name to the template.

Overriding the Cover Page Default in Outlook

To use a non-default cover page template in an Outlook fax message, choose Tools, Microsoft Fax Service Attributes in Outlook's Message window. This command is available only when you are not using Microsoft Word as your e-mail editor.

Managing the Outbox Queue

Outbound faxes pending delivery are held by Fax Console in a queue, essentially like a printer queue. You can inspect the queue by selecting Outbox in Fax Console's folder tree, and you can print, view, save, and e-mail items in the queue by choosing commands from the File menu. Once jobs have arrived in the Outbox, you can't rearrange the sequence in which they'll be sent. But you can pause an item to let the item following it be transmitted first, and then resume the paused item when you're ready to send it.

If Fax fails to complete a transmission—for example, because it retried the allotted number of times and got a busy signal on each try—the item remains in the Outbox, its icon marked with a red X. To try again, right-click the item and choose Restart.

---

tip **Clean out failed faxes**

If you find your Outbox awash in failed items, you can have Fax Console clean such items out periodically. Choose Tools, Fax Printer Configuration. Click the Devices tab, select your fax device, and click Properties. On the Cleanup tab of the device's properties dialog box, select Automatically Delete Failed Faxes After and specify an interval in days.

If Fax fails to send a job but has not used up the allotted retries, it moves on to another job in the queue and displays Retrying in the Outbox's Status column (as shown in Figure 20-12). The Scheduled Time column then displays the time of the next scheduled retry. (If these columns do not appear in your Outbox, choose View, Add/Remove Columns.) If you change your retry parameters while jobs are pending retry, Fax maintains the current retry schedule but applies your changes to subsequent retries.

Chapter 20: Sending and Receiving Faxes

Figure 20-12. The Outbox's Status, Scheduled Time, and Extended Status columns let you know when Fax will retry an unsuccessful send and why the send failed on its last try.

caution If you decide to cancel a job while Fax is sending it, don't delete the item from the Outbox. Instead, click Disconnect in Fax Monitor. (Choose Tools, Fax Monitor in Fax Console, if you don't see Fax Monitor.) Fax Console will attempt to abort a transmission if you delete it from the Outbox, but in our tests, aborting in this manner consistently locked up the computer.

Archiving Sent Faxes

When Fax has successfully sent a job, it moves it from the Outbox to the Sent Items folder, where you can manipulate it all the usual ways (double-click it to view it, for example, or choose Save As to create a copy). Fax does not include an archival procedure per se. The Sent Items folder *is* the archive for sent faxes; you can change its location by choosing Tools, Fax Printer Configuration and clicking the Archives tab. But you can't remove items from Sent Items automatically on the basis of their age or export a selection of items. The best way to preserve selected items while clearing out the Sent Items folder is to work with those items in Windows Explorer. As Figure 20-13 shows, you can

Figure 20-13. All users at a computer share common fax archival folders in Windows Explorer. Fax uses Security Identifiers (SIDs) as part of its file naming convention.

use Windows Explorer to open %AllUsersProfile\Application Data\Microsoft\Windows NT\MSFax\SentItems (or whatever folder you have chosen to use for sent items), and then you can use Windows Explorer's Filmstrip and Thumbnails views to examine faxes you've sent. Unfortunately, you'll have to cope with Fax's thoroughly unlovely file naming convention.

Receiving Faxes

If you have set Fax up to answer automatically, all you have to do to receive a fax is make sure your modem's cable is plugged into a phone jack. Fax does the rest, notifying you of a message's arrival in the manner you have selected (see "Setting Tracking Preferences," page 713). Once a fax has been successfully received, an entry for it appears in Fax Console's Inbox folder and, if requested, a copy appears at your printer or in your routing folder (see "Routing Received Faxes to a Printer or Folder," page 710).

If you've set your system up for manual answer, you can have Fax pick up the phone by clicking Answer Now in Fax Monitor (choose Tools, Fax Monitor in Fax Console if you don't see Fax Monitor), by choosing Fax Console's File, Receive A Fax Now command, or by clicking the icon that appears in your notification area when your telephone rings. You'll probably want to have a distinctive sound assigned to the Fax Line Rings sound event, so that you don't miss any calls. (See "Setting Tracking Preferences," page 713.)

---

tip **Let the telephone service use a distinctive ring**

How do you share a phone line so that you can use it for voice calls and fax calls without having to manually intercept each fax? Ask your phone service provider if they offer a service called "distinctive ring." With this service (which goes by other names as well), you pay a small extra charge to have a second phone number assigned to your existing phone line. When a caller connects to this number, your phone rings with a distinctive sound that's different from the one associated with regular voice calls. By adding the proper initialization string to the properties for your modem (AT-SDR=2 in the case of our Supra Faxmodem), you can "train" the modem to answer only calls that are identified by the distinctive ring. Give your contacts the new number as your dedicated fax line.

Reading Received Faxes

Faxes arrive in the Inbox folder as TIFF files. When you double-click an item there, Windows displays it, using whatever application is currently associated with the .tif file extension. If you have installed Microsoft Office, that application is probably Microsoft Office Document Imaging (as shown in Figure 20-14). This TIFF viewer has the virtue of providing page thumbnails for multi-page documents and also includes optical character recognition (OCR) capability. Figure 20-15 shows an OCR rendition of the first page of the fax shown in Figure 20-14. It's not perfect by any means, but it's a leg up if you need to edit the text you receive.

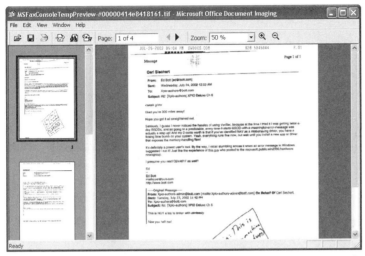

Figure 20-14. Double-click a fax in Fax Console's Inbox folder to display it in your system's default TIFF viewer.

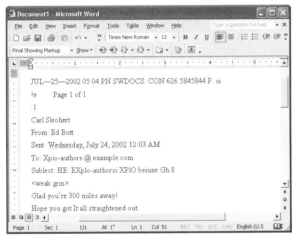

Figure 20-15. The OCR capability in Microsoft Document Imaging produced this approximation of the text displayed in Figure 20-14.

If you don't have Office, your system probably uses Windows Picture and Fax Viewer to display your faxes. This application doesn't do thumbnails. But you can move between pages of a multi-page document by clicking the Next Page and Previous Page buttons along the bottom of the window (shown in Figure 20-16 on the next page), or by pressing the Page Up and Page Down keys.

Figure 20-16. Use the Next Page and Previous Page buttons to move between pages in Windows Picture and Fax Viewer.

Archiving Received Faxes

Received faxes accumulate in your Inbox forever, unless you move them manually. Fax Console does not include a date-based archival procedure. You can delete or save (that is, copy) items individually from the Inbox. Or you can work with them in Windows Explorer, by opening %AllUsersProfile\Application Data\Microsoft\Windows NT\ MSFax\Inbox (or whatever other folder you've chosen to use for your received items).

Creating Personal Cover Pages

Using Fax Cover Page Editor, you can customize any of the four cover page templates supplied with Fax. You can also create new templates from scratch. The resulting personal cover pages become available to your own user account only.

Although the Fax folder in your Start menu includes a command to launch Fax Cover Page Editor, the simplest way to start building a personal cover page is to choose Tools, Personal Cover Pages in Fax Console. The dialog box that appears lists any personal cover pages you have already created. To edit one of these, select it and click Open. To customize one of the four common cover pages, click Copy, and select the one you want. The selected item then appears in the Personal Cover Pages dialog box, where you can rename it if you want or simply open it and begin customizing. If you want to work with a blank slate and create your own template from scratch, click New. Figure 20-17 shows Fax Cover Page Editor with the common cover page Confdent.cov, unmodified.

Chapter 20: Sending and Receiving Faxes

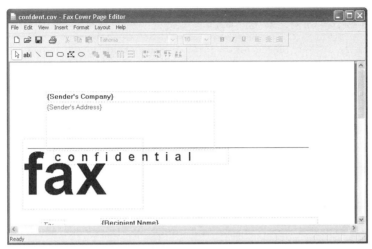

Figure 20-17. You can use Fax Cover Page Editor to modify supplied cover page templates or create your own.

Selecting, Sizing, and Moving Objects

Every element on a cover page that's bounded by a dotted line in Fax Cover Page Editor is a distinct object. To size or move an object, begin by clicking it. Black handles appear around the selected object's perimeter. To change an object's size, drag one of the handles. To move an object, position the mouse along the perimeter, but not on a handle. A four-headed arrow appears beside the normal mouse pointer. Drag the object to its new location. If you change your mind, select Edit, Undo.

To move two or more objects at once, Ctrl-click each one. The objects become temporarily grouped and will move together.

Aligning Objects

You can use View, Grid Lines to display light-blue grid lines in the editor. These might help you in positioning objects. However, it's usually easier to align objects by using Layout, Align Objects. Options on the Align Objects submenu let you line up objects flush left or flush right. You can also top align and bottom align objects or center objects horizontally or vertically.

Spacing Objects Evenly

To ensure that three or more objects have equal vertical or horizontal space between them, first Ctrl-click those objects. Then choose Layout, Space Evenly, Across or Layout, Space Evenly, Down.

Centering Objects on the Page

To center one or more objects on the page, vertically or horizontally, first Ctrl-click the objects. Then choose Layout, Center On Page, Width or Layout, Center On Page, Height.

Changing the Z-Order of Stacked Objects

If two or more objects lie atop one another, the order in which they're stacked is called the *z-order*). To change the z-order of an object relative to others, select the object and choose Layout, Bring To Front or Layout, Send To Back.

Adding Fixed Text

Fixed text is text that doesn't change (as distinguished from fields, which are replaced by information about the sender, recipient, or content of a fax). To add fixed text, follow these steps:

1 Click the Text tool on the Drawing toolbar. (If the Drawing toolbar isn't visible, choose View, Drawing Toolbar.)

2 Click one corner of the place where you want the object to go. Then drag to the diagonally opposite corner. A perimeter rectangle with black handles appears as you drag.

3 Type your text within the object perimeter. Use Format, Font and Format, Align Text (or their toolbar equivalents) to get the text looking the way you want it.

Note that new objects don't affect the placement of existing objects. If you want to insert a line of text between two lines, you must first drag objects out of the way to make room for the incoming text.

Inserting Fields, Images, and Graphics

Objects that begin and end with braces—such as {Sender's Company} and {Sender's Address} in Figure 20-17—are fields. When your fax is sent, these fields will be replaced by the appropriate data. To add fields to a cover page, use the Insert menu. The available fields appear in three submenus: Recipient, Sender, and Message.

To place an image on a cover page, first open or create that image in another application (such as Paint). Copy the image to the Clipboard, and then paste it onto your cover page. The pasted image will appear in the upper left corner, and you can use the mouse to drag it into place.

To insert lines and shapes, use the Line, Rectangle, Rounded Rectangle, Polygon, and Ellipse tools from the Drawing toolbar. To use any of these other than the Polygon tool, select the tool, and then click the cover page approximately where you want to start drawing the object and drag to the size you want. You can move and resize the objects after you first place them on the page. To use the Polygon tool, click each vertex of the polygon. When you have finished, double-click to close the polygon.

Holding down Shift while you drag constrains the Line, Rectangle, Rounded Rectangle, and Ellipse tools. Shift-dragging with the Line tool creates a horizontal, vertical, or 45-degree diagonal line. Shift-dragging with the Rectangle and Rounded Rectangle tools creates a square and rounded square, whereas Shift-dragging with the Ellipse tool creates a circle.

Previewing and Saving

The File, Print Preview command gives you a look at your work, more or less the way it will appear in a fax viewer (with fields, instead of data). The Save command puts a copy of the template in %UserProfile%\My Documents\Fax\Personal Cover Pages, the default location for personal cover pages. To save the cover page elsewhere, use File, Save As.

Managing Security

Under default permissions for a fax device, administrative accounts have complete control over all local fax resources and can view and edit security settings. Non-administrative users can view and manage (copy, print, delete) faxes that they have sent but not those sent by other users. Non-administrative accounts can view all successfully received faxes (including faxes received by other user accounts) but cannot manage any received faxes. Non-administrative users cannot see entries in Fax Console's Incoming folder—the folder that Fax Console uses while a fax reception is in progress.

To view or edit fax security settings, open the Fax Properties dialog box. You can do this by choosing Tools, Fax Printer Configuration in Fax Console or by opening Printers And Faxes in Control Panel, right-clicking Fax, and choosing Properties from the shortcut menu.

The Fax Properties dialog box includes two security tabs, labeled Security and Fax Security. The Security tab offers options that are common to all printers. To work with permissions that deal specifically with fax queues and documents, use the Fax Security tab.

Neither the Security tab nor the Fax Security tab is normally visible on a computer that is using Simple File Sharing (this includes all computers running Windows XP Home Edition). To make the Fax Security tab appear if you don't see it, close the Fax Properties dialog box and reopen it while holding down Ctrl. The Security tab is visible only on systems that are not using Simple File Sharing.

The basic permissions available for a fax device are listed in Table 20-1. In addition to these basic permissions, a much more granular set of permissions is available. To change any of these settings, click Advanced on the Fax Security tab of the Fax Properties dialog box. Then select the name of a user or security group, and click Edit. These steps display the dialog box shown in Figure 20-18.

Figure 20-18. If the basic fax permissions don't entirely meet your needs, you can micromanage permissions with the help of these advanced settings.

Table 20-1. **Basic Fax Permissions and Privileges**

Permission	Privileges
Fax	Fax a document; view all faxes in the Inbox
Manage Fax Configuration	Configure the fax device
Manage Fax Documents	Print and manage all faxes, including those owned by other users

Chapter 21

Communicating over the Internet

The ubiquity of Internet connections—many of them at broadband speeds and always on—provides an ideal medium for instant, interactive communications. E-mail is terrific for communications where you don't need an immediate response. Telephone communications are, of course, essential in business and personal intercourse. Instant messaging with a program like Windows Messenger provides a third communications method that offers a number of advantages:

● It's interactive. You can exchange questions and answers in real time instead of sending e-mail messages back and forth over a period of hours, days, or weeks.

● It's not as intrusive as telephone communications. If you choose, you can continue working in other programs or with other activities while you carry out an instant messaging session.

● It's more private. Users can control the display of their availability on other users' screens. You can block specific people from seeing your availability and from sending you messages. As with Caller ID, you can see who is trying to reach you before you answer. Strangers can't join your conversation, as they can in an Internet chat session.

● It's versatile. As with e-mail, you can send and receive text and files. You can also make voice calls as you would with a telephone. In addition, you can send and receive video, you can work collaboratively with a whiteboard or a program, and you can take control of another user's computer with that person's permission.

At Home with Windows XP

All of Windows Messenger's features are available in Windows XP Home Edition as well as Windows XP Professional. The optional Group Policy setting that prevents Windows Messenger from running is not available in Home Edition. But if you're a Home Edition user and don't want Windows Messenger to run, you can keep it from appearing by making a small registry modification. For details, see "Disabling Windows Messenger in Windows XP Home Edition," page 738.

newfeature!
Introducing Windows Messenger

Windows Messenger is the latest version of a program originally known as MSN Messenger. With Windows Messenger, after you've set up a list of contacts you can see which of your contacts is online at any time. Windows Messenger lets you engage in a conference with one or many users across the Internet or a local area network. If your computer has a sound card, a microphone, and speakers, you can talk to another person in something approximating real time. If you have a video camera connected to your computer, you can exchange video images. With or without audio and video equipment, you can "chat" with others, exchange drawings and diagrams by means of a virtual whiteboard, send and receive files, and even work together in a shared program. You can also use Windows Messenger to initiate a Remote Assistance session, in which one user can view and control the computer of another user at a remote location.

For information about using Windows Messenger for Remote Assistance, see "Connecting to Another PC with Remote Assistance," page 154.

Windows Messenger also serves as an alert service. It notifies you of new messages in your Hotmail mailbox, for example. And with Microsoft .NET Alerts, a free service, you can receive alerts about events on your calendar, changes in certain stock prices, and other events you choose.

Additional features in the latest version of Windows Messenger allow you to monitor stock prices, send text messages to electronic pagers and cell phones, and more.

note Windows Messenger can be updated through dynamic update during setup (the Windows XP Setup program can check the Internet for updates), by Windows Update, or in response to messages displayed by Windows Messenger.

Third-party enhancements to Windows Messenger offer additional functionality. Windows Messenger provides a platform that developers can use to create other services and features. Another area that's sure to be exploited is Internet games. Windows Messenger alleviates the need to know another gamer's IP address, which has been a problem in earlier multiplayer Internet games.

> **note** Don't confuse Windows Messenger with the Messenger service, a system service that you can control with the Services console (Services.msc). Despite the similar names, the two have nothing to do with each other. The Messenger service is used for broadcasting a text message to one or more computers on your network. Messenger messages are often sent by applications (to notify you that a print job is complete or that the system is running on battery backup power, for example). You can't reply to such messages; your only possible response is to close the message box by clicking OK. The Messenger service need not be running to use Windows Messenger.

Other Communications Tools Included with Windows XP

Windows Messenger provides a seamless, integrated way for users to participate in text chat, voice and video communication, and data collaboration. As such, it provides the functionality of other programs that were included in earlier versions of Windows. In addition to the chat capabilities inherited from MSN Messenger, Windows Messenger incorporates audio and videoconference capabilities of Microsoft NetMeeting and Phone Dialer.

Although they don't appear on the Start menu, NetMeeting and Phone Dialer are included in Windows XP. (Note that the version of Phone Dialer included with Windows XP is the sophisticated conferencing application introduced with Windows 2000, not the rudimentary eight-number speed dial program of the same name that was included with Windows 95 and Windows 98.) You might want to use these tools in certain situations:

- If you want to view a directory of and connect with other users whom you don't know, but who may share common interests, use NetMeeting or Phone Dialer. With both programs, you can connect to an Internet location server (ILS), which lists lots of other people who are out there waiting for your call.

(continued)

Chapter 21

Other Communications Tools Included with Windows XP *(continued)*

- If you've already stored NetMeeting conferencing information (that is, the name of the conferencing server and the address of the user) for entries in your Microsoft Outlook Express address book, use NetMeeting. You can continue working with those contacts as you always have. (On the other hand, you might want to suggest that your contacts switch to Windows Messenger so that you can both enjoy its advantages.)

- If you want to use a sophisticated speed-dial system for making voice calls over standard telephone lines, use Phone Dialer.

- If you want to hold a voice conference or videoconference with more than two people simultaneously, use Phone Dialer.

- If you want to use Whiteboard or application sharing with more than two people simultaneously, use NetMeeting.

- If you want to hold a voice or video conversation, share applications, or use Whiteboard with a user who doesn't have Windows Messenger, use NetMeeting.

NetMeeting

To start NetMeeting, open the Start menu, choose Run, and type **conf**. If you use NetMeeting regularly, you'll want to create a shortcut to its executable, %ProgramFiles%\Netmeeting\Conf.exe. The first time you run NetMeeting, a wizard asks you to provide your name and e-mail address so that you can be found in a directory. (Even if you choose not to list your name in a directory, an ILS server needs this information to know when you're online and how to route NetMeeting calls to your computer.) After completing the wizard, the main NetMeeting window opens, as shown in Figure 21-1.

To learn more about NetMeeting, open its Help menu and choose Help Topics. The Help menu also includes several links to online information but, because Windows Messenger has largely supplanted NetMeeting, some of these links no longer work. The mother lode of NetMeeting information, the NetMeeting Resource Kit, is available for download at *http://www.microsoft.com/windows/NetMeeting/Corp/reskit/default.asp*.

Phone Dialer

To start Phone Dialer, open the Run dialog box and type **dialer**. If you want to create a shortcut, you'll find Dialer.exe in the %ProgramFiles%\Windows NT folder. With Phone Dialer, you can make videoconference calls to other users on the Internet or on your local area network, as shown in Figure 21-2.

Chapter 21: Communicating over the Internet

Video image

Address bar

Place call

End call

Find someone in a directory

Start video

Picture-in-picture

Adjust volume

Names of participants in current call

Share program

Text chat

Transfer files

Whiteboard

Figure 21-1. The main NetMeeting window provides the tools to make, accept, and control your calls, along with a list of people in the current conversation and a video window.

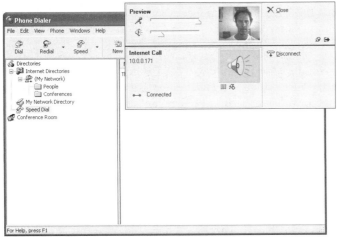

Figure 21-2. Phone Dialer offers video calls over network connections as well as voice calls over the network or telephone lines.

Chapter 21

What You Need to Use Windows Messenger

The basic requirement to run Windows Messenger is simple: You need a working Internet connection and a .NET Passport. (This is true even if you plan to use Windows Messenger only to converse with others on your local area network, because your list of contacts is available only when you're connected to the Internet.) If you want to make voice calls or video calls, you'll need some additional hardware:

- To be able to hear others speak, add a sound card and speakers or a headset.

- To add your own voice to the fray, connect a microphone to the sound card.

- To send your picture to others, add a Web camera.

> **note** For voice calls or video calls, you'll obviously get better quality with greater bandwidth. Cable or DSL connections are ideal, but you can actually get decent results with a dial-up connection. At a bare minimum, you'll need a 28,800 bps modem that's connected at 28,800 bps.

If your computer is protected from the Internet by a router other than the built-in Internet Connection Sharing, the router must support Universal Plug and Play (UPnP) if you want to use Messenger features other than instant text messaging and file transfers. For more information about router and firewall configuration, see "Punching Through a Firewall," on the facing page.

A .NET Passport provides the connection to the server where your contacts are stored. Because your contacts are stored on a central server, they're available to you no matter where you are when you sign in using your Passport. If you haven't already obtained a .NET Passport and linked it to your user account, you can do so through the User Accounts option in Control Panel. But an easier way is to simply double-click the Windows Messenger icon in the notification area.

Unless your account is already linked to a .NET Passport, this action opens the .NET Passport Wizard. The wizard helps you obtain a .NET Passport if you don't have one and then links it to your user account so that you can sign in automatically whenever you log on to your computer.

> For more information about .NET Passports, see "Setting Up a .NET Passport," page 126.

> **note** When Microsoft started its Passport service, to get a Passport you had to have an e-mail address at hotmail.com, msn.com, or passport.com. You can still use one of those addresses if you have one (or you can use the wizard to set up a Hotmail account), but you can now link a Passport to *any* e-mail address.

Punching Through a Firewall

If you have a dial-up connection or a broadband connection and your computer connects directly to the cable without passing through a router, you're probably using Internet Connection Firewall and Internet Connection Sharing to protect your network and share your Internet connection. If that's the case, you're in great shape for using all the features of Windows Messenger. This combination deals perfectly with the dynamic port assignments and supports Universal Plug and Play (UPnP).

On the other hand, if you use a router that was purchased before late 2001, it probably does not support UPnP, and therefore won't allow you to make voice calls and video calls over the Internet. In addition, you might need to open some ports to enable certain other features. If you have such a setup, check with the manufacturer of your router. Many manufacturers have promised firmware upgrades that enable UPnP, as well as incorporating UPnP support in their new products.

One of the key jobs of a router is network address translation (NAT), which converts the internal LAN address of a computer into a public IP address. NAT effectively shields your network computers from the Internet. But it also makes it difficult to connect computers on separate private networks in a peer-to-peer fashion. UPnP is a new industry standard that makes it possible for computers to detect devices on a network and work with one another. When it comes to traversing NAT devices, UPnP enables applications such as Windows Messenger to navigate the gateway. You can find more information about UPnP at *http://www.microsoft.com/WindowsXP/pro/techinfo/ planning/networking/natfaq.asp* and *http://www.upnp.org*.

Windows Messenger uses the following ports. If you're using Internet Connection Sharing (with or without Internet Connection Firewall), you don't need to do any configuration except as noted. For other firewalls, consult the device's documentation for information about opening ports.

- **Instant messaging.** Windows Messenger uses a TCP connection to port 1863 if possible. If that's not available, Messenger connects using the same connection the Web browser uses. If that's the only available connection method, you'll be limited to using Windows Messenger for instant messaging. If you're using a proxy server, open the Tools menu in Windows Messenger and choose Options. Click the Connection tab and provide the requested information, which depends on the type of proxy server you have.

- **File transfer.** Windows Messenger allows up to 10 simultaneous file transfers, each on a separate port, using TCP connections to ports 6891 through 6900. If you use Internet Connection Firewall, you need to add rules to open these ports; for details, see "Sending and Receiving Files," page 753.

- **Whiteboard and application sharing.** Like NetMeeting, Windows Messenger uses TCP connections to port 1503 for Whiteboard and application sharing.

- **Voice and video.** These services use dynamically assigned ports. (If you're curious, you can see the rules that Internet Connection Firewall uses by examining its settings while you have a voice or video conversation active. You'll see a number of services with names that begin with "msmsgs.") More important, they require UPnP support to get to an IP address on the internal network.

Troubleshooting

Windows Messenger stops working when you make a VPN connection.

You might encounter problems using Windows Messenger while you're also using a virtual private network (VPN) connection. If you have a conversation open and then connect to a VPN server, your conversation might stop. You'll receive no indication that the call has been interrupted (other than the fact that the person you're talking with no longer responds to your messages). Similarly, the person at the other end of the conversation has no indication that you're no longer in the conversation.

The reason for this is that the default configuration of a VPN connection attempts to use the default gateway on the remote network (that is, the default gateway for the VPN server) for Internet connections while the VPN connection is active. This setup is useful in situations where you're connecting to a corporate network and then using *its* ISP to connect to the Internet. If you have your own connection to the Internet, there's usually no reason to use such a setup.

To fix the problem, follow these steps:

1 In Control Panel open Network Connections.

2 Right-click the VPN connection and choose Properties.

3 Click the Networking tab, select Internet Protocol (TCP/IP) and click Properties.

4 In the Internet Protocol (TCP/IP) Properties dialog box, click Advanced.

5 On the General tab of the Advanced TCP/IP Settings dialog box, clear the Use Default Gateway On Remote Network check box.

Thereafter, you should be able to use Windows Messenger (and any other applications that access the Internet, such as Internet Explorer) while your VPN connection is active.

Setting Startup Options

By default, Windows Messenger starts each time you log on and its icon appears in the notification area. You can prevent this from happening by double-clicking the icon to open the main Windows Messenger window. (You don't need to sign in.) Open Tools, Options, and click the Preferences tab. Under General, clear the Run This Program When Windows Starts check box. Doing so removes the MSMSGS value from HKCU\Software\Microsoft\Windows\CurrentVersion\Run. (If you don't have a Passport associated with your user account, you can't open Windows Messenger to make this change until you complete the .NET Passport Wizard. However, there is a way around this roadblock without editing the registry directly. Open Outlook Express and choose Tools, Windows Messenger, Options. You can then make the change described above as well as the three that follow.)

Note, however, that the icon also appears whenever you start Outlook Express. You can prevent that from happening by making the following additional settings:

- In the Preferences tab of Messenger's Options dialog box, clear the Allow This Program To Run In The Background check box.

- In Outlook Express, open Tools, Options. On the General tab, clear Automatically Log On To Windows Messenger.

- Don't display the Contacts pane in Outlook Express. To prevent it from appearing, choose View, Layout, and clear the Contacts check box.

Before you go to great lengths to exterminate Windows Messenger, be aware that when only its icon appears, Messenger uses an insignificant amount of memory. And if you don't like seeing the icon, set it to be hidden all the time. For details, see "Removing Unneeded Icons from the Notification Area," page 320.

If you're really intent on preventing Windows Messenger from starting up—ever—you can uninstall it. The easiest way is to enter the following at a command prompt:

```
rundll32 advpack.dll,LaunchINFSection %systemroot%\inf\msmsgs.inf,BLC.Remove
```

(This command string is case-senstive.) Be aware, however, that removing Windows Messenger can affect other components; if you don't like it, you're best off leaving it in place and ignoring it.

> **tip** If you remove Windows Messenger, starting Outlook Express with the Contacts pane displayed takes an inordinately long time (because Outlook Express tries in vain to launch Windows Messenger). You can retain the Contacts pane but eliminate this delay by adding a registry value. In the HKLM\Software\Microsoft\Outlook Express key, create a new DWORD value named Hide Messenger, and then set its data to 2.

Chapter 21

If you have previously set Passport to sign in automatically on your computer and you want to change that so that when you connect to the Internet, you don't automatically sign in, follow these steps:

1 In Control Panel, open User Accounts.

2 Click your account name (if you're an administrator) and then click Manage My Network Passwords under Related Tasks in the task pane.

3 Select the Passport.Net* (Passport) entry and click Remove.

Thereafter, when you log on and connect to the Internet, you remain signed off until you explicitly sign in. If you select Sign Me In Automatically in the .NET Messenger Service sign-in dialog box, you'll again sign in automatically each time you connect to the Internet.

Using Group Policy to Disable Windows Messenger

Windows XP Professional users can prevent Windows Messenger from running as follows:

1 At a command prompt, type **Gpedit.msc**.

2 Navigate to Local Computer Policy\Computer Configuration\Administrative Templates\Windows Components\Windows Messenger.

3 Enable the Do Not Allow Windows Messenger To Be Run policy.

These steps prevent Windows Messenger from running, regardless of whether you try to start it directly or another application (such as Outlook Express) tries to run it. Note that the other policy setting, Do Not Automatically Start Windows Messenger Initially, is ineffective. If you enable Windows Messenger to run at startup by selecting Run This Program When Windows Starts in Windows Messenger's Options dialog box, Windows Messenger runs at startup, policy notwithstanding.

Disabling Windows Messenger in Windows XP Home Edition

If you're running Windows XP Home Edition, you don't have access to the Group Policy console, but you can disable Windows Messenger by modifying the registry. Proceed as follows:

1 Open HKLM\Software\Policies\Microsoft, and create a new subkey named Messenger.

2 In the Messenger key, create a new subkey named Client.

3 In the Client subkey, create a new DWORD value named PreventRun.

4 Set the data value for PreventRun to 1.

Starting Windows Messenger

If Windows Messenger is set to run at startup, you can open it by double-clicking its notification area icon. Otherwise, you can start Windows Messenger by choosing it from the All Programs menu. When you're not signed in to Passport, the icon looks like the one shown here on the left. If you are signed in, it looks like the one on the right.

Either way, Windows Messenger opens. If you have not signed in, the program prompts you to do so. Otherwise, the appearance of the window is comparable to that shown in Figure 21-3.

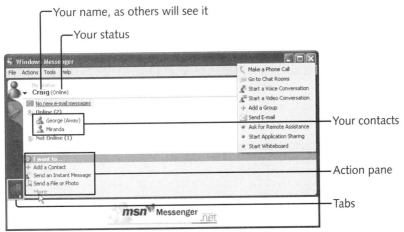

Figure 21-3. Windows Messenger's initial display shows your current status, the name and status of each contact, an action pane, and more.

The name and status that appear at the top of the window, under My Status, is what your contacts will see. You can change the name (from your e-mail address to your first name, for example) on the Personal tab of the Options dialog box (choose Tools, Options). To change your status (from Online to Be Right Back, for example), click your name.

The link below your name gives you an easy way to retrieve awaiting e-mail. (You can also use it to open your e-mail client, even if you don't have unread messages.) Below the e-mail link appear the names of your contacts. Those who have signed into their Passport accounts are listed as Online, even if they are currently away from their machines. Those who have not signed in are listed in the Not Online section.

Along the left edge of the window, you might see a panel of tabs. These provide quick access to related services, such as Microsoft .NET Alerts. To configure the tab display, choose Tools, Show Tabs.

An action pane appears near the bottom of the window, under the heading I Want To. If you click the More link, an expanded set of actions appears on the right side of the window, as shown in Figure 21-3. If you have a lot of contacts, you might want to collapse the action pane by clicking the chevron beside the I Want To heading. (All the actions are accessible via the Actions and Tools menus, in any case.)

---

tip   **Double-click to sign in**

If you sign out of Windows Messenger (or you're disconnected due to a network problem), you can sign in again by clicking (or right-clicking) the notification area icon and choosing Sign In from the shortcut menu. But when you do that, you have to reenter your password. You can bypass the password request by simply double-clicking the notification area icon. That opens Windows Messenger, which has a link you can click to sign in—without reentering your password.

Placing or Receiving a Call

Windows Messenger offers three types of calls: instant message (text), voice, and video. You can send an instant message in any of the following ways:

- Double-click the name of an online contact.

- Click Send An Instant Message in the action pane, or choose Actions, Send An Instant Message. Then choose the name of an online contact in the Send An Instant Message dialog box. To send a message to someone who's not in your contacts list, click the Other tab, and then enter the e-mail address of the person you want to reach.

- Click or right-click the notification area icon and choose Send An Instant Message.

---

tip   **Send an instant message from Outlook Express**

You don't have to open Windows Messenger to send an instant message; you can initiate a conversation from Outlook Express. Display the Contacts pane (choose View, Layout and select Contacts); your online contacts appear at the top of the list. Double-click an online contact to send an instant message.

A conversation window opens on your computer, similar to the one shown in Figure 21-4. Type your message in the box at the bottom of the window and then click Send.

Chapter 21: Communicating over the Internet

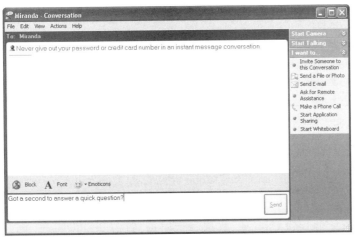

Figure 21-4. Type the text you want to send in the box at the bottom of the conversation window.

When you send your message, an alert window appears on the recipient's screen, as shown in Figure 21-5, and a sound plays. In addition, a brightly colored flashing button appears on the recipient's taskbar. (For all this to happen, of course, the recipient must have Windows Messenger running and must be signed in to Passport.) The text of the alert message is actually a link; the recipient can click the text to open a conversation

You can click the message text or the taskbar button to open a conversation window

Figure 21-5. The text of an alert window is a clickable link.

Chapter 21

window on his or her screen. The alert window, however, remains on-screen for only a few seconds. If the recipient misses that opportunity, clicking the taskbar button opens the conversation window. (The flashing, thankfully, stops after a few more seconds, but the bright color remains until the recipient opens—or closes without restoring—the conversation window.)

---

tip   Customize your alerts

Windows Messenger can display an alert window whenever one of your contacts comes online, when you receive an instant message or alert, and when you receive a message in your Hotmail Inbox. In addition, it can play a sound upon each of these events. If you want to limit the number of intrusions or change the sounds that play, open the Tools menu and choose Options. Click the Preferences tab and then make your settings in the Alerts section. (Note that you can't disable the alert window for new Hotmail messages.)

Until the recipient opens the conversation window and begins typing a response, you'll have no idea whether the person is at his or her computer, or whether the computer is even turned on. But when the person at the other end of the conversation begins typing, a message in the status bar alerts you to that fact, even before you receive a response.

---

tip   Receive other types of alerts

Microsoft .NET Alerts is a service that can send reminders of appointments, due dates, birthdays, and so on; alerts of changes in the price of stocks you're interested in; and more. You can set these alerts to arrive as instant messages when you're running Windows Messenger. (You can also set them up to be delivered to your e-mail address or pager, and you can choose different delivery options depending on your Windows Messenger status.) To learn more and to start setting reminders, visit *http://alerts.microsoft.com*.

Working with Your List of Contacts

It's easiest to initiate a conversation with someone in your contact list. First off, you can see at a glance who among your contacts is online and who is not, as shown in Figure 21-6. Secondly, you can start a conversation by double-clicking the name of an online contact or choosing the name from a menu; no typing is needed.

---

tip   Contact someone who's not online

To reach a contact who is not online—or who does not respond to an instant message— right-click the contact name and choose Send Mail.

Chapter 21: Communicating over the Internet

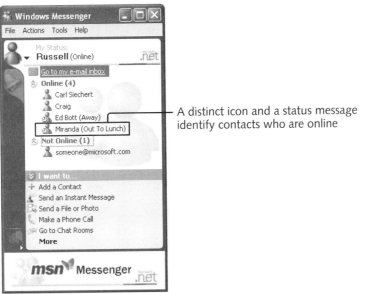

A distinct icon and a status message identify contacts who are online

Figure 21-6. The main Windows Messenger window shows which contacts are online—including those who are online but possibly unavailable.

To add someone to your contact list, click the Add A Contact link or choose Tools, Add A Contact. The Add A Contact Wizard appears, asking you to decide whether you want to type the contact's e-mail address or search for the contact. Select the default option, By E-Mail Address Or Sign-In Name.

The search option, which lets you specify a name and location, is not likely to be fruitful. It can search your own Outlook Express address book or the Hotmail member directory. However, it doesn't search the Outlook Express address book thoroughly; it includes only contacts that you have added manually, not the addresses that are added automatically when you reply to a message. The Hotmail member directory has its own limitations: It includes only a subset of Hotmail members. (For privacy reasons, many Hotmail members choose not to list their names or provide fake information.) You must enter an exact match for the directory entry; partial names won't produce hits. If you feel compelled to try anyway, leave the Country/Region box set to (Any). With a country selected, the directory search sometimes fails to produce any results.

After you enter an e-mail name (or find the match you were looking for in a name search), Windows checks the .NET Passport servers to see whether the person has a Passport. If he or she does not, the wizard can send an e-mail message on your behalf that explains how to get a Passport and set up Messenger. If your new contact already has a Passport, a dialog box, shown in Figure 21-7 on the next page, appears on your contact's computer that alerts him or her to the fact that you've added this person to your contact list. (If Messenger isn't running on the contact's computer at that time, the message appears when the contact next signs in.)

Figure 21-7. Messenger advises your new contact about your action, and offers the contact an opportunity to rebuff your advance—or to reciprocate by adding you to his or her contact list.

---

tip   **Add contacts from Outlook Express**

If you've saved e-mail contacts in Outlook Express (or in Address Book), you can quickly convert them to online contacts that appear in your Windows Messenger contact list. In Outlook Express, display the Contacts pane. (Choose View, Layout, and select Contacts.) Right-click a contact and choose Set As Online Contact. (Note that this option isn't available in the Address Book window; you must use the Contacts pane in Outlook Express.) Windows then checks to see if a .NET Passport is associated with the e-mail address of the contact you selected and reports its findings, just as the Add A Contact Wizard does.

To delete a contact you no longer want, right-click it and choose Delete Contact.

Preserving Your Online Privacy

With the increasing numbers of reports of identity theft, stalkers, cons, scams, viruses, worms, and other nasty possibilities, people are understandably wary about exposing personal information on the Internet. Windows Messenger and the supporting .NET Passport technology have a number of features that allow you to protect your privacy. To begin with, unlike Internet relay chat (IRC) programs, Windows Messenger conversations are limited to your friends and associates or, at the very least, to people who have your e-mail address and your permission to converse. You can learn about .NET Passport privacy policies, including descriptions of which personal information is available to others, by visiting *http://www.passport.com/consumer/privacypolicy.asp*.

Windows Messenger includes features that address the following privacy concerns:

Protecting your identity   You determine what name others see if you're listed in their contact list or if you're in a conversation. You can choose to use only your first name or a totally anonymous handle of your invention. To specify the name that others see, open the Tools menu and choose Options. On the Personal tab, shown in Figure 21-8, type the name that you want displayed.

Chapter 21: Communicating over the Internet

Figure 21-8. You can choose how you want to be identified to your contacts.

Protecting your e-mail address The e-mail address that's linked to your Passport appears in the conversation window while you're in a call. If you don't want that address known publicly, use another. Free e-mail addresses are available from Hotmail and a number of other online services. Changing the address associated with your existing Passport doesn't always work; you're better off obtaining a new Passport that's associated with the new address you want to use.

> **note** When you create a Passport, you can provide a phony e-mail address; Passport has no way of confirming your address during the sign-up process. However, it's not a good idea to do that. When you first sign in with your new Passport, Windows Messenger asks you to confirm your e-mail address. Passport does this by sending a message to the address you provided, to which you must respond. The message that Passport sends informs the recipient that someone has set up a password with that e-mail address. (This is done to prevent people from posing as someone else by using an address such as *president@whitehouse.gov,* for example.) Until you respond appropriately, Windows Messenger asks you to confirm your address at each logon. And although you can use Messenger to contact others without confirming your address, the text "(E-Mail Address Not Verified)" appears next to each occurrence of your name in a conversation window, alerting your correspondents to the fact that they might not be talking with the person they think they are.

Protecting your phone numbers   You can choose to make your phone numbers available to people who have you listed in their contact list. To make your phone numbers available, click the Phone tab in the Options dialog box. You can specify up to three phone numbers (identified as home, work, and mobile). If you supply one or more phone numbers, a contact can right-click your name in his or her own contact list and choose Make A Phone Call. This action allows your contact to reach you via an Internet-to-phone service. Naturally, you should publish your phone numbers only if you're willing to be called by anyone who has you in his or her contact list.

---

tip   **Use multiple Passports**

The settings you make in Windows Messenger—display name, phone numbers, and so on—are the same for everyone who reaches you through a particular Passport. You can't, for example, display one name for some contacts and a different name for others, or selectively hide your phone numbers or online status. To work around this limitation, create a different Passport for each of your "identities"—one for personal friends, one for business associates, and one for people you meet through an online special interest group, for example.

To switch between them, you must sign out (choose File, Sign Out, or click the notification area icon and choose Sign Out) and then sign back in; you can be signed in using only one Passport at a time. You can bend this rule by creating multiple user accounts as well—each with its own Passport. Use Fast User Switching to switch between them; they can all remain signed in simultaneously, although you can work with only one Passport at a time.

Blocking other users   You can prevent other users from contacting you or from viewing your online status. When you block a user, if you're in that user's contact list your status is always shown as Not Online. If the blocked user tries to send a message (by entering your e-mail address), it's immediately returned to the sender. You never receive any indication that the blocked user is trying to contact you. You can block a user in any of several ways:

- When you receive notification that the user has added you to his or her contact list (as shown in Figure 21-7), select the Block option.

- If the user is in your contact list, right-click the name and choose Block.

- If you are in a conversation with someone you want to block, click the Block button. (If you're conversing with more than one person, select the name of the person you want to block from the list that appears.) When you do this, it appears to the blocked user that you've gone offline. Conversation windows remain open on both computers.

Chapter 21: Communicating over the Internet

■ Open Tools, Options, and click the Privacy tab, shown in Figure 21-9. The lists show everyone in your contact list as well as any others you've blocked. Select a name and click Block or Allow to move the name between My Allow List and My Block List. By moving the All Other Users entry to My Block List, you prevent contact by anyone outside your circle of friends shown in My Allow List. (Others can still add you to their contact list, and you'll be notified of that action as usual. This notification allows you to add new people to My Allow List.)

Figure 21-9. Blocking users prevents them from seeing whether you're online and sending you messages.

Finding out who's watching you People who have you in their contact list can see when you're online. If you're in the habit of setting your status (letting people know when you're available and when you're not), they can track your whereabouts by knowing when you're on the phone, when you're at lunch, and so on. You can find out who's able to keep tabs on you by choosing Tools, Options, Privacy to display the dialog box shown in Figure 21-9. Then click View to see the names of all users who have added you to their contact list.

Timesaving Tips for Sending and Receiving Instant Text Messages

These tips and shortcuts will help to make your instant messaging sessions more productive:

- **Use the notification area icon.** Instead of opening the Windows Messenger window when you want to start a conversation, click the notification area icon. On the shortcut menu that appears, choose Send An Instant Message to display a menu of all your contacts who are currently online.

- **Right-size the conversation window.** If you're not going to send and receive video, hide the sidebar (the pane on the right side of the conversation window that has the Start Camera link at the top). To do that, in the conversation window choose View, Sidebar. Then adjust the window size so that the text is easy to read and the conversation easy to follow.

- **Use a distinctive font.** By using a font that's different in style and color from that used by your correspondents, it's easier to follow a conversation in the conversation window; it gives you a unique "voice." The same font appears on your screen and on the other person's screen; if he or she doesn't have the font you specify, Windows substitutes the closest available font. To change fonts while a conversation window is open, click Change Font (in the sidebar) or choose Edit, Change Font. You can set your preference in the main Windows Messenger window by choosing Tools, Options, Personal, Change Font.

- **Send hyperlinks.** If you're discussing some information that's on the Web, type or paste a URL link to the information as ordinary text. The recipient can click the link to jump immediately to the Web site.

- **Use a keyboard macro program.** If you often type the same text—whether it's your standard witty comeback or some boilerplate text that you send as part of a help desk troubleshooting process—obtain and use a keyboard macro program. Such programs look for user-defined abbreviations as you type, expanding them to their full length when it encounters them. Some keyboard macro programs even have an option that simulates typing, so your conversation partner won't know your secret.

- **Use emoticons.** Even though they're considered banal by some language purists, in casual conversation emoticons can express a lot with only two or three keystrokes. The three dozen available icons include a happy face, a smooch-ready pair of lips, a thumbs-up gesture, and more. The thirty-four most commonly used emoticons are available in the gallery that appears when you click Emoticons at the bottom of the conversation window. To see a larger list of available icons, along with the keystrokes necessary to produce each one, click the ellipsis box in the lower right corner of the Emoticon gallery. Note: if you type a keyboard shortcut for an emoticon, and the desired item doesn't appear, choose View, Enable Emoticons in the conversation window.

Chapter 21: Communicating over the Internet

Hiding your online status   Assuming that you're willing to let everyone who has added you to his or her contact list see what you're up to, you can set your status by right-clicking your name in the Windows Messenger window and selecting a description. If the Windows Messenger window isn't open, you can set your status by clicking the Windows Messenger icon in the notification area and choosing My Status. By setting your status to Appear Offline, your name appears in the Not Online list of others' contact lists. You can continue to see the status of your contacts and continue using Windows Messenger—but other users can't tell that you're online.

---

tip   Hide your online status selectively

Setting your status to Appear Offline makes you appear offline to everyone who has your name in his or her contact list. If you want to hide out from only a few individuals but remain visible to others, block certain users. The easiest way to do that is to include them in your contact list. You can then right-click their name and choose Block to go undercover. When you're ready to resurface, right-click again and choose Unblock.

Adding Other Participants to a Conversation

You can have a text chat (but not a voice call or video call) with up to five people including yourself. You initiate this type of chat by opening a conversation window, as described earlier in this chapter. (For details, see "Placing or Receiving a Call," page 740.) You then add participants—one at a time—by clicking Invite Someone To This Conversation in the sidebar or choosing Actions, Invite Someone To This Conversation.

Note that you can add participants at any time during the conversation. However, if you want all participants to be included in the conversation from the beginning, open a conversation window and invite all participants before you send your first message.

Any participant in a conversation can add others to the fray. The To box at the top of the conversation window (just below the menu bar) shows the display names and e-mail addresses of all participants other than yourself.

Saving an Online Session as a File

Windows Messenger does not have a built-in logging feature that automatically records your every word. You can, however, save the content of the conversation window at any time. Simply choose File, Save. Doing so saves the entire transcript in a plain text file with a .txt extension.

Although this method is convenient, a plain text file loses the fonts, colors, and indentation that can enhance readability. A better alternative is to select the text you want to preserve (or choose Edit, Select All to select the entire transcript), copy the text, and then paste it into an application (such as Microsoft Word or WordPad) that can accept formatted text. That way, it looks just the way it does in the conversation window. Copying and pasting has the added benefit of allowing you to include only the parts of the conversation you want to preserve.

> **note** Whether you save the transcript as a plain text file or copy it to the Clipboard, you lose all emoticons and other icons, such as the ones that appear before system-generated messages.

Using Your PC to Make Voice Calls

In the past, voice conversations over the Internet were often of such poor quality that the capability was of little value. With Windows Messenger, the quality has improved to the point where you're likely to consider it a viable alternative to telephone conversations in most cases. Windows Messenger achieves this level of quality by introducing three significant technological improvements:

- The voice delay has been reduced to as little as 70 milliseconds. A delay of that length (or only slightly greater) is hardly noticeable. You'll sometimes encounter greater delays on phone calls that are carried by satellite.

- Windows Messenger selects appropriate voice codecs (coders and decoders) based on network conditions. For communications on a local area network or a broadband connection that provides great bandwidth and minimal delay, Messenger uses codecs that provide telephone-like quality. If network throughput decreases or delay increases beyond a certain point, Windows automatically switches to a lower bit rate. When network conditions improve, Windows automatically steps up to a higher quality.

- Windows Messenger supports acoustic echo cancellation, allowing you to use an ordinary microphone and speakers. (Without acoustic echo cancellation, excessive echo can necessitate the use of a headset). Note that acoustic echo cancellation might not work on some systems. For more information, see Microsoft Knowledge Base article Q295952, "The Acoustic Echo Cancellation Technology May Not Work with Various Sound Cards."

> **note** To make voice calls over the Internet, the firewall and router that protect your computer from the Internet must support Universal Plug and Play (UPnP). The built-in Internet Connection Firewall and Internet Connection Sharing do use UPnP, but third-party products might not. Without UPnP support, you can make voice calls only over your local area network. For more information about router and firewall configuration, see "Punching Through a Firewall," page 735.

Chapter 21: Communicating over the Internet

Before you make your first voice call, you should run the Audio And Video Tuning Wizard. It helps you to select a camera, microphone, and speakers (if your computer has more than one of any of these components), and to set speaker and microphone volume. To run the wizard, in the Windows Messenger window, choose Tools, Audio Tuning Wizard. Rerun the wizard whenever you install a new camera, microphone, speakers, or headset.

To make a voice call, you can start with an existing conversation window—one in which you're exchanging instant text messages. Simply click Start Talking in the sidebar. (If the sidebar isn't visible, choose Actions, Start Talking.)

Or you can initiate a new conversation as a voice call. In the main Windows Messenger window, choose Actions, Start A Voice Conversation.

Either way, the speaker and microphone controls appear, and you'll see a message like the one shown in Figure 21-10. The recipient sees a similar message and has the choice of accepting or declining your invitation by clicking a link or pressing a shortcut key. When he or she does so, a message notifies both of you about the action. The conversation window remains open regardless of the recipient's response to your invitation. You can continue to send and receive instant messages in the conversation window while you carry out the voice conversation.

To end the voice conversation, either close the conversation window (to break off the connection entirely) or click the Stop Talking link in the sidebar (to end the voice conversation only).

Figure 21-10. The person at the other end must agree before you can have a voice conversation.

newfeature! Using Your Webcam to Make Video Calls

If your computer has a video camera attached, you can send video as well as voice. Depending on the speed of your connection, the motion may be jerky and you'll get some digital artifacts—but the quality can be surprisingly good. Even if the person at the other end of the conversation doesn't have a camera, you can send your picture.

> **note** Like voice calls, video calls over the Internet require a UPnP-compatible router. Without UPnP support, you can make video calls only over your local area network. For more information about router and firewall configuration, see "Punching Through a Firewall," page 735.

Before you make your first video call, you should run the Audio And Video Tuning Wizard. (In the Windows Messenger window, choose Tools, Audio Tuning Wizard.) The wizard shows an image from your camera, which you can review to be sure that the camera is positioned properly and that the colors look good. If the colors require adjustment, you'll need to use the software that came with your camera to change the settings.

The procedure for participating in a video conversation is almost identical to that for holding a voice conversation. Start by opening a conversation window, using any of the techniques described earlier in this chapter. Then click the Start Camera link in the sidebar. (If the sidebar isn't visible, choose Actions, Start Camera.) This link opens the video window as well as the speaker and microphone controls (because a video call always includes voice messaging also) and sends an invitation to the other person, who can accept or decline your offer. If he or she accepts, the cameras start rolling and soon you'll see the other person's picture on your screen, as shown in Figure 21-11.

To see what your own video looks like, click the Options button (right below the video image) and choose Show My Video As Picture-In-Picture. This displays your outgoing

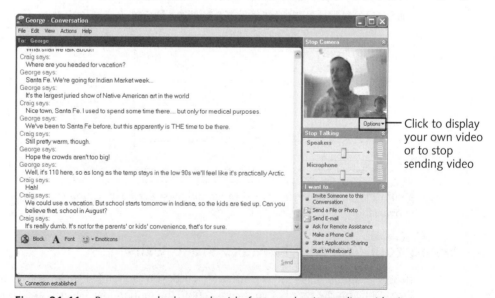

Click to display your own video or to stop sending video

Figure 21-11. Be sure you look your best before you begin sending video!

picture in a small box in the corner of the video image. To see a full-size image of your own video, you must run the Audio And Video Tuning Wizard—but you can't do that while you're in a video call.

There are several ways to stop sending video—and each way has a slightly different effect:

- If you want to stop sending video but keep the voice and instant message conversations alive, click Options and choose Stop Sending Video. You continue to receive video from the other party. To turn your camera back on, choose the same command again.

- If you want to stop the video and voice conversations but keep the conversation window open for instant messages, click Stop Camera or Stop Talking; both links shut down video and voice.

- If you want to break the connection completely, close the conversation window.

---

tip   **Find a compatible camera**

If you search the Hardware Compatibility List (*http://www.microsoft.com/hcl*) to find a suitable webcam, you'll find compatible cameras listed in the Video Capture/Camera and Video Capture/TV Tuner categories.

Sending and Receiving Files

Windows Messenger provides a convenient method of sending a file to another Passport user. Using Messenger to send files provides some advantages over sending files as e-mail attachments:

- Many e-mail client programs, including Microsoft Outlook, make it impossible to send or receive files of certain types. This is a surefire way to prevent the spread of some viruses and worms, but it becomes a hassle when you and your correspondent *know* that you're working with a safe file and would like a handy way to exchange it. Windows Messenger provides the handy way.

---

caution   Windows Messenger doesn't put up roadblocks to files the way Outlook does—but be aware of the extra risk and responsibility this incurs. With Messenger, you *can* send or receive a virus-infected file. It's up to you to know the identity of the file sender and, more important, to scan each file you receive with a virus-scanning program. (Even trustworthy and knowledgeable sources can inadvertently send you an infected file.)

- When you send a file as an e-mail attachment, the sender and the recipient each end up with two copies of the file—one that's saved in a folder and one that's saved with the e-mail message. (By default, most e-mail programs save a copy of each message you send.) The extra copy can be a problem particularly if your messages are stored on a mail server (such as Hotmail or the one at your ISP) that limits the amount of disk space you can use for stored messages. Windows Messenger copies a file directly from a folder on one computer to a folder on the other computer, without leaving extra copies lying about.

- Some mail servers limit the size of attachments. Windows Messenger imposes no such limit.

> **note** You can't send a file if your conversation includes more than one other person.

Before you can send or receive files, you must be sure that your firewall or proxy server is configured properly. Windows Messenger uses TCP connections to ports 6891 through 6900. Each port is used for transferring a single file; by opening all 10 ports you can transfer up to 10 files concurrently. If you're using Internet Connection Firewall as your firewall, follow these steps to configure it for file transfer:

1 In Control Panel, open Network Connections.

2 Right-click your Internet connection and choose Properties.

3 On the Advanced tab (the General tab if you're connected through Internet Connection Sharing on a different computer), click Settings.

4 On the Services tab of the Advanced Settings dialog box, click Add.

5 Enter a name for the service, the name of your computer, and the port numbers, as shown here, and then click OK.

Type the name of your computer

6 If you want to open additional ports for file transfer, repeat steps 4 and 5, replacing the port numbers with values from 6892 to 6900.

Chapter 21: Communicating over the Internet

To send a file, follow these steps:

1 If you haven't yet started a conversation, right-click the name of the contact you want to send to and choose Send A File Or Photo. If you already have a conversation window open, click Send A File Or Photo (in the sidebar) or choose File, Send A File Or Photo.

A standard File Open dialog box appears.

2 Navigate to the folder that contains the file you want to send, select the file, and click Open.

Messenger displays an estimate of the file transfer time and, on the recipient's computer, an invitation to accept the file.

3 The recipient must click the Accept link.

File transfer commences immediately, and displays its progress in the status bar. Either the sender or the recipient can cancel the transfer at any time by clicking the Cancel link in the status bar. When the transfer is complete, Messenger displays a notification of completion and a link to the file, as shown in Figure 21-12. The recipient can click the link to open the file with its associated program.

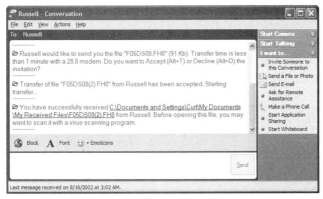

Figure 21-12. You can open a received file with a single click—but you should scan an executable program for viruses before running it.

By default, all files you receive are stored in %UserProfile%\My Documents\My Received Files. You can open that folder to work with your received files by choosing File, Open Received Files in any Windows Messenger window. If you want to change the location for received files, in the main Windows Messenger window choose Tools, Options. Click the Preference tab and then click Browse to navigate to the folder you want to use.

newfeature!
Using Windows Messenger
for Online Meetings

Windows Messenger inherits two collaboration features that were previously available only in NetMeeting: Whiteboard and application sharing.

- Whiteboard is an electronic equivalent of the whiteboard in a conference room. With it, you can enter text and draw shapes as well as create freehand drawings. It also includes a feature that's more akin to a conference-room easel than a whiteboard: the ability to create multiple pages of drawings.

- With application sharing, users in a meeting can view and control a program that's running on one participant's computer. With this capability, you can work together on a document or presentation, for example.

> **note** You won't find online help about either of these features by using the Help menu in Windows Messenger, nor will you find much in the Help And Support Center. Online help is available, however. At a command prompt, type **hh conf.chm** to display help for NetMeeting, the source of these two features.

Using Whiteboard

Whiteboard, shown in Figure 21-13, is a drawing program that functions superficially like Microsoft Paint, except that it's designed for sharing drawings, diagrams, screen

Figure 21-13. Whiteboard is a drawing program that lets you share images with another user in a Windows Messenger conversation.

Chapter 21: Communicating over the Internet

shots, and other images with another Passport user. Anything you create in the Whiteboard window is visible to both parties in the conversation, and either participant can modify the Whiteboard contents at any time.

To run Whiteboard, use any of these methods:

- If you haven't yet started a conversation, right-click the name of the contact you want to work with and choose Start Whiteboard.

- If you already have a conversation window open, click the If you already have a conversation window open, click the Start Whiteboard link in the sidebar, or choose Actions, Start Whiteboard.

- If the Sharing Session window, shown in Figure 21-14, is already open, click the Whiteboard button.

Figure 21-14. Sharing Session manages shared applications as well as Whiteboard.

A small Sharing Session window appears. A moment later, after the invitation is accepted and the two machines negotiate a connection, the Whiteboard window appears.

> **note** Closing the Sharing Session window also closes Whiteboard and stops sharing applications.

Like Paint, Whiteboard includes editing and line-width tools displayed to the left of the drawing window, and a color palette displayed below. You can enlarge the available drawing space by hiding the toolbar. (Choose Tool Bar from the View menu.) With the toolbar removed, you can use commands on the Tools menu to switch between editing tools and use the Tools menu's Line Width command to change line width. Table 21-1 provides an overview of the available tools.

Table 21-1. **Whiteboard Tools**

Tool	Description
Tools for Selecting and Editing	
	Selector. Use the Selector tool when you want to move, cut, copy, or recolor part of a drawing. Click the Selector tool, and then click anywhere on the object you want to manipulate. To select more than one object, drag a rectangle over the group of objects you want to manipulate.

(continued)

Chapter 21

Table 21-1. *(continued)*

Tool	Description

Tools for Selecting and Editing *(continued)*

	Eraser. The Eraser tool works exactly like the Selector tool except that it deletes what you select. Click an object once, and the object is gone. Although Whiteboard has no Undo command, its Edit menu does have an Undelete command. After you have deleted something, the Undelete command stays active until you use it, even if you subsequently add new objects to your drawing. However, only the last deletion can be restored.
A	**Text.** To add text, click the Text tool and then click once where you want the text to go. Whiteboard displays a small rectangle for your text and expands the rectangle as you type. Words do not wrap; to begin a new line, press Enter. To change the font, click the Font Options button that appears when you select the Text tool; to change the text's color, click a color in the palette. Note that font and color changes always affect everything in the text rectangle.
	Highlighter. The Highlighter tool works just like the Pen tool (described next), except that, if you choose an appropriate color, it creates transparent lines. Thus, for example, you can use yellow highlighting to emphasize particular words in a text object without obliterating the highlighted text. Highlighting works best with light colors.
	Pen. The Pen tool lets you add freehand elements to your drawing. Click the tool, click the line width and color you desire, click a starting point in the drawing window, and hold down the mouse button while you move the mouse.
	Line. The Line tool creates straight lines in the current width and color. Note that Whiteboard's Line tool, unlike Paint's, doesn't constrain lines to particular angles when you hold down the Shift key. If you want perfect diagonals, horizontals, or verticals, you can do your work in Paint and then paste it into Whiteboard.
	Unfilled Rectangle. The Unfilled Rectangle tool creates a rectangle in the current line width and color. Note that Whiteboard lacks Paint's ability to constrain rectangles into squares. If a perfect square is what you need, it's best to create it in Paint and paste it into Whiteboard.
	Filled Rectangle. The Filled Rectangle tool creates a solid rectangle in the current color. Note that Whiteboard has no counterpart to Paint's Fill With Color tool. If you want a rectangle filled with one color and outlined with another, use Paint and paste into Whiteboard.
	Unfilled Ellipse. The Unfilled Ellipse tool creates an ellipse in the current line width and color. If you need a perfect circle, use Paint and paste.

Chapter 21: Communicating over the Internet

Table 21-1. *(continued)*

Tool	Description
Tools for Selecting and Editing *(continued)*	
	Filled Ellipse. The Filled Ellipse tool creates a solid ellipse in the current color.
	Select Area. The Select Area tool lets you paste a selected portion of any window into your drawing, making it easy to show the state of some program or document to your conference mate. When you click the tool, Whiteboard displays a message telling you to select an area on the screen. Then it gets out of the way and lets you drag the area you want to paste. The area you select is pasted into the upper left corner of the whiteboard. Drag it to place it where you want it.
	Select Window. The Select Window tool works just like the Select Area tool except that it lets you paste an entire window into your drawing. When you click the tool, Whiteboard displays a message saying that the next window you click will be pasted into your drawing. Then it gets out of the way and lets you click the window you want to paste. Note that with some programs, you get only the client area of the window you click. If you click in a Word window, for example, the visible part of whatever Word document you're working in, along with Word's ruler (if displayed) and toolbar, is pasted into your drawing. You don't get the Word menu bar or title bar. Note also that if the window you click is displaying two or more document windows, only the active document window is pasted. To capture the entire window, click its title bar instead of clicking in the client area. After you paste your window, the window becomes a selected object. You can drag to reposition it.
	Insert New Page. Whiteboard lets you create multi-page documents. To insert a new page after the current page, click the Insert New Page button. To move between pages, click the controls next to the Insert New Page button—or press Ctrl+Page Up or Ctrl+Page Down.
Tools for Controlling the View	
	Zoom. Clicking the Zoom tool enlarges your drawing. Clicking again returns it to normal size. If you're not displaying the toolbar, you can choose Zoom from the View menu.
	Remote Pointer. Clicking the Remote Pointer tool displays a hand with an outstretched index finger. You can move the hand to draw attention to a particular part of your drawing. Click the tool a second time to make the hand disappear. Each Whiteboard participant has his or her own remote pointer that others can see but not move.

(continued)

Table 21-1. *(continued)*

Tool	Description
Tools for Controlling the View *(continued)*	
	Lock Contents. Click the Lock Contents tool to prevent others from making changes to the contents of the whiteboard. When the whiteboard is locked, click the Unlock Contents tool (it's the same button) so other users can make changes to the whiteboard.
	Synchronize. You can use the Synchronize tool to view a Whiteboard page privately. (Ordinarily, when someone switches to a different page, everyone's whiteboard changes so that everyone in the meeting is, well, on the same page.) Click Unsynchronize and move to a different page, and only your whiteboard changes. When you click Synchronize, everyone's whiteboard switches to the page you're viewing.

Whiteboard is object-oriented, rather than pixel-oriented (like Paint). When you create one object on top of another, they remain distinct objects. You can change the z (stacking) order of selected objects that lie atop one another by choosing Send To Back or Bring To Front from the Edit menu.

Collaborating on a Document over the Network

You can share any number of programs running on your computer with another person. Your program appears in a window on the other person's computer, and either person can control the shared program. You can use this ability, for example, to collaborate on a document or alternate moves in a game. Meanwhile, you can continue your conversation—via instant messages, voice, and or video—in the conversation window.

To begin sharing programs, use any of these methods:

- If you haven't yet started a conversation, right-click the name of the contact you want to work with and choose Start Application Sharing.

- If you already have a conversation window open, click the Start Application Sharing link in the sidebar, or choose Actions, Start Application Sharing.

- If the Sharing Session window, shown in Figure 21-14 on page 757, is already open, click the App Sharing button.

After the invitation is accepted and a connection is established, any of these actions displays a Sharing window similar to the one shown in Figure 21-15.

To share a program, you select it and click Share. The window for the shared application immediately opens in a window on the other person's computer, as shown in Figure 21-16. If you choose to share your desktop, the other user sees your entire

Chapter 21: Communicating over the Internet

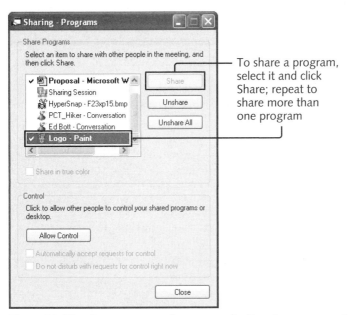

To share a program, select it and click Share; repeat to share more than one program

Figure 21-15. As soon as you share an application, it appears on the other person's screen.

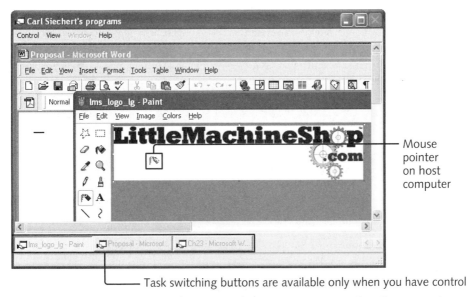

Mouse pointer on host computer

Task switching buttons are available only when you have control

Figure 21-16. As soon as you share an application, it appears on the other person's screen.

Chapter 21

desktop; you can't select individual applications to be shared. Similarly, if you share one or more applications, Desktop becomes unavailable for sharing in the list.

> **tip**   **Share your desktop**
>
> If you want to share your desktop, Windows Messenger can provide an ad hoc alternative to Remote Desktop. That feature offers a number of capabilities that are not available by sharing your desktop as an application with Windows Messenger. But it also requires some additional setup and preparation. For details, see "Setting Up a Remote Desktop Connection to Another Computer," page 1095.

The windows for the programs you share appear on the other computer exactly as they appear on your own. The other user sees your mouse pointer, insertion point, selection, and so on just as you do. If the window for a shared application is partly or completely covered by a window that is not shared, the covered portion is obscured on the other user's screen by a background pattern.

InsideOut

You might want to share Whiteboard or another application with more than one other user. Although Windows Messenger allows up to five people in an instant messaging conversation, Whiteboard and application sharing are limited to two people. If you have a two-way conversation going with Whiteboard open, for example, and you then invite another person to start Whiteboard, Sharing Session asks if you want to drop the first sharing session so that you can open another. Or, if you have a three-way conversation going and you then invite one of the other users to start Whiteboard, Windows Messenger breaks out that request into a separate two-way conversation window.

To get around the two-person limit, use NetMeeting, as follows:

1   While you're signed in to Passport (but not using Whiteboard or application sharing), open the Run dialog box and type **conf** to start NetMeeting.

2   Click the Find Someone In A Directory button. In the Find Someone window that opens, be sure that Microsoft Internet Directory is shown in the address bar. Your online contacts should appear in the window.

3   Click the name of each contact you want to invite. Note that the other users don't need to have NetMeeting running. If they're running Windows Messenger, they'll receive your invitation in Messenger, which starts NetMeeting for them.

4   Click the Share Program, Whiteboard, or Transfer Files button to open a window that lets you collaborate with all others in the call.

> **note** When you share an application, all instances of that application are shared. For example, if you have several Word documents open, sharing any one of them causes all of them to become shared. Furthermore, any additional documents you open are also shared.

To enable the other user to control shared applications running on your computer, return to the Sharing window (shown in Figure 21-15) and click Allow Control. When you've allowed control, the other user requests control by opening the Control menu and choosing Request Control. If you consent to the request by clicking Accept in the dialog box that appears, the other user takes over control of your mouse pointer, and his or her keystrokes are passed to the active application. The other user can relinquish control at any time by choosing Control, Release Control. You can retake control yourself by clicking a mouse button or pressing any key. If you press Esc while the other user has control, you not only take control, but you also immediately prevent the other user from taking control again. (This is equivalent to opening the Sharing window and clicking Prevent Control.)

> **note** When you receive a request to take control, the name might not be the same as the Windows Messenger display name of the other user. That's because this feature is actually borrowed from NetMeeting, and the name is picked up from the Options dialog box in NetMeeting.

The other options in the Sharing window deserve a little explanation:

- **Automatically accept requests for control.** When selected, the other user gains control immediately upon choosing Control, Request Control. Your permission is not required.

- **Do not disturb with requests for control right now.** If the other user requests control while this check box is selected, he or she immediately sees a message that says you're busy right now. You get no indication that the other user is trying to gain control.

Using the Internet

Advanced Internet Explorer Options

Microsoft Windows XP comes with Microsoft Internet Explorer 6 as its default tool for accessing Web pages from the Internet or a local intranet. Reflecting the range of expertise of Windows users, Internet Explorer can be used with little or no modification by novices, but it also has extensive possibilities for tailoring by expert users. In this chapter, we discuss many of these advanced configuration features.

Choosing a Default Web Browser and Java Virtual Machine

If you prefer another browser to Internet Explorer, you can (if you want) remove Internet Explorer's icons and Start menu shortcuts. To do this, choose Add Or Remove Programs in Control Panel. Click Add/Remove Windows Components. Then, when the Windows Components Wizard appears, clear the check box next to Internet Explorer, and click Next. Internet Explorer is then removed from your desktop, Start menu, and Quick Launch toolbar.

After you install another browser, you can specify it as the top choice on the Start menu's pinned items list. For details, see the sidebar "Controlling the Pinned Internet and E-Mail Items," page 274.

If you have installed Service Pack 1 for Windows XP, those options are still available, but you have another, more comprehensive tool for easing access to one browser and hiding access to others that have been installed. Use the Set Program Access

At Home with Windows XP

Internet Explorer works exactly the same way in both versions of Windows XP; Windows XP Home Edition users can apply all the information presented in this chapter.

And Defaults option within Add Or Remove Programs (you'll also find a shortcut on the Start menu) to specify which browser you want to appear on your Start menu, desktop, and elsewhere. This tool also changes the browser that's associated with HTML files (and other files normally viewed in a browser) to the one you choose.

Set Program Access And Defaults also lets you select which virtual machine (VM) you want to use for running Java applications. In the past, a Java VM has been available from Microsoft, Sun Microsystems, and others. Ongoing legal skirmishes between these companies have sometimes limited the availability of Java VMs, but if you manage to install more than one, Set Program Access And Defaults lets you specify your preference.

For more information about Set Program Access And Defaults, see "Selecting a Web Browser and Other Middleware Components," page 76.

Customizing the Internet Explorer Menu and Toolbars

Like Windows Explorer, Internet Explorer offers three optional toolbars and lets you customize each in various ways. You can add buttons to or remove them from the Standard Buttons toolbar, add links to or remove them from the Links toolbar, remove the Go button from the Address toolbar, and rearrange all of these elements to suit your tastes and optimize the space at the top of your screen. After you have positioned your toolbars (and the menu bar) to your liking, you can take advantage of the program's new toolbar-locking feature to prevent anyone (yourself included, of course) from accidentally upsetting your carefully wrought layout.

Repositioning Toolbars

Figure 22-1 shows the menu bar and three toolbars in one of their many possible arrangements. At the left edge of each of the four elements are dotted handles. To change the position of any element, drag its handle. Note that you can move the menu bar this way, as well as the toolbars. If you don't see any handles, your toolbars are locked. To unlock them, choose View, Toolbars, and then click Lock The Toolbars to toggle the lock off.

To display a toolbar that isn't currently displayed, choose View, Toolbars, and then select the name of the toolbar. Choose the same command again to hide the toolbar. Note that the menu bar is not optional; you can move it, but you can't hide it altogether.

Figure 22-1. You can rearrange toolbars by dragging their handles.

---

tip | **Press F11 for full-screen display**

Actually, you can hide the menu bar—temporarily. Pressing F11 puts Internet Explorer into a full-screen mode, in which only the Standard Buttons toolbar is visible. (It's visible in this mode, even if you've hidden it in Internet Explorer's normal display mode.) Press F11 a second time to return to a normal view.

If you really want to conserve space at the top of your screen, you can put the most essential interface elements—the menu bar, the Address bar, and the Standard Buttons toolbar—all on one line. Remove the Go button from the Address bar (pressing Enter after typing a URL in the Address bar is equivalent to clicking Go) by right-clicking it and choosing Go Button from the shortcut menu. Then reduce the Address bar to a reasonable width. If the menu bar and Standard Buttons toolbar don't fit entirely, Internet Explorer truncates them on the right and displays chevrons to indicate that it has done so. Clicking a chevron displays a small palette containing the remaining items (as shown in Figure 22-2, a picture of the screen at 800×600 resolution).

Figure 22-2. Click a chevron to show toolbar or menu bar elements that aren't otherwise visible.

Tailoring the Standard Buttons Toolbar

To edit the content of the Standard Buttons toolbar, choose View, Toolbars, Customize (or right-click the toolbar and choose Customize from the shortcut menu). To add a button to the toolbar, drag it from the Available Toolbar Buttons window of the Customize Toolbar dialog box, shown in Figure 22-3, to the location of your choice in the Current Toolbar Buttons window. To remove an item, select it in the right window and click Remove. To change the order in which toolbar buttons appear, drag them upward or downward within the Current Toolbar Buttons window. If you use a truncated toolbar like the one shown in Figure 22-2, for example, you will probably want to make sure that the buttons you use most often are in the part of the toolbar that's always visible.

Figure 22-3. The Customize Toolbar dialog box lets you populate the Standard Buttons toolbar with only those tools that you find most useful.

Note that the Standard Buttons toolbar is designed to be extensible. That is, other applications can add their own tools to it. In Figure 22-2, for example, some of the buttons on the toolbar's expanded palette were added by Microsoft Encarta. You can add and remove such application-specific buttons via the Customize Toolbar dialog box, exactly as you would add or remove an Internet Explorer button.

---

tip   **Start Internet Explorer without a home page**

To start Internet Explorer as quickly as possible, have it open without a home page. You can create a shortcut with the following command string: **iexplore –nohome**, but when you start Internet Explorer this way, some of the menu commands are unavailable until you actually load a page. If you set the program to use a blank home page by default (choose Tools, Internet Options, click the General tab, and then click Use Blank), you get a speedy start and the program's full functionality.

770

InsideOut

You can use Group Policy to configure the content of the Standard Buttons toolbar. By doing that, you can prevent non-administrative users (and administrators who don't know about Group Policy) from making changes to your custom arrangement. Type **gpedit.msc** at a command prompt to launch Group Policy. Then open User Configuration\Administrative Templates\Windows Components\Internet Explorer\Toolbars.

In the details pane, double-click Configure Toolbar Buttons. Select Enabled, select the buttons you want to include, and then click OK.

To make this policy effective, you must also enable another policy in the same folder: Disable Customizing Browser Toolbar Buttons. If you don't do that, Internet Explorer reverts to its previous toolbar settings immediately after opening. In addition, of course, enabling this policy prevents users from making changes to the toolbar arrangement.

While you're here, you might want to consider the Toolbars folder's other policy, Disable Customizing Browser Toolbars. Enabling it prevents users (including you) from selecting or repositioning toolbars as described in the preceding section. (Unfortunately, Group Policy enforces this restriction in a ham-handed way. Instead of removing the dotted handles, as when the toolbars are locked, the dotted handles remain and the mouse pointer changes to suggest that moving is possible. However, dragging the handles actually does nothing.)

For more information about Group Policy, see Appendix E, "Group Policy."

Customizing the Links Toolbar

The Links toolbar is designed to hold shortcuts to your most favorite favorites—the Web sites you use every day. Windows initially populates it with links to various Microsoft sites—which perhaps you don't need. You can replace those. To remove an item from the Links toolbar, right-click it and choose Delete from the shortcut menu. The simplest way to add a shortcut for a favorite Web site is as follows:

1 Display the Web site.

2 Drag the Internet Explorer icon at the left edge of the Address bar and drop it on the Links toolbar.

3 Right-click the new Links item, choose Rename from the shortcut menu, and then type a short name.

Chapter 22

771

The last step is optional, of course, but toolbar real estate is scarce, and you don't want to fill the space with a verbose shortcut name.

> **tip** **Put file shortcuts on the Links toolbar**
>
> You can put any kind of shortcut on the toolbar. If you're working on a project and frequently need to jump quickly from Internet Explorer to a document or folder, you can put a shortcut to that document or folder on the Links toolbar. Hold down the Alt key, drag the folder or document to the Links toolbar, and then rename it.

> **note** When you add a shortcut of any kind to your Links toolbar, Internet Explorer stores the shortcut in the folder %UserProfile%\Favorites\Links.

Configuring Internet Explorer to Work with Other Programs

Internet Explorer maintains connections with six programs related to your use of the Internet:

- An HTML editor
- An e-mail client
- A newsgroup reader
- An Internet conferencing program
- A calendar program
- A contact manager

When you click a particular kind of link on a Web page—a *mailto* link, for example—Internet Explorer opens the appropriate program. To configure these support programs, choose Tools, Internet Options, and then click the Programs tab, shown in Figure 22-4. Choose your programs from the categorized lists. If you haven't installed any programs for a certain category, you will not have any choices; for instance, the Calendar feature shown in this figure is provided by having installed Microsoft Outlook.

If you choose Hotmail as your e-mail program, clicking a *mailto* link takes you to Microsoft's Hotmail site, rather than loading an e-mail client (as happens if you select Outlook Express instead).

Figure 22-4. You can configure support programs on the Programs tab of the Internet Options dialog box.

Managing Your Favorites

Internet Explorer maintains a repository of shortcuts to your favorite Web sites in the folder %UserProfile%\Favorites. Any time you discover a site that you know you'll want to return to, you can add a shortcut for that site to the Favorites folder. To return to a favorite site, you can select it from the Favorites menu, from the Favorites Explorer bar, or from the Favorites submenu of your Start menu (if you set your Start menu to display Favorites).

To display the Favorites Explorer bar, you can do any of the following:

● Choose View, Explorer Bar, Favorites.

● Press Ctrl+I.

● Click the Favorites button on the Standard Buttons toolbar.

If the Favorites menu does not appear on your Start menu, you can put it there as follows:

1 Right-click the Start button.

2 Choose Properties from the shortcut menu.

Chapter 22

3 In the Taskbar And Start Menu Properties dialog box, click the Start Menu tab.

4 Click Customize next to the Start menu style you're using.

5 If you're using the new Windows XP Start menu, click the Advanced tab and select Favorites under Start Menu Items. If you're using the classic Start menu, click Display Favorites in the Advanced Start Menu Options list.

---

tip   Use the full Favorites menu

By default, Internet Explorer hides items on your Favorites menu that you haven't used for a while. Since many users, over time, build long Favorites lists that require scrolling, having the menu "personalized" in this manner can be a help. It minimizes clutter and lets you move quickly to the items you need regularly. (You can always click the small arrow at the bottom of the menu to reveal the temporarily hidden items.) On the other hand, some users are averse to having *anything* hidden and find the personalized menu system a major annoyance. If you're in this group, choose Tools, Internet Options, click the Advanced tab, and then clear Enable Personalized Favorites Menu.

Adding an Item to Your Favorites List

Internet Explorer makes it easy to add the currently displayed Web page to your Favorites. Any of the following methods will work:

- Press Ctrl+D.
- Display the Favorites bar; then drag the icon at the left side of the Address bar and drop it into the Favorites bar.
- Choose Favorites, Add To Favorites.
- Click the Add button at the top of the Favorites bar.
- Right-click anywhere within the current page (but not on a link), and choose Add To Favorites from the shortcut menu.

Using the Ctrl+D Keyboard Shortcut

Pressing Ctrl+D adds the current page to the top level of your Favorites folder. Because most users quickly accumulate so many favorites that they need to use subfolders to organize them (each folder representing a category of favorites), you can think of this option as a fast but temporary method for adding a favorite. After you've created a few favorites in this manner, you'll probably want to use the Organize Favorites command to put these quickly created items into subfolders.

---

tip   **Use your wheel mouse to change text size**

Internet Explorer's View, Text Size command lets you increase or decrease the size of text on a Web page—an invaluable aid if you're trying to read a page full of print in high resolution. If you have a wheel mouse, you can take advantage of a handy mouse shortcut for this command: Hold down Ctrl while you roll the wheel forward to decrease text size or backward to increase it. Note that changing the text size on screen also affects the size of text when you print.

Ctrl+D also uses the full name of the current Web page as the favorite name. Because Web pages often have verbose names (*Welcome to the Microsoft Corporate Web Site*, for example, instead of just *Microsoft*), you'll probably want to rename the resulting favorites before consigning them to appropriate subfolders.

Dragging the Current Page to the Favorites Bar

To add the current page to your Favorites bar, you can drag the icon at the left edge of the Address bar and drop it anywhere within the Favorites bar. If you want the item to go inside an existing subfolder that isn't open, pause your mouse pointer over the folder icon. After a half second or so, the folder will open, and you can position the item appropriately within the subfolder.

After you have added a favorite in this manner, you can edit its name by right-clicking it and choosing Rename from the shortcut menu.

Using the Add To Favorites Command

If you choose Favorites, Add To Favorites, or click the Add button at the top of the Favorites bar, the Add Favorite dialog box, shown here, appears. (If you don't see the lower portion of the dialog box, which shows your Favorites folder tree, click the Create In button.)

To finish creating the new favorite, follow these steps:

1 Edit the favorite name (keeping in mind that short names are easier to find on your Favorites bar or Favorites menu).

2 Select the name of the folder in which the favorite should reside. (Select a parent folder and click New Folder if the folder you want doesn't exist yet.)

3 Click OK.

---

tip   **Add folders and files to your Favorites list**

Anything stored in %UserProfile%\Favorites appears on your Favorites menu or Favorites bar. Most people use this folder exclusively for Internet shortcuts, but you can put shortcuts to files and folders there as well. Putting a shortcut to a folder or document you're currently working on makes that document easier to reach while you're working in Internet Explorer.

Editing Favorites

Favorite Web sites are recorded as Internet shortcuts in your %UserProfile%\Favorites folder. You can edit these shortcuts the same way you would edit any other kind of shortcut. Right-click the item you want to edit (on the Favorites menu, on the Favorites bar, or in the Favorites folder) and choose Properties from the shortcut menu. Figure 22-5 shows the properties dialog box for a favorite item.

You might want to edit a favorite item for the following reasons:

● To change the name of the favorite

● To change its URL

● To change its icon

● To assign it a keyboard shortcut

● To make it available offline or change its offline-update parameters

To change the name that appears in your Favorites menu, click the General tab and edit the text in the box at the top of the dialog box. To change the URL, edit the URL box on the Web Document tab. To select a different icon for this shortcut, click Change Icon on the Web Document tab.

Figure 22-5. You can edit a favorite in various ways, including adding a keyboard shortcut to activate it.

---

tip **Open Internet shortcuts in new windows**

To ensure that Internet Explorer always opens a Web shortcut in a new window, rather than replacing the material you're currently looking at, choose Tools, Internet Options and then click the Advanced tab. In the Browsing section of the Settings list, clear the Reuse Windows For Launching Shortcuts option.

Assigning a Keyboard Shortcut

Favorites, which are Internet shortcuts, can have keyboard shortcuts, just as file and folder shortcuts can. For more information about assigning keyboard shortcuts to shortcuts, see "Creating and Customizing Document Shortcuts," page 458.

Making a Favorite Available Offline

If you select Make This Page Available Offline on the Web Document tab of the favorite's properties dialog box, Internet Explorer downloads a copy of the page to your Temporary Internet Files folder (%UserProfile%\Temporary Internet Files) and updates that page at periodic intervals (every day at a particular time, for example). You can then read the page without having to reconnect to the Internet. If you use a slow dial-up connection, you might find it convenient to make favorite pages available offline, and then let Internet Explorer connect and download those pages for you at night so that you can read them at the start of your next workday.

You can also use the offline availability feature as a way of checking for changes in a favorite's content. Each time it downloads the favorite page, Internet Explorer can check the current content against the previous download and notify you via e-mail if there are differences.

---

tip   **Turn off the flash and noise**

If you're annoyed by blinking banner ads or Web pages that insist on serenading, you can hit the mute button in either of two ways. To silence the current page, simply press Esc (but wait until the content has finished loading before pressing Esc; otherwise, you might not get the whole page). To squelch the animations or sound permanently, choose Tools, Internet Options, and click the Advanced tab. In the Multimedia section, clear Play Animation In Web Pages or Play Sound In Web Pages.

When you select Make This Page Available Offline, Internet Explorer adds a Schedule tab and a Download tab to the properties dialog box. Use the Schedule tab to specify the schedule that you want Internet Explorer to use in updating the Temporary Internet Files copy of your page. (You can also indicate that you want to update only on demand.) Use the Download tab, shown in Figure 22-6, to specify additional download parameters.

Figure 22-6.   You can use the Download tab to specify a maximum size for the offline copy of your favorite—among other parameters.

If you need only the favorite page itself and none of the pages to which it is linked, leave the Download Pages value at 0. Otherwise, specify the depth to which you want Internet Explorer to go. Keep in mind that the size of your download increases dramatically as you increase this depth value; to prevent things from getting totally out of hand, you can select Limit Hard-Disk Usage For This Page To and specify a maximum file size.

To have Internet Explorer send you e-mail notification of changes in your favorite's content, select When This Page Changes, Send E-Mail To, and then supply your e-mail address and the address of your e-mail system's SMTP (outgoing mail) server. (If you're not sure what that address is, look for it in the account properties dialog box supplied by your e-mail client program, or consult your network administrator.)

Organizing Favorites

Internet Explorer provides a small dialog box, shown in Figure 22-7, that you can use to add subfolders to your Favorites tree, move items between folders, rename folders and shortcuts, and delete favorites or folders. You can open this dialog box by choosing Favorites, Organize Favorites or by clicking the Organize button at the top of the Favorites bar.

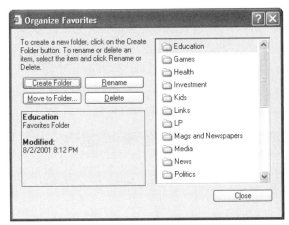

Figure 22-7. If you find this small Organize Favorites dialog box confining, you can reorganize your favorites in Windows Explorer instead.

An easier way to organize your favorites is to use Windows Explorer. In recognition of that fact, Internet Explorer provides an easy way to get to the %UserProfile%\Favorites folder: Hold down the Shift key while you open the Favorites menu and click Organize Favorites. Figure 22-8 on the next page shows the result.

> **tip** You can also get to the Favorites folder by choosing Run on the Start menu and typing **favorites**. You don't have to include %UserProfile%.

Figure 22-8. Pressing the Shift key while choosing Favorites, Organize Favorites takes you straight to the Favorites folder in Windows Explorer.

Importing, Exporting, and Sharing Your Favorites

Got a batch of favorites you want to share? Internet Explorer's File, Import And Export command lets you save any branch of your folder tree (or the entire tree) as an HTML file (named *Bookmark.htm*, by default), suitable for e-mailing to a friend, for maintaining as a backup of your Favorites folder, and for use as an alternative route to your favorite Web sites. As Figure 22-9 shows, folders in your Favorites tree become headings in the Bookmarks file, and each favorite becomes a link.

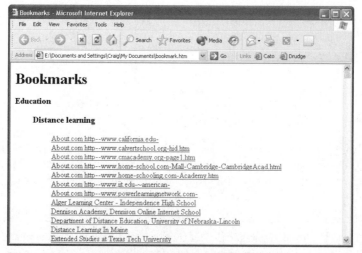

Figure 22-9. Internet Explorer can export your favorites tree (or any branch of it) to an HTML file in which each exported favorite becomes a link.

To export favorites, choose File, Import And Export. The Import/Export Wizard appears and guides you through the rest of the process.

You can use the same command and the same wizard to merge a set of links in an HTML file into your own Favorites tree. The wizard will prompt for a file name and for the branch of your current Favorites tree at which you want to import the new links.

---

tip   **Print your favorites**

To create a printed record of your favorites and the URLs to which they're linked, follow these steps:

1 Export your favorites.

2 Open the exported HTML file in Internet Explorer.

3 Choose File, Print. On the Options tab of the Print dialog box, select Print Table Of Links.

Unless you have lots of time and paper, you'll want to avoid selecting the Print All Linked Documents option, which will proceed to open all your favorites and print their contents.

Using Third-Party Favorites (Bookmark) Managers

A number of free or inexpensive third-party products are available that can help you manage your favorites and expand on features in Internet Explorer. Among the features offered by these advanced bookmark managers are the following:

- The ability to annotate favorites
- Advanced sorting capabilities
- The ability to search bookmarks for particular characteristics
- The ability to check your favorites list periodically and flag those with unreachable URLs

If you have a particularly large stash of favorites, and you have difficulty keeping tabs on them all using Internet Explorer's native feature set, you might want to check out some of these third-party products. Use Internet Explorer's searching features to look for "bookmark managers." For more information about searching the Internet, see "Searching the Internet," page 789.

Another way to manage favorites is to use services available at various Web sites. The advantage of storing your favorites list on the Web is that you can access it, use it, add to it, and so on, from any computer, anywhere. The principal disadvantage is speed. (Another disadvantage in the wake of the dot-com collapse is the possibility that the site that stores your favorites today might be gone tomorrow. Be sure you keep a local backup.) Connecting to the site that stores your bookmarks in addition to connecting to the sites to which your bookmarks take you inevitably adds overhead to the surfing experience.

newfeature!
Managing Cookies

A *cookie* is a small text file that enables a Web site to personalize its offerings in some way. The Web site downloads the cookie to your hard disk (Internet Explorer stores it in the folder %UserProfile%\Cookies), and then reads the cookie from your hard disk on your subsequent visits to the site. Cookies can be used for a variety of purposes, such as recording logon information, shopping preferences, pages at a site that you have visited, searches that you have performed, and so on. In general, cookies provide benefits to users as well as to Web content providers. They make the Web sites you visit more responsive to your needs and preferences.

Nevertheless, because cookies can provide Web sites with personal information about you (your e-mail address or telephone number, for example), and because some sites might not use this information in ways that you would regard as beneficial, cookies are a mixed blessing. A cookie can provide a Web site only with information that you supply while visiting the site (a cookie can't scurry around your hard disk, reading your address book and financial records, for example), and this information can be read only by the site that created the cookie. Nevertheless, because it's not always obvious who's sending you a cookie and what purposes that cookie will serve, many users are understandably wary about allowing cookies on their systems.

In previous versions of Internet Explorer, your cookie management options were limited to allowing all cookies, blocking all cookies, or being prompted every time a site wanted to read or write a cookie. In practice, the second and third of these options created so much inconvenience that most users gave up and accepted all cookies. (Some sites will not even allow you to log on if you block all cookies, and if you request a confirmation prompt for every cookie transaction, you spend most of your time responding to confirmation prompts.)

Perhaps the most important new feature in Internet Explorer 6 is support for the emerging (and still evolving) Platform for Privacy Preferences (P3P) standard. This enables Internet Explorer to filter cookie transactions (that is, block cookies or admit them) on the basis of the cookie's content and purposes, in accordance with your stated privacy preferences.

Sites that support P3P supply information about their use of cookies in the form of a *compact privacy statement*—special HTML tags embedded in the site's HTTP header that indicate what kind of cookies are used and for what purposes. When you access a site, Internet Explorer compares the site's compact privacy statement with your expressed privacy preferences, and then accepts, blocks, or *restricts* the cookies. (To restrict a cookie means to allow it for the current session only, deleting it from your

Chapter 22

hard disk when you leave the Web site.) Thanks to Internet Explorer's P3P support, you can now choose to block certain kinds of cookies, while allowing the rest. (You can also still choose to be prompted each time a site wants to use a cookie.)

To express your preferences regarding cookies, choose Tools, Internet Options, and then click the Privacy tab. On the Privacy tab of the Internet Options dialog box, shown in Figure 22-10, use the slider to choose one of the following settings:

● Block All Cookies

● High

● Medium High

● Medium

● Low

● Accept All Cookies

The default setting is Medium. Table 22-1, on the next page, summarizes these options.

note If you don't see a slider on your Privacy tab, you are currently using "advanced" or imported privacy settings. You can undo those settings and make the slider appear by clicking Default.

Figure 22-10. Use the slider in this dialog box to select a policy for accepting, rejecting, and restricting cookies based on their source and purpose.

> **note** Your privacy setting applies only to sites in the Internet zone. By default, all cookies are accepted in the Trusted Sites and Local Intranet zones. (You can override these defaults by importing custom privacy settings. Doing so requires knowledge of XML programming; for details, see *http://msdn.microsoft.com/workshop/security/privacy/ overview/privacyimportxml.asp*.) Cookies from sites in the Restricted Sites zone are always rejected, and you can't override that default. For more information about Internet Explorer's security zones, see "Using Security Zones," page 818.

Table 22-1. **Effects of Privacy Settings on New and Existing Cookies**

Privacy Setting	Effects
Block All Cookies	Blocks all new cookies
	Prevents Web sites from reading existing cookies
	Ignores per-site settings
High	Blocks cookies from sites that do not have a compact privacy statement
	Blocks cookies that use personally identifiable information without your explicit consent
	Allows Web sites to read existing cookies
	Can be overridden by per-site settings
Medium High	Blocks cookies from third-party sites that do not have a compact privacy statement
	Blocks third-party cookies that use personally identifiable information without your explicit consent
	Blocks first-party cookies that use personally identifiable information without your implicit consent
	Allows Web sites to read existing cookies
	Can be overridden by per-site settings
Medium (Default)	Blocks third-party cookies that do not have a compact privacy statement
	Blocks third-party cookies that use personally identifiable information without your implicit consent
	Accepts first-party cookies that use personally identifiable information without your implicit consent, but deletes those cookies when you close Internet Explorer
	Allows Web sites to read existing cookies
	Can be overridden by per-site settings

784

Table 2-1. *(continued)*

Privacy Setting	Effects
Low	Blocks third-party cookies from sites that do not have a compact privacy statement
	Accepts cookies from third-party sites that use personally identifiable information without your explicit consent, but deletes those cookies when you close Internet Explorer
	Accepts all first-person cookies
	Allows Web sites to read existing cookies
	Can be overridden by per-site settings
Accept All Cookies	Accepts all new cookies
	Allows Web sites to read existing cookies
	Ignores per-site settings

To make an informed choice, you need to understand the following terms:

- **Compact privacy statement.** Information in a Web site's HTTP header that indicates the source, purpose, and lifetime of cookies used by that site. (Some cookies, called *session cookies,* are designed to be deleted when you leave a site. Other cookies have a fixed expiration date—usually sometime in the next decade or beyond.)

- **Personally identifiable information.** Information that a site could use to contact you, such as your name, e-mail address, or home or work address; also the credentials (name and password) you use to log on to a site.

- **Explicit consent.** Giving explicit consent, also known as *opting in*, means that you have taken some kind of affirmative step to allow a site to use personally identifiable information.

- **Implicit consent.** To consent implicitly means not to have *opted out*—that is, not to have taken an affirmative step to deny a Web site permission to use personally identifiable information.

- **First-party cookie.** A cookie used by the site that you are currently viewing. First-party cookies are generally used to personalize your experience with a Web site.

- **Third-party cookie.** A cookie used by a site other than the one you're currently viewing—such as an advertiser at the site you're currently viewing.

> **note** Some Web sites will not function at all if you block their cookies. If you find that a particular site you trust does not let you on with your current privacy setting, you can make an exception for that site, and change your setting in Internet Explorer to accept all of that site's cookies, regardless of your current privacy setting. (For details, see "Overriding Your Privacy Setting for Particular Web Sites," on the facing page.)

> You can find a detailed discussion of cookies and other privacy issues in *Microsoft Windows Security Inside Out for Windows XP and Windows 2000* (Microsoft Press, 2002).

Viewing a Site's Privacy Report

When Internet Explorer blocks or restricts a cookie, it displays this icon on your status bar. (Choose View, Status Bar, if your status bar is not visible.)

To find out what cookie was blocked and why, double-click this icon. You will see the site's Privacy Report dialog box, which will indicate which cookies were blocked or restricted. To learn more about why a cookie was blocked or restricted, double-click it in the Privacy Report dialog box.

To read the privacy report for any site, whether or not Internet Explorer has blocked or restricted cookies from that site, choose View, Privacy Report. Figure 22-11 shows the Privacy Report dialog box for the MSN home page (*http://www.msn.com*). Note that a number of different sites provide content for the MSN home page, and that no

Figure 22-11. A site's privacy report provides information about all parties contributing content to that site. Double-click a site URL to read its privacy policy (if any).

site in this example has tried to serve an unacceptable cookie. If some cookies served by a site are rejected because of your privacy setting, the word *Blocked* will appear in the Cookies column next to the entry for that site. You can limit the dialog box to showing only the names of sites with blocked cookies by selecting Restricted Web Sites from the Show list.

Double-clicking the entry for the *http://www.msn.com* cookie (the third item listed in Figure 22-11) reveals the privacy policy summary for Microsoft Corporation, shown in Figure 22-12.

Figure 22-12. This Privacy Policy dialog box shows the privacy policy for the MSN site.

Overriding Your Privacy Setting for Particular Web Sites

If, after reading a site's privacy statement (or discovering that it doesn't have one that conforms to the P3P standard), you decide that you want to block or accept all cookies from that site, regardless of the privacy setting that you have chosen in the Internet Options dialog box, select either Always Allow This Site To Use Cookies or Never Allow This Site To Use Cookies in the site's Privacy Policy dialog box.

You can also specify per-site privacy settings by clicking Edit on the Privacy tab of the Internet Options dialog box. The Per Site Privacy Actions dialog box appears, as shown in Figure 22-13 on the next page. To allow or block all cookies from a site, enter the site's address and then click Allow or Block. As you add settings for individual sites, the sites will be listed in the Managed Web Sites portion of the dialog box.

Figure 22-13. The Per Site Privacy Actions dialog box lists all sites that you designate to be exceptions to your privacy policy.

Dispensing with Automatic Cookie Handling

If you want, you can tell Internet Explorer to forget about privacy settings assigned on a site-basis and institute uniform policies for all first-party and all third-party cookies regardless of their site. For example, you can tell Internet Explorer to accept all first-party cookies and to issue a prompt for all third-party cookies (allowing you to block or accept third-party cookies on a case-by-case basis). To override automatic cookie handling, click Advanced on the Privacy tab of the Internet Options dialog box. The Advanced Privacy Settings dialog box appears, as shown in Figure 22-14.

Figure 22-14. Clicking Advanced on the Privacy tab of the Internet Options dialog box lets you institute uniform policies for all first-party and third-party cookies.

This dialog box also includes a check box that tells Internet Explorer to accept all session cookies, which are cookies that a Web site will delete at the end of your current session. Session cookies are usually benign (they're used for such things as keeping track of what's in your shopping cart), so if you are planning to override automatic cookie handling, this is normally a safe option to select.

Asking Internet Explorer to prompt you for all third-party cookies is an excellent way to learn which of the sites you visit regularly rely on third-party cookies. After a few days' experience with this setting, you can return to automatic cookie handling and tell Internet Explorer always to block cookies from any particularly troublesome third parties that you notice.

> **note** Per-site settings trump advanced settings. If you decide to block either first-party or third-party cookies (or both) through the Advanced Privacy Settings dialog box, be sure to remove any per-site settings that allow cookies. Otherwise, the sites to which you gave carte blanche earlier will continue to drop cookies on your plate. To do this, click Edit on the Privacy tab of the Internet Options dialog box. Select specific sites, and click Remove, or simply click Remove All.
>
> Advanced settings don't affect cookies already stored on your computer. Be sure to back up and delete existing cookies for sites that you want to block (or to be prompted for). Otherwise, those sites will continue to read your current cookie data.

Backing Up Your Cookies

Because cookies—particularly the ones you intentionally allow your system to accept—are more likely to be beneficial than harmful, it's smart to back them up from time to time. Internet Explorer's Import/Export Wizard lets you do just that. Choose File, Import And Export, and then follow the wizard's steps to export your cookies. The wizard creates a single text file, stored by default in My Documents.

The command to export cookies was included in Internet Explorer to provide users with a way to transfer their cookies to the format used by Netscape browsers. But it works just as well as a backup tool. If you ever need to restore your cookies, choose File, Import And Export again, and point the wizard to the file you exported earlier.

Searching the Internet

Internet Explorer 6 provides the following ways to search for sites, businesses, and people on the Internet:

- Search Companion
- Classic Internet Search
- Address bar

Search Companion and Classic Internet Search provide alternative search behaviors on the Search Explorer bar. That is, you can configure Internet Explorer to use one or the other when you display the Search bar. Searching on the Address bar bypasses the Search bar. Whenever you type anything on the Address bar, Internet Explorer attempts to parse your typing into a URL (an Internet address). If it cannot do so, it hands your entry off to a search provider.

newfeature!
Using Search Companion

To summon Search Companion, display the Search bar, using any of the following methods:

● Click Search on the Standard Buttons toolbar.

● Choose View, Explorer Bar, Search.

● Press Ctrl+E.

Search Companion appears in the Search Explorer bar, the pane on the left side of Internet Explorer, as shown in Figure 22-15. If instead you see Classic Internet Search (shown in Figure 22-17 on page 793), you can switch to Search Companion as follows:

1 Click the Customize button on the Search bar.

2 Select Use Search Companion.

3 Click OK.

4 Close all Internet Explorer windows and restart Internet Explorer.

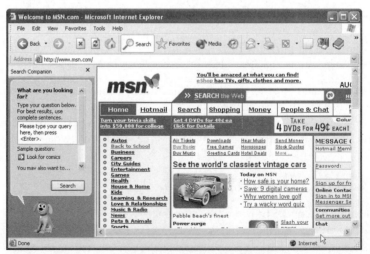

Figure 22-15. Search Companion in Internet Explorer looks, feels, and sounds like Search Companion in Windows Explorer.

790

---

tip   **Set Internet Explorer to use a favorite search provider**

Both Search Companion and Classic Internet Search are set up (initially, at least) to let you use a variety of search providers. If the current default provider doesn't satisfy a search need, you can move on to another one. If you have a favorite search service that you plan to use exclusively, this default user interface will get in your way. To set up Internet Explorer to use a single search provider in the Search bar, see "Using a Single Search Provider," page 795. Alternatively, you can simply bookmark that provider's Web site and select it from your Favorites menu, the Favorites bar, or the Links toolbar. You might even consider making that search provider's site your home page in Internet Explorer. (To do that, display the provider's site. Then choose Tools, Internet Options, click the General tab, and click Use Current.)

As it does in Windows Explorer (see "Locating Files with Search Companion," page 474), Search Companion in Internet Explorer comes with animated characters to personalize your search experience, including Rover and Merlin, among others. If you prefer, you can turn off the companions by clicking the Change Preferences link on the opening pane of Search Companion, and then clicking Without An Animated Screen Character.

Search Companion invites you to express your wishes in plain English sentences. This too is optional, of course. Whether you phrase your query like Tarzan or Henry James, Search Companion takes the significant words in your search string (ignoring conjunctions, articles, and prepositions) and passes them to the default search engine (which you can change, as you'll see in a moment).

Search Companion also presents a sample search question, drawn at random from a store of such questions. (You might see anything here from *Find comics* to *How bad is the traffic in Phoenix?* to *Read reviews of lawn tractors.*) For amusement, you can click the sample question and see what emerges in the other pane.

In most cases, after responding to your search question (by displaying the results in the right pane), Search Companion will propose some follow-up questions. Sometimes those questions will seem related to your initial query, and sometimes not. Occasionally you'll be given an opportunity to exercise your credit card (for example, *Buy a Movie*).

Forwarding Your Query to Other Search Engines

Generally, the most useful item in Search Companion's follow-up menu is Automatically Send Your Search To Other Search Engines. Clicking this link opens the menu shown in Figure 22-16 on the next page, which you can use to try your query with another search provider. (If you don't see the one you want, click Send Search To More Search Engines.)

Chapter 22

791

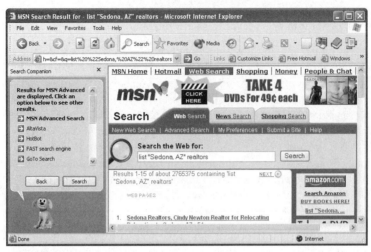

Figure 22-16. Search Companion can pass your query to other search engines, in addition to its default engine.

Changing the Default Search Engine

Search Companion's factory-default search provider is MSN. You can make a different engine the default as follows:

1 Open Search Companion and click the Change Preferences link.

2 Click Change Internet Search Behavior to see the search engines displayed here.

3 Make a selection and click OK.

Using Classic Internet Search

To use Classic Internet Search, first display the Search bar. Classic Internet Search appears in the Search bar with the title *Search* and a small toolbar that includes New, Next, and Customize buttons, as shown in Figure 22-17. If instead you see Search Companion (the Search bar's title will display *Search Companion*), you can switch to Classic Internet Search as follows:

1 Click the Change Preferences link at the bottom of the Search bar.

2 Click Change Internet Search Behavior.

3 Click With Classic Internet Search.

4 Click OK.

5 Close all Internet Explorer windows and then restart Internet Explorer.

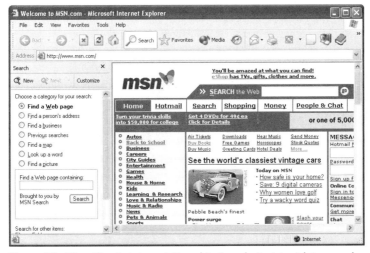

Figure 22-17. Classic Internet Search's Search Assistant lets you choose from broad categories—such as Web page, address, and business.

Classic Internet Search itself operates in either of two modes. If you use the Search Assistant (shown in Figure 22-17), you start by selecting one of seven search categories (if you don't see all seven, click the More link). After you've made this initial selection, the rest of the Search bar presents edit boxes appropriate for your selection.

If you prefer, you can dispense with Search Assistant and deploy a single search provider for all your queries in Classic Internet Search (see "Using a Single Search Provider," page 795).

Search Assistant begins by using the default search provider for the category you've chosen. (You can modify this default.) After it has completed a search using the default provider, you can click the Next button at the top of the Search bar to repeat the search with another provider. (To use a particular provider, click the arrow beside the Next button and then choose from the list.)

Changing Search Assistant's Default Providers

To change the default provider for each search category (as well as the order in which the Search Assistant cycles through available search providers when you click Next), follow these steps:

1 Click Customize.

2 In the Customize Search Settings dialog box, shown here, be sure that Use The Search Assistant For Smart Searching Is Selected.

3 In each search category (you will have to scroll the dialog box to see all the categories), select the names of the providers you want to include.

4 To change the order in which Search Assistant consults a provider, select that provider and then click the up or down arrow. For example, to make Goto.com the default provider for Web page searches (assuming that Search Assistant is currently set as shown here), select Goto.com and click the up arrow.

5 Clear the check boxes for any categories of search that you don't want Search Assistant to include. For example, if you don't think you'll ever need to search for pictures on the Internet, scroll down to Find A Picture and clear its check box.

Using a Single Search Provider

To use a favorite search provider exclusively in the Search bar, follow these steps:

1 Click the Customize button on the Search bar.

2 In the Customize Search Settings dialog box, select Use One Search Service For All Searches.

3 Select a provider and click OK.

Searching from the Address Bar

Often the simplest way to search is to type a search string directly in the Address bar. For example, if you start typing something that Internet Explorer doesn't recognize as a URL, like this.

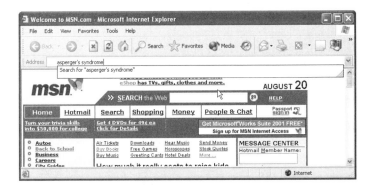

Internet Explorer passes what you have typed to the current default Autosearch provider, like this.

You can change the default Autosearch provider as follows:

1 Display the Search Explorer bar, using Classic Internet Search.

2 Click Customize.

3 In the Customize Search Settings dialog box, click Autosearch Settings.

4 In the Customize Autosearch Settings dialog box, shown here, select a search
provider.

5 To change the behavior of the search provider (for example, to switch from
showing a list of search hits to going straight to the most likely hit), choose an
option from the When Searching list. The options available vary by provider.

InsideOut

Tweak UI, one of the PowerToys that you can download from Microsoft's Web site
at *http://www.microsoft.com/windowsxp/pro/downloads/powertoys.asp*, enables
you to create your own custom Address bar searches. In Tweak UI, expand Internet
Explorer and select Search. Then click Create to define a search. For example, to provide fast access to Google, in the Prefix box, type **g**. (You can use any string you like
as an identifier; to be useful, it should be short and meaningful.) In the URL box, type
http://www.google.com/search?q=%s. Then, if you want to search Google for information about the Pacific Crest Trail, for example, in Internet Explorer's Address bar,
type **g pacific crest trail**. Internet Explorer replaces the %s parameter with the text
you type after the prefix. In this example, Internet Explorer converts your entry to
http://www.google.com/search?q=pacific+crest+trail.

You can create your own Address bar searches for all manner of Web sites that offer
some sort of search capability, including sites with weather conditions, stock quotes,
comparison shopping information, recipes, and more. The trick is to perform a search
on the site in which you're interested. Copy the resulting URL to the URL box in
Tweak UI, but replace the search terms you use with **%s**. Here are some other ideas
for custom Address bar searches you can create with Tweak UI:

● To display a Microsoft Knowledge Base article for which you know the article
ID (the "Q number"), use prefix **kb** and URL **http://support.microsoft.com/
default.aspx?scid=kb;en-us;%s**. For example, type **kb q300698** to view the

article with that ID. (Tweak UI creates this custom search when you install Tweak UI, so you needn't re-create it.)

● To automatically jump to the first result returned by Google, use prefix **gl** and URL **http://www.google.com/search?q=%s&btnI=I'm+Feeling+Lucky**. (Note that the letter following "&btn" is a capital *I*.)

● To look up a word in the Merriam-Webster dictionary, use prefix **mw** and URL **http://www.m-w.com/cgi-bin/dictionary?%s**.

● To find the meaning of an acronym or abbreviation, use prefix **abbr** and URL **http://www.acronymfinder.com/af-query.asp?String=exact&Acronym=%s &Find=Find**

By default, Internet Explorer replaces each space in your search phrase with a plus sign. If the target site uses other characters in place of spaces (many use *%20*, for example), you can specify the correct characters by making a change in the registry. Using Registry Editor, open HKCU\Software\Microsoft\Internet Explorer\SearchUrl, and then open the subkey for the prefix you saved in Tweak UI. You can then change the data for the "space" value and for any other character that needs to be replaced.

Managing the Web Cache

When you browse sites on the Internet, Internet Explorer stores copies of everything you download (including HTML pages and graphics) in a Temporary Internet Files folder. This *cache* of recently visited sites enables Internet Explorer to redisplay pages more quickly—particularly pages (such as the MSN home page) that are made up of many separate files, pages that use a lot of unchanging graphics, and so on. When you revisit a Web page, Internet Explorer checks to see if you have a current version of the page's files in your cache. If you do, the program loads what it can from the cache instead of downloading material again from the Internet.

Changing the Size of the Cache

Temporary Internet Files are stored by default in various subfolders of the hidden system folder %UserProfile%\Local Settings\Temporary Internet Files. If you're curious about the contents of the cache, you can take a look at it as follows:

1 Choose Tools, Internet Options, and click the General tab.

2 Click Settings.

3 In the Settings dialog box, shown in Figure 22-18, Click View Files.

By default, Internet Explorer reserves a maximum of about 3 percent of the space on your system disk for the Web cache. On today's gigantic disks, that's probably way more than you need. You can free up some disk space without suffering any loss of browsing functionality by reducing the cache size. To do this, display the Settings dialog box and drag the slider to the left (or enter a smaller number in the edit box).

Figure 22-18. The Settings dialog box lets you control how Internet Explorer uses its Web cache.

Moving the Cache

If you want to move the cache—to a different disk, for example—you can do that from the Settings dialog box as well. Click Move Folder. In the Browse For Folder dialog box, select the new folder and click OK.

Controlling How Internet Explorer Uses the Cache

The Settings dialog box gives you four options that control how Internet Explorer exploits its Web cache. Each option strikes a different balance between the desire for quick display and the need for current information. As you consider these options, remember that the cache is particularly critical to performance on systems that use a dial-up connection to the Internet. If you're working with a broadband connection, the benefit you receive by having Internet Explorer reload pages from the cache is considerably less significant.

The options are as follows:

- **Every Visit To The Page.** This option causes Internet Explorer to check the Web for newer versions of cached pages every time you visit those pages. If the temporary files are still current, Internet Explorer displays them. Otherwise, it downloads new pages and displays them. This option ensures that the information you see is always current, but it can slow your browsing.

- **Every Time You Start Internet Explorer.** This option causes Internet Explorer to check for newer versions once per Internet Explorer session. A check is made the first time you visit a page after you open Internet Explorer, but not again until you close and reopen the browser. If, however, you have Internet Explorer open over the course of several days and you revisit a page that you visited on a previous day, Internet Explorer does check the files again.

- **Automatically.** This option, the default, is the same as the Every Time You Start Internet Explorer option, except that Internet Explorer tabulates how often pages are actually updated. If a page is not updated frequently, Internet Explorer reduces the frequency with which it checks that page.

- **Never.** With this option, Internet Explorer never checks for newer files and always displays what is in the cache.

---

tip   **Ensure that the Web page is up-to-date**

If Internet Explorer appears to be reading from the cache when it should be downloading afresh (for example, if you find yourself looking at yesterday's headlines at a newspaper site), hold down the Shift key while you click Refresh (or press Shift+F5).

799

Emptying the Cache Automatically

Some users who are particularly concerned with privacy like to cover their tracks by having Internet Explorer purge the Web cache whenever they quit the browser. To do that, follow these steps:

1 Choose Tools, Internet Options.

2 Click the Advanced tab.

3 In the Security section of the Settings list, select Empty Temporary Internet Files Folder When Browser Is Closed.

Using Internet Explorer as an FTP Client

You can use Internet Explorer to access File Transfer Protocol (FTP) sites as well as Web sites. By default, Internet Explorer displays FTP sites in "folder view"—making them look and function almost exactly like local or network folders.

To view an FTP site that allows anonymous access, simply type the URL in the Address bar—of either Internet Explorer or Windows Explorer. To connect to an FTP server that requires you to provide your user name and password, you can include your logon information in the Address bar, like this:

```
ftp://name:password@ftp.microsoft.com
```

Alternatively, after you arrive at the site, you can choose File, Login As and provide your credentials. Regardless of who you log on as—even if you use anonymous logon—you can tell who you're logged on as by looking at the status bar (choose View, Status Bar if it isn't visible).

Internet Explorer's FTP support excludes the following functionality:

- Connecting to the Internet using a CERN proxy server or Web proxy server

- Connecting to a Virtual Address Extension (VAX) or Virtual Memory System (VMS) FTP server

- Using Internet Explorer from within a separate program or service

- Copying files from one server to another

If you prefer a non-folder approach to FTP browsing, choose Tools, Internet Options, and then click the Advanced tab. In the Browsing section, clear Enable Folder View For FTP Sites.

Securing Your Internet Connection

When you connect to the Internet, you put yourself at risk. That's undeniable, but it needn't be alarming. You can manage the risk if you understand its nature and take relatively simple precautions.

Some precautions are obvious decisions. Just as you wouldn't leave for vacation with your residence unlocked, you shouldn't leave your files and folders accessible to intruders roaming the *Wild Wild* Web. Making sure your data is not exposed in that way is not difficult and imposes no penalties on you.

Other protective measures cause moderate inconvenience and impose modest financial costs. For instance, no one who uses the Internet should be without a reliable, up-to-date virus checker. You may have to search to find one that suits your preferences and your budget (free and low-cost third-party virus scanners are available, but Windows doesn't include one), and scanning e-mail attachments for viruses can be a minor nuisance. But getting hit with a virus is dramatically more inconvenient and potentially destructive to your data, so don't even think of operating without virus protection.

The tradeoffs imposed by still other precautionary steps require judgment calls that only you can make. The use of *active content*—downloadable items such as ActiveX controls, Java applets, and scripts—makes Web sites far more interesting and usable than they would otherwise be. (Some sites won't function at all without it.) But active content supplied by a malicious or incompetent programmer can be destructive. Should you accept it, reject it, or be prompted on a case-by-case basis?

801

At Home with Windows XP

All of the tools, techniques, and protective measures we discuss in this chapter are available in Windows XP Home Edition as well as Windows XP Professional.

Microsoft Internet Explorer, by default, gives you a modest degree of protection against the possibility of downloading "rogue" content (harmful active content) without interrupting the flow of your work unduly. But you can adjust the tradeoffs in many ways. Most important, Internet Explorer encourages you to categorize Web sites according to the degree of trust you accord them. Based on a site's reputation or your own direct knowledge of it, you can apply stricter or more lenient security standards. Thus, you can deal with the Web in much the same way you deal with the world at large—giving reputable vendors and other trusted contacts the benefit of the doubt and exercising greater caution with unknown or suspicious parties.

This chapter reviews the basic Internet security options provided in Microsoft Windows XP and Internet Explorer. Because they're closely related to issues of security, we'll also discuss some measures you can take to enhance your privacy online.

Protecting Yourself Against Intruders

To use the Internet you need two-way connectivity, which means that Internet sites and other Internet users have the potential to initiate unsolicited contact with your system whenever you're connected. Specifically, unless you take measures to protect yourself, an Internet intruder could retrieve files from your computer, place unwanted files on your computer (including viruses and Trojan horses), and monitor your Internet activity.

The precautionary steps to take depend on how your system accesses the Internet. In the following sections we review some typical home and small-business scenarios. (We're assuming that if you participate in a larger, domain-based network, the responsibility for ensuring security falls to a network administrator.)

note If you used the Windows XP Network Setup Wizard to configure your network, your network should already be safely set up. For information about using this wizard, see "Using the Network Setup Wizard," page 1003.

Connecting from a Standalone Computer

Whether you use a dial-up connection or some form of broadband Internet access (DSL, cable modem, wireless, ISDN, or a T1 line), if your computer is not part of a local area network, you need to do the following:

- Activate Internet Connection Firewall (or use a third-party software firewall or a hardware firewall such as a router).

- Disable File And Printer Sharing For Microsoft Networks.

Using a firewall and disabling file and printer sharing is particularly important if you have a broadband connection. Such connections tend to be continuously active for longer periods of time than dial-up connections and are more likely to have static IP addresses (IP addresses that don't change from session to session). The longer you're connected under the same IP address, the greater the chance that some malicious party will find you and attempt to intrude. Nevertheless, even with a dial-up connection and a variable IP address, there's no good reason not to take these precautionary measures as well.

Sharing an Internet Connection

If your computer connects to the Internet, via dial-up or broadband, and other computers on your network share your Internet connection, take these measures:

- Activate Internet Connection Firewall (or use a third-party firewall program or a hardware device that includes firewall features, such as a router or residential gateway) on your own computer.

- Do not use Internet Connection Firewall on the other computers that share your connection.

> **note** If other computers on your network are sharing your Internet connection, they will lose their connection when your computer is not running. If they do not lose their connection when your computer is off, they are connected independently. See the next scenario.

Networked Computers Independently Connected to the Internet

If two or more networked computers are independently connected to the Internet—that is, if each computer retains its Internet connection even when the other computers are off—the entire network should be insulated from the Internet by means of a hardware device such as a router or residential gateway. This is a hardware device that performs network address translation (NAT) as a means of hiding the computers behind it from the Internet at large. The Internet "sees" the gateway as a network node with a public IP address, but the gateway assigns each computer behind it a private IP address, thereby making those computers invisible to the Internet.

> For more information about network address translation and private IP addresses, see "Public and Private IP Addresses," page 1017.

Chapter 23

If your network is situated behind such a gateway, you do not need to concern your-self with enabling Internet Connection Firewall or disabling file and printer sharing. If this is not the case—if your network connects to the Internet by means of a hub that does not perform network address translation, your network is open to attack via the Internet. For information about correcting this problem, see "Securing a Peer-to-Peer Network," page 1027.

newfeature!
Using Internet Connection Firewall

Internet Connection Firewall (ICF) is a software component that blocks unsolicited traffic from the Internet. It does this by monitoring all inbound and outbound com-munication involving the computers it protects. Inbound traffic (that is, communica-tion originating from the Internet, not from you or a computer on your network) is *dropped* (blocked without notification to the originating party) if ICF does not recog-nize it as a response to an outbound communication emanating from one of the com-puters on your network. You notice nothing if an inbound packet is dropped, but you can (at your option) create a plain-text log of all such events.

You can configure ICF to allow particular forms of unsolicited traffic. If you're hosting a Web site, for example, you can configure ICF to allow the HTTP Web Server service.

You should use ICF (or another firewall) on each direct Internet connection. For example, if your network is insulated from the Internet by means of a residential gate-way, but one computer on the network also connects to the Internet via a modem and dial-up account, that dial-up connection should be firewall-protected.

If you're using Internet Connection Sharing (ICS), a configuration in which one computer is directly connected to the Internet and other computers share this con-nection, enable Internet Connection Firewall only on the computer that is directly connected. If you enable ICF on the sharing computers, you will disrupt local net-work communications.

> **For more information about Internet Connection Sharing, see "Sharing an Internet Connection," page 1026.**

If your network uses another firewall or a proxy server, you do not need ICF.

> **note** Internet Connection Firewall should not be used on virtual private network (VPN) connections and is not available in Window XP 64-Bit Edition.

Enabling Internet Connection Firewall

Normally, ICF is enabled when you run the Network Setup Wizard. If you have already run this wizard and you want to manually enable ICF, follow these steps:

1 Open Network Connections in Control Panel.

2 Right-click the connection you want to firewall and choose Properties from the shortcut menu.

3 Click the Advanced tab.

4 On the Advanced tab of the properties dialog box, shown in Figure 23-1, select Protect My Computer And Network By Limiting Or Preventing Access To This Computer From The Internet.

Figure 23-1. Select the first check box to enable Internet Connection Firewall.

Enabling and Configuring a Log of Firewall Activity

ICF does not create an activity log by default. If you want to see a record of what your firewall is doing, follow these steps:

1 On the Advanced tab of the connection's properties dialog box, click Settings.

2 In the Advanced Settings dialog box, click the Security Logging tab, as shown in Figure 23-2 on the next page.

3 Select the check boxes for the kinds of events you want to log—dropped packets, successful connections, or both.

Chapter 23

Figure 23-2. Keeping a log of dropped packets can help you determine whether someone is trying to intrude.

4 Specify a file name.

5 To keep a log from getting too large, specify a maximum file size.

6 Click OK.

Logging dropped packets can help you determine whether someone is trying to scan ports in search of a security hole in your system. Logging successful connections might also be interesting, but if you use the Internet much, a log including successful connections will quickly grow to maximum proportions.

To read your log, open it in Notepad or another text editor. Figure 23-3 shows a sample of an ICF activity log.

Figure 23-3. This log creates a record for each packet that was dropped.

The log uses the W3C Extended Log format, a standard logging format that allows you to analyze data using third-party utilities. To understand what the columns mean, look at the column headers in line 4 (they don't align over the data below, but they're in the right order). The most significant columns are the first eight, listed in Table 23-1.

Table 23-1. The First Eight Columns of ICF's Activity Log

Item	Description
Date	Year-Month-Date of occurrence
Time	Hour:Minute:Second of occurrence
Action	Specifies the operation that was logged by the firewall. Possible values: OPEN, CLOSE, DROP, and INFO-EVENTS-LOST
Protocol	Protocol used for the communication. Possible values: TCP, UDP, ICMP
Source IP	The IP address of the computer that initiated the communication
Destination IP	The IP address of your computer
Source Port	The port number of the sending computer
Destination Port	The port that the sending computer was trying to access on your computer

InsideOut

Do you have Microsoft Office installed on your computer? If so, skip Notepad and use Microsoft Excel to analyze ICF log files. After converting the comma-delimited text file to Excel columns, you can sort, filter, and search the output. Try using Excel's AutoFilter capability to pick out specific IP addresses or ports from the log; this technique can help zero in on attackers quickly.

Allowing Particular Services to Pass the Firewall

By default, ICF blocks all unsolicited incoming data packets. If you run Web, FTP, or Telnet server software on your computer, or if you want to enable contact from the outside on some particular TCP port, you need to take some additional setup steps.

To enable a service, such as HTTP Web Server, click the Services tab in the Advanced Settings dialog box, as shown in Figure 23-4 on the next page. The Services tab provides check boxes for enabling a combination of predefined services. To use one of these services, all you need to do is select the appropriate check box.

Figure 23-4. The Services tab lets you configure ICF to allow particular kinds of unsolicited inbound traffic.

To add a service that isn't on this list of predefined services, click Add. In the ensuing dialog box you will be asked to provide the following:

- A descriptive name

- The IP address of the computer hosting the service

- The port number that external computers will use to access the service

- The port number that the service is using on your network

You will also be asked to indicate whether the service uses TCP or UDP.

Enabling Ping and Other Diagnostic Commands

Error correction and diagnostic commands, such as Ping and Tracert, use Internet Control Message Protocol (ICMP) rather than TCP or UDP. These functions are also disabled by default on an ICF-protected network. To enable them, click the ICMP tab of the Advanced Settings dialog box. The ICMP tab provides a set of check boxes for predefined ICMP services, along with descriptive information about each. Select the check boxes for the services you intend to use.

note For more details about Ping, Tracert, and other essential utilities, see "Network Troubleshooting Tools," page 1041.

Limitations of Internet Connection Firewall

The firewall software supplied with Windows XP provides a basic level of protection against intrusion via the Internet. You can acquire freeware and low-cost third-party software firewalls that have features not included in ICF. The most important additional feature to look for if you're shopping for a firewall is the ability to monitor outbound communication. ICF is concerned only with blocking unwanted inbound traffic. Some viruses and Trojan horses do their mischief by lodging themselves on your system, reading your address books, and then using your computer to launch denial-of-service attacks and export copies of themselves via your Internet connection, in essence making your computer the creator of mischief on others' computers. ICF does not protect you against this kind of miscreant. Some third-party products, such as ZoneAlarm (*http://www.zonelabs.com*) do provide this protection.

Disabling File And Printer Sharing For Microsoft Networks

For maximum security, you should consider disabling File And Printer Sharing on the properties dialog box of the connection you use for the Internet. Internet Connection Firewall (which is set up by default when you run the Network Setup Wizard) provides a strong first line of defense. Disabling File And Printer Sharing adds a second layer of protection that makes it much more difficult for an intruder to break into your personal files. If your computer is a standalone system without a network you have no need to enable File And Printer Sharing anyway. (If you want to set up access to your computer over the Internet, consider setting up a virtual private network connection instead, using the instructions in "Allowing Remote Access via Virtual Private Network," page 1117.)

If you connect to the Internet only via dial-up and you disable File And Printer Sharing for the dial-up connection, then you can continue to use File And Printer Sharing for your Local Area Connection, which typically uses the TCP/IP protocol. If your computer is part of a local area network in which two or more computers connect directly to the Internet, however, and if you're not protected by a gateway or other device that performs network address translation, then you face a serious security dilemma.

If your Internet connection and your LAN share the same TCP/IP connection and you have no residential gateway, you can run Internet Connection Firewall on each

Chapter 23

computer. That protects your data from outside attackers, but it also blocks all local file sharing—rendering your network nearly useless. You have three alternatives:

● Your best option is to add a router or residential gateway between the Internet connection (usually a DSL or cable modem) and your network hub (many popular routers, switches, and residential gateways include a hub, eliminating the need for a separate hardware device). The network address translation provided by the router will keep unauthorized users on the Internet from penetrating to your LAN. In this configuration, you do not need to use Internet Connection Firewall on any computer on the network and you can continue to use TCP/IP and File And Printer Sharing for local network traffic.

● An equally secure alternative is to purchase a second network interface card (NIC) for the computer you want to connect directly to the Internet. On this TCP/IP connection, you can use the Network Setup Wizard to configure Internet Connection Sharing and Internet Connection Firewall, turning this computer into the ICS host. For extra protection, you can disable File And Printer Sharing on the outside connection on this machine. Other local network computers can then use private IP addresses and the TCP/IP protocol without having to enable Internet Connection Firewall.

● If you're unwilling or unable to add extra hardware to your network, you can choose to maintain your Internet connection on the TCP/IP protocol if you enable Internet Connection Firewall (and, optionally, disable File And Printer Sharing). On all other computers on your local network, you can disable the TCP/IP protocol completely and instead use a separate protocol, such as IPX, with File And Printer Sharing enabled only on that protocol. To implement this strategy, follow the instructions in "Securing a Peer-to-Peer Network," page 1027.

To disable File And Printer Sharing For Microsoft Networks on your Internet connection, follow these steps:

1 Open Network Connections in Control Panel.

2 Right-click your connection (for example, your dial-up connection, if you're a standalone user connecting via dial-up modem), and choose Properties from the shortcut menu.

3 If you're configuring a dial-up connection, click the Networking tab of the properties dialog box. Otherwise, click the General tab.

4 Clear File And Printer Sharing For Microsoft Networks, as shown in Figure 23-5.

Figure 23-5. Clear this check box to disable File And Printer Sharing For Microsoft Networks on an Internet connection.

Using E-Mail Safely

The biggest hazard attendant to e-mail use is the potential for messages to harbor viruses or destructive active content. Viruses can be attached to messages. Rogue content can be included in an e-mail message's HTML code, if you set your e-mail program to accept HTML-formatted mail. It's not necessary to forgo attachments or HTML to be safe, however; you can take some simple measures to protect yourself.

As you undoubtedly know, your e-mail inbox can also become a receptacle for all manner of unwanted communication. Spam can be a simple nuisance if you're the only one using the Inbox. If you share your Inbox with your children, spam can be a considerably greater hazard, if only because it can present "opportunities" to your kids that you don't want them to see. (You can use identities in Microsoft Outlook Express to segregate your mail from your children's. For more information, see "Managing Identities," page 671.)

Guarding Against Hazardous E-Mail Attachments

The cardinal rules for dealing with potentially hazardous e-mail attachments are as follows:

- Don't open any attachment that's potentially executable. Save it instead, and scan it with your virus checker before running it.

- Don't open attachments from unknown parties. Save and scan them. If you can't verify that an attachment is harmless, hit the Delete key.

811

● If you receive an unexpected attachment from someone you know, be suspicious. Many viruses do their dirty work by taking over the victim's address book or by forging the return address. When in doubt, ask the supposed sender if the attachment is legitimate.

It's not always easy to tell whether an attachment contains executable code. (Data files in applications that support programming languages such as Visual Basic for Applications, for example, can include potentially harmful macros.) If you're in any doubt, save and scan.

The best way to protect yourself against dangerous attachments is to use an e-mail program that can prevent you from opening (or even saving) a potentially executable attachment. Microsoft Outlook 2002 (and the earlier Outlook 2000 with the E-Mail Security Update) and Outlook Express 6 offer slightly different implementations of this feature. Outlook Express 6, which is included with Windows XP, is set by default to prevent you from saving or opening any attachment that could possibly be a virus. If a message arrives containing such an attachment, Outlook Express notifies you that it has blocked access to the attachment. When you are so notified, you can either ignore the attachment or temporarily remove the default protection, save the attachment to disk, scan it, and then reinstate the default protection. (To remove the default virus protection, choose Tools, Options, click the Security tab, and then clear Do Not Allow Attachments To Be Saved Or Opened That Could Potentially Be A Virus. To reinstate it, select this check box.)

For more information about the security features in Outlook Express, including its ability to warn you if a virus appears to be sending mail from your system, see "Blocking Dangerous Attachments," page 694.

If your e-mail program does not offer the ability to block access to potentially infected attachments, you will need to be vigilant yourself. Get in the save-and-scan habit, and you can be reasonably sure you won't become a virus victim.

InsideOut

Many experienced Windows users believe they can hold viruses and worms at bay merely by practicing safe computing. They're wrong, as victims of Klez and other auto-executing viruses will ruefully attest. These bits of hostile code are written to exploit known security holes in Windows, and they can execute on an unpatched system, infecting the user's computer and spewing out infected e-mails, if the victim simply opens or previews the message. Any sensible e-mail security strategy must include software that blocks known viruses as well as a routine that ensures all critical updates and patches are installed as soon as they're available.

Guarding Against Rogue HTML Content

If you can receive mail formatted with HTML, you can enjoy all the graphics, sound, and formatting that HTML brings to Web content. Along with those benefits, however, comes the possibility that an e-mail sender might intentionally or unintentionally embed destructive code within the message, such as a hostile snippet of script, a link to a dangerous ActiveX control or Java applet, or a deliberately malformed URL designed to exploit a security flaw in Windows. If you use Outlook Express or Outlook, you can take advantage of Internet Explorer's security zones to protect yourself. If you use a different e-mail program, check to see whether it includes a comparable security mechanism. If you receive your e-mail exclusively through Internet Explorer (for example, if you're a Hotmail user, and you don't prefer to receive your mail in Outlook Express or another client program), you're already enjoying the protection afforded by the browser.

Outlook Express and Outlook are both set by default to use the security settings assigned to the Restricted Sites security zone. If you have not altered these settings, this means that all active controls will be disabled. If you find this stricture too confining, you can switch Outlook Express or Outlook to the Internet zone (which is, by default, much more permissive with regard to active content), or you can modify the settings associated with the Restricted Sites zone. For information about security zones, see "Using Security Zones," page 818.

Defending Yourself Against Spam

In its simplest definition, spam is unsolicited commercial e-mail. In practice, it's a nuisance that clutters up your inbox with junk mail—much of it clearly illegal and often offensive. If you're unlucky enough to get on one of the many lists that spammers use to blast out their junk e-mail, your Inbox can become so clogged with garbage that your real messages are lost in the muck.

Unfortunately, there's no foolproof way to ward off spam. The best thing you can do is to configure your e-mail program so that it filters out messages containing particular words or phrases and delete those messages from your mail server so they never appear in your Inbox. The worst thing you can do is reply to the spam sender.

Unsolicited advertising messages usually include instructions telling you how to get yourself removed from the sender's address list. Unfortunately, however, spam purveyors are not known for high ethical standards. In many cases, the spammer is sending his or her message to thousands of e-mail addresses without actually knowing which addresses are currently valid. If you respond—even to request removal—you might simply be confirming that the message has reached a live body, thereby inviting a renewed flood of spam.

If you use Outlook Express, you can apply the Block Sender command to ward off mail from a particular mailer. This tactic is usually ineffective, however, because the majority of spammers use fake e-mail addresses, and even those mass marketers who use a legitimate return address frequently change domain names to bypass filters. The best approach is to use rules to filter out messages that have particular phrases either in the subject or the body. You might occasionally lose a valid message this way—but most of your friends will know better than to send you mail containing get-rich-quick slogans or invitations to sites containing adult content.

In *Microsoft Windows Security Inside Out* (Microsoft Press, 2002), we cover basic and advanced spam-fighting techniques in detail. The following suggestions are summarized from the discussion in Chapter 11 of that book, "Blocking Spam."

1 **Guard your e-mail address as if it were gold.** Never post it in a public place, such as a Web-based discussion board. Don't use it to sign up for online contests (which are often fakes, used by spammers to harvest e-mail addresses). And don't use it with strangers until you're certain they can be trusted. Instead, set up a "throwaway" e-mail account at a free service like Hotmail and use it for any correspondence outside of your trusted circle of family and friends. If the free account is taken over by spam, shut it down and start a new one.

2 **Use server-based spam-blocking solutions, when they're available.** An increasing number of ISPs filter out spam, but most do so only if you request it. Both Hotmail and MSN offer junk-filtering features that can be set to different levels, including one that blocks all messages unless they come from contacts in your address book. Check with your e-mail provider and find out if this service is available for you.

3 **Learn to use e-mail filters effectively.** Virtually all e-mail programs allow you to set up rules to process incoming messages. The best strategy for using these filters is to define rules that identify the messages you want to receive. The first few rules in the list should allow messages from people who are in your address book and from mailing lists that you subscribe to. Use additional rules to block messages from known spammers and those containing terms associated with spam. Finally, set up a rule for everything that isn't handled by one of these rules, moving any such messages to a Possible Spam folder. Go through this folder every couple days, picking out the occasional legitimate message and deleting the rest.

Browsing the Web Safely

Your principal security concern when browsing is to ensure (insofar as it is possible) that anything you download comes with a clean bill of health. Internet Explorer can download the following kinds of active content:

- ActiveX controls
- Java applets
- Scripts

ActiveX controls are small programs that enhance the functionality of a Web site, using a technology developed by Microsoft. They're used for such things as enabling you to play games with other Internet users, displaying stock tickers, and displaying animation. ActiveX controls, like executables that you run from the Start menu or a command line, have essentially full access to your computer's resources.

Java applets are platform-independent applications written in the Java programming language. Unlike ActiveX controls, they are restricted to running in a particular area of memory—the so-called *sandbox*.

Scripts are small snippets of code, written in a scripting language such as JavaScript or VBScript, that run on the client computer (that is, *your* computer, not the Web provider's) to enhance the functionality of a Web page. (A scripting language is a simple programming language designed to perform limited tasks.) These should be distinguished from Active Server Pages (Web pages with the extension .asp), which employ a server-side scripting technology and don't, by themselves, represent a security hazard.

Of the three types of active content, ActiveX controls constitute the greatest potential threat because they have complete access to your system. They're also, for the same reason, the most useful and versatile kind of active content. Java applets and scripts are much less likely to be harmful, although a rogue script or Java applet is not out of the question.

If you'd like to take inventory of all the ActiveX controls and Java applets that you've downloaded and installed on your computer, follow these steps:

1 In Internet Explorer, choose Tools, Internet Options.

2 Click the General tab and then click Settings.

3 In the Settings dialog box, click View Objects.

As Figure 23-6 on the next page shows, these steps take you to the Downloaded Program Files folder (%SystemRoot%\Downloaded Program Files), where you can see a listing of installed ActiveX controls and Java applets, and view the properties of each item. (Scripts are embedded in Web pages, not downloaded as separate files, so they don't appear in the Downloaded Program Files folder.)

note This listing is by no means complete. Windows includes an enormous collection of ActiveX controls that it uses for various functions, and programs like Microsoft Office also install ActiveX controls that don't appear in the Downloaded Program Files folder. As the name suggests, this listing shows only ActiveX controls that you've downloaded and installed using your Web browser.

The most useful columns in this display, apart from the first column, are Status and Version. If a downloaded item stops working properly, that fact will be reported in the

Figure 23-6. The Downloaded Program Files folder lists your installed ActiveX controls and Java applets.

Status column. The Version column, meanwhile, can help you determine whether you need to update a control or utility. If you suspect that a newer version of an item is available for download, right-click its entry in the Program File column and choose Update from the shortcut menu. Internet Explorer will go to the site from which you downloaded the control or applet, check for an update, and download it if one is available.

Note that you can't tell from the icon associated with an item whether that item is an ActiveX control or a Java applet. As it happens, the last four items displayed in Figure 23-6 are Java applets, and the rest are ActiveX controls. But the only way to know which species an item belongs to is by right-clicking it and choosing Properties from the shortcut menu. (Look at the Type field on the General tab.) The properties dialog box, shown in Figure 23-7, includes information about the item's dependencies

Figure 23-7. A downloaded program's properties dialog box tells you whether it's an ActiveX control or a Java applet, in addition to other details about the item.

(other files that must be present for the item to work properly), as well as the URL from which you downloaded the item.

Determining Whether Active Content Is Safe to Download

By default, Internet Explorer displays a Security Warning dialog box, like the one shown in Figure 23-8, before downloading an ActiveX control or Java applet. Your choices are to download and install (Yes), not to download (No), or to display a boilerplate help message about these choices (More Info). Notice that because you don't have the option of downloading and *not* installing, you can't run a virus scan on the item before putting it into action.

note Although the inability to scan an ActiveX control in advance may sound like a security risk, you're safe if you've configured your antivirus software to perform real-time scanning for hostile code. If the ActiveX control contains the signature of a known virus or worm, the antivirus software will intercept it and refuse to allow the installation to proceed.)

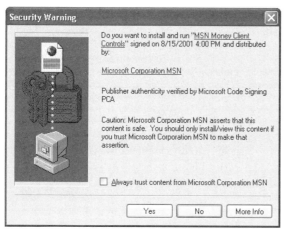

Figure 23-8. You can avoid seeing dialog boxes like this from trusted publishers by selecting the check box.

So how do you decide? You either trust or don't trust the item's publisher. Microsoft uses a digital signing technology, called *Authenticode*, to guarantee that the item comes from the publisher it says it comes from, and that it has not changed since it left the publisher's hands. If the publisher is reputable and the Security Warning message reports that the item has been digitally signed, you can be reasonably certain that it's safe to click Yes. But the deciding factor has to be your confidence in the publisher.

A digital signature doesn't promise that the signed item is healthy and benevolent. It confirms only that the bits you're about to download are the authentic work of a particular party and haven't been tampered with on their way to you. On the other hand, it's prudent to regard an unsigned item, or an item without a valid signature, as a potential threat.

Note that if you download an inactive data file (an .MP3 file, for example), a program (a shareware product, for example), or a helper application (an accessory, such as Adobe Acrobat Reader, that assists Internet Explorer to render a particular kind of content), you are given the choice between saving the item to disk and installing or running it. To be safe, you should always save and scan, rather than installing or running directly.

---

tip   **Add the known good guys to your trusted publishers list**

You probably don't want to be prompted every time you download a control from certain trustworthy parties. You can download and install their ActiveX controls or Java applets without further Security Warning dialog boxes by selecting Always Trust Content From *publisher* (see Figure 23-8). If you change your mind later, you can rescind the publisher's trusted status as follows:

1 Choose Tools, Internet Options.

2 Click the Content tab.

3 Click Publishers.

4 Select the publisher and then click Remove.

Using Security Zones

Internet Explorer's security zones let you divide the universe of Internet sites into four categories, according to sites' perceived level of trustworthiness. Internet Explorer calls the categories "zones" and gives them the following names:

- Local Intranet
- Internet
- Trusted Sites
- Restricted Sites

Internet Explorer applies to each zone a constellation of security settings (precautionary measures), appropriate to the kind of sites it includes. Initially, any sites you connect to internally (that is, your own company's sites, which you access by means of an intranet connection) are automatically assigned to the Local Intranet zone, and the Local Intranet zone is accorded a "medium-low" level of security settings. All the rest of the Internet is lumped into the Internet zone, which is given a "medium" level of security settings.

As you roam the Internet, if you come upon a site that you trust implicitly, you can move that site into the Trusted Sites zone. Internet Explorer, by default, applies a "low" level of security settings to the Trusted Sites zone. When you discover a site that warrants a high degree of wariness, you can move that site into the Restricted Sites zone. The security settings that apply there, by default, are described as "high."

Adding Sites to a Zone

To change the zone in which a site resides, or to reconfigure the security settings associated with a zone, you use the Security tab of the Internet Options dialog box (choose Tools, Internet Options, and then click the Security tab), which is shown in Figure 23-9. As the figure shows, Internet Explorer uses icons to depict each zone.

Figure 23-9. You can use this dialog box to add sites to particular zones or modify the security settings associated with a zone.

Whenever you visit a site, the icon and name of the site's zone appear at the right side of the status bar, like this.

To add a site to your Trusted Sites or Restricted Sites zone, follow these steps:

1 On the Security tab of the Internet Options dialog box (shown in Figure 23-9), select Trusted Sites or Restricted Sites.

2 Click Sites. You'll see the following dialog box (or one similar if you selected Restricted Sites).

819

3 Type the URL for the site and then click Add.

When you're adding sites to the Trusted Sites zone, you can stipulate that Internet Explorer verify that the site's server is secure before establishing a connection. To do this, select the check box at the bottom of the Trusted Sites dialog box.

By default, Internet Explorer populates the Local Intranet zone with the following:

- All intranet sites that you haven't moved into either the Trusted Sites zone or the Restricted Sites zone

- All sites that bypass your proxy server

- All network servers accessed via UNC paths

To remove one or more of those categories (so that the affected category joins the Internet zone), select Local Intranet in the Internet Options dialog box and then click Sites. You'll see the following dialog box.

Clear the appropriate check boxes.

If you want to add a site to the Local Intranet zone, click the Advanced button. Then type the site's URL and click Add.

Changing a Zone's Security Settings

Any site placed in a security zone receives the same privileges and restrictions as all other sites in that zone. You can change the overall security settings associated with the zone, however, and thereby change the security settings for all its member sites. To change the security settings associated with a zone, follow these steps:

1 Choose Tools, Internet Options, and then click the Security tab (shown in Figure 23-9).

2 Select the zone you want to adjust.

3 In the Security Level For This Zone section of the dialog box, click the Default Level button to reveal a slider control (if the slider isn't already visible).

4 Move the slider up to apply more stringent security measures, or down to be more lenient. As you move the slider from level to level, the description to the right of the slider summarizes the current level's settings.

To fine-tune the settings for a zone, or to read all the particulars about the current level of settings, click Custom Level. In the Security Settings dialog box that appears, shown in Figure 23-10, you can use the option buttons to adjust individual settings.

Figure 23-10. For most security settings, you can choose between Disable, Enable, and Prompt.

Blocking Objectionable Content

The Internet undoubtedly has something to offend every taste and moral standard. Although objectionable content is not a security issue in the sense that it threatens the

Chapter 23

well-being of your hardware and data, some users might consider it a threat to other aspects of their well-being, so we'll briefly discuss the most important features of Internet Explorer's Content Advisor. When Content Advisor is enabled, if a user tries to go to a Web page that is beyond the limits you set, Internet Explorer won't show the page. Instead it displays a warning message. Users who know the supervisor password (you supply this password when you first enable Content Advisor) can bypass the warning and view the page.

By default, Internet Explorer includes a single set of ratings, the Recreational Software Advisory Council's Internet rating system (RSACi). This system divides potentially objectionable content into four categories: language, nudity, sex, and violence. Each category has five levels, numbered 0 through 4. A higher number indicates more explicit or intense content. The RSACi system is being supplanted by the Internet Content Rating Association (ICRA) system, which has a much larger number of categories, each of which you can choose to allow or not allow. If you intend to use Content Advisor, we recommend that you install the ICRA system in addition to the default RSACi. (For details about the two systems, see the ICRA Web site at *http://www.icra.org*.)

To install the ICRA rating system and set up Content Advisor, follow these steps:

1 Download the icra.rat file (the extension is short for "ratings") from *http://www.icra.org/icra.rat* and save it to the %SystemRoot%\System32 folder.

2 Open Internet Explorer, choose Tools, Internet Options, and then click the Content tab.

3 Click Enable under Content Advisor. (If you've already enabled Content Advisor, click Settings instead.) The Content Advisor dialog box appears.

Chapter 23

4 On the General tab, click the Rating Systems button to display a list of available rating systems and categories.

> **tip** You can also install other rating systems, although RSACi and ICRA ratings are currently applied to more Web sites than any other system. To learn about other systems, click the Find Rating Systems button on the General tab

5 Click Add, select the icra.rat file you downloaded in step 1, and then click OK in the Rating Systems dialog box.

6 Click the Ratings tab, select a category, and then drag the slider to set the limits you want. As you move the slider, a description of the current setting appears below the slider. Repeat this step for each category.

7 Click Apply or OK. If you haven't already set up a supervisor password, supply and confirm your supervisor password in the Create Supervisor Password dialog box that appears.

The supervisor password is the master key that lets you change the Content Advisor settings or bypass the Content Advisor protections. Write this password down in a safe place so that if you forget it, you won't be blocked from modifying or disabling Internet Explorer's content restrictions.

> **tip** If you forget your password, don't panic. Open Registry Editor and navigate to HKLM\Software\Microsoft\Windows\CurrentVersion\Policies\Ratings. Then delete this key's Key value. Restart the computer, return to the Internet Options dialog box, and click the Disable button on the Content tab. If you're concerned that your kids might be savvy enough to make this registry fix themselves, use registry permissions to control access to that key (using the Permissions control on the Edit menu). (Exercise caution when editing the registry. For information about using Registry Editor, see Chapter 29, "Editing the Registry.")

Blocking Unrated Sites

Not all Internet content is rated. By default, Content Advisor blocks pages that don't have a rating, because Content Advisor has no way of knowing what types of content are on such pages. Just as when you attempt to view a site with unacceptable ratings, when you attempt to view an unrated site, you'll see a dialog box similar to the one shown in Figure 23-11 on the next page.

Figure 23-11. Content Advisor blocks pages with ratings beyond the limits you set and pages that aren't rated.

If you don't want this type of protection, you can change the default behavior. Open Internet Options, click the Content tab, and then click Settings. In the Content Advisor dialog box, click the General tab, shown in Figure 23-12, and select Users Can See Sites That Have No Rating.

Figure 23-12. The General tab lets you block unrated sites, bypass blocking, and change the supervisor password.

Because so many sites are unrated—including both "good" sites and "bad" ones—Content Advisor lets you create your own ratings for particular sites. To set up a list of sites that you want to allow or disallow, regardless of their claimed content rating, click the Approved Sites tab in the Content Advisor dialog box. Type each site's URL and then click Always or Never.

Turning Off Blocking

If you change your mind about blocking offensive material, simply display the Internet Options dialog box, click the Content tab, click the Disable button, and then enter your supervisor password. Blocking will remain turned off until and unless you return and click the Enable button (which alternates with the Disable button).

Protecting Your Privacy

Cookies constitute the most serious potential threat to your privacy online, because these small text files can provide unknown parties with personally identifiable information—your e-mail address, for example—as well as information about your habits and predilections. Handling cookies, like handling active Web content, requires a serious evaluation of tradeoffs—in this case, the convenience afforded by being recognizable to your regular Web haunts versus the vulnerability that comes from being (in some respects) watched.

Internet Explorer 6 (the version included with Windows XP) introduces an elaborate set of features for filtering cookies based on various parameters. For more details on how these features work, see "Managing Cookies," page 782.

Guarding Passwords and Other Sensitive Data

Windows XP provides a secure system for storing sensitive data associated with your use of the Web, such as saved user names, passwords, and Web form data you "remember" using the AutoComplete feature in Internet Explorer. The Protected Storage service, which runs as part of the Local Security Administration subsystem (Lsass.exe) manages this data store and decrypts the data only when it can verify that the request is accompanied by the correct logon credentials. Some earlier versions of Windows stored passwords in a weakly encrypted text file with the extension .pwl. In Windows XP, this data is stored in a secure portion of the registry. The saved data is encrypted using your logon credentials, and for security reasons you cannot view the hashed data directly. Instead, Windows allows programs to query the store for specific data. If you've saved your password for an Outlook Express account, for instance, it's stored here as well.

note The Protected Storage service is used only for Internet Explorer's AutoComplete details. Windows XP uses a different mechanism to store other secrets, including private keys and certificates.

Chapter 23

The AutoComplete feature in Internet Explorer allows you to save form data and user name/password combinations associated with Web pages. As you begin entering data in a field on a Web form, AutoComplete consults its list of previous entries and proposes possible matches—thereby reducing the amount of typing you have to do. Likewise, when Internet Explorer detects matching user name and password fields on a Web page, it saves the data as a matched pair. Each chunk of data gets its own 15-digit encrypted pointer, saved as a DWORD value in HKCU\Software\Microsoft\Internet Explorer\Intellliforms\SPW. The Protected Storage service uses this index to query the encrypted data store and return the saved data when a program asks for it.

When it comes to entering passwords, AutoComplete can be both a help and a hazard. If you're prone to forgetting your passwords, AutoComplete can do your remembering for you and save you time and frustration. On the other hand, AutoComplete can also make it easier for someone else to log onto one of your private accounts.

If you'd rather do without AutoComplete for user names and passwords, follow these steps:

1 Choose Tools, Internet Options.

2 Click the Content tab.

3 Click AutoComplete.

    The AutoComplete Settings dialog box appears.

4 Clear User Names And Passwords On Forms.

5 To erase Internet Explorer's memory of user names and passwords that you've already recorded, click Clear Passwords.

If you like using AutoComplete for user names and passwords but want to forgo it for particularly sensitive accounts, click Clear Passwords (to get back to an initial state, before Internet Explorer began remembering any of your passwords), and then make sure that Prompt Me To Save Passwords is selected. As you use your various accounts, you will be prompted each time you enter a password that Internet Explorer can (optionally) remember. Let it record passwords for the accounts you're not concerned about and decline its offer to remember the ones that are more critical.

You can delete individual saved entries from the AutoComplete list. To do so for a single value, go to the Web page associated with the saved data. Click in the box that contains the form field or logon name and press the Down Arrow key to select the stored item (you may need to press this key repeatedly if you have a number of items stored for that field). When you've selected the data you want to get rid of, press the Delete key. If you select a logon name that is associated with a password, Windows displays a dialog box asking if you want to delete the stored password.

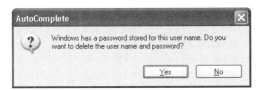

InsideOut

Windows XP doesn't include any tools for exploring and managing saved AutoComplete data. For that task, you need to use third-party utilities.

PC Magazine's free AutoWhat? 2 utility, for instance, scans the AutoComplete list and displays the names of fields for which data is stored. You can add or remove values associated with each form field, and if you remove all the stored data for a field, Windows removes the field name from the AutoComplete list. AutoWhat? 2 is available from *http://www.pcmag.com/article2/0,4149,137603,00.asp.*

A much more powerful tool, Protected Storage Explorer, allows you to view all sorts of saved data from the Protected Storage service, including passwords for e-mail accounts in Microsoft Outlook and Outlook Express, saved forms data, saved user names and passwords on Web pages, and cached logon credentials for Web sites that require authentication. Although you can view this data, you cannot change or delete individual entries. The free utility was developed by James and Jeremy Pullicino and is available from *http://www.codeproject.com/tools/PSExplorer.asp.*

The ability to see saved passwords can be a tremendous convenience if you once saved a Web site password but have since forgotten it. Using a tool like Protected Storage Explorer lets you see the saved password in plain text and write it down. Does the fact that you can view saved passwords and other data constitute a security risk? It can, if your computer is in a location that isn't physically secure. If you leave your computer unattended without logging off or locking the screen, an unscrupulous intruder can sit down and use one of these tools to inspect all your saved passwords. The moral of the story? If you want your secrets to be safe, lock your computer!

Chapter 23

827

Clearing Your History

Internet Explorer keeps track of Web sites you've recently visited and presents links to those sites in the History bar. This feature, which is convenient for retracing your steps, also makes it easy for others with access to your computer to know where you've been. If you would rather delete this information, follow these steps:

1 Choose Tools, Internet Options.

2 Click the General tab.

3 Click Clear History.

By default, Internet Explorer maintains 20 days' worth of history. You can modify that number upward or downward using the Days To Keep Pages In History box on the General tab in the Internet Options dialog box. To minimize the amount of history that Internet Explorer records, set this value to 0.

InsideOut

Internet Explorer always records the sites you visited today and lets you return to those sites via the History bar, even if you set the Days To Keep Pages In History value to 0. If you set this value to 1, Internet Explorer keeps today's sites and yesterday's sites—and so on.

Finding Additional Security Resources

Microsoft maintains a security Web site (*http://www.microsoft.com/security*) that publicizes current virus threats, any newly discovered security vulnerabilities (and their remedies), and other important matters relating to your security online. It's a good idea to visit this security site from time to time. If you want more technical details, add Microsoft TechNet Security (*http://www.microsoft.com/technet/security*) to your Favorites list and visit it regularly as well. To receive timely notice of security bulletins from Microsoft via e-mail, subscribe to the Microsoft Security Notification Service. You can do so by visiting the Microsoft Profile Center at *http://register.microsoft.com/regsys/pic.asp*, or by sending a blank e-mail message to *securbas@microsoft.com*.

You can also find valuable technical information on current security threats at *http://www.cert.org*, a site maintained by the CERT Coordination Center, a federally funded research institute operated by Carnegie Mellon University.

To test your entire system for security vulnerabilities, download the Microsoft Baseline Security Analyzer from *http://www.microsoft.com/technet/security/tools/Tools/mbsahome.asp*. Using this small application (digitally signed, of course), you can test a dozen or more different aspects of your system, including not only your settings in Internet Explorer and Outlook Express, but also your password-strength policy, your Microsoft Office macro security settings, the security settings for your operating system services, and whether you've installed all necessary service packs and hotfixes. As Figure 23-13 shows, you can use MBSA to simultaneously scan a group of computers on a network, using domain names or IP addresses to define which computers to check.

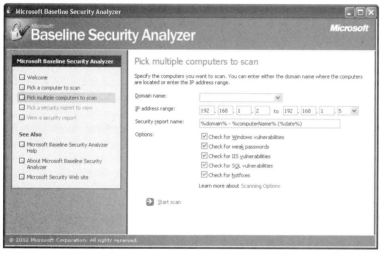

Figure 23-13. Use the Microsoft Baseline Security Analyzer to check security settings for one computer or a range of computers on your network .

Hosting a Web or FTP Site

Microsoft Windows XP Professional includes Internet Information Services (IIS) version 5.1, software that allows you to host Web and FTP sites. IIS provides a Web server, a File Transfer Protocol (FTP) server, and a Simple Mail Transfer Protocol (SMTP) virtual server. You might already be familiar with IIS; IIS 5.0 is included with Windows 2000 Professional and a scaled-down version of IIS, Personal Web Server (PWS), is included with Windows 98. IIS is not included with Windows XP Home Edition.

What You Can and Can't Do with IIS in Windows XP Professional

The version of IIS included with Windows XP Professional is not as versatile or powerful as the one shipped with server editions of Windows. Its principal limitations are that it lets you create only one Web site and one FTP site, and it allows a maximum of 10 simultaneous TCP connections. (Practically speaking, because some Web pages might require multiple connections, this might mean that no more than seven users can be accessing your Web or FTP site at any one time.) To use IIS with more than 10 simultaneous connections or to create multiple Web or FTP sites, you need one of the server editions of Microsoft Windows.

The connection limit precludes your using Windows XP Professional as a platform for hosting an e-commerce site or any other kind of site that's intended to reach the public at large. But IIS on Windows XP Professional can still be very useful in your organization.

At Home with Windows XP

Windows XP Home Edition does not include Internet Information Services. If you upgrade to Windows XP Home Edition from a version of Windows on which Personal Web Server (IIS 5.0) was previously installed, the software will no longer work. As a result, the information in this chapter applies only to users of Windows XP Professional.

First, if you're a Web developer, IIS provides a server that you can use for developing and testing your work before you move it to a larger server. Second, small and medium-sized organizations or workgroups can use IIS on Windows XP Professional to host an intranet, a private network based on Internet technology. If your workgroup needs an FTP site to use as a repository for shared files, IIS on Windows XP Professional should meet your needs more than adequately. Finally, if what you intend to create is a public Web site that will be used primarily by extended family members or a small club or school, the 10-connection limit might not present a serious obstacle.

Installing Internet Information Services

IIS is not installed by default unless you installed Windows XP Professional as an upgrade and Personal Web Server was installed on your previous system. To install IIS if it isn't already installed, follow these steps:

1 In Control Panel, open Add Or Remove Programs.

2 Click Add/Remove Windows Components.

3 In the Windows Components Wizard, select Internet Information Services (IIS), as shown in Figure 24-1.

4 With Internet Information Services (IIS) selected, click Details. A list of optional subcomponents appears.

5 Select the check boxes for the subcomponents you want to install, and clear those for subcomponents you don't want to install. Then click OK.

The following optional subcomponents are available:

- **Common Files.** This selection installs a core group of files required by other components of IIS. If you attempt to clear this check box you'll be warned that doing so will disable most of the other IIS components.

- **Documentation.** The Documentation option, selected by default, puts 9.15 MB of help files in the folder %SystemRoot%\Help\Iishelp. You'll need this

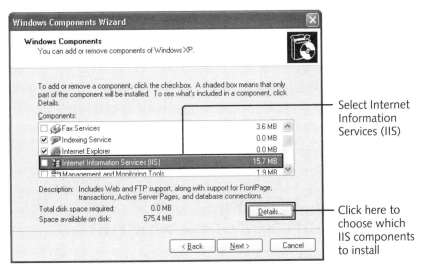

Select Internet
Information
Services (IIS)

Click here to
choose which
IIS components
to install

Figure 24-1. IIS is not installed by default. Use the Windows Components Wizard to install it.

documentation to master IIS, but if you administer several IIS-hosted Web sites from a single workstation, you might not want to install the documentation on each system.

● **File Transfer Protocol (FTP) Service.** If you're planning to set up an FTP site, be sure to select this check box.

● **FrontPage 2000 Server Extensions.** Installed by default, the Microsoft FrontPage Server Extensions are a set of server-side programs that enable you to include forms, discussion threads, hit counters, and full-text search capability on your Web site. The extensions also make it easier for you to keep your site up to date, by letting you publish revisions directly from FrontPage. Microsoft recommends that you update to the FrontPage 2002 Server Extensions, which are available online at *http://msdn.microsoft.com/library/en-us/dnservext/html/fpse02win.asp*.

note Available with Microsoft Office XP Professional Special Edition or Microsoft Office XP Developer suite, FrontPage is Microsoft's Web authoring tool. For more information about FrontPage and the FrontPage 2000 Server Extensions, see *http://www.microsoft.com/frontpage*.

● **Internet Information Services Snap-In.** The IIS snap-in gives you the ability to administer IIS via Microsoft Management Console. If you choose not to install it, you will need to use scripts to manage your server.

833

Chapter 24

- **SMTP Service.** Simple Mail Transfer Protocol (SMTP) provides you with the means to set up an intranet mail system. SMTP is not discussed in this book. For more information about SMTP, install the service and open %SystemRoot%\Mail.chm.

- **World Wide Web Service.** The World Wide Web Service allows your IIS-hosted site to serve pages over the Internet. This service isn't optional; not installing it effectively disables IIS. However, it has optional sub-components. Click Details to see the subcomponents and select the ones you want to install.

Using the Internet Information Services Snap-In

IIS 5.1 provides a Microsoft Management Console snap-in that you can use for administering all details concerning your Web and FTP sites. Figure 24-2 shows the snap-in as it appears immediately following the installation of IIS. The Internet Information Services snap-in can be opened at any time from the Administrative Tools folder (in the Performance And Maintenance category) of Control Panel.

Figure 24-2. The IIS snap-in for Microsoft Management Console lets you administer every detail of your site.

Like other MMC snap-ins, the IIS snap-in presents two panes. On the left is the console tree, on the right the details pane. (For more information about using and customizing

Microsoft Management Console, see Appendix D, "Using and Customizing Microsoft Management Console.") Sites and directories (folders) appear in the console tree. Subdirectories and files contained within the currently selected console-tree item appear in the details pane.

The console tree represents the directory structure of your Web and FTP sites, in much the same manner as the folder tree in Windows Explorer depicts the structure of your ordinary disk storage. At the highest level of the outline is the name of the computer whose IIS installation you're administering. By default, the console displays the local computer. To connect to a remote computer, select a computer name in the console tree and then choose Action, Connect. (You must have the necessary permissions, of course.)

Under the computer name entry in the console tree are Web Sites, FTP Sites, and Default SMTP Virtual Server. The Web Sites and FTP Sites entries are superfluous in Windows XP, because you are allowed to create only one of each site type.

IIS initially assigns default names to your Web and FTP sites, and these names appear at the next branch level. You can rename the sites by right-clicking their entries and choosing Rename from the shortcut menu. By default, your Web site and FTP site are located at C:\Inetpub\Wwwroot and C:\Inetpub\Ftproot, respectively, assuming that Windows XP is installed on drive C.

At the next level below your site names appear the names of folders. In IIS documentation, folders are called *directories,* following the MS-DOS and UNIX traditions. Directories are of two types: ordinary and virtual. An *ordinary directory* is just like a folder in Windows Explorer. For example, the Images directory in Default Web Site, an ordinary directory, corresponds to the folder C:\Inetpub\Wwwroot\Images on your hard disk.

A *virtual directory* is a pointer to a folder located elsewhere—on your local hard disk or another computer. The details pane of the IIS snap-in displays path information for virtual directories. In Figure 24-2, for example, you can see that IISHelp is a virtual directory whose real location is G:\Windows\Help\Iishelp.

For information about how and why to create virtual directories, see "Creating Virtual Directories," page 844.

To take an action affecting any component of this structure, the simplest approach is usually to right-click the component and choose a command from the shortcut menu. For example, you can view the properties dialog box and modify properties for your Web site by right-clicking Default Web Site and choosing Properties from the shortcut menu. Figure 24-3 on the next page shows the Documents tab of the Default Web Site Properties dialog box.

Chapter 24

Part 6: Using the Internet

Part 6: Using the Internet

Figure 24-3. The Documents tab of the Web Site Properties dialog box displays the names of possible home pages and the order in which IIS will search for them.

Accessing Your Web and FTP Sites

As you develop your sites, you can browse your work locally by pointing your browser to *protocol*://localhost, where *protocol* is *http* for your Web site or *ftp* for your FTP site. (If you set your Web site up to require an encrypted connection, use *https* instead of *http*.)

The home directories of your sites are mapped to your domain name or computer name. So to reach your sites from another computer on your local area network, you can type *protocol*://*computername*, replacing *computername* with the network name of the computer on which you're running IIS. To reach your site from outside your local area network, users type either *protocol*://*domainname* or *protocol*://*IP_address*.

Until you have created a default Web page, a trip to http://localhost generates the display shown in Figure 24-4, as well as the IIS documentation in a second browser window, shown in Figure 24-5. Users who browse your site from somewhere other than your own computer see an "under construction" page. As Figure 24-3 shows, your Web site is set initially to use the following as default home pages: Default.htm, Default.asp, Index.htm, and Iisstart.asp. When you address the root of the Web site without specifying a document, IIS displays the first of those four documents that it finds. When you first install IIS, the only one of those four pages that exists is Iisstart.asp, the script that displays the welcome page and documentation locally and the under-construction page for remote browsers. When you begin creating your own site, your home page will take priority over Iisstart.asp, so these greetings will no longer appear.

6: Using the Internet

Figure 24-4. The first time you access your site locally, you might see this welcome screen and (in a second window) the IIS documentation. Those browsing remotely will see an "under construction" screen.

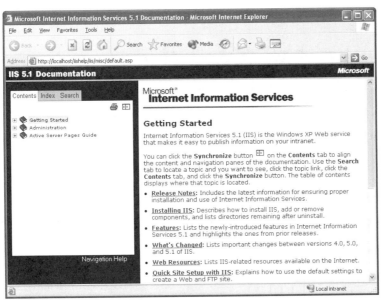

Figure 24-5. You might see this IIS documentation window in addition to the welcome screen the first time you access your site locally.

Reading the IIS Documentation

The documentation for IIS appears if you direct your browser to *http://localhost* without having created a home page for your Web site. You can get to the documentation at any subsequent time by pointing your browser to *http://localhost/iishelp*. If you're working in the IIS snap-in and want to look something up quickly in the IIS help files, you might find it simpler to open the help files within the snap-in. In either the console tree or the details pane, right-click IISHelp under Default Web Site (or the name of your site if you've created one), and then choose Browse from the shortcut menu. The help files will appear in the console's details pane. To return the console to its more conventional purposes, click on another part of the console tree, or right-click IISHelp again and choose View, Detail from the shortcut menu.

To search the IIS documentation, you must be running the Indexing Service. If the Indexing Service is not running on your system, follow these steps:

1 Choose Start, Run, and then type **services.msc**. (There are other ways to get to the Services console, but this is often the simplest.)

2 In the details pane of the Services console, double-click Indexing Service.

3 On the General tab of the Indexing Service Properties dialog box, click Start. To ensure that the Indexing Service will run each time you run Windows XP, select Automatic in the Startup Type list.

Configuring Site Properties

To inspect and configure properties that affect your entire Web or FTP site, right-click either Default Web Site or Default FTP site in the console tree. Then choose Properties from the shortcut menu. Figure 24-6 shows the Home Directory tab of the Default Web Site Properties dialog box.

Specifying a Home Directory

Your Web site and FTP site each must have a home directory. The home directory is the starting point for everything offered by your site. It contains a home page document—typically named Index.htm or Default.htm—that contains links to other pages served by your site. By default, the locations for your Web and FTP sites' home directories are %SystemDrive%\Inetpub\Wwwroot and %SystemDrive%\Inetpub\Ftproot, respectively. To locate your site somewhere else on your local hard disk, supply the appropriate path in the Local Path box on the Home Directory tab of the Web site's or FTP site's properties dialog box. To locate it on another computer on your network, select A Share Located On Another Computer. The box labeled Local Path then changes to Network Directory and the Browse button changes to a Connect As button. You can supply the appropriate server and directory information in the Network Directory box and click the Connect As button to supply your logon credentials for the network share.

Figure 24-6. On the Home Directory tab of a site's properties dialog box, you can specify the location of the home directory, enable logging and indexing, and configure IIS permissions for the site.

> **tip** For maximum control over access to your Web and FTP content, it's best to locate that content on NTFS drives.

You can also redirect your entire Web site to a different URL. If you move your site, this is a way of leaving a forwarding address for users who don't have the new URL. When you choose A Redirection To A URL, you specify the new URL and select any of the following options:

- **The Exact URL Entered Above.** This option redirects all requests for your site to the location you specify, such as *http://newsite/default.htm.*

- **A Directory Below This One.** This option redirects requests for your current home directory to the specified child directory of the current home.

- **A Permanent Redirection For This Resource.** This option causes IIS to send a 301 Permanent Redirect message to requesting browsers. Some browsers can use this information to update their bookmarks or favorites lists with the new URL.

Redirection to another URL is not an available option for your FTP site.

Specifying a Default Web Site Document

To specify the document that your Web site serves in response to a URL that references the root of the site but doesn't specify a document name, go to the Documents tab of the Web site's properties dialog box, shown in Figure 24-3 on page 836. Be sure that Enable Default Document is selected. The list of default documents can contain more than one document. IIS will search for documents following the order in which they're listed and will serve the first one it finds. To add a document to the list, click Add. To remove one, select it and click Remove. Use the arrow buttons to change the order of the listed documents.

Note that if you clear Enable Default Document, a browser that references the home directory without a document name will receive an Error 403 "You are not authorized to view this page" message.

To append an HTML-formatted footer to every document served by your site, select Enable Document Footer and specify an HTML file. Be aware that appending an HTML footer can impact the performance of your site.

Setting Connection Limits and Timeout Parameters

IIS running on Windows XP Professional allows a total of 10 simultaneous connections, counting both the connections to your Web site and those to your FTP site. You can't increase this number. On the FTP site, you can decrease the maximum, however. You might consider doing this if you run both a Web site and an FTP site and you want to reserve some of your connections for users of your Web site. You could also set this value to 0 as a way of temporarily excluding users from the FTP site.

To change the connection limit for your FTP site, right-click Default FTP Site in the console tree, choose Properties from the shortcut menu, and then click the FTP site tab. Enter a number from 0 through 10 in the Limited To box.

Both your Web site and your FTP site are set by default to maintain an inactive connection for 900 seconds (15 minutes). After this period of time has elapsed, the TCP connection is closed, freeing that connection for another user. If your sites frequently use the maximum number of connections, you might consider lowering this timeout value. That way, you'll reduce the chance that someone will be locked out of your site while another user is holding a connection open without interacting with the site. Lowering the timeout threshold unnecessarily can negatively impact users' experience with your sites, however, by forcing their browsers to reestablish connections after short periods of inactivity.

Understanding Property Inheritance

You can set properties at three levels: site, directory (or virtual directory), and file. These levels form a hierarchy, with site at the highest position and file at the lowest. Properties set at higher levels are ordinarily passed on to (inherited by) lower levels. A property change at the site level, for example, is passed on to every directory and virtual directory in the site.

If, however, you have explicitly made a property change at the directory or file level, a property change at a higher level is not necessarily passed on to the lower level. Instead, IIS presents an Inheritance Overrides dialog box like the one shown here that allows you to choose which levels should retain their current settings and which should inherit the higher-level change.

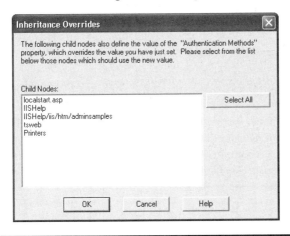

To change the connection timeout value for either your Web site or your FTP site, right-click it in the console tree, choose Properties from the shortcut menu, and go to the Web Site or FTP Site tab. Then enter a new value in the Connection Timeout box.

Enabling and Configuring Activity Logs

IIS can maintain plain-text log files of all activities on both your Web site and your FTP site. You can read these files in Notepad or another text editor to get an idea of what's going on at your sites. Analyzing activity logs can help you determine who's visiting your sites and what features are most and least used. Figure 24-7 on the next page shows an example of an FTP log.

Figure 24-7. IIS can keep plain-text logs of activities at your Web and FTP sites, allowing you to track who is visiting the sites and what features are most popular.

note It's important to distinguish IIS's activity logs from both the event logs that Windows XP maintains and the auditing of file and folder access. For information about event logs, see Chapter 36, "Monitoring System Activities with Event Viewer." For information about auditing, see Chapter 38, "Auditing Security."

By default, logging is enabled for both Web and FTP sites, and IIS creates daily logs using the W3C Extended format—a space-delimited text format developed by the World Wide Web Consortium. You can read the details about the W3C specification at *http://www.w3.org/protocols/specs.html*. To change these parameters, right-click Default Web Site or Default FTP Site, choose Properties from the shortcut menu, and then click the Web Site or FTP Site tab.

If you don't have a lot of free disk space and you don't care about activity logging, clear the Enable Logging check box. To use a different logging format, choose from the Active Log Format list. The following formats are available for Web site logging:

- W3C Extended Log File Format

- Microsoft IIS Log File Format

- NCSA Common Log File Format

The NCSA format is not available for FTP sites, and the ODBC logging format, available on IIS running on server editions of Windows, is not available in Windows XP Professional.

All three formats generate space-delimited text files. The W3C format is the most versatile of the three, because it allows you to specify which kinds of information you want to track. Its one possible inconvenience is that it records times in Greenwich Mean Time. The other two formats use local (server) time.

To specify additional options relating to activity logging, select a log format on the Web Site or FTP Site tab and then click the Properties button next to it. The corresponding logging properties dialog box will appear. Figure 24-8 shows the Extended Logging Properties dialog box for the W3C Extended format.

Figure 24-8. You can change the rollover frequency or maximum size of your log files, and if you're using the W3C Extended format, you can specify which fields to include in the log.

By default, IIS creates a new log file beginning at midnight local time each day and allows the file to grow without size limit. Files are stored in %SystemRoot%\System32\ LogFiles\W3SVC1 (for Web sites) and %SystemRoot%\System32\LogFiles\MSFTPSVC1 (for FTP sites). IIS uses a file-naming pattern based on the current (local) date. You canuse the option buttons to change the logging frequency (or to create a single log file of limited or unlimited size) or the Log File Directory box to store the files in a different location.

To specify which fields you want to include in a W3C Extended Format log, click the Extended Properties tab. Then select the Extended Properties check box and the check boxes for fields that you want to include.

Configuring Content Ratings

The Platform for Internet Content Selection (PICS) specification defines metalabels included in HTML headers that are used to describe potentially objectionable content of Web pages. To apply content ratings to your Web site, follow these steps:

1 Right-click Default Web Site and choose Properties from the shortcut menu.

2 On the HTTP Headers tab of the Default Web Site Properties dialog box, click Edit Ratings.

3 On the Rating Service tab of the Content Ratings dialog box, click Ratings Questionnaire.

4 After you complete the questionnaire and register with the Recreational Software Advisory Council (RSAC, the organization that developed the rating system), you will be given the appropriate ratings for your site. Then click the Ratings tab, select Enable Ratings For This Resource, and enter ratings for each of the four categories.

After you've done all this, all pages from your site will be sent with the appropriate header information. If the user's browser is able to interpret these headers, the browser can be set to accept or reject your content, depending on its rating.

Creating Virtual Directories

As stated earlier, a virtual directory is an alias for a conventional directory located elsewhere on the computer that hosts your Web or FTP site or on another network computer. Creating content in a virtual directory has certain advantages over creating it in an ordinary directory:

● Virtual directories enhance security by hiding the actual location of your content from users.

● Virtual directories simplify access to your content. Even if all your content is created on the same computer, the likelihood is that some of it will be deeply nested in your hard disk's folder structure. In such cases, the alias for your virtual directory will probably have a shorter path than the directory's actual location.

● Virtual directories are easier to relocate. If you reorganize your hard disk, you don't have to change the URL for the relocated content. All you have to do is change the alias so that it points to the content's new location.

● Virtual directories facilitate the distribution of effort. With virtual directories, you can delegate the creation of portions of your Web content to various employees or groups, and that content need not all reside on the same computer.

To create a virtual directory, you can do either of the following:

● Right-click an existing folder in Windows Explorer and choose either Sharing And Security or Properties (it doesn't matter which—they both take
you to the same place) from the shortcut menu. On the Web Sharing tab,
shown in Figure 24-9, make sure Default Web Site is selected in the Share
On box. Then select Share This Folder.

● In the Internet Information Services console, right-click the parent directory of the new virtual directory. Choose New, Virtual Directory from the
shortcut menu. Then follow the steps presented by the Virtual Directory
Creation Wizard.

Figure 24-9.   You can turn an existing folder into a virtual Web directory
by selecting Share This Folder on the Web Sharing tab of its Properties
dialog box.

The first method works only for local folders. The second can be used with remote as
well as local folders. To specify a remote folder, you must enter a Universal Naming
Convention (UNC) path, which takes the form *server**share*, in the Virtual Directory
Creation Wizard. (You can't specify a local drive letter that you have mapped to a
remote folder.) After you enter the UNC path, the wizard will prompt you for the
credentials you use to log on to the remote computer.

As the last step in the creation of a virtual directory (by either method), you will be asked
to specify access permissions and application permissions for the new directory. For
information about making these decisions, see "Setting IIS Permissions," page 850.

Chapter 24

Controlling Access to Your Sites

IIS and Windows XP together provide three mechanisms by which you can control access to the directories and files served by your Web and FTP sites:

- Authentication
- IIS permissions
- NTFS permissions

Authentication is the process by which Windows and IIS determine who's trying to access a resource on your site and whether that person is authorized to do so. *Permissions* are rules that determine what an authenticated user is allowed to do with a resource. IIS permissions apply uniformly to all users. NTFS permissions, in contrast, allow you to make different rules for different user accounts or groups of user accounts. NTFS permissions, of course, can be applied only to directories and files stored on NTFS drives.

> Because NTFS permissions are a feature of the NTFS file system, rather than of IIS, they are discussed elsewhere in this book. For information about setting NTFS permissions, see "Controlling Access with NTFS Permissions," page 507.

> **note** An additional authentication feature—the ability to grant or deny access to your site based on the IP address or domain name of the visitor—is available only in the server editions of Windows.

Authentication options and IIS permissions can be applied to any level of your site—the site itself, a particular directory, or a particular file. You might, for example, allow anonymous access to most of your site (making it available to the general public, without qualification) but use another form of authentication in conjunction with NTFS permissions to restrict access to private areas.

Understanding Authentication Methods

For Web sites, IIS allows you to choose anonymous access and/or three forms of authentication:

- Basic authentication
- Advanced digest authentication
- Integrated Windows authentication

Of these, basic authentication is the least secure and integrated Windows authentication is the most secure.

> **note** Client certificates can be used in place of user names and passwords in any of the authentication methods. For more information, see "Authenticating Users with Client Certificates," page 856.

You can use authentication methods in combination with one another and in combination with anonymous access. If anonymous access is enabled, IIS uses it whenever possible—that is, it logs the client on anonymously unless the client is trying to access a resource that is protected by NTFS permissions (in which case, it attempts to establish an authenticated connection). If anonymous access is not enabled and you have selected more than one authentication method, IIS uses the most secure method it can. For example, it uses integrated Windows authentication in preference to basic or advanced digest authentication, if the client computer and the computer running IIS meet the requirements for integrated Windows authentication.

The options for FTP sites are fewer than those for Web sites. FTP sites can be set up either for anonymous access or to use basic authentication. Because the methods available to FTP sites provide less security than those available to Web sites, Microsoft recommends that, if possible, you use Web Distributing Authoring and Versioning (WebDAV) as a method of sharing files over the Internet, rather than FTP. For information about WebDAV, see "Sharing Files with WebDAV," page 857.

Anonymous Access

Using anonymous access means that your site or resource is available to any client; the client is not required to provide a name or password. IIS "impersonates" anonymous visitors to your site, using a special account called IUSR_*computername* that was created when you installed IIS.

The IUSR_*computername* account has the following characteristics:

- It is a member of the Guests group.
- The user cannot change the password.
- The password never expires.

When someone attempts to reach a directory or file at your site anonymously, IIS checks to see whether NTFS permissions restrict IUSR_*computername*'s access to that resource. If they do not, an anonymous connection is established. If they do, and you have configured the resource to allow other forms of authentication, IIS tries to use that other method. If authentication is achieved, a connection is established. Otherwise, the user receives an "HTTP 403 access denied" error message.

You should use anonymous access in circumstances where the need for security is low and for resources that you want to make available to the general public.

Basic Authentication

When IIS uses basic authentication, the client's browser presents the user with a logon dialog box. The user must enter an account name and password that can be validated by the computer hosting your site (or its domain controller) to establish a connection. If the credentials are not valid, IIS gives the user two more tries before returning an "access denied" error message.

The advantage of basic authentication is that it is part of the HTTP 1 standard and therefore can be used by any browser running on any operating system. The disadvantage is that logon credentials are transmitted using Base64 encoding (sometimes called *uuencoding*) and can be intercepted and decoded.

> **note** Creating a secure connection eliminates the principal problem of basic authentication—the fact that logon credentials are transmitted without effective encryption. The drawback to using a secure connection is that it slows performance. For more information, see "Using SSL to Secure Basic Authentication," page 856.

Advanced Digest Authentication

The advanced digest authentication method eliminates the principal defect of basic authentication—the fact that client credentials are sent across the network in a form that can be intercepted and decoded. With advanced digest authentication, IIS transmits a realm name to the client browser. The client browser prompts the user for logon credentials, and then creates an MD5 *hash* (a form of encryption) from the realm name and the user's logon credentials. This hash is transmitted back to IIS, which submits the hash to your domain controller for verification.

The requirements for advanced digest authentication are as follows:

- The client browser must be Microsoft Internet Explorer 5 or later.
- The user and the computer running IIS must be members of, or be trusted by, the same domain.
- The user must have a valid Windows user account stored in Active Directory on the domain controller.
- The domain controller must be running Windows .NET Server.
- The computer running IIS must be running Windows XP.

Advanced digest authentication represents a security improvement over digest authentication, a form of authentication that was introduced with Windows 2000. If your domain controller is running Windows 2000 Server, rather than Windows .NET Server, IIS uses digest authentication instead of advanced digest authentication. The only difference between the two is that in digest authentication the user's password is stored in clear text on the server; in advanced digest authentication, the password is stored as an MD5 hash. In either case, the transmission of credentials across the network is hashed.

Integrated Windows Authentication

Using integrated Windows authentication, IIS can authenticate a user without requiring the transmission of logon credentials across the network. The authentication takes place by means of a cryptographic exchange between the client and IIS that involves hashing. Because logon credentials are not transmitted, this form of authentication is more secure than digest or advanced digest authentication. It has the following limitations, however:

● The client must be running Internet Explorer version 2 or later.

● This form of authentication does not work over HTTP proxy connections.

Specifying Authentication Methods

You can allow anonymous access and/or specify authentication methods at any level of your site: the site itself, a particular directory (including its files and subdirectories), or a particular file. For information about how settings at one level affect other levels, see "Understanding Property Inheritance," page 841.

To specify settings, follow these steps:

1 Right-click the appropriate item in the console tree or details pane of the Internet Information Services console.

2 Choose Properties from the shortcut menu.

3 Click the Directory Security or File Security tab (File Security, if you've right-clicked a file; otherwise, Directory Security).

4 In the Anonymous Access And Authentication Control section of the dialog box, click Edit.

5 Fill out the Authentication Methods dialog box, shown in Figure 24-10 on the next page.

Figure 24-10. You can use authentication methods in combination with one another.

Setting IIS Permissions

IIS permissions control what users can do after they have accessed a resource on your Web or FTP site. Unlike NTFS permissions, IIS permissions are applied uniformly to all clients. If the IIS permissions for a directory differ from the NTFS permissions, the more restrictive permissions are applied.

IIS permissions can be applied to files, directories, virtual directories, or entire sites. For information about how settings at one level affect settings at other levels, see "Understanding Property Inheritance," page 841.

To apply IIS permissions, follow these steps:

1 Right-click the appropriate item in the console tree or details pane.

2 Choose Properties from the shortcut menu.

3 In the properties dialog box, click Home Directory, Virtual Directory, or File (the tab name you see matches the selection type you made in the console tree).

Figure 24-11 shows the Home Directory tab of the Default Web Site Properties dialog box. In the figure, the highlighted controls are the ones concerned with IIS permissions.

Figure 24-11. Use the controls highlighted in this figure to set IIS permissions.

To configure IIS permissions, set or clear the following check boxes:

- **Read** (set by default). Allows users to view directory or file content and properties.

- **Write.** Allows users to change directory or file content and properties.

- **Script Source Access.** Allows users to access source files. If Read is also selected, users can read script source code. If Write is also selected, users can modify source code. If neither Read nor Write is selected, Script Source Access is unavailable.

- **Directory Browsing.** Allows users to view file directories.

The following options are available in the Execute Permissions list:

- **None.** Disables scripts (such as ASP applications) and executables.

- **Scripts Only.** Enables scripts (such as ASP applications) but disables executables.

- **Scripts And Executables.** Enables both scripts and executables.

Tightening Security with the IIS Lockdown Wizard

Adding any server software to a computer poses security risks, and IIS is no exception. By inviting other computers to connect to yours, you expose yourself to a wide range of potential problems, ranging from viruses and worms that are targeted at IIS (such as the infamous Nimda and Code Red worms), to exploits that allow outside attackers to break into your server and launch attacks against the rest of your network or the Internet at large.

How do you make sure you've installed the proper IIS updates and configured your server settings properly? We recommend using a freely available tool called the Internet Information Services Lockdown Wizard (sometimes referred to as the IIS Lockdown tool). This officially sanctioned wizard steers you through the sometimes tricky process of determining which IIS features you need, disabling the features you don't need, and eliminating common security holes. You can read about the wizard at *http://www.microsoft.com/technet/security/tools/tools/locktool.asp*, and you can download it from *http://www.microsoft.com/Downloads/Release.asp?ReleaseID=33961*.

Before using the IIS Lockdown Wizard, visit Windows Update, and install all current security patches for Windows XP and IIS. After completing this task, download the wizard, and run it by following these steps:

1 Open Windows Explorer, browse to the folder where you saved the downloaded file, and double-click the executable file, Iislockd.exe.

2 Click Next on the introduction and license agreement pages. The Select Server Template page appears.

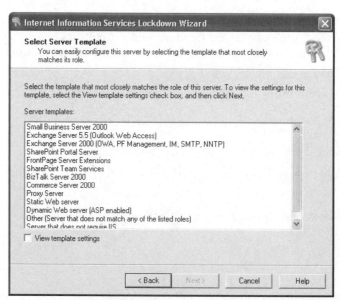

3 Select the template that most closely matches how you use IIS, and click Next.

4 Select Install URLScan Filter On The Server, and click Next. (This feature protects the Web server from attacks that use deliberately malformed URLs to try to crash the server and leave the computer in a state where it might execute arbitrary code of the attacker's choosing.) The Ready To Apply Settings page appears.

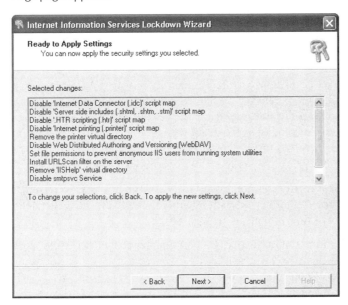

5 Review the proposed changes to be certain they're appropriate. If everything looks right, click Next. The wizard applies new, tighter security settings, disables unneeded and potentially vulnerable services, removes sample files and scripts, and so on.

6 After the changes are made, the wizard displays a summary of its actions. Click the View Report button to see a short log file. Click Next, and then click Finish to close the wizard.

caution After completing its work, the IIS Lockdown Wizard saves a concise report of its actions in %SystemRoot%\System32\Inetsrv\Oblt-rep.log. You'll find a more detailed log file in the same folder, saved as Oblt-log.log. Even if the wizard ran with no problems, do not delete these log files! You'll need them later if you need to rerun the wizard for any reason.

If you have problems accessing IIS after running the wizard, you can undo the changes it made. Just run the wizard again. You can reverse all its modifications and then lock down IIS with a different set of options. For troubleshooting purposes, you can select or clear specific options and see which option is the source of the problem you are experiencing.

Enabling a Secure (Encrypted) Connection

IIS can use Secure Sockets Layer (SSL) to create an encrypted connection between your Web site and its clients. SSL employs public-key encryption, at either 40-bit or 128-bit strength. When users log onto your Web site over a secure connection, they construct a URL using *https* instead of *http*.

Enabling SSL entails the use of *certificates,* digital documents that allow servers and clients to authenticate each other. Certificates come in three flavors:

- **Server certificates** are used to identify servers to Web browsers and to supply the public key for SSL encryption. Whenever a user connects to a resource on your server using the HTTPS protocol (as opposed to HTTP), the server first identifies itself with its server certificate. After the browser accepts the certificate, an encrypted SSL connection is established using the server's private key at the server and public key at the browser.

- **Client certificates** are used to identify Web browsers to servers. A secure site can require browsers to identify themselves with a client certificate as part of the authentication step.

- **Certification Authority (CA) certificates** provide the trust value for server and client certificates. Internet Explorer keeps a list of known and trusted CAs. When a user browses to a secure Web page, the Web server's server certificate is sent to the browser. The browser checks the CA that issued the server certificate. If the CA is in the list of trusted CAs, the certificate is accepted automatically. If the CA is not in the list, a dialog box is displayed, giving the user the option of accepting or rejecting the certificate.

To enable a secure connection to your Web site, directory, virtual directory, or file, follow these steps:

1 Right-click the appropriate object in the console tree or details pane.

2 Choose Properties from the shortcut menu and then click the Directory Security or File Security tab.

3 In the Secure Communications section of the dialog box, click Edit. (If the Edit button is not available, you need to obtain and install a server certificate. See "Obtaining a Server Certificate" on the next page.) The Secure Communications dialog box appears, as shown in Figure 24-12 on the next page.

4 Select Require Secure Channel (SSL) at the top of the Secure Communications dialog box.

Figure 24-12. To establish an encrypted connection, select Require Secure Channel (SSL).

note If you don't require SSL, users can still try to create an SSL connection to your site by using *https* instead of *http*. If your server has a server certificate installed, a secure connection is created, even though you have not required it. If your server does not have a server certificate installed, the user receives a "This page cannot be displayed" error message.

Obtaining a Server Certificate

The process for obtaining a server certificate involves creating a certificate request (in the form of a request file), submitting the request to a Certification Authority, obtaining the approved certificate, and installing the certificate on your computer. The Web Server Certificate Wizard handles most of this process.

The Web Server Certificate Wizard generates a request for a server certificate and installs the certificate after it has been granted. If you are connected to a domain server running Enterprise Certificate Services, the wizard submits your request online. The wizard also detects an out-of-date or about-to-expire certificate.

To start the Web Server Certificate Wizard, follow these steps:

1 Right-click Default Web Site.

2 Choose Properties from the shortcut menu.

3 Click the Directory Security tab.

4 Click Server Certificate under Secure Communications and complete the wizard.

Using SSL to Secure Basic Authentication

You can set up a Web site to use basic authentication and require an SSL communication link. If you do so, an SSL link is made before authentication is performed. The user name and password are therefore transmitted in an encrypted form. All user interaction with the Web site will use SSL, however, and hence will run more slowly.

You can also configure a Web site for basic authentication without requiring an SSL link, and users can request SSL themselves if they want to protect their logon credentials. The user can do this by addressing your site with *https* instead of *http*. If you have a server certificate installed, an encrypted logon occurs, and all pages on your site will use the secure link. However, if the link was created by user request, the user can manually change a URL from *https* to *http* after authentication takes place, and the remainder of his or her interaction with your site will be unencrypted and will not incur the SSL performance overhead.

Authenticating Users with Client Certificates

Client certificates can be used in place of user names and passwords in any of the authentication schemes requiring them. You accomplish this by mapping client certificates to Windows user accounts. If certificate mapping is used, when the client's certificate is received by the server, it is checked against the mapping and, if a corresponding user account exists, the user is logged on using that account.

Two ways of mapping certificates are available: one-to-one and many-to-one. In *one-to-one mapping*, each user's certificate is mapped to an account. The server must have an exact copy of each user's certificate to create the mappings.

In *many-to-one mapping*, client certificates are mapped by rules that relate a set of certificate parameters to a user account. In this scenario, copies of the certificate are not needed. However, this means that many-to-one mapping is not as secure as one-to-one mapping.

Follow these steps to enable certificate mapping:

1 Choose Accept Client Certificates in the Client Certificates section of the Secure Communications dialog box, shown in Figure 24-12.

2 Select Enable Client Certificate Mapping and then click Edit.

3 In the ensuing dialog box, choose how you want to map the certificates:

   ■ To create a one-to-one mapping, click the 1-to-1 tab and then click Add. Select a certificate to use and the user account to which it should be mapped.

   ■ To create a many-to-one mapping, click the Many-to-1 tab, click Add, and follow the wizard to select certificate fields to use in the mapping rules.

Sharing Files with WebDAV

Web Distributed Authoring and Versioning (WebDAV) is an extension of the HTTP 1.1 protocol that allows users running Windows 2000 and later (and Internet Explorer 5 or later) to read and write files on a virtual directory managed by IIS. Because a WebDAV directory, unlike an FTP site, can employ all of the authentication methods supported by IIS, Microsoft recommends the use of WebDAV in preference to FTP for sharing files among users of Windows 2000 and later.

Setting Up a WebDAV Directory

To set up a directory for sharing via WebDAV, simply create a virtual directory in your Web site. You can do this in either of two ways:

● Right-click the directory in Windows Explorer, choose Sharing And Security from the shortcut menu, select the Web Sharing tab, and then choose Share This Folder.

● Right-click Default Web Site in the Internet Information Services snap-in, choose New, Virtual Directory from the shortcut menu, and then follow the steps of the Virtual Directory Creation Wizard.

Chapter 24

As the last step in either process, you need to assign IIS permissions for the shared directory. Figure 24-13 shows the dialog box you'll see if you start in Windows Explorer. (A similar dialog box appears if you begin with the IIS snap-in.)

Figure 24-13. Read permission is enabled by default in a WebDAV directory. To provide usability comparable to that of an FTP site, select Directory Browsing as well.

Read permission is enabled by default. To provide functionality comparable to what an FTP site would offer, be sure to select Directory Browsing. If you want users to be able to modify existing files in the directory or create new ones, select Write as well. If you enable Write permission, however, you should choose None in the Application Permissions box. Otherwise, users will be able to upload and execute potentially damaging scripts or executables.

Using a WebDAV Directory

Assuming you have enabled read, write, and directory browsing permissions, users with appropriate credentials (or any user, if you enable anonymous access) can work with your WebDAV directory as they would with their own local file system. They can use the Add Network Place Wizard to create a shortcut to the directory in My Network Places and then display the shared folder in Windows Explorer. If they use Microsoft Office 2000 or later, they can create, publish, edit, and save documents in the WebDAV directory, exactly as they would with a local folder. And, if they open the directory in Internet Explorer, the directory looks and behaves just like an FTP site, as shown in Figure 24-14.

Figure 24-14. A WebDAV directory opened in Internet Explorer 5 or later looks and acts like an FTP site.

Setting Up IIS for Internet Printing

IIS supports the Internet Printing Protocol (IPP). Whenever you share a printer and you are running IIS, the shared printer becomes available over the Internet. Users to whom you've given permission can view and manage printers in a Web browser in much the same way that they can using the Printers And Faxes folder for local and network printers. In an Internet Explorer window, open *http://hostname/printers* for a list of shared printers on *hostname. Hostname* can be a computer name (for an intranet) a domain name, or an IP address. Three shared printers are shown here.

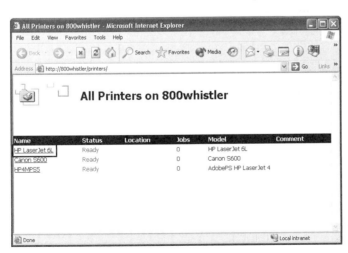

You can select one of the printers to open a page showing its status, queuing, and control options, as shown here.

You can then click the Properties link in the left pane under View to generate a page of information about the selected printer, including the estimated wait time and information about the printer's capabilities.

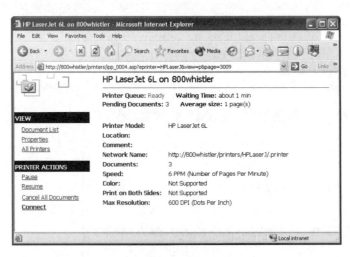

To use a printer shared via IPP, follow these steps:

1 Choose Start, Printers And Faxes.

2 In the Printers And Faxes folder, click Add A Printer under Printer Tasks.

3 When the Add Printer Wizard opens, click Next.

4 On the Local Or Network Printer page, select the second option, A Network Printer, Or A Printer Attached To Another Computer, and then click Next. The Specify A Printer page appears.

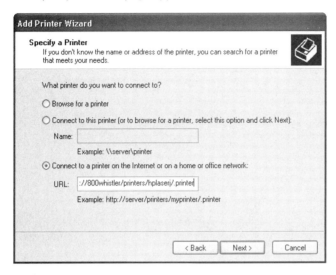

5 Select Connect To A Printer On The Internet Or On A Home Or Office Network.

6 Specify a URL of the form *http://*hostname*/printers/*printername*/.printer*, where *hostname* is the network name of the computer running IIS (you can enter a domain name, a computer name, or an IP address) and *printername* is the name under which the printer is shared. For example, for the printer shared as Hplaserj on the computer named 800whistler, you would type **http://800whistler/printers/hplaserj/.printer**. Click Next and then complete the wizard.

You might be prompted to select drivers for the printer on your local machine, or to insert a disk containing such drivers, as part of the installation process.

After the printer is installed, use the IPP printer exactly as you would any other local or networked printer.

Chapter 25

Performing Routine Maintenance

Your personal computer is a curious combination of digital data and temperamental machinery. To keep your system running smoothly, it pays to perform some regular maintenance steps. In particular, it's wise to do the following on a regular basis:

- Check your disks for file system and media errors.

- Defragment your hard disks to optimize file access.

- Make sure that you always have enough space on your hard disk by getting rid of files you no longer need and compressing files if necessary.

- Perform regular backups of data and system files.

Checking Disks for Errors

Errors in disk media and in the file system can cause a wide range of Windows problems, ranging from an inability to open or save files to blue-screen errors and widespread data corruption. Microsoft Windows XP is capable of recovering automatically from many disk errors, especially on drives formatted with NTFS. To perform a thorough inspection for errors, you can manually run the Windows XP Check Disk utility, chkdsk.exe. Two versions of this utility are available—a graphical version that performs basic disk-checking functions, and a command-line version that provides a much more extensive set of customization options.

At Home with Windows XP

With one glaring exception, the tools and techniques described in this chapter work identically in Windows XP Home Edition and Windows XP Professional. That exception is the Backup Utility program. In Home Edition, it's not installed by default, although in this chapter we explain how to install it. There's another Backup Utility gotcha for Home Edition users, however, and this one has no workaround: the Automatic System Recovery feature works only in Windows XP Professional.

To check for errors on a local disk, follow these steps:

1 Open the My Computer window, right-click the icon belonging to the drive you want to check, and then choose Properties.

2 On the Tools tab, click the Check Now button.

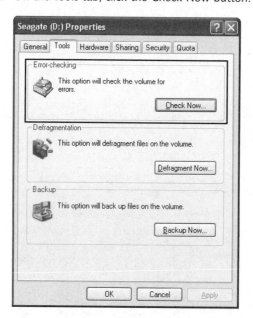

3 In the Check Disk dialog box, shown here, select from the following options.

Chapter 25: Performing Routine Maintenance

■ **Automatically Fix File System Errors.** Select this option if you want Windows to automatically repair any file system errors. If this option is not selected, the Check Disk utility reports any errors it finds but does not change them. This option is the equivalent of running the Chkdsk command with the /F switch, as described later in this section.

■ **Scan For And Attempt Recovery Of Bad Sectors.** Select this option to perform an exhaustive check of the entire disk, locate bad sectors, and recover readable information stored in defective locations. Note that selecting this option automatically repairs file system errors as well, even if the previous option is cleared. This option is the equivalent of running the Chkdsk command with the /R switch.

If you simply want to see a report of file system errors without making any changes to disk structures, leave both boxes unchecked.

4 Click the Start button to begin the disk checking process. The green progress bar provides feedback as the error-checking tool goes through several phases.

If you selected the Automatically Fix File System Errors option on a drive that currently has open files, Windows is unable to run the utility immediately. In that case, you see the message shown here.

Click Yes to schedule the disk check to run the next time you start your computer. The disk check occurs during the character-mode startup phase of Windows; during this period your computer is not available for you to perform any other tasks. When your computer restarts, Windows notifies you that it's about to perform a scheduled disk check; by default, you have 10 seconds to cancel the operation and boot normally instead.

After the Check Disk utility completes its operation, it reports its results. If the disk check turns up no errors, you see a Disk Check Complete dialog box. If the Check Disk utility uncovers any errors, it writes a message to the Event log and displays a dialog box listing the errors it found and the repairs it made.

---

caution Although the Check Disk utility is a useful tool and sometimes a lifesaver, it can cause you headaches if used indiscriminately. Once started, the Check Disk operation cannot be stopped except by pressing your computer's power switch. On very large drives (60 GB and larger), the full disk check can takes hours or even days to complete.

Longtime users of Windows 95, Windows 98, or Windows Me are probably accustomed to seeing the ScanDisk program run automatically after a power failure or other unexpected shutdown. Windows XP, however, behaves differently. The Check Disk utility runs automatically after an illegal shutdown only if a specific bit in the registry is set, indicating that the file system is "dirty"—that is, that it has data that it did not properly read or write when it was shut down. If the file system wasn't doing anything when the system shut down, the dirty bit will not be set. Because NTFS volumes keep a journal of all disk activities, they are able to recover and remain clean even if you shut down in the middle of a disk write. Check Disk is most likely to run automatically at startup only on FAT32 volumes after an unexpected shutdown.

InsideOut

Two additional and well-hidden Windows commands are crucial to the operation of the Check Disk utility. Autochk.exe runs automatically any time you specify that you want to schedule a disk check to run at startup. The Chkntfs command is especially useful if you change your mind and decide you want to cancel a scheduled check. From a command prompt, type **chkntfs /x d:** (where *d* is replaced by a drive letter) to exclude the drive specified. Chkntfs has another nifty trick: it can tell you whether a disk is dirty. At a command prompt, simply type **chkntfs d:**. For more details about these commands, see Knowledge Base article Q218461, "Description of Enhanced Chkdsk, Autochk, and Chkntfs Tools in Windows 2000."

The command-line version of the Check Disk utility gives you considerably more options. It also allows you to schedule disk-checking operations using the Scheduled Tasks folder (as described in "Scheduling Tasks to Run Automatically," page 356). To run this command in its simplest form, log on using an account in the Administrators group, open a Command Prompt window (by typing **cmd** in the Run box, for instance), and then type **chkdsk** at the prompt. This command runs Chkdsk in read-only mode, displaying the status of the current drive but not making any changes. If you add a drive letter after the command (**chkdsk d:**, for instance), the report applies to that drive.

You can use any combination of the following switches at the end of the command line to modify its operation:

- /F   Instructs Chkdsk to fix any errors it detects. This is the most commonly used switch. The disk must be locked. If Chkdsk cannot lock the drive (as is always the case with the system drive), it offers to check the drive the next time you restart the computer.

- /V   Displays verbose output, listing the name of every file in every directory as the disk check proceeds.

- /R   Identifies bad sectors and recovers information from those sectors if possible. The disk must be locked.

The following switches are valid only on NTFS volumes:

- /I   Performs a simpler check of index entries (stage 2 in the Chkdsk process), reducing the amount of time required.

- /C   Skips the checking of cycles within the folder structure, reducing the amount of time required.

- /X   Forces the volume to dismount, if necessary, and invalidates all open file handles. This option is intended for server administrators. Because of the potential for data loss, it should be avoided in normal use with Windows XP Professional or Home Edition.

- /L[:*size*]   Changes the size of the file that logs NTFS transactions (the default is 65536). If you omit the *size* parameter, this switch displays the current size. This option is intended for server administrators. Because of the potential for data loss, it should be avoided in normal use with Windows XP Professional or Home Edition.

Troubleshooting

When you run Chkdsk at the Recovery Console, some options are not available.

The Chkdsk command used when you boot to the Recovery Console is not the same as the one used within a full Windows session. Only two switches are available for this version:

- **/P**   Performs an exhaustive check of the current disk.
- **/R**   Repairs damage on the current disk.

If your system is able to boot to Windows either normally or in Safe Mode and you suspect that you have disk errors, you should use the full Chkdsk command. For more details, see "Making Repairs from the Recovery Console," page 907.

Defragmenting Disks
for Better Performance

On a relatively new system with a speedy processor and plenty of physical memory, hard disk performance is the single biggest bottleneck in everyday operation. Even on a zippy hard disk, it takes time to load large data files into memory so you can work with them. The problem is especially noticeable with databases, video clips, and CD images, which can easily consume hundreds of megabytes.

On a freshly formatted disk, files load fairly quickly, but over time, performance can degrade because of disk fragmentation. To understand how this process works, it helps to understand the basic structure of a hard disk. The process of formatting a disk divides it into *sectors*, each of which contains space for 512 bytes of data. The file system combines groups of sectors into *clusters*, which are the smallest units of space available for holding a single file or part of a file.

> For more details about how to choose a size and format for disk partitions, see "Working with Partitions, Volumes, and Disks," page 927.

On a 10-GB NTFS drive, the cluster size is 4 KB. On a FAT32 drive of the same size, clusters are 8 KB. Thus, when you save a 20-MB movie clip on that drive, Windows divides the file into approximately 2,560 pieces (NTFS) or 1,280 pieces (FAT32).

When you save this file for the first time on a freshly formatted hard disk, Windows writes it in contiguous clusters. Because all the clusters that hold individual pieces of the file are physically adjacent to one another, the mechanical components of the hard disk can work very efficiently, scooping up data in one smooth operation. As a bonus, the Windows disk cache is able to anticipate the need for data and fetch nearby clusters that are likely to contain other parts of the file, which can then be retrieved from the fast cache rather than from the relatively slow disk.

Unfortunately, hard disks don't stay neatly organized for long. When you add data to an existing file, the file system has to allocate more clusters for storage, typically in a different physical location on the disk. As you delete files, you create gaps in the once-tidy arrangement of contiguously stored files. As you save new files, especially large ones, the file system uses all these bits of free space, scattering the files over the hard disk into many noncontiguous pieces. The resulting inefficiency in storage is called *fragmentation*; each time you open or save a file on a badly fragmented disk, disk performance suffers, sometimes dramatically, because the disk heads have to spend extra time moving from cluster to cluster before they can begin reading or writing data.

Chapter 25: Performing Routine Maintenance

newfeature! The Disk Defragmenter utility improves performance by physically rearranging files so that they're stored in contiguous clusters. In addition to consolidating files and folders, the utility also consolidates free space, making it less likely that new files will be fragmented when you save them. Windows XP includes a graphical utility that works as a snap-in with Microsoft Management Console. A command-line version of this utility (new in Windows XP) allows you to schedule defragmentation so that it occurs automatically, at regular intervals. For details, see "Scheduling Tasks to Run Automatically," page 356.

---

tip   **Get a more powerful defragmenter**

Like many Windows utilities, the Disk Defragmenter utility offers a basic set of features that are sufficient for average users. If you want more bells and whistles, you'll need to pay extra for a third-party alternative. Your easiest choice is Executive Software's Diskeeper utility (*http://www.diskeeper.com*), which is a full-featured version of the exact same utility bundled with Windows XP. The full version allows you to schedule continuous defragmentation in the background and also allows you to perform boot-time defragmentation of the page file, which the built-in Windows utility doesn't touch. Defrag Manager (*http://www.winternals.com/es/*) is targeted toward network administrators, and it allows you to defragment hard disks on computers throughout your network. By some measures, Defrag Manager provides the most thorough defragmentation. (A number of fragmented files remain even after most defragmenters run.) Symantec's Norton Utilities package (*http://www.symantec.com/nu*) also includes a capable disk defragmenter, as does Raxco's PerfectDisk (*http://www.raxco.com*). Before installing any disk utility, be sure to verify that the version you've purchased is compatible with Windows XP.

A white paper published by Winternals (the publishers of Defrag Manager) discusses some of the benchmarking methods used to compare defragmenters; you can read it online at *http://www.winternals.com/es/documentation/DefragmenterPerformance.pdf*.

To open the graphical Disk Defragmenter console, use any of the following techniques:

- From the All Programs menu, choose Accessories, System Tools, Disk Defragmenter.

- From the My Computer window, right-click any drive icon and choose Properties from the shortcut menu. Then click the Tools tab and click Defragment Now.

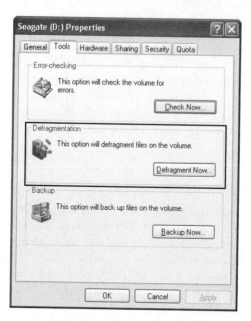

- Run Dfrg.msc from a command prompt.

- Right-click the My Computer icon on the Start menu and choose Manage from the shortcut menu. In the Computer Management console, open the Storage option in the console pane and select Disk Defragmenter.

Disk defragmentation can be a time-consuming process, so it's probably not worth the bother on a drive that is only slightly fragmented. To determine whether you need to defragment a drive, select its icon in the top half of the Disk Defragmenter window and click Analyze. As Figure 25-1 shows, Disk Defragmenter presents a graphical display of fragmentation and makes its recommendation.

In some cases, you might want to override the recommendation and defragment anyway. For instance, if you're about to copy a large number of files to CD, you might want to maximize your chances for a successful burn. Regardless of the recommendation, you can begin the defragmentation process by clicking the Defragment button. (You must be logged on as a member of the Administrators group to perform most defragmenting tasks.) While the Disk Defragmenter is running, you see a graphical display that indicates the progress of the operation, and you can use the Pause or Stop button at any time to halt the process.

For more details about the current state of defragmentation, click the View Report button, which displays detailed statistics about the overall level of fragmentation on a drive, as shown in Figure 25-2.

Chapter 25: Performing Routine Maintenance

Select a drive for analysis

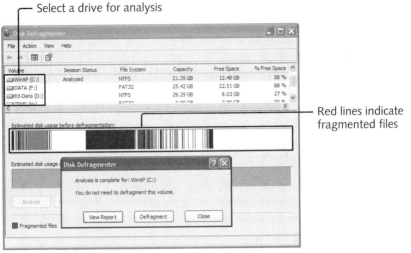

Red lines indicate
fragmented files

Figure 25-1. If the level of fragmentation exceeds a preset threshold, Disk
Defragmenter recommends defragmentation.

Figure 25-2. This report format lets you see overall fragmentation percentages and
identify files that are most widely scattered.

InsideOut

The best way to avoid disk fragmentation is to start from a completely clean slate. If you routinely work with CD images, for instance, consider creating a separate partition that's big enough to temporarily hold the files you're working with. A 2-GB partition, for instance, is big enough to hold a CD image and all temporary files associated with it. Keep that drive empty except when you plan to create a CD, at which time you can copy files to it for burning. Using this strategy, you can be certain that fragmentation won't have a deleterious impact on your CD-burning performance.

The command-line version of the Defrag utility uses the exact same program code as the graphical version. The only difference in operation is that it does not report its status or provide a final report. To use this command, type **defrag** *d*: at any command prompt, where *d* is the drive letter or mount point of an existing volume. (For an explanation of mount points, see "Assigning and Changing Drive Letters or Drive Paths," page 940.) You can use the following switches with the Defrag command:

/A   Analyzes the selected drive or volume and displays a summary of the analysis report.

/V   Displays complete (verbose) reports. When used in combination with /A, displays only the analysis report. When used alone, displays both the analysis and defragmentation reports.

/F   Forces defragmentation of the volume regardless of whether it needs to be defragmented.

Troubleshooting

The Disk Defragmenter utility does not fully defragment the drive.

A volume must have at least 15 percent free space before the Disk Defragmenter will completely defragment the volume. If you have less free space available, the operation will run, but only partial defragmentation will result. Check the value at the right of the drive entry in the Defragmenter console to confirm current free space values for the selected drive. If necessary, delete or move files to make extra room.

You cannot defragment a volume that Windows has marked as possibly containing errors. To troubleshoot this possibility, enter **chkdsk** *d*: **/f** at any command prompt, substituting the letter of the drive in question.

The Disk Defragmenter does not defragment files in the Recycle Bin. Empty the Recycle Bin before defragmenting.

The Disk Defragmenter does not defragment the following files: Bootsect.dos, Safeboot.fs, Safeboot.csv, Safeboot.rsv, Hiberfil.sys, and Memory.dmp. In addition, the Windows page file is never defragmented. (See the text following this sidebar to learn how to work around this issue.)

With some large files, it takes several passes to fully defragment the files in question. If the View Report option shows one of these stubborn files, try moving it to another drive before running a full defragmentation pass. After defragmentation is complete, move the file back to its original location. You should be able to copy the file to the newly optimized drive without any problems.

Disk Defragmenter will pass over any files that are currently in use. For best results, shut down all running programs first. For even better results, log off and log back on (using an account in the Administrators group) before continuing.

The command-line Disk Defragmenter does not provide any status indicator except for a blinking cursor. To interrupt the defragmentation process, click in the command window and press Ctrl+C.

Using Disk Defragmenter's Analysis Report, you can determine whether your page file is fragmented. (For an explanation of how the page file works, see "Making the Most of Virtual Memory," page 238.) Although page file fragmentation is normally not a serious issue, a severely fragmented page file can reduce your system's performance. Disk Defragmenter cannot consolidate your page file, because Windows holds it open while you work. However, if you have more than one volume available (even if the second volume is on the same physical hard disk as your system drive), you can work around the problem as follows:

1 Open Control Panel and double-click the System icon.

2 On the Advanced tab of the System Properties dialog box, click the Settings button under Performance.

3 On the Advanced tab of the Performance Options dialog box, click Change under Virtual Memory.

4 From the list of available drives, choose a volume other than the one that holds your current page file. This drive will hold your temporary page file.

5 Choose the Custom Size option, enter settings in the Initial Size and Maximum Size boxes to match your current page file, and click Set.

6 Select the drive that contains the fragmented page file, set the Initial Size and Maximum Size boxes to 0, and then click Set.

7 Reboot to allow your system to stop using the old page file and begin using the new one.

8 Defragment the drive that previously held your page file. This consolidates the free space on that volume so that your new page file will be stored in contiguous space.

9 Repeat steps 1 through 6, this time creating a page file on the original disk and eliminating the temporary page file you created.

10 Reboot to allow the new, defragmented page file to take over.

Managing Disk Space

In the digital era, Parkinson's Law has an inescapable corollary: Data expands to fill the space allotted to it. Gargantuan hard disks encourage consumption, and digital media files (not to mention Windows itself) supply plenty of bits to be consumed. It's surprisingly easy to run low on disk space, and the consequences can be deleterious to your system. If you run low on storage, Windows might not have enough room to expand its page file, or it might be unable to create temporary files. In addition, essential features such as Indexing Service and System Restore may stop working properly. At that point, you start seeing ominous error messages and (possibly) degraded performance.

To pare down on disk space consumption, you can do any or all of the following:

- Clear out temporary files that you no longer need
- Uninstall programs you don't need
- Uninstall Windows components you don't need
- Delete documents you don't need
- On NTFS volumes, use real-time file compression

---

tip **Shut down "low disk space" messages**

When you're running low on disk space, Windows displays a warning message in the notification area at the right of the taskbar. Clicking on the balloon opens the Disk Cleanup utility and allows you to clean out unwanted files. If you'd prefer not to see these messages, you can disable them globally by adding a value in the registry (unfortunately, this option cannot be used only on specific drives). Open Registry Editor and select the following key:

HKCU\Software\Microsoft\Windows\CurrentVersion\Policies\Explorer\

Choose Edit, New, DWORD Value, and name the new value NoLowDiskSpaceChecks. Set the data value to 1. Close Registry Editor to apply the change.

Windows will no longer display these warnings.

Cleaning Up with Disk Cleanup

The simplest way to make room on any drive is with the help of the Disk Cleanup utility, Cleanmgr.exe. If you click a "low disk space" warning, this tool opens automatically. You can start it manually at any time by choosing the Disk Cleanup shortcut (from the All Programs menu, choose Accessories, System Tools). If you use this option, Windows prompts you to select a local drive letter. To begin working directly with a local drive, right-click the drive icon in the My Computer window, choose Properties from the shortcut menu, and then click Disk Cleanup on the General tab of the properties dialog box. Figure 25-3 shows a system with nearly a gigabyte of space that can be recovered easily.

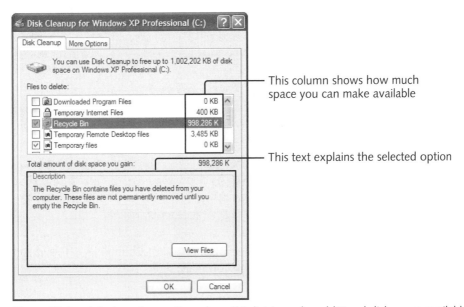

This column shows how much space you can make available

This text explains the selected option

Figure 25-3.   Select or clear options from this list to make additional disk space available on the selected drive.

Most of the Disk Cleanup options are fairly self-explanatory and merely consolidate functions scattered throughout the Windows interface. For instance, you can empty the Recycle Bin, clear out the Temporary Internet Files folder, and delete files left behind by Indexing Service. (Avoid cleaning out the Downloaded Program Files folder, which contains generally useful ActiveX and Java add-ins.) Using these default settings, the Disk Cleanup utility is strictly an interactive tool. Each time you run the utility, you must select options you want to run and then click the OK button to actually perform the cleanup.

> **caution** The Disk Cleanup utility includes one confusing option that can leave an inordinate amount of wasted space on your hard disk if you don't understand how it works. When you run Disk Cleanup, one of the available options offers to delete Temporary Files—the accompanying Help text explains that these are unneeded files in the Temp folder. Unfortunately, this option may display a value of 0, even if your Temp folder contains tens or even hundreds of megabytes of useless files. The reason? Although the Help text doesn't explain it clearly, this value lists only files in your Temp folder that are more than one week old. If you want to completely clean this folder out you'll need to do so manually. Close all running programs and type **%temp%** in the Run dialog box; from the resulting Windows Explorer window, delete everything you find. You may discover that some files are not available for deletion until you reboot.

The overwhelming majority of Windows users never realize that the Disk Cleanup utility offers two cool switches that are documented only here and in a Knowledge Base article (Q315246, "How to Automate the Disk Cleanup Tool in Windows XP").

To automate the cleanup process, use the following switches:

/D *driveletter*	Runs the Disk Cleanup utility using the drive letter you specify in place of *driveletter*, C: for example.
/Sageset:*n*	Enter a number from 0 through 65535 in place of *n*. This option opens a dialog box that lets you select Disk Cleanup options, creates a registry key that corresponds to the number you entered, and then saves your settings in that key.
/Sagerun:*n*	Retrieves the saved settings for the number you enter in place of *n* and then runs the Disk Cleanup utility without requiring any interaction on your part.

To use these switches, follow these steps:

1 Open a Command Prompt (cmd.exe) window and type the command **cleanmgr /sageset:200**. (This number is completely arbitrary; you can choose any other number from 0 through 65535 if you prefer.)

2 In the Disk Cleanup Settings dialog box, shown in Figure 25-4, choose the options you want to apply whenever you use these settings. For this example, select the Temporary Setup Files, Debug Dump Files, Old Chkdsk Files, and Setup Log Files options.

3 Click OK to save your changes in the registry.

4 Create a shortcut that uses the command **cleanmgr /sagerun:200**. Save the shortcut in the Windows folder using a descriptive name—Weekly Cleanup, for instance.

Chapter 25: Performing Routine Maintenance

5 Open Control Panel's Scheduled Tasks folder and start the Add Scheduled Task Wizard. When prompted to select the program you want Windows to run, click Browse and select the shortcut you just created. Follow the wizard's remaining prompts to schedule the command to run at regular intervals.

6 Repeat steps 1–5 for other Disk Cleanup options you want to automate.

Figure 25-4. When you use the /Sageset switch, you can work with an expanded set of options that are not available interactively.

---

tip **Make the most of Disk Cleanup shortcuts**

Disk Cleanup shortcuts can be tremendously useful for routine maintenance. For instance, you might want to create a batch file that automatically empties the Temporary Internet Files folder every time you log on to your computer and another that automatically compresses old files every week or two. If you create a shortcut that empties the Recycle Bin, it's best not to add it to the Scheduled Tasks folder, where it can inadvertently toss files you later discover you wanted to recover; instead, save this shortcut and run it as needed.

The More Options tab in the Disk Cleanup dialog box provides three more Clean Up buttons.

The top two buttons (in the Windows Components and Installed Programs sections) take you to the Add Or Remove Programs dialog box where you can remove Windows components and programs. (For details, see "Uninstalling Programs," page 186, and "Adding and Removing Windows Components," page 73.) The third button, under System Restore, lets you remove all but the most recent System Restore checkpoint—this option can recover a dramatic amount of space, but you should choose it only if you're certain you won't need to roll back your configuration to one of the saved versions you're about to delete.

Using NTFS File Compression

One of the many advantages of choosing the NTFS file system over FAT32 is that it offers on-the-fly compression. Don't confuse this capability with the clunky and unreliable DriveSpace compression schemes found in Windows 95. The NTFS version is slick and essentially seamless. All you have to do is set an attribute for an NTFS file (or an entire folder), and Windows XP compresses it, decompressing it automatically when you open it.

To compress a file or folder, right-click its icon in Windows Explorer, choose Properties from the shortcut menu, and click the Advanced button. In the Advanced Attributes dialog box, shown in Figure 25-5, select Compress Contents To Save Disk Space.

tip   **Use compression sparingly**

A little compression goes a long way. In general, NTFS compression is most effective when used on files that are not already compressed. Bitmap images, Microsoft Word documents, and database files are highly compressible. Because music files (in MP3 and WMA format) and JPEG or GIF images are already compressed, NTFS compression provides little benefit and incurs a noticeable performance hit. By all means, avoid compressing the folders that contain Windows system files and log files that the operating system uses regularly. The negative effect on performance is especially severe here.

Figure 25-5. You can compress a single file, a folder full of files, or an entire drive—but only on a drive formatted with NTFS.

To compress an entire volume at once, right-click the drive in Windows Explorer and follow the same procedure. You'll be asked to confirm that you really want to do this for every file in the volume. When you say yes, the system begins compressing files, one at a time. The process can take hours to complete; fortunately, it only needs to be done once. You can continue working while Windows is busy compressing files. If the system needs to compress an open file, you'll be notified with a dialog box. At that point, you can close the file in question and click Retry, or click Ignore or Ignore All.

Troubleshooting

When you select the encryption option, the compression button is cleared.

For security and performance reasons, encryption and compression are mutually exclusive attributes for files stored on an NTFS volume. If the file is compressed, it can't be encrypted, and vice versa. For more information about file encryption, see Chapter 14, "Encrypting Confidential Information."

(continued)

> **Troubleshooting** *(continued)*   If you need to combine compression with security, consider using password-protected Zip files, which offer good (but not great) encryption along with efficient compression capabilities. Use the third-party WinZip program (*http://www.winzip.com*) or the Compressed Folders feature in Windows XP (as described in "Using Zipped Folders," page 463).

When you compress a folder, that attribute affects files that you move or copy later, according to the following rules:

- If you create a new file in a compressed folder, the new file is compressed.

- If you copy a file into a compressed folder, the file is compressed.

- If you move a file from a different NTFS volume into a compressed folder, the file is compressed.

- If you move a file into a compressed folder on the same NTFS volume, the file retains whatever compression setting it had originally and is not automatically compressed.

- If you move a compressed file into an uncompressed folder on the same NTFS volume, the file retains the compressed attribute. However, if you move a compressed file to an uncompressed folder on a different NTFS partition, the file loses the compression attribute.

> **tip**   **Highlight compressed files**
>
> If you use on-the-fly compression, take advantage of an option in Windows Explorer that displays compressed files and folders in an alternate color. That way, you can see at a glance which files and folders are compressed. To verify that this feature is enabled, open Windows Explorer and choose Tools, Folder Options. On the View tab, make sure that Show Encrypted Or Compressed NTFS Files In Color is selected. By default, the names and other details of compressed files appear in blue within Windows Explorer.

Smart Backup Strategies

Hard disks are amazing yet fragile mechanical devices. Packed with ultra-miniature electronics that zoom along at thousands of revolutions per minute, it's no wonder that they fail more often than any other component in the average computer. When a disk crashes, it's usually impossible to recover your data without spending a small fortune at a data recovery service.

And even if your hardware never lets you down, human error can wreak havoc with data. You can press the wrong key and inadvertently delete a group of files you meant to move. If you're not paying attention, you might absentmindedly click the wrong button in a dialog box, saving a new file using the same name as an old one, wiping out an irreplaceable document in the process.

In any of those circumstances, you're almost certainly going to lose some data. When a hard disk crashes, for instance, all files you've created or saved since your last backup are gone for good. But you can avoid the worst data losses if you get into the habit of backing up regularly.

> One of our other books, *Microsoft Windows Security Inside Out for Windows XP and Windows 2000* (Microsoft Press, 2002), describes additional backup strategies and goes into much greater detail about methods for preventing data loss. Although the strategy recommended in that book (in short: use disk imaging software for periodic full backups and use the backup program included with Windows for frequent interim backups) relies on third-party software, it ends up being easier to use for many users in home and small business environments. A strategy that's easier to use is more likely to be used—an important benefit for a tedious, but essential, task such as backup.

Using the Windows XP Backup Program

Windows XP includes an enhanced version of the powerful Backup Utility (Ntbackup.exe) originally included with Windows 2000. This utility is installed by default on Windows XP Professional. Using this utility, you can back up all or part of the data on your computer's local drives and on shared network folders.

> **note** If you're running Windows XP Home Edition, you won't find Backup Utility on the Start menu or even in Add Or Remove Programs. It *is* included, though; you just need to know where to look. To install Backup Utility, you need your Windows XP Home Edition CD. Use Windows Explorer to open the Valueadd\Msft\Ntbackup folder, and then double-click Ntbackup.msi.
>
> If your computer came with only a "system recovery" CD instead of a full Windows CD, finding Ntbackup.msi is not as easy. Look on the CD that was furnished and on any additional hard disk partitions set up on your computer. Some manufacturers provide the Windows files more or less intact, whereas others embed them in compressed disk image files. (Compaq systems with Windows XP Home Edition pre-installed, for example, have Windows files stored within Drive Image files on drive D.) If you happen to have the disk imaging program that was used to create the disk image files, you can extract the Windows files you need.

Although the Backup Utility was originally designed for use on networks equipped with tape drives, the overwhelming majority of Windows users will choose the much simpler option of saving backup sets to a file, either on a second local drive, on a shared network folder, or on a high-capacity removable storage medium such as a Zip drive.

Chapter 25

---

tip   Back up to a CD

The Windows XP Backup Utility does not support backing up directly to CD recorders. However, if you plan your backups carefully you can accomplish the same goal in a two-step process. Back up to a file first, and then copy that backup file to a CD-R or CD-RW disk. If you need to restore data from your backup set, you can do so directly from the CD. For this procedure to work, you must ensure that you have enough free disk space to hold your backup files; you also have to plan your backups so that the resulting backup files will fit on a single CD, because the Backup Utility won't prompt you for multiple CDs, as it will with other removable media such as Zip drives. This might entail reorganizing your backup sets into two or more groups, with each one under 650 MB in size.

To start Backup Utility, run Ntbackup.exe from a command prompt, or choose the Backup shortcut from All Programs, Accessories, System Tools. The default view is a straightforward wizard that walks you through the backup process quickly and efficiently. Make sure you've logged on using an account in the Administrators group and then follow these steps:

1   After clicking past the Welcome screen, choose the Back Up File And Settings option and click Next.

2   The What To Back Up page, shown in Figure 25-6, presents the following four options.

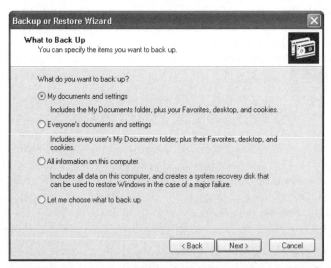

Figure 25-6.   The complete backup option can consume a frightful amount of disk space; for most Windows users, the top two options are adequate.

Chapter 25: Performing Routine Maintenance

- **My Documents And Settings.** The explanatory text is confusing; if you choose this option, you effectively back up your entire user profile, including the My Documents folder, the Application Data folder, and the contents of your desktop. This backup does not include any data stored outside your profile. (If you've moved the My Documents folder to a different location than its default, this option will not work properly. You must select the correct location manually, using the fourth option in this list.)

- **Everyone's Documents And Settings.** This option backs up all user data stored in individual profiles—in other words, the entire contents of the Documents And Settings folder.

- **All Information On This Computer.** This option backs up all data on all local drives and creates an Automated System Recovery disk (see the following section for a description of this option).

- **Let Me Choose What To Back Up.** Choosing this option lets you pick individual files, folders, and drives to back up.

3 Choose the fourth option and click Next to see the Items To Back Up page shown next. (You won't see this page if you select one of the other options.)

4 Select the check box next to each item you want to back up. Click Next to open the Backup Type, Destination, And Name page.

Part 7: System Maintenance and Recovery

5 Choose the backup type. On most systems, the File option is selected by default and no other options are available. If your system includes a tape drive that is compatible with Backup Utility, you can select it from the Select The Backup Type list. If you select a file as the destination (as most people will), select a local or network drive from the Choose A Place To Save Your Backup list and enter a name for the file. Click Next to continue.

6 On the Completing The Backup Or Restore Wizard page, you can click Finish to begin the backup immediately, or click the Advanced button to choose additional options.

Most of the Advanced options are self-explanatory. The most confusing option is the choice of five backup types:

● A *normal backup* backs up all selected files and clears their archive attributes (so that subsequent differential or incremental backups copy only those files that have changed since their normal backup).

● An *incremental backup* copies selected files that have changed since the most recent normal or incremental backup and clears these files' archive attributes. If you perform a normal (full) backup every Monday, you can perform an incremental backup on Tuesday through Friday. As part of each incremental backup, the Backup Utility will pick up only those files that have been changed since the last backup, which should take significantly less time than a full backup. In case of data loss, you would restore the normal backup and each succeeding incremental backup.

Chapter 25: Performing Routine Maintenance

- A *differential backup* copies selected files that have changed since the most recent normal or incremental backup but does not clear the files' archive attributes. Subsequent differential backups continue to copy all files that have changed since the most recent normal or incremental backup. If you perform a full backup on Monday and a differential backup on each succeeding day of the week, you could restore your data by using the full backup and the most recent differential backup.

- A *copy backup* copies all selected files but does not clear archive attributes. A copy backup is useful as a way of archiving particular files without affecting your overall backup routine.

- A *daily backup* copies all selected files that have changed on the current day, without clearing the files' archive attributes. This procedure represents a way of backing up a particular day's work without affecting the overall backup routine and is best used as part of a Scheduled Task that runs late at night, after you've quit work for the day.

---

note Backup Utility, like most backup programs, uses each file's archive attribute to determine whether to include the file in a backup. The archive attribute is a single bit in the file's directory entry. When a file is created or modified, its archive attribute is turned on. When a file is backed up using a normal or an incremental backup, the archive attribute is cleared. You can view (and set, if you like) the archive attribute for a file by right-clicking the file in Windows Explorer and choosing Properties. On the General tab, click the Advanced button; the first check box in the Advanced Attributes dialog box represents the archive attribute. On a FAT-formatted drive, the Archive check box appears on the General tab.

It's relatively easy to schedule backups so they occur effortlessly and automatically. When you complete the wizard, click the Advanced button and then click Next until you reach the When To Back Up page, where you're given the opportunity to schedule the job you just saved. Choose the Later option and enter a descriptive name for the combination of settings you just created and the schedule you're about to specify—My Documents Weekly Backup, for instance. Then click the Set Schedule button and choose the frequency, start time, and other settings for the scheduled backup, as shown on the next page.

Chapter 25

After setting the schedule, you'll need to enter and confirm the user name and password of an administrator account, and then click Finish to close the wizard. To review the backup task you've created, open Scheduled Tasks on the Control Panel.

Although we all hope we never have to deal with data loss, the law of averages says that sooner or later you'll have a disk crash. When that happens, reach for your backup disks and begin the restore process.

To restore data from a backup, start the Backup Utility in Wizard Mode and choose the Restore Files And Settings option. Follow the prompts to restore individual files or an entire backup set. At the conclusion of the wizard, click the Advanced button and choose one of the following three options from the Where To Restore page:

● **Original Location.** As the name implies, this option puts the files back in the same location as they were when you backed them up. This is the correct choice if you're restoring an entire backup set to a freshly formatted drive; if you're restoring a backup set to a drive that contains data, be careful that you don't inadvertently overwrite newer files with older ones from the backup. To avoid that potentially disastrous outcome, on the subsequent How To Restore page, specify Replace Existing Files If They Are Older Than The Backup Files.

- **Alternate Location.** Use this option to specify that you want to restore the specified files to a different location than where they were originally stored. After you finish restoring files, you can manually compare old and new files.

- **Single Folder.** Use this option when you're restoring just a few files from a backup set and you want them to be easy to find.

newfeature!

Creating an Automatic System Recovery Backup

The Backup program included with Windows XP Professional offers a new feature called Automated System Recovery (ASR). Don't be misled by the name: The procedure isn't fully automated, and it won't necessarily recover your entire system. In fact, the procedure requires a substantial amount of advance preparation, and its stated purpose is to restore your system partition in the event of a catastrophic failure. After you learn what ASR can and can't do, you can decide how you want to use this backup option or whether you want to rely on another solution.

> **caution** The Automated System Recovery feature is not available on systems running Windows XP Home Edition. Confusingly, Backup Utility allows you to create an ASR backup; however, because the option to restore this backup is not available, you're unable to use it properly.

Most people find out the hard way that Automated System Recovery works only if you prepare a complete backup in advance. Creating an ASR backup set saves the complete contents of your system drive to the backup media you select, such as a second physical disk, a network folder, or a tape drive. In addition, ASR saves information about your current arrangement of disk partitions, system files, and detected hardware, on a floppy disk. The combination can quickly and effectively restore your system configuration; however, it does not back up or restore data on drives other than the system volume. For that task, use the Backup Utility in Wizard Mode and choose the option to back up everything on the computer.

If you have a large amount of data on drives other than the system drive and you have an effective strategy to back up those files, you might decide to use the ASR Preparation Wizard to back up only the system drive. In that case, follow these steps:

1 Start the Backup Utility (Ntbackup.exe) in Advanced Mode. (If the utility starts in Wizard Mode, click the Advanced Mode link to switch views.)

2 On the Backup Utility Welcome screen shown next, click the Automated System Recovery Wizard button.

Part 7: System Maintenance and Recovery

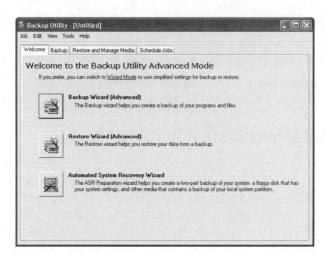

3 Click past the Welcome screen to display the Backup Destination dialog box, shown in Figure 25-7, and then choose where you want the backup file to be created.

Figure 25-7. If a compatible tape drive is available, you can select it from the Backup Media Type list. Otherwise, select a local folder or network drive as the destination.

Make sure the destination you select has at least enough room to hold all data on the system drive, minus the page file and hibernation file. Click Next to continue.

4 In the final page of the wizard, click the Finish button to begin backing up files from the system drive.

5 When prompted, insert a floppy disk to store the system recovery information.

InsideOut

At the time it begins saving a backup set, the Windows XP Backup Utility creates a "volume snapshot" using free disk space on any available NTFS drive. If you have sufficient space, you can continue to use the computer while a backup is in progress, and you don't need to close any open files. If your system is short on free space, however, Backup can't create the snapshot, and you may find that open files are not properly backed up.

Save the backup media and the recovery disk in a safe place. In the event of a catastrophic failure of your system partition, you can boot using the Windows XP CD, press F2 to run Automated System Recovery when prompted by Windows Setup, and then follow the prompts to restore your system.

Other Backup Software Options

The Windows XP Backup Utility is not your only option for safeguarding data. You can effectively use any combination of the following options as well, depending on your data, your hardware, and your personal preferences:

- **Files And Settings Transfer Wizard.** Although this utility was designed to move data and settings from an old machine to a new one, it makes a surprisingly effective backup tool as well. Follow the instructions outlined in "Saving Files and Settings to a Folder or Drive," page 55.

- **Compressed folders and other Zip utilities.** If you have a relatively modest amount of personal data, you might find it easier to zip the files using the built-in compressed folders feature or a third-party utility such as WinZip. You can then copy the resulting archive file to a safe location or to removable media.

- **Simple copies.** If you have plenty of disk space, you can open two copies of Windows Explorer and drag a folder from one location to another—to make a copy on a network drive, for instance. This option doesn't allow you to easily keep track of changed files, but it's uncomplicated.

- **Third-party file-syncing utilities.** Programs like LapLink's PCsync (*http://www.laplink.com*) and FileWare's FileSync (*http://www.fileware.com/*) allow you to set up mirror images of important data folders, typically on a network drive or an Internet-based server. The software keeps your local copy in sync with the network-based copy, replacing changed files and removing deleted files. If you inadvertently erase a local copy, or if a disk crash wipes out your local disk, you can recover your data from the network.

Chapter 26

Recovering After a Computer Crash

It's a fact of life: computers crash. Some computer crashes are unavoidable and unpredictable. An update to a software package that you've used successfully for ages might conflict with another program or with a device driver installed on your computer. If a speck of dust sneaks into a hard disk enclosure on your system, it can send your system files to never-never land. A stroke of lightning or an unexpected surge of electrical power can overwhelm a power supply, fry the sensitive traces on a motherboard, or scramble bits on a memory chip, rendering your system unstartable.

Occasionally, the flaw is within Windows itself. Despite lengthy and exhaustive testing, some bugs are inevitable in any complex operating system. The overwhelming majority of these glitches are minor annoyances, but, as Murphy's Law predicts, a few data-destroying software flaws are sure to sneak past the defenses and into a released version of Microsoft Windows. Fortunately, truly destructive Windows bugs are exceedingly rare, and when they're discovered, you can bet that a hotfix will be available via Windows Update in record time and that the same fix will be incorporated into the next Windows XP service pack.

So what do you do when your system stops working properly? Windows XP offers a wide assortment of tools you can use to find the cause of the problem and repair it quickly. Your first challenge is to figure out what caused the problem, so you can decide which tool to use.

893

At Home with Windows XP

Users of Windows XP Home Edition have access to all the same repair and recovery tools as users of Windows XP Professional. The only feature described in this chapter that is not available to Home Edition users is the ability to customize error reporting and Recovery Console using Group Policy.

After a Computer Crash: Assessing the Damage

Not every Windows crash is a catastrophe. That might be difficult to remember when you switch on your computer and are confronted by an ominous error message or a blank screen instead of the Windows logo. But if you analyze what caused your system to stop working properly, you have an excellent chance of recovering quickly and completely.

In some cases, the cause is easy to pinpoint. If you install a new scanner or update a video driver and your system hangs at a blank screen when you restart, you can safely bet that the new device or driver is to blame. Error messages sometimes point directly to a file that's causing a problem. Even without a smoking gun, you can use basic troubleshooting techniques to uncover the cause of a crash.

Windows XP provides a full assortment of troubleshooting and repair options. The circumstances and severity of the problem usually dictate which tool is most appropriate. In this chapter, we cover the following five options:

- **Safe Mode.** If Windows won't start normally, you may be able to reach the desktop by using one of three Safe Mode options available at startup. From Safe Mode, you can start and stop services, change computer settings, uninstall a program or driver that you suspect is causing your problems, or use the System Restore utility to roll back your configuration.

- **Last Known Good Configuration.** Veterans of Windows NT and Windows 2000 should be familiar with this option, which is available from the Advanced Options menu or by pressing F8 at startup. It lets you quickly reverse changes made to the CurrentControlSet registry key (which defines hardware and driver settings) since you last successfully started Windows.

- **System Restore.** This system recovery tool, a greatly improved version of a utility that debuted in Windows Me, is the next best thing to a time machine. At regular intervals, the System Restore utility takes a snapshot of your system files and settings, monitoring every change and storing compressed copies of original files in a protected location. If you can start Windows—normally or in Safe Mode—you may be able to use System Restore to undo the configuration change that's causing the problem.

- **Recovery Console.** If you're unable to boot into Safe Mode, this self-contained command-line environment is your last best hope. You can start from the Windows CD and choose the Repair option to start the Recovery Console. From the command line, you may be able to replace a corrupted file, delete a misbehaving driver file, or stop a service that's interfering with startup.

- **Reinstallation.** When all else fails, you may be able to repair serious problems by reinstalling Windows XP over your existing installation. With the right preparation (and a little luck), you can repair system files without disturbing your settings and preferences.

> A terrific tool for tracking down the cause of some sporadic, unexplained crashes is Driver Verifier Manager, which checks each device driver to see that it conforms to Windows standards. (Faulty drivers are responsible for many computer crashes.) For information about Driver Verifier Manager, see the Troubleshooting tip on page 199. You can find further details online at *http://www.microsoft.com/hwdev/driver/verifier.asp* and *http://www.compuware.co.jp/drivercentral/resources/win2k_driverver.asp*.

InsideOut

This chapter and Chapter 28, "Troubleshooting Windows Errors," deal primarily with operating system crashes—ones in which the entire system becomes unusable or, at the very least, unstable. Fortunately, such crashes are rare. A more likely occurrence in Windows is an application crash, in which a particular application locks up. Because Windows generally handles these crashes gracefully and displays explanatory messages (and because these crashes usually indicate a problem with the application and not with Windows itself), you won't find much discussion of application crashes in this book.

One of the things that Windows does when an application crashes is to display a message suggesting that you send an error report to Microsoft for analysis. (Microsoft engineers really do use this information for solving problems and for making improvements to Windows; sometimes an engineer follows up via e-mail to request more information or to offer a solution. In fact, a large number of the fixes in Service Pack 1 came as a result of submitted error reports.) If you'd rather not be bothered by the messages or if you're uncomfortable sending any information to Microsoft, you can disable the error reporting features.

To do that, right-click My Computer and choose Properties to display the System Properties dialog box. On the Advanced tab, click Error Reporting. In the Error Reporting dialog box, you can choose to disable the error reporting suggestion and, optionally, disable all notification of the error by clearing But Notify Me When Critical Errors Occur. (If you choose this route, a misbehaving application simply disappears from the screen without leaving a suicide note.) A middle-ground solution is also available: select Enable Error Reporting and then click Choose Programs to exclude reporting for certain programs.

(continued)

Inside Out *(continued)*

System Properties ? X

| System Restore | Automatic Updates | Remote |
| General | Computer Name | Hardware | Advanced |

Error Reporting ? X

You can choose to have software errors reported to Microsoft to help improve future products.

○ Disable error reporting
　☑ But notify me when critical errors occur

◉ Enable error reporting
　☑ Windows operating system
　☑ Programs　　[Choose Programs...]

[OK]　[Cancel]

[Environment Variables]　[Error Reporting]

[OK]　[Cancel]　[Apply]

Using Group Policy, you can fine-tune your error reporting options even more. (Group Policy is not available in Windows XP Home Edition.) To start Group Policy, at a command prompt type **gpedit.msc**. In Group Policy's console tree, open Computer Configuration\Administrative Templates\System\Error Reporting. The Display Error Notification policy determines whether the error message appears when an application crashes; select Enabled to display crash notifications, Disabled to suppress messages, or Not Configured to observe the setting in System Properties. (Group Policy settings override those you make through System Properties.)

The Report Errors policy works independently of the Display Error Notification policy. That is, you could configure your system to report errors to Microsoft without even displaying a notification and giving you an opportunity to opt out.

The policies in the Advanced Error Reporting folder let you specify which applications will generate error reporting notifications and which will not.

For more information about Group Policy, see Appendix E, "Group Policy."

Using Advanced Startup Options

When you experience problems at startup, you can choose from a similar set of options on two separate menus. From Windows XP Professional and Home Edition, you can access the Advanced Options menu, shown here, by pressing F8 at the menu that prompts you to choose an operating system. (If Windows starts without displaying a startup menu, press F8 after your system finishes displaying startup messages from the BIOS but before the Windows logo appears.)

```
Windows Advanced Options Menu
Please select an option:

    Safe Mode
    Safe Mode with Networking
    Safe Mode with Command Prompt

    Enable Boot Logging
    Enable VGA Mode
    Last Known Good Configuration (your most recent settings that worked)
    Directory Services Restore Mode (windows domain controllers only)
    Debugging Mode

    Start Windows Normally
    Reboot
    Return to OS Choices Menu

Use the up and down arrow keys to move the highlight to your choice.
```

If Windows hangs at startup, use the power switch or the reset button to restart your system. You should see the Startup Recovery menu, shown here, which offers most of the same troubleshooting options as the Advanced Options menu.

```
We apologize for the inconvenience, but Windows did not start successfully.  A
recent hardware or software change might have caused this.

If your computer stopped responding, restarted unexpectedly, or was
automatically shut down to protect your files and folders, choose Last Known
Good Configuration to revert to the most recent settings that worked.

If a previous startup attempt was interrupted due to a power failure or because
the Power or Reset button was pressed, or if you aren't sure what caused the
problem, choose Start Windows Normally.

    Safe Mode
    Safe Mode with Networking
    Safe Mode with Command Prompt

    Last Known Good Configuration (your most recent settings that worked)

    Start Windows Normally

Use the up and down arrow keys to move the highlight to your choice.
Seconds until Windows starts: 20
```

Using Safe Mode

As in previous Windows versions, Windows XP gives you the option to start your system in Safe Mode if you're unable to reliably start in normal mode. In Safe Mode, Windows uses only those services and drivers that are absolutely required to start your system. The operating system starts with a minimal set of drivers and services, using a generic video driver at a resolution of 640×480, with support for your keyboard, mouse, monitor, local storage, and default system services. In Safe Mode, Windows does not install support for audio devices and nonessential peripherals, including most devices connected via USB ports. (USB keyboards and mice may be used in Safe Mode only if your system BIOS includes the option to recognize and enable these devices.) In Safe Mode, Windows ignores all startup programs as well, whether they're specified in a startup group on the All Programs menu or in the registry.

> **note** Unlike previous Windows versions, the base video driver in Windows XP will display 24-bit color in Safe Mode; the 640×480 resolution, however, cannot be adjusted.

In Safe Mode, you can access most essential configuration tools, including Device Manager, System Restore, Registry Editor, and Backup. Virtually all Help And Support Center features are available in Safe Mode as well, with the noteworthy exception of the Group Policy features in Advanced System Information. You can use these tools to disable system services, device drivers, or startup applications that are preventing your computer from starting.

If Windows appears to work properly in Safe Mode, you can safely assume that there's no problem with the basic services. Use Device Manager, Driver Verifier Manager, and Event Viewer to try to figure out where the trouble lies. If you suspect that a newly installed device or program is the cause of the problem, you can remove the offending software while you're running in Safe Mode. Use Device Manager to uninstall or roll back a hardware driver; try the Add Or Remove Programs option in Control Panel to remove a program. Then try restarting the system normally to see whether that resolved the problem.

> For more details about working with device drivers, see "Managing Installed Drivers," page 215. For advice on the right way to remove a Windows program, see "Uninstalling Programs," page 186.

If you need access to network connections, choose the Safe Mode With Networking option, which loads the base set of Safe Mode files and adds drivers and services required to start Windows networking. Note that this option will do you no good on a portable computer with a PCMCIA (PC Card) network adapter, because PCMCIA peripherals are disabled in Safe Mode.

The third Safe Mode option, Safe Mode With Command Prompt, loads the same stripped-down set of services as in Safe Mode, but uses the Windows XP command interpreter (Cmd.exe) as a shell instead of the graphical Windows Explorer (Explorer.exe). This option is recommended only for diehard command-line aficionados.

---

tip   **Put Safe Mode on the menu**

If you routinely test hardware, software, and drivers that require you to switch into Safe Mode, you don't have to go through the hassle of pressing F8 at precisely the right time and choosing from the startup menu. Instead, add one or more Safe Mode options to the list of available operating systems that Windows displays at startup.

To install this option, follow these steps:

1 Right-click My Computer on the Start menu and choose Properties.

2 On the Advanced tab, click the Settings button in the Startup And Recovery section.

3 In the Startup And Recovery dialog box, click the Edit button to open Boot.ini in Notepad.

4 Under [Operating Systems], select the entire line that contains the settings for your default operating system choice and copy it to the bottom of the list.

5 Append the following set of switches to the end of the newly copied line:

`/safeboot:minimal /sos /bootlog`

(Replace *minimal* with *network* if you want the shortcut to start Windows in Safe Mode with networking.)

6 Change the description in quotation marks to "Windows XP Safe Mode" and then save the file.

Restoring the Last Known Good Configuration

Every time you successfully start Windows in normal mode, the operating system makes a record of all currently installed drivers and the contents of the registry key HKLM\SYSTEM\CurrentControlSet. This record comes in handy if you install a driver or make a hardware configuration change that causes your system to hang at startup. When Windows displays the Startup Recovery menu, you can choose the Last Known Good Configuration option. This menu choice restores the previous, working registry key, effectively removing the changes that are causing the problem.

In general, System Restore is a more reliable alternative than the Last Known Good Configuration menu choice, because it restores all Windows system files and the entire registry rather than just a single key.

> **caution** If you suspect that a driver change is causing system problems and you don't have a recent System Restore point to go back to, don't log on in normal mode. As soon as you log on in normal mode, Windows resets the Last Known Good Configuration information, effectively removing your safety net. If you suspect problems, start Windows in Safe Mode and do basic troubleshooting first. Logging on in Safe Mode does not update the Last Known Good Configuration information, so you can safely roll back to the Last Known Good Configuration if Safe Mode troubleshooting is unsuccessful.

Other Startup Options

Four additional choices on the Advanced Options menu are of use in specialized circumstances:

- **Enable Boot Logging.** When you select this option, Windows starts up normally and creates a log file that lists the names and status of all drivers loaded into memory. To view the contents of this file, look for Ntbtlog.txt in the %SystemRoot% folder. If your system is hanging because of a faulty driver, the last entry in this log file may identify the culprit.

- **Enable VGA Mode.** This option starts the computer in standard VGA mode using the current video driver (not the plain-vanilla Vga.sys driver used in Safe Mode). Use this option to recover from video problems that are caused not by a faulty driver but by incorrect settings, such as an improper resolution or refresh rate.

- **Directory Services Restore Mode.** Although this option appears on the Advanced Options menu for Windows XP Professional, it is only used with domain controllers running Windows 2000 Server or Windows .NET Server. Ignore it.

- **Debugging Mode.** This choice starts Windows XP in kernel debug mode. To take advantage of this capability, you must connect the system to another computer using a serial connection on COM2. The other computer must run a compatible debugger to perform troubleshooting and system analysis.

Undoing Configuration Mistakes with System Restore

System Restore is a Windows XP service that runs in the background, continually monitoring changes in files, folders, and settings that are essential to the correct operation of the operating system. At regular intervals, System Restore takes a "snapshot" of your system's registry as well. If you encounter a problem that causes Windows to become unstable, you can start the System Restore Wizard in normal or Safe Mode and roll back your system files and registry to those saved from a previous date—when, presumably, your system worked properly.

Chapter 26: Recovering After a Computer Crash

System Restore can't perform miracles, but it can be a lifesaver in the following situations:

- **You install a program that conflicts with other software or drivers on your system.** If uninstalling the program doesn't cure the problem, you can restore your system configuration to a point before you installed the program.

- **You install one or more updated drivers that cause performance or stability problems.** Rather than using the Driver Rollback feature from Device Manager, use System Restore to restore all previously installed drivers.

- **Your system developed performance or stability problems for no apparent reason.** This scenario is especially likely if you share a computer with other family members or coworkers who casually install untested, incompatible software and drivers. If you know the system was working properly on a certain date, you can use a restore point from that date or earlier and be reasonably confident that your system will return to proper operation.

> **caution** You cannot count on System Restore to protect you from viruses, worms, Trojan horse programs, and other malware. In fact, if your system contracts a virus, files stored in restore points created after that point might be infected also, and you run the risk of restoring the virus along with your system files. Use a reliable antivirus program, keep it up-to-date, and don't open e-mail attachments unless you're certain they're safe.

How System Restore Works

System Restore is a Windows XP service that runs automatically in the background, keeping a log of changes to file types defined in %SystemRoot%\System32\Restore\ Filelist.xml. At regular intervals, the System Restore service copies system files to hidden archives for safekeeping. In addition, the system takes regular snapshots of the *system state,* including information about user accounts, hardware and software settings, and files required for startup.

System Restore does *not* monitor the following files and folders:

- The page file (virtual memory) or hibernation file.

- Any files of any type stored in the following personal data folders: My Documents, Favorites, Cookies, Recycle Bin, Temporary Internet Files, History, and Temp.

- Image and graphics files, including bitmap and JPEG files, and files that use extensions commonly associated with data files, such as .doc, .xls, .mdb, and .pdf.

- E-mail files managed by Microsoft Outlook or Outlook Express.

InsideOut

Are you looking for a good reason to convert the drive that contains your Windows files from FAT32 to NTFS? System Restore takes full advantage of the NTFS file system in two ways: First, your backed-up files are protected from accidental deletion by NTFS permissions. The restore files are saved in the hidden System Volume Information folder, where only the System account is authorized to access them. On FAT32 volumes, by contrast, any user can undermine the effectiveness of System Restore by accidentally or deliberately deleting restore points. Second, the System Restore service uses NTFS compression to minimize the amount of space each restore point takes. This on-the-fly compression takes place in the background, when your system is idle, so it has no deleterious effect on performance.

Windows creates an initial restore point when you install or upgrade to Windows XP. You can create a restore point manually at any time. In addition, Windows XP creates restore points automatically whenever you take any of the following actions:

You install an unsigned device driver   When you attempt to install an unsigned hardware driver, Windows displays a warning message. If you choose to continue, the system creates a restore point before completing the installation. If the driver causes problems, you can use the System Restore Wizard to completely remove the driver.

For more details about driver signing, see "A Crash Course in Device Drivers," page 191.

You install an application using an installer that's compatible with System Restore   Applications that use Windows Installer (including Microsoft Office 2000 and Office XP) and InstallShield Professional version 6.1 or later fall into this category.

You install a Windows update or patch   Windows creates a restore point automatically whenever you download and install an update using Windows Update or the Automatic Updates feature.

You restore a prior configuration using System Restore   Each time you perform a restore operation, System Restore saves your current configuration, allowing you to undo the restore if necessary.

You restore data from a backup set created with the Windows XP Backup program   Each time you use the Backup program to restore files (in Advanced or Wizard mode), System Restore creates a restore point. If restoring the backed-up files causes problems with Windows system files, you can quickly restore a working configuration.

---

caution   Don't rely on System Restore to protect you from data loss or backup mistakes. Restoring a backed-up configuration can undo damage only to your Windows system files; a restore point does not protect data files. If you inadvertently delete working data files or overwrite them with out-of-date backup copies, you will not be able to recover your data files unless you have a recent backup set.

Finally, System Restore creates restore points at regular intervals, regardless of user activity: By default, System Restore creates a restore point every 24 hours if you leave your computer on. If you shut down your computer, the System Restore service creates a new restore point when you restart, if the most recent restore point was more than 24 hours ago.

---

tip   **Customize System Restore intervals**

System Restore settings and preferences are stored in the registry, in the key HKLM\SOFTWARE\Microsoft\WindowsNT\CurrentVersion\SystemRestore. Most of the values found here can be adjusted safely and easily using the System Restore tab of the System Properties dialog box. (For details, see "Configuring System Restore Options," page 78.) However, some settings can only be adjusted by editing the values stored in this registry key.

Normally, System Restore automatically creates restore points every 24 hours. To adjust this interval, change the value RPGlobalInterval from its default setting of 86,400 seconds (24 hours). Cut this figure in half, to 43,200, if you want to save restore points twice a day; triple it, to 259,200, if you want restore points created every three days.

By default System Restore deletes restore points after 90 days. To adjust this interval, change the value RPLifeInterval from its default setting of 7,776,000 seconds (90 days). A value of 2,592,000 seconds (30 days) should be sufficient.

Restoring a Previous System Configuration

To restore the system to a previous configuration, you must be logged on as a member of the Administrators group. Shut down all running programs and make sure that no other users are logged on to the machine (either in inactive local sessions or across the network) and then follow these steps:

1 From the Start menu, choose Help And Support.

2 In the Help And Support Center, under Pick A Task, click the Undo Changes To Your Computer With System Restore link.

3 In the Welcome To System Restore screen, shown on the next page, choose Restore My Computer To An Earlier Time and click Next.

Part 7: System Maintenance and Recovery

Choose the top option to restore a previous system configuration

The Undo option appears only after you've performed a restore operation

4 Select the restore point you want to use, based on the date and description, as shown here. Then click Next.

Descriptions identify automatic and manual restore points

Bold dates indicate saved restore points

Chapter 26: Recovering After a Computer Crash

5 On the Confirm Restore Point Selection page, verify the settings you've chosen. If everything is in order, click Next.

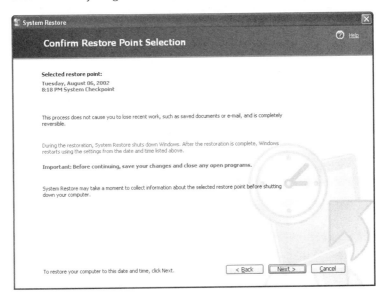

6 System Restore copies system files and settings from the System Restore archives and restarts your computer automatically. If the results are not what you expected, run System Restore again and then choose the Undo My Last Restoration option.

System Restore Dos and Don'ts

You don't have to be a science fiction fan to appreciate the potential for problems with time travel. In the case of System Restore, sending your system back in time may change more than you bargained for:

- If you create a new user account and then use System Restore to roll back your system configuration to a point before the new account was created, that user will no longer be able to log on, and you will receive no warning. (The good news is that System Restore does not wipe out data files, so if the new user created any data files, they'll still be intact.)

- If you change your computer or workgroup name or domain membership and then perform a restore operation that takes you back to a time before the change was effective, Windows warns you that you may lose access to some network resources. After the restore operation, you might need to change the name of the computer or workgroup.

Part 7: System Maintenance and Recovery

- System Restore does not uninstall programs, although it does remove executable files and DLLs. To avoid having "orphaned" program shortcuts and files, make a note of any programs that you installed after the date of the restore point you're about to roll back to. If you don't want the program anymore, uninstall it before running the restore operation. If you want to continue using the program, reinstall it after the restore is complete.

- If you use Recovery Console to make any changes to your system configuration, those changes are not monitored by System Restore. This can produce unintended consequences if you make major changes to system files and then roll back your system configuration with System Restore.

- If you upgrade from Windows Me to Windows XP or from Windows XP Home Edition to Windows XP Professional, all your existing restore points will be wiped out.

- Although you can restore your system to a previous configuration from Safe Mode, you cannot create a new restore point in Safe Mode. As a result, you cannot undo a restore operation that you perform in Safe Mode. If possible, you should always start Windows in normal mode to perform a restore operation.

- When you install a service pack, you can save or reset restore points. If you choose the reset option, all existing restore points are lost and System Restore uses the new configuration as the baseline for future restore points.

- You cannot shut down System Restore temporarily. If you use Control Panel to stop monitoring one or more drives, Windows deletes all saved restore points on the selected drives. If you then reenable System Restore monitoring, the deleted restore points are not re-created.

For more details about changing the way System Restore works, see "Configuring System Restore Options," page 78.

Chapter 26: Recovering After a Computer Crash

Making Repairs from the Recovery Console

What do you do if you can't start Windows in normal or Safe Mode? Don't give up hope. You may be able to get back to work by using the Recovery Console, a stripped-down command-line environment that provides a limited set of tools you can use to diagnose and repair problems. The Recovery Console is not for the faint of heart. But if you're experienced with working outside a graphical environment, it can be tremendously useful.

The chief advantage of the Recovery Console over Safe Mode is that it works even when your Windows system files are corrupted. Using the Recovery Console, you can perform any of the following tasks:

- Use, copy, rename, or replace Windows system files and folders
- Enable or disable services or devices (these changes take effect the next time you start Windows)
- Repair the file system boot sector or the Master Boot Record (MBR)
- Rebuild or repair the Windows boot menu
- Create and format drives

To start the Recovery Console from the Windows CD, follow these steps:

1 Insert the Windows CD and restart your computer. Follow your computer's prompts to start from the CD. (You may need to adjust settings in the computer's BIOS to enable the option to start from a CD.)

2 Follow the setup prompts to load the basic Windows startup files. At the Welcome To Setup screen, press *R* to start the Recovery Console.

3 If you have multiple options on the Windows startup menu, enter the number of the Windows installation you want to access from the Recovery Console.

caution   If you have only a single Windows installation to choose from, you might be tempted to just press Enter here. Don't do it. You must type the number of the Windows installation to start the Recovery Console. If you press Enter, Windows restarts. Also, resist the temptation to select the entry for another Windows version from this menu. Although the Recovery Console automatically detects Windows 2000 and Windows NT installations on multiboot systems, logging on to one of these operating systems is not recommended, because you risk damaging the earlier operating system's core files if you perform any repairs. To repair installations of Windows 2000, use the Recovery Console from that operating system version. To repair a Windows NT installation, use the Windows NT Emergency Repair Disk.

4 When prompted, type the Administrator password. If you're using the Recovery Console on a system running Windows XP Home Edition, this password is blank by default, so just press Enter.

5 At the command prompt, enter Recovery Console commands directly.

6 To quit the Recovery Console and restart the computer, use the Exit command.

---

tip   **Add the Recovery Console to the startup menu**

With a modest amount of advance preparation, you can add the Recovery Console to the Windows XP boot menu. In this configuration, the Recovery Console files are stored on the same drive that holds your Windows system files, and you don't need to hassle with BIOS options or boot CDs to recover from serious problems. You'll find step-by-step instructions for configuring this option in "Adding the Recovery Console," page 87.

Recovery Console Restrictions

Although the Recovery Console prompt looks identical to the command prompt that you're familiar with from MS-DOS or the Windows XP command interpreter (Cmd.exe), it's not the same. After logging on to the Recovery Console, your actions are severely limited. You may access files only in the following locations:

● The root directory of any volume.

● The %SystemRoot% folder and subfolders of the selected Windows XP installation. On a typical clean setup or an upgrade from Windows 98 or Windows Me, this is usually C:\Windows.

● The Recovery Console Cmdcons folder and any subfolders (if you installed the Recovery Console as a startup option).

● Files and folders on removable disks, including floppy disks, CDs, and Zip disks.

---

note   In addition to these security-based restrictions, technical limitations impose additional restrictions on Windows XP Professional systems that use dynamic disks. If your system is configured with one or more dynamic disks, see Knowledge Base article Q227364, "Dynamic Volumes Are Not Displayed Accurately in Text-Mode Setup or Recovery Console."

If the Recovery Console allowed unlimited access to files and folders on your hard disk, it would pose a serious security hole, especially on systems running Windows XP Home

Edition, where the Administrator password is blank. To prevent unauthorized access, the Recovery Console imposes the following limits on your actions when you log on:

- If you try to access folders other than those described in the previous list, you will receive an "access denied" message. Specifically, you cannot read from or write to the following folders: Program Files, Documents And Settings, and disks or folders containing other Windows installations. These restrictions apply on NTFS and FAT32 volumes alike.

- Write access to removable disks is disabled. This prevents you from copying files to floppy disks and other removable media. If you try to copy a file to a removable disk, you receive an "access denied" message.

- You cannot change the local Administrator account password from the Recovery Console. In fact, if you use Windows XP Home Edition you have to jump through several hoops to add a password to the local Administrator account at all, as explained in "Securing the Administrator Account," page 119.

- No text editing tools are available in the Recovery Console.

Using Recovery Console Commands

After you've logged on to Recovery Console, you can type **help** to see a list of all available commands. Type **help** *commandname* or use the /? switch after a command name to learn its syntax. Although many of Recovery Console's commands are similar to those used in the Windows XP command interpreter (Cmd.exe) and its MS-DOS predecessor (Command.com), the Recovery Console versions of each command typically offer fewer options (switches). Also, unless you tweak the Recovery Console environment as outlined in "Customizing the Recovery Console" on page 911, these commands do not accept wildcard specifications.

Table 26-1 summarizes the commands available from the Recovery Console prompt.

Table 26-1. **Recovery Console Commands**

Command	Effect
Attrib	Sets or clears attributes (Read Only, Hidden, System) for a single file or folder
Batch	Executes commands from a text file
Bootcfg	Automatically scans all local disks for Windows installations and configures and repairs entries in the operating system menu (Boot.ini)
Cd or Chdir	Changes folders

(continued)

Table 26-1. *(continued)*

Command	Effect
Chkdsk	Checks and, if needed, repairs or recovers a drive; marks bad sectors and recovers readable information; requires that the Autochk.exe command be located in the %SystemRoot%\System32 folder or on the Windows CD
Cls	Clears the screen
Copy	Copies a file
Del or Delete	Deletes a single file
Dir	Displays folder contents and attributes for all files in the specified folder, including hidden and system files
Disable	Disables a service or driver
Diskpart	Manages the partitions on basic disk volumes; note that this command is not the same as the one available at a normal command prompt and should never be used with dynamic disks
Enable	Enables a service or driver
Exit	Closes the Recovery Console and restarts the computer
Expand	Extracts a file from a compressed (.cab) file on a local disk or removable media such as the Windows CD
Fixboot	Writes a new partition boot sector onto the partition you specify
Fixmbr	Repairs the Master Boot Record of the specified disk, usually the system partition
Format	Formats a primary partition, volume, or logical drive using the file system you specify
Help	Displays a list of all available commands
Listsvc	Lists all available services and drivers and their current start types
Logon	Lists all detected installations of Windows XP, Windows 2000, and Windows NT and allows you to choose which installation you want to log on to; if you type an incorrect password three times, the system restarts
Map	Lists drive letters, file system types, partition sizes, and mappings to physical devices; intended for use with basic disks only and may return inaccurate information when used with dynamic disks

Table 26-1. *(continued)*

Command	Effect
Md or Mkdir	Creates a new folder or subfolder in the specified location
More	Displays a text file, pausing at each screenful; use the Enter key and the spacebar to scroll through a file one line at a time and one screen at a time, respectively
Rd or Rmdir	Removes a folder
Ren or Rename	Renames a file
Set	Displays or modifies Recovery Console environment variables (for details on the usage of this command, see "Customizing the Recovery Console," below)
Systemroot	Sets the current folder to the %SystemRoot% folder of the current Windows installation
Type	Displays a text file

Chapter 26

Customizing the Recovery Console

With a little advance preparation, you can overcome at least some of the Recovery Console limitations listed here when running Windows XP Professional (this technique will not work with Home Edition). Doing so requires that you use the Set command to change system variables in the Recovery Console environment. By default, the Set command is disabled. To enable it, you must change system settings using the Group Policy tool. After logging on as an administrator, follow these steps:

1 From any command prompt, type **gpedit.msc** to open the Group Policy editor.

2 In the console tree, select Local Computer Policy\Computer Configuration\ Windows Settings\Security Settings\Local Policies\Security Options.

3 In the list of policies on the right, double-click the entry for Recovery Console: Allow Floppy Copy And Access To All Drives And All Folders.

4 Select the Enabled option and then click OK.

After enabling this policy, you can start the Recovery Console, log on with the local Administrator password, and use any of the following commands to expand your

(continued)

Customizing the Recovery Console (continued)

capabilities: Note that the space around the equal signs is required. (To see the current settings for all four parameters, type **set** and press Enter.)

Set allowwildcards = true   Allows you to use the * and ? wildcards with Recovery Console commands.

Set allowallpaths = true   Permits you to use the Cd command to list files and subfolders in all folders on all local disks.

Set allowremovablemedia = true   Allows you to copy files from local drives to removable media.

Set nocopyprompt = true   Eliminates the warning message that appears when you copy one or more files that overwrite existing files using Recovery Console commands.

Repairing Damaged Boot Files

The most common cause of problems with boot files is the improper use of third-party disk utilities or failed attempts to create a multiboot system. If the setup program for another operating system is incompatible with Windows XP, it might overwrite or damage essential startup files. The following are repair techniques available from the Recovery Console for common problems:

The Boot.ini file is corrupt or missing   From the Recovery Console, type **bootcfg /scan** to list all available Windows installations on all available disks. Use **bootcfg /rebuild** to automatically replace the existing Boot.ini file; use **bootcfg /add** to append a Windows installation to Boot.ini without changing existing entries.

Critical system files are damaged or missing   You can restore Ntldr, Ntoskrnl.exe, Ntdetect.com, and driver files from the Recovery Console. If the file exists on the Windows CD, use the Copy command and enter the source and destination; Windows expands compressed files automatically. If the file is stored within a .cab file, such as Driver.cab, use the Expand command.

Another operating system replaced the Windows XP boot sector code   Start Recovery Console from the Windows CD and use the Fixboot command to rewrite the boot sector code. Restart your computer.

Enabling and Disabling Services and Drivers

Because services operate at a privileged level alongside crucial operating system components, it's possible for a poorly written third-party service to crash your system. Likewise, buggy hardware drivers can interfere with startup, in some cases so severely that you encounter Stop messages even when attempting to start in Safe Mode. If you suspect that a hardware driver or a service such as an antivirus scanner or a remote-control utility is causing your problems and you can't start Windows even in Safe Mode, use these three Recovery Console options to identify the offending service and enable or disable it:

Listsvc   Enter this command to display a complete list of all services and drivers on your system, along with their current status and any optional comments. This list is long and not exactly packed with helpful information. You might need to scroll through many screens and look carefully to identify the driver or service in question. It may help if you have documentation from the developer of the suspect driver or service that lists the names of specific driver and service files.

Disable   Enter this command followed by the name of the service or driver you want to stop and press Enter. The Disable command sets the start type of the service to SERVICE_DISABLED. Before doing so, it displays the current start type value of the service: SERVICE_BOOT_START, SERVICE_SYSTEM_START, SERVICE_AUTO_START, or SERVICE_DEMAND_START. Make a note of this value so that you can re-enable the device or service properly if necessary.

Enable   If after troubleshooting you determine that the device you disabled is not causing your problem, use this command, followed by the service or device name and the start type value you noted when you disabled the service or device.

Repairing and Reinstalling Windows

When all attempts to repair your system fail, you may be able to repair your Windows XP installation using the Windows Setup program. As a last resort, you can reinstall Windows over an existing installation and hope that the new installation will recover enough of your old settings to allow you to retrieve your data files.

The repair option is quick and painless and typically does not adversely affect user settings. To exercise this option, start from the Windows CD as if you were going to do a clean install. It's easy to become confused during this process, because the word *repair* appears in two different places when you start your computer using the Windows CD. At the Welcome To Setup screen, do not choose the option to repair your installation using the Recovery Console. Instead, press Enter, which starts the Windows Setup program. After you accept the license agreement, Windows searches your system for existing Windows installations. When you reach the screen that lists your current Windows installation, select it from the list and press *R* to start the repair process. The remainder of this procedure requires the same steps as if you were performing a clean installation; when Setup finishes, your system files should be refreshed and your existing data and settings should be accessible again.

In cases of severe disk damage or registry corruption, a repair installation will not be effective; the only alternative is to reformat the disk and install a clean copy of Windows.

Chapter 27

Managing Disks and Drives

When you get right down to it, storage defines what you can and can't do with Microsoft Windows XP. A big hard disk (or two or three) makes it possible for you to download digital media and manage it effectively. By subdividing hard disks intelligently, you can keep data and programs organized, making it easier to find data and back up copies of important files. Windows XP includes built-in support for removable media, too, most notably recordable CD drives, which you can use to create custom music CDs and data backups with relative ease.

If you've mastered hard-disk setup utilities from Windows 98 and Windows Me, prepare to unlearn everything you know. Windows XP offers new capabilities and a new set of tools. When you set up a new hard disk, you have some important decisions to make: How many partitions will you create? Do you need to combine space from multiple physical disks into a single volume? Which file system will you use to format drives? And how can you configure the built-in CD writing capability of Windows XP so that it works smoothly every time?

Hard Disk Management 101

What appears in My Computer to be a hard disk drive might or might not correlate to a single physical device. A single physical device can be subdivided into partitions, volumes, or logical drives—each appearing in My Computer as a separate drive letter. Conversely, in Windows XP (as in Windows 2000), you can combine storage space from several physical devices so that it appears as a single drive letter.

At Home with Windows XP

For the most part, disks and drives in all their permutations work the same way in both versions of Windows XP. However, computers running Windows XP Home Edition can't use dynamic disks, one of two types of disk structures. Therefore, Home Edition users can't use simple volumes, striped volumes, or spanned volumes—volume types that are available only on dynamic disks.

We mention in passing one other Professional-only feature in this chapter: file encryption. We describe that feature in depth in Chapter 14, "Encrypting Confidential Information"—but Home Edition users can save a trip to that chapter.

This chapter explains how to disable AutoPlay. The procedure is different depending on which version of Windows XP you have (we describe both), but the end result is the same.

Let's define the terms used in this chapter:

- A *disk* (or *hard disk*) refers to a physical disk drive installed in your computer. Your computer's first hard disk is identified as Disk 0. If you have additional hard disks installed, they're identified as Disk 1, Disk 2, and so on. As we'll explain in the next section, Windows XP Professional allows you to define a physical disk as a basic disk or dynamic disk, with different tools and capabilities for each one.

- A *basic disk* is a disk that is divided into one or more partitions. A *partition* is a portion of a physical disk that functions as if it were itself a physically separate disk. A *primary partition* is one that can be used for starting Windows (and other operating systems). A primary partition cannot be further subdivided. An *extended partition* can be further divided into one or more *logical drives,* each of which can be formatted separately and assigned its own drive letter.

- When a partition or logical drive is formatted for a particular file system (FAT, FAT32, or NTFS) and assigned a drive letter, it's called a *volume*. A volume appears in My Computer as a local disk.

- Whereas basic disks contain only basic volumes (that is, formatted primary partitions or logical drives), *dynamic disks* contain volumes that can be simple, spanned, or striped, with these last two types combining space from multiple dynamic disks. Unlike basic volumes, dynamic volumes can be resized.

> **note** If you use Windows XP Home Edition, or if you're running Windows XP Professional on a portable computer, you cannot create or use dynamic disks.

Windows XP includes a utility called Disk Management that provides virtually every tool you'll need to manage disks, partitions, volumes, and logical drives. The Disk

Active, System, and Boot Partitions

Three technical terms can confuse anyone who isn't thoroughly experienced with the ways in which Windows XP works with partitions.

The active partition on a basic disk is the one from which an x86-based computer boots. On these machines, one primary partition—the one containing the files needed for startup—must be marked active for the computer to start itself and an operating system. The active partition must always be on the first hard disk attached to the system (Disk 0).

If you use Windows XP exclusively, or if you use any combination of Windows XP and Windows 2000, Windows NT, Windows 95/98/Me, or MS-DOS, you do not have to change the active partition. In fact, this option will be unavailable from the Disk Management menu in this type of configuration. If you use another operating system, such as Linux or OS/2, you must mark its system partition as active and reboot in order to use the alternate operating system. If your system contains a drive (including a removable drive) that is capable of starting another operating system, you will see the Active label alongside its status in the Disk Management window.

The system partition is the one that contains the bootstrap files that Windows XP uses to start your system and display the boot menu. On the overwhelming majority of computers, this is the first primary partition on Disk 0, which is identified as drive C. The System label appears in the graphical view in the Disk management window alongside the status indicator for that drive.

The boot partition is the partition where the Windows system files are located. On most systems, this is the same as the system partition. On a multiboot system, where drive C contains files from an earlier Windows version and you've installed Windows XP to drive D or drive E, the boot partition is identified as such in the Disk Management window. (And yes, we know that it makes no sense for the system files to be on the boot partition and the boot files to be on the system partition. However, this counterintuitive nomenclature has been a part of the Windows NT family since the very earliest days and isn't likely to change any time soon. So make a mental note of these two terms and you won't be confused.)

Part 7: System Maintenance and Recovery

Management utility is a Microsoft Management Console (MMC) snap-in, and it can be accessed in either of the following ways:

- At any command prompt, enter **diskmgmt.msc**.

- Right-click the My Computer icon on the Start menu, choose Manage, and then select Disk Management from the console pane on the left side of the Computer Management window.

As Figure 27-1 shows, Disk Management provides a wealth of information about physical disks and the volumes, partitions, and logical drives in place on those disks. You can use this utility to perform virtually any disk-related task.

Figure 27-1. Use the Disk Management utility to gather information about and manage hard disks and removable disks.

If you've upgraded to Windows XP from Windows 2000, the Disk Management utility will be refreshingly familiar; the only changes are a few minor improvements to various wizards. If you've recently upgraded from Windows 98 or Windows Me, however, this set of tools will be as welcome as a breath of fresh air. Instead of the ancient and arcane Fdisk and the command-line Format utility, you can use this sleek graphical tool to perform any of the following tasks:

- Check the size, file system, status, and other properties of disks and volumes

- Create partitions, logical drives, and volumes

Chapter 27: Managing Disks and Drives

- Format volumes

- Delete partitions, logical drives, and volumes

- Assign drive letters to hard disk volumes, removable disk drives, and CD-ROM drives

- Create mounted drives

- Convert basic disks to dynamic disks, and vice versa

- Create spanned volumes and striped volumes, which combine storage space from two or more disks into a single drive letter

- Extend volumes to increase the size of a drive using free space from the same disk or another disk in the same system

For the most part, when you make changes to your disk configuration with the Disk Management utility you don't need to restart your computer. With tasks that are potentially destructive, such as deleting a partition or formatting a drive, you'll still have to click through one or two "Are you sure?" messages. But after you give your assent, Disk Management makes the changes immediately.

Some of these disk management tasks also apply to removable disks (such as Zip disks and CDs). For example, you can use Disk Management to format a Zip disk (although there's no particular reason to, because you can also format from other programs that you're more likely to have open: Windows Explorer or a command prompt). More important, you use Disk Management to assign drive letters (or drive paths for mounted drives, if you prefer) for all types of drives—a task you can't perform elsewhere.

> **note** On workstations that use 64-bit processors such as Intel's Itanium and the 64-bit version of Windows XP, Disk Management allows you to work with disks that are formatted using the GUID partition table (GPT) instead of the Master Boot Record (MBR). The basic tools for working with GPT disks are the same as those used with MBR disks, but there are some important and subtle technical differences in the newer format. For an excellent overview, search in the Help And Support Center for the "GUID partition table" topic.

newfeature! In addition, two command-line tools are brand new to Windows XP:

- **Fsutil.** This utility (presumably, the name means *file system utility*) is designed for support professionals and allows you to find files by security identifier (SID), change the short name of a file, and perform other esoteric tasks.

- **Diskpart.** This utility is actually a console application that allows you to manage disks, partitions, and volumes from a command prompt. When you run the Diskpart command, it opens a console window and dumps you at the DISKPART> prompt. If you type **Help** and press Enter, you see a screen that lists all available commands, like the one shown here.

caution These command-line tools are indisputably powerful, but they're not for the faint of heart or for casual experimentation. Both are documented thoroughly in online Help and are intended primarily to be incorporated into scripts rather than for interactive use. The Diskpart command in particular is dense and cryptic, with a complex command structure that requires you to list and select objects before you can act on them. Diskpart provides a superset of the commands available through Disk Management. Disk Management offers only those capabilities that are generally safe, whereas Diskpart also provides options that, while necessary in some instances, can destroy your data. Therefore, all but the most expert Windows users should stick with the graphical tool whenever possible. For detailed information about Diskpart, see Knowledge Base article Q300415, "A Description of the Diskpart Command-Line Utility."

NTFS or FAT32: Which Disk Format Should You Choose?

The single most important disk decision you have to make on a Windows XP system is which file system to choose for each drive or volume. On a clean install, you face this choice during Windows Setup; on an upgrade from Windows 98 or Windows Me, Setup lets you choose whether to convert the file system used on your existing drive. And you face the issue all over again if you repartition an existing drive or add a second (or third or fourth) drive to an existing system.

File-system choices available to you depend on the size of the partition or volume you create. Most of the time, the choice comes down to NTFS or FAT32. On drives that are less than 4 GB in size, the 16-bit version of the FAT file system is also an option.

> **tip** **Avoid FAT16**
>
> The 16-bit FAT file format exists in Windows XP for backward compatibility purposes only. Because it was designed in an era when hard disks were dramatically smaller, it's woefully inadequate on modern systems. In the modern era, FAT16 is appropriate for floppy disks and very small hard-disk partitions only. If you must use a FAT16 partition for compatibility reasons, try to keep its size under 511 MB.

Which file system should you choose? There's no right or wrong answer. NTFS has significant advantages in reliability, security, and flexibility, but in some system configurations FAT32 is a better choice. Make your decision based on the following factors and how they apply to your needs:

- **Compatibility.** Windows 95/98/Me cannot recognize NTFS volumes. On multiboot systems, it's essential that you use FAT32 for any local drives that you want to access when you boot the system using Windows 95, Windows 98, or Windows Me. Note that this restriction does not apply to network access. Assuming you've set up sharing properly, other network users can access your shared folders from computers running any other version of Windows, regardless of the local disk format.

- **Security.** On an NTFS volume, you can restrict access to files and folders using permissions, as described in "Controlling Access with NTFS Permissions," page 507. With Windows XP Professional, you can add an extra layer of protection by encrypting files. On a FAT or FAT32 drive, anyone with physical access to your computer can access any files stored on that drive.

- **Reliability.** By design, an NTFS volume can recover from disk errors more readily than an otherwise identical FAT/FAT32 drive. NTFS uses log files to keep track of all disk activity. In the event of a system crash, Windows XP can use this journal to repair file system errors automatically when the system is restarted. In addition, NTFS can dynamically remap clusters that contain bad sectors and mark those clusters as bad so that the operating system no longer uses it. FAT and FAT32 drives are more vulnerable to disk errors.

- **Expandability.** Using NTFS-formatted volumes, you can expand storage on existing drive letters without having to back up, repartition, reformat, and restore.

- **Efficiency.** On partitions greater than 8 GB in size, NTFS volumes manage space more efficiently than FAT32. The maximum partition size for a FAT32 drive created by Windows XP is 32 GB; by contrast, you can create a single NTFS volume of up to 16 terabytes (16,384 GB) using default settings, and by tweaking cluster sizes, you can ratchet the maximum volume size up to 256 terabytes.

---

tip **Use Fdisk for extra-large FAT32 drives**

Most of the time, it's better to use the Disk Management utility to manage partitions you plan to use with Windows XP. However, under one specific circumstance, you might want to prepare a disk using the tools from Windows 98 or Windows Me instead. Windows XP cannot create or format a FAT32 partition greater than 32 GB in size, but the Fdisk utility from those earlier Windows versions can. Boot from a startup disk prepared by either of those operating systems and use Fdisk to create the partition. After formatting the extra-large FAT32 partition using the Windows 98/Me Format command, restart Windows XP.

To view information about the file system currently used for a given drive or volume, right-click the drive icon in the My Computer window or the volume in the Disk Management window and choose Properties. As Figure 27-2 shows, the file system information appears prominently.

Figure 27-2. This dialog box tells you whether the drive is formatted with NTFS or FAT32.

Converting a FAT32 Disk to NTFS

To convert a FAT or FAT32 disk to NTFS format, use the command-line Convert utility. This utility uses the following syntax:

```
convert d: /fs:ntfs
```

where *d* is the drive letter you want to convert.

Chapter 27: Managing Disks and Drives

The Convert utility can do its work within Windows if the drive to be converted is not in use. However, if you want to convert the system volume or a volume that holds a page file, you might see an error message when you run the Convert utility. In that case, you must schedule the conversion to occur the next time you start Windows. After you restart the computer, you'll see a prompt that warns you that the conversion is about to begin. You have 10 seconds to cancel the conversion. If you allow it to proceed, Windows will run the Check Disk utility and perform the conversion automatically. During this process, your computer will restart twice.

caution Converting your system drive to NTFS makes it impossible to restore your previous operating system, a fact the Convert utility warns you about in no uncertain terms. If you have set up your system using a multiboot configuration so that you can continue to run Windows 95, Windows 98, or Windows Me, do not convert the system drive to NTFS; doing so will make it impossible to start your previous Windows version.

To improve your system's performance, run the Convert command with the /Cvtarea switch. This allows the master file table (MFT), the index of all files and folders on the selected volume, to be created in a single space, rather than being fragmented. Although the Windows XP Disk Defragmenter utility can work with the MFT, it cannot move the first fragment. This limitation practically guarantees that the MFT will be fragmented, unless you follow these steps as part of the NTFS conversion:

1 Use the Windows XP Disk Defragmenter to defragment the drive you plan to convert and consolidate free space on the drive. (For details, see "Defragmenting Disks for Better Performance," page 870.)

2 Calculate the size of the MFT to be created. The default size of the MFT equals 12.5 percent of the partition size. Thus, on a 10 GB partition, the MFT should be approximately 1.25 GB. If your partition is larger than 40 GB, use 4 GB as the MFT size.

note In the next step, you'll create a file of this calculated size. Because the drive hasn't yet been converted to NTFS, you're constrained by the limitations of FAT drives, which can't have a file larger than 4 GB.

3 Use the Fsutil command to create a new contiguous placeholder file equal in size to the MFT you want to create. This file must be created in the root of the drive to be converted. For this example, issue the following command:

```
fsutil file createnew c:\testfile.txt 1250000000
```

You can use any legal file name. For the final parameter, substitute the proper size for the placeholder file, in bytes.

Chapter 27

4   Run the Convert command, using the following syntax:

```
convert c: /fs:ntfs /cvtarea:testfile.txt
```

Substitute the correct drive letter as necessary.

5   If necessary, restart your system to complete the conversion.

InsideOut

With Windows 2000, converting a FAT32 system volume to NTFS entailed several trade-offs, most notably a reduced level of security, because the Convert utility in Windows 2000 does not adjust default security attributes as the Windows Setup program does. The Windows XP version of the Convert utility (Convert.exe) fixes this deficiency. When you convert a FAT or FAT32 drive under Windows XP, the Convert utility automatically applies the correct default permissions to all system folders. As long as you use the /Cvtarea switch to prevent fragmentation of the master file table, there's no fundamental difference in Windows XP between a converted NTFS volume and one that's created during Setup.

Basic and Dynamic Disks

As we mentioned in passing at the beginning of this chapter, Windows XP Professional supports two types of disk structures: basic disks and dynamic disks.

A basic disk is a physical disk that contains primary partitions, extended partitions, and logical drives. This is the same disk structure that has been used by all versions of MS-DOS, Windows 95/98/Me, and Windows NT 4. The partition table—which stores information about the number, type, and placement of partitions on the disk—is located in a 64-byte section of the Master Boot Record (MBR), the first sector on the disk. On a basic disk, you can create a maximum of four partitions, which can include one extended partition. Within an extended partition, you can create multiple logical drives, which are the familiar drive structures that appear in Windows Explorer as drive D, drive E, and so on.

A dynamic disk is a physical disk that contains one or more dynamic volumes, which are similar to partitions on a basic disk. Dynamic disks were introduced in Windows 2000 and are incompatible with earlier Microsoft operating systems. A dynamic disk does not have an MBR; instead, it maintains information about the layout of disk volumes in a database stored on the last 1 MB of the disk. When you create partitions using Windows XP (or Windows 2000), the operating system never uses the full space; instead, it reserves 8 MB for the dynamic disk database, so that you can convert a FAT32 disk later. Dynamic disks offer the following advantages:

● You can create an unlimited number of volumes on a disk. In this respect, a dynamic disk is like an extended partition on a basic disk, where you can create an unlimited number of logical drives. However, unlike a logical drive, a simple volume on a dynamic disk can be used as a system partition and can be extended.

● Dynamic disks allow you to combine physical disks in interesting ways. You can extend an existing volume, for instance. If you've created a 30-GB drive D on a dynamic disk for storing your data files and you add a new 60-GB physical disk to your system, you can extend that existing 30-GB volume using all or part of the new disk, effectively creating a 90-GB drive D, without requiring you to back up or restore data or change drive letters. This sort of disk structure is called a *spanned volume*. You can also create *striped volumes,* in which data is stored in equal-sized 64-KB strips across multiple dynamic volumes on separate physical disks to improve performance. And you can make these configuration changes without having to restart your computer.

● Disk configuration information for dynamic disks is stored in a database in a reserved area on the disk itself. If you have multiple dynamic disks on a single system, each one contains a replica of the dynamic disk database for the entire system. This feature makes it somewhat easier to move disks between computers and to recover data from corrupted disks.

The advantages of dynamic disks are especially pronounced in servers for large enterprises, where it's not unusual to see systems configured with five or more physical disks. On desktop systems, however, you must decide whether the possible benefits outweigh the increased complexity and the risk of data loss that can occur if one disk used in a multidisk spanned or striped volume crashes.

> **note** If you use Windows XP Home Edition, or if you're running Windows XP Professional on a portable computer, the option to convert a basic disk to a dynamic disk is not available.

> **caution** If you want to experiment with dynamic disks, do so on a disk that doesn't include important data, and don't treat this operation lightly. Although you can convert a dynamic disk back to a basic disk, all data in all volumes on that disk and on any other disks that are part of a spanned or striped volume will be irretrievably lost in the process. If you decide to convert a dynamic disk back to a basic disk, you'll need to have additional space or removable media to back up all your data so that you can restore it to the resulting empty basic disk.

To convert a basic disk to a dynamic disk, follow these steps:

1 Close any programs (other than Disk Management) that are using the disk you're converting. This includes all Windows Explorer windows.

2 In the Disk Management window, right-click the disk you want to convert and choose Convert To Dynamic Disk. (Right-click the disk icon at the left of the graphical view in the bottom of the window.)

3 If you have more than one disk, select which one(s) you want to upgrade and then click OK.

4 In the Disks To Convert dialog box shown on the next page, click Convert. Click through all warning dialog boxes to complete the conversion.

Want to reverse the process and convert a dynamic disk to a basic disk? Unfortunately, in this direction, the conversion is a destructive process. To convert a dynamic disk to a basic disk, follow these steps:

1 Back up all existing data to another drive or removable media.

2 Delete all volumes on the dynamic disk. (For details, see "Deleting a Partition, Volume, or Logical Drive," page 939.)

3 From the Disk Management window, right-click the disk you want to convert and choose Convert To Basic Disk.

4 After the conversion is complete, restore the backed-up data.

Working with Partitions, Volumes, and Disks

Before you can store data on a physical disk, you have to prepare it for use with Windows. Just as in previous Windows versions, the process of preparing a disk is twofold: First you carve out a space on the disk by creating a partition (or volume, if you're using dynamic disks) and, if necessary, one or more logical drives; then you choose a file system and format the drive. After you assign a drive letter to each newly formatted partition, volume, or logical drive, you're ready to go.

Creating Partitions from Free Disk Space

When you add a new drive to an existing system or delete partitions from an existing drive, you have a wide range of options for using the new disk space. How you choose to carve up the space is up to you. If you stick with basic disks, your options are similar to those that are familiar from earlier Windows versions. On the other hand, if you're willing to learn the ins and outs of dynamic disks, you can combine disk space in creative ways. In either case, wizards do most of the work.

Creating Partitions on a Basic Disk

To create a new partition on a basic disk, you need free space on your hard disk. (In the default Disk Management view, free space is identified by a black bar with the Unallocated label.) When you add a new hard disk to your system, the entire disk is available for use. You can choose all or part of the available space for use as a primary or an extended partition. If no unallocated space is available, you can make room by deleting an existing partition (and its data).

To create a new partition, follow these steps:

1 In the bottom half of the Disk Management window, right-click an unallocated portion of a disk and choose New Partition from the shortcut menu.

2 Click Next to advance past the Welcome screen of the New Partition Wizard.

3 On the Select Partition Type page, select Primary Partition or Extended Partition and click Next.

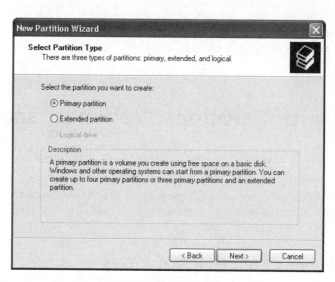

If you create an extended partition, the wizard ends here. Before you can store data on the newly created partition, you must define one or more logical drives within it, as explained in the following section. A primary partition, on the other hand, consists of a single volume, and the remaining steps of the wizard allow you to format that volume. If you select Primary Partition and click Next, the Specify Partition Size page appears, as shown here.

Chapter 27: Managing Disks and Drives

4 On the Specify Partition Size page, specify how much of the unallocated space you want to use for the new partition. The default value is the entire unallocated space. Click Next to continue. The Assign Drive Letter Or Path page appears.

On the Assign Drive Letter Or Path page, these three options appear:

- **Assign The Following Drive Letter.** By default, Windows assigns the lowest available drive letter to the partition. The list includes only drive letters that are not currently being used for local disks or for mapped network drives.

- **Mount In The Following Empty NTFS Folder.** You can create a mounted drive, which appears as a subfolder of another drive. For more information, see "Assigning and Changing Drive Letters or Drive Paths," page 940.

- **Do Not Assign A Drive Letter Or Drive Path.** Choose this option if you want to create the partition but you do not want to make it available for storage yet. Before you can use the partition to store and retrieve data, you must return to the Disk Management utility and assign a drive letter or create a mounted drive.

5 Select one of the above options and click Next to continue. The Format Partition page appears.

6 Choose Format This Partition With The Following Settings and then choose from these options:

- **File System.** Choose NTFS or FAT32 from the list. NTFS is selected by default. If the size of the volume is 4 GB (4096 MB) or less, your choices also include FAT. For more information, see "NTFS or FAT32: Which Disk Format Should You Choose?" on page 920.

- **Allocation Unit Size.** The allocation unit size (also known as the cluster size) is the smallest space that can be allocated to a file. The Default selection, in which Windows XP selects the appropriate cluster size based on volume size, is best.

- **Volume Label.** The volume label identifies the drive in the My Computer window. The default label text is New Volume. (You can change this text at any time, as explained in "Assigning or Changing a Volume Label," page 938.)

Select Perform A Quick Format if you want Disk Management to skip the sometimes lengthy disk-checking process. Select Enable File And Folder Compression if you want all data on the new volume to use NTFS compression. (This option is unavailable if you choose the FAT or FAT32 file system.)

7 Click Next, confirm your settings, and click Finish.

Creating a Simple Volume on a Dynamic Disk

On dynamic disks, simple volumes are the equivalent of primary partitions on basic disks. To create a simple volume, log on using an account in the Administrators group and follow these steps:

1 Open the Disk Management window, right-click an unallocated portion of a dynamic disk, and then choose New Volume.

2 In the New Volume Wizard, click Next to move past the Welcome screen. The Select Volume Type page appears.

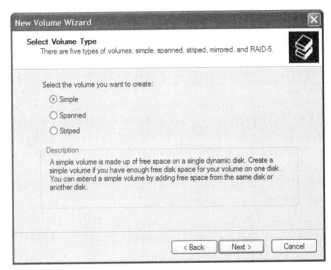

3 On the Select Volume Type page, select Simple. (If you have only one dynamic disk, this is your only choice. If you have multiple dynamic disks and you want to create a spanned or striped volume, see the instructions in the following section.)

note Don't be confused by the explanatory text in this dialog box. Although dynamic disks support five different types of volumes, only the three choices shown here are available with Windows XP Professional. The remaining two options—mirrored volumes and RAID-5 volumes—are available only on Windows .NET Server installations.

4 Click Next. The Select Disks page appears.

5 On the Select Disks page, select the disk on which you want to create the volume. By default, the disk you right-clicked in step 1 is shown in the Selected box. (To choose a different disk, click Remove, and then select a different disk and click Add.) By default, the wizard offers to create a new volume using all available unallocated space; if you want to make a smaller volume, change the value in the bottom of this dialog box. Click Next to continue.

6 On the remaining wizard pages, specify the drive letter or path and format the disk. These options are identical to those used in the New Partition Wizard; for details, see "Creating Partitions on a Basic Disk," page 927.

Combining Volumes from Dynamic Disks

If you have additional unallocated space on a dynamic disk—either the same disk or another disk—you can extend an existing volume to increase its size. If you have unallocated space on two or more dynamic disks, you can combine that space to create a volume. These combinations are subject to the following limitations:

- You can extend only simple volumes and spanned volumes on dynamic disks; you can't extend striped volumes or partitions on basic disks.

- You can extend a volume only if it's formatted with NTFS or it's unformatted; you can't extend FAT or FAT32 volumes.

- You can't extend a system volume or boot volume.

Chapter 27: Managing Disks and Drives

caution   Weigh the risks carefully before creating a volume that contains space from two
or more dynamic disks. If a catastrophic failure occurs on either physical disk, the
entire spanned or striped volume and all its data will be lost. Also, you cannot reverse
your decision and remove one chunk of space from the extended, spanned, or striped
volume. Deleting one part of the volume deletes the entire volume.

Figure 27-3 shows a system that contains four disks, two of which are dynamic disks. In
this example, Disk 0 and Disk 2 each contain significant chunks of unallocated space.
You could extend the E volume (Music) or the F volume (Backup), or both, using all or
part of this unallocated space. You could also create a new spanned or striped volume
using the two chunks of unallocated space.

Figure 27-3.   Because significant chunks of unallocated space are available on two
dynamic disks, you have a variety of options here.

Figure 27-4 on the next page shows the results after extending the two existing simple
volumes and creating a new striped volume. First, we extended the E volume (Music),
picking up 7.81 GB of space from Disk 2 and turning it into a spanned volume. Next,
we created the striped H volume, using all remaining space from Disk 2 plus an equal
chunk of space from Disk 0. Finally, we extended the F (Backup) volume, using the
remaining 8.81 GB from the end of Disk 0, making it an extended simple volume.

Part 7: System Maintenance and Recovery

This column describes the layout of volumes

Look here to see the capacity and available space on each volume

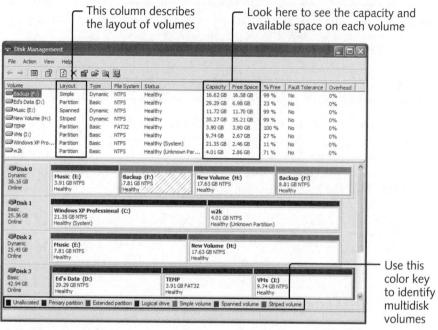

Figure 27-4. Information in the list at the top of this window, combined with color codes and volume labels from the bottom of the window, make it easy to see how storage space is arranged.

Use this color key to identify multidisk volumes

---

tip **Learn to read the numbers**

When working with extended, spanned, and striped volumes, the numbers can be confusing. In dialog boxes, values are typically listed in megabytes (MB). In the graphical view at the bottom of the Disk Management window, values are typically listed in gigabytes (GB). Because 1 GB is equal to 1024 MB, the numbers aren't always comparable. For instance, 35080 MB appears in the graphical view as 34.26 GB. As long as you're aware that the value in the graphical view will always appear a bit smaller than the one shown in dialog boxes, you should have no trouble.

To create a spanned or striped volume from unallocated space on two or more dynamic disks, use the New Volume Wizard, as described in the previous section, with the following changes:

- On the Select Volume Type page, select Spanned or Striped.

- On the Select Disks page, use the Add button to select two or more disks and specify the amount of space you want to use from each one. On a spanned volume, the portions of unallocated space on each drive can be of different sizes; in the case of a striped drive (as shown here), the two chunks of disk space must be of equal size, and the wizard will adjust the space on both disks if you change the amount at the bottom of the dialog box. In either case, the Select Disks page displays the total volume size you can expect to end up with.

The procedure for extending an existing volume is considerably simpler:

1 In the Disk Management window, right-click the volume you want to extend and choose Extend Volume. This option is available only if unallocated space exists on the same dynamic disk or another dynamic disk in the same system.

2 In the Extend Volume Wizard, click Next to skip past the Welcome screen.

3 On the Select Disks page, select which disk (or disks) you want to use by adding them to the Selected list. You can extend a simple volume to use unallocated contiguous space on the same disk, noncontiguous space on the same disk, or space on another dynamic disk. (In the latter two cases, the volume becomes a spanned volume.) At the bottom of this page, specify how much of the unallocated space you want to use.

4 Click Next and then click Finish.

After a volume is extended, you can extend it again, using additional unallocated space, but you can't reduce its size—except by deleting the entire volume.

Creating Logical Drives

A logical drive is a part of an extended partition that you subdivide and format as a separate volume. A logical drive can have its own drive letter or can be assigned as a mounted volume within an NTFS volume, as described in "Assigning and Changing Drive Letters or Drive Paths," page 940. Creating a logical drive uses the same wizard that you use to create a new partition or volume.

To create a logical drive, open the Disk Management utility and follow these steps:

1 In the graphical view at the bottom of the Disk Management window, right-click the free space within an extended partition and choose New Logical Drive from the shortcut menu.

2 In the New Partition Wizard that appears, click Next to skip past the Welcome screen. Click Next to skip the Select Partition Type page as well, where Logical Drive, the only available option, is already selected.

3 On the remaining wizard pages, specify the size, drive letter or path, and format, just as you would for a primary partition, as described in "Creating Partitions from Free Disk Space," page 927.

Formatting a Partition, Volume, or Logical Drive

Formatting a partition, logical drive, or volume deletes any existing files and prepares the volume for use. Normally, a wizard handles this task when you create a new partition, logical drive, or volume. You can reformat any drive or volume other than the current system or boot volume at any time. This option is a useful way to start fresh with a partition that you use strictly for temporary files, such as music files that you burn to CD.

To format an existing drive or volume, right-click its icon in the Disk Management utility and choose Format from the shortcut menu. You'll see a dialog box that offers the same choices as those found in the New Partition Wizard and New Volume Wizard, as shown in Figure 27-5.

You can also format any primary partition or logical drive that currently has a drive letter assigned to it from Windows Explorer. Right-click the drive icon and choose

Figure 27-5. When you format an existing primary partition or logical drive, you can choose the same options as if you were creating it from scratch with the wizard's help.

Chapter 27: Managing Disks and Drives

Format from the shortcut menu to display the dialog box shown here. Although the layout of this dialog box is different, the options are exactly the same as those found in the Disk Management window.

Finally, if you're a command-prompt fan, you can use the Format command. For volumes and partitions located on hard disks, this option doesn't provide any capabilities that aren't also available from the graphical interface. From a command prompt, use the Format Volume command. The Volume parameter specifies the drive letter (which must be followed by a colon), or the mount point or volume name. You can modify the Format command using any of the following switches:

- **/FS:*filesystem*** Specifies the file system to be used—substitute FAT, FAT32, or NTFS for *filesystem.*

- **/V:*label*** Assigns a volume label using the specified text.

- **/Q** Performs a quick format.

- **/C** NTFS only: all files and folders created on the new volume will be compressed by default.

- **/X** Forces the volume to dismount first if necessary. Caution: Using this switch may cause data loss if applications have open files with unsaved changes.

- **/A:*size*** Overrides the default allocation unit size. Use the /? switch to see details and restrictions.

Assigning or Changing a Volume Label

In Windows XP, as in previous versions of Windows, you can assign a descriptive text label to any volume. Assigning a label is purely optional, but it's a good practice, especially if you've set up separate partitions to keep your data organized. You can use Data as the label for your data drive, Music for the drive that holds your collection of digital tunes, and so on. Volume labels appear in the My Computer window alongside the drive letter for a volume, as in the example shown here.

You can enter a volume label when you format a new drive in the final step of the New Partition Wizard or New Volume Wizard, as described in "Creating Partitions from Free Disk Space," page 927. You can change a volume label at any time afterward by right-clicking a volume, choosing Properties, and entering text in the Label box on the General tab. (Or you can edit the volume label directly by clicking the label text in the My Computer window.) Regardless of how you choose to enter the label, you must follow the label rules that are specific to the file system of the underlying drive:

- **FAT/FAT32.** The volume label can be up to 11 characters long and can include spaces. On volumes originally created using DOS or Windows 95/98/Me, the label is displayed in all caps. A FAT volume label cannot include the following characters: * ? / \ | . , ; : + = [ ] < > "

- **NTFS.** The volume label can be up to 32 characters long. You can use symbols, punctuation, and special characters, and uppercase and lowercase letters are displayed exactly as you type them.

Deleting a Partition, Volume, or Logical Drive

Deleting a partition, drive, or volume is a radical step, but it's the simplest way to reorganize the layout of partitions on a disk—for instance, if you want to carve a second partition out of a disk that's currently arranged as a single large partition. The only requirement is making certain that all important programs and data have been backed up to another local or network drive, or to an alternative medium such as CD-R/CD-RW.

The most important thing to know about deleting a partition, logical drive, or volume is this: *You will lose all data stored in the partition, drive, or volume when you delete it.* For obvious reasons, you cannot use the Disk Management utility to delete the system volume, the boot volume, or an extended partition that contains logical drives. (You must delete the logical drives first and then delete the partition.)

caution If you've created any spanned or striped volumes, be especially careful when deleting a volume. Deleting one volume completely wipes out all parts of the spanned volume or stripe set. All disk regions on all disks that are part of the volume become unallocated space, immediately and irrevocably.

Troubleshooting

When you try to delete a logical drive or volume, you get an error message.

If you checked the volume first and are certain that it is completely empty, try the following techniques:

- Look at the Status line in the Disk Management window. If the word *System* or *Boot* appears in parentheses after the status indicator, you cannot remove the drive or volume from within Windows.

- Is the Windows XP page file configured to use this drive or volume? Follow the procedures outlined in "Making the Most of Virtual Memory," page 238, to view these settings and change them, if needed.

- Did you leave a Windows Explorer window open showing the contents of a folder on this volume or drive? Close all Windows Explorer windows and try again.

- Is an application program using the drive or volume? Check all running programs to see whether one of them is holding a file open on the drive or volume.

If you're certain that no files are currently in use and the drive or volume is not configured as the system or boot volume, you should see a dialog box that offers to force the deletion of the selected item. Click Yes to continue.

To delete a logical drive or a volume, first make certain that no other users are currently connected to that drive or volume, either over the network or in another session on the local computer. Then follow these steps:

1 In the Disk Management window, right-click the item you want to delete and choose Explore. Move or back up all files that you want to preserve and then close the Windows Explorer window.

2 Right-click the drive or volume again and choose Delete Logical Drive or Delete Volume.

3 Click Yes in the confirmation dialog box.

Assigning and Changing Drive Letters or Drive Paths

How does Windows XP assign letters to individual drives? On the degree-of-difficulty scale, the algorithm that Windows XP uses to assign drive letters probably falls midway between programming a VCR and Einstein's General Theory of Relativity. It's a complex subject, made more confusing by the fact that the rules for Windows XP are different from those followed by MS-DOS and Windows 95/98/Me. The following list summarizes basic facts you need to know about Windows XP and drive letters:

● On an upgrade installation, Windows XP preserves the drive letters assigned by the previous Windows version. On a clean installation, Windows XP follows the same rules as Windows 2000. (For details, see Knowledge Base article Q234048, "How Windows 2000 Assigns, Reserves, and Stores Drive Letters.")

● Assigned drive letters are persistent. Once assigned, drive letters remain the same every time you start Windows XP. This is a big change from the behavior in Windows 95/98/Me, where adding a new CD-ROM drive or hard disk or changing the number and type of partitions on existing drives can cause existing drive letters to change.

● You can assign one (and only one) letter to a primary partition, a logical drive, or a simple volume on a dynamic disk. At any time, you can change any drive letter except those assigned to the system and boot partitions, either for the sake of convenience or because it interferes with the letter mapped to a network drive. You can also remove a drive letter assignment from any volume except the system and boot partitions.

> **caution** It is possible to change the drive letter assigned to the system and boot partition in Windows 2000 or Windows XP by editing values in the registry. In general, doing so is not recommended. The only time this option makes sense is when a system configuration unexpectedly causes drive letters to change, so that the letter assigned to the system or boot partition is different from the one that was assigned when Windows XP was installed. This might be the case if you use third-party partitioning tools to alter the layout of partitions on a disk, or if you add or remove a disk controller. If this situation describes your system, read details about this tricky procedure in Knowledge Base article Q223188, "How to Change the System/Boot Drive Letter in Windows 2000." The steps are the same for Windows XP.

To change a drive letter assignment, follow these steps:

1 From the Disk Management utility, right-click the volume you want to change (in either the volume list at the top of the window or the graphical view at the bottom), and choose Change Drive Letter And Paths.

2 To replace an existing drive letter, select it and click Change. To assign a drive letter to a volume that currently has none, click Add.

3 Select an available drive letter from the Assign The Following Drive Letter list and then click OK.

4 Click OK to close the Change Drive Letter And Paths dialog box.

InsideOut

The list of available drive letters shows only those that are not currently in use. If you need to swap the drive letters for two volumes, you need to do so in three steps. To swap drive letters G and H, for instance, open the Disk Management utility and follow these steps:

1 Remove the drive letter assigned to drive H, freeing that letter for reassignment.

2 Go to drive G and change its assigned drive letter to H.

3 Return to the drive formerly designated as H and use the Add button to assign the now available letter G.

Note that the letters *A* and *B* are always reserved for removable drives and cannot be assigned to a volume on a hard disk.

In addition to (or in place of) a drive letter, you can assign one or more *drive paths* to a primary partition, a logical drive, or a simple volume on a dynamic disk. Assigning a drive path creates a *mounted volume,* which appears as a folder within an NTFS-formatted drive that has a letter assigned to it. Besides allowing you to sidestep the limitation of 26 drive letters, mounted volumes offer these two advantages:

● You can extend storage space on an existing drive that's running low on free space. For instance, if your digital music collection has outgrown your drive C, you can create a More Music folder in C:\My Music. Assign a drive path from a new partition to the More Music folder and you've increased the effective storage by the size of the new volume.

● Make commonly used files available in multiple locations. Say you have an enormous collection of clip art that you store on drive X, and each user has a folder in his or her My Documents folder where they store desktop publishing files. In each of those personal folders, you can create a subfolder called Clipart and assign a drive path to the X partition. That way, the entire clip-art collection is always available from any user's desktop publishing folder, without requiring them to manage shortcuts or worry about changing drive letters.

To create a mounted drive, follow these steps:

1 From the Disk Management utility, right-click the volume you want to change (in either the volume list at the top of the window or the graphical view at the bottom), and choose Change Drive Letter And Paths.

2 Click Add to open the Add Drive Letter Or Path dialog box.

3 Select Mount In This NTFS Folder (this is the only option available if the volume already has an assigned drive letter).

4 Click the Browse button. The Browse For Drive Path dialog box that appears
shows only NTFS volumes, and the OK button is enabled only if you select
an empty folder. Browse to the location where you want to create the drive
path and then select an empty folder, or click New Folder to create one.

5 Click OK to add the selected location in the Add Drive Letter Or Path dialog
box and then click OK to create the drive path.

You can manage files and subfolders in a mounted volume just as if it were a regular
folder. If a volume is mounted to a folder located in the root of a drive, it appears in
Windows Explorer as a drive icon. However, if the volume is mounted to a subfolder
in any other location, the mounted volume appears in Windows Explorer as a folder
icon, indistinguishable from a regular file folder. In that case, the only way to tell that
this folder is different from other folders is to right-click the folder icon, choose
Properties, and then inspect the General tab. As the example shown in Figure 27-6
illustrates, the Type field appears as Mounted Volume, and the Target field identifies
the label of the volume that actually contains the files.

If you use the Dir command in a Command Prompt window to display a folder directory, a mounted volume is identified as <JUNCTION> (for *junction point,* another
name for mounted volume), whereas ordinary folders are identified as <DIR> (for
directory, the MS-DOS term for a folder).

---

caution   When creating mounted volumes, avoid creating loops in the structure of a
drive—for example, by creating a drive path from drive X that points to a folder on
drive D and then creating a drive path on drive D that points to a folder on drive X.
Windows allows you do this, but it's invariably a bad idea, because an application that
opens subfolders (such as a search) can go into an endless loop.

To see a list of all the mounted drives on your system, open the Disk Management
utility and choose View, Drive Paths. A dialog box like the one shown in Figure 27-7
appears. Note that you can remove drive paths from this dialog box; if you do so, the
folder remains in the same spot where it was previously located, but it reverts to being
a regular, empty folder.

Part 7: System Maintenance and Recovery

Figure 27-6. The properties dialog box for a mounted drive identifies the volume that actually holds its files.

Figure 27-7. This dialog box lists all the mounted drives on a system and shows the volume label, if any, of the mounted drive.

Checking Properties and Status of a Disk or Partition

As with previous Windows versions, you can check the properties of any drive—including its volume label, file system, and the amount of free space available—from the My Computer window. Right-click the drive icon and choose Properties from the short-cut menu. You can see the same details and more by starting from the Disk Management utility. Most of the key information is visible in the volume list, shown by default at the top of the window, with slightly less information available in the graphical view at the bottom of the window. Of particular interest is information about the status of a disk or volume. Figure 27-8 shows where to look for this information.

Chapter 27: Managing Disks and Drives

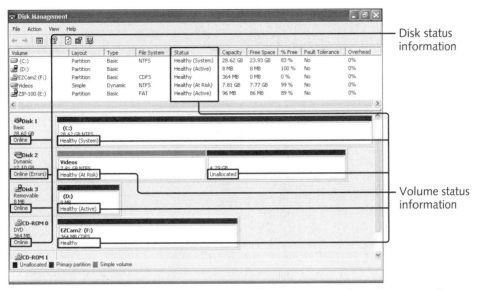

Disk status information

Volume status information

Figure 27-8. The Disk Management utility displays information about the status of each physical disk and volume.

Under normal circumstances, the status information displayed here should report that each disk is online and each volume is healthy. Table 27-1 lists all possible status messages you may see on a system running Windows XP Professional or Home Edition, along with suggested actions you should take to resolve possible errors.

Table 27-1. Disk Status

Status	Description	Action Required
Online	The disk is configured correctly and has no known problems.	None.
Online (Errors)	The operating system encountered errors when reading or writing data from a region of the disk. *(This status message appears on dynamic disks only.)*	Right-click the disk and choose Reactivate Disk to return its status to Online. If errors continue to occur, check for damage to the disk.
Offline	The disk was once available but is not currently accessible. The disk might be physically damaged or it might be disconnected. *(This status message appears on dynamic disks only.)*	Check the physical connections between the disk and the power supply or disk controller. After repairing connections, right-click the disk and choose Reactivate Disk to return its status to Online. If the damage cannot be repaired, delete all volumes, right-click the disk, and choose Remove Disk.

(continued)

Chapter 27

Table 27-1. *(continued)*

Status	Description	Action Required
Foreign	The disk was originally installed on another computer and has not yet been set up for use on your computer. *(This status message appears on dynamic disks only.)*	Right-click the disk and choose Import Foreign Disks.
Unreadable	All or part of the disk may be physically damaged, or (in the case of a dynamic disk) the dynamic disk database may be corrupted.	Restart the computer. If the problem persists, right-click the disk and choose Rescan Disks. If the status is still Unreadable, some data on the disk may be recoverable with third-party utilities.
Missing	The disk is corrupted, disconnected, or not powered on. *(This status message appears on dynamic disks only.)*	After you reconnect or power on the missing disk, right-click the disk and choose Reactivate Disk to return its status to Online.
Not initialized	The disk does not contain a valid signature. It may have been prepared on a system running a non-Microsoft operating system, such as UNIX or Linux, or the drive may be brand new.	If the disk is used by another operating system, do nothing. To prepare a new disk for use with Windows XP, right-click the disk and choose Initialize Disk.
No Media	This status, which appears only for drives using removable media (Zip drives and CD-R/CD-RW drives, for example), indicates that no disk is in the drive.	Insert a disk in the drive and choose Action, Rescan Disks.

Table 27-2 describes volume status messages you're likely to see.

---

tip   **Tackle disk problems first**

Almost without fail, a disk problem will generate a status indicator for both the disk and any volumes on that disk. For instance, if you see a disk with Online (Errors) in the Status column, you're likely to see Healthy (At Risk) as the volume's status. In this case, your best bet is to try to resolve the disk problem first. If you can successfully do so, the problems with the volume will usually clear up as a matter of course.

Table 27-2. **Volume Status**

Status	Description	Action Required
Healthy	The volume is properly formatted and has no known problems.	None.
Healthy (At Risk)	Windows encountered errors when reading from or writing to the underlying disk. Such errors are often caused by bad blocks on the disk. After encountering an error anywhere on the disk, Disk Management marks all volumes on that disk as Healthy (At Risk). *(This status message appears on dynamic disks only.)*	Right-click the disk and choose Reactivate Disk. Persistent errors often indicate a failing disk. Back up all data and run a thorough diagnostic check using the hardware manufacturer's software; if necessary, replace the disk.
Healthy (Unknown Partition)	Windows does not recognize some partitions created by other operating systems or by computer manufacturers who use the partitions to store system files. You cannot format or access data on an unknown partition.	If you're certain the partition is unnecessary, use the Disk Management utility to delete it and create a new partition in the free space created.
Initializing	The Disk Management utility cannot determine the disk status because the disk is initializing. *(This status message appears on dynamic disks only.)*	Wait. The drive status should appear in a few seconds.
Failed	The dynamic disk is damaged or the file system is corrupted.	To repair a failed dynamic volume, check to see whether the disk is online. (If not, right-click the disk and choose Reactivate Disk.) Then right-click the volume and choose Reactivate Volume. If the failed volume is on a basic disk, be sure that the disk is properly connected.
Unknown	The boot sector for the volume is corrupted, and you can no longer access data. This condition may be caused by a virus.	Use an up-to-date virus-scanning program to check for the presence of a boot-sector virus. If no virus is found, boot from the Windows XP CD and use Recovery Console's Fixmbr command to fix the Master Boot Record.

Troubleshooting

The Check Disk utility runs frequently at startup.

When your system shuts down improperly, Windows runs the Autochk program on all NTFS drives where a disk write was in process at the time of the unexpected shutdown. This problem can be exacerbated if you have write caching enabled on a hard drive connected to a standard IDE controller. Although this option improves performance by delaying the writing of data while you work on other things, it can result in an increased risk of data loss or corruption.

If this is a persistent problem on your system, you should disable write caching on the affected drive. From the graphical display at the bottom of the Disk Management window, right-click the disk icon and choose Properties. On the Policies tab, clear Enable Write Caching On The Disk. (Note that this option may not be available if your disk is connected to a high-performance ATA-66 or ATA-100 IDE controller.)

After you find the cause of the improper shutdowns and fix the underlying problem, be sure to reenable write caching.

Setting Quotas for Disk Space Use

Disk quotas allow you to monitor and limit disk-space usage on NTFS-formatted drives and volumes—a handy feature on a multiuser system where a download-happy family member can easily fill up even the most gargantuan physical disk with digital music, videos, and pictures. Using quotas, you can set storage limits for each user and each volume.

When you enable disk quotas, Windows tracks volume usage by file ownership. A file counts against a user's quota if the security identifier (SID) of the file's owner is the same as the user's SID. For an in-depth explanation of SIDs and other security issues, see "Introducing Windows XP Security," page 90.

note Disk quotas rely on the SID, not the user account name. In a workgroup environment—where each user has a separate, identically named user account on each computer—this can cause quotas to be less reliable than in a domain. That's because the user's account on each computer has a different SID. Depending on how a file is created, it might be owned by the user's account on a different computer. If your NTFS volume contains files that are owned by a user account from another computer, you'll see the owner's SID in the Quota Entries window instead of (or in addition to) the user's name.

Enabling Disk Quotas

To enable disk quotas, use the Quota tab in the properties dialog box for a volume. Log on as a member of the Administrators group and then follow these steps:

1 From the My Computer window, right-click any NTFS drive icon and choose Properties (or use the equivalent menu after right-clicking on a volume in the Disk Management window).

2 Click the Quota tab and then select the Enable Quota Management check box to enable the other items on the Quota tab.

3 Set the other options on the Quota tab as follows:

- Select Deny Disk Space To Users Exceeding Quota Limit if you want Windows to prevent users from saving files that would exceed their assigned space limit. (They'll see an "insufficient disk space" error message.) If you don't select this check box, Windows doesn't stop users from exceeding their limit—but it allows you to track disk usage by user.

- To specify a default limit for new users (that is, users who don't have an entry in the Quota Entries window, described in the following section), select Limit Disk Space To and set a limit and a warning level. (Exceeding the warning level doesn't trigger a warning to the user, but administrators can use this setting to more easily monitor users who are nearing their limit.) If you don't want to set limits on new users, select Do Not Limit Disk Usage.

949

■ If you want Windows to make an entry in the System log whenever a
user exceeds his or her quota limit or warning level, select the appropriate check box.

Managing Disk Quotas

When you enable quotas on a volume that has existing files, Windows calculates the
disk space used by each user who has created, copied, or taken ownership of the existing files. The default quota limits and warning levels are then applied to all current
users and to any new user who saves a file. To view and modify the quota entries for a
given drive, open the properties dialog box for that drive, click the Quota tab, and then
click Quota Entries. The Quota Entries window opens, as shown in Figure 27-9.

Figure 27-9.   With this list you can review disk usage and impose limits on a
per-user basis.

For each user, Quota Entries displays

● A status indicator (OK for users who are below their warning level and
quota limit, Warning for users who are above their warning level, and
Above Limit for users who are above their quota limit)

● The user's logon name

● The amount of disk space occupied by files that the user owns

● The user's quota limit and warning level

● The percentage of the quota limit currently in use

To change a user's limits, double-click his or her entry. A dialog box appears that offers
choices for this user similar to the choices offered on the Quota tab for all new users.

Chapter 27

> **note** By default, the Administrators group has no limit—meaning that while you're logged on as a member of the Administrators group, you might be able to create files that exceed the limits for your own account. Although you can set a warning limit for the Administrators group, you cannot set a quota limit.

Setting AutoPlay Options for Removable Drives

On devices that contain removable storage media, Windows is constantly on the lookout for newly inserted media. If you insert a CD or DVD into a drive, or connect a Windows XP–compatible digital camera, or pop a Compact Flash card into an external reader, Windows responds with a dialog box similar to the one shown in Figure 27-10.

Figure 27-10. When Windows detects that you've inserted a new disk (or other media) into a removable storage device, it asks you how you want to handle the content.

The Windows AutoPlay settings allow you to define different default actions for different types of content. For instance, you can specify that you want music CDs to play automatically in Windows Media Player or another application, while disks that contain mixed content open in a Windows Explorer window so that you can copy them to a local drive.

You can adjust the default AutoPlay settings at any time on a per-drive basis. If you decide that you want digital photos on a Compact Flash card to open in a Windows Explorer window instead of in the Scanner And Camera Wizard, that's your right. To adjust AutoPlay settings, open My Computer, right-click the icon for the drive in question, and then choose Properties. On the AutoPlay tab, choose different options for each type of content associated with that drive, as shown here.

InsideOut

Some people see AutoPlay as a nuisance instead of a convenience. If you're in that camp, you can disable AutoPlay altogether as explained in the following procedures.

If you're running Windows XP Professional, use Group Policy, as follows:

1 At a command prompt, type **gpedit.msc** to open Group Policy.

2 In the console tree, select Computer Configuration\Administrative Templates\System.

3 In the right pane, double-click Turn Off Autoplay.

4 Select Enabled, and then select CD-ROM Drives or All Drives. The first choice is a bit misleading; selecting CD-ROM Drives disables AutoPlay on DVD drives, removable drives, and network drives as well as CD-ROM drives. Selecting All Drives indeed disables AutoPlay on all drives, including Compact Flash cards and other non-disk drive types.

5 Click OK and then close Group Policy.

To restore AutoPlay functionality, return to the Turn Off Autoplay policy, and set the policy to Not Configured or Disabled.

If you use Windows XP Home Edition, you can't use Group Policy. However, you can edit the registry directly to achieve the same effect. Follow these steps:

1 At a command prompt, type **regedit** to open Registry Editor.

2 Navigate to the HKLM\Software\Microsoft\Windows\CurrentVersion\ Policies key.

3 Right-click the Policies key and choose New, Key. Type **Explorer** to replace the default key name, New Key #1.

4 Right-click the new Explorer subkey, and choose New, DWORD Value. Type **NoDriveTypeAutoRun** to replace the default value name, New Value #1.

5 Double-click the new NoDriveTypeAutoRun value, and type **b5** in the Value Data box. (Be sure Hexadecimal is selected in the Base box.)

6 Click OK, log off, and then log back on.

To restore AutoPlay, return to Registry Editor and delete the NoDriveTypeAutoRun value.

newfeature!
Working with Writable and Rewritable CD Drives

Windows XP includes software that allows you to copy files and folders from a Windows Explorer window onto a writable (CD-R) or rewritable (CD-RW) disk in a compatible drive. This software, which is integrated into Windows Explorer, is a light version of Roxio's Easy CD Creator program. If you have a Windows XP–compatible CD recorder, you can copy files and folders from any local folder to a writable or rewritable CD. You can also create audio CDs from Windows Media Player, read from CDs created with packet-writing software such as Roxio's DirectCD, and erase rewritable CDs so that you can reuse them.

InsideOut

The built-in CD writing capabilities in Windows XP are useful, but they're not intended for anything but occasional use. Using this software, for instance, you can't create CDs using the UDF file system. (UDF is sometimes called "packet writing.") Without UDF capability, you can't create "disk at once" music CDs, which allow music to flow smoothly from track to track without annoying 2-second gaps—a significant flaw for classical and live recordings. If you're serious about creating CDs, you should invest in full-strength CD-recording software, such as Roxio's Easy CD Creator (*http:// www.roxio.com*) or Ahead Software's Nero (*http://www.nero.com*). If you do so, be sure to disable Windows XP's built-in recording capabilities, which can cause conflicts with third-party software.

For more details about copying files and folders using a CD burner, see "Copying Files to CDs," page 467.

If you plan to use the built-in CD recording capabilities in Windows XP, check to see that CD recording is enabled on your drive. If you plan to use a third-party program instead, go to the same location to disable recording from Windows Explorer. In either case, you control this option using a check box in the properties dialog box for the CD-RW drive. From the My Computer window, right-click on the drive icon and choose Properties. Options on the Recording tab, shown in Figure 27-11, allow you to control how Windows XP works with your CD burner.

- Clear the Enable CD Recording On This Drive check box if you want to use a third-party CD-recording program. This box should remain selected if you plan to record CDs from within Windows Explorer.

- During the recording process, the CD Writing Wizard creates a CD image that is equal in size to the files you plan to copy. Using the list in the middle of the properties dialog box, you can specify which drive or volume you want to use for these temporary files.

- Normally, Windows configures your CD drive to operate at its fastest speed. If you encounter frequent errors, you might want to reduce the write speed as a troubleshooting step. Choose a speed from the Select A Write Speed list.

- After burning a CD, Windows automatically ejects it from the drive. This action is intended to alert you that the CD is done, so you can label it or insert another blank CD. Depending on your hardware, this configuration

Figure 27-11. Fine-tune CD recording options here.

may be less than ideal. If you have a tower computer that sits alongside your chair, for instance, you could inadvertently bump into the CD tray and break it if it pops out when you're not expecting it. To eliminate this possibility, clear the Automatically Eject The CD After Writing check box.

Troubleshooting

You get frequent errors when writing CDs.

The most common cause of CD writing failures is a buffer underrun, when the flow of data to the CD recorder is interrupted and the laser is unable to continue writing to the disk. When this happens, you end up with a coaster. Fixing persistent buffer underrun problems can be maddening. Here are some places to start:

- *Is your hardware fully compatible and up to date?* Check with the CD-RW drive manufacturer to see whether a firmware update is available.

- *Do you have other CD writing software installed?* If the other software works, disable the Windows XP CD writing capabilities and use the third-party program instead.

- *Are you going too fast?* Turn down the CD writing speed and see whether that helps.

- *Is your hard disk fragmented? Is it too full? Are you using your fastest hard disk for the location of the CD image?* Clean out unneeded files and defragment all drives on your system. Consider dedicating a separate volume on your fastest physical disk to the temporary files used for CD burning.

- *Are other programs interfering with the CPU?* Shut down screen savers and any background programs that might be getting in the way of the CD writing software.

- *Does the problem happen with one particular brand of blank CDs?* You could have a bad batch. Try a different brand and see whether the problem persists.

In the original release of Windows XP, certain situations resulted in several similar problems:

- The disc is unreadable.
- The disc works in Windows XP, but it's unreadable in Windows 95, Windows 98, or in an MP3 player.
- Some files are lost or missing.

These problems were resolved in Service Pack 1. If you haven't yet installed SP1, you can obtain a patch through Windows Update. For more information, see Knowledge Base article Q320174, "Compact Disc Recorded in Windows XP Is Missing Files or Folders or Is Unreadable."

Chapter 28

Troubleshooting Windows Errors

If Windows has ever suddenly and unexpectedly shut down, you've probably experienced that sinking feeling in the pit of your stomach. When Microsoft Windows XP encounters a serious problem that makes it impossible for the operating system to continue running, it shuts down immediately and displays an ominous text message whose technical details begin with the word *STOP* in capital letters. Because a Stop message typically appears in white letters on a blue background, this type of error message is often referred to as a blue-screen error or the Blue Screen of Death (BSOD). Fortunately, this type of error is rare in Windows XP, but it can occur at any time, especially when you install new hardware or software. When a Stop message appears it means that there is a serious problem that demands your immediate attention.

Windows XP includes a variety of information sources and debugging tools that you can use to identify the cause of Stop errors. Many of the tools are intended for use by developers with professional debugging tools. These topics are covered in more detail in *Microsoft Windows XP Professional Resource Kit Documentation* (Microsoft Press, 2001). If you know where to look, however, you can learn a lot from these error messages, and in many cases you can recover completely by using standard troubleshooting techniques.

Decoding Stop Messages

Stop messages may look cryptic, but they often contain detailed information about the underlying cause of the problem that can enable you to diagnose and repair the

At Home with Windows XP

All of the advice in this chapter applies equally to Windows XP Home Edition and Professional. If you use the Recovery Console to repair Windows XP Home Edition, note that the built-in Administrator account has a blank password. When you're prompted for a password, just press Enter to continue.

condition that's causing your system to fail. Stop messages may appear under any of the following circumstances:

- **During Windows Setup.** This type of Stop error is almost always caused by a faulty device driver, a piece of hardware that is in the process of failing, or an incompatible system BIOS. You may see a Stop message during Windows Setup if you attempt a clean install on a system that uses a high-speed disk controller whose drivers are not included with the Windows XP CD. To avoid encountering this Stop error, which occurs when Windows is suddenly unable to access the disk containing temporary Setup files, you must press F6 when prompted at the beginning of Setup and provide the correct drivers.

- **At startup.** If you see a Stop message during startup on a system where Windows XP previously ran properly, the cause of the error is usually an incompatible service or device driver. If you recently installed a new software application or a new device, those are the most likely culprits.

- **While Windows is running.** These Stop errors can be caused by drivers, services, or defective hardware and can be difficult to diagnose. The text of the Stop message usually provides important clues. This chapter includes a list of common Stop errors, with suggestions on how to respond to each one.

InsideOut

What should you do if your computer powers up properly but Windows hangs during startup? Find the Windows CD, use it to start your computer, and start the Recovery Console. To identify the driver or system file that may be responsible for the problem, modify Boot.ini. Add the /Noguiboot and /Sos switches, as explained in "Modifying Boot.ini," page 85. After restarting your computer, you'll see a listing for each driver and service as it loads. The last one in the list is the most likely culprit. You can then use Recovery Console's stripped-down command-line environment to disable a rogue service or replace a corrupted file. You'll find detailed instructions for working with Recovery Console in "Making Repairs from the Recovery Console," page 907.

How to Read a Stop Message

The exact text of a Stop message varies, according to what caused the error. But the format is predictable, as the example in Figure 28-1 shows.

You can gather important information from these details:

- **Symbolic error name.** This is the message that the error returned to the operating system. It corresponds to the Stop error number that appears at the bottom of the screen. In this example, the symbolic error name is DRIVER_IRQL_NOT_LESS_OR_EQUAL.

- **Troubleshooting recommendations.** This generic text applies to all Stop errors of the specified type. Depending on the error number, you may be told to check available disk space, uninstall a piece of hardware, or remove or update recently installed drivers or software.

- **Error number and parameters.** Developers call this section *bugcheck information.* The text following the word *STOP* includes the error number (in hexadecimal notation, as indicated by the 0x at the beginning of the code) and up to four parameters that are specific to each error type.

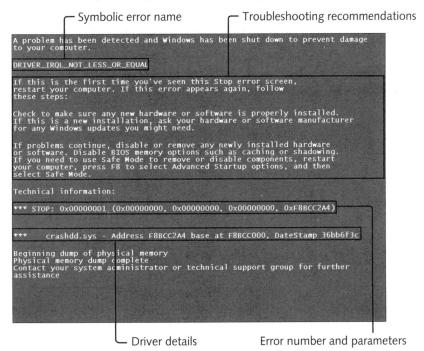

Figure 28-1. Learn to decode the information in a Stop message so you can find the underlying problem and fix it.

In this example, the error code is 0x000000D1 (or just D1), which indicates a driver that tried to use an improper memory address. In this example, the parameters, in order, identify the memory address the driver tried to access; the interrupt request level, which Windows uses to determine the order in which to respond to hardware and software requests; whether the driver tried to read from or write to memory (the 0 means this was a read operation); and the memory address from which the illegal request originated.

● **Driver information.** In some (but not all) Stop messages, this line lists the name of the driver associated with the error. If a file name appears here, check to see that the driver is digitally signed. If necessary, you can use Recovery Console or start Windows in Safe Mode to remove or roll back the driver.

> For more details about recovering from startup problems manually, see "Using Recovery Console Commands," page 909. For information about removing, disabling, and rolling back drivers, see "Managing Installed Drivers," page 215.

InsideOut

Don't automatically assume that a file listed in the driver information section of a Stop message is corrupt or needs replacing. In some cases, that reference means that another service or driver created a system instability that caused the listed program to crash when it performed a perfectly legal operation. For instance, in a Stop 1E error message you might see a reference to a system file called Win32k.sys, the Multi-User Win32 Driver. In that case, the actual cause of the crash may be a "remote control" program. Start Windows in Safe Mode and try to disable the program, or use Recovery Console to remove the service.

If the system restarts immediately after a Stop message, you may not have time to note the details of the message. However, with rare exceptions, the operating system is able to capture these details in the Event Viewer. To see the gory details, follow these steps:

1 After your system restarts, open Control Panel's Administrative Tools folder and then open Event Viewer.

2 From the console pane on the left, select the System log.

3 Scroll through the list of entries until you find one with the title Save Dump in the Source column.

4 Double-click that entry to open the event record that lists the Stop error information, as shown here.

Chapter 28: Troubleshooting Windows Errors

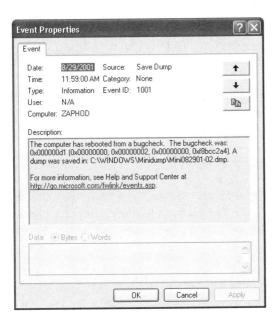

Note that the symbolic error name does not appear. However, you can use this log entry to identify the numeric error code and parameters for the error.

General Advice for Dealing with Stop Errors

If you experience a Stop error, don't panic. Instead, run through the following troubleshooting checklist to isolate the problem and find a resolution:

Look for a driver name in the error details   If the error message identifies a specific file name and you can trace that file to a driver for a specific hardware device, you may be able to solve the problem by disabling, removing, or rolling back that driver to an earlier version. The most likely offenders are network interface cards, video adapters, and disk controllers. For more details about managing driver files using Device Manager, see "Managing Installed Drivers," page 215.

---

tip   **Try an alternate driver**

Experienced support engineers recommend that you use the hardware driver that was made specifically for your device. However, if an unsigned driver causes Stop errors, you might have success by using a more recent driver for a product in the same family, even if the model name is not identical. This strategy is most likely to work with printers; it is least likely to be successful with video adapters and network interface cards.

Part 7: System Maintenance and Recovery

Don't rule out hardware problems   In many cases, software is the victim and not the cause of blue-screen errors. Damaged hard disks, defective physical RAM, and overheated CPU chips are three common hardware failures that can result in Stop errors. If the errors seem to happen at random and the message details vary each time, hardware problems are indicated.

Ask yourself, "What's new?"   Be suspicious of newly installed hardware devices and software programs. If you added a new device recently, remove it temporarily and see whether the problem goes away. Take an especially close look at software in the categories that install services or file-system filter drivers, which hook into the core operating system files that manage the file system to perform tasks such as scanning for viruses. This category includes backup programs, multimedia applications, antivirus software, and CD-burning utilities. You may need to uninstall or update the program to resolve the problem.

Search the Knowledge Base   Make a note of the error code and all parameters that appear on the same line. Search the Knowledge Base using both the full and short formats. For instance, if you're experiencing a KMODE_EXCEPTION_NOT_HANDLED error, use *0x0E* and *0x0000000E* as your search keywords.

Check your system BIOS carefully   Is an update available from the manufacturer of the system or motherboard? Stop errors are especially common in connection with Advanced Configuration and Peripheral Interface (ACPI) machines, where flaws in the BIOS may trip up the operating system. Also, check the BIOS documentation carefully—resetting all BIOS options to their default settings can sometimes resolve an issue caused by over-tweaking.

Are you low on system resources?   Stop errors are sometimes the result of a critical shortage of RAM or disk space. If you can start in Safe Mode, check the amount of physical RAM installed and look at the system and boot drives to see how much free disk space is available. You may be able to free space by running the Disk Cleanup Manager, as described in "Managing Disk Space," page 876.

Is a crucial system file damaged?   To reinstall a driver, restart your computer and press F8 when prompted to start Windows in Safe Mode. To repair a damaged system file that prevents you from starting even in Safe Mode, start from the Windows XP CD and use Recovery Console. From Recovery Console's special-purpose command prompt, the Copy command automatically expands compressed files on the fly when you copy from the CD to a local drive.

How to Troubleshoot Specific Stop Errors

The general troubleshooting steps outlined in the previous section apply to all Stop errors. Details provided by specific Stop messages, however, can help you narrow down the cause of the error and get to a solution quickly. This section lists the most common Stop error codes, with suggested troubleshooting actions and external resources to additional information.

Stop 0x0000000A or IRQL_NOT_LESS_OR_EQUAL

A kernel-mode process or driver attempted to access a memory location without authorization. This Stop error is typically caused by faulty or incompatible hardware or software. The name of the offending device driver often appears in the Stop message and can provide an important clue to solving the problem.

If the error message points to a specific device or category of devices, try removing or replacing devices in that category. If this Stop message appears during Setup, suspect an incompatible driver, system service, virus scanner, or backup program.

Stop 0x0000001E or KMODE_EXCEPTION_NOT_HANDLED

The Windows XP kernel detected an illegal or unknown processor instruction, often the result of invalid memory and access violations caused by faulty drivers or hardware devices. The error message often identifies the offending driver or device. If the error occurred immediately after installing a driver or service, try disabling or removing it.

Stop 0x00000024 or NTFS_FILE_SYSTEM

This message indicates that a problem occurred within the NTFS file-system driver. A similar Stop message, 0x23, exists for FAT32 drives. The most likely cause is a hardware failure in a disk or disk controller. Check all physical connections to all hard disks in the system, and run the Check Disk utility (Chkdsk.exe) using the instructions outlined in "Checking Disks for Errors," page 865.

Stop 0x0000002E or DATA_BUS_ERROR

Failed or defective physical memory (including memory used in video adapters) is the most common cause of this Stop error. The error may also be the result of a corrupted hard disk or a damaged motherboard.

Chapter 28

Stop 0x0000003F or NO_MORE_SYSTEM_PTES

This relatively uncommon error message appears when your system runs out of page table entries (PTEs). The cause may be an out-of-control backup program or a buggy device driver. Knowledge Base article Q256004, "How to Troubleshoot 'STOP 0x0000003F' and 'STOP 0x000000D8' Error Messages in Windows 2000," describes modifications to the Windows registry that may resolve the problem.

Stop 0x00000050 or PAGE_FAULT_IN_NONPAGED_AREA

A hardware driver or system service requested data that was not in memory, causing an exception error. The cause may be defective physical memory or incompatible software, especially remote control and antivirus programs. If the error occurs immediately after installing a device driver or application, try to use Safe Mode to remove the driver or uninstall the program.

Stop 0x00000077 or KERNEL_STACK_INPAGE_ERROR

The system attempted to read kernel data from virtual memory (the page file) and failed to find the data at the specified memory address. This Stop error can be caused by a variety of problems, including defective memory, a malfunctioning hard disk, an improperly configured disk controller or cable, corrupted data, or a virus infection.

Stop 0x00000079 or MISMATCHED_HAL

No, this message has nothing to do with Hal, the paranoid computer in the classic film *2001: A Space Odyssey*. Instead, this message identifies a mismatch between the Windows XP hardware abstraction layer (HAL) and the Windows XP system files. This error most often occurs on ACPI machines, when ACPI BIOS settings are changed unexpectedly. To disable or reenable ACPI features, reinstall Windows XP after making changes in the BIOS. For more details, read Knowledge Base article Q237556, "How to Troubleshoot Windows 2000 Hardware Abstraction Layer Issues."

Stop 0x0000007A or KERNEL_DATA_INPAGE_ERROR

This Stop error has the same underlying cause as 0x77 errors: a page of kernel data was not found in virtual memory (the page file). This might be due to incompatible disk or controller drivers or hardware problems, such as an improperly terminated SCSI device, bad blocks on the hard disk, or a conflict with the BIOS or other firmware on a disk controller. Run the Windows XP Check Disk utility as detailed in "Checking Disks for Errors," page 865. If the disk manufacturer has a more comprehensive disk utility, use it to do a thorough check of each physical hard disk on the system.

Stop 0x0000007B or INACCESSIBLE_BOOT_DEVICE

This error message means that Windows XP is unable to locate the system partition or boot volume during the startup process. The problem may occur after repartitioning disks, adding new disks, or upgrading a disk controller and its drivers. In that case, entries in the Boot.ini file no longer point to the correct partitions. If the error occurs after upgrading the disk controller, verify that the new hardware is configured properly. Then start your system with the Windows XP CD, log on to the Recovery Console, and use the Bootcfg command to scan for available Windows installations and repair the Boot.ini file automatically.

Stop 0x0000007F or UNEXPECTED_KERNEL_MODE_TRAP

Hardware failure is the most common cause of this error. You are most likely to see this Stop message if you have defective memory chips, mismatched memory modules, a malfunctioning CPU, or a failure in the fan or power supply that causes overheating. The error is especially likely to occur on systems whose CPU has been tweaked to run past its rated speed, a process known as "overclocking." The first parameter immediately after the Stop error number identifies the specific cause of the error, as explained in Knowledge Base article Q137539, "General Causes of Stop 0x0000007F Errors."

Stop 0x0000009F or DRIVER_POWER_STATE_FAILURE

A driver is in an inconsistent or invalid power state after shutting down, suspending to Standby or Hibernate mode, or resuming from either of those modes. This error is not limited to hardware drivers. It can also be caused by file-system filter drivers such as those installed by antivirus programs, backup utilities, and remote control programs. The name of the offending driver file often appears in the Stop message. As a troubleshooting technique, try uninstalling unsigned hardware drivers or the software that uses the named driver. Knowledge Base article Q266169, "How to Troubleshoot Problems with Standby Mode, Hibernate Mode, and Shutting Down Your Computer in Windows 2000," has additional suggestions for resolving this type of error.

Stop 0x000000C2 or BAD_POOL_CALLER

This Stop error occurs when a kernel-mode process or driver attempts to perform an illegal memory allocation. The problem can often be traced to a bug in a driver or software. It is also occasionally caused by a failure in a hardware device. You can find detailed debugging instructions for this error in Knowledge Base article Q265879, "How to Debug 'Stop 0xC2' or 'Stop 0x000000C2' Error Messages."

Chapter 28

Stop 0x000000D1 or DRIVER_IRQL_NOT_LESS_OR_EQUAL

This is one of the most common Stop errors. The error typically occurs when a driver tries to access an improper memory address. Check for unsigned drivers, and be especially suspicious of recently installed or updated antivirus programs, disk utilities, and backup programs, which may install a faulty file-system filter driver.

Stop 0x000000D8 or DRIVER_USED_EXCESSIVE_PTES

If a poorly written driver causes your computer to request large amounts of kernel memory, you may run out of page table entries (PTEs) and see this error message. The underlying cause of the error and troubleshooting suggestions are identical to those found in the Stop 0x3F message.

Stop 0x000000EA or THREAD_STUCK_IN_DEVICE_DRIVER

You may see this error message after you install a new video adapter or an updated (and poorly written) video driver that causes the system to pause indefinitely while waiting for the video hardware. To resolve the problem, replace the video adapter or use a different video driver.

Stop 0x000000ED or UNMOUNTABLE_BOOT_VOLUME

Windows XP was unable to gain access to the volume containing boot files. If you see this Stop message while attempting to upgrade a system to Windows XP, verify that you have compatible drivers for the disk controller, and check the drive cabling to make sure it is configured properly. If you're using ATA-66 or ATA-100 drivers, make sure you have an 80-connector cable, not a standard 40-connector IDE cable. See the troubleshooting suggestions for Stop 0x7B errors as well. In some cases, this error will spontaneously correct itself after you restart your system.

Stop 0x000000F2 or HARDWARE_INTERRUPT_STORM

This hardware-related Stop error can be extremely frustrating to experience and even more vexing to troubleshoot. The Windows XP kernel detects an *interrupt storm* when a device fails to release an interrupt request (IRQ). This error is usually caused by a poorly written device driver or a bug in firmware. To isolate the problem, try to determine which device is associated with the file name listed in the driver information section of the Stop message. Then use Device Manager or the System Information tool to identify other devices using the same IRQ, as described in "Viewing and Changing Resource Assignments," page 212. Remove all the devices identified as using that IRQ and add them back, one at a time, until the problem recurs.

Stop 0xC000021A or STATUS_SYSTEM_PROCESS_TERMINATED

This message indicates a serious security problem with Windows XP—a user-mode subsystem, such as Winlogon or the Client Server Runtime Subsystem (Csrss.exe), is compromised. The most common cause of this problem is a third-party program, and the solution is usually to remove that program. This error can also occur if a backup set has been partially restored, causing a mismatch in system files, or if system permissions have been incorrectly modified so that the System account no longer has permission to access system files and folders.

Stop 0xC0000221 or STATUS_IMAGE_CHECKSUM_MISMATCH

File or disk corruption problems (including a damaged page file) and faulty hardware are the most common causes of this type of Stop error. The Stop message usually includes the name of the damaged file at the end of the symbolic error name or on a line by itself; you might be able to restore the file from the Windows XP CD using Recovery Console. Restoring the Last Known Good Configuration might also help to resolve this problem.

Customizing How Windows Handles Stop Errors

When Windows encounters a serious error that forces it to stop running, it takes the following actions:

1 The system displays a Stop message on the screen.

2 Based on the preferences defined for the current Windows installation, the system writes debugging information to the page file. When the computer restarts, this information is saved as a *crash dump file*, which can be used to debug the specific cause of an error.

3 Again based on the current preferences, the system either pauses with the Stop message on the screen or restarts when the crash dump information has been saved.

You can customize two crucial aspects of this process by defining the size of the crash dump files and specifying whether you want Windows to restart automatically after a Stop message appears.

Part 7: System Maintenance and Recovery

By default, Windows XP automatically restarts after a Stop message. That's the pre-ferred strategy in response to a random, isolated Stop error. But if you're experiencing chronic Stop errors, you may have more troubleshooting success by reconfiguring Windows to halt at the Stop message and wait for you to manually restart the system. To make this change, follow these steps:

1 Open the System Properties dialog box from Control Panel. (As a shortcut, click the Start button, right-click My Computer, and choose Properties.)

2 Click the Advanced tab and then click the Settings button under the Startup And Recovery heading.

3 In the Startup And Recovery dialog box, clear the Automatically Restart check box.

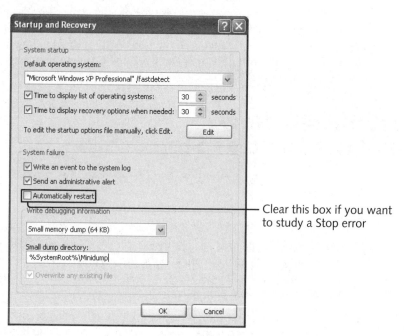

Clear this box if you want
to study a Stop error

4 Click OK to make the change effective.

From the same dialog box, you can also define the settings for crash dump files. By default, Windows XP saves the smallest possible amount of information in a 64-KB file. After recovering from a Stop error, the system displays the dialog box shown on the facing page. If you choose the Send Error Report option, the Small Memory Dump file is automatically sent to Microsoft.

Chapter 28: Troubleshooting Windows Errors

---

tip   **Clean up mini-dump files**

If you have a rash of Stop errors, mini-dump files can consume hard disk space unnecessarily. To clean the debris manually, open the %SystemRoot%\MiniDump folder and delete any files you find there. To automatically remove these files, use the Cleanup Manager options described in "Cleaning Up with Disk Cleanup," page 877.

In most cases, the information in a Small Memory Dump file is not sufficient to thoroughly debug an error. In the case of persistent Stop errors, a Microsoft support technician may ask you to create a more thorough crash dump file. To do so, open the Startup And Recovery dialog box using the steps outlined above, and change the selection in the Write Debugging Information list to one of the following options:

- **Kernel Memory Dump.** This option includes memory allocated to kernel-mode drivers and programs, which are most likely to cause Stop errors. Because it does not include unallocated memory or memory allocated to user-mode programs, it will usually be smaller in size than the amount of RAM on your system. The exact size varies, but in general you can expect the file to be approximately one-third the size of installed physical RAM. The crash files are stored in %SystemRoot% using the file name Memory.dmp.

- **Complete Memory Dump.** This option saves the entire contents of physical memory; as a result, it will be equal in size to your installed RAM. This can cause problems on systems with large amounts of RAM installed. On a system with 1024 MB of RAM installed, a crash dump file will use up 1 GB of disk space! The crash files are stored in %SystemRoot% using the file name Memory.dmp.

---

caution   Change memory dump options only when requested to do so by a support engineer, and change the options back to their default settings after troubleshooting is complete.

When It's Time to Ask for Outside Help . . .

new feature!

The Online Crash Analysis feature, which is new in Windows XP, allows the operating system to send debugging information to Microsoft Product Support Services automatically after a serious error occurs. This action occurs only with your permission. You can do so anonymously or you can use your Microsoft Passport to send an acknowledged upload. In the latter case, a support technician may contact you to request more details. With luck, the technician can suggest a course of action that allows you to recover from the error.

You can upload crash reports manually, using the Online Crash Analysis Web site. After uploading a crash report, you can check the status of your issue by returning to the site.

For more details, visit *http://oca.microsoft.com.*

Chapter 29

Editing the Registry

If you've ever read anything about the registry, you've seen the warnings: Do not try this at home—really. Making changes to the registry directly, as opposed to letting your software do it for you, is hazardous. An errant edit can bring your system down. That's why Windows is set up so that you normally don't have to get involved with the registry. When you change some detail about your system's configuration using Control Panel, Control Panel writes the necessary updates to the registry for you, and you needn't be concerned with how it happens. When you install a new piece of hardware or a new program, a myriad of registry modifications take place; again, you don't need to know the details.

But because the designers of Windows couldn't provide a user interface for every conceivable customization you might want to make, sometimes working directly with the registry is the only way to get a job done. And sometimes, even when it's not the only way, it might be the fastest way. So Microsoft Windows XP provides you with a registry editor that you should know how to use—safely. This chapter tells you how.

Understanding the Structure of the Registry

Before you begin browsing or editing the registry, it's good to know a bit about how this database is built. Figure 29-1 on page 973 shows a portion of a system's registry, as seen through Registry Editor (aka Regedit), the registry editor supplied with Windows XP. As shown in the figure, the registry consists of the following five *root keys:* HKey_Classes_Root, HKey_Current_User, HKey_Local_Machine, HKey_Users, and HKey_Current_Config. For simplicity's sake and typographical convenience, this book, like many others, abbreviates the root key names as HKCR, HKCU, HKLM, HKU, and HKCC, respectively.

At Home with Windows XP

The basic structure of the registry is identical in Windows XP Home Edition and Professional. To view and edit data in either edition of Windows XP, use the Registry Editor utility, which works exactly the same way in Home Edition as in Professional, including the ability of administrators to set permissions on individual subkeys. The only material in this chapter that does not apply to Home Edition users is the information about using Group Policy to prevent unwanted modifications to the registry, because Group Policy is not included in Home Edition.

R.I.P. Regedt32

Windows 2000 included two registry editors, Regedit.exe and Regedt32.exe. The functionality of Regedt32 has been incorporated into Registry Editor 5.1, the version shipped with Windows XP, and Regedt32 doesn't exist anymore. Typing **regedt32** at a Windows XP command prompt runs a small 4K program whose only function is to execute Regedit.exe.

In Windows 2000, Regedt32 suffered from a non-intuitive interface, but it could do a few things that the slicker-looking Regedit could not. The most important advantage of Regedt32 was that it enabled you to modify the permissions settings associated with registry keys—something that Regedit could not do. But overall, Regedit was the more versatile editor, with a Windows Explorer–style display and the ability to search for keys and values. In Windows XP, instead of using Regedit for most registry work and Regedt32 for the occasional task that Regedit can't handle, you can manage everything with a single editor. (To set permissions for a key in Regedit 5.1, right-click the key, and then choose Permissions from the shortcut menu.)

The only significant feature of Regedt32 that has not been incorporated into Registry Editor 5.1 is read-only mode. If you're accustomed to browsing the registry in Regedt32's read-only mode and don't feel comfortable without that feature, be sure to set a restore point before you begin browsing. If anything goes awry you can use System Restore to return to the restore point.

Root keys, also sometimes called *predefined keys*, contain subkeys. Registry Editor displays this structure as an outline. In Figure 29-1, for example, HKCU has been opened to show the top-level subkeys: AppEvents, Console, Control Panel, Environment, Identities, Keyboard Layout, Network, Printers, Remote, SessionInformation, Software, Unicode Program Groups, Volatile Environment, and Windows 3.1 Migration Status. A root key and its subkeys can be described as a path, like this: HKCU\Console. Root keys and their subkeys appear in Registry Editor's left pane.

Chapter 29: Editing the Registry

Figure 29-1. The registry consists of five root keys, each of which contains many subkeys.

Subkeys, which we call *keys* for short, can contain subkeys of their own. Whether they do or not, they always contain at least one *value*. In Registry Editor, that value is known as the default value. Many keys have additional values. The names, data types, and data associated with values appear in Registry Editor's right pane. As Figure 29-1 shows, the HKCU\Console key has many values—ColorTable00, ColorTable01, and so on.

The default value for many keys—including HKCU\Console—is not defined. You can therefore think of an empty default value as a placeholder—a slot that could hold data but currently does not.

All values other than the default always include the following three components: name, data type, and data. As Figure 29-1 shows, the ColorTable00 value of HKCU\Console is of data type REG_DWORD. The data associated with this value (on the system used for this figure) is 0x00000000. (The prefix *0x* denotes a hexadecimal value. Registry Editor displays the decimal equivalent of hexadecimal values in parentheses.)

A key with all its subkeys and values is commonly called a *hive*. The registry is stored on disk as several separate hive files. The appropriate hive files are read into memory when the operating system starts (or when a new user logs on) and assembled into the registry. You can see where the hives of your system live physically by examining the values associated with HKLM\System\CurrentControlSet\Control\HiveList. Figure 29-2 on the next page shows the HiveList key for one of the systems used for this book.

Chapter 29

973

Figure 29-2. You can find the names and locations of files that make up your registry in HKLM\System\CurrentControlSet\Control\HiveList.

Notice that one hive, \Registry\Machine\Hardware, has no associated disk file. This hive, which records your hardware configuration, is completely volatile; that is, Windows XP creates it fresh each time you turn your system on. Notice also the path specifications for the remaining hive files. Windows assigns drive letters after assembling the registry, so these paths do not specify drive letters.

If you explore the folders containing your hive files, you'll find hidden files with the extensions .alt and .log associated with each hive. The .log files are transaction files that record changes made to the associated hive. The .alt files are copies of the hive files. If a hive file is corrupted, Windows reconstitutes the registry using the associated .alt file.

Registry Data Types

The registry uses the following data types:

- **REG_SZ.** The SZ stands for zero-terminated string. This is a variable-length string that can contain Unicode as well as ANSI characters. When you enter or edit a REG_SZ value, Registry Editor terminates the value with a 00 byte for you. A quick scan of the registry reveals that REG_SZ is one of the most common data types and that it's often used for numeric as well as textual data. (See, for example, the values of HKCU\Control Panel\Desktop.) The default values of most keys, where defined, are of type REG_SZ.

- **REG_MULTI_SZ.** This type contains a group of zero-terminated strings assigned to a single value.

- **REG_EXPAND_SZ.** This data type is a zero-terminated string containing an environment variable, such as %SystemRoot%. If you need to create a key containing a variable name, use this data type, not REG_SZ.

- **REG_BINARY.** As its name suggests, the REG_BINARY type contains binary data—0s and 1s.

Environment Variables

As we note in the list of registry data types, the REG_EXPAND_SZ data type is used for environment variables. These strings, which contain information about the environment for the system and for the user who's currently logged on, can save time and keystrokes when used in batch files and shortcuts and at the command line. In addition, some programs use environment variables to determine where to store user data and temporary files. To use an environment variable in a command or a dialog box, surround the variable name with percent signs; this tells Windows to look up the current value for that variable in the registry and use that value in the command or path where you entered it.

Some environment variables can save a significant number of keystrokes. For instance, typing **cd %allusersprofile%** at a command prompt switches to the All Users profile folder, where shared documents and settings are stored. In a default installation, the full path name is nearly twice as long: C:\Documents and Settings\All Users. You can also use environment variables to create shared shortcuts that work differently for each user. A shortcut that points to the %UserProfile%\My Documents folder, for instance, will always open the My Documents folder of the user who's currently logged on.

Windows XP creates a group of default system variables, including several that define the location of Windows system files. Only an administrator can change a system variable. However, any user can add, edit, or remove user variables, which are exclusive to the user who created them and can be used in scripts and batch files.

To view and edit all variables, open the System option in Control Panel, and click the Environment Variables button on the Advanced tab. Click the New button to add a variable name and value; click the Edit button to change an existing variable, or use the Delete button to remove a variable. You can also see a list of all currently defined environment variables by opening a Command Prompt window and entering the **set** command.

- **REG_DWORD.** This data type is a "double word"—that is, a 32-bit numeric value. Although it can hold any integer from 0 to 2^{32}, the registry often uses it for simple Boolean values (0 or 1) because the registry lacks a Boolean data type.

- **REG_LINK.** The REG_LINK data type is a pointer to another section of the registry. For example, the HKCU root key consists of REG_LINKs to a specific user's data stored under HKU. When a user logs on, HKCU is mapped to point to the appropriate user-specific information in HKU. The REG_LINK type allows programs that need information about the current user's preferences or history to get that information from a single source, HKCU, without having to know who's logged on. You can't create REG_LINK values through Registry Editor. It can be done only through the registry application programming interfaces (APIs).

- **REG_NONE.** The rare REG_NONE type is used only in unusual circum-stances in which the presence or absence of a value is significant but the value's data is not.

- **REG_FULL_RESOURCE_DESCRIPTOR, REG_RESOURCE_LIST,** and **REG_RESOURCE_REQUIREMENTS_LIST.** These three data types pro-vide information about the resources used or required by various compo-nents of your system.

Avoiding Registry Mishaps

The two most important things to know about Registry Editor are that it copies your changes immediately into the registry and that it has no Undo command. Registry Editor doesn't wait for you to issue a File, Save command (it has no such command) before making changes permanent. And after you have altered some bit of registry data, the former data is gone forever—unless you remember it and restore it yourself or unless you have some form of backup that you can restore. Registry Editor is there-fore a tool to be used sparingly and soberly and not to be left open when not in use.

Backing Up Before You Edit

One relatively safe way to edit your registry is to back up the section you're interested in before you make any changes to it. If something goes awry, you can usually use your backup file to restore the registry to the state it was in when you backed up.

Registry Editor's File, Export command lets you save all or portions of your registry in several different formats (see "Understanding Registry Editor's Export Options," on the facing page). The best format to use before editing the registry is the registry hive format. This option saves a binary image of a selected portion of the registry. You won't be able to read the resulting file (choose one of the text-file options if that's what you need to do), but if you need to restore the keys you've worked on, you can be con-fident that this format will do the job correctly. To export a registry hive, select a key in Registry Editor's left pane, and then choose File, Export. In the Save As Type list of the Export Registry File dialog box, choose Registry Hive Files. The resulting file will include the selected key and all its subkeys and values. Note that you cannot save your entire registry as a hive file.

If you need to restore the exported hive, select the same key in Registry Editor's left pane, choose File, Import, and specify the file. You'll see a confirmation prompt letting you know that your action will overwrite (replace) the current key and all its subkeys. This is your last chance to make sure you're importing the hive into the right location, so take a moment to make sure you're in the right place before you click OK.

As an alternative to saving and restoring hive files, you can save and restore .reg files. This approach is fine if you're not going to add new values or subkeys to the section of

Understanding Registry Editor's Export Options

Registry Editor can export data in four formats: Registration Files, Win9x/NT4 Registration Files, Text Files, and Registry Hive Files. You choose these options from the Save As Type list in the Export Registry File dialog box.

The Registration Files option creates a .reg file, a text file that can be read and edited in Notepad or another similar program. A .reg file can be *merged* into a Windows XP or Windows 2000 registry. When you merge a .reg file, its keys and values replace the corresponding keys and values in the registry. Using .reg files allows you to edit your registry "off line" and add your changes to the registry without even opening Registry Editor.

The Win9x/NT4 Registration Files option also generates a .reg file, but one in an older format used by earlier versions of Windows. The principal difference between the two formats is that the current format uses Unicode and the older format does not. Use the Win9x/NT4 Registration Files option only if you need to replicate a section of your registry in the registry of an older system.

The Text Files option, like the Registration Files option, creates a file that can be edited in Notepad. But this format cannot be merged into the registry. Use it to create a record of your registry's state at a particular time. Because it cannot be merged, you won't need to worry that you'll accidentally overwrite current registry data with older data.

The Registry Hive Files option, discussed earlier (see "Backing Up Before You Edit," on the previous page) creates a binary image of a selected portion of the registry. It's the format of choice if you want to back up before working in Registry Editor.

the registry you're working with. If you do add data, however, importing an unedited .reg file that you saved before adding your new data will not remove the new data. It will return existing data to its former state but won't alter the data you've added.

For more information about using .reg files, see "Using .Reg Files to Automate Registry Changes," page 980.

Using System Restore to Save the Registry's State

The System Restore utility takes snapshots of your system's state, at prescribed time intervals or on demand, and allows you to roll your system back to an earlier state (called a *restore point*) if you experience problems. Creating a restore point before you begin working in the registry is an excellent way to protect yourself against mishap. (It's also a good idea to create a restore point before installing a new hardware device or application—in case the hardware or software creates some kind of mayhem.)

For information about using System Restore, see "Undoing Configuration Mistakes with System Restore," page 900.

Backing Up and Restoring the System State

Backup Utility, the backup program supplied with Windows XP, includes an option to back up your system state. If you exercise this option, the utility creates copies of your registry hives on your backup medium as well as in the folder %SystemRoot%\Repair. Backing up the system state—with Backup Utility or a comparable third-party program—should be part of your regular maintenance routine. In the event that your registry hive files become corrupt, you can use their backups to rebuild your system.

For details about using Backup Utility, see "Using the Windows XP Backup Program," page 883.

Browsing and Editing with Registry Editor

Because of the registry's size, looking for a particular key, value, or data item can be daunting. Fortunately, Registry Editor offers an efficient Find command (choose Edit, Find, or press Ctrl+F). Because the registry is large, finding the item you need might take a little while. Be aware that the Find command works in the forward direction only and does not wrap around when it gets to the end of the registry. If you're not sure where the item you need is located, select the highest level in the left pane (My Computer, if you're searching your own registry) before issuing the command. If you do have an approximate idea where the item you want is located, you can save time by starting at a node closer to (but still above) the target.

After you have located an item of interest, you can put it on the Favorites list to simplify a return visit. Choose Favorites, Add To Favorites, and supply a friendly name (or accept the default). If you're about to close Registry Editor and know you'll be returning to the same key the next time you open the editor, you can skip the Favorites step, because Registry Editor always remembers your position when you close and returns to that position at the next session.

InsideOut

If you prefer navigating with the keyboard, Registry Editor includes a number of time-saving shortcuts. To move to the next subkey that starts with a particular letter, simply type that letter when the focus is in the left pane; in the right pane, use the same trick to jump to the next value that begins with that letter. To open a key (revealing its subkeys), press Right Arrow. To move up one level in the subkey hierarchy, press Left Arrow. To move to the top of the hierarchy (My Computer), press Home. To quickly move between the left and right panes, use the Tab key. In the right pane, press F2 to rename a value, and press Enter to open that value and edit its data. Once you get the hang of using these keyboard shortcuts, you'll find it's usually easier to zip through the subkey hierarchy with a combination of arrow keys and letter keys than it is to open outline controls with the mouse.

Changing Data

You can change the data associated with a value by double-clicking the value in Registry Editor's right pane. Registry Editor pops up an edit window appropriate for the value's data type. So, for example, suppose you have applications that think your name is Preferred Customer (a common mistake on systems that come with Windows XP pre-installed). You can set matters aright by using Registry Editor's Find command to locate the data "Preferred Customer." Doing this will eventually take you to HKLM\Software\Microsoft\Windows NT\CurrentVersion. Selecting this key in the left pane and double-clicking the RegisteredOwner value in the right pane causes Registry Editor to display an Edit String window (shown in Figure 29-3), in which you can replace the current data with your own name.

Figure 29-3. When you double-click a data item in Registry Editor's right pane, the editor pops up an edit window appropriate for the item's data type.

Troubleshooting

You're not sure which subkey you're editing.

While you're working in the right pane, Registry Editor doesn't do much to highlight the current subkey in the left pane. The current subkey is differentiated from all the others by an open folder icon and a gray highlight, but it's not always easy to find that open folder icon at a glance. The best way to remind yourself which subkey you're working in is to look at the status bar, which always displays the full path of the current subkey. If you don't see the status bar, choose View, Status Bar.

Adding or Deleting Keys

To add a key, select the new key's parent in Registry Editor's left pane, choose Edit, New, and then choose Key from the submenu. The new key arrives as a generically named outline entry, exactly the way a new folder does in Windows Explorer. Type a new name. To delete a key, select it and then press the Delete key.

Chapter 29

Adding or Deleting Values

To add a value, select the parent key and choose Edit, New. Choose the type of value you want to add from the submenu. Table 29-1 shows the value types for each of the five data types as they appear on the Edit, New submenu. The value you select will appear in the right pane with a generic name. Type over the generic name, press Enter twice, enter your data, and press Enter once more. To delete a value, select it and press Delete.

Table 29-1. **Menu Names for Registry Data Types**

Menu Name	Registry Data Type
String Value	REG_SZ
Binary Value	REG_BINARY
DWORD Value	REG_DWORD
Multi-String Value	REG_MULTI_SZ
Expandable String Value	REG_EXPAND_SZ

InsideOut

Registry Editor isn't the only utility you can use to view and change values and data in the registry. A number of third-party software developers offer programs designed to do the same job with a little extra flair. Some offer improved search capabilities, including the ability to find and replace strings; others enable you to undo operations and compare different versions of the registry. If you're willing to accept the risks that come with more powerful tools, look at the free RegEditX (*http://www.dcsoft.com/ prod01.htm*); the Norton Registry Editor, included with Symantec's Norton Utilities (*http://www.symantec.com/nu*); or Funduc Software's Registry Toolkit (*http:// www.funduc.com/registry_toolkit.htm*).

Using .Reg Files to Automate Registry Changes

The .reg files created by Registry Editor's File, Export command are plain ASCII, suitable for reading and editing in Notepad or any other plain-text editor. Thus, they provide an alternative method for editing your registry. You can export a section of the registry, change it offline, and then merge it back into the registry. Or you can add new keys, values, and data to the registry by creating a .reg file from scratch and merging it. A .reg file is particularly useful if you need to make the same changes to the registry of

Chapter 29: Editing the Registry

several different computers. You can make and test your changes on one machine, save the relevant part of the registry as a .reg file, and then transport the file to the other machines that require it.

Figure 29-4 shows an example of a .reg file. In this case, the file was exported from the HKCU\Software\Microsoft\Windows\CurrentVersion\Explorer\Advanced key, shown in Figure 29-5.

Figure 29-4. A .reg file is a plain-text file suitable for offline editing. This one was exported from the key shown in Figure 29-5.

Figure 29-5. This key's name, values, and data are recorded in the .reg file shown in Figure 29-4.

Chapter 29

Identifying the Elements of a .Reg file

As you review the examples shown in the two illustrations, note the following:

- **Header line.** The file begins with the line *Windows Registry Editor Version 5.00.* When you merge a .reg file into the registry, Registry Editor uses this line to verify that the file contains registry data. Version 5 (the version shipped with Windows XP) generates Unicode text files. If you want to share registry data with a system running Windows NT or Windows 95/98/Me, choose the Win9x/NT4 Registration Files option from the Save As Type field in Registry Editor's Export Registry File dialog box. Otherwise, the Windows 95/98/Me or Windows NT version of Registry Editor will be unable to recognize the file's Unicode characters. (A Windows 2000 registry will be able to read the Unicode file, however.) To create a .reg file from scratch that's suitable for import into Windows 95/98/Me or Windows NT 4, use the header *REGEDIT4* instead of *Windows Registry Editor Version 5.00.*

- **Key names.** Key names are delimited by brackets and must include the full path from root key to the current subkey. The root key name must not be abbreviated. (Don't use HKCU, for example.) Figure 29-4 shows only one key name, but you can have as many as you please.

- **The default value.** Undefined default values do not appear in .reg files. Defined default values are identified by the special character @. Thus, a key whose default REG_SZ value was defined as MyApp would appear in a .reg file this way:

```
"@"="MyApp"
```

- **Value names.** Value names must be enclosed in quotation marks, whether or not they include space characters. Follow the value name with an equal sign. Notice that the value names shown in Figure 29-4 do not appear in the same order as in Figure 29-5. The .reg file displays values in the order they appear in the registry. Registry Editor, however, sorts them for your editing and browsing convenience. If you're creating a .reg file from scratch, the value order is insignificant.

- **Data types.** REG_SZ values don't get a data type identifier or a colon. The data follows directly after the equal sign. Other data types are identified as follows:

Data Type	Identifier
REG_DWORD	dword
REG_BINARY	hex
REG_EXPAND_SZ	hex(2)

Chapter 29: Editing the Registry

Data Type	Identifier
REG_MULTI_SZ	hex(7)
REG_RESOURCE_LIST	hex(8)
REG_FULL_RESOURCE_DESCRIPTOR	hex(9)
REG_RESOURCE_REQUIREMENTS_LIST	hex(a)
REG_NONE	hex(0)

A colon separates the identifier from the data. Thus, for example, a REG_DWORD value of 00000000 looks like this:

```
"Keyname"=dword:00000000
```

● **REG_SZ values.** Ordinary string values must be enclosed in quotation marks. A backslash character within a string must be written as two backslashes. Thus, for example, the path D:\Lotus\123\Addins is written like this:

```
"D:\\lotus\\123\\addins\\"
```

● **REG_DWORD values.** DWORD values are written as eight hexadecimal digits, without spaces or commas. Do not use the *0x* prefix.

● **All other data types.** All other data types, including REG_EXPAND_SZ and REG_MULTI_SZ, appear as comma-delimited lists of hexadecimal bytes (two hex digits, a comma, two more hex digits, and so on). The following is an example of a REG_MULTI_SZ value:

```
"Addins"=hex(7):64,00,3a,00,5c,00,6c,00,6f,00,74,00,00,75,00,73,00,5c,00,\
31,00,32,00,33,00,5c,00,61,00,64,00,64,00,64,00,69,00,6e,00,73,00,5c,00,\
64,00,71,00,61,00,75,00,69,00,2e,00,31,00,32,00,61,00,00,00,00,00,00,00
```

● **Line-continuation characters.** You can use the backslash as a line-continuation character. The REG_MULTI_SZ value just shown, for example, is all one stream of bytes. We've added backslashes and broken the lines for readability, and you can do the same in your .reg files.

● **Line spacing.** You can add blank lines for readability. Registry Editor ignores them.

● **Comments.** To add a comment line to a .reg file, begin the line with a semicolon.

Using a .Reg File to Delete Registry Data

.Reg files are most commonly used to modify existing registry data or add new data. But you can also use them to delete existing values and keys.

To delete an existing value, specify a hyphen character as the value's data. For example, to use a .reg file to remove the value ThumbnailSize from the key HKCU\Software\ Microsoft\Windows\CurrentVersion\Explorer, add the following lines to the .reg file:

```
[HKEY_CURRENT_USER\Software\Microsoft\Windows\CurrentVersion\Explorer]
"ThumbnailSize"=-
```

To delete an existing key with all its values and data, insert a hyphen in front of the key name (inside the left bracket). For example, to use a .reg file to remove the key HKCR\.xyz\shell and all its values, add the following to the .reg file:

```
[-HKCR\.xyz\shell]
```

Merging a .Reg File into the Registry

To merge a .reg file into the registry from within Registry Editor, choose File, Import. Registry Editor adds the imported data under the appropriate key names, overwriting existing values where necessary.

InsideOut

Sometimes it can be useful to monitor the changes that take place in your registry—particularly the changes that occur as the result of installing a new program or device. Windows XP does not provide a registry monitoring tool. You can find third-party products to do this job, however, including the freeware Regmon, developed by Mark Russinovich and Bryce Cogswell (*http://www.winternals.com/products/ monitoringtools/monitoringtools.asp*). SmartLine Software's shareware program, Active Registry Monitor (*http://www.protect-me.com/arm*), takes "snapshots" of the registry, allowing you to identify changes and experiment with different scenarios. Alternatively, you can take "before and after" shots of your registry and use the Command Prompt program Fc.exe to compare them. Before you install that program or device, use Registry Editor's File, Export command to save your entire registry as a large text file (you can choose either the .reg format or the .txt format). Repeat the process after the installation. Then, at a command prompt, type the following, substituting the actual file names of your files:

```
fc /u before.reg after.reg > regcomp.txt
```

The /U switch tells Fc to use Unicode. The > symbol saves Fc's output to a text file, which you can open in Notepad.

The default action for a .reg file is Merge—meaning merge with the registry. Therefore, you can merge a file into the registry by simply double-clicking it in Windows Explorer and answering the confirmation prompt.

> **caution** Because the default action for a .reg file is to merge it into the registry, if you want to edit the file, *don't* double-click it. Instead, right-click the file and choose Edit. (If you accidentally double-click, answer No to the confirmation prompt.)

Working with a Remote Computer's Registry

You can use Registry Editor to connect to the registry of another computer on your network. Choose File, Connect Network Registry, and then fill out the ensuing dialog box with the name of the computer to which you want to connect. The remote computer's name will appear as a top-level entry in Registry Editor's left pane, with its HKLM and HKU keys below, as shown in Figure 29-6.

> **note** To make changes to the remote computer's registry, you must be logged on as an administrator or a member of the Administrators group on both your computer and the remote computer.

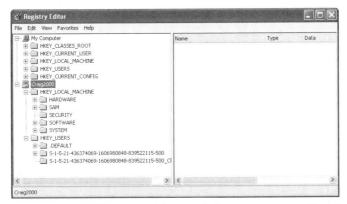

Figure 29-6. With appropriate permissions, you can use Registry Editor to work with a remote computer's registry as well as your own.

Changing Registry Key Permissions

By default, administrators and the System account have full control over all registry keys. The Creator/Owner of a key has full control over that key. (For example, a user typically has full control over HKCU while that user is logged on.) In other registry contexts, a user's default permissions allow read access but nothing more. If you attempt to change a registry key for which you have read access only, Registry Editor presents the appropriate editing dialog box but rejects your edit.

InsideOut

Compare the permissions assigned to a registry key with those available to files and folders, and you will notice one significant difference. In the Group Or User Names box for the HKEY_LOCAL_MACHINE, HKEY_CURRENT_USER, and HKEY_USERS keys, you'll find an entry called RESTRICTED. On all these keys, the Restricted SID is limited to Read permissions.

This security feature, available in both editions of Windows XP, is intended to protect you from suspicious programs. To take advantage of this protection, launch a program by using the Run As command (right-click the icon for a program or shortcut and choose Run As from the shortcut menu). If you choose to run the program using the credentials of the current user, you can then select the Protect My Computer And Data From Unauthorized Program Activity check box. This option runs the program using your credentials but adds the Restricted token, which prevents the program from making any changes to the registry. This option is especially useful when you're experimenting with a new program; by selecting this check box, you can safely run the program and see whether it generates any error messages or displays any unusual behavior. Don't use this option with programs designed to install software; setup programs are almost always designed to make changes to the registry and will invariably fail when given the permissions assigned to the Restricted SID.

You can prevent changes to an individual registry key and its subkeys (but not to individual values) by editing the permissions for that key. Registry permissions work the same way as permissions assigned to files and folders on an NTFS drive; for each account or group, you can allow full control, allow read access, deny access to the key, or set special permissions. To change permissions for a key, right-click it, and then choose Permissions from the shortcut menu. The Permissions dialog box, shown in Figure 29-7, closely resembles the Security dialog boxes available in Windows Explorer when Simple File Sharing is disabled.

Chapter 29: Editing the Registry

Figure 29-7. In most contexts, administrators have full control over data stored in the registry.

On a shared computer running Windows XP Professional, you might decide that certain users should be denied all access to registry editing tools. To enforce the ban, you can use Group Policy, as described in Appendix E, "Group Policy." From the Group Policy console, open User Configuration\Administrative Templates\System. Double-click the Prevent Access To Registry Editing Tools setting, and change it to Enabled. Unfortunately, this solution cannot be applied easily to a single user but instead locks out all users—you included.

> **note** There *is* a way to disable access to Registry Editor for individual users, but the work-around is difficult and not recommended for most users. You can read all about it in *Microsoft Windows Security Inside Out*.

Networking

Setting Up a Small Network

Setting up a network on a computer running Windows is no longer the complex and sometimes frustrating process it used to be. On a network where every computer is running Microsoft Windows XP, in fact, you may find that your network requires no configuration at all—after you finish setting up Windows, your network is available for immediate access.

You can ensure a trouble-free network setup by selecting the right hardware and configuring it properly. Even if you're a Windows networking wizard, you should use the Windows XP Network Setup Wizard to automatically set IP addresses, set workgroup names, configure the Internet Connection Firewall, and add required registry keys and values. After using the wizard, you can fine-tune network settings to suit your networking needs.

In this chapter, we focus exclusively on small networks (typically consisting of 10 computers or fewer) that don't include a system running Windows 2000 or Windows .NET Server. For details on how to work with domain-based networks, see Chapter 34, "Working with Windows Domains."

What You Can and Can't Do with a Small Network

With a minimal investment in hardware, you can connect two or more computers into a simple peer-to-peer network. Because these networks aren't built around a server, they don't allow you to manage users and shared resources centrally; instead, each computer contains its own database of authorized

At Home with Windows XP

This chapter explains how to configure a peer-to-peer network—one that is not part of a domain running Windows .NET Server or Windows 2000 Server. In this environment, the steps for setting up and configuring a network are the same whether you use Windows XP Professional or Windows XP Home Edition.

user accounts and shared folders, drives, and printers. Setting up a workgroup-based network offers the following advantages:

- **Shared storage.** By designating certain folders as shared resources, you avoid the need to swap files on floppy disks or to maintain duplicate copies of files; instead, everyone on the network can open a shared report or access a collection of digital photos or music files from a single location.

- **Shared printers.** Sharing a printer allows any authorized network user to print to that device. By setting permissions on shared printers on a home network, you can prevent your kids from wasting expensive paper and ink on a high-quality color photo printer. (This option is available only with Windows XP Professional, and only if Simple File Sharing is disabled.)

- **Shared Internet connection.** Using Internet Connection Sharing, you can set up Internet access on a single computer and allow every computer on the network to share that connection. This capability is most useful if you have a high-speed Internet connection, such as a cable or DSL modem; however, you can share a dial-up Internet connection as well and control it from any computer on the network.

For the most part, different versions of Windows can coexist quite peacefully on a network, if you plan carefully. If you plan to use Internet Connection Sharing, you'll have best results if you install Windows XP (Professional or Home Edition) on the computer that has the Internet connection. You can then use the Windows XP Network Setup Wizard to configure other systems running Windows XP, Windows 2000, Windows Me, or Windows 98.

---

tip **Set up a simple server**

If your network includes at least one computer running Windows XP Professional, you can use that machine as a workgroup server. Although this configuration doesn't come close to providing the centralized administration and security of a domain-based network, it does allow you to enforce security on a per-user basis. On the Windows XP Professional machine, disable Simple File Sharing and assign permissions to shared folders by selecting users and groups, as explained in "Controlling Access with NTFS Permissions," page 507.

Hardware, Cabling, and Connections

Before you can even think about setting up the networking software in Windows XP, you need to assemble and configure the proper hardware. In addition to two or more computers, you'll need the following components to set up a home or small office network:

- **Network adapters.** Each computer needs an adapter (also called a *network interface card*, or NIC) to communicate with the other computers on the network. Network adapters can be internal (usually installed in a PCI slot) or external (typically connected to a USB port). The overwhelming majority of network adapters conform to the Ethernet standard.

- **A central connection point.** Use a *hub* or *switch* to connect the computers in an Ethernet network. This function is sometimes integrated into a *router* or *residential gateway,* which typically adds network address translation (NAT) capabilities and security features. On wireless networks that use the 802.11b standard, a wireless access point handles these duties. Networks that use the Home Phoneline Networking Alliance (HomePNA) standard do not require a hub.

- **Cables.** On an Ethernet network, you connect each network adapter to the hub using an eight-wire Category 5 patch cable with RJ-45 connectors on each end. HomePNA networks connect to an existing telephone jack with a standard telephone connector (RJ-11). By definition, wireless networks require no cables.

---

tip   **Connect two computers without a hub**

If your home network consists of two computers and you have no plans to expand it, you can save the cost of a hub and use a crossover cable instead. A crossover cable is identical to a standard patch cable, except that two wires are reversed, simulating the connection that would take place if the wires were plugged into a hub. Using a crossover cable is an acceptable solution when you want to connect two computers directly to transfer files quickly with a minimum of hassle—using Windows Explorer and a two-computer network is much less hassle than cumbersome solutions that require null-modem cables and extra software. A crossover cable can also serve as a permanent connection between two computers if one computer has an Internet connection and the other doesn't. But as soon as you add a third computer to the network, you'll need additional hardware to serve as a hub.

Although it's not required, most networks also include one additional hardware component: a modem or other device to connect your network to the Internet.

Ethernet, Wireless, or Phone Line?

When setting up a network, you can choose from three popular technologies, all of which are supported by Windows XP:

● **Ethernet/Fast Ethernet.** This popular networking standard, developed in the mid-1970s, has stood the test of time. The original Ethernet standard (also known as 10Base-T) is capable of transferring data at maximum speeds of 10 megabits per second. The Fast Ethernet standard (also known as 100Base-T) can transfer data at 100 megabits per second. Some network adapters and hubs offer auto-switching (10/100) capabilities, allowing you to mix and match Ethernet and Fast Ethernet components on the same network. A relatively new standard called Gigabit Ethernet allows data transfers at 1 gigabit (1,000 megabits) per second. In an office or home that is wired for Ethernet, you can plug your network adapter into a wall jack and install a hub at a central location called a patch panel. In a home or office without structured wiring, you'll need to plug directly into a hub.

● **Wireless.** In recent years, wireless networking technology has enjoyed an explosion in popularity, thanks to its convenience and steadily decreasing prices. The most popular wireless networks use the IEEE 802.11b standard, adopted in 1997 and also known as Wi-Fi. Using base stations and network adapters with small antennas, Wi-Fi networks transfer data at a maximum frequency of 11 megabits per second (comparable to Ethernet speeds) using radio frequencies in the 2.4 GHz range. In theory, any network adapter certified as compatible with the Wi-Fi standard can connect to any 802.11b network, regardless of manufacturer.

A number of other wireless network standards promulgated by the IEEE's 802.11 Working Group promise benefits such as higher speed and better security. Be aware that, despite the confusingly similar names, network equipment using one of the wireless standards is generally compatible only with other equipment using the exact same standard. In addition to 802.11b, you might encounter the following:

■ **802.11a** broadcasts in a different frequency range, 5 GHz, and can reach maximum speeds of 54 Mbps, roughly five times faster than Wi-Fi.

■ **802.11g** is an alternative to the 802.11a standard that can also blast data across the network at 54 Mbps. Because this hardware uses the same 2.4 GHz frequency range as Wi-Fi adapters, manufacturers are more likely to make devices that support both standards, easing the transition for people who already have a substantial amount of Wi-Fi hardware and don't want to throw away that investment.

■ **802.1x** provides a mechanism for authenticating computers that connect to a wireless access point, typically through a Remote Authentication Dial-In User Service (RADIUS) server. This emerging standard is impractical for small networks but is ideal for large organizations that already have one or more authentication servers. (And no, the name is not a typographical error—because this standard applies to conventional wired networks as well as wireless, it contains only a single "1" in its name.)

- **802.11i** is the successor to Wired Equivalent Privacy (WEP), the authentication system built into the Wi-Fi standard that turned out to be unacceptably easy to crack. When this standard is finalized, it will probably incorporate a technique called Temporal Key Integrity Protocol (TKIP).

For the latest technical details, you can read the sometimes dense and dry commentary at the official site of the 802.11 Working Group, *http:// www.ieee802.org/11*. For a more readable summary, try the Web site run by the Wireless Ethernet Compatibility Alliance, at *http://www.wi-fi.org*.

- **Phone Line.** Networks that comply with the Home Phoneline Networking Alliance (HomePNA) standard closely resemble Ethernet networks and operate at Ethernet speeds of roughly 10 megabits per second. HomePNA networks don't require a central connection point such as a hub; instead, they employ a daisy-chain topology in which all network adapters communicate directly by plugging into existing telephone jacks and transmitting data on the same wires that carry telephone and fax signals, without interfering with those communications. For more information, visit *http://www.homepna.org*.

Installing and Configuring Network Adapters

On most systems, you don't need to take any special configuration steps to set up a network adapter. The Plug and Play code in Windows XP handles all the work of loading drivers. In the case of an internal adapter whose driver is included with Windows XP, the correct driver should be installed automatically when you restart your computer after installing the adapter (if Windows cannot find a built-in driver, you'll be prompted to supply the location of the driver files). For an external adapter connected to a USB or IEEE 1394 port, the driver loads and unloads dynamically when you attach or remove the adapter.

For more details about installing hardware, see "Setting Up a New Device," page 197.

As with all hardware devices, you can inspect the properties of a network adapter from the Device Manager window. (See "Finding Information About an Installed Driver," page 204, for details.) Most network adapters include an Advanced tab on the properties dialog box, from which you can configure specialized hardware settings. These settings are invariably hardware-specific, and they can vary dramatically, as the two examples in Figure 30-1 on the next page illustrate.

Chapter 30

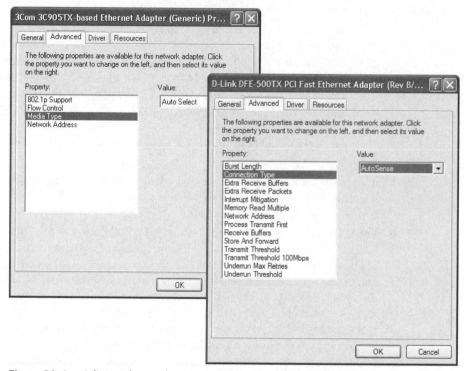

Figure 30-1. Adjust Advanced properties for a network card only when required for performance or compatibility reasons.

In general, you should accept the default settings on the Advanced tab of the network adapter's properties dialog box except when you're certain a change is required. In the examples shown in Figure 30-1, for instance, you can see by the selected Property and Value that both adapters are configured to automatically detect whether the network is operating in 10Base-T or 100Base-T mode. In some cases, this AutoSense or Auto Select capability may cause an adapter to operate at a slower speed than the rest of the network. In that case, you can force it to run at the correct speed by selecting the 100 Mbps speed from the Advanced options list.

---

tip **Check compatibility carefully**

In terms of compatibility, networking gear is among the most demanding of all hardware types. As always, your first stop before buying any networking hardware for use with a Windows XP system should be the Find Compatible Hardware And Software For Windows XP option in the Help And Support Center (under Pick A Task in the right pane). Trying to force old, incompatible network hardware to work with Windows XP is asking for trouble. Reliable, compatible, inexpensive network adapters are easy to find. If you're setting up a Windows network, don't settle for anything less.

Making Connections: Cables and Hubs

On a standard Ethernet network, all computers must be connected to a network hub. The hub is usually a small box with a row of jacks that accept RJ-45 connectors. Each jack is called a *port*. Most hubs designed for use on home networks and in small businesses have from four to eight ports. Here are some guidelines to follow when connecting your network to a hub:

- Place the hub in a central location. You must be able to run a cable from the hub to each computer on your network.

- The total length of all cables used on the network should not exceed 100 meters (328.1 feet). For most home networks, this is not an issue.

- It usually doesn't matter which ports you use on the hub, unless one is identified as *uplink*. Uplink ports are used to expand a network's capacity by connecting two hubs or sometimes to connect a hub to a router or broadband modem. On most hubs an uplink port cannot be used to connect to a computer, unless the uplink port has a switch to toggle it into a normal port mode. The uplink port achieves the same purpose as a crossover cable, and a toggle switch simply reverses the crossed-over lines to be able to accept a standard patch cable.

In addition to (or in place of) a hub, your network may use a router, switch, or residential gateway. This type of device is specifically designed to connect to an external DSL or cable, modem. Some residential gateways combine a router and hub; in this type of device, you connect your external DSL or cable modem to the Internet connector (often labeled as wide area network, or WAN) on the residential gateway and then connect each computer on the network to a port on the local area network (LAN) side. Some residential gateways are designed with a single Internet or WAN port and a single local port. If you have this type of device, connect the DSL or cable modem to the Internet connector and then connect the local port to your hub.

If you plan to use Internet Connection Sharing and you have an external DSL or cable modem, you'll need to install two network adapters in the computer with the shared Internet connection. The DSL or cable modem connects directly to one network adapter and provides the Internet connection. Connect the second network adapter to the same hub as the other computers in your home network.

If your cable or DSL modem is an internal device, or if you plan to share a conventional dial-up modem rather than a broadband connection, you need to install only one network adapter in the computer that will act as the Internet Connection Sharing host.

997

Special Considerations for Wireless Networks

In a wireless home network, you're likely to have only one access point. But in a sprawling corporate environment or on a college campus, multiple access points are available, making it possible for you to remain connected to the network as you roam from place to place. In either case, Windows XP includes automatic configuration features that help you set up your wireless network adapter automatically, without a lot of manual tweaking. These features also deal with the security problems inherent in any wireless network.

On a conventional wired network, physical security is a given: If someone plugs a computer into your hub, you'll know about it immediately, and you can trace the physical wire back to the intruder's computer. On wireless networks that use the 802.1x standard, however, anyone who comes into range of your wireless access point can tap into your network and intercept signals from it. Finding open access points has become something of a sport; participants call it *war driving*. Although some war drivers seek open access points just for fun, other users who find their way into your network present several risks:

- **Theft of service.** An intruder might be able to access the Internet using your connection, which could degrade the quality of your Internet service.

- **Denial of service.** An intruder who is unable to connect to your network can still cause some degree of havoc by flooding the network with connection requests. With enough persistence, an attacker could completely deny legitimate users access to the network.

- **Theft or destruction of data.** Outsiders who successfully connect to your network can browse shared folders and printers. Depending on the permissions assigned to these resources, they can change, rename, or delete existing files, or add new ones.

- **Network takeover.** An intruder who manages to log on to the network and exploit an unpatched vulnerability can install a Trojan horse program or tamper with permissions, potentially exposing computers on the LAN to attacks from over the Internet.

To add basic security to your system, you can and should configure Wireless Equivalent Privacy (WEP) on your network. WEP protects authorized users of a wireless network from eavesdroppers by encrypting the data flow between the networked computer and the access point. Typically, network cards use a 40-bit key (consisting of five 8-bit ASCII characters) to encrypt data. If your hardware supports it, you can add stronger encryption, such as a 13-character (104-bit) key. Even with encryption based on a 104-bit key, however, these security precautions will only keep out casual intruders. If your data is sensitive and your network is in an apartment building or office complex where you can reasonably expect other people to wander into range with wireless adapters, you need to install more robust security precautions such as IP Security (IPSec). For more information, see "IP Security and Filtering," in *Microsoft Windows XP Professional Resource Kit Documentation* (Microsoft Press, 2001). In one of our other books, *Microsoft Windows Security Inside Out for Windows XP and Windows 2000* (Microsoft Press, 2002), we provide more information about securing wireless networks and about using IPSec.

When you first install a wireless network card, Windows XP displays the Connect To Wireless Network dialog box, shown in Figure 30-2. Enter your WEP key and click the Connect button to join the network. (You must be logged in as an administrator to accomplish this task.)

Windows automatically detects available access points

Enter your encryption key here to reduce security risks

Figure 30-2. With its "zero configuration" feature, Windows XP reduces the hassle of configuring wireless networks.

Troubleshooting

You're unable to connect to your wireless network.

If you're having problems connecting to your wireless network, check the following:

● Does your wireless network adapter support automatic configuration? Check with the hardware manufacturer and, if necessary, update the drivers and firmware for the devices in question.

● Is automatic configuration enabled in Windows? Open the properties dialog box for the wireless network connection; on the Wireless Networks tab, select the Use Windows To Configure My Wireless Network Settings check box. If you are using the manufacturer's software to set up your wireless connection, clear this check box.

(continued)

Troubleshooting *(continued)*

● Is the Wireless Zero Configuration service running? Open the Administrative Tools folder in Control Panel and then double-click Services. Check the entry in the Status column for this service. If it doesn't say Started, right-click the entry and choose Start from the shortcut menu.

● Is the access point visible in the Available Networks list in the Connect To Wireless Network dialog box? If the access point does not broadcast its network name, you need to click Advanced and then click the Add button beneath the Preferred Networks list to manually enter its settings.

To set advanced options for a wireless network, follow these steps:

1 Open Control Panel, Network Connections.

2 Right-click the Wireless Network Connection icon and choose Properties.

3 On the Wireless Networks tab, shown here, you can perform any of the following tasks.

■ Enable or disable automatic wireless configuration by selecting or clearing the Use Windows To Configure My Wireless Network Settings check box.

■ Connect to a different access point by choosing an entry from the Available Networks list and clicking OK.

■ Change the settings for an existing wireless network connection by selecting its entry in the Available Networks list and clicking Configure.

> **tip**   **Network without an access point**
>
> Although the most common way to set up a wireless network is with an access point or residential gateway, you don't need this piece of hardware to set up a wireless network. By using *ad hoc mode* instead of the default *infrastructure mode,* you can connect directly to other computers on the network, as long as each one is equipped with a compatible wireless adapter. If you think of a wireless access point as a server, then a Wi-Fi network running in ad hoc mode is the equivalent of a peer-to-peer network. Wireless access points add the capability to share an Internet connection, assign IP addresses, and enforce security. To switch to ad hoc mode, open the Wireless Network Connection Properties dialog box and then click the Advanced button at the bottom of the Wireless Networks tab. In the Advanced dialog box, select Computer-To-Computer (Ad Hoc) Networks Only. Repeat this process on any other network computers equipped with wireless adapters. Your hardware may require additional configuration before an ad hoc configuration will work properly.

Configuring a Default Network Connection

After you've installed your networking hardware and powered up each of the computers on your network, Windows creates a local connection that includes the following networking components:

- **Client For Microsoft Networks.** A network client provides access to computers and resources on a network; this client allows you to connect to computers running any 32-bit or 64-bit Windows version.

- **File And Printer Sharing For Microsoft Networks.** This service allows other computers on your Windows-based network to access shared resources on your computer.

- **QoS Packet Scheduler.** This component (installed only on systems running Windows XP Professional) enables Quality Of Service features provided on corporate networks and by Internet service providers. For the most part, these advanced features will not be widely used until Internet Protocol version 6 (IPv6) is also widely used.

- **Internet Protocol (TCP/IP).** TCP/IP is the default network protocol in Windows XP. It provides easy connectivity across a wide variety of networks, including the Internet. Although TCP/IP has plenty of options you can configure, most users can safely accept the default settings without having to make any configuration changes.

For more details about TCP/IP configuration, see "Setting IP Addresses," page 1015, and "Troubleshooting TCP/IP Problems," page 1031.

Chapter 30

This default collection of clients, services, and protocols is generally all you need for working with a Microsoft network (that is, one where all computers are running 32-bit or 64-bit versions of Windows).

To see information about currently defined network connections, open Control Panel, Network Connections. Figure 30-3 shows the information and configuration options available from this window.

Use this list of tasks to work with a network connection

In Tiles view, icons and their descriptions provide useful information about connections

View summary information about the selected connection here

Figure 30-3. The Network Connections window is the starting point for configuring your network.

To see more detailed information about a network connection, double-click its icon in the Network Connections window. Figure 30-4, for instance, shows the status dialog box for the default Local Area Connection.

---

tip **Rename a connection**

Windows tags your main network connection with the Local Area Connection label. When you add connections, they get equally generic titles, like Local Area Connection 2. You can easily replace these labels with text that's more meaningful to you. For instance, on a computer that's serving as an ICS host, you might give your two network adapters distinctive names like "Media One Cable Modem" and "Home Network Connection." To edit a connection label, right-click the connection icon and choose Rename from the shortcut menu; then type the descriptive name.

Figure 30-4. The status dialog box provides basic statistics, including uptime, through-put, and the current connection speed.

newfeature!
Using the Network Setup Wizard

After you've successfully installed all the required hardware for your network, run the Network Setup Wizard. Even if your network seems to be working as it should, you should run the Network Setup Wizard anyway. This automated configuration utility sets the proper permissions on shared folders, adds required keys to the registry, configures protocols and binds them to network cards, enables or disables the Internet Connection Firewall, and adjusts system policies so that file sharing works properly over the network.

InsideOut

Are you a Windows expert? Do you have a disdain for all wizards? You're not alone. But even if you speak fluent TCP/IP and have multiple certifications in advanced networking, you should make an exception in this case and run the Windows XP Network Setup Wizard on every system that's connected to your network. Doing so is the only reliable way to ensure that your network has the proper baseline configuration. Afterward, you can manually adjust settings and enable or disable features as required.

If your network includes one computer that you want to use as an Internet Connection Sharing host, be sure to configure the Internet connection on that computer first, and then run the Network Setup Wizard on that computer. If all your networked computers have separate Internet connections, or if you use a router or residential gateway to share an Internet connection, you can start with any computer.

To start the Network Setup Wizard, open Control Panel, double-click Network Connections, and then click the Set Up A Home Or Small Office Network link under Network Tasks in the left pane. This choice is also available in the My Network Places folder. If you've turned on the Folders bar so that the task pane isn't visible in Windows Explorer, you can access the wizard from the All Programs menu—choose Accessories, Communications, Network Setup Wizard.

To use the Network Setup Wizard, follow these steps:

1 Click Next to skip past the Welcome screen. Click Next again to move past the Before You Continue screen. The Select A Connection Method page appears.

2 Choose one of these three options:

- **This Computer Connects Directly To The Internet. The Other Computers On My Network Connect To The Internet Through This Computer.** Select this option if you've already set up the Internet connection on the computer. Click Next to continue.

- **This Computer Connects To The Internet Through Another Computer On My Network Or Through A Residential Gateway.** If you use a router or residential gateway to manage shared Internet access, select this option and click Next to continue. If you use Internet Connection Sharing and you see this screen, stop and check your Internet connection. If ICS is properly set up, the wizard should display a different page of the wizard, as described at the end of this section.

- **Other.** Select this option if your computer is connected to the Internet directly or through a hub, or if your network has no Internet access. If you choose this option and click Next, you will see the Other Internet Connection Methods page shown next.

3 If you chose Other on the previous page, choose one of the following options. Otherwise skip to step 4.

■ **This Computer Connects To The Internet Directly Or Through A Network Hub. Other Computers On My Network Also Connect To The Internet Directly Or Through A Hub.** If your external DSL or cable modem is connected directly to the hub along with all networked computers, choose this option. Click Next to continue.

---

caution This configuration, in which all computers have individual Internet connections and direct access to other networked computers, potentially exposes your system to serious security risks. After the Network Setup Wizard finishes configuring your network, you must manually adjust settings to maintain network security and allow sharing. See "Securing a Peer-to-Peer Network," page 1027, for further instructions.

■ **This Computer Connects Directly To The Internet. I Do Not Have A Network Yet.** Select this option if you have only one computer and it is directly connected to the Internet. Click Next to continue.

■ **This Computer Belongs To A Network That Does Not Have An Internet Connection.** Choose this option if no computer on your network has an Internet connection you want to share. Click Next to continue.

4 If your computer has more than one network connection, one of which is directly connected to the Internet, the Select Your Internet Connection page appears.

Chapter 30

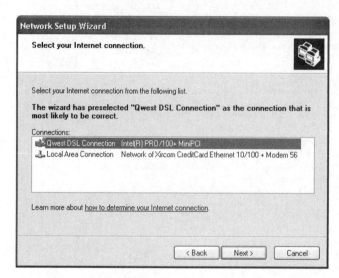

5 Confirm that the wizard has selected the correct connection and click Next to continue. The Give This Computer A Description And Name page appears.

6 Check the name of the computer listed in the Computer Name box. Adjust the name and description if necessary, and click Next to continue.

> **caution**   Under normal circumstances, you establish the computer name during Setup, and there's rarely a good reason to rename a computer. In fact, doing so can cause problems with some Internet service providers, which insist that your computer have a specific name. It can also cause inconvenience to other users who have created shortcuts to shared resources on your system. One circumstance in which it is desirable to rename a computer is if your preferred logon name is the same as your computer name. Windows XP does not allow you to create a user account whose name is the same as the computer name. In that case, it might be preferable to change the computer name so that you don't have to adopt a different user name.

7   On the Name Your Network page, enter the name of your workgroup. Note that this page is not like the previous page, in which the wizard correctly remembers your computer name. If you don't want to use the default workgroup name of MSHOME, you must manually change it here. (For more details about assigning workgroup names, see "Configuring Workgroup Settings," page 1013.) Click Next to move to the Ready To Apply Network Settings page.

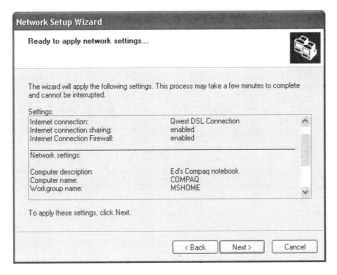

8   Scroll through the summary of changes the wizard is about to make to your network configuration. To make any changes to the settings you chose on the previous pages, use the Back button. If you're satisfied with the results, click Next to apply the changes immediately. The wizard displays an animated graphic while it works.

> **caution** When you change your network configuration, the Network Setup Wizard tempo-
> rarily shuts down your Internet connection and breaks off communication with the rest
> of your network. Do not run the wizard if you're currently in the middle of downloading
> files from the Internet or if other users are using shared resources on your computer.

9 On the final page of the wizard, you can create a network setup disk for use
on systems running previous versions of Windows that are connected to the
same network. If your network consists of Windows XP systems only, choose
Just Finish The Wizard and click Next to close the wizard.

> **tip** **Determine which connection is which**
>
> If you have two network connections defined, it can be difficult to tell which one is
> the Internet connection to be shared and which one belongs to your local network.
> The easiest way to determine which is which is to open the Network Connections
> window and then temporarily unplug the connection between your external DSL
> or cable modem and your computer. Within a few seconds, a red X should appear
> on one of the connections—note the name of that connection and select it when
> prompted by the Network Setup Wizard. (And don't forget to reconnect that cable
> before resuming the wizard!)

After running the Network Setup Wizard on the first computer, repeat the process on
other computers on the network. After you set up your shared Internet connection
using ICS, the wizard automatically detects the presence of the ICS host and becomes

considerably easier to use. Instead of the multitude of choices listed in step 2 on page 1004, you see the simplified dialog box shown in Figure 30-5.

Choose the first option: Yes, Use The Existing Shared Connection For This Computer's Internet Access. The wizard prompts you to enter or change the computer and work-group names and then automatically sets up the correct network and firewall settings.

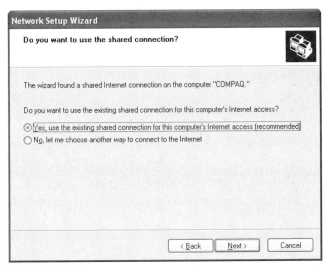

Figure 30-5. When you set up an ICS host first, the Network Setup Wizard automatically configures each additional computer to use the shared connection.

Adjusting Network Settings

Although the Network Setup Wizard is the preferred way to work with network settings, you may need to adjust settings manually under some circumstances. Windows XP allows you to add, remove, enable, and disable protocols; change network settings; and set IP addresses using options in the Network Connections folder.

Installing and Configuring Protocols

Network *protocols* are the common languages used to transfer data from point to point on a network. A few years ago, it was not uncommon for a computer running Windows to require multiple protocols, and earlier versions of Windows included a plethora of protocols developed for use on different types of networks—most of them completely irrelevant to home and small business users.

Because of the overwhelming popularity of the Internet, however, only one protocol is truly essential anymore. TCP/IP, the default protocol of the Internet, is installed on every computer running Windows XP. For virtually any networking task, TCP/IP is the preferred solution. It works equally well on tiny two-computer networks and massive multinational networks with thousands of workstations. In fact, TCP/IP is so essential to the basic operation of Windows XP that it can't be removed, although it can be disabled.

Two protocols that were once widely used in Windows networks are still available in Windows XP and can be configured for special purposes:

● **IPX/SPX.** This protocol was originally developed for use on networks running Novell NetWare. It's available in Windows XP as an installable option. As we explain later in this chapter, you should use IPX/SPX in addition to TCP/IP if you have an insecure network configuration in which all network computers share an Internet connection through a hub. For details on how to set up this configuration, see "Securing a Peer-to-Peer Network," page 1027.

● **NetBEUI.** This protocol (short for NetBIOS Extended User Interface) is available as an unsupported option in Windows XP. It was originally developed for use on small networks running Windows 3.*x*. NetBEUI can cause performance problems on some networks and should only be used when an existing network configuration requires it. In most cases, IPX/SPX is a better choice.

> **note** In most network setups, you don't need to install any additional protocols.

To install an additional protocol, follow these steps:

1 If you're going to install NetBEUI, insert your Windows CD. Use Windows Explorer to copy the following files from the CD's \Valueadd\Msft\Net\ Netbeui folder:

■ Copy Nbf.sys to the %SystemRoot%\System32\Drivers folder.

■ Copy Netnbf.inf to the %SystemRoot%\Inf folder. (This is a hidden folder. You can navigate directly to it by typing its name in the Address bar.)

2 From Control Panel, open the Network Connections folder.

3 Select the connection icon you want to edit and then click the Change Settings Of This Connection link under Network Tasks. (If this option isn't visible, right-click the connection icon and choose Properties from the shortcut menu.)

4 From the properties dialog box, click the Install button. The Select Network Component Type dialog box opens.

5 Choose Protocol and click Add. The Select Network Protocol dialog box appears.

6   Choose the protocol you want to add:

  ■ To install IPX/SPX, select NWLink IPX/SPX/NetBIOS Compatible Trans-
     port Protocol and click OK.

  ■ To install NetBEUI, select NetBEUI Protocol and click OK.

You can use the new protocol immediately.

To temporarily enable or disable the use of a protocol with a specific connection, open
the properties dialog box for that connection and select or clear the box to the left of
the protocol.

InsideOut

For performance or compatibility reasons, networking experts may want to specify the
order in which Windows should use different protocols. In Windows XP, this option is
still available, although it's well hidden. From the Network Connections folder, choose
Advanced Settings from the Advanced menu. The Advanced Settings dialog box, shown
on the facing page, lets you specify which protocols are available for clients and services on each connection and control the order in which each protocol is used. These
settings are strictly for specialized situations. Most networks will do best with the
default settings.

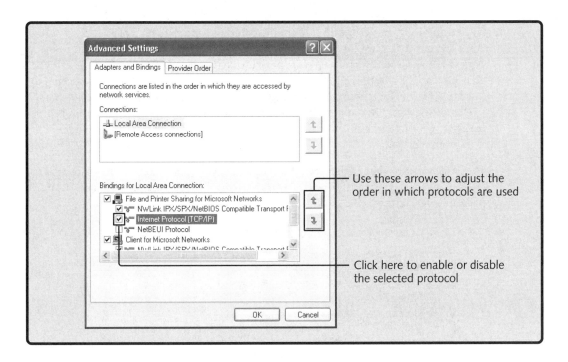

Use these arrows to adjust the order in which protocols are used

Click here to enable or disable the selected protocol

Configuring Workgroup Settings

After your network is properly configured, you should be able to see all other computers on your network by opening My Network Places in Windows Explorer. Click the
View Workgroup Computers link under Network Tasks in the left pane of My Network
Places to see a list of the computers on your network. (This option is not available if
your computer is joined to a Windows domain.)

---

tip   **Don't let the wizard change your workgroup**

Every time you run the Network Setup Wizard, you're required to pass through a page
where you enter the name of your workgroup. One usability glitch in this wizard has
the potential to temporarily cut off your workgroup if you blast through the wizard
without paying enough attention. The wizard automatically defaults to MSHOME as
the workgroup name, even if you've specified a different name during Windows
Setup, manually, or when running the wizard on previous occasions. Don't just idly
click the Next button. Be sure to enter the correct name for your workgroup.

To communicate properly with one another, all the computers on a peer-to-peer Windows network must be members of the same workgroup. "Joining" a workgroup doesn't require a secret handshake or special security settings. The workgroup name is strictly an organizational tool, which Windows uses to group computers and shared resources on the same network. As the administrator of a workgroup, you might want to change the workgroup name to something that describes your organization or family; if your network is relatively large, your network may have more than one workgroup defined.

The easiest way to change the workgroup to which your computer belongs is by using the Network Setup Wizard. However, you can also adjust this setting manually, using the following steps:

1 Open Control Panel, System, and then click the Computer Name tab.

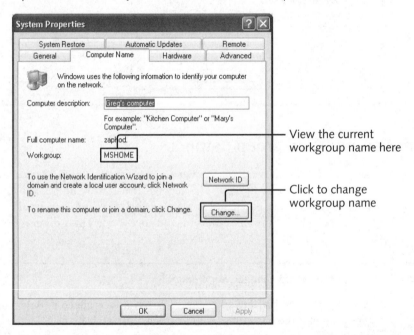

2 Click the Change button. (Don't be confused by the explanatory text for this button, which mentions domains but doesn't use the word *workgroup* at all.) The Computer Name Changes dialog box opens.

3 Select the Workgroup option and then replace the name of the current workgroup with the name of the workgroup you want to join or create.

4 Click OK to make the change. Two successive message boxes welcome you to the workgroup and remind you that you have to restart your computer to make the change effective.

> **note** A workgroup name can legally contain up to 15 characters. It cannot be the same as the name of any computer in the workgroup, and it cannot contain any of the following characters: ; : " < > * + = \ | ? ,

Setting IP Addresses

Networks that use the TCP/IP protocol rely on *IP addresses* to route packets of data from point to point. On a TCP/IP network, every computer has a unique IP address, which consists of four 8-bit numbers (each one represented in decimal format by a number between 0 and 255) separated by periods. In addition to the IP address, each computer's TCP/IP configuration has the following additional settings:

● A *subnet mask,* which tells the network how to distinguish between IP addresses that are part of the same network and those that belong to other networks.

● A *default gateway,* which is a computer that routes packets intended for addresses outside the local network.

● One or more *Domain Name System (DNS) servers,* which are computers that translate domain names (such as *www.microsoft.com*) into IP addresses.

Windows XP provides several methods for assigning IP addresses to networked computers:

● **Dynamic Host Configuration Protocol (DHCP).** This is the default configuration for Windows XP Professional and Home Edition. Most Internet service providers start with a pool of IP addresses that are available for use by their customers. ISPs use DHCP servers to assign IP addresses from this pool and to set subnet masks and other configuration details as each customer makes a new connection. When the customer disconnects, the address is held for a period of time and eventually released back to the pool so it can be reused. Many corporate networks use DHCP as well to avoid the hassle of managing fixed addresses for constantly changing resources. The Internet Connection Sharing feature in Windows XP includes a full-fledged DHCP server that automatically configures all TCP/IP settings for other computers on the network. Most routers and residential gateways also incorporate DHCP servers that automatically configure computers connected to those devices.

● **Automatic Private IP Addressing (APIPA).** When no DHCP server is available, Windows automatically assigns an IP address in a specific private IP range. (For an explanation of how private IP addresses work, see "Public and Private IP Addresses," on the facing page.) If all computers on a subnet are using APIPA addresses, they can communicate with one another without requiring any additional configuration. APIPA was first introduced in May 1998 with Windows 98 and works the same in all versions of Windows released since that time.

note For detailed technical information about APIPA, read Knowledge Base article Q220874, "Automatic Windows 98/Me TCP/IP Addressing Without a DHCP Server."

● **Static IP Addressing.** By entering an IP address, subnet mask, and other TCP/IP details in a dialog box, you can manually configure a Windows XP workstation so that its address is always the same. This method takes more time and can cause some configuration headaches, but it allows a high degree of control over network addresses.

InsideOut

Static IP addresses are essential if you plan to set up a Web server, a mail server, a virtual private network (VPN) gateway, or any other computer that needs to be accessible from across the Internet. Even inside a local network, behind a router or firewall, static IP addresses can be useful. For instance, you might want to configure the router so that packets entering your network on a specific port get forwarded to a specific computer. If you use DHCP to assign addresses within the local network, you can't predict what the address of that computer will be on any given day. But by assigning that computer a static IP address that is within the range of addresses assigned by the DHCP server, you can ensure that the computer always has the same address and is thus always reachable.

newfeature!

● **Alternate IP Configuration.** This feature, which is new in Windows XP, allows you to specify multiple IP addresses for a single network connection (although only one address can be used at a time). This feature is most useful with portable computers that regularly connect to different networks. You can configure the connection to automatically acquire an IP address from an available DHCP server, and then assign a backup address for use if the first configuration isn't successful.

Public and Private IP Addresses

Any computer that is directly connected to the Internet needs a public IP address—one that can be reached by other computers on the Internet, so that information you request (Web pages and e-mail, for instance) can be routed back to your computer properly. When you connect to an Internet service provider, you're assigned a public IP address from a block of addresses registered to that ISP. If you use a dial-up connection, your ISP probably assigns a different IP address to your computer (drawn from its pool of available addresses) each time you connect. If you have a persistent connection to your ISP via a DSL or cable modem, your IP address may be permanent.

On a home or small office network, it's not necessary to have a public IP address for each computer on the network. In fact, configuring a network with all public addresses increases security risks and usually requires an extra fee from your ISP. A safer, less costly solution is to assign a single public IP address to a single computer (or a router or residential gateway). All other computers on the network connect to the Internet through that single address. Each of the computers on the local network has a private IP address that is not reachable from the outside world. To communicate

(continued)

Public and Private IP Addresses *(continued)*   with the Internet, the computer or router on the edge of the network uses a technology called network address translation (NAT) to pass packets back and forth between the single public IP address and the many private IP addresses on the network.

The Internet Assigned Numbers Authority (IANA) has reserved the following three blocks of the IP address space for use on private networks that are not directly connected to the Internet:

- 10.0.0.0 – 10.255.255.255
- 172.16.0.0 – 172.31.255.255
- 192.168.0.0 – 192.168.255.255

In addition, the Automatic Private IP Addressing feature in all post-1998 Windows versions uses private IP addresses in the range from 169.254.0.0 to 169.254.255.255.

Routers, switches, and residential gateways that use NAT almost always assign addresses from these private ranges. The RG-1000 residential gateway from Agere, for instance, assigns addresses in the 10.0.0.*x* range (where *x* is a randomly assigned number between 1 and 255), and Linksys routers typically assign addresses starting with 192.168.1.*x*. The Internet Connection Sharing feature in Windows XP (as in previous versions of Windows) assigns private IP addresses in the 192.168.0.*x* range. If you're setting up a small business or a home network that will not be connected to the Internet, or that will be connected through a single proxy server, you can freely use these addresses without concern for conflicts. Just make sure that all the addresses on the network are in the same subnet.

To set a static IP address, follow these steps:

1 From Control Panel, open the Network Connections folder and select the connection whose settings you want to change.

2 Use any of the following techniques to open the properties dialog box for the selected connection:

- Select the connection and click the Change Settings Of This Connection link in the Network Tasks pane.

- Right-click the connection icon and choose Properties from the shortcut menu.

- Double-click the connection icon to open the Status dialog box and then click the Properties button on the General tab.

3 From the list of installed network components, select Internet Protocol (TCP/IP) and then click the Properties button.

4 In the Internet Protocol (TCP/IP) Properties dialog box, select Use The Following IP Address and fill in the blanks. Don't forget to fill in addresses for DNS servers as well. Figure 30-6 shows the dialog box with all fields filled in.

Figure 30-6. When assigning static IP addresses, you must fill in all fields correctly. Make a mistake and you'll lose your Internet connectivity.

5 Click OK to save your changes. You do not need to reboot after changing your IP configuration.

To set up an alternate IP configuration, follow these steps:

1 From Control Panel, open the Network Connections folder and select the connection whose settings you want to change.

2 Click the Change Settings Of This Connection link in the Network Tasks pane, or right-click the connection icon and choose Properties from the shortcut menu.

3 From the list of installed network components, select Internet Protocol (TCP/IP) and then click the Properties button.

Chapter 30

4 On the General tab of the Internet Protocol (TCP/IP) Properties dialog box, select Obtain An IP Address Automatically.

5 Click the Alternate Configuration tab and then select the User Configured option.

6 Enter the IP address, subnet mask, default gateway, and DNS servers for the alternate connection, as shown here.

note You can safely ignore the fields that ask you to enter a preferred and alternate WINS server. WINS stands for Windows Internet Name Service, a name resolution system that is sometimes used on large corporate networks with Windows domains. For virtually all home and small business networks, the WINS server details are unnecessary and irrelevant.

7 Click OK to save your changes. You do not need to restart after setting up an alternate configuration.

When you've configured an alternate IP configuration for a network connection, Windows XP looks first for a DHCP server to assign an IP address automatically. If no DHCP server is available, the system falls back to the static IP address defined on the Alternate IP Configuration tab.

Configuring a Dial-Up Internet Connection

Just as with previous versions, Windows XP includes a wizard that automates the process of setting up a dial-up Internet connection. If you upgrade to Windows XP, your previous connection settings should transfer to the new operating system without any problems. If you need to accomplish this task in Windows XP for the first time, be prepared for a few changes in the way you accomplish common tasks: The Dial-Up Networking folder is gone; instead, you'll find dial-up details in the Network Connections folder. Don't worry—the disorientation won't last long. The good news is that the improved setup process is straightforward and practically painless.

To set up a new Internet connection in Windows XP, start by gathering all the account information from your Internet service provider, including access numbers, logon names, passwords, and any other configuration details such as the names of e-mail servers. Then follow these steps:

1 From Control Panel, open the Network Connections folder and click the Create A New Connection link in the Network Tasks pane. Alternatively, choose File, New Connection. Click Next to skip past the Welcome screen in the New Connection Wizard.

2 From the Network Connection Type page, select Connect To The Internet and then click Next to open the Getting Ready page.

3 Choose Set Up My Connection Manually and click Next. The Internet Connection page opens, as shown on the next page.

4 Select Connect Using A Dial-Up Modem and click Next. The Connection Name page appears.

5 Enter a descriptive name for the connection in the ISP Name box. This is the label that will appear beneath the connection icon in the Network Connections folder. Click Next to continue.

---

tip **Describe your dial-up connection**

Adding extra detail to the connection name can make dial-up connections easier to use later. On portable computers, it helps to include the location along with the name of the ISP—*MSN Seattle, Earthlink Dallas,* and so on. If you set up multiple connection icons, one for your usual dial-up number and others for numbers you use when traveling, label each one clearly: MSN (Home), and MSN (Dallas), for instance.

---

6 On the Phone Number To Dial page, enter the exact number you need to dial to connect with the ISP, including any necessary prefixes or area codes. Click Next to open the Internet Account Information page.

7 Fill in the User Name and Password fields, and retype your password in the Confirm Password field. In addition, choose from the following three options:

■ **Use This Account Name And Password When Anyone Connects To The Internet From This Computer.** Select this option if you want to enable automatic dialing from all user accounts. Clear this option if you want to allow this connection to be used only when you've logged on to your account.

■ **Make This The Default Internet Connection.** Leave this option selected if this is your primary means of access to the Internet. Clear this check box if this is a backup connection.

■ **Turn On Internet Connection Firewall For This Connection.** Leave this option selected unless you have an alternate firewall program that you prefer to use.

Click Next to continue.

8 In the final page of the wizard, review your settings and click Finish to create the connection.

After you finish with the wizard, you can work with your connection by opening the Network Connections folder. To dial the connection manually, double-click the connection icon and click the Dial button.

To create a "hands free" connection that dials automatically without requiring your intervention, make sure you've saved all required information, including your user name and password, with the connection. Then follow these steps:

1 In the Network Connections folder, right-click the connection icon and choose Set As Default Connection.

2 From Control Panel, open Internet Options and select the Connections tab.

3   Select the dial-up connection from the list and then choose Always Dial My Default Connection. Click OK to close this dialog box.

4   Open Internet Explorer and browse to any page. When you see the Dial-Up Connection dialog box, shown here, select the Connect Automatically check box and click Connect.

Sharing an Internet Connection

To share an Internet connection safely on a small network, you have two options:

- **Install a router or residential gateway.** This piece of hardware sits between your network and your Internet connection (usually an external DSL or cable modem, although you can also use a conventional modem in this configuration). To the outside world, the residential gateway appears to be a computer, although it's considerably more secure because it does not have any running programs or disk storage that can be attacked by a hacker. This class of hardware typically uses network address translation (NAT) to assign private IP addresses to computers on your network. Because it's always on, any computer can access the Internet at any time through the gateway device.

> **tip** **Insist on a UPnP device**
>
> If you're shopping for a router or residential gateway for your network, look carefully. Make sure you get a model that is certified as compatible with Windows XP. In particular, make certain it supports the Universal Plug and Play (UPnP) standard, which allows programs like Windows Messenger and Remote Assistance to work seamlessly with the NAT features of the device.

- **Use Internet Connection Sharing (ICS).** In this configuration, the computer with the active Internet connection acts as the ICS host computer and shares its Internet connection. All computers on your network route their Internet traffic through the ICS host computer. ICS is most effective with high-speed (cable or DSL) connections, although it works acceptably with dial-up Internet connections. The ICS host computer must have a second network adapter to share a broadband connection; and, of course, the shared connection is only available if the ICS host computer is turned on.

To configure ICS, use the Network Setup Wizard. Run it first on the ICS host, and then on each network computer where you plan to use the shared connection. ICS works as follows:

- The shared connection on the ICS host acquires an IP address from the Internet service provider.

- The wizard enables the Internet Connection Firewall on the shared connection.

- The connection to the local network from the ICS host uses the static IP address 192.168.0.1, configured with a subnet mask of 255.255.255.0.

- The Internet Connection Sharing service runs automatically on the ICS host.

- A DHCP allocator on the ICS host automatically assigns IP addresses to other computers on the network. The default range is from 192.168.0.2 to 192.168.0.254, with a subnet mask of 255.255.255.0. A DNS proxy on the ICS host eliminates the need to specify DNS servers on other computers on the network.

- Autodial is enabled on the ICS host.

Troubleshooting

Your shared Internet connection isn't working.

Any of the following circumstances can prevent ICS from working properly:

- **The Internet Connection Sharing service is not running.** From Control Panel, open the Administrative Tools folder, double-click the Services icon, and then check to see that the Status column alongside the Internet Connection Sharing service reads Started. If necessary, right-click the Service entry and choose Start or Restart from the shortcut menu.

- **The wrong network adapter is shared.** Run through the Network Setup Wizard again and confirm that you've selected the correct adapters.

- **The settings on other network computers are incorrect.** Computers running Windows 98, Windows Me, Windows 2000, or Windows XP should be able to connect to the Internet through an ICS host, when configured to obtain an IP address automatically and obtain DNS servers automatically. Leave the default gateway field blank. If necessary, rerun the Network Setup Wizard on the other computers. (Note that this wizard will not run on Windows 95 or Windows 3.1.)

Securing a Peer-to-Peer Network

If you use Internet Connection Sharing or a residential gateway with network address translation, your network is safe from outside intruders. In the case of ICS, the Internet Connection Firewall protects the shared connection, and all remote users benefit from it. With a residential gateway, the hardware itself acts as a barrier between outsiders and computers on your network.

In one specific network configuration, however, every computer on your network is wide open to outside attacks. If you have an external DSL or cable modem and you

Chapter 30

connect it to an Ethernet hub along with other computers on your network, one of two things will happen:

● If you use the Network Setup Wizard, you'll receive a stern warning that this configuration is insecure and unsupported. The wizard sets the Internet Connection Firewall on each computer on your network. That allows every computer to access the Internet, but none of the local computers can see other local computers or access shared resources. Needless to say, this "safe" configuration defeats the purpose of having a local area network.

● If you disable the Internet Connection Firewall, every computer on your network can see the other computers and access shared resources. The trouble is, so can the entire outside world (assuming that your Internet service provider will assign a unique IP address to each computer). Anyone who can reach the IP address assigned to any computer on the network can poke around in shared resources. If you're using Windows XP Home Edition, the problem is especially serious, because Simple File Sharing allows unfettered access to shared files via the Guest account, as explained in "Introducing Windows XP Security," page 90.

If you're using this configuration for a home or small office network, you have two options:

● Replace the built-in Windows XP firewall on each networked machine with a third-party product such as ZoneAlarm or ZoneAlarm Pro (visit *http://www.zonealarm.com*). Using this configuration, you can run with a firewall, but define a local zone that includes all your local computers and allows them to punch through the firewall and access shared resources.

● Alternatively, you can disable File And Printer Sharing on the TCP/IP protocol and enable it on the IPX/SPX protocol for each computer on your network. This configuration is considerably more complex, but it's secure and doesn't entail any extra costs. To install the IPX/SPX protocol, see the instructions in "Installing and Configuring Protocols," page 1009. After adding this protocol, follow these steps to disable file and printer sharing on the TCP/IP protocol and allow it on the IPX/SPX protocol:

   1 Open the Network Connections folder from Control Panel.

   2 Choose Advanced Settings from the Advanced menu.

   3 In the Advanced Settings dialog box, select the connection that is used for Internet and local network access.

   4 In the Bindings box, locate the entry for Internet Protocol (TCP/IP) under File And Printer Sharing For Microsoft Networks, and then clear the check box to the left of it. Figure 30-7 shows what the result should look like.

Leave this check box selected to allow file sharing on your network

Clear this check box to disable file sharing over the Internet

Figure 30-7. If all your computers are exposed to the Internet, use this configuration to dramatically improve security.

note For the maximum in network security, consider installing and configuring the IP Security (IPSec) feature in Windows XP Professional. This option verifies, authenticates, and encrypts all traffic in and out of your TCP/IP-based network. For more information, see "IP Security and Filtering," in *Microsoft Windows XP Professional Resource Kit Documentation* (Microsoft Press, 2001) or "Restricting Ports Using IP Security," in *Microsoft Windows Security Inside Out for Windows XP and Windows 2000* (Microsoft Press, 2002).

Tweaking and Troubleshooting a Small Network

With Microsoft Windows XP, most simple networks of 10 computers or fewer just work. When you encounter network problems, however, the troubleshooting process can be tricky, because it's difficult to determine where the fault lies. In some cases, network problems are directly related to hardware, either on the local computer, elsewhere on your network, or at another stop on the connection between your computer and an Internet destination. But the problem is just as likely to be caused by a faulty configuration on your computer.

In this chapter, we explain how to identify and repair common network configuration problems, including TCP/IP address errors, improper subnet settings, and DNS problems.

We also explain how to identify situations where a network is performing at less than its optimum speed, and we show you how to take advantage of a new feature in Windows XP to quickly and easily bridge two networks.

Troubleshooting TCP/IP Problems

TCP/IP is the default communications protocol of the Internet, and in Windows XP it's installed and configured automatically. Most of the time, your TCP/IP connection should just work, without requiring any manual configuration. When you encounter problems with TCP/IP-based networks, such as an inability to connect with other computers on the

> # At Home with Windows XP
>
> The techniques described in this chapter work identically in Windows XP Home Edition and Windows XP Professional.

same network or problems connecting to external Web sites, the problem may be TCP/IP-related. You'll need at least a basic understanding of how this protocol works before you can figure out which tool to use to uncover the root of the problem.

Checking for Connection Problems

Anytime your network refuses to send and receive data properly, your first trouble-shooting step should be to check for problems with the physical connection between the local computer and the rest of the network. Assuming your network connection uses the TCP/IP protocol, your most potent weapon is the Ping utility. When you use the Ping command with no parameters, Windows sends four echo datagrams, small Internet Control Message Protocol (ICMP) packets, to the address you specify. If the machine at the other end of the connection replies, you know that the network connection between the two points is alive.

> **note** Where does the name *Ping* come from? Officially, it's short for Packet INternet Groper. However, it's more likely that this utility, which dates to the earliest versions of UNIX, was originally named after the sound a submarine's sonar system makes when it sends out pulses looking for objects in the sea. The "official" meaning was almost certainly made up after the fact to match.

To use the Ping command, open a Windows XP command prompt window (Cmd.exe) and type the command **ping** *target_name* (where *target_name* is an IP address or the name of another host machine). The return output looks something this:

```
C:\>ping www.example.com

Pinging VENERA.ISI.EDU [128.9.176.32] with 32 bytes of data:

Reply from 128.9.176.32: bytes=32 time=94ms TTL=242
Reply from 128.9.176.32: bytes=32 time=76ms TTL=242
Request timed out.
Reply from 128.9.176.32: bytes=32 time=81ms TTL=242

Ping statistics for 128.9.176.32:
    Packets: Sent = 4, Received = 3, Lost = 1 (25% loss),
Approximate round trip times in milli-seconds:
    Minimum = 76ms, Maximum = 94ms, Average = 83ms
```

1032

If all the packets you send come back properly in roughly the same time, your TCP/IP connection is fine and you can focus your troubleshooting efforts elsewhere. If some packets time out, the "Request timed out" message appears, as in the example above, indicating that your network connection is working, but one or more hops between your computer and the target machine are experiencing problems. In that case, repeat the Ping test using the –n switch to send a larger number of packets: ping –n 30 192.168.1.1, for example, sends 30 packets to the computer or router at 192.168.1.1. (Note that the –n switch is case-sensitive; don't capitalize it.) A high rate of timeouts, also known as *packet loss,* usually means problems elsewhere on the network and not on the local machine. (To see the full assortment of switches available for the Ping command, type **ping** with no target specified.)

If every one of your packets returns with the message "Request timed out," the problem may be the TCP/IP connection on your computer or a problem with another computer on that network. To narrow down the problem, follow these steps, in order, stopping at any point where you encounter an error:

1 Ping your own machine using either of the following commands:

```
ping 127.0.0.1
ping localhost
```

This standard IP address corresponds to your computer. If you receive an error, then TCP/IP is not configured properly on your system. For fix-it details, see "Repairing Your TCP/IP Configuration," page 1037.

2 Ping your computer's IP address.

3 Ping the IP address of another computer on your network.

4 Ping the IP address of your router or the default gateway on your network.

5 Ping the address of each DNS server on your network. (If you don't know these addresses, see the next section for details on how to discover them.)

6 Ping a known host outside your network. Well-known, high-traffic Web sites are ideal for this step.

7 Use the PathPing command to contact the same host you specified in step 6. This command combines the functionality of the Ping command with the Traceroute utility to identify intermediate destinations on the Internet between your computer and the specified host or server.

> **tip** **Choose your site carefully**
>
> In some cases, pinging an external Web site results in a string of "Request timed out" messages, even when you have no trouble reaching those sites. Don't be misled. Some popular sites, including Microsoft's home page, *http://www.microsoft.com,* block all ICMP traffic, including Ping packets, as a routine security measure. Try pinging several sites before concluding that your Internet connection is broken.

If either of the two final steps in this process fail, your problem may be caused by DNS problems, as described later in this chapter. (For details, see "Resolving DNS Issues," page 1038.) To eliminate this possibility, ping the numeric IP address of a computer outside your network instead. (Of course, if you're having DNS problems, you may have a hard time finding an IP address to ping!) If you can ping a Web site using its IP address but not by using its name, DNS problems are indicated.

If you suspect that there's a problem on the Internet between your computer and a distant host or server, use the Traceroute utility (Tracert.exe) to pinpoint the problem. Like the Ping command, this utility works from a command line. You specify the target (a host name or IP address) using the syntax **tracert** *target_name* and the utility sends a series of packets out, measuring the time it takes to reach each "hop" along the route. Timeouts or unusually slow performance indicate a connectivity problem. If the response time from your network to the first hop is much higher than the other hops, you might have a problem with the connection to your ISP; in that case, a call to your ISP's support line is in order. Problems further along in the traceroute might indicate congestion or hardware problems in distant parts of the Internet that are out of your ISP's hands and that might disappear when you check another URL that follows a different path through the Internet.

If your testing produces inconsistent results, rule out the possibility that a firewall program or network address translation (NAT) device (such as a router or residential gateway) is to blame. If you're using a third-party firewall program, disable it temporarily. Try bypassing your router and connecting directly to a broadband connection such as a DSL or cable modem. To see whether you're using the Windows XP Internet Connection Firewall (ICF), look in the Network Connections folder for a padlock icon and the word *Firewalled* on the connection icon in question. If you see these indicators, turn off Internet Connection Firewall temporarily, using these steps:

1 Right-click the firewalled connection and choose Properties from the shortcut menu.

2 Click the Advanced tab.

3 Clear the Protect My Computer And Network By Limiting Or Preventing Access To This Computer From The Internet check box.

If the Ping test works with the firewall or NAT device out of the picture, you can rule out network problems and conclude that the firewall software or router is misconfigured. After you complete your testing, be sure to enable the firewall and router again!

Diagnosing IP Address Problems

On most networks, IP addresses are assigned automatically by Dynamic Host Configuration Protocol (DHCP) servers; in some cases, you need to use static IP addresses, which are fixed numeric addresses. Problems with DHCP servers or clients can cause network connections to stop working, as can incorrectly assigned static IP addresses.

---

tip   Use these tools instead of Winipcfg

If you've recently switched to Windows XP from Windows 95, Windows 98, or Windows Me, you may be used to using the Winipcfg command to discover details about your IP connection and repair IP-related problems. That command is no longer available in Windows XP. To perform IP repairs, use the status dialog box from the Network Connections window. For detailed information about IP configuration, use the command-line based Ipconfig utility. Both techniques are described in this section.

To see details of your current IP configuration, follow these steps:

1   Open Control Panel and click Network Connections (click Network And Internet Connections if you're using Control Panel's category view).

2   Double-click the icon for the connection about which you want more information. (Alternatively, you can select the icon and click the View Status Of This Connection link in the Network Tasks pane.)

3   Click the Support tab to see the currently assigned IP address, subnet mask, and default gateway for that connection, as in the example in Figure 31-1.

Figure 31-1.   This IP address was automatically assigned by the DHCP server in a router.

If those details aren't sufficient—in particular, if you want to see information about DNS servers and when your DHCP address will expire and be renewed, click the Details button. Figure 31-2 shows the results.

Figure 31-2. This dialog box provides extra information about your network connection. Normally, DHCP addresses are renewed automatically at intervals shown here.

Want still more information? Then fire up a command prompt window (Cmd.exe) and use the IP Configuration utility, Ipconfig.exe. Used without any parameters, typing **ipconfig** at a command prompt displays the DNS suffix, IP address, subnet mask, and default gateway of your primary network connection. (It's identified as Local Area Connection in the Network Connections folder, unless you've renamed it.) To see exhaustive details about every available network connection, enter **ipconfig /all**.

note To see a full list of options for the Ipconfig command, use the /? switch.

The actual IP address you see may help you solve connection problems:

● If the address is in the format 169.254.*x.y*, your computer is using Automatic Private IP Addressing (APIPA). This means your computer's DHCP client was unable to reach a DHCP server to be assigned an IP address. Check the connection to your network.

● If the address is in one of the blocks of IP addresses reserved for use on private networks (for details, see "Setting IP Addresses," page 1015), make sure that another computer (an Internet Connection Sharing host) or a router or residential gateway is routing your Internet requests to a properly configured public IP address.

● If the address of your computer appears as 0.0.0.0, the network is either disconnected, or the static IP address for the connection duplicates an address that already exists on the network.

● Make sure you're using the correct subnet mask for computers on your local network. Compare IP settings on the machine that's having problems with those on other computers on the network. The default gateway and subnet mask should be identical for all network computers. The first one, two, or three sets of numbers in the IP address for each machine should also be identical, depending on the subnet mask. A subnet mask of 255.255.255.0 means the first three IP address numbers of computers on your network must be identical—192.168.0.83 and 192.168.0.223, for instance, can communicate on a network using this subnet mask, but 192.168.1.101 will not be recognized as belonging to the network. Likewise, with a subnet mask of 255.255.0.0, the first two numbers in each address must match—172.16.2.34, 172.16.4.56, and 172.16.83.201 are all valid addresses on a subnet with this mask. In every case, the gateway machine must also be a member of the same subnet. (If you use a router, switch, or residential gateway for Internet access, the local address on that device must be part of the same subnet as the machines on your network.)

> **note** Are you baffled by subnets and other related technical terms? For an excellent over-view of these sometimes confusing topics, read Knowledge Base article Q164015, "Understanding TCP/IP Addressing and Subnetting Basics."

newfeature!
Repairing Your TCP/IP Configuration

If you suspect a problem with your TCP/IP configuration, try any or all of the following repair options:

Run the Network Setup Wizard again   This option is especially useful if you've been tinkering with connection settings, or if you've installed a third-party utility that may have done so. Be sure to choose the correct option for your network configuration and enter the correct network name, as outlined in "Using the Network Setup Wizard," page 1003.

Use the automated repair option   Double-click the connection icon in the Network Connections folder and click the Repair button on the Support tab. Selecting this option has the same effect as typing the following commands from a command prompt:

- **ipconfig /renew.** Automatically renews your IP address from a DHCP server

- **arp –d.** Flushes the Address Resolution Protocol cache

- **nbtstat –R.** Reloads the NetBIOS name cache

- **ipconfig /flushdns.** Clears the DNS cache

- **ipconfig /registerdns.** Registers the computer's name on the appropriate DNS server

Renew your IP address If you don't want to perform the full set of repairs, use the Ipconfig /renew command to renew your IP address from the DHCP server.

Restore the base TCP/IP files Although you can't uninstall TCP/IP in Windows XP, you can reinstall all its components and reset registry keys to a clean state. To do so, type **netsh int ip reset resetlog.txt.** Note that this step is not as drastic as it sounds and will not tamper with your current network settings.

Resolving DNS Issues

The Domain Name System (DNS) is a crucial part of the Internet. (It's also at the heart of domains based on Windows 2000 and Windows .NET Server, a topic we touch on in Chapter 34, "Working with Windows Domains.") DNS servers translate host names (*http://www.microsoft.com,* for instance) into numeric IP addresses, so that packets can be routed properly over the Internet. If you can use the Ping command to reach a numeric address outside your network but are unable to browse Web sites by name, the problem is almost certainly related to your DNS configuration.

Here are some questions to ask when you suspect DNS problems:

Do your TCP/IP settings point to the right DNS servers? Inspect the details of your IP configuration and compare the DNS servers listed there with those recommended by your Internet service provider. (You may need to call your ISP to get these details.)

---

tip   **Translate names to IP addresses and vice versa**

The Nslookup command is a buried treasure in Windows XP. Use this command-line utility to quickly convert a fully qualified domain name to its IP address. You can tack on a host name to the end of the command line to identify a single address; type **nslookup ftp.microsoft.com**, for instance, to look up the IP address of Microsoft's FTP server. Or type **nslookup** to switch into interactive mode. From this prompt, you can enter any domain name to find its IP address. If you need more sophisticated lookup tools, you can find them from any search engine. Our favorite is the whimsically named Elephant's Toolbox, available at at *http://www.cotse.com/iptools.html* (you'll have to visit the site to learn how it got its name).

Is your ISP experiencing DNS problems?   A misconfigured DNS server (or one that's offline) can wreak havoc with your attempts to use the Internet. Try pinging each DNS server to see whether it's available. If your ISP has multiple DNS servers and you encounter problems accessing one server, remove that server from your TCP/IP configuration temporarily and use another one instead.

Have you installed any "Internet accelerator" utilities?   Many such programs work by editing the Hosts file on your computer to match IP addresses and host (server) names. When Windows finds a host name in the Hosts file, it uses the IP address listed there and doesn't send the request to a DNS server. If the owner of the server switches to a new service provider and changes its DNS records to point to a new IP address, your Hosts file will lead you to the wrong location.

InsideOut

A Hosts file can be useful on a mid-size network where all computers have static IP addresses. By entering computer names and IP addresses in a Hosts file, you eliminate the need to broadcast messages around the network looking for each machine. Instead, Windows finds the machine name and matching IP address in the Hosts file and goes straight to the correct address. To edit the Hosts file, use Notepad or another text editor. Open the Hosts file (it has no extension) in %SystemRoot%\System32\Drivers\Etc. The comments in this file explain its syntax and are very easy to follow.

If you suddenly and mysteriously lose the ability to connect to sites on the Internet, check to see whether you have more than one active network connection. This situation is most common if you've connected to a virtual private network and you also have a broadband Internet connection. In this case, the problem most likely occurs because the VPN connection thinks it is responsible for Internet access too. To fix this problem, follow these steps:

1 Open Control Panel, Network Connections, and click the icon for the active VPN connection.

2 In the Network Tasks pane, click Change Settings Of This Connection to open the properties dialog box for that connection.

3 On the Networking tab, choose Internet Protocol (TCP/IP) and then click the Properties button.

4 In the Internet Protocol (TCP/IP) Properties dialog box, click the Advanced button.

5 In the Advanced TCP/IP Settings dialog box, shown here, clear the Use Default Gateway On Remote Network check box.

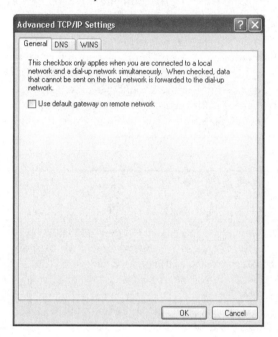

6 Click OK and then close all dialog boxes to save your changes.

Temporary DNS problems can also be caused by the DNS cache, which Windows XP maintains for performance reasons. If you suddenly have trouble reaching a single site on the Internet and you're convinced there's nothing wrong with the site, type this command to clear the DNS cache: **ipconfig /flushdns**.

Fixing Problems with My Network Places

One of the most annoying problems with any network occurs when you open the My Network Places folder and discover that none of the other computers on your network are listed there. When this happens, don't despair. Many times the problem is caused simply by a delay in the Browser service, which is used by all 32-bit Windows versions to maintain a list of computers sharing resources on the domain or workgroup in question. If you wait a few minutes, the missing computers will appear.

> **tip** **Allow time for network icons to appear**
>
> The rules that govern which computers handle browsing duties on a network are complex and occasionally Byzantine. But as a general rule, on a local network, you shouldn't have to wait longer than 24 minutes, and usually no more than 12 minutes, for the icons for network computers to appear in the My Network Places folder. If your network contains some remote segments, these periods may stretch out to 36 or 48 minutes. If you've waited more than an hour, something else is wrong. Want more details about how the Browser service works? Read Knowledge Base article Q188001, "Description of the Microsoft Computer Browser Service."

If you can't wait, then use the UNC name or IP address of the other computer and connect directly. If the other computer is named Harpo, for instance, and the Shared Documents folder is shared using its default name, you can connect to it directly by typing \\harpo\SharedDocs in the Run box.

Network Troubleshooting Tools

Windows XP contains a huge assortment of utilities you can use to diagnose, monitor, and repair network connections. Most of them are included within Windows itself. A few more are available with the Windows Support Tools collection, which you can install by running the Setup program found in the \Support\Tools folder on the Windows XP CD (Home Edition and Professional). Table 31-1 lists all the available utilities and summarizes how you can use them.

Table 31-1. **Windows XP Network Utilities**

Utility Name	What It's Used For
DHCP Server Locator Utility *Dhcploc.exe*	Displays a list of all available DHCP servers on the current subnet, so you can resolve conflicts caused by the presence of multiple DHCP servers; part of Windows XP Support Tools
Get MAC Address *Getmac.exe*	Discovers the Media Access Control (MAC) address and lists associated network protocols for all network cards in a computer, either locally or across a network
Hostname *Hostname.exe*	Displays the host name of the current computer
IP Configuration Utility *Ipconfig.exe*	Displays all current TCP/IP network configuration values and refreshes DHCP and DNS settings
Name Server Lookup *Nslookup.exe*	Displays information about Domain Name System records for specific IP addresses and/or host names, so you can troubleshoot DNS problems

(continued)

Table 31-1. *(continued)*

Utility Name	What It's Used For
Net services commands *Net.exe*	Performs a broad range of network tasks; type **net** with no parameters to see a full list of available command-line options
Netstat *Netstat.exe*	Displays active TCP connections, ports on which the computer is listening, Ethernet statistics, IP routing table, and IPv4/IPv6 statistics
Network Command Shell *Netsh.exe*	Displays or modifies the network configuration of a local or remote computer that is currently running; this command-line scripting utility has a huge number of options, which are fully detailed in Help
Network Connectivity Tester *Netdiag.exe*	Tests the status of your network connection and helps identify and isolate network problems; part of Windows XP Support Tools
Network Monitor Capture Utility *Netcap.exe*	"Sniffs" packets on a network (using Network Monitor Driver) and writes the information to a log file so you can identify suspicious or unauthorized traffic; part of Windows XP Support Tools
NWLink (IPX) Source Routing Application *Ipxroute.exe*	Displays and modifies information about the routing tables used for packets sent by the IPX protocol
PathPing *Pathping.exe*	Combines functions of Traceroute and Ping to identify problems at a router or network link
PPTP Ping Utilities *Pptpclnt.exe,* *Pptpsrv.exe*	Tests the path between virtual private network (VPN) clients and servers to verify that correct ports and protocols are in use; part of Windows XP Support Tools
TCP/IP NetBIOS Information *Nbtstat.exe*	Displays statistics for NetBIOS over TCP/IP (NetBT) protocol, NetBIOS name tables for both the local computer and remote computers, and the NetBIOS name cache
TCP/IP Ping *Ping.exe*	Verifies IP-level connectivity to another Internet address by sending ICMP packets and measuring response time in milliseconds
TCP/IP Route *Route.exe*	Displays and modifies entries in the local IP routing table
TCP/IP Traceroute *Tracert.exe*	Determines the path to an Internet address and lists the time required to reach each hop; useful for troubleshooting connectivity problems on specific network segments

Fine-Tuning Network Performance

Is your network running more slowly than it should? A fast, easy way to measure the performance of all active network connections is with the Networking tab in Windows Task Manager. To view current networking statistics, open Windows Task Manager by pressing Ctrl+Alt+Delete. (If the Welcome screen is disabled, or if your computer is joined to a domain, click the Task Manager button in the Windows Security dialog box, or use the Ctrl+Shift+Esc shortcut instead.)

In the example shown here, two network connections are active, so two graphs appear, one for each connection. Note that neither connection is even close to saturating available network bandwidth.

---

tip　**Rename network connections for clarity**

In the Network Connections folder, Windows automatically creates generic names for every connection—Local Area Connection, for instance. Get in the habit of renaming all connections in this folder with descriptive names. The names you assign will appear in Windows Task Manager graphs, notification area icons, status dialog boxes, and any other place where you can expect to see information about that connection. The descriptive name makes it much easier to troubleshoot, especially when you have multiple connections active.

On most networks, the speed of the connection to the Internet is the limiting factor for network performance. Plain Ethernet connections, with a theoretical maximum transfer speed of 10 megabits per second, run 3 to 10 times faster than even the fastest cable or DSL connections. You might see excessive network utilization on the local network connection for an Internet Connection Sharing host machine when several other computers on the network are transferring large files such as video clips directly from that machine and not from the network. Wireless connections that are having difficulty reaching a base station may also display performance problems as they automatically throttle down to lower connection speeds. Again, this slowdown will be most obvious when trying to transfer large files between two computers on the network.

For more information about how to use Windows Task Manager, see "Detecting Common Performance Bottlenecks," page 228.

---

caution   In theory, at least, you may be able to improve the performance of a TCP/IP-based network by tweaking specific settings in the registry. The TCP Receive Window (RWIN) and Maximum Transmission Unit (MTU) settings control technical details of how your TCP/IP connection transfers and receives packets. The Internet is awash with sites that claim to offer helpful advice and utilities that you can use to reset these values. Beware! Most of these articles are based on TCP/IP settings from previous Windows versions and do not apply to Windows XP, which does a generally good job of configuring connections properly. In fact, tweaking settings without understanding their consequences is a near-certain route to slower performance, and it may result in connection problems when your tweaked packets hit routers and other connection points on the Internet that can't handle them. If you feel compelled to experiment, set a System Restore checkpoint first, and read the definitive and exhaustive FAQ at the DSL Reports site, *http://www.dslreports.com/faq/tweaks*, before you fire up the Registry Editor.

newfeature!
Bridging Two Networks

As we noted in Chapter 30, "Setting Up a Small Network," Windows XP supports a variety of network media types, including Ethernet, Home Phoneline Networking, and wireless connections. In some cases, your home or small business network may consist of two or more different types of physical networks. For instance, you might have two desktop computers (we'll call them A and B) in your upstairs den connected to an Ethernet hub, with Computer A also serving as your Internet Connection Sharing host. In the basement, you have another computer (call it C) that you want to add to the network. Running coaxial cable to that distant location is impractical, but you have a phone jack in that location, so you've installed a phone-line network adapter and plugged in to that jack. Upstairs, you've installed a phone-line adapter in Computer B.

You now have two networks. Computer A and Computer B can communicate easily, and Computer B and Computer C can do so as well. But Computer A and Computer C have no way to reach each other, which means Computer C is cut off from the Internet as well. How do you bring all three computers into the same network? That's where Windows XP has a big edge over previous Windows versions. Instead of requiring you to install a hardware router and enable IP packet forwarding (a messy and complicated procedure), you can create a network bridge, which brings the two networks together seamlessly and creates a virtual connection between the separate network segments. In this example, you would bridge the two network connections on Computer B. In this configuration, Computer C could communicate directly with Computer A, even sharing its Internet connection.

caution In most home and small business setups, a network bridge is unnecessary and you should use Internet Connection Sharing or a router or residential gateway instead. If you plug a wireless access point into a router, for example, instead of hooking it directly to a broadband connection, it will join the other machines on your Ethernet network. Turn off network address translation on the wireless access point, and allow each networked computer equipped with a wireless adapter to receive its IP address directly from the router's DHCP server. This configuration requires that you dive into the access point's setup software and set some advanced options, but the results are worth it from a security and ease-of-administration point of view.

Although the steps to create a bridge are simple, the concepts behind it are potentially confusing. Here's what you need to know:

- You must be logged on as an Administrator to create a network bridge.

- You can create a bridge using any two Ethernet, IEEE-1394, or Ethernet-compatible wireless adapters. You cannot add a VPN connection, a dial-up Internet connection, or a direct cable connection to a network bridge.

- Any adapter that has Internet Connection Sharing or Internet Connection Firewall enabled cannot be added to the network bridge.

- Although it's technically possible, you should never bridge a connection that has a public Internet address with one that connects to a private network. In that configuration, you should use Internet Connection Sharing instead.

- When you use a network bridge, the machine that has the bridge enabled must be turned on to allow other computers to communicate across the virtual network. If you shut down that computer, you also shut down the bridge.

Although you can create a bridge manually, it is much easier to do so using the Network Setup Wizard. Run the wizard using the procedures outlined in "Using the Network Setup Wizard," page 1003. On the Select A Connection Method page, choose This Computer Connects To The Internet Through Another Computer On My Network

Or Through A Residential Gateway, and click Next. If you have two or more active connections that can be joined in a bridge, you will see the page shown here.

For most networks, choose the Determine The Appropriate Connections For Me option and then complete the wizard. (The only reason to use the manual option is if you have three or more network connections set up and you want to exclude one of them from the bridge.)

After the wizard finishes its work, a new device, Network Bridge, appears in the Network Connections folder, as shown here.

After you create the bridge, the settings for each individual connection are no longer available. To view details of your network configuration, double-click the Network Bridge icon and click the Support tab on the Network Bridge Status dialog box. To change details of the bridged connection, right-click the Network Bridge icon and choose Properties from the shortcut menu. The resulting dialog box, shown in Figure 31-3, lets you adjust configuration details for individual adapters or configure IP settings for the bridged connection.

Figure 31-3. To remove adapters from the network bridge, clear the appropriate check boxes in the Adapters section of this dialog box.

You can have only one network bridge on a single computer, although you can, in theory, have as many as 68 network adapters joined in a bridge. To add or remove network adapters from the bridge, right-click the connection icon in the Network Connections window and choose Add To Bridge or Remove From Bridge. If you decide you no longer want to use the network bridge, you can remove it by right-clicking the Network Bridge icon and choosing Delete from the shortcut menu.

Managing Shared Folders and Printers

By sharing your computer's resources, such as its folders and printers, you let other people on your network use these resources. With Microsoft Windows XP, using network resources and sharing your own resources with other network users is almost as simple and straightforward as using your own computer's resources. Browsing a network folder is just like browsing a folder on your own hard disk. Sending a document to a network printer is just like printing at your own computer.

Windows provides support for networks from a number of vendors and supports the simultaneous use of multiple networking protocols. This means that, assuming your network is set up properly, you should be able to work successfully in a heterogeneous network environment, which allows you to share and access resources on computers running Windows XP, Windows 2000, Windows NT, Windows Me, Windows 98, Windows 95, Windows for Workgroups, NetWare, and other operating systems.

Windows XP introduces a new wrapper on the sophisticated security settings for resource sharing that have been an integral—and often confusing—part of Windows 2000 and its predecessor, Windows NT. This wrapper, called Simple File Sharing, makes it easy to implement security appropriate for computers shared by multiple users and for many small network workgroups.

At Home with Windows XP

Because Windows XP Home Edition supports only Simple File Sharing, some of the material in this chapter will be useful only to users of Windows XP Professional. In particular, Home Edition users might want to skip over the section "Managing Shared Folders" (page 1064), which describes the Shared Folders console—a tool that is of limited utility under Simple File Sharing.

Access to folders shared by other network users is less convenient in Home Edition than in Windows XP Professional, because Home Edition is unable to retain network logon credentials. An effective and not-too-onerous workaround for this limitation is described in the Inside Out tip on page 1075.

This chapter covers the full gamut of sharing options: from the simplicity of Simple File Sharing (select one check box and immediately other network users can view and use files on your computer), to the nitty-gritty details of setting access permissions on a printer, to the arcane command-line tools that let you control shares from a batch program. It's all here.

newfeature!
Introducing Windows XP
Sharing and Security Models

Windows XP offers two distinctly different sharing models:

- **Simple File Sharing.** With Simple File Sharing, sharing folders and printers is easy, but your configuration options are limited. For example, sharing a folder in this model requires selecting a single check box, whereupon Windows XP sets appropriate shared resource permissions and NTFS file permissions. But a share created this way is available to all network users; you can't selectively set permissions for different users. With Simple File Sharing, Windows uses the Guest account for all network logons.

- **Classic sharing.** The classic sharing model is similar to the one employed by Windows 2000. When you share a folder, you must set appropriate shared resource permissions and NTFS file permissions to control the folder's use. But you can set varying permissions for individual users or groups (allowing full control to some, read-only access to some, and locking out others altogether, for example). You can also limit the number of simultaneous connections. This additional flexibility comes at the cost of complexity, however. In addition to understanding permissions and how to set them, you'll need to set up appropriate user accounts on each computer that allows network access.

Chapter 32

A Third Model: Share-Level Access in Windows 95/98/Me

If you shared folders or printers in Windows 95/98/Me, you might be familiar with a third sharing model. When not joined to a domain, those operating systems use *share-level access control*. With this type of access control, passwords (one for read-only access and one for full access) are assigned to each shared resource. When a network user tries to use a shared resource, Windows requests a password. Which password the user enters—the full control password, the read-only password, or an incorrect password—determines the user's level of access to the share. Windows makes no attempt to determine who the user is; therefore, anyone on the network who obtains (or guesses) the password has access to the share.

Windows XP, by contrast, always uses *user-level access control*, which means each shared resource allows access only by specified user accounts. To gain access to a shared resource over the network, a user must log on using an account that has access to the share.

You cannot set a password for a particular folder or printer in Windows XP; all access is controlled by permissions granted to specified users.

Windows XP Home Edition uses Simple File Sharing exclusively. Windows XP Professional can use either Simple File Sharing or classic sharing. To switch between these models, in Control Panel open Folder Options (in the Appearance And Themes category), click the View tab, and make your choice in the Use Simple File Sharing (Recommended) check box (the last item in the Advanced Settings list).

note If your computer is joined to a domain, it always uses the classic sharing model, regardless of your setting in Folder Options.

For more information about the two sharing models in Windows XP, see "Simple File Sharing vs. Windows 2000–Style Sharing," page 98.

Sharing a Folder over a Network

By sharing a folder with other network users, you enable them to access the folder (and the files it contains) directly from their own desktop. Gone are the days of "sneakernet"—copying files to a floppy disk and carrying it over to another computer. To create a shared folder, you must be logged on as a member of the Administrators, Power Users, or Server Operators group. (After a folder has been shared, however, the share is available to network users no matter who is logged on to your computer—or even when nobody is logged on.)

newfeature!
Enabling File Sharing

Sharing is disabled on a clean installation of Windows XP. That's because sharing in a workgroup environment relies on the Guest account, which is disabled by default. The easiest way to configure your computer for sharing folders, files, and printers is to run the Network Setup Wizard. The Network Setup Wizard also ensures that computers in your network share the same workgroup name; sets up a shared, firewall-protected Internet connection; and attends to other details.

> **For information about the Network Setup Wizard, see "Using the Network Setup Wizard," page 1003.**

If you haven't yet run the Network Setup Wizard, when you right-click a folder that you want to share and choose Sharing And Security, you're likely to see a dialog box similar to the one shown in Figure 32-1. (If the Network Sharing And Security box doesn't look like the one in the figure, sharing is already enabled.)

Click to run the Network Setup Wizard

Click to bypass the wizard

Figure 32-1. If sharing hasn't yet been enabled, you'll see a dialog box like this when you try to share a folder.

> **note** If the Sharing tab on your computer doesn't resemble the one shown in Figure 32-1 and the properties dialog box also has a Security tab, Simple File Sharing is not enabled on your computer. If your computer is not joined to a domain, you can enable Simple File Sharing with a visit to the View tab in Folder Options if you like. If you don't plan to use Simple File Sharing, skip ahead to "Restricting Access to Network Shares," page 1057.

You might be curious about the link that offers to bypass the wizard. Clicking it displays a dialog box similar to the one shown in Figure 32-2. Like the one before, this dialog box implores you to use the Network Setup Wizard. But if you've already configured your network so that computers are visible to each other, set up your Internet connection, and so on, you can safely choose the second option, Just Enable File Sharing.

Figure 32-2. This dialog box offers another chance to run the Network Setup Wizard.

Choosing the Just Enable File Sharing option does just two things:

● It enables the Guest account. If you prefer, you can do this manually by typing **net user guest /active:yes** at a command prompt. (Note that enabling the Guest account does not add it to the Welcome screen. To do that, you must open User Accounts in Control Panel and turn on the Guest account. This process enables Guest—if it's not already enabled—*and* removes the Deny Logon Locally user right for the Guest account.)

● It removes the Guest account from the list of accounts with the Deny Access To This Computer From The Network user right. To do this manually, you need to navigate to Local Policies\User Rights Assignment in Local Security Settings (Secpol.msc).

> **note** There's no reason to perform these tasks manually. But the online help doesn't explain what's happening "under the hood," and some users are curious (or concerned) about what changes are being made to their system.

What are the security risks that the dialog boxes shown in Figures 32-1 and 32-2 hint at? If you don't secure your Internet connection, someone on the Internet could gain access to your shared folders because the Guest account (and the folders it has access to) is available to anybody who finds his or her way into the network. The Network Setup Wizard secures the Internet connection by configuring Internet Connection Sharing and Internet Connection Firewall.

> **note** If you don't plan to use Simple File Sharing and you plan to create accounts on each computer for users who need access to shared network folders, you don't need to enable sharing in the manner described in this section. In fact, by *not* enabling the Guest account, you can create a more secure environment in which only users you designate can access your computer's shared resources. Specifically, if you don't enable sharing as described here, users on other computers must use an account that has the same name and password (the password cannot be blank) as an account on your computer. For more information, see "Restricting Access to Network Shares," page 1057.

Troubleshooting

A folder's properties dialog box doesn't have a Sharing tab.

If the folder's properties dialog box doesn't have a Sharing tab, be sure your system is set up for sharing. First, check the properties dialog box for the network connection, and be sure that File And Printer Sharing For Microsoft Networks is installed and selected. (For more information, see "Securing a Peer-to-Peer Network," page 1027.) Then use the Services tool (right-click My Computer, choose Manage from the shortcut menu, expand Services And Applications, and click Services), and be sure the Server service is started.

newfeature!
Using the Guest Account for Simple Sharing

The easiest way to set up sharing is with Simple File Sharing enabled. You can share any drive or any folder except Program Files and Windows. (You can share subfolders of these system folders, however.) To share a folder or drive, follow these steps:

1 In Windows Explorer, display the icon for the folder or drive you want to share.

2 Right-click the icon and click Sharing And Security.

If you're sharing a drive, you'll see a dialog box like the one shown below.

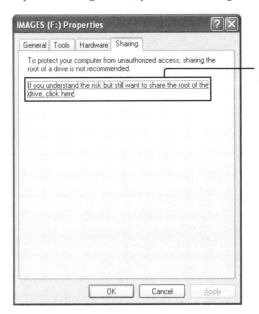

After you consider the ramifications, click here to proceed

3 Be aware that sharing a drive shares not just its root folder, but all its subfolders as well; everything on the drive is available. And because Simple File Sharing allows any network user to access your shared resources, this opens the full content of your shared drive to anyone on your network. (If the drive is formatted as an NTFS volume, NTFS permissions might be configured to restrict Guest access to some folders, however.) In general, you're better off sharing folders instead of drives; you're exposing fewer of your files to others. However, in certain situations—a CD-ROM drive or a drive dedicated to music files, for example—you might want to provide such unlimited access. If that's the case, go ahead and click the link.

4 In the Network Sharing And Security box, select Share This Folder On The Network.

5 Specify a name for the shared resource in the Share Name box. (This is the name that network users see when they browse to your shared folder.) Windows proposes the name of the folder or, for a drive, the volume name and drive letter. Making a change here affects only the name visible on the network; it doesn't change the name of the folder on your computer.

6 If you want to allow network users to view files in your shared folder and its subfolders, but not allow them to create or modify files, clear Allow Network Users To Change My Files. By default, Windows leaves this check box selected, which means network users can create and modify files in your shared folder (subject to the limitations imposed on the Guest account).

---

tip **Hide a shared folder from casual browsers**

If you append a dollar sign to the share name (for example, **Elopement$**), the folder is not visible to users who browse the network with My Network Places or Windows Explorer. Users whom you've entrusted with the name of your shared folder can still connect to it by typing its name—including the dollar sign—into any place network paths are accepted, such as the Address bar, the Add Network Place Wizard, the Map Network Drive dialog box, and so on.

Note, however, that hiding share names that end with a dollar sign is a function of the client computer, not the server. (In this context, *server* means the computer that has the shared folder.) All versions of Windows hide such shares, but if your network includes Apple Macintosh or Linux computers, users on those computers can view the "hidden" shares. Therefore, you can't rely on this method to completely secure your sensitive shared data; you must also set permissions appropriately.

1056

When you complete these steps, all network users will be able to find your shared folder in their My Network Places folder (if automatic discovery of network places is disabled, they'll need to browse to the shared folder), view its contents, and—unless you cleared the last check box—change its contents. Regardless of how they're logged onto their own computer, your computer authenticates network users as if they were using the Guest account. Within the folders you share over the network, network users have the same privileges as those granted to someone logging on locally as Guest.

Behind the scenes, here's what Windows does when you share a folder with Simple File Sharing enabled:

- It creates a share and grants shared resource permission to the built-in Everyone group. (The Guest account is a member of the Everyone group.) Depending on the choice you make in the Allow Network Users To Change My Files check box, Windows grants Read permission (if the check box is not selected) or Full Control permission to Everyone.

- If the shared folder is on an NTFS-formatted drive, Windows adds an entry for Everyone to the folder's access control list (ACL). If Allow Network Users To Change My Files is not selected, the ACL allows Read & Execute permission; otherwise, the ACL allows Modify permission. Be aware that, by default, NTFS permissions are inherited by *child objects* (that is, files and folders in the folder, as well as the files and folders they contain).

> For information about shared resource permissions vs. NTFS permissions, see "How Shared Resource Permissions and NTFS Permissions Work Together," on the next page. For information about inheritance, see "Applying Permissions to Subfolders Through Inheritance," page 517.

With Simple File Sharing, sharing is indeed simple and convenient. What Simple File Sharing lacks, however, is the ability to restrict access to certain network users or to impose different restrictions on different users. To do that, you must use classic sharing, as described in the next section.

> **note** The simple act of enabling sharing shares your computer's Shared Documents folder on the network. It appears on other computers as SharedDocs, and all network users can view, modify, and add files in this folder.

Restricting Access to Network Shares

Compared with Simple File Sharing, the classic sharing model provides a quantum leap in control over what you allow other users to do with your resources—and in complexity. Classic sharing allows you to control who can access each resource (instead of allowing access to everyone on the network) and what permissions they have (instead of allowing the same access—modify or read-only—to everyone who connects over the network).

> **note** Classic sharing is not available in Windows XP Home Edition.

> **tip** **Set different permissions for administrators and limited users**
>
> Windows provides another way to set different permissions for different users: the Create Shared Folder Wizard, which you open from the Shared Folders snap-in. For details, see "Creating a New Share," page 1066.

To enable classic sharing, in Control Panel open Folder Options (in the Appearance And Themes category), click the View tab, and clear the Use Simple File Sharing (Recommended) check box.

Classic sharing imposes three fundamental changes in the way you control network access:

- You specify shared resource permissions on a per-user basis. (Simple File Sharing, you'll recall, sets shared resource permissions only for the Everyone group.)

- If the shared folder is on an NTFS volume, you specify ACLs for each object in the share. (Simple File Sharing sets NTFS permissions only for the Everyone group, and hides the ability to view or modify ACLs.)

- Users who connect to your computer over the network are not automatically authenticated as Guest. If a network user's user name and nonblank password matches the user name and password of an account on your computer, Windows authenticates the user as the local account. If the network user's name and password do not match a local account, he or she is authenticated as Guest.

How Shared Resource Permissions and NTFS Permissions Work Together

The implementation of shared resource permissions and NTFS permissions is confusingly similar, but it's important to recognize that these are two separate levels of access control. Only connections that successfully pass through both gates are granted access.

Shared resource permissions control *network* access to a particular resource. Shared resource permissions do not affect users who log on locally. You set shared resource permissions on the Sharing tab of a folder's properties dialog box.

**How Shared Resource Permissions
and NTFS Permissions Work Together** *(continued)*

NTFS permissions apply to folders and files on an NTFS-formatted drive. They provide extremely granular control over an object. For each user to whom you want to grant access, you can specify exactly what they're allowed to do: run programs, view folder contents, create new files, change existing files, and so on. You set NTFS permissions on the Security tab of the properties dialog box for a folder or file. For more information, see "Controlling Access with NTFS Permissions," page 507.

It's important to recognize that the two types of permissions are combined in the most restrictive way. If, for example, a user is granted read permission on the network share, it doesn't matter whether the account has Full-Control NTFS permissions on the same folder; the user gets only read access when connecting over the network. In effect, the two sets of permissions act in tandem as "gatekeepers" that winnow out incoming network connections. An account that attempts to connect over the network is examined first by the shared resource permissions gatekeeper. The account is either bounced out on its caboodle or allowed to enter with certain permissions. It's then confronted by the NTFS permissions gatekeeper, which might strip away (but not add to) some or all of the permissions granted at the first doorway.

In determining the effective permission for a particular account, you must also consider the effect of group membership. Permissions are cumulative; an account that is a member of one or more groups is granted all the permissions granted explicitly to the account as well as all permissions granted to each group of which it's a member. The only exception to this rule is Deny permissions, which take precedence over any conflicting Allow permissions. For more information, see "Testing the Effect of Permissions," page 521.

Preparing for Classic Security: Setting Up User Accounts

If the computers in your network are set up as a *workgroup* (that is, they're not joined to a domain), each computer maintains its own security database of user accounts. (By contrast, in a domain environment information about global user accounts is stored on a domain controller. All computers in the domain refer to the domain controller when they need account information.) To secure resources with either type of setup, you create user accounts, and then you give those accounts permission to use specific resources. The difference is that in a workgroup, you must create user accounts on each computer instead of doing it once on a server.

On each computer in the workgroup, add a user account for each user who needs access to the computer's shared resources. For each user, if you use the same user name and password on each computer on the network, users won't have to log on to each machine individually. Logging on to their local machine allows them to access all the resources for which they have permission.

Follow these steps to add a user account:

1 In Control Panel, open User Accounts.

2 Click Create A New Account.

3 When prompted, enter a user name and then create an account.

4 After the account is created, double-click it and click Create A Password to specify a password for the account.

For each account you create, the user name and password must be identical on all computers.

> **note** Accounts that you intend to use for network access to shared folders must have a password. Except for the Guest account, Windows security prohibits network access by accounts with a blank password.

> For more information about user accounts, see "Working with User Accounts," page 100.

Sharing a Folder Using Classic Security

Provided you are logged on as a member of the Administrators, Power Users, or Server Operators group, you can share folders on your own system with other users on your network.

> **tip** Set NTFS permissions first
>
> If you're sharing a folder on an NTFS drive, you should set the NTFS permissions as you want them before you share the folder. That way, security restrictions are in place before you make the folder available on the network.

To share a folder or drive, follow these steps:

1 In Windows Explorer, display the icon for the folder or drive you want to share.

2 Right-click the icon and click Sharing And Security.

This takes you to the Sharing tab of the folder's properties dialog box, as shown in Figure 32-3.

Figure 32-3. To share a folder, choose the Sharing And Security command from the folder's shortcut menu.

3 Select the Share This Folder option.

4 Accept or change the proposed share name.

> **note** If the folder is already shared, click New Share and then type the share name. Local drives always have a default administrative share whose share name consists of the drive letter and a dollar sign (for example, C$). This share name is not visible to others, and you can't set permissions for the default share—so you'll want to create a new share.

The share name is the name that other users will see in their own My Network Places folders. Windows initially proposes to use the folder's name as its share name. That's usually a good choice, but you're not obligated to accept it. If you already have a shared folder with that name, you'll need to pick a different name.

5 Type a description of the folder's contents into the Comment box.

Other users will see this description when they inspect the folder's properties dialog box in their My Network Places folder (or use Details view).

6 To limit the number of users who can connect to the shared folder concurrently, select Allow This Number Of Users and then specify a number.

If network traffic seriously impacts your system's responsiveness, you might want to take advantage of this option. The default choice, Maximum Allowed, permits up to 10 concurrent users. (If you need to share a folder with more than 10 users at once, you must use a server version of Windows.)

For information about the Caching button, see "Setting Caching Options on the Server," page 561.

Assigning Permissions to a Shared Folder

The default shared resource permission associated with a new share is Full Control to Everyone. That means that anyone on your network can do whatever they want to your files, including delete them. (If the shared folder resides on an NTFS volume, individual folders and files can have their own access restrictions, however.) You can place limits on what particular users or groups of users can do with your shared files by clicking the Permissions button in the dialog box shown in Figure 32-3. Then you'll see the permissions dialog box, shown in Figure 32-4.

Figure 32-4. To set share permissions, right-click the shared folder in Windows Explorer and choose Sharing And Security. Then click Permissions.

> **caution** When you share a folder, you also make that folder's subfolders available on the network. If the access permissions you give for the folder aren't appropriate for any of its subfolders, either reconsider your choice of access permissions or restructure your folders to avoid the problem.

Follow these steps to view or set permissions:

1 In the Group Or User Names list, select the name of the user or group you want to manage.

The shared resource permissions for the selected user or group appear below in the permissions list.

2 Select Allow, Deny, or neither for each access control entry:

- **Full Control.** Allows users to create, read, write, rename, and delete files in the folder and its subfolders. In addition, users can change permissions and take ownership of files on NTFS volumes.

- **Change.** Allows users to read, write, rename, and delete files in the folder and its subfolders, but not to create new files.

- **Read.** Allows users to read files but not write to them or delete them.

If you select neither Allow nor Deny, the user or group can still inherit the permission through membership in another group that has the permission. If the user or group doesn't belong to another such group, the user or group is implicitly denied permission.

> **note** To remove a name from the Group Or User Names list, select it and click Remove. To add a name to the list, click Add to open the Select Users Or Groups dialog box, where you can enter the names of the users and groups you want to add. For more information about this dialog box, see "Applying Advanced Security Settings," page 509.

> **tip** **Disable Guest access to a shared folder**
>
> Setting up a share grants permission to the built-in Everyone group by default. The Guest account is included in Everyone. And because Windows authenticates as Guest network users who don't have an account on the local computer, that means that anyone on your network has access to a share. If you want to exclude anyone who does not have a user account on your computer, on the Share Permissions tab select Everyone and click Remove. Then click Add, type **Authenticated Users**, and click OK. (The built-in Authenticated Users group does not include the Guest account.) Back on the Share Permissions tab, select Authenticated Users and then select the Allow check box for Full Control.

1063

Note that shared resource permissions apply only when the folder (and its files and subfolders) are accessed over a network. They don't protect files or folders when opened locally from the computer on which they reside. If the folder you're sharing is on an NTFS volume, the NTFS permissions protect the files locally, and they also apply to network users.

> For information about NTFS permissions, see "Controlling Access with NTFS Permissions," page 507.

> **caution**   Files and folders that are created in a shared folder on an NTFS drive while Simple File Sharing is enabled are owned by the local Guest account. Ownership of files doesn't change when you disable or enable Simple File Sharing. Be aware that, even if you change to classic sharing and impose tighter security on your shared folders, users who log on as Guest (locally or remotely) continue to have full control over files that were created by *any* remote user while Simple File Sharing was enabled (assuming they still have access to the shared folder). To remedy this situation, take ownership of the folder and its contents, and remove Everyone from the ACLs of the folder and its contents.

Managing Shared Folders

Although you can manage your shared folders from Windows Explorer, the Shared Folders snap-in for Microsoft Management Console (MMC) provides a more centralized approach. With this snap-in, you can manage all the shared folders on your computer.

Start the Shared Folders snap-in by opening Computer Management (right-click My Computer and choose Manage) and then navigating to System Tools\Shared Folders. Figure 32-5 shows the Shared Folders snap-in.

Figure 32-5.   You can open Shared Folders in its own console window—without all the clutter of Computer Management—by typing **fsmgmt.msc** at a command prompt.

> **note** To use the Shared Folders snap-in, you must be a member of the Administrators or Power Users group. And to use it for anything other than merely viewing shares, sessions, and open files, you must have Simple File Sharing disabled (which means that Shared Folders is of limited use to users of Windows XP Home Edition).

Viewing and Changing Share Properties

When you open Shared Folders, all the shared folders on your computer are visible in the Shares folder. You can modify the properties of any folder by right-clicking it and choosing Properties. The associated properties dialog box appears, as shown in Figure 32-6.

Figure 32-6. Choose Properties in the Shared Folders snap-in to open a dialog box like this.

Note that if you right-click the shared folder in Windows Explorer while Simple File Sharing is disabled, you'll see nearly identical controls, as shown in Figure 32-3 on page 1061. The Permissions button shown in Figure 32-3 serves the same purpose as the Share Permissions tab shown in Figure 32-6.

Understanding Administrative Shares

Some of the shares you see in the Shared Folders list are created by the operating system. Most of these share names end with a dollar sign ($), which makes them "invisible" because they do not appear in the browse list when another Windows user looks at the shares on your computer. They are not inaccessible, however. If Simple File Sharing is disabled on your computer, any user who knows these names can connect to these shares simply by typing the share name rather than selecting it from the browse list. You can't view or set permissions on most of these shares, as you can for shares you create; the operating system restricts access to them to accounts with administrative privileges.

You can stop sharing administrative shares only temporarily. The share reappears the next time the Server service starts or you restart your computer. Table 32-1 describes the administrative shares that appear on most systems.

Table 32-1. **Administrative Shares**

Share Name	Description
C$, D$, E$, and so on	Each of these shares allows members of the Administrators and Backup Operators groups to connect to the root folder of a hard drive. You will see one of these (with the appropriate drive letter) for each hard drive on your computer. These shares are often used by backup programs.
ADMIN$	This share is used during remote administration. It maps to the %SystemRoot% folder (C:\Windows on most systems).
IPC$	This share provides the named pipes that programs use to communicate with your computer. It is used during remote administration and when viewing a computer's resources.
PRINT$	This share is used for remote administration of printers.
FAX$	This share appears on fax servers and is used by clients to send faxes and access cover pages stored on the server.

Creating a New Share

To share a folder, right-click Shares in the console tree and choose New File Share. The Create Shared Folder Wizard appears. This wizard helps you find the folder you want to share and assists in setting up basic security options, as shown in Figure 32-7. Note that unlike the default share permissions applied when you create a share in Windows Explorer (whether Simple File Sharing is enabled or not), the wizard allows you to easily set different permissions for administrators (members of the Administrators group) and other users (Everyone).

Figure 32-7. The Create Shared Folder Wizard provides an alternative to sharing a folder from Windows Explorer.

Troubleshooting

The New File Share command doesn't appear.

If sharing has not yet been enabled on your computer (by default, sharing is disabled on a new Windows XP installation), the Shared Folders snap-in is of little use. Worse, it doesn't tell you what the problem is or how to solve it. The solution, fortunately, is simple: First, be sure that Simple File Sharing is disabled. (If you disable Simple File Sharing *while* the Shared Folders snap-in is running, you might need to close and reopen the snap-in before the New File Share command appears.) If that doesn't make the command appear in Shared Folders, then run the Network Setup Wizard or share a folder using Windows Explorer; either action enables sharing. For details, see "Enabling File Sharing," page 1052.

InsideOut

You don't need to open Shared Folders to run the Create Shared Folder Wizard; you can run it by typing **shrpubw** at a command prompt. Curious users of Windows XP Home Edition will discover that they too can run Shrpubw.exe, causing them to shout, "Aha! I can use this trick to get around the all-or-nothing sharing limitations imposed by Simple File Sharing!" Alas, using the wizard to create a share with custom permissions is of no use when Simple File Sharing is enabled—which is all the time in Home Edition. That's because on a machine running Home Edition, all network users are authenticated as Guest. Therefore, it does no good to set up different permissions for different network users because all users are logged on using the Guest account.

Removing a Share

Removing a share is as easy as right-clicking the share and choosing Stop Sharing. This is equivalent to visiting the folder's properties dialog box in Windows Explorer and clearing the Share This Folder check box.

Viewing and Disconnecting Sessions

Each user who connects to your computer creates a session. You can use Shared Folders to see who is currently connected to the computer as well as what files they have open. Click Sessions in the console tree to have the current sessions appear in the details pane, as shown in Figure 32-8.

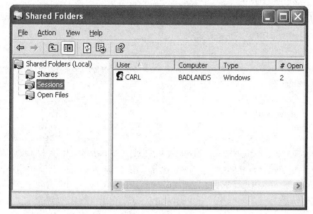

Figure 32-8. The Sessions folder shows all open connections.

---

tip **See who is authenticated**

If you're trying to determine why some users have access to certain folders and others don't, it's helpful to know whether they're being authenticated as themselves or as Guest. That's easy to do with Shared Folders. In the Sessions folder, the rightmost column is titled Guest; its value is either Yes (authenticated as Guest) or No (authenticated as named user).

Besides seeing who is connected, you can disconnect any or all sessions. Right-click a session and choose Close Session to close a single session. Right-click Sessions in the console tree and choose Disconnect All Sessions to close all the open sessions. Don't do this capriciously; you can cause users to lose information by closing a session while they have documents open.

Viewing and Closing Files

Click Open Files in the Shared Folders console tree to see a list of shared files that are currently open for other users, as shown in Figure 32-9.

You can close an individual file by right-clicking it and choosing Close Open File. You can close all the open files at once by right-clicking Open Files in the console tree and choosing Disconnect All Open Files. If you close a document file before the user has saved new information, you might cause the information to be lost.

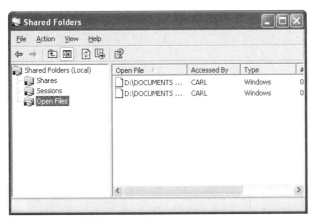

Figure 32-9. The Open Files folder shows all files that have been opened by all users.

Warning Other Users

Because closing sessions and files can cause a loss of information, you should warn users who have open sessions and files before you close them. You can send a console message directly from Shared Folders, but the command to do so doesn't appear on the shortcut menu at the location you most expect it. Because Sessions and Open Files are the places where you can most easily disrupt others' work—and therefore are the places where you'd want a way to warn users of an impending shutdown—you might expect to be able to send a message from one of those folders. You can't.

To send a console message, right-click Shared Folders or Shares in the console tree and choose All Tasks, Send Console Message. This command does not appear when you right-click Sessions or Open Files.

When the Send Console Message dialog box appears, the names of all the computers with open sessions (which includes all computers with open files) are in the Recipients list. Simply type your warning message and click Send.

Accessing Shared Folders

My Network Places is your gateway to all available network resources, just as My Computer is the gateway to resources stored on your own system. My Network Places replaces the Network Neighborhood folder that appears in earlier versions of Windows—and you'll soon see that more than the name has changed. My Network Places appears in a Windows Explorer window that contains icons for network resources you use. Network places can be shortcuts to network computers, shared folders, Web folders on the Internet or your intranet, or FTP sites.

To open My Network Places (if your Start menu doesn't already include a shortcut to it), open My Computer. Under Other Places, click My Network Places.

You can also use My Network Places to browse your network. Under Network Tasks, click View Workgroup Computers. Doing so displays the computers in your workgroup. Double-clicking a computer displays the shared resources on that computer. While viewing workgroup computers, you can click Microsoft Windows Network (under Other Places) to display a top-level view of your entire corporate network.

Troubleshooting

You can't view shared folders on other computers.

In certain network configurations (notably, if each computer on the network has a direct connection to the Internet or if network computers and a broadband modem are all connected through a hub), you might not be able to see shared folders on other computers. That's actually a sign that the Network Setup Wizard and Internet Connection Firewall are properly doing their job of protecting your network from unauthorized Internet access. In these configurations, your network has multiple paths to the Internet, so you need to be protected against other computers on the LAN as well as against other computers on the Internet. The solution in this case is to add a second network protocol and use that protocol—not TCP/IP, which can travel over the Internet—for file and printer sharing. For detailed instructions on doing this, in the Help And Support Center, search for **enable ipx sharing**. You'll find instructions for setting up IPX/SPX on computers running other versions of Windows as well as computers running Windows XP.

If your computer has separate network adapters for your Internet connection and your local area network (LAN) connection, you should be sure that Internet Connection Firewall is enabled only for the Internet connection. In Network Connections, open the properties dialog box for each connection, click the Advanced tab, and confirm that the Internet Connection Firewall check box is set appropriately. In the properties dialog box for your local area network connection, be sure that Client For Microsoft Networks is installed and selected.

Adding a Network Place

By default, Windows periodically searches your network for shared folders and shared printers. Shared resources discovered during this search automatically appear in My Network Places.

---

newfeature!

tip **Disable automatic discovery**

If your network has lots of shared resources that you don't use, you might prefer to disable the automatic discovery feature. To control this feature, follow these steps:

1 In My Network Places (or any Windows Explorer window), open the Tools menu and choose Folder Options.

2 In Folder Options, click the View tab.

3 In the Advanced Settings list, select or clear Automatically Search For Network Folders And Printers.

You can also create your own network places, such as a shortcut to a network resource, a Web site, or an FTP site. To add a network place, open My Network Places and click Add A Network Place (under Network Tasks). The Add Network Place Wizard leads you through the process.

---

note A shortcut to a Web site doesn't open the site in Microsoft Internet Explorer, as a shortcut in your Favorites folder does. Rather, it opens a Windows Explorer view of the folders within a Web site. Therefore, it's most useful as a shortcut to your own Web site or to Web folders on your intranet—where you might use or contribute files—rather than to a public Web site, which might not allow folder views.

---

tip **Go directly to the folder you want**

My Network Places can also hold shortcuts to folders and files within a shared folder. To create such a place, type the complete path (in the form *computername*\ *sharename**folder*) on the wizard's third page. Or simply drag the folder or file from a Windows Explorer window to the My Network Places icon or window.

Using Network Places with Applications

The real strength of My Network Places isn't that it allows you to peruse your network, but that it provides fast, easy access to network places that you use day in and day out, without forcing you to traverse a lengthy path to get to each one. After you create a network place, it appears in the Open dialog box or in the Save dialog box that appears in most applications when you choose one of those commands from the File menu. All you need to do is click My Network Places in the places bar at the left side of the dialog box, and shortcuts to all your network places appear, as shown in Figure 32-10.

Figure 32-10. Click My Network Places in the places bar to jump quickly to the network places you use.

Gaining Access to Shared Folders on Another Computer

To open a shared folder on another computer, double-click its icon in My Network Places. (If My Network Places doesn't contain a shortcut to the folder you want, click View Workgroup Computers or Microsoft Windows Network to navigate to it.) If you have the proper permissions, this action displays the folder's content in Windows Explorer. It's not always that easy however. If the user account with which you logged on doesn't have permission to view a network computer or resource you select, a dialog box similar to the one shown in Figure 32-11 appears. To gain access, you must provide the name of an account (and its password, of course) that has permission.

Perhaps the trickiest part of using shared folders is fully understanding what permissions have been applied to a folder and which credentials are in use by each network user. The first rule to recognize is that *all network access is controlled by the computer with the shared resources*; regardless of what operating system runs at the computer attempting to connect to a network share, it must meet the security requirements of the computer where the resource is shared. The following sections explain how to connect to shared folders on various types of servers. (In this context, *server* merely denotes the computer where the folder is shared; it might not be a dedicated server.)

Figure 32-11. Enter the name and password of a user with an authorized account on the sharing computer or domain.

Windows XP Home Edition or Windows XP Professional with Simple File Sharing Enabled

This is the easiest to use because any network user can easily open any shared folder. For the same reason, of course, it's not appropriate for all networks.

- **Share permissions.** The built-in Everyone group has Full Control or Read access, depending on the Sharing tab setting.

- **NTFS permissions.** Everyone has Modify or Read & Execute access, depending on the Sharing tab setting.

- **How to connect.** All network users are authenticated as Guest, and therefore can open any shared folder simply by double-clicking its shortcut in Windows Explorer.

Windows XP Professional with Simple File Sharing Disabled or Windows 2000

In a workgroup environment, this is more secure than Simple File Sharing, as it lets the share owner decide who to let in. Computers joined to a domain always have Simple File Sharing disabled, so this information applies to those computers as well.

- **Share permissions.** By default, Everyone has Full Control. Administrators on the sharing computer can grant or deny permissions to any user or group.

- **NTFS permissions.** By default, a folder inherits the permissions of its parent folder, but administrators on the sharing computer can grant or deny permissions to any user or group.

- **How to connect.** If your local account has the same user name and non-blank password as an account on the sharing computer, you're authenticated using that account and therefore have the access privileges granted to

Chapter 32

that account. If your local account does not match one on the sharing computer, you're authenticated as Guest and therefore have only the access privileges explicitly granted to Everyone or Guest. (If the Guest account is disabled on the sharing computer, only users with an account matching a local account can connect.)

If you're presented with a dialog box like the one shown in Figure 32-11, enter the user name and password of an account that has been granted the permissions you need. If the account you want to use is a local account on the sharing computer (always the case in a workgroup), enter the user name in the form *computername\username* (for example, **GLACIER\Jan**). To use a domain user account, use the form *domain\username* if your computer is not joined to the domain; if your computer is joined to the domain, you can enter the user name alone.

If you get an "access denied" error message instead of a user name request, you'll need to add an entry to your stored network passwords. (You can do this only if you're running Windows XP Professional.) In Control Panel, open User Accounts and, if necessary, click your name to make changes for your account. Under Related Tasks, click Manage My Network Passwords, click Add, and then provide the requested information. (If your computer is joined to a domain, the path to Stored User Names And Passwords is slightly different: in User Accounts, click the Advanced tab and then click Manage Passwords.) You might need to log off and log on before you can access the shared folder.

Click to add credentials for a network computer

Type the name of the computer to provide the same credentials for all shared folders on a computer, or append the shared folder name to provide credentials for a particular folder

InsideOut

Whether you provide a user name and password when Windows requests them or add them directly to the stored network passwords, if you're using Windows XP Professional, Windows saves the credentials so that you need never enter them again to access the same resource. Unfortunately, the same is not true of Windows XP Home Edition. With a little effort, you can work around this limitation of Home Edition, as follows:

1 Use Notepad or another plain text editor to create a batch program (a plain text file with the file name extension .bat or .cmd).

2 Enter a Net Use command on a separate line in the batch program for each network resource you want to connect to. The command takes the form net use *computername**sharename password* /user:*computername**username*, where *computername* is the name of the sharing computer, *username* is the name of an account on the sharing computer with access rights to the share, and *password* is that account's password.

For example, to make the connection shown in the figure on the facing page, you'd type the following:

```
net use "\\sequoia\budget data" WhI89dd /user:sequoia\carl
```

3 Drag a shortcut for the batch program to the Startup group on your Start menu, or set up a scheduled task so that it runs when you log on.

For more information about batch commands and scheduled tasks, see Chapter 10, "Automating Windows XP." For information about the Net Use command, see "Net Use," page 1089.

Windows 98 or Windows Me

These computers rely on passwords to protect shared resources; they don't care what user provides the password.

● **Permissions.** When a folder is shared, it can be protected with a password for read-only access, a password for full access, both, or neither.

● **How to connect.** Any network user can open any shared folder simply by double-clicking its icon in Windows Explorer. If the password for your user account matches the password assigned to the folder, the folder opens immediately. If not, Windows asks you to provide the password in a dialog box like the one shown in Figure 32-11 on page 1073. You don't need to provide a user name; that box is disabled.

Working with Mapped Network Folders

Mapping a network folder makes it appear to Windows as though the folder is part of your own computer. Windows assigns the mapped folder a drive letter, making the folder appear like an additional hard drive. You can still access a mapped folder in the conventional manner, by navigating to it through My Network Places. But mapping gives the folder an alias—the assigned drive letter—that provides an alternative means of access.

In general, drive mapping is obsolete, having been supplanted by improvements in and greater reliance on My Network Places. But mapping still offers benefits in some situations:

● **It makes the network folder available to programs that don't use the Windows common dialog boxes.** With programs that use the common dialog boxes, you can navigate to network folders just as you would with My Network Places. But to read a document from, or save a document to, a network folder using earlier programs, you will probably need to map the folder to a drive letter.

● **It makes the network folder accessible from My Computer.** Because a mapped folder becomes a virtual drive on your local computer, an icon for the folder appears in the My Computer folder, right alongside your local drives. If you do most of your work with files stored locally but need access to particular network folders, you might find it convenient to map them. That way, you won't have to bother opening My Network Places to find the network folders you need.

Mapping a Network Folder to a Drive Letter

To map a network folder to a drive letter, follow these steps:

1 In Windows Explorer, open the Tools menu and choose Map Network Drive.

2 Select a drive letter in the Drive box. You can choose any letter that's not already in use.

3 In the Folder box, type the path to the folder you want or, more easily, click Browse and navigate to the folder.

4 Select Reconnect At Logon if you want Windows to connect to this shared folder automatically at the start of each session.

5 If your regular logon account doesn't have permission to connect to the resource, click the Different User Name link, enter a user name and password, and click OK. (This capability is useful if you personally have multiple user accounts. For example, you might have an administrator account that has access to some folders that are not available to your regular logon account.)

6 Click Finish.

Unmapping a Mapped Network Folder

If you change your mind about mapping a network folder, simply right-click the folder's icon in your My Computer folder. Choose Disconnect in the resulting shortcut menu, and the tie will be severed.

Sharing a Printer

If you've figured out how to share a folder over the network, sharing a printer will be easy. You configure all options for a printer—whether you plan to share it or not—using the printer's properties dialog box. To display it, open the Printers And Faxes folder (choose Printers And Faxes in Control Panel or on the Start menu), right-click the printer you're interested in, and choose Properties.

To make a printer available to other network users, simply click the Sharing tab, select Share This Printer, and provide a share name, as shown in Figure 32-12 on the next page. Windows XP permits spaces and other characters in printer names, but if you're going to share with users of other operating systems, you should observe the following restrictions:

- Use only letters and numbers; don't use spaces, punctuation, or special characters.

- The entire Universal Naming Convention (UNC) name, including the requisite backslashes and your computer name, should be 31 or fewer characters. For example, assume that your computer name is YELLOWSTONE (11 characters). When you add slashes, the length becomes 14 characters, meaning that the share name should be 17 characters or less. This results in a UNC name something like \\YELLOWSTONE\HPLASERJET4000.

- If any MS-DOS users will connect to the printer, the share name must be no longer than 8 characters.

1077

Figure 32-12. On the Sharing tab, specify a share name.

Using a Network-Interface Printer

Your print device doesn't necessarily have to be connected directly to the computer that's acting as the print server. That is, it needn't be connected to one of the computer's local ports, such as a parallel port (LPT*x*), a serial port (COM*x*), an infrared (IrDA) port, a universal serial bus (USB) port, or a 1394 port. If your print device has a built-in Ethernet adapter (or it's connected to a network-interface device such as a Hewlett-Packard JetDirect), all you need to do is set up a standard TCP/IP port—a simple procedure in Windows XP:

1 Be sure that the print device is connected to the network and powered on.

2 Open Printers And Faxes in Control Panel. Under Printer Tasks, click Add A Printer.

3 On the Local Or Network Printer page of the Add Printer Wizard, select the local printer option and clear the automatic-detection option.

4 On the Select A Printer Port page, select Create A New Port and then select Standard TCP/IP Port. Click Next to open the Add Standard TCP/IP Printer Port Wizard.

5 On the first page of the Add Standard TCP/IP Printer Port Wizard, click Next.

6 On the Add Port page, type the IP address of the printer. (You can get that by printing a configuration report from the print device or network-interface

1078

Chapter 32

device. See the device's manual for instructions.) You can accept the Port Name that the wizard proposes or create your own. Click Next.

7 The wizard's final page shows your settings and also shows information (such as the adapter type) that confirms successful communication with the print device. Click Finish.

> **note** If you've already created a printer (if, for example, the print device was initially attached directly to a computer), you can change its port to use a network-interface device. In Printers And Faxes, open the printer's properties dialog box and click the Ports tab. Click Add Port, and in the Printer Ports dialog box that appears, select Standard TCP/IP Port and then click New Port. The Add Standard TCP/IP Printer Port Wizard then opens, and you can proceed with step 5 in the preceding procedure.

Setting Permissions on Shared Printers

Unlike shared folders, which maintain separate share permissions and NTFS permissions, a single set of permissions controls access to printers, whether by local users or by network users. (Of course, only printers that have been shared are accessible to network users.)

When you set up a printer, initially all users in the Everyone group have Print permission for documents they create, which provides access to the printer and the ability to manage their own documents in the print queue. And by default, members of the Administrators and Power Users groups also have Manage Printers and Manage Documents permission. Table 32-2 on the next page shows the basic permissions and associated privileges that Windows XP provides for printers.

Table 32-2. **Basic Printer Permissions and Privileges**

Permission	Privileges
Print	Print documents
	Control properties of owned documents
	Pause, restart, and remove owned documents
Manage Printers	Share printer
	Change printer properties
	Remove printer
	Change printer permissions
	Pause and restart the printer
Manage Documents	Pause, restart, move, and remove all queued documents

A user account that doesn't have any of these permissions can't connect to the printer, print to it locally, or view its queue.

> **note** To set permissions on a printer, you must be using Windows XP Professional, and you must have Simple File Sharing disabled.

If you have Manage Printers permission for a printer, you can change other users' permissions for that printer. To do so, click the Security tab of the printer's properties dialog box. To add another user or group to the list, click Add. After you type the names of users or groups you want in the Select Users Or Groups dialog box, return to the printer's properties dialog box. Then select each new user or group and assign permissions by clicking Allow, Deny, or neither. (If you select neither, permissions are determined by the user's group membership.)

Setting Hours of Availability and Other Options

The Advanced tab of the printer's properties dialog box, shown in Figure 32-13, includes a number of options that are both intriguing and confusing. Making changes to these options requires Manage Printers permission.

- **Always Available** and **Available From.** To restrict the availability of the printer to certain times of day, select Available From and specify the range of times. Print jobs that are sent outside of these hours are held in the queue until the appointed time.

Figure 32-13. The Advanced tab offers the ability to set the hours of operation for a printer, along with a number of unrelated options.

● **Priority.** The Priority setting has a similar purpose: if you create multiple printers for a single print device, documents sent to the printer with the higher Priority setting print ahead of those sent to the other printer. You might want to create a high-priority printer that certain users have permission to use when they need to cut in line to get a document printed quickly. Or you might want to assign Print permission to the high-priority printer to one group of users, and permission to the lower-priority printer to another group of users with different (less urgent) needs.

● **Driver.** This list includes all the printer drivers currently installed on your system; use it to select the correct driver for the print device. If the correct driver isn't in the list, click New Driver to start the Add Printer Driver Wizard.

● **Spool settings.** The four option buttons in the center of the dialog box determine whether a document should be spooled to a hard disk before sending it to the printer. (For information about specifying the location of spool files, see "Setting Server Properties," page 1085.) Spooled documents are then sent to the print device in the background. Ordinarily, you should select the first and third options, which cause fastest return of control to your application and fastest printing completion. But if you have trouble with complex print jobs being interrupted by pages from another document, select Start Printing After Last Page Is Spooled.

Chapter 32

- **Hold Mismatched Documents.** Selecting this option tells the spooler to check a document's properties against the printer properties and to hold the document in the queue if the properties don't match. A mismatched document typically occurs when an application specifies a form that's not currently assigned to a printer tray, for example. Correctly matched documents continue to print normally, bypassing any mismatched documents in the queue.

- **Print Spooled Documents First.** Selecting this option directs the spooler to print documents that have completed spooling ahead of documents that are still spooling, even if the latter documents have a higher priority. When this option is cleared, the spooler selects the next document to print based only on its priority. Selecting this option maximizes printer efficiency because the print device doesn't have to wait for an incomplete, high-priority document to finish spooling before it can begin printing a complete, lower-priority document.

- **Keep Printed Documents.** When this option is selected, the spooler doesn't delete documents from the queue after they print. You can then reprint a document from the queue rather than from the program that created it, or you can delete the document manually.

- **Enable Advanced Printing Features.** Selecting this option turns on metafile spooling for print jobs from Windows XP and Windows 2000 clients using Windows-based applications. Of more interest to most users, selecting this option enables new options in the common Print dialog box for some printers and some applications, such as Booklet Printing and Pages Per Sheet. The only reason to clear this option is if you have problems printing.

- **Printing Defaults.** Clicking this button displays the printing defaults dialog box—the same one that appears if you right-click a printer and choose Printing Preferences. In this dialog box, you specify default document settings for options such as orientation, two-sided printing, paper tray selection, and so on. Your settings here become the default settings for all users of the printer. (Another reason to create multiple logical printers for a single device: You might want to create printers with different default settings for different types of documents or for users with different needs.)

- **Print Processor.** Clicking this button opens the Print Processor dialog box, a place you'll probably never need to venture. In a nutshell, it displays the available print processors (a *print processor* tells the spooler how to alter a print job depending on the document data type) and the default data type for the selected print processor. *Microsoft Windows XP Professional Resource Kit Documentation* (Microsoft Press, 2001) provides detailed information about print processors and data types.

- **Separator Page.** Click this button to specify a separator page. For more information, see the next section.

Using Separator Pages

A *separator page* prints before each document (much like a fax cover page) and identifies the name of the user who printed the job, the date and time it was sent, and other details. Using separator pages makes finding your document among a stack of others in the printer's output bin easier. In addition, two of the separator pages furnished with Windows XP switch between PostScript and PCL (the Printer Control Language used by most Hewlett-Packard printers), which is useful for printers that don't automatically switch languages.

Windows XP includes four separator page files, which you can use ready-made or you can customize. These are the supplied files, which are stored in the %SystemRoot%\ System32 folder:

- **Sysprint.sep.** Switches the printer to PostScript and then prints a separator page that includes account name, job number, date, and time.

- **Pcl.sep.** Switches the printer to PCL and then prints a separator page that includes account name, job number, date, and time.

- **Pscript.sep.** Switches the printer to PostScript but does not print a separator page.

- **Sysprtj.sep.** A variant of Sysprint.sep that uses Japanese fonts, if available.

Separator page files are plain-text files with the extension .sep. You can create your own separator pages either by modifying the files supplied with Windows XP or by typing codes into a new plain-text document and saving that document in your %SystemRoot%\System32 folder.

The codes you can use for your separator pages are listed in Table 32-3. Each separator file must start with a single character on a line by itself; that character becomes the *command delimiter*, which identifies commands elsewhere in the file. You can use any character as a command delimiter. In Table 32-3, the @ character is used as the command delimiter. For these commands to work, the first line of your file must contain only a single @ character.

Table 32-3. Separator Page Codes

Code	Description
@N	Prints the user name of the person who submitted the print job.
@I	Prints the job number.
@D	Prints the date, in the date format specified by Regional Options in Control Panel.
@T	Prints the time, in the time format specified by Regional Options in Control Panel.

(continued)

Chapter 32

Table 32-3. *(continued)*

Code	Description
@L	Prints all characters following @L up to the next @ code or until the page width specified by @W is reached.
@F*pathname*	Prints the contents of the file specified by *pathname*.
@H*nn*	Sends a printer-specific control code, where *nn* is a hexadecimal value. For example, use @H1B to send an escape code, which has a hexadecimal value of 0x1B (27 decimal).
@W*nnn*	Sets the maximum width of the separator page to the decimal value specified by *nnn*. Any characters beyond this width are truncated. (The default width is 80; the maximum is 256.)
@B@S	Prints in single-width block characters.
@B@M	Prints in double-width block characters.
@U	Turns off block-character printing.
@*n*	Skips *n* lines. (*n* can be 0 through 9.)
@E	Ejects the current page from the printer.

Setting Up a Printer for Non–Windows XP Clients

Your network probably includes computers that are not running Windows XP. By configuring your print server properly, you can make it easy for users of the other computers to use your printers. A Windows XP–based print server includes support for the following types of clients:

- **Windows XP, Windows 2000, Windows NT, and Windows 95/98/Me.**
  To provide access for these types of clients, click the Sharing tab in the printer's properties dialog box. Click Additional Drivers and then select each of the client types you want to support. When one of these clients connects to the printer for the first time, Windows automatically sets up the printer on the client system.

- **Windows 3.*x* and MS-DOS.** These clients must install a 16-bit printer driver on their systems and must redirect a local port to the network share. For example, you'd configure a printer driver on such a machine to print to LPT1, and then issue this command to the network redirector: **net use lpt1: *server**share*.** (Replace *server* with the computer name of your print server and replace *share* with the share name of the printer.)

- **UNIX.** On the print server, install Print Services For UNIX. (Go to Control Panel, Add/Remove Programs, Add/Remove Windows Components, Other Network File And Print Services, Details, Print Services For UNIX.) You also need to set the TCP/IP Print Server service (the name of Print Services For UNIX as it appears in the Services snap-in) to start automatically. (For information about controlling services, see Appendix F, "Managing Services.") Set up an LPR port by opening the printer's properties dialog box and clicking Ports, Add Port, LPR Port, New Port. UNIX clients then connect to the printer using the Line Printer Daemon (LPD) service.

- **Internet.** Clients that support Internet Printing Protocol (IPP) can print to a Windows XP print server using HTTP. To provide access for Internet (or intranet) clients, you must install Internet Information Services (IIS). (For details about IIS, see "Setting Up IIS for Internet Printing," page 859.) To connect to a shared printer using IPP, at the client computer, type **http://** *server***/printers/** (replace *server* with the URL or the computer name of the server) in the Address bar of Internet Explorer. Users with the requisite permissions can view the queue, manage the printer, and manage documents. Clicking Connect (under Printer Action in the left frame) automatically installs the printer on the client computer if it's not already installed.

Setting Server Properties

In addition to setting properties for individual printers by using their properties dialog box, you can set other properties by visiting the Print Server Properties dialog box. To get there, open the File menu or right-click a blank area of the Printers And Faxes folder and then choose Server Properties.

The first three tabs control the list of items you see in the properties dialog box for a printer:

- The Forms tab controls the list of forms that you can assign to trays using the Device Settings tab in a printer's properties dialog box. You can create new form definitions and delete any that you create, but you can't delete any of the predefined forms.

- The Ports tab offers the same capabilities as the Ports tab in a printer's properties dialog box.

- The Drivers tab offers a list of all the installed printer drivers and provides a centralized location where you can add, remove, or update drivers.

The Advanced tab, shown in Figure 32-14 on the next page, offers a potpourri of options:

- You can specify the location of spool files. You might want to change to a folder on a different drive if, for example, you frequently run out of space on the current drive when you attempt to print large documents.

Figure 32-14. Settings you make here affect options available in all printer properties dialog boxes.

InsideOut

Your Spool Folder setting on the Advanced tab is stored in the DefaultSpoolDirectory value in the HKLM\Software\Microsoft\Windows NT\CurrentVersion\Print\Printers registry key, and it determines the spool folder for all your local printers. If you want to use a different folder for a particular printer, you must edit the registry directly. Go to the HKLM\Software\Microsoft\Windows NT\CurrentVersion\Print\Printers*printer* key (where *printer* is the name of the printer you want to modify), and set the SpoolDirectory value to the path you want to use.

- The first three check boxes on the Advanced tab determine which types of events merit entries in the Windows System log, which you can view with the Event Viewer snap-in. For more information, see Chapter 36, "Monitoring System Activities with Event Viewer."

- The two Show Informational Notifications check boxes control pop-up status messages near the notification area.

- The last two check boxes control an alternative notification method. Windows XP can cause a message to pop up to let you know when your print job has completed. If you don't select the last check box, the message goes to the first workstation at which the user who printed the job is logged on. If that user account is logged on to more than one workstation, the message might not go to the one that generated the print job. To ensure that it does, select the last check box also, which causes the message to be delivered to the computer that generated the print job.

Windows XP uses the Alerter service on a print server to send notification to users when network printing jobs are complete. By default, the Alerter service does not run automatically in Windows XP. If you plan to use this feature, you'll need to start the Alerter service using the Services snap-in in Computer Management.

To receive such a message, a computer must be running the Messenger service. Users right next to the printer might want to stop this service (and not be bothered by the pop-up messages), whereas users down the hall can leave it running.

Troubleshooting

Your document won't print.

If a document gets stuck in the print queue and you can't delete it, open the Services snap-in in the Computer Management console, and stop the Print Spooler service. Then restart the service.

Command-Line Utilities for Managing Shared Resources

Some users prefer a terse command prompt to a wizard or even an MMC window. If you're in that group, you'll want to use Net.exe for managing resource sharing.

In the following sections, we describe only the most common Net commands (and their most common parameters) for managing network connections. This isn't an exhaustive reference, however. You can get more information from online help or by typing **net help** *command,* replacing *command* with the word that follows Net in the examples. For example, to get more information about the Net Use command, type **net help use**. This provides more help than typing **net use** /?, which shows only the command syntax.

Net Share

The Net Share command lets you view, create, modify, or delete shared resources on your computer.

Viewing Share Information

Typing **net share** with no parameters causes the program to display a list of the shared resources on your computer, as shown in the following sample:

```
C:\>net share

Share name      Resource                        Remark

-------------------------------------------------------------------------------
IPC$                                            Remote IPC
D$              D:\                             Default share
C$              C:\                             Default share
print$          D:\WINDOWS\System32\spool\drivers
                                                Printer Drivers
ADMIN$          D:\WINDOWS                      Remote Admin
HyperSnap       C:\HyperSnap
SharedDocs      D:\DOCUMENTS AND SETTINGS\ALL USERS\DOCUMENTS

LJ4000          LPT1:                  Spooled   HP LaserJet 4000 Series PS
The command completed successfully.
```

If you follow Net Share with the name of a local shared resource, it displays information about that share. For example, the command **net share shareddocs** displays the following:

```
C:\>net share shareddocs
Share name         SharedDocs
Path               D:\DOCUMENTS AND SETTINGS\ALL USERS\DOCUMENTS
Remark
Maximum users      No limit
Users              JAN                  CARL
Caching            Manual caching of documents
The command completed successfully.
```

Adding or Modifying a Share

You can share the folder C:\Spreadsheets, for use by an unlimited number of users, and add the comment "Budgets" with the following command:

```
C:\>net share Spreadsheets=C:\spreadsheets /unlimited /remark:"Budgets"
Spreadsheets was shared successfully.
```

Setting a *sharename* "equal" to a folder creates a share. To modify an existing share, you use only the *sharename* (and no folder), as in the following command, which changes the remark on the Spreadsheets share to "Year 2002 Budgets":

```
C:\>net share Spreadsheets /remark:"Year 2002 Budgets"
The command completed successfully.
```

Several parameters can be used with the Net Share command, as shown in Table 32-4.

Table 32-4. Useful Parameters for the Net Share Command

Parameter	Description
/Users:*number*	Sets the maximum number of concurrent users
/Unlimited	Lets the maximum number of users connect to the share at one time
/Remark:"*text*"	Adds or changes a comment that appears in Details view in Windows Explorer
/Cache:manual, /Cache:documents, /Cache:programs, or /Cache:no	Sets the document and program caching option for offline files; for details, see "Setting Caching Options on the Server," page 561

Deleting a User Share

To remove a share, simply use the /Delete switch with the Net Share *sharename* command:

```
C:\>net share spreadsheets /delete
spreadsheets was deleted successfully.
```

Net Use

The Net Use command connects your computer to shared resources on other computers. It can also disconnect, or display, all the resources to which you are connected.

Viewing Connections

Type **net use** with no parameters to display the resources to which you are currently connected.

```
C:\>net use
New connections will be remembered.


Status       Local    Remote               Network

-------------------------------------------------------------------
OK           G:       \\everglades\programs    Microsoft Windows Network
OK           K:       \\everglades\document    Microsoft Windows Network
OK           P:       \\everglades\company     Microsoft Windows Network
OK           LPT2     \\badlands\lj4000         Microsoft Windows Network
                      \\www.msnusers.com\xxxxx@msn.com
                                               Web Client Network

The command completed successfully.
```

Adding a Mapped Network Drive

You can create drive mappings with a command like this:

```
C:\>net use e: \\badlands\spreadsheets
The command completed successfully.
```

This maps the network share Spreadsheets on the computer named Badlands to the local drive letter E. If you want to use the next available drive letter, use an asterisk (*) instead of the drive letter and colon. You can add any of the parameters shown in Table 32-5.

Table 32-5. Useful Parameters for the Net Use Command

Parameter	Description
password	Enter your password following the share name if a password is required.
/User:*domain\username*	To connect using a user name that is different from the one you are currently logged on with, you can use the /User parameter. The domain name is necessary only if you are not in the same domain as the resource you're connecting to. You can also enter the domain and user name in the format of an e-mail address (for example, *user@domain*).
/Delete	Disconnects the connection. You need only specify the drive letter and /Delete to disconnect.
/Persistent:yes or /Persistent:no	The yes option causes connections to persist so that they are reconnected the next time you log on.

Disconnecting a Mapped Drive

To disconnect a mapped drive, simply use the /Delete switch with the Net Use command:

```
C:\>net use e: /delete
e: was deleted successfully.
```

Net Session

The Net Session command lets you view or disconnect connections between your computer and clients that are accessing it.

Viewing Session Information

Type **net session** with no parameters to display the current connections to your computer:

```
C:\>net session

Computer           User name         Client Type       Opens Idle time

-------------------------------------------------------------------------

\\127.0.0.1                          Windows 2002 2600    1 01:20:24

\\GLACIER          CARL              Windows NT 1381      0 00:00:07

The command completed successfully.
```

Disconnecting a Session

Following Net Session *computername*, append /Delete to disconnect a session. If you don't include *computername*, all active sessions are disconnected.

Net File

The Net File command lets you view or close the open shared files on your computer. Typing **net file** with nothing following it causes the program to list all the open files, including a file ID, the user name of the person who has the file open, and the number of locks each has.

```
C:\>net file

ID       Path                              User name        # Locks

-------------------------------------------------------------------------

24       E:\Catalog                        JAN              0
32       C:\spreadsheets\Q1 Budget.xls     CARL             3
The command completed successfully.
```

You can close a file by following Net File with the ID of the file and /Close:

```
C:\>net file 24 /close
The command completed successfully.
```

Net Statistics

The Net Statistics command displays the statistics log for the local Workstation or Server service. Type **net statistics workstation** to view the Workstation statistics. Type **net statistics server** to view the Server statistics.

The workstation statistics log looks like this:

```
C:\>net statistics workstation
Workstation Statistics for \\SEQUOIA


Statistics since 11/17/2001 4:06 PM


    Bytes received                                232765115
    Server Message Blocks (SMBs) received         394263
    Bytes transmitted                             65653800
    Server Message Blocks (SMBs) transmitted      393773
    Read operations                               187879
    Write operations                              1258
    Raw reads denied                              0
    Raw writes denied                             0

    Network errors                                0
    Connections made                              20
    Reconnections made                            24
    Server disconnects                            7

    Sessions started                              102
    Hung sessions                                 0
    Failed sessions                               0
    Failed operations                             0
    Use count                                     126
    Failed use count                              2

The command completed successfully.
```

Remote Access Options

If you're like many twenty-first century knowledge workers, you have a computer at your office and another one at home. How many times have you arrived home, planning to catch up on some work, only to find that you don't have the files you need? Or worse, you don't have the programs you need installed on your home computer? Microsoft Windows XP offers several features that enable you to retrieve the items you need without hopping in the car and driving back to the office.

The most exciting of these features is Remote Desktop, which lets you operate your office computer from home. This goes way beyond being able to download a few forgotten files. Rather, you're able to see exactly what is displayed on the other computer's display and, more important, operate that computer as if you were sitting right in front of it. You have access to all the other computer's files, applications, and network resources.

With Remote Desktop, you can work from home using the full capabilities of your office computer. If you need to wait at home for a repair person (do they ever come within the scheduled time?!), you can continue to work just as productively as if you were at your office. If you're stuck working over the weekend, at least you can do it from the comfort of home!

Remote Desktop can work in the other direction too: If, after working all night to finish up a project at home, you forget to bring the documents to work, you can connect from your office network to your home computer. Again, using Remote Desktop, you have complete control to view and operate the computer from afar.

At Home with Windows XP

Remote access is most useful in a business setting, so it should come as no surprise that Windows XP Professional is more capable than Windows XP Home Edition when it comes to staying in touch with the office. Remote Desktop is not available in Windows XP Home Edition. If you want to set up your computer to allow access using Remote Desktop, you must be running Windows XP Professional. However, you can use Remote Desktop Connection under Windows XP Home Edition to connect to a computer running Windows XP Professional. (In fact, you can run the Remote Desktop Connection software under earlier Windows versions too).

Don't confuse Remote Desktop with the Remote Assistance capability of the Windows XP Help And Support Center, either; that feature allows a friend or help-desk professional to take over a remote computer's screen temporarily to diagnose or repair a persistent problem; this feature—which is covered in "Connecting to Another Computer with Remote Assistance," page 154—works equally well with Windows XP Professional and Home Edition.

The capability to create secure virtual private networks (VPNs) between computers is identical in both Windows XP editions. You can set up either Windows XP Professional or Home Edition to function as a VPN server. Likewise, the wizard that lets you connect to a remote VPN server is the same in both editions.

Remote Desktop can be useful within the confines of a single network as well. For example, you can use it to solve a problem on another computer without trudging over to the other computer, whether it's in the next cubicle or upstairs in the bedroom. You can manage it from your own desktop.

Windows XP can also serve as the connection point for a single virtual private network (VPN) connection. With a VPN, you use the Internet to connect a computer to your network. In effect, this makes your home computer into just another computer on your office network. You have full access to network resources, just as if your computer were physically connected to the local area network (LAN).

Both types of connections are encrypted, so your information is secure, even if you're making a connection over the public Internet.

The basic difference between Remote Desktop and a VPN is that with Remote Desktop, your computer takes over control of a remote computer, whereas with a VPN connection, your computer becomes another node on the network. With Remote Desktop, applications run on the remote computer (your computer is effectively used as a dumb terminal), but with a VPN, applications run on your computer. Both can be incredibly valuable, and in this chapter we explain how to set them up and use them.

Setting Up a Remote Desktop Connection to Another Computer

newfeature!

Remote Desktop allows you to work on your Windows XP Professional computer from any other computer. It's based on the Terminal Services technology that first appeared in server versions of Windows NT and Windows 2000.

> **note** Remote Desktop is not available in Windows XP Home Edition. However, you can use Remote Desktop Connection on a computer running Home Edition to connect to a computer running Windows XP Professional. If you want to connect to a remote computer that's running Windows XP Home Edition, you're not completely out of luck, however. Two other programs—while not as flexible and powerful as Remote Desktop—might serve your needs, at least for an occasional connection. The first is Remote Assistance; for more information, see "Connecting to Another PC with Remote Assistance," page 154. The other program is NetMeeting; for more information, see "Other Communications Tools Included with Windows XP," page 731. In addition, you can use a free third-party program called VNC (the name is short for Virtual Network Computing) to set up remote access to any computer running a 32-bit version of Windows. You'll find more details about VNC at *http://www.uk.research.att.com/vnc/index.html*.

What You Need to Use Remote Desktop

The requirements for using Remote Desktop are pretty simple: You need two computers that are connected via a local area network, the Internet, or a dial-up connection.

> **note** The computer that you want to control—the one at the remote location—is called the *remote computer*. The computer you want to use to control the remote computer is called the *client computer*.

These are the requirements for the two computers:

- **Remote computer.** You need a computer running Windows XP Professional. (Windows XP Home Edition doesn't include the required components for hosting Remote Desktop sessions.) This computer must have a connection to a local area network or to the Internet, or it must have a modem that's configured to answer incoming calls automatically. If you're going to connect to this computer over the Internet, its Internet connection must have a known, public IP address. (For ways around this last requirement, see "Finding Your Remote Computer on the Internet," page 1099.)

- **Client computer.** You need a computer running nearly any version of Windows: Windows XP (all versions), Windows 2000 (all versions), Windows Me, Windows 98, Windows 95, Windows NT, or Windows for Workgroups. You must install client software (included on the Windows XP Professional CD-ROM) on the client computer. This computer must have access to the remote computer via a network connection, a virtual private network, or a dial-up connection.

Setting Up the Remote Computer

Before you can connect to a remote computer, you must enable Remote Desktop on the remote computer. To set up a computer to accept Remote Desktop connections, follow these steps:

1 Log on as a member of the Administrators group.

2 Open the System Properties dialog box shown on the next page (press the Windows logo key+Break or, in Control Panel, open Performance And Maintenance, System) and then click the Remote tab.

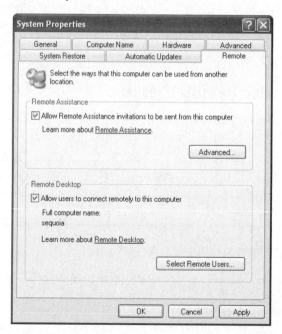

3 Under Remote Desktop, select Allow Users To Connect Remotely To This Computer.

At this point, any of the following user accounts (as long as the account has a logon password) can be used to connect remotely to the computer:

- The account currently logged on

- All members of the local Administrators group

- All members of the local Remote Desktop Users group

> **note** For security, only accounts that require a password to log on can be used to make a remote connection.

4 If you want to change which users can connect remotely, click Select Remote Users. The Remote Desktop Users dialog box appears.

- To add a user to the Remote Desktop Users group, click Add. Then type the user's name in the Select Users dialog box that appears (or click Advanced, Find Now to select names from a list). You can type the name of any local user account or, if your computer is in a domain, any domain user account. You can add multiple users by separating each user name with a semicolon.

- To delete a user from the Remote Desktop Users group, select the user's name in the Remote Desktop Users dialog box and click Remove.

If you're going to connect from another computer on your local area network, that's all you need to do to set up the remote computer.

If you're planning to connect to the remote computer via a dial-up connection, you must install a modem, configure it to answer automatically, and then set up an incoming connection.

For information about installing a modem, see "Setting Up a New Device," page 197. For information about setting up an incoming connection, see "Configuring a Remote Access Server for Dial-Up Access," page 1121.

If you're going to connect over the Internet, you must take the following additional steps:

● If the Internet connection is protected by a firewall—and it should be— you must open the port used by Remote Desktop. If you use the Internet Connection Firewall included with Windows XP, opening the port is simple:

   1 In the Network Connections folder, right-click the Internet connection and choose Properties.

   2 Click the Advanced tab and click Settings.

   3 In the Advanced Settings dialog box, select Remote Desktop.

   If you use a hardware firewall (or different software firewall), you need to configure it to allow incoming access to TCP port number 3389.

note You can use a different port for Remote Desktop connections. Although there's seldom reason to do so, changing to a different port can provide increased security because you don't expose a listening port where malevolent hackers expect to find Remote Desktop. For details about changing the port, see Microsoft Knowledge Base article Q187623, "How to Change Terminal Server's Listening Port."

● If the remote computer is on a network *and* it's not connected directly to the Internet, you must create a virtual private network. To do that, set up the computer connected to the Internet so that it allows incoming VPN connections. (For details, see "Allowing Remote Access via a Virtual Private Network," page 1117.) This is the typical setup for an office network that you want to connect to from your home.

InsideOut

To connect to a remote computer that's not directly connected to the Internet, you first establish a VPN connection to the network. Then you can start Remote Desktop Connection and connect to the desktop of any remote network computer on which Remote Desktop is enabled. You can specify the computer by its name or private IP address. You can't connect to those computers directly over the Internet because they don't have public IP addresses.

However, if you can't use a VPN for some reason, there is another way to get to the desktop of a remote network computer: Set up Remote Desktop on the computer with the Internet connection as well as the computer that you want to connect to.

Use Remote Desktop Connection to connect to the computer with the Internet connection. Then, using the remote desktop, connect to the remote desktop of the other network computer you want to use. (In other words, you'll have a remote desktop within a remote desktop.) It's a bit cumbersome and confusing, but it works! And this approach might be slightly faster because it doesn't require the overhead of VPN encryption and tunneling.

Finding Your Remote Computer on the Internet

To connect through the Internet, the remote computer (or the computer it uses to connect to the Internet, if it's part of a local area network) must have a known public IP address. Otherwise, how are you going to address this computer from elsewhere on the Internet? The best method is to have a fixed (static) IP address for your Internet connection. But your ISP might not offer static addresses for the type of Internet access account you have. Dial-up accounts, in particular, are likely to use dynamic addressing, in which your computer is assigned a different IP address each time you connect to the ISP. Many "always-on" connections, such as cable or DSL, also use dynamic addressing. (Some broadband ISPs use dynamic addressing, but as long as you maintain a connection your address *almost* never changes.)

If the Internet connection to the remote computer doesn't have a fixed IP address, you have a couple of options:

● You (or someone else with physical access to the remote computer) can type **ipconfig** at a command prompt to learn the network adapter's current IP address. (If the computer has more than one network adapter, be sure you find the one that's connected to the Internet. If you can't identify it by its description, take a look at the IP address: It's *not* the one in the 10.*x.x.x,* 169.254.*x.x,* 172.16.*x.x*–172.31.*x.x,* or 192.168.*x.x* ranges. Those addresses are reserved for private networks; if you see one of those addresses you know the adapter is not connected to the public Internet.)

● You can use a dynamic DNS service, such as those offered by TZO (*http://www.tzo.com*) and DHS International (*http://www.dhs.org*). Such services rely on software installed on your remote computer that monitors the computer's IP address. Whenever the IP address changes, the resident software notifies the service provider's dynamic domain name servers. The domain name server updates its table that correlates your domain name with an IP address—allowing you (or others) to always find your computer by using your registered domain name instead of a numeric IP address, even when the numeric address changes.

Setting Up the Client Computer

If the client computer—the one that you want to use to connect to the desktop of a remote computer—is running Windows XP, you don't need to install any additional software. Remote Desktop Connection, the client software, is installed by default in both Windows XP Professional and Windows XP Home Edition.

If you use Windows 95, Windows 98, Windows Me, Windows NT 4, or Windows 2000 on the client computer, you must install Remote Desktop Connection, which is included on the Windows XP CD. The easiest way to install it is to insert the CD. On the menu that appears, click Perform Additional Tasks, Set Up Remote Desktop Connection. (If the menu doesn't appear, open the CD in Windows Explorer. Double-click the Setup.exe icon in the CD's root folder to display the menu. Alternatively, you can start the Remote Desktop Connection setup program directly by double-clicking Msrdpcli.exe in the \Support\Tools folder.)

If the client computer is running an earlier version of Windows, the client software you need is available only with Windows 2000 Server or Windows .NET Server. If you don't have either of those operating systems, you'll need to use Remote Desktop Web Connection.

InsideOut

Because of its importance, you might not want to carry your original Windows XP CD with you—particularly if it's in its original sleeve or if you've written the CD key on the CD itself. This makes an inviting target for a thief who happens to see it on your car seat. The only file you need from the CD is Msrdpcli.exe in the \Support\Tools folder, so you might want to copy it to a CD-R disc or a Zip disk. This file is over 3 MB in size, so it won't fit on an ordinary floppy disk.

However, if the computer on which you want to install Remote Desktop Connection has Microsoft Installer support, you can get everything you need on a single floppy disk. Microsoft Installer support is built in to Windows 2000 and Windows Me, and you have it on other Windows-based computers if you've installed Microsoft Office 2000 or Microsoft Internet Explorer version 5 or later.

Open Msrdpcli.exe in a program that opens .zip archives, such as WinZip. (Msrdpcli.exe is actually a self-extracting .zip archive.) Extract the file named Msrdpcli.msi and copy it to a floppy disk; it's smaller than 800 KB. (The other files in Msrdpcli.exe merely install Microsoft Installer, so they're unnecessary if you already have it.)

Finally, you can leave the disk at home and download the Remote Desktop Connection software to the computer where you're planning to use it. If it has a good enough connection to allow remote access, you'll have no trouble with the 3.4-MB download. You'll find the file at *http://www.microsoft.com/windowsxp/pro/downloads/rdclientdl.asp*.

Configuring a Web Server for Use with Remote Desktop Web Connection

In some cases (for example, if you use a public Internet terminal while traveling), it's not feasible to install the Remote Desktop client software. That's okay; with the right setup, you can access your remote computer over the Internet using only Internet Explorer 4 or later.

To make this work, the remote computer must be on a network that has a computer configured as a Web server using Internet Information Services (IIS). (For details on installing and configuring IIS, see Chapter 24, "Hosting a Web or FTP Site.") If you didn't install it as part of the initial IIS setup, you must install the Remote Desktop Web Connection component, which you do as follows:

1 In Control Panel, open Add Or Remove Programs.

2 Click Add/Remove Windows Components.

3 Select Internet Information Services (IIS) and click Details.

4 Select World Wide Web Service and click Details.

5 Select Remote Desktop Web Connection, making sure that its check box is selected.

6 Click OK and Next, as needed, to finish the Windows Components Wizard.

After the Remote Desktop Web Connection component is installed, you must also set the appropriate permissions. To do that, follow these steps:

1 In Control Panel, open Administrative Tools, Internet Information Services.

2 Under the name of your computer in the tree pane, navigate to Web Sites\Default Web Sites\Tsweb.

3 Right-click Tsweb and choose Properties. Then click the Directory Security tab, shown in Figure 33-1 on the next page.

4 Under Anonymous Access And Authentication Control, click Edit to display the dialog box shown in Figure 33-2 on the next page.

5 Select Anonymous Access and then click OK in each dialog box.

> **note** You must still configure the remote computer—which might not be the same computer as the Web server—to allow remote connections. For details, see "Setting Up the Remote Computer," page 1096.

Figure 33-1. The name of the Tsweb Web site comes from Terminal Services, the feature now known as Remote Desktop.

Figure 33-2. At the IIS level, you want anonymous access. Remote Desktop takes care of authentication.

newfeature!

Using Remote Desktop Connection

After you've set up the remote computer to accept remote desktop connections and installed Remote Desktop Connection on the client computer, the rest is easy.

Connecting to a Remote Desktop

To use Remote Desktop Connection, the client computer must be connected to the remote computer. If they're on the same local area network (that is, you want to view the desktop of another computer on your network), that's already done. Similarly, if the remote computer has a public IP address (and the client computer is also connected to the Internet), they're connected. But if you plan to use a dial-up connection or you plan to connect to a computer that doesn't have a direct Internet connection, you must first connect the computers using a dial-up connection or a VPN connection.

Then start Remote Desktop Connection. Click the Start button and choose All Programs, Accessories, Communications, Remote Desktop Connection. A dialog box like the one shown in Figure 33-3 appears. In the Computer box, type the name of the remote computer or its IP address. Then click Connect.

note After a successful connection to a remote desktop, the name of the remote computer is added to the list in the Computer box. Thereafter, you can simply select it from the list (if it isn't already selected) instead of typing the name each time.

Figure 33-3. You can specify the computer by name or IP address.

Troubleshooting

Your firewall blocks outbound access.

If you have a firewall that blocks unknown outbound Internet traffic (such as ZoneAlarm), it prevents your initial attempt to connect to your remote desktop. Configure the firewall to enable Mstsc.exe (the file name of the Remote Desktop Connection program) to make outbound TCP connections on port 3389.

Unless you've changed the default settings, your screen goes black except for a small title bar at the top of the screen. In a moment, a logon dialog box appears, as shown in Figure 33-4. Enter the user name and password of an account that is a member of the Remote Desktop Users group on the remote computer.

Figure 33-4.   By default, Remote Desktop Connection takes over your full screen, regardless of the screen resolution of the remote computer.

If the account is already logged on to the remote computer—or no one is logged on to the remote computer—then the remote computer's display appears on your computer, either in a window or a full-screen display.

If someone else is already logged on to the computer (that is, a user account other than the one with which you're making the remote connection), Windows lets you know that you'll be forcing that person to log off. The message you see—and the effect it has—depends on whether Fast User Switching is enabled on the remote computer.

- **Fast User Switching enabled.** You'll see a message similar to the one shown in Figure 33-5. If you click Yes, a message is displayed on the remote computer, as shown in Figure 33-6, but if that user doesn't respond within a few seconds, he or she is unceremoniously bumped off. (While it sounds drastic, this allows you to connect to a desktop that someone has left logged on but is no longer using. Just as in local Fast User Switching, the other user's session remains logged on, but inaccessible.)

Figure 33-5. You'll know right away if someone else is logged on, giving you an opportunity to cancel your Remote Desktop Connection session.

Figure 33-6. If you attempt to connect while someone else is using the remote computer, they'll see this message, which allows them to reject your intrusion.

● **Fast User Switching disabled.** You'll see a more strongly worded message, as shown in Figure 33-7. If you click Yes, the person at the remote computer is logged off without warning—and without an opportunity to save any open documents.

Figure 33-7. If you connect to a remote computer on which Fast User Switching is disabled, the person currently using the computer will be logged off without warning.

While you use the remote computer, the remote computer's monitor (if turned on) does not display what you see on the client computer. If you could actually see the remote computer's screen, you'd notice that as soon as someone logs on remotely, the remote computer displays the Welcome screen. If the Welcome screen has been disabled, the remote computer displays the Unlock Computer dialog box. In either case, a person who has physical access to the remote computer can't see what you're doing (other than the fact that you have a certain number of programs running) at the client computer.

caution   It's important to note that only one user at a time can control the desktop of a computer running Windows XP Professional. If someone logs on locally to the remote computer, the remote session is immediately disconnected without warning to the users at either end of the connection. (The good news is that no data is lost when the remote user is disconnected. It works the same as when you switch users with Fast User Switching; the first session remains logged on and all applications continue running, but the new session has control of the desktop.) Particularly with the Welcome screen and Fast User Switching enabled, it's all too easy for this to happen. Someone seeing the Welcome screen on a computer with nobody around might naturally assume that the computer is not being used and is available for his or her use.

Therefore, if you use Remote Desktop and other people have physical access to your remote computer while you're connected remotely, you should disable the Welcome screen. At the very least, consider disabling Fast User Switching. Although it doesn't prevent another user from knocking you off, the user who tries to log on locally to the remote computer at least gets a message that explains who is connected remotely and warns that logging on will disconnect the remote user and cause the loss of unsaved data.

Whether you disable the Welcome screen and Fast User Switching or not, logging on locally with the same account that's currently connected remotely disconnects the remote user without warning. This is a good reason to create a separate user account for each person (and for each person to log on with his or her account only); it's not likely that one person will be in two places at once!

For information about disabling the Welcome screen and Fast User Switching, see "Controlling How Users Log On," page 107. For information about locking and unlocking a computer, see "Logging Off or Locking Your Computer," page 116.

Connecting from a Web Browser

If you set up a Web server on your network, you can connect to a remote desktop without using the Remote Desktop Connection client program; instead, the remote desktop appears in a Web browser window. For details about setting up the Web server for this purpose, see "Configuring a Web Server for Use with Remote Desktop Web Connection," page 1101.

To connect to the remote desktop, you'll need a TCP/IP connection to the network or the Internet, and you must be running Internet Explorer 4 or later. Remote Desktop Web Connection installs an ActiveX control on the client computer. To make the connection, simply type the URL for the Remote Desktop Web Connection home directory in Internet Explorer's Address bar. By default, the URL is *http://server/tsweb/*, where *server* is the name or IP address of the server. On an intranet (or if you've already made a VPN connection to your network), simply use the computer name. If you're connecting over the Internet, the server must have a registered domain name or a known IP address. Internet Explorer then displays a page like the one shown in Figure 33-8.

Figure 33-8. Your initial view of the remote computer looks like this.

In the Server box, type the name of the remote computer you want to view; it doesn't have to be the same computer as the Web server. In the Size box, select a screen size. (If you select Full Screen, Internet Explorer uses the screen resolution of the client computer; otherwise, the remote desktop appears in a resizable window.) Then click Connect. The first time you connect from a client computer, Windows displays a security warning about an ActiveX control that you must download. Click Yes to accept the download, and then the remote desktop logon dialog box appears—just as it does when you use the Remote Desktop Connection program. After you provide your user name and password, the desktop appears in your Internet Explorer window, as shown in Figure 33-9 on the next page, and you can interact with it exactly as if you were at the remote computer.

---

tip **Bookmark the remote desktop**

After you get to the remote desktop, save it as a favorite in Internet Explorer. (Open the Favorites menu and choose Add To Favorites.) That way, you can bypass the Remote Desktop Web Connection screen next time. But this method has other advantages: The server name, screen size, and user name (if you select Send Logon Information For This Connection and specify a user name before clicking Connect) are encapsulated in the stored URL—so you needn't enter this information again.

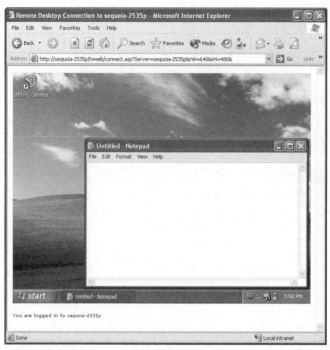

Figure 33-9. Your remote desktop in an Internet Explorer window is fully functional.

Working with Different Screen Resolutions

Whether you connect to a remote computer using Remote Desktop Connection or Remote Desktop Web Connection, by default, the remote computer takes over your entire screen. It uses the resolution of the client computer, regardless of the resolution set on the remote computer. At the top of the screen, a small title bar appears, as shown in Figure 33-4 on page 1104. This title bar lets you switch between your own desktop and the remote desktop. Table 33-1 explains each button on the title bar.

Table 33-1. Remote Desktop Connection Full-Screen Title Bar

Button	Description
📌	The pushpin locks the title bar in place. If you click the pushpin, the title bar disappears completely, retracting into the top of the screen. To make the title bar reappear, move the mouse pointer to the top edge of the screen. To keep the title bar visible, click the pushpin again.
–	The Minimize button reduces the remote desktop to a taskbar button on your own desktop.
🗗	The Restore button displays the remote desktop in a resizable window on your own desktop. To return to full-screen view, click the window's Maximize button.

1108

Table 33-1. *(continued)*

Button	Description
✕	The Close button disconnects the remote computer (but does not log off) and closes Remote Desktop Connection. You can pick up where you left off by reopening Remote Desktop Connection and reconnecting, or by logging on locally at the remote computer.

tip **Hide the title bar**

If you seldom use the Remote Desktop Connection title bar and it gets in your way, you can hide it by clicking the pushpin. (To make it visible again, "bump" the top of the screen with the mouse pointer.) If you rarely use the title bar, you can prevent it from showing up in the first place: Before you connect, click the Options button in Remote Desktop Connection. Click the Display tab and then clear the Display The Connection Bar When In Full Screen Mode check box.

You might prefer to not use your full screen for the remote desktop. You set this—along with a number of other options—before you connect to the remote computer. After you start Remote Desktop Connection, click the Options button to expand the dialog box. Then click the Display tab, which is shown in Figure 33-10. You can set the

Figure 33-10. Screen resolution is determined by the client computer.

screen resolution to any size from 640×480 up to the current resolution of the client computer (not the remote computer)—or you can set it to full screen by moving the slider all the way to the right.

> **note** Changes you make to settings that appear when you click Options become the default settings for new Remote Desktop Connection sessions. These settings are saved in a hidden file called %UserProfile%\My Documents\Default.rdp.

Troubleshooting

Colors are washed out.

The screen resolution of a Remote Desktop Connection session is determined entirely by the client computer. The number of colors, however, is set to the lowest value set on either computer. At the client computer, you specify the number of colors on the Display tab. On the remote computer, the number of colors is set by Group Policy. If this value is lower than the client setting, it prevails. The Terminal Services and Remote Desktop server in Windows .NET Server defaults to 8-bit color (256 colors). To increase the number of colors that the remote computer delivers, on the remote computer open Group Policy (Gpedit.msc). Navigate to Computer Configuration\Administrative Templates\ Windows Components\Terminal Services, and double-click the Limit Maximum Color Depth policy. Select Enabled and then specify the maximum color depth you want to allow for remote connections.

Accessing Local Resources

While you use Remote Desktop Connection, it's immediately apparent that you have control of the remote computer. You see its desktop, Start menu, and so on. That's terrific if the remote computer has everything you need. But you'll often want to use local resources and information from the client computer as well as from the remote computer. In addition, you might want to move information between the two computers. With Remote Desktop Connection, you can do so easily with the following features:

- **Clipboard.** When you copy or cut text or graphics on either the remote computer or the local computer, it's saved on the Clipboard. It's then available for pasting in documents on either computer. Similarly, you can cut or copy files or folders from a Windows Explorer window on either computer and then paste them into a folder on the other computer.

If you want to disable this capability as a security measure, you must use Group Policy on the remote computer. At a command prompt, type **gpedit.msc** to open Group Policy and navigate to Computer Configuration\Administrative Templates\Windows Components\Terminal Services\Client/Server Data Redirection. Enable the Do Not Allow Clipboard Redirection policy.

● **Disk drives.** You access your own drives through My Computer on the remote desktop. As shown in Figure 33-11, each drive on the client computer appears on the remote desktop in the My Computer's Other group. You can navigate to any folder or file on your computer, and then use any of the usual methods to copy, move, rename, open, delete, and so on.

Figure 33-11. Drives on the client computer (Glacier in this figure) appear in My Computer on the remote computer (Sequoia).

● **Printers.** Your local printers appear in the remote computer's Printers And Faxes folder. Their entries have "(from *clientcomputername*)" appended to each printer name. To print to a local printer, you simply select its name in a Print dialog box.

> **note** For Clipboard and disk drives features to work, Disk Drives must be selected on the Local Resources tab before you connect. To use the printers feature, Printers must be selected.

If you're connecting to another computer on your local area network, you might not want your local drives and printers to appear on the remote desktop. In that situation, the drives and printers you need might already be available on the remote computer; allowing Remote Desktop Connection to add an entry for each one merely clutters your windows with a lot of duplicated drive and printer icons. And if you're connecting over a slow modem connection, you might not want to show them, because using those shortcuts merely provides a slow round-trip path to your local resources. To prevent their appearance, before you make the connection, click Options in the Remote Desktop Connection dialog box. Then click the Local Resources tab, shown in Figure 33-12.

Decide where you want sounds to play

Decide which computer responds to special Windows key combinations

Decide which local devices you want displayed on the remote desktop

Figure 33-12. You control which of the client computer resources are available in the remote desktop window.

On the Local Resources tab, you also specify which computer should play the sounds generated by the remote computer. On a fast connection, you'll probably want them to play on the client computer (select Bring To This Computer). On a slow connection, you're better off selecting Do Not Play. The Leave At Remote Computer option, apparently, is to scare the wits out of anyone who happens to be sitting by the remote-controlled computer!

Troubleshooting

Sounds don't play.

Remote Desktop Connection uses UDP for transmitting audio data. If sounds don't play at all, it might be because a firewall is blocking this UDP traffic. Check your firewall logs and, if the firewall is blocking the traffic, create a rule that permits it to pass.

If a firewall isn't blocking sounds, the problem might be that the UDP packets are being dropped. Audio data is considered to be relatively unimportant, which is why it uses UDP, a protocol that, by design, permits data to be lost. If you're pushing the bandwidth limits of your connection, audio data disappears in favor of accurate transfer of screen images and other data. You can make more room in the pipe by lowering the number of colors (to 256 colors, for example).

InsideOut

You can force the setting of most items on the Local Resources, Display, Programs, and Experience tabs by using Group Policy. Dozens of other settings are also available, including a number of security-related options and the ability to automatically disconnect remote desktop sessions after a period of inactivity. To make these settings, open Group Policy (Gpedit.msc) and navigate to Computer Configuration\Administrative Templates\ Windows Components\Terminal Services and its subfolders. In the details pane, click the Extended tab, and then select a policy to see its description. For more information about Group Policy, see Appendix E, "Group Policy."

Using the Keyboard with Remote Desktop Connection

When the Remote Desktop Connection window is active, almost every key you press is passed to the remote computer. Certain key combinations, however, can be processed by the client computer, depending on the setting you make on the Local Resources tab of the Remote Desktop Connection dialog box (shown in Figure 33-12). You can specify that the key combinations shown on the next page in the first column of Table 33-2 on the next page are sent to the remote computer all the time, only when the remote desktop is displayed in full-screen mode, or never.

Table 33-2. **Special Keys in Remote Desktop Connection**

Key for Client Computer	Equivalent Key for Remote Desktop Session	Description
Alt+Tab	Alt+Page Up	Switches between programs
Alt+Shift+Tab	Alt+Page Down	Switches between programs (in reverse order)
Alt+Esc	Alt+Insert	Cycles through programs in the order they were started
N/A	Ctrl+Alt+Break	Switches the remote desktop between a window and full screen
Ctrl+Alt+Delete	Ctrl+Alt+End	Displays the Windows Security dialog box (if the remote computer is joined to a domain) or Task Manager (if the remote computer is not joined to a domain)
Ctrl+Esc	Alt+Home	Displays the Start menu
N/A	Alt+Delete	Displays the Control menu of the active window
Shift+Print Screen	Ctrl+Alt+Plus (on numeric keypad)	Captures a bitmap image of the remote desktop and places it on the Clipboard
Alt+Print Screen	Ctrl+Alt+Minus (on numeric keypad)	Captures a bitmap image of the active window and places it on the Clipboard

If you select On The Local Computer, key combinations from the first column of Table 33-2 are always applied to the client computer. To get the equivalent function on the remote computer, press the key combination shown in the second column. The same is true if you select In Full Screen Mode Only and the remote session is displayed in a window.

If you select On The Remote Computer, key combinations from the first column are applied to the remote computer. Key combinations in the second column are ignored (unless they have some function in the active application on the remote desktop). The same is true if you select In Full Screen Mode Only and the remote session is displayed in full-screen mode.

One exception is the Ctrl+Alt+Delete combination, which is always applied to the client computer. Regardless of your Local Resources tab setting, you must press Ctrl+Alt+End to obtain the same result on the remote computer. As an alternative, in the remote session open the Start menu and choose Windows Security.

Configuring Performance Options

When you first use Remote Desktop Connection, you might notice that the remote desktop doesn't display a background. Disabling the background is one of several settings you can make that affect the speed of your remote session. How you set these options depends in large measure on the speed of the connection between the two computers. If you're using a dial-up connection, you should disable as many features as possible to reduce the amount of information that must be transmitted across the wire. On the other hand, if you're connecting to another desktop on your local area network, you might as well enable all features to enjoy the full experience of working at the remote computer.

The performance-related options are on the Experience tab, shown in Figure 33-13. To quickly select an appropriate set of options, select the speed of your connection from the list box.

Figure 33-13. Remote Desktop Connection has a default collection of settings for each connection speed. Use those settings or select your own options.

The last two options on the Experience tab are not as comprehensible as the others:

- **Themes.** Clearing the Themes check box disables the Windows XP visual styles, causing everything to display using the Windows Classic visual style—the one used in earlier versions of Windows. (For information about visual styles, see "Changing Colors, Fonts, and Visual Effects," page 308.)

- **Bitmap Caching.** Unlike the other options on the Experience tab, you get the fastest performance if you *select* (not clear) Bitmap Caching. Bitmap caching can speed up your connection by storing frequently used images on a local drive.

Saving a Remote Desktop Configuration

Changes you make in the expanded Remote Desktop Connection dialog box are automatically saved in %UserProfile%\My Documents\Default.rdp, and they're automatically reused the next time you open Remote Desktop Connection. But you might want to have several different Remote Desktop Connection configurations for connections to different computers. If you have a portable computer, you might want different settings for use with different connections to the same computer (for example, dial-up versus LAN).

To save a configuration, simply make all your settings, click the General tab (see Figure 33-14), and click Save As. By default, Remote Desktop Connection offers to save your configuration file in %UserProfile%\My Documents.

Figure 33-14. Options for saving or opening saved connection settings are on the General tab.

To reuse a stored configuration at a later time, start Remote Desktop Connection, click Options, click Open, and then double-click the stored file. More simply, double-click the stored file in Windows Explorer. For the quickest access to a frequently used remote desktop configuration, drag a shortcut to your Start menu or the Quick Launch toolbar.

Disconnecting a Remote Session

When you're through with a Remote Desktop Connection session, you can either disconnect or you can log off.

If you disconnect, your programs continue to run. It's effectively like pressing the Windows logo key+L with Fast User Switching enabled: The Welcome screen is visible, and the remote computer is available for another user. If you log on later—either locally or through a remote connection—you can pick up right where you left off. To disconnect, in the remote session open the Start menu and choose Disconnect, which appears in place of the Turn Off Computer (or Shut Down, on domain-based computers) command. A simpler alternative is to click the Close button on the title bar of the remote session. Either way, a confirmation dialog box awaits your answer before Remote Desktop Connection pulls the plug.

Logging off closes all your programs before disconnecting. To log off, in the remote session open the Start menu and choose Log Off.

You can also turn off or restart the remote computer. To perform either task, in the remote session press Ctrl+Alt+End or open the Start menu and choose Windows Security. If the remote computer is joined to a domain, the Windows Security dialog box appears; click Shut Down to turn off or restart the computer. If the remote computer is not a domain member, Windows Task Manager appears. Its Shut Down menu offers Turn Off, Restart, and Log Off commands.

Allowing Remote Access via a Virtual Private Network

A *virtual private network* (VPN) is a means of connecting to a private network (such as your office network) via a public network, such as the Internet. This combines the virtues of a dial-up connection to a dial-up server (the ability to use all your network resources and protocols just as if you were connected directly to the network) with the ease and flexibility of an Internet connection. By using an Internet connection, you can travel worldwide and still, in most places, connect to your office with a local call to the nearest Internet access phone number. And if you have a high-speed Internet connection (such as cable or DSL) at your computer (and at your office), you can communicate with your office at full Internet speed, which is much faster than any dial-up connection using an analog modem.

Chapter 33

Tunneling provides a secure, cost-effective way to connect two computers (or two networks) that are each connected to the Internet. Instead of paying the phone company to use its cables and set up special protocols at each end, you leverage the existing Internet infrastructure and its transmission protocols. Tunneling protocols dig underneath the protocol of the intervening network to create the illusion of a direct path between the two separated networks.

This path is created by encrypting each IP packet or frame (depending on the protocol) and wrapping it inside another packet or frame with new header information for traveling through the intervening network. That is, when a network frame (if we're talking about a frame-based protocol) created on one of the computers is destined for a computer on the other side of the tunnel, the entire frame is encrypted and a new header that routes the encrypted frame through the intervening network is attached. When the new frame gets to the other side, the new header is stripped off, and the original frame is decrypted and routed forward just as though it had never left the original local network. When you put all these pieces together, you end up with a virtual private network. Tunneling protocols are the core of VPNs.

Three tunneling protocols are in wide use today:

- **Point-to-Point Tunneling Protocol (PPTP).** PPTP allows IP, IPX, or NetBEUI frames to be encrypted and then wrapped in an IP header to be sent across an intervening network.

- **Layer 2 Tunneling Protocol (L2TP).** L2TP allows IP, IPX, or NetBEUI frames to be encrypted and then sent over any IP, X.25, Frame Relay, or ATM intervening network.

- **IP Security (IPSec) Tunnel Mode.** IPSec Tunnel Mode allows IP packets to be encrypted and then encapsulated in an IP header to be sent across an intervening network.

Windows XP uses PPTP or L2TP for tunnel connections. Only Windows .NET Server or Windows 2000 Server can act as a VPN server using L2TP. Windows XP can, however, connect to a VPN server using L2TP. Windows XP uses IPSec to enhance the security of all network interactions.

Configuring a VPN Server

A number of third-party VPN solutions are available, and they're often appropriate for allowing VPN access to a corporate network. For a standalone computer or a small network, where you need only a single incoming connection at any time, Windows XP has everything you need built in.

You can make your computer a remote access server so that others can connect to it via a VPN and then access shared folders on your local drives. If your computer is connected to a local area network, incoming VPN connections can also browse the network and access shared resources elsewhere on the network.

> **note** To create or modify incoming connections, you must be logged on as a member of the Administrators group.

To enable others to connect to your computer, follow these steps:

1 In Control Panel, open Network Connections.

2 Under Network Tasks, click Create A New Connection. The New Connection Wizard appears.

> **note** If you have not configured a modem and a dialing location, the Location Information dialog box appears. This dialog box asks for the name of your country and the area code (or city code) that you're in. If your computer doesn't have a modem or you don't plan to ever use the computer to dial a phone number, you might be tempted to simply close this dialog box without providing the requested information. Because of a bug in Windows, however, you might not be able to complete the other steps unless you enter an area code and click OK.

3 On the New Connection Wizard's first page, click Next.

4 On the Network Connection Type page, select Set Up An Advanced Connection and click Next.

5 On the Advanced Connection Options page, select Accept Incoming Connections and click Next.

6 If a Devices For Incoming Connections page appears, simply click Next. (These options are for setting up an incoming dial-up connection, direct cable connection, or infrared connection.) This page appears only if your computer has an installed modem, serial port, parallel port, or IrDA port.

7 On the Incoming Virtual Private Network (VPN) Configuration page, select Allow Virtual Private Connections and click Next.

To receive VPN connections over the Internet, your computer's IP address (more precisely, the IP address of your connection to the Internet, if your computer has multiple network adapters) must be known on the Internet. This IP address is assigned to you by your Internet service provider. (For ways to work with dynamic addresses, see "Finding Your Remote Computer on the Internet," page 1099.)

8 On the User Permissions page, select the check box next to the name of each user you want to allow to make an incoming connection.

Windows lists all of the local user accounts on your computer. As shown below, you can add (or delete) user accounts from this page, which can save a visit to the User Accounts program.

When you're finished with the User Permissions page, click Next.

9 On the Networking Software page, select the check box next to the name of each network component you want to use for an incoming connection.

For an incoming connection to work, the calling computer and your computer have to "speak" the same network protocol. Click Install to add a new networking component. For more information about installing network components, see "Installing and Configuring Protocols," page 1009.

When you're finished with the Networking Software page, click Next and then click Finish.

---

tip   **Require encryption**

By default, the VPN connection does not require that users encrypt all transmitted data and passwords. You can improve security by requiring encryption. In the Network Connections folder, right-click the Incoming Connections icon and choose Properties. Click the Users tab and select the Require All Users To Secure Their Passwords And Data check box. Before a user can connect, he or she should open Network Connections on the client computer and open the properties dialog box for the VPN connection. On the Security tab, Require Data Encryption (Disconnect If None) must be selected.

Configuring a Remote Access Server for Dial-Up Access

If your computer—the one you want to use as a VPN server—doesn't have a full-time Internet connection and a static IP address, you might consider using a dial-up connection instead. You'll need a modem that's configured to answer automatically.

Follow the same steps just described in "Configuring a VPN Server," but replace steps 6 through 8 with these steps:

6 On the Devices For Incoming Connections page, select the modem you want to use.

7 On the Incoming Virtual Private Network (VPN) Configuration page, select Do Not Allow Virtual Private Connections.

8 On the User Permissions page, select the check box next to the name of each user you want to allow to make an incoming connection.

You might want to set callback options, which can be used as an additional security measure for dial-up connections as well as to determine who pays for the phone call. To set callback options for a particular user, select the user name, click Properties, and then click the Callback tab. If you select an option other than Do Not Allow Callback, when your computer receives a call, it authenticates the user, disconnects the call, and then dials the user's modem. Use the following guidelines to make your selection:

- Select Do Not Allow Callback if you want the remote user to make a connection with a single call to your computer.

- Select Allow The Caller To Set The Callback Number if you want the caller to be able to specify a phone number for a return call.

- Select Always Use The Following Callback Number and specify a phone number if you want your computer to call the user at a particular number. This reduces the likelihood that an intruder who has come upon a valid user name and password can access your system.

Configuring Firewalls and Other Network Settings for VPN Access

With a simple network configuration and Windows XP running at each end of the connection, your VPN should be ready to go without any further ado. If you're unsuccessful at making a connection to the VPN server or you're unable to browse network resources, a few additional configuration steps are required.

Troubleshooting

You can't connect to the VPN from another computer.

After you set up a VPN connection on another computer, you might not be able to connect. This can occur if a firewall at either end of the connection blocks VPN traffic.

At the server, when you use the New Connection Wizard to create an incoming VPN connection, the wizard automatically configures the built-in Internet Connection Firewall appropriately. You can confirm that by visiting Network Connections, opening the properties dialog box for the Internet connection, clicking the Advanced tab, and clicking Settings. You should see entries for Incoming Connection VPN (L2TP) and Incoming Connection VPN (PPTP), and they should both be selected.

If you use a different firewall—software or hardware—you'll need to configure it similarly. For PPTP connections (the type most commonly used with a Windows XP–based VPN), you must open port 1723 for TCP communication. (L2TP connections, which use port 1701, require a machine certificate for authentication and are available only when the VPN server is on a network with Windows .NET Server or Windows 2000 Server. L2TP, therefore, is a topic that's beyond the scope of this book.)

If the firewall on your client computer filters outbound traffic as well as incoming connections, you'll need to open port 1723 on that computer as well.

If you're certain that firewalls at each end are not blocking traffic, yet you still can't connect, the problem might be in between. Some ISPs block VPN traffic or allow it only with certain types of accounts. Check with your ISP for information about its policies.

Troubleshooting

You can't browse the remote network.

If you're able to connect with the VPN server but you can't see any other computers on the network, you might need to change some network settings. In particular, you need to be sure that the incoming VPN connection has an IP address in the same subnet as the rest of your local area network.

On the server, open the Network Connections folder, right-click the Incoming Connections icon, and choose Properties. In the Incoming Connections Properties dialog box shown on the next page, click the Networking tab, select Internet Protocol (TCP/IP), and click Properties.

Select if you want incoming connections to see other computers on your network

Select to allow Windows to supply an IP address

Select to specify an IP address

Select to let the client computer specify the IP address

On the client, open the Network Connections folder, right-click the icon for the VPN connection, and choose Properties. In the properties dialog box, click the Networking tab, select Internet Protocol (TCP/IP), and click Properties. If the server is set up to assign an address, select Obtain An IP Address Automatically. If the server is configured to let the client supply its own IP address, select Use The Following IP Address and specify an address in the same subnet as the VPN server.

Connecting to a Virtual Private Network

To connect to your Windows XP VPN server, you don't need to run Windows XP; you can connect with any version of Windows. To set up a VPN connection on a computer running Windows XP, follow these steps. (The steps are quite similar for users of other Windows versions.)

1 In Control Panel, open Network Connections.

2 Under Network Tasks, click Create A New Connection. The New Connection Wizard appears.

3 On the New Connection Wizard's first page, click Next.

4 On the Network Connection Type page, select Connect To The Network At My Workplace and click Next.

5 On the Network Connection page, select Virtual Private Network Connection and click Next.

Chapter 33

> **note** If you want to make a dial-up connection to a remote access server, select Dial-Up Connection instead. The rest of the wizard is straightforward.

6 On the Connection Name page, type a descriptive name for the connection and click Next.

7 If you need to dial to connect to the Internet, select Automatically Dial This Initial Connection and select your dial-up Internet connection from the list. If you have a full-time connection, select Do Not Dial The Initial Connection and click Next.

8 On the VPN Server Selection page, type the host name (for example, mycompany.com) or the IP address (for example, 123.45.67.89) of the computer you want to connect to and click Next.

Troubleshooting

Other Internet services stop working when you make a VPN connection.

When you make a VPN connection, you might find that you can no longer browse the Internet using Internet Explorer, hold conversations using Windows Messenger, or use other applications that access the Internet. This occurs when the VPN connection is configured to use the default gateway on the remote network for Internet access. When you make a VPN connection, Windows adds to the IP routing table a new default route that uses the connection to the VPN server. That new route is assigned the lowest metric, which means that it's used in place of your original default route—and therefore prevents access to some locations. Although this is a useful feature when you connect to some corporate networks, it's generally of little use when you're connecting to a single computer or a small workgroup.

To fix the problem, follow these steps:

1 In Control Panel open Network Connections, right-click the VPN connection, and choose Properties.

2 Click the Networking tab, select Internet Protocol (TCP/IP), and click Properties.

3 In the Internet Protocol (TCP/IP) Properties dialog box, click Advanced.

4 On the General tab of the Advanced TCP/IP Settings dialog box, clear the Use Default Gateway On Remote Network check box.

You should then be able to use other Internet applications while your VPN connection is active.

To connect to a VPN, open the VPN connection in your Network Connections folder. If you don't already have a connection to the Internet open, Windows offers to connect to the Internet. Once that connection is made, the VPN server asks for your user name and password. Enter them correctly, click Connect, and your network resources should be available to you in the same way they are when you connect directly to the network.

---

tip   **Share your VPN connection**

You can share a VPN connection in the same way that you share an Internet connection. For more information, see "Sharing an Internet Connection," page 1026.

Working with Windows Domains

Computers on a network can be part of a workgroup or a domain.

In a *workgroup*, the security database (including, most significantly, the list of user accounts and the privileges granted to each one) for each computer resides on that computer. When you log on to a computer in a workgroup, Microsoft Windows checks its local security database to see if you've provided a user name and password that matches one in the database. Similarly, when network users attempt to connect to your computer, Windows again consults the local security database. A workgroup is sometimes called a *peer-to-peer network*.

By contrast, a *domain* consists of computers that share a security database stored on one or more domain controllers running a member of the Microsoft Windows .NET Server, Windows 2000 Server, or Windows NT Server families. When you log on using a domain account, Windows authenticates your credentials against the security database on a domain controller.

When you have more than a handful of computers in a network, they become much easier to manage when configured as a domain. For example, instead of re-creating a database of user accounts on each computer, you create each account only once. A domain environment also offers much greater power and flexibility. For example, you can easily set up roaming user profiles, which allow users to log on at any network computer and see the same personalized desktop, menus, applications, and documents. A domain using Active Directory, a feature of Windows 2000 Server and Windows .NET Server (but not

At Home with Windows XP

By design, Windows domains are intended for use on business networks. Only the most fanatical of computer hobbyists would even consider installing a domain controller on a small home network. Thus, you shouldn't be surprised to learn that access to most domain features requires Windows XP Professional.

Computers running Windows XP Home Edition cannot join a domain. If you're running Home Edition, however, you *can* access shared domain resources, such as folders and printers. For details, see "Accessing Domain Resources from a Computer Running Windows XP Home Edition," page 1147.

Windows NT Server), also offers a fully searchable directory service, which allows network users to easily find shared resources, contacts, users, and other directory objects. In addition, these server families offer IntelliMirror, a collection of technologies that offer centralized

- User data management
- Software installation and maintenance
- User settings management

In this chapter we make no attempt to explain how to configure a domain or use its management capabilities. Those are features of the server acting as the domain controller, and they're well documented in the numerous books about server versions of Windows. Rather, our intent here is to explain how to use your computer running Windows XP in a domain environment, focusing on the differences from using Windows XP in a workgroup.

Domains vs. Workgroups

In addition to the location and use of the all-important security database, you'll notice a number of differences—some trivial and some that can have a significant effect on the way you use Windows—when your computer is joined to a domain. Many of these changes are designed to make Windows XP work the same way that Windows 2000 Professional works in a domain environment, which eases the training and support burden on administrators. A domain-based computer running Windows XP Professional differs in the following ways from a workgroup-based computer:

- Logon and logoff

    - **Logon screen.** The Welcome screen is unavailable in a domain environment. Instead, you use the "classic" logon, which prompts you to press Ctrl+Alt+Delete and then enter your user name (if it isn't already entered from your last session) and password. For more information about using the classic logon, see "Logging On to a Domain," page 1145.

- **Automatic logon.** In a workgroup environment, you can easily set up your computer to log on automatically so that you don't need to enter your password. (Ironically, you use the domain version of User Accounts to achieve this. For details, see "Bypassing the Logon Screen," page 113.) In a domain environment, you must delve into the registry to set up automatic logon. For details, see "Logging On Automatically," page 1145.

- **Logon scripts.** In a domain environment, a domain administrator can set up scripts that run automatically each time you log on to your computer. These scripts, which are typically stored and administered on the domain controller, can be used to provide software updates, new virus definitions, and other information to your computer; set up network connections; start programs; and perform other tasks. A computer that's not joined to a domain can't run domain logon scripts. Although you can create local logon scripts for workgroup computers, they're generally less powerful and, of course, they're not centrally managed for all computers on the network.

- **Forgotten passwords.** With the classic logon that's used in a domain environment, password hints aren't available. Nor can you create or use a Password Reset Disk, which allows you to set a new password if you can't remember your current one. A domain administrator can change the password for your domain account. Any user who is a member of the local Administrators group can change the password for any local account. For details about using these features in a workgroup, see "Recovering from a Lost Password," page 134.

- **Fast User Switching.** Fast User Switching, an awesome feature that allows a user to log on without requiring the current user to first log off, is not available on domain-based computers. Application compatibility and other technical issues prevent its use. For information about Fast User Switching, see "Configuring Fast User Switching," page 114.

- **Workstation locking.** On a computer that's joined to a domain, pressing the Windows logo key+L locks a workstation so that only the currently logged on user or an administrator can unlock it. (In a workgroup, Windows logo key+L invokes Fast User Switching.) For details about locking, see "Logging Off or Locking Your Computer," page 116.

- **Logoff and Shutdown screens.** Instead of the big, colorful buttons that appear when you choose to log off or shut down a workgroup computer, a computer joined to a domain displays dialog boxes similar to those in Windows 2000, as shown in Figures 34-1 and 34-2 on the next page. They serve the same function and they're no harder or easier to use; they are simply intended to ease the transition to Windows XP for corporate users.

1129

Figure 34-1. Domain users see this utilitarian Log Off Windows dialog box.

Figure 34-2. To shut down a domain-based computer, you select from a list and click OK. Windows displays your previous selection as the default option.

● File sharing and security

■ **Simple File Sharing.** Although the option to enable Simple File Sharing remains in the Folder Options dialog box (and indeed, it's selected by default), Simple File Sharing is not available in a domain environment.

Without Simple File Sharing, the Security tab appears in the properties dialog box for all printers and for all folders and files on NTFS drives. When you're logged in as a member of the local Administrators or Power Users group, the Sharing tab, with which you set network access permissions, appears in the properties dialog box for all folders.

Most important, without Simple File Sharing, network users are authenticated as themselves. To access local resources, their account must be granted appropriate permissions, either directly or through their membership in a group.

> For more information about Simple File Sharing, see "Simple File Sharing vs. Windows 2000–Style Sharing," page 98, and "Simple File Sharing vs. Advanced Permissions," page 499. For information about how sharing options affect sharing over a network, see Chapter 32, "Managing Shared Folders and Printers."

- ■ **Shared Documents.** On computers in a workgroup environment, the local Shared Documents folder, %AllUsersProfile%\Documents, occupies a prominent place in My Computer. Particularly when Simple File Sharing is enabled, it is the default and easiest location for storing folders and files that you want to share with other users on your computer or on your network.

  When your computer is joined to a domain, however, you're likely to forget that Shared Documents exists. My Computer no longer includes a Files Stored On This Computer group. If your computer was in a workgroup and you ran the Network Setup Wizard before you joined a domain, the folder continues to be shared as Shared Documents. If you have not run the Network Setup Wizard, the folder is not set up as a network share by default. Either way, by default only local users and groups have permissions to access the folders and files within Shared Documents. If you want to grant permissions to domain users, you should add the appropriate domain groups to the folder's access control list (ACL). For information about modifying the ACL, see "Controlling Access with NTFS Permissions," page 507.

- ● Networking

  - ■ **Network Setup Wizard.** The Network Setup Wizard, which is designed to help you set up a home or small office network, does not run on a computer that's joined to a domain. For information about the Network Setup Wizard, see "Using the Network Setup Wizard," page 1003.

  - ■ **Network Tasks.** When you open My Network Places, the links that appear in the task pane vary depending on whether your computer is part of a workgroup, a Windows NT domain, or an Active Directory domain, as shown in Figure 34-3 on the next page. In addition, your options for browsing and searching the network vary. For details, see "Finding Files, Printers, and Users," page 1147.

- ● Computer and user management

  - ■ **User Accounts.** When you open User Accounts in Control Panel, you get a different version depending on whether your computer is joined to a domain or not. The two versions have similar capabilities; the difference is more style than substance. The workgroup version follows the newer style of Windows XP, complete with graphics and links to wizard-like dialog boxes. For information about the work-group version of User Accounts, see "Working with User Accounts," page 100.

Figure 34-3. Note that Shared Documents appears in Other Places only in a workgroup. You can browse computers in a domain by clicking Entire Network.

The domain version uses a traditional dialog box that's nearly identical to its Windows 2000 predecessor. For information about this version, see "Advanced Account Setup Options," page 120.

- **Group Policy.** A computer in a workgroup or in a non–Active Directory domain can use the local Group Policy Object to make a large number of settings and impose a number of restrictions—but these settings and restrictions apply to only a single computer, and they apply to all users on that computer. In a domain with Active Directory, many more Group Policy settings are available. More important, they're centrally managed and they can be selectively applied to computers, users, groups, domains, and other divisions. This is a huge topic that's covered in great depth in the resource kits for the Windows 2000 Server and Windows .NET Server families. You can learn about local Group Policy—and get a hint of the power available in domain-based policy—by reviewing Appendix E, "Group Policy."

● Miscellaneous user interface elements

- **Ctrl+Alt+Delete.** In a domain environment, pressing Ctrl+Alt+Delete displays the Windows Security dialog box, shown in Figure 34-4, a time-honored path to options for locking, logging off, shutting down, and other tasks. In a workgroup that's configured to use the Welcome screen for logons, pressing Ctrl+Alt+Delete opens Windows Task Manager. (In fact, this behavior is linked to the Welcome screen, not domain membership per se.)

Chapter 34

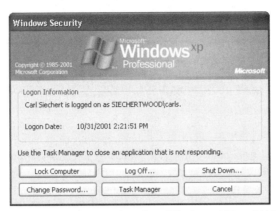

Figure 34-4. Many longtime Windows NT and Windows 2000 users are in the habit of pressing Ctrl+Alt+Delete and then Enter to lock their workstation.

■ **Time synchronization.** The appearance of an Internet Time tab in Control Panel's Date And Time Properties dialog box depends on domain membership. In a workgroup environment (or in a Windows NT–based domain), you use this tab to set up synchronization of your computer's clock with an Internet time server. This feature is unavailable on computers joined to a domain using Windows 2000 Server or Windows .NET Server.

In fact, this is not merely a user interface change, nor is it a feature that's missing from domain-based computers. It's actually related to the authentication method used by domain controllers. Windows 2000 Server and Windows .NET Server use Kerberos V5 authentication. One part of Kerberos V5 authentication relies on close synchronization between times on the client workstations and on the server; if transmitted data between them is tagged with a time that's not nearly identical, it's deemed to be invalid. For this reason, a computer that's joined to a domain that uses Windows 2000 Server or Windows .NET Server as its domain controller always synchronizes its internal clock to the domain controller—not to an external time source. The domain controller should be configured to get its time from an accurate time source.

Like local logons and workgroup logons, Windows NT Server uses the NTLM authentication protocol instead of Kerberos V5 authentication. Clients in a Windows NT domain can be configured to retrieve the time from the domain controller or another Windows time server via NetBIOS (synchronizing all computers in a domain is still a good idea, but not essential), or they can be configured to independently contact an Internet time server.

Chapter 34

1133

tip   Setting your computer's clock

If your computer is in a Windows NT domain, you can synchronize your clock to the domain controller by including this line in a batch program that runs at startup (either as a logon script or by inclusion in your Start menu's Startup group):

```
net time /domain /set /y
```

If your computer is not in a domain, synchronize your clock using Date And Time Properties. In Control Panel, open Date And Time (or simply double-click the clock in the notification area). Click the Internet Time tab, select the check box, and then click Update Now. (If you prefer a command-line utility, use W32tm /Resync. The Net Time command does *not* work with SNTP, the Internet time protocol.)

(If your computer is in an Active Directory domain, you shouldn't set the clock directly; let Windows synchronize automatically to the domain controller.)

For more information about synchronizing with an Internet time server, click the Time Synchronization link on the Internet Time tab in Date And Time Properties.

- **Start menu.** A number of trivial changes differentiate the Start menu in a domain environment: No picture appears by the user's full name at the top of the menu, and the command to quit appears as Turn Off Computer on a workgroup computer and Shut Down in a domain. Why? Simply to more closely resemble the Windows 2000 interface that's familiar to many domain users.

InsideOut

You might want to use features that are available only in a workgroup setting. (Fast User Switching is the feature that many domain users miss the most.) Depending on how your domain is configured, which domain-dependent features you need, and whether you need to share your own computer's resources with other domain users, you might decide that you're better off *not* joining a domain. You can still have access to shared files and printers; here's how:

1 If your computer is already joined to a domain, join a workgroup (doing so removes your domain membership), as explained in "Leaving a Domain," page 1143.

2 Log on using your local account.

3 Set the name of your workgroup to be the same as the domain name. (This isn't essential, but it makes browsing the network easier.)

4 In Control Panel, open User Accounts, click your account name, and then click Manage My Network Passwords under Related Tasks in the left pane.

5 In the Stored User Names And Passwords dialog box, click Add.

6 In the Logon Information Properties dialog box, type *domainname** (where *domainname* is the name of your domain) in the Server box. In the User Name and Password boxes, enter the credentials for your domain account, not your local account.

Provide the user name and password for your domain account

Adding a credential this way (instead of providing your user name and password each time you try to view the resources of a different domain computer) gives you immediate access to all domain file and printer resources for which your domain account has permissions. You have effectively linked your domain account to your local account. Be aware that your domain logon script won't run and several other domain-only features (such as Group Policy) won't be effective. The domain administrator might prevent you from logging on this way. In addition, some privileges (such as the ability to use the domain's proxy server) might be limited to members of the Domain Users group or some other global group. Your local account can't be included in a global group.

Entering Domain Credentials

When you enter your user name, Windows needs to know which security database to look in to find the name. In some dialog boxes (such as the Log On To Windows dialog box), you enter your user name in one box and select the name of the domain or computer in another box. Other dialog boxes, however, provide only a User Name box. Windows assumes that you're entering the name of an account on the resource you're trying to access, so in most cases you don't need to enter the name of a domain or computer. In some cases, however, you must provide the name of the computer or domain as well as your user name; you provide both pieces of information in the User Name box. If the security database is on a computer running Windows NT, use the form *domainname\username* (for example, **documentation\carls** or, for a local account on a computer named Sequoia, **sequoia\carls**). If the security database is on a computer running Windows 2000, Windows XP, or Windows .NET Server, you can use that form or the newer *username@domainname* form (for example, **carls@documentation.swdocs.com** or **carls@sequoia**).

Joining a Domain

To join a domain, your computer must have a computer account set up on the domain controller. You can do this before, during, or after you install Windows XP Professional on your computer:

- Before you set up Windows XP, an administrator can create the computer account on the domain controller. In Windows 2000 Server or Windows .NET Server, you use the Active Directory Users And Computers console to add a computer account; in Windows NT Server, you use Server Manager.

- During installation, the Setup program asks whether you want to join a workgroup or domain. If you elect to join a domain, you can create a computer account (if you haven't already set one up), provided that you can furnish the name and password of a domain administrative account that has authority to add domain computer accounts (typically, an account that's a member of the Domain Admins group). You can provide this information whether you run Setup in an interactive or unattended fashion.

- After installation, you can join a domain from the Computer Name tab of the System Properties dialog box. Details of this method are provided next. Again, if you haven't already set up a computer account on the domain controller, you can set one up from here—as long as you provide the name and password of a domain administrator account.

To join a domain after you've set up Windows, follow these steps:

1 Log on as a member of the local Administrators group.

2 In Control Panel, open System (in the Performance and Maintenance category). Alternatively, right-click My Computer and choose Properties.

3 In the System Properties dialog box, click the Computer Name tab.

<table>
<tr><td></td><td></td><td></td></tr>
</table>

tip **Skip the Network Identification Wizard**

The Computer Name tab has two buttons that perform essentially the same task. Clicking the Network ID button starts the Network Identification Wizard, which, over the course of a half dozen pages or more, helps you to join a domain. The Change button gets there with a single dialog box, as described in this section.

The Network Identification Wizard does offer one advantage: It helps you add a single domain user account to a local user group. For more information about this task, see "Adding Domain Accounts to Your Local Account Database," page 1139.

4 Click Change to open the Computer Name Changes dialog box, shown on the next page.

5 Select Domain, type the name of your domain, and then click OK. Another Computer Name Changes dialog box appears.

6 Type the user name and password of an account that has permission to join your computer to the domain. By default, members of the global Domain Admins group have this permission.

7 Restart your computer when prompted.

---

tip **Use resources on another domain**

Your computer can be joined to only one domain. But if you routinely use resources from another domain, you can add credentials for other domains that allow access to those domains' resources. In Control Panel, open User Accounts. Click the Advanced tab and then click Manage Passwords. Click Add and then specify the name of the other domain's computer that has the shared resources (in the form *domainname\ computername*), along with your user name and password for the other domain.

1138

Is Your Computer Joined to a Domain?

Unless you're aware of some of the subtle visual and operational differences described earlier in this chapter, your computer's domain membership status might not be immediately obvious. The most reliable way to tell at a glance is to open System Properties and click the Computer Name tab. Below Full Computer Name appears either the word *Workgroup* or *Domain,* along with the name of the workgroup or domain.

Domain or *Workgroup* appears here

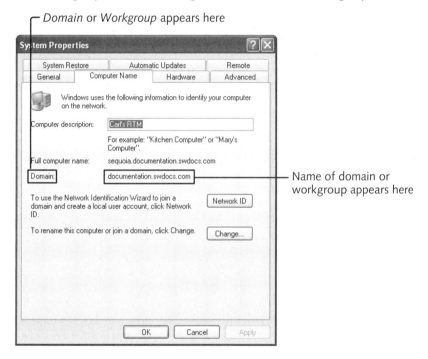

Name of domain or workgroup appears here

You can glean some other interesting information about your domain status by using the Whoami command-line utility, which you can find on the Windows XP CD-ROM in the \Support\Tools\Support.cab file. (You can install all the support tools utilities by running \Support\Tools\Setup.exe.) Open a command prompt window and type **whoami** to find out the user name of the currently logged on user; the user name is preceded by the domain name if you're logged on using a domain account or the computer name if you're using a local account. Type **whoami /groups** to see a list of all the local and global security groups to which your account belongs.

Adding Domain Accounts to Your Local Account Database

When you join a domain using the procedure described in the previous section, Windows adds two global security groups to your local account database.

● The domain's Domain Admins group is added to your local Administrators group.

● The domain's Domain Users group is added to your local Users group.

You can confirm these additions by opening Local Users And Groups (type **lusrmgr.msc** at a command prompt) and examining the properties of the Administrators group and Users group, as shown in Figure 34-5.

The Domain Admins group in the DOCUMENTATION domain is a member of the local Administrators group

Figure 34-5. Adding domain accounts gives domain users access to local resources.

Placing these groups in your local account database gives their members the same privileges on your computer as local members of the group. For example, any member of the Domain Admins group can log on to your computer locally and have all the rights and permissions accorded to local administrative accounts.

> **note** Don't worry: Membership in a local group doesn't automatically allow access to your files over a network connection. Only folders that you choose to share are available on the network. And permissions that you apply to the shared folder restrict who can access the folder and what they can do with its contents. For more information about sharing on a network, see Chapter 32, "Managing Shared Folders and Printers."

By default, your domain account is a member of the Domain Users group. Therefore, when you log on to your computer using your domain account, you'll have all the privileges of a member of the local Users group. (In other words, you won't have very many privileges; you'll be a limited user.) Therefore, you might want to add your domain account to a more high-powered group. You can do this in either of two ways:

- At the domain controller, add your account to a global group that has the privileges you need. For example, adding your account to the Domain Admins group gives you instant membership in the local Administrators group—not only of your computer, but of all computers in the domain. Depending on the size of your domain and your role in the organization, this may be entirely inappropriate, of course. But a domain administrator might choose to add your account to another group that has privileges that fall somewhere in between those of Domain Users and Domain Admins.

- At your computer, you can add your domain account (or another global group of which you're a member) to your local account database.

To exercise the second option—adding a domain account to your local account database—you can use either User Accounts or Local Users And Groups. User Accounts is the better tool for adding individual user accounts; Local Users And Groups lets you add groups more easily.

To add a user account, follow these steps:

1 In Control Panel, open User Accounts.

2 On the Users tab, click Add.

3 In the Add New User dialog box, type the user name and domain name of the account you want to add (or click Browse, Advanced, Find Now to select from a list of domain user accounts), and then click Next.

4 In the next dialog box, select the local group that you'd like to add the account to and then click Finish.

To add a global user account or global group to your local account database, follow these steps:

1 At a command prompt, type **lusrmgr.msc** to open Local Users And Groups.

2 Open the Groups folder, and then double-click the name of the group to which you want to add a user or group.

3 Click Add, Advanced. The Select Users dialog box appears.

4 Be sure the domain name appears in From This Location. If it does not, click Locations and select the domain name.

5 Click Find Now to display a list of users and groups.

6 Select the users or groups you want to add (hold down the Ctrl key as you click to select multiple names), and then click OK.

> For more information about using Local Users And Groups, see "Using the Local Users And Groups Snap-In," page 123.

Leaving a Domain

The procedure for leaving a domain and joining a workgroup is similar to the procedure for joining a domain, described earlier in this chapter. To join a workgroup, follow these steps:

1 Log on as a member of the local administrators group.

2 Open System Properties and click Computer Name, Change.

3 Select Workgroup and then type the workgroup name. A workgroup name can contain up to 15 characters. It cannot be the same as the name of any computer in the workgroup, and it cannot contain any of the following characters:

; : " < > * + = \ | ? ,

4 If you're leaving an Active Directory domain, in the dialog box that appears, enter the user name and password of a domain account that has permission to remove the computer from the domain.

Accessing Domain Resources from a Computer Running Windows XP Home Edition

A computer running Windows XP Home Edition cannot be joined to a domain. Moreover, using Home Edition you can't manually add entries to the list in the Stored User Names And Passwords dialog box. However, users of Windows XP Home Edition who have a domain user account can access shared folders and printers in a domain. If your Home Edition computer is connected to the domain, either through a local area connection or a virtual private network (VPN) connection, you can use either of the following techniques to access domain resources:

● In Windows Explorer's Address bar, type the network path to the resource you want to use, in the form *servername**sharename*. For example, to open

the Document share on a server named Everglades, type **everglades\
document**. In a few moments, a dialog box requests your user name and
password. Enter the credentials for your domain account, not the local
account you use to log on to your own computer. The folders in the share
then appear in Windows Explorer.

● Open My Network Places and click View Workgroup Computers. If your
workgroup name is the same as the domain name, other computers in the
domain become visible. (If your workgroup name is not the same as the
domain name, click Microsoft Windows Network under Other Places.
Then double-click the domain name to see its computers.) Double-click a
computer icon, and the request for user name and password appears. Enter
your domain credentials, and the computer's shared resources appear.

Credentials you enter using these methods persist throughout your session, but are
discarded when you log off. Therefore, typing an address or browsing to a network
resource works fine for ad hoc connections. But if you regularly connect to the same
resources, there's a better way, which lets you avoid the (sometimes lengthy) wait for
the password request dialog box and the requirement to enter your network credentials
repeatedly: Set up a batch program that makes your network connections, and run the
batch program each time you log on (or each time you connect to the network). To set
up such a batch program, follow these steps:

1 Start Notepad.

2 For each network resource you want to connect with, type a Net Use command on a separate line. Use the format net use *servername\sharename
password* /user:*username*, where *servername* is the name of the computer,
sharename is the name of a shared folder, *password* is the password for your
domain account, and *username* is the user name for your domain account.
For example, to connect to the Document share on the computer named
Everglades using Carl's domain account, you'd enter

```
net use \\everglades\document WdYw2Gt /user:carls
```

> **caution** Your network password is stored as plain text in this file. If you don't want to
> expose your password in this way, replace it with an asterisk (*). Then Windows
> prompts you to enter the password when you run the batch program.

3 Save the file, giving it a name with either a .cmd or .bat extension. You
might place it on the desktop or in your Startup folder.

1144

Logging On to a Domain

When your computer is joined to a domain, you'll ordinarily log on using your domain account. Doing so loads the portions of your profile stored on network servers, applies domain-based Group Policy objects, and lets you use any resources throughout the domain for which your account has requisite permissions.

Alternatively, you can log on using a local account. If you have a desktop computer that's permanently attached to the network, there's seldom any reason to do so. Even most local administrative tasks are just as easily handled—either locally or remotely— by a domain account that's a member of the local Administrators group. If you have a portable computer, you might want to use a local account when your computer is not connected to the network. It's not necessary to do that, however, because Windows uses a locally cached version of your profile if the domain controller is unavailable. Using separate accounts for local and network logons can make it more complicated to manage permissions on your locally stored documents. In this situation, you might be better off not joining the domain and instead always using a local account.

To log on, wait for the Welcome To Windows dialog box to appear and press Ctrl+Alt+Delete. Doing so displays the Log On To Windows dialog box, shown in Figure 34-6. Type the user name and password for your domain account, and be sure that your domain name is selected in the Log On To box. (To log on using a local user account, type its user name and password, and select the computer name in the Log On To box.)

Figure 34-6. If the Log On To box doesn't appear, click the Options button.

Logging On Automatically

If your computer is in a secure location where only you (and others you trust) have physical access to it, you might want to set it up so that you don't need to press Ctrl+Alt+Delete and then enter your user name and password each time you start the computer. By making some changes in the registry, you can set up your computer to log on automatically.

> **caution** With automatic logon, anyone with physical access can start your computer and log on using your credentials. An individual then has access to all your files (including encrypted files), network resources, and even Web sites for which you've cached your password.
>
> There's another risk to this scheme: Your password is stored in plain text in the registry. Authenticated users on the network who have remote access to your registry can view your password.

With those risks in mind, if you're confident that automatic logon doesn't pose a security risk for you, follow these steps to set it up:

1 Log on as a member of the Administrators group.

2 Type **regedit** at a command prompt to open Registry Editor.

3 Open the HKLM\Software\Microsoft\Windows NT\CurrentVersion\ Winlogon key.

4 Change the setting of the AutoAdminLogon value to 1.

5 Open the DefaultDomainName value and type the name of your domain.

6 Open the DefaultUserName value and type the user name of the account you want logged on automatically.

7 If the DefaultPassword value doesn't exist, create a new string value of that name.

8 Open the DefaultPassword value and type the password for the user account you specified in step 6.

After you complete these steps, the account you specified is logged on automatically each time you turn on the computer.

If you decide you no longer want to log on automatically, an easy method is available that doesn't require venturing into the registry again. Follow these steps:

1 In Control Panel, open User Accounts.

2 On the Users tab, select Users Must Enter A User Name And Password To Use This Computer.

Selecting this check box makes two essential changes in the registry: It changes the AutoAdminLogon value back to 0, and it deletes the DefaultPassword value altogether. (The other registry changes you made to enable automatic logon are quite harmless and can safely remain in place.) For more information about classic logon, see "Controlling How Users Log On," page 107.

Finding Files, Printers, and Users

In general, you can browse a domain to find its shared resources in much the same way as you browse a workgroup. Start by opening My Network Places. In a workgroup environment, the View Workgroup Computers link under Network Tasks displays all the computers in your workgroup. In a domain environment, there isn't a corresponding link. To browse the computers in your domain, click Entire Network (under Other Places) and then double-click Microsoft Windows Network. This displays an icon for each domain and workgroup in your network; double-click a domain name to see its computers. Figure 34-7 shows a small network. (Three domains in a network this size is unusual, but we use this approach to separate test systems from our production network.)

Figure 34-7. The Folders Explorer bar illustrates the network hierarchy.

If your domain controller uses Active Directory, a service included with Windows 2000 Server and Windows .NET Server, there's a better way. Instead of browsing for network objects (such as applications, files, printers, and users), you can search Active Directory. Predefined searches help you locate users, contacts, and groups; computers; printers;

shared folders; and organizational units. To start a search, click the Search Active Directory link under Network Tasks in My Network Places. Select the type of object you're searching for and then enter your criteria. The search application window, shown in Figure 34-8, is well organized and easy to figure out.

After you enter your criteria, click Find Now. The window then enlarges, and the results of your search appear in a list at the bottom of the window.

Figure 34-8. In a large organization, you can use this Active Directory search page to locate a printer that has certain features you need.

Part 9

Administering a System

Chapter 35

Managing User Profiles

As you've undoubtedly discovered, Microsoft Windows XP offers users all manner of customization possibilities. Using various settings in Control Panel and elsewhere, users can control the appearance of their desktop, taskbar, Start menu, folder windows, and other items; specify sounds that play when certain events occur; add or remove programs; and so on. This is terrific for a single computer operated by a single user who wants to master his or her working environment.

But if you have to keep more than one computer humming along and keep more than one user productive, you as an administrator might want to perform some of this customization for the user. With tools provided by Windows XP, you can make settings for users who lack the knowledge, experience, or time to make settings on their own. Just as important, you can impose restrictions that prevent inexperienced or devious users from damaging their setup.

In this chapter we describe user profiles, a feature of Windows XP that controls each user's computing environment. Administrators can work with profiles in various ways to customize a system for one or more users.

Introducing User Profiles

A *user profile* contains all the settings and files for a user's work environment. This includes the user's personal registry settings for everything from mouse pointers to view settings used in Microsoft Word and files that are specific to a user, such as cookies the user receives while using Microsoft Internet Explorer, documents in the My Documents folder and its subfolders, and shortcuts to network places.

1151

At Home with Windows XP

Because Windows XP Home Edition does not include a practical way to work with NTFS permissions or a GUI method for assigning a profile to a user account, it's impractical—although not altogether impossible—to set up and work with roaming user profiles in Home Edition. This feature, which is best suited to a domain environment, is rarely used in workgroup environments. The same limitations also prevent all but the most masochistic Home Edition users from using mandatory user profiles.

And because Windows XP Home Edition does not support Group Policy, you can't use scripts specified in Group Policy that run at logon, logoff, startup, and shutdown. You can, however, specify the location of a script to run at logon by using the Net User command-line utility.

The other features of user profiles described in this chapter apply to both versions of Windows XP.

Location and Content of User Profiles

By default, each user who logs on to a computer has a local user profile, which is created when the user logs on for the first time. Local user profiles are stored in %SystemDrive%\Documents And Settings. Each user's profile is stored in a subfolder with the user name as the folder name (for example, C:\Documents And Settings\Jan). The entire path for the current user's profile is stored in another commonly used environment variable, %UserProfile%.

note If you upgraded from Microsoft Windows NT 4 (instead of performing a clean installation or upgrading from another version of Windows), user profiles are stored in %SystemRoot%\Profiles.

Within a user's profile folder, you'll find a hierarchy of folders, as shown in Figure 35-1. The root of the profile (that is, the subfolder of Documents And Settings with the user name as the folder name) contains Ntuser.dat, which is the user portion of the registry (in other words, the HKCU hive). In addition, a computer that's a member of a Microsoft Windows NT Server domain might have an Ntuser.pol file, a file that has system policy settings. (System policy is the Windows NT predecessor to Group Policy, which was introduced with Microsoft Windows 2000.)

The profile includes the following folders:

- **Application Data.** This hidden folder contains application-specific data, such as a custom dictionary for word processing programs, junk sender lists for an e-mail program, a CD database for a program that plays music CDs, and so on. Application vendors decide what information to put in this folder.

Chapter 35: Managing User Profiles

To prevent confusion, the My Documents folder for another user is shown with that person's user name

Figure 35-1. Each user profile contains a number of folders, including several hidden ones.

- **Cookies.** This folder contains Internet Explorer cookies.

- **Desktop.** This folder contains all items stored on the user's desktop, including files and shortcuts.

- **Favorites.** This folder contains Internet Explorer favorites.

- **Local Settings.** This hidden folder contains settings and files that don't roam with the profile, either because they're machine-specific or because they're so large that it's not worthwhile to include them in a roaming user profile, which must be copied from and to a network server at each logon and logoff. (Roaming user profiles are discussed in the next section.) For example, the staging area for burning CDs—which is machine-specific *and* potentially large—is stored in a subfolder of Local Settings. The Local Settings folder contains four subfolders:

  - **Application Data.** This hidden folder contains machine-specific application data.

  - **History.** This folder contains the user's Internet Explorer browsing history.

  - **Temp.** This folder contains temporary files created by applications.

  - **Temporary Internet Files.** This folder contains the offline cache for Internet Explorer.

- **My Documents.** This folder is the default target for the My Documents shortcut that appears on the Start menu, in the Windows Explorer task pane (under Other Places), and elsewhere. My Documents is the default location for storing user documents in most applications. When you view the profile folders for another user, the user's name replaces *My*, although the actual folder name for all users is My Documents.

Chapter 35

1153

- **NetHood.** This hidden folder contains the shortcuts that appear in My Network Places.

- **PrintHood.** This seldom-used hidden folder can contain shortcuts to items in the Printers And Faxes folder.

- **Recent.** This hidden folder contains shortcuts to the recently used documents; the most recent of these can appear on the Start menu. Although it appears in Windows Explorer as My Recent Documents, the actual folder name is Recent.

- **SendTo.** This hidden folder contains shortcuts to the folders and applications that appear on the Send To submenu. Send To is a command that appears on the File menu in Windows Explorer when you select a file or folder; it also appears on the shortcut menu when you right-click a file or folder.

- **Start Menu.** This folder contains the items (such as shortcuts to applications and documents) that appear on the Start menu's All Programs submenu.

- **Templates.** This hidden folder contains shortcuts to document templates. These templates are typically used by the New command (on the File menu and the shortcut menu) in Windows Explorer and are referenced by the FileName value in the HKCR*class*\ShellNew key, where *class* refers to the extension and file type.

> **note** Group Policy settings always take precedence over user settings in user profiles. This allows administrators to foil users who have the knowledge and permissions to make changes directly in their own user profile. For more information, see Appendix E, "Group Policy."

Types of Profiles

Windows XP Professional supports three types of profiles:

- **Local user profiles.** A local user profile is stored in the %SystemDrive%\ Documents And Settings (or %SystemRoot%\Profiles) folder on the local hard disk. Windows creates a local user profile the first time a user logs on to the computer. If the user makes changes to the profile, the changes affect only the computer where the changes are made.

- **Roaming user profiles.** A roaming user profile is stored on a network server, which makes it available when a user logs on to any computer on the network. Windows creates a local copy of the user profile the first time a user logs on to a computer. If the user makes changes to the profile, Windows merges the changes into the server copy when the user logs off; therefore, the revised profile is available the next time the user logs on to any computer. Roaming profiles are easily managed by and are ideally suited to Windows .NET Server and Windows 2000 Server. With some extra effort, however, you can achieve some benefits of a roaming user profile even without a server edition of Windows. For details about this workaround, see "Using Roaming User Profiles," page 1165.

● **Mandatory user profiles.** A mandatory user profile is one that can be changed only by an administrator. Like a roaming user profile, a mandatory profile is stored on a network server, and Windows creates a local copy when a user who has been assigned a mandatory profile logs on for the first time. Unlike a roaming user profile, a mandatory profile is not updated when the user logs off. This makes mandatory profiles useful not only for individual users whom you want to severely restrict, but also for multiple users (for example, all users in a certain job classification) to whom you want to apply consistent job-specific settings. Multiple users can share a mandatory user profile without affecting others. Users who have been assigned a mandatory profile can make profile changes while they're logged on (unless prevented by policy settings), but the network copy remains unchanged. Although a copy of the profile—changes and all—remains on the computer after a user logs off, at the next logon Windows recopies the original profile from the network share. For information about assigning a mandatory user profile, see "Using Mandatory User Profiles," page 1169.

note Windows XP Home Edition uses local user profiles. As stated earlier in the At Home sidebar, it's possible, but not practical, to implement roaming or mandatory profiles in Home Edition.

Common Profiles

In the profiles folder (%SystemDrive%\Documents And Settings or %SystemRoot%\Profiles), you'll find two profiles that aren't associated with a particular user account: All Users and Default User. (The Default User folder is hidden.)

● **All Users.** The content of the All Users folder appears for all users who log on to a workstation in addition to the content of each user's own profile folder. For example, items in the All Users\Desktop folder appear on the desktop along with items that the current user has saved on the desktop. Similarly, the Start menu shows the combined contents of the All Users\Start Menu folder and the current user's Start Menu folder. The All Users\Documents folder (which appears as Shared Documents in Windows Explorer) contains documents that are available to all users. The exception is the All Users\Favorites folder, which appears to serve no purpose whatsoever.

By default, only members of the Administrators group and the Power Users group can add items to the Desktop and Start Menu folders in the All Users profile. All users can add items to Shared Documents.

Chapter 35

1155

---

tip   **View the Start Menu folder**

Windows offers a simple way to get directly to either branch of the Start menu hierarchy. Right-click the Start button and choose Open or Explore if you want to look at the Start Menu folder within the current user's profile; choose Open All Users or Explore All Users to view the All Users\Start Menu folder in Windows Explorer.

- **Default User.** When a user logs on to a computer for the first time (and his or her account is not set up to use a roaming profile or mandatory profile), Windows creates a new local profile by copying the content of the Default User folder to a new folder and giving it the user's name. Therefore, you can configure the Default User profile the way you want new users' initial view of Windows to appear. With the default security settings, only members of the Administrators group can make changes to the Default User profile.

Setting Up a Default Profile

You can populate the Default User profile with files that you want each new user to have available. In particular, you might want to supply a set of Internet links, a few desktop shortcuts, and perhaps some documents. You can easily do this simply by copying the appropriate shortcuts and files to the Favorites, Desktop, and My Documents folders. (Because the Default User folder is hidden, you'll first need to display hidden folders by opening Folder Options and selecting Show Hidden Files And Folders on the View tab.)

Be sure that you *copy* files to the Default User profile so that they inherit the appropriate permissions from the destination folder. If you *move* files to the folder, they retain their existing permissions, which will likely prevent them from being copied to the new user's profile.

Like the other user profiles, the Default User profile contains Ntuser.dat, which is the user-specific portion of the registry. The registry-controlled settings in the Default User profile become the initial settings for a new user who signs on. Therefore, you can make settings therein that become the default settings for new accounts. The trouble is that it's not as easy to make registry settings in the Default User profile as it is to copy files to it, as described in the preceding paragraphs. You can make the settings in either of two ways:

- If you know precisely what needs to be changed in the registry to implement a certain setting or feature, you can modify the Default User profile in Registry Editor. In Registry Editor, make changes to the HKU\.DEFAULT branch of the registry. From that key, navigate to the same subkey that you would use within HKCU to make a change to your own profile.

● You can create a new account, log on using that account, and make all the settings you want. Configure the desktop, menus, mouse, and other options as you want new users to see them. Then log off and log on using your administrative account. Copy the profile for the user account you created to the Default User folder. Be sure you copy as described in "Copying a User Profile," on the next page; do not use Windows Explorer to copy the profile information.

Working with User Profiles

Armed with the knowledge of where profiles reside and what they contain, you might be tempted to manipulate them directly from Windows Explorer or a command prompt. Although you can safely add, modify, or remove items such as the Start menu and desktop items, you should not move, copy, or delete entire profiles in this manner. Instead, you should use the User Profiles dialog box, shown in Figure 35-2. To get there, right-click My Computer and choose Properties (or choose System in Control Panel). On the Advanced tab, click Settings under User Profiles.

Figure 35-2. Use the User Profiles dialog box to copy or delete a user profile.

Chapter 35

note Users who are not members of the Administrators group can't see other user profiles in the User Profiles dialog box, nor can they delete, copy, or change their own profile.

Removing a User Profile

The User Profiles dialog box indicates the disk space occupied by a profile. Because each user's documents are stored in the profile, this space can be significant. To recover the space occupied by unused profiles, you can remove the profile in either of two ways (shown in order of desirability):

- Open User Accounts in Control Panel and delete the user account associated with the profile. For details, see "Deleting an Account," page 105. This method deletes the user account as well as the profile, and also offers a way to save the profile's documents.

- From the User Profiles dialog box, simply select a profile and click Delete. You cannot delete a profile that is currently logged on. Deleting profiles in this manner (instead of using Windows Explorer, for example) ensures that the appropriate profile also gets removed from the registry. (Each user profile occupies a subkey of HKLM\Software\Microsoft\Windows NT\ CurrentVersion\ProfileList.)

> **note** If you use roaming user profiles, Windows ordinarily saves the copy of the profile that has been copied to the local hard drive. Windows uses this local copy if the network copy happens to be unavailable the next time the user logs on. If you have a computer that's available to many users, this occasional convenience can cost a lot of disk space. You can force Windows to automatically delete the local copy of a roaming profile when a user logs off. To do that, open Group Policy (Gpedit.msc), go to Computer Configuration\Administrative Templates\System\User Profiles, and enable the policy named Delete Cached Copies Of Roaming Profiles. Other policies in the same folder also affect how roaming profiles are applied. For more information, see Appendix E, "Group Policy."

Copying a User Profile

Copying a user profile (by selecting a profile and clicking Copy To) doesn't add the profile to the registry; that happens the first time a user who has been assigned the profile you copy logs on. But copying from the User Profiles dialog box instead of using Windows Explorer has an important advantage: Windows assigns the proper permissions to the copy. That is, it gives Full Control permission to the user or group you specify and removes permissions for other nonadministrative users. Such permissions are necessary to allow a user access to his or her own profile—but no one else's.

> **note** You cannot copy a profile that is currently logged on, including your own. If you want to copy your own profile, you'll need to log on using a different account.

InsideOut

Because so much of your important data is stored in your profile, you might want to store two copies of the profile on different drives. By using some techniques that are intended for managing roaming profiles, you can create automatic local backups. (This procedure works only if you have Windows XP Professional.) Here's how:

1 Copy the profile you want to use to another drive. You'll need to log on using a different administrator account because you can't copy the profile you're currently using. In the User Profiles dialog box, select the profile and click Copy To. In the Copy To dialog box, specify a folder on a different drive. You don't need to change the permitted users.

2 Open Local Users And Groups (Lusrmgr.msc), open Users, and double-click your user name. On the Profile tab, specify the path to the profile copy in the Profile Path box.

Now when you log on, Windows copies the profile you created on the other drive to the Documents And Settings folder. This copy becomes your working copy, and any changes you make to settings or files are recorded there. When you log off, the profile in Documents And Settings is then copied back to the other drive. Easy backup!

Troubleshooting

An error prevents you from logging on.

If you get a profile-related error when you try to log on or if you notice such an error in the Application event log, it could be caused by one or more of the following conditions:

- Your account doesn't have sufficient access permissions. Your account must have (at least) Read access to the %UserProfile% folder, whether it's a local profile or a roaming or mandatory profile stored on another computer.

- Your account doesn't have sufficient access permissions to the profiles folder—the folder that contains the individual profiles (%SystemDrive%\Documents And Settings on most computers). The Everyone account should have Full Control access to the folder. In addition, if it's a shared folder on a network drive, the Everyone account should have Full Control access to the share.

- Your system is low on hard disk space.

- The profile has been corrupted. In most cases, the only solution to this situation is to delete the profile. Before you take that drastic step, try using System Restore to revert to a working profile. Be aware, however, that this will roll back *all* profiles to the time of the restore point.

Chapter 35

Assigning a Profile

If you want to assign a profile to a user account, you use Microsoft Management Console with the Local Users And Groups snap-in. You can find it under System Tools in Computer Management, or you can open it in its own window by typing **lusrmgr.msc** at a command prompt. In the Users folder, double-click the name of the user you want to assign the profile to and click the Profile tab, shown in Figure 35-3.

Figure 35-3. Use the Profile tab to specify a user profile, a logon script, and a home folder.

> **note** Local Users And Groups is not available in Windows XP Home Edition. You can achieve the same result, however, by using the /Profilepath switch with the Net User command. For details, type **net help user** at a command prompt.

On the Profile tab, you can specify the following:

● **The location of the user profile.** (Note that you need to do this only if you want to use a profile that's not stored in the default location, such as a roaming user profile or a mandatory user profile.) For more information, see "Using Roaming User Profiles," page 1165.

● **The location and file name of a logon script—a program that runs each time the user logs on.** For more information, see "Using Scripts That Run at Logon, Logoff, Startup, and Shutdown," page 1163. (With the Net User command, you can specify the script location with the /Scriptpath switch.)

●   **The path to the user's home folder.** The *home folder* is a folder in which a user can store his or her files and programs. Although most programs use My Documents as the default folder for File Open and File Save, some older programs use the home folder. The home folder is also the initial current folder for Command Prompt sessions. The home folder can be a local folder or on a shared network drive, and multiple users can share a common home folder. To specify a local home folder, enter a path specification in the Local Path text box. To use a folder on a network server as a home folder, select a drive letter (Windows maps the folder to this letter at each logon) and specify the full network path to the folder. (With the Net User command, you can specify the script location with the /Homedir switch.) If you don't specify a home folder, Windows uses %UserProfile% as the home folder.

Troubleshooting

Your files are missing, or you have two profiles.

A common problem with profiles is that, for one reason or another, you end up with more than one profile for a user account. The symptoms are deceiving: all of a sudden, your documents are missing, programs are missing from the Start menu, or your settings have changed. This usually occurs when you join a domain and then log on using the same user name as you used before joining the domain. In this case, you have (perhaps unwittingly) created two user accounts: a local account and a domain account. And each account is associated with its own profile.

If you haven't yet used your new profile to store any documents or make any settings and you are able to determine which account is associated with each profile, you can remedy this situation simply by assigning the correct profile to your account.

A better solution is to use the File And Settings Transfer Wizard. Log on with the account you no longer plan to use and save your files and settings. Then log on with the other account and import your information. For more information about using the File And Settings Transfer Wizard, see "Moving Windows Settings and Files," page 51.

In some cases—particularly if you just want to retrieve your documents—it's easier to use Windows Explorer to move the documents from one profile to another. (The profile folders in Documents And Settings each begin with your user name, but at least one of them will have the computer or domain name appended to make it unique.)

Whichever way you move your information, you can then remove the profile you no longer need. (Ordinarily, that would be the profile associated with the local account, assuming you normally log on with your domain account.)

Moving Folders from the Standard Profile Locations

You can easily change the location of the My Documents folder and its subfolders, My Music and My Pictures. You might want to do this if the drive where your profile is stored becomes full, for example. As an alternative to using a different location on your computer, you might consider moving these document folders to a shared folder elsewhere on the network. Storing such data on a network server apart from the user profile offers two important benefits:

- Storing user data in a central location can make backup easier.

- Separating user data from the user profile speeds up the logon and logoff process for users with roaming profiles. (If a user's documents are stored within the profile, they are copied from the network server to the local computer at each logon, and then copied back at each logoff. By storing them apart from the profile, each file is fetched only as it's needed.)

To move My Documents, follow these steps:

1 Right-click My Documents and choose Properties. On the Target tab, click Move.

2 Select the path of the folder where you want to keep My Documents, either on your own computer or in a shared network folder. Here the Data folder is selected on a network server.

3 Click OK on each screen. Click Yes if you want to move the existing documents to the new target location.

Using Scripts That Run at Logon, Logoff, Startup, and Shutdown

With user profiles or group policy, you can implement scripts that run automatically. A *logon script* is a program that runs whenever a user logs on. Any executable file— that is, a batch program (.bat or .cmd extension), a Windows Script Host (WSH) script (.vbs, .js, or .wsf extension), or a program (.exe or .com extension)—can be used as a logon script. For information about batch programs and WSH scripts, see Chapter 10, "Automating Windows XP."

Logon scripts are commonly used to map network drives to a drive letter, to start certain programs, and to perform other similar tasks that should happen at each logon. As with most tasks in Windows, you can use other methods to perform each of these—but a logon script offers a convenient, flexible method.

Note that using system environment variables such as %UserName% makes it easy to use the same script for different users. Windows substitutes the correct user name when it runs the script.

To use a logon script for a local user account, specify the script's path and file name in the Logon Script box on the Profile tab of the user's properties dialog box (shown earlier in Figure 35-3 on page 1160).

Windows XP Professional (but not Home Edition) also offers support for four other types of scripts:

- Group Policy logon scripts, which run whenever a user logs on
- Group Policy logoff scripts, which run whenever a user logs off
- Group Policy startup scripts, which run whenever the computer starts up
- Group Policy shutdown scripts, which run whenever the computer shuts down

Like ordinary logon scripts, you can use the executable file type for any of these scripts. Though you're free to store scripts anywhere you like, each type of script has a default location.

Logon script	%SystemRoot%\System32\GroupPolicy\User\Scripts\Logon
Logoff script	%SystemRoot%\System32\GroupPolicy\User\Scripts\Logoff
Startup script	%SystemRoot%\System32\GroupPolicy\Machine\Scripts\Startup
Shutdown script	%SystemRoot%\System32\GroupPolicy\Machine\Scripts\Shutdown

Note that the %SystemRoot%\System32\GroupPolicy folder is hidden.

(continued)

Chapter 35

Using Scripts That Run at Logon, Logoff, Startup, and Shutdown (continued)

To implement any of these scripts, start Group Policy (Gpedit.msc) and go to Computer Configuration\Windows Settings\Scripts (for startup and shutdown scripts) or User Configuration\Windows Settings\Scripts (for logon and logoff scripts).

When you double-click an entry in one of these folders, you'll notice some additional improvements over legacy logon scripts:

- You can specify more than one script for each of these events, and you can specify the order in which they run.

- You can specify command-line parameters for each script.

Group Policy also offers a number of policy settings that affect how scripts run—synchronously or asynchronously, hidden or visible. (In this case, *synchronously* means, in effect, that nothing else runs until the script finishes running.) You'll find these settings, along with more complete explanations of their effects, in Computer Configuration\Administrative Templates\System\Scripts and in User Configuration\Administrative Templates\System\Scripts. Some policies appear in both places; if the settings are configured differently, the one in Computer Configuration takes precedence.

newfeature!

To move My Music or My Pictures, simply use Windows Explorer to move the folder to the desired location. Windows XP automatically updates all references to the folder, including those on the Start menu.

Unless you use roaming user profiles to move them en masse, moving other profile folders isn't practical unless your computer is joined to a domain. In a domain-based network, Group Policy settings allow an administrator to use folder redirection to store on a network server the data files from a user's profile. The Folder Redirection extension in Group Policy for domain-based accounts lets administrators easily change the actual location of the Application Data, Desktop, My Documents, and Start Menu components of the user profiles—and users won't even notice the difference.

note It's possible—but not at all advisable—to move the entire Documents And Settings folder. For details, see Microsoft Knowledge Base article Q236621, "Cannot Move or Rename the Documents and Settings Folder."

Using Roaming User Profiles

A *roaming user profile* allows a user to log on to a workstation and see his or her familiar settings on the desktop, the Start menu, and so on. Roaming user profiles work by storing the user profile in a shared network folder. When the user logs on, the profile information is copied from the shared network folder to the local hard disk. When the user logs off, the profile information—which might have changed during the computing session—is then copied back to the shared folder.

If you use more than one computer, you might find roaming user profiles useful. For example, if you have a small business with a front office and a back office, you might find yourself spending equal time in each location. Although it's relatively easy to set up your data files in a shared network location for easy access, you'll probably find that your productivity suffers because little changes in settings—your personal spell-checking dictionary in Word, for example, or your list of favorite Web sites—are different in the two locations. Using roaming user profiles solves this problem.

Ordinarily, roaming user profiles are a feature of domain-based networks (that is, a network that uses a member of the Windows .NET Server, Windows 2000 Server, or Windows NT Server family as a domain controller). With a bit of extra work, however, you can enjoy some of the same benefits in a workgroup environment. In a domain environment, user accounts and computer accounts are centrally managed at the domain level, so you need to make settings only one time and in only one place. Accessing a profile for the first time from a new computer happens automatically. By contrast, with a workgroup, you must explicitly create similar user accounts on each computer where you want to log on before you're allowed to log on.

To make this work in a workgroup environment, each user whom you want to set up with a roaming profile must have an account on each computer where that user will log on, plus an account on the computer that contains the shared profiles folder. The user account on each computer must have the same user name and password.

caution   Our own experimentation showed that configuring roaming profiles and mandatory profiles in a Windows XP–only workgroup environment is difficult, at best. Because of the way settings are applied (particularly settings related to the new theme engine and new Start menu), not all settings roam properly, and operation is somewhat unpredictable if you don't configure everything correctly. If having these features perform perfectly is important to you and your business, you should seriously consider upgrading to Windows .NET Server, which makes user configuration much easier and more reliable.

Setting Up the Shared Folder for Roaming Profiles

Because you'll need to view and modify permissions, the computer where you're planning to store roaming profiles must be running Windows XP Professional, and Simple File Sharing must be disabled.

To set up the shared folder, follow these steps:

1 Log on as a member of the computer's Administrators group.

2 Using Windows Explorer, create a folder called Profiles.

3 In Windows Explorer, right-click the folder and choose Sharing And Security.

4 On the Sharing tab of the Profiles Properties dialog box that appears, select Share This Folder. The default sharing permissions, which provide Full Control share access to Everyone, are appropriate.

5 Click the Security tab (if you created the folder on an NTFS volume), and be sure that Everyone has Full Control permission.

Chapter 35: Managing User Profiles

Setting Up User Accounts

To set up the user accounts, follow these steps:

1 On each computer (including the "server" that you set up in the preceding procedure), log on as a member of the Administrators group.

2 Right-click My Computer and choose Manage.

3 In Computer Management, go to System Tools\Local Users And Groups\Users.

4 If the user account you want doesn't already exist, choose Action, New User, and create a user account. Be sure to use the same user name and password on each computer. Clear the User Must Change Password At Next Logon check box before you click Create.

5 In the right pane of the Computer Management window, double-click the name of the user to display the properties dialog box.

6 Click the Profile tab. In the Profile Path box, type the network path to the shared profiles folder, as shown in Figure 35-4. The advantage of using the %UserName% environment variable is merely convenience: You can use the same string for every user, without having to pause to figure out the correct name of the profile folder.

Figure 35-4. The %UserName% environment variable is expanded to the user name when you move to another field or click OK.

> **note** A *client* computer—not the one where the profile is stored—can run Windows XP Home Edition. Although Home Edition does not include the Local Users And Groups snap-in, you can use other tools to achieve the same results. If necessary, create a new user account and assign a password with User Accounts in Control Panel. To assign a profile path, use the Net User command. For example, to make the same assignment shown in Figure 35-4, at a command prompt type **net user josie /profilepath:\\badlands\ profiles\josie**.

Troubleshooting

Windows doesn't use the shared profile.

If you forget to set up a user account on the computer with the shared profiles folder, Windows displays a warning when the user attempts to log on. If a local copy of the user profile already exists, Windows uses that copy; if not, Windows creates a temporary profile (based on the Default User profile) in a folder called Temp, which is not saved when the user logs off.

Creating the Profile

To create a profile to be used as a roaming user profile and copy it to the shared profiles folder, follow these steps:

1 Create a profile by logging on (ideally with a temporary user account you create for the purpose) and making the settings you want.

2 Log off and then log back on as a member of the Administrators group.

> **note** If you are copying a profile from a computer other than the one that contains the shared profiles folder, the account you log on with must have the same name and password as an account that has administrative privileges on the target computer.

3 Right-click My Computer and choose Properties. In the System Properties dialog box, click the Advanced tab and then click Settings under User Profiles.

4 Select the profile you created and click Copy To.

Chapter 35: Managing User Profiles

5 In the Copy Profile To box, type the full path of the destination profile folder. For example, if you want to create a profile for a user named Josie in the Profiles share on the computer named Badlands, type **\\badlands\profiles\josie**. Be sure the destination folder you specify doesn't exist; if it does, Windows deletes its contents before copying the profile.

6 Under Permitted To Use, click Change and then type the name of the user who will use the profile.

When you click OK in the Copy To dialog box, Windows copies the user profile to the specified folder and sets permissions on the destination folder and its contents. Windows gives Full Control permission to the Administrators group, the user or group you entered in the Permitted To Use box, and the System account. This prevents non-administrative users from accessing a profile other than their own.

If you copied the profile from one computer to a shared folder on another computer, the permissions that Windows creates are not exactly right, and you must take one

Using Mandatory User Profiles

A mandatory user profile works much like a roaming user profile: When a user logs on, the profile is copied from a network location to a local folder, thereby providing familiar settings. The difference is that a mandatory profile isn't updated with user changes when the user logs off.

To assign a mandatory user profile to one or more users, follow the same procedures as described for using roaming user profiles. Then, on the computer where the shared profile is stored, make the following changes:

1 Change the folder permissions to remove Full Control, Modify, and Write permissions for the user account (or accounts) that will use the profile—leaving them with only Read & Execute, List Folder Contents, and Read permissions.

2 Change the name of the hidden Ntuser.dat file (in the profile's top-level folder) to Ntuser.man. (Be sure you change Ntuser.dat, not Ntuser.dat.log, which ordinarily has a hidden extension.) The .man extension identifies a mandatory profile.

more step to correct them. On the computer with the shared profiles folder, right-click the new profile folder, choose Properties, and click Security. If one of the names shows the security identifier of an unknown user, as shown in Figure 35-5, you must add the correct user account (Josie, in this case) and give it Full Control permission. You can remove the unknown user, although it's not necessary to do so. (The unknown account is actually the correct user name, but it's the account from the source computer, not the account on the local computer. This is one of the hazards and annoyances of relying on separate security databases—as the workgroup model does—rather than using the centralized security database used by domains. For more information, see "Local Accounts and Groups vs. Domain Accounts and Groups," page 93.)

Figure 35-5. If the permissions for the profile folder don't include the local user account, the user won't be able to log on.

Chapter 35

Troubleshooting

Certain files are unavailable to the roaming profile.

You might encounter problems if certain user profile settings rely on files that are stored on the local hard drive. For example, you might set the desktop background to a file stored on drive C. When you log on at another computer, the background doesn't appear (unless the same file happens to be in the same location on the other computer). You can alleviate such problems by redirecting My Documents to a shared network folder and then using it to store documents and other files that you want to access from different computers.

Chapter 36

Monitoring System Activities with Event Viewer

In Microsoft Windows XP, an *event* is any occurrence that is potentially noteworthy—to you, to other users, to the operating system, or to an application. Events are recorded by the Event Log service, and their history is preserved in these three log files: Security (Secevent.evt), Application (Appevent.evt), and System (Sysevent.evt). Event Viewer, a Microsoft Management Console snap-in supplied with Windows XP, allows you to review and archive these three event logs.

Why would you want to do this? The most likely reasons are to troubleshoot problems that have occurred, to keep an eye on your system in order to forestall problems, and to watch out for security breaches. If a device has failed, a disk has filled close to capacity, a program has crashed repeatedly, or some other critical difficulty has arisen, the information recorded in the event logs can help you, or a technical support specialist, figure out what's wrong and what corrective steps are required. Watching the event logs can also help you spot serious problems before they occur. If trouble is brewing but hasn't yet erupted, keeping an eye on the event logs may tip you off before it's too late. For example, if a network adapter is failing intermittently or a network cable is improperly connected, you might begin to see items in the event log showing frequent disconnections from and reconnections to the network. Finally, you can use one of the event logs to track such things as unsuccessful logon attempts or attempts by users to read files for which they lack access privileges. Such occurrences might alert you to actual or potential security problems in your organization.

At Home with Windows XP

Event Viewer works exactly the same way in both versions of Windows XP. Only certain events are recorded in the Security log, but that topic is covered in Chapter 38, "Auditing Security."

Types of Events

Security events are recorded in the Security log, Secevent.evt. Monitoring these events is called *auditing* and is the subject of Chapter 38, "Auditing Security." In the remainder of this chapter, we focus on the other two event logs, Appevent.evt and Sysevent.evt. Appevent.evt and Sysevent.evt record application events and system events, respectively.

Application events are generated by applications, including programs that you install, programs that come with Windows XP, and operating system services. For example, events relating to Microsoft Office, the backup program that comes with Windows XP, and the Windows XP Fax service are all recorded in the Application log.

System events are generated by Windows XP itself and by installed components, such as device drivers. If a driver fails to load when you start a Windows XP session, for example, that event is recorded in the System log.

(If you're curious about what elements of your system generate events and where those events are recorded, use Registry Editor to open the following registry key: HKLM\System\CurrentControlSet\Services\Eventlog. Then inspect each of the subkeys, Application, Security, and System. Each entity capable of generating an event has a subkey under one of those three keys.)

For details about using Registry Editor, see Chapter 29, "Editing the Registry."

The System and Application logs recognize three types of events, each identified by a unique icon:

Errors. These are events that represent possible loss of data or functionality. Examples of errors include events related to a malfunctioning network adapter and loss of functionality caused by a device or service that doesn't load at startup.

Warnings. These events represent less significant or less immediate problems than errors. Examples of warning events include a nearly full disk, a timeout by the network redirector, and data errors on a backup tape.

Information. These are other events that Windows XP logs. Examples of information events include someone using a printer connected to your computer and a successful dial-up connection to your ISP.

Keeping Track of Computer Events

To start Event Viewer, do one of the following:

- In Control Panel, choose Performance And Maintenance, Administrative Tools, Event Viewer.

- At a command prompt, type **eventvwr.msc.**

You can also run Event Viewer by right-clicking My Computer and choosing Manage. The Computer Management console that appears includes the Event Viewer snap-in, along with a number of other administrative tools.

Figure 36-1 shows an example of what you might see when you open Event Viewer. The console tree displays the names of the three event logs, allowing you to move from one log to another. The details pane presents a columnar view of the current log.

Figure 36-1. Event Viewer's details pane presents a columnar view of the log selected in the console tree.

Figure 36-1 shows all eight of Event Viewer's columns. You can use the Add/Remove Columns command on the View menu to hide columns you don't need or to change the order in which columns appear. By default, events are sorted chronologically, with the most recent at the top. You can change the sort order by clicking column headings.

Note that, while the details pane includes some useful information, it doesn't provide many details about what events portend or why they occurred. You can get more of that information by inspecting the details for individual events. (See "Examining Event Details," page 1175.) Here is a column-by-column rundown of what the details pane does display:

- **Type.** As mentioned, events in the System and Application logs are of three types: Information, Warning, and Error. The icon at the left side of the Type column helps you spot the event types in which you're interested.

1173

- **Date and Time.** The Event Log service records the date and time of each event's occurrence in Greenwich mean time, and Event Viewer translates those Greenwich mean time values into dates and times appropriate for your own time zone.

- **Source.** The source column reports the application or system component that generated each event.

- **Category.** Some event sources use categories to distinguish different types of events they may report. Many sources do not. As you can see, none of the four sources shown in Figure 36-1 (W32Time, Windows File Protection, Service Control Manager, and Disk) use categories.

- **Event.** All events are identified by a numerical value. This number is associated with a text description that appears when you view an event's properties. There's no systemwide code in use here—each event source's designer simply decides what numbers to use and records those numbers in a file—and there's no requirement that each event source use a unique set of numbers. After spending some time in your event logs, however, you might begin to recognize particular events by their arbitrary numbers. For example, events 6006 and 6009, generated by the Event Log service itself (listed as eventlog in the Source column), occur respectively when the Event Log service is stopped and started. Because the Event Log service is ordinarily never stopped while your computer is running, these events represent system shutdown and restart.

- **User.** The User column records the user account associated with each event. Not all events are associated with a particular user account. Many events, particularly system events, are not generated by a particular user. These events show up as N/A.

- **Computer.** The Computer column records the computer on which the event occurred.

Daylight Saving Time, Remote Computers, and Changes to the System Clock

When you move from standard time into daylight saving time or vice versa, Event Viewer changes the displayed Time (and possibly Date) values for events that have already occurred. For example, if an event occurred at 6 P.M. in standard time, after you move into daylight saving time that event will appear as if it had occurred at 7 P.M. That's because Event Viewer applies a single offset from Greenwich mean time to all events in its logs and decrements that offset by one hour when you pass from standard into daylight saving time.

If you monitor events on remote computers in other time zones, be aware that Event Viewer always displays those events' dates and times in your (local) time zone. It records occurrences in Greenwich mean time but applies your time zone's Greenwich mean time offset for display purposes. Thus, for example, an event occurring at noon in New York will be reported in Los Angeles as having occurred at 9 A.M.

If you change the clock on your system, the times reported in event logs do not change, because your offset from Greenwich mean time has not changed. If you change your time zone, however, Event Viewer applies the new offset and changes the times displayed for all events in the log.

Examining Event Details

To learn more about an event than Event Viewer's details pane tells you, you need to display individual information for the event. Select the event you're interested in and do one of the following:

- Double-click the event.
- Press Enter.
- Choose Properties from Event Viewer's Action menu.

Figure 36-2 on the next page shows the properties dialog box for an event in the System log.

The summary information in the top third of the properties dialog box is identical to the information that appears in Event Viewer's columnar details pane. The description in the middle third of the window is the plain-language description of what has occurred. For localization purposes, this information is kept separate from the log (.evt) file. Each event type is mapped to descriptive text that lives elsewhere, in whatever file the application's or component's designer chose to use. (The event message file is recorded in the EventMessageFile registry value in HKLM\System \CurrentControlSet\Services\Eventlog*logname**eventsource*, where *logname* is the name of the log—System, for example—and *eventsource* is the name of the application or component that generates the event in question.)

Some events generate binary data that can be useful to programmers or support technicians who are familiar with the product that generated the event. If binary data is available, it appears in the bottom third of the properties dialog box.

Figure 36-2. The properties dialog box for an event can provide useful diagnostic information.

If you want to view details for other events, you can do so without first returning to the details pane: Click the arrow buttons in the upper right corner of the properties dialog box to move to the previous or next event in the list.

Directly below the Next Event button, near the upper right corner of the window, is a handy Copy button, as shown in Figure 36-2. Clicking here sends the entire contents of the properties dialog box to the Clipboard, allowing you, for example, to paste the information into an e-mail message and send it to a support technician. (You can also copy some or all of the text in the dialog box by selecting it and pressing Ctrl+C. You can use this technique to selectively copy field data from the top of the dialog box as well as information in the Description and Data boxes.)

Searching for an Event

The Find command on Event Viewer's View menu allows you to locate particular items in the current log. The Find dialog box, shown in Figure 36-3, includes a Description box in which you can specify all or a portion of an event's descriptive text. To locate the most recent event that involved any kind of failure, for example, you would select the first event in the log (assuming you've kept the default chronological sort order), choose Find, type **fail** on the Description line, and click Find Next.

Chapter 36: Monitoring System Activities with Event Viewer

Figure 36-3. You can use this dialog box to find a particular event.

Filtering the Log Display

As you can see from a cursory look at your System log, events can pile up quickly, obscuring those of a particular type (such as print jobs) or those that occurred at a particular date and time. To filter a log so that Event Viewer displays only the items you currently care about, right-click the log's name in the console tree, and choose Properties. Then fill out the Filter tab of the log's properties dialog box (it looks much like the Find dialog box shown in Figure 36-3), and click OK. To restore the unfiltered list, return to this dialog box, and click Restore Defaults.

With the help of the New Log View command on the Action menu, you can switch quickly between filtered and unfiltered views of a log—or between one filtered view and a different filtered view. Simply select the log in which you're interested, right-click, and then choose New Log View. Event Viewer adds the new view to the console tree. Select the new view and filter to taste. Now you can move between views by navigating the console tree.

Working with Log Files

In general, you don't need to do anything with the log (.evt) files. But you might want to limit their size, archive their content, or clear them—tasks that are explained in the following sections.

Setting Log File Size and Longevity

Log files don't continue to pile up new events forever. If they did, they would eventually consume an unmanageable amount of disk space. By default, each log file has a maximum size of 512 KB. You can adjust that downward or upward in 64-KB increments.

Also by default, events in each log file have a minimum longevity of seven days. That means that if a file reaches its maximum size, new events overwrite the oldest ones—but only if the oldest ones are at least seven days old. That too is an adjustable parameter.

To change either a log file's maximum size or its events' minimum longevity, select the log in question in the console tree. Then choose Properties from the Action menu. Figure 36-4 shows a log file's properties dialog box. (You must have administrative privileges to use this dialog box; otherwise, all the controls appear dimmed.)

If the Event Log service is unable to add new events to a log, either because you have told it never to overwrite or because it has reached capacity before the oldest events have reached their minimum age, you'll receive a warning message. Then you can remedy the situation, either by simply clearing the log or by archiving and then clearing it.

Figure 36-4. The properties dialog box allows you to control the size and lifespan of your event logs.

Archiving and Clearing Log Files

To archive a log, select it in the console tree, and choose Save Log File As from the Action menu. In the dialog box that appears, be sure to choose the default file type, Event Log (*.evt). The resulting file includes all events (ignoring the current filter, if any) and all the recorded information (including the binary details).

To clear a log, either click the Clear Log button in the log's properties dialog box (see Figure 36-4) or select the log in the console tree and choose Clear All Events from the Action menu. You must have administrative privileges to clear a log.

Displaying an Archived Log File

After you have saved a log file in the .evt format, you can redisplay its contents at any time by using the Open Log File command on the Action menu. You need to tell the system what kind of log file—Application, Security, or System—you're reopening when you specify the file's name.

A reopened archive appears as a new entry in the console tree. You can view it, filter it, and search it, just as you would any other log file. You can also delete it—something you can't do to the default Application, Security, and System logs.

Troubleshooting

An error message says you don't have enough disk space to record events.

If you run out of space on the disk where your log files reside, the Event Log service will be unable to record new events and you will receive an error message to that effect. If you cannot create free space on the full disk, you can work around the problem by changing the default location of the log files. Doing so requires three modifications to your registry. Proceed as follows:

1 Run Registry Editor.

2 Navigate to the key HKLM\System\CurrentControlSet\Services\
Eventlog\Application.

3 Double-click the File value.

4 Change the File value's data to specify a path to a disk that isn't full.
For example, if the current data is located in %SystemRoot%\System32\
Config\Appevent.evt and you have room to put the Appevent.evt file in
E:\SomeFolder, change the File value's data to E:\SomeFolder\Appevent.evt.

The folder you specify must exist, or the change won't take effect.

(continued)

Chapter 36

> **Troubleshooting** *(continued)*
>
> **5** Repeat these steps to change the location specified by the File value in HKLM\System\CurrentControlSet\Services\Eventlog\Security and HKLM\System\CurrentControlSet\Services\Eventlog\System.
>
> **6** Close Registry Editor.
>
> **7** Restart your computer.
>
> For additional information about modifying the registry, see Chapter 29, "Editing the Registry."

Exporting Log File Information

Saving a log in its native (.evt) format creates a complete replica of the log, but you can view that replica only in Event Viewer (or a third-party application capable of reading native event logs). Event Viewer can also export log data to tab- or comma-delimited text files, however, and you can easily import these into database, spreadsheet, or even word processing programs. When you save a log in one of these formats, you get everything in the log except the binary data associated with certain events.

To save an entire log file in a text format, select the log in the console tree, choose Save Log File As from the Action menu, and then select either Text (Tab Delimited) or CSV (Comma Delimited) from the Save As Type list.

The Save Log File As command always exports all of the current log, regardless of how the log might be filtered for display purposes. If you want to generate a text report showing only particular kinds of events, first filter the log to display those events, and then use the Action menu's Export List command. Like the Save Log File As command, Export List provides tab- and comma-delimited options. It also offers the option to save in Unicode—something that could prove handy if your local language includes non-Latin characters. Do not, however, select the Save Only Selected Rows check box in the Export List dialog box unless you want a report that includes only column headers and a single event.

Backing Up Log Files

Because the Event Log service is ordinarily running at all times, the three log files—Appevent.evt, Secevent.evt, and Sysevent.evt—are generally open at all times. *Do not try to back up these log files using Windows Explorer or the command line!* Windows Explorer and the Copy command will copy your open log files without complaint, but if you copy them back to your %SystemRoot%\System32\Config folder (the default log file location), Event Viewer will find them corrupted and will be unable to display their contents.

Fortunately, Windows XP Backup Utility (Ntbackup.exe) can back up and restore log files without corrupting them in the process. You can use Backup Utility to schedule regular backups of your log files.

Troubleshooting

Your log files are corrupt.

If Event Viewer reports on startup that one or more of your log files is corrupt, you can remedy the situation as follows:

1 Disable the Event Log service. (For information about disabling a service, see "Starting and Stopping Services," page 1294.)

2 Restart Windows XP.

3 Delete the corrupt log(s)—Appevent.evt, Secevent.evt, and/or Sysevent.evt—from %SystemRoot%\System32\Config (or wherever they may be). Your existing event data will be lost, but a new log file will be created when the service is restarted, and that log will start to accumulate new events.

4 Reenable the Event Log service, and start the service.

5 If the Event Log service doesn't restart successfully, then restart Windows XP.

Note that you cannot delete or rename the log files while the Event Log service is running.

Using Third-Party Tools to Monitor Events

Several third-party tools are available to help you monitor events. While some of these tools are directed at helping monitor events across a large enterprise, others provide features useful on small networks and individual computers.

These products provide the capability to perform one or more of the following actions:

● Monitor multiple computers from one workstation

● Organize information and print reports

● Schedule monitoring activities

● Monitor other types of logs in addition to event logs, such as Web server logs

● Send reports or notifications via e-mail

● Provide real-time monitoring and notification of events

● Enable Web-based remote viewing of events

Chapter 36

Examples of programs that provide some or all of these capabilities include

- WDumpEvt (*http://www.eventlog.com*)

- EventAdmin (*http://www.aelita.com/products/EventAdmin.htm*)

- EventReporter (*http://www.eventreporter.com*)

- ELM Log Manager (*http://www.tntsoftware.com*)

---

tip The Help And Support Center offers an alternative view of the system logs. This view merges the content from all three logs, but it shows only the errors (not warnings or information events)—which are typically the most significant events. To see this view of events, click Start, Help And Support Center. From the Help And Support Center home page, click Use Tools To View Your Computer Information And Diagnose Problems, Advanced System Information, View The Error Log.

Chapter 37

Securing Your Computer with Templates

Microsoft Windows XP is rife with security options—various settings you can make to ensure that the bad guys are locked out of your computer and that people to whom you want to grant access can use your computer and its resources. You can specify user rights, which determines the accounts that are permitted to perform certain tasks. You can configure numerous settings that determine how your computer operates. You can apply permissions to every file, printer, and other resource, specifying exactly what type of access is granted to each user. And on and on. We describe in detail these security options—and many others—in *Microsoft Windows Security Inside Out for Windows XP and Windows 2000* (Microsoft Press, 2002).

Fortunately, the default settings in Windows are appropriate in most cases, and you needn't spend an inordinate amount of time reviewing and setting security options. In certain situations, you might need to grant an additional user right to a particular user account or user group—a task we explain in this chapter. Once you know how, it's quite easy. But what if you need to apply uniform, non-default security settings to all the computers on your network? Although making settings on one computer is not particularly difficult, it's not a job you want to repeat any more than necessary. Security templates provide a solution.

At Home with Windows XP

If you use Windows XP Home Edition, you might as well skip right past this chapter; the settings described here rely on MMC snap-ins that are included only with Windows XP Professional. (Don't worry about your computer's security, however. Windows XP Home Edition enjoys the same security protection as Professional; the difference is that in Home Edition you can't change the settings.)

The final topic of this chapter is Security Configuration And Analysis, a Microsoft Management Console (MMC) snap-in that allows you to compare your current security settings with those of a security template and apply the template settings if you choose.

Setting User Rights

A *user right* is authorization to perform an operation that affects an entire computer. (A *permission*, by contrast, is authorization to perform an operation on a specific object—such as a file or a printer—on a computer.) For each user right, you can specify which user accounts and groups have the user right. To review or set user rights, use the Group Policy console. (At a command prompt, type **gpedit.msc** to open Group Policy.) Navigate to Computer Configuration\Windows Settings\Security Settings\Local Policies\User Rights Assignment. Then double-click a user right to view or change the list of users and groups, as shown in Figure 37-1.

For more information about Group Policy, see Appendix E, "Group Policy."

---

tip **Use the Local Security Settings console**

The Local Security Settings console displays a subset of the Group Policy console's content, thereby providing a shorter path to User Rights Assignment. Local Security Settings is useful when you're not setting other policies, such as the ones in the Administrative Templates folders. To open Local Security Settings, double-click Local Security Policy in the Administrative Tools folder or type **secpol.msc** at a command prompt.

Ten of the user rights—Access This Computer From The Network, Allow Logon Through Terminal Services, Log On As A Batch Job, Log On As A Service, Log On Locally, and their corresponding "Deny" user rights—are known more precisely as

Chapter 37: Securing Your Computer with Templates

Figure 37-1. To review or change the local setting for a user right, double-click the user right in User Rights Assignment.

logon rights. They control how users are allowed to access the computer—whether from the keyboard ("locally") or through a network connection, or whether as a service or as a batch facility (such as Task Scheduler). You can use these logon rights (in particular, Log On Locally and Deny Logon Locally) to control who can log on to your computer. By default, Log On Locally is granted to the local Guest account and members of the Administrators, Backup Operators, Power Users, and Users groups. If you want to prevent certain users from logging on at the keyboard (but still allow them to connect via the network, for example), create a group, add those user accounts to it, and then assign the Deny Logon Locally user right to the new group. Like deny permissions, deny logon rights take precedence over allow logon rights, so if a user is a member of a group that is allowed to log on (such as Power Users) and a group that is not (such as the one described in the previous sentence), the user will not be allowed to log on. (Such users are rebuffed with an error message after they type their user name and password in the Log On To Windows dialog box.)

Microsoft Windows XP Professional Resource Kit Documentation (Microsoft Press, 2001) contains a description of each user right. Table 37-1 on the next page lists the default rights assigned to the built-in user groups.

Table 37-1. **Default Rights of Built-In User Groups in Windows XP Professional**

Group	Default Rights
Administrators	● Access this computer from the network
	● Adjust memory quotas for a process
	● Allow logon through Terminal Services
	● Back up files and directories
	● Bypass traverse checking
	● Change the system time
	● Create a page file
	● Debug programs
	● Force shutdown from a remote system
	● Increase quotas
	● Increase scheduling priority
	● Load and unload device drivers
	● Log on locally
	● Manage auditing and security log
	● Modify firmware environment values
	● Perform volume maintenance tasks
	● Profile single process
	● Profile system performance
	● Remove computer from docking station
	● Restore files and directories
	● Shut down the system
	● Take ownership of files or other objects
Backup Operators	● Access this computer from the network
	● Back up files and directories
	● Bypass traverse checking
	● Log on locally
	● Restore files and directories
	● Shut down the system
Everyone	● Access this computer from the network
	● Bypass traverse checking

Chapter 37: Securing Your Computer with Templates

Table 37-1. *(continued)*

Group	Default Rights
Guest (account)	● Deny logon locally
	● Deny access to this computer from the network[1]
	● Log on locally
Power Users	● Access this computer from the network
	● Bypass traverse checking
	● Change the system time
	● Log on locally
	● Profile single process
	● Remove computer from docking station
	● Shut down the system
Remote Desktop Users	● Allow logon through Terminal Services
Users	● Access this computer from the network
	● Bypass traverse checking
	● Log on locally
	● Remove computer from docking station
	● Shut down the system
(Not assigned to any group)	● Act as part of the operating system
	● Add workstations to domain
	● Create a token object
	● Create permanent shared objects
	● Deny logon as a batch job
	● Deny logon as a service
	● Deny logon through Terminal Services
	● Enable computer and user accounts to be trusted for delegation
	● Generate security audits
	● Lock pages in memory
	● Log on as a batch job
	● Log on as a service
	● Replace a process-level token
	● Synchronize directory service data

[1] The Guest account is removed from the list of accounts with the Deny Access To This Computer From The Network right when you enable network file sharing.

1187

Using Security Templates

If you decide to change some of the default settings for user rights or other security options, you can make the changes in Group Policy or in Local Security Settings, as described in the preceding section. If you want to apply the same changes to a number of computers in your network, however, making the settings can be tedious. In this common situation, you're better off using *security templates,* files that contain pre-configured security settings for various purposes. You can also use security templates to restore your security settings to a known condition if experimentation with various settings has compromised your secure system. A security template can contain the following types of settings:

- Account Policies, including Password Policy and Account Lockout Policy settings. (For details about these settings, see "Tightening Password Security," page 132.)

- Local Policies, including Audit Policy, User Rights Assignment, and Security Options settings. (See "Keeping an Eye on Who Uses Your Computer," page 1202, and "Setting User Rights," page 1184.)

- Event Log. (See "Working with Log Files," page 1177.)

- Restricted Groups. (See "Controlling Security Group Membership," page 1192.)

- System Services, which determines the startup type for each service. (See "Using the Services Snap-In," page 1293.)

- Registry, which sets permissions on registry keys. (See "Changing Registry Key Permissions," page 986.)

- File System, which sets permissions on folders and files. (See "Controlling Access with NTFS Permissions," page 507.)

Security templates are saved as ordinary text files with a .inf file name extension. By default, they're stored in %SystemRoot%\Security\Templates. Although you could edit these plain-text (but rather cryptic) files in Notepad or another text editor, you don't need to. The Security Templates snap-in for MMC provides a much better and easier means to view, modify, create, and delete security templates.

Each security template that comes with Windows is configured for specific purposes. You can use one of these templates as is, modify it, or create a new one from scratch. Table 37-2 describes the templates included with Windows XP Professional.

Chapter 37: Securing Your Computer with Templates

Table 37-2. **Security Templates Included with Windows**

Template Name	Description
Compatws	This template removes all users from the Power Users group and relaxes the default permissions for members of the Users group. This setting allows members of the Users group to run certain applications that aren't properly designed for Windows security, without granting them the additional administrative privileges (such as the ability to create user accounts) granted to Power Users.
Hisecdc and Hisecws	These templates are intended for configuring a highly secure domain. They include all the settings in the Securedc and Securews templates, plus additional settings that require more secure authentication, restrict security group membership, and require data signing and encryption in most network communications. Hisecdc is intended for domain controllers; Hisecws is for workstations.
Rootsec	This template applies permissions to the root folder of the system drive, using the permissions introduced with Windows XP. If you inadvertently change those permissions, this template provides a quick and easy way to restore the default permissions. The permissions propagate to all child objects that inherit permissions from the parent, but they aren't applied to child objects for which explicit permissions have been set.
Securedc and Securews	These templates configure strong password, lockout, and audit settings; require the use of strong authentication protocols; restrict anonymous users; and configure Server Message Block (SMB) packet signing. They're intended for creating secure domains. Use Securedc on domain controllers and Securews on workstations.
Setup Security	This template contains the default security settings that were applied when Windows was set up on your computer. As such, it makes a good disaster-recovery template, allowing you to easily go back to the original Windows configuration.

note Except for Setup Security.inf, none of the furnished templates includes a complete set of security settings. Instead, they're designed to modify only a specific subset while leaving other settings unchanged.

InsideOut

You can restore default NTFS permissions and other security settings with a hidden template. Windows includes a template called Defltwk.inf that includes all the default security settings (including NTFS permissions, user rights assignments, policies, registry permissions, and so on) as originally configured by Microsoft for a clean installation of Windows on a new machine. (For a number of reasons, some of these settings might be different from the settings in Setup Security.inf.) Unlike the other predefined templates, Defltwk.inf is stored in %SystemRoot%\Inf, a hidden folder. Because of its storage location, it doesn't appear by default in the Security Templates snap-in— where it's more likely to get changed inadvertently. Instead, Defltwk.inf is intended to be used only with Security Configuration And Analysis or Secedit.exe, the tools for analyzing current settings and applying settings. Read more about Defltwk.inf in Knowledge Base article Q266118, "HOW TO: Restore the Default NTFS Permissions for Windows 2000." (The article refers only to Windows 2000, but Defltwk.inf is also included with Windows XP.)

Using the Security Templates Snap-In

Security Templates is an MMC snap-in that allows you to view and edit security templates. No console furnished with Windows includes the Security Templates snap-in; you'll have to create your own, as follows:

1 At a command prompt, type **mmc**.

2 Open the File menu and choose Add/Remove Snap-In.

3 On the Standalone tab, click Add.

4 Select Security Templates, and then click Add.

5 Click Close, and then click OK in the Add/Remove Snap-In dialog box.

By default, the Security Templates snap-in displays the templates stored in %SystemRoot%\Security\Templates, as shown in Figure 37-2. To view templates stored in another folder, including those stored on a network drive, right-click Security Templates in the console tree, and choose New Template Search Path.

To create a new template, in the console tree, right-click the folder where you want to store the template, and choose New Template. Enter a name and, optionally, a description of the template. You can view the description for a template in two ways:

● In the console tree, select the folder that contains the templates. The description of each template appears next to its name in the details pane.

● Right-click a template name (in the console tree or the details pane), and choose Set Description.

Chapter 37: Securing Your Computer with Templates

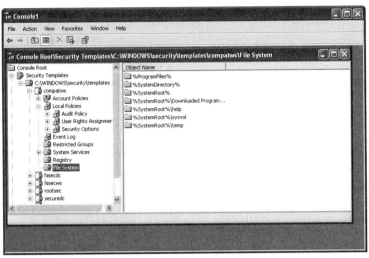

Figure 37-2. The Security Templates snap-in lets you set permissions on folders and files and make other security settings.

If you want to modify the settings in an existing template and also want to keep the original template unchanged, right-click the template name and choose Save As. After you specify a name for your copy of the template, it appears in the console tree. Note that none of the changes you make to a template are saved to disk unless you select the template and choose Action, Save or right-click a template name and choose Save. (The Save command on the File menu saves the console layout and settings—not the template settings.) If you have unsaved templates when you close the MMC console, Windows asks which of these templates you want to save. Select the ones you want to save, and click Yes.

> **note** The Security Templates snap-in is a tool for viewing and modifying templates only. Changes you make in the snap-in are saved in template files, but this snap-in does not apply template security settings to a computer. To apply the settings in a template, use the procedures described in "Applying Template Settings," page 1194.

Reviewing Account Policies, Local Policies, Event Log, and System Services Settings

You can easily review account policies, local policies, the event log, and system services settings. In the Security Templates snap-in, expand the folders in the tree pane until the policy in which you're interested is displayed in the details pane. Then double-click the policy name to open the properties dialog box; Figure 37-3 on the next page shows an example. If you want the policy to be controlled by the security template, select Define

Figure 37-3. The properties dialog box for each policy has options comparable to those in the Local Security Settings console.

This Policy Setting In The Template, and then specify the setting you want. Your choices for policy setting depend on the specific policy. (For example, some policies require you to select among two or more options, whereas others provide a text box or spinner with which you can specify a numeric value.)

Controlling Security Group Membership

With restricted groups policies, you can control membership in security groups. When you apply a security template with restricted groups policies, any user accounts that are currently members of a group whose membership is restricted are removed from that group. For example, if you create a restricted group policy for Administrators that includes only Ed and Carl in that group, applying the template adds Ed and Carl to the group (if they're not already members) and removes all other accounts. Restricting group membership in this way is a one-shot deal; administrators can subsequently add or remove members from the group.

To add a group to the list of restricted groups, right-click Restricted Groups and choose Add Group. In the Add Group dialog box, type the name of the security group you want to add, or click Browse to display a list of all security groups. In the Select Groups dialog box, click Advanced, and then click Find Now to display the list.

To control the membership of a restricted group, double-click the group name to display the properties dialog box for the group, as shown in Figure 37-4. Next to the Members Of This Group box, click Add. In the Add Member dialog box, type the user name you want, or click Browse to display a list of user names. You can separate multiple names with semicolons, or you can simply repeat the process to add other names.

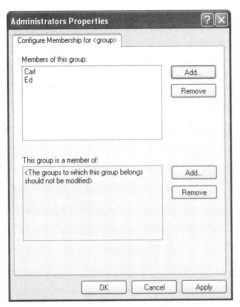

Figure 37-4. After applying the template, only user accounts listed in the top box remain in the group; if no names appear, the group is empty.

Configuring Permissions on Folders, Files, and the Registry

The File System and Registry sections of a security template let you apply permissions to folders, files, and registry keys, overriding any permissions currently protecting the items you specify. Just as you can within Windows Explorer and Registry Editor, you can specify a discretionary access control list (DACL), which grants (or denies) access permissions to users and groups. You can also specify a system access control list (SACL), which specifies the security events to be recorded in the Security log.

For information about permissions on folders and files, see "Controlling Access with NTFS Permissions," page 507. For information about applying permissions within Registry Editor, see "Changing Registry Key Permissions," page 986. For information about setting SACLs, see "Seeing Who Has Tried to Access Your Files and Folders," page 1206.

If the folder or file on which you want to configure ACLs does not appear in the details pane when you select File System, right-click File System (or right-click an empty area of the details pane), and choose Add File. The Add File command opens the Add A File Or Folder dialog box, which lets you browse all folders and files in My Computer. The steps for adding a registry key are similar: Right-click Registry and choose Add Key. In the Select Registry Key dialog box, you can expand the registry hierarchy and select the key you want to configure.

When the folder, file, or registry key of interest appears in the details pane, simply double-click it to configure it. A dialog box similar to the one shown in Figure 37-5 appears. To set ACLs, select the first option, and then specify how you want to set permissions on child objects (subfolders and files within the specified folder or subkeys within the specified registry key). The options to propagate inheritable permissions and replace existing permissions correspond to the similarly worded options in the Advanced Security Settings dialog box, which opens when you click the Advanced button on the Security tab in Windows Explorer or Registry Editor.

Figure 37-5. The dialog box for setting registry key permissions is nearly identical to this one. Minor wording variations refer to keys instead of files and folders.

Select Do Not Allow Permissions On This File Or Folder To Be Replaced if you want to ensure that permissions on this folder, file, or key are *not* changed when a security template is applied. Why not just omit this object name from the Registry or File System folder in the template? This option prevents changes that might be inflicted through inheritance by settings on a parent object.

Finally, of course, you need to specify the permissions for the object. Click Edit Security, and you'll see a dialog box that includes a Security tab just like the one in Windows Explorer or Registry Editor. This dialog box shows the object's current security settings.

Applying Template Settings

After you've configured a template to include the settings you want, you can apply the settings to your local computer. You do this with Security Configuration And Analysis, an

Chapter 37: Securing Your Computer with Templates

MMC snap-in that manages a database of security settings from one or more templates. You can also use this snap-in to compare your current settings to those in the database.

> **tip** Before you apply your template settings, you might want to analyze your configuration to see what differences exist between your current settings and the settings in your security template. For details, see "Analyzing System Security," on the next page.

To use Security Configuration And Analysis, you must add it to an MMC console. Use the same procedure as described for Security Templates; for details, see "Using the Security Templates Snap-In," page 1190. Initially, the Security Configuration And Analysis snap-in looks like no other, displaying only an empty console tree and, in the details pane, sparse instructions for tasks whose purpose isn't clear.

> **tip** To house all your security-management tools in one place, create a console that includes the Group Policy, Security Templates, and Security Configuration And Analysis snap-ins. Save the console in your Administrative Tools folder.

Go ahead and follow these instructions:

1 Right-click Security Configuration And Analysis and choose Open Database.

2 In the Open Database dialog box, type a name for a new database, and then click Open. (If you want to use a database that you've created previously, select it instead.)

3 In the Import Template dialog box, select a security template, and then click Open.

4 If you want to import another security template into the database, right-click Security Configuration And Analysis, and choose Import Template.

Now you're ready to actually apply your settings. Right-click Security Configuration And Analysis, and choose Configure Computer Now. In the Configure System dialog box, type the path and name for a log file if you don't want to accept the default file. Click OK. (Why it's called an *error* log file is another mystery of Security Configuration And Analysis; it's a log of all configuration actions, not only errors.) Windows applies your settings, and you're once again left at the same cryptic console display. To see what's occurred, right-click Security Configuration And Analysis, and choose View Log File; the log file appears in the details pane.

InsideOut

You might find it more convenient to apply template settings with Secedit.exe, a command-line utility. This utility can make applying settings on multiple computers easier. You could, for example, store the security database (.sdb) file on a shared network drive, along with a one-line batch program that applies the settings. A command-line utility also makes it easy to set up security configuration as a scheduled task.

Before you use Secedit, you must create a security database file with Security Configuration And Analysis, as described in the numbered steps in the preceding section. Then, to apply your settings, use the command **secedit /configure /db** *databasefile*, where *databasefile* is the path and name (including extension) of the database file. You can omit the path if the database is in the current directory. For example, if you leave the security database file in the default location, you'd enter the following:

```
secedit /configure /db
"%userprofile%\my documents\security\database\mysettings.sdb"
```

With additional command-line parameters, you can instruct Secedit to apply only certain types of settings specified in the database, control the location and display of the log file, and set other options. In addition, you can use Secedit to compare your computer settings with security database settings, extract a security template file from a security database, and more. For details, type **secedit /?** at a command prompt.

Analyzing System Security

The Security Configuration And Analysis snap-in has that name for a reason: In addition to applying template settings (configuration), it compares a computer's current security settings with those in a security database file (analysis). This comparison provides an easy way to comprehensively review security settings. You can see which settings have been changed, how your computer compares with one of the highly secure template configurations, and so on.

To perform an analysis, open Security Configuration And Analysis in MMC, and then create or open a security database. (See the preceding section, "Applying Template Settings," for details.) Right-click Security Configuration And Analysis, and choose Analyze Computer Now. In the Perform Analysis dialog box, modify the log file name if you want, and then click OK. After the analysis is complete, the console tree sprouts new branches, identical to those in a template in the Security Templates snap-in.

Chapter 37: Securing Your Computer with Templates

For each policy in the Account Policies, Local Policies, and Event Log folders, the details pane shows the database setting and the current computer setting. A symbol in a policy's icon indicates at a glance the results of the analysis of that policy:

A circled green check mark indicates that the two settings match.

An *X* in a red circle identifies policies in which the database setting differs from the computer setting.

A circled exclamation point or question mark indicates that the computer setting was not analyzed; this typically occurs on policies that are relevant only on a domain controller.

Double-click a policy to see its properties dialog box, as shown in Figure 37-6. The dialog box displays the current settings for the computer and in the database. If you want to change the setting in the database, select Define This Policy In The Database, make your setting, and click OK.

Figure 37-6. The properties dialog box for a policy initially shows the value in the security database. You can change the database value if you want to.

Differences between the database settings and computer settings in the Restricted Groups, System Services, Registry, and File System folders are indicated with icons similar to those just shown. Instead of displaying the settings in the details pane, however, Security Configuration And Analysis displays the word *Investigate* alongside items with differences. Double-click any such items in the Restricted Groups or System Services folder to display a properties dialog box, similar to the dialog box shown in Figure 37-6, that shows both settings and allows you to modify the database setting.

Security Configuration And Analysis has another quirk as well. Double-clicking an item in the Registry or File System folder doesn't open the properties dialog box unless the item is at the bottom of the hierarchy. To view the properties dialog box for a folder or a key that has child objects, right-click it and choose Properties.

Chapter 38

Auditing Security

As a secure operating system, Microsoft Windows XP is designed to prevent unauthorized access to a computer's files, folders, and printers. Through a user inadvertently making improper settings or through the determined efforts of an intruder, someone might gain access to resources that should be off limits. Monitoring, or *auditing*, system usage can be a helpful tool in the administration of system security. For example, repeated attempts to log on with the wrong password might be an indication that unauthorized users are trying to gain access to your system. Repeated failure to access a folder might indicate that software has been incorrectly installed or that security for the folder is set up incorrectly.

Microsoft Windows XP provides the ability to audit security events by recording attempts to access system resources. In this chapter, we describe the various auditing tools that you, as a system administrator or resource owner, can use. We examine their purpose and use and explain what information they supply when they are used properly.

About Auditing

When a user attempts to access a system resource, Windows checks the resource's access control list (ACL) to determine whether the user should be allowed access. This is the essence of Windows XP security.

At Home with Windows XP

In Windows XP Home Edition, account logon, account management, logon, policy change, and system events are audited for both successful incidents and failed attempts. You cannot enable auditing for directory service access, object access, privilege use, or process tracking events, or disable the categories that are already enabled, without additional tools.

> **note** Even if your computer is configured to use Simple File Sharing (the default configuration in standalone and workgroup environments), Windows still uses ACLs. With Simple File Sharing, the standard user interface provides fewer options for viewing and editing ACLs, but the lists—and the protection they provide—are still in place. For more information about the Simple File Sharing model, see "Simple File Sharing vs. Windows 2000–Style Sharing," page 98.

If auditing is enabled, you can also request that Windows audit access to a given resource. (For more information, see "Keeping an Eye on Who Uses Your Computer," page 1202.) Windows will then record in a log file any attempts to access that resource. You might direct Windows to record all failed print jobs on a given printer, for example, or to record all failed file-read requests for a certain folder.

Windows records this information in the Security log (Secevent.evt), one of the three systemwide logs that Windows manages. The other two are the System log (Sysevent.evt), which records events generated by components of the operating system—such as display or network drivers—and the Application log (Appevent.evt), which records events generated by applications. For example, Backup Utility generates events when you erase a tape or restore files, and records the events in the Application log.

For information about the System and Application logs, see Chapter 36, "Monitoring System Activities with Event Viewer."

Avoid auditing if you don't need it. Security audits, like IRS audits, can be time-consuming. (OK, security audits aren't *that* bad.) When you enable auditing, the system must write an event record to the Security log for each audit check the system performs. Because this can severely degrade system performance, you should audit only the events that are important to you.

Ensuring That You Don't Miss Any Security Events

By default, when the Security log fills up, Windows erases the oldest entries when it needs to make a new entry—just as it does with the System log and the Application log. But if security is critical to your operation, you can make a registry setting that ensures that events can be deleted only by a member of the Administrators group. (Even without this registry setting, only administrators—and others with the Manage Auditing And Security Log right—can view the Security log or clear its contents. To prevent people from covering their tracks, no one can delete individual entries; authorized individuals must delete all or none.)

This solution is rather drastic and should therefore be used only when it's essential that every security event be preserved. With this registry entry, the system halts when the Security log becomes full, preventing all further use—and possibly losing data if document files happen to be open when this occurs. If you want to enable this level of security, here's how it's done:

1 In Event Viewer, right-click Security and choose Properties. (Type **eventvwr.msc** at a command prompt to launch Event Viewer.)

2 On the General tab, select either Overwrite Events Older Than or, for maximum security, Do Not Overwrite Events (Clear Log Manually).

3 Use Registry Editor to change or create a DWORD value named CrashOnAuditFail in HKLM\System\CurrentControlSet\Control\Lsa. Set its value to 1.

4 Restart the computer.

After you've followed these steps, the computer will halt when the Security log becomes full. At that point, you need to restart the computer and log on as a member of the Administrators group; no other accounts are allowed to log on. Your first action after logging on should be to review, export if desired, and clear the Security log. You then need to reset the value of the registry entry to 1. (The operating system automatically sets it to 2, which is the mechanism that prevents others from logging on.) To restore the computer to normal operation (that is, it continues to run even if the Security log is full), set the value to 0.

Naturally, if you employ this trick, you should take steps to avoid having the security log fill up and lock the machine at inopportune moments. Review and then clear the log periodically. (Export the log contents first if you want to preserve them.) You might also want to increase the size of the log. For more information, see "Working with Log Files," page 1177.

Keeping an Eye on Who Uses Your Computer

No events are written to the Security log until you enable auditing, which you do via Local Security Settings. (In Windows XP Home Edition, security auditing is enabled for certain events. Because Home Edition doesn't include Local Security Settings, you cannot change which events are audited unless you use a tool like Auditpol.exe—included in the Windows 2000 Resource Kit—or a comparable third-party tool.) Even if you set up auditing for files, folders, or printers, as explained later in this chapter, those events aren't recorded unless you also enable auditing in Local Security Settings.

> **note** To enable auditing, you must be logged on with an account that has the Manage Auditing And Security Log privilege. By default, only members of the Administrators group have this privilege. For information about privileges, see "Setting User Rights," page 1184.

> **note** Like most other settings in Local Security Settings, the audit policy settings can be overridden by domain-level policy settings. If your computer is part of a Windows 2000 Server or Windows .NET Server domain, you should use domain-level Group Policy to make audit policy settings instead of using Local Security Settings.

To enable auditing, follow these steps:

1 In Control Panel, open Administrative Tools, Local Security Policy. (If you use Category view, you'll find Administrative Tools under Performance And Maintenance.) Alternatively, you can type **secpol.msc** at a command prompt.

2 Expand Local Policies and then click Audit Policy to display the list shown in Figure 38-1.

3 Double-click each policy for which you want to enable auditing, and then select Success, Failure, or both.

Figure 38-1 shows the types of activities you can audit. Some, such as account management and policy change, can provide an audit trail for administrative changes. Others, such as logon events and object access, can help you better secure your system. Still others, including system events and process tracking, can assist you in locating problems with your system. Table 38-1 provides more details.

Chapter 38: Auditing Security

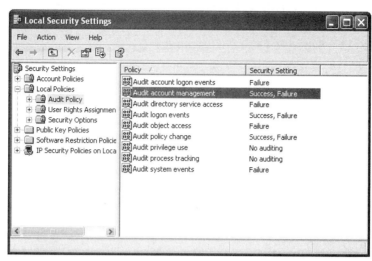

Figure 38-1. You enable auditing using the Local Security Settings console.

Table 38-1. **Events That Can Be Audited**

Audit Policy	Description
Audit account logon events	Account logon events occur when a user logs on or logs off another computer that uses this computer to validate the account. This happens only on a server running Windows 2000 or Windows .NET, and is therefore not applicable on a computer running Windows XP.
Audit account management	Account management events occur when a user account or group is created, changed, or deleted; when a user account is renamed, enabled, or disabled; or when a password is set or changed.
Audit directory service access	Directory service access events occur when a user accesses an Active Directory object that has its own system access control list. (This is the same as object access except that it applies only to Active Directory objects in a Windows domain.)
Audit logon events	Logon events occur when a user logs on or logs off a workstation or connects via a network.

(continued)

Table 38-1. *(continued)*

Audit Policy	Description
Audit object access	Object access events occur when a user accesses a file, folder, printer, registry key, or other object that is set for auditing.
Audit policy change	Policy change events occur when a change is made to user rights assignment policies, audit policies, or trust policies.
Audit privilege use	Privilege use events occur when a user exercises a user right (other than logon, logoff, and network access rights, which trigger other types of events).
Audit process tracking	Process tracking includes arcane events such as program activation, handle duplication, indirect object access, and process exit. This policy is generally not useful for everyday security concerns.
Audit system events	System events occur when a user restarts or shuts down the computer or when an event occurs that affects the system security or the Security log.

Troubleshooting

Windows requires a logon password but you don't have one.

Ordinarily, a user who has no logon password assigned can log on simply by clicking his or her name on the Welcome screen. In some cases, clicking the name displays a request for a password, and nothing you type (even just pressing Enter) satisfies the request.

New security features in Windows XP prevent users who don't have a password from logging on in certain situations. (This is done to prevent someone who knows your account name from logging on via a network or the Internet, for example—but it can affect local logons as well.) One of those situations can occur when auditing is enabled.

You can solve the problem by disabling auditing (and setting the CrashOnAuditFail value to 0 if you have changed it), but a much better solution is to assign a logon password—even a short one—to each user. To do that, visit User Accounts in Control Panel.

Viewing Security Events

Before we examine how to audit events, let's first take a look at Event Viewer—the Microsoft Management Console snap-in that allows you to examine the events that have been recorded. Event Viewer is in Computer Management, under System Tools. For the uncluttered view, go instead to Control Panel, Administrative Tools, Event Viewer, or simply type **eventvwr.msc** at a command prompt. You can use Event Viewer to examine any of the three logs: System, Security, or Application. If you select the Security log, you'll see a window similar to the one shown in Figure 38-2.

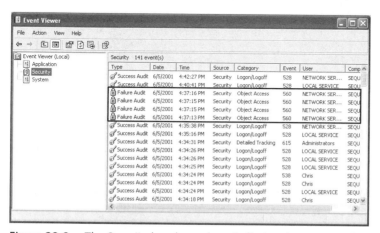

Figure 38-2. The Security log shown here indicates that an unauthorized user has apparently been attempting to use an object. These unsuccessful access events, identified with a lock icon, happened within a few seconds of each other.

> For more information about Event Viewer, see Chapter 36, "Monitoring System Activities with Event Viewer."

note You must be logged on as a member of the Administrators group to view the Security log. (A system administrator can grant Security log access to other groups and user accounts by assigning the Manage Auditing And Security Log right. For details, see "Setting User Rights," page 1184.)

If you want more information about an event in the Security log, double-click the event, or select it and then choose Action, Properties. The Event Properties dialog box appears, similar to the one shown in Figure 38-3 on the next page.

Figure 38-3. This properties dialog box indicates that Barbara has tried to open the file 37-01.bmp without permission.

By carefully examining all unsuccessful logon events, you might be able to find a pattern in attempts to gain access to the system. You can then take measures to tighten security, such as warning users to change their passwords and monitoring the Security log more closely.

Seeing Who Has Tried to Access Your Files and Folders

If you are logged on as a member of the Administrators group (or if the Manage Auditing And Security Log right has been assigned to your logon account), you can set up auditing of certain files or folders on your system. Windows XP can audit a variety of events and can audit different events for different users.

> **note** The files and folders that you want to audit must reside on an NTFS volume; FAT volumes do not support auditing.

Chapter 38: Auditing Security

Avoid auditing too many successful events. Although auditing is a useful technique for monitoring access to your system, you should be careful when auditing busy folders or files—and be particularly careful about auditing successful accesses. Each time a user successfully completes an operation on the file or folder, Windows XP writes one or more records to the Security log to reflect the access. This slows down your system and adds many events of little value to the log, thereby making it more difficult to find real security breaches. On the other hand, selectively auditing successful file access can be beneficial in some situations. For example, you might want to log all access to a payroll database file, which would allow you to track down who did what (and when) as well as find out if someone without the proper authority accessed the file.

Use the Security tab in the properties dialog box for a file or folder to display its audit settings. You can specify the users and groups whose access to the selected file or folder you want to audit. For each user and group, you can specify which types of access should generate entries in the Security log. You can specify different auditing events for each user and group.

> **note** The settings you make on the Auditing tab of the Access Control Settings dialog box (as described in the following procedure) are effective only if you also enable auditing. If you haven't done so already, visit Local Security Settings to enable auditing. Be sure to set Audit Object Access events to audit success and failure. (See "Keeping an Eye on Who Uses Your Computer," page 1202.)

To set up auditing for files and folders, follow these steps:

1 If your computer is not a member of a domain, in Windows Explorer choose Tools, Folder Options. Click the View tab and then clear the Use Simple File Sharing (Recommended) check box. Click OK.

Disabling Simple File Sharing allows the Security tab to appear when you look at an object's properties.

> **note** After you make the audit settings you want for various files and folders (as described in the following steps), you can restore Simple File Sharing by returning to Folder Options and selecting the same check box. Although the Security tab is no longer visible in the properties dialog box for files and folders, the audit settings you made remain in effect.

Part 9: Administering a System

2 Right-click a file or folder in Windows Explorer and choose Properties.

3 Click the Security tab.

note If the selected file or folder is not stored on an NTFS volume, the Security tab doesn't appear, because auditing and other security features are implemented only for NTFS volumes.

4 Click the Advanced button. The Access Control Settings dialog box appears.

5 Click the Auditing tab. For each object, you can specify different audit settings for different users.

Chapter 38: Auditing Security

6 Click Add to add a new user or group, or select an existing user or group and then click Edit to change its audit settings.

7 If you click Add, the Select User Or Group dialog box appears. In this example, the Everyone group is being selected. Click OK.

8 Whether editing an existing entry or adding a new one, in the Auditing Entry dialog box, select the types of access you want to audit for the selected user or group, in this case Everyone.

Part 9: Administering a System

The different types of access you can audit for success or failure are the same types of access for which you can set permissions.

9 If you're making audit settings for a folder, select the scope of objects you want audited from the Apply Onto list.

If you select an event's Successful check box, Windows generates a Security log record containing (among other information) the time and date of each successful attempt at the event by the specified user or group for the specified file or folder. Similarly, if you select an event's Failed check box, Windows generates a Security log record each time the specified user or group unsuccessfully attempts the event for the specified file or folder.

> **tip** You can change audit settings for multiple files or folders simultaneously. If you select more than one file or folder in Windows Explorer before you click the Security tab in the properties dialog box, the changes you make affect all the selected files or folders. If the existing security settings are not the same for all the items in your selection, a message appears, asking whether you want to reset the audit settings for the entire selection.

Seeing Who Has Tried to Use Your Printers

Windows XP can audit several printer events as well as audit different events for different users. If you have a color printer that uses expensive ink cartridges, for example, you might want to know who's causing it to run dry so frequently. You can manage all the printer security features through the Printers folder.

> **note** You must be logged on as a member of the Administrators group (or your logon account must have the Manage Auditing And Security Log right) to set up auditing of printers.

To set up printer security auditing, follow these steps:

1 Use Local Security Settings to enable auditing. Be sure to set Audit Object Access events to audit success and failure. For details, see "Keeping an Eye on Who Uses Your Computer," page 1202.

2 If your computer is not a member of a domain, in Windows Explorer choose Tools, Folder Options. Click the View tab and then clear the Use Simple File Sharing (Recommended) check box.

Disabling Simple File Sharing causes the Security tab to appear when you look at a printer's properties dialog box. (Yes, the Simple *File* Sharing setting also applies to printers.)

> **note** After you make the audit settings you want for your printers (as described in the following steps), you can restore Simple File Sharing by returning to Folder Options and selecting the same check box. Although the Security tab is no longer visible in the properties dialog box for printers, the audit settings you made are still in effect.

3 Open the Start menu and choose Printers And Faxes.

4 Right-click the icon for the printer you want to audit and choose Properties.

5 Click the Security tab.

6 Click the Advanced button. The Access Control Settings dialog box appears.

7 Click the Auditing tab.

The Auditing tab for a printer object is nearly identical to the one for a file object, as shown on the next page.

Part 9: Administering a System

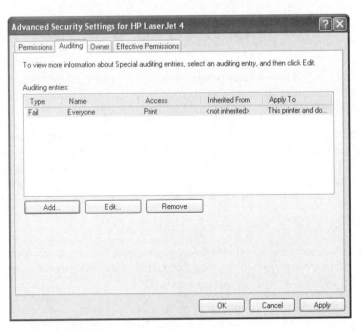

8 Click Add to add a new user or group, or click Edit to change audit settings for an existing user or group. If you click Add, specify the new user or group in the Select User Or Group dialog box that appears and then click OK.

9 In the Auditing Entry dialog box (similar to the one shown here), select the types of access you want to audit.

Chapter 38: Auditing Security

For a printer, often the most useful information comes from auditing failures rather than successes. Logging printer successes generates a large number of relatively useless log entries. You might want to do this for only a short time to identify users who should not have access to a printer. Printer failures, on the other hand, create few entries and can be used to quickly identify people who attempt to access a printer for which they do not have permission.

When Windows logs a printer event, such as successful printing or a deletion from the print queue, the event record is written to the System log. In contrast, security events, such as attempts to access a printer for which an account does not have permission, result in an event record being written to the Security log.

---

tip   It is often useful to monitor unsuccessful print jobs and deletions from the print queue, because these events might indicate a problem with the printer or difficulty using the printer. These are printer operation events, however, not security events. On the Advanced tab of the Print Server Properties dialog box, select Log Spooler Information Events. (To display the Print Server Properties dialog box, in the Printers And Faxes folder open the File menu and choose Server Properties.) For more information, see "Setting Server Properties," page 1085.

Chapter 38

Part 10

Appendixes

Professional or Home Edition: What's the Difference?

To understand the differences between the two editions of Microsoft Windows XP, remember this simple fact: Windows XP Professional contains everything included in Windows XP Home Edition and more.

Throughout this book—in the "At Home with Windows XP" sidebars that appear at the beginning of each chapter and elsewhere—we point out the features that are unavailable in Home Edition. In some cases, we provide a hidden work-around to obtain a Professional feature in Home Edition (for example, editing the registry instead of using Group Policy). But in fact, for computers in a home or small business, the differences are few.

The operating system kernel is identical in both editions. The Web browser works the same, as do all the file and folder management tools and techniques in Windows Explorer. Some default settings are different, depending on the edition in use; for instance, the taskbar is locked by default in Windows XP Home Edition but not in Professional. Regardless of which edition you use, you'll find most of the same system management utilities and troubleshooting tools, and there's no difference in the bundled applications used to manage digital media.

To discover the true differences between the two editions, you need to dig a little deeper. As Table A-1 on the next page shows, most of the differences are obvious only when you use specialized hardware or try to access advanced security and networking features and capabilities.

If you consider yourself a power user, we predict you'll prefer Windows XP Professional. But that doesn't mean you need to upgrade every machine on your network. Windows XP Home Edition and Professional coexist happily on a peer-to-peer network; in fact, both editions get along well with earlier Windows versions and even with computers running other operating systems. (If your network is set up as a domain using Windows 2000 Server or Windows .NET Server, however, you must use Windows XP Professional to join the domain.)

Table A-1. **Key Features Available Only in Windows XP Professional**

Feature	Description
Support for multiple processors	Windows XP Professional supports symmetric multiprocessor (SMP) designs that employ up to two CPUs. If you install Windows XP Home Edition on an SMP system, it will not use the second processor.
Support for 64-bit CPUs	Systems built around a 64-bit Intel Itanium processor must use a 64-bit version of Windows XP Professional; the Home Edition is unable to work with this CPU.
Advanced security features	Several sophisticated security capabilities are found only in Windows XP Professional, including support for Encrypting File System and Internet Protocol Security (IPSec) as well as the ability to assign complex access controls to files.
Automated System Recovery	The Backup program in Windows XP Professional includes tools that let you easily rebuild a system from scratch in the event of a catastrophic failure.
Internet Information Services	If you use Windows XP Professional, you can set up a personal Web server using Internet Information Services (IIS) 5; this capability is not available in Home Edition.
Remote Desktop Connection	With this feature, you can configure a Windows XP Professional machine to allow remote access, either across a local area network or over the Internet. The client machine can be running any 32-bit version of Windows, including Windows 95/98/Me, Windows 2000, or any version of Windows XP. You cannot make a remote connection to a system running Windows XP Home Edition (although it does include the similar Remote Assistance feature, which allows a remote user to share the desktop for support and training purposes).

Appendix A

1218

Table A-1. *(continued)*

Feature	Description
Offline files	The offline files feature, available only in Windows XP Professional, lets you use network files even when your computer isn't connected to the network. When you reconnect, Windows synchronizes your offline files with their network versions.
Domain membership	On a corporate network, Windows XP Professional can join domain and take advantage of domain-based management features such as group policies and roaming profiles. A system running Windows XP Home Edition can access domain resources such as printers and servers, but it does not exist as an object in the domain.
Dynamic disks	Windows XP Professional allows you to create disk volumes that span multiple hard drives; this capability allows you to increase the storage capacity and performance of drives. Windows XP Home Edition supports only basic volumes, which follow the same basic partitioning rules as disk structures created in Windows 95/98 and Windows Me.
System administration	Windows XP Professional includes a number of management tools and utilities that let you customize your system and lock it down in ways that cannot be done with Home Edition. Foremost of these tools is Group Policy, which includes myriad settings for controlling the way your system is used. Windows XP Professional also includes support for security templates, which lets you apply an assortment of security settings to your own computer and to others on your network. You'll also find a handful of Microsoft Management Console snap-ins and command-line utilities that are available only in Professional.

Appendix A

Appendix B

Windows XP Tablet PC Edition

The Tablet PC is a new type of notebook computer that uses a pen for input, including handwritten input such as notes. Microsoft Windows XP Tablet PC Edition is a version of Windows XP that includes all the features of Windows XP Professional plus features and utilities designed for the Tablet PC.

The most obvious difference between a Tablet PC and an ordinary desktop computer is its mobility. Unlike a notebook computer, a Tablet PC doesn't require you to stake out desk space and use a keyboard and mouse to input text and use the operating system. Instead, you can carry your tablet to a meeting and enter your handwritten notes directly on the screen, using an accessory application called Windows Journal. You can share those notes with other people just as you wrote them, or you can convert your handwritten notes to text (and correct the text that wasn't converted correctly, because the handwriting recognition feature isn't flawless) and then insert the information into other documents. You might create a Microsoft Word document, for example, and then send it by e-mail to a colleague or coworker who can add his or her own handwritten annotations to the document and then send it back to you.

To facilitate use of the pen, and especially its use as a writing instrument, Tablet PCs are designed so that you can change the screen orientation from landscape to portrait (and back to landscape) without rebooting. The change in orientation happens almost instantaneously. With the pen, you can use the on-screen keyboard in Input Panel to enter characters and other symbols by tapping them, or you can enter data through Input Panel's writing pad.

In this appendix, we'll outline the special features included in Windows XP Tablet PC Edition. A complete introduction to the Tablet PC is provided in *Tablet PC Quick Reference* (Microsoft Press, 2002). Also, the Help And Support Center in Windows XP Tablet PC Edition provides several animated tutorials and other help topics that cover Tablet PC basics.

Using the Pen

The pen is the device you use to write notes, enter text and other information, and interact with the user interface on your tablet. In Windows Journal, or when you're using the writing pad in Input Panel, you write with the pen as you do with any writing instrument. When the keyboard is active in Input Panel, tap the characters and symbols with the pen to enter text and numbers. You can use the pen to activate regular keyboard shortcuts as well.

You can use the pen in five basic ways:

- **Use your pen as a mouse.** The pen can be used like a mouse at any time in any application in which you would use a regular mouse. The pen can provide both left and right mouse button actions as well as other familiar mouse operations. Table B-1 compares mouse and pen actions.

- **Use your pen in lieu of a keyboard as a text input device.** With the Input Panel's keyboard, the pen can be used to input text in any application with which you would use a regular keyboard.

- **Create ink that becomes a static image.** Some applications accept pen input and convert it to images. The images can be inserted into documents or attached to e-mail messages.

- **Create ink that becomes both a static image and converted text.** Some applications can contain the image of the ink you create and the text recognized from your handwriting. For example, Word can insert your handwriting into a document and show you the results of converting the handwriting to text.

- **Create rich ink.** Currently only a few applications have this highest level of pen integration, but more are in development and will no doubt appear as the Tablet PC platform matures. In this case, you can edit, format, and even search the ink you create. Windows Journal supports this use of the pen.

Table B-1. **Comparison of Mouse and Pen Actions**

Mouse Action	Pen Action
Point	Point/hover
Single-click	Tap once
Double-click	Tap twice
Right-click	Press and hold

note *Ink* is a term for the pen strokes you create on the tablet screen. These strokes are not recorded by the computer as images. Instead they are represented by equations describing the relative sizes, angles, and directions of the lines. In different situations, your ink may be converted to text, converted to an image, or saved in its original format.

As on a desktop computer or a conventional laptop, shortcut menus save time and effort on a Tablet PC. You can use the pen as you would use a mouse to right-click. To open a shortcut menu with the pen, press the pen tip against the screen until the mouse icon appears, and then lift the pen off the screen. Point at the command you want, and then tap it.

Some pen designs incorporate a button that serves the same function as the right button on a conventional mouse; these designs make it even easier to open shortcut menus. To right-click with a pen button, hold down the pen button before you make contact with the screen, tap the item you want to right-click, and then lift the pen off the screen before releasing the pen button.

Configuring the Tablet PC Workspace

Windows XP Tablet PC Edition provides a number of ways in which you can change and customize the tablet workspace. The following sections provide some suggestions that might help you use your tablet more effectively.

Adjusting Text and Icon Size

The standard size for text and icons on your tablet is set to make the most of the limited screen space that's inevitable when designing a portable computer. If you're having trouble seeing the icons and on-screen buttons on your tablet, you can increase the size of most of your icons and on-screen text. Be sure to close any programs that are running and have your tablet in landscape screen orientation before making these adjustments.

Appendix B

Open the Display item in Control Panel. Go to the Settings tab, and then tap the Advanced button. Use the DPI Setting list on the General tab to change the DPI (dots per inch) from 96 DPI to 120 DPI. The new settings take effect after you restart Windows. The screen will appear somewhat more crowded with icons at this larger size, but you should find that legibility improves.

Customizing the Start Menu

Using a pen to navigate menus such as the Start menu, which has several layers of submenus, can take a little more time than navigating such a menu with a mouse. The extra time stems from the need to lift the pen after each tap to see the next submenu.

tip When using the Start menu, tap to open each submenu rather than hover and wait for the menu to expand on its own.

The Taskbar And Start Menu item in Control Panel provides options for adding recently used documents and favorites to the Start menu. Organizing the menu in this way puts some common items only two taps away. Open the Taskbar And Start Menu item in Control Panel. On the Start Menu tab, tap Customize. You'll see the dialog box shown here. Note that the options listed below are identical to those found on a standard desktop or notebook PC running Windows XP; however, you may choose to use different settings on a Tablet PC to make the most of limited screen real estate.

- **Small or large icons.** Using small icons lets you put more items on the Start menu without causing the menu to spill over the screen. The size of the icon labels does not change.

- **Number of programs listed.** Windows XP keeps track of the programs you use most often and places them on the first level of the Start menu for quick access. By increasing the number of programs in this list, you can save the time required to work through different layers of menus.

- **Show e-mail and Internet.** These options place items on the Start menu for the e-mail client and Web browser you choose. The items appear above the list of commonly used programs so that you can find them with ease.

Customizing the Taskbar

You might want to set up the taskbar on your tablet to conserve space and to account for the differences between pen input and using a conventional mouse. To adjust taskbar settings in Windows XP Tablet PC Edition, press and hold the pen on an empty spot on the taskbar, and select Properties from the shortcut menu. (You can also open the Start Menu And Taskbar item in Control Panel to modify the taskbar.) Here's a summary of ways you can set up the taskbar for a tablet:

- **Turn off auto hide.** The auto hide feature makes the taskbar disappear when it is not in use. The taskbar appears again when you move the pointer to the edge of the screen. On many tablets, reliably moving the pointer far enough toward the edge to display the taskbar is difficult. Although the screen area on a tablet is relatively small—so hiding the taskbar automatically would bring good benefits—having clear access to the taskbar is more important.

- **Group similar items.** Windows XP allows you to group on the taskbar items belonging to one program when more than one window is open in that program. Grouping similar items is invaluable on a tablet because the taskbar is usually restricted in size.

> **note** You can fine-tune how program items are grouped on the taskbar by using the Tweak UI utility. For more information about Tweak UI, see "Changing Views in Common Dialog Boxes," page 424.

- **Hide inactive icons.** Most of the time you don't need to see all of the system tray icons on the taskbar. Selecting the Hide Inactive Icons option will create more space on the taskbar.

- **Show Quick Launch.** The Quick Launch bar on a tablet allows for one-tap launching of your favorite programs. Add quick launch icons for the programs you use most often.

Appendix B

> **tip**   **Dock the taskbar for greater convenience**
>
> You can also dock the taskbar along the side of your tablet or at the top of the screen. In either of these locations, you might find that you have a better view of items on the Start menu and the taskbar and that the pen movements required to point and tap these items are less awkward. When you switch to the landscape screen orientation, as you do when you work with your tablet in laptop mode or when your computer is connected to an external monitor and keyboard, the taskbar will still be at the top or side. You can move the taskbar to the bottom of the screen in landscape orientation if you find that position more convenient.

Tablet and Pen Settings

In Windows XP Tablet PC Edition, Control Panel includes the Tablet And Pen Settings dialog box, shown in Figure B-1. The dialog box includes options for calibrating pen and pointer movements, setting the display orientation, assigning actions to tablet buttons, and customizing pen actions.

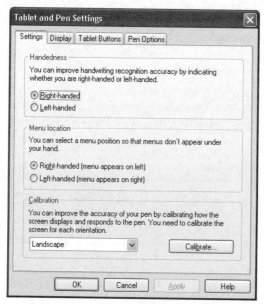

Figure B-1.   The Tablet And Pen Settings dialog box lets you assign actions to the buttons on the tablet's chassis, adjust the speed with which pen movements are recognized, and choose other options.

Screen Calibration

The purpose of screen calibration is to adjust how the pen and pointer move together on the screen. The precision with which you can control the pointer's location with the pen depends in part on how you hold the pen and your posture in relation to your tablet. The calibration tool samples four points on the screen to gauge your personal perspective. When you calibrate the screen, try to orient the tablet surface and your head so that they are in the same position they will be in when you use your tablet. You need to calibrate the screen for both landscape and portrait orientations.

After calibrating your tablet, use it for a while to see how well the pen directs the pointer. Let some time pass before calibrating again. If the pointer doesn't follow the pen well over the entire screen, hold the pen more upright. If the pointer and pen track well together over most of the screen but not in a specific area, try calibrating the tablet again.

> **note** The Settings tab in the Tablet And Pen Settings dialog box also provides options for setting up your tablet for right-hand or left-hand control. Your orientation affects the accuracy of handwriting recognition and the positioning of menus.

Display Settings

Use the Display tab to switch screen orientation (landscape or portrait) and set up the sequence in which changes in screen orientation occur. The Display tab also lets you adjust the brightness of the screen for when the tablet is plugged in and when it is operating on batteries.

Tablet Buttons

The Tablet PC chassis can include buttons that you can set up to perform a variety of actions, including standard keyboard commands (pressing Enter, for example) or running an application. The default actions for these buttons are to emulate the use of the Down Arrow, Up Arrow, Esc, Tab, and Enter keys and to change the screen orientation. You can customize these actions for your own needs by tapping the Change button and then selecting the action you want. The tablet buttons can also include a function button that allows you to assign two actions for each of the other buttons. Figure B-2 on the next page shows the Tablet Buttons tab.

By default, the tablet buttons perform the same actions for all screen orientations; however, you can assign different actions to the buttons for different orientations. Using the buttons for actions associated with the keyboard is most helpful when you're using the tablet with the pen only. Having quick access to these actions is not as helpful when the tablet's full keyboard is available. For that case, you can assign the tablet buttons actions such as running an application you use frequently or changing to the next track on the CD you're listening to.

Figure B-2. Tablet buttons give you access to your most needed keyboard commands.

Pen Options

The Pen Options tab includes settings for how the pen behaves in performing actions you are used to carrying out with the mouse. Table B-2 lists the four pen actions and the settings you can change.

Table B-2. **Settings for Pen Actions**

Pen Action (Mouse Equivalent)	Settings
Double-tap (double-click)	The duration of time that can occur between two taps and still have the tablet recognize the taps as a double-tap
	The distance that can separate two taps and still have them be recognized as a double-tap

Table B-2. *(continued)*

Pen Action (Mouse Equivalent)	Settings
Press and hold (right-click)	The amount of time you need to press and hold the pen against the screen to emulate a right-click
	The amount of time that passes while you press and hold the pen before you have to select a right-click action
Point/hover (point)	The amount of space you can move the pen and still have the pen's hovering be recognized as pointing to an object or an area on the screen
Start Input Panel gesture	The extent of the side-to-side movement you need to make with the pen to open Input Panel

tip Some pens with pen buttons have a combination button that acts as a right-click if pushed one way and an eraser if pressed differently. The Pen Options tab includes a setting for whether to use the top of the pen as an eraser. You can select this setting independently of the setting to use the pen button to right-click.

Input Panel

Input Panel is an online keyboard, writing pad, and speech recognition tool. You need to use Input Panel when you are working with another application and using only the pen. Input Panel converts your handwritten notes to text and provides its keyboard for pen input. Use the tabs, listed below, which are found at the bottom right of Input Panel, to display the writing pad or keyboard.

note We don't cover using Input Panel for speech recognition in this appendix. For information about requirements for speech recognition, see the Speech Tutorial in the Windows XP Tablet PC Edition Help And Support Center.

- **Writing Pad.** When you are using the writing pad, shown on the next page, tap where you want to insert text or other information in the document you're creating, and then use the pen to write. Tap Send to insert the text or other data in the document. Use the pad of quick keys to enter a new line in the document, delete or backspace over text, insert a tab, and so on.

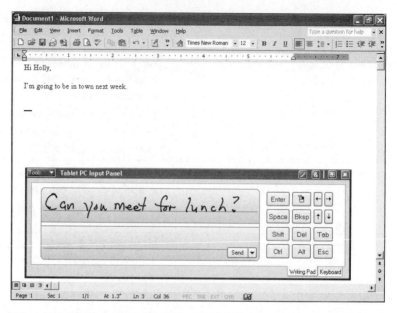

Select Text Preview on the Input Panel Tools menu to display a small pane in which you can review how well your handwriting's been recognized before inserting the information in the document. You can use the quick keys or the Input Panel keyboard to correct any text that wasn't converted correctly, or you can select the word or phrase you need to correct and then tap the caret that appears to open a menu of alternative words.

● **Keyboard.** With the keyboard, tap in the document where the information should be inserted, and then use the pen to tap the characters, numbers, and symbols you need to enter. The keyboard behaves much like a regular keyboard: tap Shift to enter an uppercase letter or other symbol, tap the arrow keys to move the insertion point, and so on. You can open the symbols key pad by tapping the ampersand icon in Input Panel's title bar. The Input Panel keyboard is shown on the facing page.

1230

In the upper left corner of the Input Panel window is the Tools menu. From this menu, you can open the speech recognition tool, open the text preview pane, dock Input Panel, open online help, and more. To set up options for Input Panel, tap Options on the Tools menu. The options you can set for Input Panel include the following:

- Change the number of lines in the writing pad—either one or two.

- Elect to have your handwriting converted to text and inserted in a document automatically after a set interval of time (.25 seconds to 10 seconds).

- Display or hide the pad of quick keys (the arrow keys, the Enter key, and other keys you use to move around in a document and work with the text you write).

- Display the Turn On Write Anywhere button on the Input Panel title bar. Write Anywhere is a feature that enlarges the area on your screen that's available for pen input. For more information about Write Anywhere, see the following section.

- Set speech recognition options.

- Set options for how Input Panel is displayed.

Write Anywhere

Write Anywhere turns most of your screen into a writing area. Word processing documents, presentation slides, and other types of documents are then available for handwritten input that is converted to text.

The first step in using Write Anywhere is to select the Show The Turn On Write Anywhere Button On The Title Bar option in Input Panel's Options dialog box. With the button displayed, open a document window—either a new document or a document you want to edit or annotate—tap in the document where you want to insert text, tap the Turn On Write Anywhere button, and then begin to write.

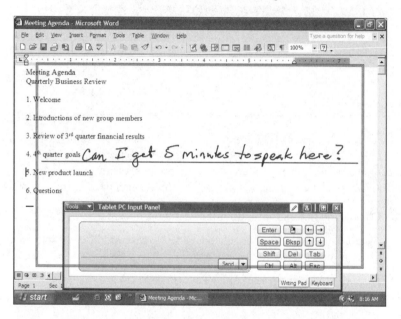

By default, the borders of the writing area are outlined. When your pen is just above the screen, Input Panel displays a straight line that you should use as a guide for handwriting. You'll see better results in the placement of text and in how accurately handwriting is recognized by writing just above this line. Your handwritten information is converted to text after a short period of time, and you can then use the text correction features in Input Panel to fix any text that wasn't converted perfectly.

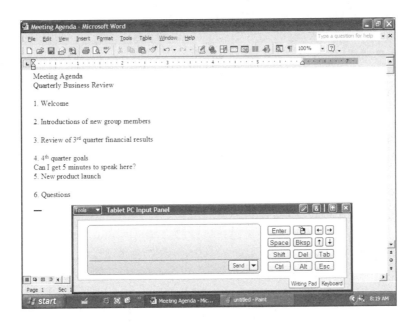

> **note** Use the Write Anywhere tab of the Options dialog box in Input Panel to adjust the thickness and color of ink, the length of time that elapses before handwriting is converted to text, and how the writing area is displayed. At this time, Write Anywhere recognizes only handwriting in English.

Windows Journal

Windows XP Tablet PC Edition includes an accessory application named Windows Journal that works like an electronic version of a legal pad with an endless supply of paper. Using Journal, you can take your tablet to a meeting and enter electronic ink notes. The operating system stores and indexes your handwritten notes, which you can then retrieve and update or edit. You can also search through a series of notes using the words and phrases you've written as the criteria.

Windows Journal appears on the Programs menu with the rest of your applications. Journal opens a new note page when it starts. To begin a note, write a name for the note in the Note Title box at the top of the page. This title will be used as the default file name for the note when you save it. You can then write on the screen with the tablet pen as if you were using pencil and paper.

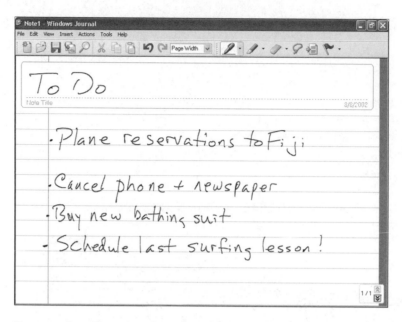

You can select all or a portion of a note and convert the handwriting to text. You can also draw by hand in Journal, include graphics files in the notes you create, print notes, and create notes that occupy multiple pages.

Writing in Journal

When you write notes in Journal, you can choose different degrees of fineness for the pen's point or use the pen as a highlighter to emphasize a portion of a note. When necessary, you can use your pen as an eraser by tapping the Eraser button on the Journal toolbar. The Pen And Highlighter Settings dialog box, shown here, supplies options for which pen point to use and other preferences. In the dialog box, you can change the width of the pen's point, the color of the digital ink, and the tip style. You can make similar selections for use of the pen as a highlighter.

To add or remove space between the information you've written in a note, use the Insert/Remove Space command. You position the dotted line and pointer where you want to adjust the white space, place the tip of your pen on the screen, and then drag.

> **note** Space is inserted or removed in one-line increments by default. You can gain finer control by clearing the option Insert Space In Full Line Increments on the View tab of the Options dialog box in Journal.

Converting Notes to Text

You can copy and paste handwritten notes into another note. Use the Selection tool on the Journal toolbar to select the portion of the note you want to reuse.

Windows Journal can also convert your handwritten notes to text. You can correct the words or phrases that Journal doesn't recognize correctly and then store the text with the note or use it in a different application.

Select the handwriting you want to convert, and then choose Convert Handwriting To Text from the Action menu. Journal displays the Text Correction dialog box, shown here.

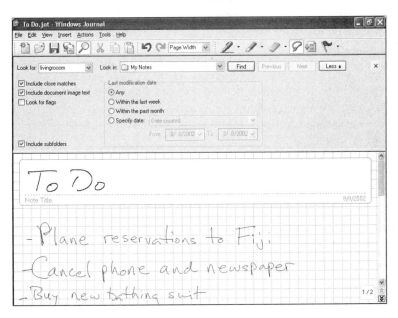

The text that Journal did not recognize is highlighted, and the corresponding handwriting from the note is displayed for comparison. Correct the text by selecting an incorrect word and choosing the word you need from the list of alternatives provided on the right. You can also tap a word or phrase you need to correct, tap the green caret that then appears, and choose a word from the menu that pops up. The list of alternative words that's displayed in the pop-up menu in Journal is the same list you would

1235

see using Input Panel. It uses the same dictionary, so vocabulary added in Journal will appear in Input Panel as well. If you choose the rewrite option from the pop-up menu, Input Panel opens automatically. The list of alternatives on the right of the Text Correction dialog box is a little longer and offers a wider range of words.

While the Text Correction dialog box is open, you can rearrange text by dragging and dropping and can add or remove line breaks. By default, the correction tool enters a line break wherever a new line appeared in the Journal note. You can remove these line breaks by tapping the Options button and clearing the option to preserve line breaks.

When you tap OK in the Text Correction dialog box, a Journal message asks whether you want to copy the converted text to the Clipboard, preserving your original ink, or replace the ink in the note by a text box containing the text.

> **note** You can use the Copy As Text command on the Edit menu to convert a handwritten note to text and place the text on the Clipboard. The Copy As Text command displays the Text Correction dialog box prior to copying the text.

How Handwriting Is Recognized in Journal

Every time you put ink on a page, Journal assesses the strokes to see whether they might form a word. If Journal recognizes the strokes as a word, the strokes are grouped and the handwriting recognizer records its guess for the word as well as several alternatives. The list of possible words is stored as part of the Journal note. The recognition process takes place in the background so that it doesn't interfere with your work. If you choose to convert your handwriting to text, the recognition is already complete.

This method of writing and handwriting recognition differs from those that users of the Pocket PC or Palm devices are used to. With those devices, you enter one character at a time or draw letters following a prescribed path. When you are using the writing pad in Input Panel, you can display a character recognizer that lets you enter text in a manner similar to these popular mobile devices.

Converting Text to Items in Microsoft Outlook

Journal's Action menu includes commands that convert text and information you select in a note to an Outlook e-mail message, appointment, contact, or task. The information you select is converted to text and displayed in a version of the Text Correction dialog box. (The dialog box is named for the Outlook item you are converting the note to.) When you tap Convert in the dialog box, a new Outlook item appears, and the converted text is inserted in the body of the item for an e-mail message, appointment, or task or in the informational area at the bottom of a contact item.

Figure B-3 shows an Outlook task created from a note in Windows Journal. You can use Input Panel to fill in other information in the item and then send it or add it to your calendar, task list, or list of contacts in Outlook.

Figure B-3. This Outlook task was created by converting a handwritten note in Journal.

Journal Page Setup Options

The Page Setup dialog box in Journal provides the means to change the line style of the Journal page. Formats range from wide- or narrow-ruled lines to variations of a quadrille grid (commonly used in engineering drawings) to custom formats you set up yourself. You can also change the color of the writing pad and choose illustrated backgrounds.

Saving and Finding Notes

The notes you write in Windows Journal can be stored in folders, just like any document, so that you can refer to them later. A note is saved by default to the My Notes folder as a Windows Journal Note file type, with a .jnt extension. Journal uses its recognized version of what you write in the Note Title box as the default file name. You can change the Windows file system name by using the regular keyboard or the onscreen keyboard in Input Panel.

To see a list of notes you've written recently, tap View Recent Notes on the Journal toolbar. You can then open a note based on its inked title.

When you need to find a note you've saved, tap File, Search to display Journal's search pane, shown here.

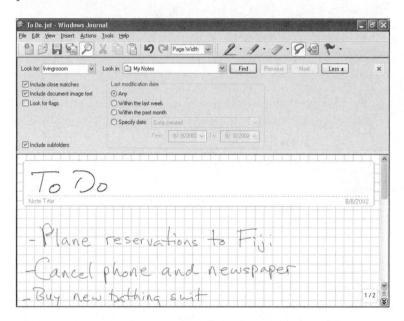

In the Look For box, pick a word or phrase you've used to search with in the past, or use Input Panel to write or tap in the term you want to search by. Select the location to search in the Look In box. The search pane displays a list of the notes in which Journal finds the word or phrase you searched for.

As mentioned earlier, Journal performs background recognition of your handwriting and stores the list of probable words and alternatives. This word list is used for both converting your ink to text and for finding words in your notes. When you search your notes, Journal shows items in which the search text matched the words it recognized as well as the main alternatives. By finding alternatives, a search is more likely to find the text you're looking for, but you will also see several near misses.

> **note** If you use the search tool on the Start menu to search for text within documents, it will find matches in handwritten words, text boxes, and imported document text in Journal notes. Search only finds the handwriting recognizer's most likely word, however, and not any of the alternates.

Text boxes and text in imported documents can be included in a search of notes, but the results depend on how the text was inserted in the note. Text boxes created from converted handwriting retain their alternative word lists, and these are included in the search. If a text box contains text copied from another program, no alternative list exists and only exact matches are found. Imported text is included in most searches but only returns exact matches. If you don't want alternative words or the imported text included in your search, tap the More button in the search pane, and clear the options for close matches or document image text.

Sharing Journal Notes

If you need to share a note with someone who also has a Tablet PC, you can send a note as an e-mail attachment in the note format. The recipient can open the note in Windows Journal to read and edit it. You can send notes as attachments in other formats to colleagues, friends, and family who don't have a tablet. These formats can be viewed in Microsoft Internet Explorer.

Annotating Office XP Documents in Journal

When you work with documents created in Microsoft Office XP or other applications, you can import the image of a document into Journal and then annotate that document with handwritten notes. Word documents, Web pages, PowerPoint slides, and pictures can all be imported. When you import a document, Journal opens the original application and creates an image of the document, which is then displayed in the Journal window, as shown here.

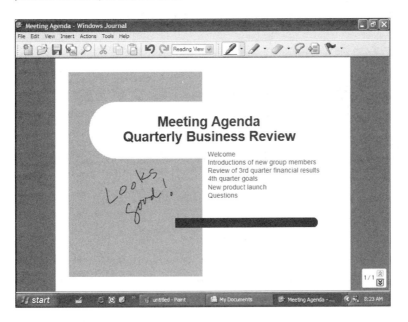

> **note** If the program that created the document is not installed on your computer, you might have trouble importing the document into Journal.

Imported documents are opened as a new note with the same page dimensions as the original document. For the files you import that are created on 8.5-by-11-inch pages, the text might appear small on the tablet screen. Adjust the view setting as you work to show the whole page, and zoom in when you need to see the text more clearly. You can write and insert text boxes or pictures on the surface of the imported material, but you cannot select or change it. Of course, the annotations you add to the document in Journal don't become part of the original document.

You can add pages to imported documents in the same way you add pages to a regular Journal note. Because the document is not editable, when you insert or remove space in the note, your ink will move but the content of the imported document is untouched.

Office XP and the Tablet PC

In the previous section, we described how you can annotate Office XP documents by importing an image of the document into Journal. You can also add ink annotations to Office XP documents in the Office application, provided you have installed the Office XP Pack for Tablet PC add-in.

In Outlook, for example, you can handwrite an e-mail message. Open a new message item, and then click the Insert Ink Canvas button on the message item's Standard toolbar.

Use your pen to compose the message within the ink canvas. A pen and ink toolbar provides handy access to pen options.

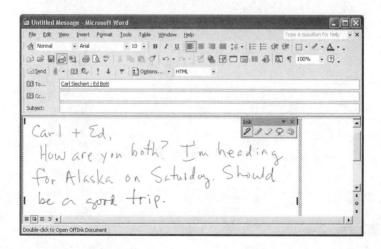

Other Office documents can also include ink annotations. Annotations in a Word document, for example, appear in an ink canvas on the page or as an ink comment, which you can view together with other comments. Annotations in Word show up even on a computer that's not a Tablet PC, as shown in Figure B-4.

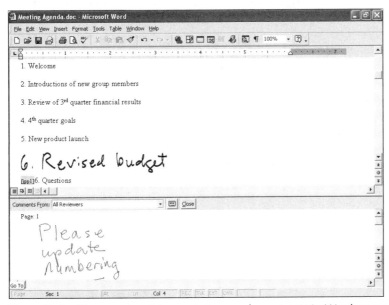

Figure B-4. You can view ink annotations and comments in Word on a computer that's not a tablet.

Working with the Command Prompt

Microsoft Windows XP allows you to enter commands, run batch programs, and run applications by typing commands at the command prompt. If you're accustomed to performing administrative tasks at the command line, you don't need to change your ways in Windows XP. You can open multiple Command Prompt sessions, with each session protected from any failures that might occur in other sessions.

Starting and Ending a Command Prompt Session

To get to the command prompt, do any of the following:

- Choose Start, All Programs, Accessories, Command Prompt.

- Choose Start, Run, and type **cmd**, with or without command-line arguments.

- Double-click the Cmd icon in your %SystemRoot%\System32 folder.

- Double-click any shortcut for Cmd.exe.

You can open as many Command Prompt windows as you like. With each additional window, you start another Command Prompt session. For example, you might want to open two Command Prompt windows to see two directories in side-by-side windows. To open another Command Prompt window, type **start** or **start cmd** at the command prompt. (These commands produce the same result. If you don't type a program name after typing **start**, Windows assumes that you want to start Cmd.exe.)

1243

At Home with Windows XP

The Command Prompt window works identically in Windows XP Home Edition and Windows XP Professional. The only disadvantage for Home Edition users is that the Help And Support Center in Windows XP Professional includes more detailed information about command-line utilities.

---

tip   **Start a command-line program with AutoRun**

By setting a registry value, you can make a particular application, command, batch file, or script run any time Command Prompt starts. For information about this feature, see "Using AutoRun to Execute Commands When Command Prompt Starts," page 1246.

When the Command Prompt window is active, you can end a Command Prompt session in any of the following ways:

- Type **exit** at the command prompt.
- Click the Close button.
- Click the Control menu icon and choose Close from the Control menu.
- Double-click the Control menu icon.

If you are running a character-based program in the Command Prompt window, you should use the program's normal exit command to quit the program before attempting to close the window and end the Command Prompt session; otherwise, it's possible that you'll lose unsaved data. However, if you are sure that the program doesn't have any unsaved files, you can safely and quickly close it using one of the last three methods in the preceding list. If a program is running, a dialog box appears asking whether you really want to terminate the program.

Starting Command Prompt at a Particular Folder

You can add a shortcut menu command to the folder file type that will allow you to right-click any folder in Windows Explorer and start a Command Prompt session focused on that folder. The easiest way to add this capability is to install the CmdHere PowerToy, available as an unsupported download from Microsoft. (For details about this and other Windows XP PowerToys, see "Customizing Windows XP with Tweak UI," page 327.) You can also add this task manually, by using the following procedure to edit the registry:

1 In Notepad or another plain-text editor, create a file with the following data:

```
Windows Registry Editor Version 5.00
[HKEY_CLASSES_ROOT\Folder\shell\Cmd Here]
```

1244

Appendix C

```
@="Command &Prompt Here"
[HKEY_CLASSES_ROOT\Folder\shell\Cmd Here\command]
@="cmd.exe /k pushd %L"
```

2 Save the file, using the extension .reg. For example, save the file as Cmdhere.reg.

3 Double-click the new .reg file, and click Yes at the prompt to add the information to the registry.

InsideOut

Cmd.exe is the Windows XP command processor. Command.com, the 16-bit command processor of MS-DOS days, is still supported, but unless you have a legacy application that requires it, you should use Cmd.exe. You can run external MS-DOS commands, batch files, and other executables with either processor, but Cmd includes a few internal commands not available in Command.com, and some of the internal commands common to both have additional options in Cmd. Only Cmd understands long file names, and most of the command-line syntax, described later in this appendix, is available only with Cmd.

These steps create a new command that appears on the shortcut menu whenever you right-click a folder in Windows Explorer. Choosing this command opens a new Command Prompt session, with the selected folder current.

Starting Command Prompt and Running a Command

The /C and /K command-line arguments allow you to start a Command Prompt session and run a command—an MS-DOS command or a batch file, for example. The difference between the two is that Cmd /C *commandstring* terminates the Command Prompt session as soon as *commandstring* has finished executing, whereas Cmd /K *commandstring* keeps the Command Prompt session going after *commandstring* has finished. Note the following:

- You must include either /C or /K if you want to specify a command string as an argument to Cmd. If you type **cmd** *commandstring*, the command processor simply ignores *commandstring*.

- While *commandstring* is executing, you can't interact with the command processor. To run a command and keep the Command Prompt window interactive, use the Start command. For example, to run Mybatch.bat and continue issuing MS-DOS commands while the batch file is running, type **cmd /k start mybatch.bat**.

- If you include other command-line arguments along with /C or /K, the /C or /K must be the last argument before *commandstring*.

> For more information about using Command Prompt's command-line syntax, see "Using Cmd's Command-Line Syntax," page 1249.

Cmd.exe and Other Command Prompts

Cmd.exe, the application whose name is Command Prompt, is only one of several forms of command prompt available in Windows XP. Others include the Run command on the Start menu, the Address toolbar, the Address bar in Windows Explorer, and the Address bar in Microsoft Internet Explorer. In many ways, these command prompts function alike. You can start a Windows-based application from any of them, for example. (If you start from Internet Explorer, you need to include an explicit path specification, or Internet Explorer will try to find a URL that matches your command string.) What's exceptional about Cmd.exe is that it allows you to execute internal MS-DOS commands (that is, commands that are not stored in discrete .exe files).

Using AutoRun to Execute Commands When Command Prompt Starts

Command Prompt's equivalent to the old MS-DOS Autoexec batch mechanism is a feature called AutoRun. By default, Command Prompt executes on startup whatever it finds in the following two registry values:

- The AutoRun value in HKLM\Software\Microsoft\Command Processor
- The AutoRun value in HKCU\Software\Microsoft\Command Processor

The AutoRun value in HKLM affects all user accounts at the current machine. The AutoRun value in HKCU affects only the current user account. If both values are present, both are executed—HKLM before HKCU.

Both AutoRun values are of data type string, which means they can contain a single string. (You can enter a multi-string value, but Windows XP ignores all but the first string.) To execute a sequence of separate Command Prompt statements, therefore, you must use command symbols or store the sequence as a batch program, and then use AutoRun to call the batch program.

To specify an AutoRun value, open a registry editor and navigate to the Command Processor key in either HKLM or HKCU. Create a new string value there, and name it AutoRun. Then specify your command string as the data for AutoRun, exactly as you would type it at the command prompt.

To disable AutoRun commands for a particular Command Prompt session, start Command Prompt with /D. For more about Command Prompt's command-line syntax, see "Using Cmd's Command-Line Syntax," page 1249.

Using Commands

In most respects, entering commands or running programs at the Windows XP command prompt is the same as using the command prompt of any other operating system—MS-DOS, OS/2, UNIX. If you've used one command prompt, you've used them all. Every operating system has a command to delete files, another to display lists of files, another to copy files, and so on. The names and details might differ, but it's the same cast of characters.

The commands and features available at the Windows XP command prompt most closely resemble those of MS-DOS 5—with some important enhancements and additions.

---

tip   **Type /? for help**

You can get help on any Command Prompt command by typing its name followed by /?. For example, to see a list and explanation of the command-line switches for the Dir command, type **dir /?**. Alternatively, type the word **help** followed by the command name—for example, **help dir**. For help with network-related commands, precede your help request with **net**. For example, type **net view /?** or **net help view** for information about the Net View command (with the Net commands, **net help** *command* provides more detailed help than **net** *command* **/?**). You can also type **help** with no arguments to get a list of the internal commands and system utilities provided with Windows XP.

Starting Programs

You can start all kinds of programs at the command prompt—programs for Windows XP, earlier versions of Windows, or MS-DOS—so you don't need to know a program's origin or type to run it. If it's on your disk, simply type its name (and path, if needed) followed by any parameters. It should run with no problem.

If you're starting a character-based program, it runs in the Command Prompt window. When you terminate the application, the command prompt returns. If you start a Windows-based program, it appears in its own window.

In early versions of Microsoft Windows NT, if you ran a Windows-based program from Command Prompt, the Command Prompt session remained inaccessible until the Windows-based program ended. To continue using Command Prompt after launching a Windows-based program, you had to launch that program with the Start command.

That behavior has changed. In Windows XP (and in Windows 2000), the Command Prompt session remains accessible by default. If you want the old behavior, launch your program with the Start command, using the Wait switch:

```
start /wait myprog.exe
```

The /Wait switch is probably not useful unless you need the old behavior for some reason. The Start command has other options that are useful, however. For Windows-based programs, you can use /Min or /Max to open the program in a minimized or maximized window. For character-based programs, you can enter (in quotation marks) the title that you want to appear on the program window. Place any parameters or switches that you use with the Start command *before* the name of the program or command you want to start. Anything after the program name is passed to the program as a command-line parameter and is ignored by Start.

For more information about the Start command, type **start /?** at the command prompt.

Using Command Extensions

Command extensions are changes or additions to the following internal commands: Del, Erase, Color, Cd, Chdir, Md, Mkdir, Prompt, Pushd, Popd, Set, Setlocal, Endlocal, If, For, Call, Shift, Goto, Start, Assoc, and Ftype. For example, with command extensions enabled, you can use Cd or Chdir to switch to a directory whose name includes space characters, without enclosing the path specification in quotation marks. For details about a particular command's extensions, type the command name followed by /?. (You can also type **help**, followed by the command name.)

Command extensions are available only in Cmd.exe, not in Command.com, and are enabled by default. Set the DWORD value EnableExtensions in HKLM\Software\ Microsoft\Command Processor to 0 to disable them for all user accounts at the current machine. Set EnableExtensions in HKCU\Software\Microsoft\Command Processor to 0 to disable them for the current user account. Start Command Prompt with /E:off or /E:on to disable or enable them for the current session, regardless of the registry settings.

Using File-Name and Directory-Name Completion

Command Prompt offers an invaluable file-name and directory-name completion feature that can save you the trouble of typing long paths or file names. If you start typing a command string and then press Tab, the default *completion character*, Command Prompt proposes the next file or directory name that's consistent with what you've typed so far. For example, to switch to a directory that starts with the letter *Q*, you can type **cd q** and press the directory-name completion character as many times as necessary until the directory you want appears.

- By default, the completion character for both file names and folders is the Tab key. You can change this setting by using Tweak UI (part of the

Windows XP PowerToys collection, described in "Customizing Windows XP with Tweak UI," page 327). To make this change manually, modify the registry values of HKCU\Software\Microsoft\Command Processor\ CompletionChar and HKCU\Software\Microsoft\Command Processor\ PathCompletionChar. These DWORD values specify the file and directory completion characters, respectively, for the current user. (To change the settings for all users, modify the same keys in HKLM.) If you decide to experiment with these registry settings, keep in mind the following: If CompletionChar is defined and PathCompletionChar is either absent or set to the hexadecimal value 0x40, the CompletionChar setting works for both file completion and directory completion. In all cases, the completion characters should be specified as hexadecimal values—for example, 0x9 for Tab, 0x4 for Ctrl+D, 0x6 for Ctrl+F, 0xC for Ctrl+L, and so on.

● Settings made via HKLM are added to those made via HKCU. In other words, you can set completion characters for all users via HKLM, and individual users can add their own completion characters via HKCU.

You can also override the registry settings for an individual Command Prompt session by starting the session with Cmd /F:on or Cmd /F:off. Cmd /F:on starts a Command Prompt session with Ctrl+D as the path-completion character and Ctrl+F as the file-completion character, disabling the completion characters set in the registry. Cmd /F:off starts a Command Prompt session with no completion characters, regardless of your registry settings. Cmd /F:on and Cmd /F:off both disable the Tab key as a completion character.

---

tip   **Use wildcards for file-name and directory-name completion**

Command Prompt recognizes wildcards in file and path specifications. Typing **cd pro***, for example, might take you to your Program Files folder (depending, of course, on where you are when you type it). Because you can include multiple wildcards in a string, you can even create formulations such as cd pro*\com*\mic* to get to Program Files\Common Files\Microsoft Shared.

Using Cmd's Command-Line Syntax

The complete command-line syntax for Cmd.exe is

```
cmd [/a | /u] [/q] [/d] [/e:on | /e:off] [/f:on | /f:off] [/v:on |
/v:off] [[/s] [/c | /k] commandstring]
```

All arguments are optional.

/A | /U   This argument lets you specify the encoding system used for text that's piped to a file or other device. Use /A for ANSI or /U for Unicode. The default is ANSI.

/Q The /Q argument starts Command Prompt with echo off. (With echo off, you don't need to include an @echo off line to suppress screen output in a batch program. To turn echo back on after starting Command Prompt with /Q, enter **echo on** at the command prompt.)

/D The /D argument disables execution of any AutoRun commands specified in the registry. (For more information, see "Using AutoRun to Execute Commands When Command Prompt Starts," page 1246.)

/E:on | /E:off The /E argument allows you to override the current registry settings regarding command extensions. (See "Using Command Extensions," page 1248.)

/F:on | /F:off The /F argument allows you to override the current registry settings regarding file- and directory-name completion. (See "Using File-Name and Directory-Name Completion," page 1248.)

/V:on | /V:off The /V argument lets you enable or disable delayed variable expansion. With /V:on, for example, the variable !var! is expanded only when executed. The default is /V:off. To turn delayed variable expansion on as a default, add the DWORD value DelayedExpansion to HKLM\Software\Microsoft\Command Processor (for all users at the current machine) or HKCU\Software\Microsoft\Command Processor (for the current user account only), and set DelayedExpansion to 1. (Delayed variable expansion is useful in conditional statements and loop constructs in batch programs. For more information, type **help set** at the command prompt.)

/S [/C | /K] commandstring The alternative /C and /K arguments allow you to run a command when Command Prompt starts—with /C terminating the session at the command's completion and /K keeping it open. Including /S before /C or /K affects the processing of quotation marks in *commandstring*. For more information, see "Starting Command Prompt and Running a Command," page 1245.

If you do not include /S, *and* there are exactly two quotation marks in *commandstring, and* there are no "special" characters (&, <, >, (,), @, ^, or |) in *commandstring, and* there are one or more white-space characters (spaces, tabs, or linefeeds, for example) between the two quotation marks, *and commandstring* is the name of an executable file, then Command Prompt preserves the two quotation characters.

If the foregoing conditions are not met and if the first character in *commandstring* is a quotation mark, Command Prompt strips the first and last quotation marks from *commandstring*.

Editing the Command Line

When working at a command prompt, you often enter the same command several times, or enter several similar commands. If you make a mistake when typing a command line, you don't want to retype the whole thing—you just need to fix the part that was wrong. Windows XP includes a feature that recalls previous commands and allows you to edit them on the current command line. Table C-1 shows the editing keys and what they do.

Table C-1. **Command-Line Editing Keys**

Key	Function
Up	Recalls the previous command in the command history
Down	Recalls the next command in the command history
PgUp	Recalls the earliest command used in this session
PgDn	Recalls the most recent command used
Left	Moves left one character
Right	Moves right one character
Ctrl+Left	Moves left one word
Ctrl+Right	Moves right one word
Home	Moves to the beginning of the line
End	Moves to the end of the line
Esc	Clears the current command
F7	Displays the command history in a scrollable pop-up box
F8	Displays commands that start with characters currently on the command line
Alt+F7	Clears the command history

The command-line recall feature keeps a history of the commands entered during the Command Prompt session. To display this history, press F7. A window appears that shows the commands you have recently entered. Scroll through the history with the arrow keys to select the command you want. Then press Enter to reuse the selected command, or press the Left Arrow key to place the selected text on the command line without executing the command. (This allows you to edit the command before executing it.)

It's not necessary to display the pop-up window to use the command history. You can scroll through the history with the Up Arrow and Down Arrow keys.

The F8 key provides a useful alternative to the Up Arrow key. The Up Arrow key moves you through the commands to the top of the command buffer and then stops. F8 does the same, except that when you get to the top of the buffer, it cycles back to the bottom. Furthermore, F8 displays only commands in the buffer that begin with whatever you type before you press F8. Type d at the command prompt (don't press Enter), and then press F8 a few times. You'll cycle through recently entered commands that start with *d,* such as Dir and Del. Now type e (after the *d*), and press F8 a few more times. You'll cycle through Del commands along with any others that start with *de*. You can save a lot of keystrokes with F8 if you know the first letters of the command you're looking for.

Using Wildcards

Windows XP, like MS-DOS, recognizes two wildcard characters: *?* and *. The question mark represents any single character in a file name. The asterisk matches any number of characters.

In MS-DOS, the asterisk works only at the end of the file name or extension. Windows XP handles the asterisk much more flexibly, allowing multiple asterisks in a command string and allowing you to use the asterisk character wherever you want.

Using Command Symbols

Old-fashioned programs that take all of their input from a command line and then run unaided can be useful in a multitasking system. You can turn them loose to do complicated processing in the background while you continue to work with other programs in the foreground. Windows XP includes features that make command-line programs easier to run and more powerful and that allow you to chain programs together so that later ones use the output of their predecessors as input.

In order to work together better, many command-line programs follow a set of conventions that control their interaction:

- By default, programs take all of their input as lines of text typed at the keyboard. But input in the same format also can be redirected from a file or any device capable of sending lines of text.

- By default, programs send all of their output to the screen as lines of text. But output in the same format also can be redirected to a file or another line-oriented device such as a printer.

- Programs are written to set a number called a return value when they terminate, to indicate the results of the program.

When programs are written according to these rules, you can use the symbols in Table C-2 to control a program's input and output, and to connect or chain programs together.

Table C-2. **Command Symbols**

Symbol	Purpose
<	Redirects input
>	Redirects output
>>	Appends redirected output to existing data
|	Pipes output
&	Separates multiple commands in a command line
&&	Runs the command after && only if the command before && is successful
||	Runs the command after || only if the command before || fails
^	Treats next symbol as a character
(and)	Groups commands

The Redirection Symbols

As in MS-DOS and UNIX, Command Prompt sessions in Windows XP allow you to override the default source for input (the keyboard) or the default destination for output (the screen).

Redirecting output　To redirect output to a file, type the command followed by a greater than sign (>) and the name of the file. For example, to send the output of the Dir command to a file instead of the screen, type the following:

```
dir /b *.bat > batch.lst
```

This command line creates a file called Batch.lst that contains the names of all the .bat files in the current folder.

Using two greater than signs (>>) redirects the output and appends it to an existing file. For example:

```
dir /b *.cmd >> batch.lst
```

This command line appends a list of .cmd files to the previously created file containing .bat files. (If you use >> to append to a file that doesn't exist, Windows XP creates the file.)

Redirecting input   To redirect input from a file, type the command followed by a less than sign (<) and the name of the file. The Sort and More commands are examples of commands that can accept input from a file. The following example uses Sort to filter the file created with the Dir command above.

```
sort < batch.1st
```

The input file, Batch.lst, contains a list of .bat files followed by a list of .cmd files (assuming you have some of each in the current folder). The output to the screen has the same list of files sorted alphabetically by file name.

Redirecting Input and Output

You can redirect both input and output in a command line. For example, to use Batch.lst as input to the Sort command and send its output to a file named Sorted.lst, type the following:

```
sort < batch.1st > sorted.1st
```

Standard output and standard error   Programs can be written to send their output either to the standard output device or the standard error device. Sometimes programs are written to send different types of output to each device. You can't always tell which is which because by default both devices are the screen.

The Windows XP Type command illustrates the difference. When used with wildcards (something you can't do with the Type command in MS-DOS or Windows 95/98/Me), the Type command sends the name of each matching file to standard error and sends the contents of the file to standard output. Because they both go to the screen, you see a nice display with each file name followed by its contents.

However, if you try to redirect output to a file like this:

```
type *.bat > std.out
```

the file names still appear on your screen because standard error is still directed to the screen. Only the file contents are redirected to Std.out.

Windows XP allows you to qualify the redirection symbol by preceding it with a number. Use 1> (or simply >) for standard output and 2> for standard error. For example:

```
type *.bat 2> err.out
```

This time the file contents go to the screen and the names are redirected to Err.out. You can redirect both to separate files with this command line:

```
type *.bat 2> err.out 1> std.out
```

The Pipe Symbol

The pipe symbol (|) is used to send or *pipe* the output of one program to a second program as the second program's input. Piping is commonly used with the More utility, which displays multiple screens of output one screenful at a time. For example:

```
help dir | more
```

This command line uses the output of Help as the input for More. The More command filters out the first screenful of Help output, sends it to the screen as its own output, and then waits for a keypress before sending more filtered output.

The Command Combination Symbols

Windows XP allows you to enter multiple commands on a single command line. Furthermore, you can make later commands depend on the results of earlier commands. This feature can be particularly useful in batch programs and Doskey macros, but you might also find it convenient at the command prompt.

To simply combine commands without regard to their results, use the & symbol:

```
copy a:file.dat & edit file.dat
```

But what if there is no File.dat on drive A? Then it can't be copied to the current drive, and the Edit command will fail when it can't find the file. Your screen will be littered with error messages. Windows XP provides two command symbols for better control over situations like this:

- The && symbol causes the second command to run only if the first command succeeds.

- The || symbol causes the second command to run only if the first command fails.

Consider this modified version of the earlier example:

```
copy a:file.dat && edit file.dat
```

With this command line, if the Copy command fails, the Edit command is ignored.

Sometimes you want the opposite effect: execute the second command only if the first fails. You can do this with the || symbol:

```
copy a:file.dat || copy b:file.dat
```

This command line tries to copy the file from drive A. If that doesn't work, it tries to copy the file from drive B.

The Escape Symbol

Some command symbols are legal characters in file names. This leads to ambiguities. You can resolve such ambiguities by using the caret (^) as an escape to indicate that whatever follows it is a character rather than a command symbol.

Consider the following command line:

```
copy f:\cartoons\Tom&Jerry
```

This copies the file F:\Cartoons\Tom to the current folder, and then executes the Jerry command—probably not what you wanted. You might think that because there is no space before or after the & symbol, the system will know that you are referring to the file name Tom&Jerry. Not true. When a command symbol appears on the command line, whatever follows it is assumed to be a command, space or no space. Use the caret as shown below to indicate that you are referring to a file name.

```
copy f:\cartoons\Tom^&Jerry
```

Alternatively, instead of using the ^ symbol, you can enclose a file specification that includes command symbols (or other troublesome characters, such as spaces) within quotation marks to achieve the same effect. For example:

```
dir "f:\cartoons\Tom&Jerry"
```

Pausing or Canceling Commands

You can pause or cancel a command that you enter at the command prompt. (Keep this in mind if you accidentally request a directory of all the files—or worse, enter a command to delete all the files—on a huge network server drive!)

To pause the output of a command, press Ctrl+S or the Pause key. To resume output, press any key.

If you have enabled QuickEdit mode for your Command Prompt window (see "Setting Other Options," page 1263), simply click in the window to pause command output. To resume output, right-click in the window.

To cancel a command, press Ctrl+C or Ctrl+Break. With either key, your command is canceled, and the command prompt returns. Be aware, though, that any action (such as deleting files) that occurs before you cancel the command is done—and cannot be undone.

Simplifying Command Entry with Doskey Macros

The Doskey utility lets you encapsulate command strings as easy-to-enter macros. For example, by typing the following at the command prompt:

```
doskey 50=mode con:lines=50
```

you create a macro named *50* that executes the command string *mode con:lines=50*. You can create as many macros as you like with Doskey, but your macros are effective only for the current Command Prompt session. To create a reusable set of Doskey macros, save them in a plain-text file, using an editor such as Notepad. Then load them from the command prompt, using Doskey's /Macrofile switch. For example, if your macros are stored in the file C:\MyMacros.txt, typing

```
doskey /macrofile=c:\mymacros.txt
```

makes those macros available for the current Command Prompt session. (If you regularly use the same macro file, consider using the AutoRun feature to load your macros. See "Using AutoRun to Execute Commands When Command Prompt Starts," page 1246.)

Doskey macros can use replaceable parameters, in much the same way batch files can. The difference between a Doskey parameter and a batch-file parameter is that the former uses a dollar-sign prefix instead of a percentage symbol. Parameters 1 through 9 thus are identified as $1 through $9. For example, the Doskey macro assignment

```
doskey lines=mode con:lines=$1
```

allows you to switch your display by typing *lines* followed by the number of lines you want.

In Doskey macros, the $* represents all the arguments passed, even if there are more than nine.

You can use redirection, piping, and command combination symbols in Doskey macros, but you must insert a caret (^) before each such symbol. For example, the following assignment creates a macro that pipes output through the More filter:

```
doskey mtype=type $* ^| more /e
```

For more information about using Doskey, type **doskey /?** at the command prompt.

Using Environment Variables

Command-prompt operating systems traditionally use environment variables as a means for programs to share information and read global settings. (Windows XP—and applications written for Windows XP—use the registry for the same purpose.) To use an environment variable in a command, program, or address, enclose it between percent signs, like this example: %UserName%.

Viewing Environment Variables

The Set command allows you to examine as well as set environment variables. To examine the current environment variables, open a Command Prompt window and type **set** (without any arguments). Windows XP displays a listing of all the current environment variables and their values, as the following typical example shows:

```
ALLUSERSPROFILE=D:\Documents and Settings\All Users
APPDATA=D:\Documents and Settings\Craig\Application Data
CommonProgramFiles=D:\Program Files\Common Files
COMPUTERNAME=FAFNER
ComSpec=D:\WINNT\system32\cmd.exe
HOMEDRIVE=D:
HOMEPATH=\Documents and Settings\Craig
LOGONSERVER=\\FAFNER
NUMBER_OF_PROCESSORS=1
OS=Windows_NT
Path=D:\WINDOWS\system32;D:\WINDOWS;D:\WINDOWS\System32\Wbem
PATHEXT=.COM;.EXE;.BAT;.CMD;.VBS;.VBE;.JS;.JSE;.WSF;.WSH
PROCESSOR_ARCHITECTURE=x86
PROCESSOR_IDENTIFIER=x86 Family 6 Model 8 Stepping 6, GenuineIntel
PROCESSOR_LEVEL=6
PROCESSOR_REVISION=0806
ProgramFiles=D:\Program Files
PROMPT=$P$G
SESSIONNAME=Console
SystemDrive=D:
SystemRoot=D:\WINDOWS
TEMP=D:\DOCUME~1\Craig\LOCALS~1\Temp
TMP=D:\DOCUME~1\Craig\LOCALS~1\Temp
USERDOMAIN=FAFNER
USERNAME=Craig
USERPROFILE=D:\Documents and Settings\Craig
windir=D:\WINDOWS
```

Modifying Environment Variables

Command Prompt gets its environment variables from three sources:

- Any variables set in your Autoexec.bat file

- System variables, as recorded in HKLM \SYSTEM\CurrentControlSet\Control\Session Manager\Environment

- User variables, as recorded in HKCU\Environment

When you log on, Windows XP scans the Autoexec.bat file in the root folder of your boot drive. At logon, the system does not actually execute Autoexec.bat; it merely scans it for environment variables initialized with Set statements. If you don't want Windows XP to scan your Autoexec.bat file for Set statements, open a registry editor and navigate to HKCU\Software\Microsoft\Windows NT\CurrentVersion\Winlogon. Then change the data associated with the ParseAutoexec value from 1 to 0.

System and user variables are both stored in the registry, but you don't need to launch a registry editor to change them. Open Control Panel, System instead. Click the Advanced tab, and then the Environment Variables button. To change system variables, you must be logged on as a member of the Administrators group.

Environment changes made via Control Panel affect your next and subsequent Command Prompt sessions (not the current ones, of course). Changes made via Autoexec.bat are not effective until the next time you log on. In case of conflicting assignments, user variables take precedence over system variables, which take precedence over variables declared in Autoexec.bat. The Path variable, however, is cumulative. That is, changes made in any venue are appended to any changes made in other avenues. (But changes made via Autoexec.bat or HKCU\Environment are not effective until your next logon.)

Within a given Command Prompt session, you can change environment variables by means of Set statements. Such statements affect only the current session and any applications (including additional Command Prompt sessions) spawned from the current session.

Predefined Environment Variables

Many of the environment variables in the example above are ones that Windows XP automatically sets with information about your system. You can use these values in batch programs, Doskey macros, and command lines—and if you're a programmer, in the programs you write. The system-defined environment variables include the following:

- **Information about your place in the network.** COMPUTERNAME contains the name of your computer, USERDOMAIN contains the name of the domain you logged on to, and USERNAME contains your logon name.

- **Information about your computer.** PROCESSOR_ARCHITECTURE contains the type of processor (such as "x86"), and PROCESSOR_IDENTIFIER, PROCESSOR_LEVEL, and PROCESSOR_REVISION provide specific information about the processor version.

- **Information about Windows XP.** SystemRoot contains the drive and folder in which Windows XP is installed; SystemDrive contains only the drive letter.

- **Information about your programs.** When you type a program name (to start the program) without typing its path, Windows XP looks first in the current folder. If the program isn't located in the current folder, Windows XP looks in each folder listed in the Path variable.

- **Information about the command prompt.** PROMPT contains codes that define the appearance of the command prompt itself. (For details, type **prompt /?** at the prompt.)

> **note** The Autoexec.nt file has no effect on the Command Prompt environment. Autoexec.nt affects MS-DOS–based applications only. Command Prompt, although it is the MS-DOS command interpreter, is itself a Windows XP–based application.

Customizing Command Prompt Windows

You can customize the appearance of a Command Prompt window in several ways. You can change its size, select a font, and even use eye-pleasing colors. And you can save these settings independently for each shortcut that launches a Command Prompt session, so that you can make appropriate settings for different tasks.

To customize a Command Prompt window, you make settings in a properties dialog box that you can reach in any of three ways:

- Right-click a shortcut that opens a Command Prompt window, and choose Properties from the shortcut menu. Changes you make here affect all future Command Prompt sessions launched from this shortcut.

- Click the Control menu icon on a Command Prompt window, and choose Properties from the Control menu. (If Command Prompt is running in full-screen mode, press Alt+Enter to switch to window display.) Changes you make here affect the current session. When you leave the properties dialog box, you'll be given the option of propagating your changes to the shortcut from which this session was launched. If you accept, all future sessions launched from that shortcut will have the new properties.

- Click the Control menu icon on a Command Prompt window, and choose Defaults from the Control menu. Changes here do not affect the current session. Instead, they affect all future sessions, except those launched from a shortcut whose properties you have modified. They also affect future sessions in character-mode, MS-DOS–based applications that do not have a program-information file (PIF) and that do not store their own settings.

Setting the Window Size and Position

To change the screen position where a newly launched Command Prompt window appears, open the window's properties dialog box and click the Layout tab (see Figure C-1).

The dialog box maintains two different sizes—the screen buffer size and the window size. The width for both sizes is specified in columns (characters); the height is specified in rows (text lines).

The screen buffer settings control the size of the "virtual screen," which is the maximum extent of the screen. Standard screen sizes are 80×25, 80×43, or 80×50, but you can set your Command Prompt screen to any size you want. (Some programs that you launch from a Command Prompt session, however, might work correctly only with standard screen sizes. In such cases, Windows XP automatically adjusts the screen buffer size to the closest size that the program understands.)

The window size settings control the size of the Command Prompt window on your screen. In most cases, you'll want it the same size as the screen buffer. But if your screen is crowded, you can reduce the window size. If you do, scroll bars are added so that you can scroll to different parts of the virtual screen. The window size settings cannot be larger than the screen buffer size settings.

Figure C-1. Settings on the Layout tab control the number of lines and characters per line that a Command Prompt window can display.

Because you size a window by specifying how many rows and columns of characters it should have, the size of those characters also affects the amount of space the window occupies on your display. For information about changing the character size, see "Selecting a Font" on the next page.

Setting the Window Size and Position Visually

Rather than guess at the settings for window size and position, you can use the following procedure:

1 Open a Command Prompt window.

2 Drag the window's borders to adjust its size and drag its title bar to adjust its position.

3 Click the Control menu icon and choose Properties.

4 Click the Layout tab and you'll see the settings that reflect the window's current condition.

5 Click OK to apply these settings.

6 Select Save Properties For Future Windows With Same Title (or Modify Shortcut That Started This Window, if you started the session from a shortcut instead of from the Run command) to retain the settings for future sessions.

Selecting a Font

Unlike most Windows-based applications, applications in a Command Prompt can display only one font at a time. Your choice is relatively limited, as you'll see if you click the Font tab in the Command Prompt window's properties dialog box. Figure C-2 shows the Font tab of the Command Prompt's properties dialog box.

You should make a selection in the Font list first because your choice here determines the contents of the Size list. If you select Lucida Console, you'll find point sizes to choose from in the Size list. If you select Raster Fonts, you'll find character widths and height in pixels.

Figure C-2. The small window at the bottom of this dialog box shows an actual-size sample of the selected font; the window at the top shows the relative size and shape of the Command Prompt window if you use the selected font.

Setting Colors

You can set the color of the text and the background of the Command Prompt window. You can also set the color of the text and the background of pop-up windows that originate from the command prompt, such as the command history.

To set colors, click the Colors tab in the Command Prompt window's properties dialog box, shown in Figure C-3.

Figure C-3. You can set separate foreground and background colors for the Command Prompt window and pop-up windows, such as the command history that appears when you press F7.

Setting Other Options

The Options tab in the Command Prompt window's properties dialog box, shown in Figure C-4 on the next page, offers a variety of options that affect how your Command Prompt window operates.

- **Cursor Size.** These options control the size of the blinking cursor in a Command Prompt window.

- **Display Options.** This setting determines whether your Command Prompt session appears in a window or occupies the entire screen.

- **Command History.** These options control the buffer used by Doskey:

  - **Buffer Size** specifies the number of commands to save in each command history.

  - **Number Of Buffers** specifies the number of command history buffers to use. (Certain character-based programs other than Cmd.exe use Doskey's command history. Doskey maintains a separate history for each such program that you start.)

  - **Discard Old Duplicates,** if selected, uses the history buffers more efficiently by not saving duplicate commands.

- **QuickEdit Mode.** This option provides a fast, easy way to copy text from (and paste text into) Command Prompt windows with a mouse. (If you don't select QuickEdit Mode, you can use commands on the Control menu for copying and pasting text.)

- **Insert Mode.** This option (on by default) allows you to insert text at the cursor position. To overstrike characters instead, clear the Insert Mode check box.

Figure C-4. You can set cursor size, the size of your command history buffer, and other specifications on the Options tab.

Appendix D

Using and Customizing Microsoft Management Console

Microsoft Management Console (MMC) is an application that hosts administrative tools. By itself, MMC performs no administrative services. Rather, it acts as host for one or more modules called *snap-ins*. The snap-ins do the useful work. MMC simply provides user-interface consistency so that you or the users you support see more or less the same style of application each time you need to carry out some kind of management task. The combination of MMC with one or more snap-ins is called an MMC *console*.

Creating snap-ins requires expertise in ActiveX programming. You don't have to be a programmer, however, to make your own custom MMC consoles. All you need to do is run MMC, start with a blank console, and add one or more of the snap-ins available on your system. (You'll find a list of these in one of MMC's dialog boxes.) Alternatively, you can customize some of the MMC consoles supplied by Microsoft or other vendors simply by adding or removing snap-ins.

At Home with Windows XP

Microsoft Management Console works identically in both versions of Windows XP. However, certain MMC snap-ins are not included in Windows XP Home Edition; see Table D-1 on page 1273 for details.

note MMC snap-ins are not stored as executable files and cannot be opened directly from a command line or from Windows Explorer unless they are first added to a console and saved using the .msc extension. Typically, snap-ins are contained in dynamic link libraries (DLLs), and details about a snap-in must be added to the registry before you can add the snap-in to an MMC console. You can view details about all available snap-ins by opening Registry Editor (Regedit.exe) and browsing to HKLM\Software\ Microsoft\MMC\SnapIns.

Why might you want to customize your MMC consoles? Because neither Microsoft nor any other vendor can anticipate your every need and desire. Perhaps you would like to take some of the functionality from two or more existing MMC consoles and combine them into a single console. (You might, for example, want to combine the Fax Service Management console with the Event Viewer console, the latter filtered to show only those events generated by the Fax service.) Or perhaps you would like to simplify some of the existing consoles by removing snap-ins that you seldom use.

You also might find MMC customization worthwhile if you support others in your organization who occasionally need to perform administrative tasks. You can set up consoles that supply only the functionality that your colleagues need, removing or disabling components that might distract or confuse. Some of the snap-ins available on your system, for example, are designed to administer remote as well as local computers. If the user you're supporting needs to be able to administer only his or her own machine, you might want to create a custom console for that person that has remote-administration capabilities disabled.

Running MMC Consoles

MMC consoles have, by default, the extension .msc, and .msc files are associated by default with MMC. Thus you can run any MMC console by double-clicking its file name in a Windows Explorer window or by specifying the file name on a command line.

MMC consoles can be run in author mode or in three varieties of user mode. Author mode gives you full access to MMC's menus and options. In its user modes, elements of MMC's functionality are removed.

By default, when you run an MMC console, the console runs in the mode it was last saved in. But you can always run any console in any mode you need to.

Running a User-Mode Console in Author Mode

To run a console in author mode, right-click it in a Windows Explorer window and choose Author from the shortcut menu. Alternatively, you can run a console in author mode using the following command-line syntax:

```
name.msc /a
```

where *name* is the filename of the console file.

Running a Console and Specifying a Target Computer

Many of the consoles supplied by Microsoft are set up to operate on the local computer by default, but—provided that you have the appropriate permissions—they can also be used to manage remote computers. To open such a console and specify a target computer, use this command-line syntax:

```
name.msc /computer=computername
```

Be aware that if you use the /Computer switch with a console that has not been set up to allow remote-computer management, you will not get an error message. Instead, you will simply get the console applied to the default (typically, the local) computer. In the console tree, you can look at the top-level entry for a snap-in to confirm that you're working with the correct target computer.

Some of the consoles supplied with Windows that are designed to work with remote as well as local computers include a menu command for connecting to a different computer. The Computer Management console (Compmgmt.msc), for example, allows you to switch from one computer to another while the console is running. Others, such as Shared Folders (Fsmgmt.msc), can be used with remote computers, but these consoles manage the local computer unless you specify a different target computer on the command line.

Using MMC Consoles

Notwithstanding the fact that MMC is intended to provide user-interface consistency across administrative applications, actual MMC consoles can take on quite a variety of appearances. Compare the Computer Management console (Compmgmt.msc) with the Disk Management console (Diskmgmt.msc), for example.

MMC is designed to be extremely flexible. Snap-ins can add elements to the MMC user interface, and console designers can hide or display UI elements as needs dictate. Nevertheless, *most* of the consoles that come with your operating system look somewhat like Figure D-1 on the next page, and we can make a few generalizations about their use.

Console tree   Details pane

Figure D-1. Most of the MMC consoles that come with Windows XP include a console tree and a details pane.

The console tree and the details pane   If the console is divided into panes vertically, the one on the left contains the *console tree* and the one on the right is called the *details pane*. The console tree shows the organization of the console and allows for easy navigation between snap-ins. Outline controls in the console tree function just the way they do in Windows Explorer. The vertical split bar between the console tree and details pane can be dragged to the left or right, like its counterpart in Windows Explorer. The details pane shows information related to the item currently selected in the console tree.

The Action and View menus   The Action menu, if present, provides commands specific to the current snap-in. In other words, this is the menu you use to carry out administrative tasks. The View menu, if present, allows you to choose among alternative ways of presenting information. In many MMC consoles, for example, the View menu offers Large Icons, Small Icons, List, and Details commands, just like the View menu in Windows Explorer. The View menu might also include a Customize command. This command presents the dialog box shown in Figure D-2, which allows you, among other things, to hide or display the console tree.

Shortcut menus   Whether or not an Action menu is present, you'll probably find that the easiest way to carry out an administrative task is to right-click the relevant item in the console tree or the details pane and choose an action from the item's shortcut menu. That's because the shortcut menu *always* includes all the actions available for the selected item. (If you don't immediately find the command you need, look for an All Tasks command; the action you want is probably on the All Tasks submenu.) The shortcut menu also always includes a Help command.

1268

Figure D-2. You can use the Customize View dialog box to control various elements of the MMC console.

Working with content in the details pane   If the details pane provides a tabular presentation, like the one shown in Figure D-1, you can manipulate content using the same techniques you use in Windows Explorer. You can sort by clicking column headings, control column width by dragging the borders between column headings (double-click a border to make a column just wide enough for the widest entry), and rearrange columns by dragging headings.

To hide or display particular columns, look for a Choose Columns command on the View menu. Here you can specify which columns you want to see, as well as the order in which you want to see them.

Exporting details pane data to text or .csv files   Many MMC consoles include Action-menu commands for saving data in binary formats. In most consoles that produce tabular displays, however, you can also use an Export List command to generate a tab-delimited or comma-delimited text file, suitable for viewing in a word processing, spreadsheet, or database program. If this command is available, you'll find it on the Action menu or any shortcut menu.

Creating Your Own MMC Consoles

Creating your own MMC console or modifying an existing one involves the following steps (not necessarily in this order):

● Running MMC with no snap-in, or opening an existing MMC console in author mode

● Displaying the console tree if it's not already visible

● Adding folders to the console tree if appropriate for your needs

1269

- Adding or removing snap-ins and, if appropriate, extensions (modules that extend the functionality of snap-ins)

- Adding or removing ActiveX controls and Internet links, if appropriate

- Adding taskpad views (customized pages that appear within the details pane of a snap-in), if appropriate

- Manipulating windows and other display elements to taste

- Adding items to the Favorites menu, if appropriate

- Naming the console and choosing an icon for it

- Choosing author mode or one of the three user modes

- Further restricting user options, if appropriate

- Using the File menu to save your .msc file

Running MMC with No Snap-In

To run MMC with no snap-in, simply type **mmc** on a command line. An empty, author-mode MMC console appears, as shown in Figure D-3.

MMC is a multiple-document-interface (MDI) application (the Console Root window is a child window), although most of the consoles supplied with Windows XP do their best to disguise this fact. You can create consoles with multiple child windows, and those windows can be maximized, minimized, restored, resized, moved, cascaded, and tiled.

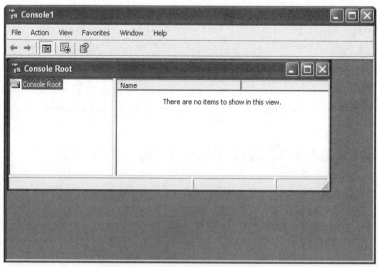

Figure D-3. An empty author-mode MMC console looks like this.

Displaying the Console Tree

If the console tree is not visible in the application you're creating or modifying, choose Customize View from the View menu. In the Customize View dialog box (see Figure D-2), select the Console Tree check box. You can also use this dialog box to control other elements of the MMC display.

Adding Folders to the Console Tree

If the console you're designing will include several snap-ins, you might want to consider using folders to create logical subdivisions within your console tree. To see how folders can be helpful, check out the Computer Management application (Compmgmt.msc). Computer Management uses three folders—System Tools, Storage, and Services And Applications. These folders allow the user to control the amount of detail shown in the console tree and simplify navigation from one point in the application to another.

To add one or more folders to an MMC application:

1 Choose File, Add/Remove Snap-In (or press Ctrl+M).

2 In the Snap-Ins Added To field of the Add/Remove Snap-In dialog box, choose the parent of the new folder. (In a brand new MMC application, this folder must be Console Root.)

3 Click Add.

4 In the Add Standalone Snap-In dialog box, select Folder and then click Add. Repeat if you want more folders; then click Close.

5 In the Add/Remove Snap-In dialog box, click OK.

6 In the console tree, right-click the new folder, choose Rename, and supply a meaningful name.

Adding Snap-Ins and Extensions

To add a snap-in to your application:

1 Choose File, Add/Remove Snap-In (or press Ctrl+M).

2 In the Snap-Ins Added To field of the Add/Remove Snap-In dialog box, choose the parent of the new snap-in. This folder can be Console Root or a folder that you've already added.

3 Click Add.

4 In the Add Standalone Snap-In dialog box, select the snap-in you want and then click Add.

If the selected snap-in supports remote management, you might see a dialog box similar to the one shown in Figure D-4.

5 Supply the name of the computer you want to manage. Also select the check box if you want the user of your custom console to be able to specify the target computer by means of a command-line switch. (This option is not available for all remote-management snap-ins.) Then click Finish.

Some snap-ins come with optional extensions. You can think of these as snap-ins for snap-ins—modules that provide additional functionality to the selected snap-in.

6 To add an extension to a snap-in, select it from the Standalone tab of the Add/Remove Snap-In dialog box, and then click the Extensions tab. There you can select the extensions that you want to use. When you have finished adding extensions, click OK.

Figure D-4. If your snap-in can manage a remote computer, you will see a dialog box similar to this.

Table D-1 lists the available snap-ins included with a base installation of Windows XP and Service Pack 1.

Table D-1. **Available MMC Snap-Ins**

Snap-In Name	Description
.NET Framework Configuration	Use this snap-in (an optional component included with SP1) to edit program settings, communication channels, and security policies for applications built using .NET Framework tools (including Microsoft Management Console). This tool is primarily of interest to developers.
ActiveX Control	Select this option to add a previously installed ActiveX control to the current console as if it were a snap-in. The list of available controls includes all installed ActiveX controls, not just those visible within Internet Explorer. Few ActiveX controls are suitable for use in an MMC console, making this option useful mostly to developers.
Certificates	Using this snap-in, you can view currently installed certificates for the current user, a service account, or a computer. Choosing any option except the current user allows you to specify additional details, including the name of a service or a remote computer. A more accessible version of this tool is available from Control Panel, Internet Options; click the Certificates button on the Content tab.
Component Services	This snap-in, also primarily intended for developers, allows you to view and manage settings for programs that use COM+ and DCOM to communicate with the operating system and with each other.
Computer Management	Use the assortment of tools in this snap-in to manage system settings, storage, and services. Most users will access this snap-in through the Administrative Tools folder or by right-clicking the My Computer icon and choosing Manage; either option opens the preconfigured Computer Management console (Compmgmt.msc), which contains only this snap-in.
Device Manager	View properties for installed hardware devices and drivers using this snap-in, which is more commonly available from the System option in Control Panel; this snap-in is also available in the Device Manager console (Devmgmt.msc) and as one node in the Computer Management console (Compmgmt.msc).
Disk Defragmenter	This snap-in, which is also accessible via the Computer Management console (Compmgmt.msc), allows you to analyze and defragment any local hard disk volume. When you select a task, this snap-in calls one of two external programs (Dfrgntfs.exe or Dfrgfat.exe) to perform any actions.

(continued)

Appendix D

Table D-1. *(continued)*

Snap-In Name	Description
Disk Management	Use this snap-in to manage partitions and volumes on local hard disks; it calls Dmadmin.exe, which actually does the work. You can also gain access to the snap-in via its own saved console (Diskmgmt.msc) and as one node in the Computer Management console (Compmgmt.msc).
Event Viewer	This is yet another snap-in that you're more likely to access from its standard saved console file (Eventvwr.msc), which is available on the Start menu (All Programs, Administrative Tools, Event Viewer) or from the Computer Management console (Compmgmt.msc). For more details on how to view and interpret event logs, see Chapter 36, "Monitoring System Activities with Event Viewer."
Folder	The sole purpose of this snap-in is to help you organize consoles that contain multiple snap-ins. By using folders to arrange complex consoles, you can simplify their use.
Group Policy	This is perhaps the most powerful and most misunderstood of all MMC snap-ins. Although Group Policy is most often used to administer Windows domains, you can also use it to tighten control over a standalone computer running Windows XP, as we explain in Appendix E, "Group Policy." This snap-in is not included with Windows XP Home Edition.
Indexing Service	Use this snap-in to enable, disable, and manage file-system indexes, which improve system performance when searching for files and folders. For more details, see "Using Indexing Service and Query Language," page 480.
IP Security Monitor	If you've enabled Internet Protocol Security (IPSec), you can monitor the status of your secure connections using this snap-in.
IP Security Policy Management	With the help of this snap-in, you can configure Internet Protocol Security (IPSec), which enables you to carry on secure communications over standard Internet connections. This feature is complex and confusing, and most people don't require this level of security; if you need in-depth explanations and step-by-step instructions, see Chapter 17, "Securing Ports and Protocols," in our other book, *Microsoft Windows Security Inside Out* (Microsoft Press, 2002).
Link To Web Address	Technically, this menu choice isn't a snap-in at all; rather, it allows you to add any URL to a console, so that you can view a Web page or access another resource via HTTP instructions. See the text that follows this table for more details.

Table D-1. *(continued)*

Snap-in Name	Description
Local Users And Groups	Manage user and group accounts on a single computer using this snap-in, which provides a range of features not accessible through the simplified User Accounts Control Panel option in Windows XP, as we explain in "Advanced Account Setup Options," page 120. This snap-in produces an error message if you try to access the user account database on a computer running Windows XP Home Edition.
Performance Logs And Alerts	Use this snap-in to set up a battery of performance data counters, trace event logs, and performance alerts. Most users will access this set of tools through the saved Performance console (Perfmon.msc), which also includes the System Monitor snap-in. For more details on this extremely useful tool, see "Advanced System Performance Measurement," page 253.
Removable Storage Management	Although its name might conjure up images of CD-RW and Zip drives, this snap-in is actually intended for managing libraries of backup tapes, typically used only in very large enterprises. Unless you have a "jukebox" style backup device, you can safely ignore this snap-in.
Resultant Set Of Policy	Use this fairly esoteric snap-in to view policies that have been applied to a particular computer and to predict what their effect will be on a specific user. This snap-in is not included with Windows XP Home Edition.
Security Configuration And Analysis	For anyone interested in advanced security, this snap-in (which is available only in Windows XP Professional and is not included with Windows XP Home Edition) is practically irresistible. It allows you to use security template files to apply consistent security policies to computers and users. For more details, see Chapter 37, "Securing Your Computer with Templates."
Security Templates	This snap-in (included only with Windows XP Professional) allows you to edit security templates used with the Security Configuration And Analysis snap-in.
Services	Using this snap-in, you can start, stop, and configure services running on a local or remote computer. Most users will access these tools using the Services console (Services.msc) or the Services And Applications node in the Computer Management console (Compmgmt.msc).

(continued)

Appendix D

Table D-1. *(continued)*

Snap-In Name	Description
Shared Folders	With the help of this snap-in, you can view and manage shared folders, monitor current sessions, and see which network users have opened files on a local or remote computer. Although this snap-in can be run from Windows XP Home Edition, it does not perform any useful functions; see "Managing Shared Folders," page 1064, for more details.
WMI Control	Windows Management Instrumentation (WMI) is an essential system service that allows remote and local monitoring of hardware and software. In theory, you can control and configure WMI settings using this snap-in; in practice, no user-configurable options are available on a default installation of Windows.

Adding ActiveX Controls and Internet Links

The Add Standalone Snap-In dialog box includes the entries ActiveX Control and Link To Web Address, as well as snap-ins. If you choose ActiveX Control, a new wizard appears, allowing you to choose and configure the control you want to add.

If you choose Link To Web Address, the dialog box that appears lets you specify a hyperlink or browse to an Internet resource. The hyperlink you enter does not have to be a Web URL. It can be another kind of Internet URL (a mailto, for example) or a link to a local or network folder. If you do specify a Web link, MMC displays the Web content in the details pane when you select the link in the console tree.

Adding Taskpad Views

A *taskpad* is a customized page that appears within the details pane of a snap-in. The main value of a taskpad is that you can create icons that encapsulate menu commands, command strings, scripts, URLs, and shortcuts to Favorites items. Navigational tabs at the bottom of a taskpad view make it easy for your user to switch between the taskpad view and a normal view of the same data. You can suppress these tabs (by means of the Customize View dialog box) if you don't want to give your console's user this freedom.

To create a taskpad view, start by selecting an item in the console tree to which you want to apply the view. As you'll see, when you create your taskpad view, you have the option of applying it only to the selected console-tree item or to all items at the same outline level.

Next, right-click that console-tree entry and choose New Taskpad View from the shortcut menu. A wizard appears. The sample table at the right side of the wizard's second page makes the options pretty self-explanatory. The default choices work well in most situations.

The default selections in the wizard's third screen apply the new taskpad view to all comparable console-tree items and make the taskpad the default view for those items. Moving on from this screen, you have the opportunity to assign a name and some descriptive text to the new view.

In the wizard's final screen, select the Start New Task Wizard check box if you want to create one or more task shortcuts. This selection summons a new wizard that walks you through the process of creating your first shortcut. On the final page of this wizard, select Run This Wizard Again if you have additional shortcuts to create.

Manipulating Windows

With the New Window From Here command on the Action menu, you can create a new child window rooted on the current console-tree selection. You might want to use this command to create multiple-window applications—for example, a console consisting of the Indexing Service in one window and a filtered list of Index Service events in a second. After you've created your windows, you can use Window menu commands to tile or cascade them.

You can also use the New Window From Here command to remove the Console Root item that appears atop your default console tree:

1 Select the first item below Console Root.

2 Choose New Window From Here from the Action menu (or right-click and choose it from the shortcut menu).

3 Close the original window (the one with Console Root).

Controlling Other Visual Elements

The Customize View command (under View) allows you to hide or display various elements of the MMC visual scene, including taskbars, menus, and the navigational tabs that appear below taskpad views. Note that selections in the Customize View dialog box take effect immediately. You don't need to hit an Apply button or leave the dialog box, so you can easily try each option and see whether you like it.

Using the Favorites Menu

The Favorites menu allows you to store pointers to places within your console tree. If you create a particularly complex MMC console, you might want to consider using Favorites to simplify navigation. To add a console-tree item to your list of favorites, select that item and then choose Add To Favorites from the Favorites menu.

1277

Naming Your Console

To assign a name to your console, choose File, Options. Your entry in the field at the top of the Options dialog box will appear on the title bar of your console, regardless of the file name you apply to its .msc file. If you do not make an entry here, MMC will replace Console1 with the console's eventual file name.

Choosing Between MMC's Three User Modes

In the Console Mode field of the Options dialog box (choose File, Options), you can choose between MMC's three user modes:

- User Mode—Full Access. In this mode, the top level menu is present but the Console menu has a single command—Exit.

- User Mode—Limited Access, Multiple Window.

- User Mode—Limited Access, Single Window.

In both limited-access modes, the top-level menu disappears, leaving users to work with only the two snap-in menus: Action and View (provided that you haven't suppressed those menus via the Customize View command). In the single-window limited-access mode, the current child (snap-in) window is maximized, and MMC essentially loses its MDI character. If you have two or more child windows open at the time you save an MMC console in single-window mode, a confirmation prompt warns you that the user will see only the current child window.

In multiple-window limited-access mode, MMC retains its MDI character (whether or not you've created multiple child windows), allowing child windows to be minimized, maximized, restored, resized, and repositioned.

Imposing Further Restrictions

If you choose one of the three user modes, the two check boxes at the bottom of the Options dialog box become available. Your choices are as follows:

Do Not Save Changes To This Console   With this check box cleared (its default), MMC saves the state of your application automatically when a user closes it. The user's selection in the console tree, for example, is preserved from one use to the next. If you always want your user to see the same thing each time he or she runs the console, select this check box.

Allow The User To Customize Views   This check box, selected by default, keeps the Customize View command available, allowing your user, for example, to hide or display the console tree. Clear the check box if you want to deny the user access to this option.

1278

Group Policy

Group Policy is a highly touted feature of Active Directory, which is part of Windows .NET Server and Windows 2000 Server. In that environment, Group Policy is indeed an enormously powerful feature that lets administrators configure computers throughout sites, domains, or organizational units (OUs). In addition to setting standard desktop configurations and restricting what users are allowed to change, administrators can use Group Policy to centrally manage software installation, configuration, updates, and removal; specify scripts to run at startup, shutdown, logon, and logoff; and redirect users' special folders (such as My Documents) to the network. Administrators can customize all these settings for different computers, users, or groups.

But Group Policy can also be a useful tool for managing computers on a small network or even for managing a single computer with multiple users. Using only the local Group Policy object on a computer running Windows XP Professional, you can

- Manage registry-based policy—everything from configuring the desktop to hiding certain drives to preventing the creation of scheduled tasks. These settings—and hundreds more—are stored in the HKLM and HKCU branches of the registry, which you can edit directly. But Group Policy provides two distinct advantages: It's much easier to use than a registry editor, and it periodically updates the registry automatically (thereby keeping your policies in force even if the registry is somehow modified by other means).

- Assign scripts for computer startup, computer shutdown, user logon, and user logoff. (For details, see "Using Scripts That Run at Logon, Logoff, Startup, and Shutdown," page 1163.)

- Specify security options.

1279

At Home with Windows XP

In a nutshell: Group Policy is not available in Windows XP Home Edition. Home Edition users can use none of the procedures described in this chapter, nor can they use the various Group Policy settings that are described elsewhere in the book.

In a domain environment, Group Policy enables an administrator to apply policy settings and restrictions to users and computers (and groups of each) in one fell swoop. With a workgroup, you must make similar Group Policy settings on each computer where you want such restrictions imposed.

Starting Group Policy

You make Group Policy settings using the Group Policy snap-in for Microsoft Management Console (MMC), which is shown in Figure E-1. Windows XP Professional includes an MMC console that shows only this snap-in, but you won't find it on the Start menu. To open the console, go to Start, Run and type **gpedit.msc**. You must be logged on as a member of the Administrators group to use Group Policy.

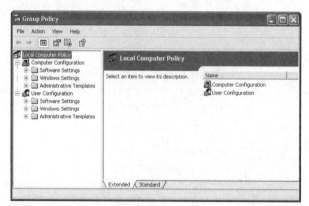

Figure E-1. Typing **gpedit.msc** at a command prompt opens the Group Policy console.

If your computer is joined to a domain with Active Directory–based policies, and if you have appropriate domain administrative privileges, you can configure Group Policy to display snap-in extensions that let you view and modify domain policies as well as extensions for the local Group Policy object. (For more information, see "How Local Group Policy Settings Interact with Active Directory–Based Group Policy Settings," page 1286.) However, because our focus in this book is Windows XP, in this chapter we explore only the local Group Policy object.

Starting Group Policy for a Remote Computer

With some MMC snap-ins (for example, Computer Management), you can use a menu command to switch from the local computer to another computer on your network. Such is not the case with Group Policy, which, once started, directs its attention toward a single computer. You can, however, start Group Policy with its gaze turned toward another computer. To do that, you must have administrative privileges on both your own computer and the other computer. Even without Windows .NET Server (or Windows 2000 Server) and Active Directory, you can administer all the computers on your network from a single console. (A key difference is that you must set local Group Policy on each computer rather than setting Active Directory–based Group Policy that automatically applies to all computers.) You can use either of two methods to start Group Policy for a remote computer: a command-line parameter or a custom MMC console.

The simplest method is to append the /Gpcomputer parameter, as we did in this example:

```
gpedit.msc /gpcomputer:"redwood"
```

The computer name that follows /Gpcomputer can be either a NetBIOS-style name (as shown here) or a DNS-style name (for example, redwood.swdocs.com), which is the primary naming form used by Windows .NET Server and Windows 2000 Server domains. In either case, you must enclose the computer name in quotation marks.

An alternative is to create a custom console that opens another computer's local Group Policy object. The advantage of this approach is that you can create a single console that can open Group Policy for each computer you want to manage. To create a custom console, follow these steps:

1 Go to Start, Run and type **mmc**.

2 Open the File menu and choose Add/Remove Snap-In.

3 On the Standalone tab, click Add.

4 Select Group Policy and click Add.

5 In the Select Group Policy Object dialog box, click Browse.

6 On the Computers tab, select Another Computer, and then type the name of the computer or click Browse, Advanced, Find Now to select it from a list.

7 Click OK and then click Finish.

8 Repeat steps 4 through 7 to add other computers to the console.

9 Click Close and then click OK.

For more information about MMC, see "Creating Your Own MMC Consoles," page 1269.

Customizing the Group Policy Window

The Group Policy console has some easily overlooked options that you won't find in other MMC snap-ins. You can add or remove administrative templates, and you can restrict the view to show only the policies that have been configured.

Adding or removing policy templates   The Administrative Templates folders (under Computer Configuration and User Configuration) are extensible. The Administrative Templates policies are defined in an .adm file. Windows XP includes several .adm files, of which four are displayed by default, as shown in Table E-1.

You might want to remove the templates that contain policies you never use, or you might want to add a custom template provided with another program. For example, the *Microsoft Office XP Resource Kit* includes policy templates for managing Microsoft Office; for details, visit *www.microsoft.com/office/ork*.

To add or remove a policy template, right-click Administrative Templates (either folder) and choose Add/Remove Templates. After you make your changes and click Close in the Add/Remove Templates dialog box, both Administrative Templates folders reflect your new selections.

1282

Table E-1. **Administrative Template Files Included with Windows XP**

File Name	Description
Conf.adm (displayed by default)	Conferencing settings for Microsoft NetMeeting that appear in Administrative Templates\Windows Components\NetMeeting (under Computer Configuration and User Configuration)
Inetcorp.adm	Microsoft Internet Explorer settings for use with Internet Explorer Administration Kit (IEAK), not Group Policy
Inetres.adm (displayed by default)	Microsoft Internet Explorer settings that appear in Administrative Templates\Windows Components\Internet Explorer (under Computer Configuration and User Configuration)
Inetset.adm	Microsoft Internet Explorer settings for use with Internet Explorer Administration Kit (IEAK), not Group Policy
System.adm (displayed by default)	A wide variety of settings for Windows XP, encompassing most of the policies that appear in Group Policy
Wmplayer.adm (displayed by default)	Windows Media Player settings that appear in User Configuration\Administrative Templates\Windows Media Player

Adding a policy template merely copies the .adm file to %SystemRoot%\System32\GroupPolicy\Adm; removing a template deletes the copy in that folder. Adding or removing policy templates does not change the underlying policy settings, if there are any; it only controls whether those policies are displayed in Group Policy.

newfeature!

Displaying only policies you want   With only the standard templates installed, Group Policy offers hundreds of policies that you can set. Many of these policies might be for areas of Windows that you never use; including them in the Group Policy console provides only clutter. Windows now offers a way to selectively filter the list of displayed Administrative Templates policies to include only the ones that might interest you.

To use this feature, right-click Administrative Templates and choose View, Filtering. In the Filtering dialog box, shown in Figure E-2 on the next page, you can choose to hide items that apply only to certain versions of Windows or Internet Explorer. (This is useful primarily when you're remotely editing policies on another computer, which might not be running Windows XP.) After you configure your local Group Policy as you want it (as described later in this chapter), you can clean up the display by hiding the myriad policies that you aren't interested in setting: select Only Show Configured Policy Settings.

Filtering the display of policies does not change the underlying policy settings, if there are any; it only controls whether those policies are displayed in Group Policy.

Figure E-2.   You can hide policies that you're not interested in.

Unlike the Add/Remove Templates command, filtering applies only to the Administrative Templates folder that you select. If you want to filter the policies in both Computer Configuration and User Configuration, you must repeat the process in each folder.

Understanding the Local Group Policy Object

A *Group Policy object* (often abbreviated as GPO) is simply a collection of Group Policy settings. In a domain based on Windows .NET Server or Windows 2000 Server, Group Policy objects are stored at the domain level and affect users and computers based on their membership in sites, domains, and organizational units. Each computer running Windows XP has a single *local Group Policy object*. Because it doesn't rely on a server version of Windows, that's the one we focus on here.

The local Group Policy object is stored as a series of files and folders in the hidden %SystemRoot%\System32\GroupPolicy folder. By default, the local Administrators group and the operating system itself have Full Control permissions for this folder and all the objects it contains; Authenticated Users has Read & Execute permissions. The GroupPolicy folder typically contains the following files and folders:

- **Gpt.ini.** This file stores information about which extensions (identified by their globally unique identifier, or GUID) contain modified settings and whether the Computer Configuration or User Configuration branch is disabled.

- **Adm.** This folder contains the administrative templates (stored as .adm files) that are in use. (See "Adding or Removing Policy Templates," page 1282.)

- **User.** This folder holds the Registry.pol file, which contains registry settings that apply to users. The User folder includes these subfolders:

1284

- Microsoft\IEAK contains settings for the items that appear in the \User Configuration\Windows Settings\Internet Explorer Maintenance folder in Group Policy.

- Scripts includes two folders, Logon and Logoff, which contain the scripts that run when a user logs on or logs off.

- **Machine.** This folder holds the Registry.pol file, which contains registry settings that apply to the computer. Within the Machine folder is a Scripts subfolder that holds two folders, Startup and Shutdown; these contain the scripts that run when the computer starts up or shuts down.

> **note** Some of these files and folders are created only when you run Group Policy and make some settings.

How Group Policy Works

The majority of the Group Policy settings are in the Administrative Templates extension of the Group Policy snap-in. (As noted elsewhere in this chapter, the content of the Administrative Templates folders is derived from the .adm files in the Group Policy object.) When you configure a policy in the Administrative Templates folder (that is, you select either Enabled or Disabled and, optionally, set a value), Group Policy stores that information as a custom registry setting in one of the two Registry.pol files. As you'd expect, Group Policy uses the copy of Registry.pol in %SystemRoot%\System32\GroupPolicy\Machine for settings you make in the Computer Configuration\Administrative Templates folder in Group Policy and uses the copy in User for settings you make in User Configuration\Administrative Templates.

Computer-related Group Policy settings—those stored in Machine\Registry.pol—are copied to the appropriate registry keys in the HKLM hive when the operating system initializes and during the periodic refresh. User-related settings (in User\Registry.pol) are copied to the appropriate keys in HKCU when a user logs on and during the periodic refresh.

> **note** Group Policy settings—either local or Active Directory–based—take precedence over user settings (that is, settings that you make through Control Panel and other methods available to ordinary users). This is because Group Policy settings are not written to the "normal" registry key for a particular setting; instead, they're written to a value in a "policies" key. For example, if you use the Taskbar And Start Menu Properties dialog box to disable personalized menus, the data in the Intellimenus value in the HKCU\Software\Microsoft\Windows\CurrentVersion\Explorer\Advanced key changes. But if you use Group Policy, the Intellimenus value in the HKCU\Software\Microsoft\Windows\CurrentVersion\Policies\Explorer key changes instead. In cases of conflicts, the value under the Policies key overrules the other.

The *periodic refresh* occurs at intervals that you define as a Group Policy setting. By default, the Registry.pol files are copied to the registry every 90 minutes plus a random offset of 0 to 30 minutes. (The random offset is intended for Active Directory–based policies; on a large network, you wouldn't want all the refresh activity occurring simultaneously. For local Group Policy, the offset serves no useful purpose but is added anyway.) By enabling and modifying the Group Policy Refresh Interval For Computers setting in Computer Configuration\Administrative Templates\System\Group Policy and the Group Policy Refresh Interval For Users setting in User Configuration\ Administrative Templates\System\Group Policy, you can change the interval and the random offset. You can set the interval to any value from 0 minutes (in which case settings are refreshed every 7 seconds) through 64,800 minutes (45 days).

To refresh Group Policy settings immediately, type **gpupdate** at a command prompt. To display a list of optional switches for Gpupdate.exe, type **gpupdate /?**.

> **note** The Gpupdate command replaces the functionality of the Secedit /Refreshpolicy command, which was introduced in Windows 2000.

How Local Group Policy Settings Interact with Active Directory–Based Group Policy Settings

If your computer is joined to a domain, it might be affected by Group Policy settings other than those you set in the local Group Policy object. Group Policy settings are applied in this order:

1 Settings from the local Group Policy object

2 Settings from site Group Policy objects, in administratively specified order

3 Settings from domain Group Policy objects, in administratively specified order

4 Settings from organizational unit Group Policy objects, from largest to smallest organizational unit (parent to child organizational unit), and in administratively specified order at the level of each organizational unit

Policies applied later overwrite previously applied policies, which means that in a case of conflicting settings, the highest-level Active Directory–based policy settings take precedence. The policy settings are cumulative, so all settings contribute to the effective policy. The effective policy is called the *Resultant Set of Policy (RsoP)*.

To see which settings are in effect for a particular user, you can use a command-line tool (Gpresult.exe). To display RSoP for yourself, simply type **gpresult** at a command prompt. Type **gpresult /?** for information about other options.

The Help And Support Center also includes a tool that shows effective Group Policy settings for the current user. To use that tool, open Help And Support Center. On the home page, click Use Tools To View Your Computer Information And Diagnose Problems in the right pane, Advanced System Information in the left pane, and View Group Policy Settings Applied in the right pane. Figure E-3 shows an example.

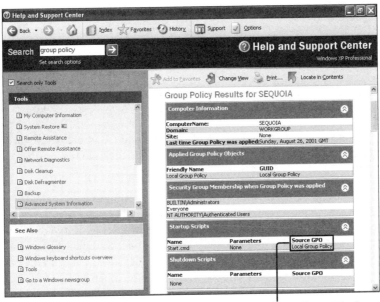

Source GPO identifies the Group Policy object that controls a particular setting

Figure E-3. The Group Policy tool in the Help And Support Center shows which settings are in effect—something that's not readily apparent in a domain environment.

Types of Settings

The Computer Configuration branch of Group Policy includes a variety of computer-related settings, and the User Configuration branch includes a variety of user-related settings. The line between computer settings and user settings is often blurred, however. Because local Group Policy settings apply to all users, your best bet for discovering the policies you need is to examine them all. You'll find a treasure trove of useful settings, including many that can't be made any other way short of hacking the registry. In the Administrative Templates folders, you'll find more than 240 computer settings and more than 440 user settings, which makes this sound like a daunting task—but you'll find that you can quickly scan the policies in each folder and ignore most of them.

new feature!

To learn more about each policy, simply select it, as shown in Figure E-4 on the next page. If you have selected the Extended tab at the bottom of the window, a description of the selected policy appears in the center pane.

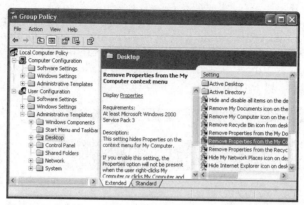

Figure E-4. The Extended tab includes a description of the selected policy.

Some settings appear in both User Configuration and Computer Configuration. In a case of conflicting settings, the Computer Configuration setting always takes precedence.

You can speed up the application of Group Policy settings by disabling those you don't use. To see at a glance which types of policies are in use, right-click Local Computer Policy (at the top of the console tree) and choose Properties. In the dialog box that appears, shown in Figure E-5, the Revisions line under Summary shows the number of Computer Configuration and User Configuration settings in use. If either value is 0 (or if you want to disable Group Policy settings for some other reason), select the appropriate check box under Disable.

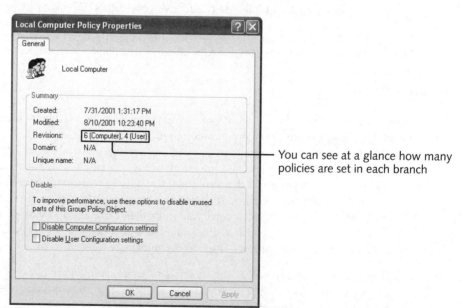

You can see at a glance how many policies are set in each branch

Figure E-5. You can selectively disable computer-related or user-related Group Policy settings.

1288

Making Settings

Each policy in the Administrative Templates folders of Group Policy has one of three settings: Not Configured, Enabled, or Disabled. By default, all policies in the local Group Policy object are initially set to Not Configured. (The policies in the Windows Settings folders do not have a Not Configured option and therefore have other default settings.)

To change a setting, simply double-click the name of the policy you want to change or click the Properties link that appears in the center pane of the Extended tab. The properties dialog box then appears. The dialog box for each policy under Administrative Templates looks much like the one shown in Figure E-6. The Setting tab includes the three options—Not Configured, Enabled, and Disabled—and a large area where you can make policy-specific settings. Controls in the center area appear dimmed and are unavailable unless you select the Enabled option. (Many simple policies leave this area blank because the policy needs no further setting.) The Explain tab provides detailed information about the policy (the same information that appears in the center pane of the Extended tab); the only place you're likely to find more information about each policy is in the Windows 2000 Group Policy Reference, available online at *http://www.microsoft.com/ windows2000/techinfo/reskit/en-us/default.asp*. (At the time of this book's writing, a version updated for Windows XP was not yet available. The information in the Windows 2000 reference applies to Windows XP as well, but it doesn't include information about the new policies added to Windows XP.) Both tabs include Previous Setting and Next Setting buttons, which make it convenient to go through an entire folder without opening and closing the properties dialog box for each policy individually.

Figure E-6. Properties dialog boxes for all Administrative Templates policies are similar to the one shown here.

> **note** Pay close attention to the name of each policy, because the settings can be counterintuitive. A number of policies begin with the word *disable* (for example, Disable Active Desktop in User Configuration\Administrative Templates\Desktop\ Active Desktop). For those policies, if you want to *allow* the specified option, you must select the *Disable* setting. (In other words, you must disable the disabling policy.) Conversely, if you want to prohibit the option, you must select Enable.

Making Different Settings for Different Users

Centrally managed Group Policy settings—that is, those that are stored in Active Directory in Windows .NET Server or Windows 2000 Server—can be applied to individual users, computers, or groups of either. You can have multiple sets of Active Directory–based Group Policy objects, allowing you to create an entirely different collection of settings for different users or computers.

Such is not the case with local Group Policy. Local Group Policy settings apply to all users who log on to the computer. (If the computer is joined to a domain, however, the local settings might be overridden by Active Directory–based settings. For details, see "How Local Group Policy Settings Interact with Active Directory–Based Group Policy Settings," page 1286.) You can't have multiple sets of local Group Policy objects.

Although you can't have customized settings for each of several different groups, you can effectively have two groups of users: those who are affected by local Group Policy settings and those who are not. This duality affects only the User Configuration settings; Computer Configuration settings are applied before anyone logs on.

You can do this because local Group Policy depends on users having Read access to the local Group Policy object, which is stored in the %SystemRoot%\System32\ GroupPolicy folder. Policies are not applied to users who do not have Read access; therefore, by denying Read access to administrators or others whom you don't want to restrict, you free those users from control by group policies. To use this method, follow these steps:

1 Make the Group Policy setting changes that you want.

2 In Windows Explorer, right-click the %SystemRoot%\System32\GroupPolicy folder and choose Properties. (GroupPolicy is a hidden folder; if you can't find it in System32, choose Tools, Folder Options, View, Show Hidden Files And Folders.)

3 On the Security tab of the GroupPolicy Properties dialog box, select the Administrators group and select the Deny check box for the Read permission. (If you want to exclude any other users or groups from Group Policy control, add them to the Group Or User Names list and then deny their Read permission.)

1290

note You must deny the Read permission rather than simply clear the Allow check box. Otherwise, all users would continue to inherit Read permission because of their automatic membership in the Authenticated Users group.

At your next logon using one of the Read-disabled user accounts, you'll find that you're no longer encumbered by Group Policy settings. Without Read permission, however, you'll find that you're also unable to run Group Policy—so you can't view or modify Group Policy settings. To regain that power, you need to revisit the Group Policy Properties dialog box and grant yourself Full Control permission.

tip **Create an account for managing Group Policy**

As an alternative to modifying permissions each time you want to work with Group Policy, consider setting up a separate user account for configuring Group Policy. Instead of denying Read permission for the Administrators group (step 3 of the preceding procedure), add your own user account to the Group Or User Names list, and deny Read permission for it. Create a new account—your Group Policy configuration account—and make it a member of the Administrators group. Finally, set up a shortcut to Gpedit.msc. When you want to review or modify Group Policy settings, right-click the shortcut, choose Run As, and enter the name and password of your configuration account.

Keep in mind that, even without the aforementioned security shenanigans, the default security settings effectively produce two groups of users. Although the local Group Policy settings apply to all users (clarification: all users who have Read access to the local Group Policy object), only members of the local Administrators group can view or change these settings.

If customizing the effects of Group Policy settings based on group membership is important to you, you should install Windows .NET Server or Windows 2000 Server and set up Active Directory. But the methods described in this section can provide an easy compromise solution.

Managing Services

A *service* is a specialized program that performs a function to support other programs. Many services operate at a very low level (by interacting directly with hardware, for example) and need to remain running even when no user is logged on; for this reason, they are often run by the System account (which has elevated privileges) rather than by ordinary user accounts. Microsoft Windows XP includes services as varied as the Event Log service, which keeps a database of event messages, and the Telnet service, which allows remote users to log on to your computer using a command-line interface.

In this appendix, you'll learn how to view the installed services; start, stop, and configure them; and install or remove them. Then we take a closer look at some of the services used in Windows XP, showing how you can configure them to your advantage.

Using the Services Snap-In

You manage services with the Services snap-in for Microsoft Management Console (MMC), shown in Figure F-1 on the next page. To view this snap-in, type **services.msc** at a command prompt.

The Extended and Standard views in the Services console are functionally equivalent. The Standard view replicates the presentation offered by the Windows 2000 version of Services.msc. The Extended view provides descriptive information of the selected service in the space at the left edge of the details pane. This space also sometimes includes links for starting, stopping, or pausing the selected service. Unless you need to constrain the console display to a small area of your screen, you'll probably find the Extended view preferable to the Standard view.

At Home with Windows XP

The procedures for managing services are identical in both versions of Windows XP. Note, however, that not all services included with Windows XP Professional are installed in Windows XP Home Edition.

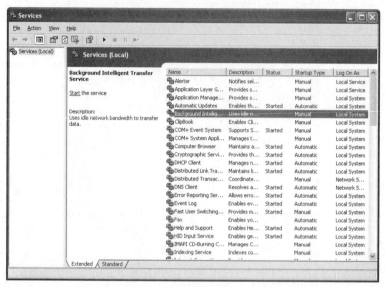

Figure F-1. Use the Services console to start, stop, and configure services.

The Services console offers plenty of information in its clean display. You can sort the display on the contents of any column by clicking the column title, as you can do with other similar lists. To sort in reverse order, click the column title again. In addition, you can

- Start, stop, pause, resume, or restart the selected service, as described in the following section

- Display the properties dialog box for the selected service, in which you can configure the service and learn more about it

Starting and Stopping Services

Most of the essential services are set to start automatically when your computer starts, and the operating system stops them as part of its shutdown process. But sometimes you might need to manually start or stop a service. For example, you might want to start a seldom-used service on the rare occasion when you need it. (Because running services requires system resources such as memory, running them only when necessary can improve performance.)

On the other hand, you might want to stop a service because you're no longer using it. A more common reason, however, for stopping a service is because it isn't working properly. For example, if print jobs get stuck in the print queue, sometimes the best remedy is to stop and then restart the Print Spooler service.

> **tip** If a service is one that allows pausing, try pausing and then continuing the service as your first step instead of stopping the service. Pausing can solve certain problems without canceling jobs in process or resetting connections.

To change a service's status, select it in the Services console. Then click the appropriate link in the area to the left of the service list (if you're using the Extended view and the link you need appears there). Alternatively, you can use the VCR-style controls in the toolbar, or right-click and choose the corresponding command.

- ▶ **Start, Resume.** Starts a service that isn't running, or resumes a service that has been paused.

- ■ **Stop.** Stops a running service.

- ‖ **Pause.** Pauses a running service. Pausing a service doesn't remove it from memory; it continues to run at a level that varies depending on the service. With some services, pausing allows users to complete jobs or disconnect from resources but does not allow them to create new jobs or connections.

- ■▶ **Restart.** Stops a running service and then restarts it.

You can also change a service's status by opening its properties dialog box and then clicking one of the buttons on the General tab. Taking the extra step of opening the properties dialog box to set the status has only one advantage: You can specify start parameters when you start a service using this method. This is a rare requirement.

Not all services permit you to change their status. Some prevent stopping and starting altogether, whereas others permit stopping and starting but not pausing and resuming. Some services allow these permissions to only certain users or groups. For example, most services allow only members of the Power Users and Administrators groups to start or stop them. Which status changes are allowed and who has permission to make them are controlled by each service's discretionary access control list (DACL), which is established when the service is created on a computer.

Configuring Services

To review or modify the way a service starts up or what happens when it doesn't start properly, view its properties dialog box. To do that, simply double-click the service in the Services console. Figure F-2 on the next page shows an example.

Figure F-2.   You specify the startup type on the General tab, where you can also find the actual name of the service above its display name.

Setting Startup Options

On the General tab of the properties dialog box (see Figure F-2), you specify the startup type:

- **Automatic.** The service starts when the computer starts.

- **Manual.** The service doesn't start automatically at startup, but it can be started by a user, a program, or a dependent service.

- **Disabled.** The service can't be started.

You'll find other startup options on the Log On tab of the properties dialog box, as shown in Figure F-3.

> **note**   If you specify a logon account other than the local System account, be sure that account has the requisite rights. Go to the Local Security Policy console (choose Start, Run, and type **secpol.msc**), and then go to Security Settings\Local Policies\User Rights Assignment and assign the Log On As A Service right to the account.

Figure F-3. On the Log On tab, you specify which user runs the service, and you can also specify which hardware profiles use the service.

Specifying Recovery Actions

For a variety of reasons—hardware not operating properly or a network connection down, to name a few—a service that's running smoothly might suddenly stop. Settings on the Recovery tab of the properties dialog box, shown in Figure F-4 on the next page, allow you to specify what should happen if a service fails.

You might want to perform a different action the first time a service fails than on the second or subsequent failures. The Recovery tab enables you to assign a particular response to the first failure, the second failure, and all subsequent failures, from among these options:

- **Take No Action.** The service gives up trying. In most cases, the service places a message in the event log. (Use of the event log depends on how the service was programmed by its developers.)

- **Restart The Service.** The computer waits for the time specified in the Restart Service After box to elapse and then tries to start the service.

- **Run A File.** The computer runs the program that you specify in the Run File box. This could be a program that attempts to resolve the problem or one that alerts you to the situation, for example.

Figure F-4. Use the Recovery tab to specify what should happen if the service fails.

- **Reboot The Computer.** Drastic but effective, this option restarts the computer after the time specified in the Restart Computer Options dialog box elapses. In that dialog box, you can also specify a message to be broadcast (using the Messenger service) to other users on your network, warning them of the impending shutdown.

Troubleshooting

Your service fails and Dr. Watson doesn't log it.

If you set up a service to log on using an account other than the local System account and the service fails, you won't get the Dr. Watson log or dump file that the failed service would otherwise generate. This occurs because Dr. Watson attempts to access the desktop of the service's logon account and it's unable to do so. To work around this problem, reconfigure the service to use the local System account and select the Allow Service To Interact With Desktop option. (Of course, this workaround doesn't help if the only way to *run* the service is by allowing it to log on with a different account.)

Viewing Dependencies

Many services rely on the functions of another service. If you attempt to start a service that depends on other services, Windows first starts the others. If you stop a service upon which others are dependent, Windows also stops those services. Before you either start or stop a service, therefore, it's helpful to know what other services your action might affect. To obtain that information, go to the Dependencies tab of a service's properties dialog box, shown in Figure F-5.

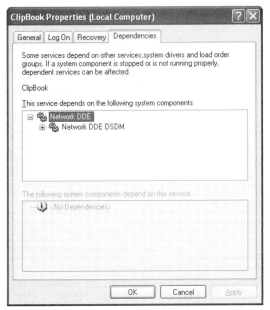

Figure F-5. The Dependencies tab shows which services depend on other services.

Determining a Service's Name

As you view the properties dialog box for different services, you might notice that the service name (shown at the top of the General tab) is often different from the name that appears in the Services console (the display name) and that neither name matches the name of the service's executable file. (In fact, the executable for many services is either Services.exe or Svchost.exe.) The General tab shows all three names.

So how does this affect you? When you work in the Services console, you don't need to know anything other than a service's display name to find it and work with it. But if you use the Net command to start and stop services (as explained in the following section), you might find using the service name more convenient; it is often much shorter than the display name. You'll also need the service name if you're ever forced to work with a service's registry entries, which can be found in the HKLM\System\CurrentControlSet\ Services*service* subkey (where *service* is the service name).

And what about the executable name? You might need it if certain users have problems running a service; in such a case, you need to find the executable and check its permissions. Knowing the executable name can also be useful, for example, if you're using Windows Task Manager to determine why your computer seems to be running so slowly. The Processes tab shows only executable names, many of which are inscrutable.

Appendix F

As mentioned earlier, you can find the actual name of each service and its executable name by looking at the General tab of the service's properties dialog box. For your reference, Table F-1 shows the names for all the services that are commonly installed with Windows XP Professional. Note that your system might have other services installed—from Microsoft or from another publisher—or it might not have all of these installed.

Table F-1. **Names of Services**

Display Name	Service Name	Executable
Alerter	Alerter	Svchost.exe
Application Layer Gateway Service	ALG	Alg.exe
Application Management	AppMgmt	Svchost.exe
Automatic Updates	Wuauserv	Svchost.exe
Background Intelligent Transfer Service	BITS	Svchost.exe
ClipBook	ClipSrv	Clipsrv.exe
COM+ Event System	EventSystem	Svchost.exe
COM+ System Application	COMSysApp	Dllhost.exe
Computer Browser	Browser	Svchost.exe
Cryptographic Services	CryptSvc	Svchost.exe
DHCP Client	Dhcp	Svchost.exe
Distributed Link Tracking Client	TrkWks	Svchost.exe
Distributed Transaction Coordinator	MSDTC	Msdtc.exe
DNS Client	Dnscache	Svchost.exe
Error Reporting	ERSvc	Svchost.exe
Event Log	Eventlog	Services.exe
Fast User Switching Compatibility	FastUserSwitching Compatibility	Svchost.exe
Fax	Fax	Fxssvc.exe
Help And Support	Helpsvc	Svchost.exe
HID Input Service	HidServ	Svchost.exe
IMAPI CD-Burning COM Service	ImapiService	Imapi.exe
Indexing Service	cisvc	Cisvc.exe

Table F-1. *(continued)*

Display Name	Service Name	Executable
Internet Connection Firewall (ICF) / Internet Connection Sharing (ICS)	SharedAccess	Svchost.exe
IPSEC Services	PolicyAgent	Lsass.exe
Logical Disk Manager	dmserver	Svchost.exe
Logical Disk Manager Administrative Service	dmadmin	Dmadmin.exe
Messenger	Messenger	Svchost.exe
MS Software Shadow Copy Provider	SwPrv	Dllhost.exe
Net Logon	Netlogon	Lsass.exe
NetMeeting Remote Desktop Sharing	mnmsrvc	Mnmsrvc.exe
Network Connections	Netman	Svchost.exe
Network DDE	NetDDE	Netdde.exe
Network DDE DSDM	NetDDEdsdm	Netdde.exe
Network Location Awareness (NLA)	Nla	Svchost.exe
NT LM Security Support Provider	NtLmSsp	Lsass.exe
Performance Logs And Alerts	SysmonLog	Smlogsvc.exe
Plug And Play	PlugPlay	Services.exe
Portable Media Serial Number	WmdmPmSp	Svchost.exe
Print Spooler	Spooler	Spoolsv.exe
Protected Storage	ProtectedStorage	Lsass.exe
QoS RSVP	RSVP	Rsvp.exe
Remote Access Auto Connection Manager	RasAuto	Svchost.exe
Remote Access Connection Manager	RasMan	Svchost.exe
Remote Desktop Help Session Manager	RDSessMgr	Sessmgr.exe
Remote Procedure Call (RPC)	RpcSs	Svchost.exe
Remote Procedure Call (RPC) Locator	RpcLocator	Locator.exe
Remote Registry	RemoteRegistry	Svchost.exe

(continued)

Appendix F

Table F-1. *(continued)*

Display Name	Service Name	Executable
Removable Storage	NtmsSvc	Svchost.exe
Routing And Remote Access	RemoteAccess	Svchost.exe
Secondary Logon	seclogon	Svchost.exe
Security Accounts Manager	SamSs	Lsass.exe
Server	lanmanserver	Svchost.exe
Shell Hardware Detection	ShellHWDetection	Svchost.exe
Smart Card	SCardSvr	Scardsvr.exe
Smart Card Helper	SCardDrv	Scardsvr.exe
SSDP Discovery Service	SSDPSRV	Svchost.exe
System Event Notification	SENS	Svchost.exe
System Restore Service	Srservice	Svchost.exe
Task Scheduler	Schedule	Svchost.exe
TCP/IP NetBIOS Helper	LmHosts	Svchost.exe
Telephony	TapiSrv	Svchost.exe
Telnet	TlntSvr	Tlntsvr.exe
Terminal Services	TermService	Svchost.exe
Themes	Themes	Svchost.exe
Uninterruptible Power Supply	UPS	Ups.exe
Universal Plug And Play Device Host	upnphost	Svchost.exe
Upload Manager	uploadmgr	Svchost.exe
Utility Manager	UtilMan	Utilman.exe
Volume Shadow Copy	VSS	Vssvc.exe
WebClient	WebClient	Svchost.exe
Windows Audio	AudioSrv	Svchost.exe
Windows Image Acquisition (WIA)	Stisvc	Svchost.exe
Windows Installer	MSIServer	Msiexec.exe

Table F-1. *(continued)*

Display Name	Service Name	Executable
Windows Management Instrumentation	winmgmt	Svchost.exe
Windows Management Instrumentation Driver Extensions	Wmi	Svchost.exe
Windows Time	W32Time	Svchost.exe
Wireless Zero Configuration	WZCSVC	Svchost.exe
WMI Performance Adapter	WmiApSrv	Wmiapsrv.exe
Workstation	lanmanworkstation	Svchost.exe

> **note** Like file names, the names of services are not case sensitive. In Table F-1, we capitalized the service names exactly as they appear in the registry. Although the capitalization style is sometimes inconsistent, you're likely to see this same capitalization whenever a particular service name is mentioned in documentation.

Recommended Startup Settings for Services

On a typical computer running Windows XP, literally dozens of services are installed by default. What do all those services do? Do you really need to have each of those running? Table F-2 lists the services you're likely to see on a base installation of Windows XP with Service Pack 1. In each case, we've included a brief description of the service, the account it uses for logon purposes, and our recommendations for setting the startup type (Automatic, Manual, Disabled).

Table F-2. Service Descriptions and Startup Settings

Service	Log On As	Description	Recommended Startup Type
Alerter	Local Service	Provides an administrative alert (a pop-up message box function that can be accessed via the Net Send command. Works in conjunction with the Messenger service. (See "Messenger and Alerter Services," page 1318, for more details.)	Manual; may be safely Disabled in most cases

(continued)

Table F-2. *(continued)*

Service	Log On As	Description	Recommended Startup Type
Application Layer Gateway Service	Local Service	Lets third-party software extend the functionality of Internet Connection Sharing (ICS) and Internet Connection Firewall (ICF).	Automatic on computers where ICS or ICF is being used; Manual on all others
Application Management	Local System	Designed for use in corporate installations, where administrators make applications available to network users, but appears to be required on standalone systems as well.	Manual
Automatic Updates	Local System	Checks for updates and patches at the Windows Update site and downloads or installs them automatically if you have selected those options.	Automatic if you use Automatic Updates; Disabled if you choose not to use this feature
Background Intelligent Transfer Service	Network Service	Lets programs download files over the Internet in a way that doesn't significantly interfere with the user's use of the available bandwidth; used by Automatic Updates feature.	Manual
ClipBook	Local System	Provides support for the obscure ClipBook Viewer application, which lets users share their Clipboard contents over the network.	Manual on computers that use ClipBook Viewer; Disabled for all other computers
COM+ Event System, COM+ System Application	Local System	System services that enable communication between applications using the Component Object Model.	Manual

Table F-2. *(continued)*

Service	Log On As	Description	Recommended Startup Type
Computer Browser	Local System	Allows a system to act as a "browse master," which maintains a list of other computers on the network. On Windows networks, computers elect a browse master.	Automatic
Cryptographic Services	Local System	Provides verification services for digitally signed files (such as device drivers and ActiveX controls), among other system-level cryptographic functions.	Automatic
DHCP Client	Local System	Acquires network settings (IP addresses and DNS names) from a Dynamic Host Control Protocol (DHCP) server at startup.	Automatic; may be set to Disabled if network settings are configured manually
Distributed Link Tracking Client	Local System	Maintains links between shortcuts and target files on NTFS volumes within a computer and on computers within a Windows domain.	Automatic on computers joined to a Windows domain; Manual on computers within a workgroup
Distributed Transaction Coordinator	Network Service	Coordinates transactions that span multiple resource managers, such as databases, message queues, and file systems, primarily with Microsoft Transaction Server and Microsoft SQL Server.	Manual
DNS Client	Network Service	Caches records of Domain Name System (DNS) lookups to improve performance. Required if using IPSec.	Automatic; may be set to Manual or Disabled if you prefer not to use DNS caching

(continued)

Table F-2. *(continued)*

Service	Log On As	Description	Recommended Startup Type
Error Reporting	Local System	Allows the operating system and applications to automatically report errors to Microsoft. To disable this feature, open Control Panel, System, and click the Error Reporting button on the Advanced tab; then select Disable Error Reporting.	Manual; Disabled if you have turned off this feature using the System Control Panel
Event Log	Local System	Maintains the system event log; this crucial service should never be disabled.	Automatic
Fast User Switching Compatibility	Local System	Supports applications when multiple users are logged on to a single computer using the Fast User Switching feature of Windows XP. (For details, see "Controlling How Users Log On," page 107.)	Manual
Fax	Local System	This optional service provides fax capabilities. (For more details, see Chapter 20, "Sending and Receiving Faxes.")	Manual; Automatic if you want your computer to receive faxes
Help And Support	Local System	Provides access to Help And Support Center in Windows XP. Most accesses will cause this service to start.	Automatic
HID Input Service	Local System	Handles the wheels and custom navigation buttons on some mice and keyboards; a standard 102-key keyboard and PS/2 mouse do not require this service.	Automatic; Manual if you have generic input hardware
IMAPI CD-Burning COM Service	Local System	Used by the built-in CD-burning feature in Windows XP.	Manual; may be set to Disabled if you don't have a CD-RW drive

1306

Table F-2. *(continued)*

Service	Log On As	Description	Recommended Startup Type
Indexing Service	Local System	Builds an index of files on your computer to speed up searches; if these indexes don't exist, file-by-file Search functions will work, albeit more slowly. (See "Using Indexing Service and Query Language," page 480, for more details.)	Automatic; set to Disabled if you prefer not to use Indexing Service
Internet Connection Firewall (ICF) / Internet Connection Sharing (ICS)	Local System	Provides Network Address Translation, address translation, and firewall services on networks.	Automatic on computers using ICS or ICF; Manual on all other computers
IPSEC Services	Local System	Manages IP Security (IPSec) policy, starts the Internet Security Key Management Protocol (ISAKMP/Oakley), and loads the IP security driver.	Automatic if you use IPSec; otherwise, set to Manual
Logical Disk Manager	Local System	Detects and monitors new hard disk drives and sends information about disk volumes to Logical Disk Manager Administrative Service	Automatic
Logical Disk Manager Administrative Service	Local System	Supports the Disk Management (Local) snap-in used in the Disk Management (Diskmgmt.msc) and Computer Management (Compmgmt.msc) consoles. Runs when needed for configuration tasks and then stops.	Manual

(continued)

Table F-2. *(continued)*

Service	Log On As	Description	Recommended Startup Type
Messenger	Local Service	Used, along with the Alerter service, by the Net Send command-line utility to send administrative alerts. Not related to Windows Messenger or MSN Messenger.	Manual; may be safely Disabled in most cases
MS Software Shadow Copy Provider	Local System	Allows the Windows Backup utility (and other compatible backup programs) to use the volume shadow copy feature, which takes a "snapshot" of open files so they can be backed up.	Manual
Net Logon	Local System	Used only for authentication of account logon events in Windows domains.	Manual
NetMeeting Remote Desktop Sharing	Local System	Supports the desktop-sharing feature of Microsoft NetMeeting. If you don't use NetMeeting, this feature is a potential security risk.	Manual on computers that use NetMeeting; Disabled on all other computers
Network Connections	Local System	Manages objects in the Network And Dial-Up Connections folder; unless you disable it, this service starts automatically when it's needed.	Manual
Network DDE; Network DDE DSDM	Local System	Supports Dynamic Data Exchange (DDE) over networks; very few modern Windows programs use Network DDE.	Disabled unless you're certain a program you use requires this service
Network Location Awareness (NLA)	Local System	Supports the ability to use multiple network configurations; used primarily on notebook computers and when ICF or ICS is in use.	Manual

Table F-2. *(continued)*

Service	Log On As	Description	Recommended Startup Type
NT LM Security Support Provider	Local System	Provides authentication for a small number of applications (notably Microsoft Exchange Server) that use remote procedure call (RPC) connections.	Manual
Performance Logs And Alerts	Network Service	Provides options to run a program and send a message when specific conditions occur. You specify alerts using the Performance console (Perfmon.msc). (Note that the "Send a network message" action requires the Alerter service to be running.)	Manual
Plug And Play	Local System	Detects and configures Plug and Play hardware devices. This service is an essential part of Windows and should never be disabled.	Automatic
Portable Media Serial Number	Local System	Retrieves the serial number of any portable music device connected to a computer running Windows XP; used to manage digital rights when transferring protected media files.	Automatic if you have a portable music player; may be set to Manual or Disabled on all other computers
Print Spooler	Local System	Manages print jobs on local and network printers. If this service is stopped, applications do not see any printers installed.	Automatic
Protected Storage	Local System	Provides encrypted storage of passwords, private keys, and other sensitive data; Internet Explorer and Outlook Express are two programs that use this service.	Automatic

(continued)

1309

Table F-2. *(continued)*

Service	Log On As	Description	Recommended Startup Type
QoS RSVP	Local System	Provides a mechanism for an application to gracefully share bandwidth with other applications. (The name stands for Quality of Service Resource Reservation Protocol.) Applications must be QoS-aware for this service to be used; the only common QoS-aware application that ships with Windows is NetMeeting.	Manual
Remote Access Auto Connection Manager	Local System	Automatically dials a connection (a connection to a dial-up ISP, for instance, or a VPN connection) when necessary to connect to a remote network.	Manual; may be set to Disabled if you never use dial-up connections of any kind
Remote Access Connection Manager	Local System	Creates network connections of all types in the Network And Dial-Up Connections folder; also required by ICF and ICS.	Manual
Remote Desktop Help Session Manager	Local System	Manages and controls the Remote Assistance feature of Windows XP.	Manual; may be set to Disabled if you have no intention of using Remote Assistance and want to reduce possible security risks
Remote Procedure Call (RPC)	Local System	Supports RPC functionality that is used throughout Windows. If this service is turned off, Windows will not start.	Automatic
Remote Procedure Call (RPC) Locator	Network Service	Manages the RPD name service database, which helps other computers find RPC-based programs.	Manual

1310

Table F-2. *(continued)*

Service	Log On As	Description	Recommended Startup Type
Remote Registry	Local Service	Lets another user at a remote computer modify the registry on your computer. This feature is typically used only in large organizations and represents a security risk if not carefully configured.	Automatic if your network uses this feature; Disabled on all other computers
Removable Storage	Local System	Poorly documented service used primarily to manage "jukebox" style tape backup devices. Rarely used on workstations.	Manual; may safely be set to Disabled on computers where no removable storage is available
Routing And Remote Access	Local System	Provides support for LAN-based routing, specifically incoming dial-up and VPN connections.	Manual if you use any such connections; Disabled on all other computers
Secondary Logon	Local System	Allows a user to start a program using an alternative user name and password; this service can be effectively used by Scheduled Tasks and by administrators.	Automatic
Security Accounts Manager	Local System	Manages security information for all local accounts. This service is essential to the proper operation of Windows and should never be disabled.	Automatic
Server	Local System	Supports network file and printer sharing and provides RPC support. To prevent all incoming access to files on this system via file and printer sharing, remove the File And Printer Sharing For Microsoft Networks component from all network connections.	Automatic

(continued)

Appendix F

Table F-2. *(continued)*

Service	Log On As	Description	Recommended Startup Type
Shell Hardware Detection	Local System	Constantly monitors for the presence of new hardware devices and sends information about newly detected hardware to the operating system and applications.	Automatic
Smart Card; Smart Card Helper	Local Service	Supports smart card authentication hardware, typically used in large, security-conscious organizations.	Manual
SSDP Discovery Service	Local Service	The Simple Service Discovery Protocol (SSDP) provides a mechanism for Universal Plug and Play (UPnP) devices to announce their presence on the network so that other computers can "discover" them. In late 2001, a buffer overflow vulnerability was patched in this service (Microsoft Security Bulletin MS01-059). ICF depends on UPnP to provide incoming connections to systems behind the firewall. If SSDP is disabled, you can't use Remote Desktop and Remote Assistance to access systems across the Internet.	Manual
System Event Notification	Local System	Tracks system events such as logon, network, screen-saver starts, and power events.	Automatic
System Restore Service	Local System	Creates and manages System Restore Checkpoints. For more details about setting up this essential safety net, see "Configuring System Restore Options," page 78.	Automatic; may be set to Disabled if you turn off System Restore completely
Task Scheduler	Local System	Runs programs in the Scheduled Tasks folder.	Automatic

1312

Table F-2. *(continued)*

Service	Log On As	Description	Recommended Startup Type
TCP/IP NetBIOS Helper	Local Service	Provides support for NetBIOS over TCP/IP and NetBIOS name management services; provided for compatibility with Windows 2000.	Automatic
Telephony	Local System	Supports programs that control telephony devices (typically modems) and IP-based voice connections. ICS and ICF also start this service.	Manual
Telnet	Local System	Allows a remote user to access a computer's resources and run programs from the command line. Most Windows users will never use Telnet and should consider it a potential security risk.	Manual on computers where Telnet access is desired; Disabled on all other computers
Terminal Services	Local System	Supports a variety of features in Windows XP that allow multiple users to connect to a computer interactively and to display desktops and applications on remote computers. This service is an essential component in Remote Desktop, Remote Assistance, and Fast User Switching.	Manual
Themes	Local System	Provides support for visual effects associated with the new look and feel of Windows XP.	Automatic; may be set to Disabled if you have chosen the Windows Classic look (Control Panel, Display, Themes) and do not intend to use any of the new interface features

(continued)

Table F-2. *(continued)*

Service	Log On As	Description	Recommended Startup Type
Uninterruptible Power Supply	Local Service	Allows an uninterruptible power supply (UPS) to notify the computer when power has failed and the battery is running low. This service requires that the UPS be connected to the computer using a serial or USB cable, and that the UPS service be configured via Control Panel, Power Options.	Manual
Universal Plug And Play Device Host	Local System	Allows the operating system to send UPnP announcements on behalf of non-computer peripherals, such as printers and cameras. The peripheral must provide the drivers and software to support UPnP.	Manual; Automatic if you use any such devices
Upload Manager	Local System	Manages synchronous and asynchronous file transfers between computers on a network.	Automatic
Utility Manager	Local System	This optional service enables a variety of tools, including Microsoft Narrator, designed to make Windows XP more accessible for users with visual impairments.	Manual
Volume Shadow Copy	Local System	Manages the volume shadow, a feature of Windows XP that backup programs can use to take a "snapshot" of volumes with open files so that they can perform a complete backup without requiring the user to shut down all running programs.	Manual

Table F-2. *(continued)*

Service	Log On As	Description	Recommended Startup Type
WebClient	Local Service	Allows Windows programs to create, access, and modify Internet files using WebDAV (uncommon in everyday use).	Automatic
Windows Audio	Local System	Manages audio devices and supports playing of sounds. You cannot stop this service from the Services console, which is a strong hint that it should always be running.	Automatic
Windows Image Acquisition (WIA)	Local System	Provides image-acquisition services for still-image devices—cameras and scanners	Manual
Windows Installer	Local System	Supports installation, repair, and removal of programs that use instructions contained in Windows Installer (.msi) files.	Manual
Windows Management Instrumentation	Local System	Provides information about your system configuration to Windows and to third-party applications; if this service is stopped, most Windows-based software will experience problems.	Automatic
Windows Management Instrumentation Driver Extensions	Local System	Communicates information between the operating system and any WSMI-compatible drivers.	Manual
Windows Time	Local System	Allows you to synchronize the date and time on a computer with a remote server using options you set on the Internet Time tab of Control Panel, Date And Time.	Automatic; may be set to Manual or Disabled if you prefer to set the time manually or use alternate synchronization software

(continued)

Table F-2. *(continued)*

Service	Log On As	Description	Recommended Startup Type
Wireless Zero Configuration	Local System	Supports automatic configuration of wireless LAN (802.11) adapters.	Automatic if your computer uses a wireless network adapter; otherwise may be safely set to Manual or Disabled
WMI Performance Adapter	Local System	Implements performance counters as part of Windows Management Instrumentation.	Manual
Workstation	Local System	Makes network connections with remote computers. Many Windows functions depend on this service being available.	Automatic

Managing Services from a Command Prompt

If you want to control services via a batch program—or if you simply prefer working at a command prompt—you can use variants of the Net command. Don't be dissuaded by the name—the Net command manages all services, not only network services. Table F-3 shows the Net commands to use for managing services.

Table F-3. Net Commands for Managing Services

Command	Description
Net Start	Displays a list of running services.
Net Start *service*	Starts the *service* service. For *service*, you can use either the service name or its display name. (For example, *net start schedule* and *net start "task scheduler"* are equivalent.) For a list of services installed by default with Windows XP Professional, see Table F-1 on page 1300. Surround multiword service names with quotation marks.
Net Stop *service*	Stops the *service* service. The service must be started before you can stop it.

Table F-3. *(continued)*

Command	Description
Net Pause *service*	Pauses the *service* service. The service must be started before you can pause it. Many services don't permit pausing.
Net Continue *service*	Resumes the *service* service. The service must be paused before you can resume it.

Services Included with Windows XP Professional

As you peruse the list of services in the Services console, you'll recognize many that relate to features described elsewhere in this book. Although those sections of the book don't specifically describe the function of the service (because there's usually no reason to change the default settings), now you know where to look. In the remaining sections of this appendix, we explain the use of a few services that aren't described elsewhere—and that often go unmentioned in discussions of Windows XP. Nonetheless, you might find them useful.

Windows Time Service

Windows XP includes a service, Windows Time or W32Time, that synchronizes the time and date of computers on a network. This is more than a convenience: Synchronized time is critical because the Kerberos version 5 protocol uses workstation time as part of the authentication process. Windows Time uses the Simple Network Time Protocol (SNTP) to synchronize a computer's time with a designated time server, known as the *inbound time partner.*

In a Microsoft Windows 2000 Server–based or Windows .NET Server–based network, workstations and member servers use their authenticating domain controller as their inbound time partner. (This happens automatically, and you don't need to do anything to configure the workstations other than ensuring that the Windows Time service is running.) In an enterprise with multiple domains and multiple domain controllers in each domain, the domain controllers follow the domain hierarchy to find their inbound time partner. The domain controller at the root of the forest is typically configured by the network administrator to synchronize its time with an authoritative outside time source, such as the United States Naval Observatory (USNO).

Workgroup computers, by default, synchronize once a week with time.windows.com. If your computer does not have a continuous Internet connection and you miss a scheduled synchronization, you can synchronize manually by opening Date and Time in Control Panel. On the Internet Time tab, click Update Now. In this dialog box, you can also select or specify an alternative time server, if you don't want to use time.windows.com.

1317

Assuming that the Windows Time service has been started (set its startup type to Automatic if it isn't already), your computer should periodically synchronize its clock with the NTP server.

> **note** SNTP uses port 123 to communicate with the time server. If you use an IPSec policy or a firewall for port blocking, be sure that port 123 is open.

> **tip** **Synchronize the time with the Net Time /Set command**
>
> If you have trouble synchronizing computers using the Windows Time service, you can use the Net Time /Set command, which was the most common method for performing a one-time synchronization in earlier versions of Windows. To synchronize your computer's clock with the clock on the computer named Glacier, for example, type **net time /set \\glacier /y** at a command prompt. To update your time regularly and automatically, put this command in your logon script or set it up as a scheduled task.

The process of setting the time on a computer is an *iterative* one at several levels, meaning that the process repeats upon itself until the required synchronization is achieved. When the computer contacts its inbound time partner, the two computers exchange packets until they determine the transmission latency between them. Then the client computer adjusts its clock. The amount of adjustment depends on how far off the clock is initially. If it's less than 2 minutes fast, the time is adjusted over a 20-minute period until the clock is synchronized; otherwise, it's immediately set to the correct time. Thereafter, the client computer periodically contacts its inbound time partner to resynchronize. The period is adjusted from 45 minutes through 8 hours, depending on how far off the clock drifts between synchronizations. Windows Time attempts to minimize the number of synchronizations while still keeping the clock within 2 seconds of its inbound time partner.

This iterative process, along with an explanation of the hierarchy of inbound time partners in an enterprise environment, is explained in Microsoft Knowledge Base article Q224799.

Messenger and Alerter Services

The Messenger service and the Alerter service provide a means of sending messages from one computer to another on your network.

Using the Messenger Service

The Messenger service allows you to receive pop-up messages sent from other computers on your network using the Net Send command. It's a crude but effective communication system that you can use for instantly alerting others. The receiving system doesn't need to have its e-mail client running; in fact, it doesn't need an e-mail client at all. The only prerequisite on the receiving end is that the Messenger service is running.

To send a message, you use the Net Send *recipient message* command. Replace *recipient* with the user name of the person you want to reach or the name of the computer where you want the message displayed. If you want to send a message to all users currently connected to your computer's shared resources (perhaps to warn them that you're going to shut down the computer), replace *recipient* with /Users. And if you want to send a message to all users in your workgroup or domain, replace *recipient* with an asterisk (*). You should, of course, replace *message* with the text you want to send. For example, at a command prompt, you could type the following:

```
net send * The pizza has arrived. Come to the lunchroom!
```

If you send a message to a computer on which the Messenger service is not running, Net Send reports its inability to send the message. In such a case, you'll see an error message whether you address your message to a computer, to a user, or to /Users. However, if you send a message to everyone in your workgroup or domain using an asterisk as the recipient, Net Send does not let you know who received the message and who did not.

Some programs other than Net Send rely on the Messenger service. For example, messages from a network printer that is configured to send notification of completed print jobs appear on your computer only if the Messenger service is running.

Using the Alerter Service

The Alerter service uses the same mechanism as the Messenger service, but it's used by Windows to send administrative alerts. Alert messages warn about security, access, printer, and other problems. To set up a computer so that it sends administrative alerts to another computer, follow these steps:

1 On the computer where the administrative alerts will originate (that is, a computer that you want to notify you when a problem arises), start a registry editor.

2 In the HKLM\System\CurrentControlSet\Services\Alerter\Parameters key, create a REG_MULTI_SZ value named AlertNames if it doesn't already exist.

3 Set the AlertNames data to the name of the computer that you want to receive the administrative alerts. You can specify multiple names if you want; type each name on a new line.

4 Use the Services console to set the Alerter service for automatic startup and start the service.

5 On the computer where you want to receive the alerts, use the Services console to set the Messenger service for automatic startup and start the service.

Viewing System Information

Whether it's for troubleshooting purposes or just curiosity, you'll occasionally need to find out more about your computer system: what kind of hardware you have, what software is installed, and so on. This appendix provides an overview of the tools included with Microsoft Windows XP for displaying information about your system.

Finding Basic Information About Your Computer

For answers to basic questions about your operating system and computer, there's no better place to start than the General tab of the System Properties dialog box, shown in Figure G-1 on the next page. No matter where you are in Windows or what your preferred input method, System Properties is only a few clicks or keystrokes away. You can open System Properties in any of the following ways:

- Press the Windows logo key+Break.

- Right-click My Computer and choose Properties. (This works just about any place that My Computer appears, including on the Start menu, on the desktop, in Windows Explorer's task pane, and in a Windows Explorer window.)

- In Control Panel, open System (in the Performance And Maintenance category).

- At a command prompt, type **sysdm.cpl**.

At Home with Windows XP

The command-line utility Systeminfo.exe is not available in Windows XP Home Edition. All the other information tools described in this appendix are available in both editions of Windows XP.

Operating system, version number, and service pack level

Processor type and speed

Installed memory

Figure G-1. System Properties provides essential information.

From System Properties, it's a short hop over to Device Manager, shown in Figure G-2. Device Manager shows detailed information about your installed hardware, including information about drivers. If you already have System Properties open, click the Hardware tab and then click Device Manager. You can open Device Manager directly, without first passing through System Properties, by typing **devmgmt.msc** at a command prompt.

Device Manager shows the devices. For details about how to use this information, see Chapter 6, "Setting Up and Troubleshooting Hardware."

1322

Figure G-2. Device Manager is an MMC snap-in that lists installed devices.

> **tip** **Use Computer Management**
>
> The Device Manager snap-in is included in the Computer Management console, along with a number of other useful snap-ins. You can open Computer Management in any of the following ways:
>
> - Right-click My Computer and choose Manage.
> - In Administrative Tools (if it's not on your Start menu, go to Control Panel's Performance And Maintenance category), open Computer Management.
> - At a command prompt, type **compmgmt.msc**.

Finding Information in the Help And Support Center

The most attractive display of system information appears in the Help And Support Center. In addition to presenting copious information in an eye-catching format, the Help And Support Center pages include links to troubleshooters, updates, and help text. Figure G-3 on the next page shows an example.

Figure G-3. The Help And Support Center offers a wealth of system information—after you find the right links.

Although the presentation in the Help And Support Center is nice, finding the information you want requires that you pick through the right links to find what you need. Start your journey at the Help And Support Center home page. On the right side, under Pick A Task, click Use Tools To View Your Computer Information And Diagnose Problems. Then, in the list of Tools that appears in the left pane, click My Computer Information. A list of links then appears in the right pane; each leads to a different report about your system.

Digging Deeper with Dedicated System Information Tools

If you want just the straight scoop about your configuration without the visual enhancements, Windows offers two tools with similar names, Systeminfo and System Information.

Systeminfo   Systeminfo.exe is a command-line utility that displays information about your Windows version, BIOS, processor, memory, and a few more esoteric items. Figure G-4 shows sample output.

To run Systeminfo, at a command prompt type **systeminfo**. In addition to the list format shown in the figure, Systeminfo offers two formats that are useful if you want to work with the information in another program: Table

1324

(fixed-width columns) and CSV (comma-separated values). To use one of these formats, include the /Fo switch. You'll also need to redirect the output to a file. For example, to store comma-delimited information in a file named Info.csv, enter the following command:

```
systeminfo /fo csv > info.csv
```

The /S switch allows you to get system information about another computer on your network. (If your user name and password don't match that of an account on the target computer, you'll also need to use the /U and /P switches to provide the user name and password of an authorized account.) When you've gathered information about all the computers on your network, you can import the file you created into a spreadsheet or database program for tracking and analysis. The following command appends information about a computer named Badlands to the original file you created.

```
systeminfo /s badlands /fo csv >> info.csv
```

> **note** Systeminfo.exe is not available in Windows XP Home Edition.

System Information System Information—often called by the name of its executable, Msinfo32.exe—is a techie's paradise. It provides all manner of information about your system's hardware and software in a no-frills window. In addition, it serves as a menu to other diagnostic tools. The following sections discuss System Information in greater detail.

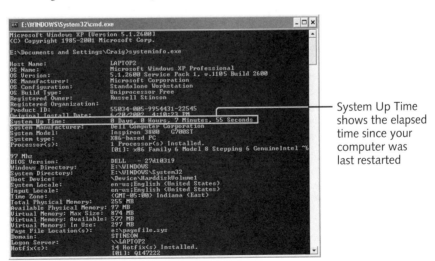

System Up Time shows the elapsed time since your computer was last restarted

Figure G-4. The command-line utility Systeminfo.exe provides an easy way to gather information on all your network computers in a single database.

Finding and Decoding Information in System Information

System Information displays a wealth of configuration information in a clear display, as shown in Figure G-5. With System Information, you can search for specific information, save information, view information about other computers, and even view a list of changes to your system.

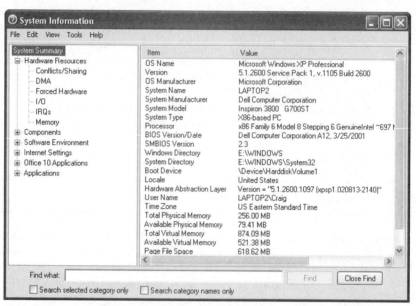

Figure G-5. System Information is for viewing configuration information only; you can't use it to make settings.

To start System Information, use any of the following methods:

- In the Run dialog box, type **msinfo32**.

- In a Command Prompt window, type **start msinfo32**.

- Click Start and choose All Programs, Accessories, System Tools, System Information.

- From the home page in the Help And Support Center, click Use Tools To View Your Computer Information And Diagnose Problems, Advanced System Information, View Detailed System Information (Msinfo32.exe).

- In the About dialog box (the dialog box you reach by choosing Help, About) of many applications, including Microsoft Office applications, click System Info.

You navigate through System Information much as you would through Windows Explorer or an MMC console: You click a category in the left pane to view its contents in the right pane. Table G-1 provides a summary of the available information. System

1326

Information is *extensible*, which means that other programs can provide information about themselves in a format that can be displayed in System Information; you might see additional categories and additional information on your system.

Table G-1. **Information Available in Msinfo32**

Category	Description
System Summary	Information similar to that provided by Systeminfo.exe: Windows version, computer name, computer make and model, processor, BIOS version and date, memory summary
Hardware Resources	Information about shared system resources, such as I/O ports and IRQs; device conflicts; DMA channels in use; devices with manually specified resources instead of system-assigned resources; I/O ports in use; IRQs in use; and memory addresses used by devices
Components	Information about each installed hardware device, including resources used, device descriptions, drivers, and current status
Software Environment	Information about drivers, environment variables, open print jobs, mapped network connections, running tasks, loaded system-level DLLs, services, Start menu program groups, programs that run at startup, file associations for OLE objects, and application crashes
Internet Settings	Information about files used by Microsoft Internet Explorer, your Internet connection, temporary Internet files, certificates, and Internet Explorer security settings
Applications	Application-specific information that can be added to System Information by your installed programs; Office, for example, lists detailed information about everything from file versions to installed fonts to default page layout settings

To find specific information, use the find feature in System Information. (If the Find bar does not appear at the bottom of the System Information window, choose Edit, Hide Find.) The find feature is basic, but effective. A couple of things you should know:

- Whenever you type in the Find What box to start a new search, Find begins its search at the top of the search range (the entire namespace unless you select Search Selected Category Only)—not at the current highlight.

- Selecting Search Category Names Only causes the find feature to look only in the left pane. When this check box is clear, all text in both panes is searched.

1327

Exporting System Information

You can preserve your configuration information—always helpful when reconstructing a system—in several ways:

- You can save the information as an .nfo file. You can subsequently open the file (on the same computer or on a different computer with System Information) to view your saved information. To save information in this format, choose File, Save. Saving this way always saves the entire collection of information.

- You can save all or part of the information as a plain text file. To save information as a text file, select the category of interest and choose File, Export. If you want to save all the information as a text file, select System Summary before you save.

- You can print all or part of the information. Select the category of interest, choose File, Print, and be sure that Selection is selected under Page Range. To print everything, select All under Page Range—and be sure to have lots of paper on hand. Depending on your system configuration, the number of installed applications, and so on, your report could top 100 pages.

Regardless of how you save your information, System Information refreshes (updates) the information immediately before processing the command.

---

tip **Save your system information periodically**

Saving system configuration information when your computer is working properly provides a useful tool when you have problems. Comparing the computer's current configuration with a known, good baseline configuration can help you spot possible problem areas. You can open multiple instances of System Information, so that you could have the current configuration displayed in one window and a baseline configuration in another.

Viewing System Information History

System Information maintains a one-month history of key parts of your configuration. It updates its history records by taking a daily snapshot, and it also records any differences from the last snapshot that it encounters whenever you run System Information. Armed with this information, you can go back and see what configuration changes occurred shortly before a problem started; this might help to isolate a problem.

You can view configuration changes by choosing View, System History. Select a date in the View Changes Since box and select a category. (Only top-level categories appear in this view.) As shown in Figure G-6, the display is rather dense, but you can use a couple of techniques to focus on information of interest:

● Click a column heading to sort the records by that field.

● Use the find feature.

Figure G-6. Here you can see that several folders were removed from the Start menu.

Using System Information to Open Other Diagnostic Tools

The Tools menu in System Information has commands that open other tools for displaying system information that can be helpful in diagnosing problems, including the following:

● **Net Diagnostics.** Network Diagnostics displays detailed information about your network connections. In addition to displaying configuration information, it performs a number of tests for network connectivity (such as pinging other computers on your network and your DNS server).

● **DirectX Diagnostic Tool.** DirectX Diagnostic Tool displays information about DirectX components, which use hardware acceleration to enhance video and audio performance. In addition, DirectX Diagnostic Tool performs several compatibility tests. You can open DirectX Diagnostic Tool directly by typing **dxdiag** at a command prompt.

Index to Troubleshooting Topics

Index to Troubleshooting Topics

Index to Troubleshooting Topics

Index to Troubleshooting Topics

Index

F

About the Authors

Ed Bott is a best-selling author and award-winning journalist who has been a part of the personal computer industry since the days when an 8-MHz 80286 was a smokin' machine. Ed's feature stories and columns about Microsoft Windows have appeared regularly in print and on the Web for more than a decade, and he has written 14 books on nearly every version of Microsoft Windows and Microsoft Office. He and Carl Siechert have collaborated on three books for Microsoft Press, including *Microsoft Windows Security Inside Out*. Ed is a three-time winner of the Computer Press Award, twice for *PC Computing*'s groundbreaking Windows SuperGuide. After spending three years living in Microsoft's neighborhood in Redmond, Washington, Ed and his wife Judy exchanged the gray and damp of the Northwest for the sunny Southwest and have never been happier.

Carl Siechert began his writing career at age 8 as editor of the *Mesita Road News*, a neighborhood newsletter that reached a peak worldwide circulation of 43 during its eight-year run. Following several years as an estimator and production manager in a commercial printing business, Carl returned to writing with the formation of Siechert & Wood Professional Documentation, a Pasadena, California firm that specializes in writing and producing product documentation for the personal computer industry. Carl is a coauthor of several books published by Microsoft Press, including *Field Guide to MS-DOS 6.2*, *Microsoft Windows 2000 Professional Expert Companion*, and *Microsoft Windows Security Inside Out*. Carl hiked the Pacific Crest Trail from Mexico to Canada in 1977 and would rather be hiking right now. He and his wife Jan live in southern California.

Craig Stinson, an industry journalist since 1981, is a contributing editor of *PC Magazine* and was formerly editor of *Softalk for the IBM Personal Computer*. Craig is the author of *Running Microsoft Windows 98* and a coauthor of *Microsoft Excel Inside Out* and *Running Microsoft Windows 2000 Professional*, all published by Microsoft Press. Craig is an amateur musician and has reviewed classical music for various newspapers and trade publications, including *Billboard*, the *Boston Globe*, the *Christian Science Monitor*, and *Musical America*. He lives with his wife and children in Bloomington, Indiana.

The authors have set up a Web site for readers of this book. At the site, you can find updates, corrections, and more useful tips. In addition, you can discuss Windows XP with the authors and with other readers. We hope you'll join us at *http://groups.msn.com/WindowsXPInsideOut*.

The manuscript for this book was prepared and galleyed using Microsoft Word 2002. Pages were composed by Microsoft Press using Adobe PageMaker 6.52 for Windows, with text in Minion and display type in Syntax. Composed pages were delivered to the printer as electronic prepress files.

coverdesigner
GIRVIN/Strategic Branding & Design

coverillustrator
Todd Daman

interiorgraphicdesigner
James D. Kramer

productionservices
Publishing.com

projectmanager
Curtis Philips

copyeditor
Erin Milnes

interiorartists
Lisa Bellomo and Jordana Glenn

pagecomposition
North Coast Publishing

proofreader
Andrea Fox

indexer
Rebecca Plunkett

Target your problem and *fix it yourself—*
fast!

When you're stuck with a computer problem, you need answers right now. TROUBLESHOOTING books can help. They'll guide you to the source of the problem and show you how to solve it right away. Get ready solutions with clear, step-by-step instructions. Go to quick-access charts with *Top 20 Problems* and *Prevention Tips*. Find even more solutions with *Quick Fixes* and handy *Tips*. Walk through the remedy with plenty of screen shots. Find what you need with the extensive, easy-reference index. Get the answers you need to get back to business fast with TROUBLESHOOTING books.

Troubleshooting Microsoft® Office XP
ISBN 0-7356-1491-1

Troubleshooting Microsoft Access Databases
(Covers Access 97 and Access 2000)
ISBN 0-7356-1160-2

Troubleshooting Microsoft Access 2002
ISBN 0-7356-1488-1

Troubleshooting Microsoft Excel Spreadsheets
(Covers Excel 97 and Excel 2000)
ISBN 0-7356-1161-0

Troubleshooting Microsoft Excel 2002
ISBN 0-7356-1493-8

Troubleshooting Microsoft Outlook®
(Covers Microsoft Outlook 2000 and Outlook Express)
ISBN 0-7356-1162-9

Troubleshooting Microsoft Outlook 2002
(Covers Microsoft Outlook 2002 and Outlook Express)
ISBN 0-7356-1487-3

Troubleshooting Your Web Page
(Covers Microsoft FrontPage® 2000)
ISBN 0-7356-1164-5

Troubleshooting Microsoft FrontPage® 2002
ISBN 0-7356-1489-X

Troubleshooting Microsoft Project 2002
ISBN 0-7356-1503-9

Troubleshooting Microsoft Windows®
(Covers Windows Me, Windows 98, and Windows 95)
ISBN 0-7356-1166-1

Troubleshooting Microsoft Windows 2000 Professional
ISBN 0-7356-1165-3

Troubleshooting Microsoft Windows XP
ISBN 0-7356-1492-X

Troubleshooting Your PC, Second Edition
ISBN 0-7356-1490-3

Microsoft®
microsoft.com/mspress

Work smarter—
conquer your software from the inside out!

Hey, you know your way around a desktop. Now dig into Office XP applications and the Windows XP operating system and *really* put your PC to work! These supremely organized software reference titles pack hundreds of timesaving solutions, troubleshooting tips and tricks, and handy workarounds in a concise, fast-answer format. They're all muscle and no fluff. All this comprehensive information goes deep into the nooks and crannies of each Office application and Windows XP feature. INSIDE OUT titles also include a CD-ROM full of handy tools and utilities, sample files, an eBook links to related sites, and other help. Discover the best and fastest ways to perform everyday tasks, and challenge yourself to new levels of software mastery!

MICROSOFT® WINDOWS® XP INSIDE OUT
ISBN 0-7356-1382-6

MICROSOFT WINDOWS SECURITY INSIDE OUT
FOR WINDOWS XP AND WINDOWS 2000
ISBN 0-7356-1632-9

MICROSOFT OFFICE XP INSIDE OUT
ISBN 0-7356-1277-3

MICROSOFT OFFICE v. X FOR MAC INSIDE OUT
ISBN 0-7356-1628-0

MICROSOFT WORD VERSION 2002 INSIDE OUT
ISBN 0-7356-1278-1

MICROSOFT EXCEL VERSION 2002 INSIDE OUT
ISBN 0-7356-1281-1

MICROSOFT OUTLOOK® VERSION 2002 INSIDE OUT
ISBN 0-7356-1282-X

MICROSOFT ACCESS VERSION 2002 INSIDE OUT
ISBN 0-7356-1283-8

MICROSOFT FRONTPAGE® VERSION 2002 INSIDE OUT
ISBN 0-7356-1284-6

MICROSOFT VISIO® VERSION 2002 INSIDE OUT
ISBN 0-7356-1285-4

MICROSOFT PROJECT VERSION 2002 INSIDE OUT
ISBN 0-7356-1124-6

Microsoft
microsoft.com/mspress

Self-paced

training that works
as hard as you do!

Information-packed STEP BY STEP courses are the most effective way to teach yourself how to complete tasks with the Microsoft Windows operating system and Microsoft Office applications. Numbered steps and scenario-based lessons with practice files on CD-ROM make it easy to find your way while learning tasks and procedures. Work through every lesson or choose your own starting point—with STEP BY STEP'S modular design and straightforward writing style, *you* drive the instruction. And the books are constructed with lay-flat binding so you can follow the text with both hands at the keyboard. Select STEP BY STEP titles also prepare you for the Microsoft Office User Specialist (MOUS) credential. It's an excellent way for you or your organization to take a giant step toward workplace productivity.

Microsoft Press also has STEP BY STEP titles to help you use earlier versions of Microsoft software.

- **Home Networking with Microsoft® Windows® XP Step by Step**
  ISBN 0-7356-1435-0

- **Microsoft Windows XP Step by Step**
  ISBN 0-7356-1383-4

- **Microsoft Office XP Step by Step**
  ISBN 0-7356-1294-3

- **Microsoft Word Version 2002 Step by Step**
  ISBN 0-7356-1295-1

- **Microsoft Project Version 2002 Step by Step**
  ISBN 0-7356-1301-X

- **Microsoft Excel Version 2002 Step by Step**
  ISBN 0-7356-1296-X

- **Microsoft PowerPoint® Version 2002 Step by Step**
  ISBN 0-7356-1297-8

- **Microsoft Outlook® Version 2002 Step by Step**
  ISBN 0-7356-1298-6

- **Microsoft FrontPage® Version 2002 Step by Step**
  ISBN 0-7356-1300-1

- **Microsoft Access Version 2002 Step by Step**
  ISBN 0-7356-1299-4

- **Microsoft Visio® Version 2002 Step by Step**
  ISBN 0-7356-1302-8

microsoft.com/mspress

Microsoft Press® Resource Kits

powerhouse

resources to minimize costs
while maximizing performance

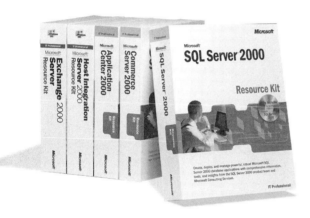

Deploy and support your enterprise business systems using the expertise and tools of those who know the technology best—the Microsoft product groups. Each RESOURCE KIT packs precise technical reference, installation and rollout tactics, planning guides, upgrade strategies, and essential utilities on CD-ROM. They're everything you need to help maximize system performance as you reduce ownership and support costs!

Microsoft® Windows® 2000 Server Resource Kit
ISBN 1-57231-805-8
U.S.A. $299.99   Canada $460.99

Microsoft Windows 2000 Professional Resource Kit
ISBN 1-57231-808-2
U.S.A. $69.99   Canada $107.99

Microsoft Office XP Resource Kit
ISBN 0-7356-1403-2
U.S.A. $69.99   Canada $99.99

**Microsoft Windows XP Professional
Resource Kit Documentation**
ISBN 0-7356-1485-7
U.S.A. $59.99   Canada $86.99

Microsoft Small Business Server 2000 Resource Kit
ISBN 0-7356-1252-8
U.S.A. $69.99   Canada $99.99

Microsoft SQL Server™ 2000 Resource Kit
ISBN 0-7356-1266-8
U.S.A. $69.99   Canada $99.99

Microsoft Exchange 2000 Server Resource Kit
ISBN 0-7356-1017-7
U.S.A. $69.99   Canada $99.99

Microsoft Application Center 2000 Resource Kit
ISBN 0-7356-1023-1
U.S.A. $69.99   Canada $99.99

Microsoft Commerce Server 2000 Resource Kit
ISBN 0-7356-1128-9
U.S.A. $69.99   Canada $99.99

Microsoft Host Integration Server 2000 Resource Kit
ISBN 0-7356-1182-3
U.S.A. $69.99   Canada $99.99

Microsoft®

mspress.microsoft.com

Get a **Free**
e-mail newsletter, updates,
special offers, links to related books,
and more when you
register on line!

Register your Microsoft Press® title on our Web site and you'll get a FREE subscription to our e-mail newsletter, *Microsoft Press Book Connections.* You'll find out about newly released and upcoming books and learning tools, online events, software downloads, special offers and coupons for Microsoft Press customers, and information about major Microsoft® product releases. You can also read useful additional information about all the titles we publish, such as detailed book descriptions, tables of contents and indexes, sample chapters, links to related books and book series, author biographies, and reviews by other customers.

Registration is easy. Just visit this Web page and fill in your information:

http://www.microsoft.com/mspress/register

Microsoft

Proof of Purchase

Use this page as proof of purchase if participating in a promotion or rebate offer on this title. Proof of purchase must be used in conjunction with other proof(s) of payment such as your dated sales receipt—see offer details.

Microsoft® Windows® XP Inside Out, Deluxe Edition
0-7356-1805-4

CUSTOMER NAME

Microsoft Press, PO Box 97017, Redmond, WA 98073-9830

MICROSOFT LICENSE AGREEMENT

Book Companion CD

user manual, in "online" documentation, and/or in other Microsoft-provided materials. Any supplemental software code provided to you as part of the Support Services shall be considered part of the SOFTWARE PRODUCT and subject to the terms and conditions of this EULA. With respect to technical information you provide to Microsoft as part of the Support Services, Microsoft may use such information for its business purposes, including for product support and development. Microsoft will not utilize such technical information in a form that personally identifies you.

- **Software Transfer.** You may permanently transfer all of your rights under this EULA, provided you retain no copies, you transfer all of the SOFTWARE PRODUCT (including all component parts, the media and printed materials, any upgrades, this EULA, and, if applicable, the Certificate of Authenticity), **and** the recipient agrees to the terms of this EULA.

- **Termination.** Without prejudice to any other rights, Microsoft may terminate this EULA if you fail to comply with the terms and conditions of this EULA. In such event, you must destroy all copies of the SOFTWARE PRODUCT and all of its component parts.

3. **COPYRIGHT.** All title and copyrights in and to the SOFTWARE PRODUCT (including but not limited to any images, photographs, animations, video, audio, music, text, SAMPLE CODE, REDISTRIBUTABLES, and "applets" incorporated into the SOFTWARE PRODUCT) and any copies of the SOFTWARE PRODUCT are owned by Microsoft or its suppliers. The SOFTWARE PRODUCT is protected by copyright laws and international treaty provisions. Therefore, you must treat the SOFTWARE PRODUCT like any other copyrighted material **except** that you may install the SOFTWARE PRODUCT on a single computer provided you keep the original solely for backup or archival purposes. You may not copy the printed materials accompanying the SOFTWARE PRODUCT.

4. **U.S. GOVERNMENT RESTRICTED RIGHTS.** The SOFTWARE PRODUCT and documentation are provided with RESTRICTED RIGHTS. Use, duplication, or disclosure by the Government is subject to restrictions as set forth in subparagraph (c)(1)(ii) of the Rights in Technical Data and Computer Software clause at DFARS 252.227-7013 or subparagraphs (c)(1) and (2) of the Commercial Computer Software—Restricted Rights at 48 CFR 52.227-19, as applicable. Manufacturer is Microsoft Corporation/One Microsoft Way/Redmond, WA 98052-6399.

5. **EXPORT RESTRICTIONS.** You agree that you will not export or re-export the SOFTWARE PRODUCT, any part thereof, or any process or service that is the direct product of the SOFTWARE PRODUCT (the foregoing collectively referred to as the "Restricted Components"), to any country, person, entity, or end user subject to U.S. export restrictions. You specifically agree not to export or re-export any of the Restricted Components (i) to any country to which the U.S. has embargoed or restricted the export of goods or services, which currently include, but are not necessarily limited to, Cuba, Iran, Iraq, Libya, North Korea, Sudan, and Syria, or to any national of any such country, wherever located, who intends to transmit or transport the Restricted Components back to such country; (ii) to any end user who you know or have reason to know will utilize the Restricted Components in the design, development, or production of nuclear, chemical, or biological weapons; or (iii) to any end user who has been prohibited from participating in U.S. export transactions by any federal agency of the U.S. government. You warrant and represent that neither the BXA nor any other U.S. federal agency has suspended, revoked, or denied your export privileges.

DISCLAIMER OF WARRANTY

NO WARRANTIES OR CONDITIONS. MICROSOFT EXPRESSLY DISCLAIMS ANY WARRANTY OR CONDITION FOR THE SOFTWARE PRODUCT. THE SOFTWARE PRODUCT AND ANY RELATED DOCUMENTATION ARE PROVIDED "AS IS" WITHOUT WARRANTY OR CONDITION OF ANY KIND, EITHER EXPRESS OR IMPLIED, INCLUDING, WITHOUT LIMITATION, THE IMPLIED WARRANTIES OF MERCHANTABILITY, FITNESS FOR A PARTICULAR PURPOSE, OR NONINFRINGEMENT. THE ENTIRE RISK ARISING OUT OF USE OR PERFORMANCE OF THE SOFTWARE PRODUCT REMAINS WITH YOU.

LIMITATION OF LIABILITY. TO THE MAXIMUM EXTENT PERMITTED BY APPLICABLE LAW, IN NO EVENT SHALL MICROSOFT OR ITS SUPPLIERS BE LIABLE FOR ANY SPECIAL, INCIDENTAL, INDIRECT, OR CONSEQUENTIAL DAMAGES WHATSOEVER (INCLUDING, WITHOUT LIMITATION, DAMAGES FOR LOSS OF BUSINESS PROFITS, BUSINESS INTERRUPTION, LOSS OF BUSINESS INFORMATION, OR ANY OTHER PECUNIARY LOSS) ARISING OUT OF THE USE OF OR INABILITY TO USE THE SOFTWARE PRODUCT OR THE PROVISION OF OR FAILURE TO PROVIDE SUPPORT SERVICES, EVEN IF MICROSOFT HAS BEEN ADVISED OF THE POSSIBILITY OF SUCH DAMAGES. IN ANY CASE, MICROSOFT'S ENTIRE LIABILITY UNDER ANY PROVISION OF THIS EULA SHALL BE LIMITED TO THE GREATER OF THE AMOUNT ACTUALLY PAID BY YOU FOR THE SOFTWARE PRODUCT OR US$5.00; PROVIDED, HOWEVER, IF YOU HAVE ENTERED INTO A MICROSOFT SUPPORT SERVICES AGREEMENT, MICROSOFT'S ENTIRE LIABILITY REGARDING SUPPORT SERVICES SHALL BE GOVERNED BY THE TERMS OF THAT AGREEMENT. BECAUSE SOME STATES AND JURISDICTIONS DO NOT ALLOW THE EXCLUSION OR LIMITATION OF LIABILITY, THE ABOVE LIMITATION MAY NOT APPLY TO YOU.

MISCELLANEOUS

This EULA is governed by the laws of the State of Washington USA, except and only to the extent that applicable law mandates governing law of a different jurisdiction.

Should you have any questions concerning this EULA, or if you desire to contact Microsoft for any reason, please contact the Microsoft subsidiary serving your country, or write: Microsoft Sales Information Center/One Microsoft Way/Redmond, WA 98052-6399.

PN 097-0002296

Solve problems, find answers, maintain systems, stay updated.

Get the support tools you need for Microsoft applications, servers and operating systems in one complete, convenient package.

TechNet is a subscription service that keeps you updated with the tools and utilities you need to keep your Microsoft products working perfectly. Your subscription begins with the portable TechNet binder and a set of up to 34 DVDs or CDs, then every month you will receive a new shipment of discs with the very latest content.

Spend less time searching for answers Take advantage of TechNet's improved search capabilities and new indexing application for convenient access to thousands of technical solutions.

Build and maintain your systems with advice from the experts Instructions and the latest tips direct from Microsoft give you long-term solutions, not band-aid remedies.

Train new users Training materials provide self-paced technical sessions to supplement your or your co-workers' knowledge.

A TechNet subscription includes service packs, technical information, drivers and patches, utilities and resource kits, training materials and deployment guides.

For more information about TechNet, and to order your subscription, visit:
www.microsoft.com/technet/buynow/xpuser